JANSON'S
BASIC HISTORY
OF
WESTERN ART

NINTH EDITION

PENELOPE J. E. DAVIES

FRIMA FOX HOFRICHTER

JOSEPH JACOBS

ANN M. ROBERTS

DAVID L. SIMON

PEARSON

Boston   Columbus   Indianapolis   New York   San Francisco   Upper Saddle River
Amsterdam   Cape Town   Dubai   London   Madrid   Milan   Munich   Paris   Montreal   Toronto
Delhi   Mexico City   Sao Paulo   Sydney   Hong Kong   Seoul   Singapore   Taipei   Tokyo

Editorial Director: Craig Campanella
Editor in Chief: Sarah Touborg
Senior Sponsoring Editor: Helen Ronan
Editorial Assistant: Victoria Engros
Vice-President, Director of Marketing: Brandy Dawson
Executive Marketing Manager: Kate Mitchell
Marketing Assistant: Paige Patunas
Managing Editor: Melissa Feimer
Project Manager: Marlene Gassler
Senior Operations Supervisor: Mary Fischer
Operations Specialist: Diane Peirano
Media Director: Brian Hyland
Senior Media Editor: David Alick
Media Project Manager: Rich Barnes
Pearson Imaging Center: Corin Skidds
Printer/Binder: Courier / Kendallville
Cover Printer: Lehigh-Phoenix Color/Hagerstown

Cover Photo: Kazimir Malevich. *Suprematist Composition: Airplane Flying*. 1915 (dated 1914).

This book was designed by Laurence King Publishing Ltd, London.
www.laurenceking.com

Editorial Manager, LKP: Kara Hattersley-Smith
Senior Editor, LKP: Sophie Wise
Production Manager, LKP: Simon Walsh
Picture Researcher: Ida Riveros
Copy Editor: Elisabeth Ingles
Designer: Ian Hunt

Acknowledgments

The authors and Prentice Hall are grateful to the following academic reviewers who helped shape this new edition:
Alyson Gill, Arkansas State University
Kathryn Keller, The Art Institute of New York City
David Nolta, Massachusetts College of Art and Design
Cory Peeke, Eastern Oregon University
Nancy Russell, Texas State Technical College
Donald Royal, Warner University
Keri Sussman Shurtliff, Fashion Institute of Design & Merchandising
Elizabeth Tebow, Northern Virginia Community College

Credits and acknowledgments borrowed from other sources and reproduced, with permission, in this textbook appear on the appropriate page within text or on the credit pages in the back of this book.

Library of Congress Cataloging-in-Publication Data
Davies, Penelope J. E.
Janson's basic history of Western art / Penelope J.E. Davies, Frima Fox Hofrichter, Joseph Jacobs, Ann M. Roberts. – Ninth edition.
pages cm
Includes bibliographical references and index.
ISBN-13: 978-0-205-24263-4 (pbk.)
ISBN-10: 0-205-24263-4 (pbk.)
1. Art–History. I. Title.
N5300.J29 2013
709–dc23
2012034215

10 9 8 7 6 5 4 3 2 1

Student Edition
ISBN 10:   0-205-24263-4
ISBN 13:   978-0-20524263-4

Instructor's Review Copy
ISBN 10:   0-205-24310-X
ISBN 13:   978-0-20524310-5

Books à la Carte
ISBN 10:   0-205-24281-2
ISBN 13:   978-0-205-24281-8

PEARSON

Contents in Brief

Contents

Preface

Welcome to the ninth edition of *Janson's Basic History of Western Art*, a concise introduction to the Western tradition in art.

Derived from the comprehensive *Janson's History of Western Art*, the *"Basic"* has always offered readers a strong focus on Western art, an important consideration of technique and style, and a clear point of view. It concentrates the discussion on the object, its manufacture, and its visual character, and considers the contribution of the artist as an important part of the analysis. In response to reviewers' requests, this edition expands the coverage of Islamic art into a discrete chapter. It also continues to maintain separate chapters on the Northern European Renaissance, the Italian Renaissance, and the High Renaissance, with stylistic divisions for key periods of the modern era. This edition thus creates a narrative of how art has changed over time in the cultures that Europe has claimed as its patrimony and that Americans have claimed through their connection to Europe.

Janson's Basic History of Western Art, ninth edition, is the product of careful revision by a team of scholars with different specialties, bringing great depth to the discussions of works of art.

Organization and Contextual Emphasis

The chapters are organized so that they integrate the media into chronological discussions instead of discussing them in isolation from one another. While connections are drawn between works of art, particular attention is paid to the patronage and function of works of art and the historical circumstances in which they were created.

The authors also explore how works of art have been used to shore up political or social power.

Interpreting Cultures

Western art history encompasses a great many distinct chronological and cultural periods, which the authors wish to treat as distinct entities. So, for example, Etruscan art is presented as evidence for Etruscan culture, not as a precursor of Roman or a follower of Greek art.

Women in the History of Art

Another important feature of the *Basic* is the visibility of women, whom the authors discuss as artists, as patrons, and as an audience for works of art. Inspired by contemporary approaches to art history, they also address the representation of women as expressions of specific cultural notions of femininity or as symbols.

Objects, Media, and Techniques

Many new objects have been incorporated into this edition. Throughout, pictures have been updated whenever new and improved images were available. The mediums discussed include not only modern art forms such as installations and earth art, but also the so-called minor arts of earlier periods—such as tapestries and metalwork. Discussions in the Materials and Techniques boxes illuminate this dimension of art history.

What's new in *Janson's Basic History of Western Art?*

Some highlights of the new edition include the following:

- Every chapter now opens with **Points of Inquiry** (key learning objectives) and concludes with a corresponding set of **Points of Reflection** that probe back to the objectives and help students think through and apply what they have learned.
- The chapters are keyed to **MyArtsLab** resources that enrich and reinforce student learning (see p. XV).
- **Newly colorized line art and 3D renderings** throughout the book allow students to better visualize architectural principles and key art processes.
- A **new series of maps** has been created to enhance the clarity and accuracy of the relationship between the art discussed and its geographical location and political affiliation.

Chapter by Chapter Revisions

The following list includes the major highlights of this new edition:

CHAPTER 1: PREHISTORIC ART

Expands discussion of *Woman from Willendorf* to explore feminist interpretations. Includes new discussion of Paleolithic dwellings constructed out of mammoth bones at Mezhirich and an account of new archaeological discoveries at Stonehenge.

CHAPTER 2: ANCIENT NEAR EASTERN ART

Incorporates an updated discussion of the Tell Asmar figures and ancient concepts of seeing. Puts added emphasis on looting issues. Includes new discussion of Hebrew architecture, focusing on the Temple at Jerusalem.

CHAPTER 3: EGYPTIAN ART

Presents updated discussion of the identity of the ruler represented by the Great Sphinx. Provides new analysis of a sculpture of Hatshepsut that explores the concept of female kingship and also updated information on the destruction of her images. Includes new section on portrait of Queen Tiy, chief wife of Amenhotep III, and its adaptation to conform to Akhenaten's monotheistic religion.

CHAPTER 4: AEGEAN ART

Offers a tighter discussion but introduces the *Flotilla Fresco* from Thera, reflecting the importance of sea transportation in the ancient Aegean.

CHAPTER 5: GREEK ART

Expands discussion of the sanctuary as a context for Greek temple architecture. Presents updated discussion on the Parthenon in light of the discovery that the *pronaos* once featured a frieze. Introduces the great lighthouse or Pharos at Alexandria.

CHAPTER 6: ETRUSCAN ART

Expands on all of its contents. Includes new artworks such as the fibula from the Regolini-Galassi Tomb and the late Classical period Anina Family Tomb, featuring demons from the funerary sphere. New discussion of residential architecture includes the monumental building complex at Murlo, and terra-cotta revetments from Acquarossa. The bronze *Chimaira* from Arezzo and *L'Arringatore* are now featured in the sculpture section.

CHAPTER 7: ROMAN ART

Features more works from the Republican period, including the Theater of Pompey, the Capitoline *She-Wolf*, and a set of terra-cotta pedimental sculptures. Includes the porphyry tetrarch portraits from San Marco, Venice, in the late antique period.

CHAPTER 8: JEWISH, EARLY CHRISTIAN, AND BYZANTINE ART

Includes a new section on Jewish art. Images of the wall paintings from the Dura-Europus synagogue and the floor mosaics from the Hammath Tiberias synagogue illustrate the new section. Now includes expanded cross-cultural coverage of the religious and artistic concerns evident during the Late Roman Empire. Section on narrative themes in icon painting now includes Byzantine icon of the Annunciation from Ohrid in addition to existing discussion of frontal representations of holy figures.

CHAPTER 9: ISLAMIC ART

Brings together discussion previously spread across several chapters to treat Islamic art as a single unit. This more coherent exploration better explains the continuities in Islamic art. Even so, regional and geographic distinctions are recognized. A new discussion of the Great Mosque of Selim II in Edirne allows for increased comparison between Islamic and Christian art, which is developed throughout the chapter.

CHAPTER 10: EARLY MEDIEVAL ART

Includes the Chi Rho Iota page from the *Book of Kells,* allowing expanded discussion of Hiberno-Saxon art. Discussion of the art of the various Early Medieval periods is more integrated.

CHAPTER 11: ROMANESQUE ART

Introduces Crac des Chevaliers, allowing for new discussion of Holy Land and crusades and development of theme of internationalization as a Romanesque phenomenon, as well as an exploration of military architecture. A new box, "Women Artists and Patrons during the Middle Ages," includes Hildegard of

Bingen and Herrad of Landsberg and raises social and cultural issues about the status of medieval women.

CHAPTER 12: GOTHIC ART
Features new illustration *of Melchizedek and Abraham*, from the *Psalter of St. Louis*, permitting a fuller discussion of the symbolic representation of kingship during the thirteenth century while also connecting to previous discussions of the crusades and the role King Louis IX (St. Louis) played in them.

CHAPTER 13: ART IN THIRTEENTH- AND FOURTEENTH-CENTURY ITALY
Distinguishes the thirteenth- and fourteenth-century Italy from the rest of Europe. Incorporates view of Pisano's Pisa pulpit. New discussion of Cimabue's Santa Trinita *Madonna Enthroned* allows for comparison with Giotto's Ognissanti *Madonna Enthroned*. Updates discussion of Lorenzetti's *Good Government* frescoes with new image. Discusses patronage of Visconti in Milan.

CHAPTER 14: ARTISTIC INNOVATIONS IN FIFTEENTH-CENTURY NORTHERN EUROPE
Includes updated discussions of key works, such as Sluter's *The Well of Moses*, Van Eyck's "Arnolfini portrait," and Van der Goes's *Portinari Altarpiece*.

CHAPTER 15: THE EARLY RENAISSANCE IN FIFTEENTH-CENTURY ITALY
Begins with a discussion of the competition panels for the Baptistery doors, to set up historical and artistic context of fifteenth-century Florence. Emphasizes patronage and the meanings for the original audiences of the works of art. New discussion of portraiture centers on Ghirlandaio's Sassetti Chapel with its narratives and portraits.

CHAPTER 16: THE HIGH RENAISSANCE IN ITALY, 1495–1520
Keeps focus on six key artists. Brings in Raphael's *Galatea* fresco as a contrast to the artist's works in religious settings. Expands discussion of Venetian High Renaissance: Titian's work updated to include the *Man with a Quilted Sleeve*; the *Venus of Urbino* now treated in this chapter.

CHAPTER 17: THE LATE RENAISSANCE AND MANNERISM IN SIXTEENTH-CENTURY ITALY
Retains stress on courtly and papal patronage, as well as the founding of the Accademia del Disegno in Florence as the context for Mannerism. Late Michelangelo is treated in this context. Includes new discussion of Pontormo's Capponi *Pietà* and Sofonisba Anguissola's *Self-Portrait*. Updates discussion of Bronzino's *Allegory of Venus* and Palladio's Villa Rotonda.

CHAPTER 18: RENAISSANCE AND REFORMATION THROUGHOUT SIXTEENTH-CENTURY EUROPE
Organizes discussion by regions of Europe and considers their responses to the double forces of Italian Renaissance style and the Reformation. Considers the movement of artists around Europe. France and Spain are discussed in connection with the Chateau of Fontainebleau and El Greco's paintings respectively. Updates discussion of Reformation in Germany with Cranach's *An Allegory of Law and Grace* woodcut. Patronage in Reformation courts is addressed with Aldorfer's *The Battle of Issos* and Holbein's *"The Ambassadors."* Netherlandish court patronage exemplified by Gossaert's *Neptune and Amphitrite*.

CHAPTER 19: THE BAROQUE IN ITALY AND SPAIN
Examines Caravaggio's and Bernini's roles in the Counter-Reformation. Discusses religious orders and the papacy, and develops an understanding of patronage, the poor, street people, and the full nature of seventeenth-century life. Spanish section is restructured with new information on Velázquez's *Las Meninas*. New works include Zurbarán's *Still Life with Oranges, Lemons, and a Rose* and Murillo's *The Immaculate Conception*.

CHAPTER 20: THE BAROQUE IN THE NETHERLANDS
Examines political and religious differences and artistic connections. The concept of an open market is treated in a discussion of the Dutch landscape, still life, and genre painting of Northern Europe. Explores importance of Rubens through an examination of his workshop. New works include Rembrandt's *Self-Portrait with a Cap, Open-Mouthed*, his *Bathsheba with King David's Letter*, as well as Frans Hals's *Malle Babbe* with documentary evidence of who its subject was and iconographic development of the painting's meaning. Extends discussion of Rembrandt's *Night Watch*.

CHAPTER 21: THE BAROQUE IN FRANCE AND ENGLAND
Considers concept of classicism in the paintings of Poussin and the architecture of Jones and Wren. New works include Claude Lorrain's *A Pastoral Landscape*, additional views of the palace and gardens at Versailles, and plans for St. Paul's.

CHAPTER 22: THE ROCOCO
Concentrates on the first half of the eighteenth century, with Gainsborough, Reynolds, and Vigée-Lebrun moved to Chapter 23. Reorganizes discussion with fuller examination of Rococo style, aspects of the Grand Tour, and growth of art market. Boucher is now included with *Portrait of Madame de Pompadour* and a new work by Chardin, *Saying Grace (Le Bénédicité)*, which was extraordinarily popular in the eighteenth century.

CHAPTER 23: ART IN THE AGE OF ENLIGHTENMENT, 1750–1789
Includes Hamilton engraving to demonstrate importance of prints for circulating images and information in the eighteenth century and to give an example of the period's new emphasis on moralistic themes. Kauffmann is represented by a work from the 1770s, allowing for exploration of eighteenth-century

women's issues. Gainsborough and Reynolds are discussed within Neoclassicism and Romanticism and with new works reflecting these styles. Vigée-Lebrun is placed in the context of Neoclassicism and her double portrait of herself with her daughter is discussed after David. Canova has been moved up from Chapter 24 to place him more squarely in the context of Neoclassicism.

CHAPTER 24: ART IN THE AGE OF ROMANTICISM, 1789–1848

Expands discussion of Goya with an etching, *The Sleep of Reason*, to reinforce importance of prints in general and to Goya specifically. Furthermore, the fantastical image underscores the role of imagination in Romantic period. David's *Bonaparte Crossing the Great St.-Bernard* has been added to emphasize importance Napoleon's personality to the Romantic era and to allow for a discussion of how Romanticism transformed Neoclassicism.

CHAPTER 25: THE AGE OF POSITIVISM: REALISM, IMPRESSIONISM, AND THE PRE-RAPHAELITES, 1848–1885

Now includes a portrait of Manet by the photographer Nadar.

CHAPTER 26: PROGRESS AND ITS DISCONTENTS: POST-IMPRESSIONISM, SYMBOLISM, AND ART NOUVEAU, 1880–1905

Offers a tighter discussion to allow for more emphasis on Realism and the chapter theme.

CHAPTER 27: TOWARD ABSTRACTION: THE MODERNIST REVOLUTION, 1905–1914

Includes a Suprematist work by Popova, reinforcing how Russian abstraction took Italian Futurism in a new and very different direction. Brancusi is now represented by *Bird in Space,* allowing for a better discussion of the pedestal in the artist's work.

CHAPTER 28: ART BETWEEN THE WARS

Now represents Rivera with a Mexican mural from the 1920s, permitting a more focused discussion of political issues and the importance of Mexican traditions, which are both central to Rivera's art.

CHAPTER 29: POSTWAR TO POSTMODERN, 1945–1980

Includes Polke and discusses his work in relation to Pop Art, while still acknowledging his important role in the development of Postmodernism.

CHAPTER 30: THE POST-MODERN ERA: ART SINCE 1980

Includes Fred Wilson's *Mining the Museum*, which allows for a discussion of the "institutional critique." More emphasis is placed on major period issues such as gender and ethnicity, as well as sexual orientation.

Give Your Students Choices

- The **Pearson eText**: available within MyArtsLab, the Pearson eText lets students access their textbook anytime, anywhere, and any way they want – including listening online or downloading to an iPad.
  MyArtsLab with eText: 978-0-205-93171-2

- **Pearson Custom Publishing** lets instructors build eBooks using the best content available. Search the Pearson eText collection for the topics and multimedia you want and seamlessly integrate your own material to create your ideal textbook. Contact your Pearson representative to get started.

- The **Books à la Carte edition** offers a convenient, three-hole-punched, loose-leaf version of the traditional text at a discounted price—allowing students to take only what they need to class. Books à la Carte editions are available both with and without access to MyArtsLab.
  Books à la Carte edition: 978-0-205-24281-8
  Books à la Carte edition plus MyArtsLab: 978-0-205-24282-5

- **Traditional Printed Text**
  Text: 978-0-205-24263-4
  Text + MyArtsLab: 978-0-205-92592-6

- The **CourseSmart eTextbook** offers the same content as the printed text in a convenient online format—with highlighting, online search, and printing capabilities.
  www.coursesmart.com
  CourseSmart eTextbook: 978-0-205-24292-4

MyArtsLab

MyArtsLab delivers **proven results** in helping individual students succeed. Its automatically graded assessments, personalized study plan, and interactive eText provide **engaging experiences** that personalize, stimulate, and measure learning for each student. A **personalized study plan** for each student promotes critical-thinking skills, and helps students succeed in the course and beyond.

■ *Art21* and *Studio Technique videos* present up-close looks at real-life artists at work, helping students better understand techniques used during different eras.

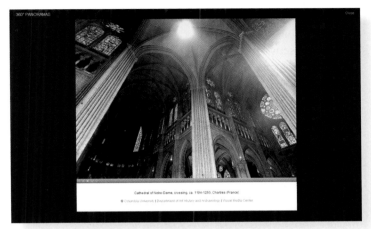

▲ 360-degree **architectural panoramas and simulations** of major monuments help students understand buildings—inside and out.

◀ *Closer Look* tours—interactive walkthroughs featuring expert audio—offer an in-depth look at key works of art, enabling students to zoom in to see detail they couldn't otherwise see—even in person.

▶ The **Pearson eText** lets students access their textbook anytime, anywhere, and any way they want—including listening online or downloading to an iPad®.

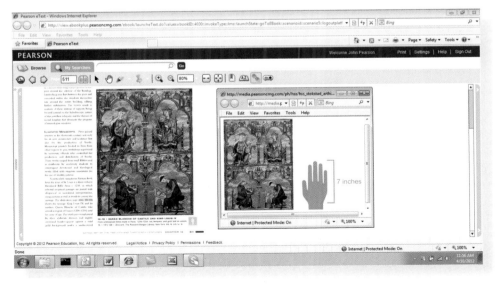

MyArtsLab lets your students experience and interact with Art.

MyArtsLab consistently and positively impacts the quality of learning in the classroom. When educators require and integrate MyArtsLab in their course, students and instructors experience success. Join our ever-growing community of 50,000 users across the country giving their students access to the high quality rich media and assessment on MyArtsLab.

"Students who use MyArtsLab perform better on their exams than students who do not."
—Cynthia Kristan-Graham, Auburn University

"MyArtsLab also makes students more active learners. They are more engaged with the material."
—Maya Jiménez, Kingsborough Community College

"MyArtsLab keeps students connected in another way to the course material. A student could be immersed for hours!"
—Cindy B. Damschroder, University of Cincinnati

"I really enjoy using MyArtsLab. At the end of the quarter, I ask students to write a paragraph about their experience with MyArtsLab and 97% of them are positive."
—Rebecca Trittel, Savannah College of Art and Design

Contemporary art is featured in *Art21* clips

Studio technique videos help students understand key techniques like lost wax casting

Powerful class presentation tools that are easy to use.

ClassPrep collects the very best class presentation resources in one convenient online destination, so instructors can keep students engaged throughout every class. With art and figures from the text, videos, classroom activities, and much more, ClassPrep makes lecture preparation simpler and less time-consuming.

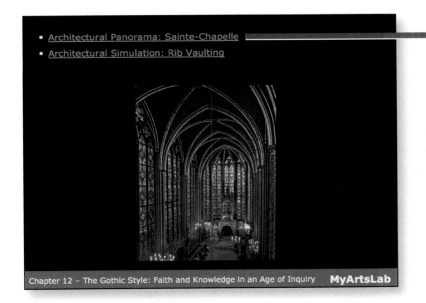

Teaching with MyArtsLab PowerPoints helps instructors make their lectures come alive. These slides allow instructors to display the very best interactive features from MyArtsLab in the classroom—quickly and easily.

Introduction

Who was Freelove Olney Scott? Her portrait (**fig. I-1**) shows us a refined-looking woman, born, we would guess, into an aristocratic family, used to servants and power. We have come to accept John Singleton Copley's portraits of colonial Bostonians, such as Mrs. Joseph Scott, as accurate depictions of his subjects and their lifestyles. But many, like Mrs. Scott, were not what they appear to be. Who was she? Let's take a closer look at the context in which the painting was made.

Copley is recognized as the first great American painter. Working in Boston from about 1754 to 1774, he became the most sought-after portraitist of the period. Copley easily outstripped the meager competition, most of whom earned their living painting signs and coaches. After all, no successful British artist had any reason to come to America. The economically struggling colonies were not a strong market for art. Only occasionally was a portrait commissioned, and typically, artists were treated like craftsmen rather than intellectuals. Like most colonial portraitists, Copley was self-taught, learning his trade by looking at black-and-white prints of paintings by the European masters.

As we can see in *Mrs. Joseph Scott*, Copley was a master at painting textures, all the more astonishing when we realize that he had no one to teach him the tricks of the painter's trade. His illusions are so convincing that we think we are looking at real silk, ribbons, lace, pearls, skin, hair, and marble. Copley's contemporaries also marveled at his sleight of hand. No other colonial painter attained such a level of realism.

But is Copley just a "face painter," as portraitists were derogatorily called at the time—capturing only the resemblance of his sitter and her expensive accouterments? And is this painting just a means to replicate the likeness of an individual in an era before the advent of photography? The answer to both questions is a resounding "no." Copley's job was not just to make a faithful image of Mrs. Scott, but to portray her as a woman of impeccable character, limitless wealth, and aristocratic status.

The flowers she holds are a symbol of fertility, faithfulness, and feminine grace, indicating that she is a good mother and wife, and a charming woman. Her expensive dress was imported from London, as was her necklace. Copley undoubtedly took her pose from one of the prints he had of British or French royalty.

Not only is Mrs. Scott's pose borrowed, but most likely her clothing is too, for her necklace appears on three other women in Copley portraits. In other words, it was a studio prop, and the dress may have been as well. In fact, except for Mrs. Scott's face, the entire painting is a fiction designed to aggrandize the wife of a newly wealthy Boston merchant, who made a fortune selling provisions to the occupying British army. The Scotts were *nouveaux riches,* commoners, not titled aristocrats. By the middle of the eighteenth century, rich Bostonians wanted to distinguish themselves from others who were less successful. Now, after a century of trying to escape their British roots (from which many had fled to secure religious freedom), they sought to imitate the British aristocracy, even to the point of taking tea in the afternoon and keeping English spaniels, a breed that in England only aristocrats were permitted to own.

Mr. Scott commissioned this painting of his wife, as well as a portrait of himself, not just to record their features, but to show off the family's wealth. These pictures were extremely expensive and therefore status symbols, much as a Rolls-Royce or a diamond ring from Tiffany's is today. The portraits were displayed in the public spaces of the house where they could be readily seen by visitors. Most likely they hung on either side of the mantel in the living room, or in the entrance hall. They were not intended as intimate, affectionate resemblances destined for the bedroom. If patrons wanted cherished images of their loved ones, they would commission miniature portraits. These captured the likeness of the sitter in amazing detail and were often so small that they could be encased in a locket for a woman to wear on a chain around her neck, or a gentleman to place in the inner breast pocket of his coat, close to the heart.

Let's move forward almost 200 years to look at a second image of a woman, Andy Warhol's *Gold Marilyn Monroe* (**fig. I-2**) of 1962, and explore the surprising stories it contains. In a sense, the painting can be considered a portrait, because it

I-2 Andy Warhol. *Gold Marilyn Monroe*. 1962. Synthetic polymer paint, silkscreened, and oil on canvas, 6′11¼″ × 4′7″ (2.12 × 1.39 m). The Museum of Modern Art, New York. Gift of Philip Johnson

portrays the famous 1950s film star and sex symbol. Unlike *Mrs. Joseph Scott,* however, the painting was not commissioned, and instead was made to be exhibited in a commercial art gallery, where it could be purchased by a private collector for display in a home. Of course, Warhol hoped that ultimately it would end up in a museum, something Copley never considered because they did not exist in his day. Because *Gold Marilyn Monroe* is not a commission, Warhol is not trying to flatter his subject. He is not even concerned about creating an illusionistic image; this image has no details and no sense of texture, as hair and flesh appear to be made of the same material—paint. Nor did Warhol painstakingly paint this picture. Instead he found a famous newspaper photograph of the film star and silkscreened it onto canvas, a process that involves first mechanically transferring the photograph onto a mesh screen and then pressing printing ink through the screen onto the canvas. He then surrounded Marilyn's head with a field of broadly brushed gold paint.

Warhol's painting is a pastiche of the public image of Monroe as propagated by the mass media. He even imitates the sloppy, gritty look and feel of color newspaper reproductions of the period, for the colors were often misregistered, not aligning properly with the image. The Marilyn we are looking at is the impersonal celebrity of the press, supposedly glamorous with her lush red lipstick and bright blond hair but instead appearing pathetically tacky because of the garish color (blond hair becomes bright yellow) and grimy black ink. Her personality is impenetrable, reduced to a public smile. The painting was prompted, in part, by Monroe's recent suicide. This was the real Marilyn—a depressed, miserable person. Warhol has brilliantly expressed the indifference of the mass media that glorifies celebrities by saturating a celebrity-thirsty public with their likenesses, but tells us nothing meaningful about them and shows no concern for them. Marilyn Monroe's image is about promoting a product, much as the jazzy packaging of Brillo soap pads or Campbell's soup cans is designed to sell a product without telling us anything about the product itself. The packaging is just camouflage. Warhol floats Marilyn's face in a sea of gold paint, imitating icons of Christ and the Virgin Mary that traditionally encase these religious figures in a spiritual aura of golden, heavenly light (see fig. 8.21). But Warhol's revered Marilyn is sadly dwarfed in her celestial gold, adding to the tragedy of this powerful portrait, which so trenchantly comments on the enormous gulf existing between public image and private reality.

Copley and Warhol worked in very different times, which tremendously affected the look and meaning of their portraits. Because art always serves a purpose, it is impossible for any artist to make a work that does not represent a point of view and tell a story, sometimes many stories. As we will see, great artists tell great and powerful stories. We will find that an important key to unraveling these stories is understanding the context in which the work was made.

The Power of Art and the Impact of Context

In a sense, art is a form of propaganda, for it represents an individual's or group's point of view, and this view is often presented as truth or fact. For centuries, art was used by the Church and the State to propagate the superiority of their powers. The *Alba Madonna* (see fig. I-16) was designed to proclaim the idealized, perfect state of existence attainable through Catholicism, and the Arch of Titus (**fig. I-3**) was erected to reinforce in the public's mind the military prowess and deification of the Roman emperor Titus. Even landscape paintings and still lifes of fruit, dead game, and flowers are loaded with messages and are far from simple attempts to capture the splendor and many moods of nature or show off the painter's finesse at creating a convincing illusionistic image.

Epitomizing the power of art is its ability to evoke entire historical periods. Say the words "ancient Egypt" and most people conjure up images of the pyramids (**fig. I-4**), the Sphinx, and flat, stiff figures lined up sideways across the face of sandstone (see fig. 56). Or look at the power of Grant Wood's famous 1930 painting *American Gothic* (**fig. I-5**), which has led us to believe

I-3 Arch of Titus, Forum Romanum. ca. 81 CE, as restored. Rome

I-4 The Great Pyramids: (from left to right) of Menkaure (ca. 2533–2515 BCE), Khafra (ca. 2570–2544 BCE), and Khufu (ca. 2601–2528 BCE). Giza, Egypt

that humorless, austere, hardworking farmers dominated the American hinterlands at the time. The painting has virtually become an emblem of rural America.

American Gothic has also become a source of much sarcastic humor for later generations, which adapted the famous pitchfork-bearing farmer and sour-faced daughter for all kinds of agendas unrelated to the artist's message. Works of art are often appropriated to serve purposes quite different from those initially intended, with context heavily influencing the meaning of a work. The reaction of some New Yorkers to *The Holy Virgin Mary* (**fig. I-6**) by Chris Ofili reflects the power of art to provoke and spark debate, even outrage. The work appeared in an exhibition titled *Sensation: Young British Artists from the Saatchi Collection*, presented at the Brooklyn Museum in late 1999. Ofili, who is British of African descent, made an enormous picture using dots of paint, glitter, map pins, and collaged images of genitalia from popular magazines to depict a black Virgin Mary. Instead of hanging on the wall, this

I-5 Grant Wood. *American Gothic*. 1930. Oil on board, 30¹¹⁄₁₆ × 25¹¹⁄₁₆″ (78 × 65.3 cm). The Art Institute of Chicago. Friends of American Art Collection. © Figge Art Museum, successors to the Estate of Nan Wood Graham/Licensed by VAGA, New York, NY

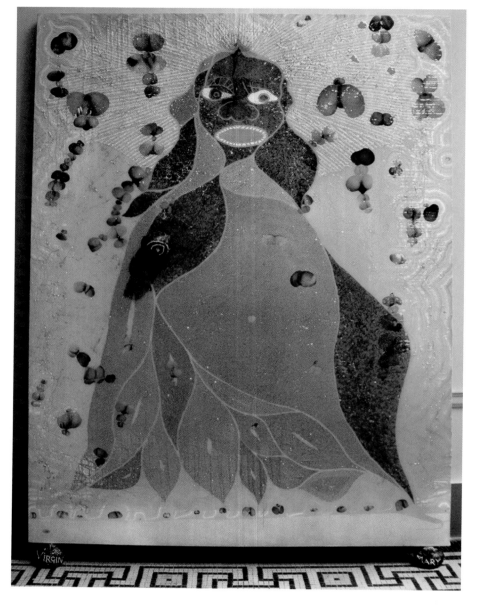

I-6 Chris Ofili. *The Holy Virgin Mary*. 1996. Paper collage, oil paint, glitter, polyester resin, map pins, and elephant dung on linen, 7′11″ × 5′11⁵⁄₁₆″ (2.44 × 1.83 m). MONA, Museum of Old and New Art, Hobart, Tasmania, Australia. © Chris Ofili, courtesy David Zwirner Gallery, New York

enormous painting rested on two large wads of elephant dung, which had been a signature of the artist's large canvases since 1991. Elephant dung is held sacred in Zimbabwe, and for Ofili, a devout Catholic who periodically attends Mass, the picture was about the elemental sacredness of the Virgin. The so-called pornographic images were intended to suggest procreation.

Many art historians, critics, and other viewers found the picture remarkably beautiful—glittering and shimmering with a delicate, ephemeral, otherworldly aura. Many Catholics, however, were repulsed by Ofili's homage to the Virgin. Instead of viewing the work through his eyes, they placed the painting within the context of their own experience and beliefs. Consequently, they interpreted

the dung and so-called pornography (and probably even a black Virgin, although this was never mentioned) as sacrilegious. Within days of the opening of the exhibition, the painting had to be put behind a large Plexiglas barrier. One artist hurled horse manure at the façade of the Brooklyn Museum, claiming "I was expressing myself creatively"; a museum visitor sneaked behind the Plexiglas barrier and smeared the Virgin with white paint in order to hide her. But the greatest attack came from New York's mayor, Rudolph Giuliani, a Catholic, who was so outraged that he tried to eliminate city funding for the museum. Ultimately, he failed, but only after a lengthy lawsuit by the museum. The public outrage at Ofili's work is one instance in a long tradition that probably goes back to the beginning of image making. Art has consistently provoked outrage, just as it has inspired pride, admiration, love, and respect, and the reason is simple: Art is never an empty container; rather, it is a vessel loaded with meaning, subject to multiple interpretations, and always representing someone's point of view.

Because the context for looking at art constantly changes, our interpretations and insights into art and entire periods evolve as well. For example, when the first edition of this book was published in 1971, women artists were not included, which was typical for textbooks of the time. America, like most of the world, was male-dominated and history was male-centric. Historically, women were expected to be wives and mothers, and to stay in the home and not have careers. They were not supposed to become artists, and the few known exceptions were not taken seriously by historians, who were mostly male. The feminist movement, beginning in the mid-1960s, overturned this restrictive perception of women. As a result, in the last 40 years, art historians—many of them women—have "rediscovered" countless women artists who had attained a degree of success in their day. Many of them were outstanding artists, held in high esteem during their lifetime, despite the enormous struggle to overcome powerful social and even family resistance against women becoming professional artists.

One of these lost women artists is the seventeenth-century Dutch painter Judith Leyster, a follower, if not a student, of Frans Hals. Over the centuries, all of Leyster's paintings were attributed to other artists, including Hals and Gerrit van Honthorst. Or they were labeled "artist unknown." At the end of the nineteenth century, however, she was rediscovered through an analysis of her signature, documents, and style, and her paintings were gradually restored to her name. It was only with the feminist movement that she was elevated from a minor figure to one of the more accomplished painters of her generation, one important enough to be included in basic histories of art. The feminist movement provided a new context for evaluating art, one that had an interest in rather than a denial of women's achievements and a study of issues relating to gender and how they appear in the arts.

A work like Leyster's ca. 1633 *Self-Portrait* (**fig. I-7**) is especially fascinating from this point of view. Because of its size and date, this may have been the painting the artist submitted as her presentation piece for admission into the local painters' guild, the Guild of St. Luke of Haarlem. Women were not encouraged to join the guild, which was a male preserve reinforcing the professional status of men. Nor did women artists generally take on students. Leyster bucked both restrictive traditions as she carved out a career for herself in a man's world. In her self-portrait, she presents herself as an artist, armed with many brushes, suggesting her deft control of the medium, which the presentation picture itself was meant to demonstrate. On the easel is a segment of a genre scene of which several variations are known. We must remember that at this time, artists rarely showed themselves working at their easels, toiling with their hands. They wanted to separate themselves from mere artisans and laborers, presenting themselves as belonging to a higher class. As a woman defying male expectations, however, Leyster needed to clearly declare that she was indeed an artist. But she cleverly elevates her status by not dressing as an artist would when painting. Instead, she appears as her patrons do in their portraits, well dressed and well off. Her mouth is open, in what is called a "speaking likeness" portrait, giving her a casual but self-assured, animated quality, as she appears to converse on equal terms with a visitor, or with us. Leyster, along with Artemisia Gentileschi and Élisabeth Vigée-Lebrun, who are also in this book, was included in a major 1976 exhibition titled *Women Artists 1550–1950*, which appeared in Los Angeles and Brooklyn, New York, and played a major role in establishing the importance of women artists.

I-7 Judith Leyster. *Self-Portrait.* ca. 1633. Oil on canvas, 29³⁄₈ × 25⁵⁄₈" (74.3 × 64.3 cm). National Gallery of Art. Gift of Mr. and Mrs. Robert Woods Bliss. 1949.6.4

What is Art?

Ask most people without a background in art and art history, "What is art?," and they will respond with "an oil painting" or "a marble or bronze sculpture." Their criterion for quality is that it be beautiful, whatever that may be, although generally they define it as the degree to which a painting or sculpture is real-looking or adheres to their notion of naturalistic. Technical finesse or craft is viewed as the highest attribute of art making, capable of inspiring awe and reverence. To debunk the myth that art is about technique and begin to get at what it is about, we return to Warhol's *Gold Marilyn Monroe.* The painting is rich with stories: we can talk about how it raises issues about the meaning of art, how it functions, and how it takes on value, both financial and aesthetic. Warhol even begs the question of the significance of technical finesse in art making, an issue raised by the fact that in some respects he leads us to believe that he did not touch the painting himself! We have already seen how he appropriated someone else's photograph of Marilyn Monroe, not even taking his own. Warhol then instructed his assistants to make the screens for the printing process. They also prepared the canvas, screened the image with the colors Warhol selected, and may even have painted the gold to Warhol's specifications.

By using assistants to make his work, Warhol is telling us that art is not about the artist's technical finesse, but about communicating an idea using visual language, even if the idea does not require the artist to actually make the art. The measuring stick for quality in art is the quality of the statement being made, or its philosophy, as well as the quality of the technical means for making this statement. Looking at *Gold Marilyn Monroe* in the flesh at New York's Museum of Modern Art is a powerful experience. Standing in front of this 6-foot-high canvas, we cannot help but feel the empty glory of America's most famous symbol of female sexuality and stardom. Because the artist's vision, and not his touch, is the relevant issue for the making of this particular work, it is of no consequence that Warhol leads us to believe that he never laid a hand to the canvas, except to sign the back. (Actually, Warhol was a workaholic, intensely involved even with the most mechanical of his works.) We will shortly see, however, that the artist's touch is often critical to the success of a work of art.

Warhol openly declared that his art was not about his technical ability when he called his mid-town Manhattan studio "The Factory." He is telling us that art is a commodity, and he is manufacturing a product, even mass-producing his product. The Factory churned out over a thousand, if not thousands, of paintings and prints of Marilyn Monroe based on the same newspaper photograph. As far as the public knew, all Warhol did for the most part was sign them, his signature reinforcing the importance people place on the signature itself as being an essential part of the work (ironically, most Old Master paintings, dating to the fourteenth through the eighteenth centuries, are not signed).

Actually, artists for centuries used assistants to help make their pictures. Peter Paul Rubens, an Antwerp painter working in the first half of the seventeenth century and one of the most famous artists of his day, had an enormous workshop that cranked out many of his pictures, especially the large works. His assistants were often artists specializing in flowers, animals, or clothing, for example,

and many went on to become successful in their own right. Rubens would design the painting, and assistants, trained in his style, would execute their individual parts. Rubens would then come in at the end and pull the painting together as needed. The price the client was willing to pay often determined how much Rubens himself participated in the actual painting of the picture, and many of his works were indeed made entirely by him. Rubens's brilliant, flashy brushwork was in many respects critical to the making of the picture. Not only was his handling of paint considered superior to that of his assistants, the very identity of his paintings, its very life, so to speak, was linked to his unique genius for applying paint to canvas, almost as much as it was to his dramatic compositions. His brushwork complemented his subject matter; it even reinforced it. The two went hand in hand, as we shall see later in the Introduction and in Chapter 20.

Warhol was not the first artist to make art that intentionally raised the issue of what is art and how it functions. This distinction belongs to the humorous and brilliant Parisian Marcel Duchamp. In 1919, Duchamp took a roughly 7- by 5-inch reproduction of Leonardo da Vinci's *Mona Lisa* in the Louvre Museum in Paris and drew a mustache and beard on the sitter's face (**fig. I-8**). Below, he wrote the letters L. H. O. O. Q., pronounced in French *elle a chaud au cul*, which translates, "She has a hot ass." Duchamp was poking fun at the public's fascination with the mysterious smile on the Mona Lisa, which had intrigued everyone for centuries and eluded suitable explanation. Duchamp irreverently provided one: She is sexually aroused, and, given the masculine facial hair, she is gay. With the childish gesture of affixing a mustache and beard to the Mona Lisa, Duchamp also attacked bourgeois reverence for Old Master painting and the age-old esteem of oil painting representing the pinnacle of art.

Art, Duchamp is saying, can be made by merely placing ink drawing on a mass-produced reproduction. It is not strictly oil on canvas or cast bronze or chiseled marble sculpture. Artists can use any imaginable medium in any way in order to express themselves. He is announcing that art is about ideas that are made visually, and not necessarily about craft. In this deceivingly whimsical work, which is rich with ideas, Duchamp is telling us that art is anything that someone wants to call art, which is not the same as saying it is good art. Furthermore, he is

I-8 Marcel Duchamp. Replica of *L. H. O. O. Q.* (*Mona Lisa*) from *Boîte-en-valise*. 1919. Rectified Readymade; pencil on a reproduction, 7 × 4⅞″ (17.8 × 11 cm). The Philadelphia Museum of Art. Louise and Walter Arensberg Collection

proclaiming that art can be small, since *L. H. O. O. Q.* is a fraction of the size of its source, the *Mona Lisa*. By appropriating Leonardo's famous picture and interpreting it very differently from traditional readings (see page 339), Duchamp suggests that the meaning of art is not fixed forever by the artist, that it can change and be assigned by viewers, writers, collectors, and museum curators, who can use it for their own purposes. Lastly, and this is certainly one of Duchamp's many wonderful contributions to art, he is telling us that art can be fun; it can defy conventional notions of beauty, and while intellectually engaging us in a most serious manner, it can also provide us with a smile, if not a good laugh.

Art and Aesthetics

L. H. O. O. Q. also raises the issue of aesthetics, which is the study of theories surrounding art, including what is beauty, and the meaning and purpose of art. Duchamp selected the *Mona Lisa* for "vandalizing" for many reasons, but one of them had to be that many people considered it the greatest and therefore the most beautiful painting ever made. Certainly, it was one of the most famous paintings in the world, if not the most famous. In 1919 most of those who held such a view had probably never seen it and knew it only from reproductions, probably no better than the one Duchamp used in *L. H. O. O. Q.* And yet, they would describe the original painting as beautiful, but not Duchamp's comical version.

Duchamp called such altered found objects as *L. H. O. O. Q.* "assisted Readymades" (for another example, see *Fountain*, fig. 28.2), and he was adamant when he claimed that these works had no aesthetic value whatsoever. They were not to be considered beautiful, and they were selected because they were aesthetically neutral. What interested Duchamp were the ideas that these objects embodied once they were declared art.

Despite his claim, Duchamp's assisted Readymades can be perceived as beautiful, in ways, of course, that are quite different from Leonardo's *Mona Lisa*, but beautiful all the same. *L. H. O. O. Q.* has an aura about it, an aura of wit and ideas that are specific to Duchamp. As a result, this slightly altered cheap reproduction is transformed into a compelling work of art, in a way that is very different from Leonardo's. And so the qualities that attract us to it, which we can describe as its beauty, could not be further from those of the *Mona Lisa*. Ultimately, beauty can be equated with quality.

Beauty is not just a pretty, colorful picture or a perfectly formed, harmonious nude marble figure. Beauty resides in content and how successfully the content is made visual. This book is intended to suggest the many complex ways that quality, and thus beauty, appears in art. Some of the greatest paintings depict horrific scenes that many people could never find acceptable, but they are nonetheless beautiful—scenes such as beheadings (see fig. 19.3), crucifixions (see fig. 18.4), death and despair (see figs. 24.9 and 24.10), emotional distress (see fig. 26.7), and the brutal massacre of innocent women and children (**fig. I-9**). Like Duchamp's *L. H. O. O. Q.*, these works possess an aura that makes them powerful and riveting, despite the repulsiveness of the subject matter. They have quality, and to those who recognize and feel this quality, that makes these works beautiful. Others will continue to be repulsed and offended by them, or at best just be uninterested.

Illusionism and Meaning in Art

The Roman historian Pliny tells the story about the competition between the Greek painters Zeuxis and Parrhasius to see who could make the most illusionistic work. Zeuxis painted grapes so real that birds tried to eat them, but Parrhasius won the competition. He had painted a curtain covering a painting. So realistic was the work that Zeuxis asked him to pull back the curtain covering his painting only to discover that he was looking at the painting. The story of this competition is interesting, because despite a recurring emphasis on illusionism in art, the ability to create illusionistic effects and "fool the eye" is generally not what determines quality in art. As we discussed, quality in art comes from ideas and execution. Just being clever and fooling the eye is not enough.

A look at the sculpture of the twentieth-century artist Duane Hanson shows us how illusionism can

be put in the service of meaning to create a powerful work of art. Hanson's 1995 sculpture, *Man on a Lawnmower* (**fig. I-10**), is a work that too often is appreciated only for its illusionistic qualities, while the real content goes unnoticed. Yet, it is the content, not the illusionism, that makes this sculpture so potent. Hanson began making his sculptures in the late 1960s. He cast his figures in polyester resin, and meticulously painted them. He then dressed them in real clothing, used real accessories (including wigs and artificial eyeballs), and placed them on real furniture. Most museum visitors are startled to discover that his sculptures are not real, and many people have tried to interact with his characters, which include museum guards, tourists, shoppers, house painters, and female sunbathers.

But Hanson's art is about more than just a visual sleight of hand. He is also a realist and a moralist, and his art is filled with tragic social content. By realist, we mean that his sculpture is not limited

I-10 Duane Hanson. *Man on a Lawnmower*. 1995. Bronze polychromed with mower, life-size. The Newark Museum, New Jersey, courtesy the O'Hara Gallery, New York. © Estate of Duane Hanson/Licensed by VAGA, New York, NY

Can a Mechanical Process Be Art?: Photography

The first edition of this book did not include photography, reflecting a prevailing attitude that photography, because it was largely a mechanical process, was not an art form. Now, three decades later, the artistic merit of photography seems self-evident. When it was invented in 1839, the art world largely dismissed it as a mechanical process with little artistic merit. Or it was perceived as not having sufficient aesthetic merit to be seen in the same lofty company with the twin peaks of art—painting and sculpture. It has struggled ever since to shed that stigma. Within the last 25 years, however, photography has been vindicated. Along with video and film, it has been elevated to an important medium used by today's artists. Pictures from the nineteenth and twentieth centuries that had interested only a handful of photography insiders suddenly became intensely sought after, with many museums rushing to establish photography departments and amass significant collections. In other words, it took well over 100 years for people to get beyond the stigma of the mechanical process and to develop an eye for the quality and beauty of the medium.

We need only look at a 1972 photograph titled *Albuquerque* (**fig. I-11**) by Lee Friedlander to see how photography matches painting and sculpture in artistic merit. In *Albuquerque*, Friedlander portrays a modern America that is vacuous and lifeless, which he suggests is due to technology. How does

to attractive, beautiful, and ennobling objects and situations but instead focuses on the base, coarse, crude, disgusting, and unseemly. In *Man on a Lawnmower*, we see an overweight man clutching a diet soda. He dwarfs the shabby riding mower he sits on. His T-shirt, baseball hat, pants, and sneakers are soiled. He is common and ordinary, and the entire sculpture is remarkably prosaic.

Man on a Lawnmower is a sad work. We see disillusionment in the man's eyes as he blankly stares off into space. The diet soda he holds suggests that he is trying to shed weight but is losing the battle. Grasscutting is another metaphor for a losing battle, as the grass is going to grow back. This work also represents the banality of human existence. What is life about? The monotony of cutting grass, Hanson is saying. In this last work, made when he knew he was dying of cancer, Hanson captured what he perceived to be the emptiness of human existence and contemporary life. The illusionism of the sculpture makes this aura of alienation and lack of spirituality all the more palpable. This man is us, and this is our life too. He embodies no poetry, nobility, or heroism. Our twentieth-century *Man on a Lawnmower* has no causes and beliefs to turn to as he confronts the down-to-earth reality of life and death.

I-11 Lee Friedlander. *Albuquerque*. 1972. Gelatin silver print, 11 × 14" (28 × 35.5 cm). © Lee Friedlander, courtesy Fraenkel Gallery, San Francisco

he do this? The picture has a haunting emptiness. It has no people, and it is filled with strange empty spaces of walkway and street appearing between the numerous objects that pop up everywhere. A hard, eerie geometry prevails, as seen in the strong verticals of the poles, buildings, hydrant, and wall. Cylinders, rectangles, and circles are everywhere. (Notice the many different rectangles on the background building, or the rectangles of the pavement bricks and the foreground wall.)

Despite the stillness and emptiness, the picture is busy and restless. The vertical poles and the strong vertical elements on the house and building establish a vibrant staccato rhythm. The energy of this rhythm is reinforced by the asymmetrical composition, which has no focus or center, as well as by the powerful intersecting diagonals of the street and the foreground wall. (Note how the shadow of the fire hydrant runs parallel to the street.) Disturbing features appear throughout the composition. The street sign—which cannot be seen because it is cropped at the top of the print—casts a mysterious shadow on the wall. A pole visually cuts the dog in two, and the dog has been separated from his attribute, the fire hydrant, as well as from his absent owner. The fire hydrant, in turn, appears to be mounted incorrectly, because it sticks too far out of the ground. The car on the right has been brutally cropped, and a light pole seems to sprout strangely from its hood. The telephone pole in the center of the composition is crooked, as though it has been tilted by the force of the cropped car entering from outside the edge of the picture (of course, the car is parked and not moving). Why do we assume this empty, frenetic quality is human-made? Because the work is dominated by the human-made and by technology. We see telephone poles, electrical wires, cross-walk signs, a banal machinelike modular apartment building, sleek automobiles, and a fire hydrant. Cropped in the lower left foreground is the steel cover to underground electrical wiring.

Everywhere, nature has been cemented over, and besides a few scraggly trees in the middle ground and distance, only the weeds surrounding the hydrant thrive. In this brilliant print, Friedlander captures his view of the essence of modern America: The way in which technology, a love of the artificial, and a fast, fragmented lifestyle are spawning alienation and a disconnection with nature and spirituality. As important, he is telling us that modernization is making America homogeneous. The title tells us we are in Albuquerque, New Mexico, but without the title we are otherwise in Anywhere, U.S.A.

Friedlander did not just find this composition. He very carefully selected it and he very carefully made it. He not only needed the sun, he had to wait until it was in the right position (otherwise, the shadow of the fire hydrant would not align with the street). When framing the composition, he very meticulously incorporated a fragment of the utility cover in the left lower foreground, while axing a portion of the car on the right. Nor did the geometry of the picture just happen; he made it happen. Instead of a soft focus that would create an atmospheric, blurry picture, he used a deep focus that produces a sharp, crisp image filled with detail, allowing, for example, the individual rectangular bricks in the pavement to be clearly seen. The strong white tones of the vertical rectangles of the apartment building, the foreground wall, and the utility box blocking the car on the left edge of the picture were probably carefully worked up in the darkroom, as was the rectangular columned doorway on the house. Friedlander has exposed the ugliness of modern America in this hard, cold, dry image, and because of the power of its message has created an extraordinarily beautiful work of art.

Can Architecture Communicate Ideas?

An art form that is basically abstract and dedicated to structuring space in a functional way might be seen as hardly able to carry a message. And yet it does, especially in the hands of great architects. We see Gianlorenzo Bernini expressing a powerful message in 1657 when he was asked by Pope Alexander VII to design a large open space, or piazza, in front of St. Peter's Cathedral in Rome. Bernini obliged, creating a space defined by a colonnade, or a row of columns, resembling arms that appear to maternally embrace visitors, welcoming them into the bosom of the Church (**fig. I-12**). His form anthropomorphized the building by emphasizing its identification with the Virgin Mary. At the same time, the French architect Claude Perrault was commissioned to design the east façade of King Louis XIV's palace, the Louvre in Paris (**fig. I-13**). To proclaim Louis's grandeur, he made the ground floor, where the day-to-day business of the court was carried out, a squat podium. The second floor, where Louis lived and held court, served

I-12 St. Peter's Cathedral. Nave and façade by Carlo Maderno, 1607–15; colonnade by Gianlorenzo Bernini, designed 1657. Rome

as the main floor and is therefore much grander and higher, resting on the "shoulders" of the staff below. Perrault articulated this elevated second story with a design that recalled Roman temples, thus associating Louis XIV with Imperial Rome and worldly power.

In our own era, an enormously wealthy businessman, Solomon R. Guggenheim, indulged his passion for modern art by commissioning the architect Frank Lloyd Wright to design a museum in New York City to house his contemporary collection. One of the boldest architectural statements of the

I-13 Claude Perrault. East front of the Louvre. 1667–70. Paris

mid-twentieth century, Wright's Solomon R. Guggenheim Museum is located on upper Fifth Avenue, overlooking Central Park (**fig. I-14**). The building, erected from 1956 to 1959, is radically different from the surrounding residential housing, thus immediately declaring that its function is different from theirs. As a matter of fact, the building is radically different from almost anything built up until that time. We can say that the exterior announces that it is a museum, because it looks as much like a gigantic sculpture as a functional structure.

Wright conceived the Guggenheim in 1945, and his goal was to create an organic structure that deviated from the conventional static rectangular box filled with conventional static rectangular rooms. Beginning in the early twentieth century, Wright designed houses that related to the landscape and nature, both in structure and material (fig. 26.16). The structure of his buildings, whether domestic or commercial, reflects the very structure of nature, which he saw as a continuous expansion. His buildings radiate out from a central core or wrap around a central void, but in either case, they are meant to expand or grow like a leaf or crystal, with one form opening up into another.

The Guggenheim is based on a natural form. It is designed around a spiral ramp (**fig. I-15**), which is meant to evoke a spiral shell. The structure also recalls a ceramic vase: it is closed at the bottom and open at the top, and as it rises it widens, until it is capped by a light-filled glass roof. When referring to the Guggenheim, Wright often cited an old Chinese aphorism, "The reality of the vase is the space inside," and for the most part, the exhibition space is one enormous room formed by the spiral viewing ramp. Wright wanted visitors to take the elevator to the top of the ramp, and then slowly amble down its 3 percent grade, gently pulled by gravity. Because the ramp was relatively narrow, viewers could not get too far back from the art and were forced to have an intimate relationship with it. At the same time, they could look back across the open space of the room to see where they had gone, comparing the work in front of them to a segment of the exhibition presented on a sweeping, distant arc. Or they could look ahead as well, to get a preview of where they were going. The building has a sense of continuity and mobility that Wright viewed as an organic experience, and looking down from the upper reaches of the ramp, we can see the undulation of the concave and convex forms that reflect the subtle eternal movement of nature. Wright even placed a pool on the ground floor, facing the light entering from the skylight high above.

Regardless of its size, no other museum has succeeded in creating a sense of open space and continuous movement as Wright did in the Guggenheim. Nor does any other museum have the same sense of communal spirit; at the Guggenheim everyone is united in one big room (see fig. I-15).

The Language of Art

As we have discussed, art is the visual expression of ideas. It has a message and makes statements. Like any language, it has a vocabulary. When discussing the Friedlander photograph, Wright's architecture, Hanson's sculpture, and the Copley and Warhol paintings, we actually touched on this vocabulary, because it is nearly impossible to talk about the messages in these works without describing how the artists brought them about. In the Friedlander photograph, for example, we discussed the artist's use of voids and harsh geometry, and how these devices had an impact on the way we viewed the print's presentation of modern technology. Friedlander used both representational motifs and abstract tools to tell his story. In painting, these abstract devices—line, color, composition, space, and form, for example—are also referred to as the formal qualities of the medium.

For most of the history of art, each period tends to share a similar vocabulary, or style. Each period has its own spirit, often called a *Zeitgeist*, meaning the spirit of the time, and it employs a similar language to convey a similar message.

Within this *Zeitgeist*, there are regional variations, and within the regional variations, individual styles. But most art is contained within the broad period style that makes it instantly recognizable as being of its time.

We can see how this concept of style operates by comparing Raphael's *Alba Madonna* of ca. 1510 (see fig. I-16) with Peter Paul Rubens's *Raising of the Cross* of 1610–11 (see fig. I-17), made roughly 100 years apart. The Raphael painting reflects a fifteenth- and early sixteenth-century view of Catholicism, whereas the Rubens painting supports a new, more fervent and emotional approach that characterizes the seventeenth century. The former period is called the Renaissance, the latter the Baroque. What concerns us now, however, is not the labeling, but rather the different languages and messages of the two artists.

In *Alba Madonna* (**fig. I-16**), Raphael presents us with a harmonious view of the Catholic Church, as represented by John the Baptist, the Christ Child,

I-16 Raphael. *Alba Madonna*. ca. 1510. Oil on panel, diameter 37¼″ (94 cm). National Gallery of Art, Washington, D.C. Andrew Mellon Collection. 1937.1.24

I-17 Peter Paul Rubens. *The Raising of the Cross.* 1610–11. Center panel of a triptych, oil on panel, 15′1″ × 11′9⅝″ (4.57 × 3.6 m). Antwerp Cathedral, Belgium. © KIK-IRPA, Brussels

and the Virgin Mary. The three figures are organized to form a stable pyramid with little sense of movement in this quiet scene. These sculpturesque monumental figures become frozen as they are aligned parallel to the picture plane. We can see this clearly in the crisp contour surrounding the group, but also in such passages as Christ's left arm and the Virgin's left shoulder and upper arm, as well as the outline of her headdress. Elements of the landscape follow the plane of the picture. Notice the buildings on the left, the earth immediately behind them, and the flat silhouette of the grouping of some of the trees. Despite this planarity, each figure is volumetric, that is, round and three-dimensional. Raphael draws the rounded outline of each figure, and then bathes it in a soft, dispersed light that gently models his forms, allowing shadow to make an arm or leg recede and light to pull it forward. Raphael's brushstrokes are virtually imperceptible as they create his sculpturesque forms. Everything is solid, settled, and rational in this image. Even color has its assigned place, carefully contained in discrete areas to form solid building blocks of composition. Raphael has presented the Church as the embodiment of perfection—rock solid, rational, serene, harmonious, and comforting.

Rubens's *The Raising of the Cross* (**fig. I-17**) is anything but. His image is filled with dramatic movement as well as physical and emotional intensity. His composition is based on a pyramid as well. But now it is asymmetrical and unstable, pushed off to the left, creating unstable motion and action. Instead of running parallel to the picture plane, his composition moves in and out of the space. The plunging diagonal of the figure pulling up the cross in the lower right corner and Christ slanting backward set the tone for fierce spatial dynamics. This straining figure actually seems to be falling out of the composition into our space, drawing us into the scene. In contrast, Raphael's perfect heavenly world was hermetically sealed from us earthbound sinners by his planar composition. Rubens's crowd of figures is composed of rippling muscles and undulating contours. A blast of light enters from the right, dramatically highlighting Christ's torso and flickering throughout the image, causing our eye to jump from one light area to the next. Spots of strong color scattered here and there have the same effect. Although not obvious from our reproduction, Rubens's brushwork is bold and dramatic, causing the surface of the painting to ripple and be in constant flux. Nothing in this painting sits still.

Clearly, Rubens's sense of the world is quite different from Raphael's. As you will learn when studying the Baroque period, the political, social, scientific, and religious landscape changed enormously by the seventeenth century. Consequently, the language of art changed as well, reflecting fresh ways of perceiving the physical world, an increased religious fervor, and an unprecedented opulence that accompanied the rise of powerful monarchies. Throughout this book, we will be looking at how the language of art changes from one period to the next, as artists express changing views of the world. We shall also explore regional, nationalistic, and individual variations within each of these periods.

Experiencing Art

You will be astonished when you see at first hand much of the art in this book. No matter how accurate the reproductions in this book—or any other—are, they are just stand-ins for the actual objects. We hope you will visit some of the museums where the originals are displayed. But keep in mind that looking at art, absorbing its full impact, takes time and repeated visits. Occasionally, you might do an in-depth reading of individual works. This would involve carefully perusing details and questioning why they are there. Ideally, the museum will help you understand the art. Often, there are introductory text panels that tell you why the art has been presented together, and labels for individual works provide further information. Major temporary exhibitions generally have a catalog, which adds yet another layer of interpretation. But text panels, labels, and catalogs generally reflect one person's reading of the art, and there are usually many other ways to approach or think about it.

Although the museum is an effective way to look at art and certainly the most efficient, art museums are relatively new. Indeed, before the nineteenth century, art was not made to be viewed in museums. Ultimately, art is everywhere: in galleries, corporate lobbies and offices, places of worship, and private homes. It can be found in public spaces, from subway stations and bus stops to plazas to such civic buildings as libraries, performing arts centers, and city halls. University and college buildings are often filled with art, and the buildings themselves are art. The chair you are sitting in and the house and building where you are reading this book are also works of art, maybe not great art, but art all the same, as Duchamp told us. Even the clothes you are wearing are art. And everywhere you find art, it is telling you something and making a statement.

Art is not a luxury, as many people would have us believe, but an integral part of daily life. It has a major impact on us, even when we are not aware of it; we feel better about ourselves when we are in environments that are visually enriching and exciting. Most importantly, art stimulates us to think. Even when it provokes and outrages us, it broadens our experience by making us question our values, attitudes, and worldview. This book is an introduction to this fascinating field that is so intertwined with our lives. After reading it, you will find that the world will not look the same.

The Ancient World

ART HISTORY IS MORE THAN the study of a stream of art objects created over time. It is inextricably bound to the study of history itself, that is, the recorded evidence of human events. History, it is often thought, began with the invention of writing by the civilizations of Mesopotamia and Egypt some 5,000 years ago. To be sure, without writing, the growth human beings have known over the millennia would have been impossible. However, writing seems to have developed over the course of several hundred years after these civilizations had evolved— roughly between 3300 and 3000 BCE, with Mesopotamia in the lead. Thus "history" was well under way by the time scribes began to use writing to create records.

For historians, the invention of writing is a huge landmark: the lack of written records is one of the key criteria that differentiates prehistoric from historic societies. Yet this raises some intriguing questions. First of all, how valid is the distinction between "prehistoric" and "historic"? Is it more about the state of our knowledge of the past (inasmuch as we know a great deal more about societies who wrote than those who did not) than about the past itself? Or was there a real change in the way things happened, and in the kinds of things that happened, after writing and

"history" began? Obviously, prehistory was far from uneventful. Yet the major events of prehistory, decisive as they may have been, seem to have unfolded sporadically and gradually when measured against the events of the last 5,000 years. Another criterion that defines "history," then, is a sudden acceleration in the occurrence of momentous events, a shift from low gear to high gear, as it were. There was also a change in the kinds of events that occurred. Historic societies literally make history. The challenges they face produce "great individuals and great deeds" (one definition of history) by demanding human effort on a large scale. Their achievements were memorable; that is, they were not only "worth remembering," but also capable of being grasped by human memory because they occurred within a short time-span, not over the course of centuries.

Of the vast prehistoric era we know almost nothing, until the last ice age in Europe began to recede, from about 40,000 to 8000 BCE. (At least three previous ice ages had alternated with periods of subtropical warmth, at intervals of about 25,000 years.) At the time, the climate between the Alps and Scandinavia resembled that of present-day Siberia or Alaska. Huge herds of reindeer and other

large plant-eating animals roamed the plains and valleys; the ancestors of today's lions and tigers preyed upon them, as did our own ancestors. These people lived in caves or under the shelter of overhanging rocks, as many sites bear witness, mostly in Spain and in southern France. Scholars call this phase of prehistory the Paleolithic or Old Stone Age, because human beings crafted their tools from stone. They lived in a manner that was suited to the conditions of a waning ice age, and as those conditions changed, so did their way of life.

The Paleolithic era came to a close with what is termed the Neolithic Revolution. Even though this was a period of transition that extended over several thousand years during the Mesolithic (Middle Stone) Age, it was indeed revolutionary, and ushered in the New Stone Age. It began in the "fertile crescent" of the Near East (an area covering what is now Turkey, Iraq, Iran, Jordan, Israel, Lebanon, and Syria) around 12,000–8000 BCE, with the first successful attempts to domesticate animals and cultivate food grains. Arriving later in Europe, the revolution then spread much more rapidly.

The production of a regular food supply was one of the most decisive achievements of human history, and scholars still struggle to understand why it came about. People

in Paleolithic societies had led the unsettled life of the hunter and food-gatherer, reaping wherever nature sowed. This placed them at the mercy of forces that they neither understood nor controlled. But having determined how to ensure the regular provision of food, they settled in permanent villages. The new way of life resulted in the introduction of a number of crafts, among them pottery, weaving, and spinning, as well as basic methods of construction in wood, brick, and stone. Around 4500 BCE, people in southeastern Europe developed metallurgy, in the form of copper-working. This was the beginning of the so-called Eneolithic era. Inasmuch as it involved use of intense heat, this technology grew naturally out of the technology used in pottery and thus it did not in itself constitute a major development; nor did it have an immediate impact.

The Neolithic Revolution placed human beings on a new level, where the forces of nature would not challenge them in the same ways as they had Paleolithic peoples. In a few places, however, a new threat emerged, posed not by nature but by human beings themselves. Symptomatic of that threat are the earliest Neolithic fortifications, built almost 9,000 years ago in the Near East. What fueled the conflict that made these defenses necessary is

uncertain; perhaps it was competition for grazing land among groups of herders or for arable soil among farming communities. Perhaps, in fact, the Neolithic Revolution had been too successful, and allowed population groups to grow beyond their available food supplies. A number of solutions might have eased this problem. Constant warfare could have checked the population, or the people could have united in larger and more structured social units bound by ambitious goals — such as building fortifications — that a loosely organized society would struggle to achieve on its own.

We do not know the outcome of the tensions in the region, though future excavations may reveal how far the urbanizing process extended. About 3,000 years later, similar conflicts, on a larger scale, arose in the Nile Valley and again in the plains of the Tigris and Euphrates rivers, and forced people in these regions to abandon Neolithic village life. Thus emerged the first civilizations. The word civilization derives from the Latin term for something pertaining to a city, *civilis*, and to be civilized means to live as a citizen, to be a city dweller. These new societies organized themselves into much larger units — cities and city-states — that were far more complex and efficient than ever

before. First in Mesopotamia and Egypt, somewhat later in neighboring areas, and in the Indus Valley and along the Yellow River in China, people would henceforth live in a more dynamic world. Their ability to survive was challenged less by the forces of nature than by human forces: by tensions and conflicts arising either within or between societies. The problems and pressures faced by historic societies thus are very different from those faced by peoples in the Paleolithic and Neolithic eras, and through the centuries, efforts to cope with them have proved to be a far greater challenge than the earlier struggle with nature.

These momentous changes also spurred the development of new technologies in what scholars term the Bronze Age and the Iron Age, which, like the Neolithic Age, are stages rather than distinct eras. People first began to cast bronze, an alloy of copper and tin, in the Near East around 3500 BCE, at the same time that the earliest cities arose there and in Egypt. The smelting and forging of iron were invented about 2000–1500 BCE by the Hittites, an Indo-European-speaking people who settled in Cappadocia (now east central Turkey), a high plateau with abundant copper and iron ore. Indeed, competition for mineral resources helped to incite the conflicts that beset civilizations throughout the world.

Atlantic
Ocean

North
Sea

IRELAND

ENGLAND

Stonehenge ○ Thames R.

N

BRITTANY

Seine R.
Trier
EUROPE
FRANCE
Loire R.

Rhine R.

Hohlenstein-Stadel
GERMANY

Vistula R.

Dnieper R.

Lake Constance
Willendorf

DORDOGNE
Lascaux
Altamira
Pech-Merle
Rhône R.
Chauvet

Po R.
Venice

DACIA

BALKANS

Danube R.
Cernavoda

Segovia ○
SPAIN

ITALY
Florence
Arno R.
Arezzo
Vulci
Tarquinia
Veii
Cerveteri
Rome
Primaporta
Praeneste
Naples
Mt. Vesuvius
Ischia
Herculaneum
Pompeii
Paestum

Tiber R.

Adriatic Sea

MACEDONI
Mt. Olympus
Vergina

Byzantium
(Constantinople) ○

Samothrace
Troy
Pergamon

GREECE
Lemnos

LYDIA

Tyrrhenian Sea

Corfu
Actium ○
Mt. Parnassus ▲

Aegean Sea

IONIA

Tral

Sicily ▲
Mt. Etna

Ionian
Sea

Athens

Rhod

Mediterranean

Carthage ○

Crete

See inset

Sea

NORTH AFRICA

LIBYA

LIBYAN DESER

The Roman Empire
at the time of Hadrian

500 km

500 miles

Inset map:

Aegean
Sea

LYDIA

Mt. Parnassus ▲
Delphi ○

Chios

IONIA

Olympia ○
Corinth
Mycenae
ATTICA
Salamis Athens
PELOPONNESUS
Aegina
Cyclades

Samos
Ephesos
Priene
Miletus
Didyma
Halikarnassos

Delos
Paros
Naxos
Amorgos
Knidos

Thera
(Santorini) Akrotiri
Siphnos

Mediterranean
Sea

Crete
Heraklion
Mt. Ida ▲
Knossos
Mallia

Phaistos

100 km

100 miles

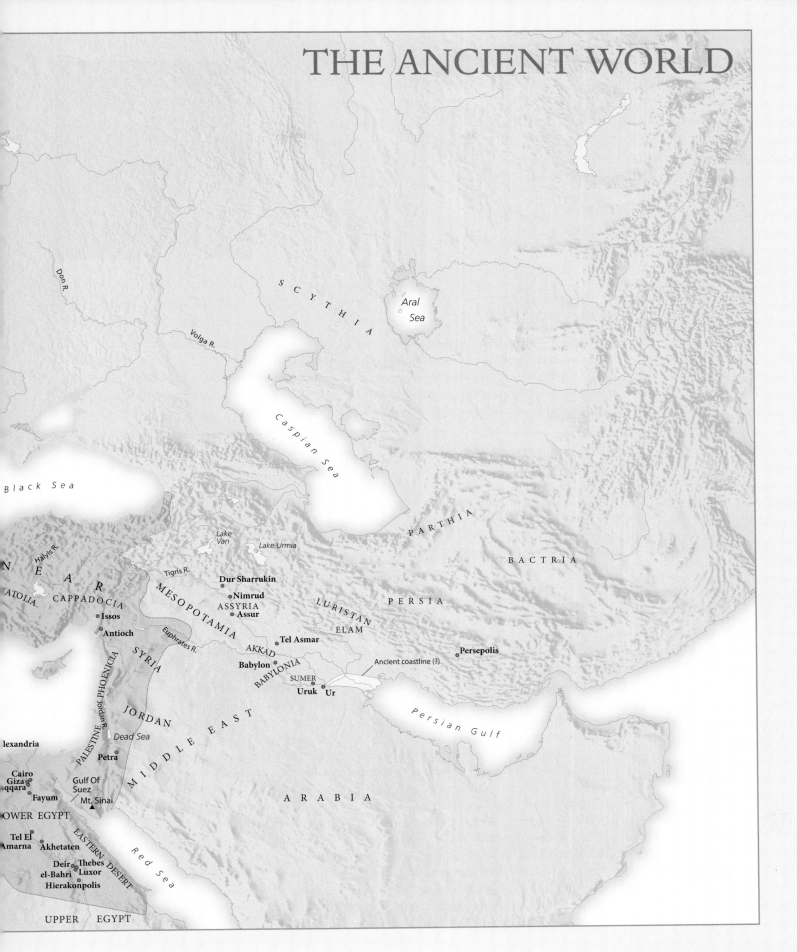

THE ANCIENT WORLD

Don R.

Volga R.

SCYTHIA

Aral
Sea

Caspian Sea

Black Sea

PARTHIA

BACTRIA

Lake
Van

Lake Urmia

Halys R.

Tigris R.

Dur Sharrukin

●Nimrud

ASSYRIA

●Assur

LURISTAN

PERSIA

ATOLIA

CAPPADOCIA

MESOPOTAMIA

ELAM

●Issos

Euphrates R.

●Antioch

AKKAD

●Tel Asmar

●Persepolis

SYRIA

PHOENICIA

Babylon●

BABYLONIA

Ancient coastline (?)

SUMER

Jordan R.

Uruk● ●Ur

JORDAN

PALESTINE

MIDDLE EAST

Persian Gulf

Dead Sea

lexandria

●Petra

Cairo
Giza●
qqara

Gulf Of
Suez

●Fayum

Mt. Sinai▲

ARABIA

OWER EGYPT

Tel El
Amarna

●Akhetaten

EASTERN DESERT

Deir ●Thebes
el-Bahri ●Luxor

Red Sea

Hierakonpolis

UPPER   EGYPT

1 Prehistoric Art

POINTS OF INQUIRY

1.1 Explore the reasons why humans first started making art in prehistoric times.

1.2 Assess the significance of cave paintings to early humans.

1.3 Consider the ways in which sculptural works functioned in Paleolithic and Neolithic life.

1.4 Investigate the developments in architecture from Paleolithic to Neolithic times and the social changes that accompanied them.

((•─Listen to the chapter audio on myartslab.com

Major Events in Prehistory

ca. 2,000,000 BCE	Earliest known tool making
ca. 70,000–8000 BCE	Last ice age in Europe
ca. 40,000–8000 BCE	Old Stone (Paleolithic) Age
ca. 40,000 BCE	Earliest known stone figures in Europe
ca. 28,000 BCE	Earliest known cave paintings
ca. 8000–2300 BCE	New Stone (Neolithic) Age
ca. 8000–1000 BCE	Plants and animals domesticated
ca. 4500–1500 BCE	Megalithic tombs and monuments
ca. 3300–3000 BCE	Earliest writing developed
ca. 3000–1000 BCE	Bronze Age

When modern humans first encountered pre-historic cave paintings in the 1870s, they could not believe the evidence of their own eyes. Although the evidence indicated that the site at Altamira in Spain dated to around 13,000 BCE, the paintings found there had been executed with such skill and sensitivity that historians initially considered them forgeries (see fig. 1.1). Since then, some 200 similar sites have been found throughout the world. As recently as 1994, the discovery of a cave in southeastern France (see fig. 1.2) brought hundreds more paintings to light, pushing back the date of the first prehistoric paintings even further, to approximately 30,000 BCE. Carved objects have been discovered that are equally old.

These earliest forms of art raise more questions than they answer. Why did prehistoric humans expend time and energy to make art? What functions did these visual representations serve? What do the images mean? Art historians often use contemporaneous written texts to supplement their understandings of art; yet prehistoric art dates to a time before writing, for which works of art are among our only evidence. Art historians deploy scientific and anthropological tools in their attempts to interpret them. With new finds being reported with regularity, the study of prehistoric art continues to develop and refine its interpretations and conclusions.

Though fully modern humans have lived on the Earth for over 100,000 years, the dates assigned to the earliest objects classed as "art" go back about 40,000 years; earlier humans crafted tools from stone and bone, but what inspired them to make detailed representations of forms found in nature? The skill with which the earliest objects were executed may have been the product of a lost period of experimentation in carving and painting techniques, making the practice of art much older than the surviving objects. Yet it has also been proposed that image making and symbolic language result from a new brain structure associated with *Homo sapiens sapiens*, when a sudden neurological mutation opened up the capacity for abstract thought. Indeed, art emerges at about the time that fully modern humans moved from Africa into Europe, Asia, and Australia, encountering—and eventually displacing—the earlier Neanderthals (*Homo neanderthalensis*). Tens of thousands of works survive from this time before history, most of which were discovered in Europe. Many are breathtakingly accomplished. Whatever led to the ability to create art, its impact on the emergence of human culture was enormous, and these prehistoric works force us to reevaluate many of our assumptions about art and the creative process.

Paleolithic Art

For the era before the written word (prehistory), historians use the activity of toolmaking as the defining feature for measuring human time. They divide the broad span of prehistory into the Paleolithic or Old Stone Age (from the Greek *palaio-*, meaning "ancient," and *lithos*, "stone"), the Mesolithic or Middle (*meso-*) Stone Age, and the Neolithic or New (*neo-*) Stone Age. The Paleolithic era spans from two million years ago to about 10,000 BCE. Within this range, scholars describe the oldest material as belonging to the Lower Paleolithic (ending about 100,000 years ago), since it lies at the lowest layer of an excavation. The Middle Paleolithic era dates from 100,000 years

ago to about 40,000 years ago, and the most recent layers reveal the Upper Paleolithic (about 40,000 BCE to around 10,000 BCE). It is in the Upper Paleolithic that the earliest works of art emerged, over a wide swath of Eurasia, Africa, and Australia (see **map 1.1**). This period falls in the Pleistocene era, also known as the Ice Age, when glaciers covered much of the northern hemisphere.

Prehistoric paintings first came to light in 1878 in a cave named Altamira, in Santillana del Mar in northern Spain. Accompanying her father, Count Don Marcelino Sanz de Sautuola, as he scoured the ground for flints and animal bones, 12-year-old Maria spied bison painted on the ceiling (**fig. 1.1**). There, and in other more recently discovered caves, painted and engraved images depict mainly animals. The greatest variety known is in the vast cave complex of Chauvet, near Vallon-Pont-d'Arc in southeastern France. Here the 427 animal representations found to date depict 17 species, including lions, bears, and aurochs (prehistoric oxen), in black

This 30,000-year-old image of an owl in the Chauvet Cave was made by pressing a flat-ended tool into the soft limestone surface of the cave wall, a process called **incising**. Most prehistoric incising produced chiseled lines that are narrower than those of this owl, but the process is the same.

Map 1.1
Prehistoric Europe

1.1 The Great Ceiling including *Wounded Bison.* ca. 15,000–10,000 BCE. Black manganese outlines with red ocher and shading on limestone. Altamira, Spain

or red outlines (**fig. 1.2**), sometimes **polychromatic** (containing several colors). In rare instances, images depict human or partly human forms.

On first assessing the Altamira paintings, experts declared them too advanced to be authentic and dismissed them as a hoax. Indeed, though cave art may represent the dawn of art as we know it, it is often highly sophisticated. The bison of Altamira and other sites were painted from memory, and their forms demonstrate the painters' acute powers of observation and skill in translating memory into image. Standing at rest, bellowing, or rolling on the ground, bison behave in these paintings as they do in the wild. Shading (**modeling**) expresses the volume of a bison's belly, and the forward contour of an animal's far leg is often rendered with a lighter hue to suggest distance.

Initially, cave paintings were assigned relative dates according to their degree of **naturalism**, that is, how closely the image resembled the subject in nature. Since naturalism was then considered the most advanced form of representation, the more naturalistic the image, the more evolved and, therefore, the more recent it was considered to be. Radiocarbon dating, developed in the mid-twentieth century, exposed flaws in this approach. Remarkable for their naturalism, some of the paintings at Chauvet might appear to be more recent in the overall sequence, yet radiocarbon dating proved them to be among the earliest known, dating to about 32,000 years ago. Indeed, it is a mistake to assume that naturalism was a Paleolithic artist's—or any artist's—inevitable or only goal.

Interpreting Prehistoric Painting

As majestic as these paintings can be, they are also profoundly enigmatic. What purpose did they serve? The simplest view, that they were merely decorative—"art for art's sake"—is highly unlikely. Most of the existing paintings and engravings are readily accessible, and many more that embellished caves opening directly to the outside have probably perished. But some, as in the cave complex at Lascaux, in the Dordogne region of France, and elsewhere, lie deep inside extensive cave systems, remote from habitation and difficult to reach (**fig. 1.3**). In these cases, the image's power may have resided in its making, rather than in its viewing: the act of creating it may have served some ritual or religious purpose.

Approaches developed by ethnographers (anthropologists who study cultural behavior) were also adopted to interpret cave paintings and engravings. Most often, the inspiration for these works was attributed to magico-religious motives. Thus early humans may have equated an image with

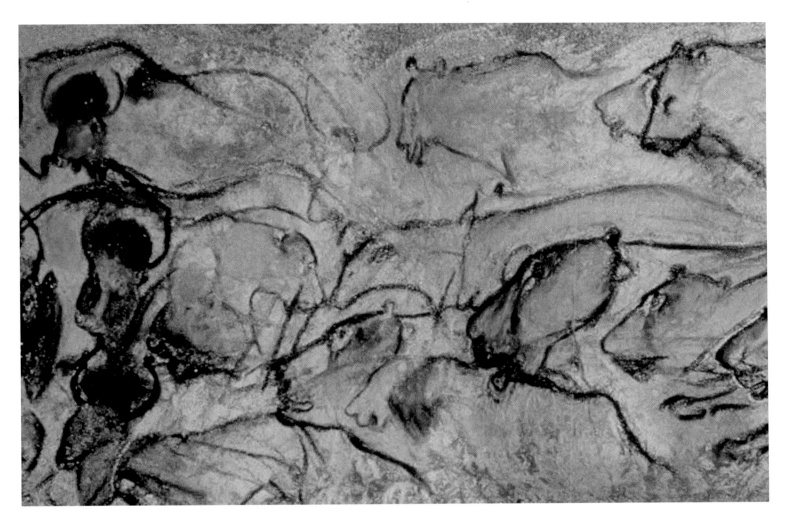

the animal it represented; to create or possess the image was to exert power over its subject, which might result in a successful hunt. Gouge marks on cave walls indicate that in some cases spears were cast at the images. Similarly, artists may have hoped to stimulate fertility in the wild—ensuring a continuous food supply—by depicting pregnant animals. A magico-religious interpretation might explain the choice to make animals appear lifelike, and to control them by fixing them within outlines.

1.2 *Lions and Bison.* ca. 30,000–28,000 BCE. Limestone End Chamber, Chauvet Cave. Vallon-Pont-d'Arc, Ardèche Gorge, France

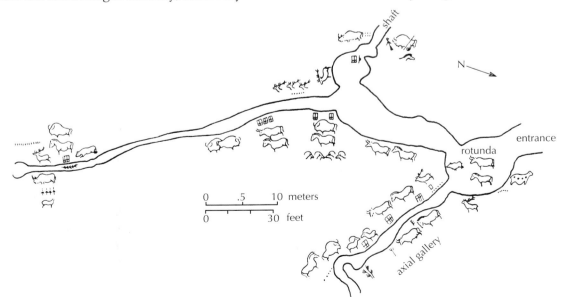

1.3 Schematic plan of Lascaux Cave system (based on a diagram by the Service de l'Architecture, Paris)

 Watch a video about the cave painting at Lascaux Cave on myartslab.com

1.4 *Spotted Horses and Human Hands.* Horses ca. 16,000 BCE; hands ca. 15,000 BCE. Limestone, approximate length 11′2″ (3.4 m). Pech-Merle Cave. Dordogne, France

The earliest Upper Paleolithic art dates to the Aurignacian period (34,000–23,000 BCE). Among the best-known works of the subsequent GRAVETTIAN period (28,000–22,000 BCE) are carved female statuettes such as the *Woman of Willendorf* (see fig. 1.6); some 130 of these have been found over a vast area from France to Siberia. The zenith of prehistoric art was reached during the Magdalenian era (18,000–10,000 BCE), the last period of the Upper Paleolithic. Its masterpieces are the magnificent cave paintings of animals in the Dordogne region of France, in the Pyrenees Mountains, and at Altamira in Spain.

More recent theories concerning shamanism—a belief in a parallel spirit world accessed through alternative states of consciousness—build upon these interpretations, arguing that an animal's "spirit" was evident where a bulge in the rock suggested its shape, as with the *Spotted Horses* (**fig. 1.4**) at Pech-Merle in southwestern France. The artist's or shaman's power brought that spirit to the surface. Some experts have cast the paintings as images for worship; others focus on a painting's physical context. This means examining relationships between figures to determine, in the absence of an artificial frame, a ground-line or a landscape, whether multiple animal images signify individual specimens or a herd, and whether these images represent a mythical past for early communities. It also means recognizing that a cave 15 feet deep is a different space from another over a mile deep, and was possibly used for different purposes, and that paintings in different spaces may have functioned differently. It means factoring in experiential aspects of caves: a precarious path, eerie flickering lights, echoes, and the musty smells that permeate subterranean spaces, all added texture to the viewing process. Most important, recent interpretations acknowledge that one explanation may not suffice across all time and place. For instance, even if sympathetic magic makes sense of some paintings, it

hardly explains those at Chauvet, where 72 percent of the animals represented were not hunted, judging by organic remains found in the cave.

Paleolithic Carving

Prehistoric artists also carved and modeled sculptures, in a variety of materials. At just under 1 foot high, a figure from Hohlenstein-Stadel in Germany (**fig. 1.5**) represents a standing creature, half human and half feline, crafted out of ivory. Although it is in a poor state of preservation, it is clear that the creation of this figure, with rudimentary stone tools, was an arduous business. It involved splitting the dried mammoth tusk, scraping it into shape, and using a sharp flint blade to incise such features as the striations on the arm and the muzzle. Strenuous polishing followed, using powdered hematite (an iron ore) as an abrasive. Exactly what the figure represents is unclear: perhaps a human dressed as an animal, possibly for hunting purposes. Some prehistorians have named these composite creatures shamans or "sorcerers," who could contact the spirit world through ritualistic behavior.

Women were frequent subjects in prehistoric sculpture, especially in the GRAVETTIAN period, when they far outnumbered men as subject material. Discovered in 1908, the hand-sized limestone carving of the *Woman of Willendorf* from Austria

dates from about 28,000–25,000 BCE (**fig. 1.6**), and still bears traces of ocher rubbed onto the surface. The artist reduced the female form to basic, abstract shapes instead of rendering it with the naturalism found in the representations of animals. Facial features are not a priority: Schematically rendered hair covers the entire head. Instead, emphasis rests on the figure's reproductive qualities: Diminutive arms sit on pendulous breasts, whose rounded forms are echoed in the bulging belly and copious buttocks. Genitalia are shown between large thighs.

The terminology applied to figures like the *Woman of Willendorf* in the past has complicated our interpretations of them. At the time of their first discovery in the mid-nineteenth century, they were named "Venus" figures after the Roman goddess of love, whom ancient sculptors portrayed as a nude female; nineteenth-century archaeologists believed the prehistoric figures to be similar to the Roman goddess, in function if not in form. Contemporary experts are still debating their meaning,

1.6 *Woman of Willendorf.* ca. 28,000–25,000 BCE. Limestone, height 4⅜" (11.1 cm). Naturhistorisches Museum, Vienna

1.5 Hybrid figure with a human body and feline head, from Hohlenstein-Stadel (Baden-Württemberg), Germany. ca. 35,000 BCE. Mammoth ivory, height 11⅔" (29.6 cm). Ulmer Museum

and avoid such anachronisms in terminology. The emphasis on reproductive features suggests that she may have been a fertility object, or was perhaps intended to ensure a successful birth rather than an increase in the number of pregnancies. According to one feminist view, the apparently distorted forms of figures like this reflect a woman's view of her own body as she looks down at it. If so, some of the figures may have served as obstetric aids, documenting stages of pregnancy to educate women toward healthy births. This may indicate that some of the artists were women.

Paleolithic Dwellings

In the Paleolithic period, people generally built huts and used caves for shelter and ritual purposes. In rare cases, traces of dwellings survive. At Mezhirich, in the Ukraine, a farmer discovered a series of oval dwellings with central hearths, dating to between 16,000 and 10,000 BCE (**fig. 1.7**), constructed out of mammoth bones: interlocked pelvis bones, jawbones, and shoulder blades provided a framework, and tusks were set across the top. Animal hides probably covered the frame. Archaeological evidence shows that inside these huts the inhabitants engaged in cold-weather occupations such as preparing foods, manufacturing tools, and processing skins, which suggests that the structures were seasonal residences for mobile groups.

Neolithic Art

Around 10,000 BCE, the climate began to warm, and the ice that had covered almost a third of the globe started to recede, leaving Europe with more or less the geography it has today. New vegetation and changing animal populations caused human habits

1.7 House at Mezhirich, Ukraine. ca. 16,000–10,000 BCE. Mammoth bone. National History Museum, Kiev

1.8 Female and male figures, from Cernavoda, Romania. ca. 3500 BCE. Ceramic, height 4½″ (11.5 cm). National Museum of Antiquities, Bucharest

to mutate. In the Neolithic period, or New Stone Age, people began to build more substantial structures than before, choosing settlement places for favorable qualities, such as a water supply, rather than moving seasonally. Instead of hunting and gathering what nature supplied, they domesticated animals and plants. This gradual change occurred at different times across the world; in some places, hunting and gathering are still the way of life.

Settled Societies and Neolithic Art

During the Neolithic period, technologies developed that suggest the beginnings of specialization. As the community could depend on a regular food supply, some members could devote time to acquiring special skills, including oven-fired pottery, weaving, and smelting of copper and lead.

In Europe, artists fashioned clay figurines, such as a woman and man from Cernavoda in Romania, of about 3500 BCE (**fig. 1.8**). Like the *Woman of Willendorf*, they are highly abstract, yet their forms are more linear than rounded: The woman's face is a flattened oval poised on a long, thick neck, and sharp edges articulate her corporeality—across her breasts, for instance, and at the fold of her pelvis.

Elbowless arms meet where her hands rest on her raised knee, delineating a triangle and enclosing space within the sculptural form. This emphasizes the figurine's three-dimensionality, encouraging a viewer to look at it from several angles, moving around it or shifting it in the hand. The abstraction highlights the pose; yet, tempting as it may be to interpret it, perhaps as coquettishness, we should be cautious about reading meaning into it, since gestures can have dramatically different meanings from one culture to another. Found in a tomb, the couple may represent the deceased, or mourners; perhaps they were gifts that had a separate purpose before burial.

Architecture: Tombs and Rituals

Neolithic dwellings were mostly framed in wood, with walls of wattle (branches woven into a frame) and daub (mud or earth), and roofs of thatch, which rarely survive. In western and northern Europe, concerns about ceremonial burial and ritual inspired monumental architecture, using huge blocks of stone known as MEGALITHS. They were usually mounted in a **post-and-lintel** arrangement (two upright stones supporting a horizontal capstone).

MEGALITHS: Generally undressed or rough-hewn stones, menhirs are often found on hilltops from southern France to Scotland and are particularly common in Brittany, in northwestern France. Dolmens, the simplest form of megalithic tomb, have several large upright stones supporting a single massive capstone. About 50,000 of these survive from Spain to Sweden. There has been much debate about how the 30- to 40-ton capstones were placed atop the standing stones.

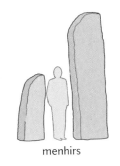

menhirs

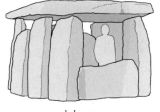

dolmen

1.9 Stonehenge (aerial view). ca. 2400 BCE. Diameter of circle 97′ (29.6 m). Salisbury Plain, Wiltshire, England

 View the Closer Look for Stonehenge on myartslab.com

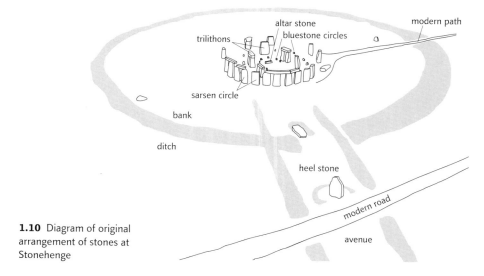

1.10 Diagram of original arrangement of stones at Stonehenge

Often, megaliths appear in circles, called cromlechs. The best-known megalithic structure is Stonehenge, on the Salisbury Plain in southern England (**figs. 1.9** and **1.10**). Its seemingly unified design is in fact the result of several construction phases, possibly beginning as early as 3000 BCE. At an early stage, a huge ditch was excavated, defining a circle some 360 feet in diameter in the white chalk ground, and an embankment over 6 feet high running around the inside. A wide stone-lined avenue led from the circle to a pointed gray sandstone (sarsen) megalith, known today as the Heel Stone. By about 2400 BCE, Stonehenge had grown into a horseshoe-shaped arrangement of five sarsen triliths (two upright stones supporting a third, horizontal one), encircled by a ring of upright blocks capped with a lintel; between the rings was a circle of smaller bluestone blocks. The entrance matched the direction of the midsummer sunrise and midwinter sunset. Recent excavations exposed remains of a similar monument built of timber two miles away, with its entrance set to mirror the midsummer sunset and the midwinter sunrise. Archaeologists believe the structures are related.

What Stonehenge—and its counterpart—signified to those who constructed them remains a tantalizing mystery. Excavations exposed burials on the site in its earliest phases, and many prehistorians believe that Stonehenge marked the passing of time. Given its monumentality, most also concur that it had a ritual function; its circular arrangement supports this conjecture, as circles are central to rituals in many societies. What is certain is that it represents tremendous manpower organization and engineering skill. The largest trilith soars 24 feet, supporting a lintel 15 feet long and 3 feet thick. A recent theory holds that the stones were not brought from afar as previously thought but from a glacial deposit nearby; still, the sarsen blocks weigh up to 50 tons apiece. The blocks reveal evidence of meticulous stone-working. Holes hollowed out of the capstones fit snugly over projections on the uprights (forming a **mortise and tenon joint**), to make a stable structure. Moreover, upright megaliths taper upward, with a central bulge, visually implying the weight they bear, and capturing an energy that enlivens the stones. The lintels are worked in two directions, their faces inclining outward by about 6 inches to appear vertical from the ground, while at the same time they curve around on the horizontal plane to make a smooth circle. This kind of refinement is usually associated with the Parthenon of Classical Athens (see fig. 5.16).

POINTS OF REFLECTION

1.1 Scholars offer a number of possible explanations for the initial development of art. Assess the relative merits of their views.

1.2 Describe the possible functions of images of animals and humans in Paleolithic cave paintings. What are the factors that complicate our understanding of their purpose?

1.3 Analyze scholars' interpretations of the Woman of Willendorf.

1.4 Describe the formal and functional differences between Paleolithic and Neolithic buildings. What prompted the construction of Neolithic monumental structures such as Stonehenge?

✔ **Study** and review on myartslab.com

ART IN TIME

● ca. 38,000 BCE—Production of the earliest objects classed as "art"

● ca. 30,000–28,000 BCE—Lions and bison at Chauvet Cave

● ca. 28,000–25,000 BCE—*Woman of Willendorf*

● ca. 16,000 BCE—**Spotted horses and human hands at Pech-Merle Cave**

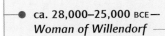

● ca. 10,000 BCE—Earth's climate gradually begins to warm

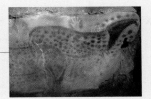

● ca. 3500 BCE—Pottery manufacturing appears in Western Europe

● ca. 3500 BCE—**Female and male figures from Cernavoda**

● ca. 2400 BCE—**Final major phase of construction at Stonehenge**

CHAPTER 2
Ancient Near Eastern Art

POINTS OF INQUIRY

2.1 Understand the intersection between art and political power in the ancient Near East.
2.2 Examine the role of art and architecture in ancient Near Eastern religion.
2.3 Compare the different narrative techniques explored by ancient Near Eastern artists.
2.4 Investigate the use of art and architecture as an expression of empire.

((•— **Listen** to the chapter audio on myartslab.com

CUNEIFORM characters were made by pressing a stylus into damp clay. Usually fashioned from a reed, the stylus was shaped on both ends. One end was wedge-shaped; the other was pointed, rounded, or flat-tipped. Scribes used the pointed end to draw lines and make punch marks. The tablets were then sun-dried or baked.

stylus

Growing and storing crops and raising animals for food, the signature accomplishments of Neolithic peoples, would gradually change the course of civilization. In the fourth millennium BCE, large-scale urban communities of as many as 40,000 people began to emerge in MESOPOTAMIA, the land between the Tigris and the Euphrates rivers. The establishment of cities had tremendous ramifications for the development of human life and for works of art.

Written, archaeological, and artistic evidence indicates that at the dawn of civilization lush vegetation covered Mesopotamia. By mastering irrigation techniques, populations there exploited the rivers and their tributaries to enrich the fertile soil even further. New technologies, including the wheel and the plow, and the casting of tools in copper and bronze, increased food production and facilitated trade. As communities flourished, they grew into city-states with distinct patterns of social organization. Specialization of labor and trade, and the mechanisms for resolving disputes, all required a central authority and government. The administration that developed in response to these needs probably generated what may have been the earliest writing system, known as CUNEIFORM. This system served for accounting, and for the Sumerian

Epic of Gilgamesh in the late third millennium BCE. With the invention of writing, we enter the realm of history.

The geography of Mesopotamia had other profound effects on developing civilizations. Unlike the narrow, fertile strip of the Nile Valley, protected by deserts on either side, where urban communities now also began to thrive, Mesopotamia is a wide trough with few natural defenses. People constantly traversed the region hoping to exploit its fertility. Indeed, throughout the history of the ancient Near East, city-states were regularly warring with one another and were only sometimes united under a single ruler. Still, Mesopotamian visual culture retains a surprisingly constant character. Two important uses of art emerge: To enable and reflect political power; and to explore strategies for telling stories in visual narratives.

Sumerian Art

The first major civilization in Mesopotamia was in the southern region of Sumer, near the junction of the Tigris and Euphrates rivers, where several city-states flourished from before 4000 BCE (see **map 2.1**) until about 2340 BCE. Who the Sumerians were

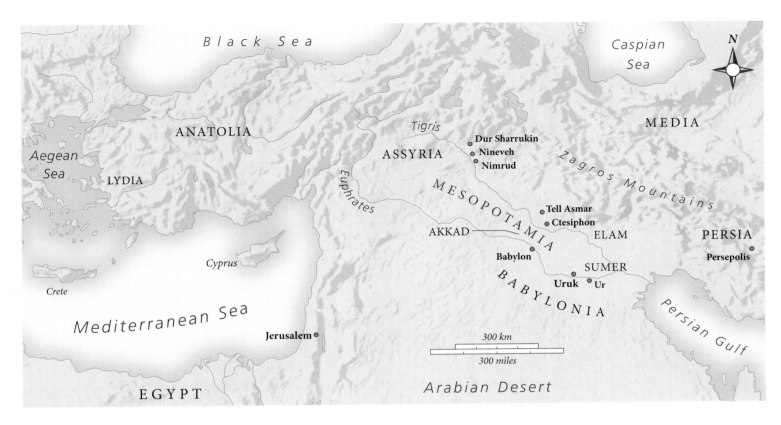

Map 2.1 The Ancient Near East

is not clear, as their language is not related to any other known tongue. Along with architecture and writing, works of art in the form of sculpture, relief, and pottery inform us about Sumerian society.

For this people, life itself depended on appeasing the gods, who controlled natural forces and phenomena such as weather and water, the fertility of the land, and the heavenly bodies. Each city had a patron deity, to whom residents owed devotion and sustenance. The god's earthly steward was the city's ruler, who directed an administrative staff based in the temple. As the produce of the city's land belonged to the god, the staff took charge of supplying farmers with seed, work animals, and tools. They built irrigation systems, and stored and distributed the harvest. Centralized food production meant that much of the population could specialize in other trades, donating a portion of the fruits of their labor to the temple. This system is known as theocratic socialism.

Temple Architecture: Linking Heaven and Earth

The temple was the city's architectural focus. Good stone being scarce, Sumerians built predominantly with mud brick, covered with plaster. Their temples stood either at ground level or raised on a platform, which was gradually transformed into a squat, stepped structure known as a **ziggurat**. The names of some ziggurats—such as Babylon's Etemenanki ("House temple, bond between heaven and earth")—suggest that they were links or portals to the heavens, where priest and god could commune. Ziggurats functioned as the equivalents of mountains, which held a sacred status for Sumerians. A source of water, mountains were also a refuge during floods, and symbolized the Earth's generative power. Significantly, raised platforms made temples more visible. Mesopotamian texts indicate that the act of seeing was paramount: In seeing an object and finding it pleasing, a god might act favorably toward those who made it. The desired response of a human audience, in turn, was wonder. Finally, there was probably a political dimension to the platform: It emphasized and maintained the priests' status by expressing their separation from the rest of the community.

Around 3500 BCE, the city of Uruk (present-day Warka and biblical Erech) emerged as a center of Sumerian culture, flourishing from trade in its agricultural surplus. One of its temples, the "White Temple," named for its whitewashed brick surfaces, probably honored the sky god Anu, chief of the Sumerian gods. It sits on a 40-foot mound constructed by filling in the ruins of older temples with brickwork, which suggests that the site itself was

Apparently independent of one another, the earliest civilizations arose along four great rivers during the fourth millennium vwB Egyptian civilization emerged in the northeast corner of the continent of Africa, nourished by the Nile River. MESOPOTAMIA is the area encompassed by present-day Iraq and its immediate neighbors, watered by the Tigris and Euphrates rivers. In roughly what is Pakistan today, drained by the Indus River, were the Indus Valley or Harappa civilizations, and in west central China, civilizations arose along the Yellow River.

2.1 Plan of the "White Temple," Uruk (Warka), Iraq (drawing after H. Frankfort)

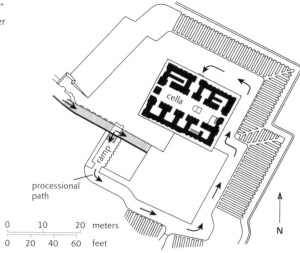

cella

ramp

processional path

0   10   20 meters

0 20 40 60 feet

N

2.2 Statues from the Abu Temple, Tell Asmar, Iraq. ca. 2700–2500 BCE. Limestone, gypsum, shell, and bitumen, height of tallest figure approx. 30″ (76.3 cm). Once in Iraq Museum, Baghdad (now unaccounted for), and the Oriental Institute Museum of the University of Chicago

ascent into a divine realm. From three sides, members of the community could also witness the ceremonial ascent of priests and leaders who had exclusive access to the temple. Enough survives of the superstructure to indicate that thick buttressed walls surrounded a rectangular hall (a **cella**) housing a stepped altar. Along the long sides of the cella, smaller rooms served as offices, priests' quarters, and storage areas, creating an overall tripartite layout typical of the earliest temples.

Sculpture

Within these temples, Sumerians often displayed sculptures to represent deities or worshipers.

sacred (**figs. 2.1**). Recessed brickwork articulated its sloped sides. A system of stairs and ramps led counterclockwise around the mound, culminating at an entrance in the temple's long north side. This indirect approach is a characteristic feature of Mesopotamian temple architecture (in contrast to the direct axial approach favored in Egypt), and the winding ascent mirrored a visitor's metaphorical

TELL ASMAR A group of limestone, alabaster, and gypsum figures was excavated in the 1930s at a temple at Tell Asmar (**fig. 2.2**). Ranging in height from several inches to 2½ feet high, these figures probably originally stood in the temple's cella. They were purposely buried near the altar along with other objects, perhaps when the temple was rebuilt or redecorated. All but one of the figures stand in a static pose, with hands clasped between chest and waist level. The style is decidedly abstract: On

most of the standing male figures, horizontal or zigzag ridges define long hair and a full beard; the arms hang from wide shoulders; hands are clasped around a cup; narrow chests widen to broad waists; and the legs are cylindrical. The male figures wear fringed skirts hanging from a belt in a stiff cone shape, while the women have full-length drapery. Their identities are controversial: The two larger figures are usually identified as cult statues of Abu, god of vegetation, and his consort. The other figures probably represent priests, since the fringed skirt is the dress of the priesthood. Similar statues from elsewhere in the region are even inscribed with the names of the dedicator and the god.

The poses and the costumes of these figures represent conventions of Sumerian art that later Mesopotamians adopted. Most distinctive are the faces, dominated by wide, almost round eyes, accentuated by dark inlays of lapis lazuli and shells set in bitumen, a tarry material used as an adhesive and by powerful eyebrows meeting over the bridge of the nose. Surviving texts imply that seeing was a major channel of communication with gods, and that the sculptures were responding to the gods' awe-inspiring nature with eyes wide open in admiration. Enlarged eyes were also a conventional means of warding off evil in Mesopotamia; this is known today as an apotropaic device.

THE ROYAL CEMETERY AT UR   At the Sumerian city of Ur (the present-day Muqaiyir and the birthplace of Abraham) in southern Mesopotamia, an extensive cemetery is preserved under the walls of Nebuchadnezzar II's later city. The cemetery contained some 1,840 burials dating between 2600 and 2000 BCE. Some were humble, but others were substantial subterranean structures that contained magnificent offerings, earning them the designation of "royal graves," even though scholars remain uncertain whether the deceased were royalty, priests, or members of another elite.

Visual Narratives

The so-called *Royal Standard of Ur*, of about 2600 BCE, found within the Royal Cemetery, offers a glimpse of the early development of visual narrative in Mesopotamia. It consists of four panels of red limestone, shell, and lapis lazuli inlay set in bitumen, originally attached to a wooden framework (**fig. 2.3**). The two principal sections show a military victory and a celebration or ritual feast, each unfolding in three superposed **registers**. Reading from the bottom,

the "war" panel shows charioteers pulled by onagers (wild asses), riding over enemy bodies. In the middle register, infantry troops engage in battle and escort denuded prisoners of war. At the top, soldiers present the prisoners to a figure whose importance the artist signals through his central position and through his larger size, a device known as **hieratic scale**; his head even breaks through the register's frame. In the "banquet" panel, figures burdened with booty accompany onagers and, in the center, animals for a feast, which is already under way in the top register. Seated figures raise cups to the sound of music from a nearby harpist and singer; a larger figure toward the left of the scene is presumably a leader or king, perhaps the same figure as on the "war" side. Thus the panels tell a story, unfolding moment by moment as the eye follows the registers, guided by the figures' motion. Together, they represent the dual aspects of kingship: the king as warrior, and the king as priest and mediator with the gods. Despite the action, the images have a static quality, emphasized by the figures' isolation; their descriptive forms (half frontal, half profile) rarely overlap. This gives the narrative an easy legibility, even from a distance. On excavating the object in the 1920s, the archaeologist Leonard Woolley envisioned it held aloft on a pole as a military standard, and named it accordingly. In fact, it is unclear how it was used; it may have been the sounding-box for a stringed instrument, an object that was commonly found in burials.

Art of Akkad

Around 2350 BCE, Sumerian city-states began to fight over access to water and fertile land. Gradually their social organization was transformed, as local "stewards of the god" positioned themselves as ruling kings. The more ambitious tried to enlarge their domains through conquest. In many places, Semitic-speaking peoples from the northern region gradually assumed positions of power in the south. Although they adopted many features of Sumerian civilization, they were less bound to the tradition of the city-state. Sargon (meaning "true king") conquered Sumer, northern Syria, and Elam (northeast of Sumer), in about 2334 BCE (see map 2.1), basing himself in the city of Akkad (probably northwest of Sumer, near modern Baghdad). Sargon's ambitions were both imperial and dynastic; his goal was to unite the region in loyalty to his absolute rule.

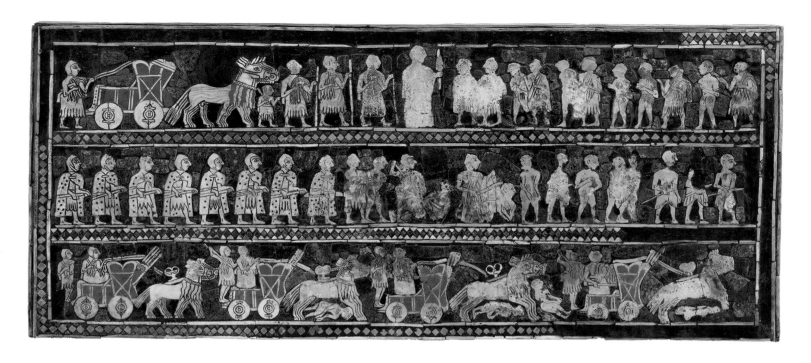

2.3 *Royal Standard of Ur,* front and back sides. ca. 2600–2400 BCE. Wood inlaid with shell, limestone, and lapis lazuli, height 8" (20.3 cm). The British Museum, London

 View the Closer Look for the *Royal Standard of Ur* on myartslab.com

Under his grandson, Naram-Sin, who ruled from 2254 to 2218 BCE, the Akkadian empire stretched from Sumer in the south to Elam in the east, and then to Syria in the west and Nineveh in the north.

Sculpture: Power

Akkadian rulers increasingly used the visual arts to establish and reflect their power, not for the last time in art history. A magnificent copper head found in a rubbish heap at Nineveh, dated between 2250 and 2200 BCE and sometimes identified as Naram-Sin

himself (**fig. 2.4**), derives its extraordinary power from a number of factors. It was designed to be seen from the front, and this **frontality** makes it appear unchanging and eternal. The abstract treatment of beard and hair contrasts with the smooth flesh to give the head a memorable simplicity and a strong symmetry, which denote control and order. The intricate, precise patterning of hair and beard testifies to the metalworker's expertise in hollow casting. Furthermore, at a time before many people understood the science of metallurgy, the use of

2.4 *Head of an Akkadian Ruler* from Nineveh (Kuyunjik), Iraq. ca. 2250–2200 BCE. Copper, height 12″ (30.7 cm). Formerly Iraq Museum, Baghdad, whereabouts now unknown

2.5 Stele of Naram-Sin. ca. 2270 BCE. Pink limestone, height 6′6″ (2 m). Musée du Louvre, Paris

> **View** the Closer Look for the Stele of Naram-Sin on myartslab.com

cast metal for a portrait demonstrated the patron's control of a technology primarily associated with weaponry. Originally, the portrait would have had eyes inlaid with precious and semiprecious materials, as other surviving figures do. The damage to the head was probably incurred during the Medes' invasion of Nineveh in 612 BCE. The enemy gouged out its eyes and hacked off its ears, nose, and lower beard, as if attacking the person represented. Many cultures, even today, practice such acts of ritualized vandalism as symbolic acts of violence or protest. War poses just as much of a threat to works of art: As a result of the looting of sites and museums during the Iraqi conflict, many works of art have vanished and valuable archaeological contexts have been destroyed. The whereabouts of this copper portrait are now unknown.

The themes of power and narrative combine in a 6½-foot **stele** (upright marker stone) erected in the Akkadian city of Sippar during the rule of Naram-Sin (**fig. 2.5**). The stele commemorates,

in relief, Naram-Sin's victory over the Lullubi, people of the Zagros Mountains in eastern Mesopotamia. This time the story does not unfold in registers; instead, ranks of soldiers, in composite view, climb the contours of a wooded mountain. Their ordered march contrasts with the enemy's chaotic rout. As the victorious soldiers trample the fallen foe underfoot, the defeated beg for mercy or lie contorted in death. Above them, the king's large scale and central position make his identity clear. He stands isolated against the background, next to a mountain peak that suggests proximity to the divine. His horned crown, formerly an exclusive accouterment of the gods, marks him as the first Mesopotamian king to deify himself (an act that his people did not unanimously welcome). The bold musculature of his limbs and his powerful stance cast him as a heroic figure. Solar deities shine auspiciously overhead, as if witnessing his victory.

Neo-Sumerian Revival

The rule of the Akkadian kings came to an end when a mountain people, the Guti, gained control of the Mesopotamian Plain. The cities of Sumer rose up in retaliation and drove them out in 2112 BCE, under the leadership of King Urnammu of Ur, who united a realm that was to last a hundred years. As part of his renewal project, he returned to building on a magnificent scale.

Part of Urnammu's legacy is the Great Ziggurat at Ur of about 2100 BCE, dedicated to the Sumerian moon god Nanna (Sin in Akkadian) (**fig. 2.6**). Its 190- by 130-foot base soared to 50 feet in three stepped stages. The base consisted of solid mud brick faced with baked bricks set in bitumen, used here as mortar. Although not structurally functional, thick **buttresses** (vertical supporting elements) articulated the walls, giving an impression of strength. Moreover, a multitude of upward lines added a dynamic energy to the monument's appearance. Three staircases, now reconstructed, converged high up at the fortified gateway. Each 100 steps long, one stood perpendicular to the temple, the other two parallel to the base wall. From the gateway, a fourth staircase once rose to the temple proper, which does not survive. The stairways may have provided an imposing setting for ceremonial processions.

Babylonian Art

The late third and early second millennia BCE were a time of turmoil and warfare in Mesopotamia. The region was then unified for over 300 years under a Babylonian dynasty. During the reign of its most famous ruler, Hammurabi (r. 1792–1750 BCE), the city of Babylon assumed the dominant role formerly played by Akkad and Ur. Combining military prowess with respect for Sumerian tradition, Hammurabi cast himself as "the favorite shepherd" of the sun god Shamash, stating his mission "to cause justice to prevail in the land and to destroy the wicked and evil, so that the strong might not oppress the weak nor the weak the strong." Babylon retained its role as cultural center of Sumer for more than a thousand years after its political power had waned.

2.6 Great Ziggurat of King Urnammu, Ur. ca. 2100 BCE. Mud brick and bitumen. Muqaiyir, Iraq

The Code of Hammurabi

Posterity remembers Hammurabi best for his LAW CODE. It survives as one of the earliest written bodies of law, engraved on a black basalt stele reaching over 7 feet in height (**fig. 2.7**). The largest portion of the text concerns commercial and property law, rulings on domestic issues, and questions of physical assault, detailing penalties for noncompliers.

At the top of the stele, Hammurabi appears in relief, standing with his arm raised in greeting before the enthroned sun god Shamash, whose shoulders emanate sunrays. The god extends his hand, holding the rope ring and the measuring rod of kingship; this single gesture unifies both the scene's composition and the implied purpose of the two protagonists. The image is a variant of the "introduction scene" found on cylinder seals, where a goddess leads a human individual with his hand raised in salute before a seated godlike figure who bestows his blessing. Hammurabi appears without the benefit—or need—of a divine intercessor, implying an especially close relationship with the sun god. Still, the smaller scale of Hammurabi compared with the seated god expresses his status as "shepherd" rather than god himself. The symmetrical composition and smooth surfaces result in a legible image of divinely ordained power that is fully in line with Mesopotamian traditions.

Assyrian Art

Babylon fell around 1595 BCE to the Hittites, who had established themselves in Anatolia (present-day Turkey), and departed leaving a weakened Babylonian state vulnerable to other invaders. By the end of the millennium, the Assyrians more or less controlled southern Mesopotamia. Their home was the city-state of Assur, sited on the upper course of the Tigris and named for the god Ashur.

Art of Empire: Expressing Royal Power

Under a series of able rulers, the Assyrian realm expanded, in time covering not only Mesopotamia but surrounding regions as well. At its height, in the seventh century BCE, the empire stretched from the Sinai peninsula to Armenia; the Assyrians even invaded Egypt in about 670 BCE (see map 2.1). They adapted the artistic achievements of the Sumerians and Babylonians to their own purpose,

The LAW CODE of Hammurabi contains 282 articles set down in 3,600 lines of cuneiform writing. Enforced throughout the empire, it aimed "to destroy the wicked and the evil, that the strong may not oppress the weak." It specifies penalties for crimes (including fines, beatings, maimings, and executions), as well as laws relating to family issues, such as divorce. The well-known phrase "an eye for an eye, a tooth for a tooth" derives from the code, and was repeated in the Bible.

2.7 Upper part of stele inscribed with the Law Code of Hammurabi. ca. 1760 BCE. Diorite, height of stele approx. 7' (2.1 m); height of relief 28" (71 cm). Musée du Louvre, Paris

 Read the document with an excerpt from the Law Code of Hammurabi on myartslab.com

2.8 Gate of the Citadel of Sargon II, Dur Sharrukin (photo taken during excavation). Gypseous alabaster. 742–706 BCE. Khorsabad, Iraq

to create an art of empire: propagandistic and public, designed to proclaim and sustain the supremacy of the Assyrian civilization, particularly through representations of military power. Their architectural emphasis shifted primarily to royal palaces, which grew to unprecedented size and magnificence, blatantly expressing a royal presence and domination.

The palace complex of Sargon II (r. 721–705 BCE) at Dur Sharrukin (present-day Khorsabad, Iraq) comprised about 30 courtyards and 200 rooms, and monumental imagery accompanied this impressive

scale. At the gateways stood huge, awe-inspiring guardian figures known as **lamassu**, in the shape of winged, human-headed bulls (**fig. 2.8**). The illustration here shows the lamassu of Khorsabad during excavation in the 1840s. Carved out of the limestone, they are, in a sense, one with the building. The addition of a fifth leg, visible from the side, reveals that the sculptor conceived of them as relief sculptures on two sides of the stone block, so that the figures are legible both frontally and in profile. With their tall, horned headdresses and deep-set eyes, and with the powerful muscularity

2.9 *Lion Hunt* relief, from Palace of Ashurbanipal at Nineveh. ca. 645 BCE. Gypsum, height 3′7″ (109.22 cm). The British Museum, London

 Watch a video about the process of sculpting in relief on myartslab.com

of their legs and bodies set off by the delicate patterning of the beard and feathers, they towered over an approaching visitor, embodying the king's fearful authority. The Assyrians may have believed the hybrid creatures had the power to ward off evil spirits.

Once inside a royal palace, a visitor would confront another distinctive feature of Assyrian architecture: the upright gypsum slabs called **orthostats** with which the builders lined the lower walls. Structurally, the slabs protected the mud brick from moisture and wear, but they served a communicative purpose as well. On their surfaces, narrative images in low relief, painted in places for emphasis, glorified the king with depictions of lion hunts and military conquests (with inscriptions giving supplementary information). Actions take place in a continuous band, propelling a viewer from scene to scene. As in Egypt, royal lion hunts were staged events within palace grounds. Earlier Mesopotamian rulers hunted lions to protect their subjects, but by the time of the Assyrians, the activity had become more symbolic than real, ritually showcasing the king's strength and serving as a metaphor for military prowess. On a section of relief from the North Palace of Ashurbanipal (r. 668–627 BCE) at Nineveh, dating to roughly 645 BCE (**fig. 2.9**), the king races forward in his chariot with bow drawn, leaving wounded and dead lions in his wake. As attendants plunge spears into its chest, a wounded lion hurls itself at the chariot, its body flat out in a clean diagonal line, its claws spread and mouth open in what appears to be pain combined with desperate ferocity. To ennoble the victims of the hunt, the sculptor contrasted the limp bodies of the slain animals with the taut leaping lion and the powerful energy of the king's party. Yet we should not conclude that the artist necessarily hoped to evoke sympathy for the beasts, or to comment on the cruelty of a staged hunt; it is more likely that by ennobling the lions the sculptor glorified their vanquisher, the king, even more.

Late Babylonian Art

The Assyrian Empire came to an end in 612 BCE, when Nineveh fell to the Medes (an INDO-EUROPEAN-speaking people from western Iran) and the resurgent Babylonians. Under the Chaldean dynasty, the ancient city of Babylon had a final brief flowering between 612 and 539 BCE, before the Persians conquered it.

The royal palace at Babylon was on almost the same scale as Assyrian palaces, with numerous reception suites surrounding five huge courtyards. For its decoration, the Late Babylonians adopted baked and glazed brick, molded into individual shapes. Glazing brick involved putting a film of glass over the brick's surface. Its coloristic effect appears on the courtyard façade of the Throne Room and the Processional Way leading to the Ishtar Gate and the gate itself, now reassembled in Berlin (**fig. 2.10**). A framework of brightly colored ornamental bands contains a procession of bulls, dragons, and other animals sacred to the gods of Babylon, set off in molded brick against a deep blue background. Unlike the massive muscularity of the lamassu, their forms are light and agile-looking, arrested in a processional stride that slowly accompanies the ceremonial parades leading to the archway.

2.10 Ishtar Gate (restored), from Babylon, Iraq. ca. 575 BCE. Glazed brick, 48′4″ × 51′6⅛″ × 14′3⅝″ (14.73 × 15.7 × 4.36 m). Staatliche Museen zu Berlin, Preussischer Kulturbesitz, Vorderasiatisches Museum

2.11 Temple of Solomon
(reconstruction), Jerusalem.
ca. 457–450 BCE

Hebrew Architecture

The Akkadians expelled the Hebrews from
Mesopotamia in about 2000 BCE. The latter settled
in Canaan, in the eastern Mediterranean region,
before moving to Egypt in around 1600 BCE. There,
they were bound into slavery. Moses led their
flight from Egypt into the Sinai desert, where
they established the principles of their religion.
Unlike other Near Eastern peoples, the Hebrews
were monotheistic—worshiping only one god.
Their worship centered on Yahweh, who provided Moses with the Ten Commandments, a set
of ethical and moral rules. After 40 years, they
returned to Canaan, which they named Israel.
King David, who ruled until 961 BCE, seized
the city of Jerusalem from the Canaanites, and
began to construct buildings worthy of a capital for Israel, including a royal palace. His son,
Solomon, completed a vast temple for worship,
now known as the First Temple. It stood within a
sacred precinct on Mount Moriah (the present-day
Temple Mount), where, according to the Scriptures,
the patriarch Abraham had prepared to sacrifice
his son, Isaac. According to the Hebrew Bible,
Solomon covered the entire temple and the altar
inside with gold. In the inner sanctuary, which
held the Ark of the Covenant (a chest containing the Commandments), sculptors created two
monumental cherubim (angels depicted as winged
children) out of gilded olive wood, and covered
the walls with carvings of cherubim, palm trees,
and flowers. Brass pillars stood at the front of the
temple, with pomegranate-shaped **capitals**. King
Hiram of Tyre (Phoenicia) is credited with providing resources for the construction of the temple,
such as materials and artisans, which is further
evidence of the close connections between Near
Eastern cultures.

Babylonian forces under King Nebuchadnezzar II destroyed the temple in 587/86 BCE,
forcing the Israelites into exile. Upon their return
in 538, they built the temple anew (**fig. 2.11**),

and under Herod the Great, king of Judea from 37 BCE to 4 CE, the Second Temple was elevated and enlarged. Roman soldiers razed this rebuilding in the reign of the emperor Vespasian, in the first century CE. The only vestige of the vast complex Herod commissioned is the western wall, known today as the Wailing Wall.

Persian Art

Alongside the successive cultures of Mesopotamia, a variety of other civilizations developed in areas beyond the Tigris and Euphrates. Some of them invaded or conquered contemporaneous city-states in Mesopotamia. Others, such as the seagoing Phoenicians on the Mediterranean coast to the west, traded with the people of Mesopotamia and in so doing spread its visual forms to Africa and Europe.

The Persian Empire: Cosmopolitan Heirs to the Mesopotamian Tradition

During the mid-sixth century BCE, the small kingdom of Parsa to the east of lower Mesopotamia came to dominate the entire Near East. Under the Achaemenid ruler Cyrus the Great (r. 559–530/29 BCE), the Persians (or Iranians) overthrew the king of the Medes, then conquered major parts of Asia Minor and Babylon. Cyrus assumed the title "King of Babylon," along with the broader ambitions of Mesopotamian rulers. The empire he founded continued to expand under his successors. Egypt fell in 525 BCE, while Greece narrowly escaped Persian domination in the early fifth century BCE. At its height, under Darius I (r. 521–486 BCE) and his son Xerxes (r. 485–465 BCE), the Persian Empire in its territorial reach far outstripped the Egyptian and Assyrian empires combined. Its huge domain endured for two centuries, during which it developed an efficient administration and monumental art forms.

The ancients classified the Hanging Gardens of Babylon as one of the Seven Wonders of the World. The others were the Pyramid of Khufu at Giza (see fig. 3.4), the Mausoleum at Halikarnassos (see fig. 5.19), the Colossus of Rhodes (a statue of the sun god Helios), the Temple of Artemis at Ephesos, the statue of Olympian Zeus by Pheidias, and the Pharos (lighthouse) at Alexandria.

0 20 50 70 100 meters

0 100 200 300 feet

2.12 Plan of Palace of Darius and Xerxes, Persepolis, Iran. 518–460 BCE. Solid triangles show the processional route taken by Persian and Mede notables; open triangles indicate the way taken by heads of delegations and their suites

Watch a video about Persepolis on myartslab.com

Persian religious beliefs were related to the prophecies of ZOROASTER (Zarathustra) and took as their basis the dualism of good and evil, embodied in Ahuramazda (Light) and Ahriman (Darkness). The cult of Ahuramazda focused its rituals on fire altars in the open air; consequently, Persian kings did not construct monumental religious architecture. Instead they concentrated their attention and resources on royal palaces, which were at once vast and impressive.

PERSEPOLIS Darius I began construction on the most ambitious of these palaces, on a plateau in the Zagros highlands at Parsa or Persepolis, in 518 BCE. Subsequent rulers enlarged it (**fig. 2.12**). Fortified and raised on a platform, it consisted of a great number of rooms, halls, and courts laid out in a grid plan. The palace is a synthesis of materials and design traditions from all parts of the far-flung empire, a clear statement of internationalism. Darius boasts in his inscriptions that the timber came from Lebanon (cedar), Gandhara, and Carmania (yaka wood), and the bricks from Babylon. To work these materials, the Achaemenid dynasty brought in craftsmen from all over the empire, who then took this international style with them on returning to their respective homes.

In marked contrast to the military narratives of the Assyrians, reliefs embellishing the platform of the huge audience hall, or *apadana*, and its double stairway proclaim a theme of harmony and integration across the multicultural empire (**fig. 2.13**). Long rows of marching figures, sometimes shown in registers one above another, represent the empire's 23 subject nations, as well as royal guards and Persian dignitaries. Each of the nations' representatives wears indigenous dress and brings a regional gift as tribute to the Persian king. Colored stone and metals applied to the relief once added richness to the wealth of carved detail. The relief is remarkably shallow, yet by reserving the figures' roundness for the edge of their bodies (so that they cast a shadow), and by cutting the background away to a level field, the sculptors created an

2.13 East stairway of the Audience Hall of Darius and Xerxes. ca. 500 BCE. Limestone. Persepolis, Iran

impression of greater depth. Most of the figures are depicted in true profile, even though some figures turn their heads back to address those who follow. Through repetition of the walking human form the artists generated a powerful dynamic quality that guides a visitor's path through the enormous space. The repetition also lends the reliefs an eternal quality, as if preserving the action in perpetual time. If, as some scholars believe, the relief represents the recurring celebration of the New Year Festival, this timeless quality would be especially apt.

The Achaemenid synthesis of traditions at Persepolis demonstrates the longevity and flexibility of the Near Eastern language of rulership. The palace provides a dramatic and powerful setting for imperial court ritual on a grand scale.

POINTS OF REFLECTION

2.1 Select a work of art and a work of architecture and analyze the ways in which they enhanced the power of those they represented.

2.2 Assess the significance of temple design in ancient Near Eastern city-states.

2.3 Contrast the narrative techniques deployed in the *Royal Standard of Ur,* Stele of Naram-Sin, and the lion hunt scene from the Palace of Ashurbanipal at Nineveh.

2.4 Describe the message of empire broadcast by the Palace of Darius and Xerxes at Persepolis.

✓•⌐**Study** and review on myartslab.com

ART IN TIME

● ca. 3500 BCE—The Sumerian city of Uruk emerges

● ca. 2900 BCE— Mesopotamians begin using cuneiform writing

● **ca. 2600 BCE—The Sumerian *Royal Standard of Ur***

● ca. 2100 BCE—King Urnammu commissions the Great Ziggurat at Ur

● ca. 1792–1750 BCE— Hammurabi rules Babylon

● **ca. 668–627 BCE—Assyrian construction of the North Palace of Ashurbanipal**

● ca. 604–562 BCE—Reign of the Late Babylonian ruler Nebuchadnezzar II

● **ca. 575 BCE—Babylonian construction of the Ishtar Gate**

● ca. 559–530/529 BCE—Rule of Cyrus the Great, who leads the Persians to overthrow the Medes

● **ca. 518 BCE—Construction of the Persian palace at Persepolis begins**

● 331 BCE—Alexander the Great defeats the Persians

CHAPTER

3 Egyptian Art

POINTS OF INQUIRY

3.1 Distinguish the different types of visual language artists deployed in ancient Egypt.

3.2 Consider the various forms of architecture used by Egyptians for funerary purposes, and the reasons behind the changes in type.

3.3 Consider Egyptian conventions for representing the human body.

3.4 Assess the relative importance of innovation and tradition to Egyptian artists and patrons.

((•─ **Listen** to the chapter audio on myartslab.com

Egypt has long fascinated the West. The ancient Greeks and the Romans knew and admired Egypt; Renaissance collectors and scholars took up their esteem. Napoleon's incursions into Egypt in the late eighteenth century brought artifacts and knowledge back to France and stimulated interest throughout Europe. European-sponsored excavations have been going on in Egypt since the nineteenth century, sometimes, as with the discovery in 1922 of the tomb of King Tutankhamun, with spectacular results.

One reason that ancient Egypt enthralls us is the exceptional quality and monumental character of its works of art. Most surviving works come from tombs, which Egyptians built to assure an afterlife for the deceased. They intended the works of art contained within them to accompany the deceased into eternity. Thus, Egyptian art is an art of permanence. Artists did not strive for innovation or originality, but adhered instead to traditional formulations that expressed specific ideas. Continuity of form and subject is a characteristic of ancient Egyptian art.

Egyptian artists executed works of art mainly for the elite patrons of a society that was extremely hierarchical. Contemporary with the Egyptian development of writing around 3000 BCE there emerged a political and religious system that placed a god-king (called a pharaoh from the New Kingdom on) in charge of the physical and spiritual well-being of the land and its people. Many of the best-known and most evocative works of Egyptian art exalted these powerful rulers, and express the multifaceted ways that Egyptians envisioned their king: as a human manifestation of the gods, as a god in his own right, as a beneficent ruler, and as an emblem of life itself. Royal projects for the afterlife dominated the landscape and provided models for elite burials.

Egyptian geography also played a formative role in the development of art. The land was established along the course of the Nile River in North Africa, with the natural protection of the surrounding desert, or "red land." The river floods annually, inundating the land on either side. As it recedes, the water leaves a dark strip of rich soil fertilized by silt, which the Egyptians called the "black land." They irrigated and farmed it, and regularly produced surplus food. This allowed them to diversify and develop a complex culture. Egypt's agrarian society depended on the Nile's flooding to survive. The king had to assure continuity of life through intercession with the gods, who often represented natural forces. The chief deity was the sun, worshiped as Ra-Horakhty. In matters concerning the afterlife, the deities Osiris, his consort Isis, and their son Horus played key roles. Gods took many forms: Ra might appear as a falcon-headed man; Osiris—who was killed and resurrected—as a mummy. Egyptians called the king himself the "son of Ra" and saw him as the human embodiment of Horus. An equal to the gods, he controlled the land, the future, and the afterlife. A large priesthood, an administrative bureaucracy, and a strong military assisted him.

Predynastic and Early Dynastic Art

The origins of Egyptian culture stretch back into the Neolithic period. By at least 5000 BCE, humans were growing crops and domesticating animals in the Nile Valley. Settlements there gradually transformed into urban centers. According to tradition, Egypt initially consisted of two regions. Upper Egypt, in the south, included the Nile Valley between present-day Aswan and the point where the river fans out into the Delta, near present-day Cairo. Lower Egypt, in the north, consisted mainly of the vast Delta, from ancient Memphis to the Mediterranean. Tradition maintained that the first king of the first dynasty founded the city of Memphis, at the mouth of the Delta (see **map 3.1**), uniting Upper and Lower Egypt. The division of Egypt into two regions was consistent with the Egyptian worldview. They saw the world as a set of dualities in opposition: Upper and Lower Egypt, the red land of the desert and the black land of cultivation, Osiris (the god of civilization) opposed to Seth (the god of chaos). The king had to balance the forces of chaos and order, and bring *ma'at* (harmony or order) to the world. Recognizing this worldview has led some scholars to question the traditional explanation that Upper and Lower Egypt were independent regions unified by King Narmer. Instead, they argue that this division was an imaginative construction of the past.

The Palette of King Narmer

The *Palette of King Narmer* (**fig. 3.1**), dated around 3000 BCE, visually expressed the concept of the king as unifier. The *Palette* is a stone tablet with a central depression for grinding the protective paint that Egyptians applied around the eyes. Its size—more than 2 feet high—suggests that it was

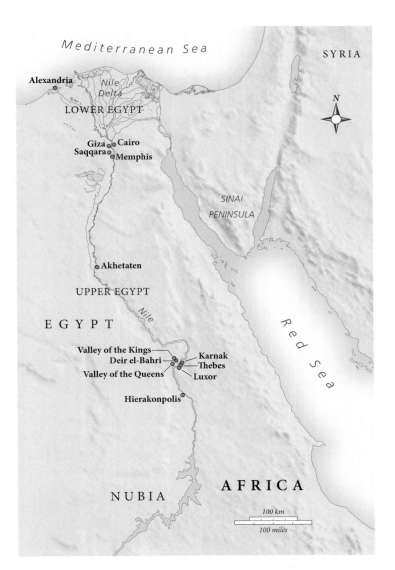

Map 3.1 Ancient Egypt

not for ordinary use, but was probably reserved for a ceremony to ornament a cult statue. This ritual function may explain its findspot in the temple of Hierakonpolis, where it had been buried along with other offerings to Horus.

Shallow relief carvings in registers (rows) decorate both sides of the *Palette*. At the top of each side, in the center, HIEROGLYPHS spell out Narmer's name, within an abstract rendering of the king's palace. The Egyptians developed hieroglyphs as a writing system at about the same time as the Mesopotamians were inventing cuneiform. Flanking the hieroglyphs, heads of cows represent the sky goddess, locating the king in the sky. On one side of the *Palette* (shown on the left), Narmer holds a fallen enemy by the hair with one hand, as he raises his mace—an emblem of kingship—with the other. The king appears in the composite view that will be the hallmark of Egyptian two-dimensional art:

amulet

The phonetic reading of this hieroglyph is, from top to bottom: *sha* (for the stand of lotus), *ba* (Egyptian for "ram"), *ka* (upraised arms meaning "spirit" or "soul"). Because a lozenge-like form, called a cartouche, encloses the signs, we know that this hieroglyph means "King Shabaka."

cartouche

3.1 *Palette of King Narmer* (both sides), from Hierakonpolis. ca. 3000 BCE. Slate, height 25" (63.5 cm). Egyptian Museum, Cairo

 View the Closer Look for the Palette of King Narmer on myartslab.com

With a frontal view of eye, shoulders, and arms, but a profile of head and legs. He wears the white crown of Upper Egypt and from his belt hangs the tail of a bull, a symbol of power that Egyptian kings would wear as part of their ceremonial dress for 3,000 years. The large scale of his figure compared with others immediately establishes his authority, according to what is termed a hieratic use of scale. For his part, the enemy, like the two defeated enemies in the bottom register, is stripped of clothing as an act of humiliation. Behind the king, and standing on his own ground-line, an attendant carries his sandals. Hieroglyphs identify both the sandal-carrier and the enemy. To the right of Narmer appears a falcon resting on a papyrus stand, which grows from a human-headed strip of land; the falcon holds a rope tethered to the face.

On the other side of the *Palette* (on the right in fig. 3.1), Narmer appears in the highest register, now wearing the red crown of Lower Egypt. Flanked by the sandal-carrier and a long-haired figure, he follows four standard-bearers to inspect the decapitated bodies of prisoners, arranged with their heads between their legs. In the larger central register, two animals, each roped in by a male figure, twist their long necks to frame a circle.

The symmetrical motif may represent *ma'at*. In the lowest register, a bull representing the king attacks a city and tramples down the enemy.

The *Palette* combines the symbols of Upper and Lower Egypt for the first time to express their unification. To communicate the message, several different types of sign come together on one object. Some of these signs—the king, attendants, and prisoners—are literal representations. Others are symbolic representations, such as the depiction of the king as a bull, denoting his strength. Pictographs, small symbols based on abstract representations of concepts, encode further information: In the falcon and papyrus group, the falcon represents Horus, whom the Egyptians believed the king incarnated, while the human-headed papyrus stand represents Lower Egypt, where papyrus grew abundantly. A possible interpretation is that this pictograph expresses Narmer's control of that region. Finally, the artist included identifying texts in the form of hieroglyphs. Together, the different signs on the *Palette* drive home important messages about the nature of Egyptian kingship: The king embodied the unified Upper and Lower Egypt, and though human, he occupied a divine office, as shown by the placement of his name in the sky, the realm of Horus.

The Old Kingdom: A Golden Age

The *Palette of King Narmer* offers an image of kingship that transcends earthly power, representing the king as a divinity as well as a ruler. The kings of the Old Kingdom (Dynasty Three to Dynasty Six, ca. 2649–2150 BCE) found more monumental ways to express this notion. Other dynasties would emulate their works of art for two millennia.

Old Kingdom Funerary Complexes

During the Old Kingdom, Egyptians fashioned buildings that housed the day-to-day activities of the living mainly out of perishable materials, with the result that little survives. The bulk of archaeological evidence comes instead from tombs. The majority of the population probably buried their dead in shallow desert graves, but the elite had the resources to build elaborate funerary monuments. The survival of these tombs is no accident; they were purposely constructed to endure.

These structures had several critical functions. As in many cultures, tombs served the living by giving the deceased a permanent marker in the landscape. They expressed the status of the dead and perpetuated their memory. They also ensured the preservation of a deceased individual's life force, or *ka*. Egyptians considered that the *ka* survived after death, and so required a place to reside for eternity. This need led embalmers to go to great lengths to preserve the body through mummification. The mummified body, usually placed within a **sarcophagus** (a stone coffin), was interred in a burial chamber, often surrounded by chambers for funerary equipment. Egyptians believed that a statue placed within the burial chamber could serve as a surrogate home for the *ka* in the event that the embalmers' efforts failed and the body decayed. They also equipped their tombs with objects of daily life for the *ka*'s enjoyment.

THE FUNERARY COMPLEX OF KING DJOSER   The first known major funerary complex is that of the Third Dynasty king Djoser (Netjerikhet), at Saqqara (**fig. 3.2**), who ruled between 2630 and 2611 BCE. On the west side of the Nile, Saqqara was the **necropolis**,

SPEAKING OF
king, kingship, kingdom, dynasty, and pharaoh

Egyptians believed their kings to combine divine and mortal qualities and thus to be quasi-divine. Kingship passed from father to son or to near kin. The early third-century BCE priest Manetho devised the dynasties, groupings of kings linked by kinship, and designated clusters of dynasties into Kingdoms and "Intermediate Periods." Three main kingdoms—the Old, Middle, and New—comprise clusters through the Twentieth Dynasty. Manetho recognized 30 dynasties to 343 BCE, after which ancient Egypt continued for another 750 years until the division of the Roman Empire in 395 CE. The word "pharaoh" derives from the Egyptian term for "royal palace." Present-day writers have used it synonymously with "king"; the Egyptians employed it to mean "king" beginning only in the Eighteenth Dynasty.

3.2 Imhotep. Step Pyramid and Funerary Complex of King Djoser. Third Dynasty. ca. 2681–2662 BCE. Limestone. Saqqara

Watch an architectural simulation about the mastaba and pyramid on myartslab.com

The Egyptians devised COLUMNS of three parts—base, shaft, and capital. The same parts are found in two of the three main Greek Classical styles, which were still to come. The PAPYRUS, both open and closed, was a favorite motif for Egyptian capitals. The shafts of columns were frequently decorated with brightly painted hieroglyphic writing in shallow or sunk relief.

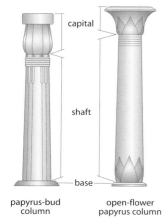

papyrus-bud column   open-flower papyrus column

Step Pyramid of Djoser with sections of Pyramid of Khufu and mastaba from the necropolis at Giza

or city of the dead, of the capital city of Memphis in Lower Egypt. Encircling the entire complex is a rectangular stone wall stretching over a mile in length and 33 feet high. The dominant feature of the complex is a stepped pyramid, which began as a 26-foot high **mastaba** (a bench tomb) and rose to its towering 204-foot height over the course of years as builders added progressively diminishing layers of masonry to its form. The layers resulted in a staircase, perhaps the means by which the dead king could ascend to the gods. The treads of the "steps" incline downward and the uprights outward, giving the structure an impressively stable appearance. A chamber cut about 90 feet into the rock beneath the pyramid contained the burial, and additional chambers held funerary provisions. North of the pyramid was a labyrinthine funerary temple, where the living performed offering rituals for the dead king.

The buildings in the burial complex reproduce the palace architecture inhabited by the living king. A large court to the south of the pyramid may have staged rituals for receiving tribute or asserting royal dominion. Shrines of Upper and Lower Egypt flanked a smaller court to its east, which may have been the site where the dead king was thought to enact the *sed* festival, which celebrated his 30-year jubilee and rejuvenated his power. Unlike palace structures, many of the buildings in the funerary complex are nonfunctional: For instance, of 14 gateways indicated in the enclosure wall, only one allows entrance; the rest are false. Furthermore, while architects chose perishable materials for palaces—primarily mud brick—they constructed the funerary complex entirely in limestone: It was built to last. Masons dressed the limestone blocks of the

enclosure wall to resemble the niched façade of a mud-brick palace. Additionally, the reconstructed façade of a shrine echoes the form of an Upper Egyptian tent building, with tall poles supporting a mat roof that billows in the wind. Engaged COLUMNS imitate the PAPYRUS stems or bundled reeds that Egyptian builders used to support mud-brick walls, with capitals shaped to resemble blossoms.

Many elements of the complex served as permanent settings for the dead king to enact rituals of kingship perpetually—rituals that maintained order among the living. The installation of a life-size seated statue of the king in a *serdab* (an enclosed room without an entrance) to the east of the funerary temple assured his presence in the complex. Two holes in the *serdab*'s front wall enabled his *ka*, residing in the statue, to observe rituals in his honor and draw sustenance from offerings of food and incense. The complex was oriented north–south, and the king's statue looked out toward the circumpolar stars in the northern sky. With these provisions, his *ka* would remain eternally alive and vigilant.

Inscriptions on statue fragments found within the complex preserve the name of the mastermind behind its construction, a high official in Djoser's court and high priest of Ra, named Imhotep. Egyptians in Imhotep's own time and beyond credited him with advancing Egyptian culture through his wisdom and knowledge of astronomy, architecture, and medicine, and they regarded him so highly that they deified him. Scholars often identify him as the first named architect in history.

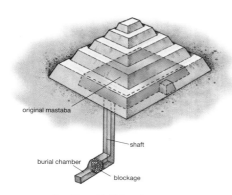

Step Pyramid of King Djoser, Saqqara

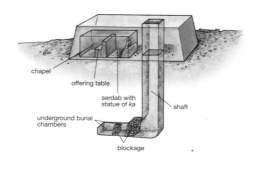

mastaba

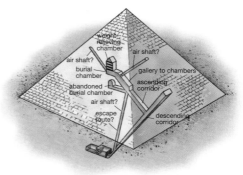

Pyramid of Khufu

3.3 Model of the Great Pyramids at Giza: Menkaure, Khafra, Khufu, shown with lower temple and Great Sphinx

The Pyramids at Giza: Reflecting a New Royal Role

Other kings followed Djoser's lead, but during the Fourth Dynasty, ca. 2575–2465 BCE, funerary architecture changed dramatically. To the modern eye, the most obvious change is the shift from a step pyramid to a smooth-sided one.

The best-known pyramids are the three Great Pyramids at Giza (**figs. 3.3** and **3.4**), commemorating Khufu (the first and largest pyramid), Khafra (a somewhat smaller one), and Menkaure (the smallest). Throughout the ages since their construction, the pyramids have continued to impress. Their grandeur derives from their sheer monumentality

3.4 The Pyramids of Menkaure, ca. 2533–2515 BCE, Khafra, ca. 2570–2544 BCE, and Khufu, ca. 2601–2528 BCE. Giza

3.5 The Great Sphinx.
ca. 2570–2544 BCE. Sandstone,
height 65′ (19.8 m). Giza

(Khafra's covers 13 acres at the base, and still rises to a height of about 450 feet), from the precision of their orientation to the cardinal points, and from the extraordinary simplicity of their form, achieved through meticulous mathematical calculation. On a square plan, their four surfaces, shaped as equilateral triangles, taper up from the desert toward the sky. At any time of day, one side will hold the sun's full glare, while another is cast into shadow. Before Islamic builders plundered their stone, each pyramid was dressed with white limestone, preserved only on the pinnacle of the Pyramid of Khafra; at the tip of each, moreover, was a thin layer of gold. The entrance to each pyramid was on its north face, and somewhere within the solid stone mass the architect concealed a burial chamber in the hope of foiling tomb-robbers. Encircling each pyramid was an enclosure wall, and clustered all around were smaller pyramids and mastabas for members of the royal family and high officials. Determining how the Egyptians constructed the pyramids continues to confound archaeologists; they believe that workers constructed ramps to raise blocks into place as the monuments grew, but still debate the ramps' design.

Like Djoser's complex at Saqqara and most subsequent royal burials, Fourth Dynasty burials took place on the Nile's west bank, the side of the setting sun, across from the habitations of the

living on the east bank. Yet, in contrast to Djoser's complex, with its compact form laid out on a north–south axis, the architects set out the monuments at Giza on an extended east–west axis. At the start of the funeral ceremony, attendants transported the body across the Nile to the valley temple, connected to the river by a canal. Beyond the valley temple, a causeway led westward into the desert for about a third of a mile to the funerary temple, adjoining the pyramid's east face. Here an embalmer preserved the dead king's body, and the living perpetuated the cult for his *ka*. Standing guard over the valley temple of Khafra is the Great Sphinx, carved from an outcropping of rock left after quarrying stone (**fig. 3.5**). Uncomfortable with human representation in art, later Islamic residents of Giza damaged the massive sculpture, obscuring details of the face, and the top of the head is missing. A question over its identity lingers: Some scholars believe that it represented Khafra, while others see a sculpture of Khufu, created before Khafra's valley temple. In either case, sculptors combined the king's portrait with the body (and thus strength) of a lion, and its vast scale proclaims the king's power.

The changes in funerary architecture suggest a shift in the way Egyptians perceived their ruler. The smooth-sided pyramid was the shape of the *ben-ben*, a sacred stone in Heliopolis, center of the sun cult.

These monumental tombs may therefore have emphasized the solar aspect of the king's person; indeed, the change coincides more or less with the king's adoption of the title "son of Ra." The change in orientation for the complexes also meant that the king's funerary temple did not face the northern stars, as before, but the rising sun in the east, which signified eternity through its daily rising and setting. The Giza complex contains no buildings for reenacting rituals of kingship. This suggests that the perpetual performance of these rituals was no longer the dead king's task. Now, his role was to rise to the sun god on the sun's rays, perhaps symbolized by the pyramid's sloping sides, and to accompany him on his endless cycle of regeneration.

Representing the Human Figure

In the hall in the valley temple of Khafra, a series of indentations in the paving shows that 23 seated statues of the king once lined its walls. Archaeologists discovered one of these almost intact and six in poorer condition, interred in the temple floor. The best-preserved statue represents the seated king in a rigidly upright and frontal pose (**fig. 3.6**), which allowed him to watch—and thus, take part in—rituals enacted in his honor; frontality gave him presence. Behind him, the falcon Horus spreads his wings protectively around his head. Like the *Palette*

Carved sculpture is subtractive in the sense that the sculptor begins with a block of raw material, such as stone, that is larger than the finished sculpture and carves away what is not needed for the form of the final piece. This drawing was copied from a wall painting decorating the tomb of Rekhmire in Western Thebes (ca. 1500–1300 BCE).

3.6 *Sculpture of Khafra*, from Giza. ca. 2500 BCE. Diorite, height 66″ (167.7 cm). Egyptian Museum, Cairo

3.7 *Sculpture of Seated Scribe*, from Saqqara. ca. 2400 BCE. Painted limestone, height 21″ (53.3 cm). Musée du Louvre, Paris

like Khafra. In the other, a paunch, rolls of fat, or slack muscles, and signs of age on the face indicate maturity. A painted limestone figure of a scribe, perhaps named Kay, from his mastaba at Saqqara, is an example of the second type (**fig. 3.7**). The scribe is rigidly upright and frontal, like Khafra, but the sallow cheeks, sagging jaw, and loose stomach show that he is aging. Since Egyptian society was mostly illiterate, a scribe occupied high status; indeed, the artist depicted the figure seated on the floor in the act of writing, the very skill in which his status resided. The image reinforces his social status: It shows an official who has succeeded in his career, eats well, and relies on subordinates to do physical work on his behalf.

These conventions of pose and appearance applied only to the highest echelons of society—royalty and courtiers. By contrast, the lower the status of the subject, the more relaxed and naturalistic their pose. Once the conventions were established, ignoring them could result in a change of meaning for a figure, even a change of status, from king or official to servant or captive. Fine low-relief paintings in the tomb chapel of Ti, a high official during the Fifth Dynasty, at Saqqara, encapsulate the correlation between rank and degree of naturalism neatly (**fig. 3.8**). In one section, Ti stands on a boat in a thicket of papyrus, observing a hippopotamus hunt. He stands in the traditional composite view, legs and head in profile, torso and eye frontal, while hunters, shown on a smaller scale, attack their prey from a second boat in a variety of active poses that more closely reflect nature. Zigzagging blue lines beneath the boats denote the river, where hippopotami and fish—on the lowest rung of the natural world—swim about in naturalistic poses. Similarly, nesting birds and predatory foxes freely inhabit the papyrus blossoms overhead.

The Middle Kingdom: Reasserting Tradition Through the Arts

The central government of the Old Kingdom disintegrated with the death of the Sixth Dynasty king Pepy II in around 2152 BCE. This led to the turbulent First Intermediate Period, lasting over a century, when local or regional overlords fostered antagonisms between Upper and Lower Egypt. The two regions reunited in the Eleventh Dynasty, as King Nebhepetra Mentuhotep or Mentuhotep II (ca. 2061–2010 BCE) reasserted regal authority

of King Narmer, this sculpture neatly expresses qualities of kingship. Horus declares the king to be his earthly manifestation and protégé, and the king's muscular form indicates his power. The smooth agelessness of his face bespeaks his eternal nature, while the sculpture's compact form gives it a solidity that suggests permanence. Intertwined plants—papyrus and perhaps sedge—carved between the legs of his chair are indigenous to Lower and Upper Egypt, indicating the territorial reach of royal authority and the unity of the land. Even the stone used for his image expresses the king's control of distant lands: Diorite came from the deserts of Nubia.

Egyptian artists used a defined CANON of proportions when depicting the human figure. Within that canon, for elite male officials there were two kinds of ideal image, each representing a different life stage. One is a youthful, physically fit image,

3.8 *Ti Watching a Hippopotamus Hunt.* ca. 2510–2460 BCE. Painted limestone relief, height approx. 45″ (114.3 cm). Tomb of Ti, Saqqara

The Egyptian CANON: In royal and elite sculpture in the round, and in relief and painting, body proportions are consistent enough that scholars believe artists relied on guidelines for designing the human image. Traces of such guidelines are still visible on reliefs and paintings. This "canon" began in the Fifth Dynasty with a grid superimposed over the human image. One vertical line ran through the body at the point of the ear, and as many as seven horizontal lines divided the body according to a standard module. Over time, the guidelines changed, but the principle of the canon remained: Although body part measurements might vary from person to person, the relationship between parts remained constant. With that relationship established, an artist could depict a human portrait at any scale, taking the proportions of body parts from copybooks. Unlike a system of perspective where a figure's size suggests its distance from a viewer, in the Egyptian canon, size signaled social status.

over all of Egypt. The late Eleventh, Twelfth, and Thirteenth Dynasties make up the Middle Kingdom (ca. 2040–1640 BCE), when much of the art of the period deliberately echoed Old Kingdom forms, especially in the funerary realm. The art asserted continuity with the golden days of the past. Sculptures of some members of the royal family, however, show breaks with tradition.

3.9 *Sculpture of Senwosret III* (fragment). ca. 1870s–1840s BCE. Quartzite, height 6½" (16.5 cm). The Metropolitan Museum of Art, New York. Purchase, Edward S. Harkness Gift, 1926 26.7.1394

Royal Portraiture: Changing Expressions and Proportions

A fragmentary quartzite sculpture of Senwosret III (r. 1878–1841 BCE) indicates a rupture with convention in the representation of royalty (**fig. 3.9**). Rather than sculpting a smooth-skinned, idealized face, untouched by time, the artist depicted a man scarred by signs of age. His brow creases, his eyelids droop, and lines score the flesh beneath his eyes. Scholars have described the image as "introspective," reading it against the background of Senwosret's difficult campaign of military expansion in Nubia to the south; they see the physical imperfections as reflections of the king's stress. Facial expressions or signs of age, however, can signify different things to different societies, and it is equally likely that the tight-lipped expression reflects a new face of regal authority, projecting firm resolve. Sculptors of this time tended to combine the aged face with a youthful, powerful body.

As central authority weakened after about 1785 BCE, local governors usurped power. During the Twelfth Dynasty, immigrants from Palestine known as the Hyksos (from the Egyptian for "rulers of foreign lands") moved into the Nile Delta, gaining control of the area and forcing the king southward to Thebes. The era of their control is known as the Second Intermediate Period.

The New Kingdom: Restored Glory

The first king of the Eighteenth Dynasty, Ahmose (1550–1525 BCE), expelled the Hyksos from Egypt. The 500 years after their expulsion, the Eighteenth,

Nineteenth, and Twentieth Dynasties, are designated the New Kingdom. They constitute a time of renewed territorial expansion and prosperity for Egypt, and a time when the arts flourished. Tremendous architectural projects were accomplished along the full length of the Nile, centering on the region of Thebes (present-day Luxor). Of these projects, many secular buildings, including palaces and forts, were made of mud brick and have perished. Stone tombs and temples, however, retain a measure of their former glory.

Royal Burials in the Valley of the Kings

Changes in burial practices expose a major difference between the Old Kingdom and the New. Having witnessed the loss of order that allowed plundering of royal burials, Eighteenth Dynasty kings abandoned the practice of marking their tombs with pyramids. Instead, they excavated tombs out of the rock face in the Valley of the

Kings west of Thebes, and their entrances were then concealed after burial. Rituals of the funerary cult took place away from the tomb, over a rocky outcropping to the east, at a temple on the edge of the land under cultivation.

HATSHEPSUT'S TEMPLE The best-preserved example of a New Kingdom funerary temple is that of the female king HATSHEPSUT (ca. 1478–1458 BCE) (**fig. 3.10**). Hatshepsut was the chief wife—and half-sister—of Thutmose II. On his death in 1479 BCE, power passed to Thutmose III, his young son by a minor wife. Designated regent for the young king, Hatshepsut ruled with him as female king until her death in 1458 BCE. She justified her unusual rule by claiming that her father, Thutmose I, had intended her to be his successor.

Nestled in the cliff side at Deir el-Bahri, Hatshepsut's temple was built beside the spectacular Eleventh Dynasty temple of Mentuhotep II, who had

3.10 Temple of Hatshepsut. ca. 1478–1458 BCE. Limestone. Deir el-Bahri

 View the Closer Look for the Funerary Temple of Hatshepsut on myartslab.com

HATSHEPSUT (ruled ca. 1478–1458 BCE) acted as regent for Thutmose III until she crowned herself king. Frequently dressing as a man and referred to as such in official records, she sent military expeditions to Nubia and Syria-Palestine. Her reign is renowned for the high quality of its art and architecture. In addition to Deir el-Bahri, her building projects include the so-called Red Chapel at Karnak and the Speos Artemidos, a rock-cut temple at Beni Hasan.

3.11 *Kneeling Figure of King Hatshepsut*, from Deir el-Bahri. ca. 1473–1458 BCE. Red granite, height approx. 8′6″ (2.59 m). The Metropolitan Museum of Art, New York. Rogers Fund, 1929 (29.3.1)

temple entrance, and paired sphinxes faced each other. Cut into the rock at the furthest reach of the temple was the principal sanctuary, dedicated to Amun-Ra, god of the evening sun.

Throughout the complex, painted relief sculptures brought the walls to life, describing battles, a royal expedition to the land of Punt in search of myrrh trees for the terraces, and scenes of Thutmose I legitimizing his daughter's rule. Sculptures of the king and deities abounded. One of eight colossal red granite statues from the third court (**fig. 3.11**) depicts Hatshepsut kneeling as she makes an offering of two spherical jars. An inscription on the base records that the king is presenting *ma'at to Amun*. Since kingship was defined as a male office, she wears the regalia of a male king: a kilt, a false beard, and the nemes headdress, the striped cloth worn by kings. Although in some images she is visibly female, in this and many others she is depicted without breasts.

Sometime after Hatshepsut's demise, Thutmose III constructed his own temple between his mother's and Mentuhotep's, with the purpose of eclipsing Hatshepsut's. He designated his temple as the destination of the divine boat carrying the statue of Amun in the Festival of the Wadi, held at Deir el-Bahri. By the 42nd year of Thutmose III, a systematic elimination of her images and removal of her name from inscriptions was under way. Still, Hatshepsut's temple remains a monument to her memory.

Temples to the Gods

Besides building their own funerary temples, Eighteenth Dynasty kings expended resources on cult temples to the gods, such as the Theban divine triad: Amun, his consort Mut, and their son Khons. At Karnak and nearby Luxor, successive kings constructed two vast temple complexes to honor this triad, and on special festivals divine boats conveyed the gods' images along waterways between the temples.

THE TEMPLE OF AMUN-RA At the temple of Amun-Ra at Karnak, a vast wall encircled the temple buildings. Entering the complex, a visitor walked through massive **pylons** or gateways built as monuments to individual kings. As a ceremonial procession moved within the buildings, these pylons marked its progress deeper and deeper into sacred space. A vast **hypostyle** hall (a building with a roof supported by columns) was the

reunited Egypt during the Middle Kingdom. Senenmut, the architect who designed Hatshepsut's temple, may have modeled some of its features after this earlier temple, with its terraces extending into the cliff face, and its crowning pyramid or mastaba. Once joined by a causeway to a valley temple beside the Nile, Hatshepsut's temple is a striking response to its physical setting. Its ascending white limestone courts, linked by wide ramps on a central axis, echo the desert's strong horizontal ground-line and the clifftop above. Meanwhile the bright light and shadows of the colonnades create a multitude of vertical lines that harmonize with the fissures of the cliff. With its clean contours, the royal structure imposes order on the less regularized forms of nature, just as the king's role was to impose order on chaos. Trees lined the way leading up to the

A simple space-spanning construction device is the post-and-lintel combination. The wider the distance spanned (and the less the "give" of the spanning material), the closer the uprights (posts) have to be. Egyptians used stone columns for posts; the weight of the rigid stone lintels forced the builders to place the columns close together.

 Watch an architectural simulation of post-and-lintel and corbel construction on myartslab.com

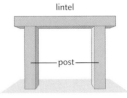

3.12 Hypostyle Hall of Temple of Amun-Ra. ca. 1290–1224 BCE. Sandstone. Karnak, Thebes

farthest point of access for all but priests and royalty (**fig. 3.12**). Here, a forest of columns would awe the mind, their sheer mass rendering the human form almost insignificant. The architect spaced the columns close together to support a ceiling of stone lintels, which had to be shorter than wooden lintels to prevent them from breaking under their own weight. Nevertheless the columns are far heavier than they needed to be, with the effect that a viewer senses the overwhelming presence of stone all around, heavy, solid, and permanent. Beyond the hall, a sacred lake allowed the king and priests to purify themselves before entering the temple proper. They proceeded through smaller halls, sun-drenched courts, and processional ways decorated with **obelisks**, tall stone markers topped by pyramid-shaped points, and chapels where they would pause to enact ceremonies. Every day the priests would cleanse and robe the images of the gods, and offer sacred meals to nourish them. The king and the priests conducted these rituals away from the public eye, gaining power for being shrouded in mystery.

Essential to the temple's ritual functioning was its metaphorical value, symbolizing the world at its inception. The columns of the hypostyle hall represented marsh plants in stylized form: Their capitals emulated the shape of both papyrus flowers and buds, so that the building evoked the watery swamp of chaos out of which the mound of creation emerged. The temple thus constituted the king's exhortation in stone to the gods to maintain cosmic order.

Akhenaten and the Amarna Style

Another Eighteenth Dynasty ruler, Amenhotep III, fostered devotion to the sun god during his reign (1391–1353 BCE). In temple complexes at Karnak and elsewhere, the king established open-air courtyards where Egyptians could worship the sun in its manifestation as a disk (or Aten) in the sky. Aten worship increased dramatically under his son, Amenhotep IV, who stressed the sun's life-giving force, and visualized the god not in the traditional guise of a falcon-headed figure, but as a disk that radiated beams terminating in hands. Enraged by the young king's monotheistic vision of Aten, a powerful conservative priesthood thwarted his attempts to introduce this new cult to traditional religious centers such as Thebes. In response, he founded a city devoted entirely to Aten on the Nile's east bank in central Egypt. He named his city Akhetaten, meaning "horizon of Aten" (it is now known as Amarna), and changed his own name to Akhenaten, meaning "beneficial to Aten." His new cult and fledgling city lasted only as long as its founder; after his death his opponents razed the city to the ground. Still, archaeological remains suggest that Akhenaten built temples in the contemporary style, using massive pylons and obelisks, as at Karnak, but with an emphasis on open-air courts beneath the sun's glare.

The Amarna Style

Sculptures of Akhenaten and his family break dramatically with long-established conventions for depicting royal subjects. In numerous representations, the figure of Akhenaten exhibits radically different proportions from those of previous kings. This is clear on a sunk relief scene on an altar stele, of the kind that Egyptians erected in small shrines in their homes and gardens (**fig. 3.13**). Beneath the disk of the sun, its life-giving beams radiate downward with hands at their terminals. Attenuated reed columns suggest that the scene is set within a garden pavilion, which is stocked with wine jars. The king and his consort Nefertiti sit facing each other on stools. The king has narrow shoulders lacking in musculature, a pot belly, wide hips, and generous thighs. His large lips, distinctive nose and chin, and narrow eyes readily identify his face. These unusual portraits are puzzling. Some experts dismiss them as caricatures, yet such expensive and prominent images must have had the king's approval. There have also been attempts to diagnose a medical condition from these representations, by reading the king's features as symptoms of Frolich's Syndrome, a hormonal deficiency that produces androgynous (both male and female) characteristics. Possibly he intended his "feminized" appearance to capture the fertile character of Aten as life-giver.

Group representations of Akhenaten with his family are remarkable for an apparent intimacy among the figures. He and Nefertiti hold three lively daughters, who clamber onto their laps and nestle in their arms, uniting the composition with animated gestures that reach across the relief, in marked contrast to the static scenes of other times. The deliberate emphasis on the daughters' childishness marks a change: In the past, artists had represented children with a hieroglyphic pictograph of

an adult in miniature, sucking a finger. The emphasis on children epitomizes the regeneration that the royal couple represent, and especially the king as manifestation of Aten.

QUEEN TIY The surprising transience implicit in the children's youthfulness and animated gestures on the altar also characterizes a one-third-life-size portrait of Akhenaten's mother Queen Tiy, chief wife of Amenhotep III (**fig. 3.14**). Using the dark wood of the yew tree, with precious metals and semiprecious stones for details, the artist achieved a delicate balance between idealized features and signs of age. Smooth planes form the cheeks and

abstract contours mark the eyebrows, which arch over striking eyes inlaid with ebony and alabaster. Yet the downturned mouth and the modeled lines running from the sides of the nose to the mouth offer careful hints of the queen's advancing years.

The sculpture went through two stages of design: Initially, the queen wore gold jewelry and a silver headdress ornamented with golden cobras, which identified her with the funerary goddesses Isis and Nephthys. A wig embellished with glass beads and topped with a plumed crown (the attachment for which is still extant) later concealed this headdress. Although excavators discovered the sculpture with funerary paraphernalia for her

3.13 *Akhenaten and His Family.* ca. 1355 BCE. Limestone, 12¾ × 15⅓″ (32.5 × 39 cm). Staatliche Museen zu Berlin, Preussischer Kulturbesitz, Ägyptisches Museum

Read the document related to Akhenaten on myartslab.com

3.14 *Sculpture of Queen Tiy*, from Kom Medinet el-Ghurab. ca. 1348–1336/5 BCE. Yew, ebony, glass, silver, gold, lapis lazuli, cloth, clay, and wax. Height 3¾″ (9.4 cm). Staatliche Museen zu Berlin, Preussischer Kulturbesitz, Ägyptisches Museum

husband, Amenhotep III, these changes indicate that it was adapted to suit the beliefs of Akhenaten's new monotheistic religion.

Tutankhamun and the Aftermath of Amarna

Shortly after Akhenaten's death, a young king ascended the throne. Married to Akhenaten's daughter, and perhaps himself even one of Akhenaten's sons, Tutankhaten was only nine or ten when he became king. Possibly under the influence of the priests of Amun, he restored the royal residence to Memphis and resurrected the orthodox religion of Egypt that Akhenaten had rejected. He changed his name to Tutankhamun to reflect the monarchy's re-alliance with Amun, before dying unexpectedly at the age of 19. His death has inspired numerous murder and conspiracy theories, but recent scientific analyses of his mummy point to natural causes.

Tutankhamun's greatest fame results not from his life, but from the discovery of his tomb in 1922 by the British archaeologist Howard Carter. Although robbers had entered the tomb twice,

3.15 Cover of the coffin of Tutankhamun. Eighteenth Dynasty (ca. 1567–1320 BCE). Gold inlaid with glass and semiprecious stones, height 72″ (182.9 cm). Egyptian Museum, Cairo

much of it was untouched. With a stairway, corridor, and four chambers, the tomb is uncharacteristically small for a royal burial, indicating the possibility that a nonroyal tomb might have been hastily co-opted for the king at the time of his unanticipated death. All the same, the offerings buried with him lacked nothing in volume or quality. The tomb contained funerary equipment, including coffins, statues, and masks, as well as items used during the king's lifetime such as furniture, clothing, and chariots. Three coffins preserved the king's mummified corpse, the innermost of which (**fig. 3.15**) is gold and weighs over 250 pounds. Even more impressive is the exquisite workmanship of its cover, with its rich play of colored inlays against polished gold surfaces.

Tutankhamun's short-lived successor, the aged Ay, continued the process of restoring the old religion. Head of the army under Tutankhamun and last king of the Eighteenth Dynasty, Horemheb completed the restoration. He set out to erase all traces of the Amarna revolution, repairing shattered images of the gods and rebuilding their temples; but the effects of Akhenaten's rule lived on in Egyptian art for some time to come.

POINTS OF REFLECTION

3.1 Describe the diverse types of sign used on the *Palette of King Narmer*, and the message they imparted.

3.2 Assess Egyptian notions of kingship in the Old Kingdom, and their impact on funerary architecture.

3.3 Discuss the different levels of naturalism in the figures depicted in the painting of *Ti Watching a Hippopotamus Hunt* from the Tomb of Ti at Saqqara. How do the royal portraits from the reign of Akhenaten compare to earlier patterns of representation?

3.4 Explain the extraordinary conservatism in Egyptian art.

✓—[Study] and review on myartslab.com

ART IN TIME

- ca. 5000 BCE—Human settlements along the Nile Valley

- ca. 3000 BCE—**The ancient Egyptian *Palette of King Narmer***

- ca. 2900 BCE— Mesopotamians begin using cuneiform writing

- 2630–2611 BCE—Rule of King Djoser; entombment at Saqqara

- ca. 2575–2465 BCE—**Ancient Egypt's Fourth Dynasty; construction of the three Great Pyramids at Giza**

- ca. 2400 BCE—Final major phase of construction at Stonehenge

- ca. 1870s–1840s BCE— **Naturalistic *Sculpture of King Senwosret III***

- 1792–1750 BCE—Hammurabi rules Babylon

- ca. 1458 BCE—King (sic) Hatshepsut dies; Senenmut designs her mortuary temple

- ca. 1353–1335 BCE—Rule of King Akhenaten; new religious center at Amarna

- ca. 1348–1336/5 BCE— ***Sculpture of Queen Tiy***

CHAPTER 4 Aegean Art

POINTS OF INQUIRY

4.1 Discover the architectural principles behind the Minoan "palace" complexes.

4.2 Explore the significance of nature to Minoan painters.

4.3 Examine the Mycenaeans' use of massive stone architecture.

4.4 Consider the impact of early archaeologists on our understanding of the ancient Aegean.

((•—**Listen** to the chapter audio on myartslab.com

Major Periods of Aegean Art

ca. 2800–1600 BCE	Cycladic
ca. 3000–1450 BCE	Minoan
ca. 1700–1100 BCE	Mycenaean
ca. 3000–2000 BCE	Early Aegean Bronze Age
ca. 2000–1600 BCE	Middle Aegean Bronze Age
ca. 1600–1100 BCE	Late Aegean Bronze Age
ca. 1600–1200 BCE	Late Helladic period

The Mediterranean was one of the primary highways that connected the cultures of antiquity. With North Africa on the south, Asia on the east, and Europe on the west and north, this body of water brought disparate cultures into contact for both trade and conflict. The Greeks named one branch of the Mediterranean, between Greece and Turkey, the Aegean Sea (see **map 4.1**), and on islands and peninsulas there several closely related but distinct cultures developed in the third and second millennia BCE. The Cycladic culture emerged on the islands forming an irregular circle between the Greek mainland and the island of Crete. The British archaeologist Sir Arthur Evans named the culture on Crete Minoan, for the legendary King Minos. That on the mainland is called Helladic, from the Greek Hellas, name of a legendary ancestor, or Mycenaean, from one of its most imposing cities.

Until the second half of the nineteenth century, Aegean civilization was known principally from the Homeric poems *The Iliad* and *The Odyssey*, which historians considered to be mostly the stuff of legend. Prompted by these stories, Heinrich Schliemann, a wealthy German businessman turned archaeologist, excavated sites in Asia Minor and Greece during the 1870s, looking for Homer's Troy. Following his lead, Arthur Evans, Keeper of the Ashmolean Museum at Oxford, began excavations in Crete in 1900. Though controversial, their work radically changed the accepted views of the ancient Aegean. Since their time a great deal more archaeological evidence has come to light, some consistent with, but much contradicting, the Homeric narratives. Writing exists from Minoan and Mycenaean contexts, but so far it is more or less indecipherable. Consequently, we understand less about Aegean civilization than we do about the cultures of Egypt or the ancient Near East.

Evidence of human habitation throughout the Aegean dates from as early as the Paleolithic period, though settlements spread and grew mainly in the Neolithic and Early Bronze Ages. The Aegean Bronze Age is divided into three phases: Early (ca. 3000–2000 BCE), Middle (ca. 2000–1600 BCE), and Late (ca. 1600–1100 BCE), each of which is subdivided into phases I, II, and III. Archaeologists often prefer these relative dates to absolute ones, because Aegean chronology is so controversial. A mass destruction of Aegean sites, from an unknown cause, led to significant depopulation in about 1200 BCE, and by 1100 BCE the Aegean Bronze Age had ended.

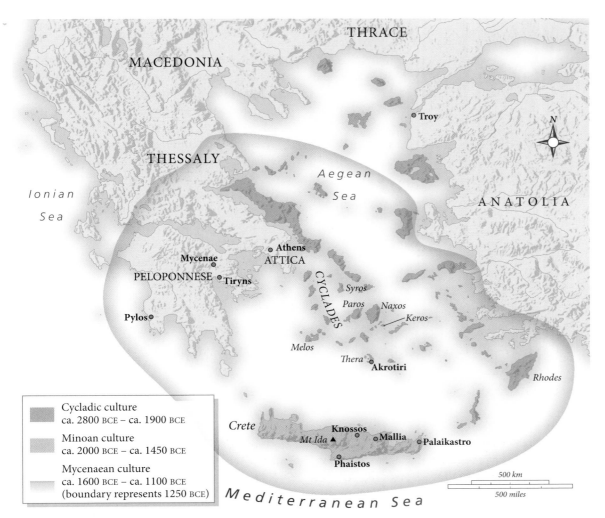

Map 4.1 The Bronze Age Aegean

THRACE

MACEDONIA

Troy

THESSALY

Aegean

Sea

Ionian

Sea

ANATOLIA

Athens

Mycenae

ATTICA

PELOPONNESE · Tiryns

CYCLADES

Syros

Paros

Naxos

Keros

Pylos

Melos

Thera

Akrotiri

Rhodes

Cycladic culture
ca. 2800 BCE – ca. 1900 BCE

Minoan culture
ca. 2000 BCE – ca. 1450 BCE

Mycenaean culture
ca. 1600 BCE – ca. 1100 BCE
(boundary represents 1250 BCE)

Crete

Knossos

Mt Ida ▲ · Mallia · Palaikastro

Phaistos

500 km

500 miles

Mediterranean Sea

Early Cycladic Art

Information about the culture of the Cyclades comes entirely from the archaeological record, which indicates that wealth accumulated there early in the Bronze Age as trade developed. Funerary practice reflects this prosperity. Near the beginning of the Early Bronze Age, around 2800 BCE, the islanders started to bury their dead in stone-lined pits known as cist graves. Some of these graves contained offerings of weapons, jewelry, and pottery, and some included striking figures, usually female, carved from the local white marble. The Early Cycladic II example illustrated here represents the prevalent type (**fig. 4.1**). The figure is nude, with arms folded across the waist, and toes extended. The flat body is straight-backed, while a long, thick neck supports a shield-shaped face at an angle. The artist used abrasives, probably emery from the island of Naxos, to distinguish details on

the figure, such as a ridgelike nose, pointed breasts, a triangular pubic area, and toes. Traces of pigments on some figures indicate that other details were painted on, including eyes, hair, jewelry, and body markings similar to tattoos. Their sizes vary, but their form is still consistent enough to provide a governing canon of proportions, as for Egyptian sculptures.

For many years, archaeologists called these figures "idols," and pictured them playing a central role in a religion focusing on a mother goddess. More recently at least two explanations have been offered for their functions. Perhaps they were manufactured purely for funerary purposes, representing servants or surrogates for human sacrifices, or even for the deceased. Alternatively, before being buried they may have functioned in daily life, possibly within household shrines. Although most have been found in a reclining position, they may also have been propped upright. The largest figures

4.1 *Figure*, Cyclades. ca. 2500 BCE. Marble, height 15¾" (40 cm). Nicholas P. Goulandris Foundation, Museum of Cycladic Arts, Athens. N.P. Goulandris Collection, No. 206

The legendary MINOS was the son of Zeus and Europa and the husband of Pasiphaë, who bore the Minotaur as a punishment after her husband had disobeyed the god Poseidon. Greek historians also speak of a King Minos as the strongest, most prosperous ruler in the Mediterranean and the first to control the area with a powerful navy.

(reaching 5 feet long) may have been cult statues. Some examples show signs of repair with wire, which indicates that they were used before being deposited in graves.

It is likely that no single explanation applies to all of them. The greatest obstacle to determining their function is our lack of knowledge about their **provenance**, that is, where and how they were found and their subsequent history. The simplicity and clear geometry of the figures appeals to a twentieth- and twenty-first-century aesthetic that favors understated and unadorned geometric forms. Those qualities and the luscious white marble used to form them have led to their widespread appearance on the art market, often without any record of archaeological context. To have a clearer sense of how to interpret these figures, archaeologists need to know their findspots, whether in a burial or in living quarters.

Minoan Art

The island of Crete, south of the Cyclades, and about 400 miles northwest of Egypt, stretches over 124 miles from east to west, divided by mountain ranges, and with a few large areas of flat, arable land (see map 4.1). Consequently, early communities were small and scattered. The island's geography, then, along with continuous migration, encouraged diversity and independence among the population, and its central location in the Mediterranean led the Minoans to become skilled seafarers. The major flowering of Minoan art occurred about 2000 BCE, when Crete's urban civilizations constructed great "palaces" at Knossos, Phaistos, and Mallia. At this time, the first Aegean script, known as Linear A, appeared. This is termed the First Palace period (Middle Minoan I and II). All three centers suffered heavy damage, probably due to an earthquake, in about 1700 BCE, and a short time later the Minoans built new and larger structures on the same sites. This phase constitutes the Second Palace period (Middle Minoan III, and Late Minoan IA–IB). An earthquake demolished these centers, too, in about 1450 BCE. After that, the palaces at Phaistos and Mallia were abandoned, but the Mycenaeans, who gained control of the island, occupied Knossos.

The Palace at Knossos

The buildings of the Second Palace period are our chief source of information for Minoan architecture. The largest is the structure at Knossos, which Evans dubbed the Palace of MINOS (**figs. 4.2** and **4.3**). In fact, Knossos may have been the most powerful Cretan center of the Middle and Late Bronze Age. The palace consisted of courts, halls, workshops, storerooms, and perhaps residential quarters, linked by corridors, staircases, and porticoes. Light wells illuminated and ventilated interior spaces.

Evans reconceived and reconstructed much of the palace in concrete. Originally, walls were framed with timbers and constructed of rubble masonry or mud brick. Some were of **ashlar masonry** (cut and dressed stone), which gave them a more ornamental appearance. Columns, often made of wood with a stone base, supported the porticoes. Their form was unusual: A smooth shaft, often oval in cross-section, tapered downward from a generous cushionlike capital. Wall paintings suggest that capitals were painted black and shafts red or white.

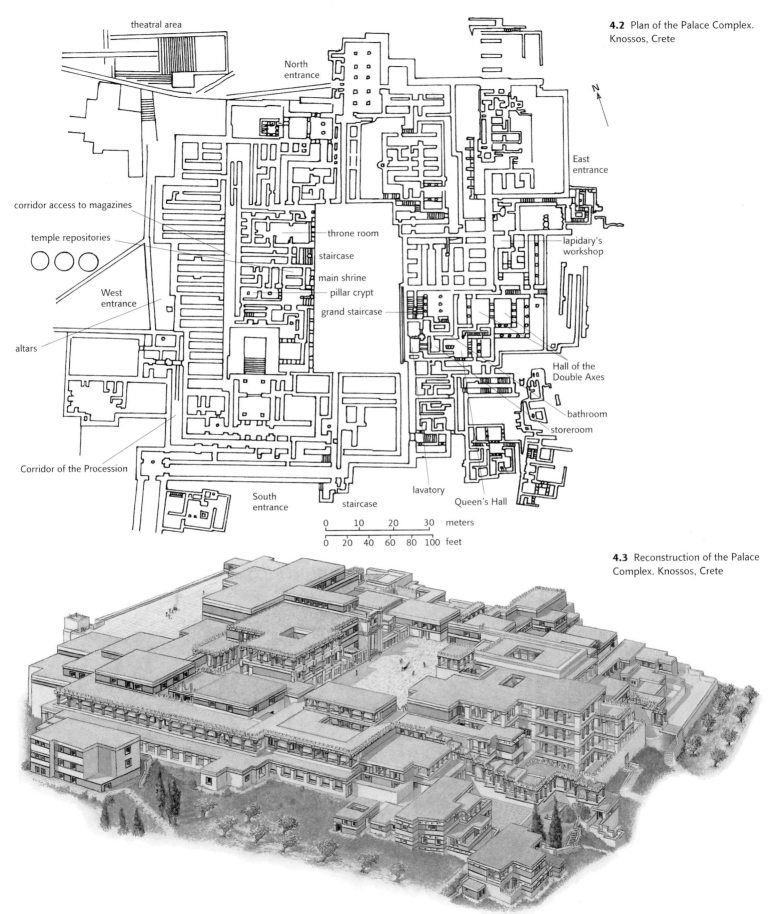

theatral area

North entrance

4.2 Plan of the Palace Complex. Knossos, Crete

N

East entrance

corridor access to magazines

temple repositories

throne room

staircase

main shrine

pillar crypt

grand staircase

lapidary's workshop

West entrance

altars

Hall of the Double Axes

bathroom

storeroom

Corridor of the Procession

South entrance

staircase

lavatory

Queen's Hall

0   10   20   30   meters
0   20   40   60   80   100   feet

4.3 Reconstruction of the Palace Complex. Knossos, Crete

4.4 The "Queen's Megaron," from Knossos, Crete. ca. 1700–1300 BCE. Archaeological Museum, Iráklion, Crete

At first glance, the palace's plan (see fig. 4.2) looks haphazard, which probably explains why later Greek legend referred to it as the LABYRINTH, home of the MINOTAUR. The mazelike arrangement may have been part of a defensive strategy; certainly no exterior fortifications protected the palace from attack, and entrances were not emphasized. Nevertheless, the design does have an underlying logic. Its core is a central court, onto which important rooms opened. The court divides the plan on an approximately north–south axis. On the west, a corridor running north–south separates narrow storerooms from rooms of less uniform shapes close to the court; the latter rooms may have performed a ceremonial role. The palace appears to grow outward from the court, and using flat (rather than pitched) roofs would have greatly facilitated the building of additions. Compared to Near Eastern palaces, such as the palace at Persepolis (see fig. 2.12), the overall effect at Knossos is modest; individual units are relatively small and the ceilings low. Still, rich decoration embellished some

of the interior walls. We should also remember that much of what remains belongs to subterranean or ground-floor levels, and archaeologists have long believed that grander rooms once existed on an upper level.

Exactly how the palaces of Crete functioned, and who lived in them, is debated. Evans described the complex as a "palace" (assigning royal names to various rooms), and the term stuck, regardless of its accuracy. He conceived of it as an elite residence for several reasons. He was reacting partly to discoveries on the Mycenaean mainland, described subsequently, and partly to the presence of a grand "Throne Room." But the social and political realities of Evans's own homeland may have been even more influential: He would have been familiar with the palaces occupied by the extensive royal family of late Victorian England. In reality, excavation of the complex at Knossos suggests that inhabitants pursued many different activities there. Extensive storage areas suggest that the palace was a center of manufacturing,

administration, and commerce. Ceremonial spaces, such as the great court, and small shrines with religious paraphernalia imply that political and ritual activities took place there too. There is no reason to believe that the Minoans segregated these activities as neatly as we often do today. Moreover, we have no evidence suggesting that the functions of the various palaces were identical, or that they remained constant over time.

Wall Paintings: Representing Rituals and Nature

Grand rooms within Minoan palaces were decorated with paintings. Most of them came to light in extremely fragmentary condition, so what we see today is the result of extensive restoration, which may not always be reliable. Painters applied vibrant mineral colors to wet or dry plaster in broad washes without shading; wide bands of geometric patterns serve as frames. Many paintings depict nature. An example restored to a wall in the room Evans called the Queen's Megaron in Knossos' east wing (**fig. 4.4**) shows sinuous blue and yellow dolphins swimming against a blue-streaked cream background, cavorting with small fish. Multilobed green forms represent plants or rocks. Curving, organic elements animate the composition. The prevalence of marine creatures in Minoan art suggests a keen awareness of and respect for the sea.

PAINTED LANDSCAPES IN A SEASIDE TOWN In the middle of the second millennium BCE, a volcano erupted on the Cycladic island of Thera (present-day Santorini), about 60 miles north of Crete. The eruption covered the town of Akrotiri in a deep layer of volcanic ash and pumice. Beginning in 1967, excavations uncovered houses dating from the Middle Minoan III phase (approximately 1670–1620 BCE) preserved up to a height of two stories. On their walls was an extraordinary series of paintings, many representing subjects from nature. One painting on the upper section of at least three walls in a large second-floor room (**fig. 4.5**) reflects the town's role as a harbor: A fleet of ships ferries passengers between islands, set within a sea full of leaping dolphins; the islands feature ports with detailed stone architecture. Crowds of people look out from streets, rooftops, and windows. The painting may represent an actual event—a memorable expedition to a foreign land, perhaps, or a nautical ceremony.

Minoan Pottery and Faience

By the Middle and Late Minoan periods, potters manufactured their vessels on the wheel. Like wall painters, they drew their inspiration from the natural world, using lively organic forms to enhance the vases' curving shapes. In the Late Minoan IB phase, marine motifs became prevalent. On a jar of eggshell-colored clay, a wide-eyed octopus with swirling tentacles stands out in black amid clumps of floating algae (**fig. 4.6**). The sea creature's rounded contours emphasize the jar's swollen belly, while the coils of the tentacles echo its curved handles. Beneath the spout, the end of a tentacle curls to define a circle of the same size as the jar's opening.

Religious life on Minoan Crete centered on natural places deemed sacred, such as caves and mountain-tops. No temples or large cult statues

4.5 *Flotilla Fresco*, from Akrotiri, Thera. ca. 1600–1500 BCE. Painted plaster. National Archaeological Museum, Athens

 View the Closer Look for the *Flotilla Fresco* on myartslab.com

4.6 *Octopus Vase*, stirrup jar from Palaikastro, Crete. ca. 1500–1450 BCE. Ceramic, height 11″ (28 cm). Archaeological Museum, Iráklion, Crete

4.7 *Faience figurine*, from the Palace Complex, Knossos. ca. 1650 BCE. Faience, height 11⅝″ (29.5 cm). Archaeological Museum, Iráklion, Crete

 View the Closer Look for the *Faience Figurine* on myartslab.com

have been discovered. Archaeologists at Knossos did find fragments of two small-scale **faience** (glazed earthenware) statuettes from the Middle Minoan III phase (about 1650 BCE). Once assembled, one shows a female figure raising a snake in each hand (**fig. 4.7**). She wears a headdress, topped by a feline creature, and a flounced skirt, and bares her breasts. Some ancient religions associated snakes with earth deities and male fertility, just as the bared breasts of this statuette suggest fecundity. Moreover, the statuettes came to light in pits (known as the Temple Repositories) sunk in the floor of a room on the west side of the central court, which has led scholars to associate them with a mother goddess. They could alternatively have represented ritual attendants.

Late Minoan Art

It is unclear what brought Minoan civilization to an end. Some scholars argue that the volcanic eruption on the island of Thera may have hastened its decline. Recent discoveries and dating of the ash from this eruption, however, indicate that Cretan culture survived this natural disaster, though perhaps in a weakened state. About 1450 BCE (Late Minoan II), invaders from the Greek mainland took over the palaces. Archaeologists call them Mycenaeans. They established themselves in the palace at Knossos until around 1375 BCE, when Knossos was destroyed and the Mycenaeans abandoned most of the island's sites. While they were in control, however, artists at Knossos worked in Minoan styles.

The fragmentary *Toreador Fresco* dates from the Mycenaean occupation (Late Minoan II–IIIA), and appears to have decorated an upper room in the northeast part of the palace (**fig. 4.8**). Against a blue background, a white-skinned figure clad in a kilt clasps the horns of a huge, curvaceous bull, painted at a full gallop. Behind the bull, a white-skinned figure stands on tiptoe with arms outstretched, while above the animal's back, a dark-skinned figure performs a backward somersault. The figures have long limbs and small waists, and they are painted in true profile. The painting's washes of color and animated though stylized poses demonstrate the continuity of Minoan practice into the Late period.

There continues to be debate about the meaning of this painting. Although it is generally agreed that bull-leaping performances had a ritual function, its purpose and the identity of the participants are not clear. Following a widespread Mediterranean convention for distinguishing gender by skin tone, Evans identified the light-skinned figures as female and the darker one as male. Others have seen all three figures as sequential representations of one person taking part in a coming-of-age initiation ceremony in which boys emerge masculine from their earlier "feminine" guise.

Mycenaean Art

By the time the Mycenaeans conquered Crete in about 1450 BCE, they had been building cities on the Greek mainland since the start of the Late Helladic period, ca. 1600 BCE. They probably made early contact with Minoan Crete, which exerted important influences on their culture. Archaeologists place the height of the culture between about 1500 and 1200 BCE (Late Helladic III). The most imposing remains are citadels at sites that Homer named: Pylos, Tiryns, and Mycenae, the legendary home of King Agamemnon, who led the Greek forces in Homer's TROJAN WAR.

Architecture: Citadels

At the beginning of the Second Palace period on Crete, growing settlements throughout the Greek mainland, including that at Mycenae (**fig. 4.9**), centered around large structures known as citadels (when fortified) or palaces. In some of them, archaeologists unearthed clay tablets inscribed with a second early writing system, dubbed Linear B because of its linear character and because it drew, in part, on Minoan Linear A. When Michael Ventris and John Chadwick decoded the system in 1952, the tablets proved to have been inventories and

4.8 *Toreador Fresco*, from the Palace Complex, Knossos. ca. 1550–1450 BCE (restored). Height including upper border approx. 24½″ (62.3 cm). Painted plaster. Archaeological Museum, Iráklion, Crete

The TROJAN WAR was a half-legendary conflict fought between a number of the Greek city-states and Troy, a city on the northwest coast of Asia Minor (present-day Turkey). Homer's epic poem *The Iliad* describes events that took place during the last year of the war, and *The Odyssey* recounts the ten-year homeward voyage of one of the Greek kings, Odysseus (Roman Ulysses), after the conflict. These poems—part history and part myth—developed gradually within the oral tradition of Greek poetry for centuries before there was a written Greek language and were passed down from one generation of poets to another.

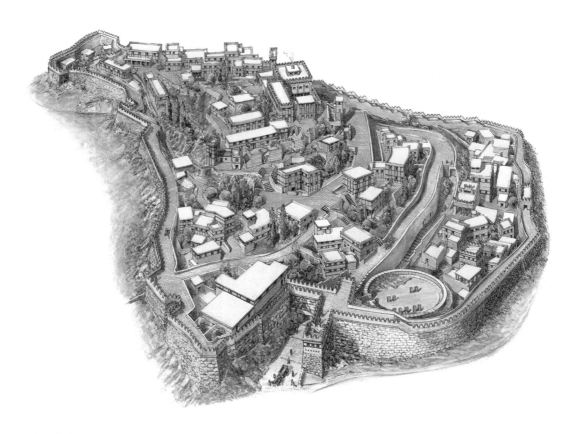

4.9 Aerial view of Mycenae, Greece. ca. 1600–1200 BCE

Corbeling as a space-spanning device relies on the downward pressure of overlapped layers of stone to lock in the projecting ends.

 Watch an architectural simulation of corbel construction on myartslab.com

corbel arch

corbel vault

4.10 The Lion Gate, Mycenae, Greece. ca. 1250 BCE. Limestone

archival documents, in a language now considered an early form of Greek. The inhabitants of these Late Bronze Age sites, therefore, were the precursors of the people we describe as the ancient Greeks.

The Linear B tablets refer to a *wanax* ("lord" or "king"), suggesting a hierarchical social order.

Indeed, Mycenaean citadels and palaces may have incorporated royal residences, centered on a **megaron**, a large rectangular audience hall. Many of them were enclosed by imposing exterior walls, often expanded and improved in several building phases, and constructed so as to exploit the site's

topography. They were built of large, irregularly shaped (or polygonal) stone blocks, and in places reached 20 feet thick. Centuries later, the massiveness of these walls so awed the Greeks that they declared them the work of the Cyclopes, a mythical race of one-eyed giants. Today, the walls are termed "Cyclopean." The walls, and tunnels leading to wells for water during a siege, have led some experts to conceive of an essential character difference between warmongering Mycenaeans and their nature-loving Minoan neighbors. Others note, however, that the fortifications date to after the destruction of Minoan centers, when the Mycenaeans may have been responding to a new set of political and social circumstances.

At entrances in the walls or at other highly visible places, masons sometimes saw-cut and dressed the stones or smoothed them with a hammer for refined visual effect. At Mycenae, when the inhabitants enlarged their city walls, they built the Lion Gate of about 1250 BCE as a principal entrance (**fig. 4.10**). Two massive stone posts support a huge lintel to form the opening. Above the lintel, which itself weighs 25 tons, a **corbel** arch directs the weight of the heavy surmounting wall to the strong posts below it: Each course of ashlar masonry projects slightly beyond the course below it, until the span is covered when the walls meet. The corbel thus relieves the vast stone lintel of weight, and is known as a relieving triangle. To seal the resulting gap, a triangular limestone slab was inserted above the lintel, carved with a pair of huge animals, probably lionesses (though they may be sphinxes or griffins). They stand in a **heraldic** pose (mirror images of each other), with their front paws on altars of a Minoan style, and flanking a tapering Minoan-style column. Dowel holes in their necks show that sculptors added their heads separately. At almost 10 feet high, this relief is the first large-scale sculpture known on the Greek mainland. The lionesses function as guardians, and their tense, muscular bodies and symmetrical design suggest a Near Eastern influence. Mycenaeans ventured throughout the Mediterranean, including Egypt and Anatolia, and Hittite records suggest contact with a people who may have been Mycenaean.

Mycenaean Tombs and Their Contents

At the end of the Middle Helladic period at Mycenae, ca. 1600 BCE, the ruling elite began to bury their dead in deep rectangular shafts, marking them at ground level with stone stelai. They distributed the

4.11 Interior of the "Treasury of Atreus," Mycenae, Greece. ca. 1300–1250 BCE. Limestone

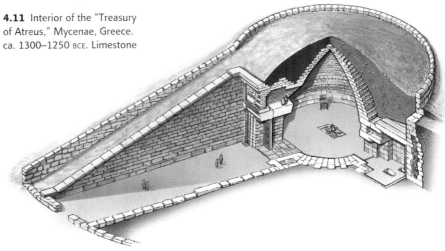

In Greek legend, ATREUS was the ancestor of the royal family of Mycenae.

Reconstruction of façade of "Treasury of Atreus," Mycenae, Greece. ca. 1300–1250 BCE

burials in two groups (known as Grave Circles A and B), which later generations set off and monumentalized with a low circular wall. As time passed, the elite built more dramatic tombs, in a round form known as a **tholos**. Archaeologists have identified over 100 tholoi on the mainland.

One of the best-preserved and largest of these tombs is at Mycenae. Dubbed the "Treasury of ATREUS," it dates to about 1250 BCE (Late Helladic III B). A great pathway, or *dromos*, lined with ashlar masonry, led to a large circular chamber excavated into sloping ground and then built up from ground level with a corbel vault (**fig. 4.11**), resulting in a beehive profile for the roof. Earth covered the structure, helping to stabilize the layers of stone and creating a small hill, which was encircled with stones. The vault rose 43 feet over a

space 48 feet in diameter. Such a large unsupported span would not be seen again until the Pantheon of Roman times (see fig. 7.20). Gilded rosettes may once have decorated the ashlar blocks of the vault to resemble a starry sky. To one side of the main room, a small rectangular chamber contained subsidiary burials.

METALWORK Like the Great Pyramids of Egypt, these monumental *tholoi* exalted the dead by drawing attention to themselves. As a result, they also attracted robbers throughout the ages, and the grave goods that once filled them have long been dispersed. Many of the earlier shaft graves also contained lavish goods, ranging from luxurious clothing and furniture to weaponry. On excavating Grave Circle A, Schliemann discovered five

4.12 *Gold mask*, from a shaft grave in Circle A, Mycenae. ca. 1600–1500 BCE. Gold, height 12″ (30 cm). National Archaeological Museum, Athens

extraordinary male death masks of hammered gold. Although far from naturalistic, each displays a distinct treatment of physiognomy: Some faces are bearded while others are clean-shaven. This suggests that the masks were individualized to correspond to the deceased's appearance. On finding the example illustrated in **fig. 4.12** in 1876, Schliemann told the press, "I have gazed into the face of Agamemnon." Since modern archaeology places the mask between 1600 and 1500 BCE, and the Trojan War—if it happened—would date to about 1300–1200 BCE, this could not be Agamemnon's mask. But given the expense of the materials it may represent a Mycenaean king of some stature.

Archaeologists continue to build up our knowledge of Minoan and Mycenaean cultures. These were central to the myths and legends of later Greek culture, which present them as an age of heroes.

POINTS OF REFLECTION

4.1 Define the design features of the great architectural complex at Knosssos. What might we deduce about Minoan society from the building?

4.2 Describe the characteristics of Minoan paintings. What does the *Toreador Fresco* represent?

4.3 Summarize the main types of project assigned to Mycenaean architects. How and why do Mycenaean and Minoan monumental buildings differ?

4.4 Assess the archaeological legacies of Heinrich Schliemann and Sir Arthur Evans. How do their views continue to inform our thinking about the ancient Aegean?

✓•—**Study** and review on myartslab.com

- ca. 2500 BCE—White marble Cycladic figurines

- ca. 2575–2465 BCE—Ancient Egypt's Fourth Dynasty; construction of the three Great Pyramids at Giza

- ca. 1792–1750 BCE— Hammurabi rules Babylon

- ca. 1700–1300 BCE—Minoan construction of the Second Palace at Knossos

- ca. 1628—Volcanic eruption on Thera

- ca. 1500–1450 BCE— *Octopus Vase*, an example of Minoan "marine style" pottery

- ca. 1450 BCE—Earthquake demolishes Knossos and other Minoan centers; Mycenaeans invade Crete

- ca. 1600–1500 BCE— Mycenaean death masks of hammered gold

- ca. 1500–1200 BCE—Height of Mycenaean culture

- ca. 1250 BCE—Construction of the Lion Gate at Mycenae

CHAPTER

5 | Greek Art

POINTS OF INQUIRY

5.1 Assess the influences at work on artists and architects in the Orientalizing and Archaic periods in Greece.

5.2 Investigate the ways in which Greek sculptors and painters explored naturalism and the depiction of movement and emotion.

5.3 Evaluate the architecture and sculpture of the Parthenon by the standards of its time.

5.4 Compare the themes of Late Classical and Hellenistic sculpture with those of the Archaic and Classical periods.

5.5 Analyze the new movements in Hellenistic architecture against the backdrop of contemporaneous political and social changes.

((•─|**Listen** to the chapter audio on myartslab.com

Greek architecture, sculpture, and civilization are instantly recognizable as the ancestors of Western culture: Government buildings, banks, and college campuses recall Greek temples, and statues of our day evoke those of the Greeks. This is not coincidental. Western civilization has carefully constructed itself in the image of the Greek and Roman worlds. Through the centuries, these worlds have represented a height of cultural achievement for Western cultures, which looked to them for artistic ideals as well as for philosophical models such as democracy. Trying to understand their visual culture presents a special challenge for the art historian: It is tempting to believe that something familiar on the surface holds the same significance for us today as it did for Greeks or Romans, but scholars have discovered time and time again that this is a dangerous fallacy.

The flowering of ancient Greek art was just one manifestation of a wide-ranging exploration of humanistic and religious issues. Artists, writers, and philosophers struggled with common questions,

still preserved in a huge body of works. Their inquiries cut to the core of human existence, and form the backbone of much of Western philosophy. For the most part, Greeks accepted a pantheon of gods, whom they worshiped in human form. Yet they debated the nature of those gods, and the relationship between divinities and humankind. Greek thinkers conceived of many aspects of life in dualistic terms. Order (*cosmos*, in Greek) was opposed to disorder (*chaos*), and both poles permeated existence. Civilization, which was, by definition, Greek, stood in opposition to an uncivilized world beyond Greek borders; all non-Greeks were "barbarians," named for the nonsensical sound of their languages to Greek ears ("bar-bar-bar-bar"). Reason, too, had its opposite in the irrational. These poles were mirrored in light and darkness, in man and woman. In their literature and in their art, the Greeks addressed the tension between these polar opposites.

There are three separate, and sometimes conflicting, sources of information for Greek art. First, there are the works themselves—reliable, but only

Major Periods of Greek Art

ca. 900–725 BCE	Geometric
ca. 725–650 BCE	Orientalizing
ca. 650–480 BCE	Archaic
ca. 480–400 BCE	Classical
ca. 400–325 BCE	Late Classical
ca. 325–30 BCE	Hellenistic

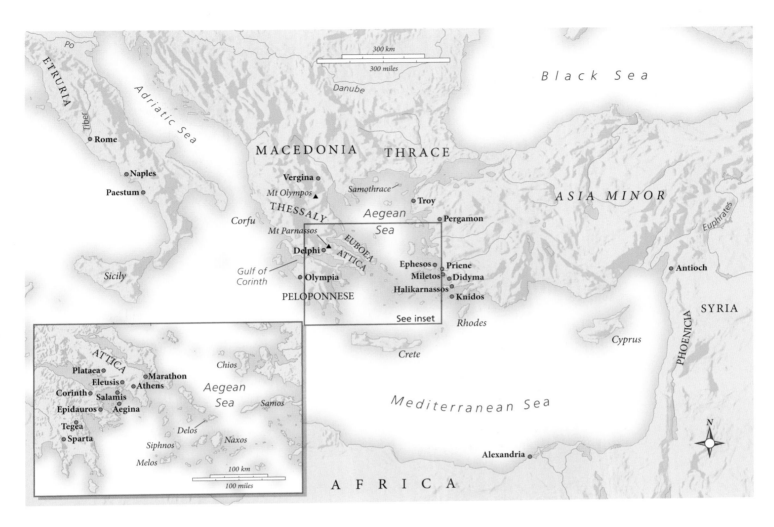

Map 5.1 Greece in the Archaic and Classical periods

a small fraction of what once existed. Secondly, there are Roman copies of Greek originals. These works tell us something about important pieces that would otherwise be lost to us, but pose their own problems. Without the original, we cannot determine how faithful a copy is, and sometimes multiple copies present different versions of a single original, because a Roman copyist's notion of a copy was quite different from ours: It was not necessarily a strict imitation, but allowed for adapting the work according to the copyist's taste or skill or the patron's wishes.

The third source on Greek art is literature. The Greeks were the first Western people to write at length about their artists. Roman writers incorporated Greek accounts into their own; many of these survive, although often in fragmentary condition. These texts offer a glimpse of what the Greeks considered their significant artistic achievements. They name celebrated artists and monuments, and often deal with lost works that we number among the greatest masterpieces of

their time. Weaving these strands of information into a coherent picture of Greek art has been the difficult task of archaeologists and art historians for several centuries.

The Emergence of Greek Art: The Geometric Style

The first Greek-speaking groups came to Greece about 2000 BCE, bringing a culture that soon encompassed most of mainland Greece and the Aegean islands. By the first millennium BCE they had colonized the west coast of Asia Minor and Cyprus (see **map 5.1**). Despite cultural differences, Greeks of different regions had a strong sense of kinship, based on language and common beliefs. From the mid-eighth through the mid-sixth centuries BCE, the Greeks spread across the Mediterranean and as far as the Black Sea in a wave of colonization. They founded settlements in Sicily, southern Italy, and North Africa.

guilloche

palmette

rosette

acanthus

meander

egg-and-dart

Some common Greek vessel forms

As pottery became an art form, Greek potters developed an extensive, if fairly standardized, repertoire of vessel shapes. Each type was well adapted to its function. Each shape presented unique challenges to the painter, and some became specialists at decorating certain types of vases. Large pots often attracted the most ambitious craftsmen because they provided a generous field on which to work. Making and decorating vases were complex processes, usually performed by different artisans. From the middle of the sixth century BCE, many of the finest vessels bear signatures of the artists who made them, indicating the pride that potters and painters took in their work. In many cases, vase painters had such distinctive styles that experts can recognize their work even without a signature, and use modern names to identify them. Dozens of vases might survive by the same hand, allowing art historians to trace a single painter's development over many years.

amphora

krater

hydria

lekythos

oinochoe

kylix

5.1 Late Geometric belly-handled amphora by the Dipylon Master, from the Dipylon Cemetery, Athens. ca. 750 BCE. Height 51″ (155 cm). Ceramic. National Archaeological Museum, Athens

After the collapse of Mycenaean civilization (see Chapter 4), art became largely nonfigural (that is, abstract) for several centuries. In the eighth century BCE, the oldest surviving style of Greek art developed, known today as the Geometric.

Geometric Style Pottery

The earliest Greek vase-painters decorated their wares with abstract designs, such as triangles, "checkerboards," and concentric circles. Toward 800 BCE, at about the time the alphabet was introduced (under Near Eastern influence) and contemporaneous with *The Iliad* and *The Odyssey*, human and animal figures began to appear within the geometric framework. In the most elaborate designs

these figures interacted in narrative scenes. The vase shown here, from a cemetery near the later Dipylon gate in Athens, dates to around 750 BCE (**fig. 5.1**). Known as the Dipylon Vase, it was one of a group of unusually large vessels Athenians used as funerary markers over burials. Holes in its base allowed mourners to pour liquid offerings (libations) to the dead during funerary rituals. In earlier centuries, Athenians had placed the ashes of their dead inside vases, choosing the vase's shape according to the sex of the deceased: They placed a woman's remains in a belly-handled amphora, a type of vase they used more commonly for storing wine or oil, and a man's ashes in a neck-amphora. Since the early first millennium, Athenians had also used kraters as burial markers, large bowl-like vessels in which they normally mixed wine with water. The shape and monumentality of the Dipylon Vase show that the deceased was a woman of considerable means.

The amphora is a masterpiece of the potter's craft. At over 5 feet tall, it was too large to be thrown in one piece. Instead, the potter built it up in sections, joined with a clay slip (clay mixed with water or another liquid). A careful proportional scheme governed the vessel's form: Its width measures half of its height and the neck measures half the height of the body. The potter placed the handles so as to emphasize the widest point of the body. Most of the decoration is given over to geometric designs dominated by a meander pattern, also known as a maze or Greek key pattern, a band of rectangular scrolls, punctuated with lustrous black bands at the neck, shoulder, and base. The decoration reflects the proportional system of the vase's shape. Single meander patterns run in bands toward the top and bottom of the neck; the triple meander encircling the neck at the center emphasizes its length. The double and single meanders on the amphora's body appear stocky by contrast, complementing the body's rounder form. On the neck, identical deer graze, one after the other, circling the vase. At the base of the neck, they recline, with their heads turned back over their bodies, like an animate version of the meander pattern, which moves forward while turning back upon itself.

In the center of the amphora, framed between its handles, is a narrative scene. The deceased lies on a bier, beneath a checkered shroud. Standing figures flank her with their arms raised above their heads in lamentation; four additional figures kneel or sit beneath the bier. The painter uses solid geometric forms to construct human bodies. A triangle represents the torso, and the raised arms extend the triangle beyond the shoulders. The scene represents the *prothesis*, part of the Athenian funerary ritual when the deceased lay in state and public mourning took place. For the living, a lavish funeral was an occasion to display wealth and status, and crowds of mourners were so desirable that families would hire professionals for the event. Thus the depiction of a funeral on the vase is not simply journalistic reportage but a visual record of the deceased person's high standing in society.

Archaeologists have found Geometric pottery in Italy and the Near East as well as in Greece. This wide distribution reflects the important role of the Greeks, as well as the Phoenicians, North Syrians, and other Near Eastern peoples, as agents of diffusion around the Mediterranean. Inscriptions on these vases show that from the second half of the eighth century onward, the Greeks had already adapted the Phoenician alphabet to their own use.

The Orientalizing Style: Horizons Expand

Between about 725 and 650 BCE, a new style of art emerged in Greece that reflects influences from the Near East and Egypt. Scholars call this the Orientalizing period. This absorption of Eastern motifs and ideas, including hybrid creatures such as griffins and sphinxes, led to a vital period of experimentation.

5.2 Griffin-head *protome* from a bronze tripod cauldron, from Kameiros, Rhodes. ca. 650 BCE. Cast bronze, 12⅝″ (32 cm) high. The British Museum, London

The ARCHAIC period stretches from the mid-seventh century to about 480 vw. Within this period, there are few secure dates for free-standing sculptures. Scholars have therefore established a dating system based upon the level of naturalism in a given sculpture: The more stylized the figure, the earlier it must be. Given the later trajectory of Greek sculpture, there is every reason to believe that this way of dating Archaic sculpture is more or less accurate (accounting for regional differences and the like). All the same, it is worth emphasizing that it is based on an assumption—that sculptors, or their patrons, were striving toward naturalism—rather than on factual data.

Among the costliest dedications to the gods in Greek sanctuaries during the Geometric and Orientalizing periods were bronze tripod cauldrons, large vessels mounted on three legs. Some of them reached truly monumental proportions, and the dedication was not only an act of piety, but also a way to display status through wealth. From the early seventh century BCE, bronzeworkers producing these vessels in the Orientalizing style attached *protomes* around the edge of the bowl—images of sirens (winged female creatures) and griffins, which were fantasy creatures known in the Near East. The cast *protome* shown here, from the island of Rhodes, is a magnificently ominous creature, standing watch over the dedication (**fig. 5.2**). The boldly upright ears and the vertical knob on the head contrast starkly with the strong curves of the neck, head, eyes, and mouth, while its menacing tongue is silhouetted in countercurve against the beak. The straight lines animate the curves, so that the dangerous hybrid seems about to spring.

Archaic Art: Art of the City-State

During the course of the seventh and sixth centuries BCE, the Greeks refined their notion of a *polis*, or CITY-STATE. Once merely a citadel, a place of refuge in troubled times, the city came to represent a community and an identity. City-states were governed in various ways, including, in Athens, democracy. With the changing ideal of the city-state came a change in its physical appearance. The art of this period is referred to as ARCHAIC, meaning "old."

The Rise of Monumental Temple Architecture

Early Greeks worshiped their gods in open-air sanctuaries. The indispensable installation for cult (religious practice) rituals was an altar, where priests performed sacrifices before the worshiping community of the *polis*. Increasingly, though, Greeks built temples to accompany these altars. Usually the temple's entrance faced east, toward

---

MATERIALS AND TECHNIQUES

Temple Plans: Reading Architectural Drawings

ARCHITECTS AND architectural historians use three types of drawings to design and study buildings: Ground plans, sections, and elevations. Together, these three views furnish a basic visual description of the building, with the parts drawn to scale.

A plan, or **ground plan**, depicts a building from above as if it were sliced horizontally about 3 feet above the ground. It usually shows solid parts in a darker tone than openings (doors and windows) and spaces. Lines may indicate changes of level, such as steps. This plan shows a typical Doric temple. It allows

us to understand how the main parts of the temple (colonnade, porches, rooms, and so on) relate to each other, and to trace the path of a typical visitor through its interior.

The **elevation** shows one exterior side seen straight on. This elevation is of the front (façade) of the Doric temple in the plan above. It gives us basic information about its height, scale, and style.

The **section** reveals the inside of a structure as if it were sliced clean through from side to side or end to end. It shows the vertical arrangement of the building's interior, indicates the levels and heights of its rooms and other spaces, and reveals technical details such as the construction of foundations, floors, walls, ceilings, and roofs. This section cuts through the middle of the Doric temple in the plan and elevation above.

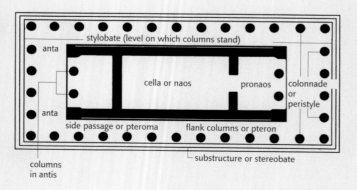

stylobate (level on which columns stand)

anta

cella or naos — pronaos — colonnade or peristyle

anta

side passage or pteroma — flank columns or pteron

columns in antis

substructure or stereobate

---

the rising sun, and the altar stood to the east of the temple. A temple's chief function was not so much to house rituals, most of which occurred outside, as to provide safe shelter for the cult image of the god to whom it was dedicated, and to store valuable dedications.

At some point in the seventh century BCE, Greek architects began to design temples in stone rather than wood. Corinthian architects were probably the first to make the change, designing in a style known as **Doric**, after the region where it originated. From there the concept spread to the mainland, then rapidly throughout the Hellenic (or Greek, from Hellas, meaning Greece) world. The **Ionic** style developed on the Aegean islands and the coast of Asia Minor. Greeks recognized the importance of this revolution as it happened: Architects wrote treatises on their buildings—the first we know of—and the fame they achieved through their work has lasted to this day.

The essential elements of Doric and Ionic temples are similar, though they vary according to the building's size or regional preferences (see box: Temple Plans: Reading Architectural Drawings). The nucleus of the building—its very reason for existing—is its main chamber, its cella or *naos*, which housed the god's image. Often, interior columns lined the cella and helped to support the roof, as well as visually framing the cult statue. Approaching the cella is a porch or *pronaos*, and in some cases architects added a second porch behind the cella, which made the design symmetrical and provided space for ritual apparatus and dedications. In large temples, a colonnade or **peristyle** surrounds the cella and porches, and the building is known as a peripteral temple. The largest temples of Ionian Greece had a double colonnade.

The peristyle added more than grandeur: It offered worshipers shelter from the elements. Being neither entirely exterior nor entirely interior space, it also functioned as a transitional zone, between the profane world outside and the sanctity of the cella. Some temples stood in sacred groves, and the columns' strong vertical form integrated the

CITY-STATES were ruled in several different ways, including monarchy (from *monarches*, "sole ruler"), aristocracy (from *aristoi* and *kratia*, "rule of the best"), tyranny (from *tyrannos*, "despot"), oligarchy (from *oligoi*, "the few," a small ruling elite), and, in Athens, democracy (from *demos*, "the people").

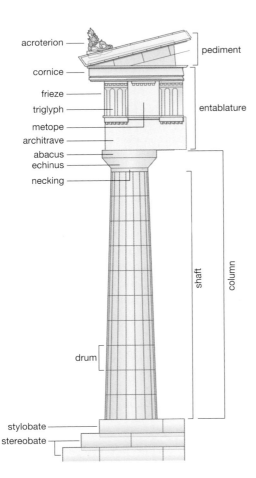

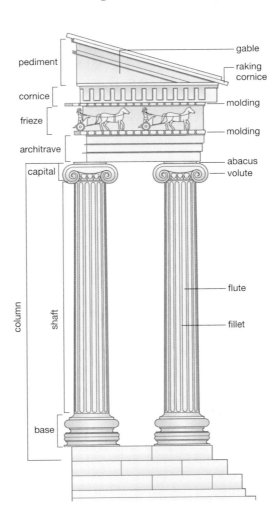

5.3 Doric (far left) and Ionic styles in elevation

building with its vegetal environment. Echoed by columns inside the cella, the peristyle also unified the exterior and interior of the building.

Differences between the Doric and Ionic styles are apparent in elevation. Many terms that Greeks used to describe parts of their buildings, shown in **fig. 5.3**, are still in common usage. The building proper rests on an elevated platform, normally approached by three steps, known as the **stereobate** and **stylobate**. A Doric column consists of a shaft, usually marked by shallow vertical grooves known as flutes, and a capital, made up of a flaring, cushionlike echinus and a square tablet called an abacus. The **entablature** includes all the horizontal elements that rest on the columns: The **architrave** (a row of stone blocks directly supported by the columns); the **frieze**, made up of alternating triple-grooved triglyphs and smooth or sculpted metopes; and a projecting horizontal cornice, or *geison*. The architrave in turn supports the triangular **pediment** and the roof elements. An Ionic column differs from a Doric column in having an ornate base. Its shaft is more slender, less tapered, and the capital incorporates a double scroll or volute. It lacks the muscular quality of its mainland cousin. Instead, it evokes a growing plant, and this it shares with its Egyptian predecessors, though it may not have

The Greek Gods and Goddesses

ALL EARLY CIVILIZATIONS and preliterate cultures had creation myths to explain the origin of the universe and humanity's place in it. Over time, these myths evolved into complex cycles that represent a comprehensive attempt to understand the world. The Greek gods and goddesses, though immortal, behaved in very human ways. They quarreled, and had children with each other's spouses and often with mortals as well. Sometimes their own children threatened and even overthrew them. The principal Greek gods and goddesses, with their Roman counterparts in parentheses, are given below.

ZEUS (Jupiter): Son of Kronos and Rhea; god of sky and weather, and king of the Olympian deities. After killing Kronos, Zeus married his own sister HERA (Juno) and divided the universe by lot with his brothers: POSEIDON (Neptune) was allotted the sea, and HADES (Pluto) was allotted the Underworld, which he ruled with his queen PERSEPHONE (Proserpina).

Zeus and Hera had several children:

ARES (Mars), god of war

HEBE (Juventas), goddess of youth

HEPHAISTOS (Vulcan), lame god of metalwork and the forge

Zeus also had numerous children through his love affairs with other goddesses and with mortal women, including:

ATHENA (Minerva), goddess of crafts, including war, and of intelligence and wisdom. A protector of heroes, she became the patron goddess of Athens, an honor she won in a contest with Poseidon. Her gift to the city was an olive tree, which she caused to sprout on the Akropolis.

APHRODITE (Venus), goddess of love, beauty, and female fertility. She married Hephaistos, and had many affairs. Her children were HARMONIA, EROS, and ANTEROS (with Ares), HERMAPHRODITOS (with Hermes), PRIAPOS (with Dionysos), and AENEAS (with the Trojan prince Anchises).

APOLLO (Apollo), god of the stringed lyre and bow, who therefore both presided over the civilized pursuits of music and poetry, and shot down transgressors; a paragon of male beauty, he was also the god of prophecy and medicine. Twin brother of ARTEMIS.

ARTEMIS (Diana), virgin goddess of the hunt and the protector of young girls. She was also sometimes considered a moon goddess and identified with SELENE. Twin sister of APOLLO.

DIONYSOS (Bacchus), god of altered states, particularly that induced by wine. Opposite in temperament to Apollo, Dionysos was raised on Mount Nysa, where he invented winemaking; he married the princess Ariadne after the hero Theseus abandoned her on Naxos. His followers, the goatish satyrs and their female companions, the nymphs and humans who were known as maenads (bacchantes), were given to orgiastic excess. Yet there was another, more temperate side to Dionysos' character. As the god of fertility, he was also a god of vegetation, as well as of peace, hospitality, and the theater.

HERMES (Mercury), messenger of the gods, conductor of souls to Hades, and god of travelers and commerce.

5.4 The Temple of Hera I ("Basilica"), ca. 550 BCE, and the Temple of Hera II ("Temple of Poseidon"), ca. 500 BCE. Limestone. Paestum, southern Italy

come directly from Egypt. Above the architrave, the frieze is a continuous band.

Greek builders created temples, whether Doric or Ionic, out of stone blocks fitted together without mortar. This required precise shaping to achieve smooth joints. Where necessary, metal dowels or clamps fastened the blocks together. With rare exceptions, they constructed columns out of sections called drums, and stonemasons fluted the entire shaft once it was in position. They used wooden beams for the ceiling, and terra-cotta tiles over wooden rafters for the roof.

Why and how either style came to emerge in Greece, and why they came together into succinct systems so quickly, are questions that still puzzle archaeologists. Remains of the oldest surviving temples show that the main features of the Doric style were already well established soon after 600 BCE. Though it is possible that the temple's central unit, the cella and porch, derived from the Mycenaean megaron (see fig. 4.4), the notion that temples should be stone and have large numbers of columns was an Egyptian one. In fact, scholars believe that the rise of monumental stone architecture and sculpture was the result of careful, on-the-spot study of Egyptian works and the techniques used to produce them. The opportunity for just such a study was available to Greek merchants living in trading camps in the western Nile delta by permission of the Egyptian king Psammetichus I (r. 664–610 BCE).

Some scholars see Doric architecture as a petrification (turning to stone) of existing wooden forms, so that stone form follows wooden function. Accordingly, triglyphs once masked the ends of wooden beams, and metopes evolved from boards that filled gaps between the triglyphs to guard against moisture. Some derivations are more convincing than others. The vertical subdivisions of triglyphs hardly seem to reflect the forms of three half-round logs, as some have suggested. The question of how far we can use function to explain stylistic features faces the architectural historian repeatedly.

DORIC TEMPLES AT PAESTUM The early evolution of Doric temples is evident in two unusually well-preserved buildings in the southern Italian *polis* of Paestum, where a Greek colony flourished during the Archaic period. The residents dedicated both temples to the goddess Hera, wife of Zeus (see box: Cultural Context: The Greek Gods and Goddesses). They built the Temple of Hera II almost a century after the Temple of Hera I, the so-called Basilica (**fig. 5.4**), and the differences in their proportions are striking. The Temple of Hera I (on the left, fig. 5.4) appears low and sprawling—and not just because so much of the entablature is missing—whereas the Temple of Hera II looks tall and compact. One reason is that the temple of Hera I is enneastyle (with nine columns across the front and rear), while the later temple is hexastyle (with six columns). Yet it is also the result of changes to the outline of the columns. On both temples, the shafts bulge outward slightly about a third of the way up, receding again at about two thirds of their height. This swelling effect, called entasis, is much stronger on the earlier Temple of Hera I. It gives the impression that the columns bulge with the strain of supporting the superstructure and that the slender tops, although aided by the flaring, cushion-like capitals, can barely withstand the weight. The device adds extraordinary vitality to the building—a sense of compressed energy awaiting release.

EARLY IONIC TEMPLES The Ionic style first appeared about a half-century after the Doric in Ionian Greece, where cities commissioned vast, ornate temples in rivalry with one another. Little survives of these early buildings. The Temple of Artemis at Ephesos gained tremendous fame in antiquity, numbering among the Seven Wonders of the Ancient World. The first monumental building constructed mostly of marble, the temple was dipteral (with two rows of columns surrounding it), and this feature emphasized the forestlike quality of the building, as did its vegetal capitals. These huge Ionic buildings had blatant symbolic value: They represented their respective city's bid for regional leadership.

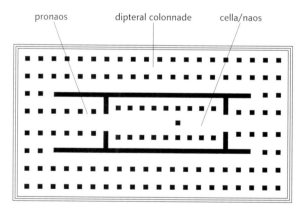

Restored plan of the Temple of Artemis at Ephesos, Turkey. ca. 560 BCE

Stone Sculpture

According to literary sources, in the eighth century BCE Greeks created simple wooden sculptures of their gods, but none of them survives. In about 650 BCE, sculptors, like architects, made the transition to working in stone, and so began one of the great traditions of Greek art.

5.5 *Kouros* (Youth). ca. 600–590 BCE. Marble, height 6′1½″ (1.88 m). The Metropolitan Museum of Art, New York. Fletcher Fund, 1932. 32.11.1

KORE **AND** **KOUROS** Early Greek statues show affinities with the techniques and proportional systems Egyptian sculptors used. Two are illustrated here, one a life-size nude male youth of about 600 BCE (**fig. 5.5**), known as the New York Kouros because it is displayed in the Metropolitan Museum of Art. The other is a female figure (**fig. 5.6**) of about 520 BCE, found on the Athenian Akropolis but probably from Chios, an island of Ionian Greece. Like their Egyptian forerunners (see fig. 3.6), the statues are rigidly frontal, and conceived as four distinct sides, reflecting the form of the block from which the sculptor carved them. The Greek youth stands with his left leg forward, and his arms by his sides. His shoulders, hips, and knees are level. Like Khafra, he is slim and broad-shouldered, his hair stylized and resembling a wig, like that of his Egyptian counterpart. Still, there are significant differences. First, the Greek sculptures are truly free-standing, without the back slab that supports Egyptian stone figures. In fact, they are the earliest large stone images of the human figure that can stand on their own. Moreover, Greek sculptures incorporated empty space (between the legs, for instance), whereas Egyptian figures remained embedded in stone, with the spaces between forms partly filled. Early Greek sculptures are also more stylized than their Egyptian forebears. This is most evident in the large staring eyes, emphasized by arching eyebrows, the smiling features, known as the Archaic smile, and the linear treatment of the anatomy: The sculptor appears to have etched the male youth's pectoral muscles and ribcage onto the surface of the stone, whereas the Egyptian sculptor modeled Khafra's. Unlike Khafra, the Greek youth is nude. Earlier cultures, like the Egyptians, forced nudity on slaves, whereas ancient Greeks considered public nudity acceptable for males, but not for females. Accordingly, like most early Greek female sculptures, this one is draped, in a light Ionian *chiton* under a heavier *himation*. The layers of the garment loop around the body in soft curves, and the play of richly differentiated folds and textures is almost an end in itself; here much of the color that played an important role in such works survives.

Dozens of Archaic sculptures of this kind survive throughout the Greek world. Scholars describe them by the Greek terms for maiden (**kore**, plural *korai*) and youth (**kouros**, plural *kouroi*), terms that gloss over the difficulty of identifying their function. Some were discovered in sanctuaries and cemeteries, but most came to light in

5.6 *Kore* (Maiden), from Chios (?). ca. 520 BCE. Marble with traces of encaustic, height 21⅞″ (55.3 cm). Akropolis Museum, Athens

Reconstruction drawing of the Treasury of the Siphnians. Sanctuary of Apollo at Delphi. ca. 525 BCE

Architectural Sculpture: The Building Comes Alive

Soon after the Greeks began to build stone temples, they started to use architectural sculpture to articulate them and bring them to life. Traces of pigment show that these sculptures were normally vividly painted—an image that is startlingly at odds with our conception of ancient sculpture as pristine white marble. Sculpture typically adorned the pediment (the triangle between the ceiling and the roof), and free-standing sculptures known as **acroteria** sometimes stood above the corners and center of the pediment, softening the severity of its outline. Sculptors also decorated the frieze. In Doric temples, they might embellish the metopes with figural scenes, whereas in Ionic temples the frieze was a continuous band of painted or sculpted decoration. Moreover, in Ionic buildings, architects might substitute female statues or caryatids for columns to support the roof of a porch.

reused contexts, which complicates any attempt to understand them. Some bear inscriptions, with the names of artists or with dedications to deities, chiefly Apollo. These, then, were votive offerings. But in most cases we do not know whether they represent the donor, a deity, or a person deemed divinely favored, such as an athletic victor. Those placed on graves may have represented the deceased. Sculptors made no clear effort to give the statues portrait features, so the images can represent individuals only in a general way. It might make sense to think of them as ideals of physical perfection and vitality shared by mortals and immortals alike, given meaning by their physical context. What is clear is that only the wealthy could afford to erect them, since many were over life-size and carved from high-quality marble. Indeed, the very stylistic cohesion of the sculptures may reveal their social function: By erecting a sculpture of this kind, a wealthy patron declared his or her status and claimed membership of ruling elite circles.

THE SIPHNIAN TREASURY, DELPHI These Ionic features came together in a building that the people of the Ionian island of Siphnos erected at Delphi shortly before 525 BCE. Although the TREASURY OF THE SIPHNIANS no longer stands, archaeologists can reconstruct its appearance from surviving blocks. Two caryatids supported the architrave of the porch. Above the architrave was a magnificent sculptural frieze, part of which depicts the mythical battle of the gods against the giants, who had challenged divine authority. At the far left of **fig. 5.7**, two lions pull the chariot of Themis and tear apart an anguished giant. In front of them, Apollo and Artemis advance together, shooting arrows, originally added in metal, into a phalanx of giants. Stripped of his armor, a dead giant lies at their feet.

5.7 *Battle of the Gods and Giants*, from the north frieze of the Treasury of the Siphnians, Delphi. ca. 530 BCE. Marble, height 26″ (66 cm). Archaeological Museum, Delphi

The tale is a cautionary one, warning mortals not to aim higher than their natural place in the order of things. Though the subject is mythical, its depiction offers detail on contemporary weaponry and military tactics.

Astonishingly, the relief is only a few inches deep. Within that shallow space, the sculptors (more than one hand is discernible) created several planes. They carved in the round the arms and legs of those nearest a viewer. In the second and third layers, the forms become shallower, yet even those farthest from a viewer do not merge into the background. The resulting relationships between figures give a dramatic sense of the turmoil of battle and an intensity of action not seen before in narrative reliefs.

The protagonists fill the sculptural field from top to bottom, and this compositional choice enhances the frieze's power. It is a dominant characteristic of Archaic and Classical art, and sculptors soon sought ways to fill the pediment, too, while retaining a unity of scale. Taking their cue, perhaps, from friezes such as that on the Siphnian Treasury, they introduced a variety of poses for figures, and made great strides in depicting the human body in naturalistic motion. The pediments of the Temple of Aphaia at Aegina, an island in the Saronic Gulf visible from Attica, illustrate this well.

PEDIMENTS OF THE TEMPLE OF APHAIA   In 490 BCE, the Persians took the island of Aegina. At that time, they probably destroyed the Temple of Aphaia's original east pediment. The Aeginetans commissioned the present one after defeating them at the Battle of Salamis in 480 BCE. It depicts the first

5.8 *Dying Warrior*, from the west pediment of the Temple of Aphaia. ca. 500–490 BCE. Marble, length 5′2½″ (1.59 m). Staatliche Antikensammlungen und Glyptothek, Munich

5.9 *Dying Warrior*, from the east pediment of the Temple of Aphaia. ca. 480 BCE. Marble, length 6′ (1.83 m). Staatliche Antikensammlungen und Glyptothek, Munich

sack of Troy, by the hero Herakles and Telamon, king of Salamis. The west pediment, which dates from about 510–500 BCE, shows the second siege of Troy (recounted in *The Iliad*) by Agamemnon, who was related to Herakles. The pairing of subjects commemorates the important role the heroes of Aegina played in both battles—and, by extension, at Salamis, where their navy helped win the day. The use of allegory to elevate historical events to a universal plane was a frequent strategy in Greek art.

5.10 *Achilles and Ajax Playing Dice.* Black-figured amphora signed by Exekias as painter and potter. ca. 540–530 BCE. Ceramic, height 2′ (61 cm). Vatican Museums

By introducing a range of action poses for the figures, the designer could fill the pediment while maintaining uniformity of scale. A comparison of a fallen warrior from the west pediment (**fig. 5.8**) with its counterpart from the later east pediment (**fig. 5.9**) exposes some of the extraordinary advances sculptors made toward naturalism during the decades that separate them. As they sink to the ground in death, both figures present a clever solution to filling the difficult corner space. Yet while the earlier figure props himself up on one arm, only a precariously balanced shield supports the later warrior, whose weight seems to pull him irresistibly to the ground. Both sculptors contorted the dying warrior's body in the agonies of death: The earlier sculptor crosses the warrior's legs in an awkward pose, while the later sculptor twists the body from the waist, so that the left shoulder moves into a new plane. Although the later warrior's anatomy does not fully respond to his pose (note, for instance, how little the pectorals stretch to accommodate the strenuous motion of the right arm), his body is more modeled and organic than the earlier warrior's. He also breaks from the head-on stare of his predecessor, turning his gaze to the ground. The effect suggests introspection: The inscrutable smiling mask of the earlier warrior yields to the suffering and emotion of a warrior in his final moments. Depictions of suffering, and how humans respond to it, are among the most dramatic developments of late Archaic art.

Vase Painting: Art of the Symposium

A similar experimentation with figural poses and emotion occurred in Archaic vase painting in Athens and other centers, where workshops produced fine wares painted with scenes from mythology, legend, and daily life. For everyday use, Greeks generally used plain, unadorned vessels for their wine. They reserved decorated vases like those illustrated here for important occasions like the symposium (*symposion*), an exclusive drinking party. Men and courtesans reclined on couches around the edges of a room, and a master of ceremonies filled their cups from a large painted mixing bowl (a krater) at the center. Music, poetry, storytelling, and word games accompanied the festivities. Often the event ended in lovemaking, which is frequently depicted on drinking cups. There was also a serious side to symposia, as described by Plato and Xenophon, which centered on debates about politics, ethics, and morality. The great issues that Greeks pondered in their philosophy, literature, and theater—the nature of virtue, or the value of an individual man's life, to name a few—were mirrored in, and prompted by, the images with which they surrounded themselves.

Toward the end of the seventh century BCE, Attic vase painters began to work in the BLACK-FIGURED technique: They painted the entire design in black silhouette against the reddish clay, and then incised internal details into the design with a needle. They added white and purple over the black to make chosen areas stand out. The technique lent itself to a two-dimensional and highly decorative effect. A fine example is an Athenian amphora signed by Exekias as potter and painter, dating to the third quarter of the sixth century BCE (**fig. 5.10**). The painting shows the Homeric heroes Achilles and Ajax playing dice, in an episode that no surviving literary source describes. The figures lean on their spears; their shields are stacked behind them against the inside of a campaign tent. The black silhouettes create a rhythmical composition, symmetrical around the table in the center. Within the black paint, Exekias incised a wealth of detail, focusing upon the warriors' cloaks; their intricately woven texture contrasts with the heroes' lustrous black weapons.

The extraordinary power of this scene derives from the tension within it. The warriors have stolen a moment of relaxation during a fierce war; even so, poised on the edge of their stools, one heel raised as if to spring into action, they are edgy. An inscription on the right reads "three," as if Ajax is calling out his throw. Achilles, who in his helmet slightly dominates the scene, answers with "four," which makes him the winner. Yet many Greek viewers would have understood the irony of the scene, for when they return to battle, Achilles will die, and Ajax will bear his friend's body back to the Greek camp before falling on his sword in despair. Indeed, Exekias himself would paint representations of the heroes' tragic deaths. This amphora is the first known representation of the gaming scene, which subsequently became popular, suggesting that vase paintings did not exist in artistic isolation; painters responded to one another's work in a close and often clever dialogue.

Despite its decorative potential, the silhouette-like black-figured technique limited artists to incision for detail, leading them to develop the reverse procedure of leaving figures red and filling in the background. This **red-figured** technique replaced the older method between 520 and 500 BCE. The effects of the change are discernible on an amphora of about 510–500 BCE, signed by Euthymides (**fig. 5.11**). No longer is the scene so dependent on profiles. The painter's new freedom with the brush translates into freedom of movement in the dancing revelers. They cavort in diverse poses, twisting their bodies and showing off Euthymides' confidence in rendering human anatomy. The shoulder blades of the central figure, for instance, one higher than the other, reflect the motion of his raised arm. The turning poses allow Euthymides to tackle foreshortening, as he portrays the different planes of the body (the turning shoulders, for instance) on one surface. This was an age of intensive and self-conscious experimentation; indeed, so pleased was Euthymides with his painting that he inscribed a challenge to a fellow painter, "As never Euphronios."

The development of BLACK-FIGURED vase painting marks the beginning of an aggressive export industry, the main consumers of which were the Etruscans (see Chapter 6). Vast numbers of black-figured vases were found in Etruscan tombs. Thus, although in terms of conception these vases (and later red-figured vessels) represent a major chapter in Greek (and specifically Athenian) art, with regard to their actual use, painted vases are a major component of Etruscan culture, both visual and funerary.

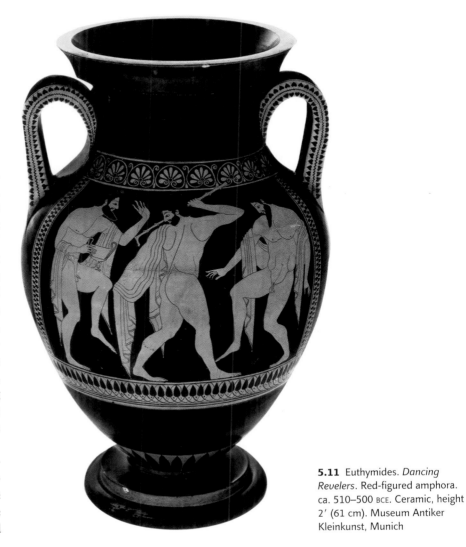

5.11 Euthymides. *Dancing Revelers*. Red-figured amphora. ca. 510–500 BCE. Ceramic, height 2′ (61 cm). Museum Antiker Kleinkunst, Munich

The Classical Age

SPEAKING OF
Classical, classical, and classic

In art history, Classical spelled with a capital C refers to Greek civilization between about 480 and 330 BCE. The term classical refers to the entire ancient Greek and Roman period and its creations. In the Western tradition, classical has also come to mean that which is moderate, balanced, excellent, and enduring. Thus, for example, serious European music is often called "classical music." The word classic describes and signifies something of lasting excellence and importance, such as Shakespeare's *Hamlet*, or a top-rank sporting event, such as a golf classic.

The beginning of the fifth century BCE brought crisis. A number of Ionian cities rebelled against their Persian overlords, and after Athens came to their support, the Persians invaded the Greek mainland, under the leadership of Darius I. At the Battle of Marathon in 490, a contingent of about 10,000 Athenians, with a battalion from nearby Plataea, repulsed a force of about 90,000 Persians. Ten years later, an even larger force of Persians returned under Darius' son, Xerxes I. They took control of Athens, burning and pillaging temples and statues. The Greeks fought them at Salamis and Plataea in 480–479, and finally defeated them. These battles were defining moments for the Greeks, who first faced destruction in their cities, and then emerged triumphant after the horrors of invasion. At least in Athens, Persian destruction of public monuments is visible in the archaeological record, and, for archaeologists and art historians, signals the end of the Archaic period. Scholars describe the period stretching from the end of the Persian Wars to the death of Alexander the Great in the late fourth century as the Classical Age.

The struggle against the Persians tested the recently established Athenian democracy. Athens emerged as the leader of a defensive alliance, which quickly evolved into a political and economic empire that facilitated numerous architectural and artistic projects. This was the time when Aristophanes, Aeschylus, Sophocles, and Euripides were penning comedies and tragedies for religious festivals, and thinkers such as Socrates, Plato, and Aristotle engaged in their philosophical quests.

Classical Sculpture

Among the many statues excavated from debris resulting from the Persian sack of the Akropolis in 480 BCE, one *kouros* stands apart (**fig. 5.12**). Archaeologists sometimes attribute it to the Athenian sculptor Kritios, and know it as the *Kritios Boy*. On account of its findspot, they date it to shortly before the Persian attack. It differs from earlier, Archaic *kouroi* (see fig. 5.5), not least because it is the first surviving statue that stands, in the full sense of the word. Although earlier figures are upright—rather than reclining or sitting—their stance is an arrested walk, with the body's weight resting evenly on both legs in a pose that is non-naturalistic and rigid. The *Kritios Boy* has one leg forward like earlier *kouroi*, yet the sculptor has shifted the youth's weight,

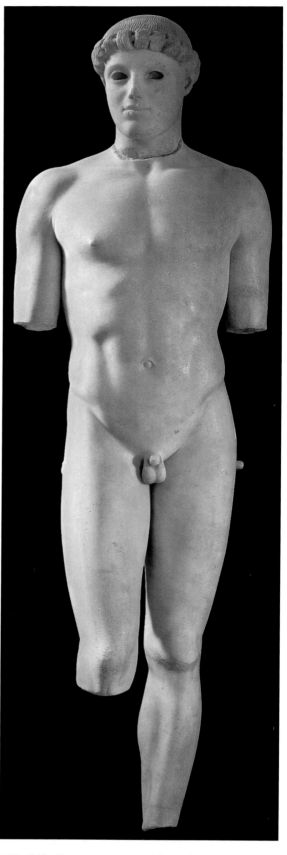

5.12 *Kritios Boy.* ca. 480 BCE. Marble, height 46″ (116.7 cm). Akropolis Museum, Athens

creating a calculated asymmetry in the two sides of his body. The knee of the forward leg is lower than the other, the right hip is thrust down and in, and the left hip up and out. The axis of the body is not a straight vertical line but a reversed S-curve. Taken together, these small departures from symmetry indicate that the youth's weight rests mainly on the left leg, while the right leg acts as a prop to help balance the body.

The *Kritios Boy* not only stands; he stands at ease. The artist masterfully observed the balanced asymmetry of this relaxed stance, which is known to historians of ancient art as a chiastic pose (from χ, the Greek letter chi), and to historians of Renaissance

5.13 *Zeus or Poseidon.* ca. 460–450 BCE. Bronze, height 6′10″ (2.08 m). National Archaeological Museum, Athens. Ministry of Culture Archaeological Receipts Fund. 15161

The Indirect Lost-Wax Process

THE *ZEUS* (fig. 5.13) is one of the earliest surviving Greek statues made by the indirect lost-wax process. This technique enables sculptors to create spatially freer forms than is possible in stone. They make projecting limbs separately and solder them onto the torso, without needing to support them with unsightly struts. Compare, for example, the freely outstretched arms of the *Zeus* with the strut extending from hip to drapery on the *Aphrodite of Knidos* (fig. 5.21).

The Egyptians, Minoans, and early Greeks had often made statuettes of solid bronze using the direct lost-wax process. The technique was simple. The sculptor modeled his figure in wax; covered it with clay to form a mold; melted away the wax; melted copper and tin in the ratio of nine parts to one in a crucible; and poured this alloy into the space left by the "lost wax" in the clay mold. Yet because figures made in this way were solid, the method had severe limitations. A solid-cast, life-size statue would have been prohibitively expensive, incredibly heavy, and prone to developing unsightly bubbles and cracks as the alloy cooled. So from the eighth through the sixth centuries BCE the Greeks developed the indirect lost-wax method, which allowed them to cast statues hollow and at any scale.

First, the sculptor shaped a core of clay into the basic form of the intended metal statue, before covering the clay core with a layer of wax to the thickness of the final metal casting, carving the details of the statue carefully in the wax. The figure was then separated into its component parts—head, torso, limbs, and so on. For each part, the artist applied a heavy outer layer of clay over the wax and secured it to the inner core with metal pegs. The package was then heated to melt the wax, which ran out. Molten metal—usually bronze, but sometimes silver or gold—was then poured into the space left by this "lost wax." When the molten metal cooled, the outer and inner molds were broken away, leaving a metal casting—the statue's head, torso, or arm—and these individual sections were then soldered together to create the statue. The sculptor completed the work by polishing the surface, chiseling details such as strands of hair and skin folds, and inlaying features such as eyes, teeth, lips, nipples, and dress patterns in ivory, stone, glass, copper, or precious metal.

 Watch a video about the process of lost-wax casting on myartslab.com

art as **contrapposto** (Italian for "counterpoise"). The leg that carries the weight is called the engaged leg, the other, the free leg. With this simple observation came recognition that, if one part of the body is engaged in a task, other parts respond. Bending the free knee results in a swiveling of the pelvis, a compensating curvature of the spine, and an adjusting tilt of the shoulders. This unified approach to the body enabled artists to represent movement with a new naturalism. Indeed, even though the *Kritios Boy* is at rest, his muscles suggest motion, and the sculpture has life; he seems capable of action. All the same, the artist recognized that strict adherence to nature would not always yield the desired result. So, as in the later Parthenon, refinements are at work. The sculptor exaggerated the line of muscles over the pelvis to create a greater unity between thighs and torso, and a more fluid transition from front to back. This emphasized the sculpture's three-dimensionality, and encouraged a viewer to move around it.

The innovative movement in the musculature gives a viewer a sense, for the first time, that muscles lie beneath the surface of the marble skin, and that a skeleton articulates the whole as a real organism. A new treatment of the flesh and the marble's surface adds to this impression: The flesh has a sensuousness that is alien to earlier *kouroi*, and the sculptor worked the surface of the marble to a gentle polish. Gone, also, is the Archaic smile, presumably as a result of close observation of a human face. The face has a soft fleshiness to it, especially marked around the chin, which is characteristic of early Classical sculpture. The head is turned slightly away from the front, removing the direct gaze of earlier *kouroi* and casting the figure into his own world of thought.

The *Kritios Boy* marks a critical point in Greek art. One of the changes it engendered was a whole-hearted exploration of the representation of movement, another hallmark of early Classical sculpture. A magnificent nude bronze dating to about 460–450 BCE, recovered from the sea near the Greek coast, illustrates this well (**fig. 5.13**). At almost 7 feet tall, it depicts a spread-eagled male figure in the act of throwing—probably Zeus casting a thunderbolt.

In a single figure, the sculptor captures and contrasts vigorous action and firm stability. The result is a work of outright grandeur, expressing the god's awe-inspiring power. The piece shows off not only the artist's powers of observation and understanding of bodies in motion, but also an expert knowledge of the strengths of bronze, which allowed the god's arms to stretch out without support (see box: Materials and Techniques: The Indirect Lost-Wax Process).

THE *DORYPHOROS*: IDEALS OF PROPORTION AND HARMONY Within half a century of the innovations witnessed in the *Kritios Boy*, sculptors were avidly exploring the body's articulation, among them Polykleitos of Argos, whose most famous work, the *Doryphoros* (*Spear Bearer*) (**fig. 5.14**), is known through numerous Roman copies. In this sculpture, the chiastic pose is much more emphatic than in the *Kritios Boy*. Polykleitos seems to delight in the possibilities the pose offers, examining how the anatomy on the two sides of the body responds to it. The "working" left arm balances the "engaged" right leg in the forward position, and the relaxed right arm balances the "free" left leg. Yet in this sculpture Polykleitos did more than study anatomy. He explored principles of commensurability (*symmetria*), and proposed an ideal system of proportions, not just for the individual elements of the body but for their relation to one another and to the body as a whole. He also addressed *rhythmos* (composition and movement). According to one ancient writer, Greeks knew this work as his *kanon*. Egyptian artists had earlier aimed to establish guidelines for depiction based on proportion. For Polykleitos the search for an ideal system of proportions was more than an artist's aid: It was rooted in a philosophical quest for illumination, and in a belief that harmony (*harmonia*)—in the universe, as in music and in all things—could be expressed in mathematical terms. Only slightly later than this sculpture, Plato would root his doctrine of ideal forms in numbers, and acknowledge that beauty was commonly based on proportion. Philosophers even referred to works of art to illustrate their theories. Moreover, beauty was more than an idle conceit for Classical Athenians; it also had a moral dimension. Pose and expression reflected character and feeling, which revealed

5.14 *Doryphoros* (*Spear Bearer*). Roman copy after an original of ca. 450–440 BCE by Polykleitos. Marble, height 6′6″ (2 m). Museo Archeologico Nazionale, Naples

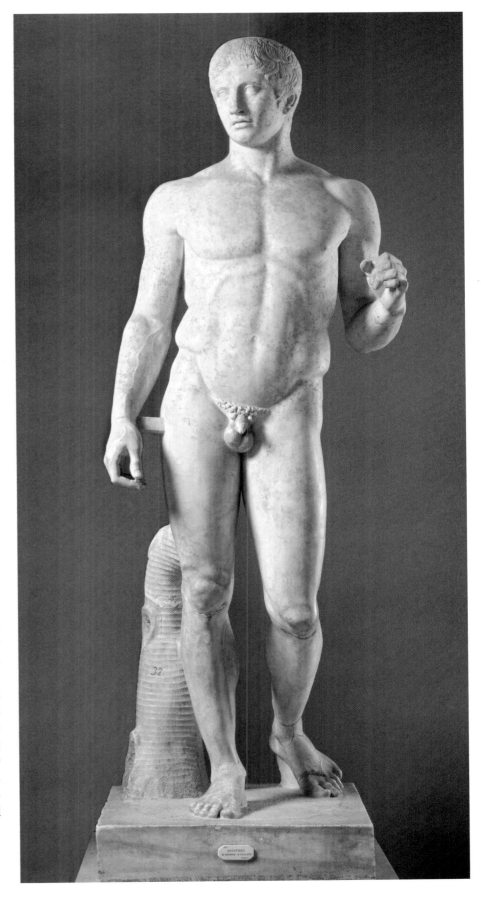

Kanon (canon) in ancient Greek meant "rule" or "measure." In art history, the canon has come to mean the large body of artworks that experts and connoisseurs have judged through the centuries to be the central, most defining works of the tradition. That canon is constantly shifting, and books like this one play a role in defining it. The term also means a normative or ideal ratio of proportions, usually based on a unit of measure (see page 55 margin note). This is why Polykleitos called the treatise that he wrote to accompany his *Doryphoros* (see fig. 5.14) the *Kanon*. "Canon" also describes the central and normative works in the fields of music, religion, and law; the central section of the Mass in the Catholic Church; and it is used in cultural fields that parallel art history, such as literature.

the inner person and, with it, *arete* (excellence or virtue). Thus contemplation of harmonious proportions could be equated with the contemplation of virtue.

Architecture and Sculpture on the Athenian Akropolis

The Athenian Akropolis, the hilltop citadel, had been a fortified site since Mycenaean times, around 1250 BCE (**fig. 5.15**). During the Archaic period, it housed at least one sizeable temple to the city's patron goddess, Athena, as well as several smaller temples or treasuries and statues. For over 30 years after the Persian sack, the Athenians left these sacred monuments in ruins as a solemn reminder of the enemy's ruthlessness. This changed in the mid-fifth century BCE with the emergence of PERIKLES into political life. His ambitions for Athens included transforming the city—with its population of about 150,000—into the envy of the Mediterranean world. His projects, which the democratic assembly approved, began on the Akropolis. The structures there expressed the ideals of the Athenian city-state, and exemplify Classical Greek art at its height.

THE PARTHENON The dominant temple on the Akropolis is the Parthenon (**fig. 5.16**). Perikles conceived it to play a focal role in the cult of Athena, though there is no evidence that Athenians used it directly for cult practices; there is no altar to the east, and the chief center of cult practice remained on the site of the Erechtheum, north of the Parthenon. Built of gleaming white marble from nearby Mount Pentelikon, the Parthenon occupies a prominent site on the southern flank of the Akropolis. It dominates the city and the surrounding countryside, a brilliant landmark against a backdrop of mountains to the north, east, and west. Contemporary building records, and a biography of Perikles written by Plutarch, indicate that two architects, Iktinos and Kallikrates, oversaw its construction between 447 and 432 BCE.

When read against the architectural vocabulary of Classical Greece the Parthenon emerges as an extraordinarily sophisticated building. Its parts integrate fully with one another, so that its spaces do not seem to be separate but to melt into one another. Likewise, its architecture and sculpture are so intertwined that discussion of the two cannot

5.15 Plan of the Akropolis at Athens in 400 BCE (after A. W. Lawrence)

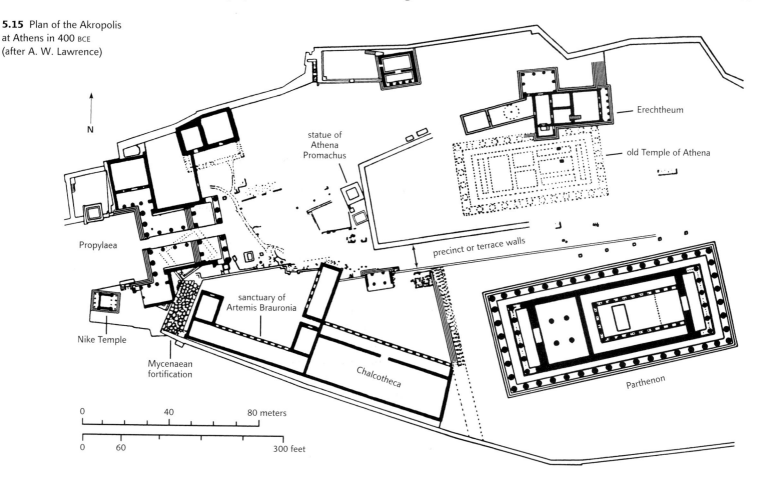

5.16 Iktinos and Kallikrates. The Parthenon (view from the west). 447–432 BCE. Marble. Akropolis, Athens

be disentangled. The temple stood near the culminating point of a grand procession that wound its way through the city and onto the Akropolis during the annual Panathenaic festival in Athena's honor, and as magnificent as it was to observe from a distance, it was also a building to experience. Imitating the grand temples of Archaic Ionia, the Parthenon featured an octastyle (eight-column) arrangement of its narrow ends. This was unusually wide, offering a generous embrace with enough space for a U-shaped colonnade in the cella and an enormous statue of Athena by the famed sculptor Pheidias. Like all peripteral temples, the encircling colonnade gave the impression that a visitor could approach the temple from all sides. In fact, a porch of six columns mediated entry to the cella, and to an *opisthonaos* (rear room) on the west, containing four tall, slender Ionic columns. The porches are unusually shallow. This allowed light into the cella, which otherwise came in through two large windows on either side of the cella's main entrance. In

its combination of a well-lit interior and the rational articulation of the interior space with a colonnade, the Parthenon initiates a new interest in the embellishment of interior space.

Compared with the Temple of Hera II at Paestum (see fig. 5.4, right), the Parthenon appears far less massive, despite its greater size. One of the reasons for this is a lightening of proportions since the Archaic period. The columns are more slender, their tapering and entasis less pronounced, and the capitals flare less. Practical necessity partly determined the diameter of the columns: For convenience and economy, the architects reused many drums from an earlier Parthenon, still unfinished at the time of the Persian sack. Yet how the columns related to the rest of the building was a matter for new design. Their spacing, for instance, is wider than in earlier buildings. The entablature is lower in relation to their height and to the temple's width, and the cornice projects less. The load the columns carry seems to have decreased, and as a

 Explore the architectural panoramas of the Parthenon on myartslab.com

The preeminent politician of Classical Greece was the Athenian PERIKLES (ca. 495–429 BCE; often Latinized to Pericles). He came to the forefront of Athenian public life in the mid-fifth century BCE, and played a critical role in the city's history until his death. During this time, Athens became the center of a wealthy empire, a highly progressive democratic society, and a vibrant hub of art and architecture. An avid patron of the arts, he focused much of his attention on beautifying the city's highest point or Akropolis.

result the supports appear able to fulfill their task with a new ease.

The governing principle behind the design was a ratio of 9 : 4 or $2x + 1 : x$. Thus, for instance, the eight (x) columns across the façades answer seventeen ($2x + 1$) columns along the sides. Additionally, the ratio of the spacing between two columns to the diameter at the lowest point of the column was 9 : 4. This was not just a matter of design convenience, but an attempt to produce harmony through numerical relationships. Iktinos and Kallikrates used the formula throughout the Parthenon, though never dogmatically. In fact, despite the precision the formula dictated, they built into the Parthenon intentional departures from its geometric regularity (as architects did in other temples). For instance, the columns are not vertical, but lean in toward the cella (the corner columns in two directions). The stepped platform on which the temple rests is not fully horizontal, but bows upward, so that the center of the long sides is about 4 inches higher than the corners. This curvature reflects up through the temple's entablature, and every column capital is slightly adjusted to fit the bowed architrave. That these irregularities were intentional is beyond doubt, as masons tailor-made individual blocks to accommodate them. Why they were desirable is less clear.

When architects first introduced irregularities into temple architecture, some 100 years earlier, they may have intended to solve drainage problems. Yet in the Parthenon, they are so exaggerated that scholars consider them to be corrections of optical illusions. For instance, when viewed from a distance, straight horizontals appear to sag, but if the horizontals curve upward, they look straight. When seen close up, a long straight line seems to curve like the horizon; by exaggerating the curve, the architects could make the temple appear even larger than it was. These two apparently contradictory theories could work in tandem, since different optical distortions would prevail depending on a viewer's vantage point. What is certain is that these refinements give the temple a highly dynamic quality. Rather than sitting quietly on its platform, the building derives energy from its swelling forms, as if it were about to burst out of its own skin; through the refinements, the temple comes alive.

THE PARTHENON SCULPTURES The largest group of surviving Classical sculptures comes from the Parthenon, which had a more extensive decorative program than any previous temple. The sculptures have a vivid and often unfortunate history. Christians converted the temple into a church, probably in the sixth century CE, and much of the decoration on the east side was destroyed or vandalized. In 1687, Venetian cannon fire ignited ammunition stored by Turkish forces in the temple. The west pediment figures survived the explosion, but not the war's aftermath. They shattered when a crane dropped them while removing them so that the Venetian commander could take them back to Venice. Over 100 years later, Lord Elgin, British

5.17 *Three Goddesses*, from the east pediment of the Parthenon. ca. 438–432 BCE. Marble, over life-size. The British Museum, London

ambassador to Constantinople, purchased what he could of the temple's decoration from the Turks and shipped it to England. In 1816 he sold the sculptures to the British Museum. Today, the Elgin Marbles, as they are known, are the focus of a heated debate on the repatriation of national treasures.

Thirteen years before the explosion in the Parthenon, an artist named Jacques Carrey executed drawings of the surviving sculptures, which, along with literary sources, have become invaluable resources for understanding the decorative program. The west pediment portrayed the struggle between Athena and Poseidon to be Athens' patron deity. The east pediment represented the birth of Athena from the head of Zeus, in the presence of other gods. The pediment figures are strikingly impressive. Like the building into which they are embedded, their forms are strong and solid, yet their implied power contrasts with their languid poses and gains strength from the contrast. A group of three female deities, usually identified as Hestia, Dione, and Aphrodite (**fig. 5.17**), is a masterpiece of swirling drapery, which disguises the sheer bulk of the marble. The garments cling to the bodies as if wet, both concealing and revealing flesh. Yet the drapery does not follow the lines of the body so much as struggle with them, twisting around the legs in massive folds. The effect is extraordinary: Although a viewer can see the deities only from a frontal vantage point, as if the figures were two-dimensional, the curves of the deeply cut folds echo their forms in section (i.e., along a plane made by an imaginary vertical slice from front to back), and thereby broadcast their three-dimensionality. The sculptor could better express nature through the appearance of truth than through truth itself. This optical device is a sculptural equivalent of the deliberate distortions in the temple's architecture.

The Parthenon is often viewed as the embodiment of Classical Doric architecture. Although this may be the impression from the outside, it is far from accurate. At architrave level within the peristyle, a continuous sculpted frieze ran around all sides of the building (see fig. 5.3). Perikles may have used this variation of the Ionic style as a deliberate symbolic gesture to unite the disparate regions of Greece. In a continuous sculpted band, some 525 feet long, the frieze depicts a procession moving from west to east, propelling a viewer around the building, drawn close to the building to read the

5.18 Frieze above the western entrance of the cella of the Parthenon. ca. 440–432 BCE. Marble, height 43" (109.3 cm). Akropolis, Athens

images. Horsemen jostle with musicians, water carriers, and sacrificial beasts. Figures overlap to create the illusion of a crowd, even though the relief is only inches deep. Frenzied animals underline the calm demeanor of the human figures (**fig. 5.18**), sculpted with the ideal proportions of the *Doryphoros*. According to the traditional view, the procession depicted in the frieze is the Panathenaic procession, part of the annual festival, held on a grander scale every four years. The figures and their groupings are typical of the participants in these processions. The frieze thus represents an idealized event, rather than a specific moment. Some scholars have suggested that this "heroicized" representation also honors the 192 Athenians slain at the Battle of Marathon, on the basis that the frieze may originally have featured 192 equestrian figures. If the frieze does represent the Panathenaic procession, it is remarkable in that it exalts mortal Athenians by depicting them in a space usually reserved for divine and mythological scenes. The recent discovery that the *pronaos* featured another frieze in its upper wall exacerbates problems of interpretation: if it was thematically connected with the frieze around the cella, we lack a crucial piece of evidence for a secure identification and interpretation of the iconography.

The Late Classical Period

By the end of the fifth century BCE, Athens' supremacy was on the wane. The Peloponnesian War of 431–404 BCE, which Athens lost, had taken its toll, and during the fourth century the Greek city-states were constantly at odds with one another. In 338 BCE, Philip II, who had acceded to power in the kingdom of Macedon to the north, exploited their disunity by invading Greece, and decisively defeated the Athenians and Thebans at the Battle of Chaironeia in central Greece.

Late Classical Architecture: Civic and Sacred

Two notable changes occurred in monumental architecture in the late fifth and fourth centuries BCE. One was a shift in emphasis: As well as constructing temples, architects explored a range of other building types. Many of these types—such as stoas (colonnaded porticoes), meeting houses for the governing council—had long existed, but now took on grander form. The other was the development of a new style, the Corinthian.

THE MAUSOLEUM AT HALIKARNASSOS In Halikarnassos (present-day Bodrum, in southwest Turkey; see map 5.1), the tendency toward monumentalization

5.19 Reconstruction drawing of the Mausoleum at Halikarnassos. ca. 359–351 BCE (from H. Colvin)

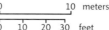

resulted in a vast tomb built for Mausolos, who ruled Caria from 377 to 353 BCE as satrap (governor) for the Persians. His wife and sister Artemisia commissioned Pytheos of Priene to design the sepulcher to commemorate Mausolos as hero-founder of Halikarnassos. Such was its renown in antiquity that the ancients counted it among the Seven Wonders of the Ancient World and by Roman imperial times its title, the Mausoleum, was used to describe any monumental tomb. It stood reasonably intact until the thirteenth century CE, when an earthquake reduced the upper sections. In the late fifteenth and early sixteenth centuries, the Knights of St. John used the site as a source of stone to refortify their castle, and in 1857, the British archaeologist Charles Newton removed many sculptural fragments to the British Museum. When coupled with literary evidence, archaeological data permits reconstructions, though none meets with universal approval. One hypothesis appears in **fig. 5.19**. The tomb was rectangular in plan, and soared 140 feet high in at least three sections, covered with sculpture: A high podium, an Ionic colonnade, and a pyramidal stepped roof supporting a statue of Mausolos or one of his ancestors in a chariot.

The Mausoleum combined the monumental tomb-building tradition of the region, Lycia, with a Greek peristyle and sculpture, and an Egyptian pyramid. The grouping of these elements in a single monument is evidence of a growing diversity in architecture. It may also have had a propagandistic function: It may have expressed Carian supremacy in the region and the symbiosis of Greek and non-Greek civilizations that might be achieved through the founding of an empire headed by Halikarnassos.

CORINTHIAN CAPITAL The other major change in architecture that took place in the late fifth century BCE was the development of the CORINTHIAN capital as an elaborate substitute for the Ionic. Its shape is an inverted bell covered with the shoots and leaves of an acanthus plant, which seem to sprout from the top of the column shaft. VITRUVIUS ascribed its invention to the metalworker Kallimachos. At first, builders used Corinthian capitals only in temple interiors, perhaps because of the conservative nature of Greek architecture, or because of the perceived sanctity of its vegetal forms. It was not until the second century BCE that Corinthian columns appeared on the exteriors of buildings.

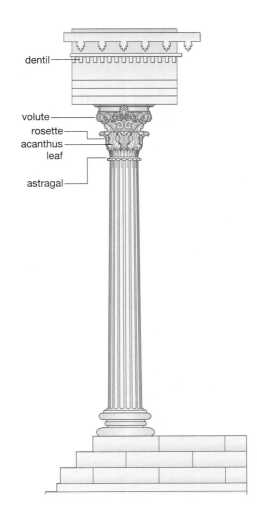

Late Classical Sculpture

The Classical style associated with Pheidias, with its apparent confidence in the transcendence of the Athenian city-state, did not survive Athens's devastating defeat in the Peloponnesian War. At the end of the fifth century BCE, a shift in mood is perceptible in sculpture, which seems to reflect a different—and less optimistic—view of man's place in the universe.

There have been attempts to match surviving sculptures with fourth-century sculptors named in literary sources. Among them is Skopas of Paros. According to PLINY THE ELDER, he was one of four masters chosen to work on the Mausoleum of Halikarnassos, and his greatest fame derives from the way he infused emotion into the faces he sculpted. A fragmentary head of Herakles or his son Telephos from a pediment of the Temple of Athena Alea at Tegea of about 340 BCE, now lost, is either by Skopas or by an artist deeply influenced

The first of the Classical styles of Greek architecture were the Doric and Ionic. The third and later major Classical style, the CORINTHIAN, is the most elaborate. The acanthus-leaf motif is distinctive of the Corinthian capital.

Watch an architectural simulation of the Greek orders on myartslab.com

Marcus VITRUVIUS Pollio (active 46–27 BCE) was a Roman architect, whose lasting fame rests on his ten-book treatise on classical architecture, *De architectura*, which is the only such work to survive from antiquity. Based heavily on Greek architectural treatises, it is our most important written source of information about Greek architecture. From the fifteenth century to the present, architects have pored over translations of Vitruvius to learn about classical principles of proportion, the Greek styles, and other matters of architectural theory and practice—often interpreting them with latitude. Our readings of his text have been mediated through early modern commentators and illustrators, who wrote of Doric and Ionic "orders" rather than "types," which is a better translation of Vitruvius' "*genera*." The distinction is important: "Order" suggests an immutable quality, a rigid building code, when in fact we find a subtle but rich variation in surviving Greek architecture.

There were two Plinys: PLINY THE ELDER (23/24–79 CE) and his nephew and adopted son, Pliny the Younger (ca. 61–ca. 112 CE). Pliny the Elder served several Roman emperors as a military officer. In midlife, he took up writing, and produced an encyclopedia that contains a history of art organized by materials—bronze, earth, and stone. This text is a prime source for our knowledge of Greek sculpture and painting. Pliny the Younger left numerous letters. One includes a detailed description of his villa and another describes his uncle's death during the eruption of Mount Vesuvius.

The labels on the figure read: dentil, volute, rosette, acanthus leaf, astragal.

5.20 *Head of Herakles* or *Telephos,* from the west pediment of the Temple of Athena Alea, Tegea. ca. 340 BCE. Marble, height 1'½" (31.75 cm). Stolen from the Archaeological Museum, Tegea, Greece

by his work (**fig. 5.20**). The smooth planes and fleshy treatment of the face are characteristic of Classical art. What is new is how the sculptor cut the marble away sharply over the eyes toward the bridge of the nose to create a dark shadow. At the outer edge, the eyelid bulges out to overhang the eye. This simple change charges the face with a depth of emotion not seen before. The slightly parted lips and the sharp turn of the head enhance the effect.

PRAXITELES If the Greeks were less confident of their place in the world in the late Classical period, they were also less certain of their relationship to fate and the gods. This is reflected in the work of Praxiteles, working at roughly the same time as Skopas. Choosing to work in marble rather than bronze, he executed several statues of divinities. Where fifth-century artists had stressed the gods' majesty, Praxiteles gave them a youthful sensuousness that suggests their willful capriciousness toward humans. Most famous is his sculpture of Aphrodite, of about 340–330 BCE (**fig. 5.21**). Pliny records that the people of Kos commissioned a cult statue of Aphrodite from Praxiteles, but rejected the nude statue he offered them in favor of a draped version. The inhabitants of Knidos purchased the nude image, and profited from the risk: Visitors came to the island from far and wide to see her. Perhaps it was her nudity that drew so much attention: She was the first nude monumental statue of a goddess in the Greek world. Yet even if artists had previously reserved female nudity principally for representations of slaves or courtesans, the clinging drapery of the fifth century BCE had exposed almost as much of the female anatomy as it concealed. Her appeal may have resided just as much in the blatant eroticism of her image. A viewer catches Aphrodite as she is about to bathe or as she rises from her bath. With her right hand, she covers her genitals in a gesture of modesty, while grasping for a robe with her left. Her head is slightly turned, so she does not engage a viewer's gaze directly, but a viewer is made complicit with the sculpture, willingly or not, by having inappropriately witnessed her in her nudity. Perhaps, in her capriciousness, Aphrodite intended to be surprised as she bathed; the uncertainty for a viewer augments the erotic quality of the image. By some accounts, the Knidians displayed Praxiteles' sculpture in a circular shrine with entrances at front and back, so that visitors could view the cult statue from all sides.

5.21 *Aphrodite of Knidos*. Roman copy after an original of ca. 340–330 BCE by Praxiteles. Marble, height 6'8" (2.05 m). Musei Vaticani, Rome

Read the document related to Praxiteles' *Aphrodite of Knidos* on myartslab.com

The Age of Alexander and the Hellenistic Period

In 336 BCE, Philip II of Macedon died, and his kingdom passed to his son ALEXANDER THE GREAT. He embarked upon a great campaign of conquest, overcoming Egypt and the Persians, then continuing to Mesopotamia and present-day Afghanistan. He died young in 323 BCE, having founded over 70 cities. His conquests changed the face of the Greek world, expanding it into unknown spheres and creating new political alignments. The years following Alexander's death were fraught with struggles between members of his family and his generals, as each tried to establish himself as his successor. By about 275 BCE, Alexander's lands had coalesced into three main kingdoms, which would dominate the Mediterranean until the Romans gradually assumed control. Ptolemy founded a dynasty in Egypt that reigned until Octavian (later the Roman emperor Augustus) defeated Cleopatra VII in 31 BCE. In the east, the Seleucids captured Babylon in 312 BCE. From Syria they ruled a kingdom which, at its largest, extended from present-day western Turkey to Afghanistan. They lost control of a small pocket of territory around Pergamon to the Attalids, who bequeathed their city to the Romans in 133 BCE. In 64 BCE, the Seleucid kingdom came under Roman control. Most coveted was Alexander's ancestral Macedon, which the Antigonids controlled until the Roman conquest in 168 BCE. Within these kingdoms, powerful cities grew—among them, Alexandria and Pergamon—with teeming populations drawn from all over the new Greek world. They vied for cultural preeminence, and art played a large part in the rivalry. Hellenistic culture was radically different from that of Classical times. The expansion of Greek dominance meant that Greek cultural institutions prevailed over a vast territory; those institutions commingled with the strong cultural traditions of the indigenous peoples to create a rich and diverse society.

Architecture: The Scholarly Tradition and Theatricality

Within the cultural centers of the Hellenistic world, academies emerged, fostering avid debate among scholars in a range of fields. They engaged, among other things, in a close analysis of the arts, and developed canons by which they could judge works of literature, art, and architecture. In architecture

Philip II (382–336 BCE), king of Macedon—present-day Macedonia—was a skilled general who, by the time of his assassination, had humbled the major powers of mainland Greece and cajoled all the Greek states except Sparta into an anti-Persian alliance. His son, ALEXANDER THE GREAT (356–323 BCE), was already an accomplished general at the age of 18 and succeeded his father two years later. He invaded Persia in 334 and within ten years created an empire that stretched to the Indus Valley. He founded many cities in the conquered territories that all bore his own name. He died suddenly in his capital, Babylon, when he was just 33. His empire disintegrated into several independent kingdoms after his death.

peristyle   cella   porch

5.22 Pytheos. Plan of the Temple of Athena. 334 BCE. Priene, Turkey

altar

this led to a heightened interest in systems of proportions, recorded in architectural treatises. Vitruvius asserts that a leading protagonist in this movement was Pytheos of Priene (**fig. 5.22**), one of the architects of the Mausoleum of Halikarnassos (see fig. 5.19). Pytheos worked in the Ionic style, as seen in his temple to Athena at Priene, dedicated in 334 BCE. The temple's colonnade had six columns by 11, and a grid of squares, each 6 by 6 feet, that dictated the proportions of all of its elements. Proportions controlled the elevation as well: For instance, the columns were 43 feet high and the entablature was 7 feet high—for a total of 50 feet, half the external length of the cella. Unlike the Parthenon and elsewhere, there were no deviations from the rule, and no refinements. The temple is a work of the intellect, the product of a didactic tradition, rather than a compromise between theory and practice. In fact, Vitruvius faults Pytheos precisely for his inability to differentiate between the two.

While this scholarly tradition flourished, the relaxation of architectural guidelines and the combination of architectural types from the late Classical period heralded another development. This was a penchant for dramatic siting, impressive vistas, and surprise revelations. This movement is termed "theatricality," and it balanced and complemented the scholarly tradition. As the glory of Athens declined, the Athenians and other Greeks came to think of themselves less as members of a city-state and more as individuals; architecture, in turn, began to cater more and more to a personal experience, often manipulating visitors toward a meaningful revelation.

THE TEMPLE OF APOLLO AT DIDYMA Begun in 313 BCE and still unfinished by the end of the Roman period, the Temple of Apollo at Didyma is a good example of architectural theatricality

(**figs. 5.23** and **5.24**). Its ground plan and design appear to have been established by the renowned architects Paionios of Ephesos and Daphnis of Miletos on the site and to the scale of an Archaic temple destroyed by the Persians in 494 BCE.

From the outside, the temple appeared similar to other large-scale dipteral Ionic buildings. A visitor would expect the interior to repeat the format of canonical temples such as the Parthenon; but, in fact, the architects constantly defied these expectations, leading visitors instead to dramatic vistas, perhaps intending to heighten their religious experience. Although the temple appeared to be accessible from all sides, its seven massive steps were too high to climb comfortably. Instead, visitors used a set of shallower steps at the front, and entered the porch between its vast columns, set to mimic the grove of sacred trees around the building. As expected, an opening led to the cella—but this cella stood approximately 5 feet off the ground, so access was impossible. From this raised threshold, scholars believe, the oracular priestess may have uttered prophecies to those standing below in the porch. The path further into the building led to the right or left of the threshold, where dark barrel-vaulted tunnels led downward. For a Greek, a barrel-vaulted tunnel evoked a dark interior such as a cave. Yet these passages led to a vast open courtyard drenched with sunlight: A revelation, it must have seemed.

At the end of the courtyard was the shrine itself, a small Ionic building dedicated to Apollo. Turning back from the shrine, a visitor faced a wide, steep staircase leading up to a pair of towering engaged (i.e., partly merged with the wall) Corinthian columns. These may have signaled that the room beyond them was the priestess's innermost sanctuary. We know little of the goings-on inside Greek temples, yet the processional quality

5.23 Paionios of Ephesos and Daphnis of Miletos. Temple of Apollo. Begun 313 BCE. Marble. Didyma, Turkey

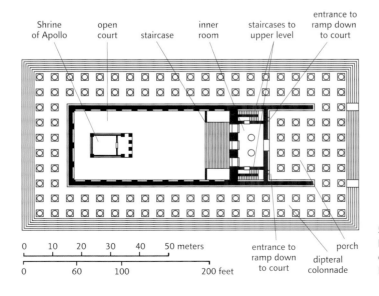

Shrine of Apollo

open court

staircase

inner room

staircases to upper level

entrance to ramp down to court

0 10 20 30 40 50 meters

0 60 100 200 feet

entrance to ramp down to court

dipteral colonnade

porch

5.24 Plan of Temple of Apollo by Paionios of Ephesos and Daphnis of Miletos. Begun 313 BCE. Didyma, Turkey

5.25 Theater at Epidauros.
Limestone. Early third to second
centuries BCE

of this staircase and the large scale of the courtyard
suggest that large crowds of worshipers could have
gathered there to witness rituals. Also unknown is
the function of the small staircases leading off from
the sanctuary and up to the roof over the colonnades. Inscriptions describe them as "labyrinths,"
and the ceilings are carved with a painted meander pattern, the Egyptian hieroglyph for a maze.
They may have provided maintenance workers
with access to the roof, but they may equally have
accommodated revelatory dramas in honor of
Apollo. As a whole, the temple manipulated visitors
along unexpected paths, and offered constant sur-
prises. This theatricality was a feature of a number
of other buildings of this time.

The Temple of Apollo is remarkable for another
reason besides the experience it offered. Inside
the courtyard, archaeologists discovered diagrams
incised (so lightly that they are visible only under a
strong raking light) upon its walls. These etchings
are scale drawings of the building's design, ranging

from capital decoration to column entasis, and provide rare insights into the design process in Greek
building. They suggest that architects drew a building's design onto its surfaces as it rose, and workers then polished them off as they finished those
surfaces. This temple's incompletion preserved the
designs in place.

THE THEATER AT EPIDAUROS   Given the propensity
for theatricality, it is no surprise that Hellenistic
architects paid close attention to theater buildings. Theaters had long been part of the religious
landscape of Greek cities, since choral performances
and plays were central to festivals of Dionysos.
The basic prerequisites were a hillside on which
an audience could sit (the *cavea*), and a level area
for the performance (the *orchestra*). However,
theaters became more formalized as their essential
components took on architectural form.

In the sanctuary of the healing god Askle-
pios at Epidauros on the Peloponnese, a

magnificent stone theater was constructed in the early third century BCE; its upper tier was completed in the second century (**fig. 5.25**). Row upon row of stone seats lined the hillside, covering slightly more than a semicircle. To facilitate circulation, the architect grouped the seats in wedgelike sections (*cunei*) separated by staircases; a wide horizontal corridor divides the upper and lower sections. Actors performed in the level circle at the center, with a stage building (*skene*) behind as a backdrop, containing utility rooms. This form is familiar to theatergoers even today, a testament to its success. Because it was open to the sky, no roof supports obstructed viewing of the performance, and many of the seats offered spectacular views across the landscape. Yet perhaps the most astonishing feature of the theater is its acoustics, which visitors can still experience: Its funnel shape carries the slightest whisper up to the highest points of the auditorium.

THE PHAROS AT ALEXANDRIA In Alexandria, on the northwest coast of the Nile delta, a vast and innovative lighthouse was a testament to the city's cosmopolitan nature and the vitality of shipping and commerce throughout the Hellenistic Mediterranean (**fig. 5.26**). Alexander the Great founded the city, but the famed lighthouse or Pharos was not begun until the reign of Ptolemy I, in ca. 279 BCE. Some sources attribute it to the architect Sostratus. The building has long collapsed, but a French team has recently recovered some of its blocks in underwater excavations. Together with mosaic depictions and medieval descriptions, archaeological evidence suggests a building with a square, slightly tapering base, an octagonal central drum, and a tholos-like element, crowned by a huge bronze statue at the dizzying height of nearly 384 feet. A hollow central tower contained the lighthouse's machinery, and around it circled an annular corridor, wide enough for mules to climb to the top with combustible materials for the fire

5.26 Sostratus (?) Reconstruction drawing of the Pharos at Alexandria. Begun ca. 279 BCE. Limestone, possibly faced with marble

5.27 Lysippos. *Portrait of Alexander the Great*, the "Azara herm." Marble, height 27" (68 cm). Roman copy after an original of the late fourth century BCE. Musée du Louvre, Paris

signal. One of the Seven Wonders of the Ancient World, the building became an icon for the city, and it was widely imitated by other cities.

Hellenistic Sculpture: Expression and Movement

Fourth-century BCE sculptors explored the portrayal of emotion and movement, and their Hellenistic successors made further strides in these directions. Both resulted in heightened drama and viewer involvement. That said, one can make only broad generalizations about Hellenistic sculpture, as it is notoriously difficult to date and to attribute to a firm place of origin.

PORTRAITURE A chief development in this period was portraiture. One of the catalysts was Alexander the Great himself. Recognizing the power of a consistent visual image, he retained the great fourth-century artist Lysippos as the exclusive creator of his sculpted portraits. No surviving original preserves Lysippos' touch, but the so-called "Azara herm" is considered relatively faithful to its model (**fig. 5.27**). To be sure, the face has an idealized quality: Its planes are smooth, especially around the brow. Yet individuality emerges in the unruly hair, raised at the front in Alexander's characteristic cowlick (or *anastole*), and in the twist of the head, which removes the portrait from a timeless realm

5.28 Epigonos of Pergamon (?). *Dying Trumpeter*. Perhaps a Roman copy after a bronze original of ca. 230–220 BCE, from Pergamon, Turkey. Marble, life-size. Museo Capitolino, Rome

and animates it with action. Moreover, Alexander does not engage with a viewer, but has a distant gaze. These characteristics would become emblematic of Alexander, and Hellenistic and Roman generals would adopt them as attributes in their own portraiture. With this image, the individual came to inhabit the sculpture.

Like architects, Hellenistic sculptors engaged their audience in the experience of their work, and favored dramatic subjects infused with emotion. The *Dying Trumpeter*, preserved in a Roman copy (**fig. 5.28**), probably belonged on one of two statue bases found in the Sanctuary of Athena on the Akropolis of Pergamon, and commemorated Attalos I's defeat of the Gauls (a CELTIC people) in about 233 BCE. Gone is the Classical tradition of referring to the enemy through mythological analogy. Instead, the sculptor identified the enemy as a Gaul through his bushy hair and moustache, and by the torque, or braided gold band, that he wears around his neck. Gone, too, is any suggestion of the inferiority of the vanquished. The Gaul dies nobly, sinking to the ground or struggling to prop himself up, as blood pours from a wound in his chest. His body is powerful, his strength palpable. He faces his agonies alone, mindless of any viewer. A viewer, in turn, is drawn in by the privateness of the moment, and drawn around the sculpture by the pyramidal composition and the foreshortening witnessed from every angle. The *Dying Trumpeter* was probably one sculpture in a group, but the victor, always present in Classical battle scenes, was absent. The monument celebrates the conqueror's valor by exalting the enemy he overcame; the greater the enemy, the greater the victory. Pliny records a famous sculpture of a trumpet player by Epigonos, and this Roman copy may reflect that work.

DRAMATIC VICTORY MONUMENTS Sculptures decorating the Great Altar of Zeus at Pergamon exemplify the highly emotional, dramatic style at its height (**figs. 5.29** and **5.30**). The monument dates to about 180 BCE, when Eumenes II built it on a terrace on the Pergamene Akropolis to commemorate territorial victories over Pontos and Bithynia and the establishment of a grand victory festival, the *Nikephoria*. The altar stood high on a podium within a large enclosure

The CELTIC tribes first appeared in the second millennium BCE in southwestern Germany and eastern France (called Gaul by the Romans), and eventually ranged over a wide territory. They spoke Indo-European dialects, were skilled in the art of smelting iron, and raided and conquered other peoples in Europe and Asia Minor well into the third century BCE. They dominated Iron Age culture in Europe until displaced by the Germans in the east and subdued by the Romans in the west. Greek and Roman writers noted that Celtic warriors were tall, light-skinned, well muscled, and ferocious; the front ranks often fought naked (see fig. 5.28).

5.29 The west front of the Great Altar of Zeus at Pergamon (restored). ca. 180 BCE. Marble, height 31'8⅓" (9.66 m). Staatliche Museen zu Berlin, Preussischer Kulturbesitz, Antikensammlung

5.30 *Athena and Alkyoneus*, from the east side of the Great Frieze of the Great Altar of Zeus at Pergamon. ca. 180 BCE. Marble, height 7′6″ (2.29 m). Staatliche Museen zu Berlin, Preussischer Kulturbesitz, Antikensammlung

defined by an Ionic colonnade, approached by a wide staircase; it is now reconstructed in Berlin. The enclosure's boldest feature is a frieze encircling the base, which extends over 400 feet in length and is over 7 feet in height. Its subject, the battle of the gods and giants—gigantomachy, was a familiar theme in architectural sculpture. Here, as before, it worked allegorically, symbolizing Eumenes' victories. Never before, however, had artists treated the subject so extensively or so dramatically. About 84 figures crowd the composition, interspersed with animals. This was no mean feat: The designer must have relied upon research by scholars in the Pergamene library to identify protagonists for this great battle. They may also have assisted with creating a balanced and resonant composition, for despite the chaotic appearance of the mêlée, guiding principles lurk behind it. Modern scholars struggle to understand these principles, even with the help of inscriptions naming some of the gods above the frieze and the giants beneath.

On the eastern frieze, facing the sanctuary's Propylon and the rising sun, were the Olympian gods, with Athena, Pergamon's patron goddess, positioned most prominently. On the south, in sunlight, were heavenly beings such as Helios, the sun god; on the shadowy north were divinities of the night. Earth and sea deities were on the west. Compositional parallels unified the four sides. The frieze is direct evidence of the Hellenistic scholarly tradition at work.

On the other hand, the frieze is deeply imbued with Hellenistic theatricality. Sculptors carved the figures so deeply, and undercut them in places so forcefully, that they are almost in the round. The high relief creates a vivid interplay of light and dark, and on the staircase, the figures seem to spill out onto the steps and climb alongside an ascending visitor. Muscular bodies rush at each other, overlapping and entwining (see fig. 5.30). The giants' snaky extremities twist and curl, echoed in their deeply drilled tendrils of ropelike hair. Wings beat and garments blow furiously in the wind or twist around those they clothe, not to reveal the anatomy beneath but to create motion; they have a life of their own and their texture contrasts with the smoothness of the giants' flesh. The giants agonize in the torment of their defeat, their brows creased in pain, their eyes deepset in an exaggerated style reminiscent of Skopas. A writhing motion pervades the design, and links the figures in a single continuous rhythm. This rhythm, and the quiet classicism of the gods' faces, so starkly opposed to those of the giants, create a unity that keeps the violence of the struggle from exploding its architectural frame—but only just. For the first time in the long tradition of its depiction, a viewer has a visceral sense of what an awesome cosmic crisis this battle would be.

HELLENISTIC REALISM The term "baroque" is used to describe the extreme emotions and extravagant gestures that characterize the Great Altar of Zeus. Art historians first used the word to describe seventeenth-century CE art, and historians of Hellenistic art borrowed it on recognizing similarities between the two styles. With its dramatic qualities, the Hellenistic baroque style has tended to eclipse the many other contemporary movements in sculpture. One of these is a penchant for works depicting unidealized and realistic everyday life. Their genre is known as Hellenistic realism, and a sculpture of a drunken old woman illustrates it well (**fig. 5.31**). Known from Roman copies, this piece has at times been ascribed to Myron of Thebes, who may have worked at Pergamon. The evidence is slim, and the figure may fit better in the cultural context

5.31 *Drunken Old Woman*. Roman copy of an original of the late third or late second century BCE. Marble, height 36″ (92 cm). Glyptothek, Munich

of Alexandria, where realism seems to have been particularly prevalent. The woman crouches on the ground, clasping a wine bottle, her head flung far back. Wrinkles cover her face, and the skin on her exposed shoulder and chest sags. She wears a buckled tunic, which identifies her as a member of an affluent social class. Other sculptures of this kind focus on the ravaging effects of a rustic life on the poor; yet in this sculpture, the artist explores drunkenness and old age. Without further insights into the cultural context for the image, it is hard to know if the sculptor intended to offer a sympathetic view of his subject, exalting her nobility, or to engage in a hard social commentary.

Hellenistic Painting

It was in the fourth century BCE that Greek wall painting came into its own. Pliny names a number of leading painters, but no surviving work can be attributed to them. All the same, paintings are preserved in Macedonian tombs, several of which have recently come—and keep coming—to light in

5.32 *The Abduction of Persephone.* ca. 340–330 BCE. Detail of a wall painting in Tomb I, Vergina, Macedonia. Painted plaster

northern Greece (in the region of Macedonia). These tombs are of great importance because they contain the only surviving relatively complete Greek wall paintings, which offer a tantalizing glimpse of what painters could accomplish. The section shown here (**fig. 5.32**) comes from a tomb at Vergina, dating to about 340–330 BCE. The subject, the abduction of Persephone, is appropriate to the funereal setting. Pluto, ruler of the underworld, abducts Persephone to be his queen. Thanks to Zeus' intervention, Persephone would be allowed to return to the world of the living for six months of every year. The artist has chosen the moment when Pluto seizes Persephone into his speeding chariot, her handmaiden rearing back in fright. This is the most harrowing moment, before Persephone knows that Zeus will find a compromise, when her futile struggle seems the only possible escape from the underworld. The painting captures all of the myth's drama. Persephone flings her body backward, while the chariot rushes onward with her captor; their bodies cross as a sign of conflict. The chariot plunges toward a viewer, its wheel sharply foreshortened. Masterful brushwork animates the scene. With swift flourishes, the artist sends hair and drapery flying, and lends plasticity to the garments. Hatchwork rounds out the bodies' flesh, as on the arms and shoulders. The colors are brilliant washes, with shading for texture. Literary sources attribute the discovery of shading (the modulation of volume by means of contrasting light and shade), known as *skiagraphia*, to a painter named Apollodorus, who used the technique perhaps as early as the fifth century BCE. They associate spatial perspective with Agatharchos, creator of stage scenery during the heyday of Athenian drama. The exploration and perfection of both devices during the course of the fourth century BCE illustrate the fascination with illusionism at this time.

POINTS OF REFLECTION

5.1 Explore the impact of Near Eastern and Egyptian culture on Greek artists and architects in the Orientalizing and Archaic periods.

5.2 Select a work from the Archaic, the Classical, and the Hellenistic periods to illustrate artists' evolving expertise in suggesting nature, motion and emotion.

5.3 The Parthenon is often regarded as the highpoint of Classical architecture and sculpture. Is this reputation justified?

5.4 Compare the subject matter and style of the gigantomachy frieze on the Great Altar of Zeus with architectural sculpture of earlier years.

5.5 Describe a visitor's experience of the Temple of Apollo at Didyma. How and why was it novel?

✓●─**Study** and review on myartslab.com

ART IN TIME

- ca. eighth century BCE — Homer writes *The Iliad* and *The Odyssey*

- ca. 750 BCE Dipylon Vase

- **late-seventh century BCE — Black-figured vase-painting technique develops**

- ca. 650 BCE — Greeks establish trading posts in Egypt

- seventh century BCE — Doric and Ionic styles develop

- ca. 500 BCE — Red-figured vase-painting technique becomes popular

- 490 BCE — Greeks defeat the Persians at the Battle of Marathon

- **ca. 480 BCE — *Kritios Boy***

- **ca. 447 BCE — Perikles orders construction of Parthenon**

- 431–404 BCE — Peloponnesian War

- 387 BCE — Plato founds the Academy in Athens

- 336–323 BCE — Reign of Alexander the Great

- **313 BCE — Construction begins on the Temple of Apollo, Didyma**

CHAPTER 6
Etruscan Art

POINTS OF INQUIRY

6.1 Explore the diverse styles of funerary architecture and art used by the Etruscans at different times.

6.2 Summarize the essential characteristics of Etruscan residential and religious architecture, inasmuch as we can reconstruct them.

6.3 Explore the importance of metallurgy in Etruscan culture.

6.4 Investigate the impact of other cultures on Etruscan artists.

(((•—**Listen** to the chapter audio on myartslab.com

Periods of Etruscan Art

ca. 700–600 BCE	Orientalizing period
ca. 600–480 BCE	Archaic period
ca. 480–300 BCE	Classical period
ca. 300 BCE	Etruscan culture is slowly absorbed into Roman culture

Early Etruscan culture, known as Villanovan, appeared on the Italian peninsula in the tenth century BCE. Who the Etruscans were remains a mystery; even in antiquity, writers disputed their origins. The Greek historian Herodotus believed that they had left their homeland of Lydia in Asia Minor in about 1200 BCE, and settled in what are now the Italian regions of Tuscany, Umbria, and Lazio (see **map 6.1**). Recent DNA sampling may support his view. Others claimed they were indigenous. Wherever they came from, the Etruscans had strong cultural links with Asia Minor and the ancient Near East. In fact, their visual culture is a rich blend of distinctly Etruscan traits with influences from the east and from Greece. Toward the end of the eighth century BCE the Etruscans began to use the Greek alphabet, and this makes it possible to read their inscriptions, which survive in the thousands; but since their language is unrelated to any other, we cannot always understand their meaning.

The Etruscans reached the height of their power in the seventh and sixth centuries BCE, coinciding with the Archaic age in Greece. They amassed great wealth by mining metals, and their territory extended from the lower Po River Valley in the north to Naples in the south. Their cities rivaled Greek cities, and their fleet dominated the western Mediterranean, protecting a vast commercial network that competed with the Greeks and Phoenicians. But, like the Greeks, the Etruscans never formed a unified nation. They remained a loose federation of individual city-states, united by a common language and religion but given to conflict and slow to unite against a common enemy. This may have been one cause of their gradual downfall. In 474 BCE, the Etruscans' archrival, Syracuse, defeated the Etruscan fleet, and during the fourth and early third centuries BCE, one Etruscan city after another fell to the Romans. By 270 BCE, all the Etruscan city-states had lost their independence to Rome, although if we are to judge by the splendor of their tombs during this period of political struggle, many still prospered.

The bulk of our knowledge about Etruscan culture comes from art, and especially from their monumental tombs. These structures elucidate Etruscan building practices, and artists often painted them with scenes that reveal a glimpse of Etruscan life. Objects found within them attest to the Etruscans' reputation as fine sculptors and metalworkers. Large numbers of Attic painted vases have also come to light in tombs, demonstrating the Etruscans' close trade ties with Greece.

Funerary Art

As with burials elsewhere in prehistoric Europe, early burials on the Italian peninsula were modest. At the beginning of the seventh century BCE, as Etruscans began to bury their dead in family groups, funerary customs became more elaborate, and the tombs of the wealthy gradually transformed into monumental structures.

Tombs and Their Contents

Named for the amateur archaeologists who excavated it, the Regolini-Galassi Tomb at Cerveteri is an early example of this more elaborate burial practice, dating to the so-called Orientalizing phase of the mid-seventh century BCE, when Etruscan arts show the marked influence of Eastern motifs. Etruscans formed tombs in the shape of mounds called *tumuli*, which were grouped together outside the living spaces of Etruscan towns to create a city of the dead, or necropolis. In the Regolini-Galassi Tomb, builders roofed the long *dromos* (plural *dromoi*; pathway, entrance corridor) leading into the tomb with corbeled vaults built of horizontal, overlapping courses of stone blocks, similar to those at Mycenae (see fig. 4.11). Among the grave goods in the tomb was a spectacular fibula (**fig. 6.1**). A fibula resembled a brooch or a decorative safety pin, and often served to hold a garment together at the neck. At 11½ inches in length, this example is a *tour de force* of the goldsmith's art and justifies the fame Etruscan goldsmiths enjoyed in antiquity. Covering the lower leaflike portion are 55 gold ducks in the round. On the upper portion, which the goldsmith shaped as a three-quarter moon, repoussé work defines pacing lions, whose profile pose and erect stance may derive from Phoenician precedents. Indeed, though the workmanship is probably Etruscan, the animal motifs suggest familiarity with the artworks of Near Eastern cultures. Also buried in tombs of this time are precious objects imported from the ancient Near East, such as ivories.

The Regolini-Galassi Tomb is but one of many tumulus tombs built at necropoleis near Cerveteri over the course of several centuries until about 100 BCE (**fig. 6.2**). The local stone is a soft volcanic

Map 6.1 Italian peninsula in Etruscan times

6.1 Fibula from Regolini-Galassi Tomb, Cerveteri. Gold. ca. 670–650 BCE. 11½″ (29.2 cm) long. Musei Vaticani, Museo Gregoriano Etrusco, Città del Vaticano, Rome

rock known as tuff, which is easy to cut and hardens after prolonged exposure to air. Those who created the tumuli excavated into bedrock, cutting away a path and burial chambers. With the excavated stone they built a retaining wall around the chambers, above which they piled up soil. Often several *dromoi* led to independent networks of chambers within a single mound. The layout of the burial chambers varies, and some scholars have supposed that these dwellings of the dead mimicked contemporary houses, often complete with chairs or beds carved out of the rock as furnishing. This is hard

6.3 Tomb of Hunting and Fishing. ca. 530–520 BCE. Painted plaster. Tarquinia, Italy

to confirm, given the scant evidence for Etruscan residences.

Farther north, at Tarquinia, tombs consist of chambers sunk into the earth with a steep underground *dromos*. Vibrant paintings cover the walls, executed while the plaster was wet. At one end of the low chamber in the Tomb of Hunting and Fishing is a marine panorama, dating to about 530–520 BCE (**fig. 6.3**). Fishermen cast lines from a boat, as brightly colored dolphins leap through waves. A sling-shot hunter on a rocky promontory aims his fire at large birds in bright red, blue, and yellow that swoop through the sky. Unlike Greek landscape scenes, where humans dominate their surroundings, here the figures form part of a larger scheme. The exuberant colors and gestures are also characteristically Etruscan. All the same, here as in most tombs, the treatment of drapery and anatomy betrays some Greek influence.

The artist seems to have conceived of the scene as a view from a tent or hut, defined by bands of color at cornice level and roofed with a tapestry. Hanging from the cornice are garlands of the kind probably used during funerary rituals. In many tombs, images of animals fill the gable—leopards, sometimes, or fantastic hybrids—perhaps used as guardian figures to ward off evil. Above the fishing scene, a man and woman recline at a banquet, with

musicians and servants. In Etruscan banquet scenes respectable women recline together with men, in contrast to Greek drinking parties (*symposia*), which were reserved for men and courtesans.

The purpose of these paintings is hard to determine. They may record and perpetuate activities the deceased once enjoyed, or rituals observed at the funeral (the games, in fact, are probably the forerunners of Roman gladiatorial contests). Or, like Egyptian tomb paintings, they may have served as provisions for the afterlife of the deceased, as part of a CULT OF THE DEAD. As enigmatic as they are, these paintings constitute a large part of our evidence for Etruscan beliefs. In a few tombs, paintings seem to reflect Greek myths, but these images merely compound the problem, since we cannot be sure that the Etruscans intended the same meaning as Greek artists.

However we interpret these archaic and classical images, it is clear that a distinct change in the content of tomb paintings begins in the late classical period during the fourth century BCE. An overwhelming sense of sadness replaces the energetic mood of the Archaic and Classical periods. The exuberant palette of the earlier periods, with their bright reds and yellows, gives way to a somber range of darker colors. At this time, funerary images often depict processions taking the

About 700 BCE Etruscans began to build and excavate tombs of stone. These contained chambers for the dead, and were covered by great conical mounds of earth. Cinerary urns, which had formerly been simple pottery vessels, gradually took on human shape (see below). The frequent depictions of funerary meals in Etruscan art, as well as the gold and other precious objects found in tombs, may be provisions for an afterlife or evidence of a CULT OF THE DEAD.

6.4 Tomb of the Anina Family. End of fourth century BCE. Painted plaster. Tarquinia, Italy

Modeled sculpture as in figure 6.5, is additive: the artist builds up the basic form from a raw material such as clay, and then finishes it by carving and smoothing the details. In large-scale work, supports or armatures are incorporated into the figure to stabilize the forms.

deceased to a world of the dead, or they are set in a shadowy underworld. In some tombs of this later period, ominous demons of death appear, painted green and blue. In the Tomb of the Anina Family at Tarquinia, dating to about the end of the fourth century BCE, two winged demons flank a door to another world (**fig. 6.4**). A hook-nosed Charun, on the left, is the soul's guide to the underworld. He holds a hammer with which he will open the door, while Vanth, on the right, bears a torch to light the darkness. It is possible that gloomy subjects reflected the downturn in Etruscan fortunes, as Rome extended its hegemony through the peninsula.

In Cerveteri, two monumental sarcophagi of the Archaic period came to light, molded in terra cotta in two separate halves. One of them, dating to about 520 BCE, is shown here (**fig. 6.5**). The artist shaped the lid to resemble a couch, and reclining side by side on top are full-length sculptures of a man and

woman, presumably a married couple. A wineskin (a canteen made from an animal skin) cushions the woman's left elbow, and the man has his arm around her shoulders. Both figures once held objects in their hands—a cup or an *alabastron* (a perfume container), perhaps, or an egg, symbol of eternity. Despite the abstract forms and rigid poses of the archaic style, the soft material allows the sculptor to model rounded forms and capture an extraordinary directness and vivacity. The artist painted the entire work in bright colors, which conservators have revealed more clearly in a recent cleaning.

The change in mood that characterizes tomb paintings between the fifth and fourth centuries BCE is also apparent in funerary sculpture. On a stone cinerary container made soon after 400 BCE, a man and woman sit at either end of a couch (**fig. 6.6**). The woman's wings identify her not as the young man's wife but as a demon from the world of the dead, and the scroll in her left hand may record his

Given the close relationship between Etruscan and Greek art forms, scholars define the stylistic periods of Etruscan art with the terms they use for Greek art: Archaic, Classical, and Hellenistic.

6.5 Sarcophagus, from Cerveteri. ca. 520 BCE. Painted terra cotta, length 6′7″ (2 m). Museo Nazionale di Villa Giulia, Rome

fate. He wears his mantle pulled down around his waist, in the Etruscan style. The two figures create a balanced composition, but their separation marks a new mood of melancholy associated with death, which each individual must face alone. Still, wealthy Etruscans continued to bury their dead together in family tombs, and the familial context for cinerary urns like this one must have gone some way toward mitigating the isolation of death.

6.6 *Youth and Female Demon.* Cinerary container. Early fourth century BCE. Stone (*pietra fetida*), length 47″ (119.4 cm). Museo Archeologico Nazionale, Florence

Architecture

According to Roman writers, the Etruscans were masters of engineering, town planning, and surveying. Almost certainly, Roman architects learned from them, especially in water management (drainage systems and aqueducts) and bridge building. How much they learned is hard to determine: Since it was built predominantly of perishable materials, relatively little Etruscan and early Roman architecture survives. Additionally, the hilltops the Etruscans favored have been inhabited more or less continually since their days, so that many of their towns lie beneath existing Italian towns, and any permanent materials employed in their construction have often been reused.

Little survives of the houses that composed Etruscan towns. Unlike tombs, they were built with a pisé technique (earth packed between molds) similar to wattle and daub or adobe, with only the base made of stone. In a few places, archaeologists have unearthed the remains of monumental building complexes that may have been palaces or large villas. An especially fine example existed at POGGIO CIVITATE (present-day Murlo) in the sixth century BCE, where numerous rooms framed a large central courtyard. This kind of architecture is conceptually linked to typically Roman atrium houses (see fig. 7.24). In order to protect the wooden fabric of their monumental buildings, Etruscans nailed terra-cotta **revetment** plaques to the exposed parts of the beams. A mid-sixth-century monumental residential building at Acquarossa yielded a fine set of molded and painted revetments. One of them shows a banquet scene, with diners on couches amid musicians (**fig. 6.7**), and others depicted Herakles accomplishing his labors. With their bright colors, the revetments enlivened the building, but they may also have equated the standing of the elite property owners with that of the Greek hero.

Etruscans built their temples, like other structures, of pisé and wood, and only the stone foundations survive. Early temples consisted of modest rectangular cellas (rooms for holding cult figures). Later temples seem to have fallen under the influence of the innovative design of the Temple of Jupiter Optimus Maximus on the Capitoline Hill in Rome (see fig. 7.1). They are characterized by a tall podium, with steps on the front. The steps lead to a deep porch with rows of columns, and to the cella beyond, which was often subdivided into three compartments. The terra-cotta tile roof hung well over the walls in wide eaves, to shield the mud bricks from rain.

Sculpture

Etruscan temples were highly ornate. Their decoration usually consisted of brightly painted terra-cotta plaques that covered the architrave and the edges of the roof, protecting them from damp. After about 400 BCE, Etruscan artists sometimes designed large-scale terra-cotta groups to fill the pediment above the porch. The most dramatic use of sculpture was on the ridgepole—the horizontal beam at the crest of a gabled roof. Terra-cotta figures at this height depicted not only single figures but narratives.

Plan of residential complex at Poggio Civitate, 6th century BCE

6.7 Revetment plaque from Acquarossa. ca. 575–550 BCE. Painted terra cotta, height 8⅓″ (21 cm). Museo Archeologico Nazionale, Viterbo

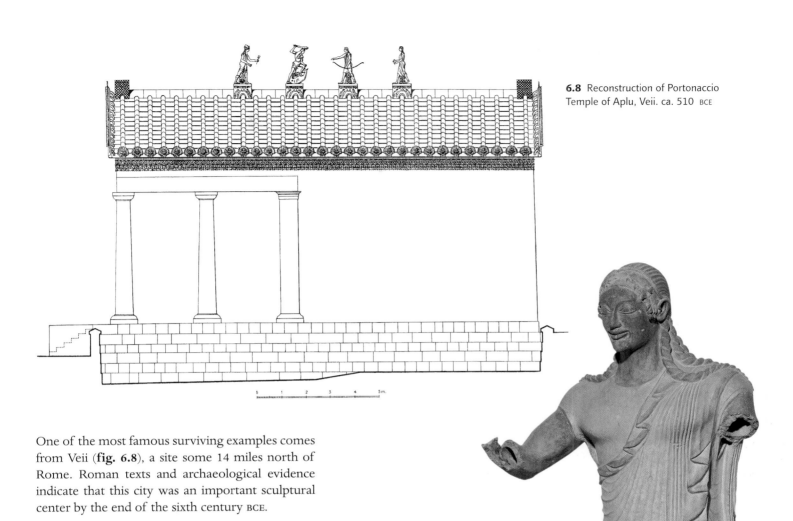

6.8 Reconstruction of Portonaccio Temple of Aplu, Veii. ca. 510 BCE

One of the most famous surviving examples comes from Veii (**fig. 6.8**), a site some 14 miles north of Rome. Roman texts and archaeological evidence indicate that this city was an important sculptural center by the end of the sixth century BCE.

Dynamism in Terra Cotta and Bronze

The late sixth-century BCE Portonaccio temple at Veii was probably devoted to the gods Menrva, Aritimi, and Turan. Four life-size terra-cotta statues crowned the ridge of the roof. They formed a dynamic and interactive group representing the contest of Hercle (Herakles) and Aplu (Apollo) for the sacred hind (female deer) in the presence of other deities. The best-preserved of the figures is Aplu (**fig. 6.9**). He wears a mantle with curved hem known to Romans as a toga. The drapery falls in ornamental patterns and exposes his massive body, with its sinewy, muscular legs. The stylistic similarity to contemporary Greek *kouroi* and *korai* signals the superficial influence of Greek sculpture. Yet this god moves in a hurried, purposeful stride that has no equivalent in free-standing Greek statues of the same date. Rendered in terra cotta, which allowed the sculptor greater freedom to experiment with poses than stone, this is a purely Etruscan energy. Art historians have attributed these sculptures to a famous Etruscan sculptor, Vulca of Veii, celebrated in Latin literary sources.

6.9 *Apollo* (*Aplu*), from Veii. ca. 510 BCE. Painted terra cotta, height 5′9″ (1.75 m). Museo Nazionale di Villa Giulia, Rome

6.10 *Chimaira*. Late fifth–early fourth century BCE. Bronze, height 31½″ (80 cm). Museo Archeologico, Florence

Etruscan sculptors also demonstrated extraordinary skill as bronze casters. A magnificent bronze sculpture of the late fifth or early fourth century BCE, found in Arezzo, depicts a chimaira, a hybrid creature combining a lion, a goat's head, and a snake (**fig. 6.10**). In Greek mythology, the hero Bellerophon killed the creature, and bleeding gashes on its body suggest that it was originally part of a larger narrative group. An inscription on the animal's right foreleg indicates that the sculpture was a votive offering. The creature snarls, crouched in anticipation of springing. The stylized tufts of its mane and raised hackles contrast with the taut, smooth muscles. Blood pumps through straining veins. The goat rears its head back, the snake writhes. The sculpture emanates energy.

Etruscan sculptors also produced fine portraits in bronze. A life-size bronze sculpture of an orator, known today as *L'Arringatore* (*The Orator*), comes from Lake Trasimene, in the central Etruscan territory (**fig. 6.11**). Most scholars place it in the early years of the first century BCE. It bears an Etruscan inscription with the name Aule Meteli (*Aulus Metellus* in Latin), presumably the name of the person it represents. The inscription shows that the workmanship is Etruscan. The high boots, however, mark the subject as Roman, or at least an official appointed by the Romans; in fact, the raised arm, a gesture that denotes both address and salutation, is common to hundreds of Roman statues. The sculpture raises important questions about the roles of artist and patron and about identity in the conquered Etruscan territories.

6.11 *L'Arringatore*. Early first century BCE. Bronze, height 5'11" (2.8 m). Museo Archeologico, Florence

POINTS OF REFLECTION

6.1 Compare and contrast the paintings of the Tomb of Hunting and Fishing and the Tomb of the Anina Family at Tarquinia. How might one explain the changes?

6.2 Describe the features of Etruscan residential complexes and temples, and the decorative forms that embellished them.

6.3 Consider the various types of work Etruscan goldsmiths and sculptors produced.

6.4 Assess the extent of the influence of Near Eastern, Greek, and Roman art and architecture on Etruscan visual culture.

✓—**Study** and review on myartslab.com

ART IN TIME

• ca. 1200 BCE — Appearance of Etruscan culture on the Italian peninsula

• ca. 600s–500s BCE — The height of Etruscan power

• ca. 530–520 BCE — **Tomb of Hunting and Fishing at Tarquinia**

• ca. 520 BCE — **Terra-cotta sarcophagi from Cerveteri**

• ca. 518 BCE — Construction of the Persian palace at Persepolis begins

• ca. 510 BCE — The Temple of Aplu at Veii

• late fifth/early fourth century BCE — ***Chimaira of Arezzo***

• ca. 450–440 BCE — *Doryphoros* of Polykleitos

• early fourth century BCE — ***Youth and Female Demon, cinerary container***

• 331 BCE — Alexander the Great defeats the Persians

• by 270 BCE — Rome controls the Italian peninsula

CHAPTER

7 | Roman Art

POINTS OF INQUIRY

7.1 Explore the possibilities opened up to Roman architects as a result of the development of concrete.

7.2 Examine the impact of politics on Roman architects and artists.

7.3 Summarize the functions and styles of Roman portraiture during the Republic and Empire.

7.4 Investigate the developments in sculptural narrative in the Roman period.

7.5 Assess the relationship between Roman and indigenous forms in art and architecture in the provinces.

7.6 Recognize the four styles of Roman wall painting, and consider the role of painting in a domestic ensemble.

((•—**Listen** to the chapter audio on myartslab.com

Of all the civilizations of the ancient world, the most accessible to modern scholars is that of ancient Rome. Romans built countless monuments throughout their empire, which are extraordinarily well preserved. A vast literary legacy, ranging from poetry and histories to inscriptions that recorded everyday events, also reveals a great deal about Roman culture. Yet there are few questions more difficult to address than "What is Roman art?"

Roman art was the art of both Republic and Empire, the art of a small city that became a vast power. It is an art created by Roman artists, but not exclusively; the greatest architect of Trajan's time may in fact have been from Damascus. Perhaps the most useful way to think of Roman art is as one of syncretism—an art that brings diverse elements together to produce something entirely new, with a powerful message-bearing potential. Syncretism, in art as in politics and religion, was a profoundly Roman attitude, and was probably the secret to Rome's extraordinary expansion. Roman civilization incorporated various other cultures and integrated them into its own culture, giving rise to a remarkably diverse world.

Some of the extant art of Rome draws heavily on Greek styles. In the nineteenth and early twentieth centuries, art connoisseurs exalted Greek Classicism as the height of stylistic achievement, and considered Roman art derivative, the last chapter, so to speak, of Greek art history. This view has changed radically, especially as connoisseurship has yielded to other branches of art history. Experts now focus, for instance, on the roles of artworks in their social and political contexts. They also recognize that Greek styles were not the first or the only ones current in the Roman world. Early Roman art shared more with the art of other Italic cities, and later works created in the provinces or by the non-elite have their own style, as do those of late antiquity. There were also phases of "Egyptianizing" in Rome.

The Roman Republic and Empire

510–27 BCE	Roman Republic
27 BCE–395 CE	Roman Empire
395–476 CE	Western Empire
395–1453	Eastern (Byzantine) Empire

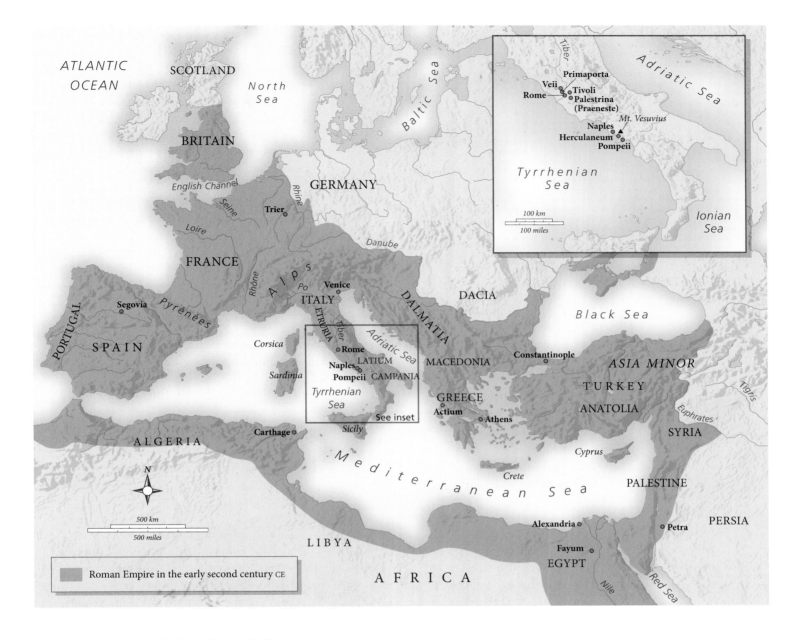

Early Rome and the Republic

According to legend, Romulus founded Rome in 753/52 BCE, in the region known as Latium, on a site near the Tiber River. Yet archaeological evidence shows that people had lived there since about 1000 BCE. From the eighth to the sixth centuries BCE, a series of kings built the first defensive wall around the settlement, drained and filled the swampy plain of the FORUM, and built a vast temple on the CAPITOLINE Hill, making an urban center out of what had been a mere group of villages. The kings established many of Rome's lasting institutions, such as priesthoods and military organization. In about 509 BCE, the elite expelled the last king, and gradually established a Republic, with an unwritten constitution.

Under the Republic, a group of elected magistrates, with an advisory Senate, managed the affairs of the growing state. Rome gradually took control of the Italian peninsula (see **map 7.1**), absorbing Etruscan cities to the north and Greek colonies to the south. After extensive wars with the Carthaginians of North Africa, Rome razed the city of Carthage in 146 BCE. During the second century Greece and Asia Minor also came under Roman control, causing an influx of Greek art and culture into Rome.

From about 133 BCE to 31 BCE, factional politics and political rivalries led to the breakdown of the

Map 7.1 Roman Empire in the early second century BCE

The FORUM was a square or rectangular market and meeting place in the heart of cities and towns built under Roman rule. Romans laid out the first forum in a marshy valley between two of Rome's seven hills, the Palatine and the CAPITOLINE (Capitol). The Capitoline was a religious center of the city from earliest times.

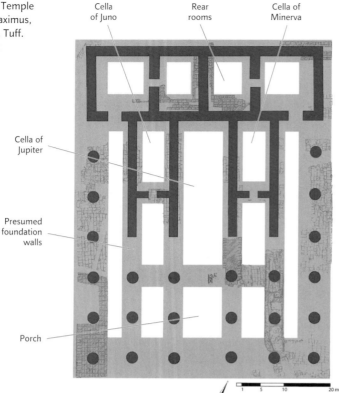

7.1 Restored plan of Temple of Jupiter Optimus Maximus, Capitoline Hill, Rome. Tuff. Dedicated ca. 509 BCE

Cella of Juno

Rear rooms

Cella of Minerva

Cella of Jupiter

Presumed foundation walls

Porch

constitution and to civil war. Julius Caesar became perpetual dictator in 46 BCE, a position that other senators could not tolerate; two years later, they assassinated him. During the course of the Republic, magistrates commissioned works of architecture and sculpture to embellish the city as well as to enhance their own careers. Conquests abroad and the development of new building technologies strongly influenced their designs.

Architecture: The Concrete Revolution

It is probably fair to say that Roman architecture has had a more lasting impact than any other ancient tradition on later Western building. It is an architecture of power, mediated through the solidity of its forms, and through the experience of those forms.

The Temple of Jupiter Optimus Maximus on the Capitoline Hill was the first truly monumental building of Rome (**fig. 7.1**), begun, so the literary tradition stated, under the sixth-century BCE kings, Tarquinius the Ancient and Tarquinius the Proud. Its scale was new to the Italian peninsula, evoking the massive Ionic temples of eastern Greece. It stood on a high masonry platform, with steps

7.2 Temple of Portunus. ca. 80–70 BCE. Tuff and travertine. Rome

Arches

ARCHES were constructed of stone or brick over a temporary wooden scaffold, called centering. Roman arches are semicircular, as opposed to later Gothic arches, which are pointed. The last stone laid in the course of building the arch is the keystone, which locks in the other stones (**voussoirs**) before the centering can be removed.

The outside curve of the arch is the extrados, the inside curve the intrados.

Built on the principle of the semicircular arch, the **barrel vault** may be thought of as a continuous arch. This vaulting is heavy and exerts enormous pressure (thrust) both outward and downward. Barrel vaulting, therefore, is usually supported by heavy walls and/or buttresses.

Also called the square vault, the **groin vault** was much favored in Roman architecture. It is formed using two intersecting vaults. The area enclosed within the four corner piers is called a bay.

● **Watch** an architectural simulation of barrel and groin vaults on myartslab.com

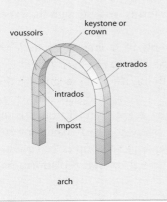

arch

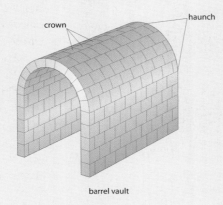

barrel vault

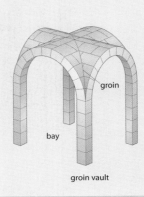

groin vault

leading up to the façade. Six columns marked the front, and six columns flanked each side. Two rows of columns supported the roof over a deep porch. Later Roman historians report that an Etruscan artist, Vulca of Veii, crafted a vast terra-cotta *acroterion* for the peak of the pediment, representing Jupiter in a four-horse chariot. A triple cella with pisé walls accommodated cult statues of Jupiter, Juno, and Minerva, and additional rooms were arranged across the rear. The rectilinear forms, the use of columns, and a gabled roof recall Greek design; yet the high podium and the emphatic frontal access set it apart. These features would characterize most Roman temples in centuries to come, as seen in the well-preserved temple to the harbor god Portunus, near the Tiber (**fig. 7.2**).

Roman architects gradually combined rectilinear designs with circular plans and with the curved form of the arch (see box: Materials and Techniques: Arches). The development of concrete, however, was the catalyst for the most dramatic changes. Concrete is a mixture of mortar and pieces of aggregate such as tufa, limestone, or brick. On adding *pozzolana* sand to the mortar, builders discovered a material of remarkable durability, and they used it with growing confidence from the second century BCE onward. They concealed it with cosmetic facings of stone and brick, which changed with the passing years and therefore provide archaeologists with an invaluable tool for dating buildings. The advantages of concrete were quickly evident: It was strong and inexpensive, and could be worked by relatively unskilled laborers. It was also extraordinarily adaptable: Builders could mold it to shapes that would have been impossible or prohibitively time-consuming to make using cut stone, wood, or mud brick. In terms of design, the history of Roman architecture is a dialogue between the traditional rectilinear forms of early Italic and Greek post-and-lintel traditions on the one hand, and the freedoms afforded by this malleable material on the other.

SANCTUARY OF FORTUNA PRIMIGENIA East of Rome, in the Apennine foothills, the town of Palestrina (ancient Praeneste) is home to a masterpiece of concrete construction (**figs. 7.3**

7.3 Sanctuary of Fortuna Primigenia. Late second century BCE. Concrete. Praeneste (Palestrina), Italy

and **7.4**). The sanctuary to the goddess Fortuna Primigenia, dated to the late second century BCE, was an oracular center where priests interpreted divine will by drawing lots. Architects used concrete to mold structures over the entire surface of a hillside and to craft spaces that controlled and heightened a visitor's experience. At the bottom stood a temple, a basilica, and a senate house. The upper terraces rose in a grand crescendo around a central axis, established by a series of statue niches and staircases. A visitor climbed lateral staircases to the third terrace, where steep ramps, roofed with sloping barrel vaults, led upward. A bright shaft of daylight beckoned from the end of the ramp, where a landing provided the first of several glorious views across the countryside.

On the fourth level, colonnaded *exedrae* (semi-circular recesses) framed the altars. Barrel vaults roofed the colonnades, forming a half-circle horizontally and vertically (annular barrel vaults). The curved forms of the *exedrae* animated the straight lines, since columns set in a semicircle shift their relationship to the environment with every step a visitor takes. A wide central staircase led upward to the next level, where shops probably sold souvenirs and votive objects (items to be consecrated in fulfillment of a vow). After the confinement of

7.4 Axonometric reconstruction of the Sanctuary of Fortuna Primigenia, Praeneste, Italy

the ramps, the exposed steps engendered a sense of vulnerability in the visitor. The next terrace was a huge open court with double colonnades on three sides, from which the visitor climbed to a small theater topped by a double annular colonnade. Here religious performances took place against the magnificent backdrop of the countryside beyond, and in full sight of Fortuna, the goddess whose circular temple crowned the complex. Its diminutive size drew grandeur from the vast scale of the whole—all accomplished with concrete. The hugely versatile material plays easily with the landscape, transforming nature to heighten a visitor's religious experience.

THEATER OF POMPEY The first century BCE was a turning point in the use of architecture for political purposes. One of the most magnificent buildings of this time was the enormous theater complex of Pompey, the first permanent theater of Rome and its most important theater throughout antiquity. Like Julius Caesar after him, Pompey maneuvered himself into a position of unconstitutional power and used architecture to express it. To commemorate his conquests, he conceived of a theater dedicated to his patron goddess Venus Victrix (the Conqueror) (**fig. 7.5**). Later buildings on the site incorporate traces of its superstructure, and the street plan reflects its curved form. Moreover, its ground plan is inscribed on an ancient marble map of the city, carved in the early third century CE, and new excavations promise additional information. The reconstruction in fig. 7.5 is therefore provisional. In some respects, Pompey's theater resembled its Greek forebears, with sloping banks of seats in a semicircular arrangement, an orchestra area, and a raised stage for scenery. In other ways, however, it was radically different. It was not, for instance, nestled into a preexisting hillside, but on an artificial slope made out of concrete, rising on radially disposed barrel vaults that buttressed one another for a strong structure: Concrete, in other words, gave the designer freedom to build independent of the landscape. The seating *cavea*, moreover, was a true half-circle, rather than the extended half-circle of Greek theaters. At its summit was a temple to Venus, and the curved façade held statues personifying the nations Pompey had subdued. Beyond the theater's stage building, porticoes defined a vast garden containing valuable works of art. Pompey's theater-portico complex dwarfed the smaller, scattered buildings that individual magistrates had commissioned up to that point, and set the precedent for the great imperial fora that would follow.

7.5 Theater Complex of Pompey, Rome. Dedicated in 55 BCE. Provisional reconstruction by James E. Packer and John Burge

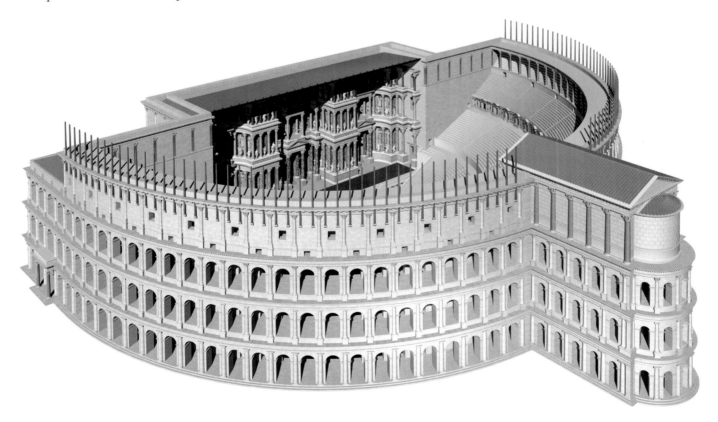

Sculpture

The Republican period saw the beginning of a rich tradition of free-standing and relief sculpture, often created in the service of politics. One of the most debated early works of sculpture is a magnificent bronze *She-Wolf* (**fig. 7.6**), which probably dates from the fifth century BCE. The twin babies Romulus and Remus beneath her were probably added by the Renaissance sculptor Antonio Pollaiuolo. The stylized, patterned treatment of the wolf's mane and hackles sets off the smoothly modeled muscularity of her body, tensed for attack. Simple lines add to her power: The straight back and neck contrast with the sharp turn of the head toward a viewer, highlighting her ferocity. So polished is the metal's surface that it almost seems wet; her

7.6 *She-Wolf*. ca. 500 BCE. Bronze, height 33½″ (85 cm). Museo Capitolino, Rome

7.7 Reconstruction of pedimental sculptures from via San Gregorio. ca. 150 BCE. Painted terra cotta. Museo Capitolino, Rome

fangs seem to glisten. The early history of this statue is unknown and it has often been considered Etruscan (and one recent hypothesis argues that it is medieval because, like church bells, it was cast in one piece, not built up out of several independently cast pieces). However, the sculpture's discovery in Rome, and the vital role of a she-wolf in Rome's foundation myth (see below), do argue for a Roman origin.

Much of the architectural sculpture produced in Republican Rome was made of terra cotta. A set of magnificent sculptures from a temple pediment demonstrates the level of expertise artists reached in the medium (**fig. 7.7**). The subject appears to be a sacrifice. The larger-scale figures probably represent divinities—Mars in the center, and two flanking goddesses. Smaller figures include a male in a toga, perhaps the presiding magistrate; a male in tunic and mantle; and several attendants. The artists modeled the figures in such high relief that they are almost in the round, and applied them to a smooth black background; they protrude toward the top, in order to be legible from below. The figures are buffed to a high polish, and as in Egypt, color conventions distinguish the female figures, with their cream skin tones, from the deeper red males. The pediment dates to the middle of the second century BCE, at the height of Greek influence. This is evident in Mars' Hellenistic breastplate, and the classicizing treatment of the drapery, the faces, and the musculature. All the same, the material and technique are distinctly Italic.

RELIEF SCULPTURE Like architecture, sculpture often commemorated specific events, as it did in the ancient Near East (see fig. 2.5). Classical Greek sculptors disguised historical events in mythical clothing—a combat of gods and giants, for instance (see fig. 5.7). Roman artists, by contrast, represented actual events, developing a form of sculpture known as historical relief—although many were not historically accurate. The reliefs shown in **fig. 7.8** probably decorated a statuary base placed near the route of triumphal processions.

7.8 Sculptural reliefs from statue base, showing sea *thiasos* and census. ca. 150–100 BCE. Marble. Musée du Louvre, Paris, and Glyptothek, Staatliche Antikensammlungen, Munich

Where Romans found the impetus to produce PORTRAITS is a mystery that art historians struggle to solve. For some, its roots lie in an Italic practice of storing ancestral masks in the home to provide a visual genealogy, in a society where a good pedigree was a reliable stepping-stone to political success. Polybius, a Greek historian of the mid-second century BCE, recounts that before burying a family member, living relatives would wear these ancestral masks in a funerary procession, parading the family's history in front of bystanders. Other scholars trace it to a Greek custom of placing votive statues of athletes and other important individuals in sacred precincts, and indeed some Roman portraits were executed in a Hellenic style.

Major Roman Emperors

Augustus	27 BCE–14 CE (in power from 31 BCE)
Vespasian	69–79
Trajan	98–117
Hadrian	117–38
Marcus Aurelius	161–80
Septimius Severus	193–211
Caracalla	211–17
Diocletian	284–305
Constantine	306/12–37

History recognizes AUGUSTUS (63 BCE–14 CE; see fig. 7.10) as the first Roman emperor. He won power in 31 BCE, and became *princeps*, or first citizen, in 27 BCE. During his long reign, he returned Rome to a form of constitutional rule, instituted a massive building program, and promoted peace and prosperity at home. His foreign policy was cautiously expansionist. The Senate and People of Rome awarded Augustus the title *Pater Patriae* (Father of His Country).

One section shows a census, a ceremony in which individuals recorded their property with the state to qualify for military service. On the left, soldiers and civilians line up to be registered. Two large figures flanking an altar represent a statue of Mars, god of war, and the officiating censor, who probably commissioned the monument. Attendants escort sacrificial animals to the altar.

On the same monument, the remaining reliefs depict a marine *thiasos* (procession) for the marriage of the sea god Neptune and the sea nymph Amphitrite. These reliefs are in an entirely different style. The swirling motion and Hellenistic forms of the marriage procession contrast dramatically with the static composition of the census relief and the stocky proportions of its figures. Moreover, the panels are carved from different types of marble. The supposition is that a triumphant general brought the sea *thiasos* reliefs as spoils from Greece to grace a triumphal monument—proof, as it were, of his conquest. By contrast, artists carved the census relief in Rome as a complement. Together, the reliefs may represent the patron's military and political achievements.

PORTRAIT SCULPTURE Literary sources reveal that the Senate and People of Rome honored political or military figures by putting their statues on display, often in the Roman Forum, the civic heart of the city. The custom began in the early Republic, took off in the late second century and the first century BCE, and continued until the end of the Empire. Many of the early PORTRAITS were bronze and were melted down for coinage or weaponry, but the majority were stone. Most represent men at an advanced age (**fig. 7.9**). Wrinkles cover their faces, etching crags into their cheeks and brows. The artist played up distinguishing marks—such as warts, or a hooked nose—rather than smoothing them over. In the example illustrated here, remnants of a veil suggest that the subject was represented as a priest. Although there is no way of knowing what the sitter looked like, the images appear overly realistic, so that scholars term the style **veristic**, from the Latin *verus*, meaning "true." For a twenty-first-century viewer, these images appear anything but idealized. Yet cultures construct different ideals; to Romans, responsibility and experience came with seniority, and most magistracies had minimum age requirements. An image marked by age therefore conveyed the requisite qualities for winning votes.

7.9 Veristic male portrait. Early first century BCE. Marble, life-size. Musei Vaticani, Rome

The Early Empire

Julius Caesar's assassination on the Ides of March of 44 BCE was a last-ditch effort to safeguard the constitution. When the Senate declared his heir Octavian as AUGUSTUS Caesar in 27 BCE, he claimed to restore the Republic. In fact, he reintroduced monarchy to Rome, and it would endure through several dynasties until the gradual transfer of imperial power to Constantinople (beginning in about 330 CE). The birth of the Roman Empire brought a period of relative stability to the Mediterranean region. Roman domination continued to spread, and at its largest extent in the time of Trajan (98–117 CE) the empire stretched through most of Europe, as far as northern England, through much of the Middle East including Armenia and Assyria, and throughout coastal North Africa. Roman institutions—political, social, and religious—mingled with indigenous ones, leading to a degree of homogenization across much of the Roman world. Increasingly, the emperor and his family became the principal patrons of public art and architecture in Rome. Often, their public monuments stressed the legitimacy of the imperial family.

Portrait Sculpture

By the time Augustus effectively became emperor, he was no more than 36. The veristic style, with its stress on maturity, might have underlined the unconstitutional nature of his status, and he turned instead to a more Hellenizing style. Until his death in his late seventies, his portraits depict him as an ageless youth, as seen in a statue discovered in the house of his wife Livia at Primaporta (**fig. 7.10**).

The statue appears to combine references to previous works of art and historical events in order to strengthen Augustus' claim to authority. The chiastic stance and the smooth facial features are so reminiscent of Polykleitos' *Doryphoros* (see fig. 5.14) that the assumption is that Augustus turned deliberately to this well-known image. There was good reason for this kind of imitation: The Classical Greek style evoked the apogee of Athenian culture, casting Augustan Rome as Greece's successor (and conqueror) in cultural supremacy. Even Augustus' hair is similar to that of the *Doryphoros*—except, that is, at the brow, where the locks part gently in a subtle reference to the youthful Alexander the Great, whose cowlick was such a distinctive feature of his portraits (see fig. 5.27). Next to Augustus' right ankle, the artist shaped a reinforcing strut as a cupid playfully riding a dolphin. Most Romans would have recognized that Cupid, or Eros, the son of Venus, symbolized Augustus' claim to descent from the goddess of love through his Trojan ancestor Aeneas. The dolphin evoked the sea, and the site off the coast of western Greece where Augustus had prevailed over Mark Antony and Cleopatra at the Battle of Actium in 31 BCE. By associating Augustus with historical or divine figures, these references projected an image of earthly and divinely ordained power.

The iconography of Augustus' breastplate serves a similar purpose by calling attention to an important diplomatic victory in 20 BCE, when the Parthians returned standards that they had captured, to Roman shame, in 53 BCE. This event took on momentous proportions in Augustan propaganda. Tiberius, Augustus' eventual successor, or the god Mars, accepts the standards from a Parthian soldier, possibly King Phraates IV. Gods and terrestrial personifications frame the scene, giving it a cosmic and eternal significance.

The Primaporta Augustus offers a good example of a tendency in Roman art to express a message through references to earlier works. Not all Romans would have understood all the references in any work, though the frequency of visual "quotations" suggests that Romans, like many other ancient peoples, were visually astute. In fact, the history of Roman portraiture, as with many other branches of Roman art, is one of constant association with or conscious turning away from past images. Portraits of Augustus' dynastic successors, for instance, look

7.10 *Augustus of Primaporta.* Possibly Roman copy of a statue of ca. 20 CE. Marble, height 6'8" (2.03 m). Musei Vaticani, Braccio Nuovo, Rome

very much like the first emperor from whom they drew their authority, even though they were rarely (or at best distantly) related by blood.

Imperial portraits exist in great multitudes. On the whole, they fall into a number of types, suggesting that there was a master portrait, often executed for a specific occasion, which sculptors would copy for dissemination within and outside of Rome; these too would be copied, creating a ripple effect around the empire. Unidentified nonimperial portraits also survive in great numbers, and are dated on the basis of similarities with imperial portraits. When dealing with female images, hairstyles are especially useful, since fashions changed relatively rapidly. Domitia Longina, wife of the emperor Domitian, wore her hair in a towering style built around a framework (**fig. 7.11**). Her coiffure was a masterpiece, and its representation in sculpture reflected her status, as well as affording the sculptor an opportunity to explore contrasts of texture between skin and hair, and to drill deep into the marble for a strong play of light and shadow.

Beginning in the second half of the second century CE, portraits gradually take on a more abstract quality. It is especially marked in the treatment of the eyes, whose heavy lids lend them a remote quality. This is perceptible in a spectacular gilded bronze portrait of MARCUS AURELIUS, which survived the melting pot in medieval times because Christians misidentified it as Constantine the Great, champion of Christianity (**fig. 7.12**). With one arm outstretched in a gesture of mercy, the emperor sits astride a spirited horse, whose raised front leg once rested on a conquered barbarian. Like the majority of second- and third-century CE male portraits, Marcus Aurelius is bearded.

7.11 *Portrait of a Woman (Flavian Woman)*. Late first century CE. Marble, height 24″ (60.8 cm). Courtesy of San Antonio Museum of Art, San Antonio, Texas. Gift of Gilbert M. Denman, Jr.

MARCUS AURELIUS (121–80 CE; see fig. 7.12), a scholar and philosopher, was constantly forced to repress rebellions and incursions by "barbarian" peoples such as the Germans and the Sarmatians (an Iranian people in western Scythia). His writings, known today as his *Meditations*, are imbued with STOIC philosophy. Stoicism expressed the ideas of the fourth-century Greek philosopher Zeno, who considered emotions to be false and deceptive; impassive detachment was the highest virtue. Sacrifice and hardship were to be endured for the sake of moral principle.

7.12 *Equestrian Statue of Marcus Aurelius.* 161–80 CE. Bronze, over life-size. Museo del Palazzo dei Conservatori, Rome

7.13 *Ara Pacis Augustae*, west façade. 13–9 BCE. Marble, width of altar approx. 35′ (10.7 m). Museum of the Ara Pacis, Rome

7.14 *Ara Pacis Augustae*, Imperial Procession, south frieze. 13–9 BCE. Marble, height 63″ (1.6 m). Museum of the Ara Pacis, Rome

Relief Sculpture

The Republican practice of commissioning narrative reliefs to record specific events continued well into the empire. They were mounted on public buildings and monuments, such as the *Ara Pacis Augustae*, or Altar of Augustan Peace (**fig. 7.13**), and the later Arch of Titus.

ARA PACIS AUGUSTAE The Senate and People of Rome vowed the MONUMENTAL ALTAR in Augustus' honor in 13 BCE and dedicated it in 9 BCE. It stood inside an open-air marble enclosure, which was richly sculpted over its entire surface. On the east and west sides, flanking two entrances, relief panels represent personifications or gods, and figures from Rome's legendary past. On the west end, a fragmentary panel shows the twin boys Romulus and Remus, legendary founders of Rome. Abandoned as babies, they were suckled by a she-wolf (see fig. 7.6), until they were found and adopted by the shepherd Faustulus, also shown in the panel. In a second relief, Aeneas (or perhaps, according to one interpretation, Numa, Rome's second king) sacrifices at a roughly hewn altar. At the east end, a relief depicting the goddess Roma seated on her weapons balances a panel with a female figure (the goddess Venus or Ceres, perhaps, or Peace, Italia, or Mother Earth) who embodies the notion of peace. Together, the panels express the message of peace that Augustus was intent on promoting, in contrast with the bleakness of the preceding civil wars. The same message was implicit in the acanthus relief that encircles the enclosure in a lower register. Vegetation unfurls in rich abundance, populated with creatures such as lizards and frogs.

On the north and south sides, the upper register contains continuous procession friezes that portray members of the imperial family interspersed with priests and senators (**fig. 7.14**). The fragmentary friezes record a particular event on the day of the altar's dedication. Most of Augustus' body is missing; his action would probably have revealed the occasion. Still, the friezes are significant for a number of reasons. In their superficial resemblance to the Greek Parthenon frieze (see fig. 5.18) they bear witness, once again, to a preference for Greek styles in the Augustan age. They also feature a number of women from the imperial family, including Livia, and small children. Their inclusion probably denotes the importance of dynasty, as well as referring to moral legislation Augustus enacted to curb adultery and promote childbirth among the elite.

COLUMN OF TRAJAN The exploration of narrative strategies comes into full bloom in the Column of Trajan (**fig. 7.15**), erected between 106 and 113 CE in a small court to the west of Trajan's Forum. Soaring about 150 Roman feet high, it supported a gilded statue of the emperor, lost in medieval times. Winding up through its shaft was a spiral staircase leading to a viewing platform, from which a visitor could see Trajan's extraordinary building accomplishments. Free-standing columns had been used as commemorative monuments in Hellenistic Greece, but the sheer scale of Trajan's Column, and its role as a belvedere, made it nothing short of a world wonder. The credit for its design often goes to Apollodorus, Trajan's military architect. However, art historians have tended to focus not on the engineering feat the column represents, but on

In writing about art, scholars use the adjective monumental to refer to architecture and artworks that give the impression of being large, grand, and permanent—like a monument. Thus, even small works can be described as monumental if they have an imposing presence. A MONUMENTAL ALTAR is a large and grand marble or stone structure, usually decorated in low relief, built to honor a divinity. A triumphal arch is a wide, round-arched, free-standing gateway, especially favored to celebrate a victor or benefactor, and carrying his portrait on top, usually in a chariot.

7.15 Column of Trajan. 106–13 CE. Marble, height 125′ (38 m). Rome

View the Closer Look for the Column of Trajan on myartslab.com

the 656-foot-long continuous narrative relief that winds counterclockwise around its shaft, celebrating the emperor's victorious campaigns against the Dacians (in present-day Romania).

The narrative begins with the Roman army crossing the Danube into Dacian territory. The river appears as a large personification. A second band shows Trajan speaking to his soldiers, and soldiers building fortifications. In the third, soldiers construct a camp and bridge as the cavalry sets out on reconnaissance; and in the fourth, foot soldiers cross a stream while the emperor addresses his troops in front of a Dacian fortress. These scenes are a fair sampling of events shown on the column. Among the more than 150 episodes, combat occurs rarely. The geographic, logistic, and political aspects of war receive more attention.

Individual scenes are not distinct from one another. Sculptors placed trees and buildings in such a way as to suggest divisions, but the scenes still merge into a continuous whole, with protagonists, such as Trajan, appearing multiple times. Thus they preserved visual continuity without sacrificing the coherence of each scene. Although Assyrian and Egyptian artists created visual narratives of military conquests, this relief is by far the most ambitious composition so far in terms of the number of figures and the narrative's density.

Understanding it is a complicated matter. Continuous illustrated scrolls make a likely inspiration for the composition, if such things existed before the column's construction. More problematic is the fact that in order to follow the narrative sequence, a viewer has to keep turning around the column. Above the fourth or fifth turn, details become hard to make out, even if added paint made the sculpture more vivid. It might have been possible to view the upper spirals from balconies on surrounding buildings, but an encircling motion would still have been required. These problems have led scholars to propose viewing strategies. They have long noted that the relief is formulaic; that is, the sculptors repeated a limited number of stock scenes. These include, for instance, sacrifices, the emperor addressing his troops, or soldiers constructing forts and dismantling enemy cities. Though not identical, the scenes are similar enough to be recognized at a distance, making the upper spirals more legible. The designer may also have aligned important and representative scenes on the cardinal axes of the column, to make an abbreviated version of the whole visible from a single standpoint. Yet there is always the possibility that the designer intended viewers to have to walk around the column in order to read its narrative. The column's base would serve as a burial chamber for Trajan's ashes after his death in 117 CE, and

7.16 Forum of Trajan, Rome. Reconstruction by Gilbert Gorski

an encircling motion would be consistent with a widespread Roman funerary ritual in which visitors walked around tombs to protect the dead within, to confine spirits to the grave, and to pay perpetual homage to the deceased.

Architecture

During the empire, emperors commissioned monumental structures with a view to currying favor with the populace. Beginning with Julius Caesar, several of them built forums as backdrops to civic and religious functions. The largest of them was Trajan's, financed with the spoils of his Dacian wars. Reconstructions of the complex give an impression of its former magnificence (**fig. 7.16**). Porticoes lined the long sides of a large open plaza. Beyond a basilica at its far end, two libraries and a temple defined a small courtyard, where Trajan's Column stood (see fig. 7.15). Colored marbles were used in great abundance, and sculpture filled the complex. In the portico attics, for instance, were statues of captive Dacians carved from exotic stone. The forum's message is clear: The Dacian Wars brought great financial benefit. As in many societies, the ruling elite hoped to dispel the starker realities of war through visual propaganda.

COLOSSEUM   As well as constructing a magnificent forum in the name of peace, Vespasian was the first to build a permanent amphitheater in Rome for the gladiatorial games and mock sea battles that were so central to entertainment and to the penal system (**fig. 7.17a**). Putting on shows for the populace was an important form of favor-gaining benefaction, and the audience assembled for diversion but also to see their emperor and to receive the free handouts that he would make on these occasions. Vespasian died before completing the Colosseum, and his son Titus inaugurated it in 80 CE with over 100 days of games, at a cost of over 9,000 animal lives. In terms of sheer mass, it was one of the largest buildings anywhere: It stood 159 feet high, 616 feet 9 inches long, and 511 feet 11 inches wide, and could hold 45,000 to 50,000 spectators. Concrete, faced with travertine, was the secret of its success. In plan, 80 radial barrel-vaulted wedges ringed an oval arena. Each barrel vault buttressed the next, making the ring remarkably stable (**fig. 7.17b**). The wedges sloped down toward the ringside to support seating, and the architects accommodated countless stairways and corridors within them to ensure a smooth flow of traffic to and from seating

areas. On the hottest days, sailors stationed nearby rigged up huge canvas sheets to shade the seating areas. On the exterior, 80 arched entrances led into the building, framed with engaged Tuscan columns (which resemble Doric columns but have simple bases). On the second story, Ionic columns framed a second set of arches, and on the third are engaged Corinthian columns. Engaged Corinthian pilasters embellish the wall on the fourth.

7.17a Colosseum. 72–80 CE. Concrete and travertine. Rome

 Explore the architectural panoramas of the Colosseum on myartslab.com

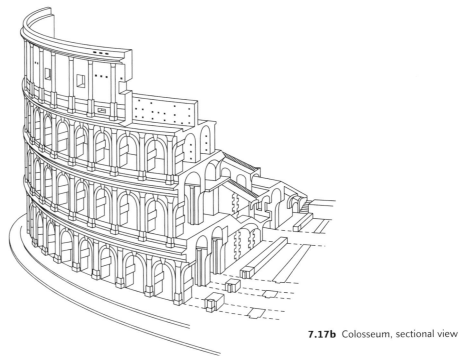

7.17b Colosseum, sectional view

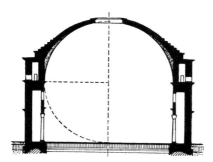

Transverse section of the Pantheon

7.18 Pantheon. Completed ca. 125 CE. Concrete, with travertine, granite, and colored marble. Rome

Explore the architectural panoramas of the Pantheon on myartslab.com

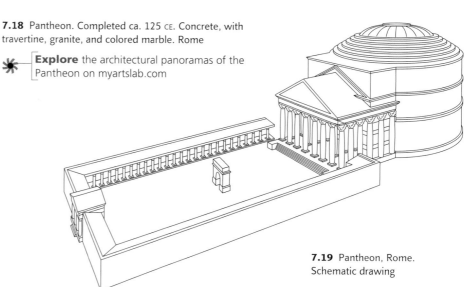

7.19 Pantheon, Rome. Schematic drawing

PANTHEON Of all the masterpieces Roman architects accomplished with concrete, the Pantheon is perhaps the most remarkable (**fig. 7.18**). As its name suggests, the temple honored all the gods. This was a Hellenistic concept, and it included living and deceased members of the ruling family among the gods. Augustus' right-hand man, Agrippa, had built the first Pantheon on the site. A fire in 80 CE destroyed this temple, and a reconstruction perished after a lightning strike. The existing Pantheon, with a substantially different design, was probably begun under Trajan, perhaps by Apollodorus; it was completed under Hadrian in about 125 CE, and Agrippa's name remained in the inscription as an act of piety. It is one of the best-preserved temples of Rome, thanks to its transformation into a church in the early seventh century CE.

The Pantheon's surroundings have changed sufficiently through the ages to alter a visitor's experience of it profoundly (**fig. 7.19**). In Roman times, it stood, raised on a podium, at the south end of a large rectangular court. Porticoes framed the three remaining sides of the court and extended on the south up to the sides of the temple's pedimented porch, hiding the circular drum from view. A visitor approaching the broad octastyle façade would have been struck by the forest of massive monolithic gray and pink granite columns soaring upward; but in most other respects the temple's form would have been familiar, evoking expectations of a rectangular cella beyond the huge bronze doors. Yet a surprise was in store. On stepping across the threshold, a visitor faced a vast circular hall with seven large niches at ground level (**fig. 7.20**). Engaged pilasters and bronze grilles decorated the attic level, and high above soared an enormous dome, pierced with a 27-foot hole or **oculus** open to the sky. Through the oculus came a glowing shaft of light, slicing through the shadows from high overhead. Dome and drum are of equal height, and the total interior height, 143 feet, is also the dome's diameter. Many ancient viewers would have associated the resultant sphere with eternity and perfection, and the dome's surface, once emblazoned with bronze rosettes in its coffers (recessed panels), must have evoked a starry night sky.

For a visitor entering the space, there was no obvious cue to point out where to go, except toward the light at the center. In fact, the dome's coffers make sense perspectively only from directly beneath the oculus. Once a visitor reached the center, molded space and applied decoration combined to provide a stunning effect. Beginning in the Renaissance, scholars have faulted the architect for neglecting to align the dome's ribs with the pilasters in the attic zone and the ground-floor columns. The design is not without logic: A void or a row of coffers aligns exactly over each central intercolumniation (space between columns) on the ground floor. All the same, the absence of a systemic network of continuous vertical lines from top to bottom means that, visually speaking, the dome appears unanchored. The optical effect is that it hovers unfettered above the

7.20 Pantheon. Interior. Rome

 Watch an architectural simulation about concrete on myartslab.com

visitor—who feels, paradoxically, both sheltered and exposed. The dome seems to be set in perpetual motion, spinning overhead in the same way as the heavens it imitates. An all-but-imperceptible rise in the floor at the center exaggerates this sensation, which can incite an unnerving feeling similar to vertigo. A visitor's instinct, in response, is to take refuge in the safety of the curved wall. The building is all experience, and photographs do it no justice. This is the place, so literary sources relate, where Hadrian preferred to hold court, greeting foreign embassies and adjudicating disputes. The temple's form cast him in the authoritative position of controller of his revolving universe, like a divine revelation before his guest, who was already awed and manipulated by the building that enclosed them.

The Pantheon is the extraordinary result of an increased confidence in the potential and strength of concrete. The architect calibrated the aggregate as the building rose, from travertine to tufa, then brick, and finally pumice, to reduce its weight. The

dome's weight concentrates on eight wide pillars between the interior alcoves, rather than resting uniformly on the drum. The alcoves, in turn, with their screens of columns, visually reduce the solidity of the walls, and colored marbles on the interior surfaces add energy to the whole. As in Trajan's Forum, the marbles were symbolic. They underlined the vast reach of imperial authority, assuming trade with or control over Egypt (gray and rose-pink granite, porphyry), Phrygia (Phrygian purple and white stone), the island of Teos (Lucullan red and black stone), and Chemtou in Tunisia (Numidian yellow stone).

Art and Architecture in the Provinces

The spread of Rome's authority had a profound impact on artistic and architectural production over a wide geographical reach. Since those in power typically construct history, it is often hard to assess

7.21 Aqueduct. First or early second century CE. Granite. Segovia, Spain

 **Watch** an architectural simulation of an arch on myartslab.com

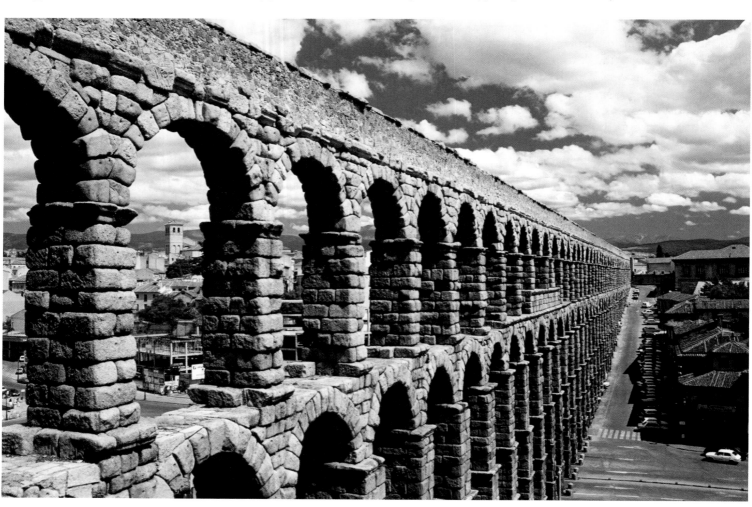

the reactions of local peoples to foreign control. To be sure, Roman rule brought some benefits. Their engineers had mastered the art of moving water efficiently, and the new aqueducts that sprang up in urban centers around the empire must have improved local standards of living immeasurably. A striking aqueduct still stands at Segovia in Spain, dating to the first or early second century CE (**fig. 7.21**). It brought water from Riofrío, about 10½ miles away, which flowed for most of its length through an underground channel. Near the town, however, architects erected a massive bridge stretching 2,666 feet long and up to 98 feet high to carry it over a valley. Some 118 arches support the water channel, built in two registers at the highest point. Like most provincial builders, the architects used a local stone, in this case granite, which they assembled without mortar and left unfinished to give it an air of strength. Despite the obvious advantages the aqueduct provided, it also illustrates how Roman architecture could effect dominion. The arches—a quintessentially Roman form—march relentlessly across the terrain, symbolically conquering it with their step.

Romans carried their way of life and their style with them across the empire, constructing theaters and amphitheaters, and temples to accommodate their rituals. Indigenous building traditions combined with Roman styles to powerful new effect. This appears to be the case with the extraordinary rock-cut façade known as El Khasneh, or the Treasury, at the site of Petra in present-day Jordan (**fig. 7.22**). This façade is the first sight to greet a visitor who wanders through the long, twisting gorge known as the Siq, leading to the town center. The Nabataeans, a nomadic people who settled this area before the Romans took control in 106 CE, buried their wealthy dead in tombs cut out of the pink sandstone cliffs, and some scholars have seen El Khasneh as one of their monuments. Most agree, however, that it belongs to the Trajanic or Hadrianic period. Carved from the living rock, it resembles a temple façade, with six columns beneath an architrave decorated with floral designs and a pediment. In a second story, lateral columns support a broken pediment. Between them is a tholos with a conical roof, surmounted by an ornamental finial. At a much later period, locals imagined that pirates had stored treasure in the finial, lending the monument its name; bullet holes show how they tried to knock it down.

The façade is a striking amalgamation of a Nabataean concept with Roman decorative features—the Corinthian columns, for instance, and the vegetal designs. The architectural elements are not structural, and this allows for a quality of freedom and fantasy in the design, not unlike the fantasy vistas of wall paintings. This playful treatment of once-structural elements became popular in the provinces and in Rome in the second century CE, and it is sometimes described as a baroque phase, for its similarities to Italian Baroque

7.22 El Khasneh. Sandstone. Probably early second century CE. Petra, Jordan

architecture. The monument's function may have changed for Roman usage as well: Relief sculptures between the columns seem to represent figures from the cult of Isis, suggesting that it was a temple. In some cases, inscriptions and other written documents indicate who commissioned monuments in the provinces; the patron might be local, a Roman official, or even the emperor himself. More often, as in this case, there is no such evidence, which makes it hard to determine meaning in a choice of design.

The greatest body of painting to survive from the Roman world is wall painting. Yet the sands of Fayum, in Lower Egypt, preserved a magnificent group of painted portraits, once covering the faces of embalmed, mummified corpses (**fig. 7.23**).

The earliest of them appear to date from the second century CE. Artists painted them on wooden panels in the **encaustic** technique, which involves suspending pigments in hot wax. The mixture can be opaque and creamy, like oil paint, or thin and translucent. The medium is durable, and the panels retain an extraordinary freshness; the wax also gives them a lustrous vitality. At their best, these portraits have a haunting immediacy, largely the result of the need to work quickly before the hot wax set. The woman pictured here wears a crimson tunic and a wealth of jewelry. Rows of black circles denote the ringlets of her hair, bound with a golden diadem. Her appearance is Roman, yet the portrait itself speaks of her local identity, since she was buried in the Egyptian, not the Roman, fashion.

7.23 *Portrait of a Woman*, from Hawara in the Fayum, Lower Egypt. ca. 110–30 CE. Encaustic on wooden panel. Royal Museum of Scotland. © Trustees of the National Museum of Scotland

Domestic Art and Architecture

Romans are one of the few ancient peoples to leave abundant evidence of domestic architecture and its decoration. The burial of Pompeii and Herculaneum after the eruption of Vesuvius in 79 CE preserved an invaluable legacy for archaeologists, and these houses tend to dominate expert commentary, as they will here; yet such was the durability of Roman domestic construction that houses survive elsewhere as well, as far afield as Morocco and Jordan, and though Roman houses have many common qualities, they also differ by region, to cater, for instance, to local climates. In any given region, there were also discrepancies between the dwellings of the rich and the poor. One should be cautious, therefore, about conceiving of a "typical" Roman house.

Elite Roman houses are called by their Latin name, *domus*, known from Vitruvius and other ancient writers. This kind of house may owe its origin, in part, to elite Etruscan residences. Its most distinctive feature is a central **atrium**, a square or oblong hall lit by an opening in the roof, answered by a shallow pool, or *impluvium*, in the ground to collect rainwater. The airy quality of the atrium confers an element of grandeur upon the house, visible here in the House of the Vettii (**fig. 7.24**), and it was where Romans kept ancestral portraits. Other rooms, such as bedrooms (*cubicula*), are grouped around the atrium, which often leads on to a ***tablinum***, a reception room where a family kept its archives. Beyond the *tablinum* is a colonnaded garden (the peristyle), and there might be additional rooms at the back of the house. Walls facing the street did not typically have windows, but it is misleading to believe that these houses were particularly private. Romans frequently used rooms flanking the entryway as shops, and the front door often stood open. At the heart of Roman society was a client–patron relationship, and clients routinely visited their patrons in their homes.

Roman domestic painting survives in great abundance, mainly from Pompeii and Herculaneum, and from Rome and its environs. Basing his analysis partly on Vitruvius' discussion of painting, the late nineteenth-century German art historian August Mau distinguished four styles of Pompeian wall painting (see box: Materials and Techniques: Wall Painting, Mural, and Fresco, page 144), dating from the end of the second century BCE to the late first century CE. They are not canonical, but prove useful as general guidelines. In the First Style, dating to the late second century BCE, artists used paint and stucco to imitate expensive colored marble paneling. Starting about 100 BCE, Second Style painters opened up the wall's flat expanse by including architectural features and figures, sometimes to suggest a fantasy realm beyond the room. In a room in the Villa of the Mysteries outside Pompeii, dating from about 60 to 50 BCE, the lower part of the wall, beneath the dado, and the upper section above the cornice level are painted in rich mottled colors to resemble exotic stone

7.24 Atrium of the House of the Vettii. Second century BCE–79 CE. Pompeii

Wall Painting, Mural, and Fresco

WALL painting is a broad descriptive term for painting in any medium on a wall-like surface, from those in caves and rock-cut tombs to those on modern buildings. A mural is a painted image made on or attached to a particular wall, such as the painting cycle in the Villa of the Mysteries (see fig. 7.25). Fresco is a specific wall-painting technique favored in Italy from Roman times through the eighteenth century. In true (*buon*) fresco, the artist paints with water-based colored pigments directly onto fresh, still-damp plaster, working in small sections and producing a stable, long-lasting image. Dry (*secco*) fresco, in which the pigments are painted on dry plaster, is far less durable than true fresco and was used mostly for details.

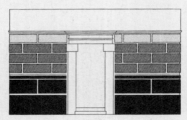

1. The First, or Incrustation, Style: The wall is painted (and molded in stucco) to imitate masonry blocks, no figured scenes. Second century BCE

2. The Second, or Architectural, Style: Characteristically featuring illusionistic architectural vistas. ca. 100–15 BCE

3. The Third, or Ornate, Style: The vistas here give way to a delicate decorative scheme, concentrating on formal ornament. ca. 20 BCE–50 CE

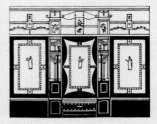

4. The Fourth, or Intricate, Style: A more extravagant painterly style, parading the whole range of decorative idioms. ca. 50 CE

7.25 *Scenes of Dionysiac Mystery Cult*, Second Style wall painting from the Villa of the Mysteries. ca. 60–50 BCE. Painted plaster. Pompeii

7.26 Fourth Style wall painting, Ixion Room, House of the Vettii. 63–79 CE. Painted plaster. Pompeii

(**fig. 7.25**). Figures interact as if on a narrow ledge set against a deep red background, articulated by upright strips of black resembling stylized columns. They are engaged in rites associated with the Dionysiac mysteries, one of the so-called mystery religions originating in Greece. The scene may represent an initiation into womanhood or marriage, in the presence of Dionysos and Ariadne with SATYRS and SILENI. The solidity and bold modeling of the near life-size figures, and their calm but varied poses, lend a quiet power and vivid drama to the room.

The Third Style dominated wall decoration from about 20 BCE until at least the middle of the first century CE. In this phase, artists abandoned illusionism in favor of solid planes of intense colors like black and red, often articulated with attenuated architectural features and imitation panel paintings. The Fourth Style, which prevailed at the time of Vesuvius' eruption, united aspects of all three preceding styles to extravagant effect. The Ixion Room in the House of the Vettii (**fig. 7.26**) combines imitation marble paneling, framed mythological scenes set into

In Greek and Roman mythology, SATYRS were phallic, goatish beings of the woods and hills. Similar to satyrs, SILENI were older, usually bald, and always bearded.

the wall, and fantastic architectural vistas receding into space.

Like the Ixion painting, many Roman paintings depicted Greek themes. The few painters' names on record show that at least some of them were of Greek origin. There are also sufficient instances of paintings (or elements of paintings) closely resembling one another to indicate that artists used copybooks; in some cases, they may have been working from a Greek original, adapting the image to their own purposes. Yet given the evident innovation in Roman painting in general, there is every reason to suppose that Roman artists were capable of creating their own compositions and narratives when they chose. In recent years, scholarship has focused on ways in which painting ensembles affected experience or dictated movement through a house and expressed the owner's status. In fact, a genre of ancient literature known as *ekphrasis* is a learned exposition on the subject of real or imagined paintings. These writings lead scholars to believe that homeowners sometimes conceived paintings as conversation pieces for their guests, who might discuss them as they dined. Designing a painting program, then, took on a new level of importance for what it might disclose about the patron's aspirations.

7.27 *Portrait Group of the Tetrarchs.* ca. 305 CE. Porphyry. Height 51″ (129.5 cm). Basilica of San Marco, Venice

The Late Empire

Portrait Sculpture

During Marcus Aurelius' reign, incursions at the empire's German and Danubian borders posed a constant threat. Succeeding him in 180 CE, his son Commodus was assassinated in 192 CE, and after a brief respite from turmoil under the Severan dynasty, Rome entered a half-century of civil war, when a succession of emperors came to power and quickly fell through violence. Imperial authority was restored in the reign of Diocletian (r. 284–305 CE), who imposed rigid order on all aspects of civil as well as military life, and divided authority between four rulers, known as tetrarchs.

During the tetrarchy, portraiture adopted a radically abstract quality. Two sculptural groups now immured in the Basilica of San Marco in Venice were probably originally mounted on columns (**fig. 7.27**). Each group shows two men in elaborate military dress. The figures are all but indistinguishable from one another (except that in each group, one is bearded, the other close-shaven). Their proportions are squat and unnaturalistic, their facial features abstract. The portraits suggest that authority resides in the office of emperor, not in the individual who holds the office. The portraits' sameness underlines the tetrarchs' equality, while their embrace stresses unanimity and solidarity. The choice of material speaks volumes too: Porphyry, a hard Egyptian stone of deep purple color, had long been reserved for imperial use.

In the early fourth century, Constantine the Great rose to sole power, overcoming his chief rival, Maxentius, at the Battle of the Milvian Bridge in Rome in 312. The colossal head of **fig. 7.28** is one fragment of a vast seated portrait that once

7.28 *Portrait of Constantine the Great.* Early fourth century CE. Marble, height 8′ (2.4 m). Museo del Palazzo dei Conservatori, Rome

BASILICAS (from the Greek *basileus*, meaning "king") had a long history in Rome. Since the Republic, they had served as civic halls, and they became a standard feature of Roman towns. One of their chief functions was to provide a dignified setting for the courts of law that dispensed justice in the name of the emperor. Vitruvius prescribed principles for their placement and proportions, but in practice they never conformed to a single type and varied from region to region. This plan shows a basilica with a nave, two side aisles, and an exedra or apse.

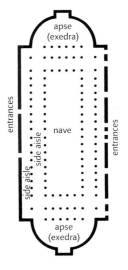

occupied an apse in a huge BASILICA (see fig. 7.31). The head alone is 8 feet tall. Its dominant features are the disproportionately large and deeply carved eyes. Combined with the stiff frontality of the face, they give the image an iconic quality. Some scholars associate changes like these with the spirituality of the later empire, exemplified by Constantine's adherence to Christianity. Perhaps the eyes gaze at something beyond this world; perhaps they are a window to the soul. At the same time, the full cap of hair, and the absence of a beard, appear to be references to Trajan and Augustus, great emperors of the past whose achievements still gave the office its authority.

7.29 Arch of Constantine. 312–15 CE. Concrete faced with marble. Rome

7.30 Constantinian relief from Arch of Constantine. Marble. Rome

Relief Sculpture

In 315 CE, the Senate and People of Rome dedicated a triple-bayed arch to Constantine to celebrate his ten-year anniversary and his conquest of Maxentius in 312 CE (**fig. 7.29**). It is one of the largest imperial arches, and what makes it unusual is that little of the sculptural relief on its surface was purposely designed for it. The free-standing Dacian captives on the attic originated in the Trajanic period, as did the Great Trajanic Frieze on the ends of the attic and inside the central bay. Eight hunting and sacrifice *tondi* (circular reliefs) above the lateral bays once adorned a Hadrianic monument, and eight panels on the attic may have decorated an arch to Marcus Aurelius. When the arch was constructed, sculptors recarved the heads of earlier emperors to resemble Constantine and his co-emperor Licinius. A modern restoration replaced some of them with heads of Trajan.

Sculptural and architectural borrowings of this kind are now termed *spolia*, from the Latin *spolium*, meaning "hide stripped from an animal," a term primarily used for spoils taken in war. The *spolia* raise all manner of questions—such as how Romans perceived the stripping of one monument in favor of another, and what became of the original monument, if it was still standing. In a renowned assault on late antique sculpture in the 1950s, the art historian Bernard Berenson condemned the use of *spolia* as evidence of a pervasive decline in form, which he attributed to a mass exodus of artists from Rome. Other experts see the *spolia* as part of a legitimizing ideology, expressing qualities of "emperorness." By leaning on "good" rulers of the past, Constantine may have hoped to harness the reputations that they had earned during their lifetimes. He had every reason to legitimize his authority: Maxentius had been a formidable opponent, and as the first openly Christian emperor, Constantine risked alienating a pagan Senate. If this interpretation is correct, it is not far from readings of the Republican statue base, partly made up of Greek reliefs, as seen in fig. 7.8.

To complement the borrowed pieces, Constantinian artists carved bases for the columns that flank the bays, a continuous relief to encircle the arch above the lateral bays, and roundels for the sides of the arch. One scene depicts Constantine addressing the Senate and people from the speaker's platform or rostrum in the Forum, after entering Rome in 312 CE (**fig. 7.30**). Figures crowd the scene. Their heads are disproportionately large, their bodies stocky, and their poses unnaturally rigid. Lines carved on the flat surface render anatomical details in place of modeling. Berenson judged the Constantinian reliefs just as harshly as the act of spoliation. Yet their abstract quality makes them unusually legible from a distance, which is how viewers would have seen them. A careful order governs the composition, with the frontal emperor occupying the center; other figures turn and focus attention on him. Buildings in the background are sufficiently distinct to make the setting recognizable even today. The artists privileged the reliefs' message-bearing potential over illusionism or naturalism.

Architecture

By the time of the late empire, architects in Rome had more or less abandoned the straightforward use of post-and-lintel construction. Their interests appear to have focused instead on exploring the interior spaces made possible by concrete. Column, architrave, and pediment became mere decoration, superimposed on vaulted brick-and-concrete cores. When Maxentius commissioned a basilica, the architects looked to the massive uninterrupted spaces of BATH BUILDINGS for inspiration. The

7.31 Basilica of Maxentius, renamed Basilica of Constantine. Begun ca. 307 CE. Concrete faced with marble. Rome

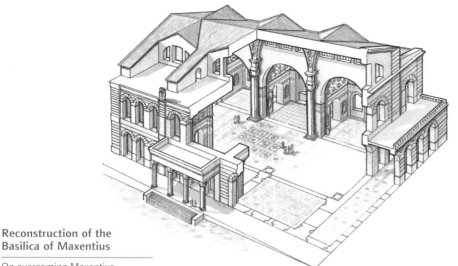

Reconstruction of the Basilica of Maxentius

On overcoming Maxentius, Constantine expropriated his basilica. He gave it his own name and placed his colossal portrait in the western apse (see fig. 7.28). Expropriations of this kind were not uncommon in Rome, and show how critical it was to have a physical presence in the city.

Basilica of Maxentius (**fig. 7.31**) was probably the largest roofed interior in Rome. It had three aisles, of which only the north one still stands. Transverse barrel vaults covered the lateral aisles, and three massive groin vaults covered the wider, taller central aisle (or nave). Since a groin vault concentrates its weight and thrust at the four corners, the architect could pierce the nave's upper walls with a large clerestory. As a result, the interior of the basilica must have had a light and airy quality despite its enormous size. Two entrances led into the building, each faced by an apse: through a transverse vestibule at the east end, and through a stepped doorway on the south, from the Roman Forum.

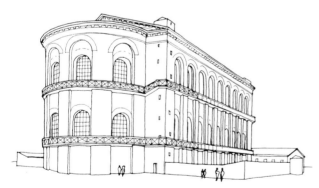

7.32 Basilica of Constantius Chlorus. Brick-faced concrete. Early fourth century CE. Trier, Germany

7.33 Interior of Basilica of Constantius Chlorus. Early fourth century CE. Trier, Germany

Late Roman Architecture in the Provinces

Developments in late Roman architecture appear to go hand-in-hand with the pervasive changes that Diocletian made to society. When he divided imperial authority, each tetrarch established a capital in a different region of the empire and embellished it with appropriate grandeur. Constantius Chlorus, father of Constantine the Great, made his seat at Trier, in present-day Germany. There he constructed a basilica, which now functions as a church (**figs. 7.32** and **7.33**). In its design, classical forms have dissolved entirely, leaving vast abstract expanses in solid and void. Elongated arches break the great mass of its walls and serve as visual buttresses to frame the windows, beneath which were balconies. As huge as the interior was, the architect aspired to achieve an illusion of even greater dimensions. The windows in the apse are significantly smaller than those in the side walls, and the apse ceiling is lower than the ceiling over the main hall. Both devices make it appear that the apse recedes farther into the distance than it does. Not only did this make the building more majestic, but the apse was where the emperor—or his image—would hold sway, and the altered dimensions would have made him appear significantly larger than life. The vocabulary of Roman building had changed, in other words, but it remained an architecture of power.

POINTS OF REFLECTION

7.1 Evaluate the importance of concrete in the construction of the Sanctuary of Fortuna Primigenia at Praeneste and the Pantheon.

7.2 Consider the role of politics in the construction of Pompey's Theater, the Altar of Augustan Peace, and the Forum of Trajan.

7.3 What might a Roman viewer have understood from the iconography of the Primaporta Augustus? How did the portrait differ from its Republican antecedents?

7.4 How did the sculptor of Trajan's Column assure its legibility?

7.5 Comment on the meeting of Roman and indigenous traditions in the aqueduct at Segovia and the portrait of a woman from the Fayum. What were the messages of such acts of syncretism?

7.6 Describe the salient features of the four styles of Pompeian wall painting. Were these paintings merely decorative?

✔●─**Study** and review on myartslab.com

ART IN TIME

- ca. 509 BCE—The Roman elite turns against the monarchy, expelling the last king

- ca. 509 BCE—**Dedication of the Temple of Jupiter Optimus Maximus**

- 100s BCE—Rome gains control of Greece and Asia Minor

- 60–50 BCE—**Paintings from the Villa of the Mysteries, outside Pompeii**

- 44 BCE—Assassination of Julius Caesar

- 27 BCE—The Roman Senate names Octavian Augustus Caesar

- 9 BCE—**Dedication of the *Ara Pacis Augustae*, the Altar of Augustan Peace**

- 79 CE—Vesuvius erupts

- early 100s CE—Aqueduct built at Segovia, Spain

- 100s CE—**The earliest painted portraits from the Fayum, Lower Egypt**

- ca. 115–25 CE—Construction of the Pantheon in Rome

- 312–37 CE (r.)—Constantine the Great

- 315 CE—**Dedication of the Arch of Constantine in Rome**

The Middle Ages

THE LABELS WE USE for historical periods tend to be like the nicknames of people: Once established, they are almost impossible to change, even though they may no longer be apt. Those who coined the term "Middle Ages" thought of the thousand years or more from the fourth to the fifteenth centuries as an empty interval between classical antiquity and its rebirth during the Renaissance in Italy. Since then, our view of the Middle Ages and of medieval art has changed greatly. (The term "medieval" is derived from the Latin *med[ium] aev[um]*, thus a synonym for the Middle Ages.) The chronological limits of the period are somewhat fluid, but for many historians, the conversion of Constantine the Great in 312 CE marks the beginning of the Middle Ages, while the Renaissance in the 1400s marks its end. The sheer breadth of its chronological span suggests the durability of its art forms, which are in fact multifaceted and varied. We now recognize this long period, not so much as one that denotes a division between two greater eras, but as one of major cultural change and creative activity in its own right.

How did these dramatic artistic changes come about? In 324 CE Constantine the Great made a fateful decision, the consequences of which are still felt today. He resolved to move the capital of the Roman Empire to the strategically located Greek town of Byzantium, which came to be known as Constantinople (and today as Istanbul). In taking this step, the emperor acknowledged the growing strategic and economic importance of the eastern provinces. The new capital also symbolized the new Christian basis of the Roman state, since it was in the heart of the most thoroughly Christianized region of the empire, far from Rome, whose senatorial elite continued to be practitioners of pagan religions.

Constantine could hardly have foreseen that shifting the seat of imperial power would result in splitting the empire. Yet, less than 75 years later, in 395, the division of the realm into the Eastern and Western Empires was complete. Eventually that separation led to a religious split as well. The differences between Eastern and Western Christianity went very deep. Roman Catholicism maintained its independence from state authority and became an international institution, reflecting its character as the Universal Church. The Orthodox Church, on the other hand, was based on the union of spiritual and secular authority in the person of the emperor, who appointed the patriarch, the head of the Eastern Church.

The two empires faced different political circumstances. The Eastern Empire was more secure, while the Western Roman Empire soon fell prey to invading Germanic tribes: Visigoths, Vandals, Franks, Ostrogoths, and Lombards. Once they had settled in their new lands, these invaders accepted the framework of Late Roman Christian civilization.

But Christianity was not the only "new" religion to affect the development of medieval art. The religion of Islam, based on the teachings of its founder, the Prophet Muhammad, was significant for the rapidity with which it spread throughout the Roman world. The African and Near Eastern parts of the empire were overrun by conquering Arab Islamic armies and by 732, only a century after the death of Muhammad, Arab armies had absorbed Spain and threatened to conquer southwestern France as well. The Eastern Empire, with its domain reduced to the Balkan peninsula, including Greece, held on until the year 1453, when the Islamic Turks conquered Constantinople itself. It is from this date that the city is known by its present-day name of Istanbul. Islam created a new civilization stretching as far east as the Indus Valley (now in Pakistan). Islamic art, learning, and crafts were to have great influence on the European Middle Ages, from **arabesque** ornament, the manufacture of paper, and Arabic numerals to the transmission of Greek philosophy and science through the studies and writings of Arab scholars. (The English language records this debt in words such as algebra.)

It should be clear from the preceding account that the medieval world was set in motion by a series of severe turmoils that present a continually shifting picture. As the major international force, religion was of critical importance in promoting a measure of stability. The rapid spread of Christianity, like that of Islam, cannot be explained simply in institutional terms, for the Church did not perfectly embody

Christian ideals. Christianity and Islam must have been extremely persuasive, in spiritual as well as in moral terms, to the masses of people who heard their messages. There is no other way to explain the widespread conversion to these religions.

Church and State gradually discovered that they could not live without each other. What was needed was an alliance between a strong secular power and a united Church. This link was forged when the Catholic Church, that is, the Roman Church, turned for support to the Germanic North. There the leadership of Charlemagne and his descendants—the Carolingian dynasty—made the Frankish kingdom the leading power during the second half of the eighth century. Charlemagne conquered most of Europe, from the North Sea to Spain and as far south as Lombardy in Italy. When Pope Leo III appealed to him for help, Charlemagne went to Rome, where on Christmas Day in the year 800, the pope bestowed on him the title of emperor—something that Charlemagne neither sought nor wanted.

In placing himself and all of Western Christianity under the protection of the king of the Franks and Lombards, Leo did not merely solemnize the new order of things. He also tried to assert his authority over the newly created emperor. He claimed that the emperor's legitimacy depended on the pope. But Charlemagne did not subordinate himself to the pope; rather, an interdependence of spiritual and political authority, of Church and State,

was established. Although the emperor was crowned in Rome, he did not live there. Charlemagne built his capital at the center of his power, in Aachen, located in what is now north Germany and close to France, Belgium, and the Netherlands.

The center of gravity of European civilization thus shifted north of the Alps, to what had been the northern boundaries of the Roman world. This shift led to dramatic cultural interchanges, which to some extent became defining features of subsequent medieval art, that is, from the period of Germanic tribal migration through the Romanesque and Gothic periods. Artistic methods, materials, and traditions were brought with migration and were combined with those customs that predominated in the regions where tribes settled, in many cases areas that had been Romanized during the height of imperial expansion. Rome would continue to be a meaningful, if shifting, construct for the developing Middle Ages.

While the early medieval dream of a unified imperial Europe to rival the height of the Roman Empire faded, new authoritative structures provided real and continued political and social stability in the Romanesque and Gothic periods. These were manifested politically through a feudal system and ecclesiastically through both a monastic system and strong bishoprics.

Although one should not undervalue the political dimensions of medieval art, the Middle Ages is generally epitomized as an era of faith and its art as an

expression of piety and devotion. It is no mere coincidence that our discussion of medieval art begins with Jewish and Early Christian works, includes the art of Islam, and ends with the creation of immense Gothic cathedrals. Even as new towns were founded and old ones fortified and strengthened, religious institutions remained the fundamental patrons of the arts throughout the Middle Ages. Certainly there was a shift inward, toward spiritualized representation, yet it would be an oversimplification to distinguish medieval from ancient art only by the medieval concentration on spiritual values. After all, the art of the ancient world also included a religious dimension, for the gods of Greece and Rome were virtually omnipresent in their art. However, whereas the ancients expressed the physical presence of their gods in naturalistic sculpture and paintings, Early Christian artists explored a different vision. In the service of their new faith, these artists concentrated on symbolic representation, using physical means to express a spiritual essence. But the change in artistic purpose was not exclusively a result of changes in religion, since, as our discussion of later Roman art has shown, the movement toward increasing stylization and abstraction also appeared in pagan contexts: witness the theories of Plotinus and the sculpture of Constantine and the tetrarchs (see fig. 7.27). Medieval art must be seen as a result of wide-ranging and shifting cultural conditions.

NORWAY

SWEDEN

Atlantic

Ocean

SCOTLAND

North

Lindisfarne

BRITISH ISLES

Sea

Durham

IRELAND

ENGLAND

SCANDINAVIA

DENMARK

Baltic Sea

N

Gloucester

Sutton Hoo

London

THE
NETHERLANDS

SAXONY

Elbe R.

POLAND

Salisbury

Thames R.

Utrecht

Hildesheim

Canterbury

Corvey

FLANDERS

Rhine R.

Cologne

GERMANY

Naumburg

Corbie

Aachen

Limbourg

HOLY

Bayeux

Laon

RHINELAND

E

Caen

Reims

Bingen

ROMAN

Nuremberg

NORMANDY

St.-Denis

Meuse R.

BOHEMIA

Chartres

ÎLE-DE-FRANCE

Paris

Verdun

Metz

Strasbourg

Schwäbisch-Gmünd

Loire R.

FRANCE

Seine R.

Fontenay

EMPIRE

Munich

Poitiers

St.-Savin-
sur-Gartempe

Cîteaux

BURGUNDY

St. Gall

Lake Constance

Lindau

Vienna

Bay

Autun

Lake
Geneva

SWITZERLAND

Reichenau

HUNG

of

Cluny

Clairvaux

A

L

P

S

Biscay

Santiago
de Compostela

Garonne R.

E

U

R

O

P

Lombardy

Milan

Po R.

Padua

Venice

Moissac

Rhône R.

Toulouse

PROVENCE

Ravenna

CROATIA

Duero R.

Pyrenees

Pisa

Florence

Adriatic Sea

Ebro R.

Arno R.

TUSCANY

Tiber R.

SPAIN

Tajo R.

Iberian

ITALY

Peninsula

Rome

Córdoba

Guadalquivir R.

Tyrrhenian Sea

APULIA

Granada

Mediterranean

Ionian

Sea

Sicily

The Byzantine Empire
ca. 1025 C.E.

NORTH AFRICA

Kairouan

500 km

500 miles

THE MIDDLE AGES

R U S S I A

Don R.

Volga R.

Dnieper R.

Caspian Sea

Black Sea

Danube R.

ARMENIA

Nerezi

Byzantium
(Constantinople)

Lake
Van

Lake Urmia

ACEDONIA

Halys R.

CAPPADOCIA

Salonica
(Thessalonika)

Mt. Athos

TURKEY

Tigris R.

GREECE

Aegean
Sea

N E A R

MESOPOTAMIA

ANATOLIA

E A S T

Mt. Parnassus

IONIA

Samarra

Daphni

Athens

Dura Europos

Baghdad

Euphrates R.

Crac des Chevaliers

S Y R I A

Crete

Jordan R.

S e a

Hammath Tiberias

Jerusalem

CHAPTER

8 Jewish, Early Christian, and Byzantine Art

POINTS OF INQUIRY

8.1 Recognize the impact of Judaism and Christianity on the production of art in the late ancient world.

8.2 Understand the parts of an Early Christian **basilica** and trace their sources.

8.3 Examine the resistance of both Jews and Christians to the making of images.

8.4 Investigate Byzantine architectural innovations.

8.5 Define the characteristics and distinguish among the achievements of Early, Middle, and Late Byzantine art.

((•—**Listen** to the chapter audio on myartslab.com

Major Dates in the Jewish, Early Christian, and Byzantine Periods

ca. 1st–6th century	Early Christian period
324	Constantine relocates capital to Constantinople
395	Roman Empire permanently divided
526–726	Early Byzantine period
ca. late 9th–11th century	Middle Byzantine period
1054	Christian Church split into Eastern (Orthodox) and Western (Catholic) churches
ca. 12th–mid-15th century	Late Byzantine period
1453	Byzantine Empire ends when Turks capture Constantinople

A spiritual crisis developed within the Roman Empire during the third century CE. Traditional value systems, including officially sanctioned religion, no longer satisfied a society weakened by inept, militaristic, or opportunistic rulers, and by threats to the borders of the empire from migrating tribes that the Romans considered barbarian. The Late Roman Empire was home to a vast melting pot of creeds—among them the ancient faith of Judaism alongside Christianity, Mithraism, Manichaeism, and Gnosticism, to name a few. These competing faiths shared several features, including an emphasis on divine revelation through a chief prophet or messiah and the hope of salvation. Additionally, they shared a belief in a cosmic struggle of good against evil, a ritual of initiation or purification (such as baptism), and, except for Judaism, the duty to seek converts. The last faith of this type to develop was Islam, which took form in the early seventh century on the Arabian peninsula and continues to dominate the Near East to this day (see Chapter 9).

The Jews of the Late Roman Empire were a Semitic people descended from the ancient Hebrews. The Hebrew people—their tradition recounts—arrived in Canaan (Israel) on the eastern shores of the Mediterranean from Egypt around the thirteenth century BCE, as a result of a long journey chronicled in the Hebrew Bible, the so-called Old Testament (see **map 8.1**). They established themselves as a United Kingdom of Israel a generation or so before 1000 BCE when Jerusalem was made the capital under King David, and it was shortly afterward that King Solomon built a temple there. The area was subsequently ruled by a series of foreign occupiers, including Babylonians, Assyrians, Persians, Greeks (under Alexander the Great), and, most significantly for our studies, Romans, who under General Pompey conquered Israel in 63 BCE. The Romans referred to this land as Palestine.

Christianity was centered on the life and teaching of Jesus of Nazareth, who himself along with many of his followers came from the ranks of the Jews. The religion spread from Palestine, first to Greek-speaking communities, notably to Alexandria, in Egypt, then reached the Latin-speaking world by the end of the second century. The

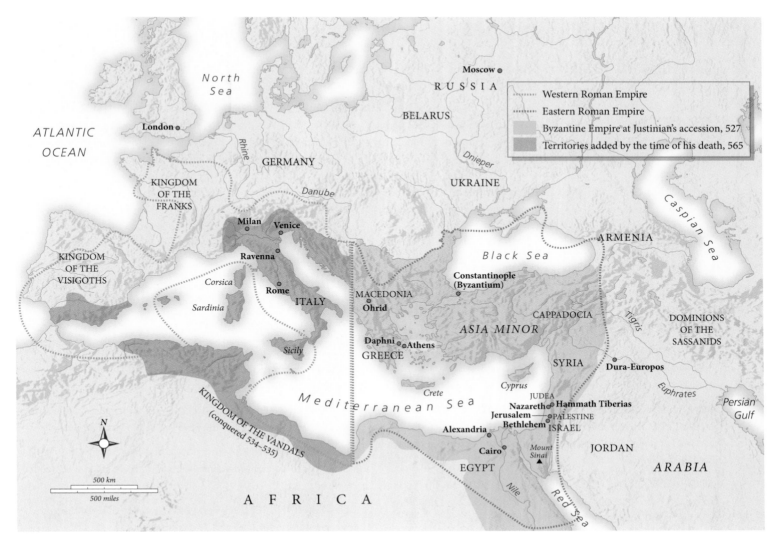

Map 8.1 Eastern and Western Roman Empire

Gospels of Matthew, Mark, Luke, and John, our principal source of information about Jesus' life, were probably written in the late first century, some decades after his death (see box: Cultural Context: The Life of Jesus, pages 158–59). The Gospels present him as a historical person and as the Son of God and Messiah or the "Anointed One." The eloquence and significance of Christ's teachings, the miracles attributed to him, and his innate goodness were considered signs of his divinity. The Roman authorities, viewing Jesus' teaching as subversive, had him arrested, tried, and ultimately punished and executed by crucifixion. By 300 CE, nearly 20 percent of the Roman Empire was Christian, though the new faith continued to have little standing until the conversion of Constantine the Great in 312.

In that year while battling his fellow tetrarch, Maxentius, for control of the Western Empire, Constantine claimed to have had a dream in which Christ himself, by a sign (reputedly the CHI RHO), assured him of his victory over Maxentius, which took place at the Milvian Bridge in Rome in 312. This triumph is commemorated by the Arch of Constantine (see fig. 7.29). Constantine accepted the Christian faith and, having consolidated imperial power, promoted Christianity throughout the empire. Claiming his political authority was granted by God, Constantine placed himself at the head of the Church as well as of the State. His choice to accept and promote Christianity was a turning point in history, as it brought about the union of Christianity with the legacy of the empire. Constantine's resolve to locate a new capital in Byzantium resulted in the division of Rome into two halves: An Eastern Empire, with its capital in Constantinople, and a Western Empire centered at Rome. Imperial might and wealth were concentrated in Constantinople, enriching and protecting the Eastern Empire. In the West, imperial authority

The CHI RHO sign, a monogram of Christ, is composed of the first two letters of Christ's name in Greek, *Christos*: Chi (χ) and rho (ρ). The monogram is often referred to as the Chrismon or the Christogram.

The Life of Jesus

IN THE CHRISTIAN RELIGION, events in the life of Jesus, from his birth through his ascension to heaven, are traditionally grouped in cycles, each with numerous episodes. The scenes most frequently depicted in European art are presented here.

Incarnation Cycle and the Childhood of Jesus

These episodes concern Jesus' conception, birth, infancy, and youth.

ANNUNCIATION. The archangel Gabriel tells Mary that she will bear God's son. The Holy Spirit, shown usually as a dove, represents the Incarnation, the miraculous conception.

VISITATION. The pregnant Mary visits her older cousin Elizabeth, who is to bear John the Baptist and who is the first to recognize the divine nature of the baby Mary is carrying.

NATIVITY. At the birth of Jesus, the Holy Family—Mary, her husband, Joseph, and the child—is usually depicted in a stable or, in Byzantine representations, in a cave.

ANNUNCIATION TO THE SHEPHERDS and ADORATION OF THE SHEPHERDS. An angel announces the birth of Jesus to shepherds in a field at night. The shepherds then go to the birthplace to pay homage to the child.

ADORATION OF THE MAGI. The Magi (also called the Three Kings), wise men from the East, follow a bright star for 12 days until they find the Holy Family and present their gifts to Jesus.

PRESENTATION IN THE TEMPLE. Mary and Joseph take the infant Jesus to the Temple in Jerusalem, where Simeon, a devout man, and Anna, a prophetess, foresee Jesus' messianic (savior's) mission and martyr's death.

MASSACRE OF THE INNOCENTS and FLIGHT INTO EGYPT. King Herod orders all children under the age of two in and around Bethlehem to be killed in order to preclude his being murdered by a rival newborn king spoken of in a prophecy. The Holy Family flees to Egypt.

Public Ministry Cycle

BAPTISM. John the Baptist baptizes Jesus in the Jordan River, recognizing Jesus' incarnation as the Son of God. This marks the beginning of Jesus' ministry.

CALLING OF MATTHEW. A tax collector, Matthew, becomes Jesus' first disciple (apostle) when Jesus calls to him, "Follow me."

JESUS WALKING ON THE WATER. During a storm, Jesus walks on the water of the Sea of Galilee to reach his apostles in a boat.

RAISING OF LAZARUS. Jesus brings his friend Lazarus back to life four days after Lazarus' death and burial.

DELIVERY OF THE KEYS TO PETER. Jesus names the apostle Peter his successor by giving him the keys to the Kingdom of Heaven.

TRANSFIGURATION. As Jesus' closest disciples watch, God transforms Jesus into a dazzling vision and proclaims him to be his own son.

CLEANSING THE TEMPLE. Enraged, Jesus clears the Temple in Jerusalem of money changers and animal traders.

Passion Cycle

The Passion (from *passio*, Latin for "suffering") cycle relates Jesus' death, resurrection from the dead, and ascension to heaven.

---

was less effective in the face of new challenges, as non-Roman groups first invaded and then settled in Europe.

Into the vacuum of power left by the decline of imperial institutions in the West stepped the bishop of Rome. Deriving his authority from St. Peter, the pope, as the bishop of Rome became known, claimed leadership of the universal Christian Church, although his Eastern counterpart, the patriarch of Constantinople, disputed this claim. Differences in doctrine and liturgy continued to develop until eventually the division of Christendom into a Western or Catholic Church and an Eastern or Orthodox Church became all but final.

The Great Schism, or final break, between the two churches occurred in the eleventh century.

The religious separation of East and West profoundly affected the development of Christian art in the Late Roman Empire. "Early Christian" does not, strictly speaking, designate a style. It refers, rather, to any work of art produced by or for Christians during the time prior to the splitting off of the Eastern Church from the Western Church, that is, roughly during the first five centuries after the birth of Jesus. "Byzantine," on the other hand, designates not only the art of the Eastern Roman Empire but also its specific culture and style, which was linked to the imperial court of Constantinople.

ENTRY INTO JERUSALEM. Welcomed by crowds as the Messiah, Jesus triumphantly rides an ass into the city of Jerusalem.

LAST SUPPER. At the Passover seder or ritual meal, Jesus tells his disciples of his impending death and lays the foundation for the Christian rite of the Eucharist: The taking of bread and wine in remembrance of Christ. (Strictly speaking, Jesus is called Jesus until he leaves his earthly physical form, after which he is called Christ.)

JESUS WASHING THE DISCIPLES' FEET. Following the Last Supper, Jesus washes the feet of his disciples to demonstrate humility.

AGONY IN THE GARDEN. In Gethsemane, the disciples sleep while Jesus wrestles with his mortal dread of suffering and dying.

BETRAYAL (ARREST). The disciple Judas Iscariot takes money to identify Jesus to Roman soldiers. Jesus is arrested.

DENIAL OF PETER. As Jesus predicted, Peter, waiting outside the high priest's palace, three times denies knowing Jesus as Jesus is being questioned by the high priest, Caiaphas.

JESUS BEFORE PILATE. Jesus is questioned by the Roman governor Pontius Pilate regarding whether he calls himself King of the Jews. Jesus does not answer. Pilate reluctantly condemns him.

FLAGELLATION (SCOURGING). Jesus is whipped by Roman soldiers.

JESUS CROWNED WITH THORNS (THE MOCKING OF CHRIST). Pilate's soldiers mock Jesus by dressing him in robes, crowning him with thorns, and calling him King of the Jews.

CARRYING OF THE CROSS (ROAD TO CALVARY). Jesus carries the wooden cross on which he will be executed from Pilate's house to the hill of Golgotha, "the place of the skull."

CRUCIFIXION. Jesus is nailed to the Cross by his hands and feet, and dies after great physical suffering.

DESCENT FROM THE CROSS (DEPOSITION). Jesus' followers lower his body from the Cross and wrap it for burial. Also present are the Virgin, the apostle John, and in some accounts Mary Magdalen.

LAMENTATION (PIETÀ or VESPERBILD). The grief-stricken followers gather around Jesus' body. In the *Pietà*, his body lies in the lap of the Virgin.

ENTOMBMENT. The Virgin and others place the wrapped body in a sarcophagus or in a rock tomb.

DESCENT INTO LIMBO (HARROWING OF HELL or ANASTASIS in the Orthodox Church). Christ descends to hell, or limbo, to free deserving souls who have not heard the Christian message—the prophets of the Hebrew Bible, the kings of Israel, and Adam and Eve.

RESURRECTION. Christ rises from the dead on the third day after his entombment.

THE MARYS AT THE TOMB. As terrified soldiers look on, Christ's female followers (the Virgin Mary, Mary Magdalen, and Mary, mother of the apostle James) discover the empty tomb.

NOLI ME TANGERE, SUPPER AT EMMAUS, and the DOUBTING OF THOMAS. In three episodes during the 40 days between his resurrection and ascent into heaven, Christ tells Mary Magdalen not to touch him (*Noli me tangere*), shares a supper with his disciples at Emmaus, and invites the apostle Thomas to touch the lance wound in his side.

ASCENSION. As his disciples watch, Christ is taken into heaven from the Mount of Olives.

Although Early Christian and Byzantine, and to some extent Early Jewish, arts have their origins in Rome, their forms differ from those of the classical world. Early Christian art refined the increasingly stylized and abstracted art forms of the Late Roman Empire into a visual language that could express both profoundly spiritual and unmistakably secular power.

Jewish Art

The relationships among various religious arts produced during the Late Roman Empire make clear that none of them was created in a vacuum and that each affected the others. Of particular interest is Jewish art, both as a subject worthy of study in its own right and because its development is closely intertwined with that of Christian art; both developed within an environment where the dominant artistic force was clearly Roman.

DURA-EUROPOS SYNAGOGUE Discoveries within the last century have forced scholars to revise their estimation of the quantity and quality of Jewish art produced in antiquity. Central to this reevaluation was the fortuitous and remarkable discovery of a synagogue in the Syrian town of Dura-Europos, a Roman outpost on the upper Euphrates. In 256 CE,

8.1 West wall of sanctuary of synagogue. Dura-Europos, Syria. 245–46 CE. Tempera on plaster. Reconstructed in the National Museum, Damascus, Syria

in order to protect itself from imminent attack by Persians, the town strengthened its protective walls, which involved filling in some adjacent streets in order to form a defensive bunker. Buried as a result, and thus preserved, were a number of buildings, including a synagogue that had been rebuilt or refurbished in 245 and 246, just a decade before the defenses against Persian attack were raised; as such, it was virtually new when buried.

The bench-lined sanctuary of the Dura-Europos synagogue (**fig. 8.1**) would have seated about 120 people. Wall murals, painted ceiling tiles, ritual objects, and other decorations, as well as the sounds of prayer and the aroma of incense embellished the synagogue and accentuated the sense of a charged space created for the enactment of the liturgy, a body of rights prescribed for public worship. More than half of the wall murals survive and, arranged in four registers of **tempera** paintings, illustrate episodes from the Hebrew Bible, including scenes with Moses and other patriarchs and prophets. The Jerusalem-facing west wall contains a centrally placed niche housing a shrine for the Torah, the **parchment** scroll containing the first five books of the Hebrew Bible. The shrine is decorated with a representation of a temple and a menorah, the seven-branched candelabrum that was housed in the Second Temple in Jerusalem, the center of Jewish worship and ritual for centuries, which was

destroyed by the Romans in 70 CE. This imagery equates the synagogues in which Jews practice their religion with the Temple in Jerusalem.

Previous to the discovery of the Dura-Europos wall paintings, it had traditionally been assumed that Jews rarely produced art, a notion based on the biblical proscription against making graven images as described in the Second Commandment (Exodus 20:4–6; Deuteronomy 5:8–10: "You shall not make to you any graven image…. You shall not bow down yourself to them, nor serve them"). Representations of God do not appear in Jewish contexts, and it is here that we should understand the significance of the edict against the production of graven images. The Second Commandment was not an injunction against representation, but rather, more specifically against making idols.

Most of the Dura-Europos scenes reveal little interest in either light or space in the Roman sense. For example, the size of objects is relative to their importance, rather than to their position in space, and figures are rendered relatively flat. Stylistically, the synagogue paintings fall within the context of the developing abstraction of later Roman art (see figs. 7.27 and 7.30).

HAMMATH TIBERIAS SYNAGOGUE In addition to wall paintings and liturgical objects, floor mosaics decorated a number of synagogues, particularly in

Palestine. Mosaics were widely used in the Roman world. Artists used them to decorate floors or outdoor spaces, where fresco would be vulnerable to deterioration. They fitted together minute colored stones or pieces of marble called tesserae to create a pattern or figured image. The fourth-century mosaic floor of a synagogue at Hammath Tiberias (**fig. 8.2**) on the shore of the Sea of Galilee contains a wheel with the signs of the zodiac between its spokes and in the center a representation of Helios, the Greek sun god, bearing a staff and globe, with rays emanating from his head and riding a quadriga, a two-wheeled chariot drawn by four horses.

Representations of the seasons fill the corners between the circle of the zodiac and the enclosing square frame, while below this section, two lions flank an inscription in Greek that praises the synagogue's builders and describes the donation of precious metals. The use of the zodiac as a central feature in a number of Palestinian synagogue mosaics might reflect the Jews' sense of themselves as distinctive in part because of their use of a calendar different from those of other peoples. The zodiac undoubtedly refers as well to God's creation of the universe. Represented above the zodiac is a Torah shrine, framed by menorahs and other ritual objects, including some used in the harvest festival, all elements from the liturgy.

The mosaic's style of representation is reminiscent of Roman mosaic work. The figures' modeling is subtle and shadows suggest solid, if squat, bodies. The Hebrew and Greek used in the mosaic—and there are inscriptions in Aramaic (a Semitic language) as well—reflect the multiple traditions at work here. Although the images at Hammath Tiberias and at Dura-Europos have special relevance to Jewish history, beliefs, and rituals, many reflect Graeco-Roman content, even if it was Judaized in accordance with the special concerns and needs of the communities the images served. A similar pattern is also evident in the development of the earliest Christian art.

Early Christian Art

Christian Art before Constantine

We do not know when or where the first Christian works of art were produced. None of the surviving paintings or sculptures can be dated earlier than about 200 CE. In fact, we know little about Christian art before the reign of Constantine the Great.

8.2 Floor mosaic. Synagogue, Hammath Tiberias, Israel. Fourth century CE

THE ART OF THE CATACOMBS   The only sizeable body of very early Christian art to survive is painted on the walls and ceilings of the Roman catacombs, underground burial places. The burial rite and the safeguarding of the tomb vitally concerned Early Christians, whose faith rested on salvation, the hope of eternal life in paradise.

The ceiling of one of the more elaborate chambers in the catacomb of SS. Pietro e Marcellino (**fig. 8.3**), in Rome, is decorated in a style that is at once formal and uncomplicated. Fixed borders control the overall organization; a central medallion or circle contains the figure of a shepherd, who is flanked by sheep and carries a lamb across his shoulders. The circle is connected to four **lunettes** (semicircular spaces), and in the four corners stand single figures, known as **orants** (worshipers), their outstretched, raised arms depicting what had long been the standard pose of prayer. The style of painting reflects Roman murals, both in the landscape settings and in the use of linear devices to divide the scenes into compartments (see fig. 7.26). But the representations

seem sketchier, less grounded in natural observation than their Roman relatives.

Catacombs would have been used only occasionally beyond the actual circumstance of burial, perhaps for a commemorative celebration. For this reason the wall paintings do not show much detail and care of execution. This sketchiness also can be attributed to their primary value as symbols. Consistent with the biblical prohibition against image making, as specified in the Second Commandment of the Hebrew Bible, Christ is generally not represented in the catacombs, except by metaphor. The shepherd with a sheep on his shoulders is a potent allusion to Christ, since in a number of biblical accounts Christ refers to himself as the Good Shepherd, concerned for the well-being of his flock and willing to sacrifice himself in order to guarantee the salvation of those who follow him (Luke 15:4–6; John 10:1–18). This Good Shepherd metaphor also builds on Hebrew Bible references, as in Psalm 23:

The Lord is my shepherd, I shall not want.
He makes me lie down in green pastures;
he leads me beside still waters;
he restores my soul.…
Surely goodness and mercy shall follow me
all the days of my life,
and I shall dwell in the house of the Lord
for ever.

The Hebrew Bible correlation reflects the fact that many of the converts to the new faith were Jewish.

The four lunettes around the Good Shepherd form a cycle dedicated to the Hebrew prophet Jonah. Here too, the symbolic references to Christian beliefs about Christ are clear: Just as it is an article of faith that Jonah spent three days within the belly of the whale, so Christ is supposed to have spent three days in the tomb, and just as Jonah was released with unharmed body, so Christ was resurrected from his tomb in physical wholeness.

Recent converts would probably have felt comfortable knowing that didactic aspects of their old faith could find a sympathetic response in the new religion. Jonah's story is presented as a **prefiguration** (foreseeing) of events in Christ's life, thus assigning the Hebrew Bible story the role of prophecy and the Christian Bible story the role of its fulfillment.

The painted ceiling in SS. Pietro e Marcellino also borrows imagery from classical sources. The Good Shepherd himself recalls pagan symbols of charity in the form of ancient sculptures of men carrying sacrificial animals on their shoulders. So, as with their Jewish counterparts, former practitioners of pagan religions who had converted to Christianity would also have been familiar with some of the images and ideas expressed in Early Christian art.

Both the Good Shepherd and Jonah are associated with messages of comfort, reminding us that Early Christian art developed during the turmoil of Rome's decline, a time of political, social, and economic instability. The allure of the new religion must have been profound indeed, suggesting that things of this world were of less significance than those of a future world, which offered the hope of eternal peace.

THE HOUSE CHURCH We have little archaeological evidence of the places where Early Christians gathered. Literary accounts, including biblical references, suggest that Christians met regularly to celebrate their shared belief in Christ as the Son of God and Savior and to observe some type of Eucharist, or spiritual union, with him by the partaking of consecrated bread and wine (representing Christ's flesh and blood). The Eucharist commemorates the Last Supper, at which Jesus and his disciples enjoyed a final communal meal. Such gatherings of Christians probably originally took place in private homes and were only later replaced by public spaces designed specifically for Christian worship. In Rome itself we know of 25 private houses—and undoubtedly there were more—reserved as places of Christian worship, although most of them were destroyed by the later building of churches on their sites.

Christian Art after the Official Recognition of Christianity

The building of churches on the sites of private Christian houses reflects a change in the nature of Christianity during the fourth century from an alternative religion to the official religion endorsed by the emperor Constantine. Almost overnight, an impressive architectural setting had to be created for the new official faith, so that the Church might be visible to all. Constantine himself devoted the full resources of his office to this task.

THE CHRISTIAN BASILICA The most important Constantinian church structures were a type of basilica, and this form provided the basic model for the development of church architecture in Western Europe. The Early Christian basilica owes its essential features to imperial basilicas (see page 147). Like them, it is characterized by a long **nave** flanked by side aisles and lit by **clerestory** windows, with an **apse** (though only at one end) and a trussed wooden roof. The Roman basilica constituted a suitable model, since it combined the spacious interior needed to accommodate a large number of people with (perhaps most important) the imperial associations that proclaimed the privileged status of Christianity. As its largely civil functions were quite different from its new uses as a house of worship, it had to be redesigned to acknowledge these changes. The longitudinal plan of the basilica was given a new focus: The **altar** was placed in front of the semicircular apse, normally at the eastern end of the nave. The significance of the altar's placement in the east, where the sun rises, reminds us that Christianity inherited many attributes of divinities from other religions. In this case, Christ shares an imagery with the Roman god Apollo, in his manifestation as sun god. This parallels the way the Greek sun god, Helios, was appropriated in the Hammath Tiberias floor mosaic (see fig. 8.2).

The greatest Constantinian church was Old St. Peter's Basilica in Rome. Torn down and replaced by the present St. Peter's Basilica, in the Vatican, during the sixteenth and seventeenth centuries, its appearance is preserved in a seventeenth-century album of copies of earlier drawings (**fig. 8.4**), and there are literary descriptions as well. Together these sources give us a clear idea of the original plan for the church. Begun as early as 319 and finished by 329, Old St. Peter's was built on the Vatican Hill next to a pagan burial ground. It stood directly over the grave of St. Peter, which was marked by a shrine covered with a *baldacchino*, a canopy that designates a place of honor. The need to orient the church in relation to the burial spot resulted in the construction of the apse at the west end, an unusual feature. Rituals were conducted

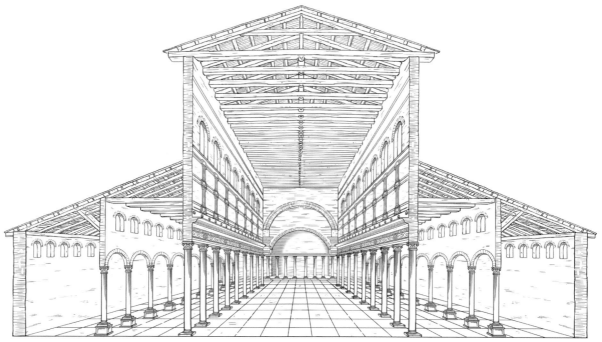

8.4 Reconstruction drawing of interior of Old St. Peter's, Rome. ca. 329 CE

Read the document related to Old St. Peter's on myartslab.com

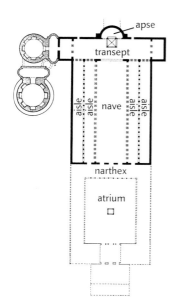

apse

transept

aisle aisle nave aisle aisle

narthex

atrium

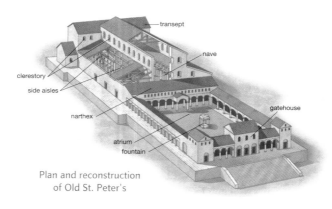

transept

nave

clerestory

side aisles

narthex

gatehouse

atrium
fountain

Plan and reconstruction of Old St. Peter's

from a portable altar placed before the shrine, using gold and silver implements donated by the emperor himself.

To enter the church the congregation first crossed a colonnaded court, the atrium, which was added toward the end of the fourth century; this feature derived from the Roman basilica. Congregants then passed through the **narthex**, an entrance hall, into the church itself. The steady rhythm of the nave colonnade would have pulled them toward the **triumphal arch**, which framed the shrine of St. Peter and the apse beyond. The shrine stood at the junction of the nave and the **transept**, a separate space set perpendicular to the nave and aisles. Spaces at the end of the transept, marked off by columns, might have served to prepare items used during church rites and to hold offerings brought by the faithful.

The main focus of Christian liturgy, a body of rites prescribed for public worship, was, and is, the Mass, which includes the sacrament of Communion, the symbolic reenactment on the altar of Jesus' sacrifice (see box: Cultural Context: The Liturgy of the Mass). The Early Christian basilica encouraged attention on the altar, making it the focal point of the church by placing it opposite the entrance and at the end of a long nave. Even beyond this general emphasis on the altar, Old St. Peter's gave special prominence to the altar zone through this church's special, additional function as a **martyrium**, a building that housed sacred relics or the remains of a holy person.

CENTRAL-PLAN STRUCTURES Buildings of round or polygonal shape capped by a dome entered the tradition of Christian architecture in Constantine's time. Roman emperors had built similar structures to serve as monumental tombs or mausoleums. Not surprisingly, therefore, the Early Christian **central-plan** building was often associated with funerary functions. Santa Costanza, in Rome, the mausoleum of Constantine's daughter Constantia (**fig. 8.5**), was built over a catacomb; it was originally attached to the now-ruined basilican church of St. Agnes Outside the Walls. The dominant central space is illuminated by clerestory windows, over which rises a dome supported by 12 pairs of columns. Four of the arches of this colonnade stand slightly higher than the others and suggest a cross inscribed within a circle. The significance of the cross in a funerary context results from its association with Christ, who, though martyred

The Liturgy of the Mass

THE CENTRAL RITE of many Christian churches is the EUCHARIST or COMMUNION service, a ritual meal that reenacts Jesus' Last Supper. Bread and wine are consecrated and consumed in memory of Christ. Catholics hold that the bread and wine actually become the body and blood of Christ through transubstantiation. In the Catholic Church and in a few Protestant churches as well, this service is known as the MASS (from the Latin words *Ite, missa est* — "Go, [the congregation] is dismissed," at the end of the Latin service). The Mass was first codified by Pope Gregory the Great around 600 CE.

Each Mass consists of the "ordinary" — those prayers and hymns that are the same in all Masses — and the "proper," the parts that vary, depending on the occasion. The "proper" of the Mass consists of prayers; two readings from the New Testament (one from the Epistles and one from the Gospels); a homily, or sermon, on these texts; and hymns, all chosen specifically for the day. There are also Masses for special occasions, such as the Requiem Mass for the dead and the Nuptial Mass for weddings.

on a cross, rose victorious over death. The Cross was meaningful to all Christians but particularly to the family of Constantine, whose personal conversion was a result of his vision of it, which had signaled his victory at the Battle of the Milvian Bridge in 312. The sarcophagus of Constantia was originally placed under the eastern, more elevated arch. Encircling the building is an **ambulatory**, a ring-shaped aisle, covered by a barrel vault (see page 125).

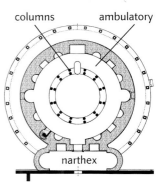

Ground plan of Santa Costanza

8.5 Interior (view through ambulatory into rotunda), Santa Costanza, Rome. ca. 350 CE

ARCHITECTURAL DECORATION: WALL MOSAICS The rapid growth of large-scale Christian architecture had a revolutionary effect on Early Christian pictorial art. All of a sudden, huge wall surfaces had to be covered with images worthy of their monumental framework. Out of this need emerged a great new art form, the Early Christian wall mosaic, which to a large extent replaced the older and cheaper medium of mural painting. The challenge of inventing a body of Christian imagery produced an extraordinary creative outpouring. Large pictorial cycles of subjects selected from the Hebrew and Christian Bibles were spread over the nave walls, the triumphal arch, and the apse. These cycles must have drawn on sources that reflected the whole range of Graeco-Roman painting as well as the artistic traditions that had surely developed in the Christian communities of North Africa and the Near East.

The pictorial embellishment of fourth-century churches is largely fragmentary or known only from literary accounts; it is in fifth-century churches that we can see the full development of mosaic decoration. Central among the Early Christian churches in which a full mosaic program survives is the basilica of Santa Maria Maggiore in Rome. Built between 432 and 440, this was the first church dedicated to Mary, begun only a year after she was declared the *Theotokos* (Greek for "the bearer of God") by the Council of Ephesus.

The exterior brick walls of the building were always much simpler than the rich interior. Having left the everyday world behind, the visitor would encounter a shimmering realm of light and color where precious marble surfaces and glittering mosaics evoked the spiritual splendor of the Kingdom of God. To some extent the building is analogous to the ideal Christian, simple in external body and glorious in inner spirit, an analogy certainly not missed by Early Christians. Roman mural painting used illusionistic devices to suggest a reality beyond the surface of the wall (see fig. 7.25), whereas Early Christian mosaics used the glitter of gold tesserae to create a luminous realm filled with celestial beings, symbols, or narrative action. Thus, Early Christian mosaics transform the illusionistic tradition of ancient painting with the new Christian message.

The apse of Santa Maria Maggiore is a later replacement, but the general outline of the original

8.6 Interior, Santa Maria Maggiore, Rome. ca. 432–40 CE

building and much of the mosaic decoration survive (**fig. 8.6**). These mosaics include the triumphal arch decoration and more than half of the 42 mosaic panels that were placed above the classically inspired entablature of the nave colonnade. Pilasters and colonnettes framed these panels. Sadly, much of this architectural decoration is now missing.

The panels above the nave colonnade illustrate scenes from the Hebrew Bible. They combine narration with a concern for structured symmetry. For instance, in the left half of *The Parting of Lot and Abraham* (**fig. 8.7**), Abraham, his son Isaac, and the rest of his family depart for the land of Canaan. On the right, Lot and his clan, including his two small daughters, turn toward the city of Sodom. The artist who designed this scene from Genesis 13 faced the same task as the ancient Roman sculptors of the Column of Trajan (see fig. 7.15). He needed to condense complex actions into a form that could be read at a distance. In fact, he employed many of the same shorthand devices, such as the formulas for house, tree, and city, and the device of showing a crowd of people as a cluster of heads, rather like a bunch of grapes.

In the Trajanic reliefs, these devices were employed only to the extent that they allowed the artist to portray actual historical events. The mosaics in Santa Maria Maggiore, by contrast, depict the history of human salvation, beginning with scenes from the Hebrew Bible along the nave and ending with the life of Jesus as the Messiah on the triumphal arch. For those who read the Bible literally, the scheme is not only a historical cycle but also a symbolic program that presents a higher reality—the Word of God. Hence the artist was not concerned with the details of historical narrative. Glances and gestures were more important than realistic movement or three-dimensional form. In *The Parting of Lot and Abraham*, the symmetrical composition, with its gap in the center, makes clear the significance of this parting. Abraham represents the way of righteousness, while Sodom, which was destroyed by the Lord, signifies the way of evil. Beneath *The Parting of Lot and Abraham* is a classically inspired but thoroughly transformed landscape, its shepherds placed on a green ground, while their sheep, as if on little islands, float in gold surroundings.

The extensive and complex wall mosaics of Early Christian art are essentially without precedent. The color scale of Roman and Jewish mosaics

8.7 *The Parting of Lot and Abraham* and *Shepherds in a Landscape*. Mosaic. ca. 432–40 CE. Santa Maria Maggiore, Rome

(see fig. 8.2), although rich in gradations, lacked brilliance because of limitations imposed by the color range found in marble. Early Christian mosaics, by contrast, consist of tesserae made of colored glass, which the Romans had known but had never fully exploited. These glass tesserae offered colors, including gold, of far greater range and intensity than marble tesserae. Moreover, the shiny, somewhat irregular faces of the glass pieces, each set slightly askew from its neighbor, act as tiny reflectors, so that the overall effect is like a glittering, immaterial screen rather than a solid, continuous surface.

What were the visual sources of the mosaic compositions at Santa Maria Maggiore and other churches like it? These were certainly not the first depictions of scenes from the Bible (see box: Cultural Context: Versions of the Bible, overleaf). For certain subjects, such as the Last Supper, models could have been found among the catacomb

Versions of the Bible

THE WORD "BIBLE" is derived from the Greek word for "books," because it was originally a compilation of a number of sacred texts. Over time, the books of the Bible came to be regarded as a unit, and thus the Bible is now generally considered a single book.

There is considerable disagreement between Christians and Jews, and among various Christian and Jewish sects, over which books should be considered canonical—that is, accepted as legitimate parts of the biblical canon, the standard list of authentic texts. However, every version of the Bible includes the Hebrew TORAH, or the Law (also called the PENTATEUCH, or Books of Moses), as the first five books. Also universally accepted by both Jews and Christians are the books known as the Prophets (which include texts of Jewish history as well as prophecy). There are also a number of other books known simply as the Writings, which include history, poetry (the Psalms and the Song of Songs), prophecy, and even folktales, some universally accepted, some accepted by one group, and some accepted by virtually no one. Books of doubtful authenticity are known as APOCRYPHAL BOOKS, or simply Apocrypha, from a Greek word meaning "obscure." The Jewish Bible or Hebrew Canon—the books that are accepted as authentic Jewish scripture—was agreed upon by Jewish scholars sometime before the beginning of the Christian era.

The Christian Bible is divided into two major sections, the HEBREW BIBLE, the so-called Old Testament, and the NEW TESTAMENT. The Hebrew Bible contains many, but not all, of the Jewish scriptures, whereas the New Testament, originally written in Greek, is specifically Christian. It contains four GOSPELS— each written in the first century CE by one of the Early Christian disciples known as the four EVANGELISTS, Mark, Matthew, Luke, and John. The Gospels tell, from slightly different points of view, the story of the life and teachings of Jesus of Nazareth. They are followed by the EPISTLES, letters written by Paul and a few other Christian missionaries to various congregations of the Church. The final book is the APOCALYPSE, by John the Divine, also called the Book of Revelation, which foretells the end of the world.

Jerome (342–420), the foremost scholar of the early Church, selected the books considered canonical for the Christian Bible from a large body of Early Christian writings. It was because of his energetic advocacy that the Church accepted the Hebrew scriptures as representing the Word of God as much as the Christian texts, and therefore worthy to be included in the Bible. Jerome then translated the books he had chosen from Hebrew and Greek into Latin, the spoken language of Italy in his time. This Latin translation of the Bible was—and is—known as the VULGATE because it was written in the vernacular (Latin *vulgaris*) language. The Vulgate remained the Church's primary text for the Bible for more than a thousand years. It was regarded with such reverence that in the fourteenth century, when early humanists first translated it into the vernacular languages of their time, they were sometimes suspected of heresy for doing so. The writings rejected for inclusion in the New Testament by Jerome are known as Christian Apocrypha. Although not canonical, some of these books, such as the Life of Mary and the Gospel of James, were nevertheless used by artists and playwrights during the Middle Ages as sources for stories to illustrate and dramatize.

murals, but others, such as the story of Joshua, may have come from illustrated manuscripts, to which, since they were portable, art historians have assigned an important role as models.

ILLUSTRATED BOOKS Because Christianity was based on the Word of God as revealed in the Bible, Early Christians, who referred to themselves as "people of the Book," sponsored duplication of sacred texts on a large scale. What did the earliest Bible illustrations look like? Because books are frail things, we have only indirect evidence of their history in the ancient world. It begins in Egypt with scrolls made from the papyrus plant, which is like paper but more brittle. Not until the second century BCE, in late Hellenistic times, did a better material become available. This was parchment (bleached animal hide) or **vellum** (a finer type of parchment), both of which last far longer than papyrus. They were strong enough to be creased without breaking and thus made possible the kind of bound book we know today, technically called a **codex**, which appeared sometime in the late first century CE.

Between the second and the fourth centuries CE, the vellum codex gradually replaced the papyrus roll. This change had an important effect on book illustration. Scroll illustrations seem to have been mostly line drawings, since layers of pigment would soon have cracked and come off during rolling and unrolling. Although parchment and vellum were less fragile than papyrus, they too were fragile mediums. Nevertheless, the codex permitted the use of rich colors, including gold. Hence it could make book illustration—or, as we usually say, manuscript **illumination**—the small-scale counterpart of murals, mosaics, and panel pictures. Some questions remain unanswered. When, where, and how quickly did book illumination develop? Were most of the subjects biblical,

mythological, or historical? How much carried over from scroll to codex?

One of the earliest surviving books to illustrate the Bible is an early fifth-century fragment, the so-called *Quedlinburg Itala* (**fig. 8.8**). The fragment is from an illustrated Book of Kings (one of the 39 books of the Hebrew Bible), which is calculated to have originally contained some 60 illustrations, each image probably comprising multiple scenes. On the **folio** (manuscript leaf) reproduced here,

8.8 Scenes from I Samuel Ch.15, the *Quedlinburg Itala*. ca. 425–50 CE. Tempera on vellum, 12 × 18″ (30.5 × 45.8 cm). Staatliche Bibliothek, Berlin

four scenes depict Saul's meeting with Samuel after the defeat of Amalekites (I Samuel 15:13–33), each scene framed so as to accentuate the overall unity of the composition. The misty landscape, architectural elements, and sky-blue and pink background are reminiscent of the antique Roman tradition of atmospheric illusionism.

Visible under the flaking paint in this badly damaged fragment are written instructions to the artist, part of which read, "You make the prophet speaking facing King Saul sacrificing." Apparently the artist was left free to interpret pictorially these written instructions, suggesting the lack of an illustrated model.

Particularly intriguing is the fact that the artist of the Quedlinburg fragment worked together in a Roman **scriptorium** (a workshop for copying and illustrating manuscripts) with an artist who illustrated the first-century BCE Roman pagan poet Vergil's *Aeneid* and *Georgics*, the so-called *Vatican Vergil*, named after the collection that houses it today. We might well ask if this is evidence of non-Christian artists working for Christian patrons and to what extent pagan motifs might have been transferred to Christian subjects. Perhaps not surprisingly, the Quedlinburg fragment and the other manuscripts produced in the same scriptorium are closely linked in style to the mosaics of the contemporaneous Santa Maria Maggiore.

SCULPTURE As we have seen, the increase in standing of Christianity profoundly affected artistic production, moving Christian art from a modest and private sphere to a public and official arena. As Early Christian architecture and its decoration demonstrated increasing monumentality as a result of its dependence on Roman imperial traditions, so too Early Christian sculpture became more impressive. This is apparent in a fine Early Christian stone coffin, the *Sarcophagus of Junius Bassus* (**fig. 8.9**).

The richly carved sarcophagus was made for a prefect of Rome who died in 359 at age 42 and who, an inscription tells us, had been "newly baptized." The front, divided by columns into ten

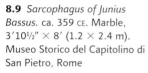

8.9 *Sarcophagus of Junius Bassus.* ca. 359 CE. Marble, 3'10½" × 8' (1.2 × 2.4 m). Museo Storico del Capitolino di San Pietro, Rome

View the Closer Look for the *Sarcophagus of Junius Bassus* on myartslab.com

compartments, contains scenes from the Hebrew Bible and the Christian one, also called the New Testament. In the upper register we see (from left to right) the Sacrifice of Isaac, St. Peter Taken Prisoner, Christ Enthroned between SS. Peter and Paul, and Jesus before Pontius Pilate (this last scene composed of two compartments). In the lower register are the Suffering of Job, the Temptation of Adam and Eve, Jesus' Entry into Jerusalem, Daniel in the Lions' Den, and St. Paul Led to his Martyrdom.

Clearly the status of Christianity has changed when a major state official proclaims, both in inscription and through representation, his belief in Christianity. The depictions of Peter and Paul, the veritable official saints of the city of Rome—each saint is commemorated by a major basilica in the city—can be related to Junius Bassus' role as a high-ranking government official. Authoritative as well is Christ's place in the central scenes. In the top register, he is enthroned with his feet treading on a personification of Coelus, the Roman pagan god of the heavens, as he dispenses the law to his disciples. Thus, Christ appropriates the emperor's role as lawgiver. Below this compartment, he enters Jerusalem in triumph. As compared to the earliest Christian representations, such as in the catacomb of SS. Pietro e Marcellino (see fig. 8.3), Christ is now depicted directly, not through allusion alone, and his imperial nature is accentuated. Daniel in the Lions' Den, the Sacrifice of Isaac, and Adam and Eve appeared in earlier representations in catacombs. Daniel's salvation is a type for Christ as well as for all Christians who hope for divine salvation; Abraham's willingness to sacrifice his beloved son Isaac parallels God's sacrifice of his only begotten son and at the same time speaks of salvation by divine grace; Adam and Eve refer to the Original Sin that led to Christ's sacrificial death and his resurrection. Thus old methods of explication are combined with new manifestations of Christianity's important role in society, particularly by stressing Christ's imperial nature.

The style of the sarcophagus also relies on imperial convention, particularly in the elements of classicism that are expressed, such as the placement within deep, space-filled niches of figures that recall the dignity of Greek and Roman sculpture. Other classicizing features include the way that the figures seem capable of distributing weight, the draperies that reveal the bodies beneath them, and the narrative clarity. However, beneath this veneer of classicism we recognize doll-like bodies with large heads and a passive air in scenes that would otherwise seem to call for dramatic action. It is as if the events and figures are no longer intended to tell their own story but to call to mind a larger symbolic meaning that unites them.

The reliance on classicizing forms on the *Sarcophagus of Junius Bassus* reminds us that Early Christian art appears throughout the Mediterranean basin in what we think of as the classical world. During the first five centuries after Jesus' death, the art of the entire area was more or less unified in content and style. Increasing political and religious divisions in the region, however, began to affect artistic production, so that it is appropriate to recognize the appearance, or, perhaps better stated, the growth of another branch of Christian art that we label Byzantine.

Byzantine Art

Early Byzantine Art

No clear-cut geographical or chronological line separates Early Christian and Byzantine art. West Roman and East Roman—or as some scholars prefer to call them, Western and Eastern Christian—traits are difficult to distinguish before the sixth century. Until that time, both geographical areas contributed to the development of Early Christian art. As the Western Empire declined, however, cultural leadership tended to shift to the Eastern Empire. This process was accomplished during the reign of Justinian, who ruled the Eastern Empire from 527 to 565. Under his patronage, Constantinople gained stature as the artistic as well as the political capital of the empire. The grandeur of the monuments he sponsored justifies the claim that his era was a Golden Age.

Ironically, the greatest number of early Byzantine monuments survives today not in the former Constantinople (now Istanbul), where much has been destroyed, but on Italian soil, in Ravenna. That town had become the capital of the West Roman emperors at the beginning of the fifth century; when Rome was sacked by the Visigoths in 410, the capital of the Western Empire moved farther north, first to Milan, then finally to Ravenna. At the end of the century Ravenna was taken by Theodoric, king of the Ostrogoths, whose tastes were patterned after those of Constantinople, where he had lived for some time.

The Ostrogothic rule of Ravenna ended in 540, when the Byzantine general Belisarius conquered the city for Justinian. Ravenna became an exarchate, or provincial capital, the main stronghold of Byzantine rule in Italy. Thus, Ravenna serves as a kind of microcosm of the transformation and divisions of the later Roman Empire.

SAN VITALE The most important building of the early Byzantine period, begun in 526 under Ostrogothic rule, was the church of San Vitale. Built chiefly during the 540s and completed in 547, it represents a Byzantine building of a type derived mainly from Constantinople, the Byzantine capital. The octagonal plan with a circular core ringed by an ambulatory derives from buildings such as Santa Costanza in Rome (see fig. 8.5), compared to which San Vitale is both larger in scale and significantly richer in spatial effect (**fig. 8.10**). In particular, below the clerestory, the nave wall turns into a series of semicircular niches that penetrate the ambulatory and thus link that surrounding aisle to the nave in a new and intricate way (**fig. 8.11**). The movement enlivens the central space so that the decorated surfaces seem to pulsate. The aisle has a second story, the galleries,

8.10 Exterior, San Vitale. 526–547 CE. Ravenna, Italy

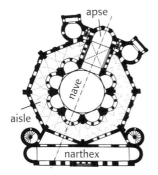

Ground plan and section of San Vitale, Ravenna, Italy

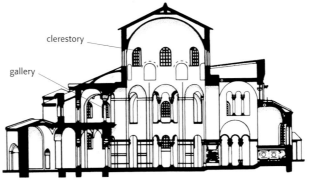

which may have been reserved for women. This reflects a practice in a number of Eastern religions, including some forms of Judaism, in which it is current even today. A new economy in the construction of the vaulting—hollow clay tubes allowing for a lighter structure—permits large windows on every level, resulting in a flood of light in the interior.

Only remnants of the longitudinal axis of the Early Christian basilica are reflected in the plan of San Vitale: Toward the east, a cross-vaulted compartment for the altar, backed by an apse; and on the other side, a narthex. How did it happen that the East favored a type of church building (as distinct from mausoleums) so different from the basilica and—from the Western point of view—so ill adapted to Christian ritual? After all, had not the design of the basilica been backed by the authority of Constantine himself? A number of reasons present themselves: Practical, religious, and political. All of them may be relevant, but none is fully persuasive. In any event, from the time of Justinian, domed, central-plan churches dominated the

world of Orthodox Christianity as thoroughly as the basilican plan dominated the architecture of the medieval West.

At San Vitale the odd, nonaligned placement of the narthex, which has never been fully explained, might be a key to helping us understand how the building functioned. Some have suggested that the narthex is turned so as to be parallel to an atrium, the axis of which was determined by site limitations. Others see it as a conscious design feature that accentuates the transition between the exterior and interior of the church. Whatever the reason, in order to enter the building visitors were forced to change axis, shifting to the right or left in order to align themselves with the main apse. The alteration of the journey into the building is unsettling, almost disorienting, an effect heightened by passing from the lighted area of the narthex to the shaded ambulatory, and then into the high and luminous domed center space. The passage from physical to spiritual realms so essential to worship manifests itself as a separation between the external world and the internal space of the building.

8.11 Interior (view from the apse), San Vitale, Ravenna, Italy

 Explore the architectural panoramas of San Vitale on myartslab.com

Lavish decoration complements the complexity of the interior architecture. Two prominent mosaics flanking the altar (**figs. 8.12** and **8.13**) link San Vitale with the Byzantine court. They depict Justinian and his empress, Theodora, accompanied by officials, the local clergy, and ladies-in-waiting, about to enter the church, as if it were a palace chapel. In these large panels, the design of which probably came from an imperial workshop, we find an ideal of beauty that differs significantly from the squat, large-headed figures seen in the art of the fourth and fifth centuries. These tall,

8.12 *Emperor Justinian and His Attendants.* ca. 547 CE. Mosaic. San Vitale, Ravenna, Italy

8.13 *Empress Theodora and Her Attendants.* ca. 547 CE. Mosaic. San Vitale, Ravenna, Italy

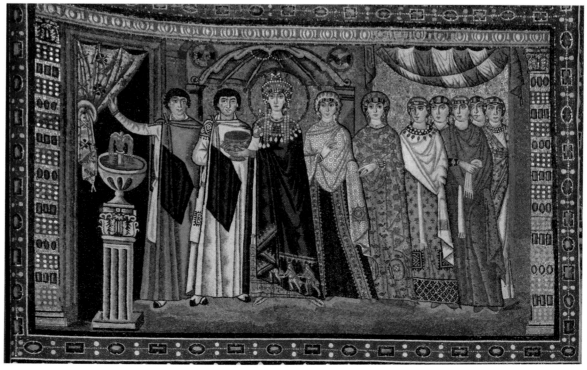

slim figures with tiny feet and small almond-shaped faces dominated by huge eyes seem capable only of making ceremonial gestures and displaying magnificent costumes. There is no hint of movement or change. The dimensions of time and earthly space, suggested by a green ground, give way to an eternal present in the form of a golden, otherworldly setting. Hence the solemn, frontal images seem to belong as much to a celestial court as to a secular one. The quality of soaring slenderness that endows the figures with an air of mute exaltation is shared by the mysterious interior space that they inhabit.

The union of political and spiritual authority expressed in the mosaics of San Vitale reflects the "divine kingship" of the Byzantine emperor and honors the royal couple as donors of the church. It is as though the mosaic figures are participating in the liturgy, despite the fact that the empress and emperor are actually hundreds of miles away. The embroidered hem of Theodora's mantle shows the three Magi carrying their gifts to Mary and the newborn King, and like them the imperial couple bring offerings. Justinian brings bread and Theodora a chalice, undoubtedly references to the Eucharist. The emperor is flanked by 12 companions, the imperial equivalent of the 12 apostles.

Moreover, Justinian is portrayed in a manner that recalls Constantine, the first Christian emperor: The shield with Christ's monogram equates Justinian's conquest of Ravenna with the divinely inspired Constantinian triumph that ultimately led to the founding of Constantinople, the court to which Justinian was heir.

HAGIA SOPHIA Among the surviving monuments of Justinian's reign in Constantinople, the most important by far is Hagia Sophia (the Church of the Holy Wisdom) (**figs. 8.14** and **8.15**). The first church on that site was commissioned by Constantine but destroyed in 532 during rioting that almost

8.14 Anthemius of Tralles and Isidorus of Miletus. Plan, Hagia Sophia, Istanbul. 532–37 CE (after V. Sybel)

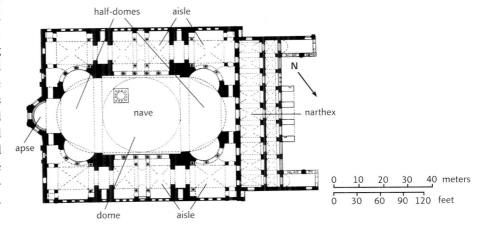

8.15 Exterior, Hagia Sophia, Istanbul

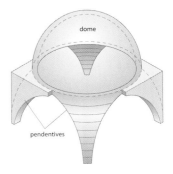

Pendentives are the curved triangular sections that arc up from the corners of a square area to form a rounded base from which a dome springs. Such a construction is called a "pendentive dome" or "dome on pendentives."

 Watch an architectural simulation of pendentives on myartslab.com

8.16 Interior, Hagia Sophia, Istanbul

Read the document related to the Church of Hagia Sophia on myartslab.com

deposed the emperor of the time; he immediately rebuilt the church, a sign of the continuity of his imperial authority. Completed in only five years, Hagia Sophia achieved such fame that the names of the architects, too, were remembered: Anthemius of Tralles, an expert in geometry and the theory of statics and kinetics; and Isidorus of Miletus, who taught physics and wrote on vaulting techniques. The dome collapsed in the earthquake of 558, and a new, taller one was built from a design by Isidorus' nephew. After the Turkish conquest in 1453, the church became a mosque. At that time the Turks added four minarets and extra buttresses to the exterior (see fig. 8.15), as well as large medallions with Islamic invocations on the interior (**fig. 8.16**). In the twentieth century, after the building was turned into a museum, some of the mosaic decoration that was largely hidden under whitewash was uncovered.

Hagia Sophia has the longitudinal axis of an Early Christian basilica, but the central feature of the nave is a vast, squarish space crowned by a huge dome. At either end are half-domes, arranged so that the nave takes the form of a great ellipse. Attached to the half-domes are semicircular apses with open **arcades**, series of arches, similar to those in San Vitale. One might say, then, that the dome of Hagia Sophia has been placed over a central space and, at the same time, inserted between the two halves of a divided central-plan church. The dome rests on four arches that carry its weight to the piers, large, upright architectural supports, at the corners of the square. Thus the brilliant gold mosaic walls below these arches, pierced with windows, have no weight-bearing function at all and act as mere curtains. The transition from the square formed by the arches to the circular rim of the dome is achieved by spherical triangles called **pendentives**. This device, along with a new technique for building domes using thin bricks embedded in mortar, permits the construction of taller, lighter, and more economical domes than the older method of placing the dome on a round or polygonal base as, for example, in the Pantheon (see fig. 7.18).

Where or when the dome on pendentives was invented we do not know. Hagia Sophia is the earliest example we have of its use on a monumental scale, and it had a lasting impact. It became a basic feature of Byzantine architecture and, later, of Western architecture as well. Its massive exterior, firmly planted upon the earth like a great mound,

rises by stages to a height of 184 feet—41 feet taller than the Pantheon—and therefore its dome, though its diameter is somewhat smaller (112 feet), stands out far more boldly in its urban setting.

Once we are inside Hagia Sophia (see fig. 8.16), all sense of weight disappears. Nothing remains but a space that inflates, like so many sails, the apses, the pendentives, and the dome itself. Here the architectural aesthetic we saw taking shape in Early Christian architecture has achieved a new, magnificent dimension. Even more than before, light plays a key role. The dome seems to float—"like the radiant heavens," according to a contemporary description—because it rests upon a closely spaced row of windows; light, both real and reflected, virtually separates the dome from the arches on which it rests. So many openings pierce the nave walls that the effect is akin to the transparency of lace curtains. The purpose of all this is clear. As Procopius, the court historian to Justinian, wrote: "Whenever one enters this church to pray, he understands at once that it is not by any human power or skill, but by the influence of God, that this work has been so finely turned. And so his mind is lifted up toward God and exalted, feeling that He cannot be far away, but must especially love to dwell in this place that He has chosen." We can sense the new aesthetic even in ornamental details such as moldings and capitals. The scrolls, acanthus leaves, and similar decorations are motifs derived from classical architecture, but their effect here is radically different. The heavily patterned butterfly-marble facing of the piers denies their substantiality, and instead of actively cushioning the impact of heavy weight on the shaft of the column, the capital has become like an openwork basket of starched lace, the delicate surface pattern of which belies the strength and solidity of the stone.

The guiding principle of Graeco-Roman architecture had been to express a balance of opposing forces, rather like the balance within the *contrapposto* of a classical statue. The result was a muscular display of active and passive members. In comparison, the material structure of Byzantine architecture, and to some extent of Early Christian architecture as well, is subservient to the creation of immaterial space. Walls and vaults seem like weightless shells, their actual thickness and solidity hidden rather than emphasized. And the glitter of the mosaics must have completed the illusion of unreality, fitting the spirit of these interiors to perfection.

8.17 *The Archangel Michael,* leaf of a diptych. Early sixth century CE. Ivory, 17 × 5½" (43.3 × 14 cm). The British Museum, London

SCULPTURE Beyond architectural decorations and some sarcophagi, Early Byzantine sculpture consists mainly of reliefs in ivory and silver, which survive in considerable numbers. An ivory relief of *The Archangel Michael* (**fig. 8.17**), from the time of Justinian, looks back to earlier classical ivories. It may have been paired with a missing panel showing Justinian, who, it has been suggested, commissioned it. The inscription above has the prayer "Receive these gifts, and having learned the cause…," which would probably have continued on the missing leaf with a plea to forgive the owner's sins, apparently a reference to the emperor's humility. In any event, this ivory must have been carved around 520–530 by an imperial workshop in Constantinople.

The majestic archangel is a descendant of the winged Victories and deities of Graeco-Roman art, down to the rich drapery revealing lithe limbs (see figs. 5.17 and 5.30). Here classicism has become an eloquent vehicle for Christian content. The power the angel heralds is not of this world, nor does he inhabit an earthly space. The niche he occupies has lost all three-dimensional reality. His relationship to it is purely symbolic and ornamental, so that, given the position of the feet on the steps, he seems to hover rather than stand. From the ankles down he appears to be situated between the columns, while his arms and wings are in front of them. It is this disembodied quality, conveyed through harmonious forms, that makes the archangel Michael's presence so compelling. The paradox of a believable figure represented naturalistically but existing within an ambiguous, indeed impossible, setting connects this work with other products of Justinian's court, such as those buildings where solid structures serve to create ephemeral spaces.

ILLUSTRATED BOOKS Illustrated books of the early Byzantine period also contain echoes of Graeco-Roman style adapted to religious narrative. The most important example, the *Vienna Genesis* (**fig. 8.18**), a Greek text of the first book of the Bible, has a richness similar to the mosaics we have seen. White highlights and fluttering drapery that clings to the bodies animate the scene. The book was written in silver (now tarnished black) and decorated with brilliantly colored miniatures on dyed purple vellum, a color reserved for the imperial court. Although some experts have suggested that an imperial scriptorium in

Constantinople produced the manuscript, recent research points to Syria as the more likely source because of parallels to manuscripts produced there and mosaics located there.

Our page shows a number of scenes from the story of Jacob. In the center foreground Jacob wrestles with the angel and then receives the angel's blessing. Hence the picture does not show just a single event but a whole sequence. The scenes play out along a U-shaped path, so that progression in space becomes progression in time. This method, known as **continuous narration**, extends back as far as ancient Egypt and Mesopotamia. Its appearance in miniatures such as this may reflect earlier illustrations created in scroll rather than book form, although this hypothesis has been highly contested. The picture certainly looks like a frieze turned back upon itself. For manuscript illustration, continuous narrative makes the most economical use of space. The painter can pack a maximum number of scenes into a small area, and the picture as a running account can be read like lines of text, rather than as a window that requires a frame.

ICONS The religious **icon** (from the Greek word *eikon*, meaning "image") provided another focus for representation at the time of Justinian. As objects of personal as well as public veneration, icons generally depicted Christ, the Enthroned Madonna, or saints. From the beginning they were considered portraits and developed in Early Christian times out of Graeco-Roman portrait panels. The potential perception of these objects as idols led to arguments about their appropriateness and their power. These discussions related to contemporary debates on the dual nature of Christ as God and man, at once both spiritual and physical. A chief argument favoring image production claimed that Christ had appeared with the Virgin to St. Luke and permitted him to paint their portrait together, and that other portraits of Christ or of the Virgin had miraculously appeared on earth by divine command. These "true" sacred images were considered sources for the later ones made by human artists, permitting a chain of copies and copies of copies, which has often made it difficult for art historians to date them.

Icons functioned as living images to instruct and inspire the worshiper. Because the actual figure—whether Christ, Mary, a saint, or an angel—was thought to reside in the image, the faithful believed

8.18 *Jacob Wrestling the Angel.* Page from the *Vienna Genesis.* Early sixth century CE. Tempera and silver on dyed vellum, 13¼ × 9½" (33.6 × 24.1 cm). Österreichische Nationalbibliothek, Vienna

the icon could intercede on their behalf. Because they were reputed to have miraculous healing properties, some were carried into battle or placed over city gates, effectively offering totemic protection to their communities. In describing an icon of the archangel Michael, the sixth-century poet Agathias writes: "The wax remarkably has represented the invisible. ... The viewer can directly venerate the archangel [and] trembles as if in his actual presence. The eyes encourage deep thoughts; through art and its colors the innermost prayer of the viewer is passed to the image."

Zealots (see below) intentionally destroyed most early examples and the resulting scarcity of these objects hinders our understanding of the origins of icons. The irony of this is particularly poignant, since early icons were painted in encaustic, the medium in which pigment is suspended in hot wax, chosen for its durability.

8.19 *Christ Icon*. Sixth century CE. Encaustic on panel, 34 × 17⅞" (84 × 45.5 cm). Monastery of St. Catherine, Mount Sinai, Egypt

Read the document about painting icons on myartslab.com

Many of the surviving early examples come from the Monastery of St. Catherine at Mount Sinai, Egypt, the isolated desert location of which aided the survival of numerous objects. A *Christ Icon* (**fig. 8.19**), generally dated to sometime in the sixth century but with later repainting, is magnificent for its freshness of color and vibrancy of brushstroke. Its link with Graeco-Roman portraiture is clear not only from the use of encaustic but also from the gradations of light and shade in Christ's face and on his neck, reminiscent of the treatment of the woman in the Roman Fayum portrait, also in encaustic (see fig. 7.23). The combination of a frontal, unflinching gaze, establishing a direct bond with the viewer, with the lively and lifelike modeling of the face suggests the kind of dichotomy between the spiritual and the physical that we have seen in so much early Byzantine art. The enormous gold halo hovering over an architectural background accentuates this dichotomy. It is as if the walls retreat into the background in response to the halo and in order to allow space for Christ.

The Iconoclastic Controversy

After the time of Justinian, the development of Byzantine art—not only painting but sculpture and architecture as well—was disrupted by the Iconoclastic Controversy. The conflict, which began with an edict promulgated by the Byzantine emperor Leo III in 726 prohibiting religious images, raged for more than a hundred years between two hostile groups. The image destroyers, called iconoclasts, led by the emperor and supported mainly in the eastern provinces, insisted on a literal interpretation of the biblical ban against graven images because their use encouraged idolatry. They wanted to restrict religious art to abstract symbols and plant or animal forms. Their opponents, the iconophiles, were led by the monks and were particularly centered in the western provinces, where the imperial edict remained ineffective for the most part. The strongest argument in favor of icons claimed that because Christ and his image are inseparable, the honor given to the image is transferred to him.

The roots of the argument went very deep. Theologically, they involved the basic issue of the relationship of the human and the divine in the person of Christ. Moreover, there was resentment that, for many, icons had come to replace the Eucharist as the focus of lay devotion. Socially and politically, the conflict was a power struggle between Church and State, organizations in theory united in the figure of the emperor. The conflict came during a low point in Byzantine power, when the empire had been greatly diminished by the rise of Islam. Iconoclasm, it was argued, was justified by Leo's victories over the Arabs, who were themselves, ironically, iconoclasts. The controversy caused an irreparable break between Catholicism and the Orthodox faith.

If the edict barring images had been enforced throughout the empire, it might well have dealt Byzantine religious art a fatal blow. It did succeed in greatly reducing the production of sacred images, but failed to wipe it out entirely, so there was a fairly rapid recovery after the victory of the iconophiles in 843.

Middle Byzantine Art

While we know little for certain about how the Byzantine artistic tradition managed to survive from the early eighth to the mid-ninth century, iconoclasm seems to have brought about a renewed interest in secular art, which was not affected by the ban. This may help to explain the astonishing appearance of antique motifs in the art of the Middle Byzantine period, sometimes referred to as the Second Golden Age. A revival of Byzantine artistic traditions, as well as of classical learning and literature, followed the years of iconoclasm and lasted from the late ninth to the eleventh century. This revival, spearheaded by Basil I the Macedonian, was underscored by the reopening of the university in Constantinople. This period is something of a renaissance, with much of its vigor credited to Constantine VII. Emperor in name only for most of his life, he devoted his energies instead to art and scholarship.

ILLUSTRATED BOOKS *David Composing the Psalms* (**fig. 8.20**) is one of eight full-page scenes in the mid-tenth century *Paris Psalter*. Illustrating the biblical King David's life, these scenes introduce the Psalms, which David was thought to have composed. Not only do we find a landscape that recalls Pompeian murals, but the figures, too, clearly derive from Roman models. David himself could well be mistaken for Orpheus charming the beasts with his music. His companions are even more surprising, since they are allegorical figures that have nothing to do with the Bible. The young woman next to David is the personification of Melody, the

one coyly hiding behind a pillar is the mountain nymph Echo, and the male figure with a tree trunk personifies the mountains of Bethlehem.

Once again style promotes meaning in the way consciously classical forms herald the revival of image making after iconoclasm. But despite the revivalist aspects, the late date of the picture is evident from certain qualities of style, such as the crowded composition of space-consuming figures and the abstract zigzag pattern of the drapery covering Melody's legs. In truth, one might well ask to what extent and how, despite iconoclasm, antique methods and forms survived—that is, how much of what we see is the result of continuities rather than revivals.

8.20 *David Composing the Psalms*, from the *Paris Psalter*. ca. 950 CE. Tempera on vellum, 14⅛ × 10¼″ (36 × 26 cm). Bibliothèque Nationale, Paris

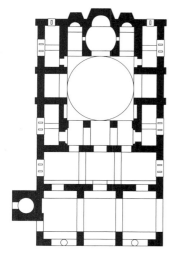

Plan of the church of the Dormition, Daphni

8.21 *Christ Pantocrator*. Late eleventh century CE. Dome mosaics. Church of the Dormition, Daphni, Greece

ARCHITECTURE AND ITS DECORATION Byzantine architecture never produced another structure to match the scale of Hagia Sophia. The churches built after the Iconoclastic Controversy were initially modest in scale and usually built for communities of monks, perhaps reflecting the fact that monks had been important in arguing against iconoclasm; later monasteries erected in Constantinople under imperial patronage were much larger and served social purposes as schools and hospitals. The monastic Church of the Dormition (meaning the "falling asleep" of Mary) at Daphni, near Athens in Greece, follows the usual Middle Byzantine plan of a Greek cross contained within a square, but with a narthex added on one side and an apse on the other. The central feature is a dome on a cylinder, or **drum**. The drum raises the dome high above the rest of the building and demonstrates a preference for elongated proportions. The impact of this verticality, however, strikes us fully only when we enter the church. The tall, narrow compartments produce both an unusually active space, with abrupt changes of light and shade, and a sense of compression. This feeling is dramatically relieved as we raise our glance toward the luminous pool of space beneath the dome, which draws us around and upward (**fig. 8.21**). The suspended dome of Hagia Sophia is clearly the conceptual precedent for this form.

The mosaics inside the church at Daphni are some of the finest works of the Second Golden Age. They show a dignity and gravity that merges harmoniously with the spiritualized ideal of human beauty evident in the art of Justinian's reign. For instance, the classical qualities of the mosaic of *The Crucifixion* (**fig. 8.22**) are deeply felt, yet they are also completely Christian. There is no attempt to create a realistic spatial setting, but the composition has a balance and clarity that are truly monumental. The heroic nudity of Christ and the statuesque dignity of the two flanking figures make them seem extraordinarily organic and graceful compared to the stiff poses in the Justinian and Theodora mosaics at San Vitale (see figs. 8.12 and 8.13).

The most important aspect of the classical heritage in Middle Byzantine depiction is emotional rather than physical. This is evident in the new interest in representing the crucified Christ, that is, the Christ of the Passion. In the Daphni *Crucifixion* mosaic, Christ is flanked by the Virgin and St. John. The gestures and facial expressions of all three figures convey a restrained and noble suffering. We cannot say when and where this human interpretation of the Savior first appeared, but it seems to have developed in the wake of the Iconoclastic Controversy. A few earlier examples of the scene survive, but none appeals to the emotions of the viewer so powerfully as the Daphni *Crucifixion*. The introduction of this compassionate view of Christ into sacred depiction ranks perhaps as the greatest achievement of Middle Byzantine art.

Alongside the new emphasis on the Christ of the Passion, the Second Golden Age accorded importance to the image of Christ Pantocrator, an oversize, awesome (though heavily restored) mosaic image of which stares down from the center of the dome at Daphni against a gold background (see fig. 8.21). In his role as Pantocrator Christ functions as both Judge and Ruler of the Universe, the All-Holder who contains everything. The type descends from images of the bearded Zeus. The bearded face of Jesus first appears during the sixth century, and we have already seen an early example in the icon from Mount Sinai (see fig. 8.19). Once again tradition and innovation mark Middle Byzantine achievements.

The decoration at Daphni, magnificent as it is, survives only in a fragmentary state. The Venetians desecrated the church in 1207 and in the 1890s earthquakes severely damaged it. As a result of these vicissitudes, the mosaics were heavily restored and the marble revetment that covered the walls is now missing, the exposed stone and brick giving the building a too-sturdy aspect. Also missing, since Daphni lacks the monastic community that was responsible for its creation—today it is a museum—is the experiential quality of chanting clergy, burning incense, and glittering liturgical objects of precious metals.

Late Byzantine Art

In 1204, Byzantium suffered an almost fatal defeat when the armies of the Fourth Crusade, instead of warring against the Turks, captured and sacked the city of Constantinople. For more than 50 years, the core of the Eastern Empire remained in Western hands. Byzantium, however, survived this catastrophe. In 1261 it regained its independence, which lasted until the Turkish conquest in 1453. The fourteenth century saw a last flowering of Byzantine painting under a series of enlightened rulers.

ICONS Because icons were objects of veneration, and because they embodied sacredness, they had to conform to strict rules, with fixed patterns repeated over and over again. As a result, most icons are noteworthy more for exacting craftsmanship than artistic inventiveness.

An icon from Ohrid, in Macedonia, though probably made in Constantinople, illustrates a type distinct from those we have seen previously in that it relates a narrative event, the Annunciation to the Virgin of her imminent role as Mother of God (**fig. 8.23**). Interest in narrative subjects for icons increases at this time and might derive from the elaborate decorative programs in Middle Byzantine churches. This icon is bilateral (or two-sided). On the other side, the Virgin Mary, to whom the church at Ohrid was dedicated, is represented holding her son. Such icons were probably meant to be mounted on a pole, both for processions and for placement within churches, where worshipers would have been able to view both sides.

The gold background heightens the tension of the spatial relationship established between the archangel Gabriel and the Virgin. The former both cuts through space and slides across it, while the latter seems boxed in by the canopy that frames

8.22 *The Crucifixion.* Late eleventh century CE. Mosaic. Church of the Dormition, Daphni, Greece

and encloses her. In the sharpness of their folds, Gabriel's garments appear almost metallic. These contrast with the dark robes of the Virgin. One can imagine how moved a viewer might have been by personal contact with this imposing icon, which measures more than 3 feet high.

MOSAICS AND MURAL PAINTING The finest surviving cycles of Late Byzantine mosaics and paintings are found in Istanbul's Kariye Camii, the former church of the Savior in the Chora Monastery. (*Kariye* is the Turkish adaptation of the ancient Greek word *chora*, which refers to the countryside, that is, outside the city walls; *camii* denotes a mosque, to which the building was converted after the Turkish conquest.) These particular mosaics and paintings represent the climax of the Humanism that emerged in Middle Byzantine art. Theodore Metochites, a scholar and poet who was prime minister to the emperor Andronicus II,

restored the church and paid for its decorations at the beginning of the fourteenth century.

The wall paintings in the mortuary chapel attached to Kariye Camii are especially impressive. Some have suggested that because of the Empire's greatly reduced resources, murals often took the place of mosaics, but at Kariye Camii they are of equal value and may even have been designed by the same artist. The main scene depicts the traditional Byzantine image of the *Anastasis* (**fig. 8.24**), the event just before the Resurrection, which Western Christians call the Descent into Limbo or the Harrowing of Hell, clearly a fitting subject for the funerary setting. Surrounded by a **mandorla**, a radiant almond shape, Christ has vanquished Satan and battered down the gates of Hell. (Note the bound Satan at his feet, in the midst of a profusion of hardware; the two kings to the left are David and Solomon.) The central group of Christ raising Adam and Eve from the dead has tremendous dramatic force; Christ moves with extraordinary physical energy, tearing Adam and Eve from their graves, so that they appear to fly through the air—a magnificently expressive image of divine triumph.

Such dynamism had been unknown in the Early Byzantine tradition, although the emotional force of Middle Byzantine painting might well have prepared the way for the vivacity of the Kariye Camii

8.23 *Annunciation to the Virgin*, from Church of the Virgin Peribleptos, Ohrid, Macedonia. Early fourteenth century CE. Tempera on panel, 36⅝ × 26¾" (93 × 68 cm). Icon Gallery, Ohrid

8.24 *Anastasis*. ca. 1310–20 CE. Fresco. Kariye Camii (Church of the Savior in the Chora Monastery), Istanbul

representations. Coming in the fourteenth century, this Late Byzantine style shows that 800 years after Justinian, when the Anastasis first appeared as a subject, Byzantine art still had all its creative powers. Thus, despite the diverse uses it served, its long chronological spread, and the different cultures and wide geographic areas it spanned, Byzantine art continued to preserve long-established traditions. Indeed, its durability verges on the immutable.

POINTS OF REFLECTION

8.1 Interpret how catacomb paintings reflect the concerns, both hopes and fears, of Early Christians.

8.2 Compare and contrast the Early Christian basilica of Old St. Peter's with a Roman basilica.

8.3 Analyze the Iconoclastic Controversy, explaining why it came about and what effect it had on artistic production.

8.4 Explain how pendentives are used in Hagia Sophia and analyze their engineering and aesthetic functions.

8.5 Compare and contrast how figures are represented on the *Christ Icon* from the Monastery of St. Catherine at Mount Sinai and the *Annunciation to the Virgin* icon from the Church of the Virgin Peribleptos in Ohrid.

✓●─ **Study** and review on myartslab.com

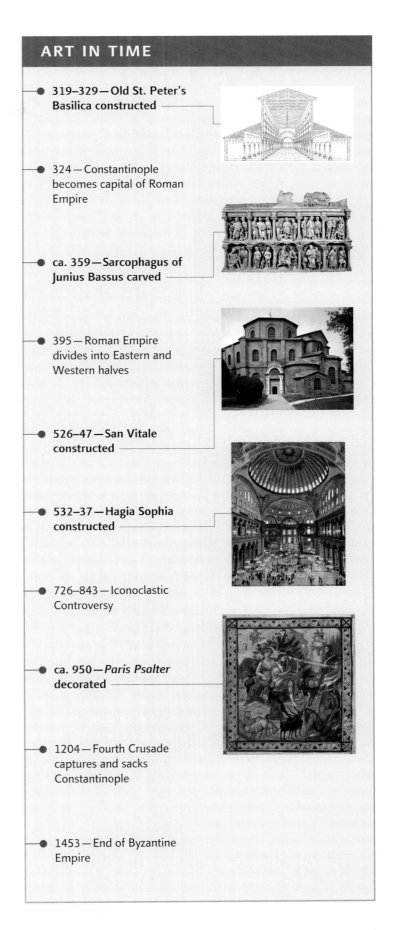

ART IN TIME

● **319–329**—Old St. Peter's Basilica constructed

● **324**—Constantinople becomes capital of Roman Empire

● **ca. 359**—Sarcophagus of Junius Bassus carved

● **395**—Roman Empire divides into Eastern and Western halves

● **526–47**—San Vitale constructed

● **532–37**—Hagia Sophia constructed

● **726–843**—Iconoclastic Controversy

● **ca. 950**—*Paris Psalter* decorated

● **1204**—Fourth Crusade captures and sacks Constantinople

● **1453**—End of Byzantine Empire

9 Islamic Art

POINTS OF INQUIRY

9.1 Identify the unifying themes that govern Islamic art.

9.2 Consider the reliance of Islamic artists on the art of other cultures and religions.

9.3 Describe the origins of the mosque as a building type.

9.4 Summarize the regional types of Islamic art.

9.5 Recognize the importance of decoration in the Islamic world.

((•—[**Listen** to the chapter audio on myartslab.com

The religion known as Islam took form in the early seventh century on the Arabian peninsula. A scant 30 years after the death of its founder, the Prophet Muhammad (also known as the Messenger), in 632, Arab warriors had carried the new faith into much of today's Middle East. A century after the death of the Prophet, Islam had spread across Africa into Spain in the west, and into the Indus Valley and Central Asia in the east. The cultural complexity of today's Islamic world existed almost from the beginning (see **map 9.1**).

Examining the formation of Islamic art gives us an intriguing look at the phenomenon of syncretism in art history, the process whereby a new artistic tradition emerges as a creative combination of previously existing artistic ideas under the impetus of a new ideology. As with Christian art, Islamic art first took form as a series of appropriations of preexisting traditions from other cultures molded into a new synthesis, in the service both of the new Islamic religion and Islamic princes.

The vast geographical and chronological scope of Islamic art means that it cannot be encompassed in simple definitions. Islam, the religion, is a significant element in Islamic culture, but Islamic art is far more than a religious art; it includes secular elements and elements frowned upon, if not actually forbidden, by some Islamic theologians. Islamic art nonetheless has certain unifying themes. The first of these is reverence for the Word—the Qur'an—and for the language of the Word—Arabic—as reflected in the art of beautiful writing. From the angular, horizontal **kufic** alphabet of early Islam to complex cursive styles developed in later times, Islamic art, both secular and religious, shows a remarkable affinity for the written word, be it scripture or secular narrative poetry (see box: Cultural Context: Islam: Beliefs and Practices, page 190). A second theme is the development of artistic expression independent of the human figure, given the mistrust of figural images in many Islamic religious traditions. Islamic art employs sophisticated and complex vocabularies of vegetal, floral, and geometric designs used in conjunction with beautiful writing. A third theme is the equality of genres. To understand and appreciate Islamic art we need to discard the notion of the primacy of (figural) painting and (figural) sculpture in the European tradition. In the Islamic world, the arts of ceramics, metalware, weaving, and carving in precious materials rank with other mediums in an artistic spectrum devoid of the formal hierarchy

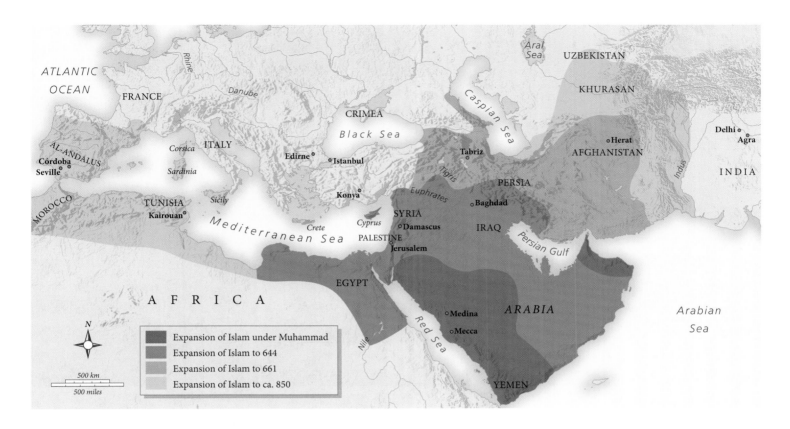

Map 9.1 The expansion of Islam to 850

that in the West led to a distinction between "fine arts" and "decorative arts."

The Formation of Islamic Art

Islamic art first took shape as a series of appropriations of preexisting Graeco-Roman, Byzantine Christian, and Sasanian (see page 194) forms. These were molded into a new synthesis to serve the needs of the new Islamic religion and the desires and political goals of Islamic princes.

Religious Architecture

The new religion required certain types of distinctive buildings, such as a place for community prayers that was visually identified with the new faith. The new Islamic rulers needed dwellings appropriate to their power and wealth. Eventually, the faith would also require commemorative buildings that memorialized great rulers, holy men, or historic events. As such, Islamic architecture came to develop a rich variety of forms and genres, and a distinctive repertoire of decoration that became emblematic of the faith itself.

The earliest major Islamic building to have survived into our time, the Dome of the Rock in Jerusalem (**fig. 9.1**), is a case in point. After the Arabian cities of Mecca and Medina, Jerusalem was the holiest Islamic site. For the first Muslims, the Temple Mount in Jerusalem marked the place where God tested Ibrahim's (Abraham's) faith by demanding the sacrifice of his first-born son Ismail. From the same site, according to later Islamic legend, the Prophet was taken by Gabriel on a *mi'raj* (spiritual journey) to experience both Heaven and Hell, Muhammad being the only mortal allowed to see these places before death. It is far from a coincidence that the Dome of the Rock is built on Mount Moriah in Jerusalem, the original site of the First (Solomon's) and Second (Herod's) Temples, the geographic center of the Jewish faith (see page 42–43). It is also far from a coincidence that the domed silhouette and ringlike plan of the Dome of the Rock echo the form of the Holy Sepulcher, a Constantinian foundation, just a few hundred yards to the west, which marked the burial place of Christ. The Dome of the Rock was constructed by artists and craftspeople, many of whom were undoubtedly local Christians or new converts to Islam, probably under orders from the Muslim caliph (from the Arabic *khalifa*, meaning "successor") Abd al-Malik sometime around the year 690. Erected on a holy place that was also one of the

9.1 The Dome of the Rock. ca. 690 CE and later. Jerusalem

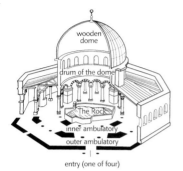

wooden dome

drum of the dome

The Rock

inner ambulatory

outer ambulatory

entry (one of four)

Cutaway drawing of the Dome of the Rock

**SPEAKING OF
pagans, infidels, heathens, and heretics**

To Early Christians and Muslims, all believers in polytheistic religions were called infidels, or unbelievers. In Early Christian Rome and during the Middle Ages, unbelievers were known either as pagans ("unenlightened ones," from the Latin *paganus*, "country dweller") or heathens (those who were not Christian, Jewish, or Muslim). Although, strictly speaking, the words pagan and heathen are synonyms, the former is often— including in this book—reserved for classical antiquity, the latter for northern Europe. Heretics, by contrast, are the faithful who hold opinions contrary to orthodox doctrine.

highest points in the city, it eloquently proclaimed that Jerusalem was under the control of Islam.

A closer look at the building shows both the nature of early Islamic appropriation of Roman and Christian forms, as well as the impact of the Messenger's views on the visual arts. The ground plan of the building, with its two ambulatories around the central bare rock, ideal for organizing visits of large numbers of pilgrims to the shrine, recalls not only the Holy Sepulcher but also Late Roman and Early Christian central-plan domed structures, such as Santa Costanza in Rome (see fig. 8.5). The dome of the shrine itself was a well-established symbol for the vault of heaven, especially appropriate given the ultimate goal of the Messenger's mystical and spiritual journey. The columns and capitals, recycled from classical monuments, convey an impression of tradition and permanence, wealth and power, to Muslim and non-Muslim alike.

The original mosaic decoration (**fig. 9.2**) consisted of Arabic script, repeating geometric motifs, and highly stylized vegetal and floral elements. Eventually, these design elements would form a distinctively Islamic repertoire of decoration: One was Arabic script, used in the many religious inscriptions. Another was a vocabulary of scrolling vines, leaves, and flowers distantly based on nature, and a third a stock of repeating geometric patterns. These were staples of the art of the classical past

and of the Sasanid Empire, which encompassed today's Iran, Afghanistan, Iraq, and neighboring areas and which was heir to Persian culture. A fourth set of motifs consisted of jewels and jeweled objects, symbols of royalty. But in marked contrast to the Graeco-Roman and Christian religious art traditions, nowhere in the Dome of the Rock do the forms of humans or animals appear. The inscriptions in the Dome of the Rock, taken from the Qur'an, were carefully chosen to underline the importance of the building itself, its symbolic location in a city holy to Jews and Christians as well as Muslims, and its place within a religion and society that saw itself as the culmination of the two earlier scriptural traditions, and which accorded tolerance toward and acceptance of both Christians and Jews (see box: Cultural Context: Islam: Beliefs and Practices, page 190).

THE HYPOSTYLE MOSQUE Of all of the pillars of Islam, the religious duty of prayer proved the most important in the development of Islamic architecture. In major cities such as Damascus, the Arab Umayyad caliphs of early Islam either built or converted from preexisting structures the first great buildings for Muslim public worship, called **mosques** in English (from the Arabic *masjid*, meaning "place of prostration"). These first mosques, designed to contain the entire male population of a

city during the noonday prayer on Friday, recall the form of the Prophet's house in Medina, with a rectangular courtyard, usually surrounded by covered arcades, and a larger hypostyle (many-columned) hall on the *qibla*, the side facing Mecca. The architecture emphasized the equality of all Muslims before God and the absence in Islam of ordained clergy. Unlike Early Christian basilican churches, such as Old St. Peter's (see fig. 8.4), there is little axiality in the early Arab mosques—no long, straight pathway leading to an architectural focus visible throughout the structure. With prayer occurring directly between each worshiper and God, and no ordained clergy or canonized saints to provide intercession, the interior space of the early mosque was essentially determined by practicality, not by

Islam: Beliefs and Practices

ISLAM WAS DEFINED by Muhammad as the culmination of a prophetic tradition that began with God's covenant with Ibrahim (Abraham). The Qur'an prominently mentions many of the major figures of the Hebrew Bible such as Ibrahim (Abraham), Musa (Moses), and Sulayman (Solomon), as well as the prophet 'Isa (Jesus) and his mother Maryam (Mary). Islamic belief is fundamentally very simple: To become a Muslim, one repeats with conviction the phrase, "There is no God but God; Muhammad is the Messenger of God." This Affirmation of Faith is the first of the so-called Five Pillars of Islam. The others are prayer (the five daily prayers and the major weekly prayer at noon on Friday, the Muslim Day of Congregation), fasting (abstention from food and drink during daylight hours for the lunar month of Ramadan), pilgrimage (in Arabic, *hajj*, a journey to Mecca during the lunar month of Dhu'l Hijja), and charity (institutionalized as a formal system of tithing, intended to benefit the sick and needy of the Islamic community).

In addition, early Islam proclaimed three other tenets that were to have a major impact on art. The first was the protected status of the "People of the Book"—Jews and Christians—in Muslim society, as ordained by God in the Qur'an. The second, based on several anecdotes from the Prophet's life, was a profound mistrust of certain images—pictures and statues of humans and animals—as potentially idolatrous, a point of view Islam shares with Judaism, and which influences the history of Christian art as well. The third, held in common with Judaism and contrasting markedly with the Christianity of that time, was a high regard for literacy and the individual's reading and study of scripture, coupled through most of Islamic history with a reverence for the written alphabet—in the case of Islam, the Arabic alphabet, which in early Islam used an angular form of script known as kufic (see illustration). The beauty of the script, with its contrasting thin and thick lines, written from right to left in an almost rhythmic visual cadence, was deemed appropriate for the poetic words of God himself. These three factors, taken in the general context of Islamic belief and early Islamic political history, were to have a profound effect on the molding of the Islamic artistic tradition.

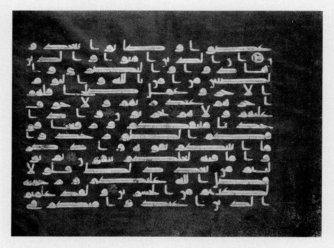

Fragment from a Qur'an with kufic, North African. Tenth century. Vellum, 11 × 14½″ (27.8 × 36.8 cm). Chester Beatty Library, Dublin

 Read the document with an excerpt from the Qur'an on myartslab.com

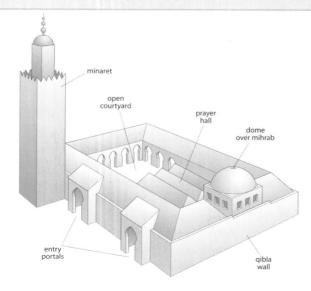

9.3 Schematic drawing of a generic Arab hypostyle mosque

minaret

open courtyard

prayer hall

dome over mihrab

entry portals

qibla wall

ceremony. Thus there was no place for music or processions, though many doors were situated for the maximum convenience of the daily coming and going of worshipers. A simple *minbar* (pulpit) served for the delivery of sermons after the Friday noon prayer, and an empty *mihrab* (niche) in the *qibla* wall was added to indicate the direction of Mecca (**fig. 9.3**). Mats of grass or rushes, and later woolen carpets, often covered the floors (see Materials and Techniques: The Oriental Carpet, opposite). These provided a clean place for the standing, bowing, kneeling, and prostration, with the brief touching of the forehead to the ground, while reciting prayers, that constitute the essence of Islamic worship.

The Oriental Carpet

NO ARTISTIC PRODUCT of the Islamic world is better known outside its original home than the pile carpet, popularly called the oriental carpet. Carpets are heavy textiles meant to be used essentially in the form in which they leave the weaver's loom. Their uses vary extensively from floor coverings to architectural decorations, from cushions and bolsters to bags and sacks of all sizes and shapes, and from animal trappings to religious objects (prayer rugs that provide a clean place for Muslim prayer). They can be used as secular or religious wall decoration. Carpet weaving is a deeply embedded art in the culture of many Islamic societies. Part of the socialization of young women, who form the bulk of Islamic artist-weavers, it is found not only in nomadic encampments and villages, but also in urban commercial weaving establishments and, in former times, in special workshops that functioned directly under court patronage in Islamic lands.

There are several different techniques for weaving Islamic carpets, but the best-known is the pile carpet, in which row after horizontal row of individual knots of colored wool are tied on vertical pairs of warp yarns, and each row of knots is then beaten in place by a beater, a tool that resembles a combination of a comb and a hammer, and subsequently locked in place by the passing of one or more horizontal weft yarns. The ends of each knot protrude vertically on the upper, or "right," side of the carpet, giving it a thick pile surface, at once highly reactive to light, conducive to rich color effects, and providing excellent insulation from cold floors or the earthen ground of a nomad's tent.

The design of a carpet, like that of a picture made on an ink-jet printer, is created out of a grid of colored dots consisting of small individual knots of colored wool that when viewed together form a design. Some carpets are fairly coarse in weave, and use a long pile; such carpets tend to use bold geometric designs and brilliant colors. Other carpets, such as those produced after designs by court or commercial artists, may use a much finer weave (in extreme cases, more than 2,000 knots in a square inch) and a short pile to reproduce curvilinear ornamental designs, calligraphy, or even depictions of humans and animals in large carpets. The symbolism of carpets may be extremely complex, varying from totemic designs of tribal significance to figural designs with arcane religious or secular meanings.

Exported to Europe since the fourteenth century, Islamic pile carpets have historically formed an East–West cultural bridge. In Europe, they not only decorated the palaces of the nobility and the houses of wealthy urban merchants, but were also used in churches, religious shrines, and as part of both secular and religious ceremonies. Islamic carpets, as prized works of art and signs of status and wealth, were frequently depicted in European paintings (see fig. 14.6). Carpet weaving continues to flourish in the Middle East today.

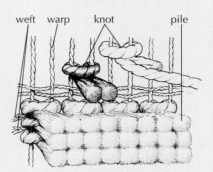

weft warp   knot   pile

The symmetrical knotting structure used in many Turkish and Transcaucasian carpets.

Rows of individual knots, tied over two vertical warps, are tied, cut, and tightly hammered in place and locked in by a pair of horizontal wefts

Village carpet in geometric design, Konya area, Turkey. Eighteenth or nineteenth century. Private collection. Courtesy of Gerard Paquin

Oil lamps provided illumination for the dawn and late evening prayers. Pools or fountains in the courtyard allowed for the ceremonial washing of hands and feet before prayers. In later times, a tower, known in English as a **minaret**, advertised the presence of the mosque and served as a place from which to broadcast the call to prayer given five times a day by a *muezzin*, an individual usually selected for the beauty and power of his voice.

The Development of Islamic Style

By 750, the Muslim Umayyad dynasty, based in Roman Syria, had been supplanted by the Abbasid dynasty, centered in Mesopotamia. Here the new caliphs built their capital, called Baghdad, on the Tigris River. The memory of the original Round City of Baghdad, the site of which lies under the present-day city, lived on in Arabic poetry and prose literature. Under Abbasid rule over the newly extensive Islamic empire the building of mosques in recently conquered areas, including North Africa and Western Europe, particularly Spain, proceeded apace.

Religious Architecture

Chief among the new structures were the large Abbasid congregational mosques that both practically and symbolically served as religious gathering places for prayers, sermons, and religious education. These mosques, many now in ruins, were built all over Iraq, and in Egypt and elsewhere. An archetypal example is the largely ninth-century congregational mosque at Kairouan, a city established under the Abbasids in what is now Tunisia.

GREAT MOSQUE OF KAIROUAN Based, like all major Arab mosques, on the house of the Prophet in Medina and the four-square Mediterranean courtyard house, examples of which today still surround the structure, the Great Mosque of Kairouan consists of a rectangular courtyard surrounded by covered halls, a large hypostyle prayer hall, and a towering minaret (**fig. 9.4**). Two domes mark the area in front of the *mihrab* and in the middle of the prayer hall facing the court. This aside, the multitude of entrances on three sides of the building, built in order to facilitate entry and exit for the five daily prayers, frees the building from the domination of a central axis for processions of clergy; it is thus the very opposite of the early Christian basilican church

9.4 Aerial view of the Great Mosque of Kairouan, Tunisia. Eighth century and later

9.5 Interior of prayer hall, Great Mosque of Córdoba. Eighth century and later

 Watch an architectural simulation of Islamic arches on myartslab.com

9.6 Carved stone grille on *qibla* wall of Great Mosque of Córdoba. Mid-tenth century

(see fig. 8.4), organized for priestly and theatrical ritual. The simplicity of the mosque reflects the simplicity of Islamic prayer, the essential lack of hierarchy among worshipers, and the absence of an ordained clergy in Islam. Each worshiper prays directly to God using a simple ritual formula usually completed in a few minutes. Artistic attention was lavished on the *mihrab*, of carved marble and ceramic tiles, and the *minbar* or pulpit, elaborately carved of Indian teak. In the Kairouan mosque, a carved wooden screen, primarily a product of security rather than ritual needs, encloses a small area near the *mihrab* called the *maqsura*, where the ruler could pray alone.

GREAT MOSQUE OF CÓRDOBA Even farther to the west, in Spain, where the sole surviving prince of the exterminated Umayyad house founded an independent state after 750, a brilliant center of Islamic culture developed in the city of Córdoba, in the southern part of Spain, referred to as al-Andalus (now Andalusia). By the tenth century, the Great Mosque of Córdoba, after a series of embellishments and enlargements, had become a virtual forest of columns (**fig. 9.5**). Its characteristic "horseshoe" arcades are composed of arches using alternating red and white voussoirs, a design which undoubtedly reflects Roman precedents. The

superimposition of one set of arches above another on elongated imposts creates an impression of almost limitless space—this space is, however, composed of relatively small architectural elements repeated again and again. Compared with a Christian structure such as Hagia Sophia (see fig. 8.16) or Old St. Peter's (see fig. 8.4), Córdoba has an equally large interior area, but there is no centralized space for the sacred theater of the Christian rite. The mosque interior, including the *maqsura* area around the *mihrab*, was lavishly decorated with mosaic and carved stone. Tenth-century marble grilles (**fig. 9.6**) on the *qibla* wall present early examples of what we sometimes call geometric arabesque: The artist carves out of marble what is essentially a single straplike line that intertwines, creating a characteristic openwork screen of stars and polygons. In the beauty of such artistic geometry many Muslims see a reflection of God's creative hand in the universe.

Luxury Arts

On the outskirts of Córdoba the Umayyads built another huge Islamic palace city, known as Medina al-Zahra. This palace complex once included royal workshops for luxury objects such as silk textiles and carved ivory, used as symbols of royal wealth

9.7 Ivory casket of al-Mughira, from Córdoba, ca. 960. Height 6″ (15 cm), diameter 3″ (8 cm). Musée du Louvre, Paris

and power and given as royal ceremonial gifts. A small, domed ivory pyxis, or box, made there for a tenth-century Umayyad prince (**fig. 9.7**), incorporates in its decoration a microcosm of Islamic royal imagery and symbolism, including depictions of falconry and hunting, sports, and court musicians, set amid lush carved vegetal ornament and a kufic inscription frieze. Such lavish objects, with their complex, many-layered iconography and their symbolism as royal gifts, had an importance far beyond their practical use as containers for jewelry or cosmetics. Despite, or perhaps because of, their Islamic origins, these luxury objects were greatly appreciated by Christians, and many of them made their way into princely collections and church treasuries. Continual Christian conquest from the north led to a dramatic decline in Muslim power in Spain and by the fourteenth century the Almohad capital of Seville had fallen to the Christian kings of Castile.

Islamic Art and the Persian Inheritance

As we have seen, in the central and western Islamic lands, Spain and the western Mediterranean shore, Islamic arts developed within the geography and culture of the Graeco-Roman tradition; in the east, however, the situation was in many respects quite different. In Mesopotamia and Iran, the Arab Muslim conquerors encountered the cultural sphere of the Sasanians, who had controlled Persia since the third century CE. This tradition included royal imagery of ceremonial pomp, warfare, and the royal sport of hunting (see fig. 2.9), as well as large and impressive palace buildings.

Architecture

In the eastern Islamic world, following pre-Islamic architectural practice, brick rather than stone was the most common construction material. In place of cylindrical columns, massive brick piers often provided vertical structural support in buildings, and heavy vaults rather than tiled wooden-beam roofs were often chosen to cover interior spaces. Islamic architecture in Mesopotamia, Iran, and Central Asia reflects the available materials, earlier cultural traditions, and even the climate of those regions in distinctive ways. It also provides a curious blending of secular and religious buildings; a new form, the *iwan*, came to define both royal and religious structures in the east.

THE FOUR-*IWAN* MOSQUE One of the first large vaulted brick structures with one open side, known as an *iwan*, was constructed by the Sasanian ruler Shapur I as an audience hall for his royal palace at Ctesiphon in Mesopotamia. The form seems originally to have symbolized royal authority in Iran, and under Islam it eventually was incorporated into a new type of prayer structure, the four-*iwan* mosque (**fig. 9.8**), by placing one massive brick recess in the middle of each of the sides of the rectangular courtyard. From the twelfth century onward the four-*iwan* courtyard was a standard feature of both mosques and religious schools of a type known as *madrasa* throughout Iran and Islamic Central Asia.

Figural Art Forms in Iran

The Iranian part of the Islamic world had inherited a rich tradition of material culture, and the successive rulers of Iran, whether themselves Arab, Persian, Turkish, or Mongol in ancestry, fell under the seductive spell of the Persian heritage, which they combined with their Islamic beliefs and traditions. From the prosperous cities of tenth- and eleventh-century Iran there have survived beautiful ceramic wares with calligraphic, figural, and vegetal decoration, as well as some exceptional silk textiles and metal objects. The Seljuk Turkish invaders, who ruled Iran from the

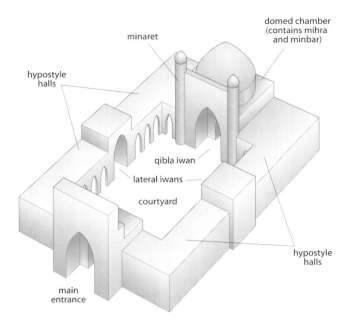

9.8 Cutaway drawing of a generic Persian four-*iwan* mosque

9.9 *Mina'i* dish with story of Bahram Gur and Azadeh, from Iran. ca. 1200. Polychrome overglaze enamels on white composite body. Diameter 8½" (22.2 cm), width 3¹³/₁₆" (9.7 cm). The Metropolitan Museum of Art, New York. Purchase, Rogers Fund and gift of the Schiff Foundation, 1957 57.36.13

mid-eleventh century onward, not only built great mosques and tomb structures, but also ruled over a prosperous urban culture that among other things produced one of the richest known traditions of decorated ceramics. Using figural images in a multitude of sophisticated techniques, including the use of a metallic pigment known as luster fired over the glaze, and polychrome enamel decoration known as *mina'i*, these ceramic wares incorporated for middle-class patrons a very diverse repertoire of scenes from Persian romances and mythology, themes from Sufism (the Islamic mystical religious tradition), and Islamic royal images of hunting and other courtly pleasures. A favorite story finding its way into ceramics, metalwork, and book illustration was that of the royal hunter Bahram Gur and his skeptical sweetheart, the harpist Azadeh. A *mina'i* plate shows two episodes of continuous narrative, with Azadeh on the camel with her royal lover, and then pushed off the beast after making a remark belittling the hero's marksmanship (**fig. 9.9**). To what do we owe this burst of figural art in seeming contradiction to strict Islamic dogma? Practical rather than dogmatic, Iranians under the Seljuks apparently believed that figural images did not necessarily have to be identified with polytheism or idolatry, but could capably serve both secular and religious purposes without morally corrupting the viewer.

The Ottoman Empire

In later Islamic times, a number of large empires, including the Ottoman Empire, formed major centers of Islamic artistic accomplishment. At the end of the thirteenth century, in a corner of Asia Minor just a dozen or so miles from the Byzantine capital of Constantinople, a vassal of the declining Seljuk sultanate named Osman (r. ca. 1281–1324) established a tiny frontier principality hosting warriors eager to expand the realms of Islam at the expense of the Christians. By 1453, what became known as the Ottoman Empire (in Italy, Osman was known as "Ottomano") claimed the elusive prize of Constantinople itself, the capital of Eastern Christianity. In this, their capital city, popularly renamed Istanbul, and in their summer and military capital of Edirne, 120 miles farther west into Europe, the Ottomans used their enormous economic power to patronize art and architecture on an unprecedented scale.

9.10 Sinan the Great. Cutaway drawing of the Mosque of Selim II (Selimiye), 1569–74. Edirne, Turkey

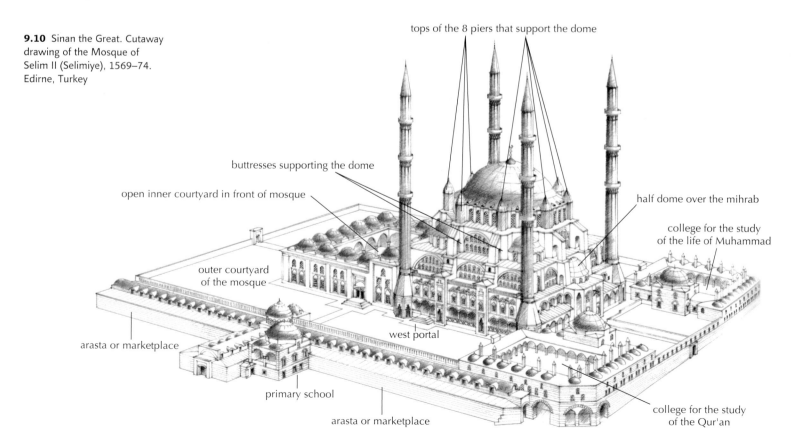

tops of the 8 piers that support the dome

buttresses supporting the dome

open inner courtyard in front of mosque

half dome over the mihrab

college for the study of the life of Muhammad

outer courtyard of the mosque

arasta or marketplace

west portal

primary school

arasta or marketplace

college for the study of the Qur'an

Architecture

To their Topkapi Palace in Istanbul flocked artists from Iran, Egypt, the Balkans, and even from Western Europe, while in the sixteenth century the architect known to posterity as Sinan the Great presided over an architectural establishment that saw the erection of hundreds of bridges, *hans* (inns), madrasas, palaces, baths, markets, and mosques. The great imperial mosques of the Ottomans paid homage to the traditional Arab mosque by incorporating an atriumlike arcaded courtyard into their design. However, the vast interior space and daring engineering of Justinian's Hagia Sophia (see figs. 8.15 and 8.16), in combination with their own well-developed traditions, provoked an architectural response that made Ottoman mosques vastly different from mosques of the Arab or Iranian traditions. In around 1572, Sinan built for Sultan Selim II (r. 1566–74) in Edirne a huge imperial mosque that the architect considered his masterpiece (**fig. 9.10**). The courtyard with surrounding arcades and central fountain recalls the typical Arab mosque plan, but the huge lead-covered dome and the four pencil-thin triple-balconied minarets proclaim the Ottoman architectural style, while the vast interior, with its eight huge piers supporting a dome almost 197 feet high and over 108 feet in diameter, shows a unified and clearly delineated space (**fig. 9.11**) that is completely different both from the Arab hypostyle mosque with its fragmented space, and from Hagia Sophia with its mysterious structural and spatial ambiguity (see fig. 8.16). In Sinan's work, the structural components—the muscles and sinews, as it were—rather than being hidden, are a primary source of the buildings' visual appeal.

The Ottoman Court Style

By 1500, the Ottomans had developed a royal design studio, called the "house of design," that served as the central focus of royal artistic patronage. It reached its zenith under the patronage of Süleyman I, "The Magnificent" (r. 1520–66), his son Selim II, who commissioned the mosque in Edirne (see figs. 9.10 and 9.11), and his grandson Murad III (r. 1576–95). Among the many artistic innovations to emerge from this complex of artists working in almost every conceivable medium and genre is a style of ornament called by some *saz*, taking its name from a legendary enchanted forest, and by others *hatayi*—that is, "from Cathay," or "China." Created in part by an émigré artist

9.11 Interior, Mosque of Selim II

from Tabriz named Shah Kulu, who was head of the Ottoman royal studio by the mid-sixteenth century, the style is typified by energetic and graceful compositions of curved leaves and complex floral palmettes linked by vines that appear to overlap and penetrate each other, sometimes embellished with birds or strange antelopelike creatures. The *saz* or *hatayi* style is found in ceramic wares, manuscript illuminations, carpets, silk textiles, freehand drawings executed for the albums of royal collectors, and some remarkable blue and turquoise paintings on tile, probably from the hand

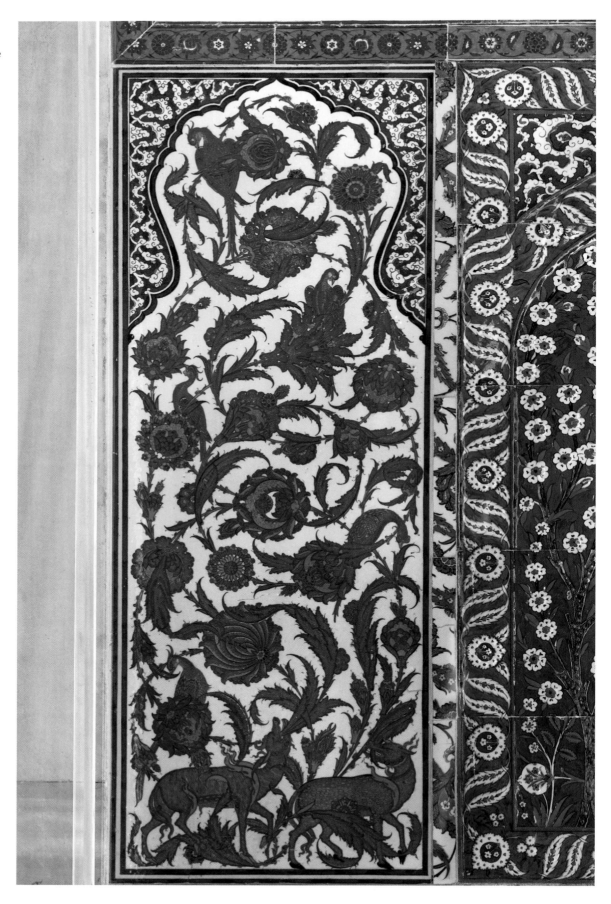

9.12 Shah Kulu (?). Tile painted in *hatayi* style with *saz* design. ca. 1525–50. Cobalt and turquoise underglaze painting on composite fritware body covered with white slip, 50 × 19" (127 × 48.5 cm). Topkapı Palace Museum, Istanbul

of Shah Kulu himself (**fig. 9.12**). Ottoman ceramics and silks were exported in large quantities to Russia and Europe, where along with the much-prized carpets from Asia Minor they were quickly absorbed into European material culture. The Ottoman regime ended in 1922 and the following year the Republic of Turkey was established as its virtual successor state.

POINTS OF REFLECTION

9.1 Analyze the reverence for the Word, the appreciation of nonfigural forms, and the equality of genres in the art of Islam.

9.2 Assess the Early Christian and Roman sources of the Dome of the Rock and interpret their significance.

9.3 Characterize the sources for the mosque as a type of building and compare and contrast its form to that of the Roman and Early Christian basilica.

9.4 Evaluate the similarities and differences in the Islamic art of Al-Andalus (Spain), Persia, and the Ottoman Empire.

9.5 Demonstrate the ways Islamic artists used ornament for decoration as well to convey meaning using three works of art or monuments in this chapter.

✔—[**Study** and review on myartslab.com

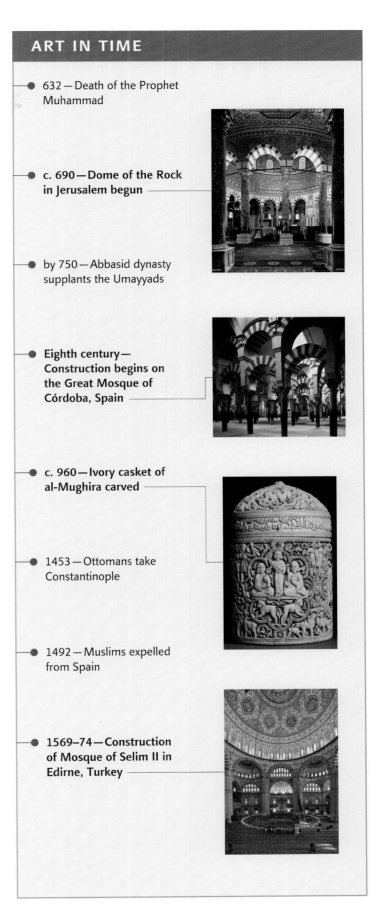

ART IN TIME

● 632—Death of the Prophet Muhammad

● c. 690—**Dome of the Rock in Jerusalem begun**

● by 750—Abbasid dynasty supplants the Umayyads

● Eighth century— **Construction begins on the Great Mosque of Córdoba, Spain**

● c. 960—Ivory casket of al-Mughira carved

● 1453—Ottomans take Constantinople

● 1492—Muslims expelled from Spain

● 1569–74—**Construction of Mosque of Selim II in Edirne, Turkey**

CHAPTER

10 Early Medieval Art

POINTS OF INQUIRY

10.1 Understand and recognize the art of Western Europe before and after the fall of Rome.

10.2 Analyze the concerns of the artists who worked for the tribal groups that migrated to Western Europe.

10.3 Recognize the way pagan and Christian art forms overlap during the early medieval period.

10.4 Assess how Carolingian art reflects Charlemagne's modeling of his rule after the Roman Empire.

10.5 Discuss the role of various institutions, both ecclesiastical and secular, in the production of art.

((•—[Listen to the chapter audio on myartslab.com

The term "early medieval" is something of a catchall phrase used to describe the art of a number of cultures and a variety of regions in Western Europe between the fall of Rome (476 CE) and the eleventh century (see **map 10.1**). The collapse of Roman institutions was in part the result of the power asserted by migrating Germanic peoples (including Franks, Visigoths, Ostrogoths, and Saxons), who moved westward into and through Europe and eventually established permanent settlements both north of the Alps and in Italy, Spain, and southern France. These were clearly tumultuous times, as invaders clashed and eventually mixed with local inhabitants, including the Celts, the descendants of the Iron Age peoples of Europe. As the invaders established permanent settlements, they adopted many customs traditional to the areas they inhabited. Overlaid on this mix of customs were Roman traditions, including those of Christianity, which in many cases had been adopted by indigenous local tribes when they were conquered by Rome.

The Church emerged as a force vitally important for European unification; even so, loyalty to family and clan continued to govern social and political alliances. Strong chiefs assumed leadership and established tribal allegiances and methods of exchange, both economic and political, that would eventually result in the development throughout Western Europe of a system of political organization known as feudalism. These social and political alignments eventually led to a succession of ruling dynasties governed by strong leaders who were able to increase the areas under their dominion. These dynasties (principally the Carolingian and Ottonian) were ambitious to reestablish a centralized authority, absent in Europe after the fall of Rome. The attempt to provide a stable political structure was based, if not in the reality of the Roman Empire, then at least in the ideals embodied in its legacy.

The art that resulted from this cultural interchange is a vibrant and vital mix. Artistic methods, materials, and traditions, introduced by migration, were combined with those customs that

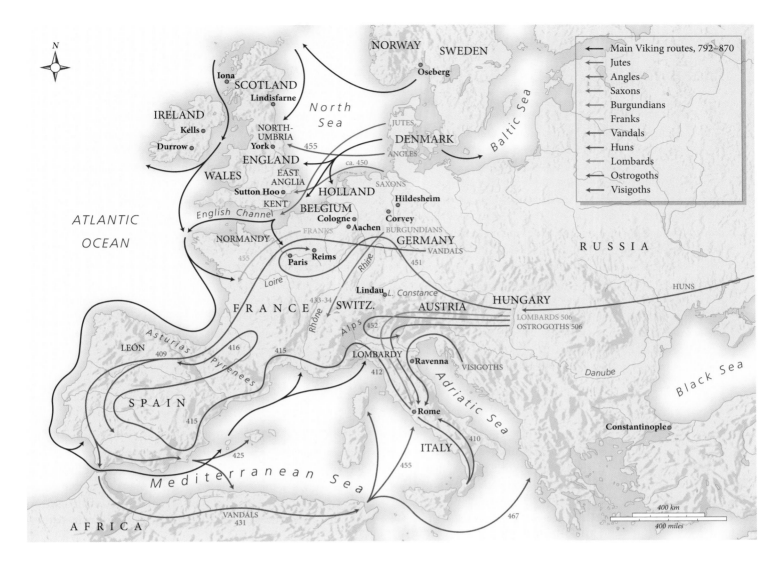

predominated in the regions where tribes settled. Thus, out of an amalgam of diverse and conflicting forces, and as new social and cultural entities developed, an art emerged that is as varied as it is exciting.

Anglo-Saxon Art

The widespread migrations of peoples transformed Europe. In 376, the Huns, who had advanced beyond the Black Sea from Central Asia, became a serious threat to Europe. They pushed the Germanic Visigoths westward into the Roman Empire from the Danube. Then in 451, under Attila (d. 453), they invaded Gaul, present-day France and Germany, and its resident Celts. Also in the fifth century, the Angles and Saxons from what are now Denmark and northern Germany invaded the British Isles, which had been colonized for centuries by Celts. Many of these Germanic tribes developed into virtual kingdoms: The Visigoths in Spain, the Burgundians and Franks in Gaul, the Ostrogoths and Lombards in Italy. The Vikings controlled Scandinavia and ventured afar, a result of their skill as sailors.

The Germanic peoples brought with them portable art forms: weaving, metalwork, jewelry, and woodcarvings. Artistic production in these media required training and skill of execution, and metalwork in particular had intrinsic value, since it was often made of gold or silver and inlaid with precious stones (see box: Materials and Techniques: Metalwork, overleaf). Metalworkers had high social status, a measure of respect for their labor and for the value of the objects they produced. In some Germanic folk legends metalworkers have abilities so remarkable that they are described as magical.

Map 10.1 Europe in the early Middle Ages

Metalwork

METAL WAS a precious commodity in the Middle Ages. Even in the ancient world patterns of interchange and colonization can be related to exploration for desirable metals. For example, the Greek settlements in Italy and the Roman settlements in Spain were partly the result of a desire for metals. Popular metals employed in the early Middle Ages were gold, silver, copper, iron, and bronze. The number of ways in which metals could be worked was undoubtedly one of their most compelling attractions. They could be flattened, drawn thin, or made into an openwork filigree design; they could be cast, engraved, punched, stamped, and decorated with colored stones, glass, or enamels.

A large buckle from the Sutton Hoo ship burial contains nearly a pound of gold, although it is only one among many gold pieces found in the burial site. That so much early medieval metalwork from gravesites is gold reflects the value attached to it.

In addition, gold is not harmed by contact with either earth or water (whereas silver and other metals are subject to progressive decay when exposed to the elements). Although gold had been mined in Europe since Roman times, the most common method of obtaining it was by collecting nuggets or small grains from rivers and streams (called placer or alluvial gold). The Rhine, Tiber, Po, Rhône, and Garonne rivers, along which the Germanic tribes settled, were major sources of this type of gold, which medieval writers refer to as "sand" gold.

The Sutton Hoo purse lid (fig. 10.1) is notable for its cloisonné decoration. Cloisonné is an ancient technique, used as early as the second millennium BCE in the eastern Mediterranean. Individual metal strips or *cloisons* (French for "partitions") are attached by their edge to a baseplate to form little walls that make cells enclosing glass or gems. The Sutton Hoo jewelry includes more than 4,000 individual garnets.

Numerous small-scale objects reflect the vitality of artistic forms produced by these migrating peoples, demonstrating an aesthetic that is quite different from the tradition deriving from Greece and Rome, yet equally rich in myth and imagery.

The Animal Style

The artistic tradition of the Germanic peoples, sometimes referred to as the animal style because of its heavy use of stylized animal-like forms, merged with the intricate ornamental metalwork of the Celts, producing a unique combination of abstract and organic shapes, of formal discipline and imaginative freedom.

SHIP BURIAL, SUTTON HOO, ENGLAND An Anglo-Saxon SHIP BURIAL in England follows the age-old tradition of burying important people with their personal effects. This custom may reflect a concern for the afterlife or it may simply be a way to honor the dead but undoubtedly a correlation was understood between a sea voyage and the journey to an eternal resting place. The double ship burial at Sutton Hoo (hoo is Anglo-Saxon for "headland" or "promontory") is of a seventh-century Anglian king, generally thought to be King Raedwald, who died around 625. Military gear, silver and enamelware, official royal regalia, gold coins, and objects of personal adornment are all part of the entombment. The Anglo-Saxon poem *Beowulf*, itself so concerned with displays of royal responsibility and obligation, includes a description of a ship fitted out for a funeral that is reminiscent of the Sutton Hoo burial. The funeral is that of Beowulf's father, King Scyld:

> They stretched their beloved lord in his boat,
> laid out by the mast, amidships,
> the great ring-giver. Far-fetched treasures
> were piled upon him, and precious gear.
> I never heard before of a ship so well furbished
> with battle tackle, bladed weapons
> and coats of mail. The massed treasure
> was loaded on top of him: it would travel far
> on out into the ocean's sway.
>
> —*Beowulf. A New Verse Translation*,
> translated by Seamus Heaney. New York:
> Farrar, Straus & Giroux, 2000

Although *Beowulf* describes events that predate the Sutton Hoo find by at least a century, the poem was probably not composed until a century or more after that burial. So, while *Beowulf* should not be taken as a documentary account, it provides a royal context within which to appreciate the Sutton Hoo site.

SHIP BURIALS originated among the Scandinavians early in the first millennium CE. The deceased was placed in the center of the ship and surrounded by grave goods (weapons, armor, and jewelry); the ship was then either buried intact beneath a mound of earth or burned before burial. Whether symbols of the soul's journey or of social status, ship burials such as those at Oseberg in Norway and Ladby in Denmark are valuable resources of material culture.

A gold, enamel, and garnet purse cover (**fig. 10.1**) was found at Sutton Hoo. The purse itself was probably a leather pouch, the whole arrangement reminiscent of the sporran that Scots wear in front of their kilts. Its original ivory or bone background does not survive and has been replaced. Each of four pairs of symmetrical motifs has its own distinctive character, an indication that they were assembled from different sources. One, the standing man between facing animals in the lower row, has a very long history indeed, first appearing in Mesopotamian art more than 3,200 years earlier. The motif of eagles pouncing on ducks brings to mind similar pairings of carnivore and victim in ancient bronzes. The upper design, at the center, is of more recent origin. It consists of fighting animals whose tails, legs, and jaws are elongated into bands that form a complex interweaving pattern. The fourth design, on the top left and right, uses interlacing bands as an ornamental device. The combination of these bands with the animal style, as shown here, seems to have been invented not long before the purse cover was made.

The Sutton Hoo objects are significant for the way they illustrate the transmission of motifs and techniques through the migration of various peoples. They show evidence of cultural interchange with Germanic peoples, combined with evidence of Scandinavian roots, but there are other noteworthy connections as well. King Raedwald was reputed to have made offerings to Christ, as well as to his ancestral pagan gods. A number of the objects discovered at Sutton Hoo make specific reference to Christianity, including silver bowls decorated with a cross, undoubtedly the result of trade with the Mediterranean.

The chief medium of the animal style was clearly metalwork, in a variety of materials and techniques. Such articles, small, durable, and often of exquisitely refined craftsmanship, were eagerly sought after, which accounts for the rapid diffusion of the animal-style repertoire of forms. These forms spread not only geographically but also from one material to another, migrating from metal into wood, stone, and even paint. They were used to convey a variety of messages, some clearly pagan and others Christian. The relevance of migration art and the animal style for the development of Christian art is particularly noteworthy in the British Isles of England, Ireland, and Scotland.

Hiberno-Saxon Art

During the early Middle Ages, the Irish (called Hibernians after the Roman name for Ireland, Hibernia) were the spiritual and cultural leaders of Western Europe. Since they had never been part

10.1 Purse cover, from the Sutton Hoo ship burial. First half of seventh century. Gold with garnets and enamels, length 8″ (20.3 cm). The British Museum, London. Courtesy of the Trustees

 View the Closer Look for the purse cover from the Sutton Hoo burial ship on myartslab.com

of the Roman Empire, the missionaries who carried Christianity to them from England in the fifth century found a Celtic society that was barbarian by Roman standards. The Irish readily accepted Christianity, which brought them into contact with Mediterranean civilization. However, because the institutional framework of the Roman Church was essentially urban, it did not suit the rural Irish way of life. Irish Christians preferred to follow the example of the desert saints of Egypt and the Near East, who had sought spiritual perfection in the solitude of the wilderness, where groups of them founded the earliest monasteries. Thus, Irish monasteries were established in isolated, secluded areas, such as islands off the mainland, places that required complete self-sufficiency. By the fifth century, monasticism had spread from its Near Eastern origins north into Italy, across the Continent, and throughout western Britain and Ireland.

10.2 *Symbol of St. Matthew*, from the *Book of Durrow*. ca. 680. Tempera on vellum, 9⅝ × 6⅛″ (24.7 × 15.7 cm). Trinity College, Dublin

Manuscripts

Irish monasteries soon became centers of learning and the arts, much energy being spent copying literary and religious texts. They also sent monks abroad to preach to nonbelievers and to found monasteries in northern Britain and Europe, from present-day France to Austria. Each monastery's scriptorium became an artistic center. Irish monks were not particularly interested in illustrating biblical events; instead, they devoted great effort to decorative embellishment. The finest of these manuscripts belong to the Hiberno-Saxon style, which combines Christian with Celtic and Germanic elements and which flourished in the monasteries of Ireland as well as those founded by Irish monks in Saxon England, Scotland, and on the Continent. These Irish monks helped speed the conversion to Christianity of Europe north of the Alps. Throughout Europe they made the monastery a cultural center and thus influenced medieval civilization for several hundred years.

In order to spread the message concerning Christ, the Kingdom of God, and salvation—called the Gospel—the Irish monasteries had to produce by hand copies of the Bible and other Christian books in large numbers. Every manuscript copy was looked upon as a sacred object containing the Word of God, its beauty reflecting the importance of its contents. Irish monks must have been familiar with Early Christian illuminated manuscripts, though they developed an independent tradition instead of simply copying the older manuscripts. The earliest Hiberno-Saxon illuminators retained only the symbols of the four evangelists from the imagery in Early Christian manuscripts, perhaps because these symbols could be readily translated into their ornamental style. The four symbols—the man or angel (St. Matthew), the lion (St. Mark), the ox (St. Luke), and the eagle (St. John)—derive from the Old Testament Book of Ezekiel (1:5–14) and the Apocalypse of St. John the Evangelist (4:6–8) and were assigned to the four evangelists by St. Jerome and other early commentators.

In the illustration of the *Symbol of St. Matthew* from the *Book of Durrow* (**fig. 10.2**) an ornamental pattern animates a figure even while accentuating its surface decoration. The body of the figure, composed of framed sections of checkerboard pattern, recalls the ornamental quality of the Sutton Hoo purse cover (see fig. 10.1). The addition of a head, which confronts us directly, and feet, turned to the side, transforms the decorative motifs into a human figure. Active, elaborate patterns, previously seen in metalwork, are here employed to demonstrate that St. Matthew's message is precious. Irish scribes and artists were revered for their abilities and achievements. A medieval account relates how, after his death, an Irish scribe's hands were preserved as relics capable of performing miracles.

THE LINDISFARNE GOSPELS   Thanks to a later colophon (a note at the end of a manuscript), we know a great deal about the origin of the *Lindisfarne Gospels*, produced in Northumbria, England, including the names of the translator, Aldred, and the scribe, Bishop Eadfrith, who presumably also painted the illuminations. Given the high regard in which Irish scribes and artists were held, it is

10.3 Cross page, from the *Lindisfarne Gospels*. ca. 700. Tempera on vellum, 13½ × 9¼" (34.3 × 23.5 cm). The British Library, London

not surprising that a bishop is credited with writing and decorating this manuscript. In Irish monasteries monks were divided into three categories: juniors (pupils and novice monks), working brothers (engaged in manual labor), and seniors (the most experienced monks), who were responsible for copying sacred books.

The Cross page (**fig. 10.3**) is a creation of breathtaking complexity. Working with the precision of a jeweler, the miniaturist (the illuminator of the manuscript) poured into the geometric frame animal interlace so dense and yet so full of movement that the fighting beasts on the Sutton Hoo purse cover (see fig. 10.1) seem simple in comparison. In order to achieve this effect, the artist had to work within a severe discipline as though he were following specific rules. The smallest motifs and the largest patterns were worked out in advance of painting. Ruler and compass were used to mark the page with a network of grid lines and with points, both drawn and pricked. In applying paint, the artist followed his drawing exactly. No mark is allowed to interfere with either the rigid balance of individual features or the overall design. The art historian Françoise Henry has suggested that artists conceived of their work as "a sort of sacred riddle" composed of abstract forms to be sorted out and deciphered. Organic and geometric shapes had to

10.4 Chi Rho Iota page, Book of Matthew (1:18), from the *Book of Kells*. ca. 800. Ink and pigments on vellum, 13 × 9½" (33 × 24.1 cm). Trinity College Library, Dublin

be kept separate. Within the animal compartments, every line had to turn out to be part of an animal's body. Other rules concerned symmetry, mirror-image effects, and repetitions of shapes and colors. Only by intense observation can we enter into the spirit of this mazelike world. It is as if these biting and clawing monsters are subdued by the power of the Cross, converted to Christian purpose just as were the Celtic tribes themselves.

The need to decorate all surfaces, evident both in manuscripts and metalwork, is traditionally referred to as *horror vacui*, a fear of empty space. But this designation imposes contemporary values on a culture alien to them. Unlike the Greeks and Romans, who used spatial illusionism to animate their art, Germanic and Celtic artists used intricate patterns to enliven the surface of their precious objects. Although the designs seem confusing and claustrophobic to us, there is, as we have seen, a consistent and intentional tightness in the way the patterns hold together.

THE *BOOK OF KELLS* The Hiberno-Saxon manuscript style reached its climax in the *Book of Kells* a hundred years after the *Lindisfarne Gospels*. It was probably made, or at least begun, at the end of the eighth or the beginning of the ninth century at the monastery on the island of Iona, off the western coast of Scotland, which had been founded by Irish monks in the sixth century. The book's name derives from the Irish monastery of Kells, where the manuscript was housed from the late ninth century until the seventeenth century. Its many pages reflect a wide array of influences from the Mediterranean to the English Channel.

The Chi Rho Iota monogram page illustrates Christ's initials, *XPI*, in Greek (**fig. 10.4**). Alongside them appear the words *Christi autem generatio*, or "now this is how the birth of Christ came about," heralding the beginning of the Book of Matthew (1:18), in which the birth of Jesus is celebrated. The Chi Rho Iota page has much the same swirling design as the Cross page from the *Lindisfarne Gospels*, and a viewer can also see parallels to contemporary jewelry. The relationship between manuscript illumination and precious metalwork is far from accidental, evidenced by the display of both on altars and their housing in church treasuries. During a period when literacy was rare and class-based, the book was a symbol of authority and dominance, an object that must have mystified many people as much as it elucidated matters for others.

On the Chi Rho Iota page, the rigid geometry of the Lindisfarne Cross page has been relaxed somewhat, and for the first time images of humans are incorporated into the design. The very top of the X-shaped Chi sprouts a recognizable face, while along its shaft are three angels with wings. And in a touch of enchanting fantasy, the tendril-like P-shaped Rho ends in a human head that has been hypothesized to be a representation of Christ. More surprising still is the introduction of the natural world. Nearly hidden in the ornamentation, as if playing a game of hide-and-seek, are cats and mice, butterflies, even otters catching fish. No doubt they performed a symbolic function for medieval readers, even if we no longer understand their meaning. The richness and intricacy of the illustration compel concentration, establishing a direct connection between the viewer and the image in much the same way as does the fixed, direct gaze of the holy figure in an Early Byzantine icon (see fig. 8.19). In each work, icon and manuscript illumination, the power of the image is so strong that the viewer virtually enters into its realm, forgetting the world outside its frame.

Carolingian Art

The wide gulf between migration and Hiberno-Saxon art, on the one hand, and the Mediterranean tradition, on the other, was bridged by the art patronized by CHARLEMAGNE and his successors, which is referred to as Carolingian (derived from Charlemagne's Latin name, *Carolus Magnus*, meaning "Charles the Great"). Charlemagne ruled from 768 as king of the Franks, one of those migrating tribes that had settled in Roman Gaul. He established an empire, which united most of Europe from the North Sea to Spain and as far south as Lombardy in northern Italy. Pope Leo III bestowed on him the title of emperor of Rome in St. Peter's Basilica on Christmas Day in the year 800, pronouncing him successor to Constantine, the first Christian emperor. Although Charlemagne was able to resist the pope's attempts to assert his authority over the newly created Catholic empire, there was now an interdependence of spiritual and political authority, of Church and State, that would define the history of Western Europe for many centuries.

The emperors were crowned in Rome, but they did not live there. Charlemagne built his

CHARLEMAGNE (742–814), king of the Franks, conquered the Saxons and the Lombards and fought the Arabs in Spain before being crowned Emperor of the West in 800 by Pope Leo III. Besides his accomplishments in the fields of art, architecture, and education, he vigorously promoted agriculture, manufacture, and commerce. After his death, the Church declared him "blessed" and he became a figure of legend, appearing, for instance, in the *Chanson de Roland*.

capital at the center of his power, in Aachen (Aix-la-Chapelle), located in what is now Germany and close to present-day France, Belgium, and the Netherlands. Among Charlemagne's goals were to better the administration of his realm and foster the teaching of Christian truths. He summoned the best minds to his court, including Alcuin of York, the most learned scholar of the day, to restore ancient Roman learning and to establish a system of schools at every cathedral and monastery. The emperor took an active hand in this renewal, which went well beyond a mere interest in the old books to include political objectives. He modeled his rule after the Roman Empire under Constantine and Justinian—rather than their pagan predecessors—and proclaimed a *renovatio imperii romani*, a "renewal of imperial Rome," his efforts

aided by the pope who had crowned him Holy Roman Emperor. The artists working for Charlemagne and other Carolingian rulers consciously sought to emulate Rome; by combining their admiration for antiquity with native Northern European features, they produced original works of art of the highest quality.

Sculpture

A bronze *Equestrian Statue of a Carolingian Ruler* (**fig. 10.5**), once thought to be Charlemagne himself but now generally assigned to his grandson Charles the Bald, conveys the political objectives of the Carolingian dynasty. The ruler, wearing imperial robes, sits as triumphantly on his steed as if he were on a throne. He holds an orb signifying his domination of the world. The statue is probably modeled on a now lost antique Roman equestrian statue of Theodoric, which Charlemagne had brought from Ravenna for the courtyard of his imperial palace. Other possible sources include the bronze equestrian statue of Marcus Aurelius (see fig. 7.12), mistakenly thought to represent Constantine, the first Christian Emperor, and thus also an appropriate model for the ambitious Carolingian rulers.

The Carolingian statue is not a slavish copy of its antique model. Compared to the statue of Marcus Aurelius, it is simpler and less cluttered with detail, yet still communicates the significant message that the Carolingian rulers were heirs to the Roman imperial throne. Most striking is the difference in size: Marcus Aurelius stands more than 11 feet high, while the Carolingian figure does not reach 10 inches. Yet the diminutive statue expresses as much majesty and dignity as the more monumental example. Given the metalwork tradition of the Franks, the miniaturization is not only appropriate, but might in itself suggest value. Unfortunately, we do not know the audience for the work or how it was used, though its scale could relate to portability.

Illuminated Books

Charlemagne's interest in promoting learning and culture required the production of large numbers of books by his SCRIPTORIA. He established an "academy" at his court and encouraged the collecting and copying of many works of ancient Roman literature. In fact, the oldest surviving texts of many classical Latin authors are found in Carolingian manuscripts that were long considered of Roman

10.5 *Equestrian Statue of a Carolingian Ruler* (Charles the Bald?). Ninth century. Bronze, height 9½" (24.4 cm). Musée du Louvre, Paris

origin. This very page is printed in letters the shapes of which derive from the script in Carolingian manuscripts. The fact that these letters are known today as Roman rather than Carolingian is a result of the confusion about the manuscripts' origins.

THE *GOSPEL BOOK OF CHARLEMAGNE* The *Gospel Book of Charlemagne* (also known as the *Coronation Gospels*, because later German emperors swore on it during their coronations) is said to have been found in Charlemagne's tomb and is thought to have been produced at his court. Looking at the page with St. Matthew (**fig. 10.6**), we can hardly believe that such a work could have been executed in northern Europe, and little more than one hundred years after the *Book of Durrow* (see fig. 10.2). Were it not for the large golden HALO, the evangelist might almost be mistaken for a Roman portrait, such is the naturalness and solidity with which he inhabits the landscape setting. The artist shows himself fully conversant with the Roman tradition of painting, from the modeling of the forms, the shading of face, hands, and feet, and the body-revealing drapery, to the acanthus ornament on the wide frame, which makes the picture seem like a window. Since the manner of painting is so clearly Mediterranean, it is possible that the artist came from Byzantium or Italy.

The HALO (or nimbus) represents light radiating around the head of a saint or divinity. The aureole is light around the body, and the glory is all the light—both halo and aureole. The mandorla is the almond-shaped form that encloses the image of a saint; it is also symbolic of the radiant light of holiness.

The monks working in the medieval SCRIPTORIA were adept at all aspects of manuscript production, from parchment preparation to binding. At first, the copying and illumination of the texts were probably performed by the same individual, but later each of these tasks was executed by a specialist. The scriptorium itself could be a large room with benches and tables or a series of individual carrels (small cubicles or studies).

10.6 *St. Matthew*, from the *Gospel Book of Charlemagne* (*Coronation Gospels*). 800–10. Ink and colors on vellum, 13 × 10″ (33 × 25.4 cm). Kunsthistorisches Museum, Vienna

THE *GOSPEL BOOK OF ARCHBISHOP EBBO OF REIMS* Less reflective of classical models, but equally reliant on them, is a miniature painted some three decades later for the *Gospel Book of Archbishop Ebbo of Reims* (**fig. 10.7**). The subject is once again St. Matthew, and the pose is similar to that in the *Gospel Book of Charlemagne* (see fig. 10.6), but the picture is filled with a vibrant energy that sets everything in motion. The thickly painted drapery swirls about the figure, the hills heave upward, and the architecture and vegetation seem tossed about by a whirlwind. Even the acanthus pattern on the frame assumes a strange, flamelike character. The evangelist has been transformed from a Roman author setting down his thoughts into a man seized with the frenzy of divine inspiration, a vehicle for recording the Word of God. The way the artist communicates this energy, particularly through the expressive use of flickering line, employing his brush as if it were a pen, recalls the endless interlaced movement in the ornamentation of Hiberno-Saxon manuscripts (see figs. 10.2, 10.3 and 10.4).

THE *LINDAU GOSPELS* COVER The Reims style is also apparent in the reliefs on the front cover of the *Lindau Gospels* (**fig. 10.8**), dating from the third quarter of the ninth century, in the expressive, near-frenetic figures that float around the image of the crucified Christ. Given the Carolingian investment in preserving and embellishing the written word, the cover was a fittingly sumptuous protection for a book. The clusters of semiprecious stones

10.7 *St. Matthew*, from the *Gospel Book of Archbishop Ebbo of Reims*. Second quarter of ninth century. Ink, gold, and colors on vellum, 10¼ × 8¾″ (26 × 22.2 cm). Bibliothèque Municipale, Épernay, France

10.8 Front cover of binding, *Lindau Gospels*. ca. 870. Gold and jewels, 13 × 9⅞″ (35 × 26.7 cm). The Pierpont Morgan Library, New York

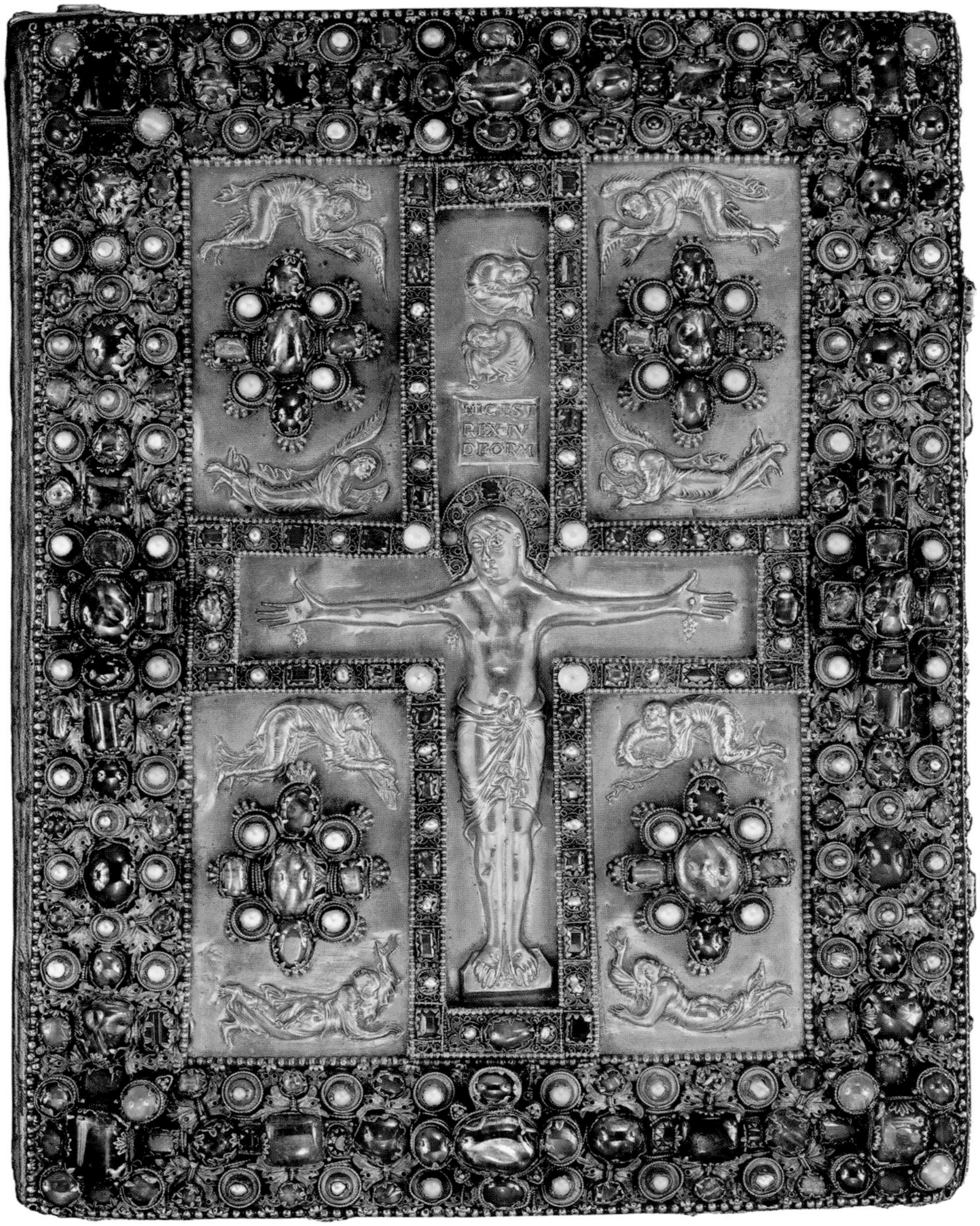

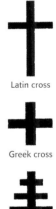

These five types of crosses are among those most often seen in Western art, though many variants exist.

Latin cross

Greek cross

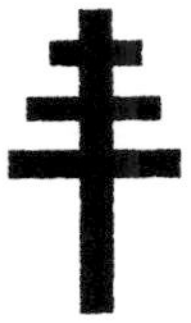

Papal cross

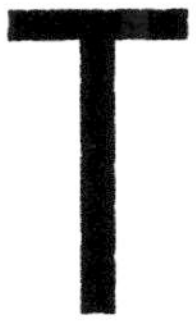

Tau, Egyptian, or St. Anthony's cross

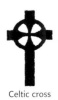

Celtic cross

are not mounted directly on the gold ground but raised on claw feet or arcaded turrets (tower-like projections), so that light can penetrate from beneath to bring out their full brilliance. Christ betrays no hint of pain or death. He seems to stand rather than to hang, his arms spread out in a solemn gesture.

Architecture

Although relatively few Carolingian buildings survive, excavations demonstrate a significant increase in building activity during the Carolingian period, reflecting the security and prosperity enjoyed during Charlemagne's reign. As was the case with his painters, Charlemagne's architects sought to revive the splendor of the Roman Empire by erecting buildings whose models were largely from Rome and Ravenna, both of which Charlemagne visited. While Rome had been the capital of the empire, Ravenna had been a Christian imperial outpost, thus a worthy prototype for what Charlemagne hoped to create in his own land.

10.9 Odo of Metz. Interior of the palace chapel of Charlemagne. 792–805. Aachen, Germany

 Watch a video about the Palace Chapel of Charlemagne on myartslab.com

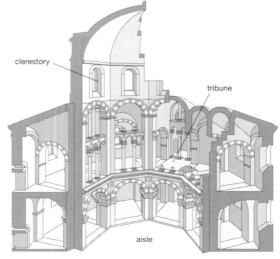

clerestory

tribune

aisle

Section of palace chapel of Charlemagne

PALACE CHAPEL OF CHARLEMAGNE, AACHEN Toward the end of the eighth century, Charlemagne erected the imperial palace at Aachen. Prior to this time, Charlemagne's court had been itinerant, moving from place to place as the political situation required. Now, to signify his position as a Christian ruler, architects modeled his palace complex on Constantine's Lateran Palace in Rome. Charlemagne's palace included a basilica, called the Royal Hall, which was linked to the palace chapel (**fig. 10.9**). The plan for the palace chapel was probably inspired by the church of San Vitale in Ravenna, which the emperor saw at first hand (see figs. 8.10 and 8.11). The building was designed by Odo of Metz, probably the earliest architect north of the Alps known to us by name. Einhard, Charlemagne's trusted adviser and biographer, supervised the project.

The debt to San Vitale is especially clear in section. The chapel design is by no means a mere echo of San Vitale but a vigorous reinterpretation of it. Piers and vaults are impressively massive compared with San Vitale, while the geometric clarity of the spatial units is very different from the fluid space of the earlier structure. To construct such a building on northern soil was a difficult undertaking. Columns and bronze gratings were imported from Italy, and expert stonemasons must have been hard to find. The columns are placed within the arches of the upper story, where they are structurally unnecessary, but where they accentuate a sense of support and create opportunities to offer Roman details. San Vitale had been designed to be ambiguous, to produce an otherworldly interior space. Aachen, by comparison, is sturdy and sober. The soft, bulging curvilinear forms of San Vitale's arcades are replaced with clear-cut piers at Aachen. They make manifest their ability to support the heavy weight of Aachen's dome, while the dome at San Vitale seems light, appearing to hover above the interior space of the building.

Equally important is Odo's scheme for the western entrance, now largely obscured by later additions and rebuilding. At San Vitale, the entrance consists of a broad, semidetached narthex with twin stair turrets, placed at an odd angle to the main axis of the church. At Aachen, these elements are molded into a tall, compact unit, in line with the main axis and attached to the chapel itself. This monumental structure, known as a westwork (from the German *Westwerk*), makes one of its first appearances here.

Charlemagne placed his throne in the tribune (the gallery of the westwork), behind the great opening above the entrance. From here the emperor could emerge to show himself to those assembled in the atrium below. The throne faced an altar dedicated to Christ, who seemed to bless the emperor from above in the dome mosaic. Thus, although contemporary documents say very little about its function, the westwork seems to have served initially as a royal compartment or chapel.

ABBEY CHURCH, CORVEY The best-preserved surviving example of a Carolingian westwork is the Abbey Church at Corvey, Germany (**fig. 10.10**), built between 873 and 885. Except for the upper stories, which date from around 1146, the westwork retains much of its original appearance. It is impressive not only because of its height but also because of its expansive surfaces, which emphasize the clear geometry and powerful masses of the exterior. The westwork provided a suitably regal entrance, which may well be its greatest significance. But it had functional benefits too. Many westworks contained chapels housing numerous relics, and on feast days, and in particular at Easter, the community positioned itself there for the beginning of an elaborate processional liturgy. Thus, to some extent the westwork functioned as a separate commemorative building. At Corvey musical notation scratched on the walls of the gallery reminds us that the boys' choir would have been positioned here, its voices spreading upward as well as throughout the church.

Unfortunately, political stability proved elusive. Upon the death of Charlemagne's son, Louis I, in 840, a bitter struggle arose among his sons for the empire built by their grandfather. The brothers eventually signed a treaty in 843 dividing the empire into western, central, and eastern parts: Charles the Bald became the West Frankish king, founding the French Carolingian dynasty in what became present-day France; Louis the German became the East Frankish king, ruling an area roughly that of today's Germany; and Lothair I became the Holy Roman emperor, ruling the middle area running from the Netherlands down to Italy. The distribution of the Carolingian domain among Louis's heirs weakened the empire, brought a halt to Carolingian cultural efforts, and eventually exposed continental Europe to attack by the Muslims from the south, the Slavs and Magyars from the east, and the Vikings from the north.

The Vikings invaded northwestern France, and through a land grant from Charles the Bald occupied the area now known as Normandy (named for the "Norsemen").

Although political stability ultimately eluded Charlemagne's heirs, the artists of the Carolingian period were able to create an enduring art that combined the northern reliance on decoration—on surface, pattern, and line—with the Mediterranean concern for solidity and monumentality. Carolingian art served as a worthy model for emulation by artists and patrons when, during the next centuries, Charlemagne's vision of a united and stable Europe would reappear.

10.10 Westwork, Abbey Church. Late ninth century, with later additions. Corvey, Germany

Ottonian Art

When the last East Frankish monarch died in 911, German kings of Saxon descent consolidated political power in the eastern portion of the former Carolingian empire. Beginning with Henry I, these kings pushed back invaders, reestablished an effective central government, improved trade and the economy, and began a new dynasty, called Ottonian after its three principal rulers: Otto I, Otto II, and Otto III. During the Ottonian period, which lasted from 919 to 1024, Germany was the leading region of Europe politically and artistically. German achievements in both areas began as revivals of Carolingian traditions but soon developed an original character.

The greatest of the Ottonian kings, Otto I, after marrying the widow of a Lombard king in 951, extended his rule over most of what is now northern Italy. Then, in 962, he was crowned emperor by Pope John XII, at whose request he conquered Rome. The emperor later deposed this pope for conspiring against him, insisting on the imperial right to designate future popes.

10.11 Interior, with view toward the east apse (after restoration of 1950–60), abbey church of St. Michael. 1001–33. Hildesheim, Germany

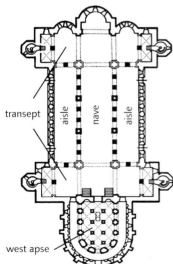

Reconstructed plan of abbey church of St. Michael, Hildesheim

Architecture

Among the most pressing concerns of the Ottonian emperors was the reform of the Church, which had become corrupt and mismanaged. They achieved this by establishing closer alliances with the papacy and by fostering monastic reforms, which they supported by sponsoring many new religious buildings. The renewal of impressive building programs effectively revived the architectural ambitions of their Carolingian predecessors, at the same time conveying and furthering the Ottonians' aspirations to restore the imperial glory of Christian Rome.

SAINT MICHAEL'S, HILDESHEIM The most ambitious patron of architecture and art in the Ottonian age was Bernward, who became bishop of Hildesheim after having been court chaplain. Bernward was also tutor of Otto III during the regency of Otto's mother the Empress Theophano, wife of Otto II and a Byzantine princess in her own right. Bernward's chief monument is the Benedictine abbey church of St. Michael at Hildesheim. The plan of this monastic church, with its two choirs and side entrances, derives from Carolingian monastic building types. However, in St. Michael's the symmetry is carried much further. There are two identical transepts, each with a tower, where the transept and the nave cross, and a pair of stair turrets at the end of each transept. But the supports of the nave arcade, instead of being uniform, consist of pairs of columns separated by square piers (**fig. 10.11**). This alternating system divides the arcade into three equal units, each with three openings. These units are equal in length to the width of the transepts, which are similarly divided into three compartments. Thus, a modular system governs the division of spaces. St. Michael's was severely damaged during World War II, but the restored interior, with its great expanse of wall space between the arcade and clerestory, formerly decorated with frescoes, retains the majestic feeling of the original design. (The capitals of the columns date from the twelfth century; the painted wooden ceiling from the thirteenth.)

Metalwork

The Ottonian emperors' reliance on church authority to strengthen their own governmental rule encouraged them not only to build new churches but also to provide sumptuous pieces of art to decorate them. They and their cohorts sponsored richly appointed works, executed in expensive, often precious materials.

BRONZE DOORS OF BISHOP BERNWARD, HILDESHEIM
For St. Michael's, Bernward commissioned a pair of extensively sculptured bronze doors (**fig. 10.12**), which were finished in 1015, the year the crypt was consecrated. According to his biographer, Thangmar of Heidelberg, Bernward excelled in the arts and "distinguished himself remarkably in the science of metalwork and the whole art of building." He must therefore have been closely involved

10.12 Doors of Bishop Bernward, Hildesheim Cathedral (originally made for abbey church of St. Michael, Hildesheim). 1015. Bronze, height approx. 16' (4.8 m). Hildesheim, Germany

10.13 *Accusation and Judgment of Adam and Eve*, from the doors of Bishop Bernward. 1015. Bronze, approx. 23 × 43″ (58.3 × 109.3 cm). Hildesheim, Germany

in the project. The idea for the doors may have come to him as a result of his visit to Rome, where he could have seen ancient Roman (and perhaps Byzantine) doors of bronze or wood. He would also certainly have been aware of the bronze doors that Charlemagne had commissioned for his palace chapel at Aachen.

Many art historians consider the doors at Hildesheim to be the first monumental sculptures created by the lost-wax process since antiquity (see page 92). Each door was cast as one piece and measures over 16 feet high. They are also the first doors since the Early Christian period to have been decorated with stories. Our detail (**fig. 10.13**) shows God accusing and judging Adam and Eve after they committed the Original Sin of eating the forbidden fruit in the Garden of Eden. (This story is known as the Temptation and Fall.) Below it, in inlaid letters notable for their classical Roman character, is part of an inscription, with the date and Bernward's name. The inscription was added around 1035, when the doors were moved from the monastery of St. Michael and attached to the westwork of Hildesheim Cathedral, where they would have been seen by a larger public than in the monastic setting of St. Michael's. The new, prominent setting indicates how valued they were in their own time.

The composition most probably derives from a manuscript illumination, since there are very similar scenes in medieval Bibles. Yet this is no mere imitation. The story is conveyed with splendid directness and expressive force. The accusing finger of the Lord, seen against a great void, is the focal point of the drama. It points to a cringing Adam, who passes the blame to Eve, who in turn passes it to the serpent at her feet.

The subjects on the left door are taken from the Hebrew Bible and those on the right from the New Testament (see fig. 10.12). The Hebrew Bible stories are presented chronologically from top to bottom, while the New Testament scenes move in reverse order, from bottom to top, suggesting that the message of the Christian Bible is uplifting. When read as horizontal pairs, the panels deliver a message of the origin and redemption of sin through a system of typology, whereby Hebrew Bible stories prefigure New Testament ones. For example, the Temptation and Fall is opposite the Crucifixion. In the center of the left panel of this pair of scenes is the tree whose fruit led to the Original Sin; in the center of the right panel is the cross on which Jesus was crucified, which medieval Christians believed was made from the wood of the tree from Eden and was therefore the instrument for redemption from the sin of that original act. Compositional similarities between the two scenes stress their typological relationship: In the left panel Adam and Eve's hands flanking the cross-shaped tree establish a visual parallel to the spears the soldiers use to pierce Christ's body on the right panel.

Manuscripts: Conveyors of Imperial Grandeur

The right of the Ottonian monarchs to call themselves Roman emperors was challenged by Byzantine rulers, who continued to claim that title as their own, even though the division of the Roman Empire into Eastern and Western empires was complete by the end of the fourth century. When Otto II married the Byzantine princess Theophano, he was able to use the full title of Holy Roman Emperor with impunity. While early Ottonian illuminators faithfully replicated features of Carolingian manuscripts for the court school, later Ottonian manuscripts, as well as ivories, blend Carolingian and Byzantine elements into a new style of extraordinary scope and power. Byzantine artists working for the court provided an impetus for new ways of presenting both religious and imperial images. Ottonian manuscripts indicate an increasing interest on the part of artists and patrons in narrative cycles of Jesus' life, which is the period's most important contribution to the field of iconography (the study of the use and meaning of images).

THE *GOSPEL BOOK OF OTTO III* Produced for the son of Otto II and Theophano, the *Gospel Book of Otto III* (**fig. 10.14**) communicates an imperial grandeur that is impressive indeed. The emperor displays the imperial regalia—a crown, an eagle scepter, and a cross-inscribed orb—while imperial lions decorate his throne. Representatives of the two domains that he controls—the military and the

ecclesiastical—flank him, reminiscent of Justinian's placement in the center of the same domains in the San Vitale mosaic (see fig. 8.12). On the facing folio, the four geographical parts of the realm—Slavinia, Germania, Gallia, and Roma—offer homage. Their stances recall traditional representations of the Magi offering gifts to Christ, such as the scene decorating Theodora's robe in the mosaic at San Vitale in Ravenna (see fig. 8.13).

The manuscript is dated to around 1000, not long after Otto III was crowned king of Germany at Aachen in 986 and Holy Roman Emperor at Rome in 993. The way Otto is represented visually in the manuscript thus parallels historical facts; he is presented here as rightful and worthy heir to Roman and Byzantine emperors as well as to Charlemagne, and his imperial dignity is enhanced by association with Christ, a reversal of the practice in Early Christian depictions, where Christ is ennobled in the fashion of a Roman emperor (see fig. 8.9). The soft pastel hues of the background recall the illusionism of Graeco-Roman landscapes and the *Quedlinburg Itala* fragment (see fig. 8.8). Such a style shows that the artist was probably aware of Roman, as well as Byzantine, manners of representation.

The *Gospel Book of Otto III* contains one of the most extensive sets of illustrations of the life of Christ. The scene of *Jesus Washing the Feet of St. Peter* (**fig. 10.15**) once again contains strong echoes of ancient painting, transmitted through Byzantine art. The architectural frame around Jesus is a late descendant of the kind of architectural perspectives

10.14 *Otto III Receiving the Homage of the Four Parts of the Empire* and *Otto III Between Church and State*, from the *Gospel Book of Otto III*. ca. 1000. Tempera on vellum. Each folio 13 × 9⅜" (33 × 23.8 cm). Staatsbibliothek, Munich

10.15 *Jesus Washing the Feet of St. Peter*, from the *Gospel Book of Otto III*. ca. 1000. Tempera on vellum, 13 × 9⅜" (33 × 23.8 cm). Staatsbibliothek, Munich

we saw in Roman wall painting (see figs. 7.25 and 7.26), and the intense gold background reminds us of Byzantine painting and mosaics, which the Ottonian artist has put to new use (see fig. 8.22). What had previously been an architectural vista now becomes the Heavenly City, the House of the Lord, filled with golden celestial space in contrast with the atmospheric earthly space outside.

The figures have also been transformed. In ancient art this composition, in which a standing figure extends an arm to a seated, supplicating figure and is watched by onlookers and assisted by others, was used to depict a doctor treating a patient. Here the emphasis has shifted from physical to spiritual action. Not only do glances and gestures convey this new kind of action, but so too does scale. Jesus and his apostle Peter, the most animated figures, are larger than the rest, and Jesus' "active" arm is longer than his "passive" one. The blending of classical and Byzantine elements results in a new style of expressive abstraction.

Sculpture

Large-scale and free-standing sculpture was rare in the early Middle Ages, in part because of the lingering fear of idol worship and because the general interest in producing portable objects virtually precluded its production. However, during the Ottonian period the scale of sculpture increased (witness Bernward's doors for St. Michael's at Hildesheim), and even many small-scale works demonstrate an imposing monumentality.

THE *GERO CRUCIFIX* The *Gero Crucifix* (**fig. 10.16**), named for Archbishop Gero of Cologne, who commissioned it around 970, is an example of a large-scale work—it is in fact life-size—with a monumental presence, indicative of the major transformation that Ottonian sculptors were able to achieve even when dealing with traditional subjects. How this happens is evident if we compare the *Gero Crucifix* with the Christ on the cover of the *Lindau Gospels* (see fig. 10.8). The two works are separated by little more than a hundred years but show marked contrast. The *Gero Crucifix* presents a sculptural image that is new to Western art, since for the first time a dead Christ is represented on the Cross. Made of painted and gilded oak, it is carved in powerfully rounded forms. Particularly striking is the forward bulge of the heavy body, which emphasizes the physical strain on the arms and shoulders, making the pain seem almost unbearable. The face, with its deeply incised, angular features, is a mask of agony from which all life has fled. The image is filled with deep feeling for Christ's suffering.

How did the Ottonian sculptor arrive at this bold conception? The *Gero Crucifix* was clearly influenced by Middle Byzantine art, which had created the compassionate view of Christ on the Cross in other media (see fig. 8.22). Yet, that source alone is not enough to explain the results. It remained for the Ottonian artist to translate the Byzantine image into large-scale sculptural terms and to replace its gentle pathos with expressive realism. Even though there were some clerics who rekindled the deep-rooted fear of idolatry, they could not restrain the newly found emphasis on the humanity of Christ or the increasing interest in relics, which were, after all, three-dimensional objects. In fact, there is a space in the back of the head of the Gero Christ to hold the Host (the bread or wafer taken during that part of the Mass referred to as Communion), transforming the sculpture into a reliquary (a container to enshrine holy remnants or relics). The marked movement toward monumentality of the *Gero Crucifix* heralds new aesthetic aims that will dominate eleventh-century sculpture throughout Europe.

10.16 *Gero Crucifix*. ca. 970. Painted and gilded wood, height 6′2″ (1.88 m). Cologne Cathedral, Germany

POINTS OF REFLECTION

10.1 Analyze the differences in the concerns of Roman imperial artists and the artists who worked for the tribes that migrated into Western Europe.

10.2 Explain how the experience of migration affected the kind of art that was made in early medieval Europe.

10.3 Distinguish forms found in Hiberno-Saxon manuscripts that derive from pagan sources from those that rely on Christian ones.

10.4 By citing specific works of art, illustrate how Charlemagne relied on the Roman past to justify and aggrandize his rule.

10.5 Demonstrate and compare how the concerns of Church and State are expressed in both Carolingian and Ottonian art.

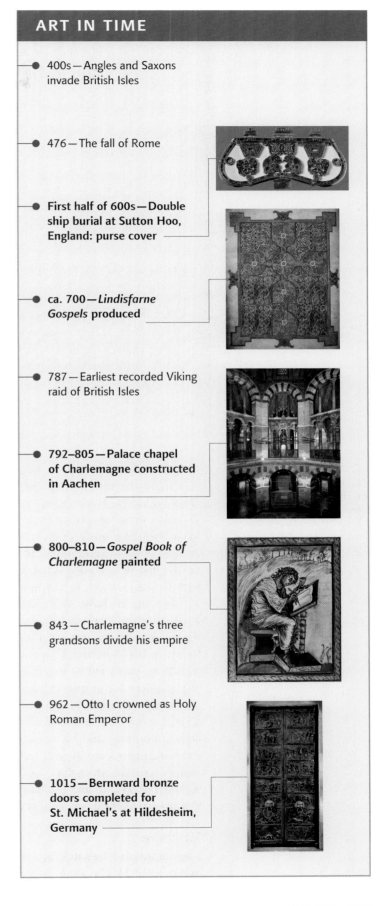

ART IN TIME

- **400s** — Angles and Saxons invade British Isles

- **476** — The fall of Rome

- **First half of 600s** — **Double ship burial at Sutton Hoo, England: purse cover**

- **ca. 700** — *Lindisfarne Gospels* produced

- **787** — Earliest recorded Viking raid of British Isles

- **792–805** — **Palace chapel of Charlemagne constructed in Aachen**

- **800–810** — *Gospel Book of Charlemagne* painted

- **843** — Charlemagne's three grandsons divide his empire

- **962** — Otto I crowned as Holy Roman Emperor

- **1015** — **Bernward bronze doors completed for St. Michael's at Hildesheim, Germany**

11 Romanesque Art

Romanesque means, literally, "in the Roman manner." We use this stylistic term today to identify the art of much of the eleventh and twelfth centuries. The borrowing of details or specific features from the antique past does not distinguish Romanesque art from the art of other post-classical periods, for Early Christian, Byzantine, Carolingian, and Islamic art also relied heavily on Rome for their formal and expressive languages. However, in Romanesque art, the aesthetic integrity and grandeur of the Roman model survive in a more vital and compelling form than in any previous periods. Yet Rome was not the style's only inspiration: Romanesque artists tapped sources in Carolingian and Ottonian art, and were influenced by Early Christian, Byzantine, migration, and Islamic traditions as well.

Romanesque art sprang up all over Western Europe at about the same time and in a variety of regional styles that are nevertheless closely related. What welded this variety into a coherent style was not any single force but several factors. For one thing, Christianity was close to triumph almost everywhere in Europe. Most of the northern tribes had entered the Catholic fold, and in 1031 the caliphate of Córdoba had broken up into many small Muslim states, opening the way for Christian conquest of the Iberian peninsula.

Another significant factor was the growing spirit of religious enthusiasm. The year 1000—the millennium—had come and gone without the apocalyptic end of the world that many had predicted from their reading of the Book of Revelation in the Bible. Chapter 20 of this New Testament book, written about 50 years after Christ's death, prophesies that the Second Coming, when Christ will return to earth and end the world as we know it, was to occur after 1,000 years. Many people, fearing the dreaded end of days, reacted to the approach of the year 1000 with terror and to its smooth passing with great relief and, in some quarters, a heightened spirituality. This was demonstrated by the large number of people making pilgrimages to sacred sites, by repeated Christian crusades against the Muslims in what was called the Holy Land, and by an increase in the number and size of monasteries, which also reflected a general growth in population and an increase in prosperity.

The reopening of the Mediterranean trade routes by the navies of Venice, Genoa, Amalfi, Pisa,

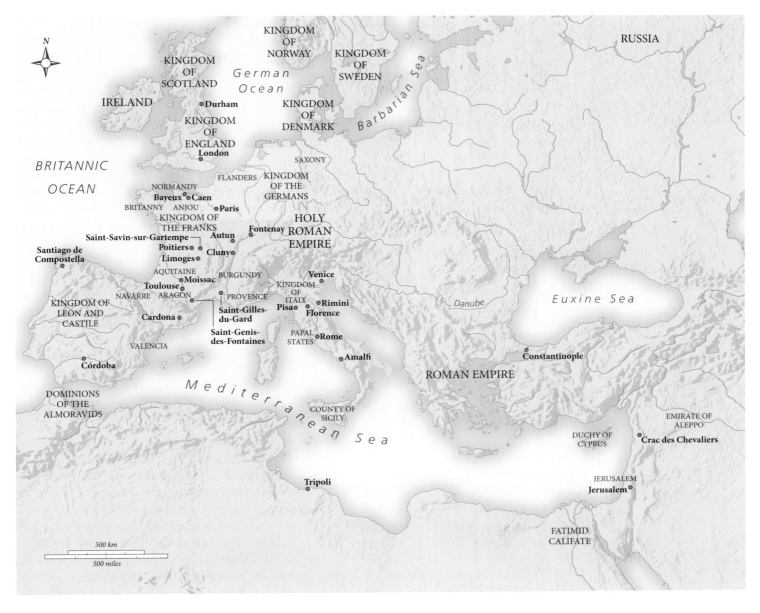

KINGDOM
OF
NORWAY
RUSSIA
KINGDOM
OF
SWEDEN
KINGDOM OF
SCOTLAND
German
Ocean
Barbarian Sea
IRELAND
Durham
KINGDOM
OF
DENMARK
KINGDOM
OF
ENGLAND
London
BRITANNIC
OCEAN
SAXONY
FLANDERS
KINGDOM
OF THE
GERMANS
NORMANDY
Bayeux Caen
BRITANNY ANJOU Paris
KINGDOM OF
THE FRANKS
Fontenay
HOLY
ROMAN
EMPIRE
Saint-Savin-sur-Gartempe Autun
Poitiers
Limoges
Cluny
Santiago de
Compostella
AQUITAINE
Toulouse Moissac
NAVARRE ARAGON
KINGDOM OF
LEÓN AND
CASTILE
Cardona
BURGUNDY
Venice
KINGDOM
OF
ITALY
PROVENCE
Saint-Gilles-
du-Gard
Pisa Rimini
Florence
Danube
Euxine Sea
VALENCIA
Saint-Genis-
des-Fontaines
PAPAL
STATES Rome
Córdoba
Constantinople
ROMAN EMPIRE
DOMINIONS
OF THE
ALMORAVIDS
Amalfi
Mediterranean Sea
EMIRATE OF
ALEPPO
COUNTY OF
SICILY
DUCHY OF
CYPRUS
Crac des Chevaliers
Tripoli
JERUSALEM
Jerusalem
FATIMID
CALIFATE
500 km
500 miles

Map 11.1 Europe in the Romanesque period

and Rimini was also significant (see **map 11.1**). The revival of trade and travel linked Europe commercially and culturally, stimulating the flowering of urban life. At the end of the early medieval period, Europe was still largely an agricultural society. A decentralized political and social system, known today as **feudalism**, had developed, mainly in France and Germany, where it had deep historical roots. In this system, landowning lords granted some of their property to knights (originally, these were cavalry officers). In return for these fiefs, or feuds, as the land parcels were called, the knights gave military and other service to their lords, to whom they were linked through a complex system of personal bonds—termed vassalage—that extended all the way to the king. A large class of generally downtrodden, virtually powerless peasants (serfs) worked the land itself. Towns that had shrunk in size during the migrations and invasions of the early Middle Ages started to regain their former importance and new towns sprang up everywhere, achieving independence via charters that enumerated a town's privileges and immunities in return for a feudal lord's guarantee of protection.

These social changes were also made possible by technological advances in agriculture. For the first time since the fall of Rome, farmers could grow more food than they needed for themselves. In many ways, then, Western Europe between 1050 and 1200 became a great deal more "Romanesque" than it had been since the sixth century. It recaptured some of the trade patterns, the urban quality, and the military strength of ancient imperial times. To be sure, there was no central political authority, for Europe was still divided into small units ruled by powerful families. Even the king of France controlled not much more than the area around Paris. However, some monasteries came to rival the wealth and power of kings, and the central spiritual authority of the pope acted as a unifying force throughout Europe.

This brief historical account underscores the number of institutions, organizations, and systems that helped to create European stability. Monasticism, feudalism, urbanism, commerce, pilgrimage, crusade, papacy, and the royal court all played their roles by setting into motion internationalizing forces that affected the transmission of artistic forms. Population growth and the increase in the number of new settlements stimulated building activity, much of it for Christian use. The development of better tools, such as saws to cut stone, resulted in improved masonry techniques. Many new constructions were made of well-cut, straight-edged blocks of stone and were monumental, built on a scale that rivaled the achievements of Rome. Heavy walls created solid and durable structures that convey a sense of enclosure and security, and the stone vaults covering these buildings enhanced their stability. These vaults, as well as the proliferation of architectural sculpture, consciously emulated the Roman manner of construction and design.

11.1 Nave and choir (looking east), Sant Vincenç. ca. 1029–40. Cardona, Spain

First Expressions of Romanesque Style

Although Romanesque art quickly spread throughout Europe, it first appeared in a zone running from Lombardy in northern Italy through southern France and into the northeastern Spanish region of Catalonia. Stone-vaulted buildings decorated with wall arcades and architectural sculpture, which are characteristic features of this early phase, survive in great numbers in these regions.

Architecture

The most striking feature of Romanesque art is the astonishing increase in building activity. An eleventh-century monk, Raoul Glaber, conveys the enthusiasm for building that characterizes the period:

> Just before the third year after the millennium, throughout the whole world, but most especially in Italy and Gaul, men began to reconstruct churches.… But it seemed as though each Christian community were aiming to surpass all others in the splendor of construction. It was as if the whole world were shaking itself free, shrugging off the burden of the past, and cladding itself everywhere in a white mantle of churches.

J. France, *The Five Books of the Histories*. Oxford, 1989

These churches were not only more numerous than those of the early Middle Ages, they were also larger, more richly ornamented, and more "Roman-looking." Their naves had stone vaults instead of wooden roofs, and their exteriors were decorated with both architectural ornament and sculpture.

CHURCH OF SANT VINCENÇ, CARDONA An excellent example of an early phase of Romanesque architecture is the collegiate church of Sant Vincenç (**fig. 11.1**), built within the walled confines of the castle at Cardona on the southern flank of the Catalan Pyrenees. The church, begun in 1029 and consecrated in 1040, is straightforward in both plan and elevation. A barrel-vaulted nave creates a continuous space marked off by transverse arches, which run across the width of the nave. These transverse arches divide the nave into units of space called **bays**. The domed bay in front of the chancel, the part of the church containing the altar and seats for the clergy and choir, focuses attention on the ceremonial heart of the building. Blind niches in the chancel walls establish a rhythmic variety that is accentuated in the nave by the staggered cadence of massive **compound piers**, solid masonry supports with rectangular projections attached to their four faces. The projections reflect the different structural elements that combine to support the building. One projection rises the full height of the nave to support the transverse arch, another forms the arch that extends across the side aisle, and two others connect to the arches of the nave arcade.

The compound pier is, in fact, a major architectural innovation of the Romanesque period.

The clarity of articulation of the architectural details at Sant Vincenç endows the building with a heightened sense of unity and harmony. Limited light and robust stone construction create an interior at once sheltering and inspiring; the sober arrangement of simple yet powerful forms is masterfully realized.

Monumental Stone Sculpture

The revival of monumental stone sculpture in the Romanesque era is as significant as the architectural achievements of the period. Free-standing statues had virtually disappeared from Western art after the fifth century and three-dimensional sculpture was rare; stone relief survived only as architectural ornament or surface decoration. Thus, the only sculptural tradition that continued through the early medieval period was that of sculpture-in-miniature such as small reliefs and occasional statuettes in metal or ivory. In works such as the bronze doors of Bishop Bernward (see fig. 10.12), Ottonian art had enlarged the small scale of this tradition but had not changed its spirit. Moreover, its truly large-scale sculptural efforts, such as the *Gero Crucifix* (see fig. 10.16), were limited almost entirely to wood.

LINTEL AT SAINT-GENIS-DES-FONTAINES The marble lintel at Saint-Genis-des-Fontaines, on the French side of the Pyrenees, is dated by inscription to between 1020 and 1021 (**fig. 11.2**). It spans the

11.2 Lintel of west portal, Saint-Genis-des-Fontaines, France. 1020–21. Approx. 2 × 7' (0.6 × 2.13 m)

Christian PILGRIMAGES began as early as the second century with journeys to Jerusalem. The pilgrim would travel to a sacred site to ask for help, to give thanks, or simply to express devotion. In medieval times, there were many pilgrimage destinations, the most popular being Rome, the Holy Land, and Santiago de Compostela in Spain. (The latter is where the remains of the apostle St. James are believed to have been buried.) Geoffrey Chaucer's classic *The Canterbury Tales* is an account of a pilgrimage to the tomb of St. Thomas Becket in Kent, England.

 Read the document with an excerpt from the *Pilgrim's Guide to Santiago de Compostela* on myartslab.com

Between 1095 and 1291, seven different armies were raised in Europe to undertake campaigns, called CRUSADES, to the Holy Land in the name of "freeing" Jerusalem from Muslim control. In fact, the Church's broad call was for war against all of its perceived opponents: Political, heretical, and schismatic. In responding to the call, however, the nobles who volunteered themselves and their loyal soldiers believed they were accumulating merit by waging a "holy war" to reclaim the lands where Jesus had lived. The crusades combined aspects of the pilgrimage as well, with crusaders making stops at holy sites along the way to their various destinations in Syria, Palestine, and Egypt.

doorway of the church and is one of the earliest examples of Romanesque figurative sculpture. The inscription cites the leaders of two stabilizing institutions of the period, *Rotberto Rege* (King Robert) and *Willelmus Aba* (Abbot William), the former a feudal lord and the latter the leader of a monastery. Six apostles flank the central motif of Christ in Majesty supported by angels; each apostle holds a book and stands under an arcade. Two intersecting circles form Christ's mandorla, one symbolizing the earth and the other the heavens, the two realms over which he presides (see page 209).

The Saint-Genis lintel is modest in size, about 2 feet high by 7 feet long. The reliance on line to indicate facial features, drapery folds, and ornamental decoration is reminiscent of early medieval manuscript illumination and reaches as far back as the Hiberno-Saxon period (see fig. 10.3). The carving, with flat surfaces marked by incision, resembles that of the decorative arts, particularly ivories and metalwork. This can be verified by comparing some of the patterns (for example, the beading around the arches) with metalwork techniques (see fig. 10.1). The correlation explains where carvers might have found their sources of inspiration after centuries during which stone sculpture had been virtually abandoned.

Although the figures are rendered with individualized hairstyles and facial features and with a variety of gestures, they are clearly stylized. Each is contained by the frame around him in such a way that it is difficult to decide if the figures are governed by their frames or if the arches swell in response to the figures. The equilibrium between frame and figure parallels the harmonious balance between form and structure that characterizes early Romanesque buildings such as Sant Vincenç at Cardona.

Mature Romanesque

Early Romanesque experiments in sturdy construction, which relied on the skills of masons and sculptors, led to buildings that employed both more sculpture and increasingly sophisticated vaulting techniques. Sculptural decoration was arranged into complicated and didactic iconographic programs.

Pilgrimage Churches and Their Art

Among the most significant social phenomena of eleventh- and twelfth-century Europe was the increased ability of people of all classes to travel. While some journeys were a result of expanded

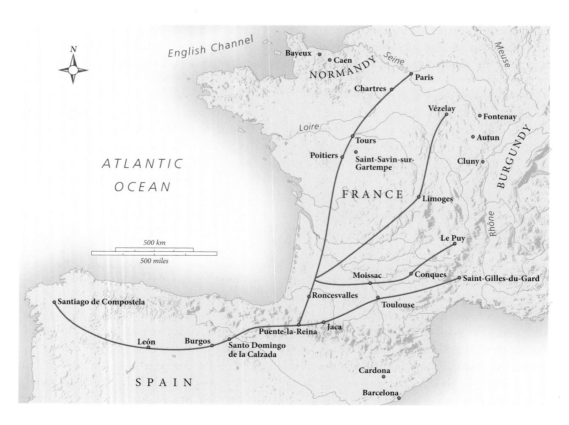

Map 11.2 The pilgrimage routes to Santiago de Compostela, Spain

trade, others, such as a crusade or pilgrimage, were ostensibly for religious purposes. Individual pilgrims made journeys to holy places for different reasons, but most shared the hope that they would find special powers or dispensations as a result of their journey. PILGRIMAGE was not a Romanesque invention. As early as the late fourth century, Egeria, a Spanish pilgrim to Jerusalem, chronicled her visit to the locations central to Christ's life. Special, often miraculous powers associated with these holy sites were transferred to relics, those body parts of holy persons or objects that had come in contact with Christ, his close followers, or other holy figures.

Partly due to the Muslim conquest of the Holy Land, travel there was difficult during the Middle Ages. This led, on the one hand, to the zeal for CRUSADE and, on the other, to the veneration of places within Europe that had important relics or that had been the site of special events. Rome, in particular, became a popular pilgrimage site, beneficiary of the aura of sanctity surrounding SS. Peter and Paul, both of whom lived and were buried there (see page 163). So did Santiago de Compostela on the Iberian peninsula.

SANTIAGO DE COMPOSTELA The tomb of St. James at Santiago de Compostela in northwest Spain (see **map 11.2**) marked the most westerly point of Christianity at the time. According to tradition, the apostle James (*Santiago* in Spanish) had preached Christianity on the Iberian peninsula and his body was returned there in dramatic circumstances after his death. Reports of the tomb's miraculous power attracted large numbers of pilgrims from all over Europe. Many had to brave a difficult sea journey or an exhausting crossing of the Pyrenees Mountains in order to reach Compostela. During the twelfth century as many as tens of thousands of people might have made the journey in a single year. The difficulty of the journey added to its allure. Since much of Spain was under Muslim control, pilgrims considered the trip to Santiago equivalent to a journey to the Muslim-held Holy Land.

The cathedral of Santiago de Compostela had much to offer those brave hearts sufficiently fortunate to reach their goal. The plan of the church (**fig. 11.3**) includes side aisles that run uninterruptedly around the church and form an ambulatory, a passage around the apse. Visitors used these aisles to circumambulate the church, even when the religious offices were being celebrated in the nave

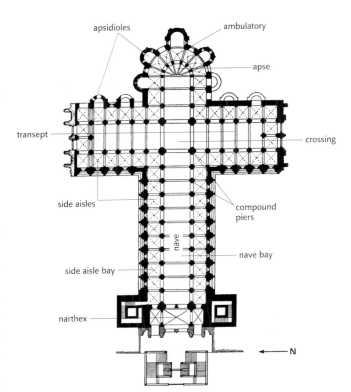

11.3 Plan of cathedral of Santiago de Compostela, Spain (after Dehio)

👁 **Watch** a video about the cathedral of St. James, Santiago de Compostela on myartslab.com

and crossing. **Apsidioles**, or small apselike chapels, arranged along the eastern walls of the transepts and around the apse, provided multiple opportunities to display the relics that pilgrims had come to venerate. As they approached the nave from the west entrance and walked through the building, pilgrims were conscious of marching step by step toward their goals in the apses, altars, and reliquaries at the east end of the church.

Passage through the cathedral was thus a microcosm of the longer journey the pilgrim had taken on the open road, and the cathedral might readily be called a **pilgrimage plan** church. Although not all pilgrimage churches have this same plan, a number of great churches of varying sizes and details, using the same plan as Santiago de Compostela, were built along the roads leading to it.

The plan of Santiago de Compostela is composed of multiple modular units. It recalls the system of architectural composition based on additive components that was employed during the early Middle Ages (see page 215). The bays of the nave and the transept are half the size of the square crossing, and the square bays of the side aisles

Seen in section, the physics of the cathedral of Santiago de Compostela are quite apparent. The walls of the nave and the aisles transfer the weight downward through the piers and outward to the lowest side walls, where it is buttressed.

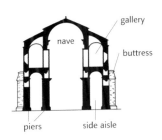

vocabulary and syntax of ancient Roman architecture to a remarkable degree.

So as not to weaken the barrel vaults at their springing, precisely where they would need the most support, Santiago de Compostela was built without a clerestory (the row of windows in the upper part of the wall). Diffused light, subtle and atmospheric, filters into the nave through the side aisles and the galleries above. The galleries provide for an elegantly elaborated interior, as the famous *Pilgrim's Guide*, written around 1130, makes clear:

> In truth, in this church no fissure or fault is found; it is admirably constructed, grand, spacious, bright, of proper magnitude, harmonious in width, length and height, of admirable and ineffable workmanship, built in two storeys, just like a royal palace. For indeed, whoever visits the naves of the gallery, if he goes up sad, after having seen the perfect beauty of this temple, he will be made happy and joyful.

> Paula Gerson, Annie Shaver Crandell, Alison Stones, and Jeanne Krochalis, *Pilgrim's Guide to Santiago de Compostela: A Critical Edition*, II. London, 1998, pp. 69–71

The Romanesque builders' ability to fuse structure and aesthetics provides the synthesis of emotional and spiritual response described in the *Pilgrim's Guide*. In both detail and execution Santiago de Compostela emulates the nobility and dignity of Roman architecture.

RELIQUARIES A twelfth-century casket, today in the Metropolitan Museum of Art in New York (**fig. 11.5**), is typical of the kinds of decorated reliquaries (containers for holy relics) that pilgrims saw on their journeys to Compostela and Rome. This one was probably made in Limoges, a major stop on the road to Compostela and a center of enamel production, where there was a large church built on the pilgrimage plan. The material and the bold areas of flat color, evident in both the foliage and the symbols of the four evangelists, relate this work to the tradition of migration and early medieval metalwork (see fig. 10.1). The method of manufacture is champlevé, which was derived from the cloisonné technique (see page 202). Instead of cells formed from thin strips of metal attached to a support, as with cloisonné, the metal surface of champlevé is gouged out to create compartments that

11.4 Nave, cathedral of Santiago de Compostela, Spain. ca. 1075–1120

Read the document related to the cathedral of St. James, Santiago de Compostela on myartslab.com

are in turn a quarter the size of the crossing and thus half the size of the nave bays. The building's interior (**fig. 11.4**) mirrors the clarity of its plan. As at Sant Vincenç at Cardona (see fig. 11.1), the four **colonnettes** (small attached columns) of the compound piers reflect the building's structural elements. In the nave of Santiago de Compostela vaults, arches, engaged columns, and pilasters (flat shafts in shallow relief) are all firmly knitted together into a coherent order that recaptures the

11.5 The Chasse of Champagnat. Reliquary casket with symbols of the four evangelists. ca. 1150. Champlevé enamel on gilt and engraved copper, 4⁷⁄₈ × 7⁷⁄₁₆ × 3³⁄₈″ (12.4 × 18.9 × 8.5 cm). The Metropolitan Museum of Art, New York. Gift of J. Pierpont Morgan, 1917. 17.190.685

contain the colored enamel. The preciousness of the enamel on the gilt copper of this reliquary and its lavish decoration suit its exceptional and holy contents, thought to be relics of St. Martial, identified by inscription on the other side of the box, since the casket comes from a church dedicated to him in Champagnat, about 60 miles from Limoges.

SCULPTURE AT SAINT-SERNIN Santiago de Compostela, like many of the other churches along the pilgrimage road, has stone sculptures decorating its interior and its portals. At Saint-Sernin at Toulouse, which is on the pilgrimage road that passes through southern France, some of the same sculptors who worked at Santiago de Compostela also carved sculpture. A series of large marble plaques, currently placed in the ambulatory of Saint-Sernin, dates to the years immediately preceding 1100. Six of these plaques depict angels and apostles, while one represents a seated *Christ in Majesty* (**fig. 11.6**). Although their original location is not certain, the plaques most likely decorated the zone around the altar and shrine of Saint-Sernin, thus embellishing an area deemed particularly holy by pilgrims.

The shallow relief and many decorative effects of the Christ plaque recall earlier metalwork and ivory objects (see fig. 10.8). The extensive use of double lines, some creating raised sections, some impressed ones, enhances the figure's volumetric presence. The treatment brings to mind manuscript illumination, particularly Carolingian and Ottonian examples, but also Byzantine ones. The emphasis on volume of the figure of Christ,

11.6 *Christ in Majesty* (*Maiestas Domini*). ca. 1096. Marble, height 50″ (127 cm). Saint-Sernin, Toulouse

Monasticism and Christian Monastic Orders

PEOPLE OF many times, places, and religious faiths have renounced the world and devoted themselves entirely to a spiritual way of life. Some have chosen to live alone as hermits, often in isolated places, where they have led harsh, ascetic existences. Others have come together in religious communities known as MONASTERIES to share their faith and religious observance. Among the Jews of the first century BCE, there were both hermits, or ANCHORITES (John the Baptist was one of these), and a kind of monasticism practiced by a sect known as the Essenes. Both forms are found in Christianity throughout most of its history as well. Their basis can be found in the scriptures. On the one hand, Jesus urged his followers to give up all earthly possessions as the road to salvation. On the other, the book of the Acts of the Apostles in the Bible records that the disciples came together in their faith after the Crucifixion.

The earliest form of a devoted religious calling practiced by Christians was the hermit's life. It was chosen by a number of pious men and women who lived alone in the Egyptian desert in the second and third centuries CE. This way of life was to remain fundamental to the Eastern Church, especially in Syria. But early on, communities emerged when colonies of disciples—both men and women—gathered around the most revered of the hermits, such as St. Anthony (fourth century), who achieved such fame as a holy man that he was pursued by people asking him to act as a divine intercessor on their behalf.

Monasteries soon came to assume great importance in early Christian life. (They included communities for women, which are often called convents or nunneries.) The earliest known monastery was founded by Pachomius along the Nile about 320 and blossomed into a community of nine monasteries and two nunneries by the time of his death a quarter-century later. Similar ones quickly followed in Syria, where monachism (monasticism) flourished until the 638 conquest by the Arabs.

Eastern monasticism was founded by Basil the Great (ca. 330–379), bishop of Caesarea in Asia Minor. Basil's rule established the basic characteristics of Christian monasticism: Poverty, chastity, and humility. It emphasized prayer, scriptural reading, and work, not only within the monastery but also for the good of laypeople in the world beyond its walls; as a result, monasticism now assumed a social role.

The most important figure in Western monasticism was Benedict of Nursia (ca. 480–ca. 553), the founder of the abbey at Monte Cassino in southern Italy. His rule, which was patterned after Basil's, divided the monk's day into periods of private prayer, communal ritual, and labor; it also required a moderate form of communal life, which was strictly governed. This was the

---

somewhat more than half life-size, hints at what may have been the main inspiration behind the revival of large-scale sculpture. A stone-carved image, being solid and three-dimensional, is far more "real" than a painted one.

Cluniac Architecture and Sculpture

During the time when the sculptural decoration of Saint-Sernin was executed, the church was under the auspices of monks from the great Benedictine monastery of Cluny (see box: Cultural Context: Monasticism and Christian Monastic Orders). Cluny was responsible for a network of dependencies; its "daughter" houses, spread across Europe, numbered more than 1,400, evidence of the order's influence and growth. The Cluniac order could determine papal elections and call for crusades against the Muslims. The rise and spread of various monastic orders was significant for the development of Romanesque art, but none was more important than Cluny.

ABBEY CHURCH OF CLUNY The rapid growth of the Cluniac order can also be seen in the fact that its original basilica church of about 910 was replaced with an ample one that itself was replaced only about 75 years later, in 1088, by the largest Romanesque church ever built, the third abbey church of Cluny (**fig. 11.7**). Unfortunately Cluny III, as it is known, was destroyed after the French Revolution, and only the south transept (the one to the right in the plan), and the octagonal tower remain from what was once the most impressive massing of towers in all of Europe. The auspicious use of towers in Carolingian buildings (see fig. 10.10) here reached its culmination. The apsidioles, apses, and towers at the east end of Cluny created a monumental gathering of ever higher forms.

The proportions of Cluny III were based on ratios of "perfect" numbers and on musical harmonies, reminding us of the importance of music to the medieval church. Monks chanted their prayers in the church eight times a day and Gunzo, one of

beginning of the BENEDICTINE order, the first of the great monastic orders (or societies) of the Western Church. The Benedictines thrived with the strong support of Pope Gregory the Great, himself a former monk, who codified the Western liturgy and the forms of Gregorian chant.

Because of their organization and continuity, monasteries were considered ideal seats of learning and administration under the Frankish kings of the eighth century. They were supported even more strongly by Charlemagne and his heirs, who gave them land, money, and royal protection. As a result, they became rich and powerful, even exercising influence on international affairs. Although they had considerable independence at first, the various orders eventually gave their loyalty to Gregory. They thereby became a major source of power for the papacy in return for its protection. Through these ties, Church and State over time became linked institutionally to their mutual benefit, thereby promoting greater stability. Important monastic orders of the West included the Cluniacs, the Cistercians, the Carthusians, the Franciscans, and the Dominicans.

The CLUNIAC order (named after its original monastery at Cluny, in France) was founded as a renewal of the original Benedictine rule in 909 by Berno of Baume. CISTERCIAN monasteries were deliberately located in remote places, where the monks would come into minimal contact with the outside world, and the rules of daily life were particularly strict. In keeping with this austerity, the order developed an architecture recognizable by its geometric simplicity and lack of ornamentation (see page 234–35).

The CARTHUSIAN order was founded by Bruno, an Italian monk, in 1084. Carthusians are in effect hermits, each monk or nun living alone in a separate cell, vowed to silence and devoted to prayer and meditation. Because of the extreme austerity and piety of this order, several powerful dukes in the fourteenth and fifteenth centuries established Carthusian houses (charterhouses; French, *chartreuses*), so that the monks could pray perpetually for the souls of the dukes after they died.

The FRANCISCAN order was founded in 1209 by St. Francis of Assisi (ca. 1181–1226) as a preaching community. Francis, who was perhaps the most saintly character since Early Christian times, insisted on a life of complete poverty, not only for the members personally but for the order as a whole. Franciscan monks and nuns were originally MENDICANTS—that is, they begged for a living. This rule was revised in the fourteenth century.

The DOMINICAN order was established in 1220 by St. Dominic (ca. 1170–1221), a Spanish monk who had been a member of the Cistercians. Besides preaching, the Dominicans devoted themselves to the study of theology. They were considered the most intellectual of the religious orders in the late Middle Ages and the Early Renaissance.

the architects of Cluny III, was noted for his musicianship. A benefit of stone-vaulted buildings was their acoustic resonance; this feature might well have encouraged the widespread use of stone vaulting or at least made the heavy financial investment acceptable to the community. Even today it is a moving experience to hear Gregorian chants sung beneath the vaults of a Romanesque church.

The interior of Cluny III (**fig. 11.8**) was as elegant as it was huge, its vaults reaching 100 feet. Below the clerestory, and in place of a gallery, was a **triforium**, a series of three-arched openings (one set per bay); this created a space within the wall that lightened it both physically and visually. The clerestory and triforium were connected by pilaster strips with Corinthian capitals, reminiscent of Roman architectural decoration. What was not Roman was the use of slightly pointed arches in the nave arcade, a device thought to derive from contact with Islamic culture. By eliminating the center part of the rounded arch, which responds the most to the pull of gravity, the two halves of a pointed arch braced each other. Because the pointed arch exerted less outward pressure than the semicircular arch, not only could it be made steeper, but the walls could be pierced and made lighter.

PRIORY OF MOISSAC The priory of Saint-Pierre at Moissac, located on the pilgrimage road close to Toulouse and also under the direction of Cluny, was another important center of Romanesque art. Four covered passageways arranged around an open garden form the cloister, which is adjacent to the church and was reserved for use by monks (**fig. 11.9**). Protected from the elements, the monks could practice their spiritual exercises here. Seventy-six sculptured capitals decorate this private zone. While they include stories from both Old and New Testaments, many are decorated with foliage, birds, animals, and monstrous creatures.

Although the Romanesque period is far removed chronologically from the Early Christian

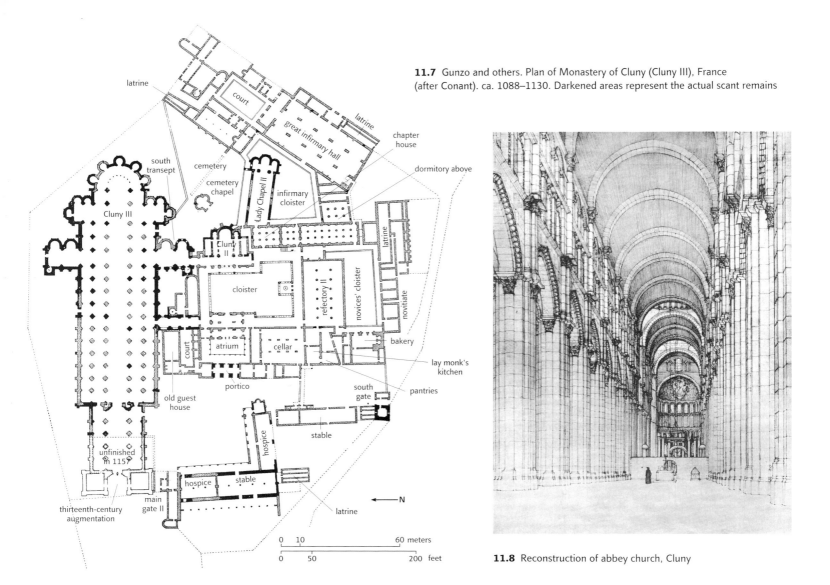

11.7 Gunzo and others. Plan of Monastery of Cluny (Cluny III), France (after Conant). ca. 1088–1130. Darkened areas represent the actual scant remains

11.8 Reconstruction of abbey church, Cluny

11.9 Cloister, priory of Saint-Pierre. ca. 1100. Moissac, France

aversion to image making, even during this period there were those who objected to the corrupting powers of visual representation. In truth, it is hard to correlate the worldly achievements of a monastery such as those at Moissac or Cluny—the wealth they acquired and the political clout they exercised—with the values to which monks traditionally aspired, which were based on the renunciation of earthly pleasures in favor of the pursuit of spiritual ideals. The pictorial representation of

Christian themes was often justified by a famous saying: *Quod legentibus scriptura, hoc idiotis ... pictura.* Translated freely, it means that painting conveys the Word of God to the unlettered.

If the Moissac monks had a profusion of sculpture to engage them, so too did pilgrims and layfolk visiting the monastery's church. Its elaborately sculptured portal (**fig. 11.10**) was executed almost a generation after the cloister was finished. Christ in Majesty takes center stage in the **tympanum**, the

11.10 South portal with *Second Coming of Christ* on tympanum, church of Saint-Pierre, Moissac, France. ca. 1115–30

 Watch an architectural simulation of a Romanesque church portal on myartslab.com

semicircular lunette above the lintel of the portal. He is shown during his Second Coming, when he returns to earth after the apocalyptic end of days, as described in the Book of Revelation (4:1–8), in order to judge mortals as saved or damned. In accordance with the biblical account, Christ is attended by four beasts, two angels and 24 elders, while wavy lines beneath the latter's feet represent "the sea of glass like crystal." The elders, relatively small compared with the other figures, and many of them gesticulating, can barely contain their excitement in the face of the remarkable vision. Abstraction and activity characterize the style of carving, in which quivering lines, borders of meandering ribbon patterns, and fluttering drapery offset a hierarchy of scale and pose. The use of abstraction in the service of religious zeal has parallels in earlier medieval art, for example the manuscript illuminations of the Ebbo Gospels (see fig. 10.7). At Moissac, however, the presentation is on a monumental and public scale.

Other parts of the Moissac portal are also treated sculpturally. Both the **trumeau** (the center post supporting the lintel) and the **jambs** (the

11.11 Trumeau and jambs, south portal, Church of Saint-Pierre, Moissac, France

sides of the doorway) have scalloped outlines (see fig. 11.10), modeled on a popular Islamic device (see fig. 9.5). By borrowing forms from the art of Islam at Moissac and other churches, Christians conveyed their admiration and regard for Arab artistic achievements. At the same time, such acts of appropriation also expressed the Christian ambition to dominate the Muslim enemy (see box: Cultural Context: Spanish Islamic Art and Europe in the Middle Ages). The pilgrimage to Santiago was a similar manifestation of anti-Islamic feeling.

The scalloped outlines framing the doorway activate and dramatize the experience of entering the church. Human and animal forms are treated with flexibility; for instance, the spidery prophet on the side of the trumeau seems perfectly adapted to his precarious perch, even as he seems to struggle to free himself from the stone (**fig. 11.11**). With legs crossed in a graceful movement, he turns his head toward the interior of the church as he unfurls his scroll. The crossed lions that form a symmetrical zigzag on the face of the trumeau "animate" the shaft in the same way that the interlacing beasts of Irish miniatures (from which they are descended) enliven the spaces they inhabit.

We cannot account for the presence of the crossed lions at Moissac in terms of their effectiveness as ornament alone. They belong to an extensive family of savage or monstrous creatures in Romanesque art that retain their demoniacal vitality even as they are forced to perform a supporting function. Their purpose is thus not only decorative but expressive; they embody dark forces that have been domesticated into guardian figures or banished to a position that holds them fixed for all eternity. One medieval bishop argued that seeing animals sculpted in churches would so terrify parishioners that they would be encouraged to refrain from sinful deeds.

A deep porch with lavishly sculptured lateral ends frames the Moissac portal. The messages at Moissac are patently didactic, meant both to command and to enlighten. When visitors on the pilgrim road faced the deep portal of the church they were virtually surrounded by the sculptural program, and this intensified the liminal experience of entering the church. The journey into the church became a veritable rite of passage, transformative both physically and spiritually.

CATHEDRAL OF SAINT-LAZARE, AUTUN Close to Cluny and dependent on it was the Cathedral of Saint-Lazare at Autun. The tympanum of its west

Spanish Islamic Art and Europe in the Middle Ages

I N 711 THE COMBINED Arab and Berber forces of the Muslim commander Tariq ibn Ziyad crossed the straits of Gibraltar, and by 716 most of Spain was in Muslim hands. Under the rule of the Umayyad dynasty (751–1017), Córdoba became the capital of a prosperous, tolerant, and powerful Muslim kingdom in Spain (see page 193), in which Christians and Jews played important roles in cultural life. During the eleventh and twelfth centuries, in the aftermath of the fall of the Umayyads, successive Berber invasions from North Africa brought new Muslim dynastic patrons into Spain, who oversaw splendid new artistic production. But they also suffered a series of military defeats at the hands of the strengthening Christian powers in the north. Of the several small Islamic kingdoms that formed in the twilight of Muslim rule in Spain, one in particular, that of the Nasrids, ruling in Granada from 1230 to 1492, saw a last glorious flowering of the arts before its defeat by the Castilians and Aragonese united under King Ferdinand and Queen Isabella.

The dominant Muslim style in the arts of southern Spain affected artistic production of non-Muslims in many complex ways. From the tenth through the twelfth centuries, i.e. throughout the Romanesque period, in the mountainside principalities of the Christian north, Christian builders built small churches and monasteries in the **mozarab** style, using the horseshoe arches, alternating colored voussoirs, and mosaics of colored stone they had seen in the Muslim south. At the same time, in the northern monasteries, artist monks illustrated manuscripts with paintings that also reflected the dominant Muslim style. Beyond the Pyrenees, along the medieval pilgrimage roads into France, aspects of the Muslim style even influenced French Romanesque art; the twelfth-century wooden doors of Le Puy Cathedral in France bore an elaborate kufic inscription in Arabic: *Mashallah*—"may God protect this place."

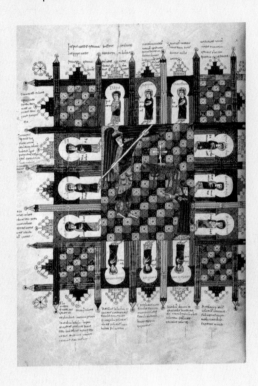

Folio of the *Silos Apocalypse*, commentary by Beatus of Liébana, illustrated by Prior Petrus, completed in 1109. Colors, gold and silver leaf on parchment, 15 × 9⅞" (38 × 25 cm)

portal (**fig. 11.12**) represents the Last Judgment, the most awe-inspiring scene in Christian art. This scene depicts Christ after his Second Coming as he separates those who will be eternally saved from those who are damned. His figure, much larger than any other, dominates the tympanum. The sculptor, Gislebertus, whose signature appears immediately under the feet of Christ in the center, treats the subject with extraordinary force. Gislebertus's style is sufficiently individual to posit convincingly that he trained at Cluny before his elevation to master's rank at Autun.

On the left side of the tympanum, apostles observe the weighing of souls, which takes place on the right side. Four angels in the corners sound the trumpets of the Apocalypse. At the bottom, the dead rise from their graves, trembling with fear; some are already beset by snakes or gripped by huge, clawlike hands. Above, their fate quite literally hangs in the balance, with devils yanking at one end of the scales and angels at the other. The saved souls cling like children to the angels for protection before their ascent to the Heavenly Jerusalem (far left), while the condemned, seized by grinning devils, are cast into the mouth of Hell (far right). These nightmarish devils are human in general outline, but they have birdlike legs, furry thighs, tails, pointed ears, and savage mouths. The hierarchical, abstract, and patterned representation of Christ conveys his formidable power more effectively than any naturalistic image could.

The Last Judgment, with its emphasis on retribution, was a standard subject for the tympana

11.12 West portal, with *Last Judgment* by Gislebertus on tympanum, cathedral of Saint-Lazare. ca. 1120–35. Autun, France

 Explore the Closer Look for the *Last Judgment* tympanum at Autun on myartslab.com

of Romanesque churches. It was probably chosen because some medieval justice was dispensed in front of the church portal, *ante ecclesium*. Thus, actual judicial proceedings paralleled the divine judgment represented here. Trial was by ordeal, whereby the accused established innocence only by withstanding grueling physical tests. The ordeals must, in reality, have been as terrifying as the scenes depicted on the tympanum.

Cistercian Architecture and Art

Cluny's very success meant that it was subject to criticism, particularly by the Cistercians, whose motherhouse was at Cîteaux in Burgundy. The Cistercians were founded in the eleventh century as an ascetic order in opposition to the increasing wealth of the Benedictines of Cluny. In addition to prayer, the Cistercians devoted themselves to hard work, which helped guarantee their own great success. Sound economic planning, skill in agriculture and husbandry, and wealthy benefactors furthered their cause. The Cistercian order and its style spread across Europe, and by the end of the

twelfth century the Cistercians controlled nearly 700 monasteries. Cistercian architecture, in its simplicity, contrasts markedly with the architecture of the Cluniac order.

ABBEY CHURCH AT FONTENAY The abbey church at Fontenay, not far from Cîteaux, was begun in 1139. Fontenay exemplifies the Cistercian reliance on simple and unadorned forms, in contrast to the opulence of Cluny. By comparison to the expansive plan of Cluny (see fig. 11.7), where the huge abbey church dominated a sprawling complex, Fontenay is precise, a pure and tightly controlled equilibrium balancing all of its constituent parts.

The east end of the church is unembellished by apses, and no towers were planned. Since Cistercians permitted neither sculpture nor wall painting, the interior of the church (**fig. 11.13**) lacks applied decoration. Clerestory and gallery are suppressed. However, in their own terms, the clean lines of the pointed transverse arches that define the nave and openings into the side aisles, and the pattern of unframed windows, create an elegant refinement of simple forms that are at once graceful and moving. Once again, the church serves as a safe, tranquil, and spiritual refuge from worldly burdens, although different in effect from the protective enclosures that other Romanesque churches offer (see figs. 11.1 and 11.4).

Wall Painting

Most Romanesque paintings on walls and ceilings, which undoubtedly were numerous, have been destroyed over the centuries. Fortunately, an impressive cycle of wall paintings still survives at the Benedictine abbey church of Saint-Savin-sur-Gartempe near Poitiers. The church was designed to offer a continuous surface for murals. *The Building of the Tower of Babel* (**fig. 11.14**) is part of an extensive cycle of Hebrew Bible scenes on the barrel vault of the nave. The intensely dramatic design is crowded with strenuous action. God himself, on the far left, participates directly in the narrative, addressing the builders of the huge structure. He is counterbalanced, on the right, by the giant Nimrod, leader of the project, who frantically hands blocks of stone to the masons atop the tower. The entire scene becomes a great test of strength between God and mortals. The heavy, dark contours and the emphatic gestures make the composition easy to read from the floor below. Elsewhere in the church the viewer can see New Testament episodes and scenes from the lives of local saints.

11.13 Nave, abbey church, Fontenay. 1139–47

11.14 *The Building of the Tower of Babel*. Early twelfth century. Detail of painting on the nave vault, Saint-Savin-sur-Gartempe, France

Book Illustration

As in the early Middle Ages, manuscript production in the Romanesque period continued to be largely the responsibility of monastic scriptoria under the supervision of monks. Manuscripts produced by Cluniac scriptoria are stylistically similar to Cluniac wall painting and often express concerns remarkably akin to those of the period's architects and sculptors. The interrelationship of monastic communities accounts for some consistency of manuscript production across various regions during the Romanesque period.

THE *CODEX COLBERTINUS* The illustration of *St. Matthew* from the *Codex Colbertinus* (**fig. 11.15**) is similar in concept and pose to a number of Romanesque carvings, particularly the pier reliefs from the Moissac cloister (see fig. 11.9). The manuscript was made at that monastery, or nearby, just when sculptors were at work in the cloister. Matthew appears at the beginning of his Gospel, next to an embellished letter L, the first letter of *Liber*, meaning "book." Figures, animals, foliage, and decorative patterns conform to the shape of the letter, recalling the way Romanesque sculptured figures correspond to their frames (see fig. 11.2).

In contrast to the small, freely disposed figures and animals in the initial, the figure of Matthew confronts us directly. Although he fills the available space of the architectural setting, a number of features deny his solidity. The heavy outlines and bold colors, reminiscent of enamelwork, in combination with a variety of juxtaposed patterns, flatten the image. These devices demonstrate to what extent forms popular during the early Middle Ages remained vital.

11.15 *St. Matthew*, from the *Codex Colbertinus*. ca. 1100. Tempera on vellum, 7½ × 4″ (19 × 10.16 cm). Bibliothèque Nationale, Paris

11.16 *St. Mark*, from a gospel book produced at the Abbey at Corbie. Early twelfth century. Tempera on vellum, 10¾ × 7⅞″ (27.3 × 20 cm). Bibliothèque Municipale, Amiens, France

THE CORBIE GOSPEL BOOK In its monumentality, the image of *St. Mark* from an early twelfth-century gospel book produced at Corbie (**fig. 11.16**) can also be likened to Romanesque sculpture. The active pose and zigzag composition bear comparison with the prophet on the Moissac trumeau (see fig. 11.11). The twisting movement of the lines, not only in the figure of St. Mark but also in the winged lion, the scroll, and the curtain, recalls Carolingian miniatures of the Reims School as well, such as the Ebbo Gospels (see fig. 10.7).

This resemblance helps us see the differences between them as well. In the Romanesque manuscript, every trace of classical illusionism has disappeared. The fluid modeling of the Reims School, with its suggestion of light and space, has been replaced here by firm contours filled in with bright, solid colors. As a result, the three-dimensional aspects of the picture are reduced to overlapping planes. The Romanesque artist has given his work a clarity and precision that had not been possible in Carolingian or Ottonian times. Here, the representational, the symbolic, and the decorative elements of the design are fully integrated.

Regional Variants of the Romanesque Style

Although consistent aesthetic aims expressed across various media link the art of diverse areas of Europe during the Romanesque period, a variety of distinct regional approaches can be identified. These distinct approaches appear in regions of what is now France as well as in other parts of Europe. Regional variety in Romanesque art reflects the political conditions of eleventh- and twelfth-century Western Europe, which was governed by a feudal, though loose, alliance of princes and dukes.

Western France: Poitou

A so-called school of sculptural decoration appears during the Romanesque period in the region of Poitou, part of the Duchy of Aquitaine in southwestern France. A notable example is Notre-Dame-la-Grande in Poitiers, seat of the lords of Aquitaine.

NOTRE-DAME-LA-GRANDE, POITIERS The broad screenlike façade of Notre-Dame-la-Grande (**fig. 11.17**) offers an expanded field for sculptural decoration. Elaborately bordered arcades house large seated or standing figures. Below them a wide band

11.17 West façade, Notre-Dame-la-Grande. Early twelfth century. Poitiers, France

of relief carving stretches across the façade. The Fall of Adam and Eve appears with scenes from the life of Mary, including the Annunciation and Nativity, juxtaposing Eve and Mary. Next to the representation of Adam and Eve, an inscription identifies an enthroned figure as Nebuchadnezzar, the king of Babylon mentioned in the Hebrew Bible. The *Play of Adam*—a twelfth-century medieval drama of a type that was traditionally performed in churches—probably served as the source for the choice and arrangement of figures at this church. Beside Nebuchadnezzar, centered above the arch on the left of the portal, there are four figures carrying either scrolls or books on which are inscribed lines from the Adam play, in which Adam and Eve figure prominently and Nebuchadnezzar is also mentioned.

Essential to the rich sculptural effect is the deeply recessed doorway, without tympanum but framed by a series of arches with multiple archivolts, decorative moldings or bands that frame the arch. The conical helmets of the towers nearly match the height of the **gable** (the triangular wall section at the top of the façade), which rises above the actual level of the roof behind it. The gable contains a representation of Christ with angels, their height in the composition denoting their heavenly place. The sculptural program spread out over this entire area is a visual exposition of Christian doctrine intended as a feast for the eyes as well as the mind.

Southeastern France: Provence

In the French region of Provence, south of Burgundy, Romanesque art benefited from its proximity to Italy. The name Provence derives from its ancient designation as *provincia romana* in recognition of its close political and cultural connections to Rome, and even today considerable vestiges of Roman art and architecture abound in the region.

SAINT-GILLES-DU-GARD The façade of the abbey church of Saint-Gilles-du-Gard (**fig. 11.18**), like that of Notre-Dame-la-Grande in Poitiers, screens the church. The inspiration for this façade, composed of three arches, can be found in the Roman triumphal arch (see fig. 7.29), connecting ancient triumphal imagery with the important liminal function of entering the church. Given contemporary concerns for Christian victory, in particular the struggle to conquer the Muslims, the formal association between the façade and a Roman triumphal monument must have seemed particularly fitting. The depiction on the lintel supporting the left tympanum of Jesus' triumphal entry into Jerusalem would have had special meaning to contemporary viewers, who were aware that the town of Saint-Gilles on the Rhône River estuary was a principal site of embarkation for French crusaders on their way to the Holy Land.

The Holy Land

The history of the crusades is a complex one and the motives of crusaders diverse. Some went for what one early twelfth-century priest described as "superficial reasons," that is, for the excitement of foreign travel and for financial gain, while others undertook the quest as a form of penance or out of

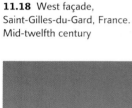

11.18 West façade, Saint-Gilles-du-Gard, France. Mid-twelfth century

deeply felt religious piety, seeking to free the places where Christ lived, taught, and died from the Muslims who had occupied them. The First Crusade, mobilized by Pope Urban II in 1095, managed to claim Jerusalem after four years, but later crusades were generally disastrous.

CRAC DES CHEVALIERS To defend territories conquered during the First Crusade, French crusaders erected a significant number of castles in the Holy Land. Among the best-preserved is in northern Syria, the Crac des Chevaliers (the name derives from the Syrian word for fortress and the French word for knight) (**fig. 11.19**). The Crac des Chevaliers guards the Homs Pass, an important commercial corridor, and rises more than 2,000 feet above the fertile pastures of the Orantes Valley. In 1110, the Franks, under Raymond IV of Saint-Gilles, count of Toulouse and subsequently count of Tripoli, occupied the site of what had been a small eleventh-century Arab fort, which was then rebuilt and expanded. The castle sits on a natural outcrop of rock, whose sharp drop protected it on the north, east, and west. The first Christian castle took the form of a trapezoidal precinct enclosed by walls with projecting rectangular towers. These towers

were later converted to rounded ones because they provided better sight-lines for defense in time of siege; and an outer enclosure, also composed of curtain walls and rounded projections, in some places more than 25 feet thick, was added. Battered (sloping) walls, difficult to scale, were added to the inner precinct. Defenses also included slits for archers as well as crenelations, notched battlements at the top of the walls that shielded warriors while allowing them to release their weapons. Projecting from the walls are machicolations providing an enclosed area supported by a row of arches and containing openings through which soldiers could drop rocks on attackers. An aqueduct brought water from the summit of a nearby mountain, filling cisterns and a reservoir built between the inner and outer walls that also served as a defense. It has been estimated that in time of siege the Crac would have been able to stock provisions for five years.

Castles were the center of authority over the local population: in the case of the Crac, a largely Muslim one. The castle proclaimed the precept of rule of the overlord and as such upheld the structure of feudal society and the relationship between lord and vassal. Romanesque castles share the same aesthetic concerns as Romanesque churches

11.19 Crac des Chevaliers, Homs Pass, Syria. Twelfth century with later additions

 View the Closer Look for the Crac des Chevaliers on myartslab.com

and other buildings and use the same system of solid stone walls, arches, and vaults. The rhythmic arrangement of curved and straight walls and the repeated patterns of wall openings suggest that similar concerns for design and proportionality were at play.

In 1271, the Crac des Chevaliers fell to the Muslims, and the chapel, which the Christians had erected within the inner precinct, was converted into a mosque.

Tuscany

During the Romanesque period, Tuscany, a region in northwestern Italy divided into several independent city-states, including Pisa and Florence, continued what were basically Early Christian architectural forms. However, they added decorative features inspired by Roman architecture. A deliberate revival of the antique Roman style in Tuscan architecture was the use of a multicolored marble "skin" on the exteriors of churches. Little of this inlay is left today on the ancient monuments of Rome because much of it was literally "lifted" to decorate later buildings. However, the interior of the Pantheon still gives us some idea of what it must have looked like (see fig. 7.20).

BAPTISTERY OF SAN GIOVANNI, FLORENCE In Florence the greatest achievement of the Tuscan Romanesque is the baptistery of San Giovanni, a domed, octagonal building of impressive size that was begun in the middle of the eleventh century (**fig. 11.20**). The green-and-white marble paneling is typical of the Florentine Romanesque in its severely geometric lines. The triple arches of the second-story blind arcades, with their triumphal-arch design, are extraordinarily classical in proportion and detail.

The individual, additive units decorating Tuscan Romanesque buildings have a conceptual parallel in

11.20 Baptistery of San Giovanni, ca. 1060–1150. Florence, Italy

11.21 *Crowds Gaze in Awe at a Comet as Harold is Told of an Omen*. Detail of the *Bayeux Tapestry*. ca. 1066–83. Wool embroidery on linen. Height 20" (50.7 cm). Centre Guillaume le Conquérant, Bayeux, France

View the Closer Look for the Bayeux Tapestry on myartslab.com

the compartmentalized bays in pilgrimage churches (see fig. 11.4) and also in the way French Romanesque portals (see figs. 11.10, 11.12, 11.17) create a unified composition of individual units. Roman elements in conscious revival—here the use of marble and the repeated arches that rest on columns topped with Corinthian capitals—unite many of these Romanesque works as well.

Normandy and England

In Normandy, Christianity was strongly supported by the Norman dukes and barons. Duke William II of Normandy actively promoted monastic reform and founded numerous abbeys. Normandy soon became a cultural center of international importance. When William invaded Anglo-Saxon England in 1066 and became its king, the country became politically allied to northern France. For that reason Norman and English art of the Romanesque period share many stylistic traits.

THE BAYEUX TAPESTRY The complex relationship between the Normans and the English is hinted at in the *Bayeux Tapestry* (**fig. 11.21**). In actuality it is not a tapestry at all, since it is not woven but, rather, an embroidered linen frieze 230 feet long. The 50 surviving scenes record the events, culminating in 1066, when WILLIAM THE CONQUEROR crossed the English Channel to claim the throne of England upon the death of King Edward the Confessor. Since a Norman patron presumably commissioned the "tapestry," the story is told from the conquerors' perspective, yet its manufacture has generally been credited to English needlewomen, justly famous during the Middle Ages for their skill (see box: Cultural Context: Women Artists and Patrons during the Middle Ages, overleaf).

The *Bayeux Tapestry* exhibits a profound interest in narrative that is also apparent in other Romanesque media (see figs. 11.14 and 11.17). The designer of the tapestry integrated narrative and ornament with complete ease. Two border strips frame the main frieze; while some of the images of these margins are decorative, others offer commentary on the tapestry's continuous narrative. In one scene (see fig. 11.21) an aide announces to a recently crowned Harold the appearance of an amazing natural phenomenon, represented in the upper border as a spinning star leaving its fiery trail. The inscription ISTI MIRANT STELLA ("These men marvel at the star") records the brilliant apparition of Halley's Comet in 1066, during the days immediately following Harold's coronation. To the medieval viewer, the prophetic significance of the natural event would have been clear,

WILLIAM THE CONQUEROR (ca. 1028–87), the illegitimate son of the duke of Normandy, claimed he was promised the English throne by his cousin Edward the Confessor. William defeated the usurper Harold Godwin at the Battle of Hastings and was crowned king on Christmas Day 1066. By the time of the Domesday Book (1086), a survey of England ordered by William, the Anglo-Saxon rebellions had been completely crushed, and a new ruling class of Normans, Bretons, and Flemings had been established.

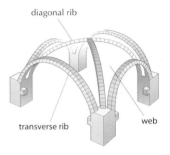

diagonal rib

transverse rib

web

Ribbed groin vault

Women Artists and Patrons during the Middle Ages

THE ROLE OF WOMEN as artists and patrons has been the subject of intense scholarly investigation during the past half-century. Even with significant ongoing research, it is hard to fully evaluate women's roles in artistic production during the Middle Ages.

The late tenth through the twelfth century witnessed a rise of women first as patrons of art and then as artists, though certainly their restricted roles in society naturally limited the opportunities available to them. In determining the capacity to patronize works of art, just as important as gender, and probably more significant, was one's social class. For the Middle Ages, the development of women patrons probably began with the Ottonian dynasty, which forged an alliance with the Church by placing members of the imperial family in prominent positions. Thus Mathilde, Otto I's granddaughter, became abbess of the Holy Trinity convent at Essen in 974, where she was credited with important gifts to the cathedral there, such as a magnificent reliquary in the form of a golden Virgin, as well as gold, enamel, and jeweled crosses. Later, the sister, daughters, and granddaughter of Otto II also served as abbesses of major convents. Hardly less important, though not of royal blood, were Hrosvitha, canoness at the monastery of Gandersheim, who was the first woman dramatist we know of, and the two abbesses of Niedermünster, both named Uota.

In truth, we have little first-hand evidence of medieval artists' identities, not only those women artists, but of their male compatriots as well. We know women produced art from the twelfth century on, although only a few of their names are known. They undoubtedly played a substantial role in the textile arts and the *Bayeux Tapestry* (see fig. 11.21) has always been credited to English embroiderers, even though there is no documentary evidence to support the claim. The role of women in manuscript production was undoubtedly significant as well, as evidenced by an initial in a manuscript that includes a nun bearing a scroll inscribed in Latin, "Guda, the sinful woman, wrote and illuminated this book." In another book, there is a depiction of Claricia, evidently a lay artist, swinging as carefree as any child from the letter Q she has decorated.

The brilliant Benedictine abbess Hildegard of Bingen (1098–1196) composed almost 80 vocal works that rank with the finest of the day. She also wrote some 13 books on theology, medicine, and science, and was known above all for her books of visions, which made her one of the great spiritual voices of her day. Although one book, the *Liber Scivias* (*To Know the Ways of God*), is now available only in facsimile (the original was destroyed in 1945) and the other, the *Liber divinorum operum* (*The Book of Divine Works*), is known only in a later version, it is likely that the originals were executed under Hildegard's direct supervision by nuns in her convent on the Rhine.

Herrad of Landsberg, abbess of Hohenberg in Alsace (1130–95), was the author of the *Hortus Deliciarum* (*The Garden of Delights*), an encyclopedia of knowledge and history compiled for the education of her nuns. But the *Hortus* was destroyed in 1870 and survives only in a 1979 reconstruction based on nineteenth-century copies of the original. Ultimately, with Herrad and Hildegard, the exact roles they played in the production of the books they wrote remain an open question, as do the larger roles of women as artists and patrons during the Middle Ages.

Page with self-portrait of the nun Guda, *Book of Homilies*, from Germany. Early twelfth century. Ink on parchment. Universitätsbibliothek Johann Christian Senckenberg, Frankfurt am Main

especially when viewed after the fact. Beneath Harold, ghostly boats await the Normans, who are preparing to cross the English Channel. The scene foreshadows the violent events to come. Although the *Bayeux Tapestry* does not use the pictorial devices of classical painting, such as foreshortening and overlapping (see fig. 5.32), its account is nonetheless vivid and detailed.

DURHAM CATHEDRAL Norman architecture is responsible for a great breakthrough in structural engineering, which took place in England, where William made donations to build in a Norman style after his conquest of the country. Durham Cathedral, begun in 1093, is among the largest churches of medieval Europe (**fig. 11.22**). Its nave is wider than Santiago de Compostela's, and its overall length (400 feet) is greater. The vault over its eastern end had been completed by 1107, in a remarkably short time, and the rest of the nave was vaulted by 1130.

This vault is of great interest. As the earliest systematic use of a ribbed groin vault over a three-story nave, it marks a fundamental advance in church construction. The groin vault, used so effectively by the Romans (see page 241), efficiently channeled thrust onto four corner points. This allowed for open space under each arch, which could be used for window openings without diminishing the strength of the vault. Looking at the plan of Durham, we see that the aisles consist of the usual almost-square groin-vaulted compartments. The bays of the nave, separated by strong transverse arches, are oblong and also groin-vaulted so that the ribs of each bay form a double-X design. Each vault of the nave is thus divided into seven sections, and they are referred to as septpartite (or seven-part) groin vaults. Since the nave bays are twice as long as the aisle bays, transverse arches occur only at the odd-numbered piers of the nave arcade. The piers therefore alternate in size. The larger odd-numbered ones are compound, with bundles of column and pilaster shafts attached to a square or oblong core, while the even-numbered ones are thinner and cylindrical.

The ribs were needed to provide a stable skeleton for the groin vault, so that the curved surfaces between them could be filled in with masonry of a minimal thickness. Thus both weight and thrust were reduced. This flexible system resulted in more efficient vault erection and greater economy of

construction. Here, the ingenious scheme remains in an experimental stage. While the transverse arches at the crossing are round, those to the west of it are slightly pointed, indicating an ongoing search for improvements.

Durham exhibits great structural strength; even so, the decoration incised in its round piers, each different from the other, and the pattern established by the vault ribs hark back to the Anglo-Saxon love of decoration and interest in surface pattern (see fig. 10.1).

SAINT-ÉTIENNE, CAEN The abbey church of Saint-Étienne at Caen in Normandy was founded by William the Conqueror a year or two after his invasion of England, but it took over a hundred

11.22 Nave (looking east), Durham Cathedral, England. 1093–1130

 Explore the architectural panoramas of Durham Cathedral on myartslab.

years to complete. Over this period of time the fruits of Durham Cathedral's ribbed groin vault system matured.

The west façade (**fig. 11.23**) offers a striking contrast with Notre-Dame-la-Grande in Poitiers (see fig. 11.17) and other Romanesque façades (figs. 11.10 and 11.12). The westwork proclaims this an imperial church. Its closest antecedents are Carolingian churches, such as the abbey church at Corvey (see fig. 10.10), built under royal patronage. Like them, it has a minimum of decoration. Four huge buttresses divide the front of the church into three vertical sections. The thrust upward continues in the two towers, the height of which would be impressive even without the tall helmets, which are later additions.

The nave of Saint-Étienne (**fig. 11.24**) was originally planned to have a wooden ceiling, as well as galleries and a clerestory. After the experience of Durham, however, it became possible in the early twelfth century to build a groined nave vault, with only slight changes in the wall design. The bays of the nave here

11.23 West façade, Saint-Étienne. Begun 1068. Caen, France

11.24 Nave, Saint-Étienne. Vaulted ca. 1115–20. Caen, France

are approximately square, whereas at Durham they were oblong. Therefore, the double-X rib pattern could be replaced by a single X with an additional transverse rib, which produced a sexpartite (or six-part) groin vault, with six sections instead of seven. These vaults are no longer separated by heavy transverse arches but instead by simple ribs. The resulting reduction in weight gives a stronger sense of continuity to the nave vault as a whole and produces a less emphatic alternation of piers. Compared with Durham, the nave of Saint-Étienne has an airy lightness.

Durham and Caen mark the culmination of Romanesque architectural experiments. The improved economic conditions and political stability of Europe, outlined at the beginning of this chapter, had their rewards in the secure structures built in the twelfth century. However, the architecture's defensive qualities also suggest a paradox: As much as the stalwart, powerfully constructed buildings express a newfound confidence, they also reveal lingering apprehension. The terrifying Last Judgment scenes (see fig. 11.12) and other Romanesque visions of monsters and diabolical beings also attest to this anxiety. The sheltering quality of Romanesque architecture must have been comforting at a time when people yearned for protection from both known and unknown dangers.

POINTS OF REFLECTION

11.1 Discuss the meaning of the term "Romanesque" and evaluate its appropriateness to describe the art of the eleventh and early twelfth centuries.

11.2 Describe the significance of monastery, pilgrimage, and crusade in the diffusion of artistic forms during the Romanesque period.

11.3 Explain in what ways the arts of Tuscany, Normandy, and England share general Romanesque characteristics and in what ways they express special concerns.

11.4 Analyze the portals of the churches of Saint-Pierre at Moissac and Saint-Lazare at Autun, differentiate the individual parts of the Romanesque portal, and explain the meanings the sculpture of these portals conveys.

11.5 Interpret the kinds of buildings that were built during the Romanesque period, consider the construction forms employed to build them, and imagine what it is like to be inside these structures.

11.6 Discuss the use of barrel and groin vaults during the Romanesque period and characterize the advantages and disadvantages of each type.

✓—[**Study**] and review on myartslab.com

ART IN TIME

- **1020/21—Carving of marble lintel at Saint-Genis-des-Fontaines, France**

- 1031—The caliphate of Córdoba breaks up

- 1040—Consecration of church of Sant Vincenç in Cardona, Spain

- **ca. 1075–1120—Cathedral built at Santiago de Compostela, Spain**

- 1099—The First Crusade warriors capture Jerusalem

- By end of 1100s—Cistercians control nearly 700 monasteries

- 1066—William the Conqueror invades England

- **ca. 1066–83—Fabrication of the *Bayeux Tapestry***

- 1088—Cluny III begun

- **1093—Construction begins on Durham Cathedral, England**

- 1204—Fall of Constantinople

12 Gothic Art

((•—**Listen** to the chapter audio on myartslab.com

We tend to think of history as the unfolding of events in time, yet we are not as aware of their unfolding in terms of place. The Gothic era cannot be defined by means of time alone—we must consider its geographic range as well. At the start, about 1140, this geographical area was small indeed, covering only the province known as the Île-de-France (Paris and vicinity), the royal domain of the French kings (see **map 12.1**). A hundred years later, most of Western Europe, from Sicily to Norway, had adopted the Gothic style, with only a few Romanesque pockets left here and there. By 1400, however, the Gothic area had begun to shrink. It no longer included Italy, and by 1550 it had disappeared almost entirely, except in England.

The term Gothic was used in the sixteenth century to describe a style of buildings thought to have descended from the Goths, those tribes that occupied northern Europe during the early Middle Ages. Although the ancestry of the style is not as direct as these early writers claimed, they were accurate about its geography, since the style is most recognizable north of the Alps. As Gothic art spread from the Île-de-France to the rest of the country and then through all of Europe, it was referred to in its

own time as *opus modernum* (modern work) or *opus francigenum* (French work). These designations are significant, because they tell us that in its own time the style was viewed as innovative and as having its origins in France. In the course of the thirteenth century, the new style gradually lost its imported flavor, and regional variety began to reassert itself.

For a century—from about 1150 to 1250, during the Age of the Great Cathedrals—architecture played the dominant role in the formation of a coherent Gothic style. Gothic sculpture, at first severely architectural in spirit, became more independent after 1200. Early Gothic sculpture and painting reflect the discipline of their monumental setting, while Late Gothic architecture and sculpture strive for more pictorial effects.

Artistic developments roughly parallel happenings in the political arena, for the Gothic was a distinctive period not only artistically but politically as well. Aided by technological advances including cannon and iron crossbow design, princes and kings conquered increasingly large territories, administered for them by vassals, who in turn collected taxes to support armies and navies. In France, the Capetian kings at first ruled only the fertile territory

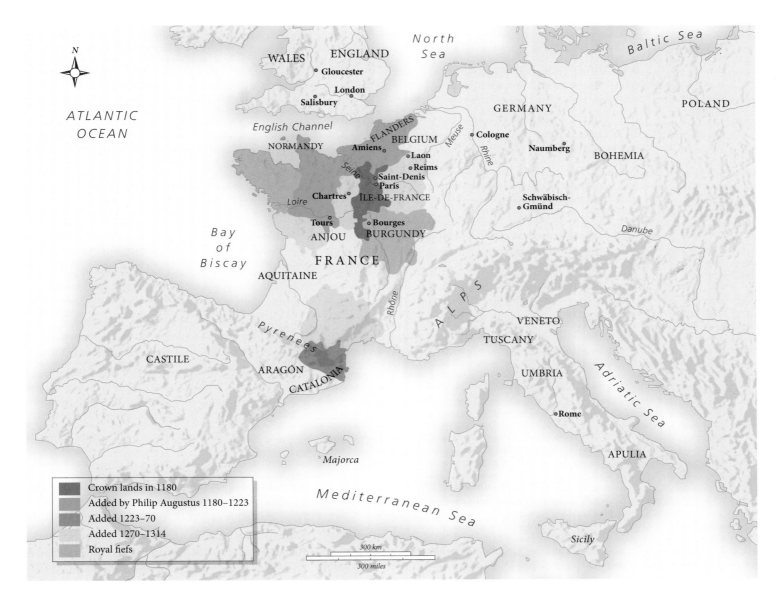

Map 12.1 Europe in the Gothic period

of the Île-de-France, but by 1300 they had added to this much of the land previously held by the Count of Flanders, as well as Bourges, Tours, and Amiens—all of which were to become the sites of important Gothic cathedrals—as well as the central province of the Auvergne and the southern province of Languedoc. The French kings also acquired Normandy and England, which gave rise to the conflicting claims over the kingship of France that led to the Hundred Years' War (1337–1453).

Germany remained a collection of independent city-states ruled by electors, who were responsible for, among other things, choosing kings. Supported by shifting alliances with the papacy, the kings of France and England emerged as the leading powers at the expense of the Germans in the early thirteenth century, generally a time of peace and prosperity. After 1290, however, the balance of power quickly broke down.

The growth of urban centers and the increasing importance of cathedrals, the seats of bishops, are formative features of the Gothic period. Universities developed out of cathedral schools as the principal centers of learning, thus taking on the role previously played by monasteries. At the same time literature written in the vernacular (as opposed to Latin) began to emerge, becoming accessible to a broader public. Romanesque art had been predominantly rural and monastic, while Gothic art, by contrast, became increasingly cosmopolitan.

Urban growth was both the result and the cause of economic, social, and demographic changes. Agriculture became more efficient, with increased acreage under cultivation, and surplus production provided commodities for sale and purchase. This produced, in turn, a money economy based on investment, profit, and trade, in place of barter. Consequently a veritable middle class arose, living in cities, the centers of trade and commerce. Once out from under the feudal yoke, merchants and artists of this middle class were free to form **guilds** to control the production and distribution of goods and services. A general and significant increase in population also spurred urban growth.

During the thirteenth century, Western European Christianity found in St. Thomas Aquinas its greatest intellect since St. Augustine and St. Jerome some 850 years earlier. Aquinas, an Italian theologian, studied in Cologne and taught in Paris. His method of argument, called scholasticism, used reason to understand and explain faith. Gothic builders shared qualities with the Scholastics. They brought the logic and clarity of engineering principles to bear on revelation, using physical forces to create a concord of spiritual experiences in much the same way the Scholastics used elucidation and clarification to build their well-constructed arguments.

Early Gothic Art in France

It is not clear why Gothic art first appeared in the area around Paris, the Île-de-France. Some art historians believe that because this region had not developed a strong local style during the Romanesque period, it was particularly open to innovation and influence from other areas. Others have suggested that it was a result of a concerted effort on the part of the kings of France to aggrandize themselves, since it was here that their domains were located. Certainly the Île-de-France is fortuitously positioned, near the center of France and thus accessible to the south and west, where major sculptural programs flourished during the Romanesque period, and adjacent to Normandy, where many structural innovations, including the ribbed groin vault, had been introduced to France (see pages 241 and 243).

Saint-Denis: Suger and the Beginnings of Gothic Architecture

The study of Gothic art begins with an examination of the rebuilding of the royal Abbey Church of Saint-Denis just outside the city of Paris. The rebuilding of this historic church was undertaken between 1137 and 1144 by its abbot, Suger. His ambitious building program was designed to

emphasize the relationship between Saint-Denis and the French monarchy. The kings of France, who belonged to the Capetian line, derived their authority from a Carolingian tradition. However, they had less power than the nobles who, in theory, were their vassals. The only area that the king ruled directly was the Île-de-France, and even there his authority was often challenged. Not until the early twelfth century did royal power begin to expand, and Suger, as chief adviser to King Louis VI, helped shape this process.

The Abbey Church of Saint-Denis, founded in the late eighth century, enjoyed a dual prestige, as the shrine of St. Denis, the Apostle of France and its patron saint, and as a chief memorial of the Carolingian dynasty. Both Charlemagne and his father, Pepin, were consecrated as kings at Saint-Denis. It was also the burial place of the kings Charles Martel, Pepin, and Charles the Bald. Suger aspired to make the abbey the spiritual center of France, a pilgrimage church to outshine all others and to provide a focal point for religious as well as patriotic emotion. To achieve this goal, the old structure had to be rebuilt and enlarged. The great abbot himself wrote two accounts of the church and its rebuilding.

AMBULATORY AND CHOIR   The ambulatory and radiating chapels surrounding the arcaded apse (**figs. 12.1** and **12.2**) are familiar elements from the Romanesque pilgrimage choir (compare fig. 11.3), but at Saint-Denis they have been integrated in a new way. The choir is as rationally planned and constructed as any Romanesque church, yet a new kind of geometric order holds together the entire plan. Seven nearly identical wedge-shaped units fan out from the center of the apse. Instead of being in separate apsidioles, the chapels merge to form, in effect, a second ambulatory. We experience this double ambulatory not as a series of individual compartments but as a continuous space, whose shape is outlined by the network of slender arches, ribs, and columns that supports the vaults. Ribbed groin vaulting based on the pointed arch is used throughout. By this date, the pointed arch (which can be "stretched" to reach any desired height regardless of the width of its base) has become an essential part of the ribbed groin vault, which is no longer restricted to square or near-square compartments. It has a new flexibility that allows it to cover areas of almost any shape, such as the trapezoids and pentagons of this ambulatory.

What most distinguishes the interior of Saint-Denis (see fig. 12.2) from earlier church interiors is its lightness, in both senses of the word. The architectural forms seem graceful, almost weightless, compared to the massive solidity of Romanesque architecture. The fluid spaciousness of the choir results from its slim columns, the use of which was made possible by the relative lightness of the vaults they needed to support. In addition, the large windows are no longer openings cut into a wall but, in effect, translucent walls, filled with stained glass. Heavy buttresses jutting out between the chapels to contain the outward pressure of the vaults make this abundance of light possible. In the plan (see fig. 12.1), they look like stubby arrows pointing toward the center of the apse. No wonder, then, that the interior appears so airy, since the heaviest parts of the structural skeleton are relegated to the exterior. In describing Suger's ambulatory and choir, we have also explained the essentials of Gothic architecture. Yet none of the elements that make up its design is really new. The pilgrimage choir plan, the pointed arch, and the ribbed groin vault can be found in regional schools of the French and Anglo-Norman Romanesque. However, they were never combined in the same building until Suger—as he himself tells us—brought together artisans from many different regions to work at Saint-Denis. We must not conclude from this, however, that Gothic architecture was merely a synthesis of Romanesque traits. If we did, we would be hard-pressed to explain the new spirit, particularly the quest for luminosity, that strikes us so forcibly at Saint-Denis. Suger's account of the rebuilding of his church stresses luminosity as the highest value achieved in the new structure. Thus, he suggests, the "miraculous" light that floods the choir through the "most sacred" stained-glass windows becomes the Light Divine, a revelation of the spirit of God. Suger also claims that harmony, the perfect relationship among parts in terms of mathematical proportions or ratios, is the source of all beauty, since it exemplifies the laws by which divine reason made the universe (see box: Cultural Context: Dionysian Theology and the Abbey of Saint-Denis, page 251).

At the heart of Suger's mysticism was his belief that the material realm is a stepping-stone for spiritual contemplation and thus that dark, jewel-like light filtering through the church's stained-glass windows would transport the viewer to "some strange region of the universe which neither exists

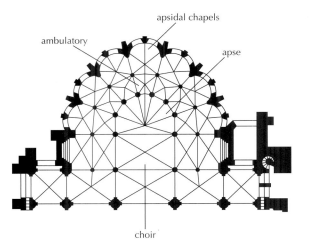

12.1 Plan of the choir and ambulatory, Abbey Church of Saint-Denis, France. 1140–44 (Peter Kidson)

12.2 Ambulatory, Abbey Church of Saint-Denis, France

Read the document related to Abbot Suger on myartslab.com

entirely in the slime of earth nor entirely in the purity of Heaven." The success of the choir design at Saint-Denis, therefore, derives from its architectural qualities as well as from its extraordinary psychological impact. Visitors, it seems, were overwhelmed by both, and within a few decades the new style had spread far beyond the Île-de-France.

WEST FAÇADE Although Abbot Suger planned to rebuild all of Saint-Denis, the only part that he saw completed, other than the ambulatory and choir, was the west façade. Its overall design (**fig. 12.3**) derived from Norman Romanesque façades. A comparison between Saint-Denis and Saint-Étienne at Caen (see fig. 11.23) reveals a number of shared

12.3 West façade, Abbey Church of Saint-Denis, France. ca. 1137–44

Dionysian Theology and the Abbey of Saint-Denis

THE INTERPRETATION of light and numerical harmony as reflecting divine reason was well established in Christian thought long before Abbot Suger's time. It derived in part from the writings of a sixth-century Greek theologian who, in the Middle Ages, was mistakenly believed to have been Dionysius the Areopagite, an Athenian disciple of St. Paul, mentioned in the New Testament book of Acts of the Apostles. In France, Dionysius was identified with St. Denis, since that is the saint's name in Latin. Not surprisingly, Suger attached great authority to the writings of Dionysius, which were available to him in the library at Saint-Denis. Dionysian light-and-number symbolism particularly appealed to him and was influential in his thinking about the design and decoration of the Abbey Church.

basic features. These include the placement of the portals, the three-story arrangement, and the pier buttresses that reinforce the corners of the towers and divide the façade vertically into three main parts. However, Saint-Denis's three portals are far larger and more richly carved than those at Saint-Étienne or any other Norman Romanesque church. From this we can conjecture that Abbot Suger attached considerable importance to the sculptural decoration of his church, although his account does not discuss it at length.

The rich sculptural decoration included carved tympana, archivolts, and jambs. The arrangement recalls the façades of southwestern France, such as Moissac (see fig. 11.10), and the carved portals of Burgundy, such as that at Autun (see fig. 11.12). These correlations corroborate Suger's claim that his workforce included artists from many regions. Unhappily, the trumeau figure of St. Denis and the statue-columns of the jambs were removed in 1770 and 1771, when the central portal was enlarged. A few years later, during the French Revolution, a mob attacked the heads of the remaining figures and melted down the metal doors. As a result of these ravages and a series of clumsy later restorations, we can gain only a general view of Suger's ideas about the role of sculpture at Saint-Denis. To envision what its west portal originally looked like we must turn to the Cathedral of Chartres, where some of the Saint-Denis sculptors subsequently worked.

Chartres Cathedral

Toward 1145 the bishop of the town of Chartres, who was a friend of Abbot Suger and shared many of his ideas, began to rebuild a cathedral in the new style, dedicated to Notre-Dame ("Our Lady,"

12.4 West façade, Cathedral of Notre-Dame, Chartres, France. (Left spire is from the sixteenth century.) ca. 1145–1220

the Virgin Mary). Fifty years later a fire destroyed all but the eastern crypt and the west façade. Our discussion of Chartres is divided into two sections: First we will discuss the west façade and later in the chapter that portion of the cathedral rebuilt after the fire of 1194.

WEST FAÇADE   Chartres's surviving west façade (**fig. 12.4**), in many ways reminiscent of Saint-Denis, is divided into units of two and three and is a model of clarity. Yet, because construction proceeded in stages and was never entirely finished, the two west towers, though similar, are by no means identical. Moreover, their **spires**, the tall top sections with tapering roofs, are very different: The spire on the left dates from the early sixteenth century, nearly 300 years later than its mate.

To judge from old drawings of Saint-Denis, the Chartres jambs (**figs. 12.5** and **12.6**) are so similar to those of the original Saint-Denis portals that the same sculptors must have worked on both buildings. Tall figures attached to columns flanked the doorways of both churches. Figures had appeared on the jambs or trumeaux of Romanesque portals (see figs. 11.10–11.12), but they seem carved from the masonry of the doorway. The Chartres jamb figures, in contrast, are essentially statues, each with its own axis. They could, in theory at least, be detached from their supports. Their roundness gives them a corporeal presence, and their heads show a gentle, human quality that indicates a naturalistic trend in Gothic sculpture, quite different from the apparent aims of Romanesque sculptors to accentuate stylization. The naturalism seen in the solemn spirit of the figures and in their increased physical bulk appears to be a reaction against the fantastic and demoniacal aspects of Romanesque art. This is apparent by comparing the Christ of Chartres's center tympanum (see fig. 12.5) with his counterpart in the tympanum at Moissac (see fig. 11.10).

12.5 West portal (Royal Portal), Cathedral of Notre-Dame, Chartres, France. ca. 1145–50

12.6 Jamb statues, west portal, Cathedral of Notre-Dame, Chartres, France

The discipline of the symbolic program underlying the entire sculptural scheme at Chartres is noteworthy. While an understanding of the subtler aspects of this program requires a knowledge of the theology that would have been taught by leading scholars of the day at the Chartres Cathedral School, its main elements can be readily understood.

The jamb statues form a continuous sequence linking all three portals (see fig. 12.5). Together they represent the prophets, kings, and queens of the Hebrew Bible. Their purpose is to acclaim the rulers of France as their spiritual descendants and to stress the harmony of spiritual and secular rule, of priests (or bishops) and kings—ideals that Abbot Suger had previously put forward. Above the main doorway symbols of the four evangelists

flank Christ in Majesty. The apostles are below, while the 24 elders occupy the two outer archivolts. Although the components are similar to those of the Moissac tympanum, the effect at Chartres is calm and comforting, whereas at Moissac it is dramatic and unsettling. The right-hand tympanum at Chartres shows Christ's Incarnation: the Birth, the Presentation in the Temple, and the infant Christ Child on the lap of the Virgin, who symbolizes the Church. The design achieves compositional and thematic unity by elevating Christ in the center of each register: on the manger, on an altar, and on the lap of his mother. In the surrounding archivolts, representations of the liberal arts as human wisdom pay homage to the divine wisdom of Christ. Finally, in the left-hand tympanum, we see the timeless Heavenly Christ (or perhaps the Christ of the Ascension) framed by the ever-repeating cycle of the year: the signs of the zodiac and their earthly counterparts, the labors of the 12 months.

Laon Cathedral

Because in 1194 fire destroyed the mid-twelfth-century church that stood behind the west façade of Chartres Cathedral, we must turn to the Cathedral of Notre-Dame at Laon to appreciate an Early Gothic interior. This cathedral was begun just before 1160.

NAVE The interior elevation of Laon Cathedral (**fig. 12.7**) includes a nave arcade, gallery, triforium, and clerestory, all features found in Romanesque architecture but never together in the same building. The four-level arrangement is a Gothic innovation that lightens the weight of the walls. The elevation develops logically and harmoniously: The single opening of the nave arcade is doubled in the gallery, then triple arches follow in the triforium, while a broad clerestory window balances the single nave arcade opening that began the vertical sequence. The rhythmical arrangement articulates a heightened sense of verticality, while the multiple openings allow increased light to enter the nave, directly from the clerestory and indirectly through galleries and side aisles. Like the uniformity in the church's plan, the vertical emphasis of the interior is a clear Gothic trait.

Sexpartite nave vaults over squarish bays at Laon continue the kind of structural experimentation begun by the Norman Romanesque builders of Saint-Étienne at Caen (see pages 243–45) and Durham Cathedral (see pages 243). Laon uses pointed

12.7 Nave, Cathedral of Notre-Dame, Laon, France. ca. 1160–1210

added to piers as well as to the wall. In the later, more westerly nave bays, the round piers are plain. Instead of the staggered rhythm created by the earlier alternating pier arrangement, the change produced a more flowing effect. However, the tradeoff for the increased uniformity of the new arrangement was a loss of structural explicitness. For other scholars, the shafts attached to the Laon nave piers mark a liturgical division in the building, the site of a screen separating the choir occupied by clerics from the spaces used by the lay congregation. Gothic churches, like earlier religious buildings, were settings for devotions and backdrops for the performance of the liturgy; as such they framed the movements and words sung in processions and practices in sacramental rites.

High Gothic Art in France

The political and economic stability of France during the thirteenth century encouraged the continued growth of cities, an ideal context for producing monumental architecture. Art historians have seen the integration of structure and design in Early Gothic art as a series of experiments that were resolved during the High Gothic period. Thus, High Gothic art is as much a continuation of Early Gothic experiments as it is their culmination. During this time the names of architects, who previously had been largely anonymous, proliferate, a reflection of the value placed on their achievements and of an increasing interest in personal identity (see box: Cultural Context: The Architect, the Master, and the Guild, opposite).

The Rebuilding of Chartres Cathedral

The rebuilding of Chartres Cathedral after the fire of 1194 (see page 252) marks an important step in the development of Gothic architecture. The new building was largely completed within the astonishingly brief span of 26 years. Its crypt houses Chartres's most important possession: remnants of a tunic said to have been worn by the Virgin Mary, to whom the cathedral is dedicated, at the time of Jesus' nativity. The relic, which miraculously survived the great fire of 1194, had drawn pilgrims from all over Europe.

The fire also spared the west façade and portals, and the decision to conserve these architectural features—which, at the time of the fire, were nearly 50 years old and certainly out of fashion—is worth

ribbed vaults, pioneered in the western bays of the nave at Durham, throughout the building. Alternating bundles of shafts rising along the wall reflect the nature of the sexpartite vaults above: Clusters of five colonnettes indicate where transverse arches cross the nave, while three colonnettes adorn the intermediate piers. Although the system develops from Romanesque building practice (see pages 244–245), the elements seem more delicate in the Gothic building.

Some experts see a change in program at Laon as revealing the evolving objectives of this cathedral's designers. At the east end of the nave, where the building work began, clustered shafts were

The Architect, the Master, and the Guild

THE WORD "ARCHITECT" derives from the Greek term for "master builder" and was defined in its modern sense of "designer and theoretician" by the Roman writer Vitruvius during the first century BCE. During the Middle Ages, it came to have different meanings. The term could apply not only to masons, carpenters, and even roofers but also to the person who commissioned or supervised a building. Not until about 1260 did Thomas Aquinas revive Aristotle's definition of "architect" as the person of intellect who leads or conducts, as opposed to the artisan who makes. Within a century the term was used by the Italian humanist Petrarch to designate the artist in charge of a project.

In the Middle Ages, the word "master" (Latin, *magister*) was a title conferred by a trade organization, or guild, on a member who had achieved the highest level of skill in the guild's profession or craft. In each city, trade guilds virtually controlled commercial life by establishing quality standards, setting prices, defining the limits of each guild's activity, and overseeing the admission of new members. Merchants formed the earliest guilds in the eleventh century. Soon, however, craftsmen also organized themselves in similar professional societies, which continued to be powerful well into the sixteenth century. Most guilds admitted only men, but some, such as the painters' guild of Bruges, occasionally admitted women as well. Guild membership established a certain level of social status for townspeople, who were not of the noble, clerical (in religious life), or peasant classes.

A boy would begin as an apprentice to a master in his chosen guild and after many years might advance to the rank of journeyman. In most guilds this meant that he was then a full member of the organization, capable of working without direction and entitled to receive full wages for his work. Once he became a master, the highest rank, he could direct the work of apprentices and manage his own workshop, hiring journeymen to work with him.

In architecture, the master mason, who was sometimes called the master builder, generally designed the building, that is, took the role of architect. In church-building campaigns, there were teams of masons, carpenters (joiners), metalworkers, and glaziers (glassworkers) who labored under the direction of the master builder.

noting. After initial despair at the damage wrought by the fire, civic and ecclesiastical authorities animated their followers by interpreting the event as an expression of the will of the Virgin herself that a new and more glorious cathedral be built. Since the west end of the church, like the famous relic of the Virgin, had also been spared, it too was treated as a relic worthy of preservation. Recognizing the divine plan in what otherwise would have been very disheartening circumstances helped to fuel enthusiasm for rebuilding, and accounts for the rapid pace of construction.

To provide room for large numbers of visitors without disturbing worshipers, a wide aisle runs the length of the nave and around the transept (**fig. 12.8**). It is joined at the choir by a second aisle, forming an ambulatory that connects the apsidal chapels. Worshipers entered the building through the old west portal and passed through a relatively low narthex. It would have taken some time for their eyes to adjust to the darkness of the interior. Once they had recovered from this disorienting effect, they would have become aware of

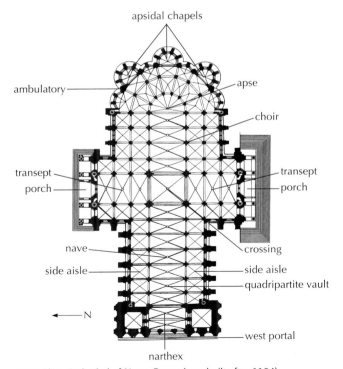

12.8 Plan, Cathedral of Notre-Dame (as rebuilt after 1194), Chartres, France

12.9 Nave and choir, Cathedral of Notre-Dame, Chartres, France. ca. 1194–1220

Explore the architectural panoramas of Chartres Cathedral on myartslab.

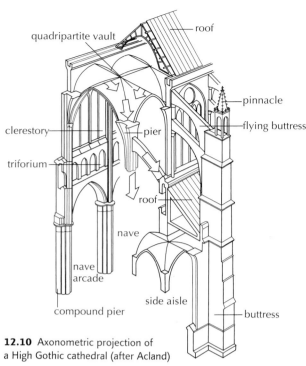

12.10 Axonometric projection of a High Gothic cathedral (after Acland)

a glimmering light, which guided them into the cavernous church. The transition, both subtle and profound, accentuated the significance of entering the church. As with entries into Romanesque and Byzantine churches (see pages 173 and 232), a liminal, or transitional, zone signaled that visitors had left the temporal world behind. Patrons, designers, and builders of a religious edifice had again found meaningful physical forms to encourage and sustain powerful spiritual experiences.

NAVE The rebuilt nave of Chartres Cathedral (**fig. 12.9**) is the first fully developed example of the mature, or High Gothic style. Several features distinguish this style (**fig. 12.10**). By eliminating the gallery, the designers of Chartres imposed a three-part elevation on the wall. Romanesque builders had used tripartite wall divisions (see figs. 11.22

and 11.24, and page 243), but the Chartres solution diminishes horizontality and treats the wall surface as a coherent vertical unit. Shafts attached to the piers stress the continuity of the vertical lines by guiding our eye upward to the vaults, which appear as diaphanous webs stretched across the slender ribs. **Quadripartite**, or four-part, vaults now replace the sexpartite vaults of Early Gothic buildings. Because quadripartite vaults cover rectangular bays, the builders no longer needed to worry about an alternating system of supports. The quickened rhythm of shorter, rectangular bays intensifies the perceived pace of propulsion down the nave. The openings of the pointed nave arcade are taller and narrower than before, and the clerestory is larger so that it is the same height as the nave arcade.

BUTTRESSES In Chartres, as in Suger's choir at Saint-Denis, the buttresses, the heavy bones of the structural skeleton, are visible only outside the building (**fig. 12.11**). The plan (see fig. 12.8) shows them as massive blocks of masonry that stick out from the building like a row of teeth. Above the aisles, these piers turn into **flying buttresses**— arched bridges that reach upward to the critical spots between the clerestory windows where the outward thrust of the nave vault is concentrated (see fig. 12.10). The flying buttresses were also designed to resist the considerable wind pressure

12.11 Cathedral of Notre-Dame, Chartres, France (from the south)

sexpartite vault

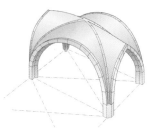

quadripartite vault

Comparison of sexpartite and quadripartite vaulting

 Watch an architectural simulation of ribbed vaulting on myartslab.com

Stained Glass

A WINDOW SUCH AS *Notre Dame de la Belle Verrière* (fig. 12.12) consists of hundreds of small pieces of tinted glass bound together by strips of lead. The size of these pieces was limited by the methods of medieval glass manufacture. The design was not "painted on glass"; rather, the window was painted with glass. Colored glass was produced by creating a molten mixture of silica (basically sand), potash (to lower the temperature at which silica melts), and lime (a stabilizer), plus the addition of metal oxides to color or "stain" the glass: The addition of cobalt oxide produced blue glass, copper oxide, red, and manganese oxide, purple. Hot iron-cutting tools were used to shape or cut the individual pieces to make up a window. It was assembled somewhat as one would put together a mosaic or a jigsaw puzzle, out of odd-shaped fragments cut to fit the contours of the forms. (See diagrams for more detail about this process.) Only the finer details, such as eyes, hair, and drapery folds, were added by painting—or drawing—in black or gray on the glass surfaces.

Stained-glass production was a costly, time-consuming, and labor-intensive activity with a marked division of labor. The artisans who made the glass supported the work of the glaziers who designed and produced the windows. Although stained glass appears throughout Europe, the most significant achievements were made in northern Europe. To produce stained glass required abundant wood, both for firing the furnaces and kilns and for making potash, and it was in the north that there were sufficient forests to support a glassmaking industry. It was also in the north that the value of light entering a building could best be appreciated. By the late thirteenth century the preference for colored glass had diminished and large areas of clear glass dominated church construction.

1. The stained-glass artist first drew the design on a large, flat surface, then cut pieces of colored glass to match the drawn sections.

2. The individual pieces of glass were enclosed by channeled strips of lead.

3. The lead strips between the individual glass pieces were an important part of the design.

on the high-pitched roof. This method of anchoring vaults, so characteristic of Gothic architecture, certainly owed its origin to functional considerations, but the flying buttress is also an integral aesthetic and expressive feature of the building. Its shape emphasizes both verticality and support, in addition to actually providing it.

STAINED GLASS Alone among all major Gothic cathedrals, Chartres still retains most of its more than 180 original stained-glass windows (see fig. 12.9). The magic of the jewel-like light from the clerestory is unforgettable to anyone who has experienced it. The windows admit far less light than one might expect. They act mainly as diffusing filters that change the quality of daylight, giving it the poetic and symbolic values so highly praised by Abbot Suger. The sensation of ethereal light dissolves the physical solidity of the church and, hence, the distinction between the temporal and the divine realms. This "miraculous light" creates the intensely mystical experience that lies at the heart of Gothic spirituality.

The majestic *Notre Dame de la Belle Verrière* (literally, "Our Lady of the Beautiful Window") at Chartres (**fig. 12.12**) appears as a weightless form hovering effortlessly in indeterminate space. This window, the only one apart from those of the west façade to survive the 1194 fire, consists of hundreds of small pieces of tinted glass held together by strips of lead. Methods of medieval glassmaking limited the maximum size of these pieces. This process encourages an abstract, ornamental style, which resists any attempt at three-dimensional appearance. Only in the hands of a great master could the maze of lead strips lead to such monumental forms (see box: Materials and Techniques: Stained Glass, page 257).

Given the way stained glass accentuates pattern and decorative effect, it is not surprising that it was so popular during the Middle Ages. Its brilliant surfaces are like the flat stones and enamelwork so highly prized in northern Europe in earlier periods (see fig. 10.1); enamel is in fact a kind of glass.

12.12 *Notre Dame de la Belle Verrière* (detail). ca. 1170 (framing panels are thirteenth-century). Stained-glass window, height approx. 14′ (4.27 m). Cathedral of Notre-Dame, Chartres, France, north portal, ca. 1210

 View the Closer Look for the rose window and lancets in the north transept of Chartres Cathedral on myartslab.com

The intensity with which the viewer engages with the image parallels the direct connection between viewer and object evident in much of the art of the earlier Middle Ages. Worthy comparisons with *Notre Dame de la Belle Verrière* are the Byzantine mosaics from the Church of the Dormition at Daphni (see figs. 8.21 and 8.22) for the way they command our attention and communicate directly with a viewer. Both use otherworldly light to convey spiritual messages: on the one hand, filtered through stained glass, and on the other, reflected off gold-glass mosaics.

TRANSEPTS AND THEIR SCULPTURE Each of the transept arms of Chartres Cathedral has three deeply recessed and lavishly decorated portals, five **lancets** (tall, narrow windows crowned by a sharply pointed arch), and an immense **rose window**, the large medallion of glass in the center of the façade (see fig. 12.11). The walls of these north and south façades have little solidity; they are so heavily pierced as to be nearly skeletal.

The north transept is devoted to the Virgin Mary. She had already appeared over the right portal of the west façade in her traditional role as the Mother of God seated on the Throne of Divine Wisdom (see fig. 12.5). Her new prominence reflects the growing importance of the cult of the Virgin, which the Church had actively promoted since the Romanesque period. The growth of Mariology, as it is known, was linked to a new emphasis on divine love, embraced by the faithful as part of the more human view that increased in popularity during the Gothic era. The cult of the Virgin at Chartres developed special meaning about 1204, when the cathedral received as a relic the head of her mother, St. Anne. This relic, in combination with the robe of the Virgin that had miraculously survived the fire of a decade earlier, gave Chartres exceptional status among those devoted to Mary.

The jamb statues of the transept portals show a discernible evolution, even among themselves since they were carved at different times. The relationship of statue and column begins to dissolve. The columns are quite literally put in shade by the greater width of the figures, by the strongly projecting canopies, and by their elaborately carved bases.

A good instance of the early dissolution of this relationship is seen on one of the south transept portal jambs (**fig. 12.13**). The three saints on the right still echo the cylindrical shape of Early Gothic

examples (see fig. 12.6), though the heads are no longer strictly in line with the central axis of the body. By comparison, the knight on the left, St. Theodore, who was carved about ten or 15 years later than his companions, stands at ease, in a semblance of classical *contrapposto*. His feet rest on a horizontal platform, rather than on a sloping shelf as before, and the axis of his body, instead of being straight, describes a slight but perceptible S-curve. Even more surprising is the wealth of carefully observed detail in his weapons and in the texture of his tunic and chain mail and, above all, the organic structure of the body. Not since imperial Roman times have we seen a figure as thoroughly alive as this. Yet the most impressive quality of the St. Theodore statue is not its naturalism but the sense of serenity and balance that it conveys. The ideal portrait of the Christian soldier, dressed as a contemporary warrior, expresses the spirit of the crusades in its most elevated form.

12.13 Jamb statues, south transept portal, Cathedral of Notre-Dame, Chartres, France. ca. 1215–20. Left-most figure (St. Theodore) ca. 1230

Reims Cathedral

Reims, as the coronation cathedral of the kings of France, was closely linked to Paris, where the kings held court, and to other cathedrals patronized by the royal family, such as Chartres.

WEST PORTAL SCULPTURE The jamb figures at Reims are not in their original positions, since some sculptures were moved between the west façade and the transept portals. As a result, continuity of style and program is difficult to assess. However, we can study here individual sculptures of distinctive style and high quality. Gothic classicism reached its climax in some of these Reims statues. The most famous of them is the *Visitation* group

12.14 *Annunciation* and *Visitation*, west portal, Cathedral of Notre-Dame, Reims, France. ca. 1230–65

(**fig. 12.14**, the two figures on the right), which was carved between 1230 and 1233. It depicts the Virgin Mary announcing the news of her pregnancy to her cousin Elizabeth.

For a pair of jamb figures to enact a narrative scene such as this would have been inconceivable in Early Gothic sculpture, where individual figures remained isolated, even within unified programs. That the *Visitation* figures are now free to interact shows how far the column has receded into the background. The S-curve, resulting from the pronounced *contrapposto*, is even more obvious here than in the St. Theodore from Chartres (see fig. 12.13) and dominates both the side and the front views of the figures. The figures gesture at each other as they communicate across the space that separates them.

Horizontal folds of cloth pulled across the women's abdomens emphasize the physical bulk of their bodies. Mary and Elizabeth remind us so strongly of ancient Roman matrons that we might wonder if the artist was inspired by large-scale Roman sculpture (compare fig. 7.10). A surviving gate attests to an earlier Roman presence in Reims, and excavations during the last century established that the first cathedral on the site was built over Roman baths. Thus, Roman models might well have been available to the Reims sculptors.

Because of the vast scale and time frame of the sculptural program at Reims (and at other cathedrals as well), it was necessary to employ a variety of sculptors working in distinct styles. Two of these styles, both clearly different from the classicism of the *Visitation*, appear in the *Annunciation* group (fig. 12.14, the two figures on the left). The difference in style within a single group derives from the fact that the angel Gabriel and the Virgin Mary were not originally intended as a pair, but were only later installed next to each other. The Virgin, from between 1240 and 1245, has a rigidly vertical axis, and her garments form straight, tubular folds meeting at sharp angles. The angel, in contrast, is remarkably graceful and was carved at least a decade later than the Virgin of the *Annunciation*, between 1255 and 1265. Features such as the tiny, round face framed by curly locks, the emphatic smile, the strong S-curve of the slender body, and the rich drapery of this "elegant style" spread far and wide during the following decades. In fact, it soon became the standard formula for Gothic sculpture. Its effect would be seen for many years to come, not only in France but also abroad.

The High Gothic cathedrals of France represent a concentrated effort rarely seen before or since. The huge cost of these truly national monuments was borne by donations and taxes collected from all over the country and from all classes of society. These cathedrals express the merging of religious and patriotic fervor that had been Abbot Suger's goal. However, the great expense and forced taxation required to construct them did produce vehement objections, and for example in 1233 construction of Reims Cathedral was suspended as a result of civil unrest directed against the cathedral authorities; it was not resumed for another three years. This cessation of building activity helps explain the variety of styles at Reims. By the middle of the thirteenth century the wave of enthusiasm for large-scale projects had passed its peak. Work on the vast structures now proceeded at a slower pace. New projects were fewer and generally far less ambitious.

Rayonnant or Court Style

One of those who still had the will and means to build on an impressive scale during the mid-thirteenth century was King Louis IX, known as St. Louis following his canonization in 1297, less than 30 years after his death. Under the king's governance and as a result of a treaty with the English that resulted in French control of Normandy, the map of Louis's possessions began to take on the shape of present-day France. The increasing importance of the monarchy and the rising importance of Paris, where the court was located, is reflected in the degree to which Louis was able to define a court style; our sense of Paris as an artistic center effectively begins under St. Louis.

Sainte-Chapelle

St. Louis's mark on the stylistic evolution of Gothic is most dramatically seen in his court chapel, called the Sainte-Chapelle, which was designed by 1241 and completed within seven years (**fig. 12.15**). The two-story building comprises a ground floor, a relatively low chapel for court officials, and an upper floor to which the royal family had direct access from their quarters in the palace. In essence, the building is a type of palatine chapel for which Charlemagne's building at Aachen (see fig. 10.9) serves as an early prototype.

The impetus for the building's construction was Louis's acquisition from his cousin, the emperor of Constantinople, of the Crown of Thorns and other relics of Christ's Passion, including a part of the True Cross, the iron lance, the sponge, and a nail. Such sacred relics required a glorious space for their display. Rich colors, elaborate patterns, and extensive amounts of gold, largely restored in the nineteenth century, cover the Sainte-Chapelle's walls, vaults, and other structural members. This decoration complements the stained glass that constitutes most of the surface of the chapel. Above the altar, an elevated shrine, destined to frame the sacred relics, was left open at the back so that filtered light would bathe the venerated objects on display. The delicate glass cage of a building, jewel-like in the intensity of the colored light that enters it, functions in effect as a monumental reliquary. The tall, thin lancets accentuate verticality to such a degree that the building conveys a sense of monumentality comparable to any cathedral despite its diminutive scale. On entering the building the viewer is virtually immersed within its aura of light, different from any normal experience of the physical world. Thus, as with Hagia Sophia (see pages 175–77), spirituality is made manifest through the materiality of architecture and its decoration.

This phase of Gothic is often referred to as *rayonnant*, from the French *rayonner*, "to radiate light." The term derives from the prevalence of raylike tracery in buildings of the period, which originally appeared in rose windows and later began to appear throughout entire churches. The style, closely associated with the court, spread through the royal domain and then through much of Europe.

Manuscript Illumination

Some art historians have been concerned that the term *rayonnant* is appropriate only for architecture. Recognizing that there were also major achievements in the pictorial arts within Louis IX's court and in the upper echelons of aristocratic society, they prefer the term court style, which they use synonymously with *rayonnant* to define the art of this time. In fact, there are many connections between the building arts and the elaborate devotional works with exquisite miniatures produced for the personal enjoyment and education of the royal family and for others who were literate and could afford them. These products of French manuscript workshops disseminated the refined taste that made the court art of Paris the standard for all Europe.

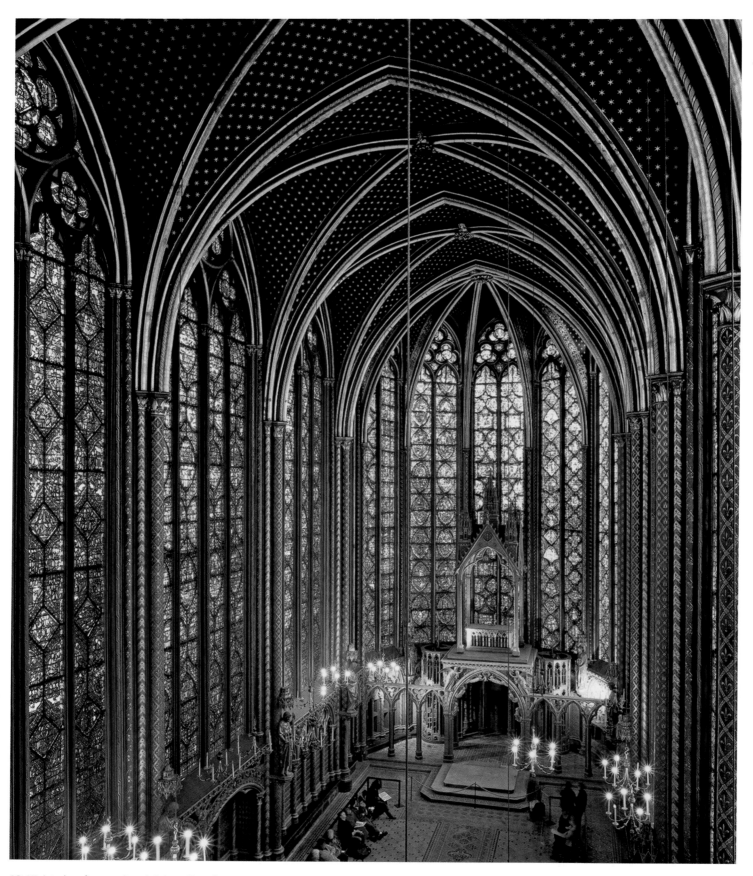

12.15 Interior of upper chapel, Sainte-Chapelle, Paris. 1241–48

PSALTER OF ST. LOUIS Perhaps the closest parallel between painting and architectural form is the *Psalter of St. Louis*, which was executed in the 1260s (**fig. 12.16**). The folio reproduced here illustrates the Genesis scene of the meeting of the sacred leaders, Abraham and Melchizedek (Genesis 14:18–20). Abraham and his troops wear crusader armor, establishing an association between contemporary struggles to free Christian lands and heroic biblical events. Louis was an eager warrior for Christianity who organized and participated in two crusades, in 1254 and 1270, the latter being the occasion of his death in Tunisia. The gold background and the banks of clouds that waft around the arcades, hovering like incense in a church, accentuate the sacral aspects of the representation.

The manuscript's painted architecture is modeled directly on the Sainte-Chapelle (see fig. 12.15). The illustration also recalls the canopies above the heads of jamb statues at Chartres (see fig. 12.13). Against the two-dimensional background of the page, the figures stand out in relief by their smooth and skillful modeling. The outer contours are defined by heavy, dark lines, reminiscent of the lead strips in stained-glass windows. The figures themselves display all the features of the elegant style seen in Gothic sculpture: graceful gestures, swaying poses, smiling faces, and neatly waved hair. (Compare the *Annunciation* angel in figure 12.14.) This miniature thus exemplifies the refined taste of the court art of Paris.

12.16 *Melchizedek and Abraham*, from the *Psalter of St. Louis*. 1260s. Ink, tempera, and gold leaf on vellum, 5 × 3½″ (13.6 × 8.9 cm). Bibliothèque Nationale, Paris

Late Gothic Art in France

Although Late Gothic art builds on earlier achievements, during this period artists felt free to deviate from previous patterns of development. Builders showed increased concern for unity of plan, but they also employed curvilinear and elaborate decorative forms that often showed little concern for the clarity of structure so important in earlier Gothic works. Decorations often take the form of undulating curves and reverse curves. Thus a late phase of Gothic architecture is labeled **Flamboyant**, literally meaning "flamelike." Late Gothic manuscripts and sculptures are also highly decorated, with rich surface treatment accentuating their precious qualities.

Manuscript Illumination

Until the thirteenth century, illuminated manuscripts had been produced in monastic scriptoria. Now, along with many other activities that were once the special preserve of the clergy, manuscript production shifted to urban workshops organized by laypeople, the ancestors of the publishing houses of today. Paris was renowned as a center of manuscript production, and it is possible even today to identify the streets on which the workshops were clustered.

HOURS OF JEANNE D'ÉVREUX The interest in depicting sculptural figures was further developed by the illuminator Jean Pucelle in a tiny, private prayer book—called a BOOK OF HOURS—illuminated in Paris between 1325 and 1328 for Jeanne d'Évreux, queen of France (**fig. 12.17**). *The Annunciation* is represented on the right page and *The Betrayal of Jesus* on the left. The delicate **grisaille** (painting in gray) adds a soft roundness to the forms. This is not Pucelle's only contribution: The architectural interior reveals a spatial recession previously unknown

Developed in the fourteenth century, the BOOK OF HOURS was a prayer book for laypersons that contained psalms and devotional meditations chosen to suit the various seasons, months, days of the week, and hours of the day. Many of these small, portable books are masterpieces of luxurious illumination, especially those made for royal or aristocratic patrons.

12.17 Jean Pucelle. *The Betrayal of Jesus* and *Annunciation*, from the Hours of Jeanne d'Évreux. 1325–28. Tempera and gold leaf on parchment. Each page 3½ × 2⁷⁄₁₆″ (8.9 × 6.2 cm). Shown larger than actual size. The Metropolitan Museum of Art, New York. The Cloisters Collection, Purchase, 1954. 54.1.2

in Northern European painting. In the *Annunciation*, Gabriel kneels in an anteroom, while angels appear in the windows of an attic, from which the dove of the Holy Spirit descends.

In representing this new pictorial space, Jean Pucelle had to take into account the special needs of a manuscript page. The Virgin's chamber does not fill the entire picture surface. It is as though it were an airy cage floating on the blank background (note the supporting angel on the right), like the rest of the ornamental framework, so that the entire page forms a harmonious unit. Many of the details are peripheral to the religious purpose of the manuscript. The kneeling queen inside the initial D is surely meant to be Jeanne d'Évreux at her prayers; it is as if her intense devotions have produced a tangible vision of the Annunciation. The identity of the man with the staff next to her is unclear, although he appears to be a courtier listening to the lute player perched on the tendril above him. The combination of scenes is a commentary on experiences that become real even if they lack physical substance: Music is at once actual and ephemeral, as is Jeanne's religious vision.

Other enchanting vignettes fill the page. A rabbit peers from its burrow beneath the girl on the left, and in the foliage leading up to the initial we find a monkey and a squirrel. These fanciful marginal designs—or ***drôleries***—are a common feature of Northern Gothic manuscripts. They originated more than a century before Jean Pucelle in the regions along the English Channel. From there they quickly spread to Paris and the other centers of Gothic art. Their subjects include a wide range of motifs, fantasy, fable, and grotesque humor, as well as scenes of everyday life, which appear side by side with religious themes. The essence of *drôlerie* is its playfulness. In this special domain, the artist enjoys an almost unlimited freedom—comparable to a jester's—which accounts for the wide appeal of these little vignettes during the later Middle Ages.

The seeming innocence of Pucelle's *drôleries* nevertheless hides a serious purpose, which is particularly evident in the one at the bottom of the right-hand page, a type of illustration referred to as a ***bas-de-page*** (French for "bottom of the page"). The four figures are playing a game of tag called Froggy in the Middle, a reference to *The Betrayal of Jesus* on the opposite page. Below *The Betrayal of Jesus*, two knights on goats joust at a barrel. This image not only mocks courtly chivalry but also suggests a parallel to Jesus' role as a "scapegoat," a spear having pierced his side at the Crucifixion.

Sculpture

Portal sculpture, the principal interest of the Early and High Gothic periods, is of relatively little consequence during the Late Gothic period. Single figures, carved in the round, many of them cult figures, are now fully detached from any architectural setting. As the individual's importance in society increased, so individual sculpted figures became prominent. Sculptors' guilds were now well established.

VIRGIN OF PARIS In an early fourteenth-century sculpture of the Virgin, we see how traces of classicism increasingly disappear from Gothic sculpture, while elegance becomes a virtual end in itself. Thus, the human figure of the *Virgin of Paris* (**fig. 12.18**) in Notre-Dame Cathedral is now strangely abstract. It consists largely of hollows, and the projections are so reduced that a viewer sees them as lines rather than volumes. The statue is quite literally disembodied—its swaying stance bears little relation to classical *contrapposto*, since it no longer supports the figure. Compared to such unearthly grace, the angel of the Reims *Annunciation* (see fig. 12.14) seems solid indeed; yet it contains the seed of the very qualities expressed so strikingly in the *Virgin of Paris*. Earlier instances of Gothic naturalism, which focused on particulars, survive here as a kind of intimate realism in which the infant Christ is no longer a Savior-in-miniature facing the viewer but, rather, a human child playing with his mother's veil.

The elegant manner of this new style was encouraged by the royal court of France and thus had special authority. It is this graceful expressive quality, not realism or classicism, that is the essence of later Gothic art.

The Spread of Gothic Art

The refined royal French style of the Paris region was enthusiastically received abroad, where it was adapted to a variety of local conditions. A number of factors contributed to the rapid spread of Gothic art. Among them were the skill of French architects and stone carvers and the prestige of French centers of learning, such as the Cathedral School of Chartres and the University of Paris. Still, one wonders whether any of these explanations really go to the heart of the matter: The basic reason for the spread of Gothic art was undoubtedly the persuasive

12.18. *Virgin of Paris*.
Early fourteenth century. Stone.
Notre-Dame, Paris

power of the style itself. It kindled the imagination and aroused religious feeling even among people far removed from the cultural climate of the Île-de-France.

England

England was especially receptive to the new style, which developed there as the influence of Gothic forms from the Île-de-France melded with Anglo-Norman Romanesque features. English Gothic, however, developed a well-defined character of its own, known as the Early English style, which dominated the second quarter of the thirteenth century.

SALISBURY CATHEDRAL The exception to the trend of multiple periods and styles in a single English Gothic church is Salisbury Cathedral, in Wiltshire, begun in 1220. One sees immediately how different the exterior of Salisbury (**fig. 12.20**) is from French Gothic churches (see figs. 12.4 and 12.11) and how futile it would be to judge it by the same

standards. Compactness and verticality have given way to a long, low, sprawling look. (The crossing tower, which provides a dramatic unifying accent, was built a century later than the rest and is much taller than originally planned.) Since height is not the main goal, flying buttresses are used only as an afterthought, not as integral design elements. The west façade is treated like a screen wall, wider than the church itself and divided into horizontal bands of ornament and statuary. The towers have shrunk to stubby **turrets** (small towers). The plan (**fig. 12.19**), with its double transept, retains the segmented quality of the Romanesque, while the square east end derives from Cistercian architecture (see page 234).

As we enter the nave (**fig. 12.21**), we recognize many elements familiar to us from French interiors of the time, such as Chartres Cathedral (see fig. 12.9). However, the English interpretation produces a very different effect. As on the façade, horizontal divisions dominate at the expense of

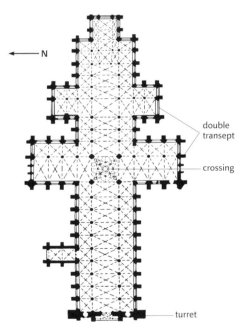

← N

double transept

crossing

turret

12.19 Plan of Salisbury Cathedral, England. 1220–65

12.20 Salisbury Cathedral, England (from the southwest). (Spire ca. 1320–30)

Explore the architectural panoramas of Salisbury Cathedral on myartslab.com

the vertical. Hence we experience the nave wall not as a succession of vertical bays but as a series of arches and supports, carved of dark stone, which stand out against the rest of the interior. This method of stressing their special function is one of the hallmarks of the Early English style. The use of bands of color also emphasizes horizontality, quite unlike the effect achieved in French Gothic buildings.

Another distinctive feature is the steep curve of the nave vault. The ribs rise all the way from the triforium level. As a result, the clerestory gives the impression of being tucked away among the vaults. At Durham Cathedral, more than a century earlier, the same treatment had been a technical necessity (see fig. 11.22). Now it has become a matter of style, in keeping with the character of Early English Gothic as a whole.

GLOUCESTER CATHEDRAL The change in the English Gothic becomes very clear if we compare the interior of Salisbury with the choir of Gloucester Cathedral, built in the second quarter of the fourteenth century (**fig. 12.22**). Gloucester is an outstanding example of English Late Gothic, also called the **Perpendicular Gothic** style. The name certainly fits, since we now find a dominant vertical accent that was absent in the Early English style. Vertical continuity is most evident at Gloucester in the **responds** that run in an unbroken line from the floor to the vault. In this respect, Perpendicular Gothic is much closer to French sources, but it

12.22 Choir, Gloucester Cathedral, England. 1332–57

 Explore the architectural panoramas of Gloucester Cathedral on myartslab.com

includes so many uniquely English features that it would look out of place on the Continent. The repetition of small, uniform tracery panels recalls the bands of statuary on the west façade at Salisbury (see fig. 12.20), and the upward curve of the vault is as steep as in the latter's nave (see fig. 12.21).

The ribs of the vaults, on the other hand, have taken on a new role. They have been multiplied until they form an ornamental network that screens the boundaries between the bays, with the result that the entire vault looks like one continuous surface. The ceiling reads as a canopy fluttering above the interior. This effect, in turn, emphasizes the unity of the interior space. Such elaboration of the classic four-part vault is characteristic of the Flamboyant style on the Continent as well, but the English started it earlier and carried it much further.

Germany

In Germany, Gothic architecture took root a good deal more slowly than in England. Until the mid-thirteenth century, the Romanesque tradition, with its persistent Ottonian elements, remained dominant, despite the growing acceptance of Early Gothic features. From about 1250 on, however, the High Gothic of the Île-de-France had a strong impact on the Rhineland. While some German sculptors relied on French models, others pursued a more independent course, unlike German architects. German Gothic sculptures are sometimes dramatic, sometimes poignant, and sometimes life-like, but they always express deep, if sometimes restrained, emotion.

HEILIGENKREUZ IN SCHWÄBISCH-GMÜND Especially characteristic of German Gothic is the hall church, or *Hallenkirche*. This type of church, with aisles and nave of the same height, stems from Romanesque architecture. Although also found in France, it was in Germany where its possibilities were explored fully. Heiligenkreuz (Holy Cross) in Schwäbisch-Gmünd (**fig. 12.23**) is one of many examples from central Germany. Heinrich Parler the Elder began Heiligenkreuz in 1317, although it was perhaps his son Peter who was responsible for the enlarged choir of 1351. The space has a fluidity and an expansiveness that enfold us as if we were standing under a huge canopy, reminiscent of the effect at Gloucester Cathedral (see fig. 12.22). There is no clear sense of direction to guide us. And the unbroken lines of the pillars, formed by bundles of shafts that diverge as they turn into lacy ribs

12.23 Heinrich Parler the Elder and Peter Parler (?). Nave and choir, Heiligenkreuz, Schwäbisch-Gmünd, Germany. Begun 1317

covering the vaults, seem to echo the continuous movement that we feel in the space itself.

NAUMBURG CATHEDRAL The growth of Gothic sculpture in Germany can be easily traced. From the 1220s on, German masters who had been trained in the sculpture workshops of the French cathedrals brought the new style back home. Because German architecture at that time was still mainly Romanesque, however, large statuary cycles like those at Chartres and Reims were not produced on façades, where they would have looked out of place. As a result, German Gothic sculpture tended to be less closely linked with its architectural setting. In fact, the finest sculptural work was often done for the interiors of churches.

This independence permitted a greater expressive freedom than in France. It is strikingly evident in the work of the Naumburg Master, whose best-known work is the series of statues and reliefs

Naumburg Master embodies the temperamental counterpart of the strained physicality demonstrated in Hellenistic art (see fig. 5.28).

The paint still visible on Naumburg's interior sculpture helps us appreciate how Gothic sculpture might have looked originally. Gothic interiors, as can be seen in the restored Sainte-Chapelle (see fig. 12.15), were elaborately painted, as was exterior sculpture; but that paint rarely survives today.

THE *ROETTGEN PIETÀ* Gothic sculpture, as we have come to know it so far, reflects a desire to give a greater emotional appeal to traditional themes of Christian art. Toward the end of the thirteenth century, this tendency gave rise to a new kind of religious image. Originally designed for private devotion, it is often referred to by the German term *Andachtsbild* (contemplation image), since Germany played the leading part in its development.

12.24 Naumburg Master. *Crucifixion*, on the choir screen, and the *Virgin* and *John the Evangelist*. ca. 1255. Stone. Naumburg Cathedral, Germany

made around 1255 for Naumburg Cathedral. The *Crucifixion* (**fig. 12.24**) forms the center of the choir screen; flanking it are statues of the *Virgin* and *John the Evangelist*. Enclosed by a deep, gabled porch, the three figures frame the opening that links the nave with the sanctuary. Rather than placing the group above the screen, as was usual, the sculptor brought the subject down to earth physically and emotionally. The suffering of Jesus thus becomes a human reality through the emphasis on the weight and volume of his body. Mary and John, pleading with the viewer, convey their grief more eloquently than ever before.

The pathos of these figures is heroic and dramatic, compared with the quiet lyricism of the Reims *Visitation* (see fig. 12.14). If the classical High Gothic sculpture of France may be compared with the calm restraint of the Classical Greeks, the

12.25 *Roettgen Pietà*. Early fourteenth century. Wood, height 34½″ (87.5 cm). Rheinisches Landesmuseum, Bonn

The most widespread type was a representation of the Virgin grieving over the dead Christ. It is called a *pietà* after an Italian word derived from the Latin *pietas*, the root word for both "pity" and "piety." No such scene occurs in the scriptural accounts of the Passion. We do not know where or when the *pietà* was invented, but it portrays one of the Seven Sorrows of the Virgin. It thus forms a tragic counterpart to the motif of the Madonna and Child, one of her Seven Joys.

The *Roettgen Pietà* (**fig. 12.25**) is carved of wood and vividly painted. Like most such groups, this large cult statue was meant to be placed on an altar. The style, like the subject, expresses the emotional fervor of lay religiosity, which emphasized a personal relationship with God, part of the tide of mysticism that swept over fourteenth-century Europe. Realism here is purely a means to enhance the work's impact. The faces convey unbearable pain and grief; the wounds are exaggerated grotesquely; and the bodies and limbs are puppetlike in their thinness and rigidity. The purpose of the work clearly is to arouse so overwhelming a sense of horror and pity that the faithful will share in Christ's suffering and identify with the grief-stricken Mother of God. The ultimate goal of this emotional bond is a spiritual transformation that grasps the central mystery of God in human form through compassion (meaning "suffering with").

At first glance, the *Roettgen Pietà* would seem to have little in common with the *Virgin of Paris* (see fig. 12.18), which dates from the same period. Yet they share a lean, "deflated" quality of form and exert a strong emotional appeal to a viewer. Both features characterize the art of northern Europe from the late thirteenth to the mid-fourteenth century. Only after 1350, as part of a change in religious outlook, do we again find an interest in weight and volume, coupled with a renewed desire to explore tangible reality.

POINTS OF REFLECTION

12.1 Classify forms that were used in the Gothic period but that have their roots in the Romanesque. Characterize what the new uses of traditional building forms reveal about Gothic concerns.

12.2 Analyze the physical and philosophical reasons why stained glass was so appreciated during the Gothic period.

12.3 Compare the interior and exterior elevations of early and mature Gothic churches and explain the changes.

12.4 Consider the role of King Louis IX (St. Louis) in the development of Gothic art and architecture.

12.5 Analyze the differences between French, English, and German Gothic art.

✔—**Study** and review on myartslab.com

ART IN TIME

- 1137–44—Rebuilding of Abbey Church of Saint-Denis, outside Paris, by Suger

- ca. 1170—Stained-glass panel of Notre Dame de la Belle Verrière created for Chartres Cathedral in France

- 1180–1223—Reign of French King Philip Augustus

- 1194—A fire destroys much of Chartres Cathedral

- 1220—Construction begins on Salisbury Cathedral in England

- 1241—Sainte-Chapelle, Paris, court chapel of King Louis IX, designed

- 1317—Nave and choir of Heiligenkreuz, Schwäbisch-Gmünd, begun by Heinrich Parler the Elder and Peter Parler (?)

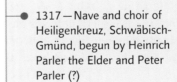

- 1325–28—Jean Pucelle illuminates a Book of Hours for Jeanne d'Évreux, queen of France

- 1337–1453—The Hundred Years' War between England and France

The Renaissance through the Rococo: Early Modern Europe

WHILE THE SACK OF ROME marked the end of the ancient world, there is no one event that signals the end of the Middle Ages and the beginning of the succeeding era, usually called the Renaissance. Some aspects of life in Europe remained unaltered from one era to the next, especially in rural areas. Yet a transformation of ideas and attitudes accompanied important social, economic, religious, and political shifts as the year 1500 approached. These cultural changes opened the door to further developments in the seventeenth and eighteenth centuries and, ultimately, the innovations of the Renaissance laid the groundwork for the modern world. As a result, many historians refer to the era from about 1400 to 1800 as the Early Modern period. But the period goes by many names and subdivisions: The Renaissance from 1300 to 1600, the Baroque from 1600 to 1700, and the Rococo in the 1700s.

Momentous events shaped the period: The fall of Constantinople and the Turkish conquest of southeastern Europe; the journeys of exploration and founding of overseas empires in the New World, in Africa, and in Asia, with the subsequent rivalry of Spain and England as the foremost colonial powers; the establishment of multinational corporations such as the Dutch East India Company; the rise of the Enlightenment in the eighteenth century.

The Renaissance, the earliest phase of the Early Modern period, finds its roots in the 1300s when intellectuals began to think of their own time as separate from the Middle Ages. Focusing their study less on the divine plan of salvation, and more on human achievements and the natural world, scholars and thinkers looked to Greece and Rome for models to imitate. These **Humanists** of the Renaissance saw classical antiquity as the era when civilization had reached the peak of its creative powers, an era that had ended abruptly when barbarian invaders destroyed the Roman Empire. During the thousand-year interval that had followed, they believed little was accomplished, but now, at last, this "time in-between" or "Middle Age" was being replaced by a revival of all those arts and sciences that had flourished in antiquity. The present could thus be fittingly labeled a "rebirth"—*rinascita* in Italian, *renaissance* in French and, by adoption, in English.

We can find this revolutionary view of history as early as the 1330s, in the writings of the Italian poet Petrarch, who thought of the new era mainly as a "revival of the classics," limited to the restoration of Latin and Greek to their former purity and the return to the original texts of ancient authors. During the next two centuries, this concept of the rebirth of antiquity grew to embrace almost the entire range of cultural endeavors, including the visual arts. The

latter, in fact, came to play a particularly important part in shaping the Renaissance, for reasons that we will explore. Humanists did not want to revive classical antiquity indiscriminately. Instead, they attempted to rediscover the secrets of ancient achievements in thought and art, while recognizing that they lived in a different world from that of the ancients.

The drive to meet the challenge of antiquity called forth an outpouring of creative energy such as the Western world had never before experienced. Paradoxically, this period's desire to return to the classics brought, not a return to antiquity, but the birth of modern ways of thinking about the world. This intellectual environment fostered a new freedom to question authority and to innovate which resulted in the profound invigoration of many areas of human activity—science, religion, the economy, and politics, to name but a few.

Freedom to explore the natural and human worlds encouraged scientific investigation and technological innovation: From the printing press to the discovery of the moons of Jupiter by Galileo. These discoveries inspired unbounded thinking, leading in the sixteenth century to challenges to the established Church in Rome—the Protestant Reformation—and the response of the Church to this challenge—the Counter- (or Catholic)

Reformation. These religious divisions produced political realignments, war, and social upheaval, as well as important artistic expressions in the seventeenth-century period we call the Baroque.

Economic and social expansion during the 1600s continued to place cities at the forefront of intellectual growth. Trade, colonization in the newly explored regions of Asia and the Americas, the birth of stock markets, and other new techniques of raising capital and growing enterprises spread wealth beyond the traditional aristocracy, thus promoting social mobility. A growing middle class of bankers, lawyers, merchants, and other professionals mimicked the tastes and spending habits of the aristocrats, even as their concerns and tastes inspired artists to experiment with subject matters and styles. The Golden Age of Dutch art most clearly illustrates this trend, as artists invented new forms and subjects for merchants in the Dutch Republic.

At the same time, hereditary rulers throughout Europe firmed up national boundaries. Monarchs in Spain, France, England, and elsewhere consolidated their power to create autocratic centralized states. The Sun King, Louis XIV of France, serves as the paradigm of this phenomenon, but such kingdoms and duchies arose in Italy, Russia, and Scandinavia too. Political boundaries

were somewhat less firm in regions of Central and Eastern Europe, but the ideal of the Holy Roman Empire persisted through the period.

By the eighteenth century, the political boundaries of Europe resembled those of today. New intellectual movements and new institutions—such as newspapers—inspired the creation of political structures that we recognize in our own forms of government. Though the artistic style called Rococo is usually associated with the eighteenth century, a variety of visual expressions responded to these conditions.

From the Renaissance to the Rococo a new idea of the individual developed. All that connects one to culture—family, sexuality, gender, identity, work, class, education, and belief—began to be viewed in the context of the individual. The visual arts of the Early Modern era in Europe give us many glimpses of the people of the period. We can see them in portraits that astonish us by their lifelikeness and in scenes from daily life that touch or amuse us.

We can respond to these images because the artists of the Early Modern era worked in a language we recognize. One of the fundamental gifts of the Renaissance to the modern world, learned from the arts of antiquity, is the emphasis, in the painted and sculptural arts, on representing the world in naturalistic terms. Artists in this

period created or discovered important new tools, such as perspective, to accomplish this goal. They experimented with these techniques to enhance the naturalism of their images and to connect the viewer with the figures they depicted. At times, artists used their skill to create illusions that, for example, stone vaults have disappeared into the sky or that the sensuous objects depicted exist in the viewer's space. Some works of the Early Modern period remain as immediate for us today as they must have been for their original viewers.

Artists contributed a great deal to the development of the Early Modern world. As geographic and scientific discovery expanded the world and the universe, artists helped their contemporaries visualize and understand it. As new forms of religious practice developed, artists devised new buildings to accommodate them. As new social structures arose, artists responded with new subjects, such as landscapes and scenes of everyday life. Early Modern paintings that depict men and women together help today's viewers to grasp not just a couple's relationship, but also to see the connectedness of figures, families, friends, workers, and larger social organizations. Although Early Modern artists often aspired to create ideal and timeless forms based on antiquity, their work is also a reflection of their own culture, social group, and time.

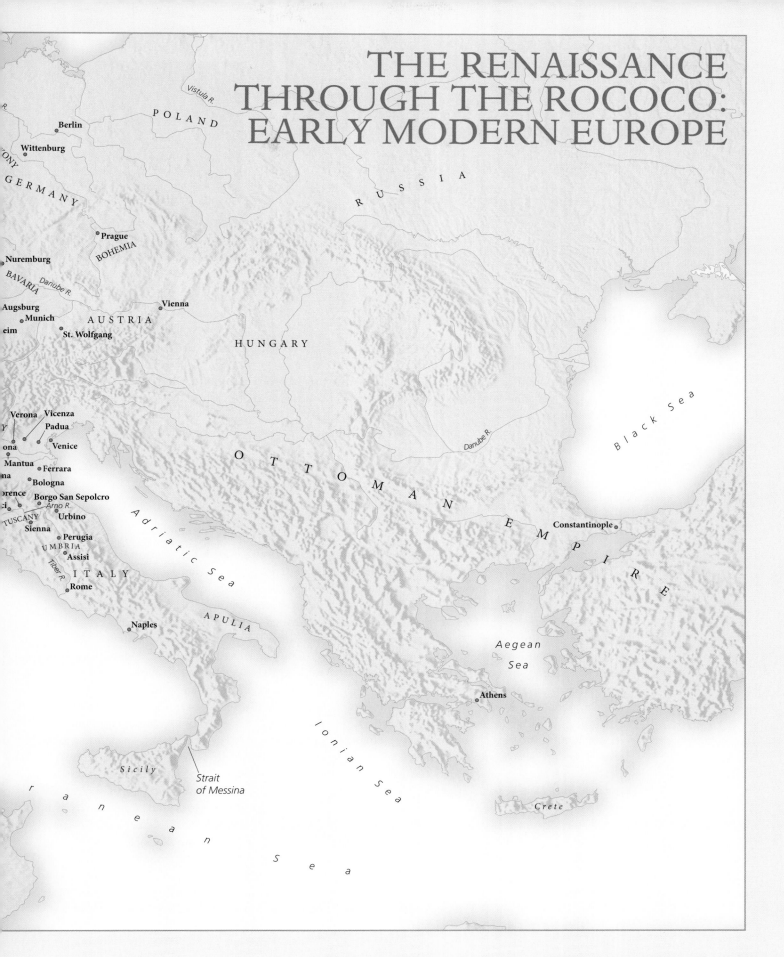

THE RENAISSANCE
THROUGH THE ROCOCO:
EARLY MODERN EUROPE

CHAPTER

13

Art in Thirteenth- and Fourteenth- Century Italy

POINTS OF INQUIRY

13.1 Investigate the visual elements that distinguish fourteenth-century Italian art from art in Northern Europe.

13.2 Explore the innovations of the celebrated artists of fourteenth-century Italy.

13.3 Understand how geography plays a role in the artistic developments that occur in Italy in this period.

13.4 Evaluate the spaces for which fourteenth-century patrons commissioned major Italian artistic programs.

13.5 Discover the cultural and historical conditions that shape Italian art in this era.

(((•─ **Listen** to the chapter audio on myartslab.com

Although Italian artists and patrons shared concerns with their contemporaries elsewhere in Europe, for geographic, historical, and economic reasons the arts in thirteenth- and fourteenth-century Italy struck out in a different direction. Many of the innovations that characterize the Italian Renaissance of the fifteenth and sixteenth centuries have their roots in the developments that took place in this period.

Throughout most of Europe in the thirteenth century, political and cultural power rested with land-holding aristocrats. Their property produced wealth and passed from one generation to the next. Even when hereditary rulers controlled large regions, they usually owed allegiance to a king or to the Holy Roman emperor. Italy, however, had few viable kingdoms or strong central authorities in this period. For most of the Middle Ages, the two international institutions of the Holy Roman Empire and the papacy dominated Italian politics. Yet the emperors generally lived north of the Alps, and sheer distance limited their control in Italy; moreover, for much of the fourteenth century,

Rome lacked a pope who could command worldly power, since the papacy had moved to France. While hereditary rulers controlled southern Italy and the area around Milan, individual city-states dominated the Italian peninsula, competing with each other for political influence and wealth.

Italy's long coastlines on the Mediterranean and Adriatic Seas (see **map 13.1**) allowed its maritime cities to become important trading centers throughout the Middle Ages. As a result new groups of merchants and artisans proliferated, as did new political institutions. The wealthiest and most influential cities were organized as representative republics; most prominent were the northern city-states of Florence, Siena, Pisa, and Venice. Tensions erupted frequently between aristocratic supporters of the emperor, and supporters of the mercantile parties, who allied themselves with the pope. In these cities, power tended to be concentrated in the hands of wealthy merchant families, who made fortunes in manufacture, trade, or banking. Members of these families would become the foremost patrons of artists in Italy.

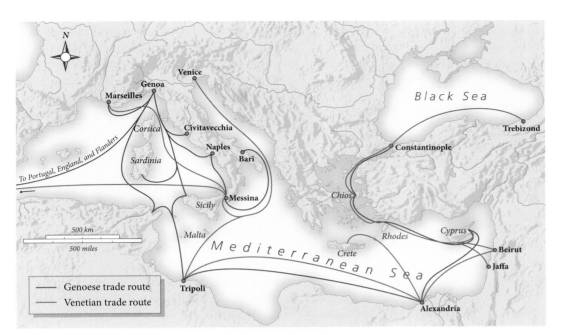

Map 13.1 The Italian peninsula's key sea-trade routes

Those artists developed their skills in a context that differed from the rest of Europe. In Italy, Roman and Early Christian art served as direct inspiration for medieval architects and sculptors, visible in such works as the cathedral of Pisa. Medieval Italy was affected by the power of western imperial forces, such as those of the Holy Roman emperor Frederick II (1194–1250), who lived for a time in southern Italy, and the eastern Byzantine Empire, with whom Italian cities traded. Added to these influences was the French Gothic style, introduced through the travels of artists, scholars, and patrons.

One of those travelers, the cleric, scholar, and poet Francesco Petrarch (1304–1374), exemplifies another aspect of fourteenth-century Italian culture: A growing interest in the creative works of individuals. Petrarch and his contemporaries, Dante Alighieri (1265–1321) and Giovanni Boccaccio (1313–1375), belonged to a generation of thinkers and writers who turned to the study of ancient works of literature, history, and art in search of beautiful and correct forms. Petrarch also sought to improve the quality of written Latin, by emulating the works of the Roman authors Vergil and Cicero. Discovering ancient thought and art inspired the analysis of the ancients' moral clarity and models of behavior, a philosophy that came to be known as humanism. Humanists valued the works of the ancients, both in the literary and the visual arts, and they looked to the classical past for solutions to modern problems. They particularly admired

Roman writers who championed civic and personal virtues, such as service to the state and stoicism in times of trouble.

The study of the art of Rome and Greece would profoundly change the culture and the art of Europe by encouraging artists to look at nature carefully and to consider the human experience as a valid subject for art. These trends found particular encouragement in the ideals and theology of the **mendicant** religious orders, that is, those who lived by collecting alms rather than owning property, such as the Dominicans, who valued classical learning, and the Franciscans, whose founder saw God in the beauty of nature.

The Cities and the Mendicants

As the lay populations increased in the rapidly growing cities, two major mendicant groups, the Franciscans and the Dominicans, established international "orders" to minister to them. Each order built urban churches where sermons could be preached to the crowds. The Dominicans, founded by Dominic de Guzmán in 1216, directed their attention to fighting heresy and promoting Church doctrine. The Franciscan order, founded by Francis of Assisi in 1209, worked in the cities to bring deeper spirituality and comfort to the poor. Taking vows of poverty, Franciscans committed themselves to teaching the laity and to encouraging them to pursue spiritual growth. Toward this goal, they told stories and used images to explain and affirm the teachings of the Church. Characteristically, Franciscans urged the faithful to visualize events such as the Nativity in tangible ways, such as erecting Nativity scenes (*crèches*) in churches as an aid to devotion.

Franciscan Churches and Paintings

Franciscan churches began to appear all over Italy as the friars ministered to the spiritual lives of city dwellers. A typical example in Florence is the church of Santa Croce (Holy Cross), begun around 1295 (**fig. 13.1**). The architect was probably the Tuscan sculptor Arnolfo di Cambio (ca. 1245–1302). Santa Croce shares some features with Gothic churches in northern Europe, but has some distinctively Italian elements. Its proportions are broad rather than vertical and the nave wall remains fairly unbroken.

Gothic elements include pointed arches in the nave arcade and vertical moldings that pull the eye up to the ceiling. Although one might expect such moldings to meet the ribs of a vaulted ceiling, Santa Croce uses wooden trusses to span the nave. Vaults cover only the apse and several chapels at the ends of the transepts, where Gothic windows pierce the wall. Since the entire nave could have been vaulted, the choice of wood for the roof seems deliberate. Recalling that the nearby Romanesque cathedral of Pisa has a wooden ceiling, we might recognize a regional preference for this kind of roof. Santa Croce's broad nave with high arches also reminds us of Early Christian basilicas, such as Old St. Peter's (see fig. 8.4). The friars may have chosen a wooden ceiling in an effort to evoke the simplicity of those basilicas and thus link Franciscan poverty with the traditions of the early Church.

13.1 Nave and choir of Santa Croce. Begun ca. 1295. Florence

Explore the architectural panoramas of the Church of Santa Croce on myartslab.com

The female branch of the Franciscans, called Poor Clares after their founder, St. Clare, built smaller churches, as the nuns did not preach. The church and convent Clare founded are still in service in Assisi in central Italy, where an early painted representation of the saint remains in place (**fig. 13.2**). A tall rectangle of wood, painted in TEMPERA, the painting was executed around 1280. The frontal figure of St. Clare fills the center of the panel; she wears the habit of her order and holds the staff of an abbess. Rather than a portrait with specific features, Clare's face has the large eyes and frontal arrangement of a Byzantine icon (see fig. 8.19), while her figure seems to exist in one plane. Eight tiny narratives flank her and tell the story of her life, death, and miracles. This image likely stood on a screen before the altar, where lay visitors could see it. Other painted panels, called ALTARPIECES, sat on the ALTARS of churches, to teach viewers about the approved route to salvation and to aid devotion.

Italian painting of the thirteenth and fourteenth centuries was dominated by fresco and tempera. Fresco (see page 144) is a wall painting technique that was known in antiquity. Pigment is mixed with water and applied to a surface of wet plaster. The pigment then bonds permanently with the plaster. The TEMPERA used in Italy at this period was a mixture of pigment and an emulsion of egg yolk and water. It was applied to wood panels that were first prepared with a coat of gesso (ground plaster or chalk and glue) and underpainted in green or brown.

ALTARS are tables, or sometimes low stones, that are the focal point of religious worship and often the site of sacrificial rites. Since the Neolithic era, they have been used at religious sites worldwide. The Christian altar traditionally is a narrow stone "table" that, in Catholic use, contains bone fragments of a martyr within or below it. Liturgical objects used in the rite of Eucharist rest on the top surface (the *mensa*). The altar frontal (*antependium*) may be plain or decorated.

An ALTARPIECE is not an altar, but is placed behind or at the back of the altar table. Early altarpieces were wingless, with painted or carved images in the central section and more images in the *predella* zone at the base of the altarpiece. Winged altarpieces were developed in the twelfth century: The wings allow the imagery to change according to the Church calendar.

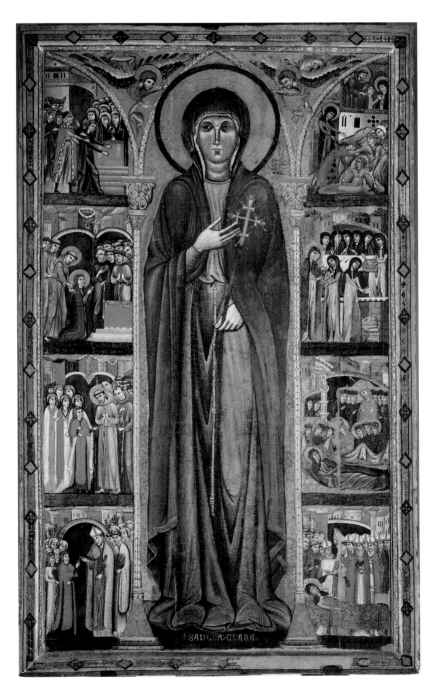

13.2 *Altarpiece of St. Clare.* ca. 1280. Tempera on panel, 9′ × 5′6″ (2.73 × 1.65 m). Convent of Santa Chiara, Assisi, Italy

Urban Churches, Baptisteries, and Civic Buildings

The growing city populations needed churches with large interior spaces; in Italy, special structures for baptismal rites stood next to the churches. For these structures, churchmen commissioned monumental pulpits with narrative or symbolic images carved onto them to focus the congregation's attention during readings of scripture or preaching. One family of sculptors who worked in Pisa, headed by Nicola Pisano (ca. 1220/25–1284), made such large pulpits a specialty. Having spent time in Naples and in Rome, Nicola had first-hand knowledge of Roman and Early Christian art. For the baptistery of Pisa, he executed an imposing marble pulpit around 1260 (**fig. 13.3**). This hexagonal structure rises to about 15 feet high, and boasts colored marble columns, classically inspired capitals, and small carved figures who represent Virtues. The six rectangular sides contain narratives, carved in relief. One of them, a densely crowded composition of the *Nativity* (**fig. 13.4**), combines the Annunciation with the Birth of Christ. The sculptor treated the scene as a shallow box filled with solid convex shapes in the manner of a Roman relief (see fig. 7.14).

13.3 Nicola Pisano. Pulpit. 1259–60. Marble, height 15′ (4.6 m). Baptistery, Pisa

13.4 *Nativity*, detail of the pulpit by Nicola Pisano. 33½ × 44½″ (85 × 113 cm). 1259–60

Nicola probably knew Byzantine images of the Nativity, for his iconography reflects that tradition. As the largest and most central figure, the reclining Virgin overpowers all the other elements in the composition. Nicola includes many details of the narrative or setting, such as the midwives washing the child and Joseph's wondering gaze, which bring the historical events closer to a viewer's own experience. At the same time, the classicizing draperies and dignified figures infuse the scene with gravity and significance.

FLORENCE CATHEDRAL AND BAPTISTERY Italian cities competed with each other by commissioning the construction and decoration of large and expensive buildings. East of Pisa along the Arno, the increasing wealth of Florence inspired its citizens to undertake major projects for its cathedral and baptistery (**fig. 13.5**). Arnolfo di Cambio designed a new cathedral (*duomo*) for Florence to replace a smaller church that once stood on the site. This project took the skills and energy of several generations. The work, begun in 1296, continued through

13.5 Florence Cathedral and Baptistery seen from the air. Cathedral begun 1296

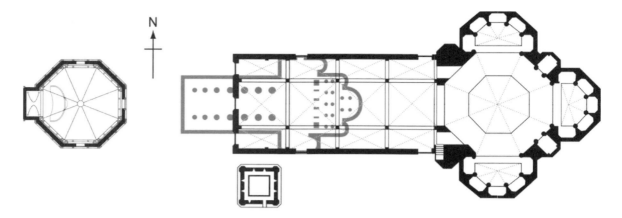

the fifteenth century as the plan grew larger and more ambitious. The west façade and other portals continued to be adorned with sculpture throughout the Renaissance period, but the Florentines did not complete the marble exterior until the nineteenth century. The citizenry intended Florence's Duomo to be a grand structure that would serve not only as the spiritual heart of the city, but also as a statement of its wealth and importance.

Arnolfo designed a broad basilica with a high arcade and trussed wooden roof like Santa Croce. Later alterations integrated ribbed groin vaults as in Northern Gothic buildings. By the mid-fourteenth century the east end of the basilica (see plan, **fig. 13.6**) had been enlarged, to terminate in three faceted arms supporting an octagonal crossing that would be covered by a dome. The scale of the proposed dome, however, presented engineering difficulties that were not solved until the early fifteenth century. Local preference tempers the Gothic elements of pointed arches and high vaults in Florence's cathedral.

Two other aspects of the plan reflect Italian tradition: instead of tall western towers incorporated into the façade, the cathedral has a free-standing *campanile* or bell tower; opposite the Duomo stands the octagonal Baptistery, built in the eleventh century on older foundations. John the Baptist is the patron saint of Florence, so the Baptistery is a focal point of civic pride. As a result, it was the site of frequent adornment in the fourteenth to fifteenth centuries, much of it focused on the doors (see Chapter 15).

PALAZZO DELLA SIGNORIA In addition to religious structures, Italian cities commissioned buildings to house their governing bodies. In Florence, the Palazzo della Signoria, also known as the Palazzo Vecchio (**fig. 13.7**), served this function. Also the work of Arnolfo di Cambio, it was begun in 1298 and completed in 1310, though it was later expanded and remodeled. The tall, blocky structure, similar to fortified castles in the region, has walls that are solid at the lowest level, and the surface is **rusticated**, left uneven and rugged, to look even stronger. Heavy battlements and a tall surmounting tower top the three stories of the building. Boasting the highest tower in the city, the Palazzo della Signoria dominated the skyline of Florence both as a defensive structure and as an expression of the power and independence of the city.

New Directions in Tuscan Painting

The stylistic beginnings of Italian painting, like those of other art forms in the thirteenth century, differ from those of the rest of Europe. Painters in Italy had access to models from Rome and Byzantium that were not available elsewhere, and these inspired them to create monumental images and render forms in naturalistic terms. Roman sculpture and relief, if not Roman painting, provided Italian artists with lessons in creating weighty and solid-looking figures in two dimensions. Many Early Christian and Byzantine mosaics and frescoes survived as well and supplied models for translating Christian narratives into memorable compositions, while Italian architectural traditions provided wall surfaces for fresco painting throughout the Middle Ages. Fresh impetus for the development of Italian painting came from an influx of Byzantine art forms and artists in the thirteenth century, as a result of the crusades. Indeed, the first historians of Italian art, among them Giorgio Vasari (1511–1574), located the beginning of Italian Renaissance style in the study of the "Greek manner," or Byzantine art. Italian artists absorbed the Byzantine tradition far more thoroughly in the thirteenth century than ever before. When Gothic style began to influence artists working in this Byzantinizing tradition, a revolutionary synthesis was accomplished in Tuscan cities by a generation of innovative and productive painters, including Cimabue, Giotto, Duccio, and Ambrogio Lorenzetti.

Florentine Painting: Cimabue and Giotto

Vasari claimed that an early master of the new style, Cimabue of Florence (ca. 1250–after 1300), was apprenticed to a Greek painter. In the 1280s, he painted a large panel depicting the *Madonna Enthroned* or *Madonna in Majesty* (*Maestà*), to sit on an altar in the church of Santa Trinita in Florence (**fig. 13.8**); the large scale of the altarpiece—it is more than 12 feet high—made it the devotional focus of the church. Its composition recalls Byzantine icons, but its scale and verticality are closer to the *Assisi St. Clare* (fig. 13.2) than to Byzantine prototypes. Mary and her son occupy a heavy golden throne, flanked by rows of angels on either side. Hebrew Bible prophets holding scrolls appear below, as if forming a foundation for Mary's throne; the relationship between the Hebrew Bible and the Christian New Testament is

an important theme in Christian art. The Virgin's towering scale and the brilliant blue of her gown against the gold-leaf background draw a viewer's eye to her; with her gesture she emphasizes the presence of her son. Like Byzantine painters, Cimabue uses linear gold elements to enhance her dignity, but in his hands the network of gold lines follows the line of her body instead of creating abstract patterns. The severe design and solemn expression are appropriate to the monumental scale of the painting.

Later artists in Renaissance Italy, such as Lorenzo Ghiberti and Giorgio Vasari, claimed that Cimabue was the teacher of Giotto di Bondone (ca. 1267–1336/37), one of the key figures in the history of art. Mentioned in Dante's *Divine Comedy*

13.8 Cimabue. *Madonna Enthroned.* ca. 1280–90. Tempera on panel, 12′7½″ × 7′4″ (3.9 × 2.2 m). Galleria degli Uffizi, Florence

 Watch a video about the egg tempera process on myartslab.com

and honored by his hometown, Giotto achieved fame in his own time, and crucially influenced the development of Italian painting. The artist formed his innovative style by synthesizing his knowledge of Byzantine traditions, the Early Christian frescoes of Rome, and the sculptural achievements of Nicola Pisano and his followers. His largest projects were monumental fresco cycles, but he also executed altarpieces, including an altarpiece of the *Madonna Enthroned* for the Church of All Saints (Ognissanti) in Florence (**fig. 13.9**). Completed by 1310, in tempera (see page 279), the altarpiece depicts Mary and her son enthroned among angels against a gold background. This is the same theme painted by Cimabue on a somewhat smaller scale, but nonetheless Giotto's painting innovates beyond the style of his supposed teacher. Like Cimabue, he paints the Virgin on a huge scale to bring a viewer's eye directly to her and to the Christ Child on her lap. Where most of Cimabue's other figures look out toward the viewer, Giotto's figures gaze at the Virgin and Child, both signaling and heightening their importance. Giotto also renders the figures as if bathed in light, recording a gradual movement from light into dark, so that the figures are molded as three-dimensional objects. Compared to the painting by Cimabue, Giotto depicts earthbound figures of the Mother and Child.

Their throne, itself based on Italian Gothic architecture, encloses them on three sides and establishes a spatial context for them. The possibility of space is further suggested by the overlapping figures, who seem to stand behind one another. This celestial assembly offers a glimpse of the court of the Queen of Heaven, for citizens then building a new cathedral in her honor.

13.9 Giotto. *Madonna Enthroned*. ca. 1310. Tempera on panel, 10′8″ × 6′8¼″ (3.35 × 2 m). Galleria degli Uffizi, Florence

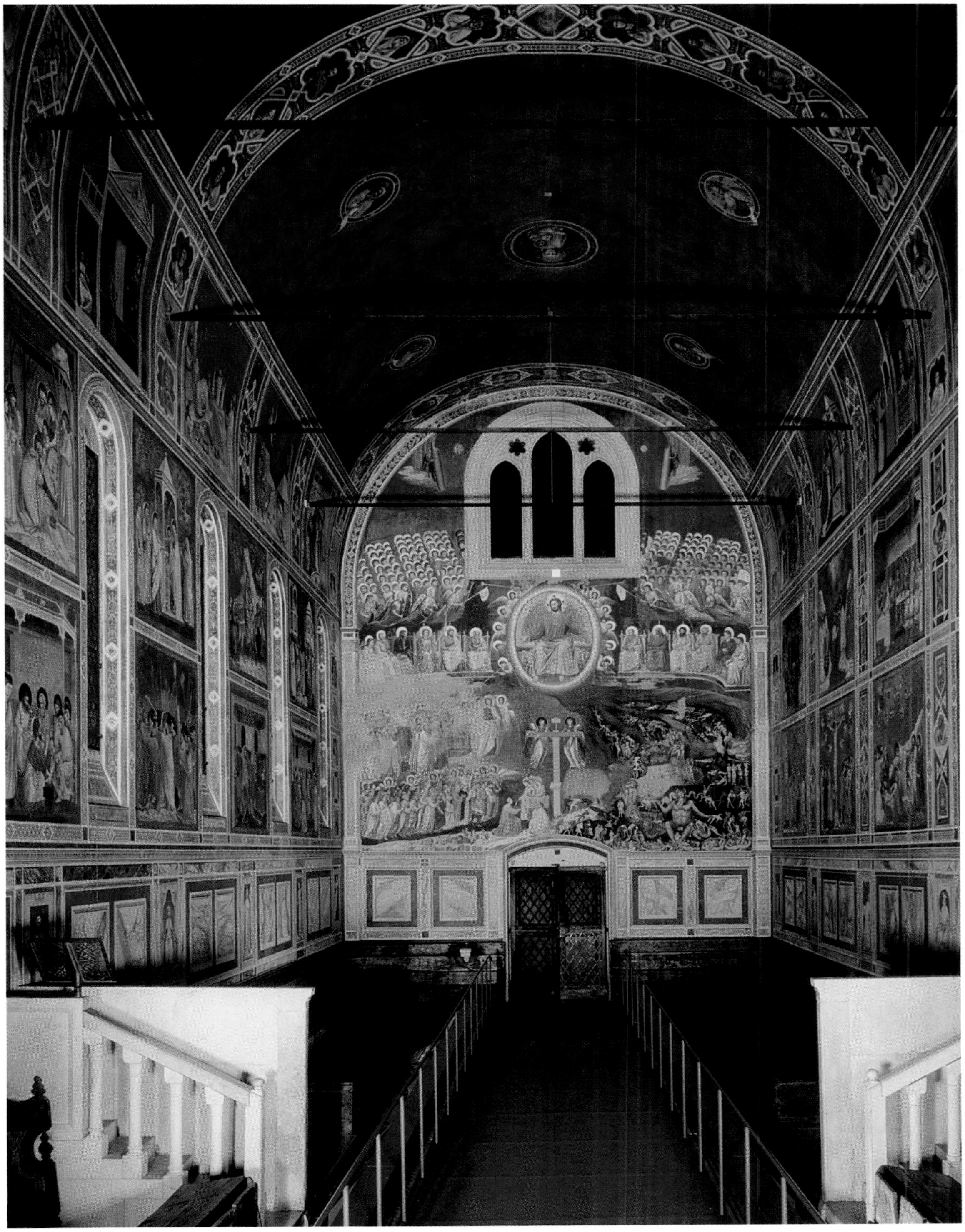

13.10 Giotto. Interior of Arena (Scrovegni) Chapel. 1305–06. Padua, Italy

THE ARENA CHAPEL The best-preserved example of Giotto's work in fresco is in the Scrovegni Chapel in Padua, next to the palace of the banker Enrico Scrovegni, painted in 1305 and 1306 (**fig. 13.10**). (It is also known as the Arena Chapel because of its proximity to a Roman arena.) The structure itself is a one-room hall covered with a barrel vault. Its limited windows left plenty of wall surface, which Giotto and his workshop painted from floor to ceiling in the fresco technique. A blue field with gold stars symbolic of heaven dominates the barrel vault, below which the walls are divided into three registers or horizontal rows. Each register contains rectangular fields for narrative scenes devoted mainly to the life of Christ. The scheme begins at the altar end with the Annunciation and culminates in the Last Judgment at the west end of the chapel. Along the length of the wall, the top register depicts stories of the early life of Mary and her parents; the middle register focuses on stories of Christ's public life and miracles; and the lowest register portrays his Passion, Death, and Resurrection. Below the narratives the walls are painted to resemble marble panels interspersed with statues symbolizing the virtues and vices.

Giotto turned each of the rectangular fields into a distinct narrative moment; at the same time, the whole program of paintings is a unity expressing a complex theological statement. The frescoes tell the story of salvation, from the incarnation of Christ to his sacrificial death and his predicted return at the end of time. Geometric bands that mimic mosaic frame each scene, while quatrefoils with small narrative scenes in them separate each story. These smaller narratives comment on the main story. One of the most memorable of these paintings depicts the Lamentation, the moment of last farewell between the dead Christ and his mother and friends (**fig. 13.11**). Although this event does not appear in the Gospels, by the end of the Middle Ages versions of it had appeared in both Byzantine and Western medieval art (see fig. 12.25).

Giotto depicts this moment in truly revolutionary terms. He conceives each figure as a separate geometric body, and renders it as a three-dimensional shape by the light washing over it. These weighty figures are arranged close to the **picture plane**, so that they dominate the foreground. (The picture plane is the theoretical plane suggested by the actual surface of a painting, drawing or relief.) The bodies overlap each other or stand behind each other and displace so much volume that they create the illusion of space in the painting. Giotto does not suggest a deep space, but a stage on which his actors can move to express the tragic narrative.

Little extraneous detail invades the scene: Even the landscape is reduced to the downward slope of a hill behind the mourners. Nothing allows the viewer's eye to avoid the anguish on the faces of Christ's followers, all of whom look toward the heads of Christ and the Virgin, together the focal point of the scene. The low center of gravity and the hunched figures convey the somber quality of the occasion, as do the cool colors and desolate sky. Giotto boldly contrasts the frozen grief of the human mourners with the frantic movement of the weeping angels among the clouds.

The composition is deceptively simple, yet profoundly moving. Even nature seems to participate in the sorrow over Christ's death, as a barren tree stands alone at the crest of the hill. This tree also refers to the Tree of Knowledge of Good and Evil, which the sin of Adam and Eve

13.11 Giotto. *The Lamentation.* 1305–06. Fresco. 6'6¾″ × 6'7⅞″ (2 × 1.85 m). Arena (Scrovegni) Chapel, Padua, Italy

had caused to wither and which Christians believed would be restored to life through Christ's sacrificial death. Further symbolic enrichment of the narrative appears in the frame element to the left, where the Old Testament prophet Jonah falls into the whale from which he would emerge three days later. The juxtaposition of the two themes draws an analogy between Jonah's three days in the body of the whale and Christ's three days in the tomb.

The Scrovegni Chapel assured Giotto's fame. He worked in Florence for 35 years after completing these frescoes, in 1334 being named the architect of the Florentine cathedral, for which he designed the bell tower. His influence over the next generation of painters was inescapable.

Sienese Painting

Giotto's slightly older contemporary, Duccio di Buoninsegna (ca. 1255–before 1319), directed another busy and influential workshop in the neighboring Tuscan city of Siena. The city competed with Florence on a number of fronts—military, economic, and cultural—and fostered a distinct identity and visual tradition. The Sienese attributed to the Virgin their victory in a key battle; once they established a republic, directed by the Nove (the Nine), Siena took the Virgin Mary as its protector and patron, and dedicated its thirteenth-century cathedral to her. The directors of the cathedral commissioned Duccio to paint a large altarpiece for the principal altar, called the *Maestà* as it depicts the Virgin and Child in Majesty (**fig. 13.12**). On its back and parts of the front, the altarpiece bears images from the life of Christ and the Virgin, and figures of prophets. The whole was designed in a form that echoes a church building, though this ensemble and its frame were dismembered in 1771.

On the front panel of the altarpiece Duccio creates a regal image on a large scale. Members of her court surround the enthroned Virgin and Child in a carefully balanced arrangement of saints and angels. She is by far the largest and most impressive figure, swathed in the rich blue reserved for her by contemporary practice. Siena's other patron saints kneel in the first row, each gesturing and gazing at her. The bodies, faces, and hands of the many figures seem to swell with three-dimensional life as the painter explores the fall of light on their forms. Like Giotto, Duccio knew Byzantine painting, with its heritage of Hellenistic–Roman illusionism. Nonetheless, Duccio's work also reflects contemporary Gothic sensibilities in the fluidity of the drapery, the appealing naturalness of the figures, and the glances by which the figures communicate with each other.

Duccio's style is distinct from Cimabue's and Giotto's. The drapery worn by Duccio's figures falls in complex, curving patterns, rather than the

13.12 Duccio. *Madonna Enthroned*, center of the *Maestà Altar*. 1308–11. Tempera on panel, central panel 7 × 13′ (2.13 × 3.96 m). Museo dell'Opera del Duomo, Siena

Read the document related to Duccio's Maestà on myartslab.com

13.13 Ambrogio Lorenzetti. *Good Government in the City and in the Country*. 1338–40. Fresco. Approximately 46 × 25′ (14 × 7 m). Sala della Pace, Palazzo Pubblico, Siena

 View the Closer Look for *Effects of Good Government in the City and in the Country* on myartslab.com

abstract lines of Cimabue's Virgin or the plain volumes of Giotto's figures; compare the figures of the Christ Child in Duccio's *Maestà* (fig. 13.12) and Giotto's *Madonna Enthroned* (fig. 13.9). Where Giotto strives to give his sturdy figures a believable spatial context, Duccio aims for splendor and lyrical elegance. Commissioned in 1308, the *Maestà* was installed in the cathedral in 1311 amidst processions and celebrations in the city. Duccio's signature at the base of the throne expresses his pride in the work: "Holy Mother of God, be the cause of peace to Siena, and of life to Duccio because he has painted you thus."

REPRESENTING GOVERNMENT Duccio's work affected many painters of the next generation, including Ambrogio Lorenzetti (ca. 1290–1348), who nonetheless spent time in Florence. As a result, his work combines the lyrical forms of Duccio with the robust naturalism of Giotto. Between 1338

and 1340, Ambrogio executed a major project in Siena's town hall; for their meeting room, Siena's ruling council (the Nine) commissioned an allegorical fresco contrasting the effects of good and bad government or War and Peace. Members of the council would be inspired by these images, for as they deliberated, they would see in these frescoes the results of both (**fig. 13.13**). Although the fresco of *Bad Government* (known originally as *War*) has been severely damaged, those depicting the positive example of *Good Government*, or *Peace*, are remarkably well preserved. On the short wall of the room, Ambrogio depicted *Good Government* as an assembly of virtues who support an enthroned personification of the City accompanied by Justice and Wisdom. Below them appear 24 Sienese judges under the guidance of Concord. On the long wall, the fresco of *Good Government in the City and in the Country* bears an inscription praising Justice and the many benefits that derive from her.

To express this idea, Ambrogio paints an architectural portrait of the city of Siena. In his fresco depicting the life of a well-ordered city-state, the artist fills the streets and houses with teeming activity: Teachers instruct, merchants sell, masons build. The figures give the architectural vista its striking reality by introducing the human scale. On the right, outside the city walls, the fresco then provides a view of the Sienese countryside, fringed by distant mountains and overseen by a personification of Security. It is a true landscape—the first since ancient Roman times. A viewer has a bird's eye view of a deep and orderly natural vista. The people here have taken full possession of nature: They have terraced the hillsides with vineyards and patterned the valleys with the geometry of fields and pastures. The peasants at their labors work toward the health and prosperity of Siena. The peace of the countryside thus supports the productivity of the city.

Late Fourteenth-Century Crises

Ambrogio's ideal vision of Siena and its countryside expresses the ideals of the rulers of the city at a moment of peace and prosperity. The first three decades of the fourteenth century in Siena, as in Florence, had been a period of relative political stability and economic expansion, as well as of great artistic achievement. In the 1340s, however, both cities suffered a series of catastrophes, the effects of which were to be felt for many years.

Upheaval and Plague

Constant warfare led scores of banks and merchants into bankruptcy; internal upheavals shook governments, and there were repeated crop failures and famine. Then, in 1348, the pandemic of bubonic plague—the Black Death—that spread throughout Europe killed more than half the population of the two cities. Popular reactions to these events were mixed. Many people saw them as signs of divine wrath, warnings to a sinful humanity to forsake the pleasures of this earth. For them, the Black Death intensified an interest in religion and the promise of heavenly rewards. For others, such as the merry company who entertain each other by telling stories in Boccaccio's *Decameron*, the fear of death intensified the desire to enjoy life while there was still time.

Among the many thousands of people who perished of the Black Death was probably Ambrogio Lorenzetti. The abrupt loss of many promising artists was but one of the effects of the plague. Worried about their mortality, patrons were even more concerned to endow chapels, tombs, and funeral Masses to ensure their souls' eternal health. Many such burials and endowments were made in mendicant churches, such as the Franciscan Santa Croce and the Dominican Santa Maria Novella in Florence. These upheavals prevented Florence from completing its cathedral in the fourteenth century. The plague returned there in 1363; the city's political elite clashed with the

papacy; and an uprising among the working classes created social and economic turmoil. Florence overcame these crises to flourish in the fifteenth century as a center of economic energy, political astuteness, and cultural leadership. As the century began, a new generation of Florentine artists would look to the art of Giotto and his contemporaries in their search for new forms of visual expression.

Northern Italy: Milan

Although also wracked by the plague, the other cities of northern Italy experienced a somewhat different situation in the fourteenth century. Unlike Florence, the city of Venice enjoyed a political stability that only increased its wealth. West of Venice in the rich agricultural region of Lombardy, a family with great dynastic ambitions took over. Having gained control of the city of Milan, the Visconti family positioned themselves among the great families of Europe through marriage ties to members of the Italian and European nobility. By 1395, Giangaleazzo Visconti had been named Duke

13.14 Giovannino dei Grassi. *Book of Hours.* ca. 1395. Tempera and gold on parchment, 9¾ × 6⅞" (24.7 × 17.5 cm). Banco Rari, Biblioteca Nazionale, Florence

of Milan, had married the daughter of the king of France, and wed his own daughter to a French duke.

Giangaleazzo used the visual arts as tools to celebrate his status. Like French aristocrats, he commissioned elaborate illuminated manuscripts with numerous personal references. His Book of Hours was begun around 1395 by Giovannino dei Grassi (active ca. 1380–1398). The page in **fig. 13.14** begins one of the Psalms with an illuminated initial D, wherein King David appears. David is both the author of the Psalms and a good biblical exemplar of a ruler, appropriate for the duke. Coats of arms and other Visconti emblems fill the page: An unfurling ribbon ornamented with the French *fleur-de-lis* forms the D; shields at the corners bear the Visconti emblem of the viper. Below the text appears a portrait of Giangaleazzo in the profile arrangement familiar from ancient coins. This naturalistic portrait is enframed by blue and purple ribbons behind which appear the rays of the sun, another Visconti emblem. Around the portrait Giovannino has painted images of stags and a hunting dog, with great attention to the accurate rendering of these natural forms. Such flashes of realism set amidst the splendor of the page reflect both the patron's and the artist's contribution to the developing International Gothic style. Commissioning such lavish books was an expression of the status and power that Giangaleazzo attempted to wield. His ambition to bring most of northern Italy under his control would profoundly affect the arts in Tuscany in the early fifteenth century.

POINTS OF REFLECTION

13.1 Review the steps taken by artists toward naturalism and spatial illusion. What inspired these changes?

13.2 Assess and explain why we know so many artists' names and biographies for this period.

13.3 Evaluate the impact of the growth of cities on art patronage at this time.

13.4 Select a civic object from this chapter and consider how its meaning is conditioned by its original location.

13.5 Outline the similarities and differences between Italian art and the art of its European neighbors during these two centuries.

✔•—**Study** and review on myartslab.com

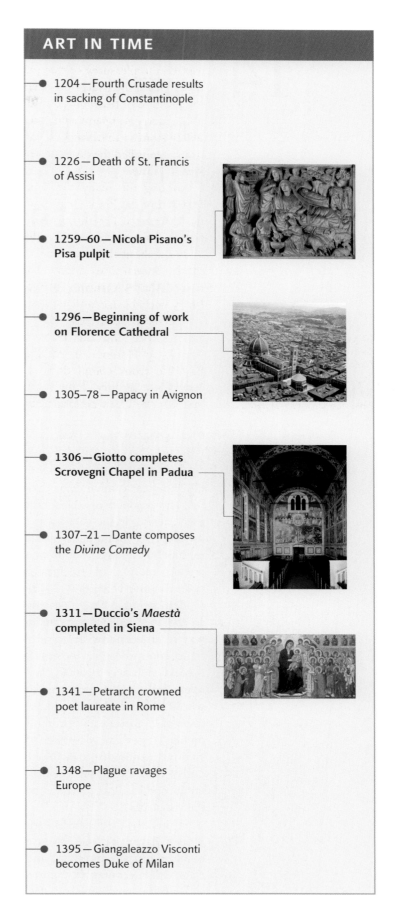

ART IN TIME

• 1204—Fourth Crusade results in sacking of Constantinople

• 1226—Death of St. Francis of Assisi

• 1259–60—Nicola Pisano's Pisa pulpit

• 1296—Beginning of work on Florence Cathedral

• 1305–78—Papacy in Avignon

• 1306—Giotto completes Scrovegni Chapel in Padua

• 1307–21—Dante composes the *Divine Comedy*

• 1311—Duccio's *Maestà* completed in Siena

• 1341—Petrarch crowned poet laureate in Rome

• 1348—Plague ravages Europe

• 1395—Giangaleazzo Visconti becomes Duke of Milan

14

Artistic Innovations in Fifteenth-Century Northern Europe

POINTS OF INQUIRY

14.1 Examine the characteristics of the luxurious International Gothic.

14.2 Discover the detailed naturalism and innovative techniques associated with Netherlandish painting in the fifteenth century.

14.3 Analyze the imagery and complex symbolism of Netherlandish paintings.

14.4 Trace the spread of Netherlandish styles into other regions of Northern Europe.

14.5 Explore the origins of print media.

((•—**Listen** to the chapter audio on myartslab.com

The great cathedrals of Europe's Gothic era—the products of collaboration among churchmen, rulers and the laity—were mostly completed by 1400. As monuments of Christian faith, they exemplify the medieval outlook. But cathedrals are also monuments of cities, where major social and economic changes would set the stage for the modern world. As the fourteenth century came to an end, the medieval agrarian economy was giving way to an economy based on manufacturing and trade, enterprises that took place in urban centers. A social shift accompanied this economic change. Many city dwellers belonged to the middle class, whose upper ranks enjoyed literacy, leisure, and disposable income. With these advantages, the middle classes gained greater social influence and cultural significance than they had enjoyed previously. This transformation had a profound effect on European culture, including the development of the visual arts.

As in Italy, cities such as Paris, London, Prague, Bruges, Barcelona, and Basel (see **map 14.1**) were home to artisans and merchants as well as aristocrats. Urban economies required bankers, lawyers, and entrepreneurs. Investors seeking new products and markets encouraged technological innovations, such as the printing press, an invention that would change Europe. Trade put more liquid wealth into the hands of merchants and artisans, and thus emboldened them to seek more autonomy from the traditional aristocracy, who themselves sought to maintain the feudal status quo.

Other forces were at work, as well. Two of the most far-reaching changes concerned increased literacy and changes in religious expression. During the fourteenth century, the removal of the papacy to Avignon and the election of two popes had created a schism in the Church that ended only in 1417. The reputation of the institutional Church suffered as a result. Many laypeople turned to religious movements—such as the mendicants—which encouraged them to read and meditate on sacred texts on their own and to seek a personal relationship with God. These religious impulses and increasing literacy among people of different social levels resulted in a demand for books in vernacular (local) languages, including translations of the scriptures. The printing press made books more readily available, further stimulating the development and spread of knowledge.

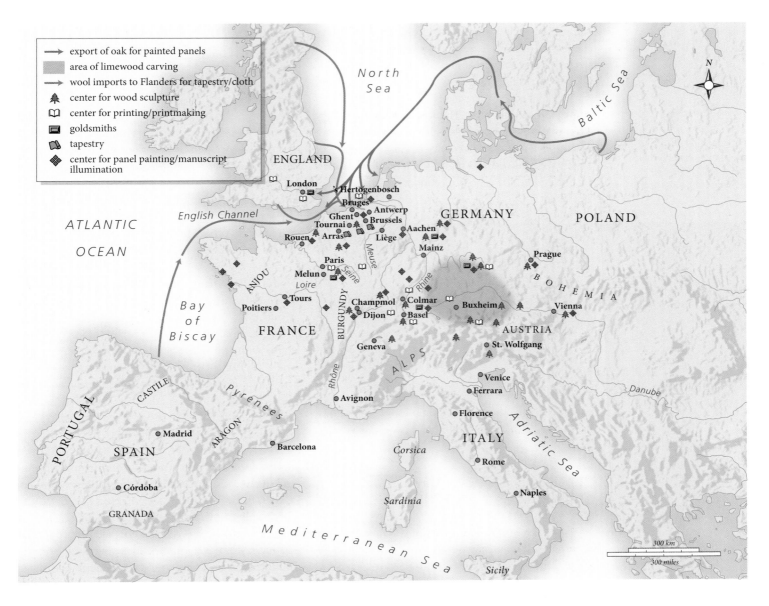

Map 14.1 Craft and manufacturing specialties in Northern Europe in the Early modern period

Political changes were shaping the modern boundaries of European nations. The end of the Hundred Years' War between France and England in 1453 allowed the French monarchy to recover, but civil war kept England politically unstable until late in the fifteenth century. French kings envied their Burgundian cousins, who controlled the trading hub of Northern Europe: The rich lands of Flanders in the Southern Netherlands (present-day Belgium) and the Northern Netherlands (present-day Holland). Indeed, Duke Philip the Good of Burgundy (r. 1419–1467) was one of the most powerful men of the century.

To the east, in Central Europe, the Holy Roman emperor had nominal control, but local rulers within this region often flouted his authority. On the Iberian peninsula, a crucial marriage between Queen Isabella of Castile and King Ferdinand of Aragon created a unified Spanish kingdom that became increasingly powerful. Competition among the powers of Europe for trade routes led to the exploratory voyages of Columbus, which would change the globe.

A new style of visual art that stressed naturalism accompanied these political and social changes. Aristocrats and churchmen continued to commission artwork, but the new ranks of society—bureaucrats and merchants—also became art patrons. For merchants and middle-class residents of urban centers, painters made images in a new medium with a new character. Using oil paints, artists in the Netherlands produced works that still astonish viewers by their close approximation to optical reality. By mid-century, this strongly naturalistic style became the dominant visual language of Northern Europe, attracting patrons from all classes and many countries.

This period of transition out of the Middle Ages was gradual and by no means universal. Faced with a growing middle class, the traditional aristocracy attempted to maintain its privileges and status. Among the aristocratic courts of Europe, many of which were linked by treaty or marriage, a preference emerged for a highly refined, courtly form of Gothic art.

14.1 Claus Sluter. *The Well of Moses*, from the Chartreuse de Champmol. 1395–1406. Stone, height of figures approx. 6′ (1.8 m)

Courtly Art: The International Gothic

As the fourteenth century came to an end, aristocratic patrons throughout Europe displayed a taste for objects made of sumptuous materials with elegant forms based on the Gothic style. Cosmopolitan courts such as Avignon and Paris attracted artists from different regions of Europe where they exchanged ideas. These circumstances produced the elegant style termed International Gothic. The chronological limits of this style are somewhat fluid, as its products are dated between the mid-fourteenth and the mid-fifteenth century.

This refined style appeared in Italy, France, Flanders, Germany, Spain, Bohemia, Austria, England, and elsewhere. For these elite patrons, artists produced works of exquisite craftsmanship, often with very complex iconographies. Their forms share with the Gothic style a level of idealization and patterning controlled by geometry, visible in the *Virgin of Paris* (see fig. 12.18). Artists added to these forms touches of directly observed nature, especially in details, like those in the Visconti Hours (fig. 13.14). Some commentators have seen the detailed naturalism of the International Gothic as a starting point for the more thoroughgoing naturalism of the painters in Flanders and their followers in the fifteenth century.

Members of the family of King Charles V of France were active patrons of the International Gothic style. His brother, Philip the Bold, became duke of Burgundy and count of Flanders. The dukes of Burgundy became powerbrokers in the military and economic battles of the fifteenth century.

Artists at the French Courts

Commissioning expensive works of art enhanced Philip's status, an example that was followed by his successors. One major project was the founding of a Carthusian monastery, the Chartreuse de Champmol, outside Dijon in Burgundy. For the creation of this building, which was almost completely destroyed in the late eighteenth century, Philip assembled a team of artists, many of them from the Netherlands. Chief among them was the sculptor Claus Sluter (ca. 1350–1406) from Brussels.

THE WELL OF MOSES Sluter's work at the Chartreuse de Champmol includes portals, tombs, pulpits, and the so-called *Well of Moses* (**fig. 14.1**). This hexagonal well, surrounded by statues of Old

Testament prophets, once supported a crucifix, which expressed visually the fulfillment by the New Testament of the Old. The majestic Moses wears a long, luxuriant beard and flowing drapery that is organized into graceful folds; his figure seems to expand into the surrounding space to interact directly with the viewer. The lifelike quality and naturalistic rendering must have been enhanced greatly by colors added to the stone by the painter Jean Malouel; these have mostly disappeared. To Moses' right stands King David, also naturalistically depicted, but with a wholly different personality; where Moses seems intensely focused on something, David has the dreamy gaze of a poet. Sluter's naturalistic style is based on specific observations such as the texture of Moses' beard or the wings of the angels and the distinct characterizations of the six prophets. A thoughtful and meditative tone imbues all the figures.

LES TRÈS RICHES HEURES DU DUC DE BERRY Jean Malouel introduced to Duke Philip his nephews Pol, Herman, and Jean de Limbourg, who came from the Netherlands. The crowning achievement of these three brothers is the luxurious Book of Hours known as *Les Très Riches Heures du Duc de Berry (The Very Rich Hours of the Duke of Berry)*. This lavish book was produced for Jean, duke of Berry, brother of Philip the Bold and the most avid art patron of his day. The brothers shared an appointment as court painters to Duke Jean, reflecting the high regard they enjoyed. Their work reflects not only the idealization inherent in French Gothic art, but the naturalistic experiments of fourteenth-century Italy.

Les Très Riches Heures was commissioned about 1413 and left unfinished when all three brothers died in 1416. The most famous pages are devoted to the calendar, depicting human activities and the cycle of nature. For each month, such calendars assigned figures to perform appropriate seasonal activities; they were an established tradition in medieval art.

The calendar page for July (**fig. 14.2**) demonstrates the Limbourgs' innovative presentation of these themes. Time's passing is noted in several ways on the page: Astrological signs and numbers identify the month, while peasants harvesting wheat and shearing sheep perform the labor of the month. These activities occur below a precisely rendered image of Jean de Berry's Château du Clain (Poitiers), now destroyed. The page depicts the orderly harvesting of a fruitful earth by the peaceful peasantry. This idealized view of the social order of feudalism is achieved by combining the portrait of the castle and naturalistic details of the peasants' work with a space that rises up the picture plane like a tapestry. The jewel-like color and splashes of gold leaf in the calendar zone contribute to the sumptuous effect of the page. The prestige of the patron and the sheer innovation of the images, especially the calendar pages, in *Les Très Riches Heures* inspired many later copies.

14.2 Limbourg Brothers. *Les Très Riches Heures du Duc de Berry*, calendar miniature for July. 1413–16. Illumination on vellum, 8⅞ × 5⅜″ (22.5 × 13.7 cm). Musée Condé, Chantilly, France

Urban Centers and the New Art

Many of the artists hired by aristocratic patrons for their projects came from the cities of the Southern Netherlands: Bruges, Brussels, Ghent, and Tournai. These towns were centers of international commerce where merchants from all over Europe gathered to do business. The cities were very jealous of their independent status, but their claims to independence often clashed with the aims of overlords who wished to control their inhabitants and tax their wealth. In addition to these social and economic shifts, the cities of Flanders witnessed the beginnings of an artistic revolution. Working either for courts or for middle-class citizens, artists began to make images in oil painting that represented sacred figures as if they existed in the natural world.

Robert Campin

One pioneer of this revolution in naturalism was Robert Campin (1378–1444) of Tournai, an important trade center in southwestern Belgium. One of the works most frequently associated with Campin and his workshop is the *Mérode Triptych* (**fig. 14.3**), dated 1425 to 1430. (The name Mérode derives from a nineteenth-century owner of the painting.) The artist represents linked images across three panels, a form called a TRIPTYCH; this was the standard format of altarpieces in the Southern Netherlands. Considered the earliest part of the triptych, the central panel depicts the Annunciation. Here the artist places Mary and the angel Gabriel in what appears to be the main room of a bourgeois house. A viewer has the sense of actually looking through the picture plane into a world that mimics reality. Campin uses several devices to create this effect. He fits the objects and figures into boxes of space, sometimes uncomfortably. He renders details in such a way as to make every object as concrete as possible in shape, size, color, and texture. He records with great sophistication the fall of light on the painted objects. He uses color to unify all three panels. His colors have richness and depth, and he achieves smooth transitions from lights into darks. To create these effects, Campin and his contemporaries expanded the possibilities of using oil paint on panels. Mixing pigments into slow-drying translucent oils allowed them to blend brushstrokes, add layers of color for greater depth, and render forms with great detail. The result is a more thorough illusion of reality than the flashes of natural detail seen in the work of earlier court artists.

Campin made these paintings for his fellow citizens, such as the two donors piously kneeling outside Mary's chamber in the wings. Although their identities are not certain, a coat of arms links

14.3 Robert Campin. *Mérode Triptych*. ca. 1425–30. Oil on panel, center section 25³/₁₆ × 24⁷/₈″ (64.3 × 62.9 cm); each wing approx. 25³/₈ × 10⁷/₈″ (64.5 × 27.4 cm). The Metropolitan Museum of Art, New York, The Cloisters Collection, 1956. 56.70

View the Closer Look for the *Mérode Triptych* on myartslab.com

them to the Engelbrecht family; they likely commissioned this triptych for their own dwelling, as it seems small for installation in a church. The Annunciation itself occurs in a fully equipped domestic interior with figures that are rendered as real people, with mass and weight. The drapery of their garments falls in deep folds, anchoring the figures to the floor, as in the sculpture of Claus Sluter (see fig. 14.1). Gabriel stands or kneels near the door. His gesture and Mary's red dress draw attention to her as she sits on the floor, book in hand. Between them a table supports another book, a vase of lilies, and a candle. On the left wing, the donors kneel in a garden, as though looking through the open door to witness this event. Campin depicts substantial bodies in a recognizably earthly setting for the eyes of the donor couple. The event takes place in their world, not in Heaven.

That earthly location extends to the right wing, where Joseph, the carpenter, works. Just what he is making has been a subject of much debate, particularly concerning the boxlike object on the ledge outside the open window. It has been identified as a mousetrap, an object that the Christian theologian St. Augustine used metaphorically to explain God's plan for salvation when he said, "The Cross of the Lord was the devil's mousetrap." Joseph's handiwork contributes to the plan for Christian salvation, which commences in the central panel. Equally puzzling is the object in Joseph's hand, identified by some historians as a firescreen (like the one in the central panel) and by others as part of a winepress (referring to the wine of the Eucharist).

Scholars read such carefully chosen details as symbols that represent concepts or ideas. Some symbols are fairly obvious: the lilies, for example, reference Mary's virginity. Yet the smoking candle next to them is more perplexing, and its symbolism less clear. The appearance in Campin's picture of so many carefully delineated objects suggests that these details constitute a symbolic program. Some commentators argue that artists consulted theologians to devise these complex programs, though it was the skill of the artist that brought the program to light.

As the moment of the Incarnation, when Christians believe God's son became human, the Annunciation has great liturgical and theological import, but it is also about the conception of a child. From the perspective of the donor couple, the triptych may reflect their own desire for children or their reverence for the Holy Family as a model for

their own. Such personalized approaches to holy figures were an important feature of religious life in this period. Believers were encouraged through sermons, by Passion plays, and in written texts to visualize the sacred in terms they could understand and to meditate on events from Christ's life. Artists like Campin may have been responding to the call to see the physical world as a mirror of divine truths and to create moving and pious images of sacred events occurring in everyday environments.

Jan van Eyck

Campin's contemporary Jan van Eyck (ca. 1399–1441) may well have known this picture. Famous in the fifteenth century, he is a figure about whom we know a good deal. He was born in Holland, in Maaseyck, and worked for the count of Holland before establishing his workshop in Bruges. Both a townsman and a court painter, Jan worked for the duke of Burgundy, who sent him on diplomatic errands. Unusually for his time, he signed and dated several surviving pictures.

GHENT ALTARPIECE Despite his court appointment, Jan was working for a townsman when he completed the *Ghent Altarpiece*, which made his reputation as a painter. Large in scale and in a prominent location in the cathedral of Ghent, the altarpiece has drawn a crowd ever since it was installed. A text once inscribed on the frame identified Jan van Eyck as the artist who finished this multipanelled altarpiece in May 1432; the inscription also alluded to the collaboration of his brother, Hubert, who died in 1426. The basic form of this complex altarpiece is a triptych but here each of the three units consists of four panels. Since the movable wings are painted on both sides, the altarpiece has a total of 20 images of various shapes and sizes. Discontinuities among the many panels suggest that alterations took place as the work progressed. It appears that Jan completed a number of panels left unfinished by Hubert, added some of his own, and assembled the whole at the request of the mayor of Ghent, Jodicus Vijd. Vijd's portrait, with that of his wife, Elizabeth Borluut, appears on the outer panels of the altar when the triptych is closed (**fig. 14.4**).

They are portrayed on the lower tier with two other figures, each in a niche framed by Gothic tracery: Here are the patrons of the cathedral, John the Baptist and John the Evangelist, painted in grisaille. The upper tier has two pairs of panels of different widths. The artist has unified all four to depict one

A TRIPTYCH has three fields for images, a diptych two. They can be fixed panels or wings that fold together and may be of any size.

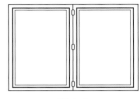

Diptych

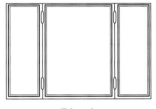

Triptych

14.4 Hubert and Jan van Eyck. *Ghent Altarpiece* (closed). Completed 1432. Oil on panel, 11'5" × 7'6" (3.4 × 2.25 m). Cathedral of St. Bavo, Ghent, Belgium

Court of Heaven, with the Lord in a bright red robe at the center. Flanking him are Mary and John the Baptist. To the left and right, choirs of angels sing and play musical instruments. At the outer edges of this upper tier stand Adam and Eve, rendered as nudes in shallow niches, below grisaille images of Abel and Cain. The artist breathes life into the almost life-size figures by rendering their textures and forms with careful attention and great anatomical accuracy, the bodies caressed by a delicate play of light and shadow.

Seeing the triptych on the altar of the Vijd Chapel in the Ghent cathedral, a viewer could not fail to be impressed by its scale and setting. The tone and majesty of this ensemble are very different from the domestic intimacy of the *Mérode Triptych*. The function of the altarpiece is to elucidate the liturgy performed in front of it. When open, its subject is the Mass itself, here shown in a paradisiacal setting. Jan's work is large in scale but full of small, naturally observed details and glowing color. His technique of building up color in layers of glazes gives a highly saturated result, while the slow methodical application of paint blends brushstrokes to a mirrorlike finish. The *Ghent Altarpiece* offers the devout viewer a glimpse into Heaven.

THE "ARNOLFINI PORTRAIT" Van Eyck also made secular paintings, fulfilling the commissions of the court and of the citizens of Flemish towns. Another signed painting represents a man and a woman standing in the richly furnished main room of a fifteenth-century house equipped with a brass chandelier, a mirror, and a canopied bed (**fig. 14.6**). Jan's signature appears not on the frame, as was his normal practice, but within the panel. Above the painted mirror, in a formal script, the inscription reads, "Jan van Eyck was here, 1434." The features of the man, if not the lady, are specific enough to be a portrait, and the image is unusual enough that later documents have identified him as Giovanni Arnolfini, an Italian merchant living in Bruges. For many years his companion was identified as Giovanna Cenami, Arnolfini's wife; recent research, however, makes this doubtful, as their marriage occurred much later than 1434.

Whatever their names, the painted couple stands with hands joined, while the man raises his right hand as if taking a solemn oath. Though they seem to be alone, the mirror behind them shows the reflection of two men entering the room. Because the signature appears right above

interior room, whose foreshortened timber ceiling extends across all four panels. Prophets and Sibyls occupy an upper story, their prophecies written in Gothic script in scrolls above their heads.

With the wings opened (**fig. 14.5**) the viewer sees a detailed rendering of a celestial assembly. Across the bottom tier, groups of figures converge on a central image of an altar, upon which stands a haloed Lamb (Christ). This assembly includes angels, apostles, popes, theologians, virgin martyrs, hermits, pilgrims, knights, and judges. A verdant landscape provides the setting for this mystic Mass, with towers of numerous churches on the skyline. Above this earthly paradise reigns an imposing

the mirror, many art historians believe that one of these men must be Jan van Eyck himself. The combination of the signature, with its flourishes and phrasing, and the image of the men in the mirror suggests to some that Jan is acting as a witness to whatever is occurring in the room.

For many years it has been argued that this panel depicts either the wedding or the engagement of the couple represented, which would have required a legal and financial contract between their two families. By this account, the painting commemorates the union of the couple. If so, one of the men in the mirror could be the bride's father, who would have made the contract for the marriage of his daughter. The woman's gesture of lifting her heavy gown may suggest her wish for children, as the bed behind her may suggest the consummation of the marriage. Given the minimal

religious imagery (only the tiny images of the Passion of Christ that surround the mirror are clearly religious), debates have raged about whether the realistic touches serve as an accurate record of an event, or whether the details in the painting carry symbolic weight. The dog, for example, may be a beloved pet, or he could stand for fidelity. (*Fides* is Latin for faithfulness, the origin of the traditional dog name Fido.) Other details are more obscure: A candle in the chandelier burns in broad daylight, pieces of citrus fruit sit near the window. A less enigmatic detail appears on the canopied bed: A tiny image of St. Margaret, the patron of child-bearing. One expert has proposed that the image commemorates a lady who died during childbirth, which may account for her somewhat generalized features. Yet, the mirror and the inscription seem to reflect Jan's own self-awareness and self-promotion

14.5 Hubert and Jan van Eyck. *Ghent Altarpiece* (open). Completed 1432. Oil on panel, 11′5″ × 15′1″ (3.4 × 4.5 m). Cathedral of St. Bavo, Ghent, Belgium

 View the Closer Look for the *Ghent Altarpiece* on myartslab.com

14.6 Jan van Eyck. *The "Arnolfini Portrait."* 1434. Oil on panel, 33 × 22½" (83.7 × 57 cm). The National Gallery, London. Courtesy of the Trustees

in this picture. The artist's rendering of many textures and details in a realistically depicted space makes this image a fascinating example of the union of technique and subject to communicate a complex idea.

Rogier van der Weyden

As a court painter, Jan van Eyck was exempt from the restrictions that governed other artists in Flemish towns. The training of artists and the market for works of art were both regulated by the guilds, professional organizations of artists and other craftsmen established to protect the interests of their members (see page 255). One famous graduate of the guild system was Rogier van der Weyden (1399/1400–1464), a painter who trained with Robert Campin, but who certainly knew the work of

Jan van Eyck. Rogier established his workshop in Brussels. His most influential work is the *Descent from the Cross* (**fig. 14.7**), dating from about 1435. It was commissioned as the center of an altarpiece by the crossbowmen's guild of Louvain (near Brussels) for a church there. Rogier depicts the moment when the body of Christ is lowered from the cross, in a composition of mourners crowded into a shallow box. His life-size forms are carefully modeled to suggest sculptural presence, and they are detailed enough to show every nuance of texture.

Rogier's goal is to increase the expressive content of his picture. He emphasizes the emotional impact of the event on its participants. Grief is etched on each figure's face, even as their postures express their sorrow. John the Evangelist on the left and Mary Magdalen on the right are bowed

14.7 Rogier van der Weyden. *Descent from the Cross.* ca. 1435. Oil on panel, 7′2⅝″ × 8′7⅛″ (2.2 × 2.6 m). Museo del Prado, Madrid

with grief. The Virgin's swoon echoes the pose and expression of her dead son. So intense are her pain and grief that they inspire the same compassion in a viewer. Rogier has staged his scene in a shallow niche or shrine, not against a landscape. This device focuses a viewer's attention on the figures. Furthermore, the emphasis on the body of Christ at the center of the composition alludes to the celebration of the Eucharist, which occurs before the altarpiece. These grief-stricken gestures and faces have their origins in Gothic sculpture like the figures on the Naumburg choir screen (fig. 12.24). Rogier's emotive painting inspired many copies, in both painting and sculpture.

Works like Rogier's *Descent from the Cross* offered powerful examples for other artists to follow, in the Netherlands and beyond. As the fifteenth century progressed, the medium of painting gained in prestige among both urban and aristocratic patrons. Large-scale sculpture continued to be made in the fifteenth-century Netherlands, though little has survived the ravages of war, social upheavals, and changes of taste.

Hugo van der Goes in Ghent

International businessmen numbered among the active patrons of artists in Flanders. They commissioned paintings as acts of piety, but also as markers of their rising social status. A good example of this phenomenon is a work by Hugo van der Goes (ca. 1440–1482). This painter, who worked in Ghent, was commissioned around 1474 by an agent of the

Medici bank in Bruges to paint a huge altarpiece to be shipped to Florence (**fig. 14.8**). The 10-foot-wide central panel represents Mary, Joseph, and the shepherds adoring the newborn Christ Child in Bethlehem. In the wings, members of the donor family, including Tommaso Portinari, his wife, Maria Maddalena Baroncelli, and their children, kneel towards the central image. A landscape unites all three wings as a continuous space, with the bare trees and December sky suggesting Flanders, not the Holy Land. Objects in the distance have taken on the blue of the atmosphere; this use of **atmospheric perspective** infuses the panel with a cool tonality. Hugo fills this setting with figures and objects rendered with precise detail in deeply saturated colors.

Yet Hugo's realistic rendering of both landscape and figures is contradicted by variations in the sizes of the figures. Mary, Joseph, and the shepherds of the Nativity dwarf the angels at the center and kneeling members of the Portinari family in the wings. This change of scale contradicts the believable pictorial space that the artist provides for his figures. Another contrast occurs between the raucous intrusion of the shepherds and the ritual solemnity of all the other figures. These rough fieldhands gaze in breathless wonder at the newborn Christ, at whom all the figures ranged around him gaze. Mary, however, sits at the physical center of the composition. Such deliberate contrasts between the pictorial and psychological focal points, between the scale of the historical and the contemporary

14.8 Hugo van der Goes. *Portinari Altarpiece* (open). ca. 1474–76. Tempera and oil on panel, center section 8′3½″ × 10′ (2.5 × 3.1 m), each wing 8′3½″ × 4′7½″ (2.5 × 1.4 m). Galleria degli Uffizi, Florence

figures, and between their static and kinetic postures contribute to a viewer's unsettled reaction to the work.

Narratives in the background support the main theme: on the left panel, Mary and Joseph travel toward Bethlehem; on the right wing, the Magi progress toward Bethlehem. In the center, the movement of angels flickers across the surface, lit by both natural and supernatural light. Strategically placed at the front of the picture are beautiful still-lifes of flowers and a sheaf of wheat: The wheat refers to the bread of the Eucharist and the flowers to Mary. Portinari brought the triptych to Florence in 1483 and installed it in the family chapel. There it proclaimed his piety, wealth, and status. Judging from their imitation of it, Italian painters who saw the work there especially admired its naturalism and its unidealized representation of the shepherds.

Hieronymus Bosch

Although many of these artists came from present-day Belgium, artists of the Northern Netherlands (present-day Holland) also contributed to the development of fifteenth-century painting. Hieronymus Bosch (ca. 1450–1516) spent his life in the town of 's Hertogenbosch, the seat of a ducal residence, from which his name derives. His famous *The Garden of Earthly Delights* (**fig. 14.9**) was acquired by King Philip II of Spain in the sixteenth century.

THE GARDEN OF EARTHLY DELIGHTS This large oil painting has the format of a triptych but a subject matter that is surprisingly unorthodox. It represents humans in the natural world. As in Hugo's triptych, a continuous landscape unites the three sections; the high horizon and atmospheric perspective imply a deep vista of the earth from an omniscient vantage point. Shades of green create an undulating topography marked by thickets of trees and bodies of water. Throughout swarm small creatures, both human and non-human. Strange rock formations, plants, and other objects appear at intervals. The left wing appears to represent the Garden of Eden, where the Lord introduces Adam to the newly created Eve. The airy landscape is filled with animals, including such exotic creatures as an elephant and a giraffe, as well as strange hybrid monsters. The central panel reveals a world inhabited by tiny humans who frolic among giant fruits, birds, and other creatures. In the middle ground, men parade around a circular basin on the backs of all sorts of beasts. Many of the humans interact with

14.9 Hieronymus Bosch. *The Garden of Earthly Delights*. ca. 1480–1515. Oil on panel, center section 7′2½″ × 6′ 4½″ (2.19 × 1.95 m); wings, each 7′2½″ × 3′2″ (2.19 × 0.97 m). Museo del Prado, Madrid

huge birds, fruits, flowers, or marine animals. The right wing depicts an infernal zone, probably Hell, where strange hybrid creatures torment the tiny humans with punishments appropriate to their sins. The reverse side of the wings depicts a crystal globe holding an image of the earth emerging from a flood, with God watching over the events from above.

Documents record that the painting belonged to Count Henry III of Nassau, in whose palace in Brussels it was reported to be in 1517, though recent research suggests it could have been painted as early as 1480. Many interpretations of it have been offered—that it represents the earth in the days of Noah, as shown by the image of a flood on the exterior; that the many swarming nudes express the views of a heretical group that promoted free love; or that the infernal landscape in the right wing demonstrates a moralizing condemnation of carnal sin.

One striking interpretation of this painting links it to the practice of alchemy as an allegory of redemption. The many strangely shaped and outsized formations refer to the tools and vessels used in this medieval approach to understanding the earth. The alchemical process required four steps: Conjunction—or mixing, for which the joining of Adam and Eve is a metaphor; child's play—the slow process of cooking diverse ingredients and letting them ferment, for which the central panel would stand; putrefaction—a step in which material is burned, related to the infernal right wing; and the final cleansing of matter—represented by the exterior flood. Bosch, who had married an apothecary's daughter, consciously used the visual symbols of that science to create an unforgettable glimpse of natural processes.

Regional Responses to the Early Netherlandish Style

Artists in many regions of Europe responded to the formal and technical achievements of the artists of the Netherlands. These regional responses were influenced by local traditions and tastes, but patrons found the naturalism of the new style useful for religious and social purposes. Many regions, including France and Central Europe, produced their own variations on the style.

France

Geographical proximity, trade routes, linguistic links, and political relationships with the Burgundian

14.10 Jean Fouquet. *Melun Diptych*. ca. 1450. Left wing: *Étienne Chevalier and St. Stephen*. Oil on panel, 36½ × 33½″ (92.7 × 85 cm). Gemäldegalerie, Staatliche Museen zu Berlin. Right wing: *Madonna and Child*. Oil on panel, 36⅝ × 33½″ (94.5 × 85 cm). Koninklijk Museum voor Schone Kunsten, Antwerpen, Belgie (Musée Royal des Beaux-Arts, Antwerp, Belgium)

Netherlands helped to spread the innovations in technique and style throughout France. Artists either traveled to Flemish cities or developed their own brand of naturalism in imitation of the effects that Rogier (see fig. 14.7) or Hugo (see fig. 14.8) had achieved. Yet French art has distinctive features and traditions. In the first half of the fifteenth century, the troubles of the Hundred Years' War limited expenditure on art. Citizens of the war-torn cities commissioned very little, but members of the Church and the court continued earlier forms of patronage.

MELUN DIPTYCH After consolidating his power in France at the close of the Hundred Years' War, King Charles VII hired Jean Fouquet (ca. 1420–1481) of Tours to work for him. Both a book illuminator and a panel painter, Fouquet traveled to Italy around 1445, where he learned some of the innovations of contemporary Italian art. His work, however, owes much to Netherlandish style in technique, color, and approach. Around 1450, the royal treasurer, Étienne Chevalier, commissioned Fouquet to paint a diptych, or two-paneled image, representing the treasurer and his patron saint, Stephen, in proximity to Mary and Christ; this is the *Melun Diptych* (**fig. 14.10**), named for the town where it was installed. Like his Flemish contemporaries, Fouquet records the specific physiognomy of the patron in his fur-lined garment. The saint carries a book and the stone of his martyrdom; his features seem as individual as those of the donor.

The two men appear in a room with marbled floors and walls framed by antique-inspired pilasters that recede to suggest space. They gaze across the frame toward an image of the enthroned Virgin and Child. According to tradition, the Virgin is also a portrait: Of Agnès Sorel, Charles VII's mistress and Chevalier's friend. If so, the panel presents an image of courtly beauty, befitting the Queen of Heaven. Fouquet deliberately contrasts the earthly and divine realms. The deep space in the left panel differs markedly from the right panel, whose composition is organized as a rising triangle, with the cool colors of the Virgin and Child set against the vivid reds and blues of the angels. Unlike his Flemish counterparts, Fouquet is not interested in suggesting specific textures here, nor does he provide elaborate details or appeal to the emotions. Rather than expressiveness, Fouquet stresses the grandeur and dignity of the Virgin.

Central Europe

Trade routes and political ties linked the Netherlands to Central Europe, where artists and patrons were also receptive to the new style. Painters, illuminators, and sculptors all responded to the naturalism of the Flemish style, but adapted it to local taste. For example, in German-speaking regions, altarpieces were usually made of wood; they were often large and intricately carved. (In the sixteenth century religious turmoil destroyed many sculpted religious images, so surviving examples are rare.)

MICHAEL PACHER The *St. Wolfgang Altarpiece* (**fig. 14.11**) by the Tyrolean (Austria) sculptor and painter Michael Pacher (ca. 1435–1498) is impressive both because of its scale and because it remains in its original setting, the pilgrimage church and monastery of St. Wolfgang. The surviving contract between the abbot who commissioned it and the painter specifies both the subject matter and the quality of the materials and workmanship, which was normal practice during this period for contracts given to artists for expensive projects.

Much as Jan van Eyck did in the *Ghent Altarpiece*, Pacher creates a vision of Heaven here: The center panel depicts the Coronation of the Virgin as Queen of Heaven, flanked by the patron saints of the monastery. Carved of soft wood that permitted the sculptor to create deep folds and sharp edges, the lavishly gilt and colored forms make a dazzling spectacle as they emerge from the shadows under Flamboyant Gothic canopies. The figures and setting in the central panel seem to converge into a pattern of twisting lines that permits only the heads to stand out as separate elements.

The complexity and surface ornamentation that dominate the center contrast with the paintings of scenes from Mary's life on the interior of the wings. Here the artist represents large figures, strongly modeled by clear light, and he suggests a deep space for them. His use of **perspective**, a system for projecting space in a painting, was inspired by developments in contemporary Italian painting. Pacher almost certainly crossed the Alps and visited northern Italy, so he had learned to use the Italian technique for projecting space. (Compare his perspective to Mantegna's in fig. 15.22.) This perspective appears only in the wings, however, where scenes from the past are set into spaces that look like the fifteenth-century present. The interior of the temple where the circumcision takes place, for example, has a vault much like those in

14.11 Michael Pacher. *St. Wolfgang Altarpiece.* 1471–81. Carved wood. Figures about life-size; wings, oil on panel. Church of St. Wolfgang, Salzkammergut, Austria

contemporary churches in the Tyrolean region. Pacher makes the historical scenes in the wings much more down to earth than the spectacle of Heaven in the center.

Printing and the Graphic Arts

Another new medium developed in fifteenth-century Europe, along with the new techniques of painting: Printmaking. History has credited Johann Gutenberg (ca. 1397–1468) with inventing movable type for printing books, but the roots of printing actually lie in the ancient Near East and China, transmitted to Europe through contact with the Islamic Middle East. This is also true of the technique for manufacturing paper, which gained ground as a cheaper alternative to parchment.

Printing on wood blocks was known in the late Middle Ages, though it was used only for ornamental patterns on cloth. The fifteenth century saw the development of a printing technology capable of producing editions of several hundred copies of relatively inexpensive books, using movable type, new inks, and the printing press. The technology quickly spread across Europe, spawning the new

Early Printmaking

PRINTMAKING primarily is used to make multiple copies of an image. In each of the printmaking techniques—woodcuts, engraving, etching—the artist works on a block or plate and then covers the design with ink to transfer it. Throughout the process, the artist must keep in mind that the resulting image will be a reverse of the original design. Typically, the artist begins with a drawing and a plan for the project.

Making a woodcut is a fairly simple method for achieving a simple design. The artist cuts away and removes wood that will not be inked. The wood left in high relief receives the ink and becomes the positive image of the print. (Potato cuts or linoleum cuts are made in the same way.) Painters or sculptors probably furnished many designs for early woodcuts. Specially trained artisans actually carved the wood blocks. Early woodcuts, like the *Buxheim St. Christopher*, emphasize contour and offer little detail, but by 1500, artists executed quite intricate woodcuts with this technique. Dürer's *Four Horsemen of the Apocalypse* (fig. 18.6) is an extraordinary example of the fine detail possible. The white space in the image corresponds to the cut-away areas of the block, and the inked lines and shapes are created by the fine wood ridges. The pressure of the press on the wood block often dulled the ridges and even split the blocks, so the number of examples of a single woodcut could be limited.

Engraving is an example of a process known as **intaglio** (the cutting or **incising** of an image into a metal plate so that the ink is held below the surface of the plate). Deep cuts are made (engraved) in the metal with a tool called a burin. The plate is inked, and the ink gathers in the grooves made by the cuts. The artist wipes the surface clean, so the only ink remaining on the plate is in the grooves. A damp sheet of paper is placed over the plate, cushioned with blankets, and then rolled through a press. (The paper is damp so that it is soft and better able to pick up the ink.) Schongauer's *The Temptation of St. Anthony* (fig. 14.13) is an especially accomplished example of an engraving.

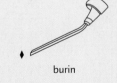

burin

Etching is a variation of intaglio printing. In this process, the artist uses acid to help make (etch) cuts in the metal plate. To begin, the plate is coated with a waxy substance. Instead of gouging to create grooves directly into the metal, the artist will

drawing on a wax-coated etching plate

lightly "draw" on the plate with a stylus, or needle, thereby removing the coating and revealing the metal beneath (see illustration). Next the plate is placed in an acid bath and the revealed metal will react to the acid; this will burn the drawing into the metal. The plate is removed from the acid, wiped off, and covered in ink. Then that is wiped off, leaving ink only in the etched grooves. As in engraving, dampened paper covers the plate and the press rolls over it. Since acid can be hard to control, the etched lines may be uneven, and depending on the length of time in the bath, the grooves can be very deep. So with etching, the actual creation is much like drawing, but the finished process includes an element of chance.

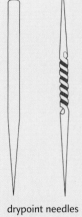

etching needle

Another intaglio technique is called **drypoint**. Drypoint is the process of cutting grooves in the metal (see illustration of tool) and leaving the metal displaced by the needle on the plate; this displaced metal or burr will then gather up the ink and print darker. This process has the possibility of creating areas of higher black density, as in Rembrandt's *Hundred Guilder Print* (fig. 20.10). Drypoint is often used in combination with etching and engraving.

Another option for creating greater tone is to wipe the plate selectively. Leaving some ink on the plate can give a darker tone to the print and create dramatic effects of light and dark. In some cases, Rembrandt seems hardly to have wiped his plate at all, for greater expressive use of tone.

drypoint needles

Changes can be made using each of the above processes. Each version of a print is called a state. After printing an example of a print, the artist can change the block or plate. That second printing, using the same plate or block, is called a second state. There can be many states for a single print. The block or plate is therefore quite valuable and can be used many years later, even after the artist's death, by family members or other owners to provide income. Sometimes the artist will deface the plate (called "striking" it) to prevent anyone else from using it.

👁 **Watch** a video about the process of intaglio on myartslab.com

14.12 *Buxheim St. Christopher*. 1423. Hand-colored woodcut, 11⅜ × 8½" (28.8 × 20.6 cm). John Rylands University Library. Courtesy of the Director and the Librarian, Manchester, England

14.13 Martin Schongauer. *The Temptation of St. Anthony*. ca. 1480–90. Engraving, 11½ × 8⅝" (29.2 × 21.8 cm). The Metropolitan Museum of Art, New York, Rogers Fund, 1920. 20.5.2

industry of bookmaking, which was stimulated by a rise in literacy in Western Europe. To compete with illuminated manuscripts, printed books included printed images, which were often hand-colored to imitate the more expensive manuscripts. Ultimately, the printed book almost completely replaced the illuminated manuscript.

The pictorial and the literary aspects of printing were closely linked from the start. The practice of inking pictorial designs carved on wood blocks and then printing those designs on paper began in Europe late in the fourteenth century. Early surviving examples of such prints, called **woodcuts**, come from France, the Netherlands, and Germany. Painters or sculptors supplied designs that were carved onto wood blocks by specialists. (For the various techniques of printing, see box: Materials and Techniques: Early Printmaking, page 307.)

An early example of a woodcut is the *Buxheim St. Christopher* (**fig. 14.12**), named for the monastery in a German town. This single-sheet, hand-colored woodcut bears the date 1423 and a prayer to the saint as well as an image. Simple, heavy lines define the forms in the print, including the fall of drapery around the figures and the contours of objects. Thin lines in parallel rows—called **hatching**—denote shadows or textures of objects, but the composition is strictly two-dimensional, as the landscape forms rise along the picture plane to surround the figures. According to legend, Christopher was a giant who ferried people across a river; he was surprised one day at the weight of a child, who turned out to be Christ. (His name derives from this encounter: "Christ-bearer.") The forms in the print owe a great deal to Late Gothic style, but the audiences for woodcuts were not aristocrats. Fifteenth-century woodcuts were popular art. A single wood block could yield thousands of copies, to be sold for pennies apiece, so that for the first time in history almost anyone could own pictures.

From the start, engravings, images printed from incised metal plates, appealed to a smaller and more sophisticated public. The oldest surviving examples, from about 1430, already show the influence of Flemish painters. Early engravers were usually trained as goldsmiths, but their prints reflect local painting styles. The artists modeled their forms with finely hatched lines and often convincingly foreshortened them, creating more complex images than woodcutters could achieve. Engravings in distinctive styles often include monograms and dates in the prints, allowing us to identify many engravers of the late fifteenth century. One such artist is Martin Schongauer of Colmar, Germany (ca. 1435/50–1491), a goldsmith and painter inspired by the works of Rogier van der Weyden. The complex designs, spatial depth, and rich textures of his engravings enable them to compete with panel paintings. Schongauer's *The Temptation of St. Anthony* (**fig. 14.13**) was known and admired throughout Europe. The print represents the climax of the hermit St. Anthony's efforts to resist the devil. Unable to tempt the monk to sin, the devil sends demons to torment him physically. Schongauer's engraving displays a wide range of tonal values, a rhythmic quality of line, and the rendering of many different textures—spiky, scaly, leathery, furry—achieved by varying the type of mark made on the plate. Without the benefit of color, Schongauer achieves a tonal and textural naturalism on a par with that of contemporary painters. Where Campin and van Eyck, working early in the fifteenth century, used deeply saturated oil colors to create powerfully naturalistic images, in the hands of Schongauer and his generation, even black and white lines printed on paper recorded the natural world to enhance the spiritual experience of the viewer.

POINTS OF REFLECTION

14.1 Compare Claus Sluter's *Well of Moses* to earlier Gothic sculpture. What are the connections between the International Gothic and the Gothic styles of earlier centuries?

14.2 Consider which social, political, or historical factors might account for an interest in naturalistic images in the fifteenth-century Netherlands. What is the role of the technique of oil painting in this development?

14.3 As you read the interpretations offered by scholars of fifteenth-century Netherlandish painting, consider why these images suggest such complex meanings. Have other art forms inspired similar interpretations? Why or why not?

14.4 Contrast the impact of Netherlandish style on a work from France and a work from Germany. What is the connection to earlier works from these regions?

14.5 Evaluate the relation of prints to the imagery and styles of paintings in this period.

✓•—**Study** and review on myartslab.com

ART IN TIME

- 1384—Philip the Bold of Burgundy inherits Flanders

- ca. 1413—Limbourg Brothers begin work on *Les Très Riches Heures du Duc de Berry*

- 1417—Papal Schism ends

- 1419—Philip the Good becomes Duke of Burgundy

- 1432—Jan van Eyck finishes the *Ghent Altarpiece*

- ca. 1435—Rogier van der Weyden's *Descent from the Cross*

- 1453—End of the Hundred Years' War between England and France

- 1455—Wars of the Roses begin in England

- ca. 1455—Gutenberg prints Bible in Mainz, Germany

- ca. 1480–90—Martin Schongauer's *The Temptation of St. Anthony*

- 1483—Hugo van der Goes's *Portinari Altarpiece* arrives in Florence

- ca. 1480–1515—Bosch's *The Garden of Earthly Delights*

CHAPTER

15 The Early Renaissance in Fifteenth-Century Italy

POINTS OF INQUIRY

15.1 Define the characteristics of Italian Renaissance style.
15.2 Summarize the intellectual and social factors that inform Renaissance art.
15.3 Discuss the spread of artistic ideas into and out of Florence.
15.4 Describe the settings for which works of art were made in the Italian Renaissance.
15.5 Recognize the most important artists and patrons of the fifteenth century.

((•—**Listen** to the chapter audio on myartslab.com

There was no single political entity called Italy in the fifteenth century (see **map 15.1**). On the Italian peninsula, regions of different sizes and political organization competed with each other economically and often on the battlefield. In the south, the Kingdom of Naples was a monarchy, while dukes, princes, and despots carved up northern Italy into city-states, such as Milan, Mantua, and Urbino. The pope returned from Avignon to Rome to reclaim control of the Papal States. The major trading cities of Florence and Venice formed republics, where mercantile elites controlled political power. Though the cultural flowering we call the Renaissance occurred throughout Italy, for many commentators the city of Florence is its birthplace.

The Inspiration of Antiquity in Florence

Florence is prominent in histories of the Renaissance, in part because many early humanists were Florentines who patriotically praised their city. Florence was an important manufacturing town, a key point for trade, and a major center for international banking, whose wealth and social dynamism attracted talented individuals. Bankers and merchants, not aristocrats, controlled the government of the city, while groups of merchants and artisans banded together in guilds to strengthen their political positions. The governing council, called the Signoria, consisted of officials elected from members of the guilds and prominent mercantile families. They called the government a republic, a word that for Florentines signaled their identity as the heirs of the ancient Roman Republic. Florentine politicians and intellectuals celebrated the city's past and urged their citizens to emulate Rome. Yet Florence was a Christian republic, so its government sponsored many religious projects. In addition, private citizens and guilds gained prestige by paying for highly visible projects for the community and the Church.

The citizens of Florence undertook programs to beautify the city by building churches and commissioning other artistic projects. A wave of such activity occurred in the opening years of the fifteenth century. Giangaleazzo Visconti of Milan (see fig. 13.14) threatened to invade Florence but his sudden death in 1402 saved it from this peril and stimulated patriotic desire to improve the city.

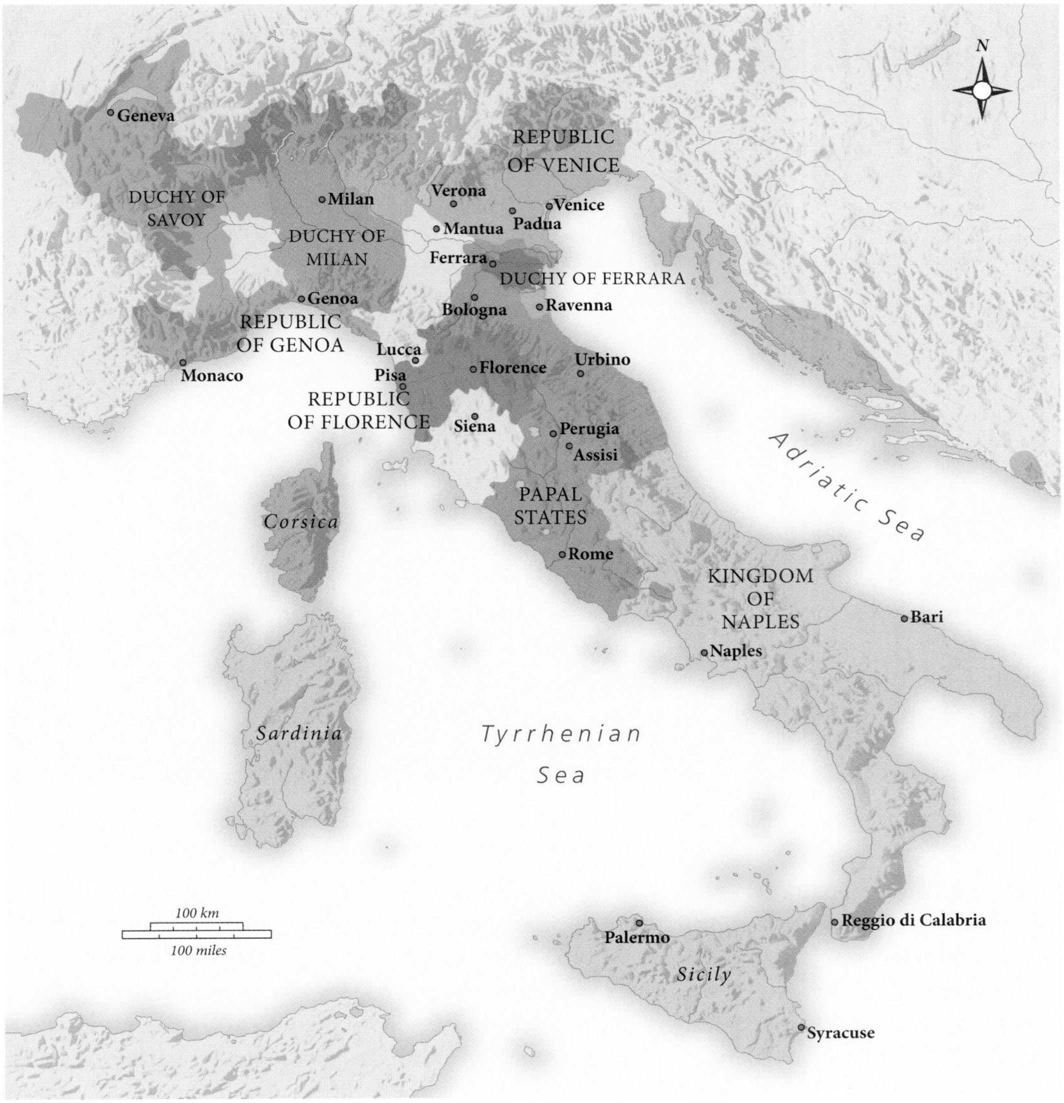

Map 15.1 Political units of the Italian Renaissance in the fifteenth century

The writings of Florentine humanists, such as the Chancellor of the city, Leonardo Bruni, encouraged these efforts. In his *Praise of the City of Florence* of 1402–03, Bruni compared the city to ancient capitals like Athens and Rome. He found the virtues of the ancients in the people and institutions of fifteenth-century Florence. The value he placed in the study of the ancients was adopted by many of his countrymen.

As practically minded individuals and businessmen, Florentine patrons were accustomed to competition. They often awarded commissions for projects after inviting artists to compete. In doing so, they could solicit the best artists to contribute designs for a project and choose among the proposals. They assigned major projects under these conditions, such as the commission for new doors for the Baptistery and the completion of the cathedral.

The Baptistery Doors

The Guild of Wool Merchants, who oversaw the Baptistery, opened a competition in 1401 for a second set of bronze doors for the structure. (Andrea Pisano had cast the first door in 1330.) Each entrant made a design on the theme of the Sacrifice of Isaac, framed in a Gothic quatrefoil shape. Each artist had to include the same figures and use the same materials. Seven artists made trial reliefs for this competition, though only two of them survive. One is by Filippo Brunelleschi (1377–1446) (**fig. 15.1**); the other is by Lorenzo Ghiberti (1381–1455) (**fig. 15.2**), whom the guild ultimately chose to execute the second set of doors.

15.1 Filippo Brunelleschi. *The Sacrifice of Isaac*. 1401–03. Panel, gilt bronze relief, 21 × 17″ (53.3 × 43.2 cm). Museo Nazionale del Bargello, Florence

15.2 Lorenzo Ghiberti. *The Sacrifice of Isaac*. 1401–03. Panel, gilt bronze relief, 21 × 17″ (53.3 × 43.2 cm). Museo Nazionale del Bargello, Florence

The subject the artists were assigned, from the Book of Genesis, recounts how God ordered Abraham to sacrifice his only son; obediently, Abraham led Isaac to an altar on a mountain and lifted his knife to slaughter him when an angel halted the sacrifice. Although Isaac is a figure for Christ in Christian theology, this is also the story of a chosen people avoiding doom through divine intervention, an issue about which Florentines felt strongly in 1402. The artists had to fill the four lobes of the quatrefoil, but also convey the narrative succinctly and naturalistically. Brunelleschi organized the forms in his relief to focus on the dynamic figure of Abraham whose arm, lifted to strike Isaac, is held by the angel rushing in from the left. Isaac struggles as his father grabs his neck, contorting his posture and increasing the drama. The ram standing next to the altar will replace him as the sacrifice. Subsidiary figures of shepherds and a donkey fill the lower portions of the quatrefoil; though their postures are complex (one of them based on an ancient work of art), they do not contribute much to the main theme. Brunelleschi gives his figures great naturalism, and the composition great drama.

In his relief, Ghiberti placed narrative details in the margins and the focal point at the center. There, Abraham gestures dramatically as he moves to sacrifice his son, bound and naked on an altar. Isaac twists to face the spectator, his beautifully formed torso contrasting with the drapery worn by his father. He does not struggle, but seems heroically to accept his fate. Ghiberti's design successfully combines movement, focus, and narrative. At the same time, his interest in the lyrical patterning of the International Gothic tempers the brutality of the scene. Abraham's drapery falls in cascades similar to those of the figure of Moses in Sluter's *The Well of Moses* (see fig. 14.1). In addition to the design, Ghiberti's entry demonstrated a technical finesse that may have persuaded the judges to select him: Unlike Brunelleschi, he cast his entry in one piece.

The casting of the doors kept Ghiberti's workshop busy for 20 years. Many of the most sought-after artists of the next generation spent time there, as he completed the doors. The competition between these two artists sets the stage for developments in both architecture and sculpture in Florence during the first half of the fifteenth century.

Brunelleschi and the Beginnings of Renaissance Architecture

Another competition, held in 1419, resulted in Brunelleschi's selection to complete the dome of Florence Cathedral. After losing the Baptistery competition, Brunelleschi traveled around the Mediterranean studying ancient structures and reportedly taking exact measurements of them. His discovery of **linear perspective** (discussed later in this chapter, page 315) may well have grown out of his search for an accurate way of recording the appearance of those ancient buildings. His own buildings reflect his study of Gothic, Roman, Byzantine, and maybe even Persian buildings.

THE DOME OF FLORENCE CATHEDRAL   In 1419, Brunelleschi won the job of building the dome (**fig. 15.3**). This large project would occupy him for most of the rest of his life. It would come to symbolize Florentine inventiveness, piety, ambition, and skill. When the cathedral, dedicated to Santa Maria del Fiore, was consecrated on March 25, 1436, the city rejoiced. Florence had demonstrated its devotion to the Virgin Mary, as well as its ambition to overawe its neighbors culturally. Florentines were justifiably proud that a native son had so cleverly accomplished what previous generations had not. Brunelleschi's forms influenced architecture far beyond Tuscany.

The basic dimensions and plans for the Cathedral of Florence had been established in the fourteenth century (see fig. 13.6). This plan included a dome at the east end for which foundations had been laid. The dome's vast size posed a difficult problem of construction: It had to cover a large area and rest on the smaller half-domes that were already in place. Brunelleschi decided to lift the dome on a drum above the level of the nave in order to reduce the weight on the walls. He also proposed to build the dome in two separate shells: This was a method more common in Islamic than Italian architecture, and one especially employed in Persia. The two shells were supported by a series of ribs, eight of them visible on the exterior but others hidden; the vertical supports were themselves linked by rows of horizontal ribs. The coffered dome of the Pantheon (see fig. 7.18) probably inspired this element. The dual shells of the dome lighten the whole mass, since their walls are thin relative to their size. Both the use of ribs and the pointed profile of the dome reflect Gothic building practices. The exterior ribs of the dome rise upward dramatically, terminating in a small marble cupola or lantern. Brunelleschi designed this lantern to tie the eight exterior ribs together and to mark the climax of that upward movement. Along with these design features, he proposed innovations in the construction

15.3 Filippo Brunelleschi. Dome of Florence Cathedral (Santa Maria del Fiore). 1420–36. Approx 295′ high (90 m), 140′ diameter (43 m)

 Watch an architectural simulation about the Florence Cathedral dome on myartslab.com

15.4 Filippo Brunelleschi. Nave of San Lorenzo. ca. 1421–69. Florence

process. Instead of the usual practice of constructing a wooden centering across the span, which required huge pieces of timber, he devised a way to construct a temporary scaffold that cantilevered out from the walls of the drum, which reduced the amount of timber needed for the project. He also designed machines to hoist materials to the required height. Brunelleschi's entire scheme reflects a bold, analytical mind that was willing to discard conventional solutions if better ones could be devised.

BRUNELLESCHI AT SAN LORENZO While he worked on the cathedral, Brunelleschi undertook commissions for prominent Florentine families to build chapels and enlarge other churches in the city. The church of San Lorenzo was the parish church of the Medici family, who became the most powerful family in the city by mid-century. The family hired Brunelleschi to build a small chapel that would serve as both a burial chapel for its members and the sacristy for the church, but they were so pleased

with the result that they asked him to develop a new design for the entire structure. Brunelleschi began work in the 1420s, but the nave was not completed until 1469, more than 20 years after his death. (The exterior remains unfinished to this day.) Nevertheless, the building in its present form

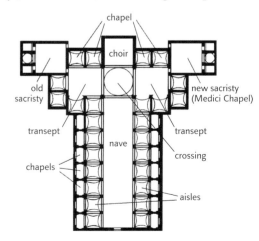

15.5 Plan of San Lorenzo, Florence

is essentially what Brunelleschi had envisioned in about 1420, and it represents the first full statement of his architectural aims (**figs. 15.4** and **15.5**).

San Lorenzo recalls Franciscan churches such as Santa Croce (see fig. 13.1); it has a square east end, an unvaulted nave, and a simple, unadorned elevation. Yet Brunelleschi placed a new emphasis on symmetry and regularity, accompanied by architectural elements, like the columns of the nave, inspired by the past. In addition to these ancient models, Brunelleschi studied Early Christian and Tuscan Romanesque churches; to

Perspective

PERSPECTIVE is a technique for making a two-dimensional surface appear to be three-dimensional. Artists have used many devices to create this illusion over the centuries, but Italian Renaissance artists systematized the projection of space, using mathematics and geometry. It is useful for paintings, prints, drawings, and relief sculptures. There are two general ways to do this: Through scientific perspective or atmospheric perspective.

The Florentine architect and sculptor Filippo Brunelleschi probably invented scientific perspective, also called linear or one-point perspective, although Leon Battista Alberti first explained it in writing. Alberti compares a painting to a window through which a viewer can see another world. Scientific perspective proposes that the viewer of a work has a single, fixed viewpoint. As a viewer's eye looks toward the distance, it can no longer make out forms at a spot on the horizon, known as the vanishing point. Starting from the edge of the picture artists project lines that converge toward that vanishing point; these are known as **orthogonals**. In some cases, those orthogonals are visible in the finished painting, though in other cases the artist simply implies the lines. We can see the orthogonals in Pietro Perugino's *The Delivery of the Keys* (fig. 15.24). The lines recede from the center foreground to the door of the church in the background. We can imagine similar lines across the walls in Leonardo's *The Luʋ vast Supper* (see fig. 16.2), focusing our attention at their vanishing point, Christ's head.

Atmospheric or aerial perspective uses changes in color to suggest depth. The decrease in intensity of color (at a horizon line) to a light blue or gray tone suggests a greater depth at the lightest point. We perceive the colors of greater intensity (as a deeper blue in the sky) as closer to us. We see this principle at work at the horizon in Piero's *Double Portrait* (fig. 15.19) and in numerous other examples. Atmospheric perspective is more subtle than scientific. It has been used by artists since Roman times.

Diagram showing the perspective in Pietro Perugino, *The Delivery of the Keys*. Fresco in the Sistine Chapel, Vatican Palace, Vatican City. See fig. 15.24

15.6 Donatello. *St. Mark.* ca. 1411–13. Marble, height 7′9″ (2.4 m). Orsanmichele, Florence (now Museo di Or San Michele, Florence)

him, these exemplified the church architecture of antiquity. They inspired his use of round arches and columns, rather than piers, in the nave arcade. The result is a well-lit space with columns that are lighter and more widely separated than in most medieval buildings.

To achieve this clarity and lightness, Brunelleschi organized his forms according to proportion. As the ground plan shows, he composed with units of space in regular square blocks, so that each bay of the nave is twice as wide as its side aisles, and the crossing and apse are each four times the size of each unit. Having studied ancient architecture Brunelleschi believed that the secret of good design lay in choosing clear and correct ratios for the major measurements of a building. His theories about proportion and design were probably shared with Leon Battista Alberti (1404–1472), whose buildings we will encounter below. In his *Treatise on Architecture*, Alberti argues that the mathematical ratios determining musical harmony must also govern architecture, for they must be divine in origin. Similar ideas, derived from the theories of the Greek philosopher Pythagoras, had been current during the Middle Ages, but they had never before been expressed so directly and simply.

In the revival of classical forms, Renaissance architecture found a standard vocabulary. The theory of harmonious proportions gave architects rules for using those forms that had been mostly absent in medieval architecture. Brunelleschi applied the lessons of classical antiquity for modern Christian ends. Furthermore, his study of the ancients and his practical application of classical geometric proportions probably stimulated his discovery of a system for rendering forms in three dimensions. This technique became known as linear or scientific perspective (see box: Materials and Techniques: Perspective, page 000).

DONATELLO AT OR SAN MICHELE The lessons of antiquity that Brunelleschi applied to the dome of Florence Cathedral and at San Lorenzo also inspired the sculptors of his time such as Donatello (1389–1466). Just as sculptors had earlier competed to earn the commission to cast the doors of the Baptistery, they vied with one another to fill the exterior niches of the building in central Florence called Or San Michele (or Orsanmichele). Begun in 1337, this structure served as both a granary and a shrine holding a locally venerated image of the Virgin and Child. Each niche on the exterior of the building was the responsibility of a Florentine guild; the sculptors hired by the guilds competed intensely to create impressive statues of their patron saints.

The Guild of Linen Weavers commissioned Donatello to fill their niche with a figure probably completed in 1413 (**fig. 15.6**). Their patron, St. Mark, stands almost 8 feet high in his niche, but that is only one of the features that make him so imposing. His large, powerful hands grip a book, probably his Gospel. His body stands in a pose Donatello learned from studying the art of the ancients: One leg is flexed while the other holds the body's weight in a *contrapposto* stance (see fig. 5.12). St. Mark's drapery falls in deep folds to reveal and emphasize his posture.

Donatello depicts the human body as capable of movement, and allows the drapery over it to reflect the shapes underneath; this contrasts with the medieval practice of depicting drapery in patterns. Following Classical precedents such as the *Doryphoros* (see fig. 5.14), Donatello carefully balances the composition, so that the elements on the left (as a viewer sees it) stress the vertical and the static, while those on the right emphasize the diagonal and kinetic. The deeply carved eyes and undulating beard give the saint a distinct personality, while the mass of drapery reminds the viewer of the Linen Weavers' products. This work reflects Donatello's deep understanding of the principles that guided the artists of antiquity and his commitment to them. *St. Mark* reveals what the sculptor learned from his studies: An emphasis on naturalistic form, the interdependence of body and drapery, a balanced but contrasting composition, the potential for movement, and psychological presence.

New Directions in Florentine Painting

Florence was home to a community of artists who knew each other's work and learned from each other. Donatello and Brunelleschi were friends and traveling companions. Both of these men are mentioned by the humanist and architect Leon Battista Alberti, who wrote treatises on architecture and painting, among other topics. Alberti's *On Painting*, finished around 1435, helped to spread Brunelleschi's ideas about perspective. Alberti's treatises codified Florentine innovations in the arts, and because the books were copied, and then printed later in the century, they contributed to the development of Renaissance art in other parts of Italy. Alberti's treatises present the artists of the fifteenth century as learned men; they encouraged patrons

and society at large to give greater respect than previously to visual artists. *On Painting* also praised the work of a young Florentine painter named Tommaso di Ser Giovanni di Mone Cassai (1401–1428), called Masaccio. Historians ever since have credited Masaccio with reviving the art of painting in Florence. At both Santa Maria Novella and the Church of Santa Maria del Carmine, the young Masaccio found employment in painting frescoes for prominent Florentine families in the 1420s.

MASACCIO AT SANTA MARIA NOVELLA Although its date is somewhat uncertain, Masaccio painted a fresco in Santa Maria Novella that depicts the Holy Trinity in the company of the Virgin, St. John the Evangelist, and two donors (**fig. 15.7**). The holy characters stand in a painted chapel; God the Father supports the figure of Christ on the Cross, with the dove of the Holy Spirit between their heads. St. John and the Virgin stand beneath the Cross; she looks out to glance at the viewer. Outside this fictive chapel kneel a man and woman, the donors, probably members of the Lenzi family. The lowest section of the fresco depicts a skeleton lying on a sarcophagus. The inscription above the skeleton reads, "What I once was, you are; what I am, you will become"; it exhorts the viewer to be prepared for death. The painting's large scale, balanced composition, and sculptural volume suggest the art of Giotto (see fig. 13.9). Giotto's art was a starting point for Masaccio, though in Giotto's work, body and drapery form a single unit, whereas Masaccio's figures, like Donatello's, are "clothed nudes," whose drapery falls in response to the body wearing it.

The setting reveals the artist's awareness of Brunelleschi's new architecture and of his system of perspective. The tall pilasters next to the painted columns recall the pilasters Brunelleschi designed for San Lorenzo, as do the moldings that define the arch and the entablature of this painted chapel. Masaccio uses Brunelleschi's device of perspective to create the illusion of depth. This barrel-vaulted chamber is not a shallow niche, but a deep space in which the figures could move freely. The picture space is independent of the figures; they inhabit the space, but they do not create it. Masaccio's perspective creates an illusion of space where none exists.

In the fresco, Masaccio expresses the theme of the Trinity by the triangular composition that begins with the donors and rises to the halo of God. The composition is carefully balanced by color, as reds and blues alternate until they meet in the

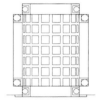

Plan of floor and ceiling derived from the painting (fig. 15.7)

Masaccio used one-point scientific perspective to create a rational picture space—the illusion that the figures are standing in a coffered, barrel-vaulted niche just above our eye.

15.7 Masaccio. *The Holy Trinity with the Virgin, St. John, and Two Donors.* ca. 1425. Fresco, detached from wall, 21'10⅝" × 10'4¾" (6.67 × 3.17 m). Santa Maria Novella, Florence

Watch a video about Masaccio's *Trinity* on myartslab.com

garments worn by God. The whole scene has a tragic air, made more solemn by the calm gesture of the Virgin, as she points to the Crucifixion, and by the understated grief of John the Evangelist. The reality of death but promise of resurrection is appropriate for a funerary monument.

MASACCIO AT THE BRANCACCI CHAPEL While we are uncertain about the identity of the donors for the *Trinity* fresco, we do know who paid for the largest group of Masaccio's surviving works. To fulfill a bequest from his uncle Pietro, the silk merchant Felice Brancacci paid for the frescoes in the Brancacci Chapel in Santa Maria del Carmine. These depict the life of St. Peter, his uncle's patron saint. Work began in the chapel around 1425, when Masaccio collaborated with a somewhat older painter named Masolino (1383 ca.–1440). (Other artists completed the work later in the fifteenth century.) These frescoes transform the space of the chapel into a display of narratives from scripture.

The most famous one is *The Tribute Money* by Masaccio (**fig. 15.8**). This fresco depicts the story in the Gospel of Matthew (17:24–27) by including several episodes in one space. In the center, Christ instructs Peter to catch a fish, whose mouth will contain money for the tax collector, who stands before them. On the far left, in the distance, Peter takes the coin from the fish's mouth, and on the right he gives it to the tax collector. Masaccio uses linear perspective, Brunelleschi's technique for spatial illusion (see box, page 315), to suggest a deep space for the narrative, but he also models the forms in the picture with light that seems to have its source in the real window of the chapel. Both perspective and this use of light connect the illusory space of the painting to the actual space in which the spectator stands. Masaccio also uses atmospheric perspective, allowing forms to blur in the distance, as the subtle tones of the landscape make the forms somewhat hazy.

The figures in *The Tribute Money*, even more than those in the *Trinity* fresco, show Masaccio's ability to create forms that have the weight and volume of Giotto's. Yet these figures also

have the possibility of movement and power like Donatello's. All the characters stand in balanced *contrapposto*. Instead of employing violent physical movement, Masaccio's figures convey the narrative by their intense glances and a few strong gestures. They express powerful emotion through their sheer physicality. Before he could finish the Brancacci Chapel, Masaccio left for Rome to work on another commission; he died there in 1428 at a very young age, but his work stimulated other painters to experiment with perspective.

Italian Art During the Era of the Medici, 1434–94

From 1434 to 1494 the Medici family dominated the city of Florence. Across four generations, Medici men worked to succeed in government and business, while Medici women contributed to the social and religious life of the city. The family's wealth came from their mercantile and banking interests and the savvy political alliances they struck both within Florence and in other Italian centers. Their status as bankers to the pope helped the Medici become leaders in the Florentine government. Ultimately they became the rulers of the city in all but name.

The family's rise began at the end of the fourteenth century. By the 1430s, Cosimo de' Medici (1389–1464) controlled the Florentine government. Cosimo's sons Piero (1416–1469) and Giovanni followed their father's example; Piero's son, Lorenzo, called "The Magnificent" (1449–1492), became one of the most celebrated and well-connected men of the century. In addition to creating links to other

prominent families in Florence, the Medici family promoted the literary and educational innovations of Florentine humanists, and actively used works of art to express their political and social status.

Many families in Florence either allied themselves with the Medici or competed with them commercially and politically. During this period, the city continued to commission artistic projects to add to its luster. The era of Medici domination saw the continued development of the stylistic innovations of the early fifteenth century along with new themes in art. Brunelleschian forms dominated Florentine architecture, along with the ideas and designs of Leon Battista Alberti. Sculptors of the first part of the century, including Donatello and Lorenzo Ghiberti, were strong presences in mid-century. Religious communities and churches acquired paintings for wall spaces or for altars by painters strongly influenced by the classicism and naturalism of Masaccio and the elegance of Ghiberti. The fame of Florence's new style quickly spread throughout Italy and patrons called these artists to other cities to work for them.

The Baptistery of Florence

Throughout the fifteenth century, the cathedral of Florence and the Baptistery remained the spiritual heart of the city. Although Brunelleschi's dome for the cathedral was completed in time for the church to be dedicated in 1436, work continued on the lantern, the façade, and the interior. In 1424 Ghiberti finally completed the bronze doors that directors of the Baptistery had commissioned in 1402. They were so impressive that the sculptor was asked to cast another set of bronze doors for a third portal.

15.8 Masaccio. *The Tribute Money.* ca. 1425. Fresco, 8′1″ × 19′7″ (2.46 × 5.96 m). Brancacci Chapel, Santa Maria del Carmine, Florence

THE *GATES OF PARADISE* These doors, begun in 1425 but not completed until 1452, were ultimately installed in the east entry of the Baptistery, facing the cathedral; this area is called the Paradise, so the doors were termed the *Gates of Paradise*. Each of the two doors contains five large panels in simple square frames; they create a larger field than the 28 small panels in quatrefoil frames of Ghiberti's earlier doors and also those by Andrea Pisano. These doors complete the program of all three sets of doors: The earliest set depicts the Life of John the Baptist, the second the Life of Christ, and this third set the Old Testament. To give the doors greater splendor, Ghiberti completely gilded the bronze. He probably consulted humanists like Chancellor Bruni in Florence to determine which stories to depict, and then organized the narratives into memorable and clear images.

In designing these reliefs, Ghiberti drew on the new devices for pictorial imagery that he and his rivals had pioneered, such as the linear perspective developed by Brunelleschi (see box, page 315) and employed by Masaccio. Yet Ghiberti's figures have more graceful proportions, elegant stances, and fluid drapery than Masaccio's or Donatello's

15.9 Lorenzo Ghiberti. *The Story of Jacob and Esau*, panel of the *Gates of Paradise*. ca. 1435. Gilt bronze, 31¼″ (79.5 cm) square. Baptistery of San Giovanni, Florence

figures. This aspect of the figures reflects Ghiberti's knowledge of the International Gothic style, which had influence in Italy as well as elsewhere in Europe (see fig. 14.1). In telling *The Story of Jacob and Esau* (**fig. 15.9**) Ghiberti has used perspective to create the illusion of a deep space defined by the arches of a building planned to accommodate the figures as they appear and reappear throughout the structure. The relief tells the story of Isaac blessing his younger son, Jacob, instead of the elder Esau. The blind Isaac sends Esau off to hunt on the left, but confers his blessing on the disguised Jacob at the right. The story unfolds in a spacious hall, itself a fine example of Early Renaissance architectural design. Perspective allows Ghiberti to present his story as a continuous narrative with unprecedented coherence, as if all seven episodes of it were taking place simultaneously.

Florentine Churches and Convents at Mid-century

Construction and renewal elsewhere in Florence accompanied the work at the cathedral, the Baptistery, and Or San Michele. Throughout the city, patrons rebuilt or enlarged churches and convents, often with corresponding commissions for their decoration. Renaissance artists and their patrons wished to put the new style to work for their faith. The naturalism and spatial effects now possible could create images that spoke powerfully to believers. Perspective and other devices could connect viewers to religious stories to evoke their empathy. New ideas coming from the study of the classics inspired artists to create balanced compositions peopled with dignified characters. Yet not all churchmen approved of the increasingly naturalistic and classicizing forms found in religious art in the fifteenth century. The tension between Christian and classical forms erupted at the end of the century with Savonarola's condemnation of "pagan" images (see page 328).

FRA ANGELICO AT SAN MARCO With Cosimo de' Medici's support, in 1436 the Dominicans established a second convent for friars in Florence. Among the members of this community was a talented painter, who came from the Florentine countryside: Fra (Brother) Giovanni da Fiesole, called Fra Angelico (ca. 1400–1455). For the friars, Angelico painted altarpieces, books, and numerous frescoes in their living quarters. His fresco of the *Annunciation*, executed between 1440 and 1445, sits

prominently at the entry to the friars' dormitory (**fig. 15.10**). Angelico places the two actors in this narrative into a vaulted space that echoes the real architecture of the convent. Brunelleschi's perspective defines the space, although the figures are too large to stand comfortably in it. Glancing across the space, Mary and the angel Gabriel humbly fold their hands, expressing their submission to divine will. Their graceful forms inhabit a spare reality: Colors are pale; the composition has been pared to the minimum; a soft light bathes all the forms. Angelico's composition has the simplicity and spatial sophistication of Masaccio, though his figures are more ethereal. An inscription at the base calls on the friars who pass by to say a prayer. The fresco surely enhanced the friars' life of prayer and contemplation, as was the goal of such imagery in religious communities.

DOMENICO VENEZIANO AT SANTA LUCIA DEI MAGNOLI
Laypeople also prayed before religious images that adorned the altars of parish churches. An important shift occurred in the design of altar panels in the 1440s, perhaps at the hands of Fra Angelico, which was soon adopted by many painters. Earlier altarpieces like Giotto's *Madonna Enthroned* (fig. 13.8) were complex ensembles with elaborately carved and arched frames, but the newer altarpieces, straightforward rectangles, placed less emphasis on gilded carpentry and more on geometric clarity. For the main altar of the parish church of Santa Lucia dei Magnoli in Florence, the painter Domenico Veneziano (ca. 1410–1461) executed the *Madonna and Child with Saints* around 1445 (**fig. 15.11**). As his name suggests, Domenico was from Venice, though he came to Florence in search of work in 1439. The altarpiece he painted for Santa Lucia depicts an enthroned Madonna and Child framed by a Gothic canopy and surrounded by saints, including Zenobius, a patron saint of Florence, and Lucy, an early Christian martyr, who holds a dish containing her eyes.

The theme of the enthroned Madonna surrounded by saints and sometimes angels is often termed a *sacra conversazione* (sacred conversation), which suggests that the image is not a narrative,

15.10 Fra Angelico. *Annunciation.* ca. 1440–45. Fresco on dormitory level of the Convent of San Marco, 7'1" × 10'6" (2.1 × 3.2 m). Museo di San Marco, Florence

15.11 Domenico Veneziano. *Madonna and Child with Saints.* ca. 1445. Tempera on panel, 6′10″ × 7′ (2.08 × 2.13 m). Galleria degli Uffizi, Florence

like Domenico Veneziano and merchant and ecclesiastical patrons, the new style, born in Florence, spread all over Italy.

The Renaissance Palace and its Furnishings, ca. 1440–90

As their fortunes rose, patrons like Cosimo de' Medici asked artists to create works of art for their families as well as for the Church. Their palaces needed to provide an appropriate setting for family life and the display of status. Sculptures and paintings proclaimed the ties between families. Works of art depicted new subjects, many of them inspired by ancient art, which displayed the humanist educations of both artists and patrons. In sculpture, the long-lived Donatello continued to innovate, and to inspire other artists. Painters sought the right style to depict imagery drawn from the ancient world. Architects built family homes that were made more splendid by their use of classical forms. For wealthy patrons with broad cultural and intellectual interests, artists developed new forms and subjects for painting and sculpture.

Patrician Palaces

Their status in Florence required that the Medici commission a lavish palace to house the family and accommodate political and diplomatic functions. The commission went to the architect Michelozzo di Bartolomeo (1396–1472), who had worked as a sculptor with both Ghiberti and Donatello. His design (**fig. 15.12**) recalls the fortress-like Florentine palaces of old. (Michelangelo added the windows on the ground floor in 1516–17, while the Riccardi family extended the whole building in the seventeenth century.)

Michelozzo borrowed the rustication and some of the window design from the Palazzo della Signoria (compare with fig. 13.7). The three stories of the palace seem to become lighter as they rise. The lowest story features rough-hewn, "rusticated" masonry; the second has smooth-surfaced blocks; and the third has an unbroken surface. On top of the structure rests, like a lid, a strongly projecting cornice such as those found on some Roman temples. Inside, the spaces of the palace open to a central courtyard defined by an arcade resting on Brunelleschian classicizing columns. The effect of the whole was to provide a splendid setting for Medici affairs: familial, social, commercial, and governmental.

but a glimpse of a heavenly court peopled by well-behaved courtiers. The convincing architecture defines an ideal space, elevated above the everyday world. Domenico probably knew Masaccio's *Holy Trinity* fresco (fig. 15.7), for his St. John the Baptist (second from left) looks at us while pointing toward Mary, repeating the glance and gesture of Masaccio's Virgin. Domenico's perspective setting emulates Masaccio's ideas, although his architectural forms look more Gothic than Masaccio's, which echo Brunelleschi's churches. Donatello's influence appears in the highly individualized faces and solidly rendered figures of the men (see fig. 15.6).

Domenico's *sacra conversazione* is as noteworthy for its color as for its composition. He uses a carefully selected range of blues, reds, greens, and grays in light tones that suggest sunlight streaming into the space. The surfaces reflect the light so strongly that even the shadowed areas glow with color. Color, light, and space come together in this painting to make a heavenly vision in which the faithful may take comfort. He is but one of many artists from around Italy who took inspiration from the innovative works created by Brunelleschi, Donatello, and Masaccio. Through the travels of artists

15.13 Donatello. *David.* ca. 1420s–60s. Bronze, height 62¼″ (1.58 m). Museo Nazionale del Bargello, Florence

👁 **Watch** a video about the process of lost-wax casting on myartslab.com

Images of Heroes for Florentine Collectors

Creating images for such palaces offered new challenges to Renaissance artists. In sculpture, painting, and other media, the artists depicted characters from past or present in clear and powerful ways. Once again, ancient works of art provided examples.

DONATELLO'S *DAVID* The courtyard of the Medici Palace once displayed one of the most innovative works of the Renaissance: Donatello's bronze *David* (**fig. 15.13**). This *David* may have been the first free-standing, life-size nude statue created since antiquity. The sheer expense of casting a whole figure of this sort in bronze, with parts gilt as well, required a patron with the wealth of the Medici to pay for it. Donatello composed the figure to be seen from every side, as the *contrapposto* stance and high finish of the work demand that the viewer walk around it.

Donatello's depiction of DAVID has offered challenges to interpreters, since much in the figure is difficult to square with the biblical story. Donatello depicts the young David standing with his

One of the greatest of Hebrew kings, DAVID (ruled ca. 1012–ca. 972 BCE) was a boy when, according to the Book of Samuel I, he killed the gigantic Philistine enemy of the Israelites, Goliath, with a stone from his slingshot. For Christians, David is both an ancestor and a prototype of Jesus, as well as the author of the Book of Psalms.

15.14 Antonio Pollaiuolo. *Battle of the Nudes*. ca. 1490. Engraving, 15¾ × 23″ (40 × 58 cm). Yale University Art Gallery, New Haven. Maitland F. Giggs, B.A. 1896, Fund 1951.9.18

left foot atop the severed head of the giant Goliath, whom he has miraculously defeated. Yet even though David has already defeated his enemy, he holds the stone that will bring the giant down. Most untraditionally, Donatello depicts David nude. The artist probably intends to suggest the youth's status as a hero in the ancient mode, although the broad-brimmed hat and knee-high boots strike a contemporary note. Instead of depicting David as a full-grown youth like the athletes of Greece, Donatello represents an adolescent boy with a softly sensuous torso. David wields Goliath's sword, which is too large for him, and his gaze seems impassive if we consider the terror he has just confronted. An inscription that once appeared on the statue's pedestal may help clarify its meaning: It identified David as the defender of the fatherland. Florentines had long venerated David as a patron of their city. Installing this work in the courtyard of their palace, the Medici took over this symbol of Florentine civic virtue to associate it with their family.

Ancient Battles in Prints

More questions of meaning surround a print by Donatello's younger colleague Antonio Pollaiuolo (1431–1498), who also made images of nudes.

He worked as a sculptor, designer, painter, and printmaker in both Florence and Rome. The Medici owned several of his works. Pollaiuolo's most elaborate design is probably his engraving *Battle of the Nudes* (**fig. 15.14**). Its subject is not known, though historians have tried to link it to ancient texts. When Pollaiuolo produced the print, between 1465 and 1470, the problem of depicting the nude in action had not been solved. Pollaiuolo realized that a full understanding of movement demands a detailed knowledge of anatomy, down to the last muscle and sinew. These naked men look almost as if their skin had been stripped off to reveal the play of muscles underneath. One purpose the engraving serves is to display the artist's mastery of the nude body in action and thus to advertise his skill. This may account for the prominent signature in the print; he signs it "The Work of Antonio Pollaiuolo of Florence." The artist wants to be sure that his name is remembered.

Paintings for Palaces

The interiors of patrician palaces served not only as private quarters and settings for family life, but as public spaces where family members performed civic roles. A visitor would be likely to find paintings and perhaps sculptures, many on religious subjects, in these places. Along with religious themes, patrons wanted images that reflected on contemporary history and demonstrated their interest in the culture and art of antiquity.

In addition to acquiring paintings in Florence, the Medici had numerous contacts with Northern Europe, not only through diplomatic exchanges, but through their banking business. Medici agents in Bruges sent many works of art to Italy, as did many of the other Italian ruling families, for Flemish art was widely admired in places as disparate as Naples, Venice, Ferrara, and Milan. Through such acquisitions, the Medici and their associates filled their palaces with panel paintings and tapestries from the North. Such objects made a profound impression on Florentine artists.

UCCELLO'S *BATTLE OF SAN ROMANO* Contemporary history, not the ancient past, was the subject of the Florentine artist Paolo Uccello's (1397–1475) painting of the *Battle of San Romano* (**fig. 15.15**). This is only one of three panels by the artist depicting a battle that took place in 1432. Recent research reveals that Lionardo Bartolini Salimbeni

commissioned the paintings for his town house in Florence around 1438, so the events were fresh in his memory. (He had been a member of the governing council of Florence during the battle.) Uccello depicts the charge of the Florentine forces led by Niccolò da Tolentino, the man on the white horse wielding a general's baton at the center of the painting. Uccello's painting looks more like a tournament than a violent battle, though, as the plastic shapes of the figures and horses march across a grid formed by discarded weapons and pieces of armor. These objects form the orthogonals (converging lines; see box, page 315) of a perspective scheme that is neatly arranged to include a fallen soldier. Spots of bright color and the lavish use of gold create a brilliant surface pattern; its splendor must have been enhanced by the gleam of armor, covered in silver foil that has now tarnished. Uccello's work owes much to International Gothic displays of expensive materials and flashes of natural observation, with the added element of perspectival renderings of forms and space.

A document of 1492 describes this series of paintings by Uccello as being in Lorenzo de' Medici's bedroom. The Medici family came to power

15.15 Paolo Uccello. *Battle of San Romano*. ca. 1438. Tempera and silver foil on wood panel, 6′ × 10′5¾″ (1.8 × 3.2 m). The National Gallery, London

 View the Closer Look for *Battle of San Romano* on myartslab.com

15.16 Sandro Botticelli. *The Birth of Venus*. ca. 1485. Tempera on panel, 5′8⅞″ × 9′1⅞″ (1.8 × 2.8 m). Galleria degli Uffizi, Florence

One of the most creative and influential philosophers of all time, PLATO (ca. 428–ca. 347 BCE) was an aristocratic Athenian, a pupil of Socrates, and founder of the Academy, on the outskirts of Athens. (Aristotle was his outstanding student.) Plato's writings are in the form of dialogues, and the ideas characterized as "Platonic thought" are those that rely on his theory of Forms, or Ideas. Expressed very simply, Plato distinguishes two levels of awareness: Opinion—based on information received by the senses and experiences—and genuine knowledge, which is derived from reason and is universal and infallible. In Platonic thinking, the objects conceived by reason exist in a pure form in an Ideal realm.

as a result of the battle commemorated in them. After the death of the original patron, Lorenzo de' Medici sought to obtain them, first by purchase and, when that failed, by force. The sons of the original owner filed a lawsuit for their return. These circumstances suggest the importance of the paintings for both families. If the image originally celebrated an achievement of the government to which Salimbeni belonged, for Lorenzo the image marked a turning point in the history of his family.

BOTTICELLI'S *BIRTH OF VENUS* Sandro Botticelli (1445–1510) became one of the favorite painters of the Medici circle—the group of nobles, scholars, and poets surrounding Lorenzo the Magnificent, the head of the Medici family and, for all practical purposes, the real ruler of Florence from 1469 until 1492. Botticelli's most famous image, *The Birth of Venus* (**fig. 15.16**), once hung in a Medici villa just outside the city. The central figure in the painting is the Goddess of Love. Born in the sea, Venus floats slowly toward the shore, where a flower-clad woman waits to enfold her in a flowered robe. The

wind god Zephyr accompanied by Chloris (Flora) aids her movement. The space behind the figures opens into the distance, with the sky and water creating a light, cool tonality for the painting. In the figures, though, shallow modeling and an emphasis on outline produce an effect of low relief rather than of solid, three-dimensional shapes. The bodies seem to be drained of all weight, so that they float even when they touch the ground.

The graceful figures depict a theme from antiquity using ideas that the artist learned from studying ancient art. Botticelli designed the figure of Venus after a Roman version of a statue by Praxiteles (see fig. 5.21). He combines ancient forms with ancient content, in an image that expresses Florentine reverence for both. The subject may derive from the Homeric *Hymn to Aphrodite*, which begins: "I shall sing of beautiful Aphrodite … who is obeyed by the flowery sea-girt land of Cyprus, whither soft Zephyr and the breeze wafted her in soft foam over the waves. Gently the golden-filleted Horae [Hours] received her, and clad her in divine garments." Yet the meaning of the image may owe as much to ancient philosophy as to ancient literature. One member of the Medici circle, Marsilio Ficino, based his philosophy on his study of the Greek philosopher PLATO. The Neo-Platonists like Ficino strove to reconcile Platonic thought with Christianity, and drew complex parallels between them. Neo-Platonists believed that Venus exists in two forms: A celestial Venus, the source of divine love, and a worldly Venus, the source of physical love. Ficino described the celestial Venus as "a nymph of excellent comeliness, born of heaven and more than all others beloved by God." In such language, Ficino likens the antique goddess to Mary. Botticelli's *Birth of Venus* may be an allegory of the origin of the celestial Venus for an audience attuned to the nuances of Neo-Platonic philosophy. The elegant forms and high finish of the painting, combined with the erudite subject matter based on ancient thought, exemplify the taste of the Medici court.

Portraiture

Images of history, of contemporary events, or of ancient myths demonstrate the expanding interest in secular themes in the art of the Renaissance. Patrons also increasingly demanded portraits. The idea of recording specific likenesses was inspired by the fifteenth century's increasing awareness of the individual, but also by the study of Roman art, where portraits abound. Artists were already making donor portraits, like Masaccio's *Trinity* fresco (fig. 15.7), and commemorations of public figures, but new forms of portraiture developed in the fifteenth century. Florentine families who commissioned works of art often included portraits of their political allies as well as themselves to make their political and social networks clear to their neighbors.

For example, the banker Francesco Sassetti and his wife paid for a chapel in Santa Trinita in Florence (**fig. 15.17**). Completed by 1485, the work included frescoes on the walls depicting stories of Sassetti's patron saint, donor portraits of himself and his wife, and an altarpiece in the new rectangular form. The commission went to Domenico Ghirlandaio (1449–1494), one of the most popular of Florentine painters in the latter years of the fifteenth century. Portraits of the donors flank the altarpiece; both Sassetti and his wife, Nera Corsi, appear in profile and direct their gaze at the events that take place there. In the frescoes above, the artist depicts events from St. Francis's life in settings that look like Florence. What is more, the

15.17 Domenico Ghirlandaio. Sassetti Chapel, with frescoes on the *Life of St. Francis* and *Altarpiece of the Adoration of the Shepherds*. 1483–85. Santa Trinita, Florence

witnesses to these historical events reveal Sassetti's social networks: The pope approves Francis's rule in the presence of Lorenzo de' Medici and his sons, and Sassetti and his son (in an image above the one shown here). The image just above the altarpiece depicts St. Francis resurrecting a boy who had died from a fall; the miracle takes place in the piazza outside Santa Trinita itself and includes portraits of other prominent men of Florence. The portraits in the frescoes describe Sassetti's commercial and political allies and proclaim his allegiance to the Medici family.

The altarpiece itself, also by Ghirlandaio, focuses on Mary and the shepherds worshiping her son. The Child is the focus of most eyes, human and animal, in the picture. He lies in front of a Roman sarcophagus, referencing the Resurrection scene in the fresco above. In a deep blue garment, Mary kneels before him, while three shepherds enter from the right. Only Joseph looks away, gazing at the Magi who approach in the distance. The composition, the rich color, and details like the flowers in the foreground echo the *Portinari Altarpiece* by Hugo van der Goes (see fig. 14.8), which had arrived in Florence in 1483. Ghirlandaio's altarpiece shows the impact that Netherlandish innovations in painting had in Italy. Antique-inspired elements appear as well: The columns that hold up the shed echo those in the frame; Roman elements appear in the form of the sarcophagus, the triumphal arch in the background, and the inscription on the frame. Like other Medici followers, Sassetti wanted to include references to Roman art, even in the Christian theme of the Nativity.

Sassetti's ally, the cultivated Lorenzo the Magnificent, established what can only be called a court in Florence, despite the claim that the city was a republic. Lorenzo was the patron of numerous humanists, philosophers, poets, and artists, including the young Michelangelo. Yet this brilliant court did not outlast his death in 1492. His son, Piero de' Medici, did not share his father's diplomatic or administrative gifts. Piero also faced an increasingly unstable economy (the bank failed in 1494) and invading armies from France and Spain. Florence expelled the Medici in 1494 as it sought to restore republican government. A vacuum of power was filled for a time by the Dominican friar Girolamo Savonarola, who attacked the "cult of paganism" and the materialism he saw in Florentine culture. Savonarola's exhortations to repentance and his strong criticism of corruption not only in Florence but in the Church hierarchy made him many enemies; he was executed in 1498. As the fifteenth century came to an end, Florence battled for its independence against the stronger powers of the papacy, Spain, and France.

The Renaissance Style Reverberates, 1450–1500

Artists from all over Italy and from other parts of Europe were inspired by the innovative styles and subject matter being created in Florence. Yet artists outside Florence responded to the new styles as individuals who were steeped in their own regional and personal differences. Additionally, patrons throughout Italy saw the advantages of expressing their authority through visual and textual references to antiquity. By mid-century, linear perspective was in widespread use, and Florentine techniques for rendering form through light were being practiced by many artists. Piero della Francesca blended his own fascination with mathematics, the ancient world, and Netherlandish painting to create a personal style that found favor in several Italian courts. The Florentine humanist and architect Leon Battista Alberti designed influential buildings in northern Italy, including one for the Marquis of Mantua, who had also attracted the services of the painter-archaeologist Andrea Mantegna. Venetian painters like Giovanni Bellini developed an influential school of Renaissance painting that rivaled the Florentine style. As the papacy regained its control in Rome, Pietro Perugino executed projects designed to celebrate papal power.

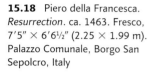

15.18 Piero della Francesca. *Resurrection*. ca. 1463. Fresco, 7'5" × 6'6½" (2.25 × 1.99 m). Palazzo Comunale, Borgo San Sepolcro, Italy

15.19 Piero della Francesca. *Double Portrait of Battista Sforza and Federico da Montefeltro*. ca. 1472. Oil and tempera on panel, each panel 18½ × 13″ (47 × 33 cm). Galleria degli Uffizi, Florence

Piero della Francesca in Central Italy

One of the most distinctive and original artists of the second half of the fifteenth century was Piero della Francesca (ca. 1420–1492), from the town of Borgo San Sepolcro. He worked for patrons throughout central Italy. Piero's choice of colors reflects his early training with Domenico Veneziano (see fig. 15.11) in Florence, while his study of Masaccio is apparent in the solidity of his forms and the solemn character of his compositions. The early fifteenth-century systemization of perspective was critical for Piero, who became such an expert that he wrote a treatise about it. It is likely that he made contact with Leon Battista Alberti, with whom he shared patrons as well as an interest in art theory.

A work that Piero made for his hometown reflects this combination of influences on his art. The city of Borgo San Sepolcro commissioned him to paint a fresco for its town hall, probably around 1463. Befitting the name of the town, which means "Village of the Holy Sepulcher," Piero's theme is the Resurrection. The fresco depicts Christ stepping out of his tomb on Easter morning (**fig. 15.18**). The figure of Christ dominates the composition: His frontality and the triangular composition may derive from the *Trinity* fresco by Masaccio (fig. 15.7), but the light of sunrise and

the pale colors show the influence of Domenico Veneziano. Piero pays special attention to the arrangement of the Roman soldiers asleep in front of the sepulcher; he treats them as variations on a theme of bodies in space. The spectator must look up to see the glorified body of Christ, so perfect in his anatomy and so serene in his aspect as he triumphs over death.

Piero's art brought him to the attention of the cultivated Duke Federico da Montefeltro, who had assembled a team of artists from all over Europe for his court at Urbino. There, Piero came into contact, and perhaps into competition, with artists not only from Italy but also from Spain and Flanders. From them, he learned the new technique of painting with oil glazes and became an early practitioner of this technique in central Italy. Piero's quiet, spatially complex paintings became thus enriched with more brilliant colors and surface textures in the style of Flemish art. The double portrait of Battista Sforza and Federico da Montefeltro that Piero painted around 1472 (**fig. 15.19**) shows his skill at rendering space and using the rich hues and varied textures made possible by oil painting. This diptych portrays both Federico and Battista in profile facing each other in front of a deep continuous landscape. Federico, whose face had been disfigured in a tournament, shows his good

15.20 Leon Battista Alberti. Interior of Sant'Andrea, Mantua. Begun 1470

 Explore the architectural panoramas of the Church of Sant'Andrea on myartslab.com

side on the viewer's right. His wife had recently died from a fever; Piero places her to the viewer's left, the place of honor. Her complicated hairstyle and elegant clothing frame her pale features, while a shadow falls over the landscape behind her. The deep red of his garments and the ruddy features of the duke give him a commanding air, in front of a well-lit and busy landscape. These naturalistic portraits sit in a frame designed in antique style and accompanied on the reverse by images of triumph and inscriptions inspired by humanist study of the past.

Alberti and Mantegna in Mantua

Mantua, in the northern Po Valley, had been dominated for more than a century by the Gonzaga. They created a brilliant court, peopled with Humanists, educators, and artists. The court was very cosmopolitan and attracted Humanists such

as Leon Battista Alberti as well as the painter Andrea Mantegna.

SANT'ANDREA Having entered the service of the Gonzaga family, Alberti designed the church of Sant'Andrea in Mantua by 1470 (**fig. 15.20**). In his architecture, Alberti aimed to merge classical temple forms with the traditional basilican church. For this church, Alberti planned only a nave ending in an apse. (Architects in the mid-eighteenth century added the transept, dome, and choir.) Following the example of the Basilica of Constantine (see fig. 7.31), Alberti replaced the usual basilica aisles with alternating large and small vaulted chapels, and eliminated the clerestory. Large arches open these vaulted chapels, the arches flanked by pilasters, like a Roman triumphal arch (see fig. 7.29). A barrel vault of impressive size covers the nave; this has coffers inspired by the dome of the Pantheon (fig. 7.18). The barrel vault rests on an unbroken entablature which is supported by pilasters reaching from floor to vault level; the large pilasters form what is known as a **colossal order**, meaning that it is more than one story high. Alberti used the same colossal order, the same proportions, and the same triumphal-arch motif on the façade of the building.

A comparison with Brunelleschi's San Lorenzo (fig. 15.4) reveals the new direction that Renaissance architecture took through Alberti. Brunelleschi's classicizing columns and contrasting colors create a much lighter and more open space, defined and controlled by the architect's judicious sense of proportion. At Sant'Andrea, Alberti focuses all attention on the nave, eliminating aisles in favor of a huge and imposing hall. He has drawn upon his study of the massive vaulted halls in ancient Roman baths and basilicas, but he interprets these models freely to create a structure that can truly be called a "Christian temple." Such a synthesis of ancient forms and Christian uses was a primary goal of fifteenth-century Humanists and their patrician sponsors. Alberti's accomplishment of this goal at Sant'Andrea would inspire many other architects to attempt the same.

MANTEGNA AS COURT ARTIST   The Humanist court at Mantua played host for many years to one of the most intellectually inclined artists of the century, Andrea Mantegna (1431–1506). Trained in Padua, but aware of artistic currents in Venice, Florence, and Rome, Mantegna became court painter to the Gonzaga in 1460, a position he held until his death at age 75. His interests as a painter, a Humanist, and an archaeologist inform his painting of *St. Sebastian* (**fig. 15.21**), probably datable to the 1450s. Sebastian was an early Christian martyr who was condemned to be executed by archers, although he recovered from these wounds. Mantegna depicts the anatomically precise and carefully proportioned body of the saint tied to a classical column. These forms are crisply drawn and modeled to resemble sculpture. Architectural and sculptural classical ruins lie at his feet and behind him, and next to him, on the left, is the artist's signature (in Greek). A road leads into the distance, traversed by the archers who have just shot the saint; through this device, Mantegna lets the perspectively constructed space denote the passage of time. Warm late-afternoon sunlight bathes the scene, creating a melancholy mood. The light-filled landscape demonstrates Mantegna's study of Netherlandish paintings, which had reached

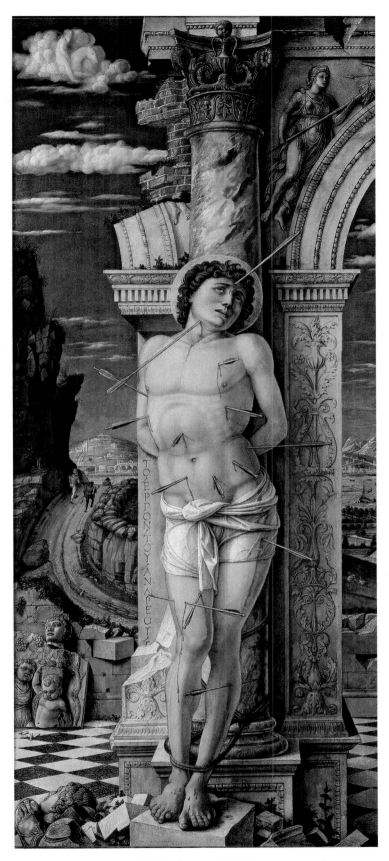

15.21 Andrea Mantegna. *St. Sebastian*. ca. 1450s. Tempera on panel, 26¾ × 11⅞″ (68 × 30.6 cm). Kunsthistorisches Museum, Vienna

15.22 Andrea Mantegna. *Camera Picta*. 1465–74. Fresco. Ducal Palace, Mantua

Florence as well as Venice by 1450, where he would have encountered them.

Mantegna's patron for the *St. Sebastian* is unknown, but as a court painter, he served the Marquis of Mantua by painting his villas and palaces. For the marquis's palace in Mantua, he began painting in 1465 a hall that has come to be called the *Camera Picta*, or painted room (**fig. 15.22**). This was a multipurpose vaulted room—sometimes bedroom, sometimes reception hall—that Mantegna finished in 1474. On the walls he painted portraits of the Gonzaga family, their retainers, their children, and their possessions. This room celebrates the marquis's brilliant court, his dynastic accomplishments, and his wealth, all in a witty display that became an attraction for visiting Humanists, politicians, artists, and princes. In such ways, princes used art to improve their social and political standing. The *Camera Picta* also celebrates Mantegna's skill, and brought him fame among his contemporaries.

Mantegna used the actual architecture of the room—the corbels supporting the vaults, the mantel over the fireplace—to create an illusionistic glimpse of the Gonzaga family at home. Through painted pilasters that flank the door, the viewer sees members of the family out of doors; above the mantel, they appear in a more formal setting, surrounded by courtiers. In addition to the specific features of the people and the naturalism of the details, Mantegna's mastery of perspective allows him to connect the painted world to the real world of the spectator. The centerpiece of this illusion occurs at the crown of the vault, where Mantegna paints an illusionistic skylight through which a spectator sees the sky. He also painted the ceiling vaults with illusionistic reliefs of Roman emperors; he thus advertises his knowledge of history, but also flatters the marquis by including him in this august company. The brilliance of the court is wonderfully captured by these splendid frescoes.

Venice

While it competed with its neighbors for territory, trade routes, and influence, Venice had a stable republican government throughout the fifteenth century. Ruled by a merchant aristocracy that was firmly established, the city suffered little internal turmoil. Its wealth and influence grew throughout the century; in these conditions, the artists of Venice developed their own form of Renaissance art. Venetian artists like Domenico Veneziano had long explored the intersection of light and color. Added to this visual tradition was an early exposure to the new technique of oil painting, in which Venetian artists excelled. Florentine ideas about perspective were exploited by artists such as Mantegna, who also brought to the region his deep study of the art of the ancients.

BELLINI AND OIL PAINTING A painter from southern Italy, Antonello da Messina, who may have traveled to Flanders to learn the oil technique, came to Venice in the 1470s and passed this knowledge on to Venetian artists. In the paintings of Giovanni Bellini (ca. 1430–1507), Mantegna's brother-in-law and a member of a family of painters, the technique of painting in oil pioneered by the Flemish is combined with Florentine spatial systems and Venetian light and color.

As the foremost artist of Venice, Bellini produced a number of altarpieces of the *sacra conversazione* type. The latest and most monumental is the *Madonna and Saints* (**fig. 15.23**), done in 1505 for the venerable Benedictine convent of San Zaccaria. This Queen of Heaven is raised up on a marble throne with her Child, while saints Peter, Catherine, Lucy, and Jerome stand before her. The prominence of the female saints may reflect the interests of the nuns for whom the altarpiece was made. Compared with Domenico Veneziano's *sacra conversazione* of 60 years earlier (fig. 15.11), the setting is simpler but even more impressive. Instead of a Gothic canopy, the saints are gathered below a semidome covered with mosaic like those that appear in numerous Venetian medieval buildings, yet the semidome rests on an antique-inspired entablature supported by Albertian pilasters. Bellini's figures stand comfortably in the space of their apse, though the structure does not appear to be a real church, for its sides are open and the scene is flooded with sunlight. He has arranged the figures in a balanced composition with Mary and her Child raised above the other figures.

What distinguishes this altar from earlier Florentine examples is not only the spaciousness of the design but its calm, meditative mood. Instead of "conversation," the figures seem deep in thought, so gestures are unnecessary. The silence is enhanced by the way the artist has bathed the scene in a delicate haze. There are no harsh contrasts. Light and shadow blend in almost imperceptible gradations, and colors glow with a new richness. Bellini creates a glimpse into a heavenly court peopled by ideal figures in an ideal space.

15.23 Giovanni Bellini. *Madonna and Saints*. 1505. Oil on panel, 16′5⅛″ × 7′9″ (5 × 2.4 m). San Zaccaria, Venice

Rome and the Papal States

The reinvigoration of the papacy after the end of the schism in 1417 allowed Rome to become a major artistic center by the end of the fifteenth century. As the papacy regained power, the popes began to rebuild both the Vatican and the city. They also reasserted their power as rulers over Rome and the Papal States. These popes believed that the monuments of Christian Rome had to outshine those of the pagan past. To achieve this goal, they called many artists from Florence and the surrounding areas to Rome, including Masaccio, Fra Angelico, Piero della Francesca, and Sandro Botticelli. Like the other courts of Italy, the papacy saw the value of spending money on adorning both ecclesiastical and domestic structures.

THE SISTINE CHAPEL Pope Sixtus IV paid for numerous architectural and artistic projects to beautify and improve Rome. One of those improvements was the building at the Vatican of a new chapel for the pope, called the Sistine Chapel, after his name. Around 1481–82, Sixtus commissioned a cycle of frescoes for the walls of the chapel depicting events from the life of Moses (on the left wall) and Christ (on the right wall), representing the Old and New Testaments. To execute them, he hired many of the important painters of central Italy, among them Pietro Vanucci, called Perugino (ca. 1450–1523). Born near Perugia in Umbria (the region southeast of Tuscany), Perugino maintained close ties with Florence. He completed the fresco of *The Delivery of the Keys* (**fig. 15.24**) in 1482.

The gravely symmetrical design of the fresco conveys the special importance of the subject in this particular setting: The authority of St. Peter as the first pope, as well as of all those who followed him, rests on his having received the keys to the Kingdom of Heaven from Christ himself. Perugino places the main figures at the center of the image with Peter kneeling before Christ. At either side, in a carefully balanced arrangement, the other apostles and a number of bystanders with highly individualized features witness the solemn event. The figures wear heavy drapery that responds to their bodies as it cascades in deep folds to the earth, in forms inspired by Donatello and his followers (see fig. 15.6).

In the background, two further narratives appear: To the left, in the middle distance, is the

15.24 Pietro Perugino. *The Delivery of the Keys*. 1482. Fresco, 11′5½″ × 18′8½″ (3.5 × 5.7 m). Sistine Chapel, Vatican, Rome

story of *The Tribute Money* (see fig. 15.8); to the right, the attempted stoning of Christ. The inscriptions on the two Roman triumphal arches (modeled on the Arch of Constantine; see fig. 7.29) favorably compare Sixtus IV to Solomon, who built the Temple in Jerusalem. These arches flank a domed structure seemingly inspired by the ideal church of Alberti's *Treatise on Architecture*. Also Albertian is the mathematically precise perspective, which lends the view its spatial clarity. The symmetry and clear space of the image express the character of the rule of Sixtus IV, in both spiritual and political terms. The new style of Renaissance art proved useful to rulers throughout Italy.

POINTS OF REFLECTION

15.1 Compare Renaissance works of art to similar Roman works. How do the works of the Italian Renaissance differ from their antique counterparts even when inspired by Roman forms?

15.2 Analyze the role of humanism in the development of early Italian Renaissance art. What did artists and patrons learn by studying antiquity?

15.3 Select individual works or artists in the chapter that exerted influence on other works of art. Using these examples, explain which factors played a role in spreading Renaissance ideas.

15.4 Investigate the differences between works of art made for church settings and those made for domestic settings by comparing the works in this chapter.

15.5 The name Medici is synonymous with lavish patronage. Consider why this family would spend so much on art, and how their patronage stimulated others to do the same.

✓—[**Study** and review on myartslab.com

ART IN TIME

- 1402 — Ghiberti wins commission to sculpt northern doors of the Baptistery of Florence

- **1420 — Brunelleschi's dome for Florence Cathedral begun**

- 1420 — Papacy returns to Rome from Avignon

- **ca. 1425 — Masaccio's frescoes in the Brancacci Chapel**

- 1444 — Medici Palace begun in Florence

- 1453 — Constantinople falls to the Ottoman Turks

- **1465 — Mantegna begins the *Camera Picta* in Mantua**

- 1469 — Lorenzo de' Medici ascends to power in Florence at the height of the Renaissance

- **ca. 1470 — Alberti's Sant'Andrea begun in Mantua**

- **ca. 1485 — Botticelli's *The Birth of Venus***

- 1498 — Girolamo Savonarola executed in Florence

16 The High Renaissance in Italy, 1495–1520

POINTS OF INQUIRY

16.1 Identify the stylistic characteristics shared across mediums by some of the world's most famous artists.

16.2 Examine the conditions in which High Renaissance artists worked in Florence, Rome, and Venice.

16.3 Recognize the ancient sources of High Renaissance forms.

16.4 Consider the new themes and topics represented in High Renaissance art.

16.5 Interpret the meaning of the human figure for the High Renaissance.

(((•—**Listen** to the chapter audio on myartslab.com

Painter, architect, and historiographer GIORGIO VASARI (1511–1574) defined Italian Renaissance art with his publication in 1550 of the history of Italian art from Cimabue through Michelangelo; in 1568 he published an expanded and corrected edition of the work. *The Lives of the Most Excellent Italian Architects, Painters, and Sculptors*, known as the *Lives of the Artists*, gives a mass of anecdotal and biographical information about Renaissance artists, and accords Florence most of the credit for the Renaissance. More significantly, Vasari's view that art should faithfully imitate nature established a standard favoring classical and Renaissance art that endured for centuries.

Looking back at the artists working around 1500, the artist and art historian Giorgio Vasari wrote in 1550 that these artists had been able to "surpass the age of the ancients." For him, the artists of this generation were paragons of their profession. Following Vasari, artists of subsequent centuries have used the works of this 25-year period between 1495 and 1520, known as the High Renaissance, as a benchmark against which to measure their own achievements. This brief period saw the creation of some of the most revered works of European art, created by the most acclaimed names in the history of art, as chronicled in VASARI's *Lives of the Artists*. Vasari's book placed the biography of the artist at the center of the study of art, and his *Lives* became a model of art-historical writing. The celebrity of artists is a distinctive characteristic of the early sixteenth century.

Patrons in early sixteenth-century Italy competed to hire Leonardo, Bramante, Michelangelo, Raphael, Giorgione, and Titian. Michelangelo and Titian were internationally celebrated during their lifetimes. This fame was part of a wholesale change in the status of the artist that had been occurring gradually during the course of the fifteenth century, and which gained impetus with these figures. No matter who their families were, or what their personalities, these artists were treated as intellectuals and, as such, accorded the same respect as were members of the great royal courts. In some cases, they were called "genius" or "divine." A few were raised to the nobility.

This period saw the coming together of demanding patrons—rulers, popes, princes—and innovative artists. The artists' own rivalries inspired them to produce innovations in technique and in expression. The prestige of the patrons and the reputations of the artists had a reciprocal effect: As the one developed, it enhanced the other. Although each artist developed a distinctive visual style that grew out of the ideas of the fifteenth century, their works share certain features: A high level of technical skill; an understanding of and reliance on the forms of antiquity; balance and clarity in their compositions; and great emotional power.

Leonardo and the Florentine High Renaissance

As the fifteenth century came to a close, events in Florence jeopardized the city's reputation as a center for the arts. After the Medici family were forced out in 1494, many Florentines heeded the warnings of the fiery preacher Girolamo Savonarola (page 328), who urged them to reform both their lives and their government. The penitential frenzy that he triggered did not survive his execution in 1498. Florence restored its republican form of government, which lasted only until another generation of Medici politicians took over in 1512. This turmoil inspired Florentine artists to look for work elsewhere in Italy, as evidenced by the careers of Michelangelo Buonarroti and Leonardo da Vinci.

Leonardo da Vinci

Leonardo (1452–1519) was at once a scientist, painter, sculptor, musician, architect, and engineer. His works are among the most famous in European art. Born in the small Tuscan town of Vinci, Leonardo trained as a painter in the Florentine workshop of Verrocchio. He left Florence around 1482 to work for Ludovico Sforza, the duke of Milan, primarily as a military engineer and only secondarily as an artist. On Sforza's removal by the French in 1499, Leonardo made his way to Venice, Rome, and back to Florence, where he executed several commissions between 1503 and 1505. From 1506 through 1516 he worked in Rome and Florence and again in Milan, whose French overlord, Francis I, invited him to retire to a chateau in the Loire Valley. Leonardo died in France in 1519.

Leonardo owes his fame to his technical skill and his constant investigations of natural and human phenomena. For Leonardo wanted to know more than the rules of perspective; he had to know all the laws of nature. He undertook a broad scientific study of natural phenomena based on careful visual observation; he believed that the eye was the perfect instrument for studying the world. The extraordinary range of his inquiries can be seen in his NOTEBOOKS, preserving the hundreds of drawings and notes that he hoped to turn into an encyclopedic set of treatises. He was fascinated by all elements of nature: Animals, water, anatomy, and the workings of the mind. He made drawing after drawing, invention after invention, his restless mind probing topics that ranged from the musculo-skeletal structure of

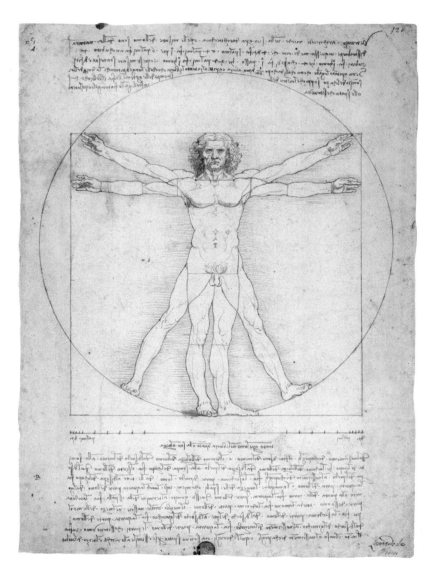

16.1 Leonardo da Vinci. *Vitruvian Man.* ca. 1487. Pen and ink, 13½ × 9½″ (34.3 × 24.5 cm). Gallerie dell'Accademia, Venice

the human body (informed by his dissection of cadavers) to the character of the sky.

Like other fifteenth-century scholars, he read ancient authorities to further his inquiries. His interest in architecture and engineering led him to the works of the Roman architect Vitruvius, whose treatise had inspired Alberti earlier in the century. A drawing from the late 1480s (**fig. 16.1**) visualizes Vitruvius' notion that the perfect geometrical forms of the circle and the square may be derived from the human body. This image expresses powerfully the value that Humanists and architects placed on these geometric elements, as carriers of meaning as well as visual forms. Like other Humanists, Leonardo was interested in the place of man in the world.

In the early 1490s, during his stay at the court of Ludovico Sforza in Milan, Leonardo made a meticulous record of his wide-ranging studies in more than 1,000 pages of NOTEBOOKS, today preserved in 31 volumes. Written backward in mirror writing, the notebooks treat four main themes—painting, architecture, mechanics, and human anatomy—and reveal the range and depth of the artist's prodigious mind. Leonardo anticipated many modern inventions: flying machines (including the helicopter), bicycles, submarines, missile launchers, and parachutes.

16.2 Leonardo da Vinci.
The Last Supper. ca. 1495–98.
Oil and tempera on plaster
(restored), 15'2" × 28'10"
(4.6 × 8.8 m). Santa Maria delle
Grazie, Milan

 Watch a video
about Leonardo da
Vinci's *The Last Supper* on
myartslab.com

THE LAST SUPPER Among Leonardo's most famous works is *The Last Supper* (**fig. 16.2**), executed between 1495 and 1498. Leonardo's patron, Duke Ludovico, commissioned him to adorn the dining hall of the Dominican monastery of Santa Maria delle Grazie in Milan, which housed the duke's family chapel. The resulting painting was instantly famous and copied numerous times by other artists, but a modern viewer can only imagine its original effect. Dissatisfied with the limitations of the traditional fresco technique, Leonardo experimented with an oil-tempera medium on dry plaster that did not adhere well to the wall. Later changes to the room (such as the piercing of the wall by a doorway) damaged the painting. Despite recent restoration, the image is merely a ghost of itself. Yet what remains is more than adequate to account for its tremendous impact.

Depicting the meal Jesus shared with his disciples on the eve of his Passion and death, the theme of the Last Supper appeared frequently in monastic refectories. Monks or nuns dined before images of the disciples and Jesus at table. In his painting, Leonardo creates a spatial setting that seems like an annex to the real interior of the room. Deeply skilled in perspective (see box, page 315), Leonardo

locates the central vanishing point behind the head of Jesus in the exact middle of the fresco. Thus even the perspective system reflects the import of Jesus' actions. The opening in the wall behind him serves as the architectural equivalent of a halo. All elements of the picture—light, composition, colors, setting—focus the attention on Jesus.

Jesus has presumably just spoken the fateful words, "One of you shall betray me." The disciples ask, "Lord, is it I?" They do not simply react to these words. Each man's response reveals his own personality. In the group to Jesus' right, Peter impulsively grabs a knife; next to him John seems lost in thought; and Judas (the figure leaning on the table) recoils from Jesus into shadow. Leonardo arranges the men into symmetrically organized groups flanking Jesus and calculates each pose and expression so that the drama unfolds across the picture plane. The figures exemplify what the artist wrote in one of his notebooks—that the highest and most difficult aim of painting is to depict "the intention of man's soul" through gestures and movements of the limbs.

Leonardo's aim, however, was not merely to tell a story. He condenses the subject, physically (by the compact, monumental grouping of the figures) and spiritually (by presenting many levels of meaning at one time). Jesus' calm presence at the center of the table suggests that in addition to announcing his betrayal, he is also instituting the Eucharist, in which bread and wine become his body and blood. Such multiple meanings would serve as spiritual food for the Dominican friars who lived in the presence of this image.

MONA LISA After the French invaded Milan, Leonardo returned to Florence. There he painted the portrait of a woman, whom Vasari identified as Lisa di Gherardo, wife of Francesco del Giocondo, the so-called *Mona Lisa* (**fig. 16.3**). If it is indeed the Lady (or Madonna) Lisa, she was about 25 when the portrait was made. For reasons that are unclear, Leonardo kept this painting throughout his life; after his death in France, it entered the collection of Francis I and thence the Louvre. This history has added to its fame.

The painting's formal qualities also make it remarkable, because in it Leonardo deployed a variety of new techniques to re-imagine the female portrait. In the fifteenth century, families commissioned portraits of elite women at their marriages, usually in a profile format that stressed the subject's expensive garments over her personality or features. (See Piero's portrait of Battista Sforza for an example, fig. 15.19.) Leonardo uses the Northern European device of the three-quarter pose; he also represents the woman at half-length, so that her hands are included in the image and her whole face is visible. This allows the entire composition to form a stable pyramid, with the crossed hands establishing a base for the rest of the figure. Light washes over her, drawing attention to her features. This method of modeling is called **chiaroscuro**, the Italian word for "light-dark." Leonardo thinks in terms of three-dimensional bodies, which he renders using dark tones to depict shadows and lighter tones for highlights. Instead of emphatic lines, he softens the contours of his forms in an atmospheric setting. In this painting, the forms are built from layers of glazes so thin that the panel appears to glow with a gentle light from within, despite the dirty varnish that obscures the painting. The lady sits before an evocative landscape, whose mountainous elements emerge from a cool, smoky backdrop, while the rivers and bridges winding through it echo the highlights on her drapery. The landscape and the woman inhabit a moist atmosphere that produces

a gentle haze around their forms. This fine haze, called *sfumato* (smokiness), lends an unusual warmth and intimacy to the portrait. Where earlier portraits paid as much attention to a woman's jewels as to her person, Leonardo concentrates on the lady's features and personality. The skill with which he renders the veil and the hands gives the woman as much character as the famous smile. Vasari helped to spread the fame of the painting, for he claimed it exemplified "how faithfully art can imitate nature." For Vasari, this skill was the root of Leonardo's genius.

16.3 Leonardo da Vinci. *Mona Lisa.* ca. 1503–05. Oil on panel, 30¼ × 21″ (77 × 53.5 cm). Musée du Louvre, Paris

 Read the document related to Leonardo da Vinci on myartslab.com

The High Renaissance in Rome

By the end of the fifteenth century, the papacy had firmly reestablished itself in Rome. Along with their spiritual control of the Church, the popes reasserted political and military control over the Papal States in the region around Rome. Although this process took decades, Pope Julius II (r. 1503–1513) intended to renew Rome to rival physically the glory of the ancient city. Julius invested vast sums in large-scale projects of architecture, sculpture, and painting, and he invited many artists to work for him. Under Julius, Rome became the crucible of the High Renaissance.

Bramante in Rome

The most important architect in Julius's Rome was Donato Bramante (1444–1514). A native of Urbino, he began his career as a fresco painter. Influenced by Piero della Francesca and Andrea Mantegna, Bramante became skilled at rendering architectural settings in correct perspective. Leonardo may have influenced Bramante too, as both men worked at the court of Milan. Bramante's architectural works started with the ideas of Brunelleschi and Alberti, but developed as he studied the architecture of ancient Rome at first hand.

After Milan fell to the French in 1499, Bramante went to Rome, where he examined ancient Roman

16.4 Donato Bramante. The Tempietto, San Pietro in Montorio. 1502–11. Rome

buildings and found new patrons. The Spanish rulers Ferdinand and Isabella, supporters of the Spanish-born pope, Alexander VI, commissioned Bramante around 1500 to build a structure to mark the supposed site of St. Peter's crucifixion, attached to the church of San Pietro in Montorio. Because it looks so much like a Roman temple, it was called the Tempietto or "little temple" (**fig. 16.4**). Yet Bramante looked back also at Early Christian buildings, for the circular plan of the structure evokes the Early Christian *martyrium*, a special chapel associated with a martyr.

Bramante designed the Tempietto as a round, domed chapel sitting on a three-step platform. It is articulated on the exterior with a plain Tuscan order, even simpler and less ornate than the classicizing columns in Alberti's or Brunelleschi's buildings. Like Brunelleschi, Bramante used the proportion of the columns as a device for designing the details of the façade. For example, the distance between the columns is four times their diameter, and they stand two diameters' distance from the wall. To this simple geometry, Bramante added an almost sculptural treatment of the wall. He placed deeply recessed niches in the upper story to balance the convex shape of the dome. He composed the upper and lower stories as alternating solids and voids, and stressed the intersection of the two stories with strongly projecting moldings and the inventive **balustrade**, or railing. As a result, the building looks much larger and stronger than it is, and recalls Roman buildings much more than any fifteenth-century structure.

ST. PETER'S Bramante's work brought him to the notice of Pope Julius II, whose goal of restoring papal authority prompted him to replace the medieval basilica of St. Peter's (see fig. 8.4) with a church so magnificent that it would overshadow all the monuments of imperial Rome. He gave the commission to Bramante and laid the cornerstone in 1506. Bramante's original design is known mostly from a sixteenth-century plan and from the medal commemorating the start of the building campaign (**fig. 16.5**), which shows the exterior in general terms.

Bramante planned a huge round dome, similar to the Pantheon's (fig. 7.18), to crown the crossing of the barrel-vaulted spaces of equal length. He intended to surround the central dome with four smaller domes, each covering a chapel that echoed the main space. As Alberti prescribed, Bramante's

16.5 Cristoforo Foppa Caradosso. Bronze medal showing Bramante's design for St. Peter's. 1506. The British Museum, London

plan begins with the circle and the square. Revered by the ancients, these perfect forms became appropriate symbols for Julius's Christian empire. Bramante envisioned four identical façades dominated by classical forms: Domes, half-domes, colonnades, and pediments. The design proposed a unified, symmetrical sculptural form, united by proportion and the interplay of geometric elements.

Along with Bramante's logical design comes the structure's huge scale, for Julius intended the church to be more than 500 feet long. Such a monumental undertaking required huge sums of money, and the construction of St. Peter's progressed so slowly that in 1514, when Bramante died, only four crossing piers had been built. For the next three decades the project was carried on by architects trained under Bramante, who altered his design in a number of ways. A new and decisive phase in the history of St. Peter's began in 1546, when Michelangelo took charge (see fig. 17.6). It was altered again in the seventeenth century (fig. 19.6). Bramante planned to put Roman imperial and Early Christian forms at the service of a Renaissance pope's spiritual and temporal ambitions.

Michelangelo in Rome and Florence

Julius's ambitions also furthered the career of one of the crucial figures in the history of art, Michelangelo di Lodovico Buonarroti Simoni (1475–1564). Acclaimed by his contemporaries,

16.6 Michelangelo. *Pietà*.
ca. 1498. Marble, height 5′8½″
(1.74 m). St. Peter's, Rome

 View the Closer Look
for the *Pietà* on
myartslab.com

hailed as "divine" by Vasari, Michelangelo is one of
the most influential and imitated artists in history.
He became the archetype of the genius, whose
intellect and talents enabled him to work in many
media; he was a sculptor, architect, painter, and
poet. Pope Julius II gave him the opportunities for
some of his most inspired works, aiding his ambition to outdo the artists of antiquity.

Michelangelo's belief in the human image as the
supreme vehicle of expression gave him a sense of
kinship with ancient sculpture, more so than any

other Renaissance artist. Among Italian masters,
he admired Giotto, Masaccio, and Donatello more
than his own contemporaries. His family came
from the nobility and they initially opposed his
desire to become an artist. Nonetheless he learned
techniques of painting from the Florentine painter
Ghirlandaio, and studied sculpture with a student
of Donatello. He came to the attention of Lorenzo
de' Medici, who invited him to study the antique
statues in the garden of one of the Medici houses.
From the beginning, however, Michelangelo was a

carver rather than a modeler. He rarely worked in clay, except for sketches; he preferred harder materials, especially marble, which he shaped with his chisel. He was a sculptor to the core.

PIETÀ Michelangelo left Florence after the Medici were exiled, eventually arriving in Rome, where in 1498 a French cardinal commissioned him to carve a *pietà* for his tomb chapel in St. Peter's (**fig. 16.6**). As a devotional theme, the *pietà*, or the Virgin Mary holding her dead son, had appeared in Gothic works such as the *Roettgen Pietà* (fig. 12.25); in narrative terms, the theme has origins in stories of the Passion, like *The Lamentation* depicted in Giotto's Arena Chapel frescoes (see fig. 13.11). Michelangelo imagines the farewell between mother and son as a calm and transcendent moment. The composition is very stable; the large figure of Mary in her deeply carved robe easily supports Jesus' weight. She seems too young to be holding her grown son, making the image an echo of the Madonna and Child theme. According to his biographer, Ascanio Condivi, Michelangelo himself intended her youth to express Mary's perpetual virginity. He does not merely tell a story, but offers viewers the opportunity to contemplate a central mystery of Christian faith—Jesus as God-made man, who offers himself as sacrifice—with the same serenity as Mary herself. To clarify the authorship, Michelangelo carved his name on the Virgin's sash. At 24, his fame was assured.

DAVID Despite his success in Rome, Michelangelo was back in Florence in 1501, where the directors of the works for Florence Cathedral commissioned him to carve a figure for the façade. The 18-foot-high block of marble for this project had been partly carved by an earlier sculptor, but Michelangelo accepted the challenge to create something memorable from it. The result was the gigantic figure of *David* (**fig. 16.7**). When it was completed in 1504, a committee of civic leaders and artists decided to install it in front of the Palazzo della Signoria, the seat of the Florentine government, then enjoying a republican phase. They placed a circlet of gilt bronze leaves around the statue's hips and a gilt bronze wreath on his head. The city of Florence claimed the figure as an emblem of its own republican virtues.

Michelangelo treated the biblical figure not as a victorious hero, but as the ever-vigilant guardian of the city. Unlike Donatello in his bronze *David* for the Medici (fig. 15.13), Michelangelo omits the head

16.7 Michelangelo. *David*. 1501–04. Marble, height 17′1½″ (5.22 m). Galleria dell'Accademia, Florence

16.8 Interior of the Sistine Chapel showing Michelangelo's ceiling fresco (1508–12) and the *Last Judgment* on the end wall (1534–41); scenes on the side walls by Perugino, Ghirlandaio, Botticelli, and others (1481–82). Vatican, Rome

Sistine ceiling

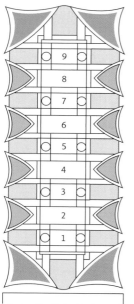

End wall with Last Judgment

☐ Scenes from Genesis

1 *Division of Light from Darkness*
2 *Creation of Sun and Moon*
3 *Division of Heaven (Earth) from the Waters*
4 *Creation of Adam*
5 *Creation of Eve*
6 *The Fall and The Expulsion*
7 *Sacrifice of Noah*
8 *The Deluge*
9 *The Drunkenness of Noah*

☐ Sibyls and prophets

☐ Ancestors of Christ

☐ Old Testament scenes

of Goliath. His David nervously fingers a slingshot, as his eyes focus on an opponent in the distance; the battle has not yet occurred. Although both Donatello and Michelangelo rendered David as nudes, the style of the later sculpture proclaims an ideal very different from Donatello's slender youth. Having spent several years in Rome, Michelangelo had been deeply impressed with the emotion-charged, muscular bodies of Hellenistic sculpture. Their heroic scale, their superhuman beauty, and the swelling volume of their forms became part of Michelangelo's own vocabulary and, through him, of Renaissance art in general. In the *David*,

Michelangelo competes with antiquity on equal terms and replaces its authority with his own. Instead of the emotionally wrought figures he saw in Hellenistic works, Michelangelo crafted the *David* to be at once calm and tense, active yet static, full of the potential for movement rather than its actual expression.

SISTINE CHAPEL CEILING Julius II summoned Michelangelo back to Rome in 1506 to enter his service. Initially commissioned to sculpt Julius's funeral monument, Michelangelo was asked by the pope to paint the ceiling of the Sistine Chapel

(see page 324). Working quickly using scaffolding of his own design, Michelangelo finished the ceiling in only four years, between 1508 and 1512 (**fig. 16.8**). In this brief period of intense creativity in a medium that he never felt was his own, Michelangelo produced a work of truly epochal importance.

The ceiling of the Sistine Chapel is a shallow barrel vault interrupted over the windows by the triangular elements (spandrels) that support it. Michelangelo treated this surface as a single entity, with hundreds of figures distributed rhythmically within an illusionistically painted architectural framework. Several different themes intersect throughout this complex structure (see diagram on opposite page). In the center, subdivided by ten illusionistic arches, appear nine scenes from the Book of Genesis, from the Creation of the World (at the altar end) to the Drunkenness of Noah (near the door); large figures of prophets and **sibyls**, ancient Greek prophetesses, flank these narratives. In the triangular spandrels sit the ancestors of Christ, who also appear in the lunettes flanking the windows. Further narrative scenes occur at the corners, depicting Old Testament heroes and prophets who prefigured Christ. There is still debate about the theological import of the whole program and whether Michelangelo consulted with advisors in its development. Except for the architecture, these themes of creation

and salvation are expressed almost entirely by the human figure. The figures convey deep drama and emotion through gesture, scale, and their physical beauty.

For example, Michelangelo depicts *The Creation of Adam* (**fig. 16.9**) not as the actual molding of Adam's body, but as the passage of a divine spark from God to Man. The design contrasts the beautiful earthbound Adam with the dynamic figure of God rushing through the sky. Adam gazes not only toward his Creator, but toward the figures in the shelter of God's left arm. The identity of these figures has occasioned much debate: The female may be Eve, awaiting her creation in the next panel; another proposal is that she is Mary, with Jesus at her knee, foreordained to redeem fallen humanity; she has also been identified as a personification of Wisdom. Adam sits in a bare landscape; nothing distracts from the figures. The entire image reflects Michelangelo's view of the human body as a divinely inspired vessel for conveying complex and deeply felt meaning.

Once this project was finished Michelangelo returned to work on the still unfinished tomb for Julius II. The return of the Medici to power in Florence, along with the election of cardinals from this family to the papacy, meant that Michelangelo was back in Florence by the end of this decade, although Rome remained his home for much of the rest of his life.

16.9 Michelangelo. *The Creation of Adam*. 1508–12. Portion of the Sistine Chapel ceiling. Fresco. Vatican, Rome

Raphael

While Michelangelo often conflicted with his patrons and struggled to complete monumental projects such as the Sistine Chapel ceiling, his younger contemporary Raphael of Urbino (Raffaello Sanzio, 1483–1520) seems to have avoided such turmoil in his professional life. Because Vasari championed Michelangelo, later generations often venerated him more than Raphael. Where Michelangelo's dramatic conflicts with his art and with his patrons made good stories, Raphael's career seems too much a success story, his work too marked by effortless grace, to match the tragic heroism of the older artist. Raphael succeeded on the strength of his technical brilliance, his intelligent approach to composing pictures, and his dialogue with the other artists of his time. By all accounts, he was also charming and diplomatic with his patrons. During his relatively brief career he created a large body of Renaissance pictorial work and oversaw a lively and large workshop, which fostered many young artists.

SCHOOL OF ATHENS   After his early training with Perugino, Raphael spent time in Florence, studying the innovations of Leonardo and Michelangelo. He painted portraits and religious pictures that synthesize these innovations and helped to establish his reputation. By 1509 Raphael had been called to Rome to paint a series of rooms in the papal apartments; he completed the Stanza della Segnatura first. The "Room of the Signature" derives its name from its later function as the place where papal bulls were signed; originally it housed Pope Julius's personal library. For this room, Raphael painted a cycle of frescoes on the walls and ceiling that refer to the four domains of learning: Theology, philosophy, law, and the arts. In attempting to represent the unity of knowledge in one grand scheme, the frescoes here reflect the ambitions of High Renaissance Humanism. The most famous of the frescoes in the Stanza della Segnatura, *The School of Athens* (**fig. 16.10**), demonstrates Raphael's commitment to surpassing antiquity while synthesizing the achievements of his

16.10 Raphael. *The School of Athens.* 1508–11. Fresco, width 19′ (5.8 m). Stanza della Segnatura, Vatican Palace, Vatican, Rome

contemporaries. Framed by illusionistic architectural and sculptural forms, the fresco depicts a gathering of philosophers from ancient Greece. Like Leonardo, Raphael crafts a persuasive illusion of space with a composition that is symmetrical and memorable. Like Michelangelo, he gives his figures powerful proportions and complex postures to express their characters. The architecture of the setting seems to reflect the innovations of Bramante. Raphael then sets the whole scene in a clear light that illuminates the complex subject matter.

The fresco became known as *The School of Athens* later, but in the scheme of the room the image stands for the study of philosophy. To embody this branch of knowledge, Raphael arranged his Greek philosophers into carefully composed groups around two central figures; at the vanishing point of the perspectival scheme, these two figures seem to be framed by the architecture. Inscriptions on the books held by these two men identify them as Plato and Aristotle, the most important Greek philosophers, according to Renaissance Humanists. The bearded figure (whose face resembles Leonardo's) is Plato, holding his book of cosmology and numerology, *Timaeus*; to his right is his pupil Aristotle, grasping a volume of his *Ethics*, which, like his science, is grounded in what is knowable in the material world. The books explain why Plato points rhetorically to the heavens, Aristotle to the earth. On the building behind them, Raphael depicts two sculptures of classical divinities in niches: Apollo, patron of the arts, with his lyre, on the left, and Athena, or Minerva, goddess of wisdom, on the right. The other figures are members of the idealist (Platonic) and empirical (Aristotelian) camps, but in some cases, Raphael's fellow artists play the roles of the philosophers. Euclid, seen drawing or measuring two overlapping triangles with a pair of compasses in the right foreground, has the features of Bramante. The man wearing a black hat behind these scientists is a self-portrait of Raphael, who places himself in the Aristotelian camp. Raphael added Michelangelo at the last minute; he cast the sculptor as Heraclitus, a sixth-century BCE philosopher, shown deep in thought sitting on the steps in the Platonic camp. Raphael not only made this figure a portrait of Michelangelo, he also adopted Michelangelo's figure style on the nearby Sistine Chapel ceiling. The inclusion of so many artists among, as well as in the guise of, famous philosophers attests to their recently acquired—and hard-won—status as members of the learned community.

GALATEA While Raphael and his workshop executed projects for Julius and his papal successors, he also found time for other commissions. Among his patrons in Rome was the powerful Sienese banker Agostino Chigi, who hired Raphael to adorn his new villa in Rome (now called the Villa Farnesina after a later owner). The building served as the setting for Chigi's interests: In the antique, in conspicuous display, and in love. Throughout the villa he commissioned frescoes on themes from the pagan past. For this setting, Raphael painted *Galatea* (**fig. 16.11**) around 1513. The beautiful nymph Galatea, vainly pursued by the giant Polyphemus, belongs to Greek mythology, known to the Renaissance through the verses of the Roman poet Ovid. Raphael's *Galatea* celebrates the sensuality of the pagan spirit as if it were a living force. Although the composition of the nude female riding a seashell recalls Botticelli's *The Birth of Venus* (see fig. 15.16),

16.11 Raphael. *Galatea.* ca. 1513. Fresco, 9′8⅛″ × 7′4″ (3 × 2.2 m). Villa Farnesina, Rome

a painting Raphael probably knew in Florence, the resemblance only serves to emphasize their profound differences. Raphael's figures are vigorously sculptural and arranged in a dynamic spiral movement around the twisting Galatea. In Botticelli's picture, the movement is not generated by the figures but imposed on them by the decorative, linear design that places all the figures on the same plane. Like Michelangelo, Raphael uses the arrangement of figures, rather than any detailed perspective scheme, to call up an illusion of space and to create a vortex of movement.

Raphael's life was cut short in 1520, when he died after a brief illness. As befitted the new status assigned to artists, he was buried in the Pantheon. Significantly, many of the leading artists of the next generation emerged from Raphael's workshop and took his style as their point of departure.

Venice and the High Renaissance

While Florence suffered political instability and Rome became the center of papal patronage, the city of Venice endured threats from its neighbors and invasions from the east. The Republic of Venice was threatened by an international military alliance aimed against it in 1509 to reduce its territory. Venice also had to defend itself against incursions

into Europe by the Turks, who had conquered the Byzantine Empire in 1453. Despite this turmoil, artists in Venice built on the traditions of the fifteenth century and the innovations of Giovanni Bellini to create a distinct visual language that appealed to wealthy patrons. Two artists in particular, Giorgione and Titian, created new subject matter, approaches to images, and techniques.

Giorgione

Giorgione da Castelfranco (1478–1510) left the orbit of Giovanni Bellini (see fig. 15.23) to create some of the most mysterious and beguiling paintings of the Renaissance. He seems to have specialized in smaller-scale paintings on secular themes for the homes of wealthy collectors. His death at a young age, probably from the plague, left the field open for his young colleague, Titian, who worked in his shop. Some of the works traditionally ascribed to Giorgione have, in fact, been reattributed to Titian in recent years.

One such work, the so-called *Concert Champêtre* or *Pastoral Concert* of about 1509 (**fig. 16.12**), has been on display in the Louvre in Paris since the nineteenth century. The painting depicts a group of young people gathered in a lush landscape to make music, when a shepherd and his flock come upon them. Attempts to find a narrative or literary subject to link to this image have proven fruitless: No single text seems to explain it. Most puzzling are the nude women, one of whom is about to play a recorder, while another takes water from a fountain. Some commentators have identified them as the **Muses**, ancient female divinities who inspire the arts. The forms of all figures are rendered in an accomplished chiaroscuro technique so that they seem to emerge from the atmospheric landscape as soft round shapes. The landscape moves from dark to light to dark passages, receding into the atmospheric distance. Instead of telling a story, the painting seems designed to evoke a mood and takes part in what was to become an important new tradition in art, the making of pictorial equivalents to poetry.

Vasari criticized Giorgione for not making drawings as part of his process of painting. Steeped in the Florentine tradition, Vasari argued that drawing or *disegno* was fundamental to good painting. The Venetians, however, valued light and color above all to create their sensual images. Vasari dismissed this as *colore*, or color, which he argued was secondary to the process of drawing. This competition

16.12 Giorgione or Titian. *Concert Champêtre (Pastoral Concert).* ca. 1509–10. Oil on canvas, 43¼ × 54⅜″ (105 × 136.5 cm). Musée du Louvre, Paris

 View the Closer Look for the *Concert Champêtre (Pastoral Concert)* on myartslab.com

between *disegno* and *colore* provided the grounds for criticizing or praising paintings well beyond the sixteenth century.

Titian

Giorgione's young colleague, Titian (Tiziano Vecellio, 1488/90–1576), who trained with Bellini and Giorgione and even repainted some of their works (possibly even the *Pastoral Concert*), would dominate Venetian painting for the next half-century. Fully aware of the innovations of other Renaissance artists, and yet committed to exploring Venetian traditions of subject matter and technique, Titian is one of the most prolific and inventive artists of the period. Throughout his long life, he earned commissions from the most illustrious patrons in Europe; he also trained many of the Venetian artists of the sixteenth century.

Titian could transform older traditions even as he respected their conventions. This ability can be seen in his *Madonna with Members of the Pesaro Family* (**fig. 16.13**), commissioned in 1519 and installed in 1526 on the altar of the Immaculate Conception of the Franciscan church of Santa Maria Gloriosa dei Frari. Here he takes a *sacra conversazione* in the tradition of Giovanni Bellini (fig. 15.23) and re-imagines both the composition and the figures. Like his predecessor, he sets the Virgin and Child at the apex of a triangular arrangement of figures, but Titian replaces the familiar frontal view with a diagonal composition that is less symmetrical and more dynamic. At the focal point of this rising diagonal stands a pudgy Infant Jesus innocently playing with his mother's veil. She and St. Peter solemnly acknowledge the donor, Jacopo Pesaro, shown kneeling in devotion at the left. This man had commanded the papal fleet in a battle against the Turks in 1502, which the Christian forces won. On the other side are the donor's brothers and sons with Sts. Francis and Anthony. The donors' portraits distinguish the ages and features of all the men gathered to venerate Mary and her son.

Titian places Mary's throne on the steps of a monumental church. The elevated columns suggest the character of the setting as the gateway to heaven. This idea is traditionally identified with Mary herself; these details imply her identity as the Immaculate Conception, a human being conceived without original sin (the sin of Adam and Eve). Because the view is diagonal, open sky and clouds fill most of the background. Brilliant sunlight makes every color and texture sparkle, in keeping with

the celebratory spirit of the altar. The only hint of tragedy is the cross that two little angels hold above a dark cloud, which adds a note of poignancy to the scene. None of the donors represented at the base of the composition, however, seems to notice it.

TITIAN AS PORTRAITIST Titian's skill at recording specific features of individuals in flattering compositions made him the most sought-after portraitist of

16.13 Titian. *Madonna with Members of the Pesaro Family*. 1526. Oil on canvas, 16′ × 8′10″ (4.9 × 2.7 m). Santa Maria Gloriosa dei Frari, Venice

the sixteenth century. His immense gifts, evident in the donors' portraits in the *Pesaro Madonna*, are equally striking in the *Man with a Quilted Sleeve*, dated about 1510 (**fig. 16.14**). In this portrait, Titian sets his sitter against a nonspecific backdrop behind a stone parapet, on which his initials ("T. V." for Tiziano Vecellio) appear. The man turns to make eye contact with a viewer. His cool glance expresses his self-confidence, as does the commanding presence of the man's projecting arm, which appears to reach out into a viewer's space. The man's fur robe indicates his elite social status. Titian records the textures of hair, cloth, and stone with great fidelity, all the while wrapping his figure in an atmospheric space through his use of chiaroscuro. Close study of the painting reveals another of Titian's innovations: The white collar of the man's shirt has a crinkly texture suggested by thick strokes of opaque white paint. In addition to defining forms with thin layers of transparent oil glazes as did Jan van Eyck (see fig. 14.5), Titian also loads thick oil paint on his brush and applies it in broad strokes. Each brushstroke sits on the canvas as one element of the whole shape; the brushstrokes only combine in the viewer's eye from a distance. Titian was to exploit this technique brilliantly throughout his career. The identity of the sitter is not known, but Titian attempts to capture

16.14 Titian, *Man with a Quilted Sleeve*. ca. 1510. Oil on canvas, 32 × 26″ (81.2 × 66.3 cm). The National Gallery, London

16.15 Titian, *Venus of Urbino*. ca. 1538. Oil on canvas, 3′11″ × 5′5″ (1.19 × 1.65 m). Gallerie degli Uffizi, Florence

his personality as well as his appearance. An early tradition identified the man as the poet Ariosto; another hypothesis identifies him as a Venetian patrician for whose family Titian worked; yet another would claim this as a self-portrait. In any case, Titian's links to Bellini and to Giorgione shine through in this image.

VENUS OF URBINO   Titian dominated painting in Venice throughout the sixteenth century; his fame was such that by the 1530s the most elite patrons of Europe sought his work. For example, in 1538, the duke of Urbino, Guidobaldo II della Rovere, commissioned him to execute the so-called *Venus of Urbino* (**fig. 16.15**). The painting, based on models by Giorgione, depicts a nude young woman lying on a bed in a well-furnished chamber. Details such as the presence of the *cassone* (wedding chest) and dog suggest that the painting commemorated a marriage. The duke, however, referred to the picture only as "the naked woman." Titian's colors record the sensuous textures of the woman's body, which has been placed on display for a viewer whose gaze she returns. Here again, Titian's technical innovations are on display, as the lady's golden hair is suggested by thick swirls of color and her pearl earring consists of a dollop of white paint. While called a "Venus," the painting may have been intended as an erotic image, not a classical theme. Titian's gift for compositions using naturalistic forms inspired by the ancient world makes him a true representative of the High Renaissance. His works had an important influence on later artists, who found in his paintings new techniques and new subject matters that inspired their own works.

POINTS OF REFLECTION

16.1   Why do the artists of the High Renaissance loom so large in art history? In what does their celebrity lie? Why were their works so influential?

16.2   Analyze the factors that led to such creative activity in Rome, Venice, and Florence. Are there similarities among all three centers?

16.3   Investigate what High Renaissance artists learned from antiquity. What did they do with antique forms?

16.4   Evaluate the traditional Christian content of Renaissance art: How do High Renaissance works compare to earlier (medieval or Renaissance) works?

16.5   Select a portrait from the High Renaissance and compare it to one from the Early Renaissance. What are the continuities and differences between these two periods?

✔—⟦**Study** and review on myartslab.com

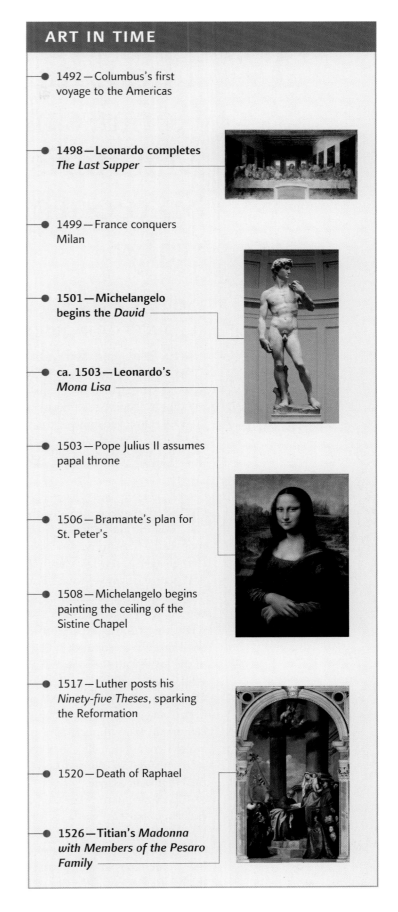

ART IN TIME

● 1492—Columbus's first voyage to the Americas

● 1498—**Leonardo completes** *The Last Supper*

● 1499—France conquers Milan

● 1501—**Michelangelo begins the** *David*

● ca. 1503—**Leonardo's** *Mona Lisa*

● 1503—Pope Julius II assumes papal throne

● 1506—Bramante's plan for St. Peter's

● 1508—Michelangelo begins painting the ceiling of the Sistine Chapel

● 1517—Luther posts his *Ninety-five Theses*, sparking the Reformation

● 1520—Death of Raphael

● 1526—**Titian's** *Madonna with Members of the Pesaro Family*

17 The Late Renaissance and Mannerism in Sixteenth-Century Italy

POINTS OF INQUIRY

17.1 Distinguish Mannerist works of art from earlier styles.

17.2 Locate the origins of Mannerism in the aristocratic courts.

17.3 Trace the movements of artists and styles across the Italian peninsula.

17.4 Compare the prevailing styles of Tuscany and Venice in the sixteenth century.

17.5 Discover some of the world's most influential buildings.

(((•—⌊**Listen** to the chapter audio on myartslab.com

The sixteenth century saw many changes in the political and cultural landscape of Italy (see **map 17.1**). The immense challenge to established Catholicism posed by Martin Luther's protest in 1517 sent shockwaves round Europe (see page 372). The great powers of France, Spain, and Germany warred with each other on the Italian peninsula, while the Turkish expansion into Europe threatened the whole continent. The spiritual challenge of the Protestant Reformation and the rise of powerful courts affected Italian artists, changing the climate in which they worked as well as the nature of patronage. No one style dominated the sixteenth century in Italy, though all the artists working in what is conventionally called the Late Renaissance were profoundly affected by the achievements of the High Renaissance.

The legacy of the High Renaissance would both challenge and nourish later generations of artists. Even though Leonardo, Raphael, Bramante, and Giorgione did not survive beyond 1520, their works had tremendous authority and influence. Two of the key figures of this generation lived to transform

their styles: Michelangelo worked until his death in 1564 and Titian worked until 1576. In addition to so weighty a visual legacy, the younger generation faced uncertainty in religious, political, and social spheres. Events such as the Sack of Rome by Habsburg troops in 1527 had immediate repercussions for artists, who scattered throughout Italy and indeed Europe (See map 17.1). Commissions came mostly from the princely courts, so artists' works reflected the taste and concerns of this powerful elite. The connections among the courts helped to spread a new style, usually labelled Mannerist, which lasted through much of the century. The style was typically used for paintings and sculptures, though some works of architecture exhibit Mannerist tendencies.

Late Renaissance Florence

Because of the connections among courts and the movement of artists, this new style appeared throughout Italy, but some of its most prominent practitioners came from or worked in Florence.

Map 17.1 Travels of some artists in sixteenth-century Italy

Legend:

→ Michelangelo
→ Parmigianino
→ Giulio Romano
→ Leonardo
→ Sofonisba
→ Primaticcio

Mannerism

The name of the new style was derived from the word *maniera*, meaning manner or style, used approvingly by contemporaries. Building on the achievements of Raphael and Michelangelo, above all, artists of the 1520s and later developed a style that emphasized technical virtuosity, erudite subject matter, beautiful figures, and deliberately complex compositions that would appeal to sophisticated tastes. Mannerism became a style of utmost refinement, which emphasized grace, variety, and virtuoso display instead of clarity and unity. Mannerist artists self-consciously explored definitions of beauty: Rather than repeat ancient forms, they experimented with proportions, ideal figure types, and unusual compositions. Like the artists of the High Renaissance, they aimed for originality and personal expression, which they considered their due as privileged creators.

With the city under Medici rule from 1512 to 1527, Florentines absorbed the innovations of the High Renaissance as artists came to the city from Rome. Pope Leo X (the son of Lorenzo the Magnificent) sent Michelangelo to Florence to work on projects for the Medici family. Despite the contributions of Florence to the development of the Early and High Renaissance, by the second decade of the sixteenth century some Florentine artists seemed to reject the serenity and confidence of High Renaissance art. Using the techniques of naturalism, chiaroscuro, and composition learned from Leonardo, Michelangelo, and Raphael, this generation of artists made images that are less balanced and more expressive than those of their immediate predecessors. In works of the 1520s, a group of Florentine artists created images of deep spiritual power in this new Mannerist style.

In the chaos after the Sack of Rome of 1527, Florentines again ousted the Medici and restored the republic of Florence. But the restoration of relations between the pope and the emperor of the Holy Roman Empire allowed the Medici to return to power by 1530. The Medici Pope Clement VII (r. 1523–1534) promoted his family interests, and worked to enhance the power of his family as the rulers of Florence. The family employed Michelangelo continually to execute works intended to glorify the Medici dynasty in Florence.

Michelangelo in Florence

Michelangelo's work for the Medici centered on the church of San Lorenzo. A century after Brunelleschi's design for the sacristy of this church (see the plan of San Lorenzo, fig. 15.5), which held the tombs of an earlier Medici generation, Pope Leo X commissioned a matching structure, the

New Sacristy. Leo wanted an appropriate space to house the tombs of his father, Lorenzo the Magnificent, Lorenzo's brother Giuliano, and two younger members of the family, also named Lorenzo and Giuliano. Aided by numerous assistants, Michelangelo worked on the project from 1519 to 1534 and managed to complete the architecture and two of the tombs, those for the later Lorenzo and the later Giuliano (**fig. 17.1**); these tombs are nearly mirror images of each other.

Michelangelo conceived of the New Sacristy as an architectural/sculptural ensemble. The influence of Brunelleschi is clear in the form of the pilasters and the colors of the stone used to articulate the walls. Thereafter, however, Michelangelo took liberties with his model, treating the walls themselves as sculptural forms in a way Brunelleschi never did. Michelangelo's plans for the Medici tombs underwent many changes while the work was underway. Other figures and reliefs for the project were designed but never executed. The present state of the Medici tombs can hardly be what Michelangelo ultimately intended, as the process was halted when the artist permanently left Florence for Rome in 1534.

Despite the chapel's unfinished state, the tomb of Giuliano remains an imposing visual unit, composed of a sarcophagus supporting two sculpted nudes, above which sits an armored figure, all framed by Michelangelo's inventive use of classical architectural elements. He designed the central niche, which barely accommodates the seated figure, to be framed by paired pilasters. These support an entablature that breaks over them. Such architectural forms defy the logic of classical architecture, even while using its vocabulary. Flanking the niche are blank windows topped by curving pediments supported by volutes; the sarcophagus below echoes these forms. The statues form a triangle that is held in place by a network of verticals and horizontals whose slender, sharp-edged forms contrast with the roundness and weight of the sculpture.

The structure has neither Christian imagery nor inscription. Instead of an effigy, two allegorical figures sit atop the sarcophagus—*Day* on the right and *Night* on the left. Some lines that Michelangelo wrote on one of his drawings suggest what these figures mean: "Day and Night speak, and say: We with our swift course have brought the Duke Giuliano to death … It is only just that the Duke takes revenge [for] he has taken the light from

17.1 Michelangelo. Tomb of Giuliano de' Medici. 1519–34. Marble, height of central figure 5′11″ (1.8 m). New Sacristy, San Lorenzo, Florence

 Explore the architectural panorama of the New Sacristy of the Church of San Lorenzo on myartslab.com

us; and with his closed eyes has locked ours shut, which no longer shine on earth." The reclining figures are themselves derived from statues of ancient river gods. The statue of Giuliano, the ideal image of the prince, wears classical military garb and bears no resemblance to the deceased. ("A thousand years from now, nobody will know what he looked like," Michelangelo is said to have remarked.) His beautifully proportioned figure seems ready for action, as he fidgets with his baton. His gaze was to be directed at the tomb of Lorenzo the Magnificent, never completed. Instead of being a commemorative monument that looks retrospectively at the accomplishments of the deceased, the tomb of Giuliano and the New Sacristy as a whole were to express the triumph of the Medici family over time.

Painters and Sculptors in Ducal Florence

Michelangelo's presence brought new energy and ideas to artists working in Tuscany. His work in painting, sculpture, and architecture inspired this and later generations of Italian artists, including many who found in Michelangelo's creative re-imagining of ancient sculptures and his brilliant color the freedom to invent themes, spaces, and color harmonies in their own works.

An important example of this phenomenon is Jacopo Carucci, called Jacopo da Pontormo (1494–1557). Born near Florence and trained there, Pontormo painted frescoes and canvases for many patrons in Florence. Ludovico di Gino Capponi, who acquired the patronage of a family chapel in the church of Santa Felicità in 1525, commissioned Pontormo to paint the altarpiece and frescoes on the walls and dome of the chapel. The altarpiece (**fig. 17.2**), completed by 1528, remains in its original location.

The subject of Pontormo's painting is unclear, as it lacks a cross or any other indications of a specific narrative, although Capponi dedicated the chapel to the *Pietà*. The Virgin swoons as two androgynous figures hold up the body of Christ for a viewer's contemplation. Pontormo's figures display an ideal beauty and sculptural solidity inspired by Michelangelo, yet Pontormo has squeezed them into an implausibly confined space. In Pontormo's painting, everything is subordinated to the play of graceful rhythms created by the tightly interlocking forms. The colors are desaturated: pale blues, pinks, oranges, and greens that may have been inspired by the colors of the Sistine Chapel ceiling (see fig. 16.8). Although they seem to act together,

17.2 Jacopo da Pontormo. *Pietà*. ca. 1526–28. Oil on panel, 10′3″ × 6′4″ (3.1 × 1.9 m). Santa Felicità, Florence

the mourners are lost in a grief too personal to share with one another. The mourners hold the body of Christ up for a viewer to see, much as the host is during the Mass; the image conveys to believers a sense of the tragic scale of Christ's sacrifice, which the Eucharist reenacts. Originally, the dome above the altarpiece depicted God the Father, to whom the body would be offered. Pontormo may have rejected the values of the High Renaissance, but he endows this image with deep spirituality.

BRONZINO Pontormo's student Agnolo Bronzino (1503–1572) worked for the court of the newly elevated duke of Florence, Cosimo de' Medici. This court was a magnet for artists from all over Europe, because the duke had inherited the Medici trait of underlining his power by means of the arts. Duke Cosimo and Duchess Eleonora commissioned works of art of many sorts, including architecture, sculpture, religious and secular paintings, and numerous portraits. To further the arts in his domain, the duke sponsored the establishment of the ACCADEMIA DEL DISEGNO, an educational institution for artists, in 1563. Many of the artists involved in the founding of the academy, like Bronzino, worked in a Mannerist style of refined technique and complex subject matter. As court portraitist, painter, and poet, Bronzino served the interests of the duke and duchess.

17.3 Agnolo Bronzino.
Allegory of Venus. ca. 1546.
Oil on panel, 57½ × 45⅝"
(146.1 × 116.2 cm).
The National Gallery, London

 View the Closer Look
for the *Allegory of Venus*
on myartslab.com

Bronzino's *Allegory of Venus* (**fig. 17.3**), which Vasari claimed was given by Duke Cosimo to Francis I of France, exemplifies the taste of the ducal court. Into a narrow plane close to the surface of the painting Bronzino crowds a number of figures who have been identified only tentatively. The bald Father Time tears back the curtain from Fraud or Oblivion, the figure in the upper left-hand corner; this exposes Venus and Cupid (figures for Love and Desire) in an incestuous embrace. The child at the right—whom Vasari called Play, though other interpretations call him Folly—throws roses at the pair in delight; the figure tearing his hair—who has been identified as either Jealousy or Pain—reacts with dismay. On the right, Pleasure, half woman and half snake, offers a honeycomb and wields a stinging tail. As this description suggests, the debate continues on both the identities of the individual figures and the meaning of the allegory.

With its cool tonalities and contorted nudes, Bronzino's painting proclaims a refined eroticism expressed by the marble-like figures (likely inspired by Michelangelo) and the mirror-like finish. The complexity of the concept matches the intricacy of the composition; the high quality of the technique matches the cleverness of the content. In Bronzino, the Medici found an artist whose technical virtuosity, complex imagery, and inventive compositions perfectly matched their taste and exemplify the Mannerist style. Cosimo's gift of a painting of such erudite imagery and accomplished technique to the king of France demonstrated his realm's achievements in the literary and visual arts.

GIOVANNI BOLOGNA A comparable combination of technical virtuosity and eroticized imagery appears in a sculpted group created by the French-born artist known as Giovanni Bologna (1529–1608). Giovanni came to Florence from France to study its artistic tradition around 1555. He created the sculpture in **fig. 17.4** to demonstrate his skill to his mentors at the Academy of Design. They challenged him to sculpt three contrasting figures united in a single action. When creating the over-life-size group, the sculptor had no specific theme in mind, but when it was finished the title *The Rape of the Sabine Woman* was suggested and was accepted by him. The duke admired the work so much that he had it installed near the Palazzo della Signoria in Florence.

The subject proposed derives from the legends of ancient Rome. According to the story, the city's

17.4 Giovanni Bologna. *The Rape of the Sabine Woman*. Completed 1583. Marble, height 13′6″ (4.1 m). Loggia dei Lanzi, Florence

founders, who came from across the sea, tried in vain to find wives among their neighbors, the Sabines. Finally, the men resorted to a trick. Having invited the entire Sabine tribe into Rome for a festival, they attacked them, took the women away by force, and thus ensured the future of their tribe. Giovanni Bologna's image sanitizes this act of raw power and violence, as the figures spiral upward in carefully rehearsed movements. He wished to display his virtuosity and saw his task only in formal terms: To carve in marble, on a massive scale, a sculptural composition that was to be seen from all sides. The contrast between form and content that the Mannerist tendency encouraged could not be clearer.

Rome Reformed

The Medici family's efforts to consolidate their power in Florence were aided by the Medici popes Leo X and Clement VII. Such papal manipulations of secular power, however, led to conflict between the papacy and the Holy Roman Empire, which resulted in the Sack of Rome in 1527 by the emperor Charles V's Habsburg troops. On Clement VII's death in 1534, the cardinals elected to the papacy a reform-minded member of a distinguished Roman family, Alessandro Farnese. As Pope Paul III, he tried to mediate among the great powers of Europe and encourage the emperor's efforts to bring German princes back to the Roman Church in the wake of the Protestant Reformation.

The spiritual crisis presented by the Reformation concerned Paul III deeply. In 1517 Martin Luther had challenged both the doctrine and the authority of the Church, and his reformed version of Christianity had taken wide hold in northern Europe (see Chapter 18). To respond to this challenge, Paul III called the Council of Trent, which began its deliberations in 1545 and issued its regulations in 1564. The council reaffirmed traditional Catholic doctrine and recommended reforms of liturgy, Church practices, and works of art.

The Catholic Church's most far-reaching and powerful weapon for combating what it considered heresy was the Roman INQUISITION, established in Italy in 1542 to investigate unapproved or suspect religious activities. Those found guilty of engaging in heresy could be imprisoned or executed. To further limit the spread of unorthodoxy, the Church compiled the Index of Prohibited Books in 1557.

Texts by suspect authors or on subjects deemed morally unhealthful could be seized or denied publication.

The reformed Catholic Church also found works of art useful to its goals. In large-scale projects in Rome, the papacy and other groups used the artistic vocabulary of the Renaissance to promote their reforms.

Michelangelo in Rome

Once elected to the papal throne, Paul III summoned Michelangelo to Rome in 1534 to execute several key projects for him. Rome remained his home for the rest of Michelangelo's life. The new mood of Rome during the Catholic Reformation (sometimes called the Counter-Reformation) may be reflected in the subject chosen for a major painting in the Sistine Chapel. Beginning in 1534, Michelangelo painted the powerful vision of the *Last Judgment* (**fig. 17.5**) on the altar wall. The fresco depicts the Catholic view of the end of the world, based on Gospel texts (Matthew 24:29–31), when Christ will return to judge mankind. It took six years to complete this huge painting, which was unveiled in 1541.

The fresco does not follow conventional representations of the theme. Images of the Last Judgment traditionally represent Hell as a place of torment; this is the way it is depicted in Giotto's *Last Judgment* at the Arena Chapel (fig. 13.10). Michelangelo's fresco de-emphasizes physical torments and stresses spiritual agony, expressed through violent physical contortions of the human body within a turbulent atmosphere. Angelic trumpeters signal the end of time, while the figure of Christ sits at the fulcrum of a wheel of action: As he raises his arm, the dead rise from the earth at the lower left and move toward Heaven where the assembly of saints crowds about him. On the right, the damned sink away from Heaven toward Charon, who ferries them to the underworld. (The presence of the pagan ferryman in a Christian image derives from Dante.) Throughout the fresco, naked human figures bend, twist, climb, fall, or gaze at Christ, their forms almost superhuman in their muscular power. Their nudity, which expresses Michelangelo's belief in the sanctity of the human body, disturbed his contemporaries, and shortly after he died in 1564 one of his assistants was commissioned to add bits of clothing to the figures. The fresco was cleaned in 1994, bringing out the brilliant colors, the compressed space, and the dramatic composition.

The INQUISITION began as a papal judicial process in the twelfth century, was codified in 1231 with the institution of excommunication, and was formalized in 1542 by Pope Paul III as the Holy Office. In Spain in 1478, it independently became an instrument of the state and was not abolished until 1834. In all its forms, its purpose was to rid the Catholic Church of heresy, though it was hardly free from political uses.

17.5 Michelangelo. *Last Judgment.* 1534–41. Fresco. Sistine Chapel, Vatican, Rome

These features link the work to the Mannerist style, though Michelangelo defies such labels.

ST. PETER'S Pope Paul III called on Michelangelo again for another project, the rebuilding of St. Peter's. The church had remained unfinished since Bramante's death in 1514, though other architects intervened at times in the project. When Michelangelo became the architect of St. Peter's in 1546, he altered Bramante's design for a centrally planned structure topped by a dome (**fig. 17.6**). Where Bramante intended four equal arms ending in identical façades, Michelangelo's plan compressed the interior spaces of the church and gave special focus to the east façade; other architects then changed these elements in the seventeenth century (see fig. 19.6). The dome and western elevations of the building preserve more of Michelangelo's design.

Where Bramante's design called for many steps and layers in the elevation (see fig. 16.5), Michelangelo unifies the tall structure by using a colossal order of pilasters across several stories of the exterior. The colossal order supports an entablature and attic story from which spring a high drum and tall dome. Michelangelo's dome has a powerful vertical emphasis that draws energy upward from the vertical pilasters of the elevation. He borrowed not only the double-shell construction but also the high curving profile of Brunelleschi's dome at Florence Cathedral (see fig. 15.3). Where Brunelleschi's dome has smooth planes and flat walls, Michelangelo surrounds his with sculptural forms. The vertical movement of the colossal pilasters is echoed by the double columns of the high drum and then continues upward over the dome to end in the tall lantern. The logic of this design is so persuasive that almost all domes built between 1600 and 1900 were influenced by it.

The Catholic Reformation and Il Gesù

As the dome for St. Peter's went up, the Council of Trent was discussing the reform of Roman Catholic hurch practices. The centralized plan Michelangelo designed for St. Peter's presented problems for the Catholic reformers, because the liturgical changes propounded by the council worked best within a basilican structure: The council decreed that believers should see the Elevation of the Host at the heart of the Mass, and this was best accomplished in a structure with a nave. Such a nave was added to St. Peter's in the seventeenth century (see page 395).

17.6 Michelangelo. St. Peter's, seen from the west. 1546–64; dome completed by Giacomo della Porta, 1590. Vatican, Rome

 Watch an architectural simulation about the plans for St. Peter's Basilica on myartslab.com

Catholic zeal for reform in the middle of the sixteenth century, which the Council of Trent exemplified, inspired the creation of a number of new religious orders. One of the most ambitious and energetic of these was the Society of Jesus, or Jesuits, founded by Ignatius of Loyola and promoted by Paul III. The order was approved in 1540. By 1550 their church, Il Gesù in Rome, was in the planning stages. The plan for the church came from one of Michelangelo's assistants, Giacomo Vignola (1507–1573), in 1568. Giacomo della Porta (ca. 1540–1602) designed the façade (**fig. 17.7**), completed in 1584. As it was the mother church of the Jesuits, Il Gesù's design must have been closely supervised so as to conform to the aims of the order. The Jesuits were at once intellectuals, mystics, and missionaries. The pope charged them to fight heresy in Europe and to spread Christianity to Asia and America. They required churches that adhered to the precepts of the Council of Trent—churches that would have impressive grandeur while avoiding excessive ornament. Their church of Il Gesù may serve as the architectural embodiment of the spirit of the Catholic Reformation.

In plan, Il Gesù is a compact basilica dominated by a high nave flanked by chapels, instead of aisles; as a result, the congregation assembles in one large, hall-like space with a clear view of the altar. Giacomo della Porta's façade is as important as the plan. He divides it into two stories with a strongly projecting entablature supported by paired pilasters; these derive from Michelangelo, with whom Della Porta had worked. The upper story repeats this idea on a somewhat smaller scale, with four instead of six pairs of supports. To bridge the difference in width between the two stories and to hide the roofline, Della Porta inserted two scroll-shaped buttresses. This device forms a graceful transition to the large pediment crowning the façade.

Della Porta masterfully integrates all the parts of the façade into a single whole: Both stories share the same vertical rhythm, which even the horizontal forms obey. For example, the broken entablature responds to the pilasters, as occurs in Michelangelo's Medici Chapel (fig. 17.1). In turn, the horizontal divisions determine the size of the vertical forms, so there is no colossal order. The sculptural treatment of the façade places greater emphasis on the main portal. Its double frame—two pediments resting on coupled pilasters and columns—projects beyond the rest of the façade and gives strong focus to the entire design. This

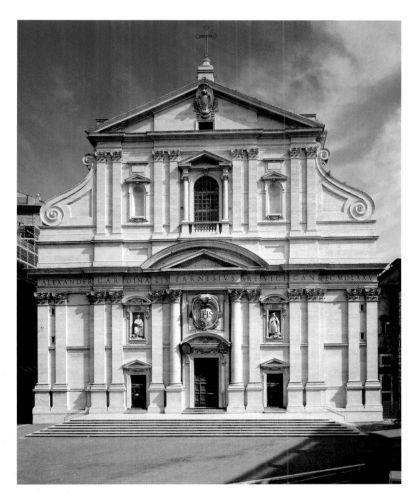

17.7 Giacomo della Porta. Façade of Il Gesù. ca. 1575–84. Rome

façade and the freedom to add movement and plastic dimension to it were an important precedent for church architecture built by the Jesuits and by others during ensuing centuries.

Cities and Courts in Northern Italy and Venice

The Papal States and the duchy of Tuscany dominated central Italy, but northern Italy comprised a number of smaller principalities and cities. Courts at Mantua, Urbino, Ferrara, and elsewhere competed for imperial titles and territorial gain. Some of the cities of the area tried to maintain their independence from the princely courts, with mixed results. France and the papacy controlled Parma as the sixteenth century opened, while Cremona belonged variously to Milan, to Venice, to France, and to Spain. Challenged at the opening of the sixteenth century by war and invasion, the republic of Venice succeeded in regaining control of northeastern Italy and reasserting its political and cultural authority.

Mantua

One of the most stable of the north Italian courts was Mantua, where the Gonzaga family retained the title of marquis into the sixteenth century. In the fifteenth century, Mantua had been host to influential artists, including Alberti and Mantegna. The family's traditions of patronage embraced women as well as men: Isabella d'Este, the wife of Francesco II Gonzaga, was one of the most active patrons of the early sixteenth century. Her son, Federico, became marquis in 1519, a title he held until Charles V created him duke in 1530. Campaigns for such titles often required displays of wealth and taste expressed through the arts. As part of his campaign, Federico II Gonzaga commissioned Giulio Romano (ca. 1499–1546) to design and decorate a villa for him outside Mantua, called the Palazzo del Te. There Federico could house his mistress and receive the emperor. Giulio Romano had been Raphael's chief assistant in Rome, but moved to Mantua in 1524.

Inside the Palazzo del Te, Giulio painted a series of rooms with illusionistic frescoes on themes drawn from antiquity. Unlike the frescoes by Mantegna in the *Camera Picta* of the Gonzaga Palace (fig. 15.22) or the frescoes of Raphael in Rome (fig. 16.10), these are not calm images of a dignified court or a distant and beautiful Golden Age, but vivid and dramatic expressions of power. In the Room of the Giants in the palazzo (**fig. 17.8**), Giulio depicted the gods expelling the giants from Mount Olympus as a cataclysm of falling bodies and columns. The viewer seems to see an entire temple collapsing. Falling architectural elements, toppled by the winds who appear as personifications in the upper corners, crush the huge figures of the giants. As if witnessing the power of the Olympian gods, the viewer feels drawn into the terror of the event. Of course, the duke himself was imagined as Zeus (Jupiter) in this concept, so the whole illusion speaks to the power of Duke Federico. Giulio uses the impact of Renaissance forms to flatter his patron.

Parma

The city of Parma became part of the Papal States in the sixteenth century, which brought it new wealth and status. The city was the birthplace of a gifted painter, Girolamo Francesco Maria Mazzola

17.8 Giulio Romano. *Fall of the Giants from Mount Olympus*, from the Sala dei Giganti. ca. 1530–32. Palazzo del Te, Mantua, Italy

(1503–1540), known as Parmigianino. He had made his reputation as a painter in Rome, Florence, and elsewhere before returning to Parma in 1530. A noblewoman there commissioned his most famous work, *The Madonna with the Long Neck* (**fig. 17.9**), in 1535 for a family chapel in the city. Parmigianino had made a deep study of Raphael, but he had a different ideal of beauty. In his painting, Mary's head appears as a perfect oval resting on a swanlike neck, while her body swells only to taper to her feet. (Her proportions resemble those of the large amphora offered by the figure at the left.) Parmigianino also replaces the High Renaissance ideal of stable compositions with more dramatic ones. Here, the sleeping Christ Child balances precariously on Mary's lap, as she lifts a boneless hand to her breast. The composition is as unbalanced as the postures: Heavily weighted to the left, open and distant to the right. All the figures have elongated limbs and ivory-smooth features, and the space is compressed. In Mannerist fashion, these elements draw attention to the artist's skill.

These choices may also reflect the meaning of the image. The large Christ Child in his mother's lap recalls the theme of the *pietà* and alludes to his death. Nor is the setting as arbitrary as it may seem. The gigantic column is a symbol often associated with the Madonna as the gateway to heaven and eternal life, as well as with her role as the Immaculate Conception (compare fig. 16.13). *The Madonna with the Long Neck* is a vision of unearthly perfection, with a cold and memorable elegance.

Cremona

The Mannerist elegance that Parmigianino achieved was but one stylistic option that artists and patrons of northern Italy could select. The work of Sofonisba Anguissola (1532–1625) of Cremona represents a different approach. The daughter of a nobleman in that north Italian city, Sofonisba received her training in painting as a professional. This was a very unusual circumstance, as most women artists of the Renaissance learned their craft at home as the daughters of artists. Sofonisba became famous in Italy as a painter; she communicated with artists all over the peninsula, including Michelangelo and Vasari. Her fame was such that Philip II of Spain hired her as his court artist. She moved to Spain in 1559 where she executed mostly portraits of imperial family members. She remained there until she married in 1573 and returned to Italy.

17.9 Parmigianino. *The Madonna with the Long Neck.* ca. 1535. Oil on panel, 7'1" × 4'4" (2.2 × 1.3 m). Galleria degli Uffizi, Florence

The reasons for her fame become clear in examining her self-portrait of about 1556 (**fig. 17.10**). Executed as a miniature, the portrait was probably a gift. In the image, the 24-year-old artist represents herself staring out at the spectator wearing sober black costume and with respectably plaited hair. Sofonisba prefers straightforward naturalism to Mannerist display. She holds a medallion with a still mysterious monogram. (It may be an anagram of her father's name, although this is not certain.) Around the medallion she claims the image as a work "by her hand done with the aid of a mirror." In the miniature, Sofonisba has wittily placed her hands next to the words "by whose hand"

17.10 Sofonisba Anguissola. *Self-Portrait*. ca. 1556. Oil on parchment, 3¼ × 2½" (8.3 × 6.4 cm). Museum of Fine Arts, Boston. Emma F. Munroe Fund, 60.155

(*ipsius manu ex*), so stressing the skill of her hands. The image advertises her skill to potential patrons.

Venice: The Serene Republic

After the crises of the beginning of the sixteenth century, Venice regained much of its territory and wealth by 1529. The city remained a nominal republic, controlled by ancient families, who commissioned works for their houses in town and for their villas in the country; artists therefore could choose from a wide variety of themes. The painters of Venice built on the achievements of Bellini, Giorgione, and Titian, while its architects experimented with classical forms.

PAINTING Titian's workshop dominated painting in the city throughout the sixteenth century. Like Michelangelo, he lived a long life, and he had numerous pupils to spread his style and techniques. Titian's creative output and reputation drew many artists to work in his shop, but he had a tremendous influence even on others. From the island of Crete (then owned by Venice), the young Domenikos Theotokopoulos, called El Greco, came to study in Titian's shop before heading to Spain (see page 371). The two leading painters in Venice after Titian, Veronese and Tintoretto, developed in different directions. Where Veronese made images that depend on early Titian works like the *Pesaro*

Madonna (fig. 16.13) and aimed for naturalism, Tintoretto exploited Titian's drama and fluid brushwork to create more dramatic and visionary images.

VERONESE Paolo Cagliari (1528–1588), called Paolo Veronese, made paintings that start from the naturalism inherent in Titian's style, but also include grand architectural frameworks and an interest in details of everyday reality, such as animals, textiles, and foodstuffs. His huge canvas called *The Feast in the House of Levi* (**fig. 17.11**), painted in 1573, exemplifies his style. The Dominicans who commissioned it for their refectory expected the painting to depict the Last Supper, following the pattern set by Leonardo's *The Last Supper* (fig. 16.2). The symmetrical composition of Veronese's image harks back to Leonardo's painting, while the festive mood of the scene echoes works of the 1520s by Titian; at first glance the picture looks like a High Renaissance work made 50 years too late. Veronese, however, is less interested than artists of that period in conveying spiritual or psychological depth or theological messages. Even its theme is ambiguous: The painting depicts a sumptuous banquet with Jesus at the center, but the scene includes so many unidentified figures, subsidiary vignettes, and noisy characters that it is unclear which event from the Gospel Veronese intended.

As with his contemporaries elsewhere in Italy, Veronese took liberties with the subject matter. For this, he was summoned by the religious tribunal of the Inquisition in 1573 on the charge of filling his picture with "buffoons, drunkards, Germans, dwarfs, and similar vulgarities" unsuited to its theme. The account of the trial shows that the tribunal thought Veronese's representation of the Last Supper was irreverent. In the face of their questions, he settled on a different title, which permitted him to leave the offending details in place. In rebuffing the Inquisition, the artist claimed the privilege to "paint pictures as I see fit."

TINTORETTO Veronese's contemporary Jacopo Robusti (1519–1594), called Tintoretto, made paintings of a more spiritual character. Tintoretto reportedly wanted "to paint like Titian and to design like Michelangelo." He did not imitate the High Renaissance phases of those artists' careers, however, but absorbed their later styles, which are more expressive and less realistic in their effects. Tintoretto's final major work, *The Last Supper*, finished in 1594 (**fig. 17.12**), seems to deny in every possible way

17.11 Paolo Veronese. *The Feast in the House of Levi*. 1573. Oil on canvas, 18′2″ × 42′ (5.5 × 12.8 m). Galleria dell'Accademia, Venice

Read the document related to Paolo Veronese on myartslab.com

17.12 Jacopo Tintoretto. *The Last Supper*. 1592–94. Oil on canvas, 12′ × 18′8″ (3.7 × 5.7 m). San Giorgio Maggiore, Venice

the balance and clarity of Leonardo's version of the theme painted almost exactly a century before (fig. 16.2). Tintoretto places Jesus at the physical center of the composition, but the small figure in the middle distance is distinguished mainly by his brilliant halo. The artist barely hints at the human drama of Judas' betrayal; Judas can be seen isolated on the near side of the table across from Jesus, but his role is so insignificant that he could almost be mistaken for an attendant. The table sits at a sharp angle to the picture plane, in exaggerated perspective. This arrangement relates the picture's space to the actual space for which it was commissioned, in the monastic church of San Giorgio Maggiore in Venice. Tintoretto used perspective to link the pictorial space to the viewpoint of the Benedictine monks who took communion before the painting.

Like Veronese, Tintoretto fills the scene with attendants, containers of food and drink, and domestic animals. At the center, Jesus offers his body and blood, in the form of bread and wine, to the disciples. The smoke from the blazing oil lamp miraculously turns into clouds of angels, who animate the upper portion of the picture and blur the distinction between the natural and the supernatural. The image becomes a magnificently orchestrated vision. Tintoretto wants to make visible the miracle of the Eucharist—the transubstantiation of earthly into divine food. During the Catholic Reformation, the central importance of this sacrament to Catholic doctrine was forcefully reasserted.

PALLADIO AND LATE RENAISSANCE ARCHITECTURE

Like patrons elsewhere in Italy, Venetian aristocrats commissioned works inspired by the ancient world. When they wanted buildings in the antique manner, they turned to Andrea Palladio (1506–1580), who dominated the field of architecture in Venice. Palladio worked mostly in his native town of Vicenza, and elsewhere in the Venetian territory, but he built many churches in Venice.

Palladio's patrons hired him to build town houses and country villas that would express their own wealth and social status. Palladio designed these structures following his own interpretation of ancient precepts that derived from his study of Vitruvius and Roman architecture. The Villa Rotonda (**fig. 17.13**), a country residence built near Vicenza beginning in 1567, exemplifies his logical approach to building. Designed on a central plan, the villa consists of a square block topped by a dome; the ancient veneration for the circle and square underlie the design. What is more, all four sides of this villa have identical porches in the shape of temple fronts. The resulting structure exhibits the balance and clarity of ancient forms, while serving the needs

17.13 Andrea Palladio. Villa Rotonda. ca. 1567–70. Vicenza, Italy

of his aristocratic patrons. Palladio's use of the temple front here reflects the period's belief that great men required houses that were dignified, beautiful, and harmonious. His design also takes advantage of the pleasing views offered in every direction by the site. Beautifully correlated with the walls behind and the surrounding vistas, the porches of the Villa Rotonda give the structure an air of serene dignity and festive grace that is enhanced by the sculptures on the façades.

Palladio's approach to architecture was inspired by his study of the ancients, but his practical exploitation of ancient ideals resulted in buildings that express Renaissance values. His design processes, based on proportion, and his innovative building techniques could be reduced to formulas for other architects to follow. When Palladio published his FOUR BOOKS OF ARCHITECTURE in 1570, his designs and the principles from antiquity that informed them would circulate his ideas around the world.

POINTS OF REFLECTION

17.1 Compare the commissions of two generations of the Gonzaga family, by comparing Mantegna's *Camera Picta* with Giulio Romano's *Fall of the Giants*.

17.2 Select a work from the chapter that is usually considered Mannerist: does the definition hold? Are all patrons of Mannerist works members of courts?

17.3 Consider how the travels of artists helped to spread stylistic innovations, not only in the sixteenth century, but also in earlier times.

17.4 Analyze the distinctive traditions of Venetian painting in the fifteenth and sixteenth centuries. What characteristics do you see carrying through these two centuries?

17.5 The architecture of the later sixteenth century proved very influential across the globe. Investigate the historical and cultural reasons why these buildings proved so inspiring for later architects.

✓—**Study** and review on myartslab.com

ART IN TIME

● **1519—Michelangelo's New Sacristy and Medici tombs begun**

● 1527—Habsburg army sacks Rome

● **ca. 1530—Giulio Romano's** *Fall of the Giants from Mount Olympus* **in Palazzo del Te**

● 1537—Cosimo I ruler in Florence

● 1540—Society of Jesus (Jesuits) approved by pope

● **1541—Michelangelo completes the** *Last Judgment*

● 1545—Council of Trent opens. Catholic Reformation begins

● **ca. 1546—Bronzino's** *Allegory of Venus*

● 1570—Palladio's *Four Books of Architecture* published

● 1571—Venetian and Spanish navies defeat Turkish fleet at Lepanto

● 1573—Veronese appears before the Inquisition

CHAPTER

18 Renaissance and Reformation throughout Sixteenth-Century Europe

POINTS OF INQUIRY

18.1 Trace the spread of Italian Renaissance style throughout Europe.
18.2 Define the impact of the Reformation on art making in Northern Europe.
18.3 Investigate sixteenth-century patrons at the courts and in urban centers.
18.4 Identify new themes and subjects in sixteenth-century Northern European art.
18.5 Recognize the works and influences on key artists of the period.

(((•—[Listen to the chapter audio on myartslab.com

In addition to the religious challenge of the Protestant Reformation and the new cultural expressions of the Renaissance, Europeans outside Italy witnessed the growing power of large centralized states in France, England, Spain, and the Holy Roman Empire, and the expansion of Europe's economic reach around the globe. The Reformation changed the map, as whole communities, cities, and even states changed their religious affiliation, fracturing the religious unity of Europe (see **map 18.1**). While France and Spain remained loyal to the Roman Catholic Church, religious sectarianism divided Germany, England, and the Netherlands.

The arts throughout Europe changed in response to these new conditions. Because Protestant reformers believed sculpture to be close to idolatry, the medium of painting increased in importance. Because religious patronage waned, artists turned to secular themes, which appealed to patrons in both the cities and the courts. To compete on the open market, artists began to specialize in particular subjects or themes. As artists absorbed Italian compositions, ideal figure

types, and admiration for antiquity, Italian Renaissance style spread across Europe. Patrons in the courts found Italian style particularly useful for emphasizing their power, while Catholic rulers often used Italianate forms to affirm their loyalty to Rome.

France and Spain: Catholic Courts and Italian Influence

France was fertile ground for the importation of Italian ideas. French kings had been intervening in Italy for centuries, and knew what was happening in its art and architecture. Francis I (r. 1515–1547) showed his admiration for Italian art by inviting Leonardo da Vinci to work for him. Francis's generous patronage made his court a magnet for many artists from Italy and from elsewhere in Europe. French traditions were maintained, too, as local architects interpreted Italian ideas.

Italian forms dominate in the chateaux, or castles, that Francis built. In 1528, he decided

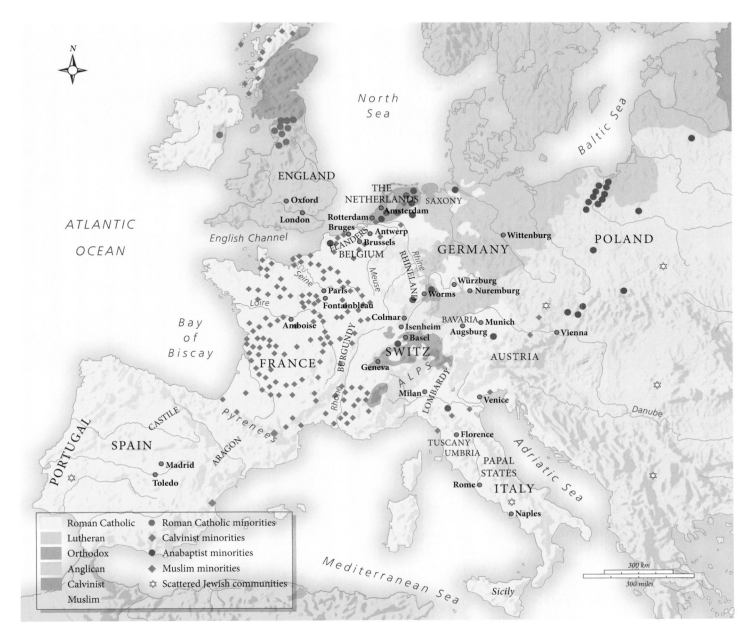

Map 18.1 The religious situation in Europe in the late sixteenth century

Legend:
- Roman Catholic
- Lutheran
- Orthodox
- Anglican
- Calvinist
- Muslim
- ● Roman Catholic minorities
- ◆ Calvinist minorities
- ● Anabaptist minorities
- ◆ Muslim minorities
- ✡ Scattered Jewish communities

300 km
300 miles

to expand a medieval hunting lodge amid the forests of Fontainebleau, south of Paris. What began as a modest enlargement soon developed into a sprawling palace. The stonemason Gilles Le Breton (d. 1553) designed the earliest sections, though many other architects worked there over the years. Le Breton established the design of the Cour du Cheval Blanc (Court of the White Horse) during Francis's lifetime (**fig. 18.1**). Generations of patrons and architects contributed to its building—the staircase in the courtyard was built by Jean Androuet Du Cerceau in 1634—yet the façade still preserves its Renaissance aspect and exemplifies the synthesis of local and Italianate ideas that occurred at Fontainebleau.

This entryway to the palace fronts a square courtyard organized by geometric plantings. Composed with rectangular pavilions at regular intervals, the façade employs a vocabulary from Italian architecture: Pilasters articulate each story and entablatures tie the whole façade together horizontally even as the pilasters on the lowest level recall the rusticated surfaces of Italian palaces (see fig. 15.12). These elements combine with a French taste for height: The rooflines and windows boast vertical proportions and distinguish the French interpretation of the palace from its Italian models. Fontainebleau set a fashion for French translations of Italianate architecture that was followed for nearly all French chateaux for the next 250 years.

18.1 Gilles Le Breton. Cour du Cheval Blanc (Court of the White Horse), Chateau of Fontainebleau. 1528–40

 Explore the architectural panoramas of Chateau of Fontainebleau on myartslab.com

18.2 Francesco Primaticcio. Detail of *Stucco Figures*. ca. 1541–45. Gallery of Francis I, designed for the Room of the Duchesse d'Étampes. Chateau of Fontainebleau, France

King Francis's love of Italian art is apparent throughout Fontainebleau. The artists, who came from all over Italy to work on the chateau, mostly worked in a Mannerist style, creating lavish interiors to flatter the king. For example, Francesco Primaticcio (1504–1570), born in Bologna and trained by Giulio Romano, combined painting and sculpted imagery for the room of the king's mistress, the Duchesse d'Étampes (**fig. 18.2**). In this room, Primaticcio surrounds his paintings with frames held by stucco nudes; these have the long, elegant proportions of figures by Parmigianino (see fig. 17.9). The willowy female figures have no specific allegorical significance, although their role recalls the nudes of the Sistine Chapel ceiling. They enframe paintings devoted to Alexander the Great, executed by assistants from Primaticcio's designs. The one shown depicts the Greek artist Apelles painting Alexander with his mistress, Campaspe; Alexander gave her to Apelles when the legendary painter fell in love with her. Roman texts of this subject characterized this gift as a mark of Alexander's great respect for his court artist. The picture draws a parallel between Alexander and Francis I, and between Campaspe and the duchess, the king's mistress, who had taken Primaticcio under her protection. Such mixtures of eroticism and power appealed greatly to the courtly audience for which Primaticcio worked.

Spain and Italianate Style

Spain became a world power in the sixteenth century, fueled by wealth from the newly colonized Americas and its rule over significant portions of Europe. The Spanish King Charles V, who was also Holy Roman Emperor, controlled the Netherlands, much of Central Europe, and parts of Italy as well as Spain. When he abdicated in 1556, he split his holdings between his son Philip and his brother Ferdinand. Ferdinand took control of the traditional Habsburg territories in Central Europe. Philip II reigned as king of Spain, the Netherlands, and New Spain in the Americas from 1556 to 1598. After fending off the Turkish advance into Europe in 1571, the very Catholic Philip took aim at Protestant regions, though less successfully. His attempts to quash the rebellion of the Calvinist Northern Netherlands ultimately produced the independent state of Holland; his attempt to invade England in 1588 strengthened England's stature.

EL GRECO Following Philip's lead, members of the Spanish court remained staunchly Roman Catholic. They commissioned churches and church furnishings throughout the century, so Italian artists moved to Spain looking for work, and Spanish artists went to Italy to study. The best-known painter of sixteenth-century Spain, Domenikos Theotokopoulos (1541–1614), called El Greco, came from Crete, then under Venetian rule. He thus came under Venetian influence, producing painterly and colorful works like those of Tintoretto; to this he fused his admiration for Raphael, Michelangelo, and Italian Mannerism. He arrived in Spain in 1576/77 and settled in Toledo.

El Greco's painting of *The Burial of Count Orgaz*, executed in 1586 in the church of Santo Tomé in Toledo (**fig. 18.3**), exemplifies his patronage and style. The painting sits above the tomb of Count Orgaz, who had died in 1323; he was so

18.3 El Greco. *The Burial of Count Orgaz.* 1586. Oil on canvas, 16′ × 11′10″ (4.9 × 3.6 m). Santo Tomé, Toledo, Spain

 View the Closer Look for *The Burial of Count Orgaz* on myartslab.com

pious, his admirers claimed, that St. Stephen and St. Augustine appeared at his funeral and lowered the body into its grave. El Greco depicts the miracle as a contemporary event: He portrays many of the local nobility and clergy of his time among the witnesses to it. With its focus on the saints and the reputation of the deceased, the painting expresses the Roman Catholic position that saints serve as intercessors with Heaven and that believers must perform good works to achieve salvation.

The display of color and texture in the armor and vestments reflects El Greco's Venetian training. An angel carries the count's soul (a small, cloudlike figure at the center) to Heaven. Where the lower half of the painting seems very concrete, the celestial assembly in the upper half looks very different. Every form—clouds, limbs, draperies—takes part in a sweeping, flamelike movement toward the figure of Christ at the top. El Greco's compressed space, unearthly light, and weightless bodies share stylistic features with Italian Mannerist works such as Pontormo's *Pietà* (fig. 17.2). The viewer standing before the actual grave of Count Orgaz sees in El Greco's painting the reenactment of the miraculous burial, so the space of the painting links directly to the space of the viewer. El Greco directs viewers from their own reality toward a vision of Heaven. His powerful works struck a chord with his orthodox Spanish patrons.

Central Europe: The Reformation and Art

While Italy, France, and Spain remained mostly Catholic, elsewhere in Europe the religious and artistic situation was more complex. Emperor Charles V headed the regions that make up present-day Germany, Austria, Hungary, and the Czech Republic. The emperor controlled these independent political units only nominally. The Reformation fractured their religious unity after 1517 (see box: Cultural Context: The Protestant Reformation, below). The spread of the reformed faiths led to wars throughout Central Europe that finally ended with the Peace of Augsburg in 1555. This compromise allowed the rulers of individual regions to choose the faith for their region's inhabitants,

The Protestant Reformation

I N OCTOBER 1517, Martin Luther, a former Augustinian friar and professor of theology at the University of Wittenberg, issued a public challenge to both the theology and the institutional practices of the Catholic Church. In his famous *Ninety-Five Theses*, which he nailed to the church door at Wittenberg Castle, Luther condemned the Catholic practice of selling indulgences—promises of redemption of sins; he argued also against the veneration of Mary and the saints. Making a fundamental critique of Catholicism, Luther claimed that the Bible and natural reason were the sole bases of religious authority, and that the intervention of clerics and saints was unnecessary for salvation, which was freely given by God. It followed, then, that religious authority depended not on the pope, but on the individual conscience of each believer. In response, the Catholic Church excommunicated him in 1521. But many Christians in Europe accepted his critique, the result of which eventually fueled political instability, rebellions, and wars. Many areas of northern Germany converted to the Protestant reform, while southern regions, like Bavaria, remained Catholic. In rethinking these basic issues of faith, Luther was joined by other religious reformers.

The Swiss pastor Ulrich Zwingli stressed individual access to the scriptures and preaching. His literal reading of the Bible led him to denounce not only the sale of indulgences, but the visual arts as well. Above all, the reformers worried about the issues of grace and free will in attaining faith and salvation. By the time of Zwingli's death in 1531, he and other reformers had defined the main elements of Protestant theology. Around mid-century, John Calvin of Geneva promoted his vision of a moral life based on a literal reading of scripture.

Studying the Bible required literacy, so reformers urged that both girls and boys be taught to read. The invention of the printing press furthered the spread of Protestantism, by putting the Bible in the hands of many believers. The implications of the Reformation were enormous for the liturgy, for social life, and for art. The Catholic Church would change as well. Luther's complaints spurred reforms beginning in the mid-sixteenth century and continuing into the seventeenth. This Catholic Reformation would have its own effects on European art and life.

furthering the spread of the reformed faiths and firming up the political divisions. The repercussions for art were equally important. While Luther saw the value of art as a tool for teaching, some of the more radical reformers considered the many forms of medieval and Renaissance religious art as idolatrous, and they encouraged ICONOCLASM, or the destruction of images. As religious commissions dried up, artists had to find new styles, new subjects, and new markets for their work.

Catholic Patrons in Early Sixteenth-Century Germany

Not all regions of Central Europe converted to the reformed faiths, and it was not until the 1520s that the Reformation took wide hold, so Catholic patrons continued to commission religious objects throughout the sixteenth century. The painter Matthias Gothart Nithart, who was known for

centuries only as Grünewald (ca. 1475–1528), executed one memorable example. Between 1509/10 and 1515, he painted a transforming triptych called the *Isenheim Altarpiece* for the monastery church of the Order of St. Anthony at Isenheim, in Alsace, France.

This church accommodated the monks of the order and the patients of their hospital, which served people suffering from a disease caused by eating spoiled rye, called St. Anthony's Fire. The painful symptoms of this disorder include intestinal disorders, gangrenous limbs, and hallucinations. Treatment consisted mostly of soothing baths and sometimes the amputation of limbs. Sitting on the high altar, Grünewald's altarpiece reflects the hospital's mission. Its painted panels enclose a carved wooden shrine of St. Anthony. Nine panels organized in two sets of movable wings open in three stages or "views." The first of these views,

ICONOCLASM comes from Greek roots that, combined, mean image-breaking. Iconoclasts destroy images for political or religious reasons. While the Byzantine Empire endured a period of iconoclasm in the seventh and eighth centuries (see Chapter 8), several waves of image destruction occurred in the wake of the Reformation in Europe. The more radical reformed faiths deplored the Catholic tradition of religious images and relics; some encouraged the destruction of images. This resulted in a great loss of works of art from earlier periods.

18.4 Matthias Grünewald. *Isenheim Altarpiece* (closed): *The Crucifixion*; predella: *Lamentation.* ca. 1509–15. Oil on panel, main body 9'9½" × 10'9" (2.97 × 3.28 m); predella 2'5½" × 11'2" (0.75 × 3.4 m). Musée d'Unterlinden, Colmar, France

when all the wings are closed, shows *The Crucifixion* in the center panel (**fig. 18.4**). Viewers saw this stage on weekdays.

Grünewald depicts Christ's body on the Cross on a heroic scale, so that it dominates the other figures and the landscape. The Crucifixion becomes a lonely event silhouetted against a ghostly landscape and a blue-black sky. Despite the darkness of the landscape, an eerie light bathes the foreground figures to heighten awareness of them. On the left, in a white garment, Mary swoons at the sight of her tortured son; St. John's red robe accenuates her paleness. Below the Cross, Mary Magdalen kneels in grief. On the right, John the Baptist points to the crucified Christ with the words, "He must increase, and I must decrease," explaining the significance of Christ's sacrifice. The lamb at his feet bleeds into a chalice, as does the lamb in the central panel of the *Ghent Altarpiece* (fig. 14.5), alluding to the Eucharist. In the **predella** below, a tomb awaits the tormented body while Christ's mother and friends bid farewell. The predella slides apart at Christ's knees, so victims of amputation may have seen their own suffering reflected in this image.

On Sundays and feast days, the outer wings were opened and the mood of the *Isenheim Altarpiece* changed dramatically (**fig. 18.5**). All three scenes in this view—*The Annunciation*, the *Madonna and Child with Angels*, and *The Resurrection*—celebrate events

as jubilant as the Crucifixion is somber. Depicting the cycle of salvation, from the Incarnation to the Resurrection, this view of the altarpiece offered the afflicted a form of spiritual medicine while reminding them of the promise of Heaven. Throughout these panels, Grünewald has depicted forms of therapy recommended for sufferers at the hospital: Music, herbs, baths, and light. The contrast of the body of the dead Jesus in the predella with the Resurrected Christ in the right panel offers consolation to the dying.

Grünewald's color draws the eye through the composition. Reds and pinks in the left panel carry through the central panels to end at the brilliant colors surrounding the Risen Christ on the right. The simple Gothic chapel in which the Annunciation takes place gives way in the next panel to a fantastic tabernacle where choirs of angels play stringed instruments and sing. Beneath that tabernacle appears a figure of the Virgin, crowned and glowing like a lit candle. The central image of the Madonna holding her child in a tender embrace gives way to a vision of Heaven, also made of pure light. These elements lead the eye to the right panel, where the body of Christ appears to float above the stone sarcophagus into which it had been placed in the predella. The guards set to watch the tomb are knocked senseless by the miracle. Their figures, carefully arranged in a perspectival display,

18.5 Matthias Grünewald. *Isenheim Altarpiece* (open): *The Annunciation; Madonna and Child with Angels; The Resurrection.* ca. 1509–15. Oil on panel, each wing 8′10″ × 4′8″ (2.69 × 1.42 m); center panel 8′10″ × 11′2½″ (2.69 × 3.41 m). Musée d'Unterlinden, Colmar, France

contrast with the weightless and transfigured body of Christ. This figure differs dramatically from the figure on the Cross; his body bears no scars and the proportions are closer to the Italian ideal seen in Piero della Francesca's *Resurrection* (fig. 15.18). Grünewald's oil technique, his brilliant use of color, and his detailed rendering of objects derive from Northern European art of the fifteenth century, but the *Isenheim Altarpiece* also demonstrates his awareness of Italian perspective. Grünewald's aim is to create an emotional response with the impact of a vision.

Albrecht Dürer as Renaissance Artist

Grünewald's contemporary, Albrecht Dürer (1471–1528), is the key figure for the Renaissance in Germany. Like Grünewald, Dürer's style began in the traditions of Northern European realism, but he also delved deeply into the innovations of the Italian Renaissance. Trained as a painter and printmaker in his native Nuremberg, he traveled in northern Europe and Venice in 1494/95; these journeys changed his view of the world and the artist's place in it. Dürer adopted the ideal of the artist as a gentleman and humanistic scholar that had taken hold in Italy. His painting technique owes much to the Flemish masters, but making copies of Italian works taught him many of the lessons of Italian art. Dürer synthesized these traditions in his paintings and graphic works (prints and drawings). His influence on sixteenth-century art spread through his prints, which circulated all over Europe.

APOCALYPSE Trained to make both woodcuts and engravings, Dürer expanded the possibilities of each. Individual patrons did not commission prints; they were made for sale on the open market. Dürer had to invest his own time and materials in these projects. He chose themes that sold well. One of his biggest successes came in 1498. As the year 1500 approached, many people believed that the Second Coming of Christ was imminent and prepared for the Millennium. With an eye to the market for things pertaining to popular fears about the end of time, Dürer produced a woodcut series illustrating the Apocalypse. This series was his most ambitious graphic work in the years following his return from Italy. The gruesome vision of *The Four Horsemen of the Apocalypse* (**fig. 18.6**) offers the viewer a frightening visualization of the text of the Book of Revelation. The woodcut depicts War, Conquest, Famine, and Death overrunning

the population of the earth. The physical energy and full-bodied volume of the figures in the *Apocalypse* woodcuts series derives partly from Dürer's experience of Italian art, although he compresses the space to present the figures in an otherworldly flatness. Dürer added to the woodcut medium some of the devices of engraving. He replaced the broad contours and occasional hatchings, used to define form in earlier woodcuts, with a wide range of hatching marks, varied width of lines, and strong contrasts of black and white, giving his woodcuts ambitious pictorial effects. (Compare, for example, the *Buxheim St. Christopher* of 1423 shown in fig. 14.12 with Dürer's woodcut.) He set a standard that soon transformed the technique of woodcut all over Europe.

18.6 Albrecht Dürer. *The Four Horsemen of the Apocalypse.* 1498. Woodcut, 15½ × 11⅙″ (39.4 × 28.1 cm). Yale University Art Gallery, 0New Haven. Library Transfer, Gift of Paul Meoon, B.A. 1929, 1956. 16.3e

ADAM AND EVE Dürer's fusion of Northern European and Italian traditions informs his engraving entitled *Adam and Eve* of 1504 (**fig. 18.7**). He depicts the biblical subject of the first parents as two ideal nudes: they look like Apollo and Venus in a densely wooded forest. Carefully detailed animals, trees, and foliage accompany the human forms. To achieve this detail, Dürer enlarged the vocabulary of descriptive marks an engraver could use: The lines taper and swell; they intersect at varying angles; marks start and stop and dissolve into dots. The result is a monochrome image with a great tonal and textural range.

Dürer chose very deliberately the animals that populate the Garden of Eden. The cat, rabbit, ox, and elk are symbols of the medieval theory that bodily fluids, called humors, controlled personality. The cat represents the choleric humor, quick to anger; the ox the phlegmatic humor, lethargic and slow; the elk stands for the melancholic humor, sad and serious; and the rabbit for the sanguine, energetic and sensual. In this moment before the fall, the humors coexist in balance and the humans retain an ideal beauty. The tonal effects balance and unify the composition. Dürer's print, which he signed prominently on the plaque by Adam's head, made an enormous impact.

Albrecht Dürer as Reformation Artist

Dürer became an early and enthusiastic follower of Martin Luther. His new faith informs the growing austerity of style and subject in his religious works after 1520. A late painting, *The Four Apostles* (**fig. 18.8**), represents the climax of this trend. In 1526, Dürer presented these two panels to the city of Nuremberg, which had joined the Lutheran camp. The four saints are fundamental to Protestant doctrine. John and Paul, Luther's favorite authors of scripture, face one another in the foreground, with Peter and Mark behind them. Quotations from their writings, inscribed below in Luther's translation into German, warn the citizenry not to mistake human error and pretense for the will of God. The heavily draped apostles have the weight and presence of figures by Raphael (see fig. 16.10). Through the power of his paintings, the portable medium of prints, and the alumni of his workshop, Dürer was the most influential artist of sixteenth-century Germany.

18.7 Albrecht Dürer. *Adam and Eve*. 1504. Engraving, 9⅝ × 7⅝″ (24.4 × 19.3 cm). Yale University Art Gallery, New Haven. Fritz Achelis Memorial Collection, Gift of Frederic George Achelis, B.A. 1907; reacquired in 1972 with the Henry J. Heinz II, B.A. 1931, Fund; Everett V. Meeks, B.A. 1901, Fund; and Stephen Carlton Clark, B.A. 1903, Fund, 1925.29

Read the document related to Albrecht Dürer on myartslab.com

18.8 Albrecht Dürer. *The Four Apostles.* 1523–26. Oil on panel, each 7′1″ × 2′6″ (2.16 × 0.76 m). Alte Pinakothek, Munich, Germany

Protestant Courts and Cities and New Forms of Art

The realignment of German culture and society produced by the Reformation required artists to adapt their styles and subject matter for the reformed faiths. The ambivalence of the reformed faiths toward images created challenges for artists throughout the century. Courtly patrons hired artists to make images on classicizing themes; these images combined local styles emphasizing detail, texture, and the natural world with forms from Italy.

The Reformation Image

The problem of the appropriate use of images for the reformed faiths concerned Lucas Cranach the Elder (1472–1553), a close friend of Martin Luther. He attempted to cast Luther's doctrines into visual form with prints and paintings that expressed his teachings. A woodcut of around 1530 entitled *An Allegory of Law and Grace* (**fig. 18.9**) contrasts the difference between the fate of a Catholic and a Lutheran. The left side depicts the Catholic doctrine that the children of Adam and Eve, stained by Original Sin, must perform specific deeds following the Law of Moses; yet at the Last

Ro. .1. Es wird offenbart gottes zorn von hymel vber
aller menschen gottlos wesen vnd vnrecht

Isaie .7. Der Herr wird euch selbs ein zeichen geben/Sihe/eine Jungfraw
wird schwanger sein vnd einen son geperen.

Text along bottom of woodcut:
Sie sind alle zumal sundere/ | Die sunde ist des todes spies/ | Durch gesetz kompt erkentnus | Der gerechte lebt seines glaus | Sihe/das ist Gottes lamb/das der | Der tod ist verschlungen ym sieg/
vnd mangeln/das sie sich | Aber das gesetz ist der sunden | der sunden Ro. .3. Das ge- | bens Ro.1.Wir halten das | wellt sunde tregt S.Joh.bap.Jo.1. | Tod/wo ist dein spies? Helle/wo
gottes nicht rhümen mugen | krafft 1.Co.15. Das gesetz | setz vnd die propheten gehen bis | ein mensch gerecht werde | In der heyligunge des geystes/zum | ist dein sieg? Danck habe Gott/
Ro.3. | richtet zorn an Ro.4. | auff Johannis zeit. Math.11. | durch den glauben/on werg | ghorsam/vnd besprengung des | der vns den sieg gibt durch Ihe-
| | | des gesetze. Ro.3. | bluts Ihesu Christi 1.Pet..1. | sum christum vnsern herrn 1.Cor.

18.9 Lucas Cranach the Elder. *An Allegory of Law and Grace.* ca. 1530. Woodcut, 10⅝ × 12¾" (27 × 32.4 cm). The British Museum, London

Judgment, the soul is consigned to Hell. The right side depicts Luther's position: the blood of Christ's Crucifixion washes over the believer, because faith in Christ alone assures salvation. Compared to Dürer's woodcuts, this image seems rather simple and straightforward, without complex tonalities, illusions of space, or an emphasis on textures. Cranach makes the image as legible and accessible as the text, subordinating artistic effects to clarity. In addition to such overtly Lutheran images, Cranach made portraits and mythologies for German courts.

Landscape

Artists in southern Germany and Austria fell under the influence of Dürer and Cranach in the first half of the sixteenth century, even as they wrestled with changes in the art market caused by the Reformation. Albrecht Altdorfer (ca. 1480–1538), who spent most of his career in Bavaria, belonged to a group of artists who chose to specialize in landscape paintings. Altdorfer's *The Battle of Issos* (**fig. 18.10**) expresses his fascination with the natural world. The painting, made in 1529, is one of a series of images depicting the exploits of historic heroes for the Munich palace of William IV, duke of Bavaria. In a sweeping landscape, Altdorfer depicts Alexander the Great's victory over Darius of Persia, which took place in 333 BCE at Issos. To make the subject clear, Altdorfer provides an

explanatory text on the tablet suspended in the sky, inscriptions on the banners, and a label on Darius' fleeing chariot. The artist follows ancient descriptions of the number and kind of combatants in the battle and alludes to the specific locale of the battle.

Altdorfer gives the spectator a viewpoint looking down on the action from a great height. From this omniscient perspective, a viewer must search for the two leaders lost in the antlike mass of their own armies. The drama of nature is more elaborated than the human actors: One can almost feel the rotation of the globe as the sun sets in the distance and the moon rises. The curve of the earth, the drama of the clouds, the craggy mountain peaks overwhelm the human figures. Altdorfer gives the battle an earthshaking importance, which may well have been the case. However, the soldiers' armor and the fortified town in the distance belong unmistakably to the sixteenth century, which encourages us to look for contemporary significance. The work dates to the period when the Ottoman Turks threatened Vienna. Altdorfer's image suggests that the contemporary battle between Europeans and Turks has the same global significance as Alexander's battle with Darius had in the fourth century BCE.

Reformation England: The Tudor Portrait

If Central Europe boasted numerous courts, the Tudor dynasty dominated sixteenth-century England. The ambitious Henry VIII, who reigned from 1509 to 1547, wanted England to be a power broker in Europe. Henry sought to annul his marriage to Catherine of Aragon, the aunt of Charles V, but the pope thwarted his plans. Henry broke away from Roman Catholicism and established himself as the head of the Church of England. Marrying often after this, he had three children, who succeeded him as Edward VI, Mary I, and ELIZABETH I. The latter ruled into the seventeenth century, and oversaw the expansion of England's navy and colonies, when England became a world power.

The Tudor court emphasized portraiture among the arts. Henry VIII appointed a German artist, Hans Holbein the Younger (1497–1543), as his court painter. Born in Augsburg, Holbein moved to Basel in search of work. But the spread of the Reformation to that Swiss city dried up opportunities for visual artists, so Holbein went to England. He found his first patrons among merchants and diplomats, who were often also Humanists. One

18.10 Albrecht Altdorfer. *The Battle of Issos.* 1529. Oil on panel, 6′2″ × 3′11″ (1.57 × 1.19 m). Alte Pinakothek, Munich, Germany

of his largest works (**fig. 18.11**) depicts two ambassadors from France, Jean de Dinteville and Georges de Selve. Painted in 1533, when the English court was in turmoil because of the king's impending break with Rome, the image displays Holbein's artistic origins and his gifts as a portraitist. The two subjects of the painting were friends, and Holbein represents them in full length, standing in a draped room with a tall double-tiered table between them. Jean de Dinteville, on the left, wears an elaborate fur-lined tunic over his velvet garment, as well as a chain identifying him as a member of the Order of St. Michael, a French chivalric order. Opposite him stands Bishop Georges de Selve, in his cleric's collar and warm gown. He bears no weapon or baton of office, as his friend does, but rests his arm on the Bible placed on the upper tier of the table. Holbein distinguishes each man's features and social station in the portrait. His rendering of textures, surfaces,

and details harks back to Jan van Eyck, as in fact the standing double portrait does (see fig. 14.6).

Holbein emphasizes the setting as well as the two figures. Objects that reflect the interests of the two men sit on the table between them. The bishop was a great patron of music, an enthusiasm alluded to by the presence of a lute. Below the lute is an open book featuring hymns written by Martin Luther. The lute itself has a broken string—making it an emblem of discord. Instruments that measure time (a sundial) or track the constellations sit on the upper tier. Two globes—a celestial globe above and a terrestrial one below—appear closer to de Dinteville. (His own town is marked on the terrestrial globe.) These objects contrast the study of earthly and heavenly subjects, with the implication that discord and division rule the earthly sphere. Before all looms an anamorphic representation of a skull: It is set into a dramatically exaggerated perspective so

18.11 Hans Holbein the Younger. *Jean de Dinteville and Georges de Selve* ("*The Ambassadors*"). 1533. Oil on panel, 6'9½" × 6'10¼" (2.07 × 2.09 m). The National Gallery, London

View the Closer Look for *Jean de Dinteville and Georges de Selve* ("*The Ambassadors*") on myartslab.com

that its form is only clearly readable from an acute angle. The skull serves as a *vanitas*, a reminder that the things of this world are fleeting. Holbein's success in recording the interests and concerns of these two men likely brought him to the notice of the court. Once he was appointed as court painter, Holbein's primary responsibility involved painting the royal family, though he also painted numerous portraits of members of Tudor society.

The Netherlands: World Marketplace

Where the courts of Europe, whether Catholic or Protestant, commissioned visual displays of power, the citizens of the Netherlands had a different taste. This region, present-day Holland and Belgium, had a very turbulent history. When the Reformation began, it was part of the empire under Charles V, who was also king of Spain. Protestantism quickly gained adherents in the Northern Netherlands; attempts by Philip II to suppress the spread of reformed faiths led to a revolt against Spanish rule. The provinces of the Northern Netherlands declared their independence in 1579. The city of Amsterdam then became a center of international trade.

The Southern Provinces (roughly corresponding to present-day Belgium) remained in Spanish hands and were committed to Roman Catholicism. The once thriving port of Bruges lost ground as a commercial center; the more strategically located Antwerp became the commercial and artistic capital of the Southern Netherlands.

Waves of iconoclasm struck the Netherlands, destroying vast numbers of medieval and Early Renaissance works of art. Since religious reformers saw large-scale sculpted works as idolatrous, commissions for such objects disappeared. As a result, painting and other two-dimensional art forms dominated artistic production. In the absence of religious commissions, artists no longer waited for patrons to hire them; they made works of art to sell on the open market. In this climate, new types of art developed that would supplement, and eventually replace, traditional religious subjects. The new Italianate style also challenged Netherlandish artists. Some saw no reason to change the Northern European visual tradition they had inherited; some grafted Italianate decorative forms to their traditional compositions and techniques; still others adopted Italian style wholesale.

Netherlandish Courts

Since the Netherlands belonged to the Habsburg Empire, imperial governors and aristocratic patrons established courts there that provided employment for a variety of artists, including Jan Gossaert (ca. 1478–1532), nicknamed "Mabuse" for his hometown of Maubeuge. He spent his early career in Antwerp, but in 1508 he accompanied Admiral Philip of Burgundy (a son of the duke) to Italy, where the Italian Renaissance and antiquity made a deep impression on him. He also worked for the regent of the Netherlands, Margaret of Austria. His paintings combine the lessons of Italian monumentality with the detailed technique of the Netherlandish tradition.

For the castle of his patron Philip of Burgundy Gossaert made images of mythological subjects, including *Neptune and Amphitrite* (**fig. 18.12**), which he signed and dated in 1516. The painting displays the painter's fascination with antiquity and Italianate perspective, as well as his skill at rendering textures, details, and rich color, in the Netherlandish tradition. Gossaert here depicts the god and his consort as nudes, basing their postures on

18.12 Jan Gossaert. *Neptune and Amphitrite*. 1516. Oil on panel, 6'2" × 4'⁴/₅" (1.9 × 1.2 m). Staatliche Museen zu Berlin

Dürer's 1504 *Adam and Eve* (see fig. 18.7). Gossaert endows these figures with bulky proportions that derive from his study in Rome of Hellenistic statues. The architecture, too, stems from ancient models, but it has a severity and a simplicity that are indebted to Bramante (see fig. 16.4). Gossaert places his figures in a temple-like structure, but he gives them an impossible scale: Neptune stands as tall as the columns. Either they are ancient cult statues come to life, or a viewer witnesses an epiphany (sudden appearance) of the pagan divinities. The subject, the god of the sea, clearly reflects Admiral Philip's interests. Gossaert brings Italianate forms to the service of his Netherlandish audience in a hybrid of the two traditions.

Urban Patronage: Antwerp

Antwerp's rise as a mercantile center brought it great wealth and a dynamic market for art. Although sculpture was produced in limited quantities, painting and printmaking dominated. The

lack of religious commissions and new market forces stimulated artists to explore other avenues for producing and selling their works. Some artists made images in anticipation of offering them for sale, instead of depending on patrons to commission them. Others developed specialties in specific kinds of painting; these GENRES, or types of art, included landscapes, portraits, still lifes, and scenes of everyday life (genre scenes). Fifteenth-century Netherlandish painting had included these elements in the backgrounds of religious paintings; in the sixteenth century, they became the principal subjects. Such themes allowed painters to sell pictures to clients of any faith.

Although born in the Northern Netherlands, the painter Pieter Aertsen (1507/08–1575) spent his early career in Antwerp. There he made numerous still-life paintings, some of which carry moralizing messages, like *The Meat Stall* (**fig. 18.13**) of 1551. He filled the foreground of this painting with products for sale in a butcher's shop, rendered in great detail;

18.13 Pieter Aertsen. *The Meat Stall.* 1551. Oil on panel, 48½ × 59″ (123.3 × 150 cm). University Art Collections, Uppsala University, Sweden

the foodstuffs obscure some tiny figures in the background. A viewer's eye meanders over these objects: some of them are items of gluttony; some, like the pretzels, are eaten during Lent. The still life is so large that the viewer almost misses the religious content: In the distance appear the Virgin and Child on the Flight into Egypt; they have stopped to give bread to the poor. By contrast, worshipers lined up to go to church ignore the poor. In the right background appears a tavern, which offers purely sensual products for sale. These background scenes suggest different choices that the viewer could make: A life of dissipation or a life of almsgiving. The painting seems to argue that Antwerp's principal economic activity of trade must be tempered by spiritual goals.

Bruegel

Aertsen's younger contemporary and fellow Antwerp resident, Pieter Bruegel the Elder (1525/30–1569), spent his career in Antwerp and Brussels.

Bruegel's personal life remains rather mysterious; yet his stylistic origins lie in the Netherlandish tradition, in particular the paintings of Hieronymus Bosch (see fig. 14.9). A trip to Italy affected him very little. Bruegel's work explores moral allegory, landscape, and peasant life.

As a painter and a designer of prints, he made pictures that demonstrate his interest in folk customs and the daily life of humble people. Highly educated, Bruegel had many friends among Humanists, intellectuals, entrepreneurs and merchants, who were his main clients. Members of the Habsburg court also collected his work, although many of his images have been interpreted as critical of Habsburg rule. During the 1560s, when Philip II of Spain attempted to quash the Protestant rebellion in the Netherlands, Bruegel apparently feared that his political imagery might cause trouble for his family, so he destroyed much of it.

Members of the urban elite collected images of the countryside and the people who worked the

18.14 Pieter Bruegel the Elder. *The Return of the Hunters.* 1565. Oil on panel, 3'10½" × 5'3¾" (1.17 × 1.6 m). Kunsthistorisches Museum, Vienna

 View the Closer Look for *The Return of the Hunters* on myartslab.com

land. For example, an Antwerp merchant probably commissioned Bruegel to paint *The Return of the Hunters* (**fig. 18.14**) as part of a series of landscapes representing the months. Such scenes had their origin in medieval calendar illustrations, like those in the *Très Riches Heures* of Jean de Berry (see fig. 14.2). In Bruegel's work, however, nature is more than a backdrop for human figures; it is the main subject of the picture. Bruegel organizes the composition of *The Return of the Hunters* with a shelf of snowy space in the foreground on which the hunters appear. The eye moves quickly into the distance through a snow-covered landscape. The human and canine members of a hunting party return to their village with their skimpy catch in the gray of a northern winter. They move down a hill toward a village, where the water has frozen into a place of recreation and where people rush to get back indoors. Human activity is fully integrated into the natural landscape in Bruegel's image. Along with the other months, the painting marks the passage of time in the natural and human domains.

Bruegel's *Peasant Wedding* (**fig. 18.15**), dated around 1568, records rural life and its ceremonies with wit and humanity. The painting depicts a gathering of peasants in a barn that has been decorated for a wedding. Bruegel's technique is as precise and detailed as that of his Flemish predecessors; his figures are weighty and solid, which adds to the impression of reality. Using Italian perspective techniques, Bruegel constructs a spacious room dominated by the table at which the wedding guests gather. The bride sits before a green curtain to distinguish her, though it is more difficult to locate the groom. Men distribute food in the foreground, though the many empty jugs in the lower left suggest that much liquid has already been consumed. Far from the expensive meats and fish depicted in Aertsen's *The Meat Stall*, diners here eat porridge. Bagpipers stand ready to play, but the noise level already seems high with so many figures talking amid the clattering of pottery.

Bruegel treats this country wedding as a serious event, and if he records the peasants' rough

18.15 Pieter Bruegel the Elder. *Peasant Wedding.* ca. 1568. Oil on panel, 44⅞ × 64″ (114 × 162.5 cm). Kunsthistorisches Museum, Vienna

 Read the document related Pieter Bruegel the Elder on myartslab.com

manners, he also records their fellowship. He treats the least of the least, like the child licking a bowl in the foreground, as worthy of observation and remembrance. Peasants themselves were hardly likely to purchase such images, so the painting expresses an urban audience's notions about country life and the ideal social order. Yet, informed by Humanist ideals about the centrality of human activity, Bruegel's images of peasant life transcend stereotypes and speak across the centuries about the human condition.

POINTS OF REFLECTION

18.1 Summarize elements from the Italian Renaissance adopted in Northern Europe. What inspired the patrons and artists to emulate the Italian works?

18.2 Consider the features of Reformation faiths that affected the market for art in this period. How did artists respond?

18.3 From this chapter, select a work commissioned for a court and one made for an urban audience. Analyze their similarities and differences.

18.4 Deduce the origins of landscape painting, still life, and paintings of everyday life by locating works in earlier chapters that contribute to their development.

18.5 Relate the work of El Greco, Albrecht Dürer, or Pieter Bruegel the Elder to the artistic traditions of the regions they lived in. What historical events affected their work?

✓—[**Study** and review on myartslab.com

ART IN TIME

- **1515—Grünewald completes** *Isenheim Altarpiece*

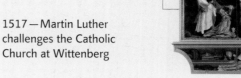

- **1517—Martin Luther** challenges the Catholic Church at Wittenberg

- **1521—Diet of Worms** condemns Luther

- **1526—Albrecht Dürer's Four Apostles presented to city of Nuremberg**

- **ca. 1528—Francis I commissions chateau in Fontainebleau**

- **1534—Henry VIII breaks with Rome and forms Church of England**

- **1551—Pieter Aertsen's** *The Meat Stall*

- **1555—Peace of Augsburg** between Catholics and Lutherans

- **1565—Pieter Bruegel the Elder's** *The Return of the Hunters*

- **1579—Establishment of Dutch Republic**

- **1586—El Greco's** *The Burial of Count Orgaz*

- **1588—Spanish Armada sails for England**

The Baroque in Italy and Spain

POINTS OF INQUIRY

19.1 Understand the characteristics of the Baroque style.

19.2 Consider how Baroque religious architecture in Rome reflects the values of the Counter-Reformation.

19.3 Investigate the evolution of ceiling painting.

19.4 Evaluate the Baroque concept of the "unification" of the arts.

19.5 Consider the qualities and innovations of Spanish seventeenth-century art.

(((•—[**Listen** to the chapter audio on myartslab.com

The Baroque

Baroque art is the dynamic, exuberant, expressive style most closely associated with the seventeenth century. The term "Baroque" may come from the Portuguese word *Barrocco*, referring to an irregular pearl; it means contorted, even grotesque, and was intended as a disparaging description of the grand, turbulent, overwhelming style of seventeenth-century art. Used for the dominant style of the seventeenth century, it also includes styles such as classicism, to which it bears a complex relationship. Some art historians include the time frame spanning 1700 to 1750, known as the Rococo, while others make the case for viewing the Baroque as the final phase of the Renaissance. Generally, Baroque art is considered to span the seventeenth century, beginning just before the turn of that century. It is the beginning of the Early Modern Period, as so many of the same concerns— issues of gender, class, and sexuality—are explored. The desire to evoke emotional states by appealing to the senses and to persuade, often in dramatic ways, underlies Baroque art. Some of the qualities that characterize the Baroque are grandeur, sensual

richness, emotional exuberance, tension, movement, and the successful unification of the various arts.

The expansive, expressive quality of the Baroque paralleled the true expansion of European influence—geographical, political, and religious—throughout the seventeenth century. The exploration of the New World that began in the sixteenth century, mobilized primarily by Spain, Portugal, and England (see **map 19.1**), developed in the seventeenth century into colonization, first of the eastern coasts of North and South America, and then of Polynesia and Asia. The Dutch East India Company developed trade with the East and was headquartered in Indonesia. Jesuit missionaries traveled to Japan, China, and India, and settled in areas of North, Central, and South America. In style and spirit, the reach of the Baroque was global.

The Baroque began in Rome and has been called a "style of persuasion," as the Catholic Church attempted to use art to speak to the faithful and to express the spirit of the Counter-Reformation (see box: Cultural Context: The Counter-Reformation, page 388). The Church celebrated its triumph over the spread of Protantism. Private influential families, some of whom would later claim a pope

as a member, other private patrons, and ecclesiastical orders all built new and often large churches in Rome in the seventeenth century. And the largest building program of the Renaissance—the rebuilding of St. Peter's—would finally come to an end and, with its elaborate decoration, would profoundly reflect the new glory of the Church.

This reinvigoration of the Catholic Church began a wave of canonizations that lasted through the mid-eighteenth century. The religious heroes of the Counter-Reformation—Ignatius of Loyola, Francis Xavier (both Jesuits), Teresa of Ávila, Filippo Neri, and Carlo Borromeo—were named saints. In contrast to the piety and good deeds of these reformers, the new princes of the Church were vigorous patrons of the arts, seeking both glory for the Church and posthumous fame for their own families.

During the first half of the seventeenth century, Europe was torn by almost continual warfare. The ambitions of the kings of France, who sought to dominate Europe, and the Habsburgs, who ruled not only Austria and Spain but also the Southern Netherlands, Bohemia, and Hungary, fueled the Thirty Years' War (1618–48). Although fought largely in Germany, the war eventually engulfed nearly all of Europe. After the Treaty of Westphalia in 1648 ended it and formally granted their freedom, the United Provinces—or the Dutch Republic, as the independent Netherlands was known—entered into a series of clashes with England and France that lasted until 1679. Yet, other than in Germany, which was fragmented into over 300 small states, many in financial ruin, there is little correlation between these rivalries and the art of the period. In fact, the seventeenth century has

Map 19.1 Western Europe ca. 1648

The Counter-Reformation

THE COUNTER-REFORMATION, also known as the Catholic Reformation, was a movement that began in the mid-sixteenth century and was created specifically to counter the attacks of the Protestant Reformation and to allow the Church of Rome both to reform and reaffirm itself.

These reforms were officially executed through the Council of Trent, which convened between 1545 and 1563 and clarified every aspect of liturgy and doctrine (including the role of art) contested by the Protestant church. The Council affirmed the role of Mary, the nature of the Eucharist, and other hotly contested points of divergence. It renewed the devotion to martyrs, developed the concept of the guardian angel and a formal sense of decorum in the Church. (Accordingly, during this time, loincloths were painted on nude figures of Michelangelo's *Last Judgment*, fig. 17.5).

The Jesuit order, founded by Ignatius of Loyola (see also page 361) and recognized by the Church in 1540, had the particular mission of defending and supporting the pope. The Church sought to gain Catholics abroad, having lost so many in Europe to the Protestant church. Through their missionary work in the East and in the Americas (aimed at converting native peoples to Catholicism), the Jesuits were central to the Reformation. Although the Council and the founding of the Jesuits date to the sixteenth century, their impact was greatest in the seventeenth. In 1622, both Loyola and Francis Xavier (also one of the first Jesuits, who was instrumental in carrying Christianity to India and Japan) became saints. In that same year, the mystic Teresa of Ávila (fig. 19.11) and Filippo Neri also achieved sainthood. Charles Borromeo, who was instrumental in the Council of Trent, had already become a saint. With these new seventeenth-century saints, who were nearly contemporary, new imagery, ideas, and a revitalization of the Church were possible. Art, with these exemplary figures as its subject, abounded and was used to spread the teachings of the saints and the Church. The worldly and spiritual splendor of the Church flourished by means of extensive building programs and elaborate commissions to furnish the churches (see fig. 19.7).

earned the label of the Golden Age of painting in France, Spain, and both the Dutch Republic and the Southern Netherlands.

The Baroque has also been identified as "the style of absolutism," reflecting the centralized state ruled by an autocrat of unlimited powers. Architecture of monumental scale emphasized massiveness, dramatic spaces and lighting, rich interior decoration from floor to ceiling, and luxurious material; and it was meant as a reflection of political and economic power. Absolutism reached its climax during the reign of Louis XIV of France, represented in his palace at Versailles, with its grandiose combination of architecture, painting, decoration, and extensive gardens. But we can also associate absolutism with the Vatican, the power of the pope, and his claim of authority won and reestablished through the Counter-Reformation. The power of absolutism suggests a style that will overwhelm and inspire awe in the spectator.

Yet this would not be a complete definition of the Baroque. A recognition of the subtle relationship between Baroque art and advances in science is essential to an understanding of the age. When scientists (most notably Galileo Galilei, 1564–1642, who was condemned for heresy in 1633) placed the sun, not the earth, at the center of the universe, they contradicted what our eyes (and common sense) tell us: That the sun revolves around the earth. Not only was the seventeenth century's worldview fundamentally different from that of the Renaissance, but its understanding of visual reality was forever changed by the new science, thanks to developments in optical physics and physiology.

The reality of seventeenth-century life is frequently suggested in genre painting—images from the everyday. These genre paintings include scenes of people drinking, smoking, and playing musical instruments. The paintings are often moralizing; that is, they often warn against the very things they are depicting. Such paintings had already emerged in the sixteenth century (see Bruegel, page 383), but they developed into a major force, along with landscape and still-life painting, in the seventeenth century in nearly every European country. Paintings of foods—plain and exotic—and landscapes of rural, urban, or far-off places were popular. Turkish carpets, African elephants and lions, Brazilian parrots, Ming vases, and peoples from Africa, India, and South America can be found in seventeenth-century art. In part, this list represents "exotica"—but the exotic was a major part of the seventeenth century as people, many of them artists, traveled to faraway places.

In the end, Baroque art was not simply the result of religious, political, intellectual, or social developments: The strengthened Catholic faith, the absolutist state, the new science, and the beginnings of the modern world combined in a volatile mixture that gave the Baroque era its fascinating

quality. The interplay of passion, intellect, and spirituality may be seen as forming a dialogue that has never been truly resolved.

Painting in Italy

Around 1600, Rome became the fountainhead of the Baroque, as it had been of the High Renaissance a century before, by attracting artists from other

19.1 Caravaggio. *The Calling of St. Matthew.* ca. 1599–1600. Oil on canvas, 11'1" × 11'5" (3.4 × 3.5 m). Contarelli Chapel, San Luigi dei Francesi, Rome

regions. The papacy and many of the new church orders (Jesuits, Theatines, and Oratorians), as well as numerous private patrons from wealthy and influential families (Farnese, Barberini, and Pamphili), commissioned art on a large scale, with the aim of promoting themselves and making Rome the most beautiful city of the Christian world "for the greater glory of God and the Church." This campaign had begun as early as 1585 (indeed, we may even date this revitalization to the reign of Julius II), and by the opening of the seventeenth century, Rome was attracting ambitious young artists, especially from northern Italy. It was they who created the innovative style.

Caravaggio and the New Style

Foremost among the young artists was the revolutionary painter Michelangelo Merisi (1571–1610), called Caravaggio after his birthplace near Milan. His style of painting, his new subjects, his use of lighting, and his concept of naturalism changed the world of painting. According to contemporary accounts, Caravaggio painted directly onto the canvas, and he worked from a live model. He depicted the world he knew, so that his canvases are filled with ordinary people. He did not idealize them as High Renaissance figures, nor did he give them classical bodies, clean clothes, and perfect features. But neither are they distorted, elongated, or overtly elegant as in Mannerism. This was an entirely new concept that was raw, immediate, and palpable. Caravaggio's style initiated the Baroque and caused a stir in the art world. He had numerous followers and imitators; and critics, both Italian and Northern European, wrote of his work, so Caravaggio and his paintings became internationally known almost immediately.

Caravaggio's first important public commission was a series of three monumental canvases devoted to St. Matthew that he painted for the Contarelli Chapel in San Luigi dei Francesi from 1599 to 1602. Of the three Contarelli paintings, one image is of the angel dictating the Gospel to St. Matthew; another is devoted to his martyrdom. The image on the left in the chapel illustrates *The Calling of St. Matthew* (**fig. 19.1**), depicting the moment he is chosen by Christ. The painting displays a naturalism that is both new and, indeed, radical. A contemporary said "he stuns the world" with this work.

Naturalism was not an end in itself for Caravaggio but a means of conveying profoundly spiritual content. The sacred subject is now depicted entirely in terms of contemporary life. Matthew, the well-dressed tax collector, sits with some armed men, his agents, in a sparse room. Two figures approach from the right. The newcomer's bare feet and simple biblical garb contrast strongly with the colorful costumes of Matthew and his companions.

We sense the religious quality in this scene and know it is not an everyday event. What identifies one of the figures on the right as Christ, who has come to Matthew and says "Follow me"? It is surely not his halo, the only supernatural feature in the picture, which is a thin gold band that we might easily overlook. Our eyes fasten instead on his commanding gesture, borrowed from Michelangelo's Adam in *The Creation of Adam* (see fig. 16.9), which bridges the gap between the two groups of people and is echoed by Matthew, who points questioningly at himself. It is also a way for Caravaggio to pun on his own given name as a reference to the older artist.

The men to the right at the table seem not to be engaged in the drama unfolding, while the ones at the left, in shadows, are blind to the entrance of Christ. One even wears eyeglasses and cannot see properly. Caravaggio uses the piercing light in this scene to announce Christ's presence, as Christ himself brought light: "I am the light of the world; he that followeth me shall not walk in darkness, but shall have the light of life" (John 8:12). Caravaggio's light here is the most dramatic gesture of all.

That beam of sunlight in the darkness above Jesus is most decisive in meaning and style. The select use of light in darkness is known as **tenebrism** (from a Latin word meaning darkness), and Caravaggio was known for his "dark paintings." Caravaggio illuminates Christ's face and hand in the gloomy interior so that we see the precise *moment* of his calling to Matthew and witness a critical piece of religious history and personal conversion. Without this light, so natural yet so charged with meaning, the picture would lose its power to make us aware of the divine presence. Caravaggio gives direct expression to an attitude shared by certain saints of the Counter-Reformation: That the mysteries of faith are revealed not by speculation but through an inner experience that is open to all people.

If this work were stripped of its religious context, the men seated at the table would seem like figures in a genre scene. Indeed, Caravaggio's painting became a source for similar secular scenes. Likewise, fanciful costumes, with slashed sleeves and feathered berets, appear in the works of his followers. Figures seen in half-length (showing only the upper half of their bodies) will also be a common element in other works by Caravaggio and his followers (see fig. 20.5).

Another aspect of Caravaggio's work is his focus on the sensual and erotic nature of both music and young men, who are depicted as seducing and soliciting. We see these elements in *The Musicians* (**fig. 19.2**), with the four androgynous, seminude youths. Actually, it may be two youths seen from two points of view. The musicians are half-length, but life-size; their blushing cheeks and full lips suggest erotic, sensual pleasures, enjoyed with each other and offered to a particular viewer. That viewer (the patron) was Cardinal del Monte, an influential, cultured patron and art collector who arranged the St. Matthew commission for Caravaggio and who commissioned other homoerotic paintings from him. The lute, the violin, the music sheets surrounding these half-draped men, and even the grapes being plucked on the side suggest a contemporary bacchanal. The erotic undertones of sensuality and passion will be explored in the Baroque and frequently imitated in later works of art by other artists.

Highly argumentative, a participant in rowdy street life, the painter carried a sword and was often in trouble with the law for fighting. When he killed a friend in a duel over a game, he fled Rome and spent the rest of his short life on the run. He went first to Naples, then Malta, then returned briefly to Naples. These trips account for both his work in these cities and his lasting influence there. He died on a journey back to Rome, where he hoped to gain a pardon. In Italy, artists and connoisseurs praised Caravaggio's work —and also criticized it. Conservative critics regarded him as lacking *decorum*: The propriety and reverence that religious subjects demanded. And many who did not like Caravaggio the man felt his influence and had to concede that his style was pervasive. The power of his style and imagery lasted into the 1630s, when it was absorbed into other Baroque tendencies.

Artemisia Gentileschi

Born in Rome, Artemisia Gentileschi (1593–ca. 1653) was the daughter of Caravaggio's friend, follower, and rival, Orazio Gentileschi, and grew up in this artistic milieu. She was a noted painter and was the first woman to be admitted to the Accademia del Disegno (Academy of Drawing) in Florence; the nobility of Venice, Florence, Naples, London, and Madrid celebrated, commissioned, and collected her work. Nonetheless, it was difficult for a woman artist to make her way professionally. In a letter of 1649, she wrote that "people have cheated me" and that she had submitted a drawing to a patron only to have him commission "another painter to do the

19.2 Caravaggio. *The Musicians.* ca. 1595. Oil on canvas, 36¼ × 46⅝" (92.1 × 118.4 cm). The Metropolitan Museum of Art, New York. Rogers Fund, 1952. 52.81

painting using my work. If I were a man, I can't imagine it would have turned out this way...."

Her best-known subjects are biblical heroines: Bathsheba, the tragic object of King David's passion, and Judith, who saved her people by beheading Holofernes. Both themes (see fig. 20.12) were popular during the Baroque era, which delighted in erotic and violent scenes. Artemisia's frequent depictions of these biblical heroines (she often showed herself in the lead role) hail the moral (and sometimes physical) strength of the female subject. The dynamic between male and female in her work may have stemmed from her own life and rape by her teacher, Agostino Tassi, who was tried in court and sentenced to banishment from Rome.

Artemisia's *Judith and Her Maidservant with the Head of Holofernes* (**fig. 19.3**) is a dramatic, large work whose darkness suggests the hushed silence of this penetrating scene. The theme is the apocryphal story of the Jewish widow Judith, who saved her people by traveling with her maid to the tent of the Assyrian general Holofernes (who was about to lead an attack on the Jews), where she made him drunk, and then cut off his head with his own sword; it yields parallels to the story of David and Goliath—might conquered by virtue and innocence. However, with the theme of Judith slaying Holofernes, the victor was not always seen positively, but with some suspicion since her triumph was achieved by deceit: The unspoken promise of a sexual encounter was never realized. Rather than the beheading itself, the artist shows the instant after. Momentarily distracted, Judith gestures theatrically as her servant stuffs Holofernes' head into a sack. The object of their attention remains hidden from view, heightening the air of suspense and intrigue. The silent, tense, candlelit atmosphere—tenebrism made intimate—creates a mood of mystery that conveys Judith's complex emotions with unsurpassed understanding. Gentileschi's rich palette was to have a strong influence on painting in Naples, where she settled in 1630.

Ceiling Painting and Annibale Carracci

The conservative tastes of many Italian patrons were met by artists who were less radical than Caravaggio, and who continued a more classical tradition steeped in High Renaissance ideals. They took their lead from Annibale Carracci (1560–1609), who arrived in Rome in 1595. Annibale came from Bologna where, in the 1580s, he and two other members of his family formed an "academy" (see also margin note page 356). He was a reformer rather than a revolutionary. Although we do not know completely what this academy entailed, it seems to have incorporated life drawing from models and drawing after ancient sculpture. As with Caravaggio, Annibale's experience of Roman classicism transformed his art. He, too, felt that painting must return to Nature, but his approach emphasized a revival of the classics, which to him meant the art of antiquity. Annibale also sought to emulate Raphael, Michelangelo, Titian, and Correggio.

Between 1597 and 1601 Annibale produced a ceiling fresco in the GALLERY of the Farnese Palace (**fig. 19.4**): *Loves of the Gods*, his most ambitious work, which soon became so famous that it ranked behind only the murals of Michelangelo and

19.3 Artemisia Gentileschi. *Judith and Her Maidservant with the Head of Holofernes.* ca. 1625. Oil on canvas, 6'1½" × 4'7" (1.84 × 1.41 m). The Detroit Institute of Arts. Gift of Mr. Leslie H. Green

 Read the document related to Artemisia Gentileschi on myartslab.com

Raphael. Although we have seen ceiling painting in the Renaissance—with works by Mantegna and of course Michelangelo—it is the Baroque period that we most associate with this form of painting.

Executed in chapels, churches, and private residences—in entranceways, hallways, and dining rooms—ceiling painting was meant to convey the power, domination, or even extravagance of the patron. One could not enter such a painted room without a certain feeling of awe. The styles from the beginning of the seventeenth century to the end become increasingly extravagant and contest even the majesty of Michelangelo. The Farnese Palace ceiling, commissioned to celebrate a family wedding, displays a humanist subject, the Loves of the Classical Gods. As on the Sistine Chapel

19.4 Annibale Carracci. *Loves of the Gods*. 1597–1601. Ceiling fresco in the Gallery. Farnese Palace, Rome

19.5 Giovanni Battista Gaulli. *Triumph of the Name of Jesus*. 1672–79. Ceiling fresco. Il Gesù, Rome

ceiling, the narrative scenes are surrounded by painted architecture, simulated sculpture, and nude youths, carefully foreshortened and lit from below so that they appear real. But the fresco does not depend solely on Michelangelo's masterpiece. The main panels resemble easel pictures, although all are frescoes. The "framed" painting, "medallions," and "sculpture" on the ceiling all in *trompe l'oeil* (deceiving the eye) are known as *quadri riportati*, pictures transported to the ceiling (singular is *quadro riportato*). This ceiling reflects the vast, actual collection of the Farnese. The figure of Polyphemus, for example, seen on the short wall, hurling the stone in the "easel painting," is based on the *Farnese Hercules*, a Hellenistic sculpture owned by the family and displayed in the courtyard. The entire ceiling displays an exuberance of brilliant and evenly lit color.

GIOVANNI BATTISTA GAULLI AND IL GESÙ It is a strange fact that few ceiling frescoes were painted after 1635. Ironically, the new style of architecture fostered by Francesco Borromini (see page 399) provided few opportunities for decoration. But after 1670 such frescoes enjoyed a revival in the decoration of older buildings, and this revival reached its peak in the interior of Il Gesù (**fig. 19.5**), the mother church of the Jesuit order (fig. 17.7). At the suggestion, late in his life, of Gianlorenzo Bernini, the greatest sculptor-architect of the century (see page 396–99), the commission for the ceiling frescoes went to his young protégé Giovanni Battista Gaulli (1639–1709). A talented assistant, Antonio Raggi (1624–1686), made the stucco sculpture. The program, which proved extraordinarily influential, shows Bernini's foresight and Gaulli's imaginative daring. As in the Cornaro Chapel (see fig. 19.11), the artist treats the ceiling as a single unit that evokes a mystical vision. The nave fresco, with its contrasts of light and dark, spills dramatically over its frame, then turns into sculptured figures, combining painting, sculpture, and architecture. Here Baroque illusionism achieves its ultimate expression. The subject of the ceiling painting is the illuminated name of Jesus—the IHS—in the center of the golden light. It is a stirring reference both to the Jesuit order, dedicated to the Name of Jesus, and to the concept that Christ is the Light of the World. The impact of his light and holiness then creates the overflowing turbulence that tumbles out of the sky at the end of days and spreads the word of the Jesuit missionaries:

"That at the name of Jesus, every knee should bow…" (Epistle of St. Paul to the Philippians, 2:10).

Architecture in Italy

The Baroque style in architecture, like that of painting, began in Rome, which was a vast construction site from the end of the sixteenth through the middle of the seventeenth century. The goals of the Counter-Reformation caused the Church to embark on a major building campaign, constructing new churches and finally completing the New St. Peter's. Although many of the building projects began during the Renaissance, they developed distinctly different characteristics as they were completed during the Baroque. Some architects continued to use a classical vocabulary but expanded or stretched it, so that the idea of perfection was not considered a circle, but an oval or ellipse (a modern concept that was frequently the object of astronomical discussions). They incorporated domes based on Michelangelo's (fig. 17.6), but which had a steeper profile to suggest greater drama in punctuating the sky; others designed buildings based on amorphous shapes that used the ornamentations but not the principles of classicism.

The Completion of St. Peter's and Carlo Maderno

In 1603, the architect Carlo Maderno (ca. 1556–1629) was given the task of completing, at long last, the church of St. Peter's (**fig. 19.6**), somewhat differently than first envisioned. Pope Clement VIII had decided to add a nave and narthex to the west end of Michelangelo's building, thereby converting it into a basilica plan covering the "footprint" of the Old St. Peter's. The change of plan, first proposed by Raphael in 1514, made it possible to link St. Peter's with the Vatican Palace to the right of the church. This decision would have consequences beyond the shape of the church: Michelangelo's dome would be difficult to see and seem to "sink," a detrimental effect that other architects would be determined not to repeat in plans of their own.

Maderno's design for the façade follows the pattern established by Michelangelo for the exterior. It consists of a colossal order supporting an attic, but with a dramatic emphasis on the portals. The total effect can only be described as a crescendo building from the corners toward the climax of the center. The spacing of the supports becomes closer, the

19.6 Aerial view of St. Peter's. Nave and façade by Carlo Maderno, 1607–12; colonnade by Gianlorenzo Bernini, designed 1657. Vatican, Rome

 Explore the architectural panorama of the colonnade of St. Peter's on myartslab.com

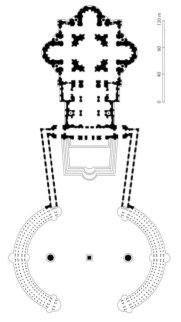

Plan for St. Peter's

pilasters turn into columns, and the façade wall projects step by step. This quickened rhythm had been hinted at a generation earlier in Giacomo della Porta's façade of Il Gesù (see fig. 17.7). Recent cleaning of the façade of St. Peter's revealed it to be of a warm cream color, which emphasizes its sculptural qualities.

Bernini and St. Peter's

After Maderno's death in 1629, his assistant Gianlorenzo Bernini (1598–1680) assumed the title "architect of St. Peter's." Considering himself Michelangelo's successor as both architect and sculptor, Bernini directed the building campaign and coordinated the decoration and sculpture within the church as well. Given these tasks, the enormous size of St. Peter's posed equal challenges for anyone seeking to integrate architecture and sculpture: The question was how to relate its vastness to the human scale and give it a measure of emotional warmth. Once the nave was extended following Maderno's design, Bernini realized that the interior needed an internal focal point in this vast space.

His response was to create the monumental composite form known as the *Baldacchino* (**fig. 19.7**), the "canopy" for the main altar, at the very crossing of the transept and the nave, directly under Michelangelo's dome (see fig. 17.6) and just above the actual crypt of St. Peter where the pope would celebrate Mass. His assistant for this elaborate work, Francesco Borromini (see page 399), who will later be his rival, may be credited for its ornate form. This nearly 100-foot object, a splendid fusion of sculpture and architecture, created mostly in bronze stripped from the ancient Pantheon (see fig. 7.18), stands on four twisted columns, reminiscent of those from the original St. Peter's (and thought, too, to replicate those of Solomon's Temple). Rather than an architectural entablature (the horizontal members—architrave, frieze, and cornice) mounted between the columns, Bernini inventively suggests fabric hanging between them. At the corners of the *Baldacchino* are statues of angels and vigorously curved scrolls, which raise a cross above a golden orb, the symbol of the triumph of Christianity throughout the world. The entire structure is so alive with expressive energy that it may be

19.7 Gianlorenzo Bernini. *Baldacchino*, at the nave crossing. 1624–33. Gilt bronze. St. Peter's, Vatican, Rome

considered as the epitome of Baroque style. We can see through the columns of the *Baldacchino* to the sculptural reliquary of the throne of St. Peter, the *Cathedra Petri* (the actual chair of St. Peter, encased in bronze, held aloft by the Four Fathers of the Church), set under stained glass in the apse of the church, and also designed by Bernini.

The papal insignia—the triple crown and crossed keys of St. Peter—and the coat of arms of the pope under whose patronage this structure was created—the Barberini bees of Urban VIII—are significant elements of the decoration. Bernini's *Baldacchino* honors not just the power and majesty of God, but that of his emissary on earth, the pope. Bernini's relationship with the pope was one of the most successful and powerful in the history of patronage. Indeed, upon his elevation to the papacy, Urban VIII was said to have told the artist: "It is your great good luck, Cavaliere, to see Maffeo Barberini pope; but We are even luckier in that Cavaliere Bernini lives at the time of our pontificate." However, the artistic aims of this pope drained the papal treasury and both the pope and, by association, Bernini took the blame for the excesses after Urban's death.

Later, under the patronage of Pope Alexander VII (r. 1655–1667), Bernini orchestrated the main entrance into St. Peter's. He molded the open space in front of the façade into a magnificent oval piazza that is amazingly sculptural (see fig. 19.6). This "forecourt," which imposed a degree of unity on the sprawling Vatican complex, acts

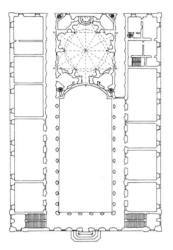

Plan of Sant'Ivo alla Sapieza

19.8 Francesco Borromini. Interior view into dome and walls of Sant'Ivo. Begun 1642. Rome

as an immense atrium framed by colonnades, while screening off the surrounding slums. This device, which Bernini himself likened to the motherly, all-embracing arms of the Church, is not new. What *was* unusual was the idea of placing it at the main entrance to a building. Also striking was the huge scale, creating a grandiose setting. Bernini's one major failure in the visual effect of St. Peter's was his inability to execute the bell towers initially planned by Bramante (see fig. 16.5). He began construction, but they turned out to be structurally unsound and physically damaging to the façade; they had to be dismantled. This failure would haunt him, but would provide a competitive resource for his rivals: Borromini in Italy and later Wren in England.

A Baroque Alternative: Francesco Borromini

Bernini's greatest rival in architecture, Francesco Borromini (1599–1667), was a secretive and emotionally unstable artist who died by suicide. The contrast between these two architects would be evident from their works alone, even without the accounts by their contemporaries. Bernini's church designs are dramatically simple and unified, while Borromini's structures are extravagantly complex. And whereas the surfaces of Bernini's interiors are extremely rich, Borromini's are surprisingly plain, relying on his phenomenal grasp of spatial geometry to achieve their total spiritual effects. Bernini himself agreed with those who denounced Borromini for flagrantly disregarding the classical tradition, enshrined in Renaissance theory and practice, that architecture must reflect the proportions of the human body. Surely, of the two, Bernini, even at the height of the Baroque, was the one more tied to a classical vocabulary. But perhaps Bernini's criticism of Borromini simply represented all-too-human rivalries.

SANT'IVO Borromini's church of Sant'Ivo alla Sapienza (**figs. 19.8** and **19.9**) was built at the end of an existing cloister for a university, which soon became the University of Rome. It is compact, but daring. Sant'Ivo is a small, central-plan church based on a star-hexagon. The six-pointed star plan represents *Sapienza* (Wisdom), although as the church was first built under Pope Urban VIII (Barberini) contemporaries suggested that the plan represented the Barberini bee, also seen in Bernini's *Baldacchino* (fig. 19.7). In designing this church, Borromini may have been thinking of octagonal structures, such

as San Vitale in Ravenna (fig. 8.10), but the result is completely novel. Inside, it is a single, unified, organic experience, as the walls extend the ground plan into the vault, culminating in Borromini's unique spiral lantern. It continues the star-hexagon pattern of the floor plan up to the circular base of the lantern (see fig. 19.8). The stars on the wall refer to the Chigi family of Pope Alexander VII, whose reign saw the building's completion.

19.9 Francesco Borromini. Exterior of Sant'Ivo. Begun 1642. Rome

Sculpture in Italy

Baroque sculpture, like Baroque painting, was vital, energized, and dynamic, suggesting action and deep emotion. The subject matter was intended to evoke an emotional response in the viewer. The sculpture was usually life-size, but with a sense of grandeur that suggested larger than life-size figures; and many figures were indeed monumental. Deeply cut, the facial expressions and clothing caught the light and cast shadows to create not just depth but drama.

19.10 Gianlorenzo Bernini. *David.* 1623. Marble, life-size. Galleria Borghese, Rome

The Evolution of the Baroque: Bernini

Bernini was a sculptor as well as an architect, and sculpture and architecture are never far apart in his work, as we have seen in the *Baldacchino* (fig. 19.7). Trained by his father, Pietro Bernini (1562–1629), a sculptor who worked in Florence, Naples, and Rome, he was also influenced by Giovanni Bologna (see fig. 17.4). Bernini's style was thus a direct outgrowth of Mannerist sculpture in many ways, but this debt alone does not explain his revolutionary qualities, which emerged early in his career.

DAVID As in the colonnade for St. Peter's (see fig. 19.6), we can often see a strong relationship between Bernini's sculpture and antiquity. If we compare Bernini's *David* (**fig. 19.10**) with Michelangelo's (see fig. 16.7) and ask which is closer to the Pergamon frieze (see fig. 5.30), our vote must go to Bernini, whose sculpture shares with Hellenistic works that union of body and spirit, of motion and emotion, which Michelangelo so consciously tempers. This does not mean that Michelangelo is more classical than Bernini. It shows, rather, that both the Baroque and the High Renaissance drew different lessons from ancient art.

Bernini's *David* suggests the fierceness of expression, movement, and dynamism of Hellenistic sculpture. In part, what makes it Baroque is the implied presence of Goliath. Unlike earlier statues of David, including Donatello's (see fig. 15.13), Bernini's is conceived not as a self-contained figure but as half of a pair, his entire action focused on his adversary. His *David* tells us clearly enough where he sees the enemy. Consequently, the space between David and his invisible opponent is charged with energy—it "belongs" to the statue.

The *David* shows us the distinctive feature of Baroque sculpture: Its new, active relationship with the surrounding space. But it is meant to be seen, as is most other Baroque sculpture, from one primary point of view. Bernini presents us with "the moment" of action, not just the contemplation of the killing—as in Michelangelo's work—or the aftermath of it, as in Donatello's. Baroque sculpture often suggests a heightened vitality and energy, while it also adheres to the Counter-Reformation concept of "decorum" and explains why the *David* is not completely nude. Because Baroque sculpture so often presents an "invisible complement" (like the Goliath of Bernini's *David*), it attempts pictorial effects that were traditionally outside the realm of monumental sculpture. Such a charging of space with energy is, in fact, a key feature of Baroque art. Caravaggio had achieved it in his *The Calling of St. Matthew* (fig. 19.1) with the aid of a sharply focused beam of light. And as we have seen in Gaulli's ceiling of Il Gesù (fig. 19.5), both painting and sculpture may even be combined with architecture to form a compound illusion, such as that seen on a stage.

THE CORNARO CHAPEL: *THE ECSTASY OF ST. TERESA*
Bernini had a passionate interest in the theater and was an innovative scene designer. A contemporary wrote that he "gave a public opera wherein he painted the scenes, cut the statues, invented the engines, composed the music, writ the comedy, and built the theatre." Thus he was at his

19.11 Gianlorenzo Bernini. *The Ecstasy of St. Teresa* (full chapel view). 1645–52. Marble, life-size. Cornaro Chapel, Santa Maria della Vittoria, Rome

 Watch an architectural simulation about the Cornaro Chapel on myartslab.com

best when he could merge architecture, sculpture, and painting and was praised by contemporaries for this unification as "marvellous." His masterpiece in this vein is the Cornaro Chapel in the church of Santa Maria della Vittoria, containing *The Ecstasy of St. Teresa* (**fig. 19.11**). TERESA OF ÁVILA, one of the great saints and mystics of the Counter-Reformation and founder of the Reformed Order of the Discalced ("shoeless," as shown here) Carmelites, was canonized in 1622. She had described how, in a vision, an angel pierced her heart with a flaming golden arrow: "The pain was so great that I screamed aloud; but at the same time I felt such infinite sweetness that I wished the pain to last forever. It was not physical but psychic pain, although it affected the body as well to some degree. It was the sweetest caressing of the soul by God."

Bernini has made Teresa's mystical experience sensuously real, as her arm and leg are limp, fabric cascades, and the saint's rapture is obvious. (In a different context the angel could be Cupid.) On a floating cloud, they appear to be levitating (as St. Teresa was known to do) toward Heaven and this transformative moment seems to cause the turbulence of their drapery. Its divine nature is suggested by the golden rays (gilt wood) which come from a source high above the altar. The scene is lit from a hidden window above and marks the first time that a sculptor has used actual, natural light as a directed focus for the viewer to experience the light as heavenly.

In an illusionistic fresco by Guidobaldo Abbatini (1600–1656) on the vault of the chapel, the glory of the heavens reveals itself as a dazzling burst of light from which tumble clouds of jubilant angels. This celestial explosion gives force to the thrusts of the angel's arrow and makes the ecstasy of the saint fully convincing.

To complete the illusion, Bernini even provides a built-in audience for his "stage." And surely his experience as a stage designer inspired him here. On the sides of the chapel are balconies resembling theater or OPERA boxes that contain marble figures depicting members of the Cornaro family, set as group portraits, who also witness the vision. Their space and ours are the same, and thus are part of our reality, while the saint's ecstasy, which is framed in a niche, occupies a space that is real but beyond our reach, as in a divine realm.

The work then is a total visual experience, not just for St. Teresa but for the viewer. Bernini uses

polychrome marbles of green, gold, black, and white to completely set the stage for us beneath the spotlight. Like the *SPIRITUAL EXERCISES* of Ignatius of Loyola, which he practiced, Bernini's religious sculpture aims to help a viewer identify with miraculous events through a vivid appeal to the senses. Theatricality in the service of faith was basic to the Counter-Reformation, which often referred to the Church as the theater of human life: It took the Baroque to bring this ideal about.

Bernini was steeped in Renaissance Humanism. Central to his sculpture is the role of gesture and expression in arousing emotion. While these devices were also important to the Renaissance, Bernini uses them with a freedom that seems anticlassical. However, he essentially followed the concept of decorum and he planned his effects carefully by varying them in accordance with his subject. Unlike the Frenchman Nicolas Poussin (see page 432–34), Bernini did this for the sake of expressive impact rather than conceptual clarity. The approaches of the two artists were diametrically opposed as well. For Bernini, antiquity served as no more than a point of departure for his own inventiveness, whereas for Poussin it was a standard of comparison.

Painting in Spain

Politics, art, and a common bond of loyalty to the Catholic Church connected Italy and Spain in the seventeenth century. Spain, still in the throes of the Inquisition (see page 358), was staunchly conservative and unflinching; its king was titled "The Most Catholic Majesty." Spain restricted the Church to only those who professed their unfaltering loyalty, and imprisoned, executed, or expelled those who did not, while the Vatican used its resources to bring reformers and the disaffected back into the fold. As we have seen, the Counter-Reformation, or Catholic Reformation (see box, page 388), began in Rome with a new style—Baroque—intended to convince viewers of the dynamism and power of the Catholic Church, its patrons, and defenders. And, at the beginning of the seventeenth century, the largest city on the Italian mainland, Naples, was under the rule of Spain, as were the region around it and the island of Sicily. So the impact of Baroque Roman art on Neapolitan and Spanish art was profound.

At the height of its political and economic power during the sixteenth century, Spain had produced great saints and writers, but no artists of the first rank. The Spanish court and most of the aristocracy held native artists in low esteem, preferring to employ foreign painters whenever possible—above all Titian. Thus the main influences came from Italy and the Netherlands, which was then also under Spanish rule. Jan van Eyck (see page 297–301) visited Spain and inspired followers there; Titian worked for Charles V of Spain; in the seventeenth century Rubens visited at least twice, and his work drew great admiration. Spanish Baroque art was heavily influenced by the style and subject matter of Caravaggio—directly and via Naples—but with a greater starkness. And his influence also spread to Seville, where many of the Spanish artists in this chapter began their education. Spanish naturalism may throw a harsher, stronger light on its subjects, but it is ultimately at least as sympathetic.

Naples and the Impact of Caravaggio: Jusepe de Ribera

Caravaggio's main disciple in Naples was the Spaniard Jusepe de Ribera (1591–1652), who settled there after having seen Caravaggio's paintings in Rome while he lived there, 1613–16. Especially popular were Ribera's paintings of saints, prophets, and ancient beggar-philosophers. Their asceticism appealed strongly to the otherworldliness of Spanish Catholicism. Such pictures also reflected the learned Humanism of the Spanish nobility, who were the artist's main patrons.

His *The Club-Footed Boy* (**fig. 19.12**) smiles openly and endearingly out at us, with a dimpled cheek, although we may be somewhat discomforted by his peasant dress, his begging, and his handicap. The words on the paper he holds state (in translation): "Give me alms for the love of God." In Counter-Reformation theory, this plea for charity indicates that only through good works may the rich hope to attain salvation. The painting, indeed, was made for the Viceroy of Naples, a wealthy collector who would have seen this as a testament to the importance of Christian charity and mercy to the poor. The boy seems almost monumental here as he stands against the broad sky with a low horizon line, like a musketeer; but instead of a weapon across his shoulder, he holds his crutch. His deformed foot appears in shadow and the viewer does not quite see it at first, but, as the leg is lit, clearly Ribera is directing our attention to it.

19.12 Jusepe de Ribera. *The Club-Footed Boy*. 1642. Oil on canvas, 5′4⅛″ × 3′5⅝″ (1.64 × 0.93 m). Musée du Louvre, Paris

The deformity may in fact not be a clubfoot but an indication of cerebral palsy. In either case, in the seventeenth century, such a deformity would have committed the sufferer to a life of begging.

Ribera executed other large paintings of beggars, of the poor, and of the blind, but created with a moral purpose. The boy himself seems an embodiment of joy as he smiles, even laughs. This was a way for the subject to withstand misfortune, for he has the ability to dispense grace: The opportunity for others to do good. This is a critical concept in the understanding of charity: Both giver and receiver benefit from it.

Ribera's use of naturalism is a hallmark of Spanish and Neapolitan painting and etching.

19.13 Francisco de Zurbarán. *Still Life with Lemons, Oranges, and a Rose*. 1633. Oil on canvas, 24½ × 43⅛″ (62.2 × 109.5 cm). Norton Simon Foundation, Pasadena

It extends Caravaggio's impact, which was felt especially in Seville, in southern Spain, the home of the most important Spanish artists: Zurbarán, Velázquez, and Murillo.

Seville as Center

Francisco de Zurbarán (1598–1664) worked in Seville throughout most of his life, and he stands out among his contemporaries for his paintings of quiet, sharp intensity and clarity with an ascetic piety that is uniquely Spanish. He is famous for his paintings for the religious and monastic orders, which were densely concentrated in this city. He depicted many individual saints; often in contemplation, sometimes in martyrdom. He also followed a tradition which became strong in Seville from the very turn of the century: still-life painting.

Zurbarán's *Still Life with Lemons, Oranges, and a Rose* of 1633 (**fig. 19.13**) sets each object on a ledge as if across a frieze. The lemons are piled up on a platter, the oranges in a tall straw basket topped by an orange branch, and the rose sits at the edge of a saucer which holds a cup of (possibly) water—perhaps signaling rosewater. There is enough space between the items to allow the eye to concentrate on a single object, and each has a unique texture that explores the full tactile qualities of the fruits and their containers. All are set against an intensely dark background, suggesting a distilled sobriety, yet breathtaking magnificence for this simple subject. The fruit and flowers are all domestic, and hence, ordinary. Yet Zurbarán treats the subject with as much reverence as martyred saints—with a quiet mystery that reminds us of Caravaggio—but deeper and perhaps with greater simplicity.

Diego Velázquez: From Seville to Court Painter

Diego Velázquez (1599–1660) painted in a Caravaggesque vein during his early years in Seville. His interests at that time centered on scenes of people eating and drinking rather than religious themes. In the late 1620s, he was appointed court painter to Philip IV, whose reign (1621–1665) was the great age of painting in Spain. Upon moving to Madrid, Velázquez quickly became a skilled courtier and a favorite of the king, whom he served as chamberlain. He spent most of the rest of his life in Madrid, painting mainly portraits of the royal family.

Velázquez discovered the beauty of the many Titians in the king's collection with the guidance of the painter Peter Paul Rubens (see pages 412–15) during the Fleming's visit to the Spanish court in 1628 while on a diplomatic mission. Rubens encouraged Velázquez to go to Rome, and some years later he was able to do so when the king dispatched him there in 1648 to purchase paintings and antique sculpture.

THE PORTRAIT OF *JUAN DE PAREJA* On his mission to Rome, Velázquez took with him Philip's permission to paint Pope Innocent X. But Velázquez's reputation seemed not to have preceded him when he arrived in 1649, and he was left waiting. It was during this interlude that he painted the portrait of his Sevillian assistant and servant of Moorish descent, Juan de Pareja (ca. 1610–1670, **fig. 19.14**), who accompanied him to Rome and was an artist himself. The portrait, stunningly life-like, was acclaimed when exhibited at an annual art show in the Pantheon in March 1650. It was said that of all the paintings, this one was "truth." Juan is shown half-length, in three-quarter view,

19.14 Diego Velázquez. *Juan de Pareja*. 1650. Oil on canvas, 32 × 27½″ (81.3 × 69.9 cm). The Metropolitan Museum of Art, New York. Purchase, Fletcher and Rogers Funds, and Bequest of Miss Adelaide Milton de Groot (1876–1967), by exchange, supplemented by gifts from Friends of the Museum, 1971. 1971.86

but facing us—a triangular format developed by Raphael and Titian in the High Renaissance, using, but simplifying, that of the *Mona Lisa* (fig. 16.3) as their point of departure. The same format used here is a powerful one, riveting our attention to his face. The feathery lace collar, brilliantly painted, picks up the white highlights that create the formidable sculptural visage. A white patch, a tear in his clothing at the elbow, reminds a viewer of his class. The success of this portrait and Velázquez's new fame in Rome may have prompted the pope to sit for him, soon after.

LAS MENINAS Velázquez's mature style is seen at its fullest in *Las Meninas* (*The Maids of Honor*) (**fig. 19.15**). Both a group portrait and a genre scene, it might be subtitled "the artist in his studio," for Velázquez depicts himself at work on a huge canvas. In the center is the Princess Margarita, who has just posed for him, among her playmates and maids of honor. The faces of her parents, King Philip IV and Queen Mariana, appear in the mirror on the back wall. This is surely a homage to Jan van Eyck's *"Arnolfini Portrait"* (fig. 14.6), then in the royal collection in Madrid. The royal couple's position also suggests a slightly different vantage point from ours, and indeed there are several viewpoints throughout the picture: the artist's, the princess's, the king and queen's, and ours. In this way, the artist perhaps intended to include the viewer in the scene by implication, even though it was clearly painted for the king and hung in the office of his summer quarters at the Alcázar Palace. As a royal family portrait it implies the notion of dynasty and hints, as well, at the vast wealth and power of Spain: the red cup handed to the princess is a contemporary ceramic from Guadalajara in the Americas, as may be the silver plate it sits on, as well as the red dye used for the color of the curtain seen in the mirror—each suggesting the global expanse of Spain.

Antonio Palomino (1655–1726), the first to discuss *Las Meninas*, wrote, "the name of Velázquez will live from century to century, as long as that of the most excellent and beautiful Margarita, in whose shadow his image is immortalized." Thanks to Palomino, we know the identity of every person in the painting. Through the presence of the princess and the king and queen, the canvas commemorates Velázquez's position as royal painter and his aspiration to the knighthood in the Order of Santiago—a papal military order to which he

gained admission only with great difficulty three years after the painting was executed. In it, he wears the red cross of the order, which was added later, after his death.

Velázquez had struggled for status at court since his arrival. Even though the usual family investigations (almost 150 friends and relatives were interviewed) assisted his claim to nobility, the very nature of his profession worked against him. "Working with his hands" conferred on Velázquez the very antithesis of noble status. Only by papal dispensation was he accepted. *Las Meninas*, then, is an expression of personal ambition; it is a claim for both the nobility of the act of painting and that of the artist himself. The presence of the king and queen affirms his status. The Spanish court had already honored Titian and Rubens (although not with the same order), and as these artists were both held in high regard, they served as models for Velázquez. They continued to have a significant impact on him, as men and because of their painterly, lush style.

The painting reveals Velázquez's fascination with light as fundamental to vision. The artist challenges us to match the mirror image against the painting. The glowing colors have a Venetian richness, but the brushwork is even freer and sketchier than Titian's. Velázquez fully explored the optical qualities of light. His aim was to represent the movement of light itself and the infinite range of its effects on form and color. For Velázquez, as for Jan Vermeer in the Netherlands (see pages 428–29), light creates the visible world.

Culmination in Devotion: Bartolomé Esteban Murillo

The work of Bartolomé Esteban Murillo (1617–1682), Zurbarán's and Velázquez's successor as the leading painter in Seville, is the most cosmopolitan, as well as the most accessible, of any of the Spanish Baroque artists. For that reason, he had countless followers, whose pale imitations obscure his real achievement. His much copied religious images, especially his depictions of the Virgin Mary (**fig. 19.16**), typified the promotion of her in the visual vocabulary of Spain in the seventeenth century. This insistence on Virgin imagery defied the Protestant influence in much of Europe. One of these themes, the Immaculate Conception, was controversial even among Catholics; the doctrine, promoted by Franciscans (Murillo was a lay member of the order), professes that the Virgin

19.15 Diego Velázquez. *Las Meninas (The Maids of Honor)*. 1656. Oil on canvas, 10'5" × 9' (3.2 × 2.7 m). Museo del Prado, Madrid

View the Closer Look for *Las Meninas* on myartslab.com

19.16 Bartolomé Esteban Murillo, *The Immaculate Conception*. ca. 1645–50. Oil on canvas, 7′8″ × 6′5″ (2.35 × 1.96 m). State Hermitage Museum, St. Petersburg, Russia

was conceived without Original Sin. Its detractors, led by the Dominicans, thought that she had been cleansed of sin in the womb after conception, but before birth. Paintings on this subject were used as propaganda to promote the Virgin's status so that the concept would, through art, become church dogma (accepted as true on the basis of faith); it was finally decreed as dogma in 1854. However, already in the seventeenth century there were spectacles of the "Immaculata" (processions carrying the image of the Immaculate Virgin) in Seville and papal declarations (notably by Alexander VII in 1661) that urged this change. Murillo was one of the major painters of this theme.

The haunting expressiveness of the Virgin's face and of the cherubs or angels has a gentle pathos that is emotionally appealing. This human warmth reflects a basic change in religious outlook. The Virgin's piety is shown by her hands folded in prayer and her upward glance to Heaven; she stands on a crescent moon, an attribute of the Immaculate Conception ("And there appeared a great wonder in Heaven: a woman clothed with the sun and the moon under her feet"—Revelation 12:1). The extraordinary sophistication of Murillo's brushwork and the subtlety of his color show the influence of Velázquez. Murillo succeeded so well that the vast majority of religious paintings in Spain and its South American colonies for the next 150 years were derived from his work. Although genre and still-life painting were also popular, the promotion of the Virgin in Spanish art defined Spain's Catholic and conservative art and its role in defying the Reformation of Northern Europe.

POINTS OF REFLECTION

19.1 Select a work in each of three different media and discuss how they reflect the stylistic qualities of Baroque art.

19.2 Discuss the ways in which St. Peter's, when completed, differed from the original plans. Where are Baroque elements visible? How do the interior and exterior reflect the values of the Counter-Reformation?

19.3 Assess how ceiling painting reflected the values of its patrons. Discuss why ceiling painting, rather than wall painting, could better achieve these goals.

19.4 Analyze the unification of the arts of architecture, sculpture, and painting in the work of Bernini.

19.5 What innovations in royal portraiture are evident in Velázquez's *Las Meninas*?

✓● **Study** and review on myartslab.com

ART IN TIME

● **1599–1600—Caravaggio's** *The Calling of St. Matthew*

● 1605—Miguel de Cervantes Saavedra writes *Don Quixote*

● 1607—First surviving opera still performed, *L'Orfeo* by Claudio Monteverdi

● 1609—Galileo Galilei refines astronomical telescope

● 1622—Ignatius Loyola, founder of the Jesuit Order, Francis Xavier, Teresa of Ávila, Filippo Neri all canonized

● **1629—Bernini commissioned to complete St. Peter's Basilica**

● 1633—The Inquisition forces Galileo Galilei to recant

● **1642—Borromini's Sant'Ivo**
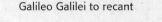

● 1642—Ribera's *The Club-Footed Boy*

● 1645–52—Bernini's *The Ecstasy of St. Teresa*

● **1656—Velázquez's** *Las Meninas*
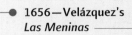
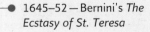

20 | The Baroque in the Netherlands

POINTS OF INQUIRY

20.1 Assess the influence of Caravaggio on Northern Baroque artists.

20.2 Explore the variations of Baroque art in the Northern and Southern Netherlands and the reasons for this difference.

20.3 Discover how Dutch artists explored new subject matter to cater to the needs of new patrons.

20.4 Explore the changing concept and use of self-portraiture.

20.5 Evaluate the role of light in the art of Rembrandt and Vermeer.

((•—Listen to the chapter audio on myartslab.com

The seventeenth century brought a division of the Netherlands into two parts (see **map 20.1**): The Northern Netherlands (now the Netherlands) and the Southern Netherlands (present-day Belgium and part of France). Each is often known by the name of its most important province: Holland (North) and Flanders (South). The Catholic Spanish Habsburgs had ruled the Netherlands in the sixteenth century, but Philip II's repressive measures against the Protestants and his attempts to curtail their local government led to a rebellion that lasted 15 years. In 1581, the northern provinces of the Netherlands, led by William the Silent, prince of Nassau, of the House of Orange, declared their independence from Spain. Spain soon recovered the Southern Netherlands, maintaining Catholicism as the official religion. After a long struggle, the seven major provinces of the North, inhabited predominantly by members of the Reformed Church, became the United Provinces with their autonomy officially recognized in a 1609 truce. Although hostilities broke out once more in 1621, the freedom of the Dutch was never again seriously in doubt. The Treaty of Münster ratified their independence and

ended the Thirty Years' War in 1648; the Dutch Republic then became an independent state.

The division of the Netherlands had very different consequences for the respective economies, social structures, cultures, and religions of the North and the South. Yet, throughout the seventeenth century, people crossed back and forth between the two regions, ensuring much social and cultural fluidity. After its sacking by Spanish troops in 1576, Antwerp, the leading port of the Southern Netherlands, lost half its population. Many migrated to the North. The city gradually regained its position as Flanders's commercial and artistic capital, although Brussels prevailed as the seat of government. As part of the Treaty of Münster, however, the Scheldt River leading to Antwerp's harbor was closed to shipping, thus crippling trade for the next two centuries. Because Flanders continued to be ruled by Spanish regents, the Habsburgs, who viewed themselves as the defenders of the "true" (i.e. Catholic) faith, its artists relied primarily on commissions from Church and State, but the aristocracy and wealthy merchants also functioned as important patrons.

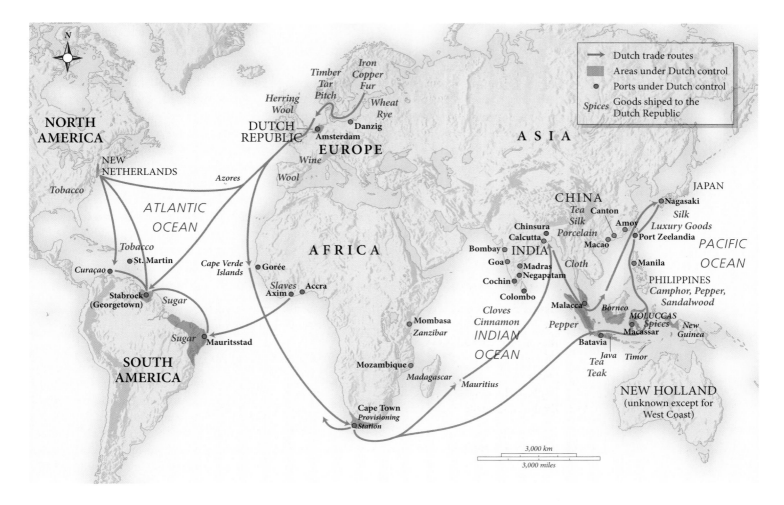

Map 20.1 Map of seventeenth-century Dutch trade routes

Holland, in contrast, was proud of its hard-won freedom. Although the predominant religion was the Reformed Church, the Dutch were notable for their religious tolerance. Even Catholicism continued to flourish, and included many artists among its ranks, while Jews, too, found a haven from persecution. Unlike Flanders, where most artistic activity radiated from Antwerp, Holland had a number of local schools of painting. Besides Amsterdam, the commercial capital, important artists worked in Haarlem, Utrecht, Leiden, and Delft (see map 20.1).

The new nation was one of merchants, farmers, and seafarers, who may have earned their living from local commerce such as the fishing trade, but who had the opportunity for more distant adventures with the development of the famous DUTCH EAST INDIA COMPANY (known as the VOC from its Dutch initials), established in 1602, and its counterpart, the DUTCH WEST INDIA COMPANY, established in 1621. These companies developed trade in East Asia (China, Japan, and Indonesia), and in the Americas, bringing home

exotic wares, strange creatures, and fabulous flora and fauna, as well as engaging in exploration, map making, and the creation of colonial settlements. Such adventures rippled through the economy: While experienced directly by the merchant sailors, there also was a direct impact on the directors and governors of the companies, who made their fortunes from these enterprises. Even the townspeople, who stayed home, purchased or at least saw some of the wonders brought back from faraway places. From this time forward, the Dutch—even those who did not travel—would consider themselves worldly.

As the Reformed Church was iconoclastic, Dutch artists rarely had the large-scale church altarpiece commissions available throughout the Catholic world. While the House of Orange in The Hague, city governments, and civic bodies such as militias offered a certain amount of art patronage, their demands were limited. As a result, private collectors became the painters' chief source of support. In both regions, North and South, a new class of patron arose—the wealthy merchant.

The DUTCH EAST INDIA COMPANY was founded in 1602, initially for the development of the spice trade (primarily pepper) and later expanded for the importation of porcelain and tea, while the DUTCH WEST INDIA COMPANY, founded in 1621, largely traded in sugar and sugar cane. They harvested these sweets through the inauguration of the slave trade through Africa to the Americas. The Netherlands and its new colonies were the portal through which these goods from East and West passed to the rest of Europe.

Flanders

The art of the great painter Peter Paul Rubens (1577–1640) defined art in seventeenth-century Flanders. Rubens brought Flanders, really Antwerp, to international notice and the art of the Western world to Flanders, accomplishing this through his commissions, his own extensive workshop, and his own travels, from which he brought ideas back.

Baroque art in Flanders thrived on commissions. Its many churches could now, with the truce of 1609, be rebuilt and redecorated. The Habsburg archduke and archduchess, their family, and private patrons provided these commissions. Rubens's own interests largely focused on painting, but he played a significant role in sculpture and sculptural decoration, architecture, costumes, and illustrated books (published by the famous Plantin Press in Antwerp), all of which were directly affected by him and his art.

The subjects of Flemish art, and of Rubens's paintings, were primarily religious—frequently large altarpieces with life-size figures. But portraits, landscapes, still lifes, or game pieces were also popular, and many were executed by other artists in collaboration with Rubens.

Peter Paul Rubens and Defining the Baroque

Although it was born in Rome, the Baroque style soon became international through the work of Rubens. He epitomized the Baroque ideal of the virtuoso artist, acting as diplomat, royal emissary, and advisor, with *entrée* to the courts of Europe—Paris, London, and Madrid. Widely read and widely traveled, he acquired a knowledge of classical literature, and spoke several languages. Acclaimed for his intellect, he had a vitality that enabled him to unite the natural and supernatural and to attain a Baroque theatricality and drama that Bernini also demonstrated (see Chapter 19). Trained by local painters, Rubens became a master in 1598, but he developed a personal style only when he went to Italy two years later.

During his eight years in the art and patronage centers of Mantua, Genoa, Florence, and Rome, he absorbed the Italian tradition far more completely than had any Northern European before him. He eagerly studied ancient sculpture, the masterpieces of the High Renaissance, and the work of Caravaggio and Annibale Carracci. He obtained major commissions in Italy for both portraits and altarpieces.

The term CYCLE refers to a number of scenes, usually painted, that illustrate a story or a series of episodes or events.

RUBENS AND THE ALTARPIECE Upon Rubens's return to Antwerp in 1609, he secured a commission to paint *The Raising of the Cross* (**fig. 20.1**) as the central panel for the high altar of the church of St. Walburga (now destroyed). Its very subject speaks to the dynamism of the Baroque and it shows how much he owed to his Italian experience. The muscular figures, modeled to show their physical power and passionate feeling, recall the antique, Hellenistic sculpture that Rubens saw, drew, and collected, and the figures from the Sistine Chapel ceiling that he also copied. These works of art served as models for his heroic figures throughout his life. He also gathered inspiration from the Farnese Gallery (see fig. 19.4), while the lighting suggests Caravaggio's work (see fig. 19.1). The altarpiece's rich color and luminosity are ultimately due to the influence of Titian (compare with fig. 16.13). Thus, it owes much of its success to Rubens's ability to combine Italian influences with Netherlandish ideas such as the realistically indicated foliage, the armor of the soldier, and the curly-haired dog in the foreground. These varied elements are integrated into a composition of tremendous force. The unstable pyramid of bodies, swaying precariously under the strain of the dramatic action, bursts the limits of the frame in a typically Baroque way, making a viewer feel like a participant in the action. Christ is shown parallel to the plane, so that we fully see him being raised to the Crucifixion. The "raising" implies movement and action happening at that moment. The entire scene is dramatic, powerful, and monumental.

The altarpiece would have been 35 feet high in its final form—a triptych (the wings are not shown here). It also included a now lost painting of God the Father above, explaining Christ's heavenward imploring glance. Placed on the high altar at the top of 19 steps, the entire altarpiece ensemble would have towered above all else.

Rubens's epic canvases defined the scope and the style of Baroque painting. They possess a seemingly boundless energy and inventiveness, which, like his heroic nudes, express life at its fullest.

MARIE DE' MEDICI CYCLE Rubens exhibited his virtuoso talent in portraits and monumental historical works in the 1620s with a prized commission, his CYCLE of paintings known as the *Marie de' Medici Cycle*. The paintings glorified the career of Marie de' Medici of France, widow of Henry IV and mother of Louis XIII, in the Luxembourg Palace in Paris. The cycle consists of 21 paintings at least 13 feet

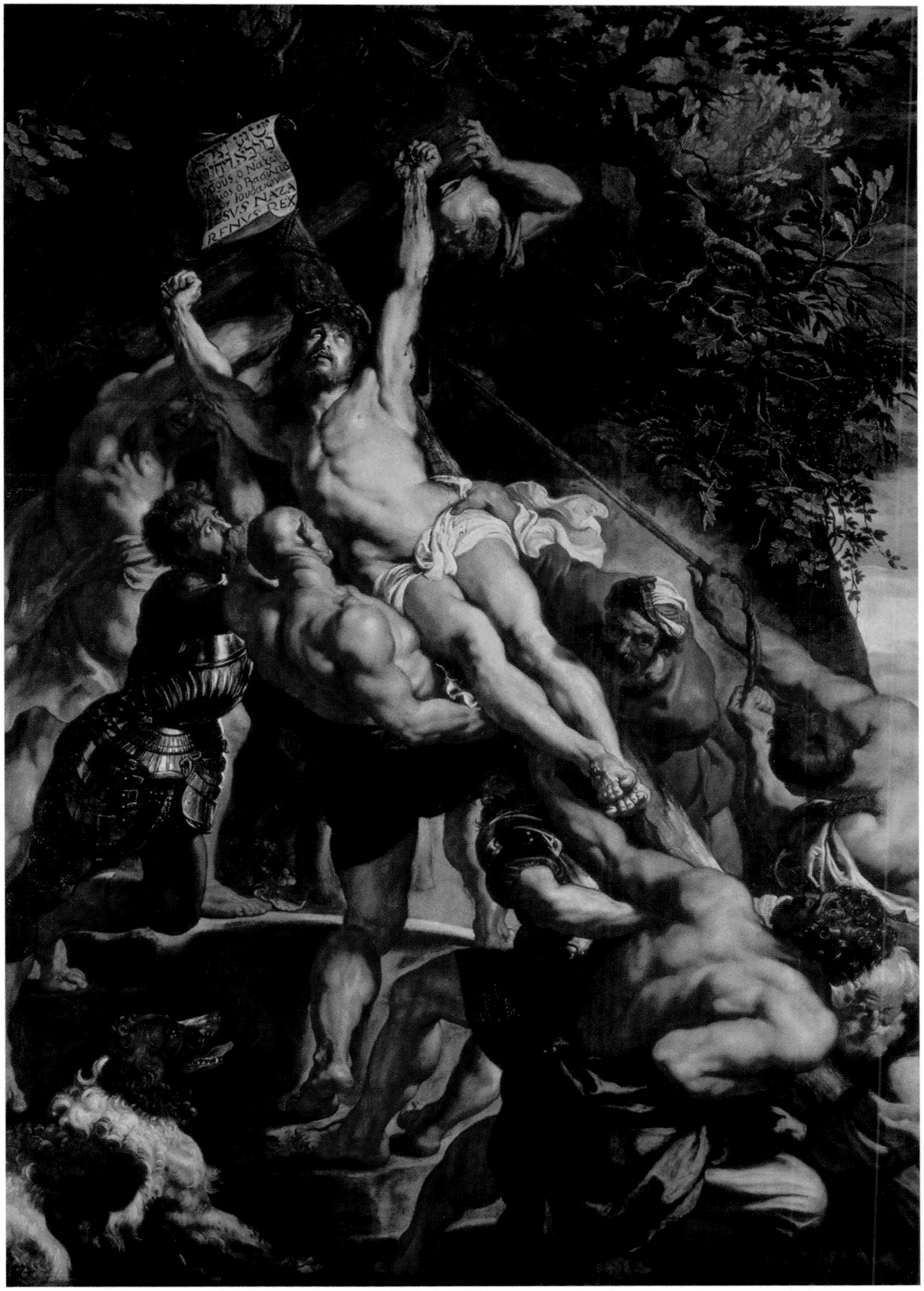

20.1 Peter Paul Rubens. *The Raising of the Cross.* 1610–11. Center panel of a triptych, 15′1″ × 11′9⅝″ (4.6 × 3.4 m). Antwerp Cathedral, Belgium. © KIK-IRPA, Brussels

high, with some as much as 28 feet wide. Our illustration shows one episode: The young queen landing in Marseilles (**fig. 20.2**). Rubens has turned this uneventful passage into a spectacle of unparalleled splendor, combining both reality and allegory. As Marie de' Medici walks down the gangplank to enter France, having already married Henry IV by proxy in Florence, she has not yet met her husband. (They will meet later in Lyons.) Accompanied by her sister and aunt as Fame flies overhead sounding triumphant blasts, she is welcomed by France, draped in a *fleur-de-lis* cape. Neptune and his fish-tailed crew, the Nereids, rise from the sea; having guarded the queen's journey, they rejoice at her arrival. Everything flows together here in swirling movement: Heaven and earth, history and allegory.

20.2 Peter Paul Rubens. *Marie de' Medici, Landing in Marseilles (3 November 1600)*. 1622–25. Oil on canvas, 12′11½″ × 9′7″ (3.94 × 2.95 m). Musée du Louvre, Paris

Read the document related to Peter Paul Rubens on myartslab.com

RUBENS'S WORKSHOP To produce these grand commissions—large paintings, painting cycles, ceilings, and altarpieces—Rubens initially worked on a small scale, with oil sketches, small paintings on wood. He used them to try out ideas and share them with his assistants. Most of the Flemish artists working in the early seventeenth century studied with Rubens in his large workshop. They often traveled where he did, worked on paintings he began or sketched, or started paintings that he completed. Many continued with Rubens for years of collaboration; others moved out on their own.

Anthony van Dyck: Portraiture at the English Court

Only one other Flemish Baroque artist, Anthony van Dyck (1599–1641), won international stature. A child prodigy, before he was 20 he had become Rubens's most valued assistant. And, like Rubens, he developed his mature style only after a stay in Italy.

Van Dyck's fame rests mainly on the life-size, stately, and elegant portraits he painted at the English court between 1632 and 1641. Using Rubens and Titian as his points of departure, Van Dyck developed a distinctive style of portraiture that would influence generations of artists and the depiction of the very wealthy.

The *Portrait of Charles I Hunting* (**fig. 20.3**) shows the king standing near a horse and two grooms in a landscape. Rather than a formal, authoritarian state portrait it represents the sovereign at ease. Yet Charles remains in full command of the state, symbolized by the horse, which bows its head toward its master. The fluid movement of the setting complements the self-conscious elegance of the king's pose. Charles's position, however, was less secure than his confidence suggests. His reign ended in civil war and his beheading in 1649. His successor, the Puritan leader Oliver Cromwell, and his followers were known as the "Roundheads" in reference to their short cropped hair. In contrast, note that in the painting Charles I's tresses drop below his shoulder in the French (Catholic) manner. His wife was Catholic and his own allegiance suspect.

Van Dyck died eight years before the beheading of Charles I and so never worked for the subsequent courts. But he had created the aristocratic portrait tradition, eventually termed "Van Dyckian," that continued in England until the late eighteenth century and which had considerable influence on the Continent as well.

Still-Life Painting

Still-life painting in seventeenth-century Flanders took many forms—depictions of flowers, game, food, and precious objects. Experts usually do not know who commissioned these works and presume they were for the homes of private patrons. At first predominantly simple paintings, by mid-century this genre explores the elaborate and dramatic explosion of objects collected at that time.

THE FLAMBOYANT STILL LIFE: JAN DAVIDSZ. DE HEEM By about the 1650s, the still-life painting was often a lavish display, known as the *pronk* still life for its visual splendor, as *pronk* means "showy" or "ostentatious." This type reached its peak in the work of Jan Davidsz. de Heem (1606–1684). De Heem began his career in Holland but soon moved to Antwerp,

20.3 Anthony van Dyck. *Portrait of Charles I Hunting*. ca. 1635. Oil on canvas, 8′11″ × 6′11½″ (2.7 × 2.1 m). Musée du Louvre, Paris. Inv.1236

20.4 Jan Davidsz. de Heem. *Still Life with Exotic Birds*. Late 1640s. Oil on canvas, 59¼ × 45½″ (150.5 × 115.5 cm). Collection of the John and Mable Ringling Museum of Art, the State Art Museum of Florida, Sarasota, Florida. Bequest of John Ringling, 1936. SN289

where he transformed the still life with his unique, flamboyant style. In *Still Life with Exotic Birds* (**fig. 20.4**), he depicts sumptuous commodities—delicious food, exotic birds, and luxurious goods—from around the world (see map 20.1): Conch and nautilus shells from the West Indies, an African gray parrot, a scarlet macaw from Brazil, and brilliant lobsters probably from the New World; Seville oranges, plums, figs, melons, pomegranates, oysters; gilt goblet and silver ewer, all imported and commanding high prices in the marketplace. It is the whole world in one picture.

Both abundance and extravagance are suggested by the food piled up on unstable pewter platters. De Heem intends this to be wondrous and theatrical, drawing back a curtain for us to see. Even the

column in the background is meant to suggest a heroic work. This stunning, celebratory display of virtuosity defines the elements of a *pronk* still life.

The Dutch Republic

Art in the Dutch Republic, unlike that of Flanders, did not depend largely on church or state commissions, but was created primarily though private patronage and the open art market, as a commodity. Many artists produced for the market rather than for individual patrons. As such, even the greatest masters could not fully support themselves with the money earned from their art. It was not unusual for an artist to keep an inn or run a small business on the side. Yet they survived—less financially secure, but freer as a community of artists.

Many artistic communities proliferated—in Haarlem, Utrecht, Amsterdam, and Delft, to name but a few. Artists frequently traveled between these cities and may have known each other's work, but most of them usually lived in only one place—Terbrugghen worked primarily in Utrecht; Frans Hals and Judith Leyster in Haarlem; Rembrandt in Amsterdam; Vermeer in Delft. Some paintings depicted religious themes, but secular images dominated: Individual portraits, group portraits commissioned by civic groups, landscapes, cityscapes, architectural paintings, still lifes, and genre paintings. And the paintings ranged from large to small—small enough to hold in the hand or for ordinary people to hang on the walls of their homes.

The *Caravaggisti* in Holland: Hendrick Terbrugghen

The Baroque style arrived in Holland from Antwerp through the work of Rubens, and from Rome through contact with the *Caravaggisti*, Caravaggio's followers. Although most Dutch painters did not travel to Italy, the majority of those who journeyed there in the early years of the century were from Utrecht, a town with strong Catholic traditions. One of these, Hendrick Terbrugghen (1588–1629), worked in Italy for several years and was one of the first of the *Caravaggisti* to return to the North. He adapted Caravaggio's style for religious painting, but also for single-figured genre painting. Terbrugghen's *Singing Lute Player* (**fig. 20.5**) of 1624 takes its inspiration from Caravaggio's painting of the same subject, his *The Musicians* (fig. 19.2), and others like it, such as the young men in *The Calling of*

20.5 Hendrick Terbrugghen. *Singing Lute Player*. 1624. Oil on canvas, 39⅝ × 31″ (100.5 × 78.7 cm). The National Gallery, London

St. Matthew (fig. 19.1), who wear slashed doublets and feathered berets. Deeply engaged, the musician leans in, plucks the strings of the lute, and sings with a full, rounded, open mouth. Terbrugghen's portrayal of a life-size, half-length figure, filling the entire canvas, became a common one in Utrecht painting, and grew popular elsewhere in Holland. The Utrecht School transmitted the style of Caravaggio to other Dutch masters, such as Frans Hals.

The Haarlem Community and Frans Hals

One of the first to profit from these new ideas permeating the Dutch Republic was the Haarlem artist Frans Hals (ca. 1585–1666), who was born in Antwerp. Capturing his contemporaries in both portraiture and genre painting, Hals excelled at combining both by animating his portraits and setting their poses in somewhat relaxed or even casual stances. He is famous for his six Civic Guard group portraits of life-size figures as well as hundreds of individual portraits, none of which repeated the same pose. His genre painting, usually of single figures, portrayed characters that seem to be drawn from real life.

A WEDDING PORTRAIT Hals's only double portrait, *Married Couple in a Garden, probably a Portrait of Isaac Massa and Beatrix van der Laen* (**fig. 20.6**), commemorates the couple's wedding in 1622. It combines the relaxed, informal, spontaneous atmosphere of genre painting with the likeness and formal attire of portraiture. This life-size couple modestly display their mutual affection for each other by sitting close together. Ingeniously, Hals set the couple off-center, which adds to the sense of spontaneity, punctuated by the sense that Massa is open-mouthed and speaking to us. Beatrix smiles broadly, her arm looped over his elbow, displaying her ring (customarily worn on the index finger). They both wear expensive clothing. Isaac sports a broad-brimmed hat in the French fashion and she an embroidered and ribboned cap, usually worn

20.6 Frans Hals. *Married Couple in a Garden, probably a Portrait of Isaac Massa and Beatrix van der Laen*. ca. 1622. Oil on canvas, 4'7" × 5'5½" (1.4 × 1.66 m). Rijksmuseum, Amsterdam

indoors or under another hat. Beatrix's silk skirt and *vlieger* (bodice) of velvet with broad shoulders is a style worn only by married women, thus identifying her status. Their eyes twinkle with enjoyment, as they sit in a garden—an imaginary Garden of Love—surrounded by ivy, a symbol of steadfast love and fidelity. The vine clinging to the tree and the thistle in the foreground are also symbols of marital love and fidelity. Indeed, they seem to be in love. His right hand touches his chest (his heart) as a show of his intended affection. Isaac Massa (1586–1643), an important and wealthy diplomat, geographer, and a cartographer of Siberia, was active in the fur trade. But his worldliness is only suggested in this wedding portrait set in his own garden.

The painting can be seen in sharp contrast to the standing couple in Jan van Eyck's *The "Arnolfini Portrait"* (fig. 14.6). We can see that the emotional tie between the Arnolfini couple was not Van Eyck's concern. This is more than a difference in personal artistic style; it is the difference between the Renaissance and the Baroque, occurring over the course of 200 years. Between Van Eyck and Hals also stood Rubens, who had executed a wedding portrait of himself and his first wife that may have served as an example to Hals, who may have seen it on a visit to Antwerp years earlier.

HALS AND GENRE PAINTING While Hals's portraits display the spontaneity of a genre painting—the quality of actual people responding to each other naturally—his genre painting suggests a sense of portraiture. The people who laugh, drink, or sing in his paintings seem so real that we assume he actually knew them, as in the case of the *Malle Babbe* (**fig. 20.7**), the so-called "Witch of Haarlem." This cackling, wild woman, whether drunk (it is a very large tankard she hauls) or just a bit deranged, might say loud and inappropriate things. The words "Malle Babbe" were written on the painting's old stretcher (inner wood foundation upon which the canvas is wrapped) and indeed there is a record of a person described as "Malle Babbe," confined to the Haarlem House of Correction in 1653. So this genre painting may have been inspired by an actual person in the town. Hals suggests her vivacity and even instinctive, animal-like movement by the slapdash, almost fevered brushstrokes, a strong contrast to the controlled, but still vivid quality of Beatrix van der Laen (fig. 20.6).

The prominent owl perched on Malle Babbe's shoulder may seem a confusing element as we

associate this bird with wisdom. But this was not its only meaning in the seventeenth century. Its appearance may reflect its relationship to demonic forces, as an owl prefers darkness to light; it is also a symbol of foolishness and vulgarity. A common saying, still used today in the Netherlands for someone who imbibes too much, is "drunk as an owl." And this phrase ties together the tankard, the owl, and the wild force of *Malle Babbe*. Whatever her nature, the painting is a vibrant *tour de force* of spontaneity.

Hals, like Rembrandt van Rijn and Jan (Johannes) Vermeer—artists of the next generation, epitomized the period referred to as the Golden Age of Dutch art. Individually, these three artists created and developed from their Northern heritage the unique style of seventeenth-century Dutch art in Haarlem, Amsterdam, and Delft respectively. None of them traveled to Italy.

20.7 Frans Hals. *Malle Babbe*, c. 1633–35. Oil on canvas, 29½ × 25⅕″ (75 × 64 cm). Gemäldegalerie, Staatliche Museen zu Berlin, Preussischer Kulturbesitz

The Next Generation in Haarlem: Judith Leyster

The most important follower of Hals was Judith Leyster (1609–1660), who was responsible for a number of works that once passed as Hals's own. She painted portraits and still lifes, but mostly genre paintings. Her *Self-Portrait* (**fig. 20.8**) shows Leyster as both portrait and genre painter and was executed no doubt to demonstrate her mastery of both. It was probably her presentation or master's piece to the Guild of St. Luke in Haarlem in 1633, when she became accepted as a master and had her own students. The painting on the easel is a detail of a popular work of hers, and so she is advertising her diverse talents. The portrait reveals her technical skill as she wields numerous brushes and a palette while she sits in her studio, open-mouthed and casually conversing with us. Many women artists, as Leyster does here, showed themselves painting—indicating their new professional status and their unique position (see Artemisia Gentileschi,

page 391–92). Leyster signed many of her paintings with a monogram, a conjoined J, L, and star, as Leyster means "leading star." Indeed, punning on her name, she was referred to during her lifetime as a "leading star" in art.

Rembrandt and the Art of Amsterdam

Like Hals and Leyster, Rembrandt Harmensz. van Rijn (1606–1669) felt the influence of Caravaggio indirectly through the Utrecht School. While he rivaled Rubens as the most famous artist of his age, Rembrandt is perhaps better known to us today. A painter, draughtsman, and printmaker, he is equally significant in each medium and established himself in the growing and prosperous city of Amsterdam. Rembrandt is known both for the intimacy and poignancy of images that convey personal relationships and emotions—an aspect seldom explored before—as well as for producing individual portraits, large group portraits, and history pieces. He had an active workshop for four decades and many of his followers became significant artists in his native Leiden or in Amsterdam.

REMBRANDT AS PRINTMAKER An innovative and experimental printmaker, Rembrandt chose to work primarily in the medium of etching (see box, page 307), and he remains perhaps the greatest proponent of this process. Etching begins as light drawing on a prepared plate and so Rembrandt was able to be relatively spontaneous and fresh in his many small examples. Among his most notable subjects at the beginning of his career, his self-portraits are experimental in the early Leiden years, theatrically disguised in the 1630s, and frank and sober toward the end of his life. Experts have suggested many reasons for their execution—as models for other paintings, as explorations of different expressions, and as possible advertisements for his craft and to many collectors who wanted to own representations of artists.

His small (less than 2 inches square) *Self-Portrait with Cap, Open-Mouthed* (**fig. 20.9**) provides us with a startling and even funny example. It makes one laugh—or at least smile—and that was surely one of its points: To get a reaction from the viewer. It appears that Rembrandt and the viewer have startled each other. His eyes are wide open and with lips parted it seems an instantaneous response. He "comes in" from one side and so is off-center, adding to the Baroque quality of "at the moment." Rembrandt etched over 20 self-portraits, half of

20.8 Judith Leyster. *Self-Portrait.* ca. 1633. Oil on canvas, 29³/₈ × 25³/₈" (72.3 × 65.3 cm). National Gallery of Art, Washington, D.C. Gift of Mr. and Mrs. Robert Woods Bliss. 1949.6.4

which are quick sketches like this one; the others are more formal and finished.

A master storyteller, Rembrandt demonstrates this ability in his biblical etchings of both the Hebrew Bible and New Testament themes, which he executed throughout his career. In his hands, these narratives evince deep empathy and pathos. His famed *The Hundred Guilder Print* (**fig. 20.10**), which derives its name from the large price of 100 guilders supposedly paid for it at a contemporary auction, was executed in stages over many years. The etching, interpreted as a depiction of the entire nineteenth chapter of the Gospel of St. Matthew, combines various aspects of Christ's preachings, including the healing of the multitude, and the gathering of children and those who had forsaken all to come to him. Poignant and filled with pathos, it reveals a humble world of bare feet and ragged clothes. The scene is full of the artist's deep compassion for the poor and outcast, who comprise the audience in the scene. It has been suggested that viewing the print in reverse (as it was drawn) puts the tormented (the poor, the sick, and the children) in the "correct" order. The setting suggests some corner in Amsterdam

20.9 Rembrandt van Rijn. *Self-Portrait with Cap, Open-Mouthed.* ca. 1630. Etching, 2 × 1⅘″ (54 × 46 mm), actual size as shown here. Rijksmuseum, Prentenkabinet, Amsterdam

where the Jews had found a haven; they are included here to provide an "authentic" background for Christ's teachings. Rembrandt had a special sympathy for them, both as heirs of the biblical past and as victims of persecution, and they were often his models, as well as, occasionally, his patrons. Rembrandt incorporates observations of life from the drawings he made throughout his career. As in Caravaggio's *The Calling of St. Matthew* (see fig. 19.1), it is the magic of light and dark here created with the velvety tone of drypoint (see box, page 307) that gives *The Hundred*

20.10 Rembrandt van Rijn. *The Hundred Guilder Print.* ca. 1649. Etching and drypoint, 11 × 15¼″ (27.8 × 38.8 cm). Yale University Art Gallery, New Haven. Fritz Achelis Memorial Collection, Gift of Frederic George Achelis, B.A. 1907, 1925.130

 Watch a video about the process of intaglio on myartslab.com

Guilder Print its spiritual significance. And, like Caravaggio, he infuses the story with the same lay Christian spirit that reveals God's ways with his human creations.

REMBRANDT AND THE CIVIC GUARD By the 1640s, Rembrandt had become Amsterdam's most sought-after portrait painter, and a man of considerable wealth. He executed portraits, mostly life-size, and sometimes full-length, of individuals or couples, as well as history and religious paintings. He painted for the court in The Hague, and for private patrons.

The famous group portrait known as *The Night Watch* (**fig. 20.11**), because of its old, darkened varnish (now removed), was painted in 1642. A Civic Guard company of musketeers is assembling, possibly for the 1638 visit of Marie de' Medici of France to Amsterdam. Founded in the fourteenth century, the Civic Guard functioned as local voluntary militia groups. Although militarily active in successfully defending their cities from the Spanish in the 1580s, with the truce of 1609 the Guard became more like civic fraternities, with civic and religious duties. They began commissioning portraits in the early sixteenth century, and this painting is one of six (by six different artists) made for their new building. Although the members of the company had each contributed toward

20.11 Rembrandt van Rijn. *The Night Watch (The Company of Captain Frans Banning Cocq)*. 1642. Oil on canvas, 12'2" × 14'7" (3.8 × 4.4 m). Rijksmuseum, Amsterdam

the cost of this huge canvas (originally it was even larger), Rembrandt did not give them equal weight pictorially. He avoided the mechanically regular designs of group portraits by many earlier artists (although Frans Hals did several outstanding ones).

Instead, the picture is full of movement and dramatic lighting, as the men stride out to meet the French monarch and demonstrate their new firearms. The focus is on Captain Frans Banning Cocq, whose hand extends toward us with such strong three-dimensional illusion that it creates a shadow across the yellow jacket of his lieutenant. Light strikes the little girl at left, one of three children (another girl nearly hidden by her and a boy just next to her with his back to us) who rush through this crowd of older men. They probably are mascots who carry the sign of the Civic Guard, as they may have done in real life. The highlighted girl carries—really wears—claws (of a chicken) tied to her belt; the claws were the symbol of the building, the Kloveniersdoelen, in which the painting hung. With the rush of figures and contrast of light and shadow, Rembrandt captures the excitement of the moment and gives the scene unique drama.

Because some figures are brightly lit and others are plunged into shadow or hidden by overlapping, legend has it that those whose portraits Rembrandt had obscured were dissatisfied with the painting, but there is no evidence for this claim. On the contrary, we know that the work was much admired in its time, and Rembrandt continued to receive major public commissions in the 1650s and 1660s.

MATURE WORK Rembrandt is known best today for his mature and late work because of its psychological insight and qualities of introspection. Both poignant and "from life," Rembrandt's monumental painting of *Bathsheba with King David's Letter* (**fig. 20.12**) is a stunning example from this period. We know nothing of its commissioning or later purchase. The subject, from 2 Samuel 11:2–27, was familiar to seventeenth-century viewers: The biblical King David noticed the beautiful, but married, Bathsheba at her bath and summoned her. Thus began a series of events culminating in her pregnancy, the death of her husband, specifically sent to the front lines of battle to be killed, her marriage to King David, and the birth of her son, who would be King Solomon. Although in the biblical account Bathsheba does not actually receive a letter, this prop became part of the visual tradition along with the attendant performing the pedicure at left.

The large nude, so close to our space, confronts us—even though *she* does not. Bathsheba with deep sadness and melancholy looks down at David's letter, contemplating its consequences and the loss of her own innocence. Indeed, Bathsheba, in the seventeenth century, was not considered innocent but complicit in allowing the king to see her body and therefore in betraying her marriage vows. The painting itself is not eroticized, but the sheer fleshiness and palpability of her body make the sensual difficult to ignore. This work brings to mind the many life-size nudes by Titian (see fig. 16.15), but our painting is of a flawed human, while Titian's is that of a goddess. Formed of flesh and light, in contrast to the color of Titian's subject, Rembrandt's Bathsheba is not at all an idealized figure an contemporary criticism faults Rembrandt in this regard. "Fat swollen belly, hanging breasts, garter marks" were descriptions associated with Rembrandt's nudes. We cannot escape her disturbing reality and get lost in the narrative of the painting—as there isn't one. Indicative of the psychological depth of Rembrandt's mature works, the painting remains an icon of vulnerability.

20.12 Rembrandt van Rijn. *Bathsheba with King David's Letter*. 1654. Oil on canvas, 55¹⁄₁₀ × 55¹⁄₁₀″ (142 × 142 cm). Musée du Louvre, Paris

The Market: Landscape, Still Life, and Genre Painting

Art in Northern Europe was largely made for an open market. Of course, portraits and group portraits, like those for the Civic Guard (Rembrandt's *The Night Watch*), were commissioned works, but a great number of paintings were made "on spec"—that is, with the hope that they would be purchased on the open market from dealers, fairs, stores, and lotteries. We know that Rubens kept many paintings in stock for his own use—even very large works available for princely patrons. But in the Dutch Republic, paintings were often small, cabinet-size, and with subjects suitable for a middle-class home. Most art buyers in Holland preferred subjects within their own experience: Landscapes, architectural views, still lifes, and genre (everyday) scenes. These subjects, we recall, emerged in the latter half of the sixteenth century (see Chapter 18).

The richest of the newly developed "specialties" was landscape, both as a portrayal of familiar views and as an imaginative vision of nature. Landscapes—frequently with only small human figures or none at all—became a staple of seventeenth-century Dutch painting. We can see the beginnings of this in the work of Pieter Bruegel the Elder (see page 383–85) and in Italy as well. But in the Netherlands, the sense of reality, almost a "portrait of the land," was a common theme. As the land is below sea level and only an elaborate system of canals and dikes can reclaim it, there is a strong sense of appreciation for it that is expressed in its depictions. A contemporary said of these paintings: "Nothing is lacking except the warmth of the sun and the movement caused by the gentle breeze."

20.13 Jacob van Ruisdael. *Bleaching Grounds Near Haarlem.* ca. 1670. Oil on canvas, 21⅔ × 24½" (55.5 × 62 cm). Royal Cabinet of Paintings, Mauritshuis, The Hague, Netherlands

Landscape Painting: Jacob van Ruisdael

Identifiable city views—panoramic landscapes with the outlying countryside and picturesque sand dunes, showing Amsterdam, Haarlem, or other cities—became popular throughout the century. In the art of Jacob van Ruisdael (ca. 1628–1682), these views become testaments to the city skyline—and to the sky of this flat, low land. The sky might occupy three-quarters of the painting, as it does in this work, *Bleaching Grounds Near Haarlem* (**fig. 20.13**). Ruisdael rendered many paintings of Haarlem, known as *Haarlempjes* (little views of Haarlem), in the 1670s. The church spires, windmills, and ruins are all identifiable, as is the major church, the Grote Kerk (Great Church), known before the Reformation as St. Bavo. In the foreground are the bleaching fields, where both domestic and foreign linen was washed and laid out to be bleached by the sun. Haarlem water was well known for its purity and so the city was famous for its linen-bleaching and its beer production. Haarlemmers took pride in their city, in their artists—and in their artists' painted views of the city and its surrounding countryside.

Still-Life Painting: Willem Claesz. Heda

Dutch still lifes may depict the remains of a meal, of food and drink and luxury objects, such as crystal goblets, glasses of different sizes, and silver dishes, chosen for their contrasting shapes, colors, and textures. Flowers, fruits, and seashells may also be represented.

Still Life with Oysters, a Roemer, a Lemon, and a Silver Bowl (**fig. 20.14**), of 1634, by the Haarlem artist Willem Claesz. Heda (1594–1680), showcases the artist's fascination with various surfaces and reflections—the rough edge of the lemon, the liquid, slimy quality of the oysters, the engraving on the silver, the sparkling light on the *roemer* (glass), its multiple reflections of the window, and its *prunts* (glass drops). Heda achieved fame for these light effects, which are heightened by the **tonal** quality (various tones of the same color) of the painting in greens and silvery grays, making it largely **monochromatic**. These contrast markedly with the colorful Flemish works of Jan Davidsz. de Heem (fig. 20.4). The table is set with white wine, beer (back right), lemon, and a paper cone of pepper to use with the oysters, known then as an aphrodisiac.

20.14 Willem Claesz. Heda. *Still Life with Oysters, a Roemer, a Lemon, and a Silver Bowl.* 1634. Oil on panel, 16⅞ × 22⅞" (43 × 57 cm). Museum Boymans-van Beuningen, Rotterdam, Netherlands

Yet the broken glass and overturned silver *tazza* suggest a hasty departure or some upheaval on a narrative level. Whoever sat at this table was suddenly forced to leave the meal. The stability of the physical composition contradicts the psychological notion of haste and suggests transience—a *vanitas*—similar to the intent of the still life in Holbein's *The Ambassadors* (fig. 18.11).

Flower Painting and Rachel Ruysch

The independent floral still life seems to have begun in Flanders, but it developed in both the Northern and Southern Netherlands. Rachel Ruysch (1664–1750), one of the leading and respected Dutch flower painters of the day, had a long and prolific career working in Amsterdam, The Hague, and Düsseldorf, where she and her husband Juriaen

Pool II (1665–1745), a portraitist, became, as a team, court painters to the Elector Palatine until his death. One could even say she was born to be a flower painter, as her father was a professor of anatomy and botany. Ruysch knew every blossom, every butterfly, moth, and snail she painted. We know from the inclusion of flowers in earlier paintings, such as the lilies in a vase in the altarpiece of the *Mérode Triptych* (fig. 14.3), that they can have meaning beyond their beauty. The flowers in **fig. 20.15**, some with stems, wild and impossibly long, that stretch across the diagonal of the canvas, are arranged to create an extravaganza of color. Yet the fallen, drooping flowers, like the broken glass in the Heda (fig. 20.14), again suggest a theme of the shortness of life, a *vanitas*, common in Dutch still-life painting.

20.15 Rachel Ruysch. *Flower Still Life*. After 1700. Oil on canvas, 29¾ × 23⅞″ (75.5 × 60.7 cm). Toledo Museum of Art, Ohio. Purchased with funds from the Libbey Endowment, Gift of Edward Drummond Libbey. 11956.57

Genre Painting: Jan Steen

Genre painting continued throughout the century, but revealed a more complex narrative by mid-century. The human figures are often no longer half-length; they are now full-length, even when the paintings are small and create a sense of intimacy. Interior scenes of homes and taverns are common. The paintings of Jan Steen and Jan Vermeer provide a range of subject matter from the comical to the deeply introspective, and offer glimpses into the home, family, relationships, and even fashion of the seventeenth century.

The Feast of St. Nicholas (**fig. 20.16**) by Jan Steen (1626–1679), a scene of both comical circumstance and family intimacy, depicts a feast still celebrated in much the same way today in Holland. St. Nicholas has just paid his pre-Christmas visit to the household, leaving toys, candy, and cake for the children, who have set their shoes out for gifts. Delighted with her presents, the little girl holds a doll of St. John the Baptist and a bucket filled with sweets, while the boy, equally delighted, plays with a *kolf* (a kind of golf) club and ball. Everyone is jolly except their brother, on the left, who has received

20.16 Jan Steen. *The Feast of St. Nicholas.* ca. 1665–68. Oil on canvas, 32¼ × 27¾″ (82 × 70.5 cm). Rijksmuseum, Amsterdam

in his shoe, held by the maidservant, only a birch rod for caning naughty children. Soon his tears will turn to joy, however: His grandmother, in the background, beckons to the bed, where surely a toy is hidden.

Steen tells the story with relish, embroidering it with many delightful details. *The Feast of St. Nicholas* also conveys a serious message as well: The doll of St. John the Baptist is a reminder of the importance of spiritual matters over worldly possessions, no matter how pleasurable. Steen drives his style of storytelling with a moral from the tradition of Pieter Bruegel the Elder (see fig. 18.15).

Intimate Genre Painting and Jan Vermeer

In the genre scenes of the Delft artist Jan Vermeer (1632–1675), by contrast, there is no clear narrative. Single figures, usually women, are seemingly engaged in everyday tasks at secluded, still

moments. Vermeer's paintings appear magical, hypnotic, and truly original. His women exist in a timeless "still-life" world, as if becalmed by a spell. In *Woman Holding a Balance* (**fig. 20.17**), a young woman, richly dressed in the at-home wear of the day, contemplates a balance in her hand, with strings of pearls and gold coins spread out on the table before her. The pearls, gold, a painting, and fur all magically help provide an eternal, yet momentary, glance into a private realm where, in fact, our view is not acknowledged. The painting on the wall depicts Christ at the Last Judgment, when every soul is weighed. This may be a reference to the soul of her unborn child, and it parallels the woman's own activity, now contemplating the future with the scales she holds. Experts once thought that the pans of the balance contained gold or pearls but scientific analysis of the painting indicates that they actually contain nothing, only

20.17 Jan Vermeer. *Woman Holding a Balance*. ca. 1664. Oil on canvas, 16¾ × 15" (42.5 × 38.1 cm). National Gallery of Art, Washington, D.C. Widener Collection. 1942.9.97

Watch a video about Vermeer's *Woman Holding a Balance* on myartslab.com beads of light. The painting is intensely private, quiet, yet also highly sensual, created with optical effects that make the surface shimmer.

Vermeer's work is marked with his use of light, frequently from a window at the left, with flecks of light on fabric, and with reflections. To achieve these effects, he may have employed mechanics that are both old and new, including a *camera obscura*, an experimental optical device (a forerunner of the photographic camera) that created an image by means of a hole for light on the inside of a dark box. The hole acts as a primitive lens and a scene from outside the box is visible, inverted, inside it. Vermeer would not have copied such scenes, but he may have taken inspiration from them. They often have a sparkling quality, as visible in the pearls and in the light on the balance. These sparkling areas are known as "disks of confusion." The *camera obscura* was well known, and there is considerable evidence that Dutch artists used it.

This new way of looking is paired with an old way—a one-point perspective view with a vanishing point. It has been shown that a hole (for a pin and string) was set in a number of Vermeer's paintings to create a one-point perspective system. The vanishing point in fig. 20.17 is just to the left of the little finger of the hand that holds the balance. It sets the balance of all elements of the painting.

Vermeer is a master of the expressive qualities of light. Concerned with all of light's visual and symbolic possibilities, his paintings reveal a world of introspection. His arrangement of figures, space, and light, while looking incredibly simple, was complex, yet the complexities remained hidden. Vermeer makes the quiet moment an intimate drama, distilled with natural light, and captures the character of the Dutch Baroque. It seems far away from the dark paintings of Caravaggio made for church patrons, but both are concerned with drama and light effects—yet worlds apart.

POINTS OF REFLECTION

20.1 Discuss the influence of Caravaggio on Rubens, Terbrugghen, and Rembrandt.

20.2 Explain how Baroque art in the Southern Netherlands differs from that in the Northern. In what ways are they similar?

20.3 Explain the role of commissions from middle-class Northern patrons on the development of new subject matter, including genre, still life, landscape, and portraiture. Use specific examples.

20.4 Using the self-portraits of Judith Leyster and Rembrandt, discuss how artists employed this theme in connection with social status and marketing.

20.5 Analyze Rembrandt's use of chiaroscuro in his *The Hundred Guilder Print*.

✓—**Study** and review on myartslab.com

ART IN TIME

● 1602—Dutch East India Company founded

● **1610–11—Peter Paul Rubens, *The Raising of the Cross***

● **1621**—Philip IV becomes king of Spain

● 1626—New Amsterdam (New York City) founded by the Dutch West India Company

● 1634—Willem Claesz. Heda, *Still Life with Oysters, a Roemer, a Lemon and a Silver Bowl*

● **ca. 1635—Anthony van Dyck, *Portrait of Charles I Hunting***

● 1639—Japan enforces policy of isolation from Europeans; permits a Dutch trading post

● **1642**—Rembrandt, *The Night Watch*

● 1648—Treaty of Münster legally recognizes the Dutch Republic

● **ca. 1664—Jan Vermeer, *Woman Holding a Balance***

● **ca. 1670—Jacob van Ruisdael, *Bleaching Grounds Near Haarlem***

● 1676—Anthony van Leeuwenhoek first to record bacteria under a microscope

CHAPTER

21 | The Baroque in France and England

POINTS OF INQUIRY

21.1 Investigate the relationship between classicism and Louis XIV's concept of power and style.

21.2 Explore Poussin's principles of the Grand Manner of painting.

21.3 Discover how the political theory of the *absolute monarch* translates into architecture.

21.4 Assess the development of landscape painting as evidenced in the works of Poussin and Claude.

21.5 Analyze the development of the new city of London as a result of the Great Fire.

(((•—Listen to the chapter audio on myartslab.com

During the course of the tumultuous seventeenth century, the great monarchies of France and England dominated as patrons of the arts. Expanding civic projects, particularly architecture, expressed the wealth of each nation. France, led by an absolute ruler, and England, governed by a king who shared power with Parliament, underwent dramatic change. Yet both countries suffered from the devastation of the previous era's religious wars, dynastic struggles, and contemporary famines and disease; further, by mid-century, increased colonial expansion sorely drained the treasuries. Their societies were bitterly divided, with Catholicism becoming the dominant religion in France and Protestantism in England. Each successive French and English monarch sought to strike a delicate balance between these competing religious forces while attempting to favor the religion of his choice.

England faced continual upheaval (**map 21.1**) and its situation degenerated in 1642 into a civil war that led to the trial of King Charles I, who was convicted of treason and beheaded in 1649. Named head of state and Lord Protector, the Puritan Oliver

Cromwell restored political stability, but upon his death in 1658 his government foundered. Two years later, in 1660, Parliament offered the throne to the son of the beheaded king, Charles II (r. 1649–1685), thus ushering in the period known as the Restoration. Unfortunately, old religious rivalries and economic crises persisted, and jeopardized the reign of Charles II's successor and brother, James II (r. 1685–1688). In the so-called Glorious Revolution of 1688, a relatively peaceful and bloodless event, members of the governing classes of Whigs and Tories proclaimed the prince of Orange, the stadholder or ruler of the Dutch Republic, as king of England; he and his wife, James's daughter, reigned jointly from 1689 as William III and Mary II (Mary died in 1694, William in 1702). The Bill of Rights (1689) established Parliament's supremacy and created a unique form of government that would gradually influence nations worldwide, notably the North American British colonies.

In France, which by mid-century had emerged as Europe's most militarily and culturally powerful nation, Louis XIV (r. 1643–1715) consolidated his power. Louis evoked the age-old divine right of kings—the idea that the monarch received his authority directly from God—and increased the state's power over the nobility and over local authorities, amassing revenue through taxation. This form of royal government, known as absolutism, gave full power to the monarch. The ABSOLUTE MONARCHY in France differed from England's constitutional monarchy, which divided power between the ruler and other institutions. Louis XIV embarked on a series of military campaigns from 1688 to 1713 against his rivals, Spain, the Dutch Republic, Germany, and England in his quest to assert the preeminence of France. Despite eventual defeat, France remained a world power upon Louis's death in 1715.

The art of these two nations was dominated by **classicism**—the style derived from the ancient Greek and Roman civilizations. Through its use of classical vocabulary—from columns, capitals, and pediments in architecture to styles of dress in painting—classicism represents a response to the ancient world. It suggests authority, order, and enduring tradition in its evocation of the imperial grandeur of Rome, an association highly desired by the reigning monarchs; and thus classicism would become the hallmark of the Baroque in France and England.

In France, classicism achieved status as the official court style of painting between 1660 and 1685, the climactic phase of Louis XIV's reign. Classical principles also dominated architecture, with the new Louvre and Versailles representing the most visible accomplishments of Baroque Classicism in France.

In England, too, classicism dominated art and architecture, notably the hospitals, churches, and country houses designed by Inigo Jones and Sir Christopher Wren. Architecture thrived as massive reconstruction projects were undertaken to rebuild the city in the wake of the Great Fire of London in 1666. Yet England's lasting artistic successes in the seventeenth century were in literature, with notable works by William Shakespeare, John Donne, and John Milton as well as the royal committee's translation of what would become known as the King James Bible.

France: The Style of Louis XIV

By the late seventeenth century, Paris was vying with Rome as Europe's art center. The French kings Henry IV (r. 1589–1610), Louis XIII (r. 1610–

Map 21.1 Political resistance and unrest in France and England in the seventeenth century

1643), and Louis XIV—aided by ambitious and able ministers and advisors such as the duc de Sully, cardinals Richelieu and Mazarin, and Jean-Baptiste Colbert—created the climate for this exciting turn of events. The rulers and their officials recognized the power of art to convey the majesty and strength of the monarchy, and they set out to create a massive program of patronage of all the arts and sciences—painting, sculpture, architecture, landscape design, decorative arts, theoretical and applied science, philosophy, and literature. Louis XIV especially manipulated art to serve as propaganda for his absolutist policies. He adopted the symbolic imagery of the sun as manifested by the Greek god Apollo, and came to be called the "Sun King". This symbolism provided an ancient lineage for Louis that would serve his principle as absolute ruler. The ideal of *gloire* (glory), seen in the portraits and architecture he commissioned, reflected his desire to give concrete form to the majesty of his rule, and thus of France.

Scholars often describe the period's art and literature as "classic." In this context, the word

The political system that gives rise to an ABSOLUTE MONARCHY is absolutism, in which full, unlimited, and unchecked power to rule a nation is in the hands of a single individual (an absolute monarch) or a group of rulers (oligarchs). Absolutism emerged in Europe near the end of the fifteenth century and is most clearly embodied by the reign of Louis XIV of France.

has three meanings. It is a synonym for "highest achievement," which suggests that the Louis XIV Style (art created under his reign) is the equivalent of the High Renaissance in Italy or the age of Perikles in ancient Greece. It also refers to the imitation of the forms and subject matter of classical antiquity. Finally, it suggests qualities of balance and restraint shared by ancient art and the Renaissance. Because the Style of Louis XIV reflects Italian Baroque art, although in modified form, we may call it Baroque Classicism.

Painting in France

While many foreign artists worked in France, French artists often traveled to Italy and the Netherlands to work. In the hopes of creating a nucleus of artists who would determine the Baroque in France, Louis XIII began officially recalling these artists to Paris. The influences of foreign art and experience largely defined seventeenth-century French art. Whether directly or indirectly, Caravaggio, Carracci, Van Dyck, and Titian all had an effect on it.

21.1 Georges de La Tour. *Joseph the Carpenter*. ca. 1642. Oil on canvas, 51⅛ × 39¾" (130 × 101 cm). Musée du Louvre, Paris

GEORGES DE LA TOUR AND THE INFLUENCE OF CARAVAGGIO Many French painters in the early seventeenth century came under the influence of Caravaggio, although it remains unclear how this happened. The paintings of Georges de La Tour (1593–1652), who was named painter to King Louis XIII and received important commissions from the governor of Lorraine, his hometown, suggest a unique interpretation of Caravaggio. His use of light and his reliance on detailed naturalism derived largely from Caravaggio's northern European followers (see page 417), whom he may have visited in the Dutch Republic.

La Tour's mature religious pictures effectively convey the complex mysteries of the Christian faith. *Joseph the Carpenter* (**fig. 21.1**) might initially be mistaken for a genre scene, with its carefully observed details and seemingly humble subject, but its devotional spirit soon overwhelms us. Set in profile, the two figures yield little in their expressions. La Tour lends maximum significance to the juxtaposition of the old man and the innocent youth. The boy Jesus holds a lit candle, a favorite device of the artist, the large and hypnotic flame of which reinforces the devotional mood and imbues the scene with intimacy and tenderness. The painting has the power of Caravaggio's *The Calling of St. Matthew* (fig. 19.1), but the simplified forms, warm palette, and arrested movement are characteristic of La Tour's restrained and focused vision.

NICOLAS POUSSIN AND BAROQUE CLASSICISM Nicolas Poussin (1594–1665), one of the most influential French painters of the century, contributed most to the rise of classicism in France. Aside from an ill-fated two-year sojourn in Paris (he was one of the artists "recalled" by Louis XIII), Poussin spent his entire career in Rome. There, he hosted and taught visiting French artists, absorbing the lessons of Raphael and Carracci's classically ordered paintings and developing his own style of rational classicism. Patrons brought Poussin's paintings back to Paris, where they influenced the royal court. Indeed, when establishing the curriculum of the French ROYAL ACADEMY, Jean-Baptiste Colbert, the king's chief advisor, and the artist Charles Le Brun, the first president of the Academy, chose Poussin's classical style to serve as a model for French artists.

POUSSIN AND HISTORY PAINTING: ANCIENT THEMES IN THE GRAND MANNER Poussin arrived in Rome via Venice in early 1624 and there studied perspective, anatomy, and examined ancient sculpture, the reliefs on ancient sarcophagi and vases, and the paintings of Raphael. His *The Death of Germanicus* (**fig. 21.2**) reflects these studies. The work, a model for artistic depictions of heroic deathbed scenes for the next two centuries, may be the first example of this subject in the history of art.

As a history painting, the work relates the powerful themes of death, loyalty, and revenge. The story, from Tacitus and set in 19 CE, tells of Germanicus, a Roman general who led campaigns against the Germanic tribes. At the urging of Tiberius, Germanicus' adoptive father, the governor of Syria poisoned the powerful general. Poussin depicts him on his deathbed, flanked on the left by his loyal soldiers swearing revenge and on the right by his mournful family. The promise to avenge is

set at the center, commanding attention, as figures gesture their grief, loyalty, and suffering. Framed by the two groups, Germanicus becomes the focus of the composition, which is based on antique death scenes. The architecture sets the stage for the figures, which are arranged horizontally in a rectangular space, as in a classical frieze. The deep blue curtain behind them restricts the action to a shallow space, heightening the drama and creating a more intimate environment.

Poussin believed the highest aim of painting was to represent noble and serious human actions (the foundation of history painting), which he called the Grand Manner and which is exemplified here. The dramatic poses and expressions communicate abundant emotion, but these stylized gestures lack spontaneity. The scene has a theatrical

21.2 Nicolas Poussin. *The Death of Germanicus.* 1627–28. Oil on canvas, 4'10¼" × 6'6" (1.48 × 2 m). Minneapolis Institute of Art, Minneapolis, Minnesota. The William Hood Dunwoody Fund. 58.28

air, and for good reason. Before beginning the painting, Poussin arranged small wax figures on a miniature stagelike setting until he was satisfied with the composition. He believed that the viewer must be able to "read" the emotions of each figure as they relate to the story. Such beliefs later proved influential for his student, Charles Le Brun, who established the approved court style for painting at the French Royal Academy.

POUSSIN AND THE IDEAL LANDSCAPE The "ideal" landscape, serene and balanced, does not represent a particular locale, but rather a generalized and often beautiful place. This austere beauty and somber calm is manifest in Poussin's *Landscape with St. John on Patmos* (**fig. 21.3**), which continues the classical landscape tradition established by Annibale Carracci. The ancient landscape strewn with architectural ruins suggests both the actual site and the concept of antiquity. Trees on either side balance the composition, and many of the ruins are depicted parallel to the picture plane. St. John, who at the end of his life lived on the Greek island of Patmos, reclines in profile facing left. Poussin's pendant (paired) painting, *Landscape with St. Matthew*, shows the saint facing right. Poussin executed both paintings in Rome for the secretary to Pope Urban VIII. The composition suggests the physical, rational arrangement of a spiritual, eternal world—a concept best explored by Baroque Classicism. Poussin's mythological landscapes show a similar blend of the physical, rational, and mythic.

CLAUDE LORRAIN AND THE IDYLLIC LANDSCAPE While Poussin developed the heroic qualities of the ideal landscape, the great French landscapist Claude Lorrain (Claude Gellée, also called Claude;

21.3 Nicolas Poussin. *Landscape with St. John on Patmos.* 1640. Oil on canvas, 39½ × 53¾″ (100.3 × 136.4 cm). Art Institute of Chicago. A.A. Munger Collection. 1930.500

Read the document related to Nicolas Poussin on myartslab.com

1604/05?–1682) brought idyllic aspects to both landscapes and seascapes. He, too, spent nearly his entire career in Rome, beginning as a pastry chef! Like many northern Europeans, Claude thoroughly explored the surrounding countryside, the *campagna*, of Rome, and his countless drawings made on site reveal his powers of observation. He is also the first artist known to have painted oil studies outdoors. Such sketches, however, were only the raw material for his landscapes. His international reputation resulted in commissions such as *A Pastoral Landscape* (**fig. 21.4**) of 1648, made for a Swiss collector, probably through an agent in Rome.

Claude evokes the poetic essence of a countryside filled with echoes of antiquity. Often, as in this painting, the hazy, luminous atmosphere of early morning or late afternoon permeates the composition. One can refer to Claude as painting "into the light." That is, his sunlight (often sunset) is at the center and at the horizon line of the painting so that the architecture and other elements in the foreground or middleground appear almost as silhouettes. The surface of this landscape is luminous, a result of it being painted on copper, a material seventeenth-century artists frequently employed for small works.

Unlike Poussin's paintings, figures in Claude's are very small, slight, and thus not thought to be significant in terms of the historic narrative. Indeed, as in this example, we don't even know the story. His patrons appear to have admired the vague quality in favor of hints of nostalgia for an ancient past. Traditionally, artistic theory had ranked the rendering of common nature at the bottom of the hierarchy of painting genres, with landscape only just above still life as merely copying from life. Claude succeeded in elevating the status of landscape painting.

21.4 Claude Lorrain. *A Pastoral Landscape.* ca. 1648. Oil on copper, 15½ × 21″ (39.3 × 53.3 cm). Yale University Art Gallery, New Haven, Connecticut. Leonard C. Hanna, Jr., B. A. 1913, Fund. 1959.47

HYACINTHE RIGAUD AND THE SPLENDOR OF LOUIS XIV The monumental *Portrait of Louis XIV* (**fig. 21.5**) by Hyacinthe Rigaud (1659–1743) conveys the power, drama, and splendor of the absolutist ruler. Shown life-size and full-length, the image of Louis recalls Charles I in Van Dyck's portrait (fig. 20.3). This intentional resemblance follows the then formulaic nature of royal portraiture: advocating power and authority through the use of the insignia of rulership and the symbols of the opulence of the monarch's reign. Draped in his velvet coronation robes lined with ermine and trimmed with gold *fleurs-de-lis*, Louis appears self-assured, powerful, majestic, and also tall—an illusion created by the artist, for his subject measured only 5 feet 4 inches. The portrait proudly displays the king's shapely legs (emphasized by the high heels Louis himself designed to increase his height), which were his pride as a dancer. Indeed, the king danced in the ballets of the composer Jean-Baptiste Lully (1632–1687) from the 1650s until his coronation. All the arts, from the visual to the performing, fell

21.5 Hyacinthe Rigaud. *Portrait of Louis XIV*. 1701. Oil on canvas, 9′2″ × 6′3″ (2.8 × 1.9 m). Musée du Louvre, Paris

 View the Closer Look for *Portrait of Louis XIV* on myartslab.com

under royal control—a fact exemplified in Rigaud's painting, which expresses Louis's dominance and unequaled stature as the center of the French state.

French Classical Architecture

Large, ostentatious, and public, building projects, even more than painting, transmitted the values of the royal court to a wide audience. In French architecture, the Classical style expressed the grandeur and authority of imperial Rome and confirmed the ideals of tradition, omnipotence, absolutism (see page 431), strength, and permanence embraced by the monarchy. Mammoth scale and repetition of forms evoke these broad concepts, which were embodied in royal structures erected in the heart of Paris as well as outside the city, in the palace and gardens of Versailles.

In 1655, Louis XIV declared *"L'état, c'est moi"* ("I am the State"). This statement was not just political but represented an artistic and aesthetic intention as well. Louis's projects for his palace and court took on colossal proportions and represented, not a single individual, or even a single monarch, but the entirety of France. He started by renovating the Louvre Palace in Paris, a project initiated by his father. Louis, however, soon decided it would be preferable to move his entire royal court to a more

isolated location where he could control them more efficiently, and so he began the construction of the palace and gardens of Versailles, a few miles outside Paris. These complex building projects all share a single style—that of Baroque Classicism.

THE LOUVRE Work on the palace had proceeded intermittently for more than a century, following Pierre Lescot's original design under Francis I; what remained was to close the square court on the east side with an impressive façade. Bernini was invited to Paris, where he spent several months in 1665, in the hope that the most famous artist of the Roman Baroque (page 396–99) would do for the French king what he had done for the popes in Italy. While in Paris, Bernini had a singular influence on sculpture, but after much argument and intrigue, Louis XIV rejected his three proposals for the building and turned over the problem to a committee: Charles Le Brun, his court painter; Louis Le Vau (1612–1670), his court architect; and Claude Perrault (1613–1688), a student of ancient architecture. "Design by committee," rather than a competition, as was common in the Renaissance, was a new concept and this means that even today we cannot decipher their individual contributions. All three men were responsible for the structure (**fig. 21.6**),

21.6 Louis Le Vau, Claude Perrault, and Charles Le Brun. East front of the Louvre. 1667–70. Paris

21.7 Aerial view of the Palace of Versailles, France. Begun 1669

 **Watch** a video about Versailles on myartslab.com

21.8 Louis Le Vau and Jules Hardouin-Mansart. Garden front of the center block of the Palace of Versailles. 1669–85

but Perrault was credited by his contemporaries with the major share of the new Louvre.

Perrault based the center pavilion on a Roman temple front and the wings look like the sides of the temple folded outward. Controversial because of its unique use of paired columns, this innovative colonnade quickly established itself as a characteristic of the new style.

The east front of the Louvre signaled the victory of French classicism over the Italian Baroque as the royal style. It further proclaimed France as the new Rome, both politically and culturally, by linking Louis XIV with the glory of the Caesars. This revitalization of the antique, both in its concept and its details, was Perrault's most significant contribution.

THE PALACE OF VERSAILLES Louis XIV's largest enterprise was the Palace of Versailles (**fig. 21.7**), located 11 miles from the center of Paris. By forcing the aristocracy to live under royal scrutiny outside Paris, the king hoped to prevent a repeat of the civil rebellion known as the Fronde, which had occurred in 1648–53 during his minority.

Le Vau began the project in 1669 and designed the garden front elevation (**fig. 21.8**), but within a year he died. Jules Hardouin-Mansart (1646–1708) succeeded him and greatly expanded the structure to accommodate the ever-growing royal household. The garden front, intended by Le Vau to be the main view of the palace, was stretched to an enormous length but with no change in the architectural elements. As a result, Le Vau's original façade design looks repetitious and out of scale.

THE HALL OF MIRRORS The center block contains a single room measuring 240 feet long, the spectacular *Galerie des Glaces*, or Hall of Mirrors (**fig. 21.9**), today still used for ceremonial events; it is where

21.9 Jules Hardouin-Mansart, Louis Le Vau, and Charles Le Brun. Galerie des Glaces (Hall of Mirrors), Palace of Versailles. Begun 1678

the Treaty of Versailles was signed, ending World War I. The use of so many full-length mirrors was unique and their manufacture in France, along with the use of colored marble that surrounds them—also quarried in France—promoted French nationalism. Placed to reflect the gardens outside, the mirrors cause the room to appear larger by day. As they reflect sunlight, historians have suggested that they were also emblematic of Louis as the Sun King. At night, the myriad reflections of candlelight illuminated the grand space. Whether day or night, the effect was, and is, impressive. Louis XIV had insisted that Versailles be a public space—open to all but for the truly private quarters. Guidebooks were printed as early as 1674. In addition to members of the court, ordinary people (with the exception of monks, "loose women," and those who displayed recent evidence of smallpox) could stroll through the Hall of Mirrors and also enjoy the gardens.

THE GARDENS OF VERSAILLES   Apart from the magnificent interior, the most impressive aspect of Versailles is the park extending west of the garden front for several miles (see figs. 21.7 and 21.8). The vast landscaped environment was designed by André Le Nôtre (1613–1700), who had become director of the gardens of Louis XIII in 1643 and whose family had served as royal gardeners for generations. Le Nôtre transformed an entire natural forest into a controlled park, a massive and expensive enterprise that reflected the grandeur of the king. The spirit of absolutism is readily apparent in Le Nôtre's plan: Forests were thinned to create stately avenues; plants were shaped into manicured hedges; water was pumped into exuberant fountains and serene lakes. The formal gardens consist of a multitude of paths, terraces, basins, and mazes that create a unified geometric whole. An especially important aspect of the landscape design was the program of sculpture, much of which incorporated images of Apollo, the sun god, adopted as the symbol of Louis XIV.

The completed palace and park covers almost 18,000 acres (the wall around it is 27 miles long). In concept, the landscape is as significant as the palace—perhaps more so, for it suggests the king's dominion over Nature. The gardens formed a series of "outdoor rooms" for the splendid fêtes and spectacles that functioned as an integral part of Louis's court and as reflections of his power.

Baroque Architecture in England

The English contribution to the Baroque came mostly in the form of architecture as painters from Italy, Flanders, and the Dutch Republic (Orazio Gentileschi, the father of Artemisia, Artemisia Gentileschi herself, Anthony van Dyck and Peter Paul Rubens—the latter two knighted during their stays) dominated the English royal court through the century. Orazio Gentileschi and Rubens worked for James I, while Charles I's court painter Van Dyck executed both portraits (see fig. 20.3) and allegorical paintings. After Van Dyck's death, many artists continued his style of portraiture for wealthy patrons, initiating little in the visual arts until the Restoration. After the Great Fire of London in 1666, the rebuilding of the city gave precedent and impetus to English architectural achievements.

Inigo Jones and the Impact of Palladio

The first significant English architect was Inigo Jones (1573–1652), architect to James I and Charles I as well as the era's leading English theatrical designer. Upon returning from his second trip to Italy, in 1614 (he also went in 1597–1603 and to Paris in 1609), Jones was appointed surveyor of the king's works, a post he held until 1643. An affirmed disciple of Andrea Palladio (see page 366–67), whose work he saw in Venice and whose treatises (along with those of Alberti) he owned and annotated, Jones introduced Palladio's Renaissance Classicism to England.

The Banqueting House that Jones built at Whitehall Palace in London (**fig. 21.10**) conforms to the principles in Palladio's treatise, although it does not copy any specific Palladian project. Originally intended for court ceremonies and performances called masques (spectacles combining dance, theater, and music), the Banqueting House is designed like a Palladian villa and resembles a Renaissance palazzo more than any building north of the Alps constructed at that time. Jones uses an ordered, classical vocabulary and the rules of proportion to compose the building in three parts. The Ionic and composite orders of the pilasters add an understated elegance, and alternating segmental and triangular pediments over the first-floor windows create a rhythmic effect. The sculpted garland below the roofline and the balustrade above decoratively enhance the overall structure. The

21.10 Inigo Jones. West front of the Banqueting House, Whitehall Palace. 1619–22. London

building, today, is perhaps starker than originally conceived; it once bore colored stones for each of the stories, but the façade was later resurfaced. Jones's spare style stood as a beacon of classicist orthodoxy in England for 200 years.

Sir Christopher Wren

If it had not been for the destruction caused by the GREAT FIRE OF LONDON of 1666, Sir Christopher Wren (1632–1723), the most important English architect of the late seventeenth century, might have remained an amateur. Wren may be considered the Baroque counterpart of the Renaissance artist-scientist. He first studied anatomy and then physics, mathematics, and astronomy, and was highly esteemed by Sir Isaac Newton, the discoverer of gravity, for his understanding of geometry. Wren, who did not turn to architecture until the age of 30, held the position of chair in the astronomy department at Gresham College, London, and then was professor of mathematics at Oxford University. His technological knowledge in geometry and mathematics may have affected the shape of his buildings; certainly, no previous architect went to such lengths to conceal a building's structural supports.

The GREAT FIRE OF LONDON of 1666 lasted for five days in early September and destroyed 373 acres, four-fifths of the city, with 100,000 made homeless, although only 16 people lost their lives. One observer famously wrote: "London was, but is no more." To help rebuild the city, Sir Christopher Wren designed a plan within days of the destruction, largely based on focal points and wide avenues that he saw in Paris; but this was, in the end, rejected. He designed more than 51 new churches, including St. Paul's Cathedral.

ST. PAUL'S CATHEDRAL Wren favored central-plan churches and originally conceived of St. Paul's in the shape of a Greek cross with a huge domed crossing, based on Michelangelo's plan of St. Peter's. This idea was also inspired by a previous design by Inigo Jones, who had been involved with the restoration of the original Gothic structure of St. Paul's earlier in the century. Wren's proposal was rejected by the church authorities, however, who favored a conventional basilica. In the end, the plan is that of a Latin cross (see below), the same followed for most Catholic churches, including St. Peter's. This was an ironic outcome given that the building program could have provided an opportunity to create a new vocabulary for the Protestant Church of England.

On his only journey abroad, in 1665–66, Wren visited France and met Bernini in Paris (see page 437). The influence of this trip can be seen on the façade of St. Paul's (**fig. 21.11**), where the impact of contemporary architecture in Paris can be

21.11 Sir Christopher Wren. Façade of St. Paul's Cathedral. 1675–1710. London

Read the document related to Sir Christopher Wren on myartslab.com

Plan of St. Paul's

discerned—as in the double columns of the Louvre. In contrast to St. Peter's, St. Paul's dome rises high above the building and dominates the façade; it looks like a much enlarged version of Bramante's Tempietto (fig. 16.4). St. Paul's is an up-to-date Baroque design that reflects Wren's thorough knowledge of contemporary Italian and French architecture.

POINTS OF REFLECTION

21.1 Describe how classicism in seventeenth-century France differs from the classical ideals of the Renaissance.

21.2 Using Poussin's *The Death of Germanicus*, describe the Grand Manner.

21.3 Analyze the architecture of the east front of the Louvre and the Palace of Versailles in terms of the relationship between classicism and absolutism.

21.4 Examine the differences between Dutch and French landscape painting.

21.5 Analyze the impact of both the New St. Peter's and the Louvre on London's new St. Paul's Cathedral.

✓•— **Study** and review on myartslab.com

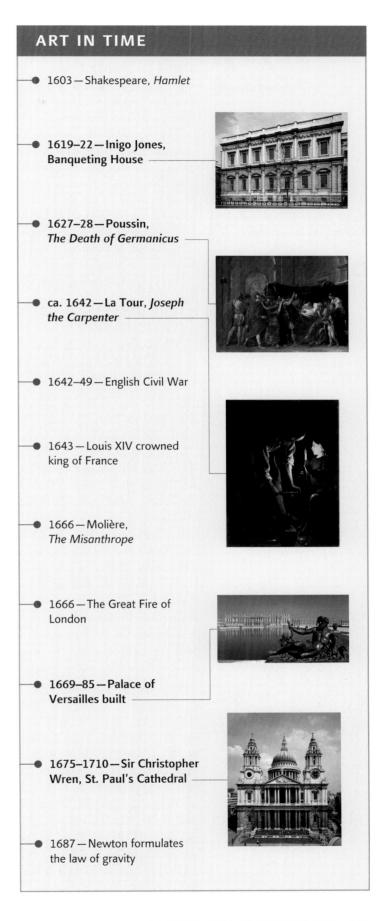

ART IN TIME

● 1603 — Shakespeare, *Hamlet*

● 1619–22 — Inigo Jones, **Banqueting House**

● 1627–28 — Poussin, ***The Death of Germanicus***

● ca. 1642 — La Tour, *Joseph the Carpenter*

● 1642–49 — English Civil War

● 1643 — Louis XIV crowned king of France

● 1666 — Molière, *The Misanthrope*

● 1666 — The Great Fire of London

● 1669–85 — **Palace of Versailles built**

● 1675–1710 — **Sir Christopher Wren, St. Paul's Cathedral**

● 1687 — Newton formulates the law of gravity

CHAPTER

22 | The Rococo

POINTS OF INQUIRY

22.1 Define the characteristics of the Rococo style in art.

22.2 Consider the role of fantasy and eroticism in painting and sculpture.

22.3 Describe the nature of the Rococo portrait.

22.4 Investigate the qualities of the Rococo interior.

22.5 Understand the continuation of Baroque ideals in Central Europe.

((•— **Listen** to the chapter audio on myartslab.com

In France the Rococo style is linked with Louis XV (1710–1774) because it corresponds roughly to his lifetime—the heart of the eighteenth century. A fundamental difference exists between the Baroque and the Rococo styles: In a word, it is fantasy. If the Baroque presents theater on a grand scale, the Rococo stage is smaller and more intimate. Its artifice evokes an enchanted realm that presents a diversion from real life. In some ways the Rococo in France manifests a shift in taste among aristocrats, who reasserted their power as patrons and began to favor stylized motifs from nature and a more domestic art—private rather than public—to decorate their new homes in Paris.

"Rococo" was coined in the nineteenth century as a disparaging term, taken from the French word *rocaille* (meaning "pebble") and the Portuguese *barrocco* ("baroque"), to refer to the perception, then current, of the taste of the early eighteenth century as excessive and ornate. The word Rococo refers to the playful, irregular pebbles, stones, and shells that decorated the grottoes of Italian gardens and became the principal motifs of French interior designs.

Artists developed new subjects of love and loss and inspired a growing interest in the poetic genre of the pastoral. Patrons were increasingly taken with the notion of "simple man" existing in an idealized nature. The French Royal Academy was still important and even provided lectures on Raphael and Poussin. Yet it recognized this new Rococo style by establishing a new category called the *fête galante*, a type of painting introduced by Jean-Antoine Watteau. The style celebrated eroticism and the tradition of love, and broadened the range of human emotion depicted in art.

Although most directly associated with France, the Rococo exerted a wide geographical influence that affected the arts in England as well as most of Western and Central Europe (see **map 22.1**). In Germany and Austria, the devastation of the Thirty Years' War (1618–1648) was followed in the eighteenth century by a period of rebuilding that often reflected the style of Italy from earlier in the century. Italian artists such as Tiepolo, with his assistants, painted ceiling frescoes in central European churches and palaces in this new elaborate and elegant style; he produced similar works for his native city of Venice as well. There, Canaletto painted **vedute**, or scenes of the city, as souvenirs (see page 454). In the performing arts, the Venetian composer Antonio Vivaldi (1678–1741) produced

Map 22.1 Western Europe in the eighteenth century

innumerable operas and the German composer Johann Sebastian Bach (1685–1750) wrote much extraordinary choral music, while London became home to the establishment of legitimate theater, notably in the Haymarket and the Drury Lane–Covent Garden district.

European colonization of the New World continued in the 1700s. Armies battled to secure these distant lands, depleting their nations' treasuries, yet succeeding in sending back to their homelands exotic objects including the feathers, jewels, and metals that collectors coveted and artists used in the creation of new art.

France: The Rise of the Rococo

After the death of Louis XIV in 1715, the nobility, previously attached to the court at Versailles, were now freed from royal control. Louis XV, only five years old at his great-grandfather's death, would not be crowned until 1723. This early period of the Rococo—between 1715 and 1723—is known as the Regency, so called because France was governed by Louis's cousin Philip, duke of Orléans, acting as regent. With a nobleman as effective king, the aristocracy regained much power and authority, and abandoned the strict, demanding court life of Versailles. Rather than returning to their chateaux in the provinces, many chose to live in Paris, where they built elegant townhouses or *hôtels* with small, intimate rooms. These were decorated with paintings, porcelain, and small sculptures that created a lavish, light-hearted mood. Paintings, therefore, played just one part in the creation of the ambience of refinement that permeated pre-Revolutionary France. These paintings, as well as interior designs, would influence the decor of Western and Central Europe throughout the century.

Painting: Poussinistes versus Rubénistes

Toward the end of the seventeenth century, a dispute arose among the members of the French Academy, who then formed two factions: The Poussinistes and the Rubénistes. Yet neither Poussin nor Rubens was still alive at the time of this debate, which focused on the issue of drawing versus color. French artists were familiar with Poussin's paintings, which had been sent from Rome to Paris throughout his career, and they knew Rubens's work from the *Marie de' Medici Cycle* (see fig. 20.2) in the Luxembourg Palace. The conservative Poussinistes defended Poussin's view that line, which appealed to the mind, was superior to color, which appealed to the senses. The Rubénistes (many of whom were of Flemish descent) favored color, rather than drawing, as being truer to nature. They also pointed out that drawing appeals only to the expert few, whereas color appeals to everyone. This argument had important implications. It suggested that the layperson should be the judge of artistic values and this challenged the Renaissance notion that painting, as a liberal art, could be appreciated only by the educated mind.

JEAN-ANTOINE WATTEAU The greatest of the Rubénistes was Jean-Antoine Watteau (1684–1721). Born in Valenciennes, which had been part of the Southern Netherlands, Watteau showed an affinity with Rubens, the region's most renowned artist. Watteau, who moved to Paris in 1702, became a significant contributor to the new Rococo style as well as to the new subjects associated with it. His painted visions of fantasy show idyllic images of aristocratic life, with elegant figures luxuriously dressed in shimmering pastel colors and set in dreamlike outdoor settings. His carefully posed figures evoke forlorn love, regret, or nostalgia, and imbue his scenes with an air of melancholy. The popularity of this theme soon spread from France throughout Europe.

Because Watteau's fantasies had little historical or mythological basis, his paintings broke many academic rules and did not conform to any established category. To admit Watteau as a member, the French Academy created the new classification of painting called *fêtes galantes* (meaning "elegant fêtes" or "outdoor entertainments"). His reception piece for the Academy (the painting he was required to give upon becoming a member) was *A Pilgrimage to Cythera* (**fig. 22.1**). The painting is an evocation of love and includes elements of classical mythology. Cythera, which came to be viewed as an island of love, was one of the settings for the Greek myth of the birth of Aphrodite (Venus), who rose from the foam of the sea. The painting appears

22.1 Jean-Antoine Watteau. *A Pilgrimage to Cythera*. 1717. Oil on canvas, 4′3″ × 6′4½″ (1.3 × 1.9 m). Musée du Louvre, Paris

in the Academy records as a *fête galante*, perhaps the first use of this term.

Watteau has created a delightful yet slightly melancholic scene. It is unclear whether the couples are arriving at or leaving the island. The action unfolds in the foreground from right to left like a continuous narrative, which suggests that the figures may be about to board the boat. Two lovers remain engaged in their amorous tryst; behind them, another couple rises to follow a third pair down the hill as the reluctant young woman casts a longing look back at the goddess's sacred grove. Young couples, accompanied by swarms of cupids, pay homage to Venus, whose garlanded sculpture appears on the far right. The delicate colors—pale greens, blues, and pinks—suggest the gentle nature of the lovers' relationships. The subtle gradations of tone displayed Watteau's debt to Rubens and helped establish the supremacy of the Rubénistes.

Yet, Watteau's figures are slim, graceful, and small in scale; they appear even more so when compared with most Baroque imagery. The landscape does not overwhelm the scene but echoes its idyllic mood. Watteau produces a sense of nostalgia with implications of longing and unrealized passion. He achieves this not only with the figures and their gentle touching and hesitancy, but also through the sympathetic parallel found in Watteau's landscape and the sculptures in it.

Although Watteau's use of color planted him firmly in the Rubéniste camp, his innovations and creativity as a draughtsman (which would have implied a Poussiniste status) combined both color and line. Earlier artists, including Rubens, may have drawn with red or black chalk heightened with white; Watteau excelled in the technique known as *trois crayons* or three chalks. In *Seated Young Woman* (**fig. 22.2**), he uses the chalks so that the red color defines her body—legs, hands, parts of her face

22.2 Jean-Antoine Watteau. *Seated Young Woman*. ca. 1716. *Trois crayons* (three chalks) drawing: Red, black, and white chalks on cream paper, 10 × 6¾″ (25.5 × 17.1 cm). The Pierpont Morgan Library, New York

 Read the document related to Jean-Antoine Watteau on myartslab.com

(lips, tip of nose), nape, breast—and suggests a vivacious quality while contrasting with the black and white of her clothing, eyebrows, and upswept hair. The colors enliven and add a spontaneity to this life drawing. In numerous sketches Watteau often worked out poses, movements, gestures, and expressions, many of which (although not this drawing) served as studies for figures in his paintings.

FRANÇOIS BOUCHER Following the untimely death of Watteau in 1721, François Boucher (1703–1770) rose to prominence in French painting. Boucher built his reputation on his imaginative compositions, pastoral landscapes, and scenes of bourgeois daily life. He served as court painter to Madame de Pompadour (1721–1764), who has been called the "godmother of the Rococo." She was Louis XV's mistress, as well as his long-term political advisor, and a major patron of the arts.

Boucher painted her portrait numerous times and with his 1756 life-size painting *Portrait of Madame de Pompadour* (**fig. 22.3**) he established—even orchestrated—her self-fashioning as a *femme-savante*—an educated, cultured, accomplished woman who was also elegant, beautiful, and sophisticated. Born Jeanne-Antoinette Poisson,

22.3 François Boucher. *Portrait of Madame de Pompadour*. 1756. Oil on canvas, 6′7⅛″ × 5′1⅞″ (2.01 × 1.57 m). Alte Pinakothek, Munich

she became the Royal Mistress (an actual title) in 1746. She had come from a nonaristocratic family, but because of her relationship with the king had been made a duchess, a marchioness, and in the year this painting was executed (when she was 35 years old and no longer his mistress, but lifelong confidante), she was named Lady-in-Waiting to the queen, the highest nonroyal title at court. There has even been a suggestion that the background clock indicates the actual time she received this title (although 8:20 is often the time set on old clocks for display purposes).

Madame de Pompadour is shown amid luxurious surroundings wearing a dress that signals opulence. The voluminous nature of the shimmering fabric, its turquoise blue color, and the intricacy of its more than 100 bows and sewn roses also show off her small, narrow waist. She sits in her boudoir/library, which reflects the range of her accomplishments. The rosewood writing table set with pen, ink, and envelopes and the well-used book in her hand as well as the many in the cabinet and on the floor (truly an overflow) further confirm—even define—her level of literacy and qualify her as an educated woman. She also identified herself with Venus. The cupid by the clock, the roses on her dress and at her feet, and the pearl bracelets (pearls from the sea in which Venus was born) are each attributes that suggest her affinity with the love goddess. She does not sit formally upright on the day bed (*chaise longue*), but leans on its pillows. The pose suggests a relaxed, casual mood—the nonchalance and luxury of the leisured aristocracy.

JEAN-SIMÉON CHARDIN Although perhaps best known, today, for his still lifes, in the eighteenth century Jean-Siméon Chardin (1699–1779) achieved fame for his genre paintings. The artist drew inspiration from the many Dutch and Flemish seventeenth-century paintings then in France, and often received commissions from the important connoisseurs of this art.

These collectors, members of the rising bourgeoisie in France, desired genre scenes and domestic still lifes that proclaimed the virtues of hard work, frugality, honesty, and devotion to family. Chardin's quiet household scenes struck a chord with his sophisticated patrons, and demand for them was so high that he often painted copies of his most popular subjects. He was particularly praised in print for the way he captured these qualities—although some of these eulogies, such as

those by Denis Diderot (see page 477)—were not published until the nineteenth century when his posthumous reputation expanded. Chardin's paintings were also reproduced as prints, making them affordable to those who lacked the means to buy an original work.

The artist produced several copies of *Saying Grace* (*Le Bénédicité*, **fig. 22.4**). After submitting this example for the Academy exhibition of 1740, Chardin presented it to Louis XV at Versailles for his collection. We do not know if the choice of this gift was the king's or Chardin's. *Saying Grace* became especially popular at the turn of the twentieth century when praised by Marcel Proust (1871–1922), who poetically suggested it yielded a world "between beings and objects, past and present, light and dark."

22.4 Jean-Siméon Chardin. *Saying Grace (Le Bénédicité).* 1740. Oil on canvas, 18½ × 14¾" (47 × 37.5 cm). Musée du Louvre, inv. # 3202, Paris

22.5 Jean-Honoré Fragonard. *The Swing.* 1767. Oil on canvas, 32⅝ × 26″ (82.9 × 66 cm). The Wallace Collection, London

Watch the videos about the process of oil painting and grinding oil paint on myartslab.com

The painting reveals a simply furnished, yet intimate, interior with a woman (mother or servant) who has placed bowls of steaming soup on the table between the boy saying grace and the girl eyeing him, perhaps impatiently. The detailed figures, their soft pastel colors, fabrics, and the positioning and frame of the sharp-faced, yet delicate woman suggest the influence of Watteau. But the tiled floor, still-life objects, and middle-class setting recall Dutch scenes. The work provides a vivid contrast to the noisy household of Jan Steen (fig. 20.16) and his Baroque contemporaries.

JEAN-HONORÉ FRAGONARD Transforming fantasy into reality in paint was the forte of Jean-Honoré Fragonard (1732–1806)—or at least that was his reputation. A brilliant colorist, an artistic descendant of Watteau, and student of Chardin, who also worked with Boucher, Fragonard won the distinguished Rome Prize in 1752 and spent five years in the city from 1756. Upon his return to Paris, he worked mostly for private collectors. Fantasy, flirtation, and licentiousness—in short, the spirit of the Rococo, a continuous tradition beginning with Watteau—coalesce in *The Swing* (**fig. 22.5**). An anecdote provides an interpretation of the painting. According to the story, another artist, Gabriel-François Doyen, was approached by the Baron de Saint-Julien to paint his mistress "on a swing which a bishop is setting in motion. You will place me in a position in which I can see the legs of the lovely child and even more if you wish to enliven the picture." Doyen declined the commission but directed it to Fragonard.

The painting, an example of an "intrigue," suggests a collusion in erotic fantasy between artist and patron, with the clergy as their unwitting dupe. This "boudoir painting" offers the thrill of sexual opportunity and voyeurism, but here in a stage-like outdoor setting. The innocence of the public arena heightens the teasing quality of the motion of the swing toward the patron-viewer. The painted sculpture of a cupid to the left, holding a finger to his lips, suggests the conspiracy at the erotic escapade in which we as viewers are now participants. Fragonard used painted sculpture in many of his works to echo or reinforce their themes. The dense and overgrown landscape, providing secrecy, lit by radiant sunlight, invokes the warmth of spring or summer and overtones of sexuality and fertility. The glowing pastel colors create an otherworldly haze that enhances the sensuality of this fantasy spun by the artist.

The French Rococo Interior

The Palace of Versailles (see page 439), still splendid and even augmented in the eighteenth century, was not the only measure of the upper-class social world. It is in the intimate spaces of early eighteenth-century interiors that the elegance and charm of the Rococo are shown to their full extent. The Parisian *hôtels* of the nobility soon developed into social centers. The field of "design for private living" took on new importance at this time. Because these city sites were usually cramped and irregular, they offered few opportunities for impressive exteriors. Hence the layout and decor of the rooms became the architects' main concern. The *hôtels* demanded an intimate style of interior decoration that gave full scope to individual fancy, uninhibited by the classicism seen at Versailles.

Crucial to the development of French décor was the important role of interior designers. They collaborated with architects, who, in turn, became more involved in interior decoration. Along with sculptors, who often created the architectural ornamentation, and painters, who decorated the areas over doors, architects helped to raise the DECORATIVE ARTS to the level of the fine arts, thus establishing a tradition that continues today. The decorative and fine arts most clearly mingled in furniture. Gilt, metals, and enamels were often applied to interior décor to create the feathery ornamentation associated with the Rococo. Many of these artisans came originally from the Netherlands, Germany, or Italy.

The decorative arts played a unique role during the Rococo. *Hôtel* interiors were total environments assembled with extraordinary care by discerning collectors and the talented architects, sculptors, decorators, and dealers who catered to their exacting taste. A room, like an item of furniture, could involve the services of a wide variety of artisans: Cabinet-makers, wood carvers, gold- and silversmiths, upholsterers, and porcelain makers.

NICOLAS PINEAU Few of these Rococo rooms survive intact; the vast majority have been destroyed or greatly changed, or the objects and decorations have been dispersed. Even so, we can get a good idea of their appearance through the reconstruction of one such room (perhaps from the ground floor behind the garden elevation) from the Hôtel de

SPEAKING OF
fine arts, minor arts,
decorative arts, applied arts,
and crafts

It was in the West in the late eighteenth century, led by the European academies and fueled by the intellectual environment of the Enlightenment, that the FINE ARTS (painting, sculpture, drawing, and architecture) were elevated at the expense of the so-called MINOR ARTS, which included ceramics, textiles and weaving, metalwork and gold- and silversmithery, furniture, glassware and stained glass, and enamel work. DECORATIVE ARTS and APPLIED ARTS have been used interchangeably with MINOR ARTS ever since. Another term, CRAFTS, has been in and out of favor for a long time. Until the late Middle Ages in the West, crafts were art; they were art again in Rococo Europe and during the Arts and Crafts Movement at the turn of the twentieth century.

Varengeville, Paris (**fig. 22.6**), designed about 1735 by Nicolas Pineau (1684–1754) for the Duchesse de Villars. His room for the duchess incorporates many contemporary Rococo features. To create a sumptuous effect, he has encrusted the white walls with gilded stucco ornamentation in arabesques, C-scallops, S-scrolls, fantastic birds, bat's wings, and acanthus foliage sprays. The elaborately carved furniture is embellished with gilt bronze. Everything swims in a sea of swirling patterns united by a sophisticated sense of design and materials. No clear distinction exists between decoration and function in the richly designed fireplace and the opulent chandelier. The paintings, too, have been completely integrated into the decorative scheme, and are set over two of the doors.

Porcelain, and especially porcelain by Sèvres, the manufactory established by Louis XV and closely associated with the tastes of Madame de Pompadour, would have once been one of the prominent decorations within the interior, from the dinner and tea services to containers for playful bowls of pot-pourri.

CLODION AND FRENCH ROCOCO SCULPTURE Used to adorn interiors, French Rococo sculpture took many forms and was designed to be viewed at close range. A typical example is the miniature *Nymph and Satyr Carousing* (**fig. 22.7**) by Claude Michel (1738–1814), known as Clodion, a successful sculptor of the Rococo period who later effectively adapted his style to the more austere Neoclassical manner. Clodion began his studies at Versailles and won the prestigious Rome Prize. His greatest contribution to the Rococo was to transform its fantasies into three-dimensional works of coquettish eroticism.

The open and airy composition of this sculpture is related to a work by Bernini, but its miniature scale produces a more intimate and sensual effect. Although Clodion undertook several large sculptural cycles in marble, he reigned supreme in the intimate medium of terra cotta.

Western European Rococo Outside France

The French Rococo exerted a major influence across the English Channel. Foreign artists—Holbein, Gentileschi, Rubens, Van Dyck—had already flourished for generations in England, and the works of Dutch and Italian artists were widely collected. Printmaking also played a key role in disseminating ideas. As we have seen with the works of Chardin and Rubens, among others, artists not only created new compositions in print form but also reproduced painted works, giving them a larger audience and broader appeal. Landscapes and genre paintings, areas of great interest to, and increasingly collected by, the British public, especially benefited from the distribution of prints.

Painting for an English Market

We can even speak of a growing English market, as indeed the major auction houses of Sotheby's and Christie's were founded in London in 1744 and 1766 respectively, to take control of the rapid sale of foreign paintings and other collections. This was the beginning of a formalized, yet active, secondary market—that is, works not directly commissioned from patrons but resold. It was largely fueled by the thirst of the well-traveled English gentleman to compete with his wealthy Continental counterpart, as well as to acquire mementos, in the form of landscapes, of his trips (see page 454). Other works provided a knowing humor for the lapses of the lower classes and their strivings, and thus genre paintings and prints, along with landscape (as well as portraits of long-dead nobility), increased the popularity of this growing independent market.

William Hogarth

The first major native English artist since the Elizabethan period, William Hogarth (1697–1764) began his career as an engraver and soon took up painting. He made his mark in the 1730s with a new kind of genre painting, which he described as "modern moral subjects … similar to representations on the

stage." He created these pictures, and the prints made from them for sale to the public, in series and repeated certain details in each scene to unify the sequence. Hogarth's morality paintings teach, by *bad example*, solid middle-class virtues and reflect the desire for a return to simpler times and values. They proved enormously popular among the newly prosperous middle class in England.

Hogarth's *He Revels* (*The Orgy*, **fig. 22.8**), Scene III from his series *The Rake's Progress* (also executed in painting), shows a young man, Tom Rakewell, who has just received an inheritance and is now spending his fortune by overindulging in wine and women. He is seen disheveled and drunk. This scene is set in a famous London brothel, the Rose Tavern. The young woman adjusting her shoe in the foreground is a stripper preparing for a vulgar dance involving the mirror-like silver plate and the candle behind her; to her left, a chamber pot spills

22.8 William Hogarth. *He Revels (The Orgy)*, Scene III of *The Rake's Progress*. 1735. Engraving, 14 × 16¼" (35.5 × 41.3 cm). Guildhall Library & Art Gallery, London. Harris Brisbane Dick Fund, 1932. 32.35(30)

its foul contents over a chicken dish (a pun on fowl/ foul); and in the background, a singer holds sheet music for a bawdy song of the day. A candle held to a map on the back wall indicates that Tom's world will burn—as did Nero's, the only Roman emperor whose image is not defaced in the paintings in the room. The scene is full of witty visual clues to its overall meaning, which the viewer would discover little by little, adding a comic element to this satire of social evils. Later in the series, the rogue enters into a marriage of convenience, is arrested for debt, turns to gambling, goes to debtors' prison, and dies in Bedlam, the London insane asylum.

Hogarth's bawdy humor and sense of narrative can be compared to Jan Steen's (fig. 20.16), from which it drew inspiration. Of course, the "progress" of the rake was really his downfall. This series was the counterpart to Hogarth's earlier set, *The Harlot's Progress* (1731), where an innocent girl, Molly Hackabout, upon coming to London is tricked into becoming a prostitute, leading to her demise. Hogarth's moral narratives were so entertaining and popular that viewers were not overwhelmed by the stern message.

Canaletto

The paintings of the Venetian artist Canaletto (Giovanni Antonio Canal, 1697–1768), known for his *vedute* (meaning "views"), garnered great popularity as souvenirs with the British, particularly young men on the Grand Tour (planned trips through

Europe to complete their education) after their formal schooling. This new subject can be traced back to the seventeenth century, when many foreign artists, such as Claude Lorrain (see fig. 21.4), specialized in depicting the Roman countryside, or to the *Haarlempjes*, the local Dutch landscapes of Ruisdael (see fig. 20.13). After 1720, however, *vedute* took on a specifically urban identity, focusing more narrowly on buildings or cityscapes. During the eighteenth century, landscape painting in Italy evolved into a new form in keeping with the character of the Rococo.

The Bucintoro at the Molo (**fig. 22.9**) is one of a series of paintings of Venice commissioned by Joseph Smith, an English entrepreneur living in the city who later was appointed British consul there. Smith subsequently issued the paintings as a suite of etchings to meet the demand for mementos from those who could not afford an original canvas by the artist. The scene represents a subject frequently depicted by Canaletto: The Doge returning on his magnificent barge to the Piazza San Marco from the Lido (the city's island beach) on Ascension Day after the Marriage of the Sea, an annual celebration that "wedded" Venice to the Adriatic Sea. Canaletto captured the pageantry of this great public festival, which is presented as a brilliant theatrical display.

Canaletto's landscapes are, for the most part, topographically accurate. However, he usually made slight adjustments for the sake of the composition, and sometimes treated scene details freely or created composite views. Contemporaries mention that he used a *camera obscura*, a forerunner of the photographic camera (see page 429), to more accurately provide a credible perspective and wide-angle view. Scholars also suggest that the liveliness and sparkle of his pictures, his sure sense of composition and the speed with which he created these images sprang in large part from his training as a scenographer, or set painter, for operas—including those by Vivaldi. Indeed several Italian *vedute* painters were also scenographers; so perhaps painting large, operatic, sweeping vistas for the stage prepared them for this smaller-scale enterprise. As in our example, Canaletto often included vignettes of daily life in Venice that lend greater human interest to his scenes and make them fascinating cultural documents as well.

One of several Venetian artists to spend long sojourns in London, Canaletto created views of that city's new skyline dotted with the church towers

22.9 Canaletto. *The Bucintoro at the Molo.* ca. 1732. Oil on canvas, 30½ × 49½″ (77 × 126 cm). The Royal Collection, London. © 2008 Her Majesty Queen Elizabeth II

of Christopher Wren (see page 441–43). Other Venetian artists, such as Giovanni Battista Tiepolo (see page 457) and painters from his workshop, had significant careers outside Italy, in Germany and Austria, where the Rococo flourished.

The Rococo in Central Europe

Rococo architecture was a refinement in miniature of the curvilinear, "elastic" Baroque of Borromini. It fused readily with the architecture of Central Europe, where the Italian Baroque had firmly taken root. It is not surprising that the Italian style received such a warm response there. In Austria and southern Germany, ravaged by the Thirty Years' War, patronage for the arts was limited and the number of new buildings remained low until near the end of the seventeenth century. By the eighteenth century these countries, especially the Catholic areas, were beginning to rebuild. The Baroque was an imported style, practiced mainly by visiting Italians. Not until the 1690s did native architects come to the fore. There followed a period of intense activity that lasted more than 50 years and

gave rise to some of the most imaginative creations in the history of architecture. The purpose of these monuments was to glorify princes and prelates who are otherwise generally remembered only as lavish patrons of the arts. Rococo architecture in Central Europe is larger in scale and more exuberant than that in France. Moreover, painting and sculpture are more closely linked with their settings. Palaces and churches feature ceiling frescoes and sculpture unsuited to domestic interiors, however lavish, although they reflect the same taste that produced the Rococo French *hôtels*.

Balthasar Neumann

The work of Balthasar Neumann (1687–1753), who designed buildings exuding lightness and elegance, is the culmination of the Rococo in Central Europe. Trained as a military engineer, he was named a surveyor for the Residenz (Episcopal Palace) in Würzburg after his return from a visit to Milan in 1720. The basic plan was already established and although Neumann greatly modified it, he was required to consult the leading architects of Paris and Vienna in 1723. The final result is a skillful blend of the latest German, French, and Italian ideas. The breathtaking Kaisersaal (**fig. 22.10**) of the Residenz is a great oval hall decorated in the favorite color scheme of the mid-eighteenth century: White, gold, and pastel shades. Neumann has minimized the structural importance of the columns, pilasters, and architraves in favor of their decorative role. Continuous, ribbonlike moldings frame the windows and vault segments, and irregular ornamental designs cover the white surfaces. These lacy, curling motifs, the hallmark of the French style (see fig. 21.6), are now matched with the lightness of the soaring oval hall to create a more grand, spectacular, almost visionary experience that became characteristic of German Rococo architecture. The painted decoration by Giovanni Battista Tiepolo completes the rich and organic structure. The abundant daylight, the play of curves and countercurves, and the weightless grace of the stucco sculpture give the Kaisersaal an airy lightness far removed from the Roman Baroque. The vaults and walls seem thin and pliable, like membranes easily punctured by the expansive power of space.

22.10 Balthasar Neumann. Kaisersaal, Residenz, Würzburg, Germany. 1719–44. Frescoes by Giovanni Battista Tiepolo, 1751–52

Giovanni Battista Tiepolo and Illusionistic Ceiling Decoration

The last and most refined stage of Italian illusionistic ceiling decoration manifests itself in the works of Giovanni Battista Tiepolo (1696–1770). He spent most of his life in Venice, where his works defined the Rococo style. His mastery of light and color, his grace and masterful touch, and his power of invention made him famous far beyond his home territory. He lived for two years in Germany, and in the last years of his life he worked for Charles III in Spain as the last in a long line of Italian artists who were invited to the Royal Palace in Madrid. Tiepolo painted the Würzburg frescoes (see fig. 22.10) at the height of his artistic power. The tissuelike ceiling gives way so often to illusionistic openings, both painted and sculpted, that we no longer feel it to be a spatial boundary.

Unlike Baroque ceilings (compare with fig. 19.5), these openings do not reveal avalanches of figures, as in Gaulli's, propelled by dramatic bursts of light. Rather, pale blue skies and sunlit clouds are dotted with an occasional winged creature soaring in the limitless expanse. Only along the edges of the ceiling do solid clusters of figures appear. Tiepolo's vast and fluid series of paintings is here set within an extravagant, curvilinear, molded ceiling, in parts framed in white trimmed with gold, so that the pale, sunlit colors of the central themes seem ethereal and suggest the pastel heavens we now expect from the age of Rococo.

POINTS OF REFLECTION

22.1 How does the Rococo differ from, yet continue, some of the principles of the Baroque?

22.2 Assess the role of Watteau and the development of the *fête galante*.

22.3 Compare Boucher's *Portrait of Madame de Pompadour* to examples of portraiture from the Baroque and the High Renaissance.

22.4 How does the Rococo interior reflect the goals and needs of its patrons?

22.5 Using the ceiling paintings of Tiepolo, examine the influence of the Italian Baroque on Central European Rococo. Assess the differences as well.

✓—Study and review on myartslab.com

ART IN TIME

● 1703 — St. Petersburg founded by Peter the Great. It serves as the Russian capital until 1918

● 1715 — Louis XIV dies

● 1717 — Watteau's *A Pilgrimage to Cythera*

● 1718 — New Orleans founded by the French

● 1719 — Daniel Defoe publishes *Robinson Crusoe*

● ca. 1732 — Canaletto's *The Bucintoro at the Molo*

● 1735 — Hogarth's *The Rake's Progress*

● 1751–52 — Tiepolo's frescoes for Kaisersaal of the Residenz

● 1756 — Boucher's *Portrait of Madame de Pompadour*

● 1767 — Fragonard's *The Swing*

● 1776 — American Colonies declare independence from Great Britain

A most remarkable change in our ideas is taking place, one of such rapidity that it seems to promise a greater change still to come. It will be for the future to decide the aim, the nature and the limits of this revolution, the drawbacks and disadvantages of which posterity will be able to judge better than we can.
— Jean d'Alembert (1717–1783)

WHEN THE FRENCH PHILOSOPHER and scientist Jean d'Alembert made this prophetic statement in 1759, the Western world was indeed embarking on a revolution, one that is still unfolding today. This revolution ushered in a radically new way of viewing the world, one that would lead to the social, scientific, economic, and political values that govern our present lives. Little did d'Alembert realize that he was witnessing the birth of the modern world.

This new world was heralded by twin revolutions: The Industrial Revolution, which began first in Britain in the middle of the eighteenth century and gradually spread worldwide in the nineteenth, and the political revolutions of the United States and France in 1776 and 1789, respectively. Democracy, personal liberty, capitalism, socialism, industrialization, technological innovation, urbanization, and the "doctrine of progress," that is, a continuous upward march toward an improved life through science and knowledge, are just some of the many modern concepts that emerged from this period.

The force behind this transformation was the Enlightenment, a term that refers to the modern philosophy that surfaced in Britain, France, Germany, and the United States in the eighteenth century (see map 22.1). The foundation for this new thought lay in late seventeenth-century Britain with the philosopher John Locke (1632–1704) and the physicist and mathematician Isaac Newton (1642–1727), perhaps the two most influential thinkers of their age. Both stressed empiricism — the deriving of knowledge from sense-experience — as the basis for philosophy and science, and they advocated rational thought. For Newton, empiricism meant proceeding from data and observation — not superstition, mysticism, religion, hearsay, or whimsy — and applying this information in a logical fashion. For Locke, empiricism established experience as the only basis for formulating ideas. No longer could ideas be considered innate or ordained by God. Locke upset the fundamental Christian notion of original sin when he declared that all humans are born good and have a natural right to life, liberty, and property. He defined the function of government as the obligation to protect these natural rights; failure to do so granted citizens the license to remove their government, even if that required revolution.

What began as a trickle of influence evolved into a torrent as the basic premises behind the innovative ideas of Locke and Newton produced an explosion of treatises and theories throughout the eighteenth century. Leading this philosophical charge were the *philosophes*, as the French intellectuals are commonly referred to. Among the best known are Voltaire (the assumed name of François-Marie Arouet, 1694–1778), Jean-Jacques Rousseau (1712–1778), and Denis Diderot (1713–1784), who, along with d'Alembert, edited the 28-volume *Encyclopédie*, the world's first encyclopedia, which in its attempt to document the world and all knowledge epitomizes Enlightenment empiricism.

In addition to establishing basic human rights, logic, and a new moral order, Enlightenment thought also ushered in modern science. Electricity and oxygen were discovered, for example, and chemistry and natural science as we know them today were established. Science helped launch the Industrial Revolution. By mid-century the first mills were churning out yards of fabric at an unimaginable rate in the north of England, and the notion of labor was redefined as the first factory workers, the new working class or proletariat, employed at subsistence wages, were tethered to clattering looms in enormous spaces filled with a deafening noise. Miners excavated coal and ore to produce iron, permitting construction of the first iron structures. Perfection of the steam engine by the Scottish engineer James Watt from 1765 to 1782 aided the mining and textile industries

and enabled Robert Fulton, in 1807, to send a steamboat chugging up the Hudson River against the swift current, arriving in Albany from Manhattan in unimaginably quick time, to public incredulity.

Not only did industrialization give rise to the new proletariat who had little if any identification with or pride in the product of the factories where they worked, but it also produced a new dominant class, the bourgeoisie, the group that controlled capital and production and would gradually rival and replace the privileged aristocracy at the apex of society toward the end of the nineteenth century. The bitter conflict between bourgeoisie and proletariat, between employer and employee, caused Karl Marx and Friedrich Engels to publish the *Communist Manifesto* in 1848, a book that argued for communal property in order to rectify the disparity between the classes. The same year a workers' revolution spread across Europe, toppling, if only temporarily, numerous governments.

Accompanying industrialization was urbanization, the rapid growth of cities as millions of people during the course of the nineteenth century abandoned their agrarian communities and the comfort of millennia-old rural tradition to seek employment in factories in metropolitan areas. Cities were generally unable to accommodate the rapid growth, resulting in severe dislocation for the country migrants and physical and psychological hardship. Urbanization was so rapid that almost as

many people lived in urban centers as outside them by 1900, and by 1920, city-dwellers outnumbered the remainder of the population in the United States.

The complexion of the Industrial Revolution took on a different face toward the end of the nineteenth century as the Modern Era entered a new phase, generally labeled "modernity." The improved steam engine, the gasoline combustion engine, electricity, and the advent of steel as we know it today elevated Western civilization to a new technological plane; telephones, electric lights, skyscrapers, the safety elevator, electric trains and subways, airplanes, x-rays, and machines and appliances of all kinds dramatically transformed the world, making it increasingly smaller and life increasingly faster and more harried. The term "rush hour" was coined about the turn of the century, and psychoanalysis, purveyed by the great Viennese psychologist Sigmund Freud, emerged to treat the traumas inflicted on the deep recesses of the mind by the stress of civilization. The reliance on machines increased so exponentially in the opening decades of the twentieth century that the post-World War I period is often referred to as "The Machine Age." Technological invention further intensified after World War II with the development of jet planes, helicopters, the atomic and hydrogen bombs, commercial television, transistor radios, satellites, and ultimately spacecraft that launched humankind into

space, circling the earth and in 1969 taking astronauts to the moon.

The Modern Era, however, evolved into yet another phase, often called "Post-Industrial." In the closing decades of the twentieth century, microchips, personal computers, the Internet, mobile and camera telephones, text-messaging, barcodes, satellite communication and surveillance, as well as global position satellites, have taken humankind into a world long imagined by science fiction. The planet has become a global village, with information and images circling the earth almost instantaneously, connecting people as never before, in effect giving humans a new freedom, and yet paradoxically depriving them of privacy and even identity. Ironically, people now "experience" the world, not first hand, but instead through the media, through television, film, and most importantly the Internet. Today's world would appear incomprehensible to an eighteenth-century European or American colonist and certainly the eighteenth century is like a foreign country to us. Nonetheless, the world we live in, including a worldwide quest for personal liberty—represented, for example, in recent times by the 2011 "Arab Spring" uprisings in North Africa and the Middle East—is a continuation of the Modern Era unleashed in the eighteenth century by men who wore gray wigs, powdered their faces, sported calf-length britches with stockings, and dined and read at night by the light of candles.

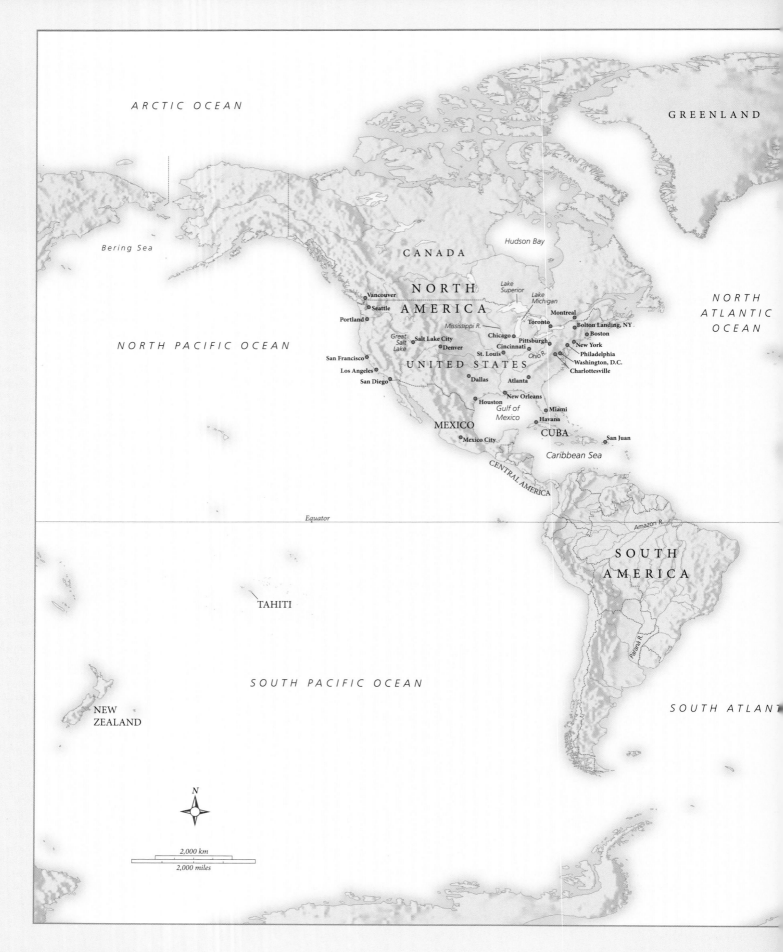

ARCTIC OCEAN

GREENLAND

Bering Sea

CANADA

NORTH
AMERICA

Hudson Bay

NORTH
ATLANTIC
OCEAN

Lake
Superior

Lake
Michigan

Montreal

Toronto

Bolton Landing, NY

Vancouver

Seattle

NORTH PACIFIC OCEAN

Portland

Mississippi R.

Chicago

Pittsburgh

Boston

New York

Great
Salt
Lake

Salt Lake City

Denver

Cincinnati

Ohio R.

Philadelphia

San Francisco

St. Louis

Washington, D.C.

Los Angeles

UNITED STATES

Charlottesville

San Diego

Dallas

Atlanta

Houston

New Orleans

Miami

Gulf of
Mexico

Havana

MEXICO

Mexico City

CUBA

San Juan

CENTRAL AMERICA

Caribbean Sea

Equator

Amazon R.

SOUTH
AMERICA

TAHITI

SOUTH PACIFIC OCEAN

Paraná R.

NEW
ZEALAND

SOUTH ATLANT

N

2,000 km

2,000 miles

THE MODERN WORLD

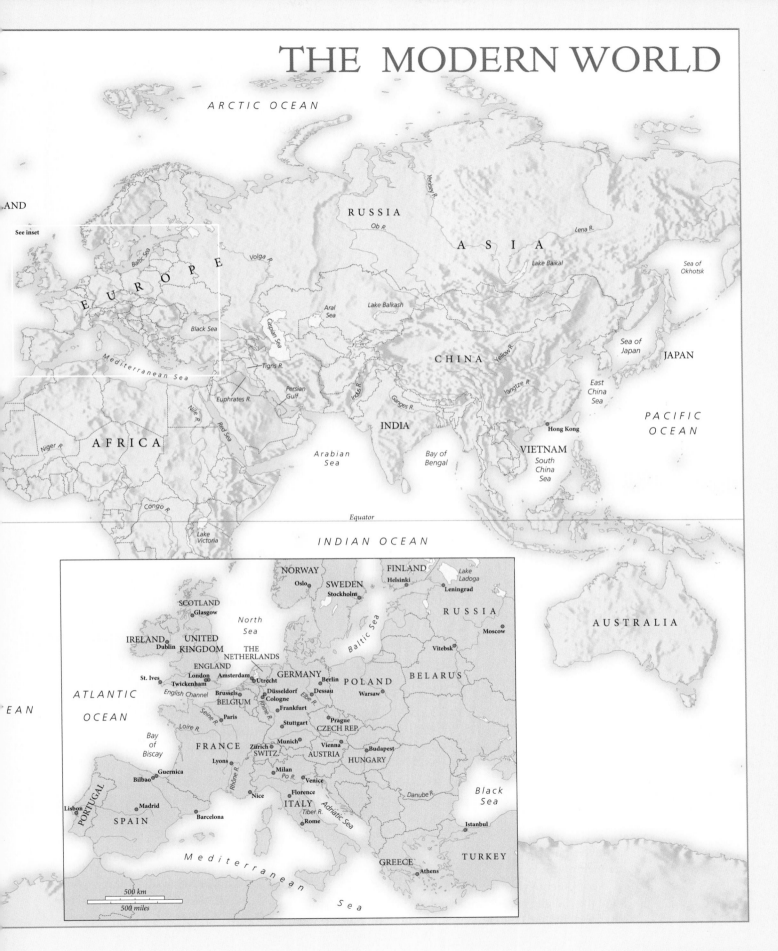

ARCTIC OCEAN

RUSSIA

ASIA

Ob R.

Volga R.

EUROPE

Baltic Sea

Lena R.

Yenisey R.

Lake Baikal

Sea of
Okhotsk

Black Sea

Caspian Sea

Aral
Sea

Lake Balkash

Sea of
Japan

JAPAN

Mediterranean Sea

Tigris R.

Euphrates R.

Persian
Gulf

CHINA

Yellow R.

East
China
Sea

PACIFIC
OCEAN

Nile R.

Red Sea

Indus R.

Ganges R.

Yangtze R.

AFRICA

Niger R.

INDIA

Arabian
Sea

Bay of
Bengal

VIETNAM

South
China
Sea

Hong Kong

Congo R.

Lake
Victoria

Equator

INDIAN OCEAN

See inset

AND

NORWAY

Oslo

SWEDEN

Stockholm

FINLAND

Helsinki

Lake
Ladoga

Leningrad

RUSSIA

AUSTRALIA

SCOTLAND

Glasgow

North
Sea

Baltic Sea

Moscow

IRELAND

Dublin

UNITED
KINGDOM

ENGLAND

THE
NETHERLANDS

Amsterdam

GERMANY

Berlin

POLAND

Vitebsk

BELARUS

St. Ives

London

Utrecht

Düsseldorf

Dessau

ATLANTIC
OCEAN

Twickenham

English Channel

Brussels

BELGIUM

Cologne

Elbe R.

Warsaw

EAN

Seine R.

Paris

Rhine R.

Frankfurt

Loire R.

Stuttgart

Prague

CZECH REP.

Bay
of
Biscay

FRANCE

Zürich

SWITZ.

Munich

Vienna

AUSTRIA

HUNGARY

Budapest

Lyons

Guernica

Bilbao

Rhône R.

Milan

Po R.

Venice

Danube R.

Black
Sea

Nice

Florence

Lisbon

PORTUGAL

Madrid

SPAIN

Barcelona

ITALY

Tiber R.

Rome

Adriatic Sea

Istanbul

Mediterranean

Sea

GREECE

Athens

TURKEY

500 km

500 miles

CHAPTER
23 | Art in the Age of the Enlightenment, 1750–1789

((•──Listen to the chapter audio on myartslab.com

The rise of the Enlightenment, which emerged in the mid-eighteenth century as discussed in the introduction to this section of the book, ushered in the Modern Era. As a result the second half of the eighteenth century was a period of transition as the world moved from the old to the modern, from rule by aristocracy and Church to democracy, from privilege to meritocracy, from agriculture to industry, from rural life to urban, and from superstition and myth to logic. The art of the period reflects this transformation, for it is often changing and complex, with several almost contradictory attitudes existing in a single work. The style generally associated with the period is Neoclassicism, meaning the "New Classicism," which often illustrated what were considered the virtuous actions and deeds of the ancient Greeks and Romans. As we shall see, however, numerous attitudes, if not styles, coexisted with Neoclassicism.

Neoclassicism was based on the logic and morality of the Enlightenment, which were perhaps best expressed by the *PHILOSOPHE* Voltaire. In his

plays, poems, novels, and tracts, Voltaire used logic to attack what he called "persecuting and privileged orthodoxy," mainly meaning Church and State, but any illogical institution or concept was fair game for his satire. He believed science could advance civilization, and that logic presumed a government that benefited the people, not just the aristocracy. It is from him that we get the "doctrine of progress." The models for Voltaire's new civilization were the republics of ancient Greece and Rome, which in addition to being the first democracies provided the first rationalist philosophers. Neoclassicism took its vocabulary from ancient art, as well as from the classically inspired Renaissance and the great seventeenth-century classical French painter Nicolas Poussin (see page 432–34).

Simultaneously, a second and seemingly contrary thread appeared in art, Romanticism, which was the flip side of the Enlightenment coin since it was equally preoccupied with morality and individual freedom. As we shall see in the next chapter, Romanticism came of age about 1800, when the

PHILOSOPHE is the French word for philosopher, but the eighteenth-century *philosophes* were not philosophers per se but simply an international community of intellectuals writing from roughly 1740 to 1789 and dedicated to using Enlightenment empiricism to deal with the problems facing the world. While many wrote treatises, they expressed their ideas in a wide variety of literary formats, including plays, novels, and even political documents, the last best represented by Thomas Jefferson's Declaration of Independence.

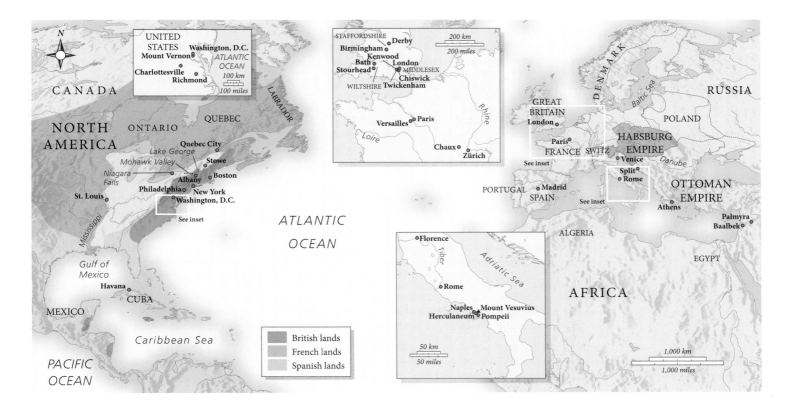

Map 23.1 Europe and North America in 1763

term itself was invented in order to describe the sweeping change in worldview then occurring. But its origins date to mid-century. Instead of Neoclassicism's logic and its desire to control the forces of nature through science, Romanticism valued emotion and intuition and believed in the supremacy of raw, unrestricted nature. Jean-Jacques Rousseau was the principal proponent of this view, which he articulated in his *Discourse on the Arts and Sciences* (1750). Here he advocated a return to Nature, arguing that humans are born good, not in sin, and that they use their innate sense or instincts to distinguish between good and bad, that is, between what makes them happy and what makes them sad. Feeling determines their choices, not rational thought, which is used to explain choices, not to make them. Society, he believed, through its mores, values, and conventions, eventually imposes its own rationalized standards on humans, distracting them from their first true and natural instincts. Rousseau praised what he called the sincere "noble savage," steeped in Nature, and he denounced contemporary civilization for its pretensions, artificiality, and, in general, those social restraints that prevent us from tapping into the power of our basic virtuous emotions. While Romanticism's emotionalism may seem antithetical to Enlightenment logic, it nonetheless similarly championed the individual

and freedom and relied on empiricism and observation to arrive at its conclusions, thoroughly rejecting religious beliefs, including Judeo-Christian mythology, as well as hearsay, superstition, and all thinking and values based merely on tradition.

The rational and the emotional survived side by side in art, and sometimes elements of each appeared within the same work, though usually not in equal proportions. Proponents of both attitudes aggressively rejected Rococo art (see Chapter 22), which they perceived as licentious, frivolous, even immoral, and which was generally associated with aristocracy and privilege, the twin evils condemned by the Enlightenment. While there was a call for a new art, one based on classical values, no one was sure what it should look like. Not until the 1780s, with the paintings of Jacques-Louis David and the sculpture of Antonio Canova, did the Neoclassical style reach full flower. In the meantime, Neoclassicism would appear in many guises, sometimes even containing elements of Rococo elegance, a reminder that the Rococo still persisted deep into the century. Simultaneously, the Romantic fascination with strong emotions, with the irrational and inexplicable, and with the powerful forces of Nature was developing, which ironically would overshadow Neoclassicism by the 1790s, the decade following David's rise and the French Revolution of 1789.

While England and France dominated art in the second half of the century and are the focus of our discussion, Neoclassicism, like the Enlightenment, was an international movement, well represented in Scandinavia, Austria, Germany, and Russia.

Rome Toward 1760: The Font of Neoclassicism

Rome was the center of the art world in the eighteenth century, and virtually anyone aspiring to become a painter, sculptor, or architect felt compelled to study there, experiencing the Roman antiquities and the riches of the Renaissance and Baroque periods at first hand. Not just artists came to Rome: No gentleman's education was complete without making a Grand Tour of Italy, including the north (Florence, Tuscany, Umbria, and Venice, see **map 23.1**) and Naples, the jumping-off point for Herculaneum and Pompeii, perfectly preserved Roman cities that were excavated beginning in 1738 and 1748, respectively. These archaeological excavations, as well as those in Athens, Palmyra, Baalbek, Split, and Ionia, fueled an interest in antiquity and fired the imagination of artists, largely through illustrations published in a large folio format. But the climax of the Grand Tour was Rome, which itself was an enormous archaeological site.

Equally responsible for creating a renewed pre-occupation with antiquity were the writings of the German scholar Johann Joachim Winckelmann (1717–1768), librarian to the great antiquities collector Cardinal Albani, whose Villa Albani in Rome was one of the antiquities museums—along with the Villa Borghese and the Capitoline Hill—that every gentleman on the Grand Tour had to visit. In 1755, Winckelmann published *Reflections on the Imitation of Greek Art in Painting and Sculpture*, and in 1765 he produced his *magnum opus*, *History of Greek Art*. In both publications, he elevated Greek culture to a position of supremacy that it had never quite held in the classical tradition: An era of perfection that was followed only by imitation and decline in the Roman era. But Winckelmann did not just see beauty in Greek art; he also saw moral qualities that paralleled Enlightenment thought: "The general and predominant mark of Greek masterpieces is *noble simplicity and calm grandeur*, both in gesture and in expression.... The expression of all Greek statues reveals even in the midst of all passions a great and grave soul [italics added]." He concludes that "the only way for us to become great, and if possible, even inimitable, is through imitation of the ancients." In response to Winckelmann's influence, the rallying cry of Neoclassicism would be the creation of moral works embodying "noble simplicity and calm grandeur."

While the ancient and Italian artistic past was revered by the Western world, there was little respect for present-day Italy, culturally, economically, or politically. Instead, every country considered it inferior and competed to inherit its artistic mantle of greatness, which had peaked in the seventeenth century.

Artistic Foundations of Neoclassicism: Mengs and Hamilton

Influenced by the revived interest in antiquity, several artists working in Rome, headed especially by Anton Raphael Mengs and Gavin Hamilton, began to lay the foundation for Neoclassicism. Mengs (1728–1779), a German who worked in Rome on and off from 1740 to 1765, gained notoriety when Cardinal Albani, at Winckelmann's urging, commissioned him to paint a ceiling fresco for the Villa Albani. Completed in 1761 and with Winckelmann assisting with the iconography, his *Parnassus* (**fig. 23.1**) depicts the naked cardinal as Apollo surrounded by the female muses, most of whom can be identified as the cardinal's friends. The composition is based on Raphael's Vatican fresco of the same title. Stylistically, Mengs drew on Raphael as well as ancient sources. His painting combines Raphael's **planarity** (objects and figures are parallel to the picture plane) with **linearity** (objects and figures have crisply drawn contours). The figures themselves are copied from Raphael and from the recently unearthed murals at Herculaneum and Pompeii. Apollo's pose recalls the *Apollo Belvedere*, a work in the Vatican collection made famous by Winckelmann. For the sake of planarity, Mengs dispensed with the Baroque device of an illusionistic ceiling (see fig. 19.5), one that opens up to the sky. Instead he made his ceiling look like a wall painting by Raphael, simply hung on a ceiling. Instead of the lush Rococo brushwork then in style, Mengs daringly used tight brushmarks that dissolve into a smooth, hard surface. All of these elements—planarity and linearity, austere, imperceptible brushwork, and classical figures and themes—played a prominent role in the Neoclassical style.

The one element missing from Mengs's painting that would be crucial for the development of

Neoclassicism is an austere, moralistic subject. This would be provided by the Scottish painter and antiquities dealer Gavin Hamilton (1723–1798), who in the early 1760s began making deathbed scenes, such as *Andromache Bewailing the Death of Hector*, a subject taken from Homer and showing the widow Andromache bent over the body of Hector while his generals take an oath to avenge his death. This painting was reproduced in a widely circulated engraving (**fig. 23.2**) of 1764, a reminder of the importance of prints in giving currency to

images before the invention of photography, as well as an additional way for artists to earn a living. Everyone who went to Rome would have seen this picture in Hamilton's studio, since at the time he was one of the must-see painters. For those who did not see the work in Rome, it was available for viewing at a 1764 exhibition of the Society of Artists in London, an organization providing an annual exhibition for members and considered the premier venue in the British capital until the Royal Academy opened in 1768. This image of mourning

23.2 Gavin Hamilton. *Andromache Bewailing the Death of Hector.* 1764. Engraving by Domenico Cunego, after a painting of ca. 1761, 17⅓ × 24¾″ (44 × 63 cm). Private collection

must have shocked eyes accustomed to Rococo gaiety, fantasy, and pleasure. Its moral is matrimonial devotion as opposed to matrimonial indiscretion, unwavering dedication rather than titillating deception, virtue not vice. Elements of the composition were inspired by reliefs on Roman sarcophagi and sepulchral buildings, but Hamilton's prime source was Poussin's *The Death of Germanicus* (see fig. 21.2), then in the Palazzo Barberini in Rome, which has the same receding barrel vault on the left and planar composition of the bed in the foreground.

Today neither Hamilton nor Mengs is generally considered a great or major artist, but they were quite famous and extremely influential in their day. Mengs's awkward and stilted *Parnassus* was a stylistic eye-opener during the heyday of the Rococo, while Hamilton's emphasis on moral virtue, largely circulated through the increased commercialization of prints, would gradually become the preferred subject as the second half of the century unfolded.

Rome Toward 1760: Romanticism

A second art current coming out of Rome in the 1750s was an emphasis on evoking powerful emotions in a viewer, a quality that is called Romantic. The source of this current is Giovanni Battista Piranesi (1720–1778), a printmaker who by this time was renowned for his *vedute*, or views, of Rome, which gentlemen on the Grand Tour took home as souvenirs of their visit. (In Venice, they would buy *vedute* by Canaletto and other artists; see page 454). Winckelmann's glorification of the Greeks and belittling of Romans had infuriated Piranesi, and he set out to defend his Roman heritage, which he did by producing *Roman Antiquities*, a four-volume work completed in 1756 and illustrated with several hundred etchings of ruins. These prints are hardly mere documentation of the sites. Often presenting the structures from a

23.3 Giovanni Battista Piranesi. *Tomb of the Metalli*, Plate XV from *Antichità Romane III*. ca. 1756. Etching, 16¾ × 18⅜″ (42.5 × 46.5 cm). The Metropolitan Museum of Art, New York. Rogers Fund, 1941, transferred from library. 41.71.3(15)

worm's-eye view (**fig. 23.3**), Piranesi transformed them into colossal looming monuments that not only attested to the Herculean engineering feats of the ancient Romans but also the uncontested might and supremacy of Roman civilization. The frightening scale of the monuments dwarfs the awestruck tourists who wander among the dramatically lit ruins. These structures seem erected not by mere humans, but by a civilization of towering giants who have mysteriously vanished. Time has taken a toll on their monuments, now crumbling and picturesquely covered by plants.

These images embody Piranesi's own sense of awe in the face of Roman civilization and constitute a melancholic meditation on the destructive ability of time to erode that once great empire. The prints are not intended just to inform; they are also meant to evoke a sense of astonishment, even fright. In them we see the beginning of a sensitivity that is at odds with the noble simplicity and calm grandeur of Neoclassicism.

Before the eighteenth century was out, the awe that Piranesi was trying to induce would be identified as being caused by what the period called the "**sublime**." The sublime is not a style, but a quality or attribute. Interestingly, the word became current in 1757, at about the same time as Piranesi's publication, when the British statesman Edmund Burke (1729–1797) published a treatise titled *A Philosophical Inquiry into the Origin of Our Ideas of the Sublime and Beautiful*. Burke's study was directed more toward psychology than aesthetics, but its impact on the world of art was tremendous. He defined beauty as embodying such qualities as smoothness, delicacy, and grace, which produced feelings of joy, pleasure, and love. The sublime, however, was obscurity, darkness, power, vastness, and infinity, anything that generated feelings of terror, being overwhelmed, and wonder. The sublime produced "the strongest emotion which the mind is capable of feeling." As the century progressed more and more artists embraced the sublime, catering to viewers' demand to be awed or moved by paintings, sculpture, and architecture.

Neoclassicism in Britain

It almost seems as though the British were predisposed to embracing Neoclassicism, not only because the Enlightenment first developed in Britain but also because the nation already had an intense involvement with antiquity in literature, which dated to the opening decades of the eighteenth century. The Augustan or Classical Age of English poetry was in full bloom by then, with its leading authors, such as John Dryden, Alexander Pope, and Samuel Johnson, emulating the form and content of the writers active during the reign of the first Roman emperor, Augustus (63 BCE–14 CE), many of whom these same British poets translated. Britain at this time was enjoying unprecedented peace and prosperity, which, in part, was responsible for the identification with Augustus' reign, similarly marked by stability, economic prosperity, and the flourishing of culture. The liberal faction of the British aristocracy modeled itself on ancient Rome, relating the British parliamentary government that shared power with the king to the democracy of the Roman Republic that preceded the Caesars. As we shall see, by the 1720s, these liberals, who compared themselves with Roman senators, wanted country homes based on Roman prototypes.

Painting: Historicism, Morality, and Antiquity

The British were particularly receptive to the Neoclassical foundation established by Mengs and Hamilton. Hamilton's moralistic scenes set in antiquity especially had a major impact, and the list of artists inspired by them is extensive, starting with a handful in the 1760s and extending to dozens in the following decades. However, the taste for the classical could also be just that, a taste for a style or look, with little consideration for a moralistic message. This was especially true in the decorative arts.

ANGELICA KAUFFMANN Angelica Kauffmann (1741–1807) was among the most important artists in the development of Neoclassicism in England. She was born in Switzerland, studied in Rome in the 1760s, and moved to London in 1766. She befriended the portrait painter Joshua Reynolds and was a founding member of the ROYAL ACADEMY in 1768, of which Reynolds was president. Prior to the twentieth century, she was one of only two women admitted into the academy, a statistic that on a negative note reflects male prejudice and on a positive one the high international esteem in which the 27-year-old Kauffmann was held. As a woman, she was denied access to studying the male nude, then considered critical to a history painter's success, and this made her accomplishments all the more remarkable.

In 1768 King George II founded the ROYAL ACADEMY OF ART in London in order to encourage the visual arts in Great Britain. The academy was inspired by the French Royal Academy (see page 432). In addition to honoring and educating artists, the academy offered an annual exhibition for its members. This exhibition became the primary vehicle for artists to present their work to the public and advertise themselves, since there were few commercial galleries. Previously, artists showed at the Society of Artists, founded in 1761 and hosting exhibitions until 1791. Joshua Reynolds, who helped establish the Society of Artists, was the first president of the Royal Academy.

 Read the document related to the opening of the Royal Academy in 1769 on myartslab.com

Like so many of her contemporaries, Kauffmann raided Greek and Roman literature for her subjects. In 1769 at the first Royal Academy exhibition she presented *Hector Taking Leave of Andromache*, and three years later she showed *Andromache and Hecuba Weeping over the Ashes of Hector*, two pictures portraying unwavering marital fidelity, both as wife and widow. A classic example of Kauffmann's moralistic pictures is her 1775 *Papirius Praetextatus Entreated by His Mother to Disclose the Secrets of the Deliberations of the Roman Senate* (**fig. 23.4**), which shows a Roman matron beseeching her son to reveal that day's confidential Senate discussions, which he had attended with his father. Women were not allowed in the Senate or even to know the secret proceedings, and the moral is that Papirius did not violate the Senate's trust. To placate his mother, he concocted a story that the Senate had debated whether it was more expedient for husbands to have two wives, or wives to have two husbands. The next day, throngs of women showed up at the senate demanding that it be the wives who would be permitted to have two husbands, the senators puzzled by this bizarre request that came from nowhere.

23.4 Angelica Kauffmann. *Papirius Praetextatus Entreated by His Mother to Disclose the Secrets of the Deliberations of the Roman Senate*. 1775. Oil on canvas, 24¹/₁₆″ (62.75 cm) diameter. Denver Art Museum, Berger Collection

Generally artists produced pendants to present this story, one painting showing the mother's beseeching, the second the matrons, looking like fools, confronting the bewildered senators at the doors to the Senate. Kauffmann only made the one picture, which allows for a second interpretation of her painting: that women were treated as second-class citizens, and furthermore that they were deceived by men. In effect, her painting is probably a subversive protest painting, arguing for women's rights, which Kauffmann was particularly sensitive to, since she had been ostracized from academic training and encouraged to champion human rights by Enlightenment thought. (Furthermore she would not have been able to attend a university; only men went.) Her support of women's issues is reflected in her prominent membership in London's Blue Stockings Society, a loose organization formed in the early 1750s by wealthy women dedicated to furthering their education. Many of Kauffmann's paintings champion women, such as *Cornelia Presenting Her Children as Her Treasures* from 1785, which presents a Roman matron as a nurturing figure responsible for the future political success of her two sons.

In *Papirius Praetextatus* Kauffmann crafts a Roman setting of grand columns and toga-clad figures, who are presented in classical profile. Columns, the socle they rest upon, the bench, and the figures are aligned parallel to the picture plane, the same planarity as we saw in Mengs's *Parnassus*. This planarity is reinforced by the circular two-dimensional outline of the two figures, which echoes the tondo shape of the image. But Kauffmann, like so many Neoclassical artists of this decade, retains elements of the Rococo in her work. The figures, both male and female, have a Rococo elegance as well as delicate facial features, hands, and feet. Kauffmann's palette is still lush, her fabrics glistening with a Watteau-like sensuousness.

The Birth of Contemporary History Painting

Enlightenment empiricism had a major impact on history painting in two ways. One was the strong emphasis on historicism—when portraying a scene set in the historical past, costume, setting, and props all had to be convincing and true to the period. The second impact affected the presentation of major contemporary events that the future would perceive as historically important. Until now, such moments were generally presented using allegory and symbols, not by portraying the actual scene, or figures were dressed in classical garb in order to give them the sense of decorum and importance that the event apparently required. But with the Enlightenment, paintings had to be logical and real and every bit as convincing to contemporaries as we expect period films to be today. This applied not only to the historical past but to contemporary events as well.

BENJAMIN WEST The artist perhaps most responsible for popularizing contemporary history painting is Benjamin West (1738–1820), one of the most successful British Neoclassical history painters. A Quaker born and raised just outside Philadelphia, West went to Rome in 1760 where he studied with Mengs, befriended Gavin Hamilton, and immersed himself in antiquity and the classically influenced Renaissance masters, especially Raphael. By 1763 he had permanently settled in London, and within three years he was a success, in part because of his innovative Neoclassicism. He was a founding

member of the Royal Academy in 1768, and he became its president upon Joshua Reynolds's death in 1792. Throughout his life, he was a mentor for many American artists, and always remained proud of his New World heritage, even supporting the American Revolution. (For a discussion of British colonial portraiture and John Singleton Copley, see Introduction, page 52–3.)

West shocked the London art world in 1770 when he announced that he was working on a contemporary history painting, *The Death of General Wolfe* (**fig. 23.5**), and placing the event in a realistic setting: 1759 Quebec during the FRENCH AND INDIAN WAR. The British general won the Battle of Quebec, which became a turning point in the war, making him a national hero. Upon hearing of West's plan, King George III declared he would never purchase a picture with his soldiers in modern uniforms, and Reynolds frowned on the picture's breach of convention, which required an allegorical apotheosis scene, that is, Wolfe dressed like a saint rising to Heaven. But when exhibited

France and England fought over possession of North America for 150 years. Tension culminated in a nine-year conflict called the FRENCH AND INDIAN WAR. Waged in New York State, New England, and Quebec, it ended in 1763 when Canada was ceded to England. The war transformed Britain into the world's dominant military power, setting the stage for the development of the British Empire. Because of the war's significance in the rise of Britain's world importance and because the Battle of Quebec was the turning point of the war, General James Wolfe was recognized as a national hero.

23.5 Benjamin West. *The Death of General Wolfe*. 1770. Oil on canvas, 59½ × 84″ (1.51 × 2.13 m). National Gallery of Canada, Ottawa. Gift of the Duke of Westminster

at the Royal Academy, the painting was immediately applauded by the public. The scene was so convincing that the audience felt as though it were indeed witnessing its great national hero at the very moment he sacrificed his life for his country in a far-off land, an exotic touch that fascinated the public, which went to look at pictures the way we view movies today. The painting was also successful because West aggrandized and classicized his figures and the event, in effect creating a modern classic. Contemporary viewers recognized that they were in the presence of what amounted to a traditional Lamentation scene (for instance, see fig. 14.7), and that their hero was a modern-day Christ or martyr. The surrounding "apostles" express remorse and concern, but their powerful emotions,

worthy of Poussin, are noble and controlled, in keeping with the classical rule of decorum. Figures strike *contrapposto* poses, stand in profile, and have the sculptural quality of an ancient low-relief or Raphael saint, apostle, or Greek philosopher (see fig. 16.10)—they are simultaneously modern and classical. West took the cue for his painting technique from Mengs, for he first drew and then colored in the figures, allowing crisp contours to ennoble them.

Grand Manner Portraiture in the Neoclassical Style: Joshua Reynolds

Portraiture dominated British painting, for it was extremely difficult to earn a living as a history painter—there just was not much demand for it. Nonetheless, it was a fashionable "face painter," as portraitists were derogatorily called, who played a major role encouraging British artists to turn to working in a Grand Manner that aspired to match the great accomplishments of the ancients and their classical heirs in the Renaissance and Baroque. This proselytizer was Joshua Reynolds (1723–1792), who studied in Rome from 1750 to 1752 and returned to London determined to elevate British art in the mold of the great masters. Working behind the scenes, Reynolds played a role in establishing the Royal Academy of Art in 1768, and as a favorite of George III, he was appointed the institution's first president. From 1769 to 1790, Reynolds delivered his Fifteen Discourses on Art, in which he laid out theories similar to those of Charles Le Brun, the first director of the French Royal Academy (see page 000). He advocated history painting in the Grand Manner, emulation of the great masters, and an idealization in art.

While Reynolds was financially forced to spurn history painting for portraiture, he elevated the genre by encasing his figures in classical poses and layering the images with recondite references of the kind that could be found in great history painting. In his 1765 portrait *Lady Sarah Bunbury Sacrificing to the Graces* (**fig. 23.6**), Reynolds fills his picture with classicisms. The presentation of the Three Graces on an antique pedestal at the upper left of the picture is based on a well-known Hellenistic sculpture. Lady Sarah's gown is not contemporary dress but rather ancient drapery, pinned at the shoulder and with a band at the waist. The brazier, urn, and architecture are also antique.

Like history painters, Reynolds loaded his image with traditional symbols taken from books

23.6 Joshua Reynolds. *Lady Sarah Bunbury Sacrificing to the Graces*. 1765. Oil on canvas, 7'11¼" × 5' (2.42 × 1.53 m). The Art Institute of Chicago, Mr. and Mrs. W.W. Kimball Collection, 1922.4468

of symbols that they used. The Three Graces, for example, represent the three stages of friendship—giving, receiving, and constant exchange of friendship between friends. The intertwined arms represent this exchange, and the nudity the openness of friendship. The myrtle wreath held by the central figure signified friendship's self-propagation, while the roses on the pedestal represent its beauty and pleasure. Art historians have identified the figure pouring a sacrificial libation as a lifelong friend of Lady Sarah, and the painting is believed to be a dedication to their friendship as much as it is a portrait.

In the 1750s and 1760s, Reynolds made countless portraits that could be described as Neoclassical, pictures filled with classical references and executed in a style that has a strong linear quality as well as smooth lighting that sculpturally forms figures and objects. But in his quest to emulate the Old Masters, Reynolds was a stylistic chameleon, taking his cue at one moment from Raphael, the next Rubens, and the next Rembrandt. One artist lurking behind most of his pictures in some form, however, is Anthony van Dyck, the Flemish painter who ended his brief career painting royalty in London. His enormous full-length portraits with grandly yet elegantly posed figures (see fig. 20.3) challenged most portraitists in eighteenth-century Britain, and despite the Neoclassical look of Lady Sarah Bunbury, the almost 8-foot-high canvas reflects the scale and grandeur of Van Dyck's work.

Architecture and Interiors: The Palladian Revival

In England a classical revival began much earlier in architecture than it did in painting and sculpture. Its origins date to the architectural treatises of Anthony Ashley Cooper, 3rd Earl of Shaftesbury, and Colen Campbell, published in the 1710s. Both writers argued for a British architecture based on antiquity (see pages 366–67) and Andrea Palladio's classically inspired villas, which not only evoked antiquity but projected a perfect harmony using geometry, mathematics, and logic. Sounding much as Winckelmann did when discussing sculpture some 50 years later, Shaftesbury wrote that the proportions and geometry of ancient architecture reflected the nobility and beauty of the Greek and Roman soul, which have a powerful effect on the enlightened "man of taste." Architecture was beauty and morality, not just function.

Both Campbell and Shaftesbury reflect a British antagonism toward Roman Catholicism. In Britain, Baroque architecture was associated with two evils: Papist Rome and French royalty. Shaftesbury, a patron and student of John Locke, was an advocate of individual freedom, and he equated ancient architecture with democracy. He was also a WHIG, a member of the liberal antimonarchy political party. In 1714, the Whig party came to power, ending 13 years of political turmoil. Its democratic members especially identified with classical-revival architecture, for they saw themselves as the modern equivalent of Roman senators, who had country villas in addition to their city houses. Campbell, who was virtually unknown prior to the publication of his architectural treatise, was hardly able to fill single-handedly the demand from Whigs who wanted Palladian-style country houses.

THE COUNTRY VILLA: CHISWICK HOUSE We can see the impact of Campbell's ideas on his patron, Lord Burlington, who after a trip to Italy in 1719 became an amateur architect and eventually supplanted Campbell as the leading Palladian figure. In 1725 Burlington with the landscape painter William Kent (1684–1748) designed Chiswick House (**fig. 23.7**), located on Burlington's estate near London and one of the most famous Palladian-revival houses. This stately home is based on Palladio's Villa Rotonda (see fig. 17.13), which Lord Burlington had studied on his Grand Tour.

Chiswick House is distinguished by its simplicity and logic, which make it easy to understand why Lord Burlington was such a success. The building is a cube. Its walls are plain and smooth, allowing for a distinct reading of their geometric shape and the form of the classically pedimented windows. The Greek temple portico protrudes from the wall, again creating a simple and clear form. Even the prominent domed octagonal rotunda is geometric, as are its tripartite semicircular clerestory windows, based on windows in Roman baths. Here we have reason and logic clearly stated, and placed in the service of the ideals of morality, nobility, and republican government. Like Shaftesbury, Burlington believed architecture to be an autonomous art dealing in morality and aesthetics, not just function.

THE NEOCLASSICAL INTERIOR The British taste for the classical extended to interior design, and this was largely due to one man, Robert Adam (1728–1792). Adam was a wealthy Scottish architect

TORY and WHIG were the terms applied in the seventeenth and eighteenth centuries to Britain's two chief political parties. *Tory* was originally a name for Irish outlaws. Later, it became associated with the political supporters of James II (1633–1701, r. 1685–1688), the Roman Catholic Stuart king. The name *Whig* was used for those who opposed James II's succession to the crown. More important, they opposed absolute rule by a king and instead supported constitutional monarchy.

23.7 Lord Burlington and William Kent. Chiswick House. Begun 1725. Chiswick, London

23.8 Robert Adam. The Library. 1767–69. Kenwood House, London

who undertook the Grand Tour from 1754 to 1758. Upon returning to Great Britain, he began practicing in London and was soon the city's most fashionable architect. Although he designed several houses, his specialty was renovating interiors and designing additions, especially for country homes.

A fine example of his work is the library wing at Kenwood (**fig. 23.8**), on what were then the northern outskirts of London; it was built in 1767–69. The ceiling of the room is a Roman barrel vault, and at either end is an apse separated from the main room by Corinthian columns. This concept comes largely from Palladio. The decoration is based on classical motifs, which Adam could copy from the many archaeological books then being published. On the one hand, the library is quite classical, not just because of the motifs, but also because it is symmetrical, geometric, and carefully balanced. On the other hand, it is filled with movement, largely because of the wealth of details and shapes that force the eye to jump from one design element to the next. Adam's palette is pastel in color and light in tone; light blues, white, and gold prevail. Curving circles, delicate plant forms, and graceful fluted columns with ornate capitals set a festive, elegant, and refined tone closer to Rococo playfulness than to severe Neoclassical morality.

Early Romanticism in Britain

Edmund Burke's 1757 treatise on beauty and the sublime (see page 467) marked the beginning of growing interest in dark themes that elicited powerful responses. These themes could occur in painting, sculpture, decorative arts, or architecture.

Architecture: Strawberry Hill and the Gothic Revival

An interest in generating strong emotional responses in the viewer first emerged in architecture and landscape design. Instead of planning symmetrical formal gardens for Chiswick, which would have been standard at the time, Kent surrounded the house with a natural-looking landscape of rolling, hilly lawns, irregularly arranged stands of trees, and naturalistic serpentine lakes. The British began using the word **picturesque** to describe the irregularity of these designs, which because of their variety provided endless interest for the eye. By the 1740s, Kent was sprinkling his landscapes with classical structures and Gothic ruins, which were meant to evoke a feeling of nostalgia for a distant past, thus adding a hint of the sublime (see page 467) to his designs.

This combination of the picturesque and the sublime can be found in architecture as well, especially in the style known as Gothic Revival.

While Roman or Palladian country houses were springing up all over Britain, a Gothic Revival was taking place as well. An interest in Gothic architecture—which was then perceived as a national architecture because it was believed, wrongly, to have originated in England—was sparked in part by the appearance of some of the first literature on the style. But its appeal in large part lay in its sublime qualities. The cathedrals were cold, dark, and gloomy, and contained vast, overwhelming spaces. Gothic ruins, which could be seen everywhere, evoked associations of death, melancholy, and even horror. In 1764, the Gothic novel emerged as a genre with the publication of Horace Walpole's *The Castle of Otranto: A Gothic Story*, set in a haunted castle. The book started a medieval craze that peaked with Victor Hugo's 1831 *The Hunchback of Notre-Dame*, in which the dark, forbidding cathedral of the title is the home of the terrifying hunchbacked recluse Quasimodo.

Horace Walpole (1717–1797) also deserves credit for making the Gothic Revival fashionable when, with a group of friends, he redesigned Strawberry Hill (**fig. 23.9**), his country house in Twickenham, just outside London. Started in 1749, the renovation took over 25 years to complete. The house is distinctly medieval; the walls are capped with crenelated battlements and pierced by tracery windows. For Walpole, Gothic meant

23.9 Horace Walpole, with William Robinson and others. Strawberry Hill. 1749–77. Twickenham, England

picturesque, and consequently the L-shaped building is irregular, asymmetrical, and looks like an accretion of additions from different periods, which it actually is because the home was erected piecemeal over a long time, with each section designed by a different person. But there is little of the sublime on the exterior, which actually has a Rococo delicacy. The crenelations are petite, not massive, the whitewash of one of the wings is bright and not gloomy, and the windows sit near the surface, making the walls look fine and paper-thin, not thick and fortresslike.

Painting: The Coexistence of Reason and Emotion

Just as the Gothic Revival thrived alongside the revival of classicism in Britain, Romantic painting coexisted with the Neoclassical. Romantic undercurrents even appeared in pictures that are essentially classical, a paradox that underscores the limitations of labeling. Like a moth to a flame, the taste of the period was increasingly drawn to the awesome power of Nature, the experience of unfettered elemental emotions and instincts, and even the wonder of the irrational. In effect, the Enlightenment at moments could deny its very foundation of logic and empiricism and permit itself to be swept away by the emotional pull of the exotic, wondrous, terrifying, and inexplicable. The thirst for sublime experiences would prevail by the end of the century.

GEORGE STUBBS George Stubbs (1724–1806), who specialized in portraits of horses, is generally described as a Neoclassical painter, in part because his early images had a somewhat hard, frozen

23.10 George Stubbs. *Lion Attacking a Horse*. 1770. Oil on canvas, 38 × 49½″ (96.5 × 125.7 cm). Yale University Art Gallery, New Haven, Connecticut. Gift of the Yale University Art Gallery Associates 1955.27.1

look, since they were carefully drawn and tightly painted, with the objects aligned parallel to the picture plane. At the same time, he made some of the earliest Romantic pictures, and is one of the first artists who directly responded to Burke's treatise on the sublime and the beautiful. In the early 1760s, Stubbs began a series of approximately 21 paintings portraying a horrifying natural event that would evoke a sublime emotion in a viewer: a lion attacking either a horse or a stag, an example of which is the 1770 *Lion Attacking a Horse* (**fig. 23.10**). His protagonists are animals, who, unlike humans, are immersed in nature and at one with it, virtual personifications of unleashed natural forces. We identify with the horse, which is white, a symbol of goodness and purity. Its mouth, eye, mane, and legs are taut with fear and pain. Evil is represented by the lion's dark, powerful legs, which seem almost nonchalant as they rip into the horse's back, pulling the skin to expose a skeletal rib cage. The lion's body disappears into the blackness of the landscape, identifying its destructive force with a frightening darkness and elemental powers that surge from the earth. Ominous storm clouds announce the horse's fate as they threaten to cast the entire scene into dark shadow at the moment, we assume, that the doomed horse expires. West, in *The Death of General Wolfe*, similarly harnessed the forces of nature through his dramatic clouds and windswept hair to reinforce the emotional intensity and psychology of his figures.

Romanticism in Grand Manner Portraiture: Thomas Gainsborough

Just as we saw that Neoclassicism affected portraiture in, for example, the work of Sir Joshua Reynolds, so too did burgeoning Romanticism. It is best exemplified in the portraits of Reynolds's nemesis, Thomas Gainsborough (1727–1788). Gainsborough was born into a prosperous Sudbury manufacturing family, and after studying painting in London with a French Rococo painter in the 1740s, he returned to his native Suffolk, initially painting landscapes. But to earn a living, he soon turned to portraiture, and in 1759 he moved to Bath to take advantage of the wealthy clientele who came there to vacation. He did not move to London until 1774, but the appearance of his works first at the Society of Artists from 1761 and at the Royal Academy after 1769 established him as one of the leading artists of his day.

Like Reynolds, Gainsborough took his cue from Van Dyck, and his forte was enormous, life-size, full-length portraits, the figures often having elegant proportions and poses. While Reynolds created bold, modeled forms, Gainsborough dissolved figures and objects in lush, feathery brushwork, as can be seen in his 1785–87 *Portrait of Mrs. Richard Brinsley Sheridan* (**fig. 23.11**), the sitter a celebrated soprano. Not only does Gainsborough's gossamer-thin touch give an elegance to the surface, it also animates it, making it seethe with motion and tying all of the objects together. More important, Gainsborough has integrated Mrs. Sheridan into the landscape. Her hair is windswept, following the pattern of the tree above and behind her, which forms a halo of sky around her head. Her body also echoes the thrust of the land, her drapery rippling in the same direction as the leaves, clouds, and rock. Mrs. Sheridan is steeped in Nature, virtually swept away by it. Here we see demonstrated Rousseau's return to Nature, the locus of innocence, beauty, and moral perfection.

23.11 Thomas Gainsborough. *Portrait of Mrs. Richard Brinsley Sheridan*. 1785–87. Oil on canvas, 7′2⅝″ × 5′3⅜″ (2.2 × 1.54 m). National Gallery of Art, Washington, D.C. Andrew W. Mellon Collection (1937.1.92)

Neoclassicism in France

As in Britain, the reaction against the Rococo in France first appeared in architecture, but it surfaced in the 1750s and 1760s, rather than the 1710s and 1720s. At first elegant and rational and largely based on seventeenth-century French classical architecture, this new style moved into an austere, awe-inspiring, and even visionary stage by the late 1770s. This "sublime" phase even had a profound impact on painting. Despite repeated appeals from numerous sources, including Enlightenment exponents and the government, painters were slow to meet the challenge to create a new moralistic art based on antiquity. It was not until the late 1770s that large numbers of painters took up the cause, and it was not until the 1780s, with the advent of Jacques-Louis David and his austere brand of Neoclassicism, that a new style emerged, one that thrived well into the nineteenth century.

Architecture: Rational Classicism and the Neoclassical Sublime

The first phase of French Neoclassical architecture was a reaction to the excesses of the Rococo, which had been about asymmetry, graceful movement, decorative flourishes, and curvilinear elegance. The new architecture was about rational design, and hence was often called "Rational Classicism." All components of a building had to be geometric, symmetrical, and logical in the sense that they were essential to the structure. While this phase of Neoclassical architecture was theoretically based on nature, it nonetheless took its lead from the seventeenth-century style. French architecture moved into a new, more austere phase in the 1770s, one less interested in following the rules of the ancients and more preoccupied with reducing architecture to elemental geometric forms that operated on a monumental scale and created a Piranesian sense of awe and power.

THEORETICAL BEGINNINGS AND RATIONAL CLASSICISM
Launching the attack on the Rococo was the architect Jacques-François Blondel (1705–1774), who in a speech at the Royal School of Architecture in 1747 condemned the ornate flamboyance of the style. Here, and in his later publications, he called for a return to the classicism of great seventeenth-century architects, such as Claude Perrault (see page 437). Blondel demanded that buildings be logical, simple, functional, and symmetrical, and

that they should be constructed with right angles, not curves. Blondel's theories were seconded in several major treatises by the influential writer Abbé Marc Antoine Laugier (1713–1769). Another major force for the development of Rational Classicism was the marquis de Marigny, the brother of Madame de Pompadour (see page 448). He was sent on the Grand Tour from 1749 to 1751 to study classical architecture in preparation for becoming the director-general of buildings upon his return, a position that gave him artistic control over France, as well as the Academy. He immediately hired the architect Jacques-Germain Soufflot (1713–1780), who had accompanied him to Italy, to finish Perrault's Louvre (see fig. 21.6), which at the time was a ruin slated for demolition. After the completion of the Louvre, he instructed Ange-Jacques Gabriel (1698–1782), the newly appointed first architect to Louis XV, to erect two enormous government buildings on the north side of what is today the Place de la Concorde, where they can still be seen: two huge identical façades framing the Rue Royale. Gabriel had never been to Rome, and for him classicism largely meant seventeenth-century French classicism. His two buildings are so similar to Perrault's Louvre that they almost do not need illustrating. Instead of double columns, Gabriel used single, and he removed the pedimented portico in the center of the building to either end, where each functioned as "book-ends" framing the colonnade.

SUBLIME NEOCLASSICAL ARCHITECTURE: CLAUDE-NICOLAS LEDOUX Rational Classicism, based largely on the classicism of Perrault and the Louvre, gave way to an austere sublime architecture beginning in the 1770s. The architect most responsible for this development was Claude-Nicolas Ledoux (1736–1806). He was a student of Blondel but was also heavily influenced by Piranesi's publications of Roman ruins. By the mid-1760s he was a fashionable Parisian architect, designing many of the most prestigious *hôtels*, as large private town houses were called, and by the 1770s he was designing austere Palladian residences, buildings that were stripped down to a geometric essence with austere Tuscan columns, which were unfluted and without bases.

One of Ledoux's greatest public projects was the 50 or more tax gates, or customs houses, he designed for the new 15-mile (24-kilometer) wall surrounding Paris. Each gate was different, although like the Barrière de l'Étoile, reproduced

The SALON was an exhibition of art by members of the Royal Academy held in the Louvre. While conceived in the seventeenth century, it was held only a handful of times before 1737, when it was first instituted as an annual show that gradually evolved into a biennial presented in the *Salon carré* of the Louvre, hence its name. The Salons, which opened August 25, the feast-day of St. Louis, and lasted between three and six weeks, were attended by some 20,000 to 100,000 people from all strata of society, from bakers and blacksmiths to dukes and duchesses. With the Salon, art critics emerged, their commentaries, often scathing, appearing in brochures that were generally published anonymously. Increasingly, public opinion would replace aristocratic patronage as the major influence on art.

here (**fig. 23.12**), they were all colossal, severe, and strictly geometric, based on cylinders, cubes, triangles, and circles and often using architectural motifs introduced in his *hôtels* in the previous decade. The Barrière de l'Étoile, which consisted of two identical buildings framing a road at the present site of the Arc de Triomphe, is a perfect square, with square blocks alternating with round cylinders to create imposing massive columns, an unadorned pediment forming a distinct triangle, and an enormous mysterious cylinder projecting through the roof that suggests the drum for a dome. Windows have no moldings and are reduced to rectangular holes punched out in the massive walls. While this uninviting fortresslike building is classical in its use of pediments and columns, Classical proportions and harmony have given way to an exaggerated, daunting scale and a bizarre juxtaposition of architectural motifs culled from different historical periods to create a brutal monumentality designed to generate a sense of awe-inspiring power.

Painting and Sculpture: Expressing Enlightenment Values

There was no parallel in French painting and sculpture with the swing toward Classicism occurring in French architecture in the 1750s and 1760s. Until the 1780s, the Enlightenment emphasis on reason and morality was best presented not by history painting but by the lower stratum of genre painting.

JEAN-BAPTISTE GREUZE One artist alone virtually created a vogue for genre painting, Jean-Baptiste Greuze (1725–1805), and from 1759 until the 1770s his scenes of everyday life were the sensation of the Paris SALONS. Greuze emerged from a working-class background in the Lyons region and went to Paris in the mid-1750s to make his mark at the Royal Academy. A wealthy collector sponsored a trip to Italy for him from 1755 to 1759, but Greuze left Paris a genre and portrait painter and returned as one as well.

Nonetheless, Greuze became the rage of Paris with *The Village Bride* (**fig. 23.13**), his submission to the Salon of 1761, which shows a Protestant wedding the moment after a father has handed his son-in-law a dowry, dutifully recorded by a notary, seated on the right. The scene seethes with virtue as the various members of this neat, modest, hardworking religious family express familial love, dedication, and respect. Here is the social gospel of Rousseau: The naïve poor, in contrast to the more

23.12 Claude-Nicolas Ledoux. Barrière de l'Étoile (Étoile Customs House), Paris (now destroyed). 1785–98. Bibliothèque Nationale, Paris

cultivated, yet immoral aristocracy, are closer to nature and thus full of "natural" virtue and honest sentiment. Greuze draws a parallel between the family of humans and the family of the hen and her chicks, each with one member separated, thus reinforcing this point about the natural instinct of common folk. Critics and public alike raved about the authenticity of the gestures and emotions, comparing them favorably with those of the noble figures by Poussin (see fig. 21.2).

While Greuze was certainly attempting to match the intensity of emotion and gesture found in history painting, especially in Poussin, he was also inspired by contemporary theater, which accounts for the arrangement of the figures in a *tableau vivant* (a "living painting," when actors onstage freeze as if in a painting to portray a pregnant moment) just when the father is declaiming his poignant speech about the sanctity of marriage. He was particularly influenced by a new realistic form of theater, *drame bourgeois* (middle-class drama), promoted by his good friend DIDEROT. But equally influencing his sense of detail and attention to texture was the increasingly popular seventeenth-century Dutch and Flemish genre and still-life painting, as well as Chardin's down-to-earth imagery (see fig. 22.4). Even Greuze's figures are individualized, rather than portrayed as ideal types. They are so real that when Greuze used them again in later

A genius in many fields, including natural science, and a novelist, dramatist, poet, and art critic, Denis DIDEROT (1713–1784) is still best known as the compiler and editor of the great French *Encyclopédie* (1751–80), a staggering 28-volume compendium of the natural and physical sciences, law, and what would today be called political science. His fellow *philosophe* Jean-Jacques Rousseau was a contributor to the *Encyclopédie*.

23.13 Jean-Baptiste Greuze. *The Village Bride*, or *The Marriage, The Moment When a Father Gives His Son-in-Law a Dowry*. 1761. Oil on canvas, 36 × 46½″ (91.4 × 118.1 cm). Musée du Louvre, Paris

By the mid-eighteenth century, sculptors not only first executed a work in PLASTER, which was inexpensive and easy to use, they increasingly exhibited these plasters. If a patron liked the sculpture, it would then be executed in a more prestigious medium, such as marble, or even at a different scale.

paintings, the public decided it was witnessing the continuation of the story of the same family. As we shall see, Greuze's realism and morality as well as his pregnant *tableau vivant* moment will figure prominently in French Neoclassicism when it emerges some 20 years later.

JEAN-ANTOINE HOUDON The French sculptor who perhaps best exemplifies Enlightenment empiricism is Jean-Antoine Houdon (1741–1828). Both Greuze and Houdon used realism in their works, but Houdon, unlike Greuze, incorporated realism into a façade of classicism, instead of the other way round. While a pensioner at the French Academy in Rome from 1765 to 1768, Houdon studied realistic Roman portrait busts, and in 1767 he executed in PLASTER a life-sized flayed male torso revealing in detail every muscle of the body while it leans against a support in perfect Greek *contrapposto*.

As would be expected of such an empirical mentality, Houdon specialized in portraits, and he became the portraitist to the Enlightenment, depicting virtually every major personality, including Diderot, Rousseau, Louis XVI, Catherine II of Russia, and Benjamin Franklin. Houdon's uncanny ability to capture both the look and the personality of his sitter is apparent in *Voltaire Seated* (**fig. 23.14**), here a terra cotta cast from the original plaster, which is lost. The sculptor classicizes his sitter by dressing him in a Roman toga and headband, and seating him in an antique-style chair. But he portrays Voltaire realistically by showing the sagging folds of skin on the neck, the sunken toothless mouth, the deep facial wrinkles, and the slumping shoulders, all of which mark the sitter's age and frailty. Houdon has also brilliantly seized the *philosophe*'s sharp intellect and wit: The head is turning and the mouth smiling, and while one hand droops over the arm of the chair, reflecting age, the other grasps it firmly, reflecting his mental tenacity (see page 462).

The Climax of Neoclassicism: Jacques-Louis David's Paintings

The reign of genre painting in Enlightenment France was short, with Greuze's popularity peaking by 1765. The tide began to turn toward history painting in 1774 when Charles-Claude d'Angiviller, the new director-general in charge of buildings and art in France and overseer of the Royal Academy of Painting and Sculpture, made it his personal mission to snuff out what he considered Rococo licentiousness and replace it with moralistic history painting. Beginning in 1777, he regularly commissioned "grand machines," as these enormous oils were called because of the elaborate equipment needed to install them, and many were based on the noble and virtuous deeds of the ancients as well as exemplary moments from French history. The project triggered a quest, and even a heated competition, among artists to produce *the* great history painting. The fruit of this program appeared in the mid-1780s with the emergence of Jacques-Louis David (1748–1825), whose images were so revolutionary that they have virtually come to epitomize Neoclassicism, thus simplifying a very complex period and a very complicated term that encompasses much more than David's style.

David discovered his mature artistic voice while studying in Rome from 1775 to 1781, and it came as a result of copying a painting of a *Last Supper* by Valentin de Bologne, a French follower of Caravaggio (see page 432), in 1779. He was especially attracted to de Bologne's powerful naturalism and dramatic lighting, which carved out crisp sculptural figures and objects. D'Angiviller liked David's new style so much that he gave him a major commission.

It took David three years to complete this painting, *The Oath of the Horatii* (**fig. 23.15**), and he finished it in Rome in 1783–84, where it would be first seen by an international audience. When David unveiled *The Oath* in his Rome studio, it instantly became a sensation, with an endless procession of visitors filing through to see this revolutionary work. *The Oath* arrived in Paris from Rome a few days after the opening of the 1784 Salon, its delayed grand entrance enhancing the public clamor.

The theme for the picture comes from a Roman seventh-century BCE story found in both Livy and Plutarch, recounting how a border dispute

23.14 Jean-Antoine Houdon. *Voltaire Seated*. 1781. Terra cotta model for marble original, height 47″ (119.3 cm). Institut et Musée Voltaire, Geneva, Switzerland

between Rome and neighboring Alba was settled by a sword fight by three soldiers from each side. Representing Rome were the three Horatii brothers, for Alba the three Curiatii brothers. Complicating the story, a Horatii sister, Camilla, was engaged to a Curiatii brother, while one of the Horatii brothers was married to a Curiatii sister. Only Horatius of the Horatii brothers survived the violent fight, and David had been instructed to paint the moment when Horatius returns home and slays his sister after she curses him for killing her fiancé. Instead, David painted a scene that does not appear in the literature: The Horatii, led by their father, taking an oath to fight to the death. The composition is quite simple and striking: David contrasts the virile, stoic men, their bodies locked in rigorous determination, with the slack, curvilinear heap of the distressed women, Camilla and the Curiatii wife, who, either way, will lose a brother, husband, or fiancé.

23.15 Jacques-Louis David. *The Oath of the Horatii*. 1783–84. Oil on canvas, 10'10" × 13'11" (3.3 × 4.25 m). Musée du Louvre, Paris

 Read the document related to Jacques-Louis David on myartslab.com

David was undoubtedly inspired by the many oath-taking paintings that had appeared since Gavin Hamilton made an *Oath of Brutus* in 1764. The dramatic moment, which David made one of the hallmarks of Neoclassical history painting, allowed him to create a *tableau vivant* championing noble and virtuous action dedicated to the supreme but necessary sacrifice of putting the state before family. The severity of the Horatii's dedication is reinforced by the severity of the composition. It is clear in the austerity of the shallow space, and even in David's selection of stark, baseless Tuscan columns, which Ledoux had made fashionable in France the decade before. It also appears in the relentless planarity that aligns figures and architecture parallel to the picture plane and in the harsh geometry of the floor, arches, and grouping of the warriors. It surfaces as well in the sharp linear contours of the figures, making them seem as solid and frozen as statues. In this planarity and linearity, David is more "Poussiniste" than his idol Poussin, from whom he borrows figures. Line and geometry,

the vehicles of reason, now clearly prevail over the sensual color and brushwork of the Rococo.

But it is the Caravaggesque naturalism and intensity that make this image so powerful and distinguish it from Renaissance and Baroque classicism. Sharpening edges and heightening the drama of the painting is a harsh light that casts precise shadows, an effect derived from Caravaggio (see fig. 19.1), as is the attention to textures and such details as chinks in the floor marble. The picture is startlingly lifelike, with the setting and costumes carefully researched to recreate seventh-century BCE Rome.

While *The Oath* is generally perceived as the quintessential Neoclassical picture, one of several David made that came to define the style and give it a new severity and virility, it is filled with undercurrents of Romanticism. It is a horrific scene, one that frightened onlookers, sending chills up their spines. This is not just an image of moral resolve and logic, reflecting Cassius who declares in Voltaire's play *Death of Caesar* that "a true republican's only father and sons are virtue, the gods, law, and country." Under the frozen Neoclassical stillness of this scene lies the tension of the bloodbath soon to come. We see this tension in the father's brightly lit fingers, which echo the stridency of the swords. This enormous 14-foot painting is about the impending violence, from which the nurse in the ominous background shadow tries to shield the children. The picture is a reminder that within 20 years, the Western world will have entered into the Age of Romanticism, as we will see in our next chapter.

Neoclassical Portraiture: Marie-Louise-Élisabeth Vigée-Lebrun

The impact of David's Neoclassicism was powerful, not just on history painting but portraiture as well. We can see this impact on the 1789 *Self-Portrait with Daughter* (**fig. 23.16**) by Marie-Louise-Élisabeth Vigée-Lebrun (1755–1842). Born in Paris to a father who was a minor painter and who died when she was 12, Vigée-Lebrun, as a woman, was denied access to the Royal Academy. Consequently, she was essentially self-taught. In her teens, she began painting portraits, which were illegal since she did not have a license from the Academy; this forced her to seek admission to the less prestigious Academy of St. Luke, where she exhibited in 1774. The following year, in a marriage of convenience, she wed Jean-Baptiste-Pierre Lebrun, a painter and prominent art dealer, who gave her access to powerful contacts. Her exceptional talent, vibrant personality, and sophistication soon had her circulating among the aristocracy and the wealthy, and she became a favorite of Queen Marie-Antoinette, whose portrait she painted many times, beginning in 1778. Through the queen's influence, the Royal Academy in 1783 accepted her as a painter of historical allegory.

Lebrun is generally labeled a Rococo painter; her portraits having an affability, liveliness, intimacy, and colorful palette associated with the style (see pages 446–51). But throughout her career, Vigée-Lebrun was attuned to the latest artistic fashions, and she was a forceful arbiter in the world of couture, introducing, for example, shawls, and making "an arrangement with broad scarves lightly intertwined around the body and on the arms, which was an attempt to imitate the beautiful drapings of Raphael...." Vigée-Lebrun's 1789 portrait of herself with her daughter reflects the taste for the classical that was then becoming so pervasive in Paris. In this portrait, we see the sitters attired *à l'antique*, wearing togas, Vigée-Lebrun's cinched above the waist with a scarf. The artist wears an antique headband and sports a Roman-style coiffure. Instead of a lavish Rococo interior, she and her daughter pose against an austere, although warm, wall.

Vigée-Lebrun loved her daughter, but the powerful intimacy and affectionate nature of the scene should also be seen as a reflection of the new Rousseauian attitude toward children that called for greater parental involvement in child-rearing, a quality that was increasingly apparent in portraiture in the second half of the century as young children began to be featured more frequently in portraits with their parents. But despite these Neoclassicisms and Enlightenment influences, this spectacular painting still retains an undercurrent of the Rococo, seen in its warm colors, affable glances, soft Correggioesque contours, and curvilinear patterning of arms and drapery. We are far removed from the hard-edge austerity of David's Neoclassicism.

23.16 Marie-Louise-Élisabeth Vigée-Lebrun. *Self-Portrait with Daughter*. 1789. Oil on canvas, 47⅔ × 35½" (121 × 90 cm). Musée du Louvre, Paris

Italian Neoclassicism Toward 1785

This chapter began in Rome toward 1760, and our story comes full circle by ending there as well, toward 1785, no longer looking at foreigners, such as Mengs and Hamilton, but at an Italian sculptor. It took over 20 years for Neoclassical painting to crystalize into a distinctive style in the work of David, and the same happened almost simultaneously in sculpture in the work of Antonio Canova. Canova emerged in Rome in the 1780s, and by the 1790s he was the most famous sculptor in the world, receiving commissions from all over Europe and America. He was the artist whom the majority of sculptors in both the Old and the New World emulated and tried to equal, far into the nineteenth century.

Neoclassical Sculpture: Antonio Canova

Antonio Canova (1757–1822) came from a family of stonecutters in the region around Venice. When he was nine his artistic talent was brought to the attention of a Venetian senator, under whose patronage he was able to study sculpture in Venice, becoming a teenage prodigy. By 1780 he was in Rome, financed by the Venetian senate, and the following year he took the city by storm with his marble sculpture *Theseus Vanquishing the Minotaur*. The work was a sensation in part because it looked Classical, like an excavated sculpture, although it was not based on a specific antique source—it was entirely Canova's creation.

We can see Canova's originality in *Cupid and Psyche* (**fig. 23.17**), commissioned in 1787 by a tourist for his home in Britain. Canova first modeled the work in plaster, and then had assistants rough it

23.17 Antonio Canova. *Cupid and Psyche*, 1787–93. Marble, 6'1" × 6'8" (1.55 × 1.73 m). Musée du Louvre, Paris

out in marble. Afterward he completed the carving, which included creating an impressive variety of surface textures, especially the remarkable cold-perfect finish for flesh that was often copied but never equaled by his many imitators. Nor did anyone match his exquisite compositions of continuous elegant contours, which in *Cupid and Psyche* are visible in the curving pattern of the sensuous arms and legs, as well as in the flowing drapery and oval mound gently elevating the figures.

Canova delivers more than beautiful idealized classical models, more than noble simplicity and calm grandeur—he also presents intense emotion. Here, he portrays the moment when Cupid, having fallen in love with the human Psyche, gives her a kiss that awakens her from the eternal sleep into which she has been cast by the jealous Venus. With this kiss, she becomes immortal, like Cupid. Canova captures a tenderness and passion in both expression and gestures that was virtually unthinkable before 1780. As we shall see in the next chapter, this psychological intensity anticipates the Romantic era.

POINTS OF REFLECTION

23.1 In what ways do works such as Angelica Kauffmann's *Papirius Praetextatus Entreated by His Mother to Disclose the Secrets of the Deliberations of the Roman Senate*, Joshua Reynolds's *Portrait of Lady Sarah Bunbury*, Jean-Antoine Houdon's *Voltaire Seated,* and David's *The Oath of the Horatii* reflect both Enlightenment values and the Neoclassical style?

23.2 How does Jean-Baptist Greuze's genre painting *The Village Bride* reflect Neoclassical values, and as a result, how does it differ from such earlier genre paintings as William Hogarth's *He Revels (The Orgy)* from *The Rake's Progress* (fig. 22.8) and Jan Steen's *The Feast of St. Nicholas* (fig. 20.16)?

23.3 What makes the following very diverse works Romantic, and which can be considered sublime: Giovanni Battista Piranesi's *Tomb of the Metalli*, George Stubbs's *Lion Attacking a Horse*, Thomas Gainsborough's *Portrait of Mrs. Richard Brinsley Sheridan*, and Claude-Nicolas Ledou's *Barrière de l'Étoile*?

23.4 In what ways do the following works combine Neoclassical and Romantic elements: Benjamin West's *The Death of General Wolfe* and Jacques-Louis David's *The Oath of the Horatii*? What style seems to prevail in each painting? And what are the Rococo elements in such Neoclassical works as Robert Adam's library at Kenwood and Angelica Kauffmann's *Papirius Praetextatus Entreated by His Mother*?

✔—**Study** and review on myartslab.com

ART IN TIME

- **1725—Burlington and Kent begin constructing Chiswick House**

- 1738—Excavation of Herculaneum begins; of Pompeii begins in 1748

- **1749—Walpole begins redesigning Strawberry Hill**

- ca. 1750—Industrial Revolution begins in England with emergence of textile industry

- 1754–63—French and Indian War, which spread worldwide and established Great Britain as a major world power

- 1751—Diderot and d'Alembert publish the *Encyclopédie*

- 1762—Jean-Jacques Rousseau publishes *The Social Contract*

- 1765–82—James Watt perfects the steam engine

- **1770—Stubbs, *Lion Attacking a Horse***

- **1770—West, *The Death of General Wolfe***

- 1775–84—The American Revolution

- 1776—Adam Smith publishes *The Wealth of Nations*, which advocates a free market economy

- **1783–84—David, *The Oath of the Horatii***

- 1789—French Revolution begins

- 1792—Mary Wollstonecraft publishes *A Vindication of the Rights of Women*, launching feminist theory

Art in the Age of Romanticism, 1789–1848

((•—Listen to the chapter audio on myartslab.com

There is no precise moment when Neoclassicism died and Romanticism was born. Just as Neoclassical and Romantic elements—the rational and the emotional—coexisted in the arts of the Enlightenment era (see Chapter 23) from 1750 to 1789 (and sometimes in the same work), Neoclassicism and Romanticism also thrived side by side from 1789 to 1848, the years bracketed by the French Revolution and the European workers' revolts. If rational Neoclassical components prevailed in the earlier period, then emotional, Romantic components did in the later one. No matter how Neoclassical in look or style, a work produced during this later period is still imbued with Romanticism.

A fundamental change in consciousness in the Western world occurred toward 1800. It was in part triggered by the upheavals accompanying the French Revolution, which resulted in the overthrow of both the monarchy and the Catholic Church and the execution of 17,000 people in France. The Revolution was followed by the Napoleonic Wars,

which wreaked havoc throughout Europe until 1814. These momentous events were accompanied by the disorienting rise of industrialization and urbanization, which saw huge migrations from the countryside to the city, where the poor lived in miserable conditions and were forced to work interminable hours for subsistence pay. Complementing the rise of this new proletariat was the continued development of the bourgeoisie, as the new wealthy middle class was labeled (see page 459). This group threatened the dominance of the aristocracy. In response to these developments, Marx and Engels published their *Communist Manifesto* in 1848, the year that saw the outbreak of European-wide revolution by the workers.

The Enlightenment seemed to have failed. Instead of social reform and progress, there was turmoil and dislocation. With this seemingly endless succession of crises, the West found a need to believe in something other than the Enlightenment values of logic and scientific empiricism. Thus arose a belief in the subjective emotion of the individual,

Map 24.1 Europe and North America in 1815

first promoted by Jean-Jacques Rousseau in France (see Chapter 23). What had been a strong undercurrent in the eighteenth century now surfaced as the defining psychology of the Western world. Artists, writers, composers, and intellectuals now placed a premium on powerful emotion, intuition, and unrestrained creative genius. The era itself is often described as being dedicated to the "Cult of the Individual." For the intellectual and cultural elite, total liberation of imagination and creative freedom replaced rules, standards, and logic. As expressed by the French Romantic writer Victor Hugo, "All systems are false; only genius is true." From this perspective, the mind was the conduit of nature, the only means of accessing elemental universal forces, and the goal of the artist was to tap into this reservoir of higher reality and express it. Sincerity and truthfulness were therefore now critical. Enlightenment morality was not applicable. Powerful emotions in response to violence, suffering, chaos, and ugliness, or just the exotic and wondrous, replaced virtuous and noble actions and the perfection associated with ideal beauty. Uniqueness became a strong value in art; copying someone else's genius, originality, or individualism was the manufacture of something false. Consequently, Romanticism was not a style, but an attitude. It was a license to abandon logic and to follow one's genius wherever it led.

Painting

Of all the visual arts, painting is most closely associated in our minds with Romanticism because, unlike sculpture and architecture, it allowed for a spontaneous outpouring of emotion. In fact, many art historians think of the study or sketch, whether painted or drawn, as the quintessential Romantic medium. While some of the most famous examples of Romantic painting are Baroque in their dramatic handling of paint and energetic compositions, Romantic works can just as readily be tightly painted and composed in accordance with Neoclassical planes, resulting in frozen images that project chilling emotions.

Spain: Francisco Goya

In the opening decades of the nineteenth century, Spanish art was dominated by Francisco Goya y Lucientes (1746–1828), an artist whose work in many ways encapsulates the new psychology and the issues pervading Europe. Charles III (r. 1759–1788) appointed Goya royal painter in 1786, putting him directly in the tradition of Velázquez (see pages 404–06). For Goya, there was not necessarily a conflict between supporting the monarchy and advocating liberal reform. The king recognized the need to bring a stagnant Spain into the eighteenth century and permitted a degree of economic and social development, which gave hope to the progressives. Goya was a member of this progressive group. He was an enlightened Spaniard who admired the French *philosophes*. His social circle, which included many of his aristocratic clients, was like-minded. But the French Revolution terrified heads of state throughout Europe and ushered in reactionary oppression, for now the Enlightenment was associated with revolution, not reform. Both Church and State suppressed the liberal reformers. Spain went to war with France, forging an alliance with its old enemy England. On top of these reversals, Goya fell mysteriously ill in 1793, barely surviving and going deaf in the process. Now, Goya's art focused on exploring the human condition and the emerging modern psychology, on exposing wanton cruelty, misery, ignorance, and greed as universal constants, and on expressing the reality of death as a frightening, unknown void.

THE SLEEP OF REASON We can get some idea of Goya's reaction to the period's crises by looking at *The Sleep of Reason Produces Monsters* (**fig. 24.1**), one of 80 etching-and-AQUATINT prints from the series *Los Caprichos* (*The Caprices*), conceived by the artist in 1797 and published at his own expense at a financial loss. Here, we see the artist asleep on the geometric block of reason, while behind him rises an ominous disarray of owls and bats, symbols of folly and ignorance respectively. In the margin of a study for this image, Goya wrote, "the author's intention is to banish harmful beliefs commonly held, and with this work of *caprichos* to perpetuate the solid testimony of truth." But it is just as easy to interpret *The Sleep of Reason* as exposing a second, non-Enlightenment side to Goya's personality—the emotional and illogical rather than the rational. We sense that the owls and bats, rather than being real, are released from the inner recess of Goya's mind, so that this nightmarish scene becomes an expression of the artist's own emotional state of despair or horror at the terrible turn of events transforming the Western world. In effect, in *The Caprices* Goya is announcing his right to abandon reason and use his imagination to express his deepest feeling, his innermost psychology—to free his demons and employ whatever stylistic tools and symbols he needs in order to do so. We are now far from Neoclassicism and the Rococo as we enter a dramatic graphic world energized by Baroque contrasts of light and dark, asymmetrical composition, the febrile patterning of the wings of bats and owls, and the rasping lines of Goya's rich intaglio process.

ROYAL COMMISSIONS Goya continued to work for Church and State, which, in addition to painting portraits, is how he earned a living. The sense of futility and despair that dominates so much of his work can be seen in *The Third of May, 1808* (**fig. 24.2**), painted on royal commission in 1814, one of many paintings, drawings, and prints the artist made between 1810 and 1815 in response to the French occupation of Spain in 1808. The corruption of his administration forced Charles IV, the son

24.1 Francisco Goya. *The Sleep of Reason Produces Monsters*, from *Los Caprichos*, ca. 1799. Etching, aquatint, drypoint and burin, 8⅞ × 6″ (21.5 × 15.2 cm). Metropolitan Museum of Art, New York. Gift of M. Knoedler & Co. 1918. (18.64(43))

 View the Closer Look for *The Sleep of Reason Produces Monsters* on myartslab.com

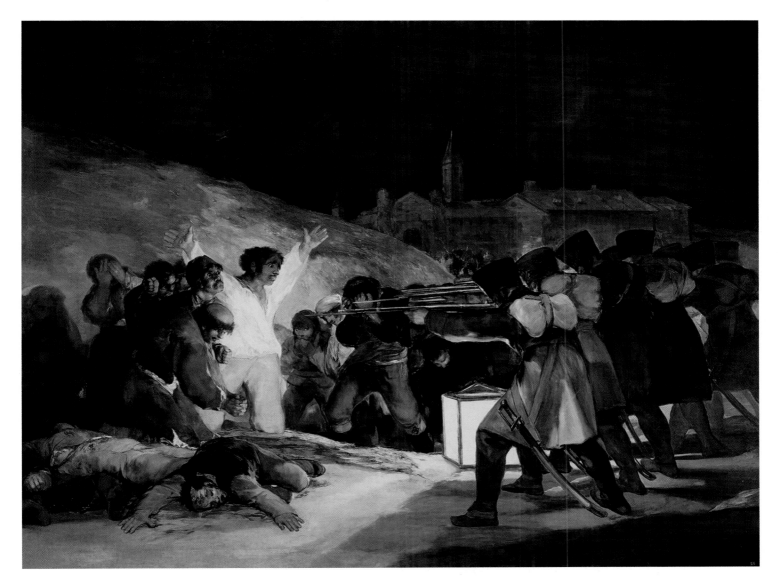

of Charles III, to abdicate in 1807. He was replaced by his son Ferdinand VII, who was deposed in 1808 when NAPOLEON's troops marched into Madrid and put the emperor's brother, Joseph Bonaparte, on the throne. Enlightened Spaniards were initially optimistic that the enlightened French would reform their nation. But in Madrid a people's uprising spurred by nationalism resulted in vicious fighting and wholesale slaughter on both sides, within days fanning out across the entire country and then dragging on for six years. Goya's enormous, dramatic picture, painted after Napoleon had been deposed and Ferdinand reinstated, shows the mass execution of Spanish rebels that took place on May 3, 1808, on a hill outside Madrid.

How different this picture is from Neoclassical history painting, which presented great and famous exemplars of nobleness, morality, and fortitude.

Goya presents anonymous nobodies caught up in the powerful forces of history. Here we see the mechanical process of the slaughter. One rebel with raised arms has the pose of Christ on the Cross. His right hand has a wound suggesting the stigmata. But, ironically, Goya denies the rioters status as martyrs. They are consumed by the fear of death, not the ecstasy of sacrifice. No divine light materializes to resurrect them, and the church in the background of this imaginary scene remains dark. When the stable lantern—which in its geometry and light could be construed as an emblem of Enlightenment logic and progress—is extinguished, there will be only eternal night, symbolized by the inert foreground body, whose face is reduced to a gory mass of paint. The faceless executioners, also small cogs in the wheel of history, are indifferent to their victims' fear of death and

24.2 Francisco Goya. *The Third of May, 1808*. 1814. Oil on canvas, 8'9½" × 11'4½" (2.68 × 3.47 m). Museo del Prado, Madrid

A brilliant military strategist with an insatiable appetite for glory, grandeur, and empire, NAPOLEON Bonaparte (1769–1821) dominated European life from about 1802 to 1815. After a decade of astonishing military successes, he came to power in 1799 as first consul of France. In 1804, he had himself crowned Emperor Napoleon I of France. He held that title until his final military defeat at Waterloo (in Belgium) in 1815 at the hands of allied British, Dutch, and German forces and the Prussian army. In the interim, he conquered most of Europe.

frantic pleas for mercy. Goya whips up the horror and emotional turmoil of his scene by abandoning Neoclassical tight paint handling, linearity, planarity, and evenly lit scenes, replacing this aesthetic with flashy **painterly** brushwork (that is, broad paint handling), dramatic contrasts of light and dark, and compositional turmoil on the left and a dramatically receding Baroque line of soldiers on the right.

Goya painted *The Third of May, 1808* at a time when he was desperate for work and wanted to gain royal favor with this picture, hence his scripting it so that it could be read as being about the sacrifice of the Spanish to the agents of political tyranny. But the real themes of the image are the anonymity of death, the senseless brutality of war, and the atrocities perpetrated by humans. Its power lies in its ability to instill in a viewer an intense sense of terror that makes one confront the inescapable knowledge of one's own mortality.

Britain: The Bond with Nature

Many British painters during the Romantic era followed the lead of such poets as William Wordsworth (1770–1850) and Percy Bysshe Shelley (1792–1822) and steeped themselves in nature, emotionally swept away by its beauties and moods or awed by its sublime power and intimations of the infinite.

JOHN CONSTABLE   Landscape gradually became a major vehicle of the search for the truth. This is not surprising considering the importance of nature in Romantic ideology—the need to bond with it and to express its essence as personally experienced. John Constable (1776–1837) is one of two British artists who stand out in this period for their landscapes. Constable was born and raised in the village of East Bergholt, in the Stour Valley of Suffolk, and spent most of his life painting its rich farmland, which until then had been considered too ordinary and thus not suitable subject matter. Instead of working at the family's prosperous farm and mill, Constable,

24.3 John Constable. *The Haywain* (*Landscape: Noon*). 1821. Oil on canvas, 4′3¼″ × 6′1″ (1.3 × 1.85 m). The National Gallery, London

Read the document related to John Constable on myartslab.com

in 1799, received parental support to study at the Royal Academy School in London. He eventually realized that he was just learning to replicate painting conventions, and returned to Bergholt to make "laborious studies from nature," drawings and oil sketches that he worked up into finished pictures in the studio but that retained the freshness and details of the original source. Constable even considered landscape scientific: "Painting is a science, and should be pursued as an inquiry into the laws of nature. Why, then, may not landscape painting be considered as a branch of natural philosophy, of which pictures are but experiments?" He was especially adept at capturing the ephemeral properties of nature—clouds, light, and atmosphere.

Constable's pictures are packed with the emotion that welled within him when experiencing the beauty of the Stour Valley—"Painting is but another word for feeling," he claimed. His pictures were both scientific and subjective, as in *The Haywain* (*Landscape: Noon*) (**fig. 24.3**) of 1821, shown at the Royal Academy, where he had been exhibiting since 1811. We sense a blue sky pushing out darker clouds, and an atmosphere of moisture that makes everything glisten. Vibrant flecks of paint and color dissolve the material world and make the atmosphere sparkle. The sky is a symphony of subjectivity, presenting a range of emotion, as does the land. It can be dark and undulating, as in the dramatic, energized twisting of tree branches, or bright and placid, as in the horizontal spread of the distant hayfield. Constable fills his picture with detailed anecdote: Besides the haywain, there is the dog, the boat, the harvesters in the distant field, and the puffs of smoke coming from the mill. This is no perfect world, representing ideal beauty or a classical Arcadia. Rather, it is a particular site presented in all of its heartfelt specificity. And it is intentionally an English scene, reflecting the welling nationalism that was overtaking all of Europe as artists now painted their own countryside, not classical Italy.

JOSEPH MALLORD WILLIAM TURNER The second major British landscape artist in this period is Joseph Mallord William Turner (1775–1851). In their basic operating premises Constable and Turner could not be further apart. Whereas Constable painted with scientific accuracy the land he knew intimately, Turner aspired to rival great history painting and consequently invested his views with a rich overlay of historical motifs, references to the Old Masters, and metaphorical themes.

Turner began his career in the early 1790s as a topographical watercolorist for hire, and by 1799, at the unheard-of age of 24, he became an associate of the Royal Academy. While he made numerous landscape studies of specific rural scenes as Constable did of the Stour, his drive to artistic greatness led him to take on the great landscape and marine painters of the past—Claude Lorrain and Jacob Ruisdael—whose works his landscapes resemble in composition, subject, and atmosphere. The reason for this mimicry was to outdo them at their own game; his sun was brighter, atmosphere moister, haze hazier, and perspectival space deeper. Like Constable's, his handling of the intangible properties of nature—wind, light, reflections, atmosphere—was magical.

Turner's quest for the grandiose and his rich imagination led him to embed spectacular mythological and historical moments in his landscapes, creating historical landscape on an epic, sublime scale. However, the direct experience of nature became stronger in his late work. Now the image begins to disappear, replaced by an atmospheric blur of paint and color that seems to sit on the surface of the canvas, making the viewer feel immersed in it. Today, Turner is best known for his late, more abstract style, which he developed toward 1838 and which is seen in *The Slave Ship* or *Slavers Throwing Overboard the Dead and Dying— Typhoon Coming On* (**fig. 24.4**) of 1840. These late works were condemned in Turner's own time. His contemporaries thought he had gone mad, for they found the works virtually unreadable, and certainly unintelligible. Furthermore, his epic stories were no longer drawn from mythology or history but from seemingly minor contemporary events. His earlier work may have been atmospheric, but there was always enough drawing to suggest precise objects and legible spatial recession and relationships. Later this readability evaporates in a haze of color and paint that represents the essence of mist, light, and atmosphere.

In *The Slave Ship* Turner shows the sick and dying human cargo thrown into the sea during a typhoon. He was inspired by James Thomson's *The Seasons*, where the poet describes how sharks follow a slave ship during a typhoon, "lured by the scent of steaming crowds, or rank disease, and death." He was also influenced by a recent newspaper account of a ship's captain who jettisoned slaves in order to collect the insurance, which paid for cargo lost at sea but not for death from illness.

24.4 Joseph Mallord William Turner. *The Slave Ship (Slavers Throwing Overboard the Dead and Dying—Typhoon Coming On)*. 1840. Oil on canvas, 35¼ × 48″ (90.8 × 122.6 cm). Museum of Fine Arts, Boston. Henry Lillie Pierce Fund, Purchase. 99.22

Turner gives us a close-up of human suffering. Outstretched hands pleading for help, a leg about to disappear into the deep for a last time, the gruesome blackness of flailing chains and manacles, the frenzied predatory fish, and bloodstained water all dominate the immediate foreground. In the background is the slave ship, heading into the fury of the typhoon and its own struggle for survival, its distance and silence a metaphor for the callous indifference of the slavers. The searing brilliance of the sun bathes the sky in a blood-red aura, its seemingly infinite reach complementing the omnipotence of the raging sea.

This is a tragic, horrific scene, painted a few years after Britain banned the slave trade. Turner certainly makes us feel the callous inhumanity of the slavers, encouraging us to despise them. And yet, the picture has a haunting thematic and moral ambiguity: Birds eat fish and human carcasses, fish feed on other fish and discarded humans, and slavers fight for their lives in the face of a storm. The picture is as much about the struggle of daily life and the role of fate as it is about the immorality of the slavers, the only constant being the frightening power of nature.

Germany: Friedrich's Pantheistic Landscape

Human destiny is treated with a chilling bleakness and unsettling silence in the sublime landscapes of the German artist Caspar David Friedrich (1774–1840). While Turner focuses on the insignificance of all life and endeavors in the face of the all-powerful cosmos, Friedrich's concern is the passage from the physical way-station of earth to the spiritual being of eternity. His landscapes virtually express PANTHEISM, an especially German phenomenon, and he invests his detailed, realistic scenes with metaphysical properties that give them an aura of divine presence.

Friedrich was born into a prosperous bourgeois family of candle and soap manufacturers in the Baltic harbor town of Greifswald, then part of Sweden. Here he found the austere landscape that served as the source material for his drawings, which formed the foundation of many of his paintings. He studied drawing at the Academy of Copenhagen from 1794 to 1797 and then continued his training in Dresden, where he would maintain a studio throughout his life. Until 1807, he worked exclusively in drawing, shunning historical themes and instead making topographical landscapes, including many of the Baltic region. His paintings would retain the hard linear draughtsmanship that he developed in these years.

Gradually, his landscape drawings became metaphorical, often presented in pairs with cyclical themes, such as the times of the day or the seasons. He continued this practice in his early paintings, which include *Monk by the Sea*, paired with *Abbey in an Oak Forest* (**fig. 24.5**), made in 1809–10. The former, which would be hung on the left and read first, pits the small vertical figure of a standing monk, his back to us, against the vastness of an overwhelming, explosive sky. Traditionally, art historians interpret the funeral depicted in *Abbey* as that of this monk. If the first picture depicts life contemplating death, this second is an image of death, as suggested by a frozen snow-covered cemetery, a lugubrious funeral procession, twisted, barren oak trees, the skeletal remains of a Gothic abbey, and a somber winter sky at twilight. The abbey and oaks, obviously equated, form a gate that the burial cortège will pass under. Religious hope is stated in the Crucifixion mounted on the portal. The oval at the peak of the tracery window is echoed by the sliver of new moon in the sky, a symbol of resurrection. We sense a rite of passage, a direct connection, between abbey and sky. Just as the moon goes through a cycle as it is reborn, twilight yields to night followed by sunrise and day, and winter gives way to spring, summer, and fall; so also, it is suggested, death will be followed by an afterlife or rebirth. And yet, this is a very gloomy picture that leaves our fate after death in doubt, making us dread the unknown on the other side of the horizon.

America: Landscape as Metaphor

Art had not been a priority for the struggling British colonies in America during the seventeenth and eighteenth centuries, and the only art market that existed was largely for portraiture. Sculpture was mostly limited to weathervanes and tombstones. This did not change dramatically in the Federalist period (1789–1801) and the opening decades of the nineteenth century, although the first academies and galleries were founded in the first quarter of the century—the Pennsylvania Academy of the Fine Arts (1802), the Boston Atheneum (1807), and New York's National Academy of Design (1825). By 1825 New York surpassed Philadelphia as the largest and wealthiest city in the nation, and simultaneously it became the nation's art capital. Consequently, our discussion of American art will center on New York well into the twentieth century.

In the 1820s, landscape painting began to acquire status, and by the 1840s it had eclipsed portraiture as the most esteemed form of American art. A young nation with little history, the United States became preoccupied with a search for its own

24.5 Caspar David Friedrich. *Abbey in an Oak Forest.* 1809–10. Oil on canvas, 3′7″ × 5′7⅓″ (1.1 × 1.7 m). Nationalgalerie, Staatliche Museen zu Berlin

identity, one that would distinguish it from its Old World roots. Literary figures such as William Cullen Bryant (1794–1878) and Ralph Waldo Emerson (1803–1882) identified the land itself as America's wealth and contrasted its unspoiled virginity to the densely populated, resource-impoverished lands of Europe. America was overflowing with natural resources, a veritable Garden of Eden. These writers also interpreted this pristine land as a manifestation of God, whose presence was to be seen in every blade of grass, ray of sun, and drop of water. To meditate on nature was to commune with God, a theory promoted by American Transcendentalists, such as Emerson in *Nature* (1836) and Henry David Thoreau in *Walden* (1852). The landscape became the symbol of young America.

THOMAS COLE AND THE HUDSON RIVER SCHOOL

America's first art movement, based on landscape painting and born in the 1820s, is called the Hudson River School, because the artists, most with studios in New York, were initially centered on the Hudson River Valley before fanning out through all of New England in the 1830s through 1850s. Spring through fall, the artists traveled through New York and New England making studies, generally drawings, of this unique land, sketches which they then developed into large paintings in their New York studios during the winter. The lead figure in this group was Thomas Cole (1801–1848), who produced his first major landscapes after an 1825 summer sketching trip up the Hudson. Initially, his views were filled with the sublime, presenting a wild, primordial nature, often with storms pummeling the forests, dark clouds blackening the earth, and lightning-blasted trees. Despite depicting specific sites, his style relied on European landscape conventions and formulas, with little attention given to detail.

By the 1830s, however, Cole's paint handling became tighter, his pictures less formulaic and

24.6 Thomas Cole. *The Oxbow (View from Mount Holyoke, Northampton, Massachusetts, after a Thunderstorm)*. 1836. Oil on canvas, 4′3½″ × 6′4″ (1.3 × 1.9 m). The Metropolitan Museum of Art, New York. Gift of Mrs. Russell Sage, 1908. 08.228

more specific, embracing a Romantic truth to nature that we saw in Constable. This is apparent in *The Oxbow* (**fig. 24.6**), made in 1836 for exhibition at the National Academy of Design. In this breathtaking view from atop Mount Holyoke in western Massachusetts, Cole presents the natural wonder of the American landscape. The foreground is sublime wilderness, with blasted, windswept trees and dark storm clouds dumping sheets of rain. Except for the representation of Cole next to his parasol looking up at us (and in effect declaring his preference for primordial nature), there is no sign of humans in the foreground. Far below in the sunlit valley are the Connecticut River and its plain. Closer inspection reveals not just a natural plain but also cultivated fields and settlements. But they are in such harmony with nature that they seem to blend in. Here is the "Garden of Eden," as Americans described their land, blessed by the divine light breaking through the clouds. Cole underscores God's presence in the land by roughly etching, under the guise of cleared forest, the name *Noah* into the distant hill; upside down, these same letters become Hebrew letters for *Shaddai*, meaning "the Almighty." First and foremost, the picture is a paean to the glory of the American land. Cole captures the immense scale of the American landscape and its many moods, from the wild sublimity of the foreground, to the pastoral tranquility of the valley, to the majestic vastness of the distant hills.

The Oxbow was also a political painting, which viewers at the 1836 exhibition would have recognized. While most Hudson River School painters depicted the glory of God as manifested in the American land, a handful, following Cole's lead, used landscape painting also to comment on the economic and social issues consuming the nation. An 1829–32 trip to Europe gave Cole first-hand knowledge of Turner's paintings and reinforced his interest in using landscape as a vehicle for themes of historical significance. In 1836, for example, he painted a five-picture series titled *The Course of Empire*, which traced the transformation of the same site from a primitive state, to an agrarian society, to a thriving empire, to a decadent empire, and lastly to a state of ruin. Cole's audience would recognize in *The Course of Empire* a statement reflecting the heated debate about progress then consuming the country. On one side were those Americans arguing for a Jeffersonian agrarian America; on the other were the advocates of Jacksonian *laissez-faire* economics, which embraced

unrestricted industrial, commercial, and financial development—in other words, the development of an empire. Cole, who like the novelist James Fenimore Cooper (1789–1851) was an early environmentalist, found the rapid destruction of the wilderness and disrespect for the land disheartening. His vision of healthy development stopped at Jeffersonian agrarian society, where Americans lived in harmony with the land. He equated Jacksonian politics with empire, which would result in not only the destruction of the land but also the eventual downfall of America.

France: Neoclassical Painting in the Romantic Era

Neoclassicism dominated French art in the late eighteenth and early nineteenth centuries, largely because of Jacques-Louis David's powerful impact on painting (see pages 479–81). In his lifetime, David had some 400 students, and after 1800 his most gifted followers from the 1790s began to rival him for public attention. Although David convinced the new republican government to abolish the Royal Academy of Painting and Sculpture—which was eventually replaced and redefined—the biennial Louvre Salon exhibitions were still held during the Directory (1794–99) and the Napoleonic era (1799–1814) and remained critical to an artist's success.

JACQUES-LOUIS DAVID: NAPOLEON'S FIRST PAINTER

As we saw in the last chapter (see page 479), David rose through the Royal Academy School to become an academician who received commissions to make paintings for the king. With the Revolution, he abandoned the monarchy and became a fierce advocate of democracy, even becoming a powerful figure in the new republican government. And with the political rise of Napoleon he once again changed his allegiance, now to serve the emperor. Napoleon, the most powerful man in the world, one who carefully controlled his image both in print and art, employed the most famous artist in the world to portray his heroics. And Napoleon was tailor-made for the Romantic era. His dramatic military exploits—glamorous campaigns in North Africa and throughout Europe, including Russia, all reported in detail in the rising press—provided endless material for the Romantic imagination.

We can see the impact of Romanticism on Neoclassicism looking at David's enormous 1801

Bonaparte Crossing the Great St.-Bernard (**fig. 24.7**), which shows the mounted general, by then also one of the four consuls ruling France, leading his troops in May 1800 through the pass in the Swiss Alps to reconquer Italy. Incised into the rocks in the foreground is Napoleon's name along with that of two predecessors, Hannibal and Charlemagne, who similarly led a surprise attack on their enemies by using this treacherous trans-Alpine route. Following Charlemagne's name are the initials IMP, for imperial, a status that Napoleon himself aspired to and would attain in 1804, when he declared himself emperor. The portrait was commissioned by Charles IV of Spain as a gift to Napoleon to celebrate a rapprochement between Spain and France, Charles keeping this version and giving a second to the general. Napoleon dictated the equestrian composition, declaring he was to be presented "calm, on a fiery horse." He refused to sit for David, saying it was his genius that was to be represented, not his likeness, and forcing David to work from existing portraits of him.

David captures this genius through the powerful energy that courses throughout the composition. We see it in the rearing horse with open mouth and a charged bulging eye, the dramatic upward cant of the rocks, and the windswept clouds, horse's mane and tail, and Napoleon's hair and cape. (No matter that Napoleon made the trip on a sure-footed mule led by a guide on a calm sunny day.) This Romantic energy, which we associate with Napoleon's passionate drive and intense personality, is locked into a Neoclassical composition that has the compositional elements run parallel to the picture plane and frozen in carefully delineated sculptural relief, qualities we saw in *The Oath of the Horatii* (see fig. 23.15). But now rational moral resolve has been replaced by a Romantic spirit of unfettered genius and raw emotion, emanating from Napoleon and infusing the surrounding world.

JEAN-AUGUSTE-DOMINIQUE INGRES The greatest painter to come out of David's studio was Jean-Auguste-Dominique Ingres (1780–1867), who would inherit the mantle of Neoclassicism from David and carry it well into the nineteenth century. Ingres entered David's studio in 1797, and in 1801 he won the Rome Prize, which allowed him to study in Italy. In part because of the Napoleonic Wars he could not take advantage of his award until 1806. Once in Rome, Ingres studied ancient art and fell in love with the classicism of Raphael. But as a Romantic, his interests were broad, even exotic, and led him to medieval, Byzantine, and Early Renaissance art. After his four-year stipend expired, Ingres stayed on in Italy at his own expense for an additional 14 years, often impoverished and, like a Romantic

artist, painting what he wanted. Periodically, he sent pictures back to Paris for exhibition, where they were generally met with derision. An example is *Grande Odalisque* (**fig. 24.8**), commissioned in 1814 by Caroline Murat, Napoleon's sister and queen of Naples; it was submitted to the Salon of 1819.

At the time, this was considered a very exotic picture, for it represents a Turkish concubine and is one of the earliest painted examples of ORIENTALISM. (Byron's Romantic poem *The Corsair*, also featuring a harem slave, was published the year the painting was commissioned.) Orientalism reflects European imperialism and its accompanying sense of superiority, which viewed non-Christian Arab culture as not only different and exotic but also inferior—backward, immoral, violent, and barbaric. Here, the exotic subject gave Ingres license to paint a female nude who was not a Greek goddess, although she recalls numerous Renaissance and Baroque paintings of a reclining Venus (see fig. 16.15) and sculptures of Ariadne from antiquity. To make his figure more appealing to a Paris audience, Ingres gave his odalisque European features, even a Raphael face and coiffure. Although the figure is alluringly sensual, and the hashish pipe, incense burner, fan, and turban "authenticate" the exotic scene, the painting as a whole projects a soothing sense of cultivated beauty, refinement, and idealization that seems classical.

**SPEAKING OF
Oriental**

ORIENTALISM, the nineteenth-century Western fascination with the culture of the Muslim world of North Africa and the Near East, was spurred in part by Napoleon's campaign in Egypt in 1798–99, the first archaeological excavations, and the detailed description of the region and its culture and customs in the 24-volume government-sponsored publication *Description de l'Égypte*, which appeared from 1809 to 1822. "Oriental" derives from the Latin *oriri*, which means "to rise," and it was thus long employed in the Western world to describe the East, the area in which the sun rises. Responding to Orientalism, Europeans invested the Middle East with several false stereotypes. It was seen as a sensual paradise, full of mysterious, enticing pleasures but also primitive and ripe for colonization by the "superior" Western nations.

24.8 Jean-Auguste-Dominique Ingres. *Grande Odalisque*. 1814. Oil on canvas, 2′11⅞″ × 5′3″ (0.9 × 1.6 m). Musée du Louvre, Paris

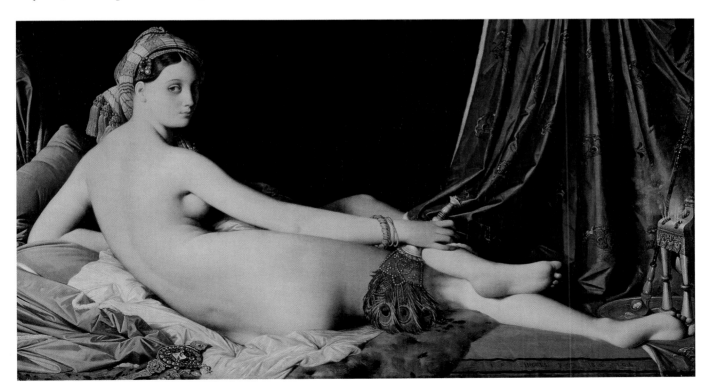

Ingres's trademark is a beautiful classical line, which we can see as he focuses on the odalisque's flesh. Bathed in a caressing chiaroscuro, the body gently swells and recedes with delectable elegance. Its contours languidly undulate with sensuality, the sharply defined edges and tan color contrasting with the objects around it. The opulent color of the objects and the lush fabrics and peacock feathers enhance the sensual aura of the picture. Salon viewers noted that the concubine's back had too many vertebrae and certainly her elbowless right arm is too long; but as far as Ingres was concerned, the sweeping curves of both were essential components of the graceful composition, the line of the right arm even being continued into the folds of the drapery.

In 1821, Ingres received a commission to make an enormous painting of *The Vow of Louis XIII* for the cathedral in Montauban, his hometown. Ingres, penniless, otherwise forgotten, and living in Florence, found that this commission turned his life around. He showed the picture at the Salon of 1824 to favorable reviews and was hailed as the great savior of the classical tradition. With the final fall of Napoleon in 1815, David, who had been named painter to the emperor in 1801, was exiled to Brussels, and the careers of all of his students had stalled at the same time, displaced by a new generation of painterly Romantic artists. Almost by default, then, Ingres was crowned the protector of classicism, the champion of line over color, and the savior of the "wholesome traditions of great art" and ideal beauty over the unfettered emotionalism of the Romantics. In 1825, he was elected to the French Academy, and soon became its director. He was also awarded the Legion of Honor. His studio became the destination of choice for aspiring young history painters.

France: Painterly Romanticism and Romantic Landscape

While Ingres was taking Neoclassicism deep into the nineteenth century, although in a Romantic vehicle, Antoine-Jean Gros, a second student of David's, opened up an alternative course, one that would abandon line, order, clear rational space, evenly diffused light, and classical repose for bold brushstrokes, dazzling color, impetuous drama, confused space, irrational lighting, and extreme emotions. In his wake came Théodore Géricault and Eugène Delacroix, who brought painterly Romanticism to the fore in the 1820s, with the result that the word Romanticism, previously reserved for literature and music, was now applied also to art. In the 1820s as well, landscape painting in France began to emerge from under the shadow cast by Neoclassicism. French Romantic landscape painting was never as apocalyptic as its British counterpart nor as pantheistic as in Germany and America. Instead it was more serene and poetic.

ANTOINE-JEAN GROS Gros (1771–1835) entered David's studio in 1785. During the turmoil of the French Revolution, David was able to secure a pass for Gros to go to Rome, although by the time he arrived the city was closed to the antipapist French. Through circumstance, he met Napoleon in Milan, traveled with his army, and impressed the general with his art. Napoleon charged Gros with painting his battles and glorifying his campaigns. Bonaparte, who was as brilliant at propaganda as he was at military strategy, carefully controlled his public image and relied heavily on art to reinforce his political position. He made sure his commissions were shown at the Salons, where they would be seen by everyone and reported in the press.

The Napoleonic era was a catalyst for French Romanticism. The drama, glory, valor, and adventures of the Napoleonic Wars provided endless material for the artistic imagination. The North African campaigns took Europeans into the forbidden Arab world and introduced them to a wondrous, exotic subject matter, which they brought back to Europeans anxious for new experiences. Gros's first commission, *Napoleon in the Pesthouse at Jaffa, 11 March 1799* (**fig. 24.9**), came in 1804 and was exhibited in that year's Salon to huge acclaim. This 23-foot-wide picture was commissioned not only to promote the emperor's bravery and leadership but to reinforce his humanitarian image, which was propagandistically essential considering the enormous human loss tallied in many of his battles, especially in Jaffa, then in Palestine but today a section of Tel Aviv, Israel. During the campaign, bubonic plague broke out among the French ranks. Legend has it that to calm his troops, Napoleon fearlessly entered the pesthouse and walked among the patients. Here we see the general, like Christ healing the sick, courageously touching the open sore of a victim, his presence virtually willing the dying to rise. The painting ignores the fact that Napoleon poisoned these same sick troops when he retreated from Jaffa.

While Gros's drawing and brushwork are relatively tight and Davidian, the picture has an overt, turbulent drama, created by the dark shadows, bursts of light, splashes of bright red, the rapidly receding perspective of the arcades, and the cloud-filled sky. Chaos prevails. Although Napoleon is placed in the center as a compositional anchor, he is momentarily lost in the turmoil of the scene. Our eye goes to the circle of the dead, dying, and sick surrounding him, which includes the Michelangelesque figures in the foreground shadows and the "resurrected" nudes next to him. The male nude is no longer heroic, as in David, but helpless and disturbing. Napoleon's courageous act has to vie for a viewer's attention with the dark mood of psychological and physical suffering and the exoticism, to Western eyes, of the Arab attendants and Islamic architecture. (This picture helped launch the vogue for Oriental subjects that we saw in Ingres's *Grande Odalisque*, see fig. 24.8) The monumental arches may pay compositional homage to David's *Oath of the Horatii* (fig. 23.15), but instead of supporting a narrative of Neoclassical stoicism and clarity they contribute to a passionate, Romantic exoticism and a foreboding of horrifying uncertainty.

THÉODORE GÉRICAULT Without the Napoleonic campaigns to feed his imagination, Gros's career soon waned. David's other outstanding students and followers were simultaneously eclipsed. The future was now represented by Théodore Géricault (1791–1824) and those who followed him. Géricault was independently wealthy and largely self-taught, frequenting the Napoleon Museum, where he copied the great colorists: Rubens, Van Dyck, and Titian. Gros, however, was his role model, and Gros and Rubens were clearly the artistic sources for Géricault's submission to the Salon of 1812, *Charging Chasseur*, a work filled with energetic brushwork, sharp diagonal recessions, bold contrasts of light and dark, rippling contours, and flashes of color, all of which could not be further from David or closer to Rubens. Completely gone is the Davidian planarity that structured the turmoil of Gros's pesthouse.

24.9 Antoine-Jean Gros. *Napoleon in the Pesthouse at Jaffa, 11 March 1799.* 1804. Oil on canvas, 17′5½″ × 23′7½″ (5.32 × 7.20 m). Musée du Louvre, Paris

24.10 Théodore Géricault. *The Raft of the "Medusa."* 1818–19. Oil on canvas, 16'1" × 23'6" (4.9 × 7.16 m). Musée du Louvre, Paris

But *Charging Chasseur* revealed Géricault's lack of formal training, namely his inability to draw. Continuing his independent study, he now worked from classical models, copying High Renaissance painters at the Royal Museum, as the Louvre was called after the second fall of Napoleon in 1815 and with the establishment of LOUIS XVIII's Restoration monarchy. In 1816, Géricault went to Italy, stopping in Florence to draw Michelangelo's Medici tombs (see fig. 17.1), before going to Rome to study the antiquities. Not long after his return to Paris in late 1817, he began thinking about the third painting he would exhibit at the Salon, *The Raft of the "Medusa"* (**fig. 24.10**), painted between 1818 and 1819 after many studies. In 1816 the *Medusa*, a government vessel, foundered off the West African coast with approximately 400 people aboard. The captain commandeered the six lifeboats for government officials and officers, with the remaining 150 passengers set adrift by the crew, consigned to a makeshift raft at the mercy of the sea. When the passengers were finally rescued some two weeks later, only a handful had survived. The callous captain was incompetent, an aristocrat who had

been politically appointed by the government of Louis XVIII, and the headline-making event was condemned in the press as a reflection of the corruption of Louis's administration.

Géricault decided to paint the moment when the survivors first sight a ship, not the more politically charged moment when the captain sets the raft adrift. The painting is thus about the harrowing mental and physical experience of survival rather than an accusation of injustice. Géricault seems to have latched onto his subject after revisiting Gros's *Napoleon in the Pesthouse*, for the foreground is littered with Michelangelesque nudes. From the bodies of the dead and dying in the foreground, the composition recedes in a dramatic Baroque diagonal (see fig. 20.1), climaxing in the group supporting the frantically waving black man. As our eye follows this line of writhing, twisting bodies, we move from death to hope. But this is not a painting just about hope. There are no heroes, no exemplary moral fortitude. Rather the theme is the human species against nature, and Géricault's goal was to make a viewer feel the trials and tribulations of the castaways. The academic, classically

proportioned monumental figures are a catalogue of human misery, reflecting the death, cannibalism, fighting, insanity, sickness, exhaustion, hunger, and thirst that tormented the victims. The stark realism, obtained in part through somewhat tight brushwork, heightens our visceral connection to the dramatically lit event; we too are on the crude raft, pitched about in the high seas, and aimlessly buffeted by the wind. Géricault would never exhibit again in a Salon and, weakened by chronic consumption, died five years later at the age of 32.

EUGÈNE DELACROIX In 1822 Eugène Delacroix (1798–1863) emerged as the standard-bearer of painterly Romanticism, the position Géricault so dearly coveted. Delacroix was seven years younger than Géricault and came from a similar background—Parisian and wealthy. Like Géricault, he was essentially independent and self-taught, studying the great masterpieces at the Louvre, especially Rubens, Titian, and Veronese. His greatest excitement came when visiting the studios of Gros and Géricault. He befriended the latter in 1818 and posed for one of the figures in *The Raft of the "Medusa."* His submission to the Salon of 1824, *Scenes from the Massacre at Chios* (**fig. 24.11**), presents a compendium of misery and suffering in the foreground and was obviously inspired by the groupings of the dead and dying in Gros's *Pesthouse at Jaffa* (fig. 24.9) and Gericault's *The Raft of the "Medusa"* (fig. 24.10). In 1821 the Greeks had revolted against the ruling Ottoman (Turkish) Empire, launching the GREEK WAR

The Ottoman Empire had occupied Greece since the fifteenth century when the GREEK WAR OF INDEPENDENCE, also known as the Greek Revolution, began in 1821 as the Greeks rebelled against their Turkish rulers. The struggle was supported by the United Kingdom, Russia, and France, with people from all over the Western world individually volunteering to fight as well. Among them was the great British Romantic poet Lord Byron, who spent some £4,000 of his own money outfitting the Greek navy. The war epitomized Romanticism, for it reflected the ideals of freedom and nationalism so essential to the period.

24.11 Eugène Delacroix. *Scenes from the Massacre at Chios*. 1824. Oil on canvas, 13′8″ × 11′7″ (4.17 × 3.54 m). Musée du Louvre, Paris

OF INDEPENDENCE, and the following year the Turks raided the Greek island of Chios, destroying villages and either massacring or enslaving virtually the entire populace of 20,000. Delacroix's painting was based upon this event and was, in part, made to show support for Greek independence as well as to express the Romantic passion for democracy and individual freedom.

Burning and slaying take place in a blur of smoke and confusion in the middle- and background of the painting, while the foreground, which focuses on a group of Greeks gathered up for execution or enslavement, is remarkably devoid of violence. Instead, resignation, desperation at the impending loss of loved ones, and hopelessness reign, this pessimism symbolized by the forbidding silhouette of the armed Ottoman guard. Delacroix reinforces the turmoil of the violence in the background through the twisting and turning of the foreground figures and their undulating contours as well as by the chaotic piling up of bodies. The intense colors of the painting have darkened considerably over time, especially the blues and reds, which originally created an optical snap of light and dark that was reinforced by the bravura of the brushwork. Clearly, Rubens is behind these qualities as well as the two asymmetrical compositional pyramids organizing the foreground group and the diagonal recession into deep space. (Delacroix, however, subverts the traditional device of putting a hero at the apex of the pyramids by instead placing villains, the Turkish guards, there.) Delacroix was also influenced by the color and brushwork of Constable, who had three landscapes, including *The Haywain* (see fig. 24.3), in the same Salon. Upon seeing them, Delacroix repainted the sky at the last minute, giving it a brilliant luminosity, and he worked vivid colors into the garments.

This "terrifying hymn in honor of doom and irremediable suffering," as the poet and critic Charles Baudelaire (1821–1867) described the work, established Delacroix as the great Romantic painter. It was the first time the term Romantic was applied to a visual artist, making him the artistic equivalent of the composer Hector Berlioz (1803–1869) and the writer Victor Hugo (1802–1885), both of whom would rise to fame in the next decade. The year 1824 therefore was a critical one. It was the year Géricault died, Constable was introduced in Paris, and Ingres returned from Italy, unaware that he would be anointed the guardian of the classical tradition.

Romantic Landscape Painting

David's Neoclassicism was so dominant in the opening decades of the nineteenth century that it even cast its shadow over French landscape painting, which was planar and stylized, largely modeled on Poussin and Claude Lorrain. The exhibition of Constable's landscapes at the pivotal Salon of 1824 opened up new possibilities, and a younger generation impressed by his powerful naturalism and Romantic moods made it the foundation of their work. By the following decades, landscape was established as a viable genre in France, one that could rival history painting in popularity and pave the way for the rise of Impressionism in the 1860s.

THÉODORE ROUSSEAU AND THE BARBIZON SCHOOL

A group of academically trained painters known as the Barbizon School took their aesthetic lead directly from Constable, augmenting his direct impression of nature with a study of the great seventeenth-century Dutch landscapists, such as Ruisdael (see fig. 20.13), who were exhibited in the Louvre. The group emerged in the 1830s and took its name from the village of Barbizon, bordering the Forest of Fontainebleau, where the artists painted and many settled. The forest had been a royal hunting preserve, and as a result it offered nature in a relatively unspoiled state, undisturbed by the Industrial Revolution smoldering just 40 miles away in Paris. The best-known Barbizon painter is Pierre-Étienne-Théodore Rousseau (1812–1867). He learned the rudiments of painting from two academically trained artists and by copying landscapes in the Louvre. In the early to mid-1830s, his work was occasionally accepted at the Salons, from which he was banished from 1837 to 1848, his view of nature deemed too unseemly. He led a rather bohemian existence and permanently settled in Barbizon in 1848.

Under the Birches (**fig. 24.12**) of 1842–43 is a fine example of Rousseau's work, which is perhaps the most diverse of all the Barbizon School. Produced in the studio from studies made on a seven-month trip to the Berry region in central France, the painting, like that of Constable, avoids artificial compositional and stylized motifs and instead captures the essence of nature. We readily sense that this is a specific site; each tree seems individualized, for example, and each wisp of cloud unique. We can feel the onset of twilight and the cool, damp atmosphere of autumn. While the blue-green sky and brownish-orange foliage offer a touch of color,

Rousseau's palette is somber and earthy, evoking soil, decaying plant and animal matter, and the interior gloom of a thicket. Like Constable's, Rousseau's brushwork is stippled, applied in small flecks that make the landscape pulse with energy, reinforced by the nervous outline of trees and bushes. We sense growth and the constant movement of nature. It is little wonder that Rousseau was rejected at the Salons. His dark, honest pictures with their turgid brushwork must have been considered ugly and depressing by conservative tastes.

Sculpture

Compared with painting, sculpture was a severely limiting medium for an artist at the opening of the nineteenth century. In its most monumental form, free-standing historical sculpture, it was generally limited to the human figure, and since the Renaissance the sculpted figure had been largely based on antique models. Nineteenth-century sculptors throughout Europe would overwhelmingly follow the classical paradigm of one or two figures that are based on Greek and Roman prototypes and embody some notion of timeless virtue, nobility, perfection, or beauty. The dominant Neoclassical sculptor during this period was Antonio Canova, discussed in the last chapter (see pages 482–483). Yet in France a dramatic change in the artistic climate toward 1830 allowed a small gap for experimentation. The rise of Delacroix and Romantic painting in the 1820s was followed by the new, more liberal constitutional monarchy of LOUIS-PHILIPPE, which emerged with the 1830 Revolution and the abdication of Charles X, Louis's successor. The bourgeoisie had more of a presence in the new government and in society in general, ushering in an era of middle-class taste. Nonetheless, it took both daring and considerable imagination for a sculptor to break away from the Neoclassical prototype and explore new subjects, feelings, and compositions. One of the more radical new sculptors was François Rude.

FRANÇOIS RUDE: BREAKING AWAY FROM THE CLASSICAL MODEL Rude (1784–1855) brought nationalistic fervor to his figurative sculpture and is best

24.12 Pierre-Étienne-Théodore Rousseau. *Under the Birches.* 1842–43. Oil on wood panel, 16⅝ × 25⅜″ (42.2 × 64.4 cm). Toledo Museum of Art, Ohio. Gift of Arthur J. Secor. 1933.37

LOUIS-PHILIPPE ascended to the French throne after the July 1830 Revolution and the abdication of Charles X. His reign, which lasted until the Revolution of 1848, was called the "July Monarchy." He was known as the "King of the French," suggesting that he had popular support, and he walked a narrow path appealing to the monarchists, or Bourbon supporters, the Bonapartists, who supported Napoleon's family, and liberal Republicans. He especially appealed to a rising middle class. But he ignored the new working classes, which led to his downfall in 1848.

24.13 François Rude. *The Departure of the Volunteers of 1792 ("La Marseillaise").* 1833–36. Stone, approx. 42 × 26' (12.8 × 7.9 m). Arc de Triomphe, Paris

remembered for *"La Marseillaise"* (**fig. 24.13**) on the Arc de Triomphe in Paris. Rude enrolled in the ÉCOLE DES BEAUX-ARTS in 1809, studying sculpture, and as a Napoleon sympathizer fled to Brussels when Bonaparte was defeated in 1815. He returned to Paris in 1827, and, with a nationalistic zeal that we associate with the Romantic era, he began studying French sculptural history—first the French Renaissance tradition of the School of Fontainebleau and Giovanni Bologna (see fig. 17.4), and then delving deeper into the past, to Claus Sluter (see fig. 14.1).

It was a perfect match, then, when in 1833 Rude received one of the four sculptural commissions on the Arc de Triomphe, since the works were about patriotic fervor. The arch had been left unfinished when Napoleon was exiled in 1815, and Louis-Philippe and his minister of the interior saw the monument's completion as an opportunity to demonstrate that the new government supported national reconciliation. Hence the sculptural

program consisted of four works by different artists, each surrounding the arch opening and offering something to every segment of the French political spectrum. Rude received the assignment based on the success of a rather Neoclassical-looking sculpture of a nude Neapolitan fisherboy playing with a turtle, which he had submitted to the Salon of 1833. The Salon submission hardly anticipated the chaotic explosion we see in *The Departure of the Volunteers of 1792*, the formal title for *"La Marseillaise."*

The scene honors the volunteers who rallied to defend the new French Republic from an Austro-Prussian threat in 1792. A winged allegorical figure representing both France and Liberty leads a selection of soldiers from different periods of the nation's past. Rather than a specific event, Rude evokes an eternal, all-powerful, nationalistic spirit that emanates from the people and arises when called upon. While the figures have a classical anatomy, strike classical poses, and are aligned parallel to the wall in shallow relief, the composition is frenetic, a whirligig of arms, legs, and twisted bodies that energizes the outpouring of patriotism swept along by Liberty above. When unveiled in 1836, *The Departure* was unanimously hailed as the best of the four works on the Arc de Triomphe and was nicknamed *"La Marseillaise"* because it so successfully embodied the national spirit. Rude himself attained no lasting fame from the project, and without commissions, which sculptors, unlike painters, rely on, he had no opportunity to develop further the innovative aesthetic implications of *The Departure.*

Romantic Revivals in Architecture

The social and political turmoil that rocked Europe from 1789 to 1848 resulted in a search for stability and comfort, which in architecture came in the form of revival styles. Instead of developing new forms, architects resurrected the past, its familiarity providing solace and continuity in a world that otherwise seemed fractured, uncertain, and in constant flux. Architects appropriated every known architectural style, selecting them for their associations, picturesque qualities, or exoticism. Egyptian, Greek, Roman, Romanesque, Gothic, Renaissance, Baroque, Chinese, Turkish, Queen Anne, rustic thatched cottage—everything and anything could be found revived in nineteenth-century European architecture. It was not unusual for an architect to submit several proposals for a single project, each in a different style. Nor was it unusual to find several periods represented in a single building. But by far the most popular revival styles were Gothic and classical.

The Gothic Revival: The Houses of Parliament

Perhaps the most famous Gothic Revival building is the Houses of Parliament in London (**fig. 24.14**) by Sir Charles Barry (1795–1860) and A. W. N. Pugin (1812–1852). It was commissioned in 1836 after the former building burned down, and the competition required the new Houses to be designed in one of two "English" styles, Gothic or Elizabethan—91 of the 97 entries were Gothic. Barry was the head architect and was best known for his work in classical or Renaissance revival styles. Predictably, he laid out the building in a symmetrical, orderly fashion. He wisely hired Pugin, Britain's leading expert on the Gothic, to draw every Gothic detail on both the interior and exterior, which he designed with meticulous historical accuracy in the florid Perpendicular style (see page 268). The picturesque towers are believed to be Pugin's contribution as well. Instead of being sublime, Gothic Revival now is largely picturesque and associational, the style having been specifically selected to conjure up a sense of nationalistic pride and the Romantic emotions that come with this realistic evocation of the distant past.

The Classical Revival

Classical Revival architecture was ubiquitous in America, since the new republic modeled itself on the democracies of ancient Greece and Rome. The White House and the nation's Capitol are Neoclassical, and most churches, banks, and government buildings were designed with a Graeco-Roman temple façade, although the Gothic was very popular as well, especially for churches.

AN ANCIENT STYLE FOR A NEW REPUBLIC: THOMAS JEFFERSON'S UNIVERSITY OF VIRGINIA In addition to being a politician, farmer, and major Enlightenment thinker, Thomas Jefferson was an amateur architect, who, working in a classical style, designed his home, Monticello (1770–82), as a Palladian villa, and the Virginia State Capitol (1785) as a version of the Maison Carrée, a Roman temple in Nîmes, France. His best-known project in the Romantic era is the University of Virginia campus in Charlottesville (**fig. 24.15**). Like Monticello and the Virginia State Capitol, the campus is based on antiquity in order to evoke the democratic heritage from Greece and Rome as well as the grandeur of these two great civilizations, which form the bedrock of Western art and culture. Designed between 1804 and 1817, the campus consists of two rows of five Palladian villas connected by a roofed colonnade, off which are rooms for students. Each of the ten villas, which housed the professors and classrooms, was different, symbolizing individualism and aesthetically introducing picturesque variety.

24.14 Sir Charles Barry and A. W. N. Pugin. The Houses of Parliament. Begun 1836. London

24.15 Thomas Jefferson. University of Virginia. Designed 1804–17, constructed 1817–28. Charlottesville, Virginia

Watch a video about Monticello on myartslab.com

Each has a different classical association: One with a Doric order refers to the Baths of Diocletian in Rome, a second with an Ionic order to the Temple of Fortuna Virilis, also in Rome. At one end of the two rows and tying them together is a Pantheon-like Rotunda, the library, suggested by fellow architect Benjamin Latrobe and built in 1823–26. Lastly, the tree-lined lawn separating the two rows of villas imbues the complex with the naturalism of a picturesque English garden. Jefferson's genius in Charlottesville was to use Neoclassicism to create a metaphor for the new republic that expresses both the individualism and the unity defining the new nation, while simultaneously producing a Romantic bridge to antiquity and its noble and democratic values.

CREATING A NEW ATHENS IN PRUSSIA: KARL FRIEDRICH SCHINKEL While the Prussian architects were as eclectic as their English, French, and American counterparts, they designed some of the finest Classical Revival buildings. The most renowned architect is perhaps Karl Friedrich Schinkel, named

state architect in 1815 by Friedrich Wilhelm III. Like many architects of the day, Schinkel (1781–1841) worked in every imaginable style—classical, Romanesque, Gothic, and Renaissance. He began as a Neoclassicist, however, as can be seen in the Altes Museum in Berlin (**fig. 24.16**), his second major commission. Designed in 1824, it was modeled on a Greek temple, in part with the intention of endowing the building with the aura of a temple of aesthetic treasures, a place where one came not to worship the gods but to contemplate art. The entrance is on what looks like the side of a temple (the real sides—their edges seen at either end of the colonnaded façade—are plain stone walls with rectangular windows), a brilliant device to suggest a temple without actually copying one, and avoiding the use of the pedimented façade so common in the Classical Revival. The museum is raised on a high podium and accessed by a centralized staircase, which along with the colossal Grecian order gives the building a serene monumentality and strong sense of axis. The width of the staircase is echoed above by a second-floor attic, which encases

24.16 Karl Friedrich Schinkel. Altes Museum. 1824–30. Berlin

a domed room for the display of sculpture. Schinkel is a master of perfect proportions and scale, and the symmetrical and logical interior echoes the exterior harmony.

Prussia emerged as a major political force at the Congress of Vienna, held after the fall of Napoleon in 1815, and the ambitious building program instituted by Friedrich Wilhelm III was designed to reinforce his imperial ambitions. Part of the charisma of the Altes Museum was to link Berlin with the glory and grandeur of ancient Athens.

POINTS OF REFLECTION

24.1 What impact did Napoleon have on the development of Romantic art, and how is it expressed in works like Jacques-Louis David's *Bonaparte Crossing the Great St.-Bernard* and Antoine-Jean Gros's *Napoleon in the Pesthouse at Jaffa*? How do both paintings differ from David's Neoclassical masterpiece, *The Oath of the Horatii*?

24.2 How does nationalism figure as a Romantic component in such diverse works of art as David's *Bonaparte Crossing the Great St.-Bernard*, Eugène Delacroix's *Scenes from the Massacre at Chios*, François Rude's *The Departure of the Volunteers of 1792*, and Sir Charles Barry's and A. W. N. Pugin's Houses of Parliament?

24.3 How do landscapes like John Constable's *The Haywain*, Caspar David Friedrich's *Abbey in an Oak Forest*, and Thomas Cole's *The Oxbow* reflect the Romantic spirit?

24.4 Works such as Théodore Géricault's *The Raft of the "Medusa"*, J. M. W. Turner's *The Slave Ship*, and Francisco Goya's *The Sleep of Reason*, on the one hand, and Jean-Auguste-Dominique Ingres's *Grande Odalisque* and Friedrich's *Abbey in an Oak Forest*, on the other hand, could not stylistically look more different. Why can they all be described as Romantic, embracing a similar mood or sensitivity despite using very different stylistic means?

24.5 What is the range of emotions evoked in such works as Goya's *The Third of May, 1808*, Constable's *The Haywain*, Ingres's *Grande Odalisque*, P. E. T. Rousseau's *Under the Birches*, and Thomas Jefferson's University of Virginia?

✓—[Study and review on myartslab.com

ART IN TIME

- 1792—New York Stock Exchange founded
- 1793—The Terror phase of the French Revolution, resulting in the execution of 17,000 people
- 1798—William Wordsworth and Samuel Taylor Coleridge publish *Lyrical Ballads*

- 1804—Ludwig von Beethoven composes Symphony No. 3, *The Eroica*
  —Napoleon crowns himself emperor of the French
  —Lewis and Clarke's Expedition of Louisiana
- **1809–10—Friedrich, *Abbey in an Oak Forest***
- **1814—Goya, *The Third of May, 1808***

- 1815—Final defeat of Napoleon at Waterloo, ending the Napoleonic Wars
- 1821–32—Greek War of Independence
- 1824—Salon of 1824, Paris, where Delacroix exhibits *The Massacre at Chios*, Ingres *The Vow of Louis XIII*, and **Constable *The Haywain***
- 1825—National Academy of Design founded in New York

- 1828—Andrew Jackson elected president of U.S.A., ushering in era of Jacksonian democracy
- 1830—July Revolution in Paris, with Louis-Philippe replacing Charles X as king of France and popular sovereignty replacing hereditary right
- **1836—Barry and Pugin begin Houses of Parliament in London**
- 1848—Europe-wide workers' revolutions

CHAPTER

25 | The Age of Positivism: Realism, Impressionism, and the Pre-Raphaelites, 1848–1885

POINTS OF INQUIRY

25.1 Define the word Positivism, and describe how the rise of Positivism, as well as the study of sociology, reflect the dramatic changes occurring in Western civilization.

25.2 Assess the differing responses found in English and French art to the social transformations brought about by the Industrial Revolution toward 1850.

25.3 Track how French Realism changed as it developed from Gustave Courbet to Édouard Manet and Edgar Degas, and lastly to Claude Monet.

25.4 Describe the different attitudes toward the new medium of photography that surfaced in the 1840s, both by artists and the public in general, and explain how, in some respects, photography was the perfect visual medium for the Age of Positivism.

25.5 Identify the period's attitude toward the use of iron in architecture.

(((•—[**Listen** to the chapter audio on myartslab.com

Romanticism began to dissipate in Europe as an intellectual attitude and stylistic trend after 1848 and was gradually superseded by Realism. Increasingly, people came to rely on the physical, physiological, empirical, and scientific as a way to understand nature, society, and human behavior. Hard facts, not feelings, became the bricks and mortar of knowledge. Positivism is the term often used to describe the new mentality of pragmatism and materialism that emerged in the 1840s. The word was coined by the French philosopher Auguste Comte (1798–1857), who in 1830 began to write a multivolume series called *Positive Philosophy*. Comte called for social progress to be based on observable fact and tested ideas—in other words, on science. This new scientific approach to studying society came to be called sociology.

Paralleling Comte's sociology was the appearance in the 1830s and 1840s of popular and widely distributed pamphlets called *physiologies*. These were short essays that analyzed in tremendous detail different niches of French society, not just professions and types, such as the Lawyer, the Nun, the Society Woman, but such specific categories as the Suburban Gardener and the Woman of Thirty. In a world undergoing tremendous flux because of rapid industrialization and urbanization, the *physiologies* were a means of understanding the dramatic transformations that were occurring.

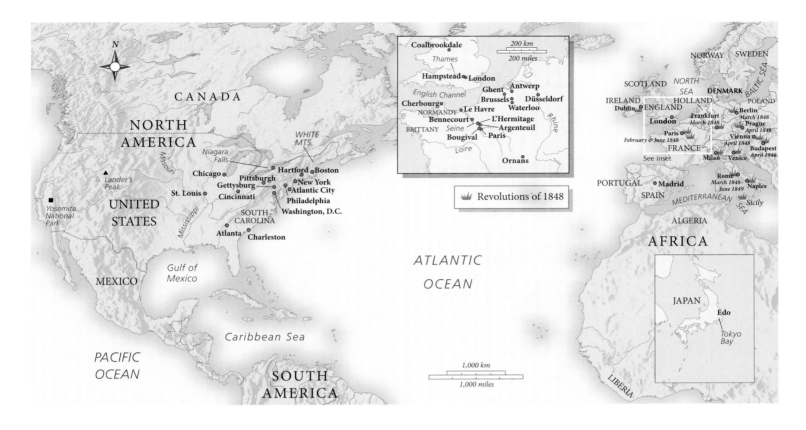

Map 25.1 Europe and North America in 1848

In the arts, Positivism resulted in Realism. Now, artists and writers did not idealize or fantasize life but instead presented it unembellished and unidealized. As early as 1846, the poet and critic Charles Baudelaire called for an art based on modern life. By the 1850s, *réalisme* was the rallying cry of the new art and literature. Instead of valuing wild flights of imagination, the exotic, and the sublime, Realists planted both feet firmly on the ground and, generally without emotion, bluntly depicted the changes in society. This ranged from the grim existence of country peasants and the downtrodden urban poor to the leisure activities of the rapidly growing metropolitan middle class and *nouveaux riches* (new rich). In landscape painting, this Realism evolved into Impressionism, a style that documented the dramatic social changes occurring in the growing suburbs surrounding Paris. The Impressionists empirically captured the world before their very eyes, the shimmering sketchiness of their finished paintings reflecting the impermanence of a constantly changing contemporary world.

While the Impressionists were committed to creating an empirical representational art—a realistic art—a by-product of their stylistic developments was the advent of Modernism. To the following generations, their bright color and broad brushwork, that is, the abstract qualities, seemed to challenge the representational components as the subject matter of their paintings. In the twentieth century, critics and historians would label this shift in art toward abstraction as "Modernism." Impressionism also marked the appearance of the **avant-garde**: The notion that certain artists and ideas are strikingly new or radical for their time. This meant, in effect, that artists began making art that was understood by only a handful of people, namely other avant-garde artists and a few art experts, including collectors. The disconnection between the avant-garde and the general public, including the working class, who felt comfortable attending the highly publicized Academy exhibitions, is reflected in the rise of commercial art galleries as the principal venue for the display of new art and the corresponding decline in the power of academic salons throughout the Western world. While Realism served as a springboard for the abstraction of Modernism, we must remember that first and foremost it was a movement preoccupied with the dramatic changes occurring in society, and that its birth coincided with the great European-wide Revolution of 1848.

Realism in France

Socialism is the name of an economic and social doctrine that advocates state ownership and control of the basic means of production together with the egalitarian distribution of wealth. A SOCIALIST, therefore, is one who believes in socialism. In France in the mid-nineteenth century, socialism was a sincerely considered alternative to monarchy, empire, and unstable republics, and the goal of ending economic and social oppression by one class or group over another paralleled the impulse that fueled the Revolution of 1848 in Paris.

The 1848 uprisings began in France. War raged in the streets of Paris as the working class demanded more political representation, and 10,000 people were killed or wounded. This proletarian rebellion produced shockwaves of class revolution that radiated throughout Europe, resulting in similar outbreaks in major cities.

The forces of conservatism ultimately prevailed everywhere. In France, Louis Napoleon Bonaparte (1808–1873), the emperor's nephew, was overwhelmingly elected president of the Second Republic, largely on name recognition. In 1852, however, he dissolved the parliament and arranged to have himself "elected" emperor as Napoleon III, thus establishing the Second Empire. France prospered under his reign, which ended in 1870 with the Franco-Prussian War. The pace of the Industrial Revolution, which had not gained momentum in France until the 1840s, now increased dramatically, and new financial systems instituted by Louis Napoleon created unprecedented wealth. Dominated by financiers, industrialists, manufacturers, lawyers, and merchants, the bourgeoisie flourished, as did their desire for material possessions. In Paris, the new wealth and increased leisure time gave rise to grand restaurants, cafés, department stores, theaters, clubs, parks, and racetracks, where people, often from different social classes, congregated and shopped.

Realism in the 1840s and 1850s: Painting Contemporary Social Conditions

French Realism developed simultaneously with the Revolution of 1848. Especially in the hands of Gustave Courbet, the self-proclaimed banner carrier of this art movement, Realism was often a highly political style expressing SOCIALIST ideals. It championed laborers and common country folk, groups that challenged the authority and privilege of the Parisian aristocracy and bourgeoisie and that were in part responsible for the upheavals of 1848.

GUSTAVE COURBET Gustave Courbet (1819–1877) came from Ornans, a town at the foot of the Jura Mountains near the Swiss border. He went to Paris in 1839 to study painting, and by the late 1840s became a dominant figure in the cafés on the Left Bank. Courbet met the literary avant-garde, befriending Baudelaire and the critic and writer Champfleury (the pen name of Jules-François-Félix Husson, 1821–1889). It was Champfleury who converted him to Realism. Champfleury, who collected folk art and was interested in such non-elitist art forms as popular prints, children's art, and caricature, convinced Courbet that he should go back to his rural roots and paint the simple world of Ornans.

In the fall of 1849, Courbet returned to his hometown, where he painted the 22-foot-wide *Burial at Ornans* (**fig. 25.1**). It was accepted at the Salon of 1850–51, and was an affront to many viewers.

25.1 Gustave Courbet. *Burial at Ornans*. 1849–50. Oil on canvas, 10′3½″ × 21′9½″ (3.13 × 6.64 m). Musée d'Orsay, Paris

 View the Closer Look for *Burial at Ornans* on myartslab.com

It presented common provincial folk, portrayed in a coarse, heavy form, without a shred of elegance or idealization. The people of Ornans posed for Courbet, and the artist not only documented their clothes and bearing but their distinguishing facial features, which included bulbous noses, grotesquely wrinkled faces, and unkempt hair. Courbet's Realism extends to the democratic presentation of the figures. Despite bold brushwork and a chiaroscuro vaguely reminiscent of his favorite artists, Rembrandt and Velázquez, the picture has no Baroque drama and no compositional structure designed to emphasize one figure over another—the dog is as important as the priest or mayor. Nor does it use classical formulas, as Benjamin West did in his pyramidal groupings in *The Death of General Wolfe* (see fig. 23.5). Instead, the image embraces the bold, simple compositions found in such popular art as broadsides, almanacs, and song sheets—the art of the people, not the Academy.

The picture seems so matter-of-fact that it is difficult to know what it is about. We see pallbearers and the coffin on the left, then a priest and assistants, followed by small-town patricians, and, to the right, womenfolk. An open grave is in the center foreground. We do not even know whose funeral it is. Nor is it clear that this is a statement about the finality of death, although it is the strongest candidate for the theme. Clearly, the picture is a document of social ritual that accurately observes the distinctions of gender, profession, and class in Ornans. More important, it brazenly elevates provincial bourgeois events to a lofty status equal to historical events. In effect, it was an assault on the highly esteemed genre of history painting.

The Realist Assault on Academic Values and Bourgeois Taste

By presenting provincial bourgeoisie and peasants on a scale reserved for history painting, Courbet launched an assault on the values of the French Academy and bourgeois taste. In effect, he declared contemporary life, and especially contemporary social conditions, just as valid (if not more valid) a subject for painting as historical events, and his emergence signals the death knell of the hierarchy of the genres that can be traced back to the establishment of the academies. Courbet's rejection of academic values in order to depict the social conditions of the modern world was taken up by Édouard Manet (1832–1883) in the early 1860s, followed shortly thereafter by Edgar Degas. Focusing on urban rather than rural life, they depicted musical gatherings in the Bois de Boulogne, the new park on the western outskirts of Paris where the upper classes came to be seen, and showed the fashionable throngs who congregated at Longchamp, the new racetrack in the Bois. They painted chic masked balls held at the Opéra, courtesans with their clients, and the new leisure activities at the new cafés, dance halls, and restaurants.

ÉDOUARD MANET Manet's pictures are often complex, loaded with references, and densely layered with multiple readings. They are so rich that he could comment on academic values while capturing the energy and psychology of contemporary society, and the changes occurring in it. What were these academic values? While it is dangerous to characterize any one kind of art as being academic and taught at the École des Beaux-Arts in the 1860s, most of the academicians still believed in the supremacy of history painting, the Graeco-Roman tradition, and the highly finished Neoclassical style of paint handling epitomized by Ingres, who was still alive at the time. Among the more popular subjects was the female nude, and images of nudes plastered the walls of the Salons. However, they were not ordinary nudes, for they were all Venuses, Dianas, bacchantes (followers of Bacchus), or nymphs. In other words, they were noble beings with a classical pedigree. These academic values were especially embraced by the bourgeoisie, who viewed academic art as the epitome of high culture and acquired it in part to gain social status.

Manet's *Luncheon on the Grass* (**fig. 25.2**) was a condemnation of bourgeois values and academic taste as well as a statement of what art should be about—the modern world. Manet himself came from a Parisian bourgeois background, and he studied with a famous academician. His true masters, however, were the painterly artists he copied at the LOUVRE—Hals, Titian, and the Spaniards Velázquez and Goya. He was a regular at the Parisian cafés, especially befriending Courbet, who was his role model.

Out of this background Manet produced the *Luncheon*, which shows two couples picnicking in the Bois de Boulogne. The painting was rejected by the 1863 Salon jurors. But that year they rejected a record number of artists, causing such an uproar that Louis Napoleon decided to present a *Salon des refusés* (Salon of the Refused), an exhibition of the rejected artists to be held in conjunction with the

The MUSÉE DU LOUVRE, located in the Louvre Palace (see fig. 21.6) in Paris, is one of the world's great encyclopedic museums. The collection was originally based on the royal collection, which was confiscated from Louis XVI in 1792 and given to the people of France in the form of a public museum, the Musée du Louvre. With the rise of Napoleon, the museum was named the Musée Napoléon, and its holdings dramatically increased by artwork confiscated as spoils of the Napoleonic Wars. The rise of public museums parallels the rise of democracy as political and economic power shifted from the aristocracy to the people.

25.2 Édouard Manet. *Luncheon on the Grass* (*Le Déjeuner sur l'Herbe*). 1863. Oil on canvas, 7′ × 8′10″ (2.13 × 2.69 m). Musée du Louvre, Paris

View the Closer Look for *Luncheon on the Grass* on myartslab.com

official Salon of 1863. Many of these artists preferred not to participate in what was perceived as an inferior exhibition; Manet, however, did.

The public showed up in record numbers to laugh at the rejects, and especially to view Manet's *Luncheon*, which created a scandal by presenting a contemporary scene of a naked woman in a park with two nattily dressed men. The public was outraged, for obviously the nude had to be a prostitute. It did not matter that critics acknowledged that the composition of the painting was based on that of major works by Titian and Raphael.

As far as the critics were concerned, referencing these august sources was not enough to overcome Manet's flagrant lack of decorum, a crime he brazenly committed on a roughly 7- by 9-foot scale. So, why did Manet base his contemporary scene on historical sources? The answer may lie in the artificiality of his figures, who fail to interact convincingly. As pointed out by one art historian, they look like art school students posing to recreate a famous Raphael painting. In effect, Manet is telling us that the present cannot live in the past, which many academicians chose to do. As trumpeted by Baudelaire in 1846, Manet was declaring that artists

must find their subject matter, their heroes, in the modern world. Furthermore, he was exposing the disguised eroticism that the tradition of the classical nude had now stooped to. It is possible, as well, that Manet used historical sources as a device to put himself into the long tradition of great art. In effect, he is announcing that his Realism is not only the most valid direction for art to take, but also that it is as important and vital as the great art of the past.

What convinced the jurors and public that Manet was an incompetent sensationalist who deserved to be relegated to the *Salon des refusés* was his style. To their academically focused eye, he could neither model nor create convincing space. The picture looked like a preliminary sketch, not a finished work. The figures are two-dimensional cutouts, flattened by their crisp, silhouetting contours and a flourish of broad brushstrokes that dispenses with the halftones between dark and light needed to mold volume. A shadow indicating a fold on a pants leg, for example, is rendered with one bold, black sweep of the brush. The woman wading in the background is too large for her recessed location and seems to float directly over the seated group. All of the objects—figures, trees, the colorful still life of clothes and basket—hover in space, failing to connect and assemble into a coherent spatial structure.

Manet has undermined the spatial order of the illusionistic Renaissance window and replaced it with a new unifying logic—a sensual sea of brushstrokes composed of lush, oily, and thickly applied paint that dramatically covers the entire surface of his canvas. Our eyes delight in the lusciousness of his brushwork, the wonderful variety of his Velázquez- and Goya-inspired blacks, the range of greens in the grass, and the deft play of darks next to lights that makes our eyes jump from one light area to another and from one dark patch to the next. These abstract qualities—paint handling and value contrasts, for example—are the new structure of painting, not illusionistic space and modeling. With *Luncheon on the Grass*, Manet began what twentieth-century critics would consider the Modernist tradition, a tradition that emphasized the abstract qualities of art and that would continue for the next hundred years. Manet undoubtedly delighted in how the unfinished, sketchy look of his paintings irreverently countered the slick drawing and modeling of academic tradition and shocked bourgeois taste. Additionally, he used it to create a fleeting, momentary quality that reflected the quickly changing modern world.

EDGAR DEGAS AND *JAPONISME* Like Manet, Edgar Degas (1834–1917) came from a wealthy background. Initially he aspired to be a history painter. He studied with an Ingres follower and emphasized drawing and modeling in his early work, retaining line even when his art became more painterly. By 1865, Degas entered Manet's and Baudelaire's orbit at the Café Guerbois, and he turned to capturing modern Paris. Degas developed a Manet-inspired painterly approach to his subject, as well as innovative compositional devices that give his images a spontaneous, transitory quality and effectively transform the viewer into a voyeur.

A classic work from the 1860s is *The Orchestra of the Paris Opéra* (**fig. 25.3**) of 1868–69. The picture is a genre scene, in which we see not only the members of the orchestra but also the ballet dancers onstage. Yet the subject is not just the talented, toiling performers but the intensity, excitement, and fragmentation of contemporary life itself, which is presented in a matter-of-fact way. Degas has put us virtually in the pit, and we feel like anonymous members of the audience. Our view is not head-on

but at an angle, which was unusual for a painting at the time but certainly typical for a theatergoer. The double-bass player is arbitrarily cropped on the right, suggesting that we are only looking at the left side of the orchestra, seeing only a fragment of a complete view. The same is true of the ballet dancers, whose heads are chopped off.

Building on this movement and energy are the planes of the wall, the stage, the front row of the orchestra, and the ballet dancers, all of which are slightly skewed, along with the angular thrust of instruments and the dancers' legs and arms. Space seems compressed, as far and near are dramatically juxtaposed, for example in the dark double bass head and brightly colored tutus or ballet skirts. The image seems to climb up the picture plane rather than recede in space, making it appear flattened out. A precise line defines figures and objects, but a sporadic spray of dashing brushwork, best seen in the dancers' tutus, adds spontaneity, giving us a feeling of a passing moment.

Scholars often attribute Degas's innovative compositions to the influence of Japanese prints,

25.3 Edgar Degas. *The Orchestra of the Paris Opéra*. 1868–69. Oil on canvas, 22¼ × 18³⁄₁₆″ (56.5 × 46.2 cm). Musée d'Orsay, Paris

25.4 Andō Hiroshige. *Plum Estate, Kameido*, from the series *One Hundred Famous Views of Edo*. 1857. Wood-block print, 13⅜ × 9″ (34 × 22.8 cm). Brooklyn Museum of Art, New York. Gift of Anna Ferris 30.1478.30

which flooded the Parisian market in the late 1850s after Japan was opened up to the West in 1854. The French were especially taken by Japanese culture, and their infatuation was called *Japonisme*, a term also used by the English and Americans. Especially intriguing for artists were the prints, works that first arrived in France as packing material for fragile Japanese objects but were nonetheless collected by the late 1850s by the artists in Manet's circle, who found them aesthetically fascinating.

As can be seen in *Plum Estate, Kameido* (**fig. 25.4**) by Andō Hiroshige (1797–1858), Japanese image-making was quite foreign to a Western way of see-ing. Forms are flat with sharp contours, while space is compressed, the foreground pressed up against the viewer's nose, the background pulled right into the foreground space. There is no transition between near and far. Just the concept of situating a viewer in a tree from which to see the main activity miniaturized in the distance would have been radi-cal to the eye of a Western artist. However, the flat contours, abrupt cropping, and spatial contraction

of Japanese prints certainly influenced Degas and Manet, although in a far from obvious manner and never approaching direct copying.

Impressionism: A Different Form of Realism

The label "Impressionism" was coined by a hostile conservative critic in 1874 when reviewing the first exhibition of an artists' collaborative called the *Société anonyme des artistes* (Artists, Inc.), an organization that sought to provide an alternative to the Salon. We now refer to that show as the first Impressionist exhibition (there would be eight alto-gether between 1874 and 1886). Like the general public, the writer found the paintings so sketchy that he felt they were just impressions, not finished paintings.

Impressionism shares with the Realism of Manet and Degas a sketchy, unfinished look, a feeling of the moment, and a desire to appear modern. It too presents its subjects matter-of-factly. Many scholars even apply the term Impressionism to the work of Manet and Degas, in part to distinguish their Real-ism from the earthy, rural Realism of Courbet and to indicate how Impressionism often shares with them a sense of the urbane and the modern. Like Manet and Degas, the Impressionists were inter-ested in recording the transformations occurring in French society, especially the leisure pursuits of the *nouveaux riches*. While they, too, painted city scenes and genre, they focused more on the evolu-tion of the sleepy rural villages surrounding Paris, now easily accessible by train, into bustling suburbs containing, on the one hand, factories, commercial wharves, and railroad trestles, and on the other hand restaurants, regattas, and boating for Parisian weekenders. Rather than the figure, the Impres-sionists focused more on landscape and cityscape, and instead of constructing their compositions in the studio using models, they worked empirically, out of doors, where they recorded the landscape and weather conditions that they witnessed at a fleeting moment in time. They painted not so much objects as the colored light that bounced off them. In effect, they painted what they saw, not what they knew.

CLAUDE MONET The leader in developing Impres-sionism was Claude Monet (1840–1926), who was born and raised in Le Havre in Normandy. He casually studied with an accomplished local land-scape painter, who painted outdoors, *en plein air*. But in order to get financial support from his grocer father, he was forced to study in Paris with an academically minded but liberal painter. In this studio he met Pierre-Auguste Renoir, who would also become a core member of the Impressionists. Throughout the 1860s, Monet and his friends painted the landscape surrounding Paris, meeting the Barbizon artists, who further encouraged them to paint outdoors. For the Impressionists, however, these paintings were not small studies but large finished products. Painting rapidly in the landscape with bold brushwork, they sought to capture light, and the color it carried, as it bounced off objects. Monet's extensive use of primary and secondary colors, the principal hues on the traditional COLOR WHEEL, was also influenced by recent scientific research into color, demonstrating that the intensity of complementary colors is increased when they are placed next to one another.

We can see the effectiveness of Monet's palette in *On the Bank of the Seine, Bennecourt* (**fig. 25.5**), painted in 1868 in a small town downriver from Paris, similar to many of the Seine and Oise river locations that Parisians visited by train on summer weekends, or where they built impressive summer homes. The artist works with glaring sun-drenched whites and bright blues and greens accented with touches of red and yellow. Objects in shadow, such as leaves and grass, retain color and do not go black. Browns are not muddy but a light-filled tan. Monet maintains the strength of his colors by keeping the imagery close to the picture plane, not allowing it to disappear into a dull atmospheric haze to suggest depth. There is no chiaroscuro to model forms. The tree foliage is a two-dimensional silhouette, while the blue sky behind is equally flat. The reflection of the house on the water runs up and down the picture plane, reinforcing the two-dimensionality of the broad smears of light and dark blue in the river just below. The solid blue sky is virtually the same shade as the darker blue in the water, a correlation that momentarily pulls the sky to the foreground. Also asserting the surface of the canvas is Monet's

The COLOR WHEEL is a circle that is anchored at three points by the primary colors yellow, blue, and red. In between these colors are the colors made by mixing these primary colors together, that is, the secondary colors, orange (red and yellow), violet (blue and red), and green (yellow and blue). The complementary colors are red and green, yellow and violet, and blue and orange. Put the complements next to one another and the colors will be intensified, a red looking more red and a green looking more green, for example.

25.5 Claude Monet. *On the Bank of the Seine, Bennecourt.* 1868. Oil on canvas, 32⅛ × 39⅝″ (81.5 × 100.7 cm). The Art Institute of Chicago. Mr. and Mrs. Potter Palmer Collection

bold, variegated brushwork, which changes character from one object to the next and gives the picture a shimmering quality that suggests we are witnessing a split second of time. The only motif that suggests depth is the rowboat running diagonally back in perspective.

Equally important, contemporaries realized that the brushwork represented the unstable, rapidly changing qualities of modern life. These pictures looked nothing like previous landscapes; they lacked the classical look of Claude Lorrain, the Baroque conventions of the Dutch landscape painters and their earthy palette, and the emotional constructions of the Romantics. Their very look was considered modern, as was their subject matter. We can safely assume that the fashionably dressed woman (actually Monet's wife) is not a local, but rather a Parisian, up from the city by train, who has been boating.

PIERRE-AUGUSTE RENOIR After meeting Monet and befriending him, Pierre-Auguste Renoir (1841–1919) also developed an Impressionist style

of bright color, bold paint handling, and modern subjects. Often working beside Monet, Renoir painted landscapes. But he was attracted to the figurative tradition as well, and his career straddles the two genres.

Among his best-known figure paintings is *Luncheon of the Boating Party* (**fig. 25.6**) of 1880–81. The picture's setting is the Restaurant Fournaise on an island in the Seine at Chatou, a small village nine miles from Paris and accessible by train. Chatou was especially popular with boaters, and restaurants like this catered to Parisians. In the background, on the river, we can just barely see sailboats, a rowboat, and a commercial barge. There is also a glimpse of a railroad bridge.

The restaurant party consists of urban types, with the exception of Alphonse Fournaise, the restaurant owner's son, who leans against the railing, his muscular biceps reflecting his task of putting rental boats into the water. Renoir portrays a colorful, sun-drenched scene of suburban leisure, presenting it as pleasurable, relaxed, and sensuous, qualities enhanced by the lavish spread on the table

25.6 Pierre-Auguste Renoir. *Luncheon of the Boating Party.* 1880–81. Oil on canvas, 4'3" × 5'9" (1.3 × 1.76 m). The Phillips Collection, Washington, D.C. Acquired 1923

and the glorious lush brushwork of the tablecloth. The picture has the momentary quality we associate with Realism, achieved in part by the flickering, feathery brushwork and the asymmetrical composition that runs off the right side of the canvas, the picture cropped and fragmented as in Degas's *The Orchestra of the Paris Opéra* (fig. 25.3).

MARY CASSATT Another key figure in the Impressionist group was Mary Cassatt (1844–1926), who approached Impressionism from a woman's perspective, her Realism even reflecting the social concerns of the women's movement. Cassatt was an American, born into a wealthy family and raised in Pittsburgh. In 1866 she went to Paris and first studied with an artist who offered classes for women. She also studied in Parma and Rome before returning to Paris in 1874, where she befriended Degas and abandoned her academic style for Realism. Invited by Degas, she participated in the fourth Impressionist exhibition in 1879. Now she displayed a bright palette, strong brushwork that hugged the surface, and the Realist compositional devices of asymmetry and cropping.

Like Degas and Manet, Cassatt was a figure painter, and her most famous themes from the late 1870s include women in *loges* (boxes) at the opera, a subject treated by Renoir and Degas as well. She also painted women at home: reading, visiting, taking tea, sewing, or bathing an infant. She presented the modern woman, sophisticated in dress, manners, and leisure activities. In the 1880s, she abandoned her *loge* theme and focused increasingly on domestic scenes, especially of women and children.

Art historians often attribute Cassatt's subject matter to the restrictions she faced as a female: As a respectable woman, she could not go unattended to the same places as her male counterparts. But more at issue was her belief in the importance of women in society, even if this importance was largely restricted to the home. Her views coincided with developments then occurring in the women's movement. In 1878, the International Congress of Women's Rights was held in Paris, and at the top of its agenda was the need for better education for women, which would not only allow them to become professionals but also to better manage the home and family. The Congress also focused on the important role that women played in nurturing children, advocating that mothers nurse and care for their offspring rather than hiring wet-nurses. This position reflects the increased importance that sociologists placed on the care of children in general in the 1870s, which in part stemmed from a concern about the high infant mortality rate in Europe, especially in France. The path to a healthier society and nation, many argued, began in the home and was in the hands of the mother who nurtured her children, both physically and emotionally, and paid attention to hygiene.

Cassatt's many domestic scenes of mothers tending their children, such as *The Child's Bath* (**fig. 25.7**) of 1893, came out of this context. Regular bathing was a modern phenomenon for late nineteenth-century Paris, when people generally

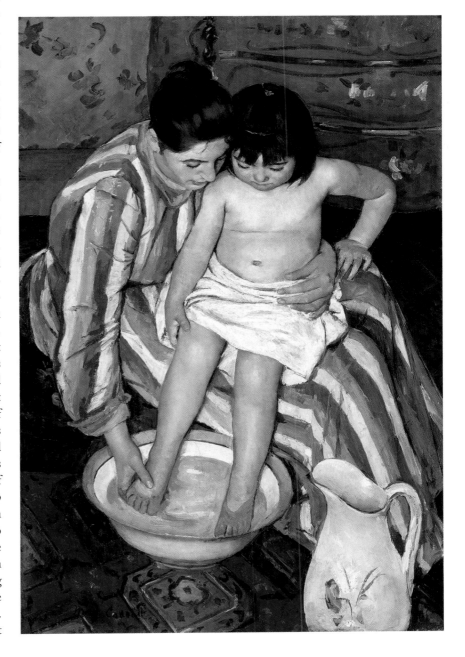

25.7 Mary Cassatt. *The Child's Bath*. 1893. Oil on canvas, 39½ × 26″ (100.3 × 66 cm). The Art Institute of Chicago. Robert A. Waller Fund. 1910.2

bathed only once a week. Not only is the picture about health, but also about intense emotional and physical involvement, as is reflected in the sensual yet tender manner in which the caregiver touches the child.

The picture contains all the ingredients we associate with Realism—the fashionable bourgeois décor, the bright colors, and the sense of spontaneity in the brushwork and skewed composition with its high viewpoint. The style of the picture reflects Cassatt's intense attraction to Japanese prints at this point in her career, an interest reflected in the overhead viewpoint as well as in the boldness of her forms and contours. Cassatt also absorbed the influence of her studies of Renaissance art, as seen

25.8 William Holman Hunt. *The Awakening Conscience.* 1853–54. Oil on canvas, 29½ × 22″ (76.2 × 55.9 cm). Tate Britain, London

in the strong line-defining contours that have the crispness found in quattrocento painting (Italian art of the 1400s). Many of Cassatt's presentations of a mother and child even resemble Renaissance depictions of a Madonna and Child, an allusion that sanctifies the important role of women in creating a better society. But it also reflects the direction that Realism took after 1880, as many of the Impressionists changed course and began to make a more monumental art that recalled the Classical art of the past.

British Realism

Realism took a very different form across the English Channel, although the word itself was never applied to art. There Positivism produced a detailed naturalism, an intense truth to nature, and an interest in social types. In Britain, the Industrial Revolution had an almost hundred-year headstart over France. Industrialization and urbanization accounted for the poverty and other social ills so familiar to us today from the serialized novels of Charles Dickens (1812–1870), which were set in a cruel, corrupt London suffocated by grime and soot. Materialism and greed were rampant. Cheap, ugly, mass-produced objects replaced the highly refined handmade products that the aristocracy and upper class had once demanded. No longer was the worker a highly trained artisan with pride in his or her product, but a human machine suffering the drudgery of dawn-to-dusk, mindless labor to turn out an inferior product without personal identification, all for a bare minimum wage.

It was the artist, educator, writer, art critic, and environmentalist John Ruskin (1819–1900) who took the lead in attempting to arrest this decline into industrial hell. Among Ruskin's most prominent beliefs was the need for contemporary society to aspire to a new spirituality and moral pride, which required adherence to truth and identification with the divinity of nature. He advocated art education for all social classes, for the working-class producers as well as the bourgeois consumers. He firmly believed that art was a necessity, not a luxury, for it molded people's lives and moral values; great art made great people. And by art, Ruskin meant not only painting, sculpture, and architecture but also the decorative arts, all of which had to be well crafted, beautiful, honest, and even spiritual, as in the Middle Ages.

Ruskin's emphasis on nature and religion marks the beginning of the nineteenth-century search for a simpler life, one that rejected the advances of urbanization and industrialization, and the theme was to dominate the art of the closing decades of the century.

The Pre-Raphaelite Brotherhood

Ruskin championed the Pre-Raphaelite Brotherhood, a society started in 1848 by three students enrolled in the Royal Academy School: William Holman Hunt, John Everett Millais, and Dante Gabriel Rossetti, the leader and spokesperson. The PRB, as they initially signed their paintings, denounced the art of the Royal Academy and most painting since the Italian Renaissance after Raphael's early period. They found the work decadent in that it clouded truth and fact with a muddy chiaroscuro and placed a premium on such artificial, formal qualities as elegant contours or pleasing compositional patterning. Like Ruskin, the Pre-Raphaelites abhorred bourgeois materialism and taste. Their heroes were the fifteenth-century Italian and Netherlandish "primitives," such as Jan van Eyck (see page 297–300), whose work they perceived as simpler, more direct, and hence sincere in its attempt to represent Nature. They also considered this work more spiritual and moral because it was identified with the intensely religious Late Gothic period.

WILLIAM HOLMAN HUNT The most religious of the Pre-Raphaelite Brotherhood was William Holman Hunt (1827–1910), who came from a poor working-class family. His work is characterized by a combination of Victorian moral didacticism and intense naturalism. *The Awakening Conscience* (**fig. 25.8**) of 1853–54 was inspired by a passage in Charles Dickens's *David Copperfield* when David's friend, the simple fisherman Peggotty, goes searching for his beloved Emily, who has run off with an amoral dandy. Hunt tells the tale of one of the thousands of poor women appearing in the Realist literature of the period who perceived prostitution as their only hope of financial security even though it would inevitably lead to ruin. While sitting on her lover's lap and singing a song, a kept woman becomes aware of the lyrics, thinks of her family, and suddenly abhors her sinful situation, from which she must then immediately escape.

Hunt renders the room, cluttered with the shiny, vulgar products of crass consumerism, with a microscopic attention to detail worthy of Jan van Eyck. As in a Van Eyck painting, every object seems to function symbolically. The cat chasing the bird under the table reflects the kept woman's position as prey, and the clock approaching high noon denotes that the time left for decisive action is quickly expiring. The background mirror reflects an open window—redemption—since beyond we see the purity, beauty, and spirituality of nature gloriously bathed in a bright divine light. The density of objects and figures in the painting eliminates the compositional patterning and pleasing aesthetic contours that the PRB disliked.

WILLIAM MORRIS About 1856, William Morris (1834–1896) became involved with the Pre-Raphaelites. He would dabble in architecture and become a renowned poet, but his true calling was implementing Ruskin's theories about replacing shoddy mass-produced products with well-designed handcrafted ones that, as in the Middle Ages, would reconnect workers and their commodities. In 1865 he opened a design company, which eventually was called Morris & Co. It manufactured beautifully crafted fabrics, wallpaper, tapestries, carpets, tiles, furniture, and stained glass, with Morris himself designing most of the wallpaper and fabrics.

The motifs and palette of Morris and his company were organic and Gothic, projecting an aura of nature and spirituality. This aesthetic is apparent in the dining room (**fig. 25.9**) that he designed in 1867 for a new applied arts museum in South Kensington, London, known today as the Victoria and Albert Museum. The gold-ground panels represent the 12 months of the year. Morris's wallpaper, laboriously hand-printed from wood blocks, is a flat abstract pattern based on an olive branch. The chest is designed in Late Gothic/Early Renaissance style. Morris's impact on the applied arts was far-reaching, launching what is known as the Arts and Crafts Movement, which soon spread to the United States.

The Aesthetic Movement: Personal Psychology and Repressed Eroticism

While William Morris kept the moral and spiritual program of Ruskin alive with his Arts and Crafts Movement, the Pre-Raphaelite group had dissolved by 1860. Rossetti, who had not been very productive in the 1850s, gravitated toward a visionary art set in a medieval guise and expressing his own personal psychology, not social morality. Running through his paintings is an undercurrent

25.9 William Morris (Morris & Co.). Green Dining Room (William Morris Room). 1867. Victoria and Albert Museum, London

of repressed sexuality, a reflection of the strict moral codes of mid-Victorian Britain that did not allow for a display of sexual appeal or even the discussion of sex. Most important, Rossetti's painting became about mood, which was produced not through narrative but through the abstract aspects of painting. The catalyst for this new attitude was the English poet Algernon Charles Swinburne (1837–1909), who in turn was influenced in the 1850s by the French critic Théophile Gautier. Gautier was a leading advocate of "art for art's sake," a theory maintaining that art's function was first and foremost to be beautiful, to appeal to the senses and not project moral values or tell stories. Rossetti came under Swinburne's spell. But the most famous, indeed notorious proponent of the Aesthetic Movement is the American painter James Abbott McNeill Whistler.

JAMES ABBOTT McNEILL WHISTLER Raised in New England and Russia, Whistler (1834–1903) studied painting in Paris from 1855 to 1859, enrolling in the same studio as Monet, whom he met. He also befriended Courbet and initially made his mark as a Realist, painting scenes of contemporary life that captured the underbelly of the city. After moving to London in 1859 (he never returned to America),

he continued to spend long periods in Paris, and traveled back and forth between the two cities into the 1860s, maintaining his Parisian connections and friendships and submitting work to the Salons. He knew Gautier through Courbet and Manet, and in London he befriended Swinburne.

By 1863, Whistler renounced French Realism to pursue Aestheticism, an example of which is his *Symphony in White No. I: The White Girl*, a title probably inspired by Gautier's poem "Symphony in White Major." Whistler submitted the picture to the 1863 *Salon des refusés*, where it hung not far from Manet's *Luncheon on the Grass* (fig. 25.2). Like Gautier's poem, which is a complex interfacing of different white visions, the painting orchestrates a range of whites, soft yellows, and reds in a full-length portrait of the artist's mistress Jo Hiffernan, who is dressed in white against a largely white ground. While Gautier and Swinburne conceptually influenced Whistler, visually the artist came under the spell of *Japonisme*, an influence that is more clearly stated in *Symphony in White No. II: The Little White Girl* (**fig. 25.10**) of 1864. Here, Jo leans on the mantelpiece of Whistler's London home, surrounded by a Japanese blue-and-white vase, fan, and a spray of cherry blossoms, often identified with Japan. At one level, the painting is a sensual display of abstract color, shape, and composition. Using thin, delicate brushstrokes and almost transparent layers of paint, Whistler creates a symphony of whites, yellows, reds, pinks, and blues that gracefully dance across the picture plane. He plays the softness of his paint and such forms as Jo's dress against the rectangular linearity of the mantel, mirror, and reflected picture frames. The flowers entering the composition on the right are another delicate touch, a Japanese compositional device used earlier by Degas to create fragmentation and spontaneity but here to make the petals seem to float magically. Whistler's use of "symphony" in the title reflects how the artist drew a parallel between painting and music, viewing his art as an abstract arrangement of color and form. (In the following decade, his work would become increasingly abstract, especially in a series of works entitled *Nocturnes*, a title again reflecting a musical parallel.) The sensuous, languid, even ethereal elegance of the painting mirrors Jo's reflective pose, giving the painting powerful yet mysterious psychological overtones, for which Whistler provides no narrative—just aesthetic beauty and an erotic mood. Whistler moved art into a subjective, nonempirical realm, far removed from the world of Realism.

Realism in America

The ripple effect of the revolutions of 1848 did not reach America, although it did produce waves of new immigrants. A more defining benchmark for the United States is the Civil War of 1861–65, which had a devastating physical, psychological, and economic impact on the nation. The Garden of Eden was ravaged. After the war, that metaphor was replaced by the *Gilded Age*, a term coined by Mark Twain and his co-author for an 1871 book of that title describing the robber barons, the new industrialists and financiers who made vast fortunes, often exploiting workers. The period is also defined by continued Western expansion, fulfilling what the nation saw as its God-given manifest destiny to overrun the North American continent. Survey teams mapped the new territories, and poorly paid workers completed the Transcontinental Railroad, connecting East and West, in 1869. By 1890, the government had subdued the Native American nations, either by containment in restricted territories or by violent annihilation.

Scientific Realism: Thomas Eakins

Thomas Eakins (1844–1916), a Philadelphian, was among the earliest and most powerful Realist painters in America. His scenes of the modern world included not only middle-class leisure activities and the popular sports and pastimes of post-Civil War America but also surgery clinics portraying surgeons as modern heroes and highlighting new scientific techniques such as anesthesia and antiseptic surgery. Eakins even brought a scientific approach

25.10 James Abbott McNeill Whistler. *Symphony in White No. II: The Little White Girl.* 1864. Oil on canvas, 30⅛ × 20⅛" (76.7 × 51.3 cm). Tate Britain, London

 Read the document related to James Abbott McNeill Whistler on myartslab.com

to his Realism, which made it quite different from the Realism of Manet and Degas that he witnessed in Paris from 1866 to 1869 while studying with a renowned academician.

Among Eakins's first works upon returning to Philadelphia was a series of sculling pictures, among them *Max Schmitt in a Single Scull* (also called *The Champion Single Sculls*) (**fig. 25.11**), a painting that reflects the rising popularity of the sport and presents Schmitt, the winner of a championship race on the Schuylkill River in Pennsylvania, as a hero of modern life. While the picture looks like a *plein-air* painting, we do not see a quickly recorded Impressionist moment but a painstakingly reconstructed event in time. Eakins's paintings are grounded in intense scientific inquiry designed to ensure the accuracy of his Realism. He made numerous perspective studies of the boats and oars, which result in the river receding with breathtaking mathematical precision, firmly locking the boats in place in space. He carefully studied light effects and anatomy, and as a teacher at the Pennsylvania Academy of Art outraged his colleagues and suffered public scorn by having his students, including women, work from the nude model, rather than imitate plaster casts of Classical figures. His quest for realism drove him to record minute details, including a steamboat behind the distant bridges and a train on a railroad bridge, details beyond the reach of normal vision.

Iconic Image: Winslow Homer

Winslow Homer (1836–1910) was in Paris at about the same time as Eakins. He was already disposed toward painting the modern world, for he began his career in 1857 as a magazine illustrator, recording the latest fashions and social activities and later covering the Civil War. He was in Paris in 1866–67, where he saw the work of Courbet and Manet, but he was too early to experience the full impact of Impressionism. Upon returning to New York, he made outdoor scenes of the middle class engaged in leisure activities of contemporary life, such as playing croquet, swimming at the newest shore resorts, and taking horseback tours in the White Mountains of New Hampshire, diversions now accessible by train.

Rather than portraying a fleeting moment, however, Homer created iconic symbolic images of American life and issues. We can see this emblematic

25.11 Thomas Eakins. *Max Schmitt in a Single Scull* (*The Champion Single Sculls*). 1871. Oil on canvas, 32¼ × 46¼" (82 × 117.5 cm). The Metropolitan Museum of Art, New York. Alfred N. Punnett Endowment Fund and George D. Pratt Gift, 1934. 34.92

approach in his *Snap the Whip* (**fig. 25.12**) of 1872. This visual record of a children's game appears at first glance to be an Americanization of Impressionism, for the image is a sun-filled scene rendered with fairly strong color and flashy passages of brushwork. But Homer's color is not as intense as the Impressionists', nor is his brushwork as loose. The picture is not about color and light and empirically capturing a specific scene and transient moment. This image is frozen. The figures are carefully outlined, modeled, and monumental, their solidity reinforced by the geometry of the one-room schoolhouse and the bold backdrop of the mountain, which parallels the direction of the boys' movement. The barefoot children in their plain country clothes, like the one-room schoolhouse behind them, are emblems of simplicity and wholesomeness, their youth projecting innocence and future hope for a recently reunified country. The game itself is symbolic of union, since the chain depends on reliance and strength. At a time when the nation was staggering under the weight of the disillusionment brought on by the Civil War and the turmoil of rampant industrialization, *Snap the Whip* embodied the country's lost innocence and was a nostalgic appeal for values that were quickly fading into memory.

Photography: A Mechanical Medium for Mass-Produced Art

In 1839 the new medium of photography was commercially introduced in both France and England. As a mechanical process that would eventually lend itself to mass production and popular culture, it was a perfect fit with the Industrial Revolution and seems a natural consequence of it. It was also a perfect tool for the Positivist era, for initially it was largely perceived as a recording device for cataloguing, documenting, and supporting scientific inquiry. It had the appearance of being objective, paralleling the matter-of-fact presentation of much Realism and Impressionism.

First Innovations

In 1838, Louis-Jacques-Mandé Daguerre (1787–1851) unveiled the **daguerreotype**, a photographic process that exposed light on a silver iodide-coated copper plate, and later a glass plate, and allowed for one image, which remained on that plate. Meanwhile, in England, William Henry Fox Talbot (1800–1877) announced in 1839 that he could fix an image on a paper negative, rather than on metal or

25.12 Winslow Homer. *Snap the Whip*. 1872. Oil on canvas, 22¼ × 36½" (56.5 × 92.7 cm). The Butler Institute of American Art, Youngstown, Ohio

glass, and in 1841 he took out a patent for the new negative–positive photograph that he called a **calotype**, a salted paper print that allowed for infinite printing of the same image.

Both the daguerreotype and the calotype were displaced in the early 1850s by the simultaneous invention in France and Britain of the **wet-collodion process**, which cut exposure time to under a second and produced a sharp, easily reproducible negative. At about the same time, the **albumen print** was developed, which used salted egg white on paper, creating a smooth, more refined surface that revealed greater detail with less graininess. For the next 30 to 40 years, photographers used wet-collodion plates for recording images and then printed them on albumen paper.

Recording the World

By the 1850s the most prevalent use of photography was for recording the world: People, sights, and objects. These pictures were generally viewed as fact, which is ironic since, as we shall see, photographers could manipulate images in various ways, including the selection of motif and the objects to be included or excluded in a photograph.

25.13 Nadar. *Édouard Manet.* ca. 1865. Albumen salted paper print, mounted on Bristol board. Musée d'Orsay, Paris

PORTRAITURE Portraiture was perhaps the most popular form of photography. By the 1840s, photographic studios appeared throughout the Western world, especially in the United States, with most towns having at least one photographer and large cities many. Portrait photography epitomized the rise of the middle class and democracy in the nineteenth century, for unlike painted portraits, it was inexpensive, with virtually anyone being able to afford it. Especially in Europe, the role of photography was to aggrandize the sitter, transforming ordinary folk into important people by presenting them, for example, with an imposing classical column and a dramatic swag of drapery, the exact same set being used from one client to the next.

While the vast majority of portraits were routinely cranked out and far from artistic, a handful of photographers distinguished themselves through innovative compositions or an ability to capture a sitter's personality. Among the most celebrated early portraitists was the Parisian Gaspard-Félix Tournachon (1820–1910), known simply as Nadar. He began cashing in on the public infatuation with celebrities by mass-producing albumen prints of the famous, specializing in writers, actors, performers, and artists of bohemian Paris. His background as a caricaturist proved invaluable in setting up his shots, enabling him to create incisive portraits that captured the essence of his sitter's mystique.

We can see this skill in Nadar's 1860s portrait of the painter Édouard Manet (**fig. 25.13**). Although of bourgeois origin, Manet is not presented as moneyed. The sitter may wear expensive clothes and be seated in a lavish chair, but there is no pretentious Classical column or billowing drapery. Instead the emphasis is on Manet's forceful personality. He has turned his chair around in a businesslike, if not argumentative manner, grasping the top with his right hand, and with a gesture of confidence placing the other hand on his hip. His meticulously trimmed beard and mustache and dapper clothes confirm his renown as a dandy. Nadar, especially noted for his lighting, has backlit Manet's head, making the entire figure seem to thrust forward and reinforcing the intensity of the painter's stare.

VIEWS Along with portraits, views dominated photography, for they allowed people to travel the world without leaving their living room. Books of photographs of exotic, and not so exotic, places began to appear, such as *Egypt, Nubia, Palestine and Syria*, published in 1852. More popular than such albums, which could be quite expensive, were **stereocards**, which by the 1860s were as prevalent as musical compact discs are today. Stereocards are side-by-side photographs of the same image taken by a camera with two lenses, replicating human binocular vision. When put into a special viewer, the twin flat pictures appear as a single three-dimensional image. To accommodate the tremendous demand for these cards, distributing companies stocked as many as 300,000 different images at one time.

Among the views popular with Americans were those of the frontier. A large contingent of American photographers, like their fellow painters, specialized in landscape, traveling west, often with survey teams, to record the sublime wilderness that symbolized the nation (see page 491–93). One of the first and most famous of this group is Carleton Watkins (1829–1916), who beginning in 1861 made hundreds of glass stereographic views of Yosemite along with about a thousand 18- by 22-inch albumen prints.

The results, as seen in *Yosemite Valley from the Best General View* (**fig. 25.14**), made on a second trip to Yosemite in 1865–66, were so breathtaking that when shown to President Lincoln they helped convince him and Congress to preserve Yosemite as a park. Continuing the romantic tradition of Thomas Cole, Watkins captures the sublime scale of the American wilderness, the mountain peaks dramatically dwarfing Yosemite Falls, one of the highest falls in America. Watkins produced a lush image by working up extremely rich textures in the developing process and a sense of drama by creating powerful value contrasts and a composition of forceful diagonals descending from both right and left. To keep the sky from going a monotonous white, Watkins used a second negative to add clouds. In other words, Watkins dramatically manipulated his images, and most important, considered his photographs art, not mere documentation. Not only did he sell them nationally, as large photographs in addition to stereoscopic views, he also exhibited them in art galleries, including a prominent one in New York.

Reporting the News: Photojournalism

Early photography also recorded famous events, and these images can be considered the forerunner of photojournalism. Among the most riveting examples are images of the Civil War, such as *A Harvest of Death, Gettysburg, Pennsylvania, July 1863*

(**fig. 25.15**) by Timothy O'Sullivan (ca. 1840–1882), who like Watkins became one of the great photographers of the West. Before setting off to document the Civil War, O'Sullivan began his career as an apprentice to Mathew Brady (1823–1896), owner of the most famous photographic portrait gallery in America, located in New York. (Abraham Lincoln sat for Brady over 30 times and credited Brady's flattering 1860 portrait for helping him win that November's presidential election.) In 1862–63, O'Sullivan signed up with the photographic team of Alexander Gardner and contributed 44 images to the album *Gardner's Photographic Sketchbook of the War* (1866).

In *A Harvest of Death*, we feel the power of the documentary reality of photography, which a painted image can never have. We see *real* people and *real* death—images of an actual event on a definite date, the Battle of Gettysburg on July 3, 1863—not a fictitious image. Although we know that the war photographers often moved objects and bodies for the sake of their image, we have no evidence that O'Sullivan did so here. In any case, he conveys the grim reality of war. The anonymous corpses are as lifeless as bales of hay waiting to be collected, their dark forms hauntingly contrasted with the void of the overcast sky. The cropped bodies at the right and left add to the brutality of the scene,

25.14 Carleton E. Watkins. *Yosemite Valley from the Best General View*. 1865–66. Albumen print, 16⅛ × 20½" (85 × 113 cm). Courtesy Janet Lehr Inc., New York/Vered Gallery, East Hampton, New York

25.15 Timothy O'Sullivan. *A Harvest of Death, Gettysburg, Pennsylvania, July 1863*, from Alexander Gardner's *Gardner's Photographic Sketchbook of the War*. 1866. Albumen print (also available as stereocard), 7 × 8¹¹/₁₆″ (17.8 × 22 cm). Library of Congress, Washington, D.C. Brady Civil War Collection

so convincingly registered with the gaping mouth on the face of the dead soldier in the foreground. The living are pushed deep into the background, shrouded in the morning mist, as though life during this seemingly endless national conflict is itself dissolving into just the barest memory.

Photography as Art: Pictorialism and Combination Printing

Not all nineteenth-century photographers saw the new medium as primarily a tool to document reality. Some, like Carlton Watkins, viewed it as high art and deliberately explored photography's aesthetic potential, confident that it was as valid an art form as painting and sculpture. This attitude, which some critics found threatening, was more prevalent in Europe than America in the first 50 years following the advent of photography.

ENGLISH PICTORIALISM In London, a group of photographers began making composite pictures designed to look like Old Master or esteemed contemporary painting. They used as many as 30 negatives to make their patchwork images and experimented with cut-and-paste assemblage. The results were heavy-handed photographs that were far from seamless and did not look lifelike. Their style is called Pictorialism, because the staged images were meant to look like paintings.

The most successful Pictorialists to a modern eye were those who did not make composite images and instead manipulated the camera and printing process to meet their needs. Although far less famous during her lifetime, Julia Margaret Cameron (1815–1879) is perhaps the most celebrated today of the British Pictorialists. Her trademark was an out-of-focus blurring of images to make them seem painterly, as in *Sister Spirits* (**fig. 25.16**) of about 1865. Like the other Pictorialists, she staged scenes using actors, costumes, and sets, and she illustrated such literary sources as the Bible, Shakespeare, and the then poet laureate Alfred, Lord Tennyson (1809–1892). Stylistically, her images recall artists as diverse as Rembrandt and Perugino, Raphael's teacher.

Sister Spirits reflects the impact of the Aesthetic Movement, less the paintings of Whistler, such as *Symphony in White No. II* (fig. 25.10), than those of Rossetti, as seen in his images of sensual, yearning women in religious robes. The scene in Cameron's photograph evokes a spiritual late medieval or early Renaissance past. The women look as though they have stepped out of a quattrocento painting and suggest such saints as Mary and Anne; the two children look like angels, and the sleeping child like the Christ Child. One can also view the picture as the three ages of woman, since the title suggests that the baby is most likely female. Cameron's blurred foreground is more than just a gimmick to give the image a painterly touch. It also carries psychological and symbolic meaning, for by dissolving the flowers and baby, leaving them unformed, Cameron makes the focused women consciously aware of the undetermined fate of the sleeping infant. Concern, pensiveness, and questioning are registered on the faces, and we sense a spiritual female bonding in this tight grouping of figures, who are closed off in the background as the image again goes out of focus. While the picture has sensual elements, it does not present women as objects meant for a male viewer, nor as appendages to a male world. Instead it reflects a powerful female vision as it embraces a female spirituality.

Cameron was generally criticized not only for her blurry images, which were attributed to incompetence, but also for just making photographs. As a female photographer in a sexist society, she found it difficult getting men to pose for her. She was criticized for exhibiting, which was a rare event for respectable British women in the Victorian era, and she was admonished for selling her photographs through a major London print dealer because it was deemed inappropriate for women to earn money. By redefining focus, Cameron challenged not only what was becoming the normative approach to photographic vision but also a vocation that was specifically male. Ironically, by the end of the century, men adopted her vision.

Architecture and the Industrial Revolution

Iron was another product of the Industrial Revolution, and its relationship to architecture was as nebulous as that of photography to fine art. Initially, in the late eighteenth and early nineteenth centuries, iron was used for civil engineering, in such projects as bridges and factories. Soon, it was used for the columns in textile factories and by 1796–97 for an entire internal structure. Revival styles continued

to dominate architecture up to the closing decades of the nineteenth century, but the use of iron, while quite limited, freed buildings and civic structures from historicism because form (design) was now determined by the material and by engineering principles, thus setting the stage for the advent of modern architecture in Chicago in the 1880s, as we shall see in the next chapter. The pragmatism of iron construction and the blunt presentation of the medium's structural properties parallel the pragmatism and realism of the Age of Positivism.

Ferrovitreous Structures: Train Sheds and Exhibition Palaces

In the early nineteenth century, builders often used cast iron for the columns of Gothic Revival churches, and in the 1830s, with the rise of railroads, they employed it for train sheds as well. The sheds had to span parallel tracks and platforms and be high enough to allow steam and smoke to dissipate. The cast-iron skeleton supported a roof of

25.16 Julia Margaret Cameron. *Sister Spirits*. ca. 1865. Albumen print, 12$^{7}/_{16}$ × 10$^{1}/_{2}$″ (31.6 × 26.6 cm). George Eastman House, Rochester, New York. Gift of Eastman Kodak Company

25.17 Sir Joseph Paxton.
The Crystal Palace, London. 1851;
reerected in Sydenham 1852,
as shown here; destroyed by
fire 1936

25.17 Sir Joseph Paxton.
The Crystal Palace, London. 1851;
reerected in Sydenham 1852,
as shown here; destroyed by
fire 1936

25.18 Gustave Eiffel. Eiffel
Tower. 1887–89. Paris

 Explore the architectural
panoramas of the Eiffel
Tower on myartslab.com

31 Mars 1889

glass, and this combination of iron and glass is often called ferrovitreous.

Perhaps the most famous ferrovitreous building of the nineteenth century is the Crystal Palace (**fig. 25.17**), built in London in 1851 to house the first great international trade fair, the Great Exhibition of the Works of Industry of All Nations. The exposition was not just a trade fair but a celebration of Western industrialization. England's preeminent greenhouse architect, Sir Joseph Paxton (1801–1865), designed the building and with engineers erected what was essentially a giant greenhouse. While the ferrovitreous materials were the same as in Paxton's earlier greenhouses, the form was not, for it resembled an English cathedral, with a long, barrel-vaulted center nave, a lower barrel-vaulted transept, and stepped-down side aisles. (After the exhibition closed, the structure was dismantled and moved to Sydenham in South London, where another transept was added. It later burned down.) The building was a cathedral of industry, which had become the new religion.

Announcing the Future: The Eiffel Tower

The most famous iron structure from the period is the Eiffel Tower (**fig. 25.18**), erected by the French engineer Gustave Eiffel (1832–1923) in 1887–89 as an entrance to the 1889 Paris International Exposition. To create his tower, Eiffel basically appropriated a **trussed pylon** from the many bridges he had already constructed. At 984 feet (300 meters) high, twice the height of any other structure then in the world, it dominated the city, and because its design was largely due to its structural integrity and not to a standard architectural style, it initially affronted the Parisians, who declared it an eyesore. The lacework tower was so thin that it looked fragile and unstable, and Eiffel added arches at the base and organic decoration on the two platforms (removed in the 1930s) to make visitors more comfortable with his radical, visionary structure. The tower anticipated the Modernist architecture of the next century, one that would shed historical references and instead allow style to reflect the nature and geometry of the new building materials.

POINTS OF REFLECTION

25.1 How does Gustave Courbet's *Burial at Ornans* reflect the Age of Positivism, and why did so many visitors to the Salon of 1848 find the work to be so radical and offensive? How did it abandon most of the basic premises of Romanticism, which can be seen, for example, in Eugène Delacroix's *The Massacre at Chios*?

25.2 The Realism in Édouard Manet's *Luncheon on the Grass* and Edgar Degas's *The Orchestra of the Paris Opéra* is very different from that found in William Holman Hunt's *The Awakening Conscience*. How do these works reflect the differences between French and British Realism?

25.3 How does Monet's approach to nature and Realism as seen in *On the Banks of the Seine, Bennecourt* differ from Courbet's Realism in *Burial at Ornans* and Manet's in *Luncheon on the Grass*? What doubts about the Impressionist style are seen in such works as Renoir's *Luncheon of the Boating Party* and Mary Cassatt's *The Child's Bath*?

25.4 How do Timothy O'Sullivan's *A Harvest of Death, Gettysburg* and Julia Margaret Cameron's *Sister Spirits* reflect two very different approaches to photography? What social issues does each image reflect?

25.5 The Crystal Palace and the Eiffel Tower are often identified as two major icons that led to the rise of modern architecture. How do they anticipate modern architecture, and how are they different from such Revival-style buildings as the Houses of Parliament or the University of Virginia?

✓—**Study** and review on myartslab.com

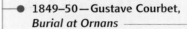

CHAPTER 26

Progress and Its Discontents: Post-Impressionism, Symbolism, and Art Nouveau, 1880–1905

POINTS OF INQUIRY

26.1 Describe the modernity that emerged in the closing decades of the nineteenth century, the many complex issues surrounding it, and the broad impact that modernity had on avant-garde art.

26.2 Discuss the different ways American and European modern architecture of this period both broke away from the previously dominant revival styles and also was spiritual, thus sharing some of the concerns of the Post-Impressionists and Symbolists.

26.3 Identify the qualities that the Post-Impressionists and Symbolists took from the Impressionists, and the qualities they abandoned or rejected.

26.4 Explain why fine art photographers were so preoccupied with establishing their medium as a major art form, and how their work reflects the same issues found in painting, sculpture, and architecture of the late nineteenth/early twentieth century.

((•—[**Listen** to the chapter audio on myartslab.com

The closing decades of the nineteenth century presented a cultural dichotomy. On one side were those who optimistically reveled in the wealth, luxury, and technological progress of the industrialized world. On the other were those who perceived these same qualities as signs of decadence, excess, and moral turpitude. The former experienced exuberance and pride, the latter despair and anxiety. Depending on one's viewpoint, the period was either La Belle Époque, "the beautiful era," or La Fin de Siècle, "the end of the century."

The close of the century, as well as the 14 years leading up to World War I in the twentieth, indeed constituted a period of unprecedented economic growth and prosperity, nurtured by virtually 40 years of peace following the 1870 Franco-Prussian War. National consolidation was largely complete, with many countries functioning as republics.

Germany and France joined Britain and Belgium as truly industrialized nations, with Germany producing twice as much steel as Britain by 1914. The United States was included as well in this exclusive group. Spurred by both capitalism and a heated nationalism was a dramatic increase in imperialism, which resulted in the carving up of Africa as well as parts of Asia and the Pacific islands into fiefdoms to be economically exploited.

The modern era, which began in the eighteenth century, now evolved into a new phase called modernity, often labeled the "New Industrial Revolution." The steam engine was refined and improved. Electricity, the telephone, the internal combustion engine, automobiles, submarines, airplanes, oil, moving pictures, and machines increasingly defined modern life, whose pace quickened even as it became more comfortable and efficient.

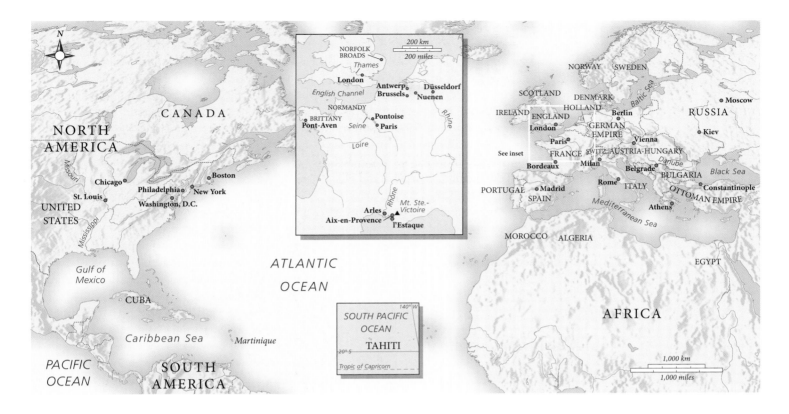

In 1901, Guglielmo Marconi sent a wireless signal across the Atlantic, further shrinking the globe.

These accomplishments resulted in a dramatic increase in a European sense of superiority. Many cultural anthropologists, however, refused to label any society as better than any other, and found tribal societies to be just as complex as Western civilization. The mores and values of any culture, they argued, were appropriate to its environment and circumstances. Those Europeans who lamented industrialization and who were suspicious of unchecked progress perceived the newly colonized, exploited territories as unspoiled utopias, havens from the materialistic evils of modern civilization. Continuing the tradition launched by Jean-Jacques Rousseau in the eighteenth century (see page 463), they viewed these so-called primitive societies as still steeped in Nature and thus virtuous and pure, as well as connected to universal spiritual forces.

Also arising in the late nineteenth century in reaction to modernity was a renewed search for the spiritual, with a growing number of people fleeing progress by embracing an intense spirituality. People were drawn to orthodox Western religions as well as to Eastern-inspired practices such as Theosophy. Many were also drawn to animism and the occult.

The late nineteenth century marks the rise of psychology. The German physiologist Wilhelm Wundt (1832–1920) transformed psychology from a philosophy to a natural science by basing it on scientific method, while the research of the Russian Ivan Pavlov (1849–1936) sparked an intense interest in how human behavior is conditioned by experience and environment. And in Vienna, the neurologist Sigmund Freud (see page 551) began to formulate his theories of the unconscious, publishing his *Interpretation of Dreams* in 1900. This interest in the mind and the elemental forces driving human responses went well beyond science to permeate popular and high culture, and artists as diverse as Auguste Rodin and Edvard Munch increasingly focused on the unseen forces residing deep within the unconscious that produced such outward manifestations as sexual urges and anxiety.

In many respects progress was the watchword of the late nineteenth century, and the force to which some artists responded. The vast majority, however, rejected it, seeking a spiritual, utopian, or primitive alternative. The result was a range of styles or movements, chief among them Post-Impressionism, Symbolism, and Art Nouveau. Most of the artists built on the brilliant formal innovations of Manet and the Impressionists and created work that was more abstract than representational.

Map 26.1 Europe and North America 1904–14

Their art was also highly personal, not reflecting a group vision. Consequently many artists, such as Vincent van Gogh and Paul Cézanne, cultivated their own distinctive form of mark making. Often their work was visionary, depicting fantasies and dream worlds, and often it was spiritual, as it sought relief from the crass, empty materialism of modernity and a more meaningful explanation for existence. Many artists found their subject matter in the sanctuary of the classical, medieval, and biblical past, which the Realists had so fiercely rejected. Even modern architecture indulged in fantasy and spirituality. While Realism and Impressionism had sought to capture the essence of the modern world, Post-Impressionism, Symbolism, and Art Nouveau largely struggled to escape it and provide an antidote.

Post-Impressionism

The early twentieth-century British art critic Roger Fry coined the term Post-Impressionism to describe the avant-garde art that followed Impressionism, work that became a springboard to take art in new directions. Each of the four major Post-Impressionist artists—Paul Cézanne, Georges Seurat, Vincent van Gogh, and Paul Gauguin—developed a unique style. Still, there are artistic conditions that unify the period from 1880 to 1905. The Post-Impressionists rejected the empiricism of Realism and Impressionism in order to create art that was more monumental, universal, and even visionary. The Post-Impressionists also rejected a collective way of seeing, which we saw in Impressionism; instead, each artist developed a personal aesthetic. Like the Impressionists, however, many Post-Impressionists continued to mine Japanese art for aesthetic ideas. They also maintained the antibourgeois, antiacademic attitude of the Impressionists, similarly turning to artists' cooperatives and private galleries to promote their art.

Paul Cézanne: Toward Abstraction

Cézanne (1839–1906) is actually the same generation as the Impressionists, developing his Post-Impressionism in tandem with their art. Born into a wealthy but socially isolated family in Aix-en-Provence in southern France, he went to Paris to study art in 1861. He enrolled at a drawing academy, but was essentially self-taught, copying paintings in the Louvre by Delacroix and Courbet,

among others, and developing dark, emotional, painterly work. His mature style began to evolve in 1872, when he started looking at Impressionism. The emotionalism of his early work dissipated, his palette lightened, even becoming colorful, and his compositions took on a powerful structural integrity, which had been suggested in his earlier work but now blossomed. As he would state later in life, he wanted "to make of Impressionism something solid, like the art in the museums."

We can see how Cézanne achieved this goal in a work from the next decade, *Mont Sainte-Victoire* (**fig. 26.1**), painted around 1885–87 in Provence, where he would spend the remainder of his life. Typical of Impressionism, this canvas presents a light-filled landscape painted with broad brushstrokes and fairly bright color. The picture seems to shimmer at first, then it freezes. Cézanne has locked his image into a subtle network of shapes that echo one another. The curves and bends of the foreground branches can be found in the distant mountain and foothills. The diagonal lines on the edges of the green pastures reverberate in the houses, mountain slopes, and the directionality of the clusters of parallel dashlike brushstrokes, perhaps best seen in the green pine needles. Just as the building to the right of the tree has a solid cubic presence, combinations of contiguous flat green pastures and ocher fields cause blocklike forms to emerge from the earth, before they dissolve once again in thin planes of color. A fair number of vertical stresses, often quite minute, are tucked into the landscape and play off strong horizontals to suggest an underlying grid.

Many aspects of the picture can be read in two diametrically opposed ways. There is an Impressionistic flicker, but a structurally frozen image. The picture is a deep panoramic view, and yet it is also flat and compressed, for the distant sky sits on the same plane as the foreground tree branches. This conflation is in part due to the tapestry of aligned, off-white brushstrokes that seem simultaneously to encase the pine needles and be woven into the sky. Every brushstroke sits on the canvas as a flat mark asserting the surface; and yet the strokes overlap one another, causing a sense of space or depth to exist between them. Even line has a dual function, for it can be read as shadow, as on the top of the mountain, making depth happen, or it can be seen as flat contour line. There is a conflict between representation and abstraction, for while the picture obviously depicts a real world, we are never

allowed to forget that we are looking at flat paint, lines, and patches of color applied to a flat canvas. We can sense the enormous amount of time that went into resolving all of these conflicts and achieving a balance of two- and three-dimensional space. Most pictures took Cézanne years to paint as he meticulously pondered every mark.

In the succeeding decades, Cézanne's art became increasingly abstract and the space from foreground to background even more compressed. With Cézanne, we meet the painter most responsible for freeing the medium from a representational role and giving artists license to invent images that instead adhered to painting's own inherent laws. The Paris gallery Durand-Ruel began exhibiting Cézanne in the late 1890s, and the public exposure had a powerful influence on other artists, especially Pablo Picasso and Henri Matisse.

Georges Seurat: Seeking Social and Pictorial Harmony

Like Cézanne, Georges Seurat (1859–1891) wanted to make of Impressionism something more like the great art of the past. He studied briefly in 1878 at the École des Beaux-Arts with a follower of Ingres, and after a year of compulsory military service in Brittany in northwest France returned to Paris, where he spent the rest of his short life. He set up a studio, and in 1884 he unveiled his new style with a large picture called *A Bathing Place, Asnières*, which depicts a group of workers swimming in the Seine in a working-class suburb of Paris, not far from where Seurat grew up. The picture, refused at the Salon, was shown in 1884 at the first exhibition of the Independent Artists, a new artists' cooperative whose shows were unjuried, like those of the Impressionists' Artists, Inc. Seurat next participated

26.1 Paul Cézanne. *Mont Sainte-Victoire*. ca. 1885–87. Oil on canvas, 25½ × 32″ (64.8 × 92.3 cm). Courtauld Institute of Art Gallery, London. The Samuel Courtauld Trust

Watch a video about Paul Cézanne's *Mont Sainte-Victoire* on myartslab.com

in what would be the last Impressionist exhibition, in 1886, submitting *A Sunday Afternoon on the Island of La Grande Jatte* (**fig. 26.2**). The dates of the two shows are significant, for they mark the end of the Impressionist era and the rise of Post-Impressionism.

La Grande Jatte's roots in the realism of Manet and in Monet's impressionistic canvases are obvious, since it is a scene of the lower and middle class taking its Sunday leisure on a sunny, color-filled afternoon. The painting presents a compendium of types that contemporaries would have easily recognized, such as the courtesan, shown walking a monkey, and the boatman, who is the sleeveless man smoking a pipe in the left corner. (Seurat's cataloguing of types extends to the dogs in the foreground and boats on the Seine.) Seurat renders his figures as icons, for each is silhouetted in profile, frontally, or in three-quarter view, following the prescription of the famous Roman architect Vitruvius for the arrangement of sculptural figures on temples.

Seurat declared that he wanted "to make the moderns file past like figures on Pheidias' Pan-Athenaic Frieze on the Parthenon, in their essential form...." And this was no idle claim. The 6- by 10-foot canvas was meant to function on the scale of great history painting and to be seen in the tradition of Poussin and David. Like a history painter, Seurat made detailed studies for every component of his work, even making a painting of the landscape alone, before the insertion of the figures, like a stage set.

Despite thematic similarities, Seurat's agenda was quite different from that of Manet, Degas, or Monet, for example. Instead of an objective presentation of his scene, his goal was to create a utopian present, a poetic vision dedicated to showing middle- and working-class tranquility and leisure. His religion was not just classicism, but also science. Familiar with the color theory of the American physicist Ogden Rood, he believed that colors were more intense when mixed optically by the eye rather than on the palette. Consequently,

26.2 Georges Seurat. *A Sunday Afternoon on the Island of La Grande Jatte*. 1884–86. Oil on canvas, 6'10" × 10'1¼" (2.08 × 3.08 m). The Art Institute of Chicago. Helen Birch Bartlett Memorial Collection. 1926.224

 View the Closer Look for *A Sunday Afternoon on the Island of La Grande Jatte* on myartslab.com

he worked by putting small dots of color next to one another, believing that the eye would then mix these colors together, the color thus stronger than if mixed on the palette. Actually, this optical mixing was not true. It does not matter, however, that he misinterpreted Rood. Seurat believed his colors were more luminous than the Impressionists', and certainly his technique, which he called "Chromoluminarism" and experts later labeled "Pointillism" or "Divisionism," created a uniform, if vibrant, surface that was a systematized Impressionism. Like the figures, the regularized dot surface of Seurat's pictures seems mechanical, as though the subjective hand–eye reaction of the Impressionists has been replaced by a machine capable of recording color and light with uniform dots of paint.

In his review of the Impressionist show, the critic Félix Fénéon labeled Seurat's style Neo-Impressionism, the "New Impressionism," and before the decade was out, it had an army of practitioners who were attracted to its scientific approach, monumentality, and modern look. Many of them worked well into the twentieth century. As distinctive as the technique is, it would be a mistake to emphasize it at the expense of the meaning of the art. Seurat was a socialist sympathizer, and his socialist vision of a harmonious, perfect world and belief in science as the force to achieve this characterize his method. This passionate faith in science, technology, and machines as the tools to attain progress and equality would be shared by later generations of artists, as we shall see in the following chapters.

Vincent van Gogh: Expression through Color and Symbol

Before becoming a painter, the Dutch artist Vincent van Gogh (1853–1890) had tried his hand at preaching and teaching. Drawn to these vocations by his desire for a life both spiritually fulfilling and socially useful, Van Gogh determined that art alone could provide access to the ideal world he

26.3 Vincent van Gogh. *Starry Night*. 1889. Oil on canvas, 28¾ × 36¼" (73 × 93 cm). Museum of Modern Art, New York. Acquired through the Lillie P. Bliss Bequest (472.1941)

sought. After receiving rudimentary art training, he spent the years 1883–85 painting at the family's vicarage (his father was a pastor) in the village of Nuenen in Holland, where he was deeply affected by the dignity, spirituality, and stolid sturdiness of the impoverished peasants, and made dark, earthy, expressionist paintings heavily influenced by Rembrandt. He then briefly enrolled at the Academy of Fine Arts in Antwerp, where he studied Rubens's paintings and collected Japanese prints. Unhappy in Belgium, Van Gogh went to Paris to be with his brother, Theo, who handled the contemporary painting department at an art gallery. Here, from 1886 to 1888, he experienced Impressionism and Neo-Impressionism at first hand, consuming their lessons with the same fervor that he applied to everything else and developing a bright palette to add to the bold brushwork of his earlier period. He soon started hounding fellow painters to join him in setting up an artists' commune in the sun drenched south of France, a "Studio of the South" that he envisioned as an Occidental Japan.

Only Paul Gauguin acquiesced in this dream, although he lasted but two months. Alone in Arles, Van Gogh thrived in the Provençal landscape, fiercely generating from 1888 to 1889 his strongest body of work. His intense, uncontrollable emotions took over and his painting became increasingly expressionistic, using color to convey emotion rather than to document reality and employing a personal symbolic vocabulary. The personality that prevailed in the majority of Van Gogh's pictures from this time belongs to the secular evangelist who celebrated all life and longed for universal harmony.

This can be seen in *Starry Night* (**fig. 26.3**). Here we see, snugly ensconced in a valley, the inviting hearth-lit homes of plain rural folk. The yellow glow from their rectangular windows unites them with yellow round stars in the universe above, their contrasting shapes a YIN and YANG of elemental harmony. An upwardly spiraling cypress tree filled with life dominates the foreground. It parallels the church steeple, and both penetrate the fiery, star-filled sky, linking earth with the transcendental. The sky is alight with spectacular cosmic fireworks—haloes of stars and joyous tumbling clouds echo the undulation of the mountains and trees below. Harnessing his expressionistic vocabulary, Van Gogh painted the primitive world and utopia he dreamed of: The peaceful tranquility of simple, unpretentious people, nurtured by Nature and in

harmony with universal forces. Yet, despite his frenetic output and his humanitarian yearnings, he was a deeply troubled and depressed man. Within a year of painting *Starry Night*, he died from what many believed to be a self-inflicted gunshot wound.

Paul Gauguin: The Flight from Modernity

Paul Gauguin (1848–1903), the fourth of the major Post-Impressionists, shared Van Gogh's distaste for advanced civilization and likewise yearned for a utopian alternative. His abandonment of society, however, was perhaps the most radical of any artist of his time. A stockbroker, he was attracted to art, collected the Impressionists, and by the early 1870s had taken up painting himself. He lost his job in 1882 and began to paint full-time. He studied with his friend, the Impressionist Camille Pissarro, who introduced him to the work of Cézanne, and participated in the last four Impressionist exhibitions between 1881 and 1886. In the latter year, he abandoned Paris to begin a nomadic search for a more meaningful existence, which he believed could be found in a simpler society steeped in nature. He went first to the village of Pont-Aven, a remote, rural community in Brittany, where locals wore a distinctive regional costume and displayed an intense, charismatic piety.

After briefly leaving Brittany for the Caribbean island of Martinique in 1887, Gauguin returned to Pont-Aven, where he painted with a colleague, Émile Bernard. Together they developed a style they called **Synthetism**, a reference to their synthetic production—the combining of flat planes of abstract color and line to express emotions and ideas—as opposed to trying to replicate on canvas what they saw in the real world. In their search to produce an authentic, direct art, as free of civilized influences as possible, they turned to a variety of vernacular and primitive sources, including crude popular illustrations (especially religious) and folk, children's, and medieval art. They were also attracted to such archaic styles as fourteenth-century Italian painting and both Egyptian and Mesopotamian art. Especially appealing were medieval stained-glass windows, because of their spiritual function and saturated colors, and cloisonné enamels, which similarly use curvilinear metal dividers to separate areas of flat color.

All of these qualities can be found in Gauguin's Tahitian work. Despite its provincial charm and distance from Paris, Brittany for Gauguin was geographically far too close to modern civilization

In Chinese philosophy, YIN and YANG are complementary energies: Yang is bright, assertive, and male, while yin is dark, receptive, and female.

and its decadent materialism and artificial social conventions. In 1891, he left for the French colony of Tahiti in the South Pacific, convinced that on this remote island he would find Jean-Jacques Rousseau's "noble savage," an elemental, innocent human, a "primitive" steeped in nature and in harmony with the universe. He expected to live in a tropical Garden of Eden, uncovering the most basic truths about human existence. And a Garden of Eden is what he depicts in *Where Do We Come From? What Are We? Where Are We Going?* (**fig. 26.4**) of 1897–98. Fruit hangs from the trees for the picking, while a statue of a god oversees the welfare of the islanders, bestowing blessings and an intense spirituality on every aspect of daily life, as he points to Heaven and the afterlife. The tropical landscape is dense, lush, and sensuous, an abstract tapestry of deeply saturated, flat, curvilinear forms in which everything seems as if gently floating. Here life is languorous and untroubled, and time has stopped.

As the title suggests, the painting represents the three stages of life seen in Renaissance art; birth is pictured on the right, youth in the center, and old age at the far left. The center figure is obviously a Tahitian Eve. The statue of the deity is a composite of the Tahitian goddess Hina, a Javanese Buddha, and an Easter Island megalith. Torsos are twisted so that they resemble Egyptian figures, and the bright gold upper corners with title and signature recall Byzantine and early Renaissance icons. The old woman on the left is derived from a Peruvian mummy that Gauguin saw at a Paris ethnological museum. Pervading the image is the spirituality and look of medieval stained glass and cloisonné, as well as the bold forms and colors of Japanese prints. The entire painting is a remarkable synthesis of cultures, religions, and periods, testifying to Gauguin's desire to portray the elemental mythic forces underlying all humanity and his belief that the renewal of Western art and civilization as a whole must come from outside its traditions.

Symbolism

Although Gauguin devised the label Synthetism to describe his art, he was soon heralded as a Symbolist. Symbolism was a literary movement announced in a manifesto issued by the poet Jean Moréas (1856–1910) in the newspaper *Figaro Littéraire* in 1886. Another poet, Gustave Kahn, succinctly encapsulated the movement's essence when he wrote shortly after Moréas that the writer's goal was to "objectify the subjective … instead of subjectifying the objective," meaning that the everyday, contemporary world was rejected, replaced by one of dreams that abstractly expressed sensations, moods, and deep-seated fears and desires. The label was soon extended to art, and Gauguin's name always topped anyone's list of important Symbolists. Van Gogh, with his expressionist fantasies, was considered a Symbolist as well.

The Nabis

Gauguin's impact was tremendous, and by the 1890s, flat, curvilinear, organic patterning was ubiquitous. Gauguin was the formative influence on the Nabis, a secret organization founded in 1888

26.4 Paul Gauguin. *Where Do We Come From? What Are We? Where Are We Going?* 1897–98. Oil on canvas, 4′5¾″ × 12′3½″ (1.39 × 3.74 m). Museum of Fine Arts, Boston. Tompkins Collection, Arthur Gordon Tompkins Fund, 36.270

 Read the document related to Paul Gauguin on myartslab.com

Nineteenth-century THEOSOPHY originated with the Theosophical Society, founded in New York in 1875 by the Russian *émigrée*, occultist, medium, and mystic, Madame Helena Blavatsky. The Theosophical Society basically claimed that all religions were essentially the same and sought to reveal the mystical connectedness of all things.

by young Parisian artists, including Édouard Vuillard and Pierre Bonnard, who were stunned by the novelty and spirituality of Gauguin's Pont-Aven paintings. *Nabi* is Hebrew for "prophet," and as the name suggests, the members immersed themselves in religion, which was perhaps an easier way to flee modernity than by going into voluntary exile in Tahiti.

The group's spiritual interests were extremely broad and included the occult and the supernatural, concerns sweeping Europe and America at the time as people sought refuge from the blunt materialism of modernity. Besides Near and Far Eastern religions, many of the Nabis were taken up by the craze then current for THEOSOPHY and Rosicrucianism. Like Gauguin, whose *Where Do We Come From?* attempted to give pictorial form to a synthesis of diverse spiritual and cultural influences, the Nabis sought to convey Theosophical mysticism through their art. But instead of seeking transcendent imagery in far-off places, Vuillard and Bonnard

turned to scenes of domestic life, leisure activities, and views of their native French landscape.

Although the Nabis as a group lost momentum in the later 1890s, Édouard Vuillard (1868–1940) and Pierre Bonnard (1867–1947) developed into prominent artists. Abandoning the group's religious thrust, they retained its emphasis on emotion expressed through abstraction. Reality dissolving into an abstraction of meditative calm can be seen in Vuillard's small, intimate oil of 1893, *The Suitor* (**fig. 26.5**). Here we see the artist's favorite theme, interiors, which are magical, not mundane. He presents his dressmaker mother, his sister, and her husband, a respected painter and member of the Nabis. The real world disappears into a poetry of paint. Lush, dappled brushwork and a subdued but rich palette create a tranquil, sensuous mood. Tables, chairs, figures, and bolts of fabric are two-dimensional ghosts floating in an enchanting sea of paint, color, and form that embodies the sweet intimacy and languid pace of bourgeois domesticity.

Other Symbolist Visions in France

Several artists predating Symbolism were embraced by the movement, especially Gustave Moreau, who emerged in the 1860s. He, along with a second artist, Odilon Redon, gained notoriety when they were featured in Joris-Karl Huysmans's Symbolist novel *À Rebours* (*Against Nature*) of 1884. Huysmans's protagonist is a jaded eccentric who retreats into a strange dream world, a lavish house filled with such surreal items as a tortoise with a jewel-encrusted shell, and artworks by Moreau and Redon.

GUSTAVE MOREAU   The imagery of Gustave Moreau (1826–1898) combined exotic Romantic motifs with an unsettling, mysterious psychology set in a supernatural world. In his large watercolor *The Apparition* (**fig. 26.6**) of about 1876, the biblical Salome is presented with the head of St. John the Baptist, as she requested. But instead of appearing on a plate, as is traditional, the head, gushing blood and encased in a bright halo, magically levitates. We see a bold confrontation between good and evil and between the sexes, since it was Salome's physical lust that resulted in John's beheading—if she could not have him in life, then she would in death. The setting and costumes are vaguely Oriental, and the vast hall dazzles with imperial opulence. Flowers, clothing, columns, and walls are created with minute, gemlike brushstrokes that are reminiscent of Delacroix and make everything sparkle. In Moreau's hands the story of Salome is not simply illustrated, but becomes a macabre hallucination of sex and death, presented through a dazzling haze of jewel-like marks and a strange, smoldering light.

Symbolism Beyond France

Strange dreamlike imagery was not unique to Paris. By the late 1880s, a Symbolist otherworldly aesthetic of fantasy, escapism, and psychology could be found throughout the Western world.

26.6 Gustave Moreau. *The Apparition* (*Dance of Salome*). ca. 1876. Watercolor, 41¾ × 28⅜" (106 × 72 cm). Musée du Louvre, Paris

26.7 Edvard Munch. *The Scream*. 1893. Tempera and casein on cardboard, 36 × 29″ (91.4 × 73.7 cm). The National Museum of Art, Architecture and Design, Oslo

had moved to Berlin. Clasping hands to a skull-like head, a grotesquely compressed, writhing figure gives voice to a base fear that appears funneled into it from the oozing, hysterical landscape behind. The violent perspective of the uptilted walkway and the Van Gogh-like brushwork elevate the hysteria to a frightening fever-pitch. The scene was perhaps in part prompted by the 1883 eruption of the Indonesian volcano Krakatoa, which was so violent that it generated the loudest sound heard by any human (the soundwaves traveled 1,500 miles) and spewed forth ashes that circled the globe, immersing Europe in frightening blood-red or blue sunsets for some six months. After witnessing such an apocalyptic display of color in Christiania (now Oslo), Munch, already in a melancholic mood, wrote in his diary, "… I sensed a great, infinite scream pass through nature."

AUBREY BEARDSLEY While a morbid, fear-of-the-infinite psychology appears in much of Munch's work, perhaps his most prevalent subject is the

26.8 Aubrey Beardsley. *Salomé*. 1892. Pen drawing, 11 × 6″ (27.8 × 15.2 cm). Private collection

EDVARD MUNCH Much Symbolist painting was influenced by Gauguin's mysterious, sinuous patterning and abstraction as well as by a quest to explore visually the most elemental psychological forces underlying modern civilization. Perhaps no one did this better than the Norwegian painter Edvard Munch (1863–1944), whose style matured in the early 1890s after he spent time in Paris. There he experienced first-hand Gauguin's Pont-Aven paintings and the intense brushwork and color of Van Gogh's Arles pictures. Munch's themes were similar to those of his Scandinavian friends, the playwrights Henrik Ibsen and August Strindberg, whose investigations of sexuality and inquiries into the meaning of existence plumbed the deepest recesses of the mind to tap into primordial forces.

Munch crafts an image of horrifying anxiety in *The Scream* (**fig. 26.7**), painted in 1893 after he

uncontrollable yearnings of the libido, along with the sexual conflict it produces, especially as expressed by the femme fatale (fatally attractive woman). In part, this theme reflects the increased interest in psychology emerging at the time. But it is also a product of the rise of worldwide movements that appeared toward mid-century demanding greater rights and freedoms for women. In America, for example, it gave rise to the "New Woman," an athletic, independent female who went out in public by herself, attended college, and even went so far as to wear male-style clothing. Most men found these liberated women threatening, set on overturning their male-dominated society. Often, artists and writers alike reflected this fear in the femme fatale theme, which became prevalent at the turn of the century.

One of the most famous examples of the theme is Oscar Wilde's French play *Salomé*, which launched a vogue for Salome images. One example (**fig. 26.8**) is by the British illustrator Aubrey Beardsley (1872–1898), which was commissioned for the play's publication in 1894. Salome possessively holds John's severed head, which although dead still projects disdain. His snakelike hair and her octopus coif transform each into an irrational Medusa driven by a base hatred. John's blood drips into a black pool of phallic plants that, like an insidious vine, slither around Salome. Their nightmarish confrontation takes place in an abstract world of curvilinear elegance, one so precious that the line virtually disappears at times as it twists in a sultry rhythm. As we shall shortly see, this tendril-like quality is characteristic of Art Nouveau (see page 542), an architectural and decorative arts style that emerged in the 1890s.

GUSTAV KLIMT A fascination with organic patterns and the psychological meanings they can convey also pervades the work of Gustav Klimt (1862–1918), whose career unfolded primarily in Vienna. Beginning in 1902, Klimt made a series of paintings centering on "the kiss," the best-known version of which dates from 1907–08 (**fig. 26.9**). Although

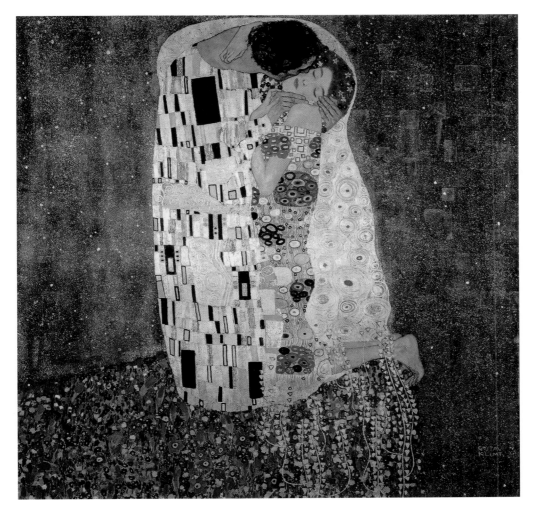

26.9 Gustav Klimt. *The Kiss*. 1907–08. Oil and gold leaf on canvas, 5′10⅞″ × 5′10⅞″ (1.8 × 1.8 m). Österreichische Nationalbibliothek, Vienna

reflecting Klimt's own personal life (the woman is his lover), the theme is Symbolist-inspired and relates directly to an 1897 painting by Munch of the same title. (In turn, both pictures were inspired by Auguste Rodin's sculpture *The Kiss*.) Munch's image presents a couple in a similarly unified form, but they are a simple dark mass, with the lovers' faces frighteningly merging as if consuming one another. Klimt's version of the theme, with its rich surface patterning, shows a faceless, lustful male losing his identity as he is lured by passion and consumed by an enticing but indifferent femme fatale, who appears about to pull him over the edge into the abyss below.

Formally inspired by the divine shimmer of Byzantine mosaics, which he studied at first hand in Ravenna, Klimt cloaks his figures in richly patterned gold-leafed robes and encases them in a halo of bright light. In his intricate designs and shifting surfaces, Klimt hints at the instability inherent in individual subjectivity and social relations. Set on a mountain carpet of wild flowers floating high above a celestial neverland, the painting simultaneously suggests the beauty and the spiritual pull of passion as well as its fleeting nature and its painful consequences.

Symbolist Currents in American Art

In the 1880s, a significant number of American artists began to make more ethereal, otherworldly

26.10 Henry Ossawa Tanner. *Angels Appearing before the Shepherds*. ca. 1910. Oil on canvas, 25¾ × 31⅞" (65.3 × 81.1 cm). Smithsonian American Art Museum. Gift of Mr. and Mrs. Norman Robins

pictures. Their imagery was more poetic and music-inspired, in many respects reflecting Whistler's aestheticism. Americans are generally not labeled Symbolists. Henry O. Tanner, for example, tends to be associated with the Realism of Thomas Eakins, reflecting his training in Philadelphia. Nonetheless, their art has the dreamlike, visionary, and spiritual qualities found in Symbolist art, and if not Symbolists per se, their art is highly influenced by the movement, to the point of sharing its spirit if not its abstract look.

HENRY O. TANNER The African-American artist Henry O. Tanner (1859–1937) fell under the spell of Symbolism in Paris. He studied in the 1880s under the liberal and supportive Thomas Eakins in Philadelphia, becoming a Realist. With little hope of achieving artistic parity in racist America, he went to Paris in 1892, where he settled permanently. There, his work began to show the influence of Symbolism as he experimented with a more abstract style and pursued new themes, even producing several Salome paintings. Tanner was the son of a preacher, and his work is dominated by religious imagery, such as *Angels Appearing before the Shepherds* (**fig. 26.10**). The composition is ingenious, for Tanner positions the viewer in the sky with the angels. From this vantage point we see the Holy Land, a breathtaking abstraction of lines and marks that nonetheless unmistakably contains hills, terraces, walls, and a city. We can even make out the shepherds' fire, the only note of color in what is otherwise a blue symphony. This spiritual blue pervades earth, sky, and angels, linking them together. Although the paint handling is rich and lush, everything in the image seems ethereal and ephemeral, the material world as transitory and weightless as the transparent angels.

The Sculpture of Rodin

The Symbolist desire to penetrate and portray the innermost essence of being had a parallel in the work of Auguste Rodin (1840–1917), the most influential sculptor of the late nineteenth century, who single-handedly laid the foundation for twentieth-century sculpture. Rodin's career started slowly: He was rejected at the École des Beaux-Arts, and was forced to attend the Petite École, which specialized in the decorative arts. His big break came in 1880, when he won a prestigious commission to design the bronze doors for a new decorative arts museum. Although the project eventually fell through, Rodin continued to work on it right up to his death. Called *The Gates of Hell* (**fig. 26.11**), the 18-foot-high doors were inspired by Charles Baudelaire's *Flowers of Evil* and Dante's *Inferno* from the *Divine Comedy*, and at one point the thinker sitting in the tympanum contemplating the chaotic, ghoulish scene below was to be Dante. Ultimately, the doors became a metaphor for the futility of life, the inability to satisfactorily fulfill our deepest uncontrollable passions, which is the fate of the sinners in Dante's second circle of hell, the circle that preoccupied Rodin the most. It is the world after the Fall, of eternal suffering, and Adam and Eve are included among the tortured souls below. Despite Rodin's devotion to the project, the work was never cast during his lifetime.

Rodin made independent sculptures from details of the *Gates*, including *The Thinker*, pondering the turmoil below, and *The Three Shades*, the group mounted at the very peak of the *Gates*, which shows the same figure merely turned in three positions. While his figures are based on familiar models—*The Thinker* (**fig. 26.12**), for example, recalls the work of Michelangelo, his favorite artist—they have an unfamiliar, organic quality. Rodin preferred to mold, not carve, working mostly in plaster or terra cotta, which artisans would then cast in bronze. We see where Rodin's hand has worked the malleable plaster with his fingers, for his surfaces undulate. His medium, instead of being smoothed out, remains intentionally rough and uneven, unlike classical sculpture. With Rodin, we

26.11 Auguste Rodin. *The Gates of Hell*. 1880–1900. Plaster, height 18 × 13 × 3′ (5.52 × 4 × 0.94 m). Musée d'Orsay, Paris

26.12 Auguste Rodin. *The Thinker*. 1879–87. Bronze, height 27½″ (69.8 cm). Musée Rodin, Paris

are made to feel privy to the creation of the figure, as if watching God making Adam out of clay. This primal quality is reinforced by his figures' nudity, which is less a classical reference than a device to present an elemental figure, a creature that has been stripped down to the very core of its humanity to expose basic fears and passions.

For the sake of expression, Rodin does not hesitate to distort his figures, shattering classical notions of idealized form and beauty. Look, for example, at *The Shades* atop the doors of the *Gates*. Their Michelangelesque musculature has been yanked and twisted, endowing these specters with a form that is at once familiar and unfamiliar. These uncanny messengers have arisen from tombs and now cast their message of eternal gloom on the teeming humanity below. We can even see this distortion to a lesser degree in *The Thinker*. Here, massive hands and feet project a ponderous weight that underscores the thinker's psychological load, while his elongated arm is draped limply over his knee, suggesting inertia and indecision. Clearly, Rodin's preoccupation with expressing elemental fears and passions related him to the Symbolist quest to plumb the depths of the mind, as did his interest in investigating the psychic toll exacted on the individual by civilization.

Art Nouveau and the Search for Modern Design

In 1895, a German entrepreneur, Siegfried Bing, opened a decorative arts shop called La Maison de l'Art Nouveau (The House of New Art) in Paris. He had made a fortune importing Japanese art and furnishings, and now sought to promote the Japanese principle of total design: Every detail of an interior space would be integrated into a single style. Aiming to eliminate any distinction between the fine and the decorative arts, he hired famous architects, artists, and designers to design not only individual products, including furniture, vases, tiles, and stained-glass windows, but also entire rooms, which were displayed in his shop. This new style was called Art Nouveau, after Bing's shop. Elsewhere in Europe it took on different names, such as Jugendstil (Youth Style) in Germany and the Secession Style in Vienna. Though varying somewhat from one country to the next, the style is usually characterized by organic forms and arabesques.

Art Nouveau can be seen as a response to William Morris's Arts and Crafts Movement, and certainly the emphasis on handcrafted, finely designed products reflects this. Important differences exist between the Arts and Crafts Movement and Art Nouveau. For instance, many Art Nouveau artists embraced mass production and new, industrial materials. Also, it is important to note that Art Nouveau designs, though clearly organic, are often purely abstract rather than based on identifiable botanical specimens, as is the case in Morris's designs.

The Public and Private Spaces of Art Nouveau

Compared with dark, ponderous Victorian interiors, the buoyant naturalism of Art Nouveau was a breath of fresh air, exuding youth, liberation, and modernity. It shared with Symbolism the element of fantasy, in this case a biomorphic fantasy (decoration based on living forms), which is especially obvious in architecture. Art Nouveau designers concerned themselves equally with exterior finish and interior space. The typically complex, animated façades endow Art Nouveau buildings with a sculptural quality that engages viewers on approach. This energetic dialogue continues in the interior, for Art Nouveau spaces pulse with a sense of movement: Interior decoration and furnishings give the impression of having germinated and grown *in situ*. This effect is often enhanced by the admission of sunlight through glass ceilings or skylights, lending the space the fecundity of a greenhouse where everything seems to have grown spontaneously.

VICTOR HORTA The first architectural exponent of the style was the Belgian architect Victor Horta (1861–1947). Born in Ghent, Horta studied drawing, textiles, and architecture there at the Académie des Beaux-Arts, and worked in Paris before returning to Belgium to start his own practice. In 1892, he designed the Tassel House in Brussels. The centerpiece of the design is the ironwork of the stairwell (**fig. 26.13**), malleable wrought-iron columns and railings easily shaped into vines that evolve into whiplash tendrils on the walls, ceiling, and mosaic floor. The supporting columns have been made as slender as possible. In a play on the Corinthian capital, they sprout ribbonlike tendrils that dissolve into arches. The linear patterns extend to the floor and wall, a device that further integrates the space visually. Sunlight filters through the glass ceiling,

heightening the organic quality of the stairwell. The curvilinear patterning derives from a variety of sources, including Japanese prints and Gauguin's cloisonnism. Everything has an organic fluidity, a springlike sense of growth and life, which has the effect of destroying the conventional boxlike quality of interior space.

ANTONI GAUDÍ Among the most bizarre Art Nouveau creations are those that sprang from the wild imagination of Antoni Gaudí (1853–1926). Gaudí worked in Barcelona, the last major stop for the short-lived style, and his work reflects the fervent nationalism of the period, drawing heavily upon Mediterranean architectural traditions. His

26.14 Antoni Gaudí. Casa Milá Apartments. 1905–10. Barcelona

remarkable Casa Milá (**fig. 26.14**), a large apartment house, expresses one person's fanatical devotion to the ideal of "natural" form, one quite different from Horta's plantlike designs. The building conjures up the Spanish Baroque, the Plateresque (indigenous Renaissance architecture suggesting elaborate silver plate), and the Moorish mosques of southern Spain. Believing that there are no straight lines in nature, Gaudí created an undulating façad and irregularly shaped interior spaces, in effect destroying the architectural box. With its huge stone blocks, the exterior evokes austere seaside cliffs, while the wrought-iron balconies resemble seaweed and the scalloped cornice mimics ocean waves. The chimneys evoke, among other things, sandcastles. These references to the seashore elicit Barcelona's distinctive geographic, cultural, and economic relationship to the Mediterranean. As the capital of Catalonia, Barcelona held a special significance for Gaudí, who supported Catalan nationalism.

American Architecture: The Chicago School

Little did anyone know that Chicago's devastating Great Fire of 1871 would launch modern architecture and make American architects for the first time the most advanced in the world. Once the flames were extinguished, the issue at hand was not just one of rebuilding. Chicago had been growing rapidly, which put a premium on real estate, and now there was a need to maximize land use by building vertically. This was made possible by the invention of the safety elevator, perfected in New York in the 1850s and 1860s by Elisha Otis. Ambitious construction was delayed for ten years, however, due to the national financial collapse of 1873, which lasted through the decade. When rebuilding finally proceeded, it was dominated by young designers, largely trained as engineers with virtually no architectural background. Unhampered therefore by strong preconceived notions of what buildings should look like, they were open to allowing their structures to reflect the new technologies and materials they employed. They abandoned the historicism of revival architecture and designed abstract structures as they allowed function to dictate form.

Louis Sullivan and Early Skyscrapers

An important influence on the rise of Chicago architecture was the advent of new technical developments. As the Chicago fire clearly demonstrated, iron is not fire resistant; intense heat makes it soften, bend, and, if hot enough, melt. To avoid towering infernos, it was necessary to fireproof the metal, cladding iron, and shortly thereafter steel (which was developed as we know it today only in the early twentieth century), with terra cotta tiles and later with a coating of concrete (modern concrete, called Portland cement, was invented in England in 1825). The insulation also prevented corrosion.

An equally important technological development was the invention of the curtain wall. Unlike a self-supporting wall, a curtain wall hangs from the lip of a horizontal I-beam. Without this innovation, the base of the wall for a tall building would have had to be extremely thick in order to support the weight of the wall above, severely limiting the number of floors. Furthermore, the curtain wall allowed for entire walls to be made of glass.

The architect generally credited with playing the main role in developing the aesthetic implications of the steel skeleton into powerful architecture is Louis Sullivan (1856–1924). His early masterpiece is the Wainwright Building (**fig. 26.15**), erected in St. Louis in 1890–91. Using the curtain wall, Sullivan designed a building that reflects the grid structure of the steel skeleton, although for aesthetic purposes he has doubled the number of external piers, with only every other one having a structural beam behind it. The major problem for the early architects of skyscrapers was how to design a building that rose so many floors, while maintaining a visually interesting exterior that did not rely on outmoded revival styles. Sullivan's solution was ingenious. He widened the end piers, thus dramatically framing the building, and he recessed the spandrels (the decorated horizontal panels between piers), giving the building a monumental sculptural quality and a sense of its evolution from a solid block. The seven-story

colossal piers and the enormous one-story cornice added to this grandeur.

While the building's exterior presented a compilation of abstract, geometric forms, largely reflecting the substructure, Sullivan did not hesitate to design terra cotta panels for the cornice and spandrels, featuring a pattern based on an antique *rinceau* motif (an ornamental vine, leaf, or floral design). These biomorphic decorations symbolized his belief that architecture should utilize new technologies to promote social harmony and progress and to be part of a natural organic evolution of the world. He believed in the mystical ideals of the eighteenth-century Swedish philosopher, theologian, and scientist Emanuel Swedenborg

26.15 Louis Sullivan. Wainwright Building, St. Louis, Missouri. 1890–91. Destroyed

 View the Closer Look for the Wainwright Building on myartslab.com

whose theory of correspondence declared that a spiritual force emanating from God flowed throughout the universe uniting all things that were otherwise unique and individual. The decoration distinguished the various parts of the building, giving each a separate identity (e.g., the upper story, the spandrels); yet at the same time, all of these distinctive parts were tightly woven together into a unified whole. The flowering plant life energized the building, reflected the vitality of the human element within, and related both to the universal current. Although he was down-to-earth, practical, and functional—it was Sullivan who issued the famous dictum that "form ever follows function"—he was also a visionary Symbolist.

Frank Lloyd Wright and the Prairie House

After studying engineering at the University of Wisconsin, Frank Lloyd Wright (1867–1959) worked for Sullivan from 1888 until 1893. His sensitivity and strengths, however, could not have differed more from Sullivan's. While his employer specialized in commercial buildings, Wright's forte was domestic architecture, although his public buildings are brilliant. Sullivan's innovations were largely in façades, whereas Wright's were in space, including

interior space and its relationship to the exterior. Wright's architecture, like Sullivan's, is based on nature, and his reputation was established with what are known as his Prairie Houses, so-called because their strong horizontal sweep echoes the planarity of the Midwest landscape where they were built.

The crowning achievement of Wright's Prairie Houses, which he began designing in the early 1890s, is the Robie House (**fig. 26.16**), designed in Chicago in 1908. The building was so shockingly modern that it would take architects a good ten to 20 years to understand it and develop its implications. As can be readily seen from the exterior, the house is an abstract play not only of horizontals and verticals, but also of open spaces and enclosed volumes. The dramatic cantilevered roofs (which are not flat as suggested by our reproduction, but slightly sloping) define one space, while the floor of the terrace, or the balcony below, charts another. The interior spaces flow into one another, for the rooms, especially communal rooms, generally do not have doors or four walls.

As abstract and geometric as the Robie House is, it resonates with nature and the organic. The house, constructed of a horizontal brick made to

26.16 Frank Lloyd Wright. Robie House. 1908–10. Chicago

Wright's specifications (the face is 1½ by 5 inches), appears perfectly integrated into the land, its lateral spread paralleling the surrounding plains. The Robie House, like many of his homes, radiates from a large masonry fireplace, which Wright saw as a domestic altar to the "gods of shelter." The rest of the house develops organically from this fulcrum, evolving much as a crystal develops or a tree grows, with one room naturally flowing into another and into the exterior, which in turn is integrated into the surrounding land. This sense of growth can be readily seen from the exterior, where the lateral spread of roofs, terraces, and balconies seems to be in constant movement. The picturesque variety of overhangs and recesses, in part inspired by Japanese buildings, creates a play of light and shadow that we do not normally associate with architecture, but rather with nature. As much as we may want to see early Wright as an abstract, machine-age thinker conceptually playing with spaces and completely breaking with tradition, his theories and sensitivity are very much of the 1890s—he still has one foot planted in the Symbolist nineteenth century that advocated a retreat from modernity into the arms of nature and its rejuvenating spiritual forces.

Photography

The primary preoccupation of photographers at the end of the century was the ongoing debate about whether photography was art. Complicating this was the dramatic increase in nonart photography. The invention of the halftone printing process was one reason for this upsurge, for it resulted in photographs being directly printed in newspapers, magazines, and books using either lithographic or relief printing. It also brought about the rise of the picture postcard, which during the height of its popularity in 1907–08 resulted in some 667 million of them being sent through the U.S. mail. Another reason for the proliferation of photographs was the invention of dry plates, which replaced the awkward and impractical wet-plate process. Now photographers could work faster and go anywhere. The process reduced exposure time to one-fiftieth of a second, and hand-held cameras with shutters were invented. Tripods were no longer necessary, and cameras could now record movement. In 1888, the Eastman Dry Plate Company of Rochester, New York, introduced the Kodak camera. It came loaded with a paper roll containing 100 frames which, once exposed, were sent back in the camera to the company for developing and printing. Also appearing about this time was the single-lens reflex camera, which had a mirror that allowed the photographer to see the image in a viewfinder. Suddenly, everyone was taking pictures, and the word "snapshot" came into common parlance. Toward 1890, there were 161 photographic societies worldwide and 60 photographic journals. The medium became so popular that newspapers had an amateur photography column.

Pictorialist Photography and the Photo Secession

To counter the image of photography as a ubiquitous, mindless, popular tool best suited for documenting the visual world, organizations sprang up dedicated to promoting the medium as high art. The first was the Wien Kamera Klub (Vienna Camera Club), founded in 1891, soon followed by the Linked Ring in London and the Photo-Club de Paris (1894). In 1902, Alfred Stieglitz quit the conservative Camera Club of New York to form the Photo Secession. All of these organizations had international membership, often with the same members, and mounted exhibitions and published magazines. And they all promoted a Pictorialist aesthetic, placing a premium on a painterly look, countering the sharp focus that characterized postcard, stereoscope, newspaper, and magazine images and the single fixed focus of the Kodak camera. Photographs by art photographers were taken out of focus, like those of Julia Margaret Cameron, whose work underwent a resurgence of interest. Pictorialist photographs were often highly textured, an effect accomplished by brushing gum onto the printing paper before exposure, or through the use of a rough, pebbly paper.

GERTRUDE KÄSEBIER   The international Pictorialists took their lead from earlier Pictorialist photographers, such as Cameron, and similarly created painterly, dreamlike images. The New Yorker Gertrude Käsebier (1852–1934) was one of the more prominent figures, becoming a member of the Linked Ring in 1900, less than five years after taking up photography, and one of the founding members of Stieglitz's Photo Secession in 1902. Fleeing a wretched marriage, she enrolled in art classes at Pratt Institute in 1889, and soon took

up the camera with the intention of making art, although she supported herself through studio portraiture. In *Blessed Art Thou Among Women* (**fig. 26.17**), an 1899 platinum print on Japanese tissue, we see Käsebier displaying all of the hallmarks of Pictorialism: A soft, grainy image, slightly off focus, with a spectacular range of lush grays that only a platinum print can provide, made all the more delicate by being printed on a gossamerlike Japanese tissue. The mother wears a white Pre-Raphaelite robe and conspicuously stands before an image of the Annunciation on the back wall. The daughter, who is about to cross the threshold to go out into the world, is encased in a mandorla-like divine light created by the brilliant white that surrounds her, especially defined by the small gap between her and her mother. The scene has a spiritual quality, set within a sanctum dedicated to maternal protection and nurturing. In a modern urban society becoming increasingly fast, fragmented, and materialistic, Käsebier creates a tranquil domestic sanctuary based on the nurturing care of a mother, as suggested by the title, a line from the Catholic prayer to the Virgin, *Hail Mary*. Käsebier's image shares with Mary Cassatt's *The Child's Bath* (see fig. 25.7) the late nineteenth-century feminist belief in the important role of women in the development of children, and with Cameron's *Sister Spirits* (see fig. 25.16) a female bonding or spiritual sisterhood designed to protect the rights and future of their gender.

26.17 Gertrude Käsebier. *Blessed Art Thou Among Women*. 1899. Platinum print on Japanese tissue, 9½ × 5¹/₁₆″ (24.2 × 14.8 cm). The Museum of Modern Art, New York. Gift of Mrs. Hermione M. Turner

26.18 Edward Steichen. *Rodin with His Sculptures "Victor Hugo" and "The Thinker."* 1902. Gum print, 14¼ × 12¾″ (36.3 × 32.4 cm). Courtesy George Eastman House. © Joanna T. Steichen

EDWARD STEICHEN Along with Käsebier and Stieglitz, Edward Steichen (1879–1973) helped to found the Photo Secession. Steichen's early contributions to this movement were painterly and moody, with tonalist, mystical qualities. His early style can be seen in his 1902 portrait *Rodin with His Sculptures "Victor Hugo" and "The Thinker"* (**fig. 26.18**), a gum print. Using the painterly effect of the gum combined with the fuzziness of the focus, he created an image that looks more handcrafted than mechanically reproduced, demonstrating that the photographer made aesthetic decisions profoundly affecting the meaning of the image. Picturing together the brooding silhouettes of Rodin and *The Thinker*, Steichen uses them to frame a brightly lit, phantomlike *Victor Hugo*, which he printed from a second negative. Clearly, Steichen identifies Rodin with *The Thinker*. One of the readings of the famous sculpture is that it is meant to represent Rodin and the daunting creative process and mental struggle behind the development of a work of art. This interpretation certainly accounts for this image, as suggested by the light striking Rodin's "brain" and the emergence of Victor Hugo as an apparition, a figment of the sculptor's imagination.

POINTS OF REFLECTION

26.1 How were Paul Gauguin, Georges Seurat, and Vincent van Gogh affected by modernity, and how is a new Western world psychology expressed in the work of Edvard Munch, Auguste Rodin, and Aubrey Beardsley?

26.2 Antoni Gaudí's Art Nouveau Casa Milá could not appear to be more different from the Chicago style of Louis Sullivan's Wainwright Building and Frank Lloyd Wright's Robie House. And yet all buildings were reacting to the same forces and reflecting the same concerns, which resulted in very different responses. What were these concerns and responses? And how do they parallel the art of such artists as Gauguin, Van Gogh, and Henry O. Tanner?

26.3 Paul Cézanne's *Mont Sainte-Victoire* and Seurat's *La Grande Jatte* rely on the stylistic developments of such artists as Édouard Manet and Claude Monet. What did they take from these artists, and what did they reject?

26.4 How do such photographic prints as Gertrude Käsebier's *Blessed Art Thou Among Women* and Edward Steichen's *Rodin with His Sculptures "Victor Hugo" and "The Thinker"* reflect the prevailing concern of fine art photographers toward the turn of the century? What issues in their work can be found in the painting and sculpture of their contemporaries?

● 1878 — First International Congress of Women's Rights, Paris

● 1882 — The Edison Illuminating Electric Company provides electricity to Lower Manhattan

● 1884 — First exhibition of the Independent Artists, Paris

● **ca. 1885–87 — Paul Cézanne, *Mont Sainte-Victoire***

● 1886 — Jean Moréas publishes a Symbolist manifesto in *Figaro Littéraire*

● ca. 1887 — High-speed elevator perfected

● 1888 — Karl Benz begins manufacturing a combustion-engine automobile in Germany

● **1892–93 — Victor Horta, Tassel House, Brussels**

● **1893 — Edvard Munch, *The Scream***

● 1895 — Siegfried Bing opens La Maison de l'Art Nouveau in Paris

● 1897 — Vienna Secession forms

● 1888 — Kodak camera introduced

● **1890–91 — Louis Sullivan, Wainwright Building**

● 1895 — Auguste and Louis Lumière invent the *cinématographe*, the first moving pictures

● 1900 — Sigmund Freud publishes *The Interpretation of Dreams*

27 | Toward Abstraction: The Modernist Revolution, 1905–1914

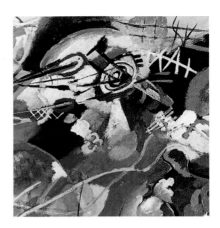

POINTS OF INQUIRY

27.1 List the new ways of perceiving, understanding, and experiencing the world that surfaced toward 1900 and the dramatic impact they had on art.

27.2 Explain why abstraction became such an appealing style for some artists in the opening decade of the twentieth century.

27.3 Describe the ways in which the German Expressionism of Die Brücke and Der Blaue Reiter differ from the Fauvism and Cubism produced in Paris.

27.4 Discuss how the architecture of Walter Gropius and Bruno Taut reflect two very different approaches to architecture, and how these contrasting approaches correspond to similar contrasting developments in painting and sculpture.

27.5 Explain why the Russian avant-garde was so heavily influenced by the Italian Futurists, and why Suprematism ultimately broke away from Futurism.

27.6 Discuss the rise of Theosophy in the late nineteenth and early twentieth centuries, its influence in the opening decades of the new century, and its impact on art.

((•—**Listen** to the chapter audio on myartslab.com

The opening decades of the twentieth century saw the continued upward march of modernity. But, as in the preceding decades, artists both embraced and fled from progress. In some instances, they even clung to tradition while they purveyed the new, which we will see in the case of Pablo Picasso and Henri Matisse, for example, two artists who successfully knitted together the new and revolutionary in style with the familiar and enduring in subject matter.

The period is marked by landmark scientific developments that artists, like the public at large, could not ignore. Max Planck (1858–1947), in 1900, proved that energy was not distinguishable from matter. He also showed that energy was emitted and absorbed in bundles called quanta, disproving the idea that it existed in a stable, uniform state. Energy and, hence, matter were in constant flux. This concept was fundamental to the discovery of radioactivity in 1902 by Ernest Rutherford (1871–1937). In 1913, the atom itself was further redefined when Niels Bohr (1885–1962) declared that it consisted of protons and neutrons, and was thus in constant movement. But the greatest amendment to classical physics was proposed by Albert Einstein (1879–1955). Einstein's revolutionary concepts appeared in a series of papers published in 1905 and 1916, and they included his Theory of Relativity, which claimed that time, space, and motion were not fixed but all relative, especially in relation to the observer's own position. The Newtonian world order, based on

Map 27.1 Europe and North America in August 1914

notions of energy and matter that remained stable, was now supplanted by a more complex and contingent notion of the universe.

Similar ideas emerged in accounts of human behavior by philosophers and psychologists. The French philosopher Henri Bergson (1859–1941) was so influential in the first years of the twentieth century that he was well known even to the general public. Bergson postulated that we experience life not as a series of continuous rational moments, but as intuited random memories and perceptions that we then piece together to form ideas. The world, therefore, was complex and fractured, or as expressed by the Harvard philosopher and psychologist William James (1842–1910), whose theories independently paralleled Bergson's, a "booming buzzing confusion." Only intuition transcended this chaos. The mind, according to Bergson, was pure energy, an *élan vital* ("vital force") that penetrated the essence of all things. While Bergson was philosophically redefining consciousness, the Austrian neurologist and founder of psychoanalysis Sigmund Freud (1856–1939) continued to refine his ideas of the unconscious through observations made during clinical practice, an approach that he felt gave his conclusions a scientific basis. Despite taking a different approach, Freud likewise developed a model of human consciousness as fragmented and conflicted.

Artists pursued similar lines of inquiry, testing traditional approaches to art making against new ideas. Their work incorporated the new vision of a fractured, constantly-in-flux world as described by scientists and psychologists and reflected in the fast pace of technological development. Some artists, such as Pablo Picasso and Georges Braque, virtually emulated scientists, treating their studios like laboratories where each creative breakthrough served as a stepping-stone to the next, as they sought to develop a new model of visual perception. Others, such as the Italian Futurists, embraced modernity and used the radical stylistic developments of Picasso and Braque to capture the technological wonders and new psychology of the modern world. Still others, however, like the German Expressionists, sought an antidote for the cold, impersonal tenor and crass materialism of modernity and tried to invest contemporary life with spirituality. Continuing Gauguin's quest to find a spiritual peace in a primitive world that was in tune with nature, many artists turned to the direct, more abstract vocabulary of tribal art as well as children's, folk, and medieval art. Many of these artists were heavily influenced by Theosophy (see page 536) and believed in the mystical interpenetration of all things, which they sought to capture in their art and architecture. For artists attempting to visualize the spiritual, the essence of which is abstract, the new stripped-down vocabulary of art was the perfect vehicle.

Fauvism

The rise of Fauvism, the first major style to emerge in the twentieth century, is part of a colorist tradition traceable through Van Gogh, Gauguin, Monet, and Delacroix back to Titian and the Venetians. The Fauves, however, took the free, expressive use of color to new heights. Van Gogh and Gauguin had the greatest impact on the Fauves, as is readily apparent in the work of Henri Matisse (1869–1954). Matisse was well aware of the aesthetic traditions with which he was wrestling. Trained in the studio of Gustave Moreau (see page 537), Matisse had received an exacting academic education at the École des Beaux-Arts. He understood his departure from tradition when, in 1905, he presented his latest pictures at the Salon d'Automne, or Autumn Salon, an important venue for vanguard artists. Strongly influenced by the Post-Impressionists' use of color

for formal and expressive ends, Matisse pushed even further the independence of color. His experiments proved too radical for some. The art critic Louis Vauxcelles was so shocked by the "orgy of pure colors" he encountered in the work of Matisse and his colleagues at the Salon d'Automne that he declared the pictures *fauves*, or wild beasts.

We can see Matisse's wild Fauve palette in his 1905–06 painting *Le Bonheur de Vivre* (*The Joy of Life*) (**fig. 27.1**). This work presents intense nonrealistic coloring, and in its artificial curvilinear patterning it reflects Matisse's awareness of Gauguin. As innovative as the color, however, is Matisse's daring suspension of logical space and scale, which increases the abstraction of the painting, a move that took him beyond both his own work and that of the Fauves of the year before. No matter how abstract and flat Matisse's earlier Fauvist pictures were, they still projected a rational progression of

27.1 Henri Matisse. *Le Bonheur de Vivre* (*The Joy of Life*). 1905–06. Oil on canvas, 5'8" × 7'9¾" (1.74 × 2.38 m). The Barnes Foundation, Merion, Pennsylvania

space. Now, that space is gone, as two enormous reclining nudes in the middle ground are as large if not larger than the pipe player and kissing couple in the foreground. Figures dissolve into one another and so do trees into sky and hills, so that it is nearly impossible to tell which sits in front of which. Reality gives way to a joyous abstract orchestration of colored lines and planes, which takes its hedonistic cue from the classical idyll of dance, passion, and music making of ancient, Renaissance, and Baroque art. But if the theme is traditional, reflecting an escape from modernity, the style is radical, reflecting the groundbreaking scientific investigations making front-page news during the period.

Cubism

The second major style to emerge in the new century was Cubism, largely under the leadership of Pablo Picasso and Georges Braque. Cubism sparked new ways of thinking about the appearance and even the purpose of art. But the journey to Cubism was a long one, starting only after both artists had fully absorbed the lessons offered by Post-Impressionism and Fauvism. Picasso was the first to push further the limits of abstraction developed by Cézanne and Matisse.

Reflecting and Shattering Tradition: *Les Demoiselles d'Avignon*

Pablo Picasso (1881–1973) was born in the Spanish town of Málaga, on the Mediterranean coast, and at age 15 he moved to Barcelona. He was soon a major figure in the city's art community, working primarily in a Symbolist style. After roughly four years of shuttling back and forth between Barcelona and Paris and leading a desperate, abject existence, he settled permanently in Paris, living in the bohemian neighborhood of Montmartre, the hill overlooking the city. This was a center for the impoverished cultural avant-garde, and Picasso quickly became part of the group's inner circle. In 1907 he shocked even his closest companions when he unveiled in his studio *Les Demoiselles d'Avignon* (*The Young Ladies of Avignon*) (**fig. 27.2**). The painting's style departed sharply from Picasso's previous work. To his contemporaries, this large, frightening picture seemed to come out of nowhere.

Of course, the painting did not emerge from an aesthetic vacuum. Among Picasso's sources were the great French history paintings of the seventeenth and eighteenth centuries, especially of classical nudes, and its large scale is meant to evoke a serious Salon picture. A more immediate influence was Matisse, for he was responding to the innovative spatial ambiguity of *The Joy of Life*, which Picasso felt compelled to upstage.

The title of the painting refers to a street in the "red-light" district in Barcelona. Preliminary studies for it show a sailor in a brothel, seated before a table with a plate of fruit and surrounded by prostitutes. The sailor is now gone, but the theme remains, for we, the viewers, are seated in his place at the table in front of the fruit, a traditional symbol of lust. Coming through the brothel curtains and staring directly at us are five of the most savage, confrontational nudes ever painted. Thematically, then, the picture began as a typical Symbolist painting about male lust and castrating women.

Instead of relying on conventional forms of pictorial narrative to tell his tale, Picasso allowed the abstract qualities of the medium to speak for him, which resulted in the creation of a new artistic language that would change the course of art. The formal qualities are threatening and violent. The space is incoherent and jarring, virtually unreadable. The entire image is composed of what looks like enormous shards of glass that overlap in no comprehensible way. Instead of receding, they hover on the surface of the picture plane, jostling each other. Sometimes the facets are shaded, as in the diamond-shaped breast of the harlot parting the curtain on the right, but Picasso has reversed the shading, in effect detaching the breast from the body. Even more incomprehensible is the seated figure below her, who has her back to us yet simultaneously faces us. The table with fruit is tilted at such a raking angle that it would shock even Cézanne, who provided the most immediate model for this spatial distortion.

The use of conflicting styles within a single picture is another disturbing quality. The three nudes to the left with their almond-shaped eyes and severe facial features were inspired by ancient sculptures from the Iberian peninsula (Spain and Portugal), which Picasso collected. But the frightening faces on the right are entirely different. At this point in the creation of the painting, Picasso's Fauve friends took him to the Trocadéro Museum of ethnographic art, where he saw African masks, providing the source for the ski-jump noses, facial scarifications, and lopsided eyes. This seems logical enough, for we know that Matisse

27.2 Pablo Picasso. *Les Demoiselles d'Avignon* (*The Young Ladies of Avignon*). 1907. Oil on canvas, 8′ × 7′8″ (2.44 × 2.34 m). The Museum of Modern Art, New York. Acquired through the Lillie P. Bliss Bequest

 View the Closer Look for *Les Demoiselles d'Avignon* (*The Young Ladies of Avignon*) on myartslab.com

was already collecting African art, and that Picasso and Matisse had known one another since 1905. Direct sources for Picasso's borrowings can be found in African sculpture, and the abstraction and frightening "barbarism" of the masks must have appealed to the artist's sensibility. Interestingly, however, Picasso, up to his death, denied having been influenced by African art in this picture, and scholars in the 1990s discovered doodles he had made of heads and bodies that anticipated his African-looking figures.

Regardless of his sources, what is most important about *Les Demoiselles* is the new freedom it announced for painting, for now line, plane, color, mass, and void were freed from their representational role to take on a life all their own. The picture laid the foundation for Analytic Cubism.

Analytic Cubism: Picasso and Braque

It may seem incredible that *Les Demoiselles* owes anything to the methodical, highly structured paintings of Cézanne, but Picasso had carefully studied

Cézanne's late work and found in his abstract treatment of volume and space the basic units from which to derive the faceted shapes of Analytic Cubism. Picasso did not arrive at this style on his own, however, and even seemed creatively stalled after *Les Demoiselles*. To help him move beyond this point, the emotional artist needed a rational interlocutor, a steadying force, someone with whom he could discuss his ideas and experiment. This intellectual partner was the French artist Georges Braque (1882–1963), who conveniently lived around the corner from him in Montmartre. From 1908 to 1910 the two fed off each other, their styles developing from a representational picture of fractured forms and space like *Les Demoiselles* to a more geometrically structured, shimmering, evanescent mirage of abstract lines and brushwork like Braque's *The Portuguese* (**fig. 27.3**) of 1911. Picasso and Braque were so intertwined that their styles began to merge by 1910.

The Portuguese is a classic example of the Analytic Cubism that had emerged in 1910. Gone are the emotional terror and chaos of *Les Demoiselles*. Braque arranged a grid of lines following the shape of the canvas and an orderly, geometric pattern of diagonal lines and curves, all recalling Cézanne's vision of a tightly structured world. Despite being abstract, however, these lines and shapes also

27.3 Georges Braque. *The Portuguese*. 1911. Oil on canvas, 45⅞ × 32⅛″ (116 × 81.6 cm). Kunstmuseum, Basel. Gift of Raoul LaRoche, 1952

function as signs. The circle at the lower center is the sound hole of a guitar, and the horizontal lines are the strings, although Braque used the same sign to indicate fingers, a confounding or visual punning of objects that is characteristic of Picasso's and Braque's Cubism. The stenciled letters and numbers are borrowed from a poster that probably read "Grand Bal" and listed the price of admission (10 francs, 40 centimes). The lines and shadows suggest arms, shoulders, and the frontal pose of a figure tapering toward the head. Behind the figure hangs a poster and, in the upper right, we see the harbor through a window. By providing these subtle visual clues, Braque prompts the viewer to recognize that the painting shows a guitar player in a Marseilles bar. Once again, we find a conventional subject—a genre scene—presented with a radical new artistic language. The atmosphere and light that flood the

27.4 Pablo Picasso. *Guitar and Wine Glass*. 1912. Charcoal, gouache, and pasted paper, 18⅞ × 14¾" (45.9 × 37.5 cm). The McNay Art Museum, San Antonio, Texas. Bequest of Marion Koogler McNay

picture and fall on individual facets seem real or naturalistic but fail to create coherent space and volume. Ultimately everything is in a state of flux without absolutes, including a single interpretation of reality. The only reality is the pictorial world of line and paint. In a 1909 review of Braque's earlier work, Louis Vauxcelles, who had named Fauvism, labeled the paintings Cubism, influenced by Matisse's description of earlier Cubist works as appearing to be made of little cubes.

Synthetic Cubism: The Power of Collage

To focus on structure and line, Picasso and Braque painted monochrome images, thus removing the problem of color from their Analytic Cubism. This situation changed in 1912, however, when they began working in collage, pasting flat objects, generally paper, onto the canvas. Picasso made the earliest known example in May 1912, when he glued onto the surface of a painting a sheet of imitation chair caning, a product not unlike contact paper. (These oilcloth sheets with a chair-caning pattern printed on them were normally pasted on wood as an inexpensive way to repair a broken seat.) This device allowed him to complicate notions of the real and the illusionistic, for the chair caning was simultaneously real—a piece of real imitation chair caning—and illusionistic, a picture of chair caning.

Picasso and Braque realized immediately the broader implication of this daring move. The pasted image now literally sat on top of the canvas. Once and for all, the Renaissance conception of the picture plane as a window into an illusionistic world was shattered. Instead of a window, the picture surface became a tray on which art was served. Art occurred in front of, not behind, the canvas, a fact Édouard Manet had implied some 50 years earlier (see pages 509–11).

Collage completely changed the way in which Braque and Picasso made their images. Instead of breaking down or abstracting an object into essential forms, the artists now synthetically constructed it by building it up or arranging it out of cut pieces of paper, hence the name Synthetic Cubism. Constructing the image out of large, flat shapes meant that they could introduce into Cubism a variety of textures and colors, as seen in Picasso's *Guitar and Wine Glass* (**fig. 27.4**) of 1912. Because music is abstract, like their art, it became a favorite theme for the Cubists, who wished to establish parallels between the two art forms. Picasso built his composition on a background of real wallpaper that, like the imitation chair caning used earlier, serves as a visual pun on illusion and reality.

Picasso puns with solid forms and intangible space as well. The guitar sound hole, an element that should be negative space but appears as a solid circle of paper, contrasts with the wine glass in the drawing, which should be three-dimensional and solid but instead consists of lines on a flat piece of off-white paper that has more physical presence than the drawn glass. Picasso even tells us he is punning, for he has cropped the newspaper collage at the bottom to read LE JOU, a shortening of *Le Journal*, or "newspaper," which in French sounds like the verb *jouer*, meaning "to play." The headline for the newspaper article is *"La Bataille s'est engagé,"* which translates as "The Battle Has Started," and refers to the violent war then raging in the Balkans, with Greece, Serbia, Bulgaria, and Montenegro fighting for independence against the Ottoman Empire (see **map 27.1**). Picasso uses the announcement to signal the friendly rivalry between himself and Braque.

The logical peak of Cubism occurred when Picasso extended Synthetic Cubism to sculpture and created the first **construction**, a three-dimensional assemblage of materials. Although his earliest construction was made in 1912 (and evidence suggests that Braque had made some even earlier), Picasso did not produce a large number of these sculptures until 1914–15. Most were musical instruments, such as *Violin* (**fig. 27.5**) of 1915. Instead of pasting paper to canvas, he assembled flat or slightly bent sheets of painted metal into a low relief. Just as he had for painting, he now redefined sculpture. Instead of being carved, chiseled, or molded, his sculpture was assembled, and, unlike most sculpture since the Renaissance, it was painted. He used paint perhaps with a bit of irony, since the cross hatching used to represent shading in painting is unnecessary for a sculpture, the three-dimensional form not requiring illusionistic shadow. Again Picasso creates puns about the medium. Without knowing the title, a viewer could not know for certain that this work represents a violin. That is not the issue, however, for Picasso is more concerned with creating a visual equivalent to music—here a staccato rhythm of shape, color, and texture—transforming the individual metal pieces into playful musical notes that we can almost hear.

The outbreak of war in 1914 disrupted daily life, bringing to an end the brilliant visual game between Picasso and Braque. By then, the two

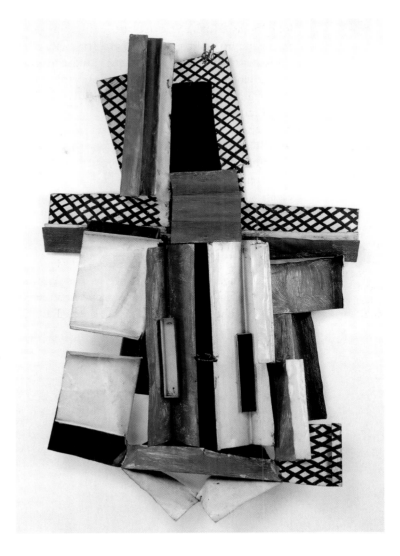

27.5 Pablo Picasso. *Violin*. 1915. Construction of painted metal, 37½ × 25⅝ × 7½" (94.5 × 65 × 19 cm). Musée Picasso, Paris.

artists had completely transformed painting, undermining some 700 years of tradition by destroying notions about what art forms could be. By making art that analyzed art and had as its very subject the way in which art functioned as an abstract visual language, Braque and Picasso sparked a revolution in the perception of reality as radical as those of Freud and Einstein.

The Impact of Fauvism and Cubism

Matisse's and Picasso's liberation of color, line, and space from illusionistic roles marked important steps in the development of modern art. As innovative as their achievements were, their interests and sensitivity during these years were limited. Their works were rational, intellectual, and pleasurable, and they focused on such traditional subjects as still life, portraiture, and the figure. Yet they provided a new artistic vocabulary for artists with very different interests and concerns, artists who used this new language to project powerful emotions, spirituality, and the intensity of modernity.

German Expressionism

The long tradition of Expressionism in German art extends back to the grotesque physical and psychological tensions of such Renaissance artists as Matthias Grünewald (see fig. 18.4) and Albrecht Dürer (see fig. 18.6). German Expressionism surfaced as a cohesive movement, however, toward 1905, and although it encompassed a range of issues and styles, it can be characterized as tortured, anguished, and brutally primitive on the one hand, or passionately spiritual, reflecting elemental cosmic forces, on the other.

27.6 Paula Modersohn-Becker. *Self-Portrait.* 1906. Oil on canvas, 24 × 19¾" (61 × 50.2 cm). Öffentliche Kunstsammlung Basel, Kunstmuseum, Basel, Switzerland

A precursor of the first German Expressionist movement is Paula Modersohn-Becker (1876–1907), whose career was cut short by her early death. Her artistic activity was limited to two mature years, during which she produced remarkable pictures that promised a brilliant future. In 1898, she settled in the commune of Worpswede, just outside Bremen in north Germany, a haven for artists and intellectuals seeking escape from modern urban life. There, she befriended two major Symbolist writers who urged her to seek the spiritual in her art and to reject the naturalistic. Modersohn-Becker visited Paris regularly, and in 1905–06 she was especially influenced by exhibitions of works by Gauguin and Cézanne.

The emergence of her individual style is represented by her 1906 *Self-Portrait* (**fig. 27.6**). In this revolutionary work, the artist presents herself nude and as an emblem of fertility, an earth goddess. Showing herself frontally, like an icon, she reduces her contours to a Gauguin-like curvilinear simplicity. Her awkward yet charming pose suggests the primitive, recalling especially Gauguin's Tahitian women (see fig. 26.4). Her amber necklace even resembles a *lei* (a Tahitian flower necklace). She poignantly displays two small flowers, symbols of fertility, which she has colored and shaped like her nipples. Also symbolic of fecundity is the garden in which she depicts herself. A celestial blue halo deifies her and reinforces her elemental presence.

What is revealing about the image is Modersohn-Becker's German primitivism, which differs radically from that of Gauguin or Picasso. There is a cultivated crudeness throughout the picture, reflected in the pasty application of paint, particularly in the masklike face and neck, and the awkward gestures, especially of her left hand. It appears as well in the ungainly flat ear and the coarse fingers of the right hand. Despite the beautiful, colorful palette, we sense a raw, primal energy and an earthiness, characteristics of much German Expressionism.

DIE BRÜCKE Scholars generally assert that German Expressionism began with Die Brücke (The Bridge), a group conceived in 1903 when four Dresden architecture students, including Ernst Ludwig Kirchner (1880–1938), decided to form an art alliance "to clear a path for the new German art." In 1905, the group officially formed and went public with no artistic program other than to oppose "older well-established powers" and create a "bridge" to the future.

The initial problem confronting these largely self-taught artists, who shared a communal studio in a former butcher's shop, was to find subject matter and a way to express it. Initially they focused on the unsettling psychology of modern Germany and turned to intense color to express it. Kirchner, the leader of Die Brücke, was among the first to mature artistically, about 1907, as seen in his *Street, Dresden* (**fig. 27.7**) of 1908. The group's love of Van Gogh and their recent discovery of Matisse are reflected in the intense Fauvist color liberated from a representational role. As important is the impact of Edvard Munch (see fig. 26.7), who exhibited throughout Germany and often resided in Berlin after 1892. The disturbing psychological undertones and arabesque patterning are decidedly Munch-like, and Kirchner's crowded street evokes a claustrophobic anxiety worthy of the Norwegian artist. Like most Munch images, this one focuses on sexual confrontation. Wraithlike women stare out. One, dressed in yellow, lifts her dress to reveal her petticoat. Searing pinks, yellows, and oranges contrast with electrifying blues and greens, creating

a disturbing dissonance and sexual excitement. This unsettling picture could never be mistaken for one by Matisse. For the Bridge artists, prostitutes were emblems of the decadence of urban life, embodying the immorality and materiality of the city.

DER BLAUE REITER The second major German Expressionist group, Der Blaue Reiter (The Blue Rider), developed in Munich, in southern Germany. It lasted but four months, from December 1910 to March 1911. Like their Brücke counterparts, the artists associated with Der Blaue Reiter drew on art forms from Western art history as well as non-Western and folk art traditions to create images that reveal their skepticism toward modern, industrial life. The group focused on visually expressing a spirituality they believed resided beneath the surface of the visual world.

The key figure in Der Blaue Reiter was the Russian artist Vasily Kandinsky (1866–1944). He left Moscow in 1896 to study art in Munich and took with him Russian influences, namely the spirituality of native religious icons and the robust, emotional

27.7 Ernst Ludwig Kirchner. *Street, Dresden.* 1908 (dated 1907 on painting). Oil on canvas, 4′11¼″ × 6′6⅞″ (1.51 × 2 m). The Museum of Modern Art, New York. © Ingeborg and Dr. Wolfgang Henze-Ketter, Wichtrach/Bern, Switzerland

27.8 Vasily Kandinsky. *Sketch I for "Composition VII."* 1913. Oil on canvas, 30¾ × 39⅜" (78 × 100 cm). Private Collection

 Read the document related to Vasily Kandinsky on myartslab.com

colors of folk art. His interest in folk culture was rekindled when, in 1908, he moved to Murnau, just south of Munich in the Bavarian Alps. There he immersed himself in folk culture and was deeply affected by the powerful colors and the simple directness of paintings on glass, a medium that he adopted. He also lived in the Schwabing neighborhood of Munich, a bohemian enclave of cafés and liberalism. The area was a breeding ground for explorations of spirituality and the occult, where Theosophy cropped up in daily conversation (see page 536). Inspired in part by Theosophy, Kandinsky in 1910 wrote *Concerning the Spiritual in Art*, published the next year and read worldwide. He proclaimed the need to paint one's connectedness with the universe and to use an abstract vocabulary, one that functioned much like music, to portray the abstract qualities of spirituality.

It was not until 1911 that Kandinsky began making totally abstract pictures, as seen in *Sketch I for "Composition VII"* (**fig. 27.8**). Painted in 1913, this was one of numerous preliminary studies for a large final version that retains some of the same compositional elements but has a very different palette. Drawing a parallel with music, Kandinsky titled many of his works "composition," "improvisation," and "concert." He was especially influenced by RICHARD WAGNER in his conjuring of universal forces and a sense of musical abstraction. These qualities differ greatly from the lyrical, refined imagery of James Abbott McNeill Whistler, who similarly aspired to create visual music (see page 519). In *Sketch I for "Composition VII,"* the references to horses, riders, figures, buildings, and specific landscape motifs that had appeared in *Compositions I* and *II* of 1910 are now gone, these motifs yielding to an abstract play of color and painted line and form that still nonetheless recalls the deep saturated colors of medieval stained-glass windows, reverse glass painting, and Russian folk art. The image may appear apocalyptic and chaotic, but these dynamic qualities are meant to capture the relentlessness of universal forces, not to portend a catastrophic future.

Austrian Expressionism

Another major center for German Expressionism was Vienna. Home of Sigmund Freud, it was an especially repressive city, socially and culturally dominated by a conservative bourgeoisie and a decadent aristocracy resistant to change. Not surprisingly, Viennese artists generated some of the era's most neurotic and disturbing visual imagery.

OSKAR KOKOSCHKA Perhaps the most prominent Viennese artist is Oskar Kokoschka (1886–1980), who initially specialized in portraiture. In 1908 he exhibited with avant-garde artists at the Vienna *Kunstschau*, an exhibition for cutting-edge art, where his violent portraits, inspired by Van Gogh, generated so much controversy that he was expelled from art school. Kokoschka called his expressionistic portraits "black portraits," and the sitters appeared to be so troubled that he became known as "the Freud of painting" who "paints the dirt of one's soul."

We can get a sense of how expressionistic these portraits looked from the figures in *The Bride of the Wind* (**fig. 27.9**), Kokoschka's 1914 self-portrait with his lover Alma Mahler, the notoriously beautiful and sophisticated widow of the famous Austrian composer Gustav Mahler. By 1914, their passionate relationship was threatened, and it ended the following year. *The Bride of the Wind* visually encapsulates the artist's distress. Originally, Kokoschka intended to disguise this personal dilemma as *Tristan and Isolde*, based on Wagner's opera about tragic lovers. Kokoschka expresses his anxiety through coarse, violent brushstrokes and a seething, swirling composition. Oblivious to this turmoil, Mahler is shown peacefully sleeping, while Kokoschka restlessly worries, his body transformed into a flayed corpse, his hands grotesquely gnarled. The couple is cradled in a monstrous shell-like berth adrift in a landscape that is bleak, uncontrollable, and subject to cosmic forces, as suggested by the gravitational pull of a distant moon.

27.9 Oskar Kokoschka. *The Bride of the Wind*. 1914. Oil on canvas, 5'11¼" × 7'2⅝" (1.81 × 2.20 m). Öffentliche Kunstsammlung Basel, Kunstmuseum, Basel, Switzerland

27.10 Robert Delaunay. *Homage to Blériot.* 1914. Tempera on canvas, 8′2½″ × 8′3″ (2.5 × 2.51 m). Öffentliche Kunstsammlung Basel, Kunstmuseum, Basel, Switzerland. Emanuel Hoffman Foundation

Cubism in Paris after Picasso and Braque

In France, Cubism was thoroughly entrenched by 1911–12, expanding well beyond Picasso and Braque. A handful of individual painters had closely followed Picasso's and Braque's developments in 1909–10, and in late 1910 they began exhibiting together at the large Paris salons and at a private gallery, calling themselves the Section d'Or (Golden Section). In 1912, two Cubists in the group, Albert Gleizes and Jean Metzinger, published *Du Cubisme* (On Cubism), the first book on the style.

ROBERT DELAUNAY Of the Section d'Or, Robert Delaunay (1885–1941) was among the most influential members. Unlike concurrent Analytic Cubist works by Braque and Picasso, Delaunay's 1910 Cubist paintings of the Eiffel Tower, an icon of modern technology, incorporated color. They also differed in their subject: The movement and energy of modernity and the constant flux of the contemporary world.

Delaunay's preoccupation with the dynamism of the modern world is evident in his 1914 *Homage to Blériot* (**fig. 27.10**), honoring the French aviator Louis Blériot (1872–1936), inventor of the modern single-wing airplane and the first pilot to fly across the English Channel. Delaunay integrates emblems of modernity—airplanes, propellers, and the Eiffel Tower—into a kaleidoscope of floating balls and rotating disks suggesting the whirling of the propellers and blazing suns. He creates movement not only through the ambiguity of Cubist space but also through the use of what Delaunay called "simultaneous contrasts," the placement of flat planes of primary and secondary colors next to one another, not only creating movement but also light and space, none of which is illusionistic. Two years before, Delaunay had even exhibited total abstractions called *Simultaneous Disks* or *Simultaneous Contrasts*, paintings consisting entirely of the multihued circles seen in *Homage to Blériot*. While Delaunay's color theory was derived from the same nineteenth-century color theorists who had influenced Seurat, his move into total abstraction was prompted by his contact with Kandinsky. (Delaunay had been included in the first Blaue Reiter exhibition.) In his 1913 review of the Salon des Indépendants, the art critic Guillaume Apollinaire labeled Delaunay's abstract work Orphism, a reference to the mythological lyre player Orpheus and evoking a parallel between abstract art and music.

Italian Futurism: Activism and Art

In January 1909, Filippo Tommaso Marinetti (1876–1944), a free-verse poet based in Milan, launched the Futurist movement when he published his *Manifesto of Futurism*, a pamphlet sent to thousands of artists and poets. On February 20, it appeared on the front page of the Parisian newspaper *Le Figaro*. Marinetti called for a rebirth of Italy, a country he saw as mired in the dusty, anachronistic classical past. He advocated an uncompromising acceptance of modernity in all its manifestations, including electricity, automobiles, and machines, writing that "all subjects previously used must be swept aside in order to express our whirling life of steel, of pride, of fever and of speed."

For Marinetti, Futurism was a continual process, a permanent revolution. Toward this end, he arranged Futurist evenings, where from a stage he expounded upon his theories, often provoking, if not insulting, the audience in his attempt to incite them to action or even violence, which he perceived as socially cleansing and productive. Marinetti was intent on generating constant activism, which he saw as the conduit for a cultural *Risorgimento*, or rebirth, of Italy.

After a 1909 lecture in Milan presented to the avant-garde art group Famiglia Artistica (Artistic Family), Marinetti enlisted a handful of its members, including Umberto Boccioni (1882–1916), to become Futurists. In 1909, these artists were mostly Neo-Impressionists (see page 533), who transformed the color and energy of Divisionism to portray contemporary dynamism. Their manifesto claimed that "Motion and light destroy the materiality of bodies" and that their concern would be the visualization of movement and energy. For their visual vocabulary, they rejected anything redolent of classical Italian culture and instead turned to science: The sequences taken by late nineteenth-century photographers that served as motion studies, the physicist and philosopher Ernst Mach's (1838–1916) graphic representations of shockwaves, and the physicist Wilhelm Konrad Röntgen's (1845–1923) x-rays, which proved the dematerialization of all things.

By the end of 1911, the group had turned from Neo-Impressionism to Cubism. Their interest in Cubism, however, departed from the concerns of Braque and Picasso because the Futurists wanted to convey motion, dynamic energy, and social progress. After visiting Paris and seeing Cubist works in 1911, Boccioni painted *States of Mind I: Farewells* (**fig. 27.11**). Embedded in a fractured world of Cubist facets is an eruption of steam, sound, moving objects, and psychic energy. The white curving lines over the locomotive reflect Mach's lines of thrust, whereas the repetition of the vaguely rendered, green-tinted embracing couple is inspired by nineteenth-century motion sequences, multiple pictures of, for example, a running horse taken within one second of one another. Boccioni is championing not just modern technology, as represented by the train, electric railroad signals, and trussed steel towers, but the perpetual movement of all objects and energy.

27.11 Umberto Boccioni. *States of Mind I: Farewells.* 1911 (second version). Oil on canvas, 28 × 37⅞" (70.7 × 96 cm). The Museum of Modern Art, New York. Gift of Nelson A. Rockefeller.

In a May 1911 lecture in Rome, he proclaimed that painting had to capture the energy in all matter, energy in perpetual motion that dissolves the object while fusing it with surrounding space, an effect he called "plastic dynamism."

In *States of Mind I: Farewells*, we sense not only the dematerialization of the train and figures through time and movement, in part created by Boccioni's application of Divisionism, but also the simultaneous presence of space as something plastic and as vital as form. Also swirling throughout the chaotic image is an emotional energy—a sense of painful separation and disappearance—which the title reveals as a theme of the work.

Cubo-Futurism and Suprematism in Russia

Of the major European countries in the 1910s, Russia was the least industrialized. Nevertheless, it became an important center for avant-garde art.

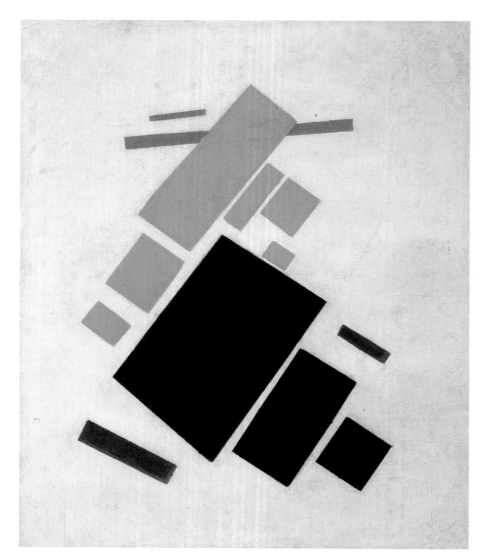

27.12 Kazimir Malevich. *Suprematist Composition: Airplane Flying*. 1915 (dated 1914). Oil on canvas, 22⅞ × 19" (58 × 48.3 cm). The Museum of Modern Art, New York. Purchase. Acquisition confirmed in 1999 by agreement with the Estate of Kazimir Malevich and made possible with the funds from the Mrs. John Hay Whitney Bequest (by exchange). 248.1935

 Read the document related to Kazimir Malevich on myartslab.com

Most of the population were former serfs ruled by an indifferent czar and dominated by the Orthodox Church. Despite a rush to modernize, Russia in some respects remained trapped in the Middle Ages. In a culture dominated by folk art and icon-painting traditions, how did radical art emerge? Part of the explanation may lie in the country's desperate need for reform. In 1917 the October (or Bolshevik) Revolution, led by Vladimir Ilyich Lenin (1870–1924), overthrew the regime and established a Communist state, finally bringing about a degree of modernization and social improvement. Change was far more radical than it had been in eighteenth-century America or France, largely because Russia was such a backward state to begin with. The transformation was so dramatic that it even embraced equality for women, who had proved integral to developing the radical art of the years preceding the revolution.

THE RUSSIAN AVANT-GARDE: KAZIMIR MALEVICH In Moscow, Sergey Shchukin and Ivan Morozov, two of the greatest collectors of contemporary art, made their extraordinary holdings of works by such major artists as Picasso and Matisse available to Russian artists to study. In response to these works and to growing ties with the Western European avant-garde, Russian artists began to explore Cubism and other approaches to abstraction, and by 1912 they were heavily influenced by Futurism as well. These groups embraced the modern, often emphasizing the pace and psychology of modern life as well as machines and industry, which were critical to bringing Russia into the twentieth century.

By 1913 many of the Russian artists were calling themselves Cubo-Futurists, a term coined by Kazimir Malevich (1879–1935) that reflects the dual origins of the style. Gradually, some of the artists moved away from modern subject matter in search of more spiritual or elemental experiences. In 1913 Malevich designed Cubo-Futurist costumes and sets for what was cited as the "First Futurist Opera" and titled *Victory over the Sun*. Presented in St. Petersburg, this radical "opera" embraced the principle of **zaum**, a term invented by progressive Russian poets. Essentially, *zaum* was a language based on invented words and syntax, the meaning of which was supposedly implicit in the basic sounds and patterns of speech. The intention was to return to the nonrational and primitive basis of language that, unencumbered by conventional meaning, expressed the essence of human experience. In *Victory over the Sun*, performers read from non-narrative texts often consisting of invented words while accompanied by the clatter of an out-of-tune piano. Malevich's geometric costumes and sets were equally abstract. A stack of triangles ran up and down the legs of one costume, while one backdrop was a square divided in half to form two triangles, one white, the other black.

It took Malevich two years to realize the implications of *zaum* for his art, namely that art could be entirely abstract. In 1915, after working in a Cubo-Futurist style, Malevich presented 39 nonobjective geometric paintings in a St. Petersburg exhibition entitled *0, 10 (Zero–Ten): The Last Futurist Exhibition*. The best-known work in the show was *Black Square*, simply a large black square floating on a white ground, most of which the square covered. In his 1920s Suprematist treatise *The Non-Objective World*, Malevich explained that Suprematism is the supremacy of feeling. This feeling is not just personal or emotional but revelatory, for the abstract essence of the world is translated into painting using an entirely new abstract language, stripped of any vestiges of realism. Like his fellow Russian Kandinsky, Malevich was a mystic, searching for cosmic unity, even a utopian world, as would supporters of the Bolshevik Revolution of 1917. *Black Square* embodies both the legacy of simple, otherworldly Russian icons and the mysticism of folk art.

Malevich's abstract language included different geometric shapes and colors. In *Suprematist Composition: Airplane Flying* (**fig. 27.12**), also painted in 1915, he used red, yellow, and blue shapes in addition to black to create a sensation of movement and floating. Color, size, and shape produce a unique rhythm against the white ground. From one composition to the next, Malevich altered the rhythm by changing these characteristics. Although the title includes the word airplane and suggests an infatuation with technology, the image itself relates to the experience of air travel and the new relationship to the universe brought about by this new and exciting mode of transportation.

Unfortunately, reproductions of Malevich's paintings almost never show their organic quality. The shapes in *Airplane Flying* may appear to be hard-edged and geometric, but on the actual painting one can see that their boundaries waver

ever so slightly and a degree of brushwork is present, giving the picture a sense of a human touch. Malevich's geometric paintings thus contain the human presence evident in the work of Kandinsky. Like Kandinsky, Malevich powerfully projects a serene mystical connection with the universe, which he accomplishes through the use of the white ground extending beyond the canvas into infinity.

LYUBOV POPOVA Another major Cubo-Futurist was Lyubov Popova (1889–1924), who studied in Paris in 1912 and in Italy in 1914, experiencing first hand the latest developments in Cubism and Futurism. In Moscow, she presented powerful pictures that combined the fracturing of Cubism with the energy and movement of Futurism. Influenced by Malevich's Suprematism, she, along with many other Russian colleagues, became a Suprematist by 1916, creating nonrepresentational works that she called "Painterly Architectonics." She removed any references to the real world from her images, creating totally abstract work that looked quite different from that of Malevich. As can be seen in this later *Painterly Architectonics* picture (**fig. 27.13**) of 1918,

27.13 Lyubov Popova. *Painterly Architectonics*. ca. 1918. Oil on linen burlap, 27¾ × 27¾″ (70.5 × 70.5 cm). Thyssen-Bornemisza Museum, Madrid

Popova does not float her planes of color on an infinite white field; she instead allows them to fill the entire canvas. Furthermore, her planes are not flat, since they are lit with what appears to be a naturalistic light, making them seem temporarily round and three-dimensional. But there is no logic to the lighting; it does not come from a single source and the planes jostle each other in Popova's illogical space. Also, some planes intersect, one plane becoming transparent and seeming to recede and pass through another. It is easy to read something mystical or spiritual into Popova's light and space, but the artist never intended such an interpretation. For her, the Painterly Architectonics, as the title itself implies, were nothing more than abstract representations of the physical presence of the material world, with each painting simply being a formalist exercise, largely based on Cubist aesthetics, in pure abstraction.

27.14 Giorgio de Chirico. *Mystery and Melancholy of a Street*. 1914. Oil on canvas, 34¼ × 28½″ (87 × 72.4 cm). Private collection

Cubism and Fantasy: Giorgio de Chirico

In his abstract compositions, Malevich stripped down Cubist geometry to the point that Cubist structure itself virtually disappeared. Other artists, such as Giorgio de Chirico (1888–1978), took the linear structure and spatial convolutions of Cubism and adapted them to a distinctly representational format, using the distortions of the style to create dreamlike fantasy imagery.

The Italian De Chirico arrived in Paris in 1910. While studying in Munich from 1905 to 1909, he was heavily influenced by German Romantic and Symbolist artists, Theosophy, and the philosophy of Friedrich Nietzsche, who described life as a "foreboding that underneath this reality in which we live and have our being, another and altogether different reality lies concealed." He moved back to Italy in 1909, settling in Florence in 1910, where, influenced by the strong southern light and the arcades of the Piazza Santa Croce, he made the first of his "Metaphysical Town Squares," images of an empty piazza formed by austere buildings rendered as bold simple forms and carefully delineated by strong line. His compositions and use of space became increasingly complex after his return to Paris in 1911, as seen in *Mystery and Melancholy of a Street* (**fig. 27.14**), made after his permanent return to Italy in 1914. His reliance on strong diagonal lines, such as the receding buildings and shadows, and his use of unstable disjointed space make his works vaguely echo Cubism, which surely influenced his change in style.

And yet, De Chirico's pictures are stylistically conventional, even suggesting stage sets. Unlike his Futurist compatriots, De Chirico idolized rather than rejected the classical past, although he subverted its austere authority by evoking a Romantic melancholy, using ominous shadows, intense light, and skewed perspective to create an unsettling eeriness. In *Mystery and Melancholy of a Street*, railroad tracks, darkened windows and arches, the empty moving van, and the girl with the hoop seem to be symbols, but De Chirico provides no clues about their meaning, insisting that none existed. Instead, the painting offers a dreamscape that can be interpreted uniquely by each viewer, just as individuals respond differently to the symbolic narratives of their dreams. De Chirico called his works metaphysical paintings, and his psychologically disturbing poetic reveries would serve as a springboard for representational Surrealism in the next decade.

Modernist Sculpture: Constantin Brancusi

The sculptures of Constantin Brancusi (1876–1957) were among the most innovative artworks being produced before World War I. Indeed, Brancusi's work is so minimal-looking and abstract that it has come to symbolize modern sculpture itself. Ironically, his background could not have been more removed from the modern world. The son of Romanian peasants, he grew up herding sheep in the remote village of Tîrju-Jiu in the Carpathian Mountains. The region had a long tradition of ornate folk carving, in which he excelled, and just as these folk carvings were often intended to capture a spiritual essence, Brancusi, in his modern minimal sculptures, would seek to evoke an elemental property. Brancusi's introduction to fine art first came in Bucharest, and after passing through Munich in 1903, he settled in Paris and became an assistant to Auguste Rodin (see page 540–42). Declaring that "Nothing can grow under big trees," he struck out on his own.

Escaping the far-reaching shadow of Rodin and his strong ties to nineteenth-century art, Brancusi steered a radical course that, aesthetically if not thematically, broke with sculptural tradition and laid a foundation for much twentieth-century sculpture. His mature style began to evolve toward 1907, and the stripped-down minimal style that he then developed can be seen in his 1928 *Bird in Space* (**fig. 27.15**), a subject that he reworked for decades in different materials. Brancusi first introduced the bird motif as early as 1910 in a work titled *Maiastra*, which was based on a Romanian legend about a magical golden bird whose song held miraculous powers. By the 1920s, Brancusi showed the same bird soaring, as in *Bird in Space*, instead of perched. The elegantly streamlined form balances on a short tapering column, the pinched section suggesting the junction of legs and body. But of course we do not really see a bird. Instead Brancusi has presented us with the essence of flight, as suggested by the smooth aerodynamic form that seems to gracefully and effortlessly cut through the air. As Brancusi explained, "Simplicity is not an end in art, but one arrives at simplicity in spite of oneself in approaching the real sense of things." Like Malevich, but using an entirely different vocabulary, Brancusi sought unseen universal essences, not visual realities.

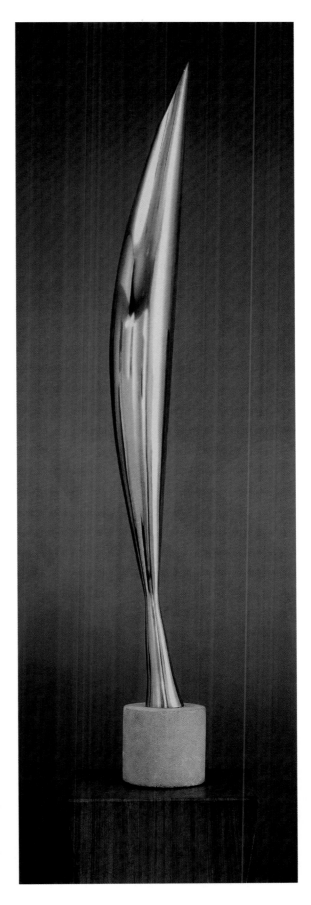

27.15 Constantin Brancusi. *Bird in Space*. 1928 (unique cast). Bronze, stone, and wood, 54 × 8½ × 6½" (137.2 × 21.6 × 16.5 cm). The Museum of Modern Art, New York. Given anonymously

Brancusi's sculpture focuses on only a handful of themes, which he repeated numerous times, often in different mediums, including bronze, wood, stainless steel, and stone of different kinds. The shift in mediums allowed the artist to explore both the visual and psychological associations of his material. His meticulous control over his work included designing the bases and pedestals, as can be seen in *Bird in Space*, where the sculpture includes the cylindrical stone base and the hourglass-shaped wood pedestal. This stacked system of presentation has the effect of distancing the sculpture from the space of the room and placing it within its own perfect world. Brancusi also realized that the height of the presentation of his sculpture affected a viewer's physical and psychological relationship to it, and thus the reading of it. A work titled *The Newborn*, which is an egg-shaped oval with an oval depression suggesting an open wailing mouth, he exhibited on a low pedestal, forcing viewers to lean over the piece, finding themselves in the position of an adult looking down at an infant in a cradle. In contrast, *Bird in Space* is presented very high, like a soaring bird, forcing viewers to look up.

27.16 Arthur Dove. *Plant Forms*. ca. 1912. Pastel on canvas, 17¼ × 23⅞" (43.8 × 60.6 cm). Whitney Museum of American Art, New York. Purchase with Funds from Mr. and Mrs. Roy R. Neuberger 51.20 © The Estate of Arthur G. Dove, courtesy Terry Dintenfass, Inc

American Art

Modernism did not come to America until the second decade of the twentieth century, when it first appeared in New York at the Little Galleries of the Photo Secession, commonly referred to as "291" after its Fifth Avenue street number and owned by Alfred Stieglitz (see page 547). Beginning in 1909, Stieglitz started featuring such seminal Modernists as Picasso, Matisse, Henri Rousseau, Rodin, and Brancusi as well as African art and children's art. The momentous Modernist event in New York was the 1913 International Exhibition of Modern Art, known as the Armory Show after the 26th Street armory where it was held. Exhibited were over 400 European works, mostly French, from Delacroix through Courbet, Monet, Gauguin, Van Gogh, and Cézanne to Picasso, Brancusi, and Matisse. Three times as many American artists were represented, but by comparison their work looked provincial and was largely ignored.

Ruthless newspaper reviews lambasted the radical contemporary French art, and the public came out in droves—75,000 people attended the

four-week show. The exhibition's slogan was "The New Spirit," and its symbol was the pine tree flag of Revolutionary Massachusetts. The American organizers intentionally set out to create their own revolution to jolt conventional bourgeois taste and bring about an awareness and appreciation for contemporary art. Despite the public's derision, the show spawned several modern art galleries and collectors adventurous enough to dedicate themselves to supporting radical art.

America's First Modernists: Arthur Dove and Abstraction

American artists digested European Modernism almost as quickly as it was made, but those in Europe, especially in Paris, absorbed most rapidly the new movements of Fauvism and Cubism. In 1908 a young Arthur Dove (1880–1946) was in Paris, where he saw work by Matisse and the Fauves. When he returned to New York, he met Stieglitz and began showing at "291."

While remaining involved in the New York art world throughout his life, Dove lived in rural areas in New York State and Connecticut, even spending several years on a houseboat anchored off Long Island. His art focused on Nature, not modernity, and on capturing universal forces. By 1910 he was painting complete abstractions, two years before Kandinsky. In *Plant Forms* (**fig. 27.16**), from a series of pastels titled *The Ten Commandments*, Dove has supplied all the components of Nature without painting it illusionistically.

As with Cubism, the composition of *Plant Forms* is made up of abstract components, although they overlap in a logical, consistent fashion to suggest continuous recession in space. The work has light and atmosphere as well as an organic quality, largely due to the elliptical, oval, and round forms and the biomorphic shapes suggestive of plants and trees. The curved white and yellow forms evoke suns, moons, and hills, and although the frondlike shapes recall plants and trees, they are also symbols of an unidentifiable burst of energy. We feel the powerful surge of Nature and an elemental life force, and because each form suggests many different objects, Dove is able to convey the universal interconnectedness of all things. The picture is cosmic in its scope, yet it provides an intimate view of nature. Dove's preoccupation with portraying potent natural forces will become a major theme in American art and, as we shall see, one of the major issues for artists in Stieglitz's circle.

Early Modern Architecture in Europe

In the last chapter, we saw the emergence of two distinct approaches to modern architecture, one in the United States and another in Europe. American architects like Louis Sullivan and Frank Lloyd Wright challenged historicism and conventional revivalism when they eliminated the distinction between the form of a building and its proposed function. In Europe, we also saw a rejection of revival styles when Art Nouveau defined modern architecture as an organic style of growth and movement. Throughout the twentieth century, modern architecture often followed these opposite poles set by the Chicago School and Art Nouveau—the rational, geometric, and functional versus the personal, referential, organic, and expressive.

German Modernist Architecture

Germany played a major role in shaping architectural developments in the opening decades of the century, largely because the German government and industry nurtured Modernist architecture. In 1896, government officials sent the architect Hermann Muthesius to London, then the world leader in quality mass production, to study British industry and design. Upon returning in 1904, Muthesius was appointed to the Prussian Trade Commission and given the task of restructuring education in the applied arts. To dominate world markets, he advocated mass production of functional objects executed in a well-designed machine style. In 1907, he was instrumental in establishing the Deutsche Werkbund, an association of architects, designers, writers, and industrialists whose goal was "selecting the best representatives of art, industry, crafts, and trades, of combining all efforts toward high quality in industrial work." In architecture he called for a new monumental style based on Schinkel's classicism (see fig. 24.16), but reflecting modern industrial values. More important, this industrial architectural style had to be a machine style—one that was based on a *Typisierung*, meaning a type or a basic unit, which permitted the development of a mass-produced modular building that would be usable by all architects.

WALTER GROPIUS The Werkbund architect who fulfilled Muthesius's goal was Walter Gropius (1882–1969). With his associate Adolf Meyer, he was commissioned in 1911 to design the Fagus

27.17 Walter Gropius and Adolf Meyer. Fagus Factory. 1911–13. Alfeld-an-der-Leine, Germany

27.18 Bruno Taut. Glass Pavilion, Werkbund Exhibition. 1914. Cologne

Factory (**fig. 27.17**), a shoe plant in Alfeld-an-der-Leine, Germany. In this building, Gropius reached back to the Chicago School architects and utilized their steel-grid skeleton, sheathed in a ferrovitreous curtain wall. The factory's glass façade appears to be magically suspended from the brick-faced entablature above. It even turns corners unobstructed, making it appear to float. The building feels light and transparent, the window mullions thin and elegant. Horizontal opaque panels, the exact size and shape of the glass, indicate each of the three floors and continue the modular composition of the windows. Here was the machine style Muthesius was seeking: An unadorned building that adheres to a grid skeleton. As we shall see, this building type was sufficiently efficient and reproducible to serve as the prototype for the glass-box structures that would dominate world architecture in the second half of the century.

German Expressionist Architecture

Not all German architects embraced technology, the machine age, and Muthesius's concept of the *Typisierung*. Others instead designed expressive spiritual structures meant to counter the cold, impersonal impact of modernity.

BRUNO TAUT An overt spiritual contribution to the 1914 Werkbund Exhibition was the Glass Pavilion (**fig. 27.18**) built by Bruno Taut (1880–1928) for the glass industry and reflecting his belief in the mystical properties of crystal. The guru of glass was the poet Paul Scheerbart, whose 1914 essay *Glasarchitektur* (Glass Architecture) had a tremendous impact on artists and architects. The entablature of Taut's Glass Pavilion is even etched with Scheerbart's sayings about the power of glass.

Scheerbart claimed that only a glass architecture that opened all rooms to light could raise German culture to a new spiritual level. Consequently, Taut used glass brick for the walls and floors. The bulbous dome, which resembles a giant crystal, is made of two layers of glass; the outer one reflective, the inner a myriad of colored glass pieces resembling medieval stained glass. Taut also considered his cupola to be Gothic, its facets evoking the vital force of Flamboyant ribbing (see page 263). The ceiling of the main space had a central oculus that emitted a shower of mystical colored light.

POINTS OF REFLECTION

27.1 Pablo Picasso and Georges Braque were heavily influenced by Cézanne, and yet their view of the world was in many ways entirely different from his. How was it different, and how did it reflect the dramatically different way in which Braque and Picasso on the one hand, and Cézanne on the other, experienced and understood the world?

27.2 In what ways do Constantin Brancusi's *Bird in Space* and Pablo Picasso's assemblage *Violin* radically differ from any sculpture that came before, and in what ways are these two works by Brancusi and Picasso so different from one another, reflecting entirely different issues, both thematic and stylistic? Similarly, why are the paintings of Vasily Kandinsky and Kazimir Malevich so radical compared to earlier painting, and how do they use abstraction both similarly and differently from Brancusi and Picasso?

27.3 While heavily influenced by Paul Gauguin, Paula Modersohn-Becker's art differs in ways that we think of as being distinctly German. Why? How does the German Ernst Ludwig Kirchner use color differently from Henri Matisse?

27.4 Walter Gropius's Fagus Factory clearly builds on the innovations of the Chicago architects and a building such as Louis Sullivan's Wainwright Building (**fig. 26.15**) What are these innovations, and how does Gropius develop them, especially reflecting the German preoccupation with mass production?

27.5 How does Umberto Boccioni's Futurist painting *States of Mind I: Farewells* differ conceptually from Georges Braque's Cubist painting *The Portuguese*, and what happens to the Cubist tradition and Futurism in the hands of such Russian Suprematists as Kazimir Malevich and Lyubov Popova?

ART IN TIME

- **1905**—Albert Einstein introduces his Theory of Relativity

- —Critic Louis Vauxcelles names Fauvism

- —Die Brücke formed

- —Alfred Stieglitz opens his gallery "291"

- **1906**—Paula Modersohn-Becker, *Self-Portrait*

- **1907**—Pablo Picasso, *Les Demoiselles d'Avignon*

- —Henri Bergson publishes *Creative Evolution*

- **1909**—Filippo Tommaso Marinetti issues a *Manifesto of Futurism*

- —Louis Blériot flies across English Channel

- **1911**—Georges Braque, *The Portuguese*

- **1911–13**—Walter Gropius and Adolf Meyer, Fagus Factory

- **1913**—Armory Show in New York City

- **1914**—World War I begins

CHAPTER

28 | Art Between the Wars

POINTS OF INQUIRY

28.1 Discuss why World War I was a determining influence on the art and architecture made between the wars.

28.2 Assess why certain Dada artists were so appealing to the Surrealists and understand the forces that brought about Surrealism.

28.3 Describe how a utopian vision is embraced in much of the European art, architecture, and design of the period and the variety of ways it was expressed in Russia, the Netherlands, Germany, and France.

28.4 Explain how the post-World War I role of the United States as technological and financial world leader is reflected in the nation's art and the way in which this work differs from the art produced in Europe.

28.5 Discuss how African-American and Mexican artists transformed the image of non-Europeans in Western art, laying a foundation for the multicultural art in the second half of the century.

((•—**Listen** to the chapter audio on myartslab.com

Physically and psychologically, World War I devastated Western civilization. The destruction and loss of life were staggering, with hundreds of thousands of soldiers dying in single battles. The Enlightenment-based logic, science, and technology that many thought would bring about a better world had gone horribly awry. Instead of a better world, the advancements of the nineteenth century had produced such high-tech weapons as machine guns, long-range artillery, tanks, submarines, fighter planes, and mustard gas.

To many, the very concept of nationalism now seemed destructive, and the rise of the first Communist government in Russia in 1917 offered the hope of salvation. Around the world, branches of the Communist Party sprang up, with the goal of creating a nationless world united by the proletariat, the working class that provided the

labor force for the capitalist system. Others maintained that a new world order could not be attained without first destroying the old; they advocated anarchy (a complete lack of any form of government or control), which remained a constant threat in the postwar decades. Despite this drive to create a nationless and classless world, by the 1930s it was fascism that dominated European politics. Fascism, a totalitarian political system that exalts the nation over the individual and demands allegiance to a single leader, held a special appeal for nations defeated in World War I. The Germans gradually fell under the spell of Adolf Hitler (1889–1945) and his National Socialist (Nazi) party, who skillfully used economic crises and anti-Semitism to consolidate power. In Italy and Japan as well, fascists took control. Armed with new technological tools of destruction, these

Map 28.1 Europe and North America in the 1920s and 1930s

nations would plunge the world into another great war by 1939.

While fascism, communism, anarchy, and democracy jockeyed for dominance in Europe, America enjoyed unprecedented prosperity in the 1920s. Historians have called the economic and cultural exuberance of the postwar years the Roaring Twenties; it was a time of jazz, speakeasies (illicit drinking clubs), radio, and film. The 1920s also saw the rise of the city as the emblem of the nation. Technology and machines were king in America, where the world's largest skyscrapers could be erected in a year. This economic exhilaration came to a screeching halt with the stockmarket crash of October 1929, which sent the entire world into a downward economic spiral known as the Great Depression, lasting throughout the 1930s. A reactionary backlash then occurred in both Europe and America (see **map 28.1**): Fascism in the former, and a conservative regionalism and isolationism in the latter. Nonetheless, the 1930s marked the advent in America of liberal social and economic programs, instituted by Franklin Delano Roosevelt's administration (1932–44). Believing that economic markets were inherently unstable, Roosevelt advocated the New Deal, which created millions of government-sponsored jobs, including many for artists.

Perhaps the strongest defining influence for artists between the wars was the Great War itself and the technology, science, and Enlightenment rationalism that enabled it to be so devastating. A direct result of the war was Dada, a movement that created a nonsensical, nihilistic art attacking bourgeois values and conventions, including faith in technology. The Dadaists aimed to wipe the philosophical slate clean, leading the way to a new world order. Other artists embraced the modernity of the Machine Age (as this interwar period is sometimes called), seeing it as a means to create classless utopias; still others rejected it, seeking higher truths or a meaningful spirituality in an increasingly materialistic, soulless world. Both groups often turned to abstraction to implement their vision. Those supporting technology embraced the geometry and mechanical look of the Machine Age, while those who rejected it sought higher truths using an organic or biomorphic vocabulary.

A second major force between the wars was Sigmund Freud (see page 551), whose theories about the unconscious and dreams were a formative influence on Surrealism, a prevailing movement in the 1920s and 1930s. Like many abstract artists, the Surrealists sought to reveal invisible, not spiritual realities, but nonetheless the elemental universal forces that drive all humans. These unseen realities are deeply embedded in the mind and symbolically revealed in dreams. Freud maintained that the conventions of civilization had repressed the elemental needs and desires shared by all people, and that this suppressed, invisible world of desires and sexual energy was fundamental to human behavior. For Surrealist artists, as well as writers and intellectuals, Freud's theory of the unconscious confirmed the existence of realities unseen by the eye or not perceived by the conscious mind, and they served as the springboard for the development of Surrealist imagery and style.

Politics also strongly shaped the art of the period. Many if not most avant-garde artists were socialists and Communists, or at least sympathizers, and their utopian dreams and aesthetic visions stemmed in part from these political ideologies. Rarely did avant-garde art engage in overt political discourse. Among the exceptions are the Berlin Dadaists and the Mexican muralists, the latter directly championing communism, especially when paired with science, as the vehicle for creating a classless utopian society. With the rise to power of Hitler and the Nazis, some avant-garde artists turned their attention to making antifascist imagery and exposing the insane thinking and sadistic brutality of the new German government.

This era also saw a growing interest in racial and ethnic identity, which was expressed in Mexican as well as African-American art. The Mexican muralists were preoccupied with national identity, which they associated with the indigenous population, not the Euro-Mexicans, while African Americans looked to uncover their heritage and culture. Just as Mary Cassatt and Julia Margaret Cameron sought to present women from a female as opposed to a male viewpoint, obtaining very different results, so the Mexicans and African Americans did the same for their own societies. These artists presented a very different image of and attitude toward non-European cultures.

Dada

The Great War halted much art making, as many artists were enlisted in their country's military service and a great number were killed. But the conflict also produced one art movement: Dada. Its name was chosen at random, the story goes, when two German poets, Richard Huelsenbeck and Hugo Ball, plunged a knife into a French–German dictionary and its point landed on *dada*, the French word for "hobbyhorse." The word's association with childishness as well as the random violence of the poets' act of word choice fit the war-influenced spirit of the movement perfectly. As the birth story of Dada suggests, the foundations of the movement lay in chance occurrences and the absurd. Reason, the Dada artists concluded, had led only to war. For them the nonsensical and the absurd became tools to jolt their audience out of their bourgeois complacency and conventional thinking. The movement was profoundly committed to challenging the status quo in politics as well as in culture. Dada began in 1916 in Zürich, in neutral Switzerland, where a large number of writers and artists had sought refuge from the war.

Zürich Dada: Jean (Hans) Arp

In Zürich, the poet Hugo Ball founded the Cabaret Voltaire in 1916 as a performance center where writers and artists could protest the absurdity and wastefulness of the Great War. Ball was soon joined by the Romanian poet Tristan Tzara, who became Dada's most vociferous proponent. Through absurd art, literature, and performances, they hoped to produce anarchy, a *tabula rasa* or clean slate that would provide a new, fresh foundation for an understanding of the world.

The Zürich Dadaists exhibited a broad range of avant-garde art, such as paintings by De Chirico

28.1 Jean (Hans) Arp. *The Entombment of the Birds and Butterflies (Head of Tzara).* 1916–17. Painted wooden relief, 15¾ × 12¾″ (40 × 32.5 cm). Kunsthaus, Zürich.

(see fig. 27.14)—as long as it undermined bourgeois taste and standards. Most of the art was abstract. Among the strongest visual artists in the group was Jean ("Hans" in German) Arp (1886–1966), whose abstract collages hung on the walls of the Cabaret Voltaire on opening night. He made his collages by dropping pieces of torn rectangular paper on the floor; where they fell determined the composition. Although he claimed that chance alone arranged the papers, Arp probably manipulated them.

Arp believed that chance itself replicated nature. For him, life, despite the best-laid plans, was pure happenstance. Arp had been in Munich with Kandinsky (see pages 559–60), and there he adopted a mystical view of the world that envisioned a life force running through all things, binding them together in no particular order. Like Kandinsky, Arp sought to capture abstract universal forces. This spiritual outlook can be seen in the low-relief sculptures that he began making at about this time, such as *The Entombment of the Birds and Butterflies (Head of Tzara)* (**fig. 28.1**). The different shapes were determined by doodling on paper. He then had carpenters cut these shapes out of wood, which he painted and assembled into abstract compositions evoking plant and animal forms as well as clouds, cosmic gases, and celestial bodies. The title came last, and, as it suggests, the image can also be seen as a head, suggesting an elemental connection between humans and nature.

New York Dada: Marcel Duchamp

In New York, Dada was centered on Marcel Duchamp (1887–1968). The New York artists had no Cabaret Voltaire, no manifestos, and no performances. The word Dada was never used at the time to describe their art; it was applied only in retrospect because their spirit was similar to that found in Zürich. Similarly they used chance processes and the absurd and outrageous to challenge bourgeois sensitivity and the status quo.

One of the highlights of New York Dada is Duchamp's *Fountain* (**fig. 28.2**). The French artist submitted his sculpture to the 1917 exhibition of the Society of Independent Artists, an organization set up several decades earlier to provide exhibition opportunities for artists who did not conform to the conservative standards of New York's National Academy of Design, which had been the most prestigious exhibition venue. Duchamp labeled his *Fountain* an "assisted readymade." He took the term from American readymade clothing, and

applied it to sculptures that simply re-presented a found object, such as a snow shovel, which he hung from the ceiling and entitled *In Advance of a Broken Arm*. Duchamp called "assisted readymades" those objects that he "assisted," by combining two found items, for example, as in *Bicycle Wheel* (made in Paris in 1913), in which he mounted a bike wheel on a bar stool, or by falsely signing, as in *Fountain*.

Fountain was, in fact, a urinal manufactured by J. L. Mott Iron Works in New York. Duchamp selected it, purchased it, turned it 90 degrees, set it on a pedestal, and crudely signed it with the fictitious name of "R. Mutt"—a reference not only to the manufacturer but also to the character in the popular *Mutt and Jeff* comic strip. The work was submitted to the society's exhibition under Mutt's name, not Duchamp's. According to the society's rules, those paying the $6 admission fee would have their work accepted. But Duchamp knew the hanging committee would not allow Mutt's *Fountain* to go on view, and when it was removed at the opening, his friends formed a rowdy removal procession that drew attention to its rejection.

28.2 Marcel Duchamp. *Fountain*. 1917. Photograph by Alfred Stieglitz, from *The Blind Man*. May 1917. Philadelphia Museum of Art, Louise and Walter Arensberg Collection

 Watch a video about Marcel Duchamp on myartslab.com

Duchamp continued the hoax of R. Mutt's authorship of the piece when he wrote an article about it in his small newspaper, *The Blind Man*. The article was illustrated by a Stieglitz photograph of it placed before a painting by the American artist Marsden Hartley, as seen in our illustration, thus asserting that the proper context for *Fountain* was the art world. The article defended Mutt's right to create a Readymade: "Whether Mr. Mutt with his own hands made the fountain or not has no importance. He chose. He took an ordinary article of life, placed it so that its useful significance disappeared under a new title and point of view … [creating] a new thought for that object."

Like all of Duchamp's works, *Fountain* is rich in ideas, and it stands as one of the seminal works of twentieth-century art, although the original has disappeared. The sculpture is all about idea. A viewer of *Fountain* must ask, what is the work of art? Is it the urinal, the provocation of submitting it to the exhibition, the boisterous parade when it was removed from the show, or the article in *The Blind Man*? Obviously, it is all of these things. Even the title is essential to the work, since it is an essential part of the sculpture, allowing Duchamp to make it clear that he is attacking a revered art form, the fountain, the centerpiece of many European towns and city squares and, in some respects, a symbol for the tradition of fine art. The satirical title also reinforces the humor of the piece, an ingredient found in much of Duchamp's work. He is telling us that art can defy conventional notions of beauty, and while intellectually engaging us in a most serious manner, can also make us smile or laugh. He challenges the notion of what is art and the importance of technique or craft, as well as the artist's signature. He also asks how a work of art takes on meaning. Here, Duchamp emphasizes the relationship between context and meaning: By taking a urinal out of its normal context he has changed its meaning. (For a more extensive discussion of Duchamp, see the Introduction, pages 8–9.) He even allows a viewer to assign meaning to the work, underscoring how this is a reality for all art. Duchamp declared that, unlike all art before him, his Readymades have no aesthetic value and theoretically no intended meaning. They are merely a device to launch ideas.

Because *Fountain* is industrially manufactured and can be easily replaced if broken or lost, Duchamp also questions the significance attached to the uniqueness of a work of art. As we shall see, in the second half of the twentieth century, Duchamp will become the dominant figure in art as artists worldwide make what will be called Conceptual Art. For those artists, an idea or conceptual premise is an important component of their work, often the most important.

Berlin Dada

With the end of the war, the Dada poet Richard Huelsenbeck (1892–1974) left Zürich for Berlin. There he found a moribund city, which like all of Germany was without food, money, medicine, or a future. Germans, especially the working class, loathed the military-industrial machine, which they felt had betrayed their interests by leading them into war. With the surrender, conditions worsened as Germany was punished by harsh and, some thought, unrealistic reparation demands. Inflation was rampant, and the value of the currency, the German Mark, plunged. Open class conflict in 1919 resulted in Communist-led worker uprisings in Berlin and Munich that were brutally repressed by right-wing armed units. The Weimar Republic government, which had replaced the emperor

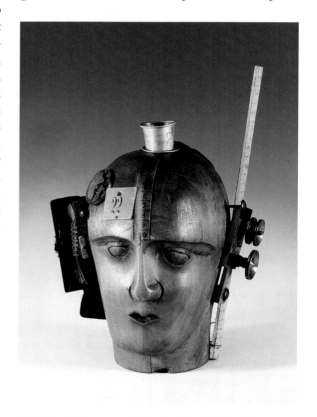

28.3 Raoul Hausmann. *Mechanical Head (Spirit of the Age)*. ca. 1920. Assemblage, height 12¾" (32.5 cm). Musée National d'Art Moderne, Centre Georges Pompidou, Paris. © ADAGP, Paris and DACS, London 2008

and represented Germany's first experience with democracy, failed to revive the economy.

For many, hope lay in the East, in Russia, where the Bolshevik Revolution established the prospect for a nationless world governed by the proletariat. The artists and writers in Berlin Dada looked to international worker solidarity as Germany's salvation. Here was a situation where Dada anarchy and nihilism could be put to practical use. Almost without exception, the Berlin Dada contingent made political art and were political activists, with some members joining the Communist Party.

RAOUL HAUSMANN Raoul Hausmann (1886–1971) quickly became the leader of the Berlin Dadaists, and was perhaps the most visually inventive, as can be seen in his 1920 assemblage *Mechanical Head (Spirit of the Age)* (**fig. 28.3**). He used found objects, which at the time were so foreign to the art world that they were considered junk: A mannequin's head, a collapsible cup, a wallet, labels, nails, and rulers. But now we see a new approach to making sculpture: The found objects are assembled together, for the purpose of making a statement condemning materialism and the loss of individuality and personal identity. Hausmann, however, is best known for his use of language, in Dada poems and in collage, which he called photomontages and which evoke a machine-made, mass-produced, antiart aesthetic.

HANNAH HÖCH Some of the most elaborate and powerful Dada collages from the period were also created by Hannah Höch (1889–1978). They mimic manipulated photographic portraits made for the German military. Individuals or entire battalions hired photographers to create fictitious portraits by photographing the patron or patrons, then cutting out their heads and pasting them onto preexisting pictures of, for example, mounted militia.

Cut with the Kitchen Knife Dada Through the Last Weimar Beer Belly Cultural Epoch of Germany (**fig. 28.4**) speaks volumes about the agenda of Berlin Dada. Using a chaotic, cramped composition of crowds, words, machinery, and lettering of different sizes and styles, Höch captures the hectic social, political, and economic intensity of the Weimar Republic. Her photomontage represents the reality captured by photographers for the popular press. To Höch and her Dada colleagues, the camera was another machine, related to the technological advances and a propagandistic tool that had led to

the war. With her "kitchen knife," she rearranged the imagery to create a handmade photograph, thus forcing the machine to be subject to the human rather than vice versa. The result is a spinning, gearlike composition with a portrait of the radical antiwar female artist Käthe Kollwitz at the center. German masses and the new leaders of their government, the Weimar Republic, are pushed to the sides and villainously labeled as the "anti-Dada," meaning against Dada and leftist politics.

Cologne Dada

In the city of Cologne, Dada initially took its lead from Berlin, but it was never as overtly political. Dada artists here were intrigued by Freud's theory of the unconscious and favored figures that combined mechanical and human forms (sometimes called **mechanomorphic** art). The key Cologne

28.4 Hannah Höch. *Cut with the Kitchen Knife Dada Through the Last Weimar Beer Belly Cultural Epoch of Germany*. ca. 1919. Collage, 44⅞ × 35⅜″ (114 × 90.2 cm). Staatliche Museen zu Berlin

 Read the document related to Hannah Höch on myartslab.com

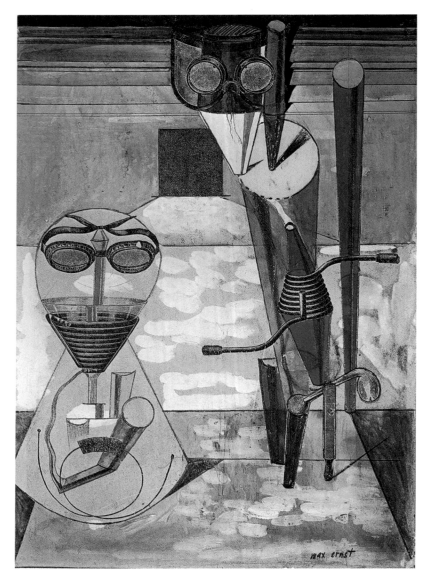

heavy psychological overtones. Not surprisingly, Ernst was fascinated by Freud's theories about the unconscious and the importance of dreams.

Through Arp, Ernst was put in contact with two leaders of the Paris Dada movement, the poets André Breton and Paul Éluard, both of whom had also come under Freud's spell, entranced by the idea that the unconscious contained elemental realities suppressed by civilization. In 1922, Ernst emigrated to Paris, and in 1924 Breton issued a *Surrealist Manifesto*, anointing a 1921 Paris show of Ernst's collages as the first Surrealist exhibition.

Paris Dada: Man Ray

The transition from Dada to Surrealism was well underway by 1922, and it occurred in Paris. Dada had established a foothold in the French capital with the return of Duchamp at the end of 1918.

One of the artists who moved in and out of the Paris Dada circle and would soon be labeled a major Surrealist was the American Man Ray (1890–1976). He had befriended Duchamp in New York, participated in New York Dada, and followed Duchamp to Paris in 1921. Best known as a photographer, Man Ray was extraordinarily inventive and worked in many media, some, such as airbrush painting, being quite innovative. Most important, Man Ray was the first artist to use photography consistently within a Dada context, and helped establish it, at least within Dada and Surrealist circles, as a medium on a par with painting and sculpture.

In 1922, Man Ray had a major impact on the development of photography, as well as on Dada and abstract art, when he popularized the photogram—a one-of-a-kind cameraless photograph made by putting objects directly on photographic paper and then exposing both object and paper to light. Solid objects block light from striking the white paper, so they appear white in the image, while the spaces between and around them become black, since there is nothing to prevent the light from exposing the paper. Tzara dubbed Man Ray's print a "rayograph."

Reproduced here is a photograph of one of these first rayographs, *Champs délicieux* (Delightful Fields), which contains the silhouettes of a brush and comb, a sewing pin, a coil of paper, and a strip of fabric, among the identifiable items (**fig. 28.6**). The image, like much of Man Ray's work, helps demonstrate the close relationship between the random and defiant art of Dada and the evocative, often sensual, art of Surrealism. The objects appear

Dada artist was Max Ernst (1891–1976), who appropriated the Berlin artists' collage technique.

Typical of Ernst's work from this very productive period is *1 Copper Plate 1 Zinc Plate 1 Rubber Cloth 2 Calipers 1 Drainpipe Telescope 1 Piping Man* (**fig. 28.5**), a collage with gouache, ink, and pencil made on an illustration from a 1914 book about chemistry equipment. With a line here and a dab of paint there, Ernst transformed the picture of laboratory utensils into bizarre robotic figures set in a stark symbol-filled landscape. Perhaps we should say dreamscape, for the glazed-over stares, and the skewed De Chirico-like perspective that culminates in a mystifying square, give this little collage an elemental power suggesting some otherworldly sphere—one of the imagination. The dreamlike quality of Ernst's image endows his figures with

ghostlike and mysterious, in a strange environment where darks and lights have been reversed and where a haunting overall darkness prevails. Shapes and lines move in and out of dark shadows, sometimes vibrating, as with the brush and comb silhouette, at other times crisply stated, as in the center oval. Man Ray's photograms, as with the Surrealistic art that would follow, have a magical blend of the real and nonreal. We feel the presence of a real comb and sewing pin, and yet they seem to exist in a dream world. Just as impossible to explain is the relationship of these objects and shapes to one another.

Surrealism

Surrealism had existed in spirit, if not in name, well before 1924, but the movement was formally launched by Breton that year when he issued his *Surrealist Manifesto*. Surrealism, Breton wrote, is "pure psychic automatism, by which it is intended to express, either verbally, or in writing, or in any other way, the true functioning of thought. Thought expressed in the absence of any control exerted by reason, and outside all moral and aesthetic considerations." Banished was the Neoclassical god of reason, the sureness of logic, and the need to portray an observable reality. Also gone was Dada nihilism, replaced by an intensive, positive exploration of the unconscious.

Surrealists argued that we see only a surface reality. More important was uncovering the reality that, as Freud maintained, resided in the deep-seated secrets and desires of the unconscious mind. Breton's manifesto proposed several ways to tap into the unconscious. He encouraged the use of dreamlike images, the juxtaposition of unrelated objects, and, for writers, stream-of-consciousness writing. He emphasized the concept of creating "the marvelous," images, either verbal or visual, that are mysterious, chance, and poetic, and jolt the audience into a new, unknown plane of reality, a surreality. But visual art had little place in Breton's manifesto, and artists were mentioned only as a footnote, appearing in a single sentence. Among those listed were Ernst, Man Ray, De Chirico, and Picasso. Perhaps the most surprising name on Breton's list is Picasso's, but Breton saw Picasso's Cubism as the first step toward loosening the grip of reality on the artistic imagination, and he especially admired *Les Demoiselles d'Avignon*.

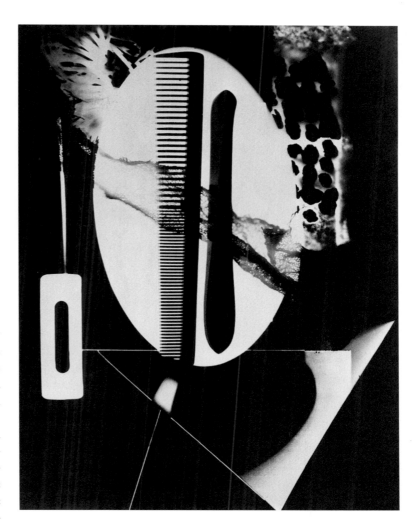

Surrealism in Paris

In 1924, Breton, like everyone, had doubts about the possibility that there could even be Surrealist art. Many argued that the visual arts, unlike writing, did not allow for a stream of consciousness. The imagery could seem surreal, but the method was not. Initially, many of the visual artists championed by Breton relied on automatic drawing and chance to produce their images. The Parisian André Masson is best known for developing automatic drawing, producing a wiry automatic line while in a trancelike state. He then allowed the initial chance drawing to spur his imagination, fleshing out the composition from there. Not to be outdone, Max Ernst developed the technique of *frottage*, which consisted of placing paper on top of an object, say, a piece of wood, and then rubbing graphite or charcoal over the surface to obtain an image, which like Masson's automatic drawing would spur his imagination to create a fantasy world.

28.6 Man Ray. *Champs délicieux*. 1922. Rayograph gelatin silver print

28.7 Joan Miró. *Composition*. 1933. Oil on canvas, 4'3⅜" × 5'4⅛" (1.3 × 1.63 m). Wadsworth Atheneum, Hartford, Connecticut. The Ella Gallup Sumner and Mary Catlin Sumner Collection Fund

Another artist championed as a Surrealist by Breton was Joan Miró (1893–1983), born in Catalonia, who came to Paris in 1920. He adopted Masson's wiry line to make abstractions of biomorphic and geometric forms set against a minimal color field that suggested a landscape or watery environment. Miró's paintings became increasingly abstract, as seen in *Composition* (**fig. 28.7**), a 1933 oil. The work was one of a series based on collages on cardboard made from images cut out of product catalogues, with the idea that the shape and even details of the objects would fire his imagination. The setting of *Composition* is a hazy atmospheric environment of washes, suggesting a kind of primeval landscape. This eerie dream world is populated by strange curvilinear floating forms that suggest prehistoric and microscopic creatures, as well as spirits, ghosts, or souls. We can even find a story in places, such as two figures playing with or fighting over a ball in the upper left corner. Or are they? Regardless, they suggest play or fighting, as other features in the painting express sex, struggle, and fear. Miró uses a minimal vocabulary, which includes color as well as form, to create a mythic image evoking primal conditions.

Representational Surrealism: Salvador Dalí

Initially, Breton's strongest support was for an abstract Surrealism based on chance, spontaneity, and trance. Over the next decade, however, artists with all kinds of styles would move in and out of the movement, and representational Surrealism in particular became popular.

One of the major Surrealists working in a representational style was Salvador Dalí (1904–1989). He came to Paris from Madrid, where he had already developed a meticulously detailed realist style heavily based on the psychological complexes that Freud described in his writings. Dalí made his paintings using a process he called "paranoiac-critical"—"[a] spontaneous method of irrational knowledge based upon the interpretative-critical association of delirious phenomena." He created in a frenzy, a self-induced paranoid state where he would begin a painting with a single object in mind. Then, he would respond to that object and so on, developing a mysterious image reflecting an irrational process that released the unconscious. *The Persistence of Memory* (**fig. 28.8**) began with the strange amorphous head with an elongated trailing neck lying on the ground. Looking at a plate of soft Camembert cheese at dinner, he was then inspired to paint the soft pocket watches. While allowing no certain reading, the picture evokes a host of associations, such as male impotency, and most obviously the crippling passage of time that leads to inevitable deterioration and death. Dalí has created a provocative image of mysterious objects that can be read as

 28.8 Salvador Dalí. *The Persistence of Memory*. 1931. Oil on canvas, 9½ × 13″ (24.1 × 33 cm). The Museum of Modern Art, New York. Given anonymously (162.1934)

 View the Closer Look for *The Persistence of Memory* on myartslab.com

metaphors for the deepest desires, fears, and anxieties, especially sexual, of the mind, and that can unleash multiple interpretations from a viewer's own unconscious.

The Surrealist Object

When Miró began work on his *Composition*, he started with an image that, like a dream, took him on a journey of psychological exploration and formal invention. Surrealists also created objects that would initiate such journeys for viewers as well as for themselves. In fact some of the most succinct Surrealist artworks were fetishistic objects, mysterious poetic things that were found or created, and had no narrative, but jolted the unconscious and spawned infinite associations, mostly sexual and often violent.

Probably the most famous Surrealist object was made by Meret Oppenheim (1913–1985). Born in Germany, she went to Paris as an 18-year-old in 1932. Inspired by an off-hand comment she made when lunching with Picasso in 1936, she covered a teacup, saucer, and spoon with gazelle fur and called it *Object* (**fig. 28.9**), although Breton, when he included it in a Surrealist exhibition, retitled it *Luncheon in Fur*, punning on Manet's sexually fraught *Luncheon on the Grass* (see fig. 25.2).

Oppenheim presents us with eroticism offered and eroticism denied, for individually, fur and beverage are sensual, but juxtaposed as they are, they are disconcerting, if not outright repulsive. The fur anthropomorphizes the porcelain and spoon, and suggests pubic hair. The work is designed to trigger the unconscious, to evoke infinite associations that deal with the repressed realities of eroticism,

28.9 Meret Oppenheim. *Object (Luncheon in Fur)*. 1936. Fur-covered teacup, saucer, and spoon; diameter of cup 4¾″ (12.1 cm); diameter of saucer 9⅜″ (23.8 cm); length of spoon 8″ (20.3 cm). The Museum of Modern Art, New York

View the Closer Look for *Object (Luncheon in Fur)* on myartslab.com

sensuality, desire, and anxiety. Using minimal means, Oppenheim created the "marvelous" that takes a viewer into the realm of the surreal.

Organic Sculpture

The abstract Surrealism of Miró and Arp inspired many artists to search for universal truths beneath the surface of things. As did the Romantic landscape painters of the previous century, they focused on Nature, trying to pry loose the unseen pulse of the cosmos that coursed through the natural world. To reveal these higher truths and realities, a number of artists, including Alexander Calder in Paris and Henry Moore in England, turned to working with abstract organic forms. Often, they showed in Surrealist exhibitions and were occasionally labeled Surrealists, especially since their work dealt with hidden realities. But despite many parallels, their interests were quite different from Breton's as they evolved in the 1930s. Breton was more concerned with the psychology of anxiety, desire, and sex; the artists working with abstract organic forms were interested in the powerful forces of the universe.

Alexander Calder in Paris

The American Alexander Calder (1898–1976) went to Paris in 1926, where he befriended Miró and the abstract Dutch painter Piet Mondrian. In the early 1930s he started making mobiles, a name that Duchamp gave his kinetic sculpture (work involving movement). Each mobile was constructed of painted sheet metal attached to wires that were hinged together and perfectly balanced. With the slightest breath of air, the mobile seems to glide, tilting and turning in space. The mobiles vary in size from tabletop models to others with a 30-foot span that hang from a ceiling.

Taking his lead from Miró and Arp, Calder generally used organic shapes, as seen in *Lobster Trap and Fish Tail* (**fig. 28.10**) of 1939. The forms suggest marine life, but generally they are abstract, and like Miró's paintings, simultaneously suggest

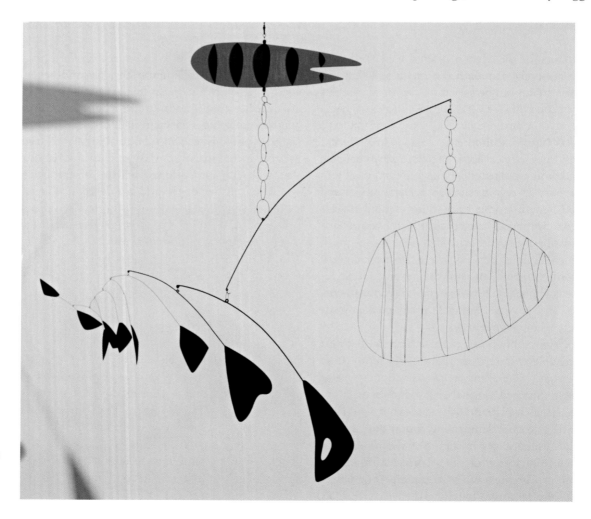

28.10 Alexander Calder. *Lobster Trap and Fish Tail*. 1939. Painted steel wire and sheet aluminum, approx. 8′6″ × 9′6″ (2.59 × 2.89 m). The Museum of Modern Art, New York. Commissioned by the Advisory Committee for the Stairwell of the Museum

28.11 Henry Moore. *Recumbent Figure*. 1938. Green Hornton stone, length approx. 54" (137.2 cm). Tate Britain, London

the microscopic and macroscopic. The black forms in *Lobster Trap* can be seen as a school of fish, but viewed together they can suggest something skeletal, even primeval. Calder was in part inspired to develop kinetic sculpture to suggest growth and cosmic energy. He kept his colors basic, generally using primary and secondary colors, as well as black and white. All colors stem from these, so Calder's palette symbolized the basic building blocks of life, a notion that he took from Mondrian, whose Paris studio he visited in 1930.

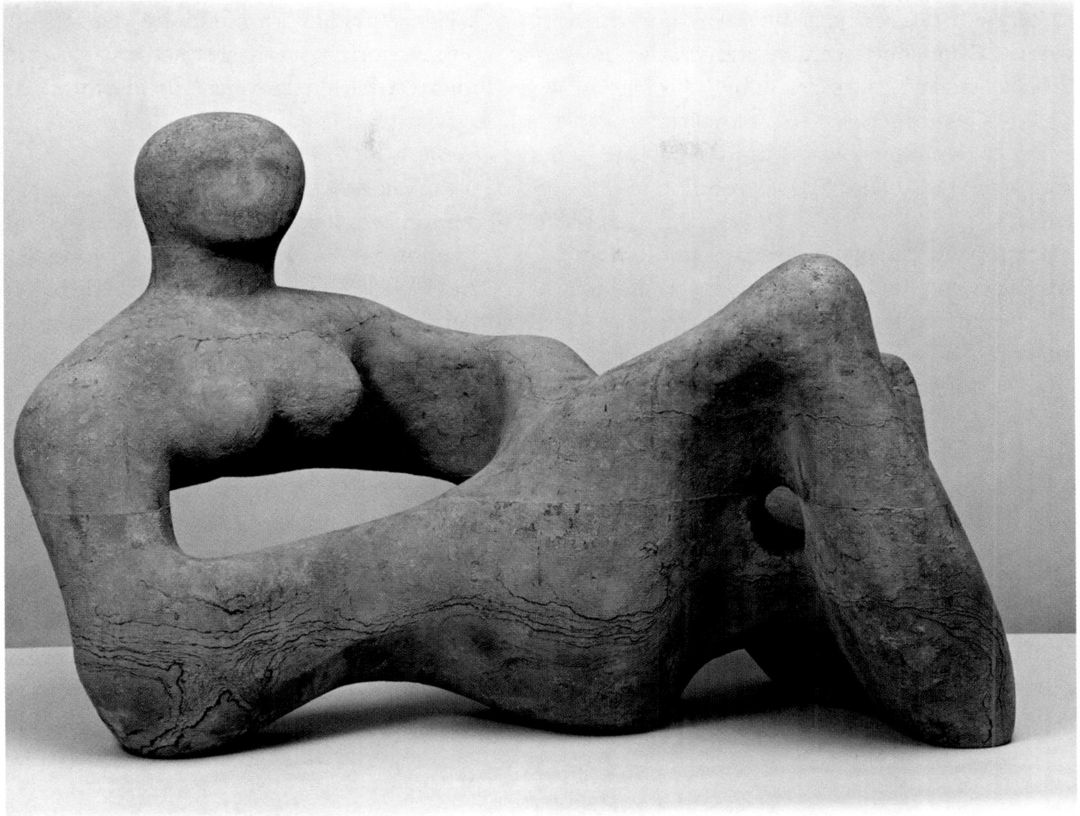

Henry Moore in England

The organic abstract style favored by Miró jumped the English Channel in the 1930s, surfacing in the work of Henry Moore (1898–1986). Moore's mature style emerged by the early 1930s, represented here by *Recumbent Figure* (**fig. 28.11**), made in 1938. The work is reminiscent of a classical reclining river goddess, although based more directly on Pre-Columbian figures. Moore is more interested in projecting the elemental and universal than in classical antiquity as he explores the associations between the forms of nature and the shapes of the figure. We see a woman, but the stone retains its identity as stone, looking like a rock that has been eroded by the elements for millions of years. Moore ingeniously suggests that figure and rock are one and the same, even making the female form harmonize with the striations of the stone. The universal forces present in the rock are transferred to the figure, which becomes an earth goddess or fertility figure. The undulation of her abstract body virtually transforms her into a landscape. Adding to the mystical aura is Moore's brilliant interplay between solid and void, each having the same weight in the composition and evoking the womb-like mystery of caves or tidal pools embedded in seashore rocks.

Creating Utopias

While Dada and Surrealism constituted a major force for the period between the wars, there were other major movements. Many twentieth-century artists remained committed to exploring abstract art. Dadaists, Surrealists, and abstract artists often shared similar socialist and communist goals: These groups championed individual freedom, and wished to undermine bourgeois values, to eradicate nationalism, to destroy capitalism, and to create a classless society. Many abstract artists viewed abstract art itself as a vehicle for creating a utopian society.

Two major centers of geometric abstraction emerged simultaneously: Constructivism, which appeared with the Russian Revolution in 1917, and De Stijl (The Style), which appeared in Amsterdam. A third center was the Bauhaus in Germany, an art school founded in 1919 that succeeded as a significant force in the following decade and was often influenced by Constructivist refugees from Russia and De Stijl artists.

Russian Constructivism: Productivism and Utilitarianism

The most direct connection between abstract art and radical politics came in the revolutionary society that developed in Russia. There, before and after the October Revolution of 1917, artists committed themselves to developing new art forms that they hoped would bring about a new utopian

28.12 Vladimir Tatlin. *Project for "Monument to the Third International."* 1919–20. Wood, iron, and glass, height 20′ (6.10 m). Destroyed; contemporary photograph

society. Building on the innovations of Malevich's Suprematism (see page 564–65), several movements followed, each attempting to put art at the service of the new revolutionary society.

VLADIMIR TATLIN As Malevich was developing his Suprematist painting in Moscow, a fellow Russian, Vladimir Tatlin (1885–1953), was working in Berlin and Paris. In 1914, Tatlin visited Picasso's Paris studio and saw his constructions (see pages 000–000). Upon returning to Russia, he then made his own constructed reliefs. Like Malevich's Suprematism, these were entirely abstract, and eventually his geometric abstract style, which had many Russian followers, became known as Constructivism.

With the Bolshevik Revolution in 1917, Tatlin's attitude toward his art changed. He embraced Communism and focused his effort on supporting the party's goal of creating a utopian society. He worked for the Soviet Education Commissariat and turned his attention to architecture and engineering. A major component of his teachings was his passionate belief in the utility of modern machinery, the democratic quality of mass-produced objects, and the efficiency of industrial materials. Technological modernity was the future and the new religion, and industrial efficiency and materials had to be incorporated into art, design, and architecture, where they would produce a new, better, classless world. In other words, the social revolution had to be complemented with an aesthetic revolution. According to Tatlin's theory called Constructivist Productivism, everything—from appliances to clothing, from living space to theater—now had to be machinelike and streamlined. Form must follow function and objects were to be stripped of all ornamentation, which was associated with bourgeois values and aristocratic ostentation.

Tatlin's most famous work is his *Project for "Monument to the Third International"* (**fig. 28.12**), begun in 1919 and exhibited in Petrograd (St. Petersburg) and Moscow in December 1920. The "monument" was designed as a construction of geometric forms. It was to be 1,300 feet high, which would have made it the tallest structure in the world at that time. It was to have a metal spiral frame tilted at an angle and encompassing a glass cube, cylinder, and cone. These geometric steel and glass units, housing conferences and meetings, were to revolve, making a complete revolution once a year, month, and day, respectively. The industrial materials of steel and glass and the dynamic, kinetic nature of the work symbolized the new Machine Age and the dynamism of the Bolshevik Revolution. The tower was to function as a propaganda center for the Communist Third International, an organization devoted to world revolution, and its rotating, ascending spiral symbolized the aspirations of Communism.

De Stijl and Universal Order

In 1917 in Amsterdam, the artist Piet Mondrian (1872–1944) founded a movement called De Stijl (The Style) with several other artists and architects, and they were joined by the architect Gerrit Rietveld (1888–1964) in 1919. Though not backed by a revolutionary government, as were the Russian artists, their goal was every bit as radical and utopian, for De Stijl artists sought to create, through abstraction, total environments so perfect that they embodied a universal harmony. Unlike their Russian counterparts, their mission was actually spiritual. Driven by Mondrian's intense commitment to Theosophy (page 536), De Stijl, like the Communists, sought a universal order that would make nationalism obsolete. They called their style the International Style, applying it most often to a new architecture of glass and steel that was modern, pure, and universal, and with no national identification.

PIET MONDRIAN In the magazine *De Stijl*, the group's publication, Mondrian published his theory of art in a series of articles. His philosophy was based on Theosophy, which he was interested in before his move to Paris in late 1911. After returning to neutral Amsterdam during the Great War, he was further influenced by the ideas of the mystical lay philosopher and his close acquaintance M. H. J. Schoenmaekers. Schoenmaekers argued that there was an underlying mathematical structure to the universe that constituted true reality and that an artist could access and present this structure through the rational manipulations of geometric forms. Mondrian developed an art based on such geometry, which he called Neo-Plasticism, meaning "new plasticism." By "plastic" in painting, he meant that the world of the painting had a plastic, or three-dimensional, reality of its own corresponding to the harmonious plastic reality of the universe. In other words, he sought to replicate in his art the unseen, underlying structure of the universe.

Beginning in 1917, Mondrian struggled to achieve this using total geometric abstraction,

and only succeeded upon returning to Paris in 1919. Once having established his style, he pretty much retained it for the rest of his life, as seen in *Composition No. II/Composition I//Composition with Red, Blue, and Yellow* of 1930 (**fig. 28.13**). His paintings, which are always asymmetrical, are remarkable for their perfect harmony. Mondrian very precisely gives every element equal weight. Each line and rectangle in this square canvas is assigned its own identity; every line exists in its own right, not as a means of defining the color rectangles. (The thickness of the lines often varies in his paintings, a function of individual identity.) Each component sits on the same plane on the surface—there is no foreground or background, no one object sitting on top of another. Despite this perfectly interlocking surface, the painting has a feeling of tremendous space, even of infinity, largely because the rectangles expand off the edge of the canvas. Space and mass have merged into a harmonious whole of what Mondrian called "dynamic equilibrium," where everything is energized yet balanced. Mondrian has attempted to capture the complexity of the universe—the

28.13 Piet Mondrian. *Composition No. II/Composition I//Composition with Red, Blue, and Yellow.* 1930. Oil on canvas, 20⅛ × 20⅛" (51 × 51 cm). The Fukuoka City Bank Ltd, Japan © 2012 Mondrian/Holtzman Trust. c/o HCR International USA

individuality of its infinite components and the harmony that holds everything together.

Mondrian made endless variations of these motifs. Even the color did not change, since these elementary hues, from which all colors are derived, are symbolic of the building blocks of the cosmos. But in principle, painting was not the end product of Mondrian's aesthetic program. He considered it just a stop-gap measure until perfect abstract environments of architecture, furniture, and objects embodying all of these same principles could be achieved.

GERRIT RIETVELD Mondrian's De Stijl colleagues sought to implement his theories in architecture and interior design. Once they discovered and understood the radical work of Frank Lloyd Wright (see page 546–47), they were able to apply architectural solutions to the theoretical ideas of Neo-Plasticism. They recognized that Wright had destroyed "the box," and declared "the new architecture will be anticubic." Combining the color and floating planes of Mondrian and the fluid spaces of Wright, Rietveld produced the definitive De Stijl building in 1924, the Schröder House in Utrecht (**fig. 28.14**), which was built onto the end of existing row houses. On the façade, we can find Mondrian's "floating" rectangles and lines. Even the

Wright-like cantilevered roof appears to float. The interior is designed along the same principles, with wall-to-ceiling sliding panels allowing for a restructuring of the interior space. Both inside and out, the Schröder House is ethereal, buoyant, and harmonious, embodying dynamic equilibrium.

The Bauhaus: Creating the "New Man"

As we have seen, most Dadaists, Surrealists, and abstract artists were socialists or Communists who believed that the Bolshevik Revolution in Russia would save the world from bourgeois materialism and decadence and would establish a worldwide utopian society. Left-wing artists regularly held conferences in Germany, attempting to commit to a social program that would put art at the service of restructuring society. All of these attempts came to naught. Instead, it was the Bauhaus, an art and design school, that gradually emerged as the strongest center for advocating social progress through art.

The Bauhaus was founded in Weimar, Germany, in 1919 by Walter Gropius. In many respects, the Bauhaus School was the embodiment of Muthesius's German Werkbund (see page 569), since the goal of the workshops was to design modern high-quality production-line products. Its guiding principle, however, was more utopian and less

28.14 Gerrit Rietveld. Schröder House, Utrecht, Holland. 1924

commercial, for the Bauhaus (meaning House of Building) was dedicated to the creation of utilitarian design for "the new man" through the marriage of art and technology. The school was formed by the merger of two Weimar arts and crafts schools, and designed to combine the fine and applied arts, giving each equal weight. The artists were called artisan/craftspeople, and their mission was to create an abstract environment of the most progressive modernity. Their design ethic was based on "the living environment of machines and vehicles." Only "primary forms and colors" could be used, all in the service of creating "standard types for all practical commodities of everyday use as a social necessity." Like De Stijl, this was a philosophy oriented toward environments, not just painting and sculpture, and the Bauhaus is often more associated with the work that came out of the textile, metal, and ceramic workshops, such as Marcel Breuer's 1927 aluminum tubular chairs and Anni Albers's abstract textiles, than the paintings of Kandinsky, who also taught at the school.

MARCEL BREUER   We can see the Bauhaus machine aesthetic at work in the living room of a Gropius house built in 1927 for a Werkbund housing

development in Stuttgart (**fig. 28.15**). The furniture and lighting were designed by Marcel Breuer (1902–1981), a former Bauhaus student who became a faculty member in 1925, heading the furniture workshop. All of Breuer's objects are geometric, made of modern materials, and easily mass-produced. On the far right is perhaps his most famous product, the "Wassily" armchair, made of polished, nickel-plated tubular steel and cotton fabric. In its planarity, the design was clearly influenced by De Stijl aesthetics. But now the heavy wood favored by De Stijl has been replaced by a strong but light metal tube that is geometrically structured in an airy, open pattern. The feeling that results echoes the transparency and weightlessness of Suprematist painting and Constructivist sculpture, qualities that can even be seen in Tatlin's *Project for "Monument to the Third International"* (see fig. 28.12).

WALTER GROPIUS   Many scholars consider the crowning aesthetic achievement of the Bauhaus to be the building itself, designed by Gropius in 1925 when the school moved from Weimar to Dessau. The building consists of three L-shaped wings coming off a central hub, one of which is

28.15 Marcel Breuer. Furniture for a living room in one of two houses desgined by Walter Gropius for the Werkbund housing development Am Weissenhof, Stuttgart, Germany. 1927

the Shop Block, a workshop wing (**fig. 28.16**). The entire complex is dominated by a clearly articulated geometry, making it look like an enormous Constructivist sculpture. The workshop wing looks like an empty glass box, the glass curtain wall on two sides continuing around corners and flush with the stuccoed parapet above and the socle (the projecting molding under the wall) below. Instead of mass, we feel a weightless volume as defined by the metal and glass wall. And because the building projects over a setback half-basement, it appears suspended.

Gropius's Bauhaus came to epitomize High Modernist architecture—the architecture that evolved out of early Modernism (see pages 569–70) in the period between the two wars. With High Modernism, buildings became more severely geometric and so light that they seemed to float. Their unadorned geometric shapes represented volume, not mass. Their walls were thin membranes of a taut veneer that encased the building, and, as with the Bauhaus Workshop, often this veneer was a curtain of glass. But High Modernism was more than just a style; it was a social movement predicated on utopian socialist philosophy and a rationalist belief in progress. Life could be improved, the theory went, by creating a Machine-Age environment. The movement was reduced to a style in 1932 when the architect Philip Johnson and the historian Henry-Russell Hitchcock organized an exhibition entitled "The International Style"

at the newly opened Museum of Modern Art in New York. Their concern was with the look of the architecture, not its social premises. The exhibition brought the style to the attention of Americans, and resulted in the label "International Style" being used to describe High Modernist architecture.

The Machine Aesthetic

The machine aesthetic and the utopian dream that accompanied it also made their way to Paris, where they found a rather different voice in the architecture of Charles-Édouard Jeanneret, called Le Corbusier (1886–1965). Unlike Moscow, Amsterdam, and Dessau, Paris had no art schools or major artistic movements pushing for a utopian vision. Instead, the cause there was undertaken by individuals.

LE CORBUSIER'S IDEAL HOME Le Corbusier was Swiss, and settled in Paris after briefly working in 1910 with Walter Gropius in the Berlin office of a leading German architect. With a third Modernist architect, Mies van der Rohe (see page 000), they talked about creating a machine-based, easily reproduced architecture.

In 1922, Le Corbusier opened an architectural firm with his cousin, and by 1923 he had developed the principles for his ideal home, which he published in an article entitled "Five Points of a New Architecture." His five points were as follows:

28.16 Walter Gropius. Shop Block, The Bauhaus. 1925–26. Dessau, Germany

28.17 Le Corbusier. Villa Savoye. 1928–29. Poissy-sur-Seine, France

 Explore the architectural panoramas of the Villa Savoye on myartslab.com

(1) No ground floor, with the house raised on columns called *pilotis*; (2) a flat roof, which would be used as a garden terrace; (3) an open floor plan, with partitions slotted between supports; (4) free composition of the exterior curtain walls; and (5) preferably ribbon (horizontal) windows. The raised house allowed for privacy and light and made the outdoors accessible by putting a garden on the roof. Much later, Le Corbusier remarked that "a house is a machine for living in," which suggested—wrongly—to many critics that he advocated a brutal functionalism that was not concerned with beauty and comfort. In fact, Le Corbusier wanted to create a classical purity based on geometry: His houses would have a Machine-Age look and efficiency, using the latest technology. And they would be filled with light. His emphasis was on the human being and "living." Machine-Age values and technology were to be at the service of humans.

The 1928 Villa Savoye (**fig. 28.17**) in Poissy-sur-Seine, outside Paris, is Le Corbusier's best-known house, and here we can see most of the elements called for in his "Five Points": The *pilotis*, the raised living space, the ribbon windows, and the flat-roof terrace, which is protected behind the enormous cylindrical windscreens that look like ocean-liner smokestacks. The main floor, the second, has an open-space plan using partition walls, and it faces into a court, from which a ramp leads up to the roof. Everywhere we look we see a beautiful classicizing geometry, the building blocks of Le Corbusier's design aesthetic. The building is a perfect square box precisely defined by its taut skin of concrete; the *pilotis* are cylinders, and the windbreakers are enormous arcs. Like the Bauhaus and Schröder House, the house appears light, virtually floating on its *pilotis*.

Art in America: Modernity, Spirituality, and Regionalism

Perhaps more than Europe, the United States could embrace the machine as the emblem of progress, for after World War I, America was the undisputed technological leader of the world. In contrast to the European avant-garde, and its search for a classless, nationless world, Americans were

28.18 Joseph Stella. *The Voice of the City, New York Interpreted.* 1920–22. Oil and tempera on canvas, five panels, 8'3¾" × 22'6" (2.53 × 6.86 m). The Newark Museum, New Jersey. 37.288 a–e. © Estate of Joseph Stella

preoccupied with national identity. American artists, living in a politically stable country, generally did not have a utopian vision. Instead they viewed skyscrapers, factories, and machines as symbols of the nation's technological superiority. But not everyone embraced modernity. As the economy boomed in the postwar years, culminating in the dizzying exuberance of the Roaring Twenties, many artists rejected materialism and sought the spiritual. While some artists turned to Nature in search of universal truths, others sought strength in old-fashioned American values that could be found in the country's heartland, especially in the lifestyle of its hearty, hard-working, God-fearing farmers.

The City and Industry

In 1915, arriving in New York harbor for the first time, Marcel Duchamp marveled at the towering skyscrapers and pronounced them the epitome of modernity. He saw in America the future of art. The skyscraper and modern industry did indeed become the emblems of America in art, replacing landscape, which had dominated painting in the previous century. The symbol of the nation for many artists and intellectuals was New York, and its defining feature the skyscraper, often described as the "cathedral of capitalism" or "commerce."

JOSEPH STELLA Perhaps the greatest single visual icon of the city was made by the Italian immigrant Joseph Stella (1877–1946). Entitled *The Voice of the City, New York Interpreted* (**fig. 28.18**) and completed in 1922, it is an 8-foot-high, five-panel work that features in the center panel an abstraction of the

city's towers, with the famous Flatiron building in the foreground, surrounded by both actual and fictitious buildings. The panels flanking the center panel represent the "Great White Way," Broadway's theater district, which has been reduced to an abstraction of color and light. The far left panel presents the harbor on the Hudson River on the west side of Lower Manhattan, while the right panel shows the Brooklyn Bridge on the east side. Every image features the technological wonders of Manhattan. We see communication towers, air venting systems, and elevated trains in the harbor picture. The Great White Way panels present the dazzling illumination of Times Square at night, which at the time had no equivalent anywhere else in the world. In effect, these two panels are a homage to electricity and the energy of the city. And even 35 years after opening, the Brooklyn Bridge still remained one of the world's great feats of engineering.

Stella moved to America in 1896, but returned to Italy to study in 1910, where he met the Futurists (see pages 562–64). Through the Stieglitz "291" Gallery and his friendship with Duchamp and Man Ray, among others, he kept in touch with European trends, with Cubism becoming his primary artistic language in the 1910s. The Great White Way panels especially reflect the tenets of Futurism, for here we see the soundwaves and Mach-like indications of motion that we saw in Boccioni's *States of Mind* (see fig. 27.11). Their dizzying kaleidoscope of color powerfully captures the intense visual experience of Times Square at night. But in the skyscraper and Brooklyn Bridge panels, Stella is not only representational, he is iconic, centering his motifs and transforming them into emblems of modernity. His palette is deeply saturated, and color is often encased in heavy black-line drawing, in effect transforming his image into a "stained-glass window." He reinforces the religious motif by adding a predella at the bottom (see page 279), which itemizes the different tunnels and utility tubes running beneath the city. Stella is declaring technology and modernity to be the religion of the twentieth century.

PAUL STRAND Photography, it turns out, was especially well suited to capturing the triumphs of the Machine Age. But first the medium had to break away from Pictorialism (see pages 524–25) and its romantic portrayal of the world. This occurred when the young Paul Strand (1890–1976) between 1915 and 1917 made a large body of work of sharply focused, high-contrast photographs. Stieglitz immediately recognized their importance and showed a selection of them at "291." *Wire Wheel* (**fig. 28.19**) is from this period. Its abstracted subject is a Model T Ford, an icon of the Machine Age since it marked the advent of the assembly line. The picture rejects the "painterliness" of turn-of-the-century Pictorial photography. In its place is a new compositional style based on the Cubism that Strand saw displayed at Stieglitz's "291" Gallery and the Armory Show. By taking a close-up of the car, Strand created a skewed perspective and tight cropping, resulting in a difficult-to-read image with a flattened and complicated space.

MARGARET BOURKE-WHITE Strand's hard-edged aesthetic transformed photography, not only in America, but eventually throughout the world. His style was especially appropriate for technological and industrial images, reinforcing the machine-made precision of the subject. The photojournalist Margaret Bourke-White especially embraced this new aesthetic and was drawn to technological imagery, as seen in *Fort Peck Dam, Montana* (**fig. 28.20**), the cover image for the very first issue of *Life*, a picture-essay magazine published on November 23, 1936. The photograph's power lies in its severe austerity, which reinforces the mammoth scale of the dam, dwarfing the antlike workers below. Each of the dam's pylons is identical, looking as though they were pressed out of an enormous machine mold, and because the photograph of the dam is cropped on either side, these gigantic

28.19 Paul Strand. *Wire Wheel*. 1917. Platinum print from enlarged negative, 12⅝ × 10¼" (32.4 × 25.8 cm). George Eastman House, Rochester, New York. © Aperture Foundation, Inc., Paul Strand Archive

28.20 Margaret Bourke-White. *Fort Peck Dam, Montana*. From *Life* magazine, 1936

assembly-line towers seem endless as well. But they take on the grandeur of ancient Assyrian or Egyptian monuments, and again we find an artist declaring modern technology to be the new classicism.

Seeking the Spiritual

In the 1910s, much of the American creative community turned its attention to producing an American art. Writers, musicians, artists, and poets all felt that American culture was derived from Europe; now they would seek to discover what was unique about the American experience and try to express it in an indigenous way. For some artists, like Stella in *The Voice of the City, New York Interpreted* (fig. 28.18), the answer lay in American modernity. Others looked to Nature, going back to the pantheistic Romanticism of the Hudson River School and its successors (see page 492). Stieglitz especially became preoccupied with this issue of an American art, deciding in the 1920s to represent only American artists and naming his last gallery, which he opened in 1928, "An American Place." The artists

that Stieglitz showed from the early 1920s until his death in 1946 were generally, but not always, preoccupied with finding a higher meaning in life within a materialistic modern world, often focusing on Nature. One of them was Georgia O'Keeffe.

GEORGIA O'KEEFFE When Stieglitz first showed her work in 1916, Georgia O'Keeffe (1887–1986) was making small, abstract, minimalist watercolors that evoked sublime landscape. Toward 1920, her presentation of nature evolved into close-ups of flowers, as seen in *Black Iris III* (**fig. 28.21**) of 1926, where the image is so magnified that it virtually becomes abstract. We do not have to look far to find the pictorial source for O'Keeffe: Paul Strand. O'Keeffe briefly fell in love with the young, handsome Strand in 1917 and was smitten as well by the power of his photography, especially the use of the close-up image. This compositional device, she wrote, forced a viewer to see flowers with the same intensity that she did. But by abstracting the close-up, O'Keeffe accomplished much more: The forms of the flowers morph into the parts of a woman's body, and the iris is redolent of female sexuality. The petals ethereally dissolve into their surroundings, seeming to become one with the rest of nature.

Partly because of Stieglitz's marketing and of course because of the subject of flowers, traditionally associated with women artists, critics labeled O'Keeffe a distinctly female artist, one who works from emotion and the womb rather than the mind or the intellect, as is the case with men. They also described O'Keeffe's flowers as overtly erotic and sexual. This sexist characterization outraged O'Keeffe, who as a result did a series of New York skyscraper paintings in the 1920s to demonstrate that she could paint "male" subjects. Further, she denied that her pictures were about sexuality per se. And they are not. As with the banned, sexually explicit novels of her friend the English author D. H. Lawrence, her paintings were not about lust but the uncontainable surging force of Nature, particularly the urge to procreate. Sexuality was portrayed as being natural, beautiful, and as essential as a flower blossoming, disseminating pollen, and reproducing. And if her wonderful organic flower, which seems to be growing before our very eyes, begins to take on the look of other objects, such as clouds, smoke, buttocks, and flesh, it only increases the sense of universal equivalence that she, like Arthur Dove (see page 569), who also exhibited

28.21 Georgia O'Keeffe. *Black Iris III*. 1926. Oil on canvas, 36 × 29⅞" (91.4 × 75.9 cm). The Metropolitan Museum of Art, New York. The Alfred Stieglitz Collection, 1949. 60.278.1

with Stieglitz, believed ran through all things. In this microcosm of an iris, O'Keeffe presents a macrocosm so large that it encompasses the entire universe.

Regionalism and National Identity

While the New York avant-garde sought a national identity and spirituality using either images of modernity or compact abstract styles, a group of Midwest artists, headed by Grant Wood, Thomas Hart Benton, and John Stewart Curry, intentionally turned to "old-fashioned" representational art and regional imagery. Although trained in modern art centers (Benton and Wood studied in Europe as well as in New York and Chicago), they generally preferred to work in the Midwest, where they came from and with which they identified.

The most famous image produced by this group is *American Gothic* (**fig. 28.22**) by Grant Wood (1891–1942) of Cedar Rapids, Iowa. The picture was shown at the Art Institute of Chicago in 1930, where it caused a stir and brought Wood to national attention. It was intended as a window into the Midwest world in which the artist grew up and lived. A fictitious father and spinster daughter are presented as the God-fearing descendants of stalwart pioneers who first worked the soil. They are dressed in traditional, even old-fashioned, clothes and stand firmly against the march of progress. The style of their house, from which the title of the painting is taken, is called Carpenter Gothic, a nineteenth-century style evoking both the humble modesty and old-fashioned ways of the residents as well as their religious intensity, which parallels the fervor of the medieval period, when Gothic cathedrals were built. The characters' faith is emphasized by the numerous crosses embedded within the façade, and by the church steeple in the distant background.

Wood tells us his figures are orderly and clean, as suggested by the crisp drawing and severe horizontal and vertical composition. This propriety also stems from the primness of the woman's conservative dress and hair and the suggestions that she carefully tends to the house, as she does to the plants on the front porch. The figures' harsh frontality, the man's firm grasp on his pitchfork, and his overalls suggest that they are hardworking and strong. There is no hint of modernity, and the simplicity and the austerity of the setting suggest that they are frugal. Nonetheless, many critics viewed Wood as ridiculing his sitters and their lifestyle, and indeed the picture does contain humor, such as the woman warily looking off to the side as if to make sure nothing untoward is occurring. But, regardless of the interpretation, no one seemed to deny that it appeared to capture something fundamentally American, and especially Midwestern.

The Harlem Renaissance

In the 1910s and 1920s, hundreds of thousands of African Americans fled the racism and poverty of the rural South for the cities of the industrial North, where they hoped to find jobs, justice and equality. This confluence of blacks in New York's Harlem and Chicago's South Side resulted in a cultural flourishing devoted to self-discovery and to establishing a black identity, something white America had methodically denied African Americans. The movement was then called the New Negro Movement, although today it is generally known as the

Harlem Renaissance, after its primary center, often described as its "capital."

Leading this movement in literature, music, theater, and art was the Howard University philosopher Alain Locke (1886–1954), who called for a distinctive style that evoked a black sensibility and perspective. He advocated recapturing the African past and its art and encouraged representations of African Americans and their lives as well as a portrayal of the distinctive physical qualities of the race, just as African masks often stressed black physiognomy. In effect, he was advocating that artists and writers declare "black is beautiful." In his promotion of a black aesthetic, he encouraged artists to depict a distinct African-American culture, one that departed from the Euro-American tradition and reflected the enormous contributions Americans of African descent had made to American life and identity.

JACOB LAWRENCE   One of the most famous painters to emerge from the Harlem Renaissance was Jacob Lawrence (1917–2000), who received his training as a teenager in the 1930s at the federally sponsored Harlem Art Workshop and Harlem Community Art Center. Lawrence was a regular visitor at the Museum of Modern Art and the Metropolitan Museum of Art, studying everything from African Art to Mexican textiles, to all of the latest European styles. In the late 1930s, he began making large narrative series dedicated to black leaders, including the slavery abolitionist Harriet Tubman (1820–1913), the Haitian revolutionary Toussaint L'Ouverture (1745–1803), and the abolitionist Frederick Douglass (ca. 1817–1895). The images were small and modest, made of poster paint on cardboard or posterboard.

Lawrence is best known for his *Migration* series, begun in 1940. In 60 images, he presented the black migration and the African-American experiences in both North and South. While the series is anecdotal, the images do much of the talking through their abstraction, as seen in no. 58, *In the North the Negro Had Better Educational Facilities* (**fig. 28.23**). Three girls write numbers on a blackboard, but we do not see their faces, which would make them individual. Instead they represent the race and human vitality. We see numbers and arms rising higher, suggesting elevation through education, and we see a clean slate for a clean start. The girls' brightly colored dresses affirm life and happiness, while the jagged and pointed edges in their hair and skirts impart an energy and a quality of striving. Lawrence's sparse and beautifully colored pictures embody a remarkable psychology, which is often reinforced by the Modernist space of his pictures. Here a flat field pushes the figures to the surface, prominently displaying them.

28.23 Jacob Lawrence. *The Migration of the Negro* Series, number 58: *In the North the Negro Had Better Educational Facilities*. 1940–41. Casein tempera on hardboard, 12 × 18″ (30.5 × 45.7 cm). The Museum of Modern Art, New York. Gift of Mrs. David M. Levy

Mexican Art: Seeking a National Identity

The Mexican Revolution, which began in 1910 with the overthrow of the dictatorship of General Porfirio Díaz and ended in 1921 with the formation of the reformist government of Alvaro Obregón, triggered a wave of nationalism within the cultural community, one that focused on indigenous traditions while rejecting European influences. A government building campaign resulted in a large number of impressive mural commissions, which in turn gave rise to a school of muralists headed by Diego Rivera, among others. Either socialists or Communists, the muralists proclaimed murals as the true art of the people. The Mexican muralists gained international renown and were especially popular in the United States, where they received enormous commissions, ironically often from major capitalists, such as the Rockefeller family.

Diego Rivera

Diego Rivera (1886–1957) is perhaps the best-known Mexican muralist. He lived in Europe, primarily in Paris, from 1907 to 1921, and became an accomplished Cubist. By the late 1910s, he was consumed by the idea of creating a nationalistic revolutionary art through mural painting, and he traveled to Italy to study Renaissance murals. Upon returning to Mexico, he jettisoned his elite esoteric Cubism for the straightforward representational art of the Quattrocento (fifteenth-century Italian painting), giving it a monumentality that often also echoed the strong, simple forms of Mayan art. Furthermore, he shunned easel painting, declaring it a bourgeois capitalistic art form, a commodity for the rich. Like his fellow muralists he viewed his fresco murals as a public art, an art for the masses. He also felt his art should be about the indigenous people, not the Mexicans of European blood and their European customs. Consequently, many of his

28.24 Diego Rivera. *The Arsenal (Distributing Arms)*. ca. 1928. Fresco, 8'5¾" × 11'9" (2.56 × 3.58 m). Secretaría de Educación Pública, Court of Fiestas, Mexico City

mural commissions are about national identity and the uniqueness of Mexican customs and tradition.

Rivera was a Communist, and his politics, especially his championing of the common folk and labor, appear in his murals, as can be seen in the mural program of well over 125 frescoes he executed from 1924 to 1928 for the Secretaría de Educación Pública in Mexico City. These works were executed in traditional fresco (see page 144) as well as in a fresco technique Rivera believed was based on an ancient Mayan formula. Illustrated here is *The Arsenal,* also known as *Distributing Arms* (**fig. 28.24**), which is located on the top floor of the three-floor Court of Fiestas. For the ground floor, Rivera illustrated the different festivals found throughout Mexico, festivals he felt continued the spirit of ancient indigenous rituals and which he carefully researched. On the second floor, he had other muralists paint the escutcheons of the Mexican states. On the third floor, he painted two series that he called the "Corrido of the Agricultural Revolution" and the "Corrido of the Proletarian Revolution." Corrido is a reference to Mexican peasant ballads, which he wanted to evoke in his painted cycles, similarly designed with a mythic scope. In *The Arsenal,* a mural from the Agricultural Corrido, we see fellow artists Frida Kahlo, Tina Modotti, and David Siqueiros helping to hand out rifles to peasants and workers, their presence symbolizing the important role of art in supporting the working classes and the revolution. (The series ends with the triumph of the great revolutionary leader Emiliano Zapata.) In the left foreground is a Soviet soldier with a rifle, and in the background a red banner with the Soviet hammer and sickle, representing the union of labor and agriculture.

Stylistically, these murals reflect the influence of early Renaissance frescoes, works similarly designed to educate and spiritually inspire. Rivera's images are not only representational, they are carefully drawn (objects delineated by strong line) and modeled, often giving them a monumentality and sense of importance. By the 1930s, Rivera was receiving numerous prestigious mural commissions in the United States, which because of Roosevelt's New Deal Federal Art Project was employing artists to paint murals for government buildings. As a result, Rivera had an enormous impact on American art in the 1930s. Most important, however, was Rivera's willingness to defy so many of the tenets of Modernism. He very consciously rejected abstraction, at which he had become quite adept, and instead worked in a reactionary representational style, one going back to the fourteenth century. As he did in Mexico, he made art for the people, presenting it not primarily in art galleries and museums (which he did as well), but in public venues. Furthermore, he presented the native people with dignity and

28.25 Edward Hopper. *Early Sunday Morning.* 1930. Oil on canvas, 2'11" × 5' (0.89 × 1.5 m). Whitney Museum of American Art, New York. Purchase with funds from Gertrude Vanderbilt Whitney. 31.426

beauty and praised their mores, as opposed to appropriating their art forms and ignoring their culture, as did the Cubists and German Expressionists, for example. As we shall see in the last chapter of the book, Rivera's rejection of so many Modernist values—such as an emphasis on abstraction, individual genius, creating new art forms, making art that deals with mainstream issues, and making precious objects—anticipates the art that surfaced in the 1980s and will be called Postmodernism.

The Eve of World War II

In October 1929, the New York stock market crashed, unleashing the Great Depression that fanned out around the globe. The deprivation it inflicted lasted an excruciating 16 years. Europe was also subjected to fascism as Germany, Italy, and Spain came under the rule of charismatic totalitarian leaders, who brought about a politics of repression, ruthlessly imprisoning and often executing anyone perceived as unfriendly to their regimes. A dark cloud was cast over the Western world, which was reflected in much art.

America: The Failure of Modernity

The avant-garde continued to work in abstraction through the 1930s, but, in an era dominated by the terrible social ills of the Great Depression, it grew increasingly difficult for artists not to be socially concerned. Many avant-garde artists became involved by becoming socialists or Communists and by supporting the labor movement, even forming their own unionlike organizations. But for many artists, political activity was not enough. Now, more and more artists worked in a style called Social Realism, a representational format that focused on such pervasive problems as poverty, labor oppression, the suffering of migrant workers, alienation resulting from increased urbanization and industrialization, and racism, especially as seen in the Ku Klux Klan lynchings.

EDWARD HOPPER   One of the most powerful representational painters of the period was Edward Hopper (1882–1967), who was based in New York. His pictures are saturated with the alienation associated with life in the big city, and more generally with modern America. A classic Hopper is *Early Sunday Morning* (**fig. 28.25**) of 1930. The image is frightening in its uncanny quiet and emptiness,

qualities reinforced by the severe, frozen geometry of the composition. The second-floor windows suggest a different story for each apartment, but none is forthcoming as their inhabitants remain secreted behind curtains and shades. A strange relationship exists among the fire hydrant, the barbershop pole, and the void of the square awning-framed window between them. The harsh morning light has a theatrical intensity. Hopper's only love outside of art was film and theater, and his paintings have a cinematic or staged quality that intimates that something is about to happen. His pictures are shrouded in mystery, and because their settings are distinctly American, the troubling psychology he portrays becomes distinctly American as well.

DOROTHEA LANGE   The largest art patron during the Great Depression was the United States government, which put tens of thousands of unemployed artists to work through the Works Project Administration and Federal Art Project, important components of Franklin Delano Roosevelt's New Deal. What was so remarkable about these programs was their lack of racial, ethnic, or gender discrimination,

28.26 Dorothea Lange. *Migrant Mother, California*. 1936. Gelatin silver print. Library of Congress, Washington, D.C.

and the result was financial support for women and minorities. One especially influential project, the Farm Security Administration (FSA), was designed to document the suffering and poverty of both rural and urban Americans. It hired about 20 photographers to record the desperate conditions of the poor. These images were then distributed to the media.

One of the most famous images from the FSA project is Dorothea Lange's *Migrant Mother, California* (**fig. 28.26**). Using the sharp-focus photography that had become commonplace by the 1930s, Lange created a powerful image that in its details captures the sitter's destitution, and in its complex composition of hands, arms, and turned heads, the family's emotional distress. Because of this photograph and an accompanying news story, the government rushed food to California, and eventually opened relief camps for migrant workers. The immediate impact of this poignant photograph testifies to the overpowering credibility projected by the medium of photography.

Europe and Fascism

While some of the most powerful antifascist works came from the German Expressionists and Dada artists, the most famous work of this kind was made by the Parisian-based Spaniard Pablo Picasso.

GUERNICA In 1936 civil war broke out in Spain when conservatives loyal to the king and under the leadership of Franco (the Nationalists) tried to overthrow the popularly elected, leftist, republican government (the Republicans or Loyalists). In some ways, this conflict was a rehearsal for World War II. Hitler and Mussolini provided military and political support for the Nationalists, while the Loyalists consisted of Communists, socialists, and Catalan and Basque separatists, as well as the International Brigade, made up of volunteers from all over the world. On April 26, 1937, Hitler's Nazi pilots used saturation bombing to attack the undefended Basque town of Guernica, killing thousands of civilians. Picasso, like most of the free world, was outraged, and responded by painting *Guernica* (**fig. 28.27**), an enormous black, white, and gray mural that he exhibited as a protest at the Spanish Republican Pavilion of the 1937 Paris International Exposition. He pulled every artistic device out of his Cubist and Surrealist arsenal to create a nightmarish scene of pain, suffering, grief, and death. We see no airplanes and no bombs, and the electric light bulb is the only sign of the modernity that made the bombing possible.

The symbolism of the scene resists exact interpretation, despite several traditional elements: The mother and her dead child are descendants of the *pietà* (see page 271), the woman with the lamp who vaguely recalls the Statue of Liberty suggests enlightenment, and the dead fighter clutching a broken sword is a familiar emblem of heroic resistance. Other symbols include the menacing

28.27 Pablo Picasso. *Guernica*. 1937. Oil on canvas, 11'6" × 25'8" (3.51 × 7.82 m). Museo Nacional Centro de Arte Reina Sofia, Madrid. On permanent loan from the Museo del Prado, Madrid

 View the Closer Look for *Guernica* on myartslab.com

human-faced bull, which we know Picasso intended to represent the forces of brutality and darkness, and the dying horse, which stands for the people, although Picasso, since the early 1930s, had used these symbols from the bullfight to represent sexual conflict. The figure resembling a Mary Magdalen at the Cross also brings to mind Goya's supplicating rebel in *The Third of May, 1808* (see fig. 24.2).

Picasso denied that this was an antifascist picture, and he may very well have meant in part that this monumental mural was more than just mundane propaganda against Franco and his ilk. Instead, this horrifying image is meant to portray the psychology of a world in perpetual conflict and misery, capturing the mood of the black cloud hanging over Europe.

POINTS OF REFLECTION

28.1 New York Dada during World War I was very different in motivation from that produced in Switzerland during the war and in Berlin shortly after. Explain this difference as seen in Marcel Duchamp's *Fountain*, Jean Arp's *The Entombment of the Birds and Butterflies*, and Hannah Höch's *Cut with the Kitchen Knife Dada.*

28.2 Why could Dada works like Max Ernst's 1920 collages and Man Ray's *Champs délicieux* be appropriated by the Surrealists? Explain the differences between Dada and Surrealism.

28.3 Piet Mondrian's Neo-plastic paintings and Gerrit Rietveld's Schröder House share a utopian vision with Bauhaus architecture and design, as seen in Walter Gropius's and Marcel Breuer's living room for a 1927 Werkbund house. How do these two groups, one Dutch, the other German, differ in spirit? Would you describe the Russian Constructivism of Tatlin and his circle as closer to the Dutch or the Germans?

28.4 The presentation of modernity could not be more different in the work of such Americans as Joseph Stella, Paul Strand, and Margaret Bourke-White on the one hand and the Europeans Le Corbusier, Tatlin, and Gropius on the other. How do the spirit and intentions differ between the two groups?

28.5 Compare the presentation of indigenous people in Diego Rivera's *The Arsenal* to Paul Gauguin's *Where Do We Come From?* Why is Rivera's painting, which is very conservative in style, so radical in concept?

✓—⎡**Study** and review on myartslab.com

ART IN TIME

- 1910–20 — Mexican Revolution
- 1910–40 — The Great Migration, as 1.6 million African Americans move from the South to the North, Midwest, and West
- 1914–18 — World War I
- **1917 — Marcel Duchamp, *Fountain***

- 1917 — Russian Revolution
- 1919 — Walter Gropius founds the Bauhaus, which is relocated to Dessau in 1925
- 1920 — First Dada International Fair, Berlin
- 1923–25 — France and Belgium occupy the Ruhr when Germany fails to make reparation payments
- 1924 — André Breton publishes his first *Surrealist Manifesto*
- 1925 — Alain Locke publishes *The New Negro*

- 1926 — Georgia O'Keeffe, *Black Iris III*
- **ca. 1928 — Diego Rivera, *The Arsenal (Distributing Arms)***

- 1929 — Stockmarket crash
- **1930 — Edward Hopper, *Early Sunday Morning***

- 1933 — Adolf Hitler establishes Nazi dictatorship in Germany
  — Franklin Roosevelt launches the New Deal
- **1936 — Meret Oppenheim, *Object (Luncheon in Fur)***
  — Spanish Civil War
- **1937 — Pablo Picasso, *Guernica***

- 1939 — Outbreak of World War II

Postwar to Postmodern, 1945–1980

POINTS OF INQUIRY

29.1 Describe how the art made in the late 1940s and early 1950s reflects the attitude held by many following the devastation of World War II, that life could no longer be controlled or understood.

29.2 Discuss how art also was affected by the unprecedented prosperity and consumerism of post-World War II America and Europe as well as by the technological developments brought on by the Cold War and Space Race.

29.3 Discuss the impact on art of the social revolution that challenged the status quo, beginning in the 1950s and gaining momentum in the 1960s and 1970s.

29.4 Explain why Minimal Art became such an iconic movement that artists felt compelled to react to and against it, in part giving rise to the term Postminimal Art and calling the 1970s the pluralistic decade.

29.5 Explain why many art historians describe the Dada artist Marcel Duchamp as a major force in the art of the second half of the twentieth century.

((•—**Listen** to the chapter audio on myartslab.com

Scholars traditionally view World War II (1939–1945) as a turning point for the art world, the time when its focus shifted from Paris to New York (see **map 29.1**) with the rise of Abstract Expressionism. In fact, the 1950s, not the 1940s and Abstract Expressionism, were the watershed for the second half of the century. Now Duchamp's preoccupation with how art functions and his questioning of the importance of craft became a driving force as the decade progressed. Likewise, many artists became obsessed with the concept, rooted in the early Cubism of Picasso and Braque, that art and image making were a form of language, and they dedicated their work to revealing the structure of this visual language and the complex ways it could be used to present ideas and opinions, even to deceive and manipulate.

Artists also realized that art need not be limited to the traditional mediums, such as oil on canvas, cast bronze, or chiseled marble. It did not have to hang on a wall or sit on a pedestal. Artists could use anything to make art, and by the late 1950s and the 1960s, they did. They used televisions, film, earth, fluorescent lights, steel tiles, acrylics, entire environments, postcards, words, and junk. Performance Art, earthworks, Conceptual Art, happenings, and video art are just a handful of the movements and concepts that sprang up from the mid-1950s through the 1970s.

In part, this burst of new mediums reflects the expansive spirit of the period, especially in the United States. World War II ended 16 years of financial depression and deprivation in America, and by the 1950s, the country had become a nation of consumers. Returning soldiers, eager to resume

Map 29.1 Cold War Alliances

normal life, married and had children in record numbers, creating the baby-boom generation. They moved from cities to new cookie-cutter tract houses in the suburbs. And, as never before, Americans shopped—for cars, televisions, labor-saving household appliances, boats, and movie cameras. Americans were fascinated by everything technological, symbolized by the Cold War space race.

The new postwar American lifestyle, however, was not equally available to all. Magazines, newspapers, and television depicted a distinct hierarchy within American democracy, with white males heading up a patriarchal society that viewed women and people of color as second-class citizens. In response, Beatniks, Zen Buddhists, underground improvisational jazz musicians, bikers, and urban gangs of juvenile delinquents established alternative lifestyles in the late 1940s and the 1950s.

But it was the civil rights movement that first seriously challenged accepted norms in the second half of the 1950s, gaining tremendous momentum in the following decade. Spurred also by the Vietnam War (1964–73), which generated persistent antiwar protests, the mid-1960s saw the start of a period of social upheaval that produced the feminist movement, Gay Pride, Black Power, Gray Power, and environmental groups such as Greenpeace. It was an age of liberation aimed at shattering the status quo and questioning the validity of any claim to superiority or fixed truth. And in the forefront was

art. But before this artistic revolution could occur, the center of the art world had to move from Paris to New York. This "coup," often referred to as the "Triumph of New York Painting," coincided with the rise of Abstract Expressionism in the late 1940s.

Existentialism in New York: Abstract Expressionism

Abstract Expressionism grew out of Surrealism, which traced its roots to the Dada movement of the 1910s (see pages 574–79). Like the Surrealists, the Abstract Expressionists were preoccupied with a quest to uncover universal truths. In this sense, their heritage goes back to Kandinsky (see page 559–60), Malevich (see page 564–65), and Mondrian (see page 585–86). In many respects, Abstract Expressionism is the culmination of artists' concerns in the first half of the twentieth century. But the Abstract Expressionists were also driven by a despondent view of the human condition that accompanied the atrocities and devastation of World War II. The war shattered not only faith in science and logic, but even the very concept of progress, the belief in the possibility of creating a better world. Life was now perceived as uncontrollable, a mere reflection of chance or fate.

This new worldview was reflected in the rise of Existentialism in the 1940s. Existentialism maintained that there were no absolute truths—no ultimate knowledge, explanations, or answers—and that life was a continuous series of subjective experiences from which each individual learned and then responded to in a personal way. Essential to this learning process was facing the direst aspects of human existence—fear of death, the absurdity of life, and alienation from individuals, society, and nature—and taking responsibility for acts of free will without any certain knowledge of what is right or wrong, good or bad. The Abstract Expressionists, like so many intellectuals after the war, embraced this subjective view of the world. Their art was a personal confrontation with the moment, reflecting upon their physical, psychological, and social being.

Abstract Expressionism: Action Painting

Just as Dada developed into Surrealism, New York Surrealism seamlessly evolved into Abstract Expressionism. The transformation occurred when all of the symbols and suggestions of myths and primordial conditions disappeared, and images dissolved into a complete abstraction containing no obvious references to the visible world. Furthermore, the Abstract Expressionists often worked on an enormous scale, a scale that overwhelmed the viewer and would characterize much of the art of the remainder of the century. Two artists are largely responsible for this new art. One is Jackson Pollock, who, in 1947, made the physical act of energetically applied paint—the gesture—the undisputed focus of painting, and the second is Willem de Kooning.

JACKSON POLLOCK Through the 1930s, Jackson Pollock (1912–1956) was a marginal figure in the New York art world. In the early 1940s, just when he started Jungian psychoanalysis, he became a hardcore Surrealist, making crude but powerful paintings filled with slapdash hieroglyphs ("letter-pictures"), totems, and references to primitive myth, whipped about in a swirling sea of paint.

In 1947, he unveiled at Peggy Guggenheim's Art of This Century gallery his first **gesture** or action **paintings**. The latter term was coined in the 1950s by the art critic Harold Rosenberg (1906–1978) and is represented here by *Autumn Rhythm: Number 30* (**fig. 29.1**) of 1950, an 8- by 17-foot wall of house paint applied by dripping, hurling, and splattering when the unstretched canvas was on the floor. Pollock had worked on it from all four sides, and he claimed that its source was his unconscious. Despite the apparent looseness of his style, Pollock exerted great control of his medium by changing the viscosity of the paint, the size of the brush or stick he used to apply it, and the speed, size, and direction of his own movements, and he rejected many paintings when he did not like the results.

29.1 Jackson Pollock. *Autumn Rhythm: Number 30.* 1950. Enamel on canvas, 8′8″ × 17′3″ (2.64 × 5.26 m). The Metropolitan Museum of Art, New York, George A. Hearn Fund, 1957 (57.92)

 Watch a video of Jackson Pollock painting on myartslab.com

The energy of the painting is overwhelming, and when hanging on the wall it looms above us like a frozen wave about to crash, although unlike a wave, the work really does not have a sense of gravity, since it had been painted on from four sides. Our eye jumps from one stress to another—from a white blob, to a black splash, to a Surrealistic automatic line, and so on. There is no focus upon which the eye can rest. Because of these even stresses throughout the image, Pollock's compositions are often described as **allover paintings**.

Pollock constructed his picture as he went along, with each new move playing off the previous one, and emotional intuition dictating the next gesture. The resulting image is not just a record of the physical self, but also of the psychological being. Because every artist must face the challenge of the bare canvas and the risk-taking responsibility of making each mark, painting becomes a metaphor for the challenges of the human condition and the risks inherent in taking responsibility for one's actions, particularly in an Existentialist world. World War II dashed the blind belief in the superiority of science, progress, and utopian societies. The one thing that could be trusted and believed in was the self, and *that* became the sole subject of Abstract Expressionist painting.

WILLEM DE KOONING Pollock's style was too personal to spawn significant followers. The gesture painter who launched an entire generation of artists was Willem de Kooning (1904–1997), a Dutch immigrant, who quietly struggled at his art for decades in New York's Greenwich Village. De Kooning made Picasso-inspired Cubist-Surrealist paintings in the 1940s, mostly of women. He finally obtained a one-person show in 1948, at the Egan Gallery, when he was 44. The radical works that he presented appeared to be total abstractions of dramatically painted curving lines and shapes, entirely covering the canvas with the same evenness as in Pollock's allover paintings.

Despite the spontaneity implied by the bravura paint handling, the pictures were laboriously crafted, often using methods similar to those of the Surrealists. For example, De Kooning fired his imagination by pinning line drawings (that he eventually removed) on his canvas, not only at the beginning but throughout the process. He jumpstarted other paintings by inscribing large letters across the canvas. Like Pollock, he constructed the paintings through a continuous process of gestural

reactions based on intuition and emotion, with the resulting marks reflecting his presence, feeling, and uncontrollable urges. Unlike Pollock, his paintings were not so allover but instead retained a Cubist compositional structure of a push–pull space or overlapping planes.

De Kooning shocked the art world with his second exhibition, held at the Sidney Janis Gallery in 1953. He did the unthinkable for an Abstract Expressionist: He made representational paintings, depicting women, as seen in *Woman I* (**fig. 29.2**), a work he struggled with from 1950 to 1952. It now became clear that the curvilinear patterning of the earlier abstractions was as sexual as everyone had suspected it was, the pink swelling forms were his emotional response to female flesh. De Kooning reportedly painted and completely repainted *Woman I* hundreds of times on the same canvas, and he made numerous other paintings of women in the summer of 1952. The other paintings in the *Women* series show a compendium of female types,

29.2 Willem de Kooning. *Woman I*. 1950–52. Oil on canvas, 6'3⅞" × 4'10" (1.93 × 1.47 m). The Museum of Modern Art, New York. Purchase

29.3 Mark Rothko. *No. 61 (Rust and Blue)* (also known as *Brown, Blue, Brown on Blue*). 1953. Oil on canvas, 9′8″ × 7′8″ (2.94 × 2.32 m). The Museum of Contemporary Art, Los Angeles. The Panza Collection

Abstract Expressionism: Color-Field Painting

Abstract Expressionism had a flip side. If one side was gestural painting, then the other was **color-field painting**. Instead of bombastic brushstrokes and the overt drama of paint, these painters used large, meditative planes of color to express the innermost primal qualities that linked them to universal forces. The objective of the color-field painters, like that of their gestural counterparts, was to project the sublime human condition as they themselves felt it. The principal color-field painters all started out by making myth-inspired abstract Surrealist paintings in the 1940s and were close friends until 1952.

MARK ROTHKO Mark Rothko (1903–1970) ranks among the best-known painters in this group. His Surrealist work in the 1940s drew heavily on Greek tragedy, such as Aeschylus' *Agamemnon Trilogy*, and on Christ's Passion cycle and death—scenes with a harrowing psychology where the lone individual faces ultimate truths about existence, death, and spirituality. But all suggestion of figuration disappeared in 1947. In 1949, Rothko arrived at his mature style, from which he did not deviate for the remainder of his life.

Now, Rothko's paintings consisted of flat planes of color stacked directly on top of one another, as in the 10-foot-high 1953 work *No. 61 (Rust and Blue)* (**fig. 29.3**). There is no longer any storytelling, nor any hieroglyphics or symbols, not even in the title. The artist has painted what he himself has confronted, the inevitable void of our common future and our sense of mystical oneness with unseen cosmic forces, a theme reminiscent of Caspar David Friedrich's in *Abbey in an Oak Forest* (see fig. 24.5). Rothko's subject, he explained, was "tragedy, ecstasy, doom, and so on." His ethereal planes are so thin that color glimmers through from behind and below, creating a shimmering spiritual light. Their edges are ragged, and like clouds dissipating in the sky, they seem precariously fragile. Although the painting is not about gesture, we feel Rothko's hand building up the planes with individual marks, giving the work a poignant organic quality. Space is paradoxically claustrophobic and infinite. On the one hand, the planes literally crowd the picture to the edges and hover at the very front of the picture plane, while on the other hand, the pervasive blue ground seems to continue forever, uncontained by the edge

not just the hostile-looking creature of our picture. The process of making the painting was almost as important as the final product, as though it were a ritualistic catharsis of sorts. *Woman I* is by far the most violent and threatening of the series, with the others that followed having a more neutral appearance and embodying a broad range of attributes.

Woman I was meant to be as unfixed in meaning, or as open to interpretation, as the other women in the series. De Kooning was surprised that viewers did not see the humor in his threatening, wide-eyed, snarling figure, which was based as much on contemporary advertisements of models smoking Camel cigarettes as on primitive fertility goddesses, such as the Paleolithic *Woman of Willendorf* (see fig. 1.6), both of which the artist cited as sources. In the *Women* series, as in all of his paintings, De Kooning played out his own emotions, which, because they constantly changed, allowed him to keep repainting his figure.

of the canvas and suggesting infinity. Enormous shifts in scale give a sense of the sublime. Note, for instance, the tiny, thin wisp of soft white on the bottom of the middle plane, which seems so insignificant in comparison to the enormous planes and the vast size of the canvas.

Regardless of the palette, whether bright yellows and oranges or the more moody blues and browns in *No. 61*, the colors in a Rothko painting have a smoldering resonance that makes the image seem to glow from within and evoke a spiritual aura. Rothko wanted viewers to stand close to his enormous iconic images, which would tower over them, and where they would be immersed in this mystical void of the unknown future, as if standing on the precipice of infinity and death.

Rejecting Abstract Expressionism: American Art of the 1950s and 1960s

By the mid-1950s other styles were already beginning to overshadow Abstract Expressionism. The 1950s planted the seeds of a cultural revolution, producing a thirst for a freedom of expression that required the invention of radically new art forms. Combines, environments, happenings, Minimal Art, and Conceptual Art took art into uncharted territory, breaking down the barriers that had narrowly restricted it to certain standard media. While all of these styles rejected Abstract Expressionism, they often retained the new scale that Abstract Expressionism had introduced.

Re-Presenting Life and Dissecting Painting

No one person or event triggered the dramatic change that occurred in art in the 1950s, but Robert Rauschenberg and Jasper Johns certainly played major roles. While both artists created paintings that had the gestural mark making of the Abstract Expressionists, these works were an intellectual, impersonal analysis of art rather than an explosion of feelings and primal urges. Both artists sought to escape the hold that Abstract Expressionism had on the art world.

ROBERT RAUSCHENBERG Rauschenberg (1925–2008) was a Texan from a working-class family who ended up in New York studying painting by 1947. A critical component of his development was attending the avant-garde Black Mountain College

in North Carolina in the fall of 1948, and again in 1951 and 1952. The art department at the small liberal arts school encouraged experimentation, which turned Rauschenberg away from pure painting toward an analysis of the very concept of art. At Black Mountain in 1951, he made, for example, a series of White Paintings. These were large canvases painted a solid white, with no

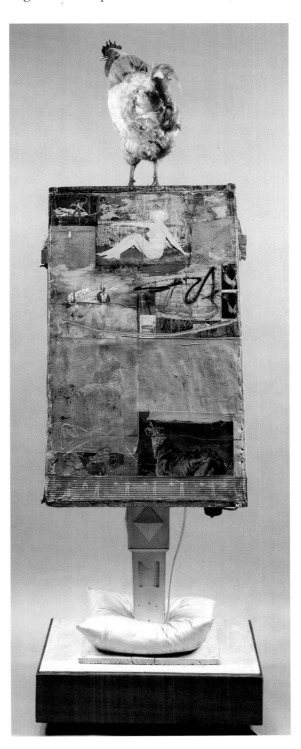

29.4 Robert Rauschenberg. *Odalisk*. 1955–58. Mixed media, 6′9″ × 2′1″ × 2′1″ (2.06 × 0.63 × 0.63 m). Museum Ludwig, Cologne. © Robert Rauschenberg Foundation/Licensed by VAGA, New York, NY

evidence of brushwork. Viewers wondered what they were supposed to see. Themselves for one thing, for their shadows were cast on the canvases, which also caught reflected colored light and accumulated dust and dirt. These canvases captured real life, which was presented without comment or meaning. Viewers could read anything into them that they wanted. Like Duchamp, Rauschenberg was making conceptual art, determined by chance, and aimed at capturing the world without attaching any firm meaning to the art. He was also trying to incorporate life into art directly.

In 1955 Rauschenberg actively incorporated the real world into his artwork when he began making what he called "**combines**," innovative works that combined painting, sculpture, collage, and found objects, as in his *Odalisk* (**fig. 29.4**) of 1955–58. This four-sided "lamp"—there is an electric light inside—is crowded with collaged material culled from contemporary magazines and newspapers as well as detritus from the street and thrift shops. Even the title is part of this busy collage, for it has to be considered when we try to construct a narrative for the work. But is there a narrative in this poetic collage of disparate material? Obviously, *Odalisk* has a subject, for it is filled with sexual innuendo: The phallic pole jammed into the pillow on the bottom, the cock mounted above

the nude pinup while the dog howls at her from below, the comic strip of a woman in bed being surprised by a man (on a side of the sculpture not pictured here). Even the title can be interpreted sexually, for it is a pun on *odalisque* (see fig. 24.8), a female, and *obelisk*, a possible phallic symbol. But the artist places no value on the material, suggests no interpretation, makes no grand statement. The work just is. It is our content, our time, our life. Rauschenberg re-presents it with extraordinary formal powers and with a poetry of paint and collage. In its energy and fragmentation, the work powerfully captures the spirit of the constantly changing world and the fractured way we experience it.

JASPER JOHNS In 1954 Rauschenberg met Jasper Johns (b. 1930) and moved into a loft in the same run-down building in lower Manhattan. Johns is primarily a painter, and his works are literally about painting. This can be seen in *Three Flags*, a work of 1958 (**fig. 29.5**). Because of the Americana theme, many writers talk about this painting as Pop Art, a style that in New York emerges in the early 1960s and derives its imagery from popular culture. *Three Flags*, however, is not about popular culture, for it is part of a series in which the artist repeatedly painted flat objects, such as numbers, targets,

29.5 Jasper Johns. *Three Flags.* 1958. Encaustic on canvas, 30⅞ × 45½ × 5" (78.4 × 115.6 × 12.7 cm). Whitney Museum of American Art, New York, 50th Anniversary Gift of the Gilman Foundation, A. Alfred Taubman, an anonymous donor and purchase. 80.32. © Jasper Johns/Licensed by VAGA, New York, NY

and maps, with the intention of eliminating the need to paint illusionistic depth. Here he has painted a flat object (a flag) on a flat surface (the canvas), so we are not tempted to read, for example, a white star as sitting on top of a blue field because we know it does not. Furthermore, Johns does not place the flag in any context that allows us to read specific meaning or emotion into it. His flag is a sign to which he has attached no specific meaning or emotion. In other words, he has created a nonillusionistic, impersonal image. What we are left to look at is *how* the picture was made. Johns's very beautiful and methodical application of wax-based encaustic paint reminds us that a painting consists of paint on canvas. And, of course, painting can be about color, here red, white, and blue. Lest we forget that a painting is a three-dimensional object, Johns has stacked three flag paintings one atop another. We see their sides and hence their depth. Lastly, he reminds us that painting can produce an image. However, he does not give us an illusionistic image; we would never mistake Johns's flag for an illusion of a real flag. In this way, Johns tells us that an image is a sign, that painting is an abstract language, just like verbal language. Just as a word is a sign, standing for something else and not the real thing, so too is painting: It signifies something else, just as numbers and maps are signs for something else.

While the intellectual gymnastics in Johns's paintings are complex and rigorous, the works themselves are objective, devoid of any emotion. Like Rauschenberg, Johns paved a way for artists to break away from the subjectivity and vocabulary of Abstract Expressionism. His powerful assertion of the properties of painting and its inherent flatness would inspire numerous artists in the following decade.

Environments and Performance Art

Rauschenberg's combines played a major role in setting off a chain reaction that caused an explosion of art making, redefining art entirely. Art was no longer just painting, sculpture, and work on paper; now it took on the form of limitless mediums and moved out of galleries and museums into the real world, sometimes interacting with daily life, at other times taking place in locations so remote that few people ever got to see it. Art was often no longer an object; rather, it could be temporary and ephemeral, something that could not be bought and sold.

ALLAN KAPROW In 1958, influenced by Rauschenberg's use of found objects and the enormous scale of Jackson Pollock's paintings, Allan Kaprow (1927–2006), a painter teaching at Rutgers University, began to make what he called **environments**. These were constructed installations that a viewer could enter. His most famous environment, *Yard* (**fig. 29.6**), came in 1961. Filled with used tires, the work, seen from above, had the allover look and energy of a Pollock painting. But visitors to the town-house gallery garden where it was installed were expected to walk through it, experiencing it physically, including the smells. They could also rearrange the tires, interacting with the work and playing an artistic role, in effect becoming co-artists. Kaprow was challenging the notion of who the artist is and how viewers interface with art, as well as the idea that art was fixed or permanent and a precious commodity meant to be owned and viewed. (The townhouse garden contained several major sculptures, today worth many millions of dollars, that Kaprow had wrapped in tar paper for protection but nonetheless were part of his piece.) Like Rauschenberg in his combines, Kaprow attached no firm meaning to his

29.6 Allan Kaprow. *Yard*. 1961. Environment of used tires, tar paper, and barrels, as installed at the Martha Jackson Gallery, New York. Life-size. Destroyed. Courtesy Allan Kaprow Estate Hauser & Wirth Zürich. Photo © Estate of Robert R. McElroy/ Licensed by VAGA, New York, NY

29.7 George Segal. *The Gas Station*. 1963. Plaster figures, Coca-Cola machine, Coca-Cola bottles, wooden Coca-Cola crates, metal stand, rubber tires, tire rack, oil cans, electric clock, concrete blocks, windows of wood and plate glass, installation 8′6″ × 24′ × 4′ (2.59 × 7.32 × 1.22 m). National Gallery of Canada, Ottawa. © The George and Helen Segal Foundation/ Licensed by VAGA, New York, NY

works, although the discarded synthetic materials suggested a modern industrial urban environment, as well as a sense of waste, even death.

Kaprow had earlier added the live human figure to his environments, which initially were made of a variety of collaged nonart materials that ran from floor to ceiling, vaguely resembling a Rauschenberg combine. He unveiled his new art form to the New York art world in 1959 at the Reuben Gallery with *18 Happenings in 6 Parts*. Using polyfilm walls, Kaprow divided his collaged environment into three rooms, in which seated spectators watched, listened, and smelled as performers carried out such tasks as painting (Rauschenberg and Johns participated), playing records, squeezing orange juice, and speaking fragments of sentences, all determined by chance. In a sense the work was like a Rauschenberg combine that took place in time and space and with human activity. Because of the title of Kaprow's innovative work, a **happening** became the term for this new visual art form in which many of the major artists of the day, including Rauschenberg, started working. While many artists accepted this term, others used different labels, all of which can be grouped under the umbrella term **Performance Art**, distinguished from theater in that it takes place in an art context.

GEORGE SEGAL Living down the road from Kaprow in rural New Jersey was George Segal (1924–2000), who responded to his friend's environments and happenings by creating representational, not abstract, environments out of real objects and populated by plaster figures, as in *The Gas Station* (**fig. 29.7**) of 1963. Now the performers are frozen, reduced to ghost-white mannequins. To create them, Segal used real people, making castings of them by using medical plaster bandages. Like Rauschenberg and Kaprow, he was breaking down the barrier between art and life. But his art is far from neutral; it is emotional and makes a statement. Segal's work condemns the alienation he perceived in contemporary life. This alienation can be seen in his figures, which are left white, as though drained of life. Generally they are lethargic, exhausted, and alone, and seem trapped by the harsh geometry of the horizontals and verticals of their settings.

The works even contain symbols used in more traditional art. *The Gas Station*, for example, is dominated by a Bulova clock, a *memento mori* ("reminder of death") motif, which floats in a 10-foot expanse of darkness. Its shape mysteriously resonates with the tire on the floor. The vending machine, tires, cans of high-performance oil, and the gas station itself suggest modernity, technology, and fast, efficient living. Missing from this materiality, however, is something meaningful—human interaction and spirituality. Segal retains the Existential angst of his Abstract Expressionist background by questioning the meaning of modern existence. Although he often used contemporary branded objects, such as Coke bottles, to give his environments the look of reality and modernity, Segal never celebrated the products of consumer culture, nor questioned how mass-media imagery, including advertising, manipulates its audience. His sculpture is closer in spirit and style to the paintings of Edward Hopper (see fig. 28.25) than to Pop Art, with which he has been mistakenly associated.

Pop Art: Consumer Culture as Subject

Pop Art is a movement that emerged in New York in the early 1960s, although it had appeared in a very different guise in Britain a decade earlier. The movement earned its name because it derives its imagery from popular or vernacular culture. Like Rauschenberg and Kaprow, Pop artists re-presented the artifacts of the world they lived in, namely the imagery of the mass media, although they did it using conventional painting rather than new mediums. Unlike Johns and Segal, both of whom occasionally used popular imagery, Pop artists focused on the products of popular culture by taking what art historians often describe as a *low* art form, that is, commercial art, and incorporating it into one that is considered *high*, meaning fine art. By doing so, however, they subversively revealed the manipulative impact of the mass media. Among the best-known Pop artists are the Americans Roy Lichtenstein and Andy Warhol.

ROY LICHTENSTEIN Another close friend of Kaprow's, Roy Lichtenstein (1923–1997), came to Rutgers University to teach in 1960. When he arrived he was an Abstract Expressionist painter. Within a year, however, he was making what would be considered Pop paintings, in part influenced by Kaprow's dictum: To make art that did not look like art.

The contemporary life that Lichtenstein scavenged and represented was not that of the urban streets, as was the case with Kaprow, Rauschenberg, and Segal, but the crude black-and-white advertisements of telephone books and newspapers and the prosaic drawings in comic books. These he cropped and adjusted into visually riveting images,

like *Drowning Girl* (**fig. 29.8**). Traditionally, Lichtenstein is appreciated for seeing the beauty of "low art" and elevating it to "high art," in effect celebrating popular culture, and in particular American culture.

Lichtenstein's work does more than just blur the distinctions between fine art and mass culture. Like Johns, whose *Flag* paintings had a profound impact on him, Lichtenstein was interested in the language of art, particularly issues of perception. He does not just imitate the comic strip, he also plays with that genre's technique of making an image out of benday dots, the small dots that when massed together create color and shading in printed material. He was intrigued by how an illusion of three-dimensional volume could be made using flat dots and flat black lines. When viewed from close up, Lichtenstein's large images dissolve into a flat abstract pattern, virtually becoming Abstract Expressionist compositions.

Lichtenstein's work does far more than just appropriate popular culture images, for it also reveals the gender stereotyping embedded in them. His paintings from 1961 to 1964 fall into a distinct pattern: Men are portrayed as strong, virile soldiers and fighter pilots, whereas women are shown as emotionally distraught, dependent on men, and

29.8 Roy Lichtenstein. *Drowning Girl*. 1963. Oil on canvas, 5′7⅝″ × 5′6¾″ (1.72 × 1.69 m). The Museum of Modern Art, New York. Philip Johnson Fund and Gift of Mr. and Mrs. Bagley Wright. © The Estate of Roy Lichtenstein

Read the document related to Roy Lichtenstein on myartslab.com

happily slaving around the house doing domestic work. With deadpan brilliance, Lichtenstein made his paintings a mirror of contemporary society, revealing how the media reinforces social perceptions of the sexes. But the paintings themselves appear objective and unemotional, giving little suggestion of a polemical agenda or a sense of the artist's presence, whether his hand (brushwork) or emotions.

ANDY WARHOL Andy Warhol (1928–1987) was making art based on comic books at exactly the same time as Lichtenstein, and when the dealer Leo Castelli decided to represent Lichtenstein and not him, he turned to other kinds of popular imagery, namely product design and newspaper photographs. Among his most famous motifs are Campbell's soup cans, as seen in *32 Campbell's Soup Cans* (**fig. 29.9**), begun in 1961. Warhol produced 32 soup can images for his first exhibition, held at the Ferus Gallery in Los Angeles in 1962. Campbell's offered 32 soup varieties at the time, hence 32 paintings, which Warhol hand-painted himself. He installed the works as monotonously as possible, evenly spacing them and placing them on a shelf, as soup cans would be in a supermarket. Just as the

soup came off a mass-production assembly line, Warhol, soon after his Ferus Gallery exhibition, began mass-producing his paintings in his studio, which he called "the Factory." Assistants made the works to his specifications using a silkscreen process to print a photographic image onto canvas, or onto paper, as he did to make prints. While he was intensely involved in the entire process, the works nonetheless appeared to be factory-produced, with Warhol simply signing the back. With a Duchampian gesture, he tells us that paintings are commodities, that people are buying a name product—that is, a Warhol—and that art is about idea, not necessarily about technique or craftsmanship. But he also comments on the camouflaging function of product design, on how it tells us nothing about the mass-produced commodity it promotes and how the packaging lures us into buying it. Warhol's message is that Campbell's soups are everywhere, having penetrated to the farthest reaches of the country, and that mass-production uniformity and consumerism dominate American society. In effect, these soup cans are a portrait of modern America. As with Lichtenstein, Warhol neither praises nor condemns. (For a further discussion of Warhol, see the Introduction, pages 3–4 and 7–8.)

29.9 Andy Warhol. *32 Campbell's Soup Cans*. 1961–62. Acrylic on canvas, 32 works, each 20 × 16″ (50.8 × 40.6 cm). The Museum of Modern Art, New York. Gift of Irving Blum; Nelson A. Rockefeller Bequest, gift of Mr. and Mrs. William A. M. Burden, Abby Aldrich Rockefeller Foundation

The Impact of Pop Art in Germany: Sigmar Polke

American Pop Art had an impact on art made in France, Italy, and Germany, with Germany becoming the most important for the art of the following decades, as we shall see in the next chapter. This German art, which came out of Düsseldorf, gained very little attention at the time as the art world was largely focused on New York. (Similarly, much Pop Art from Los Angeles received little attention.) It was not until the 1980s that a broad audience discovered Sigmar Polke (1941–2011), an East German transplant, who, along with several other Düsseldorf painters, toward 1963 cultivated a kind of German Pop Art. Influenced by paintings by Lichtenstein and Warhol reproduced in art magazines

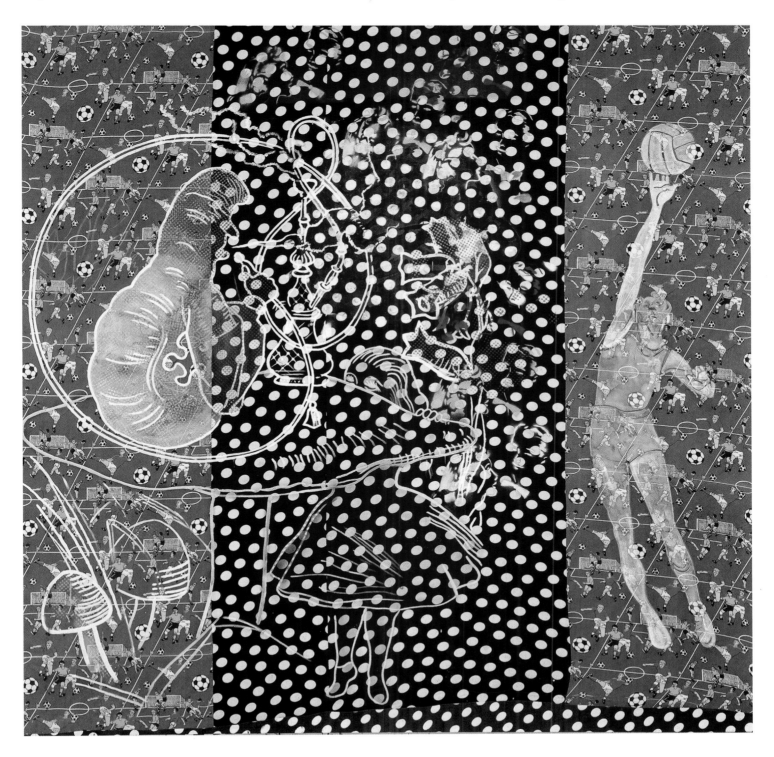

29.10 Sigmar Polke. *Alice in Wonderland*. 1971. Acrylic, spray, and poster paint on printed fabric, 10′2″ × 9′4″ (3.1 × 2.86 m). Private collection

and the consumerism resulting from a dramatic economic recovery (due to the Marshall Plan and a government embracing social democracy), a handful of Düsseldorf artists became preoccupied with mass-media imagery, commodity culture, and analyzing art and image making in general, revealing how it functions and takes on meaning. For a brief period they called their art "Capitalist Realism," a pun on Socialist Realism, the official representational propaganda art of East Germany and the rest of the Soviet bloc. In the 1960s Polke made countless drawings based on images found in magazines and advertising for common products. He used a range of styles, from a slick deadened illustrational look to a crude cartoony style. He often used nonart materials, such as blue ballpoint pen on notebook paper. The works were a rejection of the refinement of the high art tradition, and at the same time they were quite cynical, not only toward artistic values but also the mass media and how it transformed commercial products into appealing objects: The objects in Polke's drawings were not appealing.

Before the decade was out, Polke was creating art on a wide range of surfaces and with a wide range of materials, as suggested by *Alice in Wonderland* (**fig. 29.10**) of 1971, which is paint on store-bought printed fabric, not canvas. One fabric is covered with soccer players and the other with polka dots, the latter a visual pun on the artist's name but also a reference to his use of Raster dots, and thus the media. Like Warhol, Polke printed appropriated images on his fabric—a ghost-white image of a basketball player, pirated from a magazine, and the caterpillar with a hookah and Alice biting into a mushroom, taken from the illustrations by Sir John Tenniel for Lewis Carroll's 1865 *Alice in Wonderland*. Difficult to see in reproductions are the appropriated 1950s-style outlines of the heads of a man and woman, hand-stamped several times in red and yellow. Polke bombards us with a variety of pilfered images, images executed in a range of styles and from many different periods. In effect, he is telling us that we both see and know the world through images, and that this pictorial world becomes the real world, our reality. He also raises the issue of how context structures meaning: The juxtaposition of unrelated motifs, each without any clear or expected context, allows for a very broad interpretation of their significance. Ultimately, it is virtually impossible to attach a fixed meaning to *Alice in Wonderland*, allowing us to assume that

Polke saw art, and images in general, as not having fixed meanings—only interpretations depending on context and who is doing the interpreting.

Polke and his circle did not consider their art Pop Art, and despite Polke re-presenting media images, as did Warhol and Lichtenstein, there is no mistaking his art for theirs. There is no sense of fun or light humor and no sense of celebrating low art, even if the Americans were actually being subversively ironic in their celebration. His work has a sense of parody, loss, and sadness, as evoked by the ghostlike figures and the chaos of the imagery. Unlike American Pop, his art is emotional and subjective. As we shall see in the next chapter, Polke anticipated many of the fundamental issues of Postmodernism of the 1980s.

Formalist Abstraction of the 1950s and 1960s

The most influential art critic in the 1940s and well into the 1960s was Clement Greenberg (1909–1994). He began by championing Pollock's formalism, but as the 1940s progressed he increasingly promoted an art that was totally abstract and dealt with just those qualities inherent in the medium, that is, color, texture, shape of field (meaning shape of the picture), and composition. This work, which emphasized the formalist or abstract qualities of the medium, could make no reference beyond itself. Greenberg's theories had an enormous impact on the way painters, sculptors, and critics thought about art. His criticism helped lay a foundation for the Hard-Edge painting and Minimalist art that emerged in the 1950s and 1960s.

Formalist Painting and Sculpture

Formalist painting emerged in the heyday of Abstract Expressionism, the early 1950s, and in large part was a reaction to it. Just as Rauschenberg, Johns, Kaprow, and the Pop artists rejected the subjective components of Pollock and De Kooning, the formalist painters sought to make unemotional art. They replaced bold, gestural brushwork with smooth surfaces that gave no hint of the artist's hand or feelings. Instead of the push–pull Cubist space of De Kooning's style of Abstract Expressionism, they powerfully asserted the flatness of the canvas, virtually eliminating any sense of space. Led by Greenberg, they were attracted to the formalist implications of Abstract Expressionism, not its emotional content. They also embraced the style's enormous scale. Among the formalist abstraction styles of the period are Hard-Edge Abstraction, typified by Ellsworth Kelly, and Minimalism, exemplified by Donald Judd.

ELLSWORTH KELLY Ellsworth Kelly (b. 1923) developed a distinctly American brand of abstract painting in Paris between 1948 and 1954. During those years, he began to reduce painting to a bare-bones simplicity, which some critics called Hard-Edge Abstraction. To free his mind from earlier art, he based his abstractions on the shapes that he saw in the world around him, especially negative spaces, such as the opening under a bridge, a shadow, or a window. His paintings use just a handful of geometric shapes in solid primary and secondary colors, and with these explore how forms move through space, colors interact, and "figure" relates to "ground," that is, how image relates to background. Kelly generally locks his figure and ground so tightly into a single unit that they seem to coexist on the same spatial plane.

In *Red Blue Green* (**fig. 29.11**), a 1963 work, Kelly plays a red rectangle and a blue curved shape off against a green ground. The left side of the painting appears fixed, whereas the right has movement. When standing in front of this enormous work,

which is more than 11 feet wide, a viewer can feel at one moment the green ground consuming the blue and at the next moment the blue plunging down into the green. In other words, the figure–ground relationship is reversed. But never to be forgotten is the sheer intensity of the color, especially as presented on such a large scale. Kelly's genius is his simple gesture: He strips everything else away, including any sense of himself, to make a painting that is about color—in this case red, blue, and green—and movement.

Formalist Sculpture: Minimal Art

A group of sculptors emerged in the early 1960s who generally composed their work using a mathematical or conceptual premise. The reliance upon geometry in this new work emphasized conceptual rather than emotional content and favored the means and materials of mass production. Their sculpture came to be known as Minimal Art. The artists generally did not make their objects themselves, preferring to send specifications to an artisan, or more likely a factory, for production. Like Pop paintings, Minimal sculpture lacks the evidence of the artist's touch that traditionally served as the sign of personal emotion and expression as well as proof of the artist's technical accomplishment. There is no sign of the artist at all.

29.11 Ellsworth Kelly. *Red Blue Green*. 1963. Oil on canvas, 6′11⅝″ × 11′3⅞″ (2.12 × 3.45 m). Collection of the Museum of Contemporary Art, San Diego. Gift of Dr. and Mrs. Jack M. Farris. © Ellsworth Kelly 1963

Furthermore, the artists used unconventional non-art materials to make art—Plexiglas, fluorescent tubes, galvanized steel, magnesium tiles—continuing the exploration of new materials that characterized so much of the art-making of the late 1950s and 1960s. Similarly, one of their concerns was to make art that did not look like art. They wanted their artworks to be perceived as independent objects, having no reference to anything beyond themselves.

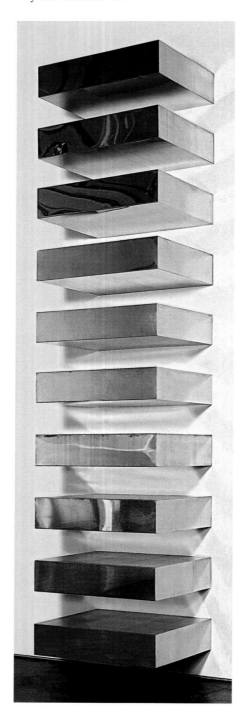

29.12 Donald Judd. *Untitled.* 1969. Copper, ten units, 9 × 40 × 31″ (22.8 × 101.6 × 78.7 cm) each, with 9″ (22.8 cm) intervals; 14′2″ × 40″ × 31″ (4.32 × 1.02 × 1.07 m) overall. Solomon R. Guggenheim Museum, New York. Panza Collection. 91.37.13. © Judd Foundation/Licensed by VAGA, New York, NY

DONALD JUDD The characteristics of Minimalism are apparent in *Untitled*, a 1969 sculpture of copper boxes (**fig. 29.12**) by Donald Judd (1928–1994), one of the leading Minimalists. The sculptor determined the shape and spacing of the boxes by mathematical premise (each box is 9 × 40 × 31 inches, with 9 inches between boxes), not by intuition or artistic sensitivity. Judd's work was constructed by serial repetition of elements, so there is no hierarchy of composition and no evocation of emotion. A viewer can take in and readily understand his composition at a glance. The sculpture is a real object, a "specific object" as Judd called it to distinguish Minimalism from traditional art, and critics admired it for its precision, consistency, color, texture, and scale.

In addition to possessing the properties of a well-made "real thing," Judd's boxes occupy space like ordinary things as well. They are not presented on a base or pedestal, and there is no glass case to protect them. By relinquishing the props that announce an object to be a work of art, Minimalism heightens our awareness of the spaces in which we view art. In other words, the actual space around the object becomes an integral part of the work and of the art experience.

The Pluralist 1970s: Post-Minimalism

The cold objectivity of Minimalism and formalist abstraction dominated contemporary art in the mid-1960s, overshadowing styles that focused on subjectivity and the human figure. Even Pop Art seemed unemotional and machine-made. But as the 1960s progressed, so did an interest in an art based on emotion, the human being, and referential and representational subject matter. In the midst of the Vietnam War and the civil rights-led social revolution that challenged the status quo, artists began to view formalist abstraction as an escapist indulgence. With Minimalism, the Modernist avant-garde seemed to many in the art world to have completely lost touch with society, retreating into a hermetic world of its own. By the mid-1960s, artists could no longer remain removed from their emotions and the hotly contested social and political issues of the day. By the late 1960s, American artists began to put the human component back into art, and many addressed the issues tearing the nation apart. The responses were diverse, with artists using what seemed like an endless array of media to deal with an endless array of issues. Now, many artists made art that was temporary or conceptual and could not be collected, in effect, dematerializing the art object.

While often driven by aesthetic premises, these artists nonetheless reflected the antimaterialistic stance of the 1960s social revolution and its anticapitalist stance. Led by women, African Americans, and Latinos, minority groups, generally ignored by the white-male-dominated art establishment, protested their exclusion from the art world. They picketed museums, denouncing the prejudices of those organizations, and made art that dealt with issues not considered mainstream or valid aesthetic concerns by museum curators and directors—issues such as gender, ethnic and racial identity, and sexual orientation. Disenfranchised artists, like the Impressionists 100 years earlier, began opening their own galleries to provide an alternative to museums. Because the pluralism of the 1970s came on the heels of Minimalism, and in many respects is a response to its hermetic aesthetics, the art from this decade is often called Post-Minimalism.

Post-Minimal Sculpture: Geometry and Emotion

Some of the first Post-Minimal sculptors retained the geometry of Minimalism, but they were hardly creating insular objects. To the contrary, their geometric forms were loaded with powerful emotional issues.

EVA HESSE One of the outstanding Post-Minimalists in the 1960s was Eva Hesse (1936–1970). Her accomplishment is astonishing when one considers that her career was cut short by her death from a brain tumor at age 34. Born in Hamburg, Germany, she was raised in New York after her Jewish parents fled Nazi persecution. Hesse worked with a variety of unusual materials, such as acrylic paint on papier-mâché over balloons. Her works were abstract and had a basis in geometry. Because her sculptures reveal the dripping, pooling, flowing, stretching, and drying by which they took shape, they suggest organic forms and processes, as well as growth and sexuality. In 1968 she began using fiberglass, which became her trademark material and was perhaps responsible for her brain cancer.

A classic work is *Untitled* (**fig. 29.13**), which has as its starting point the geometric form of

Minimalism. The four rectangular units of which it is composed imply boxes or framed paintings because of their curled edges. Contradicting their geometry are the uneven, rippling surfaces and sides, which transform the fiberglass into an organic substance, recalling especially skin. The strange ropelike latex appendages eccentrically flopping from either side of center suggest arms or legs, although they ultimately are nothing more than abstract elements, like the rectangular units. The work is full of contradictions: It is simultaneously funny and morbid, geometric and organic, erotic and repulsive, abstract and referential. Perhaps the most powerful quality in Hesse's sculptures is the sense of frailty, wear, decay, and aging—best expressed in *Untitled* by the wobbly "legs."

Earthworks and Site-Specific Art

By the late 1960s, the Post-Minimal aesthetic operated on an enormous scale, not only far beyond the confines of the gallery but far away from the art world, and in many instances in uninhabited, remote areas. Several artists began sculpting with earth, snow, volcanoes, lightning, and deep-sea sites, their work by definition often temporary and existing today only in photographs and drawings. Usually the work had a strong geometric component, reflecting the influence of Minimal Art and Hard-Edge Abstraction. But in contrast, this sculpture generally was filled with references, including environmental, ontological (concerned with the nature of being), and political issues, as we can see in the work of Robert Smithson.

29.13 Eva Hesse. *Untitled*. 1970. Fiberglass over wire mesh, latex over cloth and wire (four units), 7'6⅞" × 12'3⅝" × 3'6½" (2.31 × 3.75 × 1.08 m) overall. Des Moines Art Center, Iowa. Purchased with funds from the Coffin Fine Arts Trust, Nathan Emory Coffin, Collection of the Des Moines Art Center, 1988 (1988.6.a-d). © The Estate of Eva Hesse. Courtesy Hauser & Wirth

 Read the document related to Eva Hesse on myartslab.com

ROBERT SMITHSON One of the most famous **earthworks**, works of art created by manipulating the natural environment, is *Spiral Jetty* (**fig. 29.14**), made by Robert Smithson in 1970. Smithson (1938–1973) became a prominent figure in the New York art world in the mid- to late 1960s because of his articles on art, which often took an environmental approach to discussing land and nature.

Like Hesse's sculpture, Smithson's Minimalist-looking work is full of references and issues, which is apparent in *Spiral Jetty*. The work is 1,500 feet long, 15 feet wide, and involved moving 6,650 tons of mud and black basalt. It is located at Rozel Point, a remote area of Utah's Great Salt Lake that looks like an industrial wasteland because of the rusting, discarded mining equipment littering the surrounding area. Just as time consumes civilization, and all things for that matter, so too will the jetty eventually disappear as it erodes into the lake. The spiral form, as it wraps around itself, going nowhere, accumulating salt on its sides, and

trapping microorganisms that turn the water red, seems like the relic of a prehistoric civilization. Rather than just a minimal geometric shape to be admired for its own sake, *Spiral Jetty* is a powerful sculpture that utilizes time as a major component to speak about the entropy of all things.

Conceptual Art: Art as Idea

Although the Frenchman Marcel Duchamp had made ideas the focus of art, beginning in the 1910s (see Chapter 28), the term Conceptual Art did not become commonplace until the 1960s, when a large number of artists started producing art that emphasized ideas rather than the aesthetics of style. Of course, ideas appear in all art, but the ideas are closely tied to the formal qualities of the art and cannot exist without them. In Conceptual Art, the art generally exists solely as an idea, with no visual manifestation other than words. Or the idea or information can appear as a graph, chart, map, or documentary photograph.

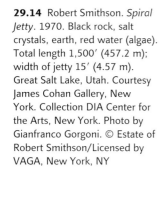

29.14 Robert Smithson. *Spiral Jetty*. 1970. Black rock, salt crystals, earth, red water (algae). Total length 1,500′ (457.2 m); width of jetty 15′ (4.57 m). Great Salt Lake, Utah. Courtesy James Cohan Gallery, New York. Collection DIA Center for the Arts, New York. Photo by Gianfranco Gorgoni. © Estate of Robert Smithson/Licensed by VAGA, New York, NY

JOSEPH KOSUTH   By the late 1960s, more and more artists were making art based on ideas, and one of the leading figures in this movement was Joseph Kosuth (b. 1945). Characteristic of Kosuth's work is *One and Three Chairs* (**fig. 29.15**) of 1965, in which he combined a large gelatin silver print of a folding chair with the real chair and a photograph of a dictionary definition of a chair. By using words instead of just an image, Kosuth tells us how cerebral and nonaesthetic his intentions are.

The work appears to be a textbook study in semiotics, the science of signs—a popular topic in universities and in a small segment of the art community at the time. In the language of semiotics, the real chair is the "signified," the photograph is the "signifier," signifying that particular chair, and the dictionary definition is the idealized nonspecific chair. By arranging three versions of a chair in this particular way, Kosuth has determined their context, which leads a viewer to consider issues of language and meaning, rather than such typical art issues as beauty and expression. Reading the definition, we tend to think of the real chair next to it. If it were not present, we would probably think of some other chair from our own experience. If we look only at the photograph of a chair, we may even think that the subject of the photograph is not necessarily the chair but the absence of a person sitting in the chair. The title is an important part of the work, for it too provides context, suggesting that we can view the chairs as the same chair (one chair) or as three different chairs with very different stories. In other words, this work is about ideas as much as it is about the aesthetics of the visual presentation, which is as unemotional and straightforward as Minimalism. Ultimately, the task of establishing meaning is the viewer's.

One and Three Chairs also reflects a new approach to photography that appeared in the mid-1960s: The medium was no longer the sacred preserve of professional photographers, who worked on a modest scale, carefully took their own photographs, and meticulously made their own prints. Now photographs were used by installation, earthwork, Performance, and Conceptual artists, who in their primary medium often worked on a large scale. They now made photographs based on their work that functioned at a similar size, even rivaling painting. Generally, they did not take their own pictures, and few if any did their own printing. Most shocking to traditional photographers, they often integrated photography into other media, as

Kosuth did in *One and Three Chairs*, thus violating the time-honored integrity of the medium.

JOSEPH BEUYS   Joseph Beuys (1921–1986) was a German Conceptual artist who produced work so complex and rich in ideas that it is nearly impossible to pin down exactly what his art is. His objects, diagrams, photographs, and performances interrelate so tightly that no one piece can comfortably stand on its own. He was based in Düsseldorf, a city that by the 1970s was home to many of the world's leading artists, its art scene perhaps second only to New York's (see pages 611–12). Beuys played a major role in developing this artistic climate. His impact included spurring German artists to confront their Nazi past, to rediscover the German Romantic tradition, and to invest their art with spirituality, much as the German Expressionists had done in the early twentieth century.

Two key factors in Beuys's development were his experiences in World War II as a fighter pilot in Hitler's Luftwaffe and the 1963 arrival in Düsseldorf of the Fluxus artists, highly Conceptual artists noted for, among other things, their Performance art, which had been influenced by Kaprow. Beuys propagated a myth that his plane was shot down in 1943 in a snowstorm over the Crimea, and that nomadic Tartars saved him from freezing to death by covering him in animal fat and layers of felt, materials that became a foundation for much of his sculptural work.

29.15 Joseph Kosuth. *One and Three Chairs*. 1965. Wooden folding chair, photographic copy of chair, and photographic enlargement of dictionary definition of chair; chair, 32³⁄₈ × 14⁷⁄₈ × 20⁷⁄₈" (82.2 × 37.8 × 53 cm); photo panel, 36 × 24¹⁄₈" (91.5 × 61 cm); text panel, 24 × 24¹⁄₈" (61 × 61.2 cm). The Museum of Modern Art, New York. Larry Aldrich Foundation Fund

In 1961 Beuys was teaching at the Düsseldorf Art Academy, and two years later he was introduced to Fluxus, joining them for a segment of their European performance tour. In 1965 he performed *How to Explain Pictures to a Dead Hare* (**fig. 29.16**). For three hours he moved his lips as if silently lecturing the dead hare cradled in his arm about the pictures surrounding him on the walls. Attached to his left sole was felt, and to his right, steel, the one representing "spiritual warmth," the other "hard reason." Honey and gold paint covered Beuys's head, transforming him into a shaman, a high priest who uses magic to cure ills. The honey represented a life force. This mysterious ritualistic performance was about the meaninglessness of conventional picture-making—art that had to be explained—and about the need to replace it with a more spiritual and natural form of communication, an art the meaning of which could be felt or intuited by a viewer rather than understood intellectually. The performance was designed to create a magical art that would cause people to invest their own lives with spirituality. Anyone who watched the performance found it riveting and unforgettable, even if they did not understand it. His objects, too, such as a worn wooden chair with a pile of fat on its seat, affected people similarly.

Television Art: Nam June Paik

Another artist who participated in Fluxus activities in Düsseldorf in the early 1960s was the Korean-born musician, Performance artist, and sculptor Nam June Paik (1932–2006). Living in Düsseldorf in 1963 and performing in the Fluxus program, he began making art using television monitors. He called television the "electronic superhighway" and declared it the medium of the future, dedicating his life to working with it. The following year he moved to New York, and with the launch of the first affordable video camera by Sony, he often used video as well. As a result, he is often labeled a "video artist."

Paik's work in the 1970s became increasingly grand and complex. Typical of the more elaborate structure of the later work is a piece from 1995, *Electronic Superhighway: Continental U.S.* (**fig. 29.17**). Fed by numerous computer-controlled video channels, this installation consists of dozens of monitors inserted in a neon map of the 48 continental states. The rapidly changing images generally relate to the respective states, except for New York, which was fed from a live camera in the Holly Solomon Gallery in Manhattan, where the work was shown and from where our reproduction originates.

In the *Electronic Superhighway*, Paik reaffirms the prevalence of television in American society, presenting it with the fast-paced continuous stream of information characteristic of broadcast television. The work celebrates American vernacular culture, both in its use of neon and television as media and in the Americana presented on the videos. Television is America, Paik tells us. It is, in effect, real life, because most Americans experience the world through their television screens.

29.16 Joseph Beuys. *How to Explain Pictures to a Dead Hare.* 1965. Performed at Galerie Schmela, Düsseldorf, Germany

Art with a Social Agenda

Most of the postwar artists discussed thus far did not have a social agenda. Even some who did, such as Lichtenstein and Warhol, subversively buried

29.17 Nam June Paik. *Electronic Superhighway: Continental U.S.* 1995. Installation: 47-channel closed-circuit video installation with 313 monitors, laser disk images with sound, steel structure, and neon, 15 × 32 × 4′ (4.57 × 9.75 × 1.2 m). Courtesy of the Artist and Holly Solomon Gallery, New York. © Estate of Nam June Paik

their message so that it was not readily visible, especially to the groups they criticized. While an atmosphere of counterculture dominated the vanguard art world that paralleled the social revolution taking place in America and worldwide by the late 1960s, few artists made political art. By the 1970s the trickle of artists making work that dealt with social issues began to swell into a torrent. So great was its influence that we think of social issues playing a major role in avant-garde art for the last 40 years. An art with a social agenda became a key component of 1970s Post-Minimalism.

African-American Art: Ethnic Identity

In the 1960s, a handful of artists began doing what had been unthinkable in the art world: Turning their backs on both Minimalism and abstraction in general and instead making art about the nation's problems and issues, particularly those concerning race, ethnic background, gender, and sexual orientation. Because of the civil rights movement, African-American artists were challenged to make art about their heritage. At universities and in art schools, they were trained like everyone else to make abstract art. But their communities pressured them to do the exact opposite: Make narrative art and take up the black cause. To balance both claims was a challenge.

ROMARE BEARDEN   In New York in 1963, a number of African-American artists formed a loose group called Spiral, dedicated to supporting the civil rights movement. They met in the studio of Romare Bearden (1911–1988), a New York University-educated mathematician and philosopher who in the 1940s increasingly became a committed artist. Inspired by Martin Luther King, Jr.'s 1963 March on Washington, D.C., Bearden suggested a collaborative project for Spiral that involved the members all contributing to a large photo collage about black identity. When no one turned up, Bearden undertook the project by himself, cutting up newspapers and magazines to make collages, for which he became famous.

29.18 Romare Bearden. *The Prevalence of Ritual: Baptism.* 1964. Collage of photochemical reproduction, synthetic polymer, and pencil on paperboard, 9⅛ × 12″ (23.2 × 30.5 cm). Hirshhorn Museum and Sculpture Garden, Smithsonian Institution, Washington, D.C. Gift of Joseph H. Hirshhorn, 1966. Art. © Romare Bearden Foundation/ Licensed by VAGA, New York, NY

The composition of Bearden's collages is based on Cubism, as seen in *The Prevalence of Ritual: Baptism* (**fig. 29.18**), created in 1964, but the subject matter is distinctly African American. Bearden grew up in Charlotte, North Carolina, before moving to New York City's Harlem, and the fractured image shows a baptism, reflecting the importance of religion in black culture. The faces not only express the African physiognomy but in some instances also suggest African masks. This work has the effect of tracing American culture back to its African roots and reinforcing the continuous importance of ritual and community. The collage composition has a wild syncopation, and even a sense of improvisation, that seem to relate to the black jazz musicians of the period, such as Charlie Parker or John Coltrane. The power of Bearden's work lies in the artist's ability to pack so much information and energy into a single image that it overflows with the vitality and essence of the African-American experience.

Feminist Art: Judy Chicago and Gender Identity

Betty Friedan's 1963 book *The Feminine Mystique* signaled the start of the feminist movement. Almost simultaneously a number of women artists began making work that dealt with women's issues. Nancy Spero (1926–2009), for example, made simple but powerful expressionistic drawings depicting violence toward women.

The most famous work emerging from the women's movement is *The Dinner Party* (**fig. 29.19**), orchestrated by Judy Chicago (b. 1939) and made by over 400 women between 1974 and 1979. By the late 1960s, Chicago was a dedicated feminist, who in the early 1970s established a Feminist Art Program, the first of its kind, at California State University at Fresno. Shortly thereafter, with the artist Miriam Schapiro (b. 1923), she started a second similar program at the California Institute of the Arts in Valencia. The thrust of these courses was to encourage women to make art and deal with gender issues, which the art world, including university and art school faculties, said she could not do because the work did not conform to the aesthetic norms of Modernist formalism that signified serious art. The Feminist Art Program was designed to provide support for women artists and to redefine aesthetic values in contemporary art.

The Dinner Party reflects Chicago's shift from a maker of abstract Minimalist objects and paintings to works on feminist themes in alternative media and installations. It pays homage to the many women who, she felt, were ignored, underrated, or omitted from the history books. Chicago laboriously researched these lost figures. She then designed a triangular table with 39 place settings, 13 to a side, each honoring a significant woman, ranging from ancient goddesses to such twentieth-century icons as Georgia O'Keeffe. In addition, 919 other women's names are inscribed on the white floor tiles lying in the triangular enclosure of the tables. Each place setting included a hand-painted ceramic plate that pictured a vagina executed in a period style. The American poet Emily Dickinson's reproductive organ, for example, is surrounded by lace, and the medieval queen Eleanor of Aquitaine's is encased in a *fleur-de-lis*. Under each place setting is an embroidered runner, often elaborate and again in period style.

Instead of using bulldozers, chain saws, hoists, and welding equipment as men did for their environments and installations, Chicago intentionally turned to media associated with women—painted china, ceramics, and embroidery—and created an elegant, beautiful work that subtly operates on an epic scale, spanning millennia. Also present is a sense of community and ritual, for we feel as though Chicago has appropriated and transformed the Christian male theme of the Last Supper into a spiritual communion of women.

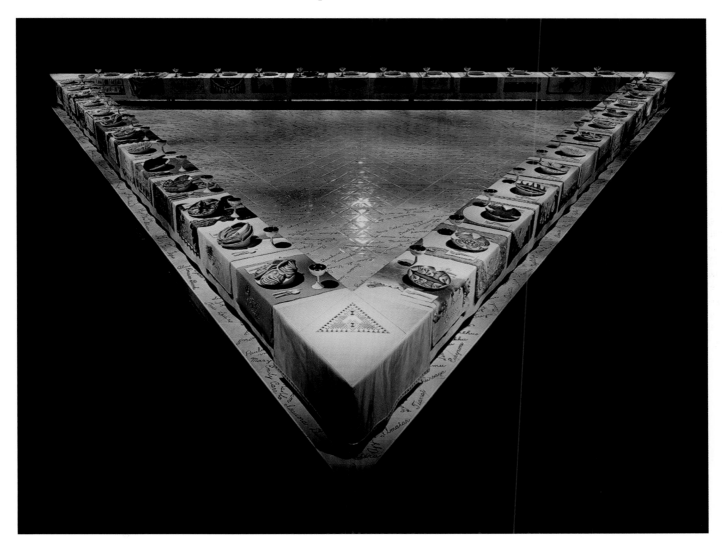

29.19 Judy Chicago. *The Dinner Party*. 1979. Mixed media, 3 × 48 × 42′ (0.9 × 17.6 × 12.8 m). Brooklyn Museum of Art, New York. Gift of the Elizabeth A.

Late Modernist Architecture

Modernist architecture thrived after World War II, especially in America, which previously preferred traditionalist architecture (skyscrapers, for example, in a Gothic style). But now Modernist architecture was only a look or style. It no longer had the utopian vision and revolutionary zeal to improve the world that we saw in the High Modernism of De Stijl and the Bauhaus (see pages 585–88), and in

29.20 Ludwig Mies van der Rohe and Philip Johnson. Seagram Building, New York. 1954–58

the art and design of Constructivist Productivism (see pages 584–85). However, some of the most influential buildings of the period continued to be designed by the great Early and High Modernist architects: Wright, Le Corbusier, and Mies van der Rohe, not discussed in the last chapter. While Mies continued the International Style aesthetic of light, floating geometric buildings with taut, thin glass walls, Frank Lloyd Wright and Le Corbusier developed a sculptural architecture that emphasized mass and the physical presence of a building, and they were not afraid to be referential.

Continuing the International Style: Ludwig Mies van der Rohe

Postwar Late Modernism resulted in glass boxes sprouting up in urban centers and dotting the beltways that circled American cities, especially beginning in the 1960s and 1970s. The glass box became the required image for corporate headquarters, as seen in the Seagram Building (**fig. 29.20**) in New York by Ludwig Mies van der Rohe (1886–1969), built from 1954 to 1958, with interiors by Philip Johnson (1906–2005). If one were to choose a single building to epitomize the Late Modernist skyscraper, it would be this tower. This is the building that was imitated worldwide. But rarely did the imitations begin to approach the perfection that Mies achieved with his aesthetic of "Less is more," which he developed in the 1920s when stripping buildings down to a pure, simple geometric essence that projected an image of breathtaking elegance.

We can see these minimal gestures in the Seagram Building. Mies began by removing the building from its urban environment, placing his 38-story tower on a plaza elevated above street level. The plaza is simple but sumptuous; it is made of pink granite, has two shallow pools placed symmetrically on either side of the building, and is surrounded by a low, serpentine marble wall. The weightless, tinted glass-and-bronze tower sits on a colonnade of *pilotis*, or pillars, that leaves the first floor open, and every detail, including the paving stones, is carefully proportioned to create a sense of perfection and elegance. With the rise of Hitler in Germany, Mies had joined the new Bauhaus in Chicago, and in the Seagram Building we can see the influence of the nineteenth-century Chicago School in the emphasis on its skeletal grid. To acknowledge the functionalism of the grid, Mies used thin I-beams for the mullions, or solid spaces, between windows. They provide the vertical accent that the proportions of the horizontal spandrels so perfectly counterbalance with their thin ridges at top and bottom. Inside and out, lavish, beautifully harmonized materials embellish the building's exquisite proportions.

Sculptural Architecture: Referential Mass

Mies's architecture was essentially nonreferential, just like Minimalist sculpture. However, his contemporaries Frank Lloyd Wright (see page 546–47) and Le Corbusier (see page 588–89) took Late Modernist architecture in a different direction. Their buildings contain historic references and are organic, if not outright expressionistic. Made of poured concrete, they are massive monumental buildings that have a powerful sculptural presence. For a discussion of Frank Lloyd Wright's Solomon R. Guggenheim Museum, built at virtually the same time as the Seagram Building and 36 blocks north of it in Manhattan, please see the Introduction, pages 13–15.

POINTS OF REFLECTION

29.1 Why is Jackson Pollock's 1950 *Autumn Rhythm: Number 30* closer in spirit and concerns to Vasily Kandinsky's 1913 *Sketch I for "Composition VII"* (fig. 27.8) or Piet Mondrian's 1930 *Composition No. II* (fig. 28.13) than to Robert Rauschenberg's *Odalisk* or Andy Warhol's *32 Campbell's Soup Cans*, American works made not long after Pollock's painting?

29.2 How do works such as Andy Warhol's *32 Campbell's Soup Cans*, Roy Lichtenstein's *Drowning Girl*, and Sigmar Polke's *Alice in Wonderland* comment on the mass media, marketing, and consumerism?

29.3 What are the many art forms and artistic materials that emerged after 1950, giving specific examples? Be sure to include the new attitude to photography.

29.4 Why is a work like Eva Hesse's 1970 *Untitled* labeled Post-Minimal, and why is it so different from a Minimal work like Donald Judd's 1969 *Untitled* copper boxes?

29.5 Discuss the very different ways in which Robert Rauschenberg's *Odalisk*, Jasper Johns's *Three Flags*, Allan Kaprow's *Yard*, Joseph Kosuth's *One and Three Chairs*, and Nam June Paik's *Electronic Superhighway: Continental U.S.* all reflect the impact of Marcel Duchamp.

✓• **Study** and review on myartslab.com

ART IN TIME

- 1945–49 — Jean-Paul Sartre publishes his trilogy *Les Chemins de la liberté*
- 1948 — First McDonald's restaurant opened
- **1950 — Jackson Pollock, *Autumn Rhythm: Number 30***
- **1955–58 — Robert Rauschenberg, *Odalisk***
- 1955–68 — First phase of civil rights movement
- 1956 — Tunisia gains independence from France, launching the independence movement in Africa
- 1957 — Jack Kerouac publishes *On the Road*, a Beat classic
  - — Russia launches *Sputnik*
- **1958 — Jasper Johns, *Three Flags***
- 1961 — John F. Kennedy becomes President of the United States of America
- 1963 — Betty Friedan publishes *The Feminine Mystique*
- 1964 — United States enters the Vietnam War
- ca. 1965 — Commercial portable video cameras become available
- 1961 — Allan Kaprow, *Yard*
- 1968 — Assassination of Martin Luther King, Jr.
- 1969 — Woodstock Festival, Bethel, New York
  - — Stonewall riots, New York, which launches gay and lesbian rights movements
  - — *Apollo 11* astronauts land on the moon
- **1970 — Eva Hesse, *Untitled***
  - — Robert Smithson, *Spiral Jetty*
- **1979 — Judy Chicago, *The Dinner Party***

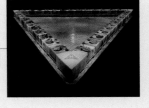

The Postmodern Era: Art Since 1980

((•—**Listen** to the chapter audio on myartslab.com

The art that came to the art world's attention toward 1980 is generally known as Postmodern. The term was coined in the mid-1960s by a circle of European literary critics that included the French philosophers Jacques Derrida (1930–2004) and Jean Baudrillard (1929–2007), and was first applied to literature. (The group's theories are also called Deconstructionism or Post-Structuralism.)

At the heart of European Postmodernism is the premise that all literature and art is an elaborate construction of signs, and that the meaning of these signs is determined by their context. A Raphael altarpiece, for example, meant one thing to a sixteenth-century Catholic viewing it in its original context, a church, but it conveys a different message today when it is presented as a fine art object in a prestigious museum. Context can also change as viewers bring their personal experiences to the work. Postmodernists claimed that there can be no fixed meaning, and thus no fixed truths. By the late 1970s, artists and critics had digested this theory and applied it to art. Postmodern theory now became the driving force behind much art

making and art criticism, and a self-consciousness about entering a new era arose in the art world in the late 1970s. Now a large number of artists and critics asked more overtly and persistently: How do signs acquire meaning? What is the message? Who originates it? What—and whose—purpose does it serve? Who is the audience and what does this tell us about the message? Who controls the media—and for whom? More and more artists began using familiar images in new contexts, revealing—or deconstructing—their deeper social, political, economic, and aesthetic meanings. The preferred mediums for many of these artists were those of the mass media, namely photography, electronic signs, billboards, and video.

While this Postmodernist attitude signified a major thrust in art toward 1980, it has been only one of numerous issues that have preoccupied the art world in the last 30 years. The period is characterized by pluralism, in effect continuing the pluralism associated with 1970s Post-Minimalism. Now, however, it had a philosophical foundation in Postmodern theory. By denying any one system,

Map 30.1 Europe and North America in the twenty-first century

reading, interpretation, or truth, Postmodern theory destroyed the credibility of the authoritarian hierarchies of styles, media, issues, and themes, and it opened the door for everything and everyone.

In effect, Postmodernism marked the end of the Modernist era. Modernism viewed modern art as a linear progression of one style building upon the last, with artist-geniuses continuously advancing art toward the "new." By the 1980s, artists had license *not* to be new, nor to be innovative geniuses, instead working in teams and collaborating. Not only did they appropriate art in every imaginable style and medium from the history of civilization and combine it as they saw fit, many of the leading artists, such as Felix Gonzalez-Torres and Kiki Smith, did not even concern themselves with cultivating a distinguishable style as they jumped from one medium to the next, relying on a theme rather than a look to tie their work together. Message was more important than having a readily identifiable, single style, a quality that had been one of the hallmarks of Modernism.

The Postmodern era also redefined the nature of the art world itself. The art establishment widened to embrace artists of all ethnicities and races, accepting all kinds of media, styles, and issues without placing a value on one over another. In this new multicultural environment, artists who had been marginalized in the 1970s became mainstream. Furthermore, artists from all over the world, not just America and Europe, molded contemporary art. The acceptance of artists worldwide mirrors the global restructuring of the last 30 years. Political and economic realignments resulted as first the U.S.S.R. and then China abandoned a strict adherence to Communism, experimented with capitalism, and opened up to foreign trade and investment. In the 1990s, Europe formed the European Union, and the United States, Mexico, and Canada signed the North American Free Trade Agreement (see **map 30.1**). Barriers were falling everywhere, with people crossing borders more readily than ever before. Another important force behind the creation of a world art is the long-term impact of the American civil rights movement and the independence movements, especially in Africa and Asia, of the post-colonial 1950s and 1960s. These movements asserted their cultural traditions as viable and valuable alternatives to mainstream culture, and in the last 30 years they have increasingly been woven into the fabric of a world culture. But perhaps the communications field more than anything else has been responsible for the creation of the "Global Village." Television, cellular phones, satellites, computers, and the Internet have linked the world. The Post-Industrial era is also the Information Age. Today, the world's leading artists come from countries as varied as Lebanon, Iran, Israel, Cambodia, Thailand, Korea, Japan, China, South Africa, Mali, Russia, Colombia, Brazil, Cuba, and Iceland.

Map 30.1 Europe and North America in the twenty-first century

In this world of complex media and changing interpretations, scholars do not always agree on the meaning of Postmodernism. While the term initially was applied specifically to the European philosophy that emerged in the 1960s, today scholars and historians use the term quite loosely, to encompass all of the art made since 1980. In effect, they use it to mean art made after Modernism. We will use it in the same way.

Architecture

Postmodernism appeared in architecture in the 1960s and was accompanied by a manifesto of sorts, a book titled *Complexity and Contradiction in Architecture*, by the Philadelphia architect Robert Venturi. In it, Venturi called for a new architecture, one that rejected the cold, abstract Modernist International Style. The new architecture would be referential, that is, buildings would recall earlier architectural styles, or contain motifs that referred to the past and present. Furthermore, architects would be free to design buildings without following a set of rules or principles. They were free, too, to be entertaining and witty. Venturi's message was gradually absorbed by the architectural community, and by the 1980s, an architecture that it

labeled "Postmodern" emerged. The term was used specifically to describe work that made references to earlier periods and styles.

Since fundamental to European literary Postmodernism is the concept that no one authoritative style or set of principles can prevail, architecture since the 1980s reflects a broad range of issues and interests going well beyond just designing referential buildings. Among them is a revised Modernism, one strain of which we can call Hi-Tech because of its highly technological appearance. Another strain is Deconstructivism, a concept relating to Derrida's theories of Deconstruction and embracing the notion that architecture should not have a fixed structure, conceptual premise, or logic, thus being wide open to interpretation.

Postmodern Architecture

Robert Venturi (b. 1925) upset the architectural establishment by attacking Modernist architecture in *Complexity and Contradiction*. He challenged Mies van der Rohe's dictum "Less is more" with "Less is a bore" and argued that architecture could be whatever the architect wanted it to be. By the late 1970s his writing triggered the rise of a referential architecture, an architecture often referred to as "Postmodern."

30.1 Robert Venturi. Vanna Venturi House. 1962. Chestnut Hill, Philadelphia. Venturi, Scott Brown and Associates, Inc.

ROBERT VENTURI Venturi practiced what he preached. In 1962, he designed a house for his mother in Chestnut Hill, Philadelphia (**fig. 30.1**). The structure resembles a Modernist abstraction of flat planes, strict geometry, clean lines, and a play of forms and spaces, notably in the enormous cleft in the center of the façade. But the house is also referential, for it is a parody of a conventional American home, complete with a slanted gable (the roof is much lower), a front porch, and behind that a large rectangular block that looks like a chimney. (It is a false chimney, which dwarfs the real chimney inserted within it.) Venturi then complicates the house with endless architectural references—the "lintel" that seems to support the two halves of the façade and the interrupted "segmental arch," floating over and framing the entrance, recall an Egyptian pylon. Venturi has imbued the

over-scaled house with humor, irony, and allusions, transforming the traditional American home into a rich architectural statement.

MICHAEL GRAVES Postmodern architecture did not become prevalent until the late 1970s. A fine example is the Public Services Building (**fig. 30.2**) of 1980–82 in Portland, Oregon, designed by the Princeton, New Jersey architect Michael Graves (b. 1934). The building is complex and quite difficult to interpret, and furthermore, it is filled with paradox, as every design on its surface begs to be seen in several ways: Flat and sculptural, representational and abstract, historical and modern. The form of the building is a Palladian cube sitting atop a platform, with the square or near-square motif echoed in the outline of the façade and in additional squares within (for example, the enormous mirror-glass window, which encases a square defined by the maroon vertical piers). The individual windows are each 4 feet square. The wall can be read as a flat mural, a thin Modernist membrane stretched over the metal skeleton; but suddenly it becomes three-dimensional and sculptural, an effect heightened by the maroon-colored vertical shafts in front of the large mirror window. These mullionlike shafts become the fluting of pilasters, topped with bracket capitals, which support an enormous keystone above. Yet, if we read the keystone with the beige-colored wall, it becomes part of a flat arch framing the mirror window. The façade can even be described as anthropomorphic, for the pilasters and keystone can be read as a huge face, the capitals as eyes, and the pilasters as legs. The building has a whimsical sense of play, but it is also serious, recalling such great historical models as Palladio and Mannerism.

New Modernisms: Hi-Tech Architecture

Major Postmodern architecture in the vein of Venturi faded in the 1990s, superseded by an exhilarating diversity that expanded architecture to a true Postmodernism, that is, a pluralism that the term Postmodernism generally refers to. Many architects began to revisit Modernism, reinvigorating it with the new artistic license that had emerged during the late 1970s. An extreme version of this New Modernism is Hi-Tech, a style whose buildings resemble powerful industrial machines. Perhaps the most famous prototype for the Hi-Tech Modernism that became fashionable in the following decades is the 1971–77 Pompidou Center (**fig. 30.3**) in Paris. Its architects, Richard Rogers (b. 1933) and Renzo Piano (b. 1937), exposed the building's utilities—instead of being buried within the interior, they are displayed on scaffolding around the perimeter of what is otherwise a classical Modernist glass box.

30.3 Richard Rogers and Renzo Piano. Centre National d'Art et Culture Georges Pompidou. 1971–77. Paris

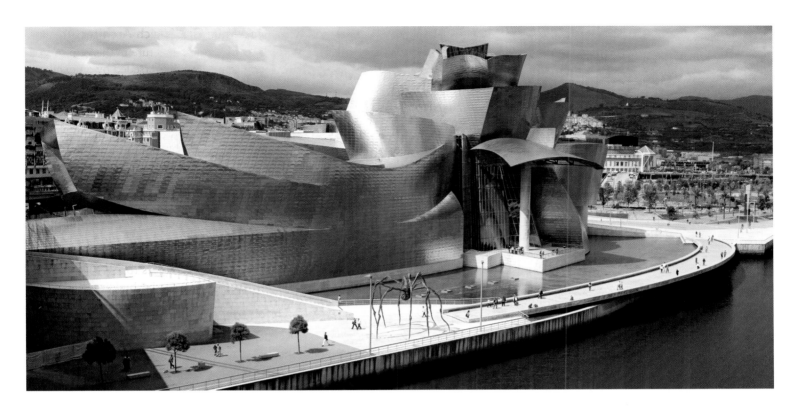

Elevators and escalators, plumbing, electrical and ventilation ducts are all prominently displayed as exterior "ornament." Besides challenging architectural aesthetics, this device has the advantage of completely opening up the interior space, allowing for any necessary configuration.

Deconstructivism: Countering Modernist Authority

In 1988 the Museum of Modern Art in New York mounted an exhibition titled *Deconstructivism*. The show presented seven architects whose work displayed a Constructivist geometry and planarity that created an architecture of "disruption, dislocation, deviation, and distortion," as the curators for the show wrote. The term Deconstruction caught on, and a major trend emerged in the 1980s challenging the idea that architecture had to adhere to any single concept or ideal and the notion that architecture had to aspire to some kind of perfection, order, or logic.

FRANK GEHRY Frank Gehry (b. 1929) was one of the seven architects included in the *Deconstructivism* show, but he views himself as an independent, refusing to be associated with any style or group. Nevertheless, his projects share with those of the other artists in the exhibition a sense of disorder, fragmentation, and energy, as seen in his

most famous building, the Guggenheim Museum Bilbao, Spain (**fig. 30.4**). Its unique forms and vocabulary make it impossible to establish any specific meaning or architectural references, although people have described its forms as a boat, a fish, and a blossoming flower (Gehry's own description). Ultimately the structure is an exploration of the abstract sculptural play of enormous volumes, and it shows clearly the architect's pure delight in architectural freedom.

The building's curvilinear masses are contrary to orthodox Deconstructivism, which emphasizes flat planes and angularity. Gehry designed the complex forms using computer technology, an integral tool in the fabrication of the building as well. The museum even feels Hi-Tech, for covering the steel skeleton is a thin skin made up of thousands of tiny titanium shingles. These shimmer in the light, changing color—silver, blue, gold—according to the time of day or the weather.

The Guggenheim Bilbao is an example of the architectural diversity that had emerged by the end of the twentieth century, when all rules about design were suspended. As important, it reflects how architecture has moved beyond just being about designing buildings. Architects have, once again, begun to create prominent symbols for a city. From its conception, the museum was intended to be more than just a museum; it was

30.4 Frank Gehry. Guggenheim Museum. 1992–97. Bilbao, Spain meant to change the image of this industrial Spanish port, giving it cultural cachet and transforming it into a tourist destination. That is precisely what happened.

Post-Minimalism and Pluralism: Limitless Possibilities

Beginning in the late 1960s, the Post-Minimalists had rejected the austerity of Minimalism (see pages 614–15) and once again returned the human figure, the artist's hand, subjectivity, and references back into art. The reaction to Minimalism was accompanied by the rise of a broad range of issues, styles, and media in the 1970s. During the 1980s this pluralism began to gain widespread acceptance as it moved from marginalized art to the mainstream. At the same time, Postmodern theory provided a philosophical basis for pluralism, as it argued against all authoritative aesthetics and philosophical positions. The Modernist notion that one and only one style was correct and could move art forward at any given moment was dead. Indeed, if a single

word could encapsulate the art made since the 1980s, it would be "diverse."

Among the many developments of the last 30 years are a revival of interest in painting, the popularity of installation art, and the ascendance of photography and video as leading media. Among the more popular themes are racial, ethnic, and gender identity, a preoccupation with the body and death, and a Postmodern analysis, or Deconstruction, of how images and art take on meaning. But if there is anything that unites this period, it is the belief that Modernism and its authoritarian posturing is dead, and that the possibilities of what art can be and be about are limitless.

The Return of Painting

Painting was back by 1980. Not that it had disappeared, but in the late 1960s and 1970s it had been overshadowed by Conceptual, video, Performance, and earth art. The Derrida-influenced art critics of the late 1970s associated painting with Modernism and were talking about "the death of painting," even though a stream of shows featuring the medium opened in London, New York, Germany, and Italy in the late 1970s and the 1980s.

The new type of painting that emerged came to be known as Neo-Expressionism, an appropriate label for works that are both painterly and expressionistic. Neo-Expressionism appeared first in Germany and Italy in the 1970s and then migrated to New York. In Germany, painters self-consciously recalled the Northern Romanticism and Expressionism so deeply ingrained in that nation's culture. Joseph Beuys, through his mystical performances, was the catalyst for this resurrection of the German past. Among the themes he and other artists began to explore was the legacy of Hitler's Third Reich.

ANSELM KIEFER Among Beuys's students at the Düsseldorf Art Academy was Anselm Kiefer (b. 1945). Kiefer created images of mythical themes and epic scope that evoke centuries of German history. His enormous painting *To the Unknown Painter* (**fig. 30.5**) explodes with the energy of flailed paint and the dramatic perspective of crop furrows rushing toward an eerie monumental tomb. Cold, bleak, and lifeless, the neutral-colored image seems to exude an atmosphere of death. Or does it? Crops lying fallow in the winter will be reborn in the spring; the cycle of life continues. Kiefer's expressive use of paint and dramatic composition can be interpreted as a metaphor for the constant

30.5 Anselm Kiefer. *To the Unknown Painter*. 1983. Oil, emulsions, woodcut, shellac, latex, and straw on canvas, 9′2″ × 9′ × 2″ (2.79 × 2.74 m × 5 cm). The Carnegie Museum of Art, Pittsburgh. Richard M. Scaife Fund; A. W. Mellon Acquisition Endowment Fund. © Anselm Kiefer

movement and force of nature. Inspired by Beuys's use of symbolic objects, Kiefer often incorporated real materials into his paintings, imbuing them with a similar ritualistic magic. In this work, he embedded straw into the paint, and viewers could smell its scent for years. Nature is not just illustrated in this work, it is physically present. Yet unlike crops in a field that are continually rejuvenated, the straw in this painting will eventually disintegrate.

How does the tomb fit into this image? As the title suggests, the mausoleum is for painters. We deduce that they are German because the tomb is not painted but rendered by a large woodcut, a medium associated with German art since being widely used by Northern European artists during the Renaissance as well as by Expressionists such as Kirchner (see page 558–59) in the early twentieth century. The bunkerlike shape suggests a shelter, and the isolated but well-anchored monument seems to be surrounded by the swirling forces of nature, representing not only the German mythical past but also the Romantic spirit that has driven German artists for centuries. We know from other works by Kiefer that these destructive forces are meant to symbolize Hitler's perversion of the German Romantic tradition, which he manipulated to serve his racist agenda.

In a painting about national identity, Kiefer's Expressionistic style and his use of Romantic themes proclaim his place within the Northern European Romantic tradition. He assures us that this tradition is once again in safe hands. With its wealth of symbols, metaphors, and overlapping and interlocking interpretations, the resulting image is varied and complex, reflecting the epic scale Kiefer covers and the mythical themes he evokes.

JEAN-MICHEL BASQUIAT Of the many American Neo-Expressionists to emerge in the 1980s, among the most exciting was Jean-Michel Basquiat (1960–1988), born in New York to a middle-class family. Basquiat's father was Haitian and his mother was of Puerto Rican descent. He dropped out of school at age 17, first writing poetry and then becoming a street artist. By studying art books, he became knowledgeable about art history and began painting. By the time he was 22, he had achieved international stardom. He died of a drug overdose at age 27.

In *Horn Players* (**fig. 30.6**) of 1983, Basquiat combines both poetry and graffiti. More important, he draws upon the lessons of the pluralistic 1970s by brilliantly incorporating the era's strategies of using texts, making process art, working with narratives, and dealing with social politics, here racial identity. Basquiat also owes a debt to Abstract Expressionism, seen in his dynamic handling of paint, and to Pop Art, visible in his cartoonlike imagery and popular-culture references.

Basquiat was prolific, working quickly and with the stream-of-consciousness intensity sensed here. We can feel him painting, writing, crossing out. He draws us into the canvas by forcing us to read and piece it together. He makes us experience the sounds coming out of the saxophone, think about the repetition of words and the rhythms they make, and analyze his masterful use of color—a brilliant pink and blue here, yellow and green there. Because they are so powerfully presented, we cannot dismiss Basquiat's use of the words,

30.6 Jean-Michel Basquiat. *Horn Players*. 1983. Acrylic and oil paintstick on canvas, three panels, overall 8′ × 6′5″ (2.44 × 1.91 m). The Broad Art Foundation, Santa Monica, California

such as *alchemy* (a reference to the alchemy of jazz), *ornithology* (a nod to the jazz musician Charlie Parker, nicknamed "Bird"), and *ear* (an allusion to musical instinct). His works evoke the raw energy of the 1950s: Beat poetry, improvisational jazz, and Abstract Expressionism. But 1980s hip-hop also comes to mind. Basquiat creates a powerful, sensuous experience as he shares his passionate feelings about the black musicians Dizzy Gillespie and Charlie Parker, with whom he clearly identifies. Much of his work features African-American musicians, singers, and athletes, and is a reflection of the importance artists were now giving to racial, ethnic, and gender identity.

Sculpture

The Post-Minimal aesthetic in sculpture, the combination of the geometry of Minimalism with references and emotion that we saw in the work of Eva Hesse (see fig. 29.13), continued unabated into the 1980s and 1990s.

MAYA LIN   One of the great Post-Minimal sculptures of the 1980s is the *Vietnam Veterans Memorial* (**fig. 30.7**) by Maya Lin (b. 1959). Lin received the

commission while still a student in the architecture program at Yale University. This was a daunting project because of the strong emotions and opinions surrounding the Vietnam War, but Lin's solution proved beautiful in its simplicity, ingenious in its neutrality, and sublime in its emotional impact. She presents the names of the dead and missing in action in a chronological list from 1959 to 1975. The names are etched into slabs of black granite that together carve out a V-shaped gash in the earth. Viewers start reading from the left, representing the year 1959, where the first killed are listed and the granite rises out of the ground. The name-laden stone gradually rises along its 247-foot length as more and more Americans die. The names keep coming, and the viewer soon becomes emotionally overwhelmed by their number.

At its 10-foot peak, the granite turns at a 130-degree angle and then descends along another 247-foot length, with fewer soldiers listed as the 1973 withdrawal from Vietnam approaches. At the end, as the granite again disappears into the ground, many viewers are left with a feeling of existential nothingness. Adding to this sense of

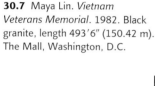

30.7 Maya Lin. *Vietnam Veterans Memorial*. 1982. Black granite, length 493′6″ (150.42 m). The Mall, Washington, D.C.

loss is the impact of the granite's polished surface, which acts like a mirror, casting reflections of the living onto the names of the dead. This memorial is a sharp departure from traditional representational monuments to heroism, like Rude's *La Marseillaise* (see fig. 24.13), which glorified nationalistic spirit and dedication. In a sense, the granite wall acts as an enormous tombstone. While the structure takes the form of Minimal sculpture, it has been transformed through references into a brilliant Postmodern monument of powerful emotions.

Deconstructing Art: Context as Meaning

By 1980 many artists were making art that analyzed how images functioned. We saw Warhol and Lichtenstein doing this in the 1960s (see Chapter 29), by appropriating mass-media images to comment on how they influence public perception. Now, influenced by Postmodern Deconstruction theory, even more artists were exploring how images function and how context affects meaning. They were also influenced by the Post-Structuralist philosopher Jean Baudrillard, and especially by his theory of simulacrum. Baudrillard wrote that contemporary American culture was based on a notion of hyperreality—that Americans, especially through the mass media, including films and television, had constructed an artificial, perfect, timeless world that was more "real" than reality itself. In effect, the copy had replaced authenticity, and looking at images and experiencing the world through images had become a simulacrum, or visual substitute, for real experience. Artists now began representing this simulacrum, borrowing images from the mass media—a process often referred to as appropriating—and analyzing the effect of context on meaning.

In effect, their art was about deconstructing images as used in the social environment. Often they recontextualized and layered the appropriated images and designs with the intention of exposing, or deconstructing, the social, aesthetic, political, and economic systems that the original images presented. Suddenly Sigmar Polke (see page 611–12) and other Düsseldorf Pop-inspired artists of the 1960s who had been largely ignored in the United States were discovered, their appropriation and layering of images as well as their analysis of the role of context providing inspiration for many artists who viewed their work as central to the art of the 1980s. But by the second half of the 1980s

it was photography, not painting, that came to the fore. Often, these photographs were large-scale, the size of a Jackson Pollock or a Mark Rothko, clearly indicating that photography was now considered as major as painting. But photography was considered so important because after World War II it played such a powerful role in influencing society—in the proliferation of newspapers and magazines that accompanied postwar consumerism, and in the form of films and television. In part influenced by Baudrillard, artists realized that the world was now viewed through a lens, not through drawn and painted images, and they now used the same mass-media vehicles to make their art. By the late 1980s, many in the art world were pronouncing painting as dead, which while hardly true reflected a shift in focus. Painting was associated with Modernism, while photography was viewed as a Postmodern medium.

But Deconstruction appeared in many mediums and in many contexts, one of which was the institutional critique, art aimed at revealing how museums, the supposedly august pinnacles of culture, were like the mass media, guilty of having an agenda and similarly manipulating their message. While this kind of art surfaced in the 1960s, it came to the fore in the 1980s with the rise of Postmodernism.

PHOTOGRAPHY: CINDY SHERMAN Among the first artists to challenge the painters was a group of New York Postmodern photographers, which included Cindy Sherman (b. 1954). As was the case with Joseph Kosuth and the many other vanguard artists who started using the camera in the 1960s and 1970s (see pages 617), most are not interested in the mechanics of taking and processing pictures. Some of them do not handle the camera, and almost none do their own printing. What interests these artists is revealing how the context of an image determines its meaning, and how the mass media subversively structure content to manipulate viewers. Many of these artists were women, and they were heavily influenced by feminist theory as well as by the psychoanalytic premises of the French writer Jacques Lacan, who described how women were served up by society for the pleasure of men, specifically for the male gaze.

All of these issues can be found in Cindy Sherman's photographs, although in addition to the power of the mass media, especially

30.8 Cindy Sherman. *Untitled Film Still #15*. 1978. Gelatin silver print, 10 × 8" (25.4 × 20.3 cm). Courtesy of the artist and Metro Pictures, New York. © Cindy Sherman

Watch a video about Cindy Sherman on myartslab.com

than it does about the picture itself, which remains ambiguous. Her "babe" could very well be dressed for a costume party instead of a date, and her look of concern could be for something occurring on the street below. Innumerable stories can be spun from this image, taking into account such details as her cross pendant or the old-fashioned spindle-back chair and brick wall. Remove any one of these motifs, and the story would change.

THE INSTITUTIONAL CRITIQUE: FRED WILSON AND GUERRILLA GIRLS   Fred Wilson (b. 1954) is a New York Conceptual artist who generally works with found objects that he puts into new contexts in order to reveal the hidden meanings or agendas of their previous uses. He is especially renowned for deconstructing museums by reinstalling collections to reveal how institutions have an agenda when they present art and how the interpretation of this art can change when it is put into a new context. Generally his work reflects his own African-American background and how African-American identity is manipulated. His best-known work is *Mining the Museum* (**fig. 30.9**), a commission from the Museum of Contemporary Art in Baltimore. For this project, Wilson "mined" the collection of the nearby Maryland Historical Society, pulling works out of storage that probably had not seen the light of day in decades, and then inserting them into existing installations, the new item creating a new context for the display and powerfully deconstructing the arrangement of the original objects. Wilson, for example, discovered slave manacles in storage, which he then inserted in a case of fine silver from roughly the same period. Silver pitchers, teapots, and goblets, originally presented as objects of fine craftsmanship and design, were now seen as valuable commodities, their production and acquisition made possible by the proceeds of slave labor. The manacles raised a second issue, which is that without the manacles, African Americans, who constitute a large portion of Baltimore's populace, would not be presented at all in the museum. The unadorned, painfully functional iron manacles sit in powerful contrast to the glistening polished silver, creating a new context that radically undermines the story formerly told by the historical society.

movies, she is also interested in revealing a viewer's participation in determining meaning. In 1977, Sherman began a series called *Film Stills*, in which she photographed herself in situations that resemble an 8- by -10-inch advertising still from a B-grade movie. For each, she created a set and a female character that she played herself, wearing different clothes, wigs, and accouterments so that she is unrecognizable as the same person from one still to the next. That she is always the actress is conceptually important, for her metamorphosis represents the transformation women undergo subliminally as they conform to societal stereotypes reinforced, if not actually determined, by the mass media. In *Untitled Film Still #15*, Sherman plays the "sexy babe" who seems to be anxiously awaiting the arrival of a date or lover (**fig. 30.8**). But is this really what is happening? Sherman leaves the viewer guessing. She may suggest a narrative, but she never provides enough information to determine one securely. In effect, the story viewers imagine tells more about their own backgrounds, experiences, and attitudes

In contrast to Wilson's subtle subversion of museum presentations is the bold propaganda of the Guerrilla Girls, a group founded in New York in 1985 and with cells throughout the

United States. Their collaboration, i.e. the idea of many artists working together to make art, was very Postmodern, undermining the cult of individual genius associated with Modernism. They produced printed matter, especially posters, and gave presentations wearing gorilla masks, a feminist ploy meant to undermine the Modernist emphasis on the single artist. They especially spotlighted how women were marginalized by the art establishment. Among their most famous posters, which appeared on city buses and reflect how Postmodern artists often work in public nonart environments, is one made in 1989 presenting Ingres's *Grande Odalisque* (see fig. 24.8) wearing a gorilla mask, above which is printed "Do women have to be naked to get into the Met. Museum? Less than 5% of the artists in the Modern Art sections are women, but 85% of the nudes are female."

The AIDS Pandemic and a Preoccupation with the Body

One of the most embattled fronts in the 1980s artistic war with right-wing politics was the struggle to bring about government support to deal with the AIDS epidemic, a disease of the immune system first identified in 1981 that to date has affected over 33 million people worldwide. The Reagan government of the 1980s did nothing to counter the disease. Artists, many gay, and often working in collaborative groups and in a public forum, attacked the administration. One group, Gran Fury, its name taken from the Plymouth automobile used by the then repressive New York Police Department, made posters, such as the 1988 "The Government Has Blood on Its Hands," the bold type of the title appearing above and below a large blood-red handprint.

THE AIDS CRISIS: FELIX GONZALEZ-TORRES Felix Gonzalez-Torres (1957–1996), a member of the collaborative Group Material, produced some of the most powerful AIDS-related art, although his work encompasses a wide range of social issues. Gonzalez-Torres, who was born in Cuba and came to Florida in 1981 in the mass exodus called the Mariel boatlift, can be described as a Conceptual artist working in a Minimalist mode. He is the quintessential Postmodern artist, since his art is issue-driven as opposed to style-driven. His many mediums include, for example, two identical wall clocks hung side by side, which can be viewed

as lovers who fade and die as the batteries wear out; a string of lightbulbs hanging from the ceiling, the lights evoking tears, or even souls; enormous public billboards of an empty unmade bed with two pillows that can evoke a sense of absence and even death; and a pile of brightly wrapped candy, weighing the same as the ideal weight of the artist's lover, which visitors may take and eat, the gradual disappearance of the candy, reflecting, among other things, the lover's body being consumed (*"Untitled,"* **fig. 30.10**). Typical of Postmodern art in this last work is viewer participation, which we first encountered in Allan Kaprow's *Yard* of 1960 (see fig. 29.6).

30.9 Fred Wilson. "Metal Work, 1793–1880," from *Mining the Museum: An Installation by Fred Wilson*. The Contemporary Museum and Maryland Historical Society, Baltimore, April 4, 1992–February 8, 1993. Photograph courtesy of PaceWildenstein, New York

30.10 Felix Gonzalez-Torres. *"Untitled."* 1991. Candies individually wrapped in cellophane. © The Felix Gonzalez-Torres Foundation Courtesy of Andrea Rosen Gallery, New York

KIKI SMITH The death and suffering of AIDS victims brought about a new awareness of the body, especially its vulnerability and frailty. One artist to explore the vulnerability of the body and the brevity of life was the New Yorker Kiki Smith (b. 1954). In the 1980s, she created a work consisting of eight identical jars of blood, and another presenting silver-coated water-cooler bottles etched with the names of such bodily fluids as tears, milk, saliva, vomit, semen, urine, and sweat, which a viewer is led to believe are in the jars. Because these works contain repeated elements, they resemble Minimal art. Yet the conceptual component—the thoughts we have when confronting the blood, for example—packs a strong visceral response and the emotional punch of Baroque art or German Expressionism. Smith has reduced existence to an elemental essence, stripping away individuality and uniqueness to reveal the basic building blocks of life.

Toward 1990, Smith began constructing entire figures, usually using such impermanent materials as paper, papier-mâché, and wax, which served as a metaphor for the fragility of the body and the transience of life. In the 1990 untitled wax work reproduced here (**fig. 30.11**), she cleverly revives the classical tradition of the nude figure. However, we are viewing neither Greek gods and goddesses nor heroic athletes and soldiers. Rather, she portrays flesh-and-blood mortals. The woman oozes milk from her breast and the man semen from his penis, attributes of nourishment, procreation, and life. But death dominates, in the form of the limp figures slumped on their poles and the jarring discoloration of the skin. Smith presents the entire life cycle, but it is the sadness of deterioration and our ultimate fate of death that prevails.

The Power of Installation and Video Art

Installation art had existed since the late 1950s (when the work was called environments), but its popularity surged dramatically in the 1980s, when it became a featured medium, just as photography had. As we saw in Kiefer's incorporation of actual materials into his canvases, a thirst for the real features prominently in much art since 1980.

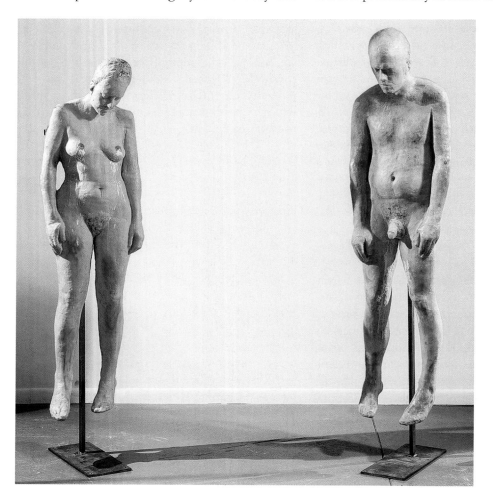

30.11 Kiki Smith. *Untitled.* 1990. Beeswax and microcrystalline wax figures on metal stands, female figure installed height 6′4¹⁵⁄₁₆″ (1.95 m). Collection Whitney Museum of American Art, New York. Purchase, with funds from the Painting and Sculpture Committee. 91.13 (a–d). © Kiki Smith

ILYA KABAKOV Of the many installation artists who emerged in the 1980s, one of the most engaging is the Russian Ilya Kabakov (b. 1933), who emigrated from Moscow to New York in 1988. In Russia between 1981 and 1988 he made a series of rooms called *Ten Characters* that replicated the types of seedy communal apartments assigned to people by the Russian state under the Communist regime. Each was inhabited by an imaginary person with an "unusual idea, one all-absorbing passion belonging to him alone." One spectacular cubicle was *The Man Who Flew into Space from His Apartment* (**fig. 30.12**). We see the room after its occupant has achieved his dream of flying into space, hurled through the ceiling from a catapult suspended by springs, an allusion to the space race between the U.S.A. and Russia. Like the other rooms, this one is accompanied by a grim story, worthy of the Russian novelist Fyodor Dostoevsky. The text, the collapsed ceiling, limp sling, and clutter become a tableau of life in Communist Russia, where claustrophobic squalor has brought about a hopeless delusional state, and flights of fantasy are the only escape from the drudgery of daily life. The ruin we are witnessing in *The Man Who Flew into Space* is not just the devastation of one man's life, but rather the shattered dream of the utopia in which Tatlin, the Constructivists, the Dadaists, and the Communist world in general had so firmly believed (see Chapter 28). Kabakov's installation is presented as a relic of an actual event, and like any relic, it possesses a powerful aura, almost impossible to achieve in conventional painting and sculpture.

BILL VIOLA An especially popular form of installation is video or film installation, which had its roots in the film and video art of the 1960s and 1970s, particularly in the work of Nam June Paik (see page 618). Among the best-known practitioners of the medium to emerge in the early 1980s is Bill Viola (b. 1951), who was also one of the first major artists to specialize in video. He started working with the medium in the 1970s after graduating from Syracuse University and by the early 1980s was incorporating it into installations or environments containing real objects. Although Viola's work does not always have a clear sequential narrative, it always has a theme, usually an unsettling, intense questioning of the meaning of existence.

One of Viola's best-known—and simpler—works is *The Crossing* (**fig. 30.13**). In two

simultaneous, approximately ten-minute projections, shown side by side, or on either side of a single screen, a plainly dressed man approaches from the distance, passing through an empty, darkened space and stopping when his body, now nearly 12 feet tall, fills the screen. In one projection, water begins to drip on him, eventually becoming a deluge that washes him away. In the other, a small fire erupts at his feet, increasingly swelling into a bonfire that ultimately consumes him. The projections end with water hauntingly dripping in one, and a fire mysteriously smoldering in the other. Both videos are accompanied by a deafening soundtrack of pouring water and crackling fire, which intensifies the force of the imagery and heightens its visceral impact. Viola's elemental symbols of fire and water seem to have destroyed the figure. Or perhaps the

30.12 Ilya Kabakov. *The Man Who Flew into Space from His Apartment*, from *Ten Characters*. 1985. Mixed-media installation, life-size. Centre Pompidou, Paris

 Read the document related to Ilya Kabakov on myartslab.com

30.13 Bill Viola. *The Crossing.* 1996. (Video still.) Video/sound installation. First exhibited at the West Bank Gallery, Savannah College of Art and Design, Georgia. Courtesy of Bill Viola Studio. Photo Kira Perov

30.14 Cai Guo-Qiang. *Light Cycle: Explosion Project for Central Park.* New York. 2003. Fireworks: tiger tail, titanium solutes fitted with computer chips, shells with descending stars. © Cai Guo-Qiang. Commissioned by Creative Time in conjunction with the city of New York and Central Park Conservancy for the 150th anniversary of the creation of Central Park

and then suddenly leaves us in an existential void. In an era when technology and science were and still are extending life and providing hope for cures for deadly diseases, artists such as Bill Viola were returning to the early twentieth-century quest for the spiritual.

A World Art: Cai Guo-Qiang

The closing decades of the twentieth century have marked the rise of a world art, although this phenomenon has its roots in the 1950s. With the Internet and satellite communications and jet travel, the entire world is artistically bound together, transforming it into one large art gallery and making it nearly impossible to talk about art in one hemisphere without talking about developments occurring everywhere else. Now, artists worldwide use the same art language, deal with similar issues, and avidly follow each other's work.

It seems only fitting to end this book with Cai Guo-Qiang (b. 1957), a Chinese artist living in New York since 1995. Among the most visible artists today, Cai brings to this new global art a Chinese background and perspective, enriching the world's visual language. Like Gonzalez-Torres, Cai is primarily a Conceptual artist working in a broad range of media. His oeuvre is dominated by installation art and the use of explosions, namely

two forces have brought about a transformative process, as the body dissolves into a spiritual state, crossing into a higher reality and becoming one with the unseen universal forces. The video relentlessly instills a sense of the physical and sensory

fireworks, which have become his signature style. Explosives, including fireworks, are a Chinese invention, and through his use of this medium, Cai highlights his cultural identity. Yet his choice of explosives is motivated by other aesthetic and conceptual concerns. As the artist explains: "Explosions make you feel something intense at the very core of your being because, while you can arrange explosives as you please, you cannot control the explosion itself. And this fills you with a great deal of freedom." Cai "draws" with the explosives, sometimes evoking Chinese calligraphy. And like the work of the Abstract Expressionists, his drawing contains sublime references or represents an attempt to tap into universal forces. He even discusses the yin and yang of the explosions, the way in which the work, in a split second, presents both creation and destruction.

In 2003 Cai was commissioned by New York City and the Central Park Conservancy to create an explosion piece in Central Park. Titled *Light Cycle: Explosion Project for Central Park* (**fig. 30.14**), the work lasted four minutes and was divided into three parts: "Signal towers" (pillars of light), "The Light Cycle" (a series of haloes), and "White Night" (small-shell explosions of brilliant white light). The degree to which Cai controls the explosions is remarkable. He draws and paints with the medium. Through his work, Cai seeks to capture a spiritual essence. He has said that his work is for extraterrestrials, and he has subtitled many of his explosions "Project for Extraterrestrials." Just as the art world has become global, so Cai, perhaps with a little wink, is looking beyond earth, seeking to create art for the universe.

POINTS OF REFLECTION

30.1 How do such works as Fred Wilson's *Mining the Museum* and Cindy Sherman's *Untitled Film Still #15* reflect Postmodern theory?

30.2 Why is Michael Graves's Public Services Building in Portland, Oregon, considered a Postmodern building and how does it differ from Mies van der Rohe's Modernist icon the Seagram Building (fig. 29.20) in New York City?

30.3 Which works of art in this chapter exemplify multiculturalism and why? Why does so much Postmodern art deal with political and social issues, and what are these issues?

30.4 How does Bill Viola's use of video in a work such as *The Crossing* and Ilya Kabakov's use of installation in *The Man Who Flew into Space from His Apartment* allow artists to do things that could not be done with traditional painting or sculpture?

✓—**Study** and review on myartslab.com

ART IN TIME

1978—**Cindy Sherman,** ***Untitled Film Still #15***

1979–90—Margaret Thatcher is Prime Minister of the United Kingdom

1981—First AIDS cases reported

1981–89—Ronald Reagan is President of the United States

1982—**Maya Lin,** ***Vietnam Veterans Memorial,*** **Washington, D.C.**

1989—Berlin Wall torn down, followed by the collapse of the Soviet Union in 1991

—Student protests in Tiananmen Square, Beijing

1991—European Union formed

1991–92—Republic of South Africa repeals apartheid

1992–97—**Frank Gehry,** **Guggenheim Museum** **Bilbao**

1994—World Wide Web launched

1996—**Bill Viola,** ***The Crossing***

2001—Al Qaeda terrorists attack the United States, which wages war in Afghanistan

2003—**Cai Guo-Qiang,** ***Light Cycle***

2008—Barack Obama is elected the first African-American president of the United States

2010—Start of the Arab Spring uprisings

Glossary

Cross references are indicated by words in SMALL CAPITALS.

ACROTERION Decorative ornaments placed at the apex and the corners of a pediment.

ACTION PAINTING See GESTURE PAINTING.

ALBUMEN PRINT A process in photography that uses the proteins found in eggs to produce a photographic plate.

ALLOVER PAINTING Painting that has even stresses throughout the image.

ALTAR A mound or structure on which sacrifices or offerings are made in the worship of a deity. In a Catholic church, a tablelike structure used in celebrating the Mass.

AMBULATORY A passageway to the outside of the nave that forms a walkway around the apse of a church.

ANDACHTSBILD German for "devotional image." A late medieval image, either painted, engraved, or carved, that was designed to inspire pious feelings in the viewer as he or she contemplated it.

APSE A large architectural niche facing the NAVE of a BASILICA or church, usually at the east end. In a church with a TRANSEPT, the apse begins beyond the crossing.

APSIDIOLE A small apse or chapel connected to the main APSE of a church.

ARABESQUE A type of linear ornamentation characterized by flowing, organic shapes, often in the form of interlaced vegetal, floral, and animal motifs.

ARCADE A series of arches and their supports.

ARCHITRAVE The lowermost member of a classical entablature, such as a series of stone blocks that rest directly on the columns.

ASHLAR MASONRY Carefully finished stone that is set in fine joints to create an even surface.

ATMOSPHERIC PERSPECTIVE Means of showing distance or depth in a painting by lightening the tones of objects that are far away from the PICTURE PLANE and by reducing in gradual stages the contrast between lights and darks.

ATRIUM In ancient architecture, a room or courtyard with an open roof; or the vestibule, usually roofed, in an Early Christian church.

AVANT-GARDE Meaning "advance force" in French, the artists of the avant-garde in nineteenth- and twentieth-century Europe led the way in innovation in both subject matter and technique, rebelling against established conventions.

BALDACCHINO A canopy usually built over an altar.

BALUSTRADE (1) A railing supported by short pillars called balusters. (2) Occasionally applied to any low parapet.

BARREL VAULT A semicylindrical vault.

BAS-DE-PAGE Literally "bottom of the page." An illustration or decoration that is placed below a block of text in an illuminated manuscript.

BASILICA During the Roman period, a large meeting hall, its exact form varying according to its specific use as an official public building. The term was used by the Early Christians to refer to their churches. An Early Christian basilica had an oblong plan, a flat timber ceiling, a trussed roof, a NAVE, and an APSE. The entrance was on one short side, and the apse projected from the opposite side, at the far end of the building.

BAYS Compartments into which a building may be subdivided, usually formed by the space between consecutive architectural supports.

BUTTRESS A masonry support that counteracts the thrust exerted by an arch or a vault. See FLYING BUTTRESS.

CALOTYPE Invented in the 1830s, calotype was the first photographic process to use negatives and positive prints on paper.

CAPITAL The uppermost member of a column or pillar supporting the ARCHITRAVE.

CELLA A rectangular hall in ancient temple architecture, housing an altar or cult image.

CENTRAL-PLAN CHURCH The standard design used for churches in Eastern Orthodox Christianity, in which symmetrical chambers radiate from a central primary space.

CHIAROSCURO Italian for "light and dark." In painting, a method of MODELING form primarily by the use of light and shade.

CLASSICISM Art or architecture that harkens back to and relies upon the style and canons of the art and architecture of ancient Greece or Rome, which emphasize certain standards of balance, order, and beauty. See sidebar page 90.

CLERESTORY A row of windows piercing the NAVE walls of a BASILICA or church above the level of the side aisles.

CODEX (pl. **CODICES**) A manuscript in book form made possible by the use of parchment instead of papyrus. During the first to fourth centuries CE it gradually replaced the *rotulus*, or "scroll," previously used for written documents.

COLONNETTE A small, often decorative, column that is connected to a wall or pier.

COLOR-FIELD PAINTING A technique of Abstract painting in which thinned paints are spread onto an unprimed canvas and allowed to soak in with minimal control by the artist.

COLOSSAL ORDER Vertical supports in a structure, usually in the form of columns, piers, or pilasters, that span two or more stories.

COMBINES A term applied to the three-dimensional work of Robert Rauschenberg that combines painting and sculpture.

COMPOUND PIER A pier with columns, pilasters, or shafts attached.

CONSTRUCTION A type of sculpture, developed by Picasso and Braque toward 1912, and popularized by the Russian Constructivists later in the decade. It is made by assembling such materials as metal or wood.

CONTINUOUS NARRATION Portrayal of the same figure or character at different stages in a story that is depicted in a single artistic space.

CONTRAPPOSTO Italian for "set against." The disposition of the parts of the body so that the weight-bearing, or engaged, leg is distinguished from the raised, or free, leg, resulting in a shift in the axis between the hips and shoulders. Used first by Greek sculptors as a means of showing movement in a figure.

CORBELING A space-spanning technique in which each layer of stone increasingly tapers inward to form an arch or a vault.

DAGUERREOTYPE Originally, a photograph on a silver-plated sheet of copper that had been treated with fumes of iodine to form silver iodide on its surface and, after exposure, was developed by fumes of mercury. The process, invented by L.-J.-M. Daguerre and made public in 1839, was modified and accelerated as daguerreotypes gained worldwide popularity.

DORIC An architectural style characterized by columns that have a simple cushionlike abacus and the absence of a base. One of three styles consistently used by Greek and Roman architects.

DRÔLERIES French word for "jests." Used to describe the lively animals and small figures in the margins of late medieval manuscripts and in wood carvings on furniture.

DRUM Cylindrical wall supporting a dome; one of several sections composing the shaft of a column.

DRYPOINT A type of INTAGLIO printmaking in which a sharp metal needle is used to carve lines and a design into a (usually) copper plate. The act of drawing pushes up a burr of metal filings, and so, when the plate is inked, ink will be retained by the burr to create a soft and deep tone that will be unique to each print. The burr can only last for a few printings. Both the print and the process are called drypoint.

EARTHWORKS Very large-scale, outdoor artwork produced by altering the natural environment.

ENCAUSTIC Method of painting in colors mixed with wax and applied with a brush, usually while the mixture is hot. The technique was practiced in ancient times and in the Early Christian period, and has been revived by some modern painters.

ENGRAVING A graphic-arts process in which a design is INCISED in reverse on a copper plate; this is coated with printer's ink, which remains in the incised lines when the plate is wiped off. Damp paper is placed on the plate, and both are put into a press; the paper soaks up the ink and produces a print of the original. Also, a print made by this process. See box, page 307.

ENTABLATURE (1) In classical order, the entire structure above the columns; this usually includes the ARCHITRAVE, FRIEZE, and cornice. (2) The same structure in any building of a classical style.

ENVIRONMENT In art, environment refers to the earth itself as a stage for Environmental art, works that can be enormously large yet very minimal and abstract. These works can be permanent or transitory. The term Earth art is also used to describe these artworks.

ETCHING (1) A print made by coating a copper-plate with an acid-resistant resin and drawing through this ground, exposing the metal with a sharp instrument called a stylus. The plate is bathed in acid, which eats into the lines; it is then heated to remove the resin and finally inked and printed on paper. (2) The technique itself is also called etching. Like ENGRAVING, etching is an incising graphic-arts process. However, the design is drawn in reverse with a needle on a plate thinly coated with wax or resin. The plate is placed in a bath of nitric acid, which etches the lines to receive ink. The coating is then removed, and the prints are made as in engraving. Also, a print made by this process.

FAIENCE (1) A glass paste fired to a shiny opaque finish, used in Egypt and the Aegean. (2) A type of earthenware that is covered with a colorful opaque glaze and is often decorated with elaborate designs.

FLAMBOYANT GOTHIC A style of Late Gothic architecture in which the bar tracery supporting the stained-glass windows is formed into elaborate pointed, often flamelike, shapes.

FLYING BUTTRESS An arch that springs from the upper part of the pier buttress of a Gothic church, spans the aisle roof, and abuts the upper NAVE wall to receive the thrust from the nave vaults; it transmits this thrust to the solid pier buttresses.

FOLIO A leaf of a manuscript or a book, identified so that the front and the back have the same number, the front being labeled *recto* and the back *verso*.

FRIEZE (1) A continuous band of painted or sculptured decoration. (2) In a Classical building, the pat of the entablature between the ARCHITRAVE and the cornice. A Doric frieze consists of alternating triglyphs and metopes, the latter often sculptured. An Ionic frieze is usually decorated with continuous relief sculpture.

FRONTALITY Representation of a subject in a full frontal view.

GABLE Triangular part of a wall, enclosed by the lines of a sloping roof.

GESTURE PAINTING A technique in painting and drawing where the actual physical movement of the artist is reflected in the brushstroke or line as it is seen in the artwork. The artist Jackson Pollock is particularly associated with this technique. Also called ACTION PAINTING.

GRISAILLE Monochromatic painting in grays that simulates sculpture (often used on the outer wings of altarpieces).

GROIN VAULT Vault formed by the intersection at right angles of two BARREL VAULTS of equal height and diameter so that the groins form a diagonal cross.

GUILD Economic and social organization that controlled the making and marketing of given products in a medieval city. To work as a painter or sculptor in a city, an individual had to belong to a guild, which established standards for the craft.

HALLENKIRCHE German word for "hall church." A church in which the NAVE and the side aisles are of the same height. The type was developed in Romanesque architecture and occurs especially frequently in German Gothic churches.

HAPPENING A type of art that involves visual images, audience participation, and improvised performance, usually in a public setting and under the loose direction of an artist.

HATCHING A series of parallel lines used as shading in prints and drawings. When two sets of crossing parallel lines are used, it is called *crosshatching*.

HERALDIC Relating to a system of elaborate symbols used to designate family membership. Heraldic symbols were often employed to decorate the homes and armor of noble families.

HIERATIC SCALE An artistic technique in which the importance of figures is indicated by size, so that the most important figure is depicted as the largest.

HUMANISM A philosophy emphasizing the worth of the individual, the rational abilities of humankind, and the human potential for good. During the Italian Renaissance, humanism was part of a movement that encouraged study of the classical cultures of Greece and Rome; often it came into conflict with the doctrines of the Catholic Church.

HYPOSTYLE A hall whose roof is supported by columns.

ICON A panel painting of Christ, the Virgin, or saints; regarded as sacred, especially by Eastern Christians.

ILLUMINATION A painting technique combining rich pigments, gold, and other precious metals to produce dazzling color effects. A term used generally for painting in manuscripts. Illuminated manuscripts may contain separate ornamental pages, marginal illustrations, ornament within the text, entire miniature paintings, or any combination of these.

INCISING Technique of cutting into a hard surface with a sharp instrument to create a linear image.

INTAGLIO A printing process using the principle of cutting into a plate (see also ENGRAVING).

IONIC An architectural style characterized by columns that have a base and a capital with two volutes. One of three styles consistently used by Greek and Roman architects.

JAMB Side of a doorway or window frame.

KORE Archaic-period Greek statue of a draped maiden.

KOUROS Archaic-period Greek statue of a standing nude youth.

KUFIC One of the first general forms of Arabic script to be developed, distinguished by its angularity; distinctive variants occur in various parts of the Islamic world.

LAMASSU An ancient Near Eastern guardian of a palace; often shown in sculpture as a human-headed bull or lion with wings.

LANCET A tall, pointed window common in Gothic architecture.

LINEAR PERSPECTIVE Also known as scientific perspective. See PERSPECTIVE.

LINEARITY The use of obvious line to define forms.

LUNETTE A semicircular zone, either painted or sculpted, usually above a window or doorway.

MANDORLA Italian for "almond." An almond-shaped radiance of light surrounding a holy figure.

MARTYRIUM A church, chapel, or shrine built over the grave of a martyr or upon the site of a great miracle.

MASTABA Aboveground tomb building with a flat roof and inward-sloping walls, linked by a deep shaft to an underground burial chamber. A tomb form popular in ancient Egypt.

MECHANOMORPHIC A mechanical form made to look human, or a human made to look mechanical.

MEGARON From the Greek word for "large." The central audience hall in a Minoan or Mycenaean palace or home.

MENDICANT From a Latin word for begging, having to do with late medieval religious groups which lived on charitable donations. The two most important mendicant groups were the Franciscans and the Dominicans.

MENHIR A megalithic upright slab of stone, sometimes placed in rows by prehistoric peoples.

MIHRAB A niche in the center of the QIBLA wall.

MINARET A tower on or near a mosque, varying extensively in form throughout the Islamic world, from which the faithful are called to prayer five times a day.

MINBAR A type of staircase pulpit, found in more important mosques to the right of the MIHRAB, from which the Sabbath sermon is given on Fridays after the noonday prayer.

MODELING An additive sculptural process in which a malleable material is molded into a three-dimensional form. In painting or drawing, the means by which the three-dimensionality of a form is suggested on a two-dimensional surface, usually through variations of color and the play of lights and darks.

MONOCHROMATIC Term used to describe a painting or drawing created by shades of black and white or values of a single color.

MORTISE AND TENON JOINT A joining technique used primarily in stonemasonry and carpentry, where a projection (the tenon) on one piece of stone or board is inserted into a hole (the mortise) in a second piece.

MOSQUE A building used as a center for community prayers in Islamic worship; it often serves other functions, including religious education and public assembly.

MOZARAB Term used for the Spanish Christian culture of the Middle Ages that developed while Muslims were the dominant culture and political power on the Iberian peninsula.

MUSES In Greek mythology, the nine goddesses who presided over various arts and sciences. They are led by Apollo as god of music and poetry and usually include Calliope, muse of epic poetry; Clio, muse of history; Erato, muse of love poetry; Euterpe, muse of music; Melpomene, muse of tragedy; Polyhymnia, muse of sacred music; Terpsichore, muse of dancing; Thalia, muse of comedy; and Urania, muse of astronomy.

NARTHEX The vestibule at the main entrance of a BASILICA or church.

NATURALISM A style of art that aims to depict the natural world as it appears.

NAVE The central aisle of a BASILICA or church; also, the section of a church between the main entrance and the choir.

NECROPOLIS Greek for "city of the dead." A burial ground or cemetery.

OBELISK A tall, tapering four-sided stone shaft with a pyramidal top. First constructed as megaliths in ancient Egypt; certain examples have since been exported to other countries.

OCULUS The Latin word for "eye." (1) A circular opening at the top of a dome used to admit light. (2) A round window.

ORANT A standing figure with arms upraised in a gesture of prayer.

ORTHOGONAL Term used in describing a spatial projection according to linear perspective. It refers to a line that runs perpendicularly from the lower edge of the picture plane to the vanishing point established in the projection.

ORTHOSTAT An upright slab of stone constituting or lining the lowest courses of a wall, often in order to protect a vulnerable material such as mud brick.

PAINTERLY The use of strong or obvious brush-work.

PARCHMENT From Pergamon, the name of a Greek city in Asia Minor where parchment was invented in the second century BCE. (1) A paper-like material made from bleached animal hides used extensively in the Middle Ages for manuscripts. VELLUM is a superior type of parchment made from calfskin. (2) A document or miniature on this material.

PEDIMENT (1) In Classical architecture, a low gable, typically triangular, framed by a horizontal cornice below and two raking cornices above; frequently filled with sculpture. (2) A similar architectural member used over a door, window, or niche. When pieces of the cornice are either turned at an angle or interrupted, it is called a broken pediment.

PENDENTIVES Among the supports for a dome, the triangular segments of a wall leading from the square base to the circular drum.

PERFORMANCE ART A type of art in which performance by actors or artists, often interacting with the audience in an improvisational manner, is the primary aim over a certain time period. These artworks are transitory, perhaps with only a photographic record of some of the events.

PERISTYLE Colonnade (or arcade) around a building or open court.

PERPENDICULAR GOTHIC The third style of English Gothic architecture, in which the bar tracery uses predominantly vertical lines. The fan vault is also used extensively in this style.

PERSPECTIVE A system for representing spatial relationships and three-dimensional objects on a flat two-dimensional surface so as to produce an effect similar to that perceived by the human eye. In atmospheric or aerial perspective, this is accomplished by a gradual decrease in the intensity of color and value and in the contrast of light and dark as objects are depicted as farther and farther away in the picture. In color artwork, as objects recede into the distance, all colors tend toward a light bluish-gray tone. In scientific or LINEAR PERSPECTIVE, developed in Italy in the fifteenth century, a mathematical system is used based on orthogonals receding to vanishing points on the horizon. Transversals intersect the ORTHOGONALS at right angles at distances derived mathematically. Since this presupposes an absolutely stationary viewer and imposes rigid restrictions on the artist, it is seldom applied with complete consistency. Although traditionally ascribed to Brunelleschi, the first theoretical text on perspective was Leon Battista Alberti's *On Painting* (1435).

PICTURE PLANE The imaginary plane suggested by the actual surface of a painting, drawing, or relief.

PICTURESQUE Visually interesting or pleasing, as if resembling a picture.

PIETÀ In painting or sculpture, a representation of the Virgin Mary mourning the dead Jesus, whom she holds.

PILGRIMAGE PLAN The general design used in Christian churches that were stops on the pilgrimage routes throughout medieval Europe, characterized by having side aisles that allowed pilgrims to ambulate around the church.

PLANARITY The arrangement of objects so that they run parallel to the picture plane.

POLYCHROMY, POLYCHROMATIC (adj.) The decoration of architecture or sculpture in multiple colors.

POST-AND-LINTEL CONSTRUCTION A space-spanning technique in which two or more vertical beams (posts) support a horizontal beam (lintel).

PREDELLA In an altarpiece, the predella is a base or panel at the bottom; predellas are often adorned with small images that make reference to the main theme of the altarpiece.

PREFIGURATION The representation of Old Testament figures and stories as forerunners and foreshadowers of those in the New Testament.

PROVENANCE The place of origin of a work of art and related information.

PYLON In Egyptian architecture, the entranceway set between two broad, oblong towers with sloping sides.

QIBLA The direction Muslims face when praying. A wall in each mosque marks this direction (toward Mecca).

QUADRIPARTITE A quadripartite vault is one whose ribs divide the vault into four compartments.

QUADRO RIPORTATO (pl. *quadri riportati*) Meaning "a painting taken somewhere else" in Italian. The illusion of a framed painted scene arranged in a ceiling vault.

RED-FIGURE A type of Greek vase painting in which the design is outlined in black and the background painted in black, leaving the figures and the reddish color of the baked clay after firing. This style replaced the black-figure style toward the end of the sixth century BCE.

REGISTER A horizontal band containing decoration, such as a relief sculpture or a fresco painting. When multiple horizontal layers are used, registers are useful in distinguishing between different visual planes and different time periods in visual narration.

RESPOND A projecting and supporting architectural element, often a pier, that is bonded with another support, usually a wall, to carry one end of an arch.

REVETMENT Retaining wall supporting a rampart.

ROSE WINDOW A round window decorated with stained glass and tracery, frequently incorporated into façades and TRANSEPTS of Gothic churches.

RUSTICATION In masonry, a style of cutting stones that leaves the surface of cut blocks rough and uneven.

SARCOPHAGUS (pl. *sarcophagi*) A coffin made of stone, marble, or terra cotta, and, less frequently, of metal. Sarcophagi are often decorated with paintings or reliefs.

SCRIPTORIUM (pl. *scriptoria*) A workroom in a monastery reserved for copying and illustrating manuscripts.

SECTION An architectural drawing presenting a building as if cut across the vertical plane at right angles to the horizontal plane.

SIBYL In Greek and Roman mythology, any of numerous women who were thought to possess powers of divination and prophecy. They appear on Christian representations, notably in Michelangelo's Sistine ceiling, because they were believed to have foretold the coming of Christ.

SPIRE A tall tower that rises high above a roof. Spires are commonly associated with church architecture and are frequently found on Gothic structures.

STELE (pl. *stelae*) A vertical stone slab decorated with a combination of images in relief and inscriptions; often used as a grave marker.

STEREOBATE A solid mass of masonry as a foundation for a building

STEREOCARD A single card with side-by-side photographs of the same image taken by a camera with two lenses, replicating human binocular vision. When put into a special viewer, the twin flat pictures appear as a single three-dimensional image.

STYLOBATE A continuous base supporting a row of columns.

SUBLIME In Romanticism, the ideal and goal that art should inspire awe in a viewer and engender feelings of high religious, moral, ethical, and intellectual purpose.

SYNTHETISM A style associated with Paul Gauguin when he was working in Pont-Aven, France. The word is a reference to the synthetic production of images based on imagination and emotion as opposed to a mimetic, empirical replication of reality.

TABLINUM The Latin word meaning "writing tablet" or "written record." In a Roman house, a room at the far end of the ATRIUM and the second courtyard, used for keeping family records.

TEMPERA Medium for painting in which pigments are suspended in egg yoke tempered with water or chemicals; this mixture dries quickly, reducing the possibility of changes in the finished painting.

TENEBRISM Meaning "dark/darkness" in Italian and referring to intense darkness and its contrast in painting.

THOLOS A dome-shaped tomb.

TONE, TONAL A reference to the color, darkness, depth, or brightness of a pigment.

TRANSEPT In a cross-shaped church, the arm forming a right angle with the NAVE, usually inserted between the latter and the choir or APSE.

TRIFORIUM An arcade running along the walls of a church above the NAVE, and usually pierced by three openings per BAY.

TRIUMPHAL ARCH A massive, free-standing ornamental gateway; originally developed by the ancient Romans to honor a military victory. Also, a monumental arch inside a structure.

TROMPE L'OEIL Meaning "trick of the eye" in French, it is a work of art designed to deceive a viewer into believing that the work of art is reality, an actual three-dimensional object or scene in space.

TRUMEAU A central post supporting the lintel of a large doorway, as in a Romanesque or Gothic portal, where it was frequently decorated with sculpture.

TRUSSED PYLON A steel pylon composed of trusses.

TURRET (1) A small tower that is part of a larger structure. (2) A small tower at a corner of a building, often beginning some distance from the ground.

TYMPANUM The semicircular panel between the lintel and arch of a medieval portal or doorway; a church tympanum frequently contains relief sculpture.

VANITAS From a Latin word for "emptiness," the term refers to works of art that remind the viewer of the transience of life.

VEDUTA (pl. *vedute*) A "view," a painting, drawing, or print of an actual city.

VELLUM Thin, bleached calfskin that can be written, printed, or painted upon.

VERISTIC From the Latin *verus*, meaning "true." Describes a hyperrealistic style of portraiture that emphasizes individual characteristics.

VOUSSOIRS Wedge-shaped stones forming an arch.

WET-COLLODION PROCESS A photographic technique that involves coating a plate in collodion, a very sensitive material consisting of gun-cotton dissolved in alcohol ether. This process, invented shortly after 1850, resulted in camera exposure times being reduced to under a second, as opposed to the DAGUERREOTYPE, which required minutes.

WOODCUT A printing process in which a design or lettering is carved in relief on a wooden block; the areas intended not to print are hollowed out.

ZAUM A term invented by progressive Russian poets in the early twentieth century to refer to a language based on invented words and syntax, the meaning of which was supposedly implicit in the basic sounds and patterns of speech. The poets' intention was to return to the non-rational and primitive base of language that, unencumbered by conventional meaning, expressed the essence of human experience.

ZIGGURAT An elevated platform, varying in height from several feet to the size of an artificial mountain, built by the Sumerians to support their shrines.

Books for Further Reading

This list includes standard works and the most recent and comprehensive books in English. Books with material relevant to several chapters are cited only under the first heading.

Introduction

Broude, Norma, and Mary D. Garrard, eds. *Feminism and Art History: Questioning the Litany*. Harper & Row, New York, 1982.

Holt, Elizabeth Gilmore, ed. *A Documentary History of Art*. 3 vols. Vols. 1–2, Princeton University Press, Princeton, 1981–86; vol. 3, Yale University Press, New Haven, 1986.

Kostof, Spiro. *A History of Architecture: Settings and Rituals*. 2nd edn. Oxford University Press, New York, 1995.

Panofsky, Erwin. *Meaning in the Visual Arts*. Reprint of 1955 edn. University of Chicago Press, Chicago, 1982.

Taylor, Joshua C. *Learning to Look: A Handbook for the Visual Arts*. 2nd edn. University of Chicago Press, Chicago, 1981.

Trachtenberg, Marvin, and Isabelle Hyman. *Architecture: From Prehistory to Post-Modernism*. 2nd edn. Upper Saddle River, NJ, 2003.

PART ONE
The Ancient World
1 Prehistoric Art

Chauvet, Jean-Marie, Éliette Brunel Deschamps, and Christian Hillaire. *Dawn of Art: The Chauvet Cave*. Trans. Paul Bahn. Harry N. Abrams, New York, 1996.

Clottes, Jean. *Chauvet Cave: The Art of Earliest Times*. Trans. Paul Bahn. University of Utah Press, Salt Lake City, 2003.

———. *The Shamans of Prehistory: Trance and Magic in the Painted Caves*. Harry N. Abrams, New York, 1998.

Cunliffe, Barry, ed. *The Oxford Illustrated Prehistory of Europe*. Oxford University Press, New York, 1994.

Fowler, Peter. *Images of Prehistory*. Cambridge University Press, New York, 1990.

McCold, C. H., and L. D. McDermott. "Toward Decolonizing Gender: Female Vision in the Upper Palaeolithic." *American Anthropologist* 98, 1996.

Ruspoli, Mario. *The Cave of Lascaux: The Final Photographs*. Harry N. Abrams, New York, 1987.

Sandars, Nancy K. *Prehistoric Art in Europe*. Reprint of 1985, 2nd integrated edn. Pelican History of Art. Yale University Press, New Haven, 1992.

Saura Ramos, Pedro A. *The Cave of Altamira*. Harry N. Abrams, New York, 1999.

White, Randall. *Prehistoric Art: The Symbolic Journey of Humankind*. Harry N. Abrams, New York, 2003.

2 Ancient Near Eastern Art

Amiet, Pierre. *Art of the Ancient Near East*. Harry N. Abrams, New York, 1980.

Aruz, Joan, ed. *Art of the First Cities: The Third Millennium BC from the Mediterranean to the Indus*. Exh. cat. Metropolitan Museum of Art, New York; Yale University Press, New Haven, 2003.

Collon, Dominique. *Ancient Near Eastern Art*. University of California Press, Berkeley, 1995.

Curtis, John, and Nigel Tallis. *Forgotten Empire: The World of Ancient Persia*. Exh. cat. British Museum Press, London, 2005.

Feldman, Marian. *Diplomacy by Design: Luxury Arts and an "International Style" in the Ancient Near East, 1400–1200 BCE*. Chicago: University of Chicago Press, 2006.

Frankfort, Henri. *The Art and Architecture of the Ancient Orient*. 5th edn. Pelican History of Art. Yale University Press, New Haven, 1997.

Leick, Gwendolyn. *A Dictionary of Ancient Near Eastern Architecture*. Routledge, New York, 1988.

Lloyd, Seton. *The Archaeology of Mesopotamia: From the Old Stone Age to the Persian Conquest*. Rev. edn. Thames & Hudson, New York, 1984.

Reade, Julian. *Mesopotamia*. 2nd edn. Published for the Trustees of the British Museum by the British Museum Press, London, 2000.

Zettler, Richard, and Lee Horne, eds. *Treasures from the Royal Tombs of Ur*. Exh. cat. University of Pennsylvania, Museum of Archaeology and Anthropology, Philadelphia, 1998.

3 Egyptian Art

Arnold, Dieter. *Building in Egypt: Pharaonic Stone Masonry*. Oxford University Press, New York, 1991.

———. *Egyptian Art in the Age of the Pyramids*. Harry N. Abrams, New York, 1999.

Davis, Whitney. *The Canonical Tradition in Ancient Egyptian Art*. Cambridge University Press, New York, 1989.

El Mahdy, Christine, ed. *The World of the Pharaohs*. Thames & Hudson, London, 1990.

Málek, Jaromir. *Egypt: 4000 Years of Art*. Phaidon, London, 2003.

Parry, Dick. *Engineering the Pyramids*. Sutton, Stroud, England, 2004.

Robins, Gay. *The Art of Ancient Egypt*. Harvard University Press, Cambridge, MA, 1997.

Schulz, Regine, and Matthias Seidel. *Egypt: The World of the Pharaohs*. Könemann, Cologne, 1998.

Smith, William Stevenson. *The Art and Architecture of Ancient Egypt*. Rev. edn. Pelican History of Art. Yale University Press, New Haven, 1999.

Tiradritti, Francesco. *Ancient Egypt: Art, Architecture and History*. British Museum Press, London, 2002.

Wilkinson, Richard. *Reading Egyptian Art: A Hieroglyphic Guide to Ancient Egyptian Painting and Sculpture*. Thames & Hudson, New York, 1992.

4 Aegean Art

Akurgal, Ekrem. *The Aegean, Birthplace of Western Civilization: History of East Greek Art and Culture, 1050–333 BC*. Metropolitan Municipality of Izmir, Izmir, Turkey, 2000.

Dickinson, Oliver T. P. K. *The Aegean Bronze Age*. Cambridge University Press, New York, 1994.

Elytis, Odysseas. *The Aegean: The Epicenter of Greek Civilization*. Melissa, Athens, 1997.

German, Senta C. *Performance, Power and the Art of the Aegean Bronze Age*. Archaeopress, Oxford, 2005.

Getz-Preziosi, Pat. *Sculptors of the Cyclades: Individual and Tradition in the Third Millennium BC*. University of Michigan Press, Ann Arbor, 1987.

Hood, Sinclair. *The Arts in Prehistoric Greece*. Pelican History of Art. Yale University Press, New Haven, 1992.

Preziosi, Donald, and Louise Hitchcock. *Aegean Art and Architecture*. Oxford University Press, New York, 1999.

Renfrew, Colin. *The Cycladic Spirit: Masterpieces from the Nicholas P. Goulandris Collection*. Thames & Hudson, London, 1991.

5 Greek Art

Beard, Mary. *The Parthenon*. Harvard University Press, Cambridge, MA, 2003.

Boardman, John. *Greek Art*. 4th edn., rev. and expanded. The World of Art. Thames & Hudson, New York, 1996.

———. *The History of Greek Vases: Potters, Painters, and Pictures*. Thames & Hudson, New York, 2001.

Carratelli, Giovanni P., ed. *The Greek World: Art and Civilization in Magna Graecia and Sicily*. Exh. cat. Rizzoli, New York, 1996.

Fullerton, Mark D. *Greek Art*. Cambridge University Press, New York, 2000.

Haynes, Denys E. L. *The Technique of Greek Bronze Statuary*. P. von Zabern, Mainz am Rhein, 1992.

Hurwit, Jeffrey M. *The Acropolis in the Age of Pericles*. Cambridge University Press, New York, 2004.

———. *The Art & Culture of Early Greece, 1100–480 BC*. Cornell University Press, Ithaca, NY, 1985.

Lawrence, Arnold W. *Greek Architecture*. Rev. 5th edn. Pelican History of Art. Yale University Press, New Haven, 1996.

Neils, J. *The Parthenon Frieze*. Cambridge University Press, Cambridge, UK, 2006

Osborne, Robin. *Archaic and Classical Greek Art*. Oxford University Press, New York, 1998.

Pedley, John G. *Greek Art and Archaeology*. 5th edn. Pearson Prentice Hall, Upper Saddle River, NJ, 2012.

Pollitt, Jerome J. *Art and Experience in Classical Greece*. Cambridge University Press, New York, 1972.

———. *Art in the Hellenistic Age*. Cambridge University Press, New York, 1986.

Ridgway, Brunilde S. *Hellenistic Sculpture: Vols. I–III*. University of Wisconsin Press, Madison, Wisconsin, 1990–2002.

Stafford, Emma. *Life, Myth, and Art in Ancient Greece*. J. Paul Getty Museum, Los Angeles, 2004.

6 Etruscan Art

Boëthius, Axel. *Etruscan and Early Roman Architecture*. 2nd edn. Pelican History of Art. Yale University Press, New Haven, 1992.

Bonfante, Larissa, ed. *Etruscan Life and Afterlife: A Handbook of Etruscan Studies*. Wayne State University, Detroit, MI, 1986.

Brendel, Otto. *Etruscan Art*. Pelican History of Art. Yale University Press, New Haven, 1995.

Haynes, Sybille. *Etruscan Civilization: A Cultural History*. J. Paul Getty Museum, Los Angeles, 2000.

Spivey, Nigel. *Etruscan Art*. The World of Art. Thames & Hudson, New York, 1997.

Steingräber, Stephan, ed. *Etruscan Painting: Catalogue Raisonné of Etruscan Wall Paintings*. Johnson Reprint, New York, 1986.

Torelli, Mario, ed. *The Etruscans*. Exh. cat. Bompiani, Milan, 2000.

7 Roman Art

Beard, Mary, and John Henderson. *Classical Art: From Greece to Rome*. Oxford University Press, New York, 2001.

Claridge, Amanda. *Rome: An Oxford Archaeological Guide*. 2nd edn. Oxford University Press, New York, 2010.

Clarke, John R. *The Houses of Roman Italy, 100 BC–AD 250. Ritual, Space and Decoration*. University of California Press, Berkeley, 1991.

Elsner, Jas. *Imperial Rome and Christian Triumph: The Art of the Roman Empire, AD 100–450*. Oxford University Press, New York, 1998.

Kleiner, Diana. *Roman Sculpture*. Yale University Press, New Haven, 1992.

———, and Susan B. Matheson, eds. *I, Claudia: Women in Ancient Rome*. Yale University Art Gallery, New Haven, 1996.

Kleiner, F. S. *A History of Roman Art*. Wadsworth, London, 2010.

Lancaster, L. C. *Concrete Vaulted Construction in Imperial Rome: Innovations in Context*. Cambridge University Press, Cambridge, UK, 2005.

Ling, Roger. *Ancient Mosaics*. British Museum Press, London, 1998.

———. *Roman Painting*. Cambridge University Press, New York, 1991.

Pollitt, Jerome J. *The Art of Rome, c. 753 BC–AD 337: Sources and Documents*. Cambridge University Press, New York, 1983.

Ramage, Nancy H., and Andrew Ramage. *Roman Art: Romulus to Constantine*. 5th edn. Pearson Prentice Hall, Upper Saddle River, NJ, 2009.

Richardson, Lawrence. *A New Topographical Dictionary of Ancient Rome*. Johns Hopkins University Press, Baltimore, MD, 1992.

Vitruvius. *The Ten Books on Architecture*. Trans. I. Rowland. Cambridge University Press, Cambridge, UK, 1999.

Ward-Perkins, John B. *Roman Imperial Architecture*. Reprint of 1981 edn. Pelican History of Art. Penguin, New York, 1992.

Zanker, Paul. *The Power of Images in the Age of Augustus*. University of Michigan Press, Ann Arbor, 1988.

PART TWO
The Middle Ages

Alexander, Jonathon J. G. *Medieval Illuminators and Their Methods of Work*. Yale University Press, New Haven, 1994.

Calkins, Robert G. *Medieval Architecture in Western Europe: From A.D. 300–1500*. Oxford University Press, New York, 1998.

Coldstream, Nicola. *Medieval Architecture*. Oxford History of Art. Oxford University Press, New York, 2002.

Duby, Georges. *Art and Society in the Middle Ages*. Blackwell Publishers, Polity Press, Malden, MA, 2000.

Kessler, Herbert. *Seeing Medieval Art*. Broadview Press, Peterborough, Ont. and Orchard Park, NY, 2002.

Luttikhuizen, Henry, and Dorothy Verkerk. *Snyder's Medieval Art*. 2nd edn. Prentice Hall, Upper Saddle River, NJ, 2006.

Stokstad, Marilyn. *Medieval Art*. Westview Press, Boulder, 2004.

8 Jewish, Early Christian, and Byzantine Art

Cormack, Robin. *Byzantine Art.* Oxford History of Art. Oxford University Press, New York, 2000.

———. *Icons.* British Museum Press, London, 2007.

Evans, Helen C., ed. *Byzantium: Faith and Power, 1261–1557.* Metropolitan Museum of Art, New York, 2004.

Evans, Helen C., and William D. Wixom, eds. *The Glory of Byzantium: Art and Culture of the Middle Byzantine Era, A.D. 843–1261.* Metropolitan Museum of Art, New York, 1997.

Kitzinger, Ernst. *Byzantine Art in the Making: Main Lines of Stylistic Development in Mediterranean Art, 3rd–7th Century.* Harvard University Press, Cambridge, 1995.

Krautheimer, Richard, and Slobodan Curcic. *Early Christian and Byzantine Architecture.* 4th edn. Pelican History of Art. Yale University Press, New Haven, 1992.

Lowden, John. *Early Christian and Byzantine Art.* Phaidon, London, 1997.

Mango, Cyril. *The Art of the Byzantine Empire, 312–1453: Sources and Documents.* Reprint of 1972 edn. University of Toronto Press, Toronto, 1986.

Mathews, Thomas F. *The Clash of the Gods: A Reinterpretation of Early Christian Art.* Princeton University Press, Princeton, 1993.

———. *Byzantium from Antiquity to the Renaissance.* Perspectives. Harry N. Abrams, New York, 1998.

Weitzmann, Kurt. *Late Antique and Early Christian Book Illumination.* Braziller, New York, 1977.

9 Islamic Art

Blair, Sheila S., and Jonathan M. Bloom. *The Art and Architecture of Islam 1250–1800.* Pelican History of Art. Yale University Press, New Haven, 1996.

Brookes, John. *Gardens of Paradise: The History and Design of the Great Islamic Gardens.* New Amsterdam, New York, 1987.

Denny, Walter B. *The Classical Tradition in Anatolian Carpets.* Textile Museum, Washington D. C. , 2002.

Dodds, Jerrilynn D. *al-Andalus: The Art of Islamic Spain.* Metropolitan Museum of Art, New York, 1992.

Ettinghausen, Richard, Oleg Grabar, and Marilyn Jenkins-Madina. *Islamic Art and Architecture, 650–1250.* 2nd edn. Pelican History of Art. Yale University Press, New Haven, 2003.

Grabar, Oleg. *The Formation of Islamic Art.* Rev. and enl. edn. Yale University Press, New Haven, 1987.

Hilldenbrand, Robert. *Islamic Architecture: Form, Function and Meaning.* New edn. Columbia University Press, New York, 2004.

10 Early Medieval Art

Barral i Altet, Xavier. *The Early Middle Ages: From Late Antiquity to A.D. 1000.* Taschen, Cologne, 1997.

Conant, Kenneth J. *Carolingian and Romanesque Architecture, 800–1200.* 4th edn. Pelican History of Art. Yale University Press, New Haven, 1993.

Davis-Weyer, Caecilia, ed. *Early Medieval Art, 300–1150: Sources and Documents.* Reprint of 1971 edn. University of Toronto, Toronto, 1986.

Dodwell, C. R. *The Pictorial Arts of the West, 800–1200.* New edn. Pelican History of Art. Yale University Press, New Haven, 1993.

Kitzinger, Ernst. *Early Medieval Art, with Illustrations from the British Museum.* Rev. edn. Indiana University Press, Bloomington, IN, 1983.

Lasko, Peter. *Ars Sacra, 800–1200.* 2nd edn. Pelican History of Art. Yale University Press, New Haven, 1995.

Mayr-Harting, Henry. *Ottonian Book Illumination: An Historical Study.* 2 vols. Oxford University Press, New York, 1991–93.

Nees, Lawrence. *Early Medieval Art.* Oxford History of Art. Oxford University Press, New York, 2002.

Sekules, Veronica. *Medieval Art.* Oxford History of Art. Oxford University Press, New York, 2001.

Stalley, Roger A. *Early Medieval Architecture.* Oxford History of Art. Oxford University Press, New York, 1999.

11 Romanesque Art

Barral i Altet, Xavier. *The Romanesque: Towns, Cathedrals, and Monasteries.* Taschen, Cologne, 1998.

Bowie, Fiona, and Oliver Davies, eds. *Hildegard of Bingen: Mystical Writings.* Crossroad, New York, 1990.

Focillon, Henri. *The Art of the West in the Middle Ages.* Ed. Jean Bony. 2 vols. Reprint of 1963 edn. Cornell University Press, Ithaca, 1980.

Hearn, M. F. *Romanesque Sculpture: The Revival of Monumental Stone Sculpture in the Eleventh and Twelfth Centuries.* Cornell University Press, Ithaca, 1981.

Petzold, Andreas. *Romanesque Art.* Perspectives. Prentice Hall, Upper Saddle River, NJ, 2003.

Schapiro, Meyer. *Romanesque Art.* Braziller, New York, 1993.

Stones, Alison, Jeanne Krochalis, Paula Gerson, and Annie Shaver-Crandell. *The Pilgrim's Guide: A Critical Edition.* 2 vols. Harvey Miller, London, 1998.

Toman, Rolf, and Achim Bednorz. *Romanesque: Architecture, Sculpture, Painting.* Könemann, Cologne, 2008.

12 Gothic Art

Bony, Jean. *French Gothic Architecture of the Twelfth and Thirteenth Centuries.* California Studies in the History of Art. University of California Press, Berkeley, 1983.

Camille, Michael. *Gothic Art.* Perspectives. Prentice Hall, Upper Saddle River, NJ, 2003.

Erlande-Brandenburg, Alain. *Gothic Art.* Harry N. Abrams, New York, 1989.

Frisch, Teresa G. *Gothic Art, 1140–c. 1450: Sources and Documents.* Reprint of 1971 edn. University of Toronto Press, Toronto, 1987.

Toman, Rolf, and Achim Bednorz. *The Art of Gothic: Architecture, Sculpture, Painting.* Könemann, Cologne, 1999.

Williamson, Paul. *Gothic Sculpture, 1140–1300.* Pelican History of Art. Yale University Press, New Haven, 1995.

Wilson, Christopher. *The Gothic Cathedral: The Architecture of the Great Church, 1130–1530.* 2nd rev. edn. Thames & Hudson, London, 2005.

PART THREE

The Renaissance through the Rococo: Early Modern Europe

Campbell, Lorne. *Renaissance Portraits: European Portrait-Painting in the 14th, 15th, and 16th Centuries.* Yale University Press, New Haven, 1990.

Harbison, Craig. *The Mirror of the Artist: Northern Renaissance Art in its Historical Context.* Harry N. Abrams, New York, 1995.

Harris, Ann Sutherland. *Seventeenth-Century Art & Architecture.* 2nd edn. Pearson Prentice Hall, Upper Saddle River, NJ, 2008.

Hartt, Frederick, and David G. Wilkins. *History of Italian Renaissance Art: Painting, Sculpture, Architecture.* 7th edn. Pearson Prentice Hall, 2011.

Hults, Linda C. *The Print in the Western World: An Introductory History.* University of Wisconsin Press, Madison, WI, 1996.

Landau, David, and Peter Parshall. *The Renaissance Print, 1470–1550.* Yale University Press, New Haven, 1994.

Millon, Henry A. *The Triumph of the Baroque: Architecture in Europe, 1600–1750*. Rizzoli, New York, 1999.

Paoletti, John T., and Gary M. Radke. *Art in Renaissance Italy*. 4th edn. Pearson Prentice Hall, Upper Saddle River, NJ, 2012.

Pope-Hennessy, J. *An Introduction to Italian Sculpture: Vol. 1, Italian Gothic Sculpture. Vol. 2, Italian Renaissance Sculpture. Vol. 3, Italian High Renaissance and Baroque Sculpture*. 4th edn. Phaidon Press, London, 1996.

Smith, Jeffrey Chipps. *The Northern Renaissance*. Art & Ideas. Phaidon, London and New York, 2004.

Snyder, James. *Northern Renaissance Art: Painting, Sculpture, the Graphic Arts, from 1350 to 1575*. 2nd edn. Harry N. Abrams, New York, 2005.

Welch, Evelyn S. *Art in Renaissance Italy, 1350–1500*. New edn. Oxford University Press, Oxford, 2000.

Wittkower, Rudolf. *Architectural Principles in the Age of Humanism*. 5th edn. St. Martin's Press, New York, 1998.

13 Art in Thirteenth- and Fourteenth-Century Italy

Derbes, Anne, and Mark Sandona, *The Usurer's Heart: Giotto, Enrico Scrovegni, and the Arena Chapel in Padua*. The Pennsylvania State University Press, University Park, PA, 2008.

Meiss, Millard. *Painting in Florence and Siena After the Black Death: The Arts, Religion, and Society in the Mid-Fourteenth Century*. Princeton University Press, Princeton, 1978, © 1951.

Norman, Diana, ed. *Siena, Florence and Padua: Art, Society and Religion 1280–1400*. Yale University Press, New Haven, 1995.

Stubblebine, James H. *Assisi and the Rise of Vernacular Art*. Harper & Row, New York, 1985.

Vasari, Giorgio. *The Lives of the Artists*. Trans. with introduction and notes by J. C. Bondanella and P. Bondanella. Oxford University Press, New York, 1998.

White, John. *Art and Architecture in Italy, 1250–1400*. 3rd edn. Pelican History of Art. Yale University Press, New Haven, 1993.

14 Artistic Innovations in Fifteenth-Century Northern Europe

Borchert, Till-Holger. *From Van Eyck to Dürer: The Influence of Early Netherlandish Painting on European Art 1430–1530*. Thames & Hudson, London, 2011.

Cuttler, Charles D. *Northern Painting from Pucelle to Bruegel: Fourteenth, Fifteenth, and Sixteenth Centuries*. Rev. and updated. Holt, Rinehart, and Winston, New York, 1972.

Dixon, Laurinda. *Bosch*. Art & Ideas. Phaidon, London, 2003.

Friedländer, Max J. *Early Netherlandish Painting*. 14 vols. Praeger, New York, 1967–73.

Inglis, Erik. *Jean Fouquet and the Invention of France: Art and Nation after the Hundred Years War*. Yale University Press, New Haven, 2011.

Nash, Susie. *Northern Renaissance Art*. Oxford University Press, New York, 2008.

Nuttall, Paula. *From Flanders to Florence: The Impact of Netherlandish Painting, 1400–1500*. Yale University Press, New Haven, 2004.

Panofsky, Erwin. *Early Netherlandish Painting*. 2 vols. Harvard University Press, Cambridge, 1971.

Stechow, Wolfgang. *Northern Renaissance Art, 1400–1600: Sources and Documents*. Northwestern University Press, Evanston, IL, 1989.

15 The Early Renaissance in Fifteenth-Century Italy

Baxandall, Michael. *Painting and Experience in Fifteenth Century Italy: A Primer in the Social History of Pictorial Style*. Oxford University Press, New York, 1988.

Borsook, Eve. *The Mural Painters of Tuscany: From Cimabue to Andrea del Sarto*. 2nd edn., rev. and enl. Oxford University Press, New York, 1980.

Brown, Patricia Fortini. *Private Lives in Renaissance Venice: Art, Architecture and the Family*. Yale University Press, New Haven, 2004.

Burckhardt, Jacob C. *The Civilization of the Renaissance in Italy*. Penguin Classics. Penguin, Harmondsworth, UK, 1990.

Cole, Bruce. *The Renaissance Artist at Work: From Pisano to Titian*. Harper & Row, New York, 1983.

Gilbert, Creighton E. *Italian Art, 1400–1500: Sources and Documents*. Reprint of 1980 edn. Northwestern University Press, Evanston, IL, 1992.

Gombrich, E. H. *Norm and Form: Studies in the Art of the Renaissance*. 4th edn. University of Chicago Press, Chicago, 1985.

Heydenreich, Ludwig Heinrich, and Wolfgang Lotz. *Architecture in Italy, 1400–1500*. Rev. edn. Pelican History of Art. Yale University Press, New Haven, 1996.

Huse, Norbert, and W. Wolters. *The Art of Renaissance Venice: Architecture, Sculpture, and Painting, 1460–1590*. University of Chicago Press, Chicago, 1990.

Janson, H. W. *The Sculpture of Donatello*. 2 vols. Princeton University Press, Princeton, 1979.

Kent, Dale. *Cosimo de' Medici and the Florentine Renaissance*. Yale University Press, New Haven, 2000.

Seymour, Charles, Jr. *Sculpture in Italy, 1400–1500*. Pelican History of Art. Penguin, Harmondsworth, UK, 1966.

16 The High Renaissance in Italy, 1495–1520

Brown, Patricia Fortini. *Art and Life in Renaissance Venice*. Prentice Hall, Upper Saddle River, NJ, 1997.

Cole, Alison. *Virtue and Magnificence: Art of the Italian Renaissance Courts*. Perspectives. Harry N. Abrams, New York, 1995.

Freedberg, Sydney J. *Painting of the High Renaissance in Rome and Florence*. New rev. edn. 2 vols. Hacker Art Books, New York, 1985.

Hall, Marcia B. *The Cambridge Companion to Raphael*. Cambridge University Press, New York, 2005.

Kemp, Martin. *Leonardo da Vinci: Experience, Experiment and Design*. Princeton University Press, Princeton, 2006.

Partridge, Loren W. *The Art of Renaissance Rome*. Perspectives. Harry N. Abrams, New York, 1996.

Pope-Hennessy, John. *Italian High Renaissance and Baroque Sculpture*. 3 vols. 3rd edn. Oxford University Press, New York, 1986.

Rowland, Ingrid D. *The Culture of the High Renaissance: Ancients and Moderns in Sixteenth Century Rome*. Cambridge University Press, New York, 1998.

Steinberg, Leo. *Leonardo's Incessant Last Supper*. Zone Books, New York, 2001.

Wallace, William E. *Michelangelo: The Complete Sculpture, Painting, Architecture*. Hugh Lauter Levin, Southport, 1998.

17 The Late Renaissance and Mannerism in Sixteenth-Century Italy

Barkan, Leonard. *Unearthing the Past: Archaeology and Aesthetics in the Making of Renaissance Culture*. Yale University Press, New Haven, 1999.

Franklin, David. *Painting in Renaissance Florence, 1500–1550*. Yale University Press, New Haven, 2001.

Freedberg, Sydney J. *Painting in Italy, 1500–1600*. 3rd edn. Pelican History of Art. Yale University Press, New Haven, 1993.

Klein, Robert, and Henri Zerner. *Italian Art, 1500–1600: Sources and Documents*. Reprint of 1966 edn. Northwestern University Press, Evanston, IL, 1989.

Partridge, Loren W. *Michelangelo—The Last Judgment: A Glorious Restoration*. Harry N. Abrams, New York, 1997.

Rosand, David. *Painting in Sixteenth-Century Venice: Titian, Veronese, Tintoretto*. Cambridge University Press, New York, 1997.

Shearman, John K. G. *Mannerism*. Reprint of 1967 edn. Style and Civilization. Penguin, Harmondsworth, UK, 1986.

Smyth, Craig Hugh. *Mannerism and Maniera*. 2nd edn. Bibliotheca artibus et historiae. IRSA, Vienna, 1992.

Wundrum, Manfred. *Andrea Palladio, 1508–1580. Architect Between the Renaissance and the Baroque*. Taschen, Cologne, 2004.

Enggass, Robert, and Jonathan Brown. *Italy and Spain, 1600–1750: Sources and Documents*. Reprint of 1970 edn. Northwestern University Press, Evanston, IL, 1992.

Garrard, Mary D. *Artemisia Gentileschi: The Image of the Female Hero in Italian Baroque Art*. Princeton University Press, Princeton, 1989.

Marder, Tod A. *Bernini and the Art of Architecture*. Abbeville Press, New York, 1998.

Montagu, Jennifer. *Roman Baroque Sculpture: The Industry of Art*. Yale University Press, New Haven, 1989.

Puglisi, Catherine R. *Caravaggio*. Phaidon, London, 1998.

Schroth, Sarah, Ronnie Baer, *et al*. *El Greco to Velazquez: Art during the Reign of Philip III*. MFA Publications, Boston, New York, 2008.

Varriano, John. *Italian Baroque and Rococo Architecture*. Oxford University Press, New York, 1986.

Wittkower, Rudolf. *Art and Architecture in Italy, 1600–1750*. 4th edn. Pelican History of Art. Yale University Press, New Haven, 2000.

18 Renaissance and Reformation throughout Sixteenth-Century Europe

Ainsworth, Maryan W., ed. *Man, Myth, and Sensual Pleasures: Jan Gossart's Renaissance; The Complete Works*. Metropolitan Museum of Art, New York, 2010.

Baxandall, Michael. *The Limewood Sculptors of Renaissance Germany*. Yale University Press, New Haven, 1980.

Eichberger, Dagmar, ed. *Dürer and His Culture*. Cambridge University Press, New York, 1998.

Foister, Susan. *Holbein and England*. Yale University Press, New Haven, 2005.

Hayum, Andrée. *The Isenheim Altarpiece: God's Medicine and the Painter's Vision*. Princeton University Press, Princeton, 1989.

Kavaler, Ethan Matt. *Pieter Bruegel: Parables of Order and Enterprise*. Cambridge University Press, New York, 1999.

Koerner, Joseph Leo. *The Moment of Self Portraiture in German Renaissance Art*. University of Chicago Press, Chicago, 1993.

———. *The Reformation of the Image*. University of Chicago Press, Chicago, 2004.

Mann, Richard G. *El Greco and His Patrons: Three Major Projects*. Cambridge University Press, New York, 1986.

Panofsky, Erwin. *The Life and Art of Albrecht Dürer*. 4th edn. Princeton University Press, Princeton, 1971.

Wood, Christopher S. *Albrecht Altdorfer and the Origins of Landscape*. University of Chicago Press, Chicago, 1993.

Zerner, Henri. *Renaissance Art in France: The Invention of Classicism*. Flammarion, Paris, 2003.

19 The Baroque in Italy and Spain

Bacchi, Andrea, Catherine Hess, and Jennifer Montagu, eds. *Bernini and the Birth of Baroque Portrait Sculpture*. J. Paul Getty Museum, Los Angeles, 2008.

Bissell, R. Ward. *Masters of Italian Baroque Painting*. Detroit Institute of Art in association with D. Giles Ltd., Detroit, MI; London, 2005.

Brown, Jonathan. *Painting in Spain, 1500–1700*. Pelican History of Art. Yale University Press, New Haven, 1998.

———. *Velázquez: The Technique of Genius*. Yale University Press, New Haven, 1998.

Delbeke, Maarten, and Evonne Levy and Steven Ostrow, eds. *Bernini's Biographies, Critical Essays*. The Pennsylvania State University Press, University Park, PA, 2006.

Dempsey, Charles. *Annibale Carracci and the Beginnings of Baroque Style*. 2nd edn. Cadmo, Fiesole, Italy, 2000.

20 The Baroque in the Netherlands

Alpers, Svetlana. *The Art of Describing: Dutch Art in the Seventeenth Century*. University of Chicago Press, Chicago, 1983.

Bruyn, J., *et al*., with the collaboration of L. Peese Binkhorst-Hoffscholte; trans. D. Cook-Radmore. *A Corpus of Rembrandt Paintings*, Stichting Foundation Rembrandt Research Project. 5 vols. M. Nijhoff Publishers, The Hague; Boston, 1982–2011.

Chapman, H. Perry. *Rembrandt's Self-Portraits: A Study in Seventeenth-Century Identity*. Princeton University Press, Princeton, 1990.

Franits, Wayne E. *Dutch Seventeenth-Century Genre Painting: Its Stylistic and Thematic Evolution*. Yale University Press, New Haven, 2004.

Hochstrasser, Julie Berger. *Still life and Trade in the Dutch Golden Age*. Yale University Press, New Haven, 2007.

Kiers, Judikje, and Epco Runia, eds. *The Glory of the Golden Age: Dutch Art of the 17th Century*. 2 vols. Exh. cat. Waanders, Rijksmuseum, Amsterdam, 2000.

Schama, Simon. *The Embarrassment of Riches: An Interpretation of Dutch Culture in the Golden Age*. University of California Press, Berkeley, 1988.

Schwartz, Gary. *The Rembrandt Book*. Abrams, New York, 2006.

Slive, Seymour. *Dutch Painting. 1600–1800*. Pelican History of Art. Yale University Press, New Haven, 1995.

_____. *Frans Hals*. Prestel, Munich, 1989.

_____. *Jacob van Ruisdael: Master of Landscape*. Royal Academy of Arts, London, 2005.

Sluijter, Eric-Jan. *Rembrandt and the Female Nude*. Amsterdam University Press, Amsterdam, 2006.

Sutton, Peter. *The Age of Rubens*. Exh. cat. Museum of Fine Arts, Boston, 1993.

Vlieghe, Hans. *Flemish Art and Architecture, 1585–1700*. Pelican History of Art. Yale University Press, New Haven, © 1998.

Westermann, Mariët. *Art and Home: Dutch Interiors in the Age of Rembrandt*. Exh. cat. Waanders, Zwolle, 2001.

———. *A Worldly Art: The Dutch Republic 1585–1718*. Perspective. Harry N. Abrams, New York, 1996.

Wheelock, Arthur K., ed. *Johannes Vermeer*. Exh. cat. Yale University Press, New Haven, 1995.

21 The Baroque in France and England

Blunt, Anthony. *Art and Architecture in France, 1500–1700*. 5th edn. Pelican History of Art. Yale University Press, New Haven, 1999.

Lagerlöf, Margaretha Rossholm. *Ideal Landscape: Annibale Carracci, Nicolas Poussin, and Claude Lorrain*. Yale University Press, New Haven, 1990.

Mérot, Alain. *French Painting in the Seventeenth Century*. Trans. Caroline Beamish. Yale University Press, New Haven, 1995.

Porter, Roy. *London, A Social History*. Harvard University Press, Cambridge, 1995

Rosenberg, Pierre and Keith Christiansen, eds. *Poussin and Nature: Arcadian Visions*. Yale University Press, New Haven, 2008.

Summerson, John. *Architecture in Britain, 1530–1830*. Rev. 9th edn. Pelican History of Art. Yale University Press, New Haven, 1993.

Tinniswood, Adrian. *His Invention So Fertile: A Life of Christopher Wren*. Oxford University Press, New York, 2001.

Whinney, Margaret D. *Wren*. The World of Art. Thames & Hudson, New York, 1998.

22 The Rococo

Bailey, Colin B. *The Age of Watteau, Chardin, and Fragonard: Masterpieces of French Genre Painting*. Yale University Press, New Haven, in association with the National Gallery of Canada, 2003.

Kalnein, Wend von. *Architecture in France in the Eighteenth Century*. Pelican History of Art. Yale University Press, New Haven, 1995.

———. *Painting in Eighteenth-Century Venice*. 3rd edn. Pelican History of Art. Yale University Press, New Haven, 1993.

Rosenberg, Pierre. *Chardin*. Exh. cat. Royal Academy of Art, London; Metropolitan Museum of Art, New York, 2000.

Scott, Katie. *The Rococo Interior: Decoration and Social Spaces in Early Eighteenth-Century Paris*. Yale University Press, New Haven, 1995.

Wintermute, Alan. *Watteau and His World: French Drawing from 1700–1750*. Exh. cat. Merrell Holberton, London; American Federation of Arts, New York, 1999.

PART FOUR
The Modern World

Arnason, H. Harvard, and Elizabeth C. Mansfield. *History of Modern Art*. 7th edn. Pearson Prentice Hall, Upper Saddle River, NJ, 2013.

Bergdoll, Barry. *European Architecture 1750–1890*. Oxford History of Art. Oxford University Press, New York, 2000.

Chipp, Herschel B., ed. *Theories of Modern Art: A Source Book by Artists and Critics*. University of California Press, Berkeley, 1968.

Colquhoun, Alan. *Modern Architecture*. Oxford University Press, New York, 2002.

Craske, Matthew. *Art in Europe 1700–1830, A History of the Visual Arts in an Era of Unprecedented Urban Economic Growth*. Oxford University Press, Oxford and New York, 1997.

Documents of Modern Art. 14 vols. Wittenborn, New York, 1944–1961.

Doss, Erika. *Twentieth-Century American Art*. Oxford University Press, Oxford and New York, 2002.

Marien, Mary Warner. *Photography, A Cultural History*. Pearson Prentice Hall, Upper Saddle River, NJ, 2011.

McCoubrey, John. *American Art, 1700–1960: Sources and Documents*. Prentice Hall, Englewood Cliffs, NJ, 1965.

Newhall, Beaumont. *The History of Photography from 1830 to the Present Day*. Rev. and enl. 5th edn. Museum of Modern Art, New York; dist. by Bullfinch Press/Little, Brown, 1999.

Patton, Sharon F. *African-American Art*. Oxford History of Art. Oxford University Press, New York, 1998.

Robinson, Hilary. *Feminism-Art-Theory: An Anthology 1968–2000*. Blackwell, Oxford, UK, and Malden, MA, 2001.

Stiles, Kristine, and Peter Selz. *Theories and Documents of Contemporary Art*. University of California Press, Berkeley, 1996.

23 Art in the Age of Enlightenment, 1750–1789

Crow, Thomas. *Painters and Public Life in Eighteenth-Century Paris*. Yale University Press, New Haven, 1985.

Eitner, Lorenz. *Neoclassicism and Romanticism, 1750–1850: Sources and Documents*. Reprint of 1970 edn. Harper & Row, New York, 1989.

Honour, Hugh. *Neoclassicism*. Reprint of 1968 edn. Penguin, London, 1991.

Irwin, David G. *Neoclassicism*. Art and Ideas. Phaidon, London, 1997.

Miles, Ellen G., ed. *The Portrait in Eighteenth-Century America*. University of Delaware Press, Newark, NJ, 1993.

Ottani Cavina, Anna. *Geometries of Silence: Three Approaches to Neoclassical Art*. Columbia University Press, New York, 2004.

Rosenblum, Robert. *Transformations in Late Eighteenth Century Art*. Princeton University Press, Princeton, 1967.

Saisselin, Rémy G. *The Enlightenment Against the Baroque: Economics and Aesthetics in the Eighteenth Century*. University of California Press, Berkeley, 1992.

Solkin, David. *Painting for Money: The Visual Arts and the Public Sphere in Eighteenth-Century England*. Yale University Press, New Haven, 1993.

24 Art in the Age of Romanticism, 1789–1848

Boime, Albert. *The Academy and French Painting in the Nineteenth Century*. New edn. Yale University Press, New Haven, 1986.

Brown, David B. *Romanticism*. Art and Ideas. Phaidon, New York, 2001.

Chu, Petra ten-Doesschate. *Nineteenth-Century European Art*. 3rd ed. Pearson Prentice Hall, Upper Saddle River, NJ, 2012.

Hartley, Keith. *The Romantic Spirit in German Art, 1790–1990*. Exh. cat. South Bank Centre, London © 1994.

Herrmann, Luke. *Nineteenth Century British Painting*. Giles de la Mare, London, 2000.

Honour, Hugh. *Romanticism*. Harper & Row, New York, 1979.

Middleton, Robin. *Architecture of the Nineteenth Century*. Electa, Milan, © 2003.

Noon, Patrick J. *Crossing the Channel: British and French Painting in the Age of Romanticism*. Exh. cat. Tate, London, 2003.

Novak, Barbara. *Nature and Culture: American Landscape and Painting, 1825–1875*. Rev. edn. Oxford University Press, New York, 1995.

25 The Age of Positivism: Realism, Impressionism, and the Pre-Raphaelites, 1848–1885

Broude, Norma. *Impressionism: A Feminist Reading*. Rizzoli, New York, 1991.

Clark, Timothy J. *The Painting of Modern Life: Paris in the Art of Manet and His Followers*. Rev. edn. Princeton University Press, Princeton, 1999.

Herbert, Robert. *Impressionism: Art, Leisure, and Parisian Society*. Yale University Press, New Haven, 1988.

House, John. *Impressionism: Paint and Politics*. Yale University Press, New Haven, 2004.

Jenkyns, Richard. *Dignity and Decadence: Victorian Art and the Classical Inheritance*. Harvard University Press, Cambridge, MA, 1991.

Mainardi, Patricia. *The End of the Salon: Art and the State in the Early Third Republic*. Cambridge University Press, Cambridge, UK, 1993.

Nochlin, Linda, ed. *Impressionism and Post-Impressionism, 1874–1904: Sources and Documents*. Prentice Hall, Englewood Cliffs, NJ, 1976.

———. *Realism and Tradition in Art, 1848–1900: Sources and Documents*. Prentice Hall, Englewood Cliffs, NJ, 1966.

Novak, Barbara. *Nature and Culture: American Landscape and Painting, 1825–1875*. Oxford University Press, New York, 1995.

Prettejohn, Elizabeth. *The Art of the Pre-Raphaelites*. Princeton University Press, Princeton, 2000.

Rewald, John. *Studies in Impressionism.* Harry N. Abrams, New York, 1986, © 1985.

Werner, Marcia. *Pre-Raphaelite Painting and Nineteenth-Century Realism.* Cambridge University Press, New York, 2005.

26 Progress and Its Discontents: Post-Impressionism, Symbolism, and Art Nouveau, 1880–1905

Denvir, Bernard. *Post-Impressionism.* The World of Art. Thames & Hudson, New York, 1992.

Dorra, Henri, ed. *Symbolist Art Theories: A Critical Anthology.* University of California Press, Berkeley, 1994.

Gibson, Michael. *The Symbolists.* Harry N. Abrams, New York, 1988.

Herbert, Robert L. *Georges Seurat, 1859–1891.* Metropolitan Museum of Art; dist. by Harry N. Abrams, New York, 1991.

Silverman, Debora. *Art Nouveau in Fin-de-Siècle France.* University of California Press, Berkeley, 1989.

Troy, Nancy J. *Modernism and the Decorative Arts in France: Art Nouveau to Le Corbusier.* Yale University Press, New Haven, 1991.

27 Toward Abstraction: The Modernist Revolution, 1905–1914

Behr, Shulamith. *Expressionism.* Movements in Modern Art. Cambridge University Press, Cambridge, 1999.

Bowlt, John E., ed. *Russian Art of the Avant-Garde: Theory and Criticism, 1902–1934.* Thames & Hudson, New York, 1988.

Edwards, Steve. *Art of the Avant-Gardes.* Yale University Press in association with the Open University, New Haven, 2004.

Golding, John. *Cubism: A History and an Analysis, 1907–1914.* 3rd edn. Harvard University Press, Cambridge, MA, 1988.

Herbert, James. *Fauve Painting: The Making of Cultural Politics.* Yale University Press, New Haven, 1992.

Rosenblum, Robert. *Cubism and Twentieth-Century Art.* Harry N. Abrams, New York, 2001.

Taylor, Brandon. Collage: *The Making of Modern Art.* Thames & Hudson, London, 2004.

Washton, Rose-Carol, ed. *German Expressionism: Documents from the End of the Wilhelmine Empire to the Rise of National Socialism.* The Documents of Twentieth-Century Art. G. K. Hall, Boston, 1993.

Weiss, Julie. *The Popular Culture of Modern Art: Picasso, Duchamp and Avant Gardism.* Yale University Press, New Haven, 1994.

28 Art Between the Wars

Corn, Wanda. *The Great American Thing: Modern Art and National Identity, 1915–1935.* University of California Press, Berkeley, 2001.

Durozoi, Gerard. *History of the Surrealist Movement.* University of Chicago Press, Chicago, 2002.

Fer, Briony, *et al. Realism, Rationalism, Surrealism: Art Between the Wars.* Modern Art—Practices and Debates. Yale University Press, New Haven, 1993.

Gale, Matthew. *Dada & Surrealism.* Art and Ideas. Phaidon, London, 1997.

Gössel, Peter, and Gabriele Leuthäuser. *Architecture in the Twentieth Century.* Taschen, Cologne, 1991, 1999.

Haskell, Barbara. *The American Century: Art & Culture, 1900–1950.* W. W. Norton, New York, 1999.

Hochman, Elaine S. Bauhaus: *Crucible of Modernism.* New York: Fromm International, © 1997.

Hopkins, David. *Dada and Surrealism: A Very Short Introduction.* Oxford University Press, New York, 2004.

Lane, Barbara. *Architecture and Politics in Germany, 1918–1945.* New edn. Harvard University Press, Cambridge, MA, 1985.

Lodder, Christina. *Russian Constructivism.* Yale University Press, New Haven, 1983.

Silver, Kenneth E. *Esprit de Corps: The Art of the Parisian Avant-Garde and the First World War, 1914–1925.* Princeton University Press, Princeton, 1989.

29 Postwar to Postmodern, 1945–1980

Archer, Michael. *Art Since 1960.* World of Art. Thames & Hudson, New York, 2002.

Beardsley, John. *Earthworks and Beyond: Contemporary Art in the Landscape.* 3rd edn. Abbeville Press, New York, 1998.

Carlson, Marvin A. *Performance: A Critical Introduction.* 2nd edn. Routledge, New York, 2004.

Causey, Andrew. *Sculpture Since 1945.* Oxford History of Art. Oxford University Press, New York, 1998.

Crow, Thomas. *The Rise of the Sixties: American and European Art in the Era of Dissent.* Laurence King, London, 2005.

Fineberg, Jonathan. *Art Since 1940, Strategies of Being.* 3rd edn. Pearson Prentice Hall, Upper Saddle River, NJ, 2010.

Hopkins, David. *After Modern Art: 1945–2000.* Oxford University Press, New York, 2000.

Sandler, Irving. *Art of the Postmodern Era: From the Late 1960s to the Early 1990s.* Icon Editions, New York, 1996.

30 The Postmodern Era: Art Since 1980

Belting, Hans. *Art History After Modernism.* University of Chicago Press, Chicago, 2003.

Broude, Norma, and Mary Garrard., eds. *Reclaiming Female Agency: Feminist Art History After Postmodernism.* University of California Press, Berkeley, 2005.

Brunette, Peter, and David Wills, eds. *Deconstruction and the Visual Arts: Art, Media, Architecture.* Cambridge University Press, New York, 1994.

Foster, Hal, ed. *The Anti-Aesthetic: Essays on Postmodern Culture.* New Press; dist. by W. W. Norton, New York, 1998.

Harris, Jonathan. *The New Art History: A Critical Introduction.* Routledge, New York, 2001.

Jencks, Charles. *What Is Post-Modernism?* 4th rev. edn. Academy Editions, London, 1996.

Picture Credits

I-1 Photo The Newark Museum / Art Resource / Scala, Florence

I-2 Digital image, The Museum of Modern Art, New York / Scala, Florence. © 2012 The Andy Warhol Foundation for the Visual Arts, Inc. / Artists Rights Society (ARS), New York

I-3 akg-images / Erich Lessing

I-4 © Dallas & John Heaton / Free Agents Ltd / Corbis

I-5 Photograph © The Art Institute of Chicago.

I-7 Courtesy National Gallery of Art, Washington

I-8 Digital image, The Museum of Modern Art, New York / Scala, Florence. © 2012 Artists Rights Society (ARS), New York / ADAGP, Paris / Succession Marcel Duchamp

I-9 © 2012 Estate of Pablo Picasso / Artists Rights Society (ARS), New York

I-12 © Alinari Archives / Corbis

I-13 akg-images / Erich Lessing

I-14 David Heald © The Solomon R. Guggenheim Foundation, New York

I-15 Ben Mangor / SuperStock. © 2012 Frank Lloyd Wright Foundation, Scottsdale, AZ / Artists Rights Society (ARS), NY

I-16 Courtesy National Gallery of Art, Washington. Photo Jose A. Naranjo

1.1 Jean Vertut Collection, Courtesy Yvonne Vertut

1.2 French Ministry of Culture and Communication, Regional Direction for Cultural Affairs - Rhone Alpes, Regional Department of Archaeology

1.4 Photo Scala, Florence / BPK, Bildagentur fuer Kunst, Kultur und Geschichte, Berlin

1.5 Thomas Stephan, © Ulmer Museum

1.6 Erich Lessing / akg-images

1.8a Erich Lessing / akg-images

1.8b Erich Lessing / akg-images

1.9 © English Heritage (Aerofilms Collection)

2.1 The Art and Architecture of the Ancient Orient, Yale University Press (1997) fig 3.2

2.2 Courtesy of The Oriental Institute of the University of Chicago

2.3a © The Trustees of the British Museum

2.3b © The Trustees of the British Museum

2.4 Photo Scala, Florence

2.5 © Photo Josse, Paris

sidebar, page 38 © The Trustees of the British Museum, London

2.6 © Michael S. Yamashita / Corbis

2.7 © RMN (Musée du Louvre) / Hervé Lewandowski

2.8 World Tourism Organization, Iraq

2.9 © The Trustees of the British Museum

2.10 Photo Scala, Florence / BPK, Bildagentur fuer Kunst, Kultur und Geschichte, Berlin

2.11 © ALAN ODDIE / PhotoEdit

2.13 © Gérard Degeorge / Corbis

3.1a Werner Forman Archive, London.

3.1b Werner Forman Archive, London.

3.2 Iberfoto / Archivi Alinari

3.3 Courtesy of the Semitic Museum, Harvard University, © President and Fellows of Harvard College for the Semitic Museum. Photo by Carl Andrews

3.4 © Dallas & John Heaton / Free Agents Ltd / Corbis

3.5 © Paul M.R. Maeyaert

3.6 Jürgen Liepe

3.7 © RMN (Musée du Louvre) / Franck Raux

3.8 akg-images / Interfoto

3.9 Image © The Metropolitan Museum of Art / Art Resource / Scala, Florence

3.10 © Radius Images / Corbis

3.11 Photograph Schecter Lee / © 1986 The Metropolitan Museum of Art

3.12 Dagli Orti / Art Archive

3.13 Photo Scala, Florence / BPK, Bildagentur fuer Kunst, Kultur und Geschichte, Berlin

3.14 Photo Scala, Florence / BPK, Bildagentur fuer Kunst, Kultur und Geschichte, Berlin

3.15 Boltin Picture Library / Bridgeman Art Library

4.1 John Bigelow Taylor

4.2 from John Griffiths Pedley, Greek Art and Archaeology, 2e, Prentice Hall, 1998, fig 3.1, p.65

4.3 Courtesy McRae Books Srl, Florence

4.4 © Studio Kontos / Photostock

4.5 akg-images / Nimatallah

4.6 © Craig & Marie Mauzy, Athens mauzy@otenet.gr

4.7 © Craig & Marie Mauzy, Athens mauzy@otenet.gr

4.8 © Craig & Marie Mauzy, Athens mauzy@otenet.gr

4.9 Maltings Partnership © Dorling Kindersley

4.10 © Studio Kontos / Photostock

4.11 © Craig & Marie Mauzy, Athens mauzy@otenet.gr

sidebar, page 73 © Dorling Kindersley

sidebar, page 74 from John Griffiths Pedley, Greek Art and Archaeology, 2e, Prentice Hall, 1998, fig 3.40, p.95

4.12 © Craig & Marie Mauzy, Athens mauzy@otenet.gr

5.1 akg-images / Nimatallah

5.2 © The Trustees of the British Museum

5.4 © Marco Cristofori / Corbis

5.5 Image © The Metropolitan Museum of Art / Art Resource / Scala, Florence

5.6 © Craig & Marie Mauzy, Athens mauzy@otenet.gr

5.7 © Craig & Marie Mauzy, Athens mauzy@otenet.gr

5.8 Photo Studio Koppermann

5.9 Photo Studio Koppermann

5.10 © Vatican Museums

5.11 Photo Studio Koppermann

5.12 Craig & Marie Mauzy, Athens mauzy@otenet.gr

5.13 © Craig & Marie Mauzy, Athens mauzy@otenet.gr

5.14 akg-images / Nimatallah

5.16 © Craig & Marie Mauzy, Athens mauzy@otenet.gr

5.17 © The Trustees of the British Museum

5.18 © Studio Kontos / Photostock

5.19 From Howard Colvin, Architecture and the After Life, Yale University Press, 1991, fig 31, p.35

sidebar, page 99 From Howard Colvin, Architecture and the After Life, Yale University Press, 1991, fig 31, p.35

5.20 Hirmer Fotoarchiv

5.21 akg-images / Nimatallah

5.22 From Jerome Pollitt, Art in the Hellenistic Age, Cambridge University Press, 1986, fig 258 on p. 243. Reprinted with the permission of Cambridge University Press

5.23 © Georg Gerster / Panos

5.24 From Jerome Pollitt, Art in the Hellenistic Age, Cambridge University Press, 1986, fig 250 on p. 237. Reprinted with the permission of Cambridge University Press

5.25 © Craig & Marie Mauzy, Athens mauzy@otenet.gr

5.26 akg-images

5.27 © RMN (Musée du Louvre) / Hervé Lewandowski

5.28 Photo Scala, Florence

5.29 Photo Scala, Florence / BPK, Bildagentur fuer Kunst, Kultur und Geschichte, Berlin

5.30 Photo Scala, Florence / BPK, Bildagentur fuer Kunst, Kultur und Geschichte, Berlin

5.31 Photo Studio Koppermann

5.32 © Studio Kontos / Photostock

6.1 INDEX / Ricciarini

6.2 National Georgraphic / Getty Images

6.3 © Soprintendenza Etruria Meridionale / Ikona

6.4 Soprintendenza Beni Archeologici Etruria Meridionale

6.5 Soprintendenza per i Beni Archeologici dell'Etruria Meridionale

6.6 Photo Scala, Florence

sidebar, page 118 Bonfante, Larissa. Image of "Plan of Tomb Residential Complex. 6th Century BCE. Murio (Poggio Civitate), Italy" Etruscan Life and Afterlife: A Handbook of Etruscan Studies, Copyright © 1986 Wayne State University Press, with the permission of Wayne State University Press

6.7 Photo Scala, Florence

6.8 Soprintendenza per i Beni Archeologici dell'Etruria Meridionale

6.9 © Vincenzo Pirozzi, Rome fotopirozzi@inwind.it

6.10 Photo Scala, Florence - courtesy of the Ministero Beni e Att. Culturali

Kunst, Kultur und Geschichte, Berlin

14.10b © Koninklijk Museum voor Schone Kunsten, Antwerp / Lukas

14.12 Reproduced by courtesy of the Librarian and Director, The John Rylands Library, The University of Manchester

14.13 Image copyright The Metropolitan Museum of Art / Art Resource / Scala, Florence

15.1 © Studio Quattrone, Florence

15.1 © Studio Quattrone, Florence

15.3 © Vanni Archive / Corbis

15.4 © Quattrone, Florence

15.6 Canali Photobank, Milan Italy

15.7 © Studio Quattrone, Florence

15.8 © Studio Studio Quattrone, Florence

15.9 © Studio Quattrone, Florence

15.10 © Studio Quattrone, Florence

15.11 © Studio Quattrone, Florence

15.12 Photo Scala, Florence

15.13 © Studio Quattrone, Florence

15.15 Photo © The National Gallery, London

15.16 © Studio Quattrone, Florence

15.17 Seat Archive / Alinari Archives

15.18 © Studio Quattrone, Florence

15.19 © Studio Quattrone, Florence

15.20 Canali Photobank, Milan Italy

15.21 Erich Lessing / akg-images

15.22 akg-images / Electa

15.23 © Cameraphoto Arte, Venice

15.24 Canali Photobank, Milan Italy

16.1 © Cameraphoto Arte, Venice

16.2 © Studio Quattrone, Florence

16.3 © RMN (Musée du Louvre) / Hervé Lewandowski

16.4 © Vincenzo Pirozzi, Rome fotopirozzi@inwind.it

16.5 © Trustees of The British Museum

16.6 Canali Photobank, Milan Italy

16.7 © Studio Quattrone, Florence

16.8 Musei Vaticani / IKONA

16.9 Canali Photobank, Milan Italy

16.10 Vatican Museums and Galleries, Vatican City

16.11 © Vincenzo Pirozzi, Rome fotopirozzi@inwind.it

16.12 © Photo Josse, Paris

16.13 © Cameraphoto Arte, Venice

16.14 The National Gallery, London / akg

16.15 © Studio Quattrone, Florence

17.1 © Studio Quattrone, Florence

17.2 © Studio Quattrone, Florence

17.3 The National Gallery, London / akg

17.4 © Studio Quattrone, Florence

17.5 © Vatican Museums

17.6 © James Morris, London

17.7 Photo Scala, Florence

17.8 Photo Scala, Florence - courtesy of the Ministero Beni e Att. Culturali

17.9 © Studio Quattrone, Florence

17.10 Photograph © 2012 Museum of Fine Arts, Boston

17.11 © Cameraphoto Arte, Venice

17.12 © Cameraphoto

17.13 © Cameraphoto Arte, Venice

18.1 De Agostini / Getty Images

18.2 Photograph by Patrick Muller © CMN, Paris

18.3 Photo Scala, Florence

18.4 Photo Scala, Florence

18.5 Photo Scala, Florence

18.8 © Bayer&Mitko - ARTOTHEK

18.9 © Trustees of The British Museum

18.10 Photo Scala, Florence / BPK, Bildagentur fuer Kunst, Kultur und Geschichte, Berlin

18.11 © The National Gallery, London / Scala, Florence

18.12 Photo Scala, Florence / BPK, Bildagentur fuer Kunst, Kultur und Geschichte, Berlin

18.13 Bo Gyllander

18.14 Erich Lessing / akg-images

18.15 Erich Lessing / akg-images

19.1 © Studio Quattrone, Florence

19.2 Image copyright The Metropolitan Museum of Art / Art Resource / Scala, Florence

19.3 The Bridgeman Art Library

19.4 Canali Photobank, Milan Italy

19.5 © Vincenzo Pirozzi, Rome fotopirozzi@inwind.it

19.6 © Alinari Archives / Corbis

19.7 Photo Scala, Florence

19.8 © Achim Bednorz, Cologne

19.9 © Achim Bednorz, Cologne

19.10 Photo Scala, Florence

19.11 © Vincenzo Pirozzi, Rome fotopirozzi@inwind.it

19.12 Erich Lessing / akg-images

19.14 Image © The Metropolitan Museum of Art / Art Resource / Scala, Florence

19.16 Photograph © The State Hermitage Museum / photo by Vladimir Terebenin, Leonard Kheifets, Yuri Molodkovets

20.2 © Photo Josse, Paris

20.3 © RMN (Musée du Louvre) / Christian Jean

20.4 The John and Mable Ringling Museum of Art

20.5 The National Gallery, London / akg

20.6 © Corbis

20.7 Photo Scala, Florence / BPK, Bildagentur fuer Kunst, Kultur und Geschichte, Berlin

20.8 Courtesy National Gallery of Art, Washington

20.12 © RMN (Musée du Louvre) / Jean Schormans

20.13 Photo Scala, Florence

20.14 Museum Boijmans Van Beuningen, Rotterdam. Photography: Studio John Tromp, Rotterdam

20.15 Photo: Toni Marie Gonzalez, Toledo Museum of Art

20.17 Courtesy National Gallery of Art, Washington. Photo Richard Carafelli

21.1 © RMN (Musée du Louvre) / Gérard Blot

21.3 Photograph © The Art Institute of Chicago

21.5 © RMN (Musée du Louvre) / Hervé Lewandowski

21.6 akg-images / Erich lessing

21.7 Stéphane Compoint

21.8 © Paul M.R. Maeyaert

21.9 © RMN (Château de Versailles) / Michel Urtado

21.10 akg-images / A.F.Kersting

21.11 © Angelo Hornak Photo Library

22.1 © RMN (Musée du Louvre) / Gérard Blot

22.2 Photo Pierpont Morgan Library / Art Resource / Scala, Florence

22.3 © Blauel / Gnamm - ARTOTHEK

22.4 © Photo Josse, Paris

22.5 © Wallace Collection, London, UK / The Bridgeman Art Library

22.6 Image © The Metropolitan Museum of Art / Art Resource / Scala, Florence

22.7 Image © The Metropolitan Museum of Art / Art Resource / Scala, Florence

22.8 Photo Scala Florence / Heritage Images

22.9 The Royal Collection © 2011 Her Majesty Queen Elizabeth II / The Bridgeman Art Library

22.10 Bayerische Verwaltung der Staadlichen Schloesser

23.1 akg-images / Electa

23.2 The Bridgeman Art Library

23.3 Image © The Metropolitan Museum of Art

23.4 Image courtesy of the Denver Art Museum

23.5 Photo © National Gallery of Canada, Ottawa. Transfer from the Canadian War Memorials, 1921

23.6 Photograph © The Art Institute of Chicago

23.7 Archivision

23.8 Photo Scala Florence / Heritage Images

23.9 © Kilian O'Sullivan / VIEW

23.11 Courtesy National Gallery of Art, Washington

23.13 Erich Lessing / akg-images

23.14 Erich Lessing / akg-images

23.15 © RMN (Musée du Louvre) / Gérard Blot / Christian Jean

23.16 © RMN (Musée du Louvre) / Gérard Blot

23.17 © RMN (Musée du Louvre) / Christian Jean

24.1 Bibliotheque Nationale, Paris, France / The Bridgeman Art Library

24.3 Photo The Print Collector / Heritage-Images / Scala, Florence

24.4 Photograph © 2012 Museum of Fine Arts, Boston

24.5 Photo Scala, Florence / BPK, Bildagentur fuer Kunst, Kultur und Geschichte, Berlin

24.6 Image © The Metropolitan Museum of Art / Art Resource / Scala, Florence

24.7 © RMN (Château de Versailles) / Gérard Blot

24.8 © RMN (Musée du Louvre) / Hervé Lewandowski

24.9 © RMN-Grand Palais (Musée du Louvre) / Thierry Le Mage

24.10 akg-images / Erich lessing

24.11 © RMN (Musée du Louvre) / Thierry Le Mage

24.12 Photo: Photography, Incorporated, Toledo, Ohio

24.13 © Paul M.R. Maeyaert

24.14 © Stewart McKnight / Alamy (RF)

24.15 Tom Hoover Photography

24.16 © Achim Bednorz, Cologne

25.1 The Bridgeman Art Library

25.2 © RMN (Musée du Louvre) / Hervé Lewandowski

25.3 © RMN (Musée d'Orsay) / Hervé Lewandowski

25.4 Brooklyn Museum of Art, New York, USA / Gift of Anna Ferris / The Bridgeman Art Library

25.5 Photograph © The Art Institute of Chicago

25.7 Photograph © The Art Institute of Chicago

25.8 ©Tate, London 2012

25.9 © Victoria and Albert Museum, London

25.10 ©Tate, London 2012

25.11 Image © The Metropolitan Museum of Art / Art Resource / Scala, Florence

25.12 © Butler Institute of American Art, Youngstown, OH. Museum Purchase 1918 / Bridgeman Art Library

25.13 © Ministère de la Culture - Médiathèque du Patrimoine, Dist. RMN-GP / Atelier de Nadar

25.15 Library of Congress, Prints and Photographs Division, Washington, DC

25.16 Courtesy George Eastman House, International Museum of Photography and Film

25.17 Art Archive

25.18 Getty Images

26.1 © Samuel Courtauld Trust, The Courtauld Gallery, London, UK / The Bridgeman Art Library

26.2 Photograph © The Art Institute of Chicago

26.3 Digital image, The Museum of Modern Art, New York / Scala, Florence

26.4 Photograph © 2012 Museum of Fine Arts, Boston

26.5 © 2012 Artists Rights Society (ARS), New York

26.6 © RMN (Musée d'Orsay) / Jean-Gilles Berizzi

26.10 Photo Smithsonian American Art Museum / Art Resource / Scala, Florence

26.7 Art Archive / Nasjonal Galleriet, Oslo / Joseph Martin. © 2012 The Munch Museum / The Munch-Ellingsen Group / Artists Rights Society (ARS), NY

26.8 Stapleton Collection / Bridgeman Art Library

26.9 ÖBN / Wien, 95.262-C

26.11 © RMN (Musée d'Orsay) / Droits réservés

26.12 Musée Rodin, Paris / Bridgeman Art Library

26.13 © 2013 Bastin & Evrard / SOFAM, Belgium

26.14 Gala / SuperStock

26.15 © Art on File / Corbis

26.16 Andrea Jemolo / Scala, Florence

26.17 Image © The Metropolitan Museum of Art / Art Resource / Scala, Florence

26.18 Courtesy George Eastman House, International Museum of Photography and Film

27.1 The Bridgeman Art Library. © 2012 Succession H. Matisse / Artists Rights Society (ARS), New York

27.2 Digital image, The Museum of Modern Art, New York / Scala, Florence. © 2012 Estate of Pablo Picasso / Artists Rights Society (ARS), New York

27.3 The Bridgeman Art Library. © 2012 Artists Rights Society (ARS), New York / ADAGP, Paris

27.4 McNay Art Museum / Art Resource, NY / Scala, Florence. © 2012 Estate of Pablo Picasso / Artists Rights Society (ARS), New York

27.5 © RMN / Béatrice Hatala. © 2012 Estate of Pablo Picasso / Artists Rights Society (ARS), New York

27.6 akg-images

27.7 Digital image, The Museum of Modern Art, New York / Scala, Florence

27.8 © 2012 Artists Rights Society (ARS), New York / ADAGP, Paris

27.9 © Hans Hinz - ARTOTHEK. © 2012 Fondation Oskar Kokoschka / Artists Rights Society (ARS), New York / ProLitteris, Zürich

27.10 akg / De Agostini Pict.Lib.

27.11 Digital image, The Museum of Modern Art, New York / Scala, Florence

27.12 Digital image, The Museum of Modern Art, New York / Scala, Florence

27.13 © Museo Thyssen-Bornemisza, Madrid

27.14 © 2012 Artists Rights Society (ARS), New York / SIAE, Rome

27.15 Digital image, The Museum of Modern Art, New York / Scala, Florence. © 2012 Artists Rights Society (ARS), New York / ADAGP, Paris

27.16 Photograph Geoffrey Clements / Whitney Mseuem of American Art

27.17 © Vanni Archive / Corbis

27.18 French Governement Tourist Office

28.1 © 2012 Artists Rights Society (ARS), New York / VG Bild-Kunst, Bonn

28.2 Photo The Philadelphia Museum of Art / Art Resource / Scala, Florence. © 2012 Artists Rights Society (ARS), New York / ADAGP, Paris / Succession Marcel Duchamp

28.3 © Centre Pompidou, MNAM-CCI, Dist. RMN / Droits réservés. © 2012 Artists Rights Society (ARS), New York / ADAGP, Paris

28.4 Photo Scala, Florence / BPK, Bildagentur fuer Kunst, Kultur und Geschichte, Berlin. © 2012 Artists Rights Society (ARS), New York / VG Bild-Kunst, Bonn

28.5 © 2012 Artists Rights Society (ARS), New York / ADAGP, Paris

28.6 Telimage - Paris, 2004. © 2012 Man Ray Trust / Artists Rights Society (ARS), NY / ADAGP, Paris

28.7 Wadsworth Atheneum Museum of Art / Art Resource, NY / Scala, Florence. © 2012 Successió Miró / Artists Rights Society (ARS), New York / ADAGP, Paris

28.8 Digital image, The Museum of Modern Art, New York / Scala, Florence. © Salvador Dalí, Fundació Gala-Salvador Dalí, Artists Rights Society (ARS), New York 2012

28.9 Digital image, The Museum of Modern Art, New York / Scala, Florence. © 2012 Artists Rights Society (ARS), New York / ProLitteris, Zürich

28.10 Digital image, The Museum of Modern Art, New York / Scala, Florence. © 2012 Calder Foundation, New York / Artists Rights Society (ARS), New York

28.11 ©Tate, London 2012. Reproduced by permission of The Henry Moore Foundation. © The Henry Moore Foundation. All Rights Reserved, DACS 2012 / www.henry-moore.org

28.12 Moderna Museet, Stockholm

28.14 © Bildarchiv Monheim GmbH / Alamy

28.15 Bauhausarchiv-Museum fur Gestaltung, Berlin. © 2012 Artists Rights Society (ARS), New York / VG Bild-Kunst, Bonn

28.16 © Vanni / Art Resource, NY

28.17 White Images / Scala, Florence

28.18 Photo The Newark Museum / Art Resource / Scala, Florence

28.19 Courtesy George Eastman House, International Museum of Photography and Film

28.20 Time & Life Pictures / Getty Images

28.21 Image © The Metropolitan Museum of Art / Art Resource / Scala, Florence © 2012 Georgia O'Keeffe Museum / Artists Rights Society (ARS) New York

28.22 Photograph © The Art Institute of Chicago.

28.23 Digital image, The Museum of Modern Art, New York / Scala, Florence. © 2012 The Jacob and Gwendolyn Lawrence Foundation, Seattle / Artists Rights Society (ARS), New York

28.24 Photo Art Resource / Bob Schalkwijk / Scala, Florence

28.25 Photograph by Geoffrey Clements / Whitney Museum of American Art

28.26 Library of Congress, Washington, DC

28.27 © 2012 Estate of Pablo Picasso / Artists Rights Society (ARS), New York 29.1 The Metropolitan Museum of Art / Art Resource / Scala, Florence. © 2012 The Pollock-Krasner Foundation / Artists Rights Society (ARS), New York 29.2 Digital image, The Museum of Modern Art, New York / Scala, Florence. © 2012 The Willem de Kooning Foundation / Artists Rights Society (ARS), New York

29.3 © 1998 Kate Rothko Prizel & Christopher Rothko / Artists Rights Society (ARS), New York

29.4 Museum Ludwig, Rheinisches Bildarchiv, Museen der Stadt, Cologne

29.5 Photograph by Geoffrey Clements / Whitney Museum of American Art

29.6 The Getty Research Institute, Los Angeles (980063)

29.8 Digital image, The Museum of Modern Art, New York / Scala, Florence

29.9 Digital image, The Museum of Modern Art, New York / Scala, Florence. © 2012 The Andy Warhol Foundation for the Visual Arts, Inc. / Artists Rights Society (ARS), New York

29.10 Courtesy Galerie Michael Werner. © 2012 The Estate of Sigmar Polke, Cologne / ARS, New York / VG Bild-Kunst, Bonn

29.11 © Ellsworth Kelly, all rights reserved. Photograph by Philipp Scholz Ritterman

29.12 Photograph by David Heald / Solomon R. Guggenheim Museum

29.15 Digital image, The Museum of Modern Art, New York / Scala, Florence. © 2012 Joseph Kosuth / Artists Rights Society (ARS), New York

29.16 © Ute Klophaus, D-Wuppertal. © 2012 Artists Rights Society (ARS), New York / VG Bild-Kunst, Bonn

29.18 Photographer: Lee Stalsworth

29.19 Photograph © Donald Woodman. © 2012 Judy Chicago / Artists Rights Society (ARS), New York

29.20 Andrew Garn

30.1 Photo: Matt Wargo, courtesy of Venturi, Scott Brown and Associates, Inc.

30.2 Courtesy of Michael Graves & Associates

30.3 Centre Pompidou

30.4 © Visions of America, LLC / Alamy

30.5 Photograph © 2012 Carnegie Museum of Art, Pittsburgh

30.6 Photography: Douglas M. Parker Studio, Los Angeles. © 2012 The Estate of Jean-Michel Basquiat / ADAGP, Paris / ARS, New York

30.7 © Frank Fournier

30.9 © Fred Wilson, courtesy The Pace Gallery

30.11 © Kiki Smith, courtesy The Pace Gallery. Photograph by Jerry L. Thompson / Whitney Museum of American Art

30.12 Photo James Dee. © 2012 Artists Rights Society (ARS), New York / VG Bild-Kunst, Bonn

30.13 Courtesy of Bill Viola Studio, Photo: Kira Perov

30.14 Photo by Hiro Ihara, courtesy Cai Studio

Index

Figures in *italics* refer to illustrations; artists and architects are shown in **bold**

Caravaggio (Michelangelo Merisi) 390–1,
403–4, 432;
The Calling of St. Matthew 389, 390–1, 401,
417–8, 421;
The Musicians 391, *391*
Caravaggisti 391, 417, 479
Cardona, Spain: Sant Vincenç *222*, 223
Carolingian dynasty 200, 207–8;
architecture 211–3, 228, 244;
illuminated books 208–11;
sculpture 208
carpets, Islamic 190–1, *191*
Carracci, Annibale 392;
Loves of the Gods 392–3, *393, 395*
Carter, Howard 62
Carthage 123;
see also Phoenicians
Carthusian order 229
Cassatt, Mary 515, 574;
The Child's Bath 515, 515–6, 548
Catacombs, Rome 161–3, *162*, 167–8
Catelli, Leo 610
Catherine II ("the Great") 478
cave paintings, prehistoric 22, 23–6, *24–6*
Celtic tribes 107, 200–2
ceramics/pottery: Greek vases 78, *78–9*, 88,
88–9, 89;
Minoan 69–70, *70*;
Neolithic 29, *29*;
Persian (*mina'i*) *195*, 196;
Sèvres porcelain 452
Cernavoda, Romania: ceramic figures 29, *29*
Cerveteri, Italy: sarcophagi 116, *117*;
tombs and grave goods 113, *113–5, 114*
Cézanne, Paul 530–1, 534, 554–5, 558;
Mont Sainte-Victoire 530–1, *531*
Chadwick, John 71
Chaldeans 41
Champion Single Sculls, The (Eakins) 520, *520*
champlevé enamel 226–7, *227*
Champs délicieux (Man Ray) 578–9, *579*
Chardin, Jean-Siméon 449, 451;
Saying Grace 449, *449*, 451
Charging Chasseur (Géricault) 497–8
Charlemagne, Emperor 153, 207–8, *209*, 211,
212–3, 216, 229, 248
Charles I, of England 415, 430, 440;
Portrait of Charles I Hunting (van Dyck)
415, *415*
Charles II, of England 430
Charles III, of Spain 485–6
Charles IV, of Spain 486–7, 494
Charles V, Emperor 358, 362, 371–2, 378,
381, 403
Charles the Bald 208, 213, 248
Charlottesville, Virginia: University of Virginia
(Jefferson) 503–4, *504*
charterhouses 229
Chartres, France: Cathedral *251*, 251–2, 254–6, *255,
256, 257*;
jamb statues 252–3, *253*, 259, *259*, 263;

stained glass 257, *258*, 258–9;
Cathedral school 265
Chartreuse de Champmol, France: *The Well of
Moses* (Sluter) *294*, 294–5
Chaucer, Geoffrey: *Canterbury Tales* 224
Chauvet, France: cave paintings 22, 23–4, *25*
Chestnut Hill, Philadelphia: Vanna Venturi House
(Venturi) *626*, 627
Chevalier, Étienne: *Étienne Chevalier and St.
Stephen* (Fouquet) *304, 305*
Chi Rho sign 157;
Iota monogram *206*, 207
chiastic poses 91, 93, 131
Chicago, Ill. 525, 544–5, 569, 593;
New Bauhaus 622;
Robie House (Wright) *546*, 546–7
Chicago, Judy 620–1;
The Dinner Party 620–1, *621*
Chicago School 570, 622
Chigi, Agostino 347
Child's Bath, The (Cassatt) *515*, 515–6, 548
Chimaira (Etruscan bronze) 120, *120*
Christ *see* Jesus of Nazareth
Christ in Majesty (Romanesque sculpture) *227*,
227–8
Christians/Christianity, early 132, 147, 149, 152,
153, 156–7, 159, 171, 190, 200, 203;
basilicas 163–4;
catacomb paintings 161–3, 283;
churches 163–5;
liturgy 164–5;
mosaics 166–7, 283;
sculpture 170–1;
see also Bible(s);
monasticism
Cimabue 283;
Madonna Enthroned 283, *283*
Cistercian monasteries 229, 234–5, *235*
city-states: Etruscan 112;
Greek 81, 94;
Italian 310
Clare, St. 279
Claricia 242
classic, classical, Classical 90
Classical period (Greece) 90–100
classicism 431
Claude Lorrain 434–5, 489;
A Pastoral Landscape 435, *435*
Clement VII, Pope 354, 358, 395
Cleopatra VII, of Egypt 101, 131
Clodion (Claude Michel) 452;
Nymph and Satyr Carousing 452–3, *453*
Club-Footed Boy, The (Ribera) 403, *403*
Cluniac order 229, 236;
see below
Cluny, France: Abbey Church 228–9, *230*
Codex/codices 168–9
Codex Cobertinus 236, *236*
Colbert, Jean-Baptiste 431–2
Cold War, the 601;
map *601*

Cole, Thomas 492–3;
The Course of Empire 493;
The Oxbow 492, 493
collages 556–7, 577–8, 619–20
Cologne, Germany: Dada 577–8;
Cathedral (*Gero Crucifix*) 218, *219*;
Werkbund Exhibition (Glass Pavilion) (Taut)
570, 570–1
color wheel, the 513
colossal order 331
Colosseum, Rome 137, *137*
combines 605, 606
Commodus, Emperor 146
Communism 572, 573, 576–7, 584–6, 625, 637
Communist Manifesto (Marx and Engels) 459, 484
Composition (Miró) 580, *580*, 581
*Composition No. II...Composition with Red, Blue, and
Yellow* (Mondrian) 585, 585–6
Comte, Auguste 506: *Politive Philosophy* 506
Conceptual Art 600, 605, 616–8, 634
Concert Champêtre (Giorgione or Titian) 348, *348*
concrete, Roman 125–7, 137, 140, 149
Condivi, Ascanio 343
Constable, John 488–9, 500;
The Haywain 488, 489, 500
Constantine the Great, Emperor 132, 146, 148,
149, 152, 157, 161, 163, 165;
Head 146–7, *147*
Constantine VII, Emperor 181
Constantinople 152, 157–8, 171, 183, 196, 272;
university 181;
see also Istanbul
Constantius Chlorus, Emperor 151
constructions 557, *557*
Constructivism, Russian 584–5
contrapposto 91–2, 317, 319, 323
Cooper, James Fenimore 493
Copley, John Singleton 2;
Mrs. Joseph Scott 2, 2–3, 4
corbeling *72*, 73
Corbie, France: gospel book *236*, 237
Córdoba, Spain 220, 233;
Great Mosque *193*, 193–4;
Medina al-Zahra 194
Corinthian capitals/columns 99, *99*, 102, 137,
141, *141*
Cornelia Presenting Her Children as Her Treasures
(Kauffmann) 468
Corvey, Germany: abbey church 213, *213*, 244
Counter-Reformation/Catholic Reformation
272–3, 358, 360–1, 366, 372, 386–7, 388,
390, 395, 402
Courbet, Gustave 508–9, 512, 518;
Burial at Ornans 508, 508–9
Course of Empire, The (Cole) 493
Crac des Chevaliers, Syria 239, 239–40
"crafts" 451
Cranach, Lucas, the Elder 377;
An Allegory of Law and Grace 377–8, *378*
Creation of Adam, The (Michelangelo) 345, *345*, 390
Cremona, Italy 361, 363

Neptune 82;
  Neptune and Amphitrite (Gossaert) *381*, 381–2
Neri, St. Filippo 387–8
Netherlands, the 387, 410–1;
  15th-c. art 293–4, 297–304;
  16th-c. art 381–5;
  17th-c. art 416–29;
  19th-c. art 533–4;
  20th-c. architecture 586;
  20th-c. art 585–6;
  see also Flemish art
Neumann, Balthasar: Residenz, Würzburg
  455–6, *456*
New Deal 573, 596, 597
New Negro Movement 593
"New Woman," the 539
Newborn, The (brancusi) 568
Newton, Charles 99
Newton, Sir Isaac 458
New York 491, 590, 601;
  "An American Place" (gallery) 592;
  Armory Show (1913) 568;
  Art of This Century gallery 602;
  Dada 575–6;
  National Academy of Design 491, 493;
  Guggenheim Museum 13–5, *14*;
  Janis (Sidney) Gallery 603;
  Museum of Modern Art 8, 588, 629;
  Seagram Building *622*, 622–3;
  "291" Gallery 568–9, 590–1
New York Kouros *84*, 85
Nietzsche, Friedrich 566
Night Watch, The (Rembrandt) *422*, 422–3
Nineveh 36, 37;
  relief *40*, 41
Norman architecture 243–5, 250–1, 253–4
Normandy 241, 247, 261
No. 62 (Rust and Blue) (Rothko) 604, 604–5
Nymph and Satyr Carousing (Clodion) 452–3, *453*

O

Oath of Brutus (Hamilton) 480
Oath of the Horatii, The (David) 479–81, *480*
obelisks 60
Object (Luncheon in Fur) (Oppenheim) *581*, 581–2
Obregón, Alvaro 595
Octopus Vase (Minoan) 69, *70*
oculus 139
Odalisk (Rauschenberg) *605*, 606
Odo of Metz: palace chapel, Aachen 212, 212–3
Ofili, Chris: *The Holy Virgin Mary* 5–6, *6*
oil painting 293, 333
oinochoe 78
O'Keeffe, Georgia 592–3, 621;
  Black Iris III 592, *592*
On the Bank of the Seine, Bennecourt (Monet) *513*, 513–4
One and Three Chairs (Kosuth) *617*, 617
1 Copper Plate... (Ernst) *578*, 578
opera 402

Oppenheim, Meret 581;
  Object (Luncheon in Fur) *581*, 581–2
Orator, The (Etruscan bronze) 120, *121*
Orchestra of the Paris Opéra, The (Degas) 511, *511*
Orgy, The (Hogarth) 453–4, *454*
Orientalism 495, 497
Orientalizing style (Greece) 79–80
Orphism 562
Orthodox Christianity 152, 158, 173
orthogonals 315, 325
orthostats 41
Osman 196
Ostrogoths 152, 171–2, 200–1
O'Sullivan, Timothy 523;
  A Harvest of Death, Gettysburg... 523–4, *524*
Otis, Elisha: elevator 544
Otto I, Emperor 214, 242
Otto II, Emperor 214–5, 217, 242
Otto III, Emperor 215, 217
Ottoman Empire/Turks 152, 183, 195–6, 199,
    272, 371, 378, 499–500, 557;
  architecture 197;
  ceramics 197, *198*, 199;
  court style 197
Ottonian dynasty 200, 214;
  architecture 215;
  manuscripts 217–8;
  metalwork 215–6;
  sculpture 215–6, 218, 223
Oxbow, The (Cole) 492, *493*

P

Pacher, Michael: *St. Wolfgang Altarpiece*
    305–6, *306*
Pachomius 228
Padua: Arena (Scrovegni) Chapel frescoes (Giotto)
    285, 285–7, *286*
Paestum, Italy: Temples of Hera *83*, 83–4
pagans 188
Paik, Nam June 618, 637;
  Electronic Superhighway: Continental U.S.
    618, *619*
Painterly Architectonics (Popova) 565, 565–6
painting(s) *see* cave painting;
  encaustic painting;
  landscapes;
  oil painting;
  portraiture;
  still-life painting;
  tempera;
  wall paintings/frescoes
Paionios of Ephesos and **Daphnis of Miletos**:
    Temple of Apollo, Didyma 102, *103*, 104
Paleolithic Age 18–9, 23, 65;
  art 23–8;
  dwellings 28
Palestrina, Italy: Sanctuary of Fortuna Primigenia
    125–7, *126*
Palette of King Narmer 47–8, *48*
Palladian Revival 471–2

Palladio, Andrea 366, 440;
  Four Books of Architecture 366–7;
  Villa Rotonda, Vicenza 366, 366–7, 471
Palomino, Antonio 406
pantheism 490
Pantheon, Rome *138*, *139*, 139–40
papacy 158, 276, 292, 310, 328, 334, 340, 358,
    361, 388
Papirius Praetextatus... (Kauffmann) *468*, 468
Pareja, Juan de: portrait (Velázquez) *405*,
    405–6
Paris 261, 292, 432, 508, 553;
  Arc de Triomphe *502*, 502;
  Barrière de l'Étoile 476–7, *477*;
  Café Guerbois 511;
  École des Beaux-Arts 502, 531;
  Eiffel Tower *526*, 526–7;
  hôtels 445, 451–2, *452*, 476, 477;
  Louvre 12–13, *13*, 339, 349, 433, 437, *437*, 439,
    476, 498, 509;
  Photo-Club 547;
  Pompidou Center *628*, 628–9;
  Sainte-Chapelle 261, *262*, 263;
  University 265;
  Virgin of Paris 265, *265*, 271, 294;
  see also Saint-Denis;
  Salons
Paris Psalter 181, *181*
Parler, Heinrich, the Elder (and Peter(?)):
    Heiligenkreuz, Schwäbisch-Gmünd
    268–9, *269*
Parma, Italy 361–2
Parmigianino (Girolamo Mazzola) 362–3;
  The Madonna with the Long Neck 363, *363*
Parnassus (Mengs) 464–5, *465*, 466
Parrhasius 10
Parthenon *see* Akropolis
Parthians 131
Parting of Lot and Abraham, The (mosaic)
    167, *167*
Passion plays 297
Pastoral Concert (Giorgione *or* Titian) 348, *348*
Pastoral Landscape, A (Claude Lorrain) 435, *435*
Paul III, Pope 358, 360–1
Pavlov, Ivan 529
Paxton, Sir Joseph: Crystal Palace, London
    526, *526*
Peasant Wedding (Bruegel the Elder) 384, 384–5
Pech-Merle, France: cave paintings 26, *26*
Peloponnesian War 99
Pennsylvania Academy of the Fine Arts 491
Performance Art 600, 608, 617
Pergamon 101, 107, 109;
  Great Altar of Zeus 107, 107–9, *108*
Perikles 94–5, 97
peristyles 81
Perpendicular Gothic architecture 269
Perrault, Claude 437, 476;
  Louvre, Paris 12–3, *13*, 437, *437*, 439
Persephone 82, 111
Persepolis: Palace *43*, 44, 44–5

Weimar Republic 576–7;
  Bauhaus 586–7
Well of Moses, The (Sluter) *294*, 294–5
West, Benjamin 469;
  The Death of General Wolfe 469, 469–70
westworks 212–3, *213*, 244
wetcollodion process (photography) 522
Weyden, Rogier van der 301, 305;
  Descent from the Cross 301, 301–2
*Where Do We Come From? What Are We? Where Are
  We Going?* (Gauguin) 535, *535*, 536
Whistler, James Abbott McNeill 518;
  Symphony in White No. 1: The White Girl
    518–19, *519*
Whitman, Walt 490
Wilde, Oscar: *Salomé* 539
William I ("the Conqueror") 241, 243
Wilson, Fred 634;
  Mining the Museum 634, *635*
Winckelmann, Johann Joachim 464
Wire Wheel (Strand) 591, *591*
Woman I (De Kooning) 603, *603*, 604
Woman Holding a Balance (Vermeer) 428, 428–9
Woman of Willendorf 26–8, *27*
Women series (De Kooning) *603*, 603–4
Wood, Grant 592;
  American Gothic 4–5, *5*, 593, *593*
woodcuts 306, 307, 308, *308*, 375, *375*, 377–8, *378*
Woolley, Leonard 35

Wordsworth, William 488
World War I 528, 557, 572–4
World War II 600–1, 603, 617
Wren, Sir Christopher 431, 441, 454–5;
  St. Paul's Cathedral, London *442*, 442–3
Wright, Frank Lloyd 546, 569, 586, 622–3;
  Guggenheim Museum, New York
    13–5, *14*;
  Prairie Houses 546;
  Robie House, Chicago *546*, 546–7
writing/scripts 18;
  Arabic 188, 190;
  cuneiform 32;
  Egyptian hieroglyphs 47–8;
  Greek alphabet 78–9, 112;
  kufic alphabet 186, 190, *190*;
  Minoan (Linear A) 64, 66;
  Mycenaean (Linear B) 64, 71–2;
  Roman 209
Wundt, Wilhelm 529
Würzburg, Germany: Residenz (Neumann)
    455–6, *456*;
  frescoes (Tiepolo) *456*, 457

X

Xavier, St. Francis 387–8
Xenophon 88
Xerxes I, of Persia 43, 90

Y

Yard (Kaprow) 607, *607*, 635
Yellow River civilization, China 19, 33
yin and yang 534
Yosemite Valley... (Watkins) 523, *523*

Z

Zaum 564, 565
Zealots 179
Zeitgeist 15
Zeno 133
0, 10 (exhibition) 565
Zeus 82, 111
Zeus (bronze) *91*, 92–3
Zeuxis 10
ziggurats, Sumerian 33, 38, *38*
Zoroaster/Zoroastrianism 44
Zurbarán, Francisco de 404;
  Still Life with Lemons, Oranges, and a Rose
    404, *404*
Zürich: Cabinet Voltaire 574–5;
  Dadaists 574–5
Zwingli, Ulrich 372